# Handbook
# of Modern
# Personality Theory

# THE SERIES IN CLINICAL AND COMMUNITY PSYCHOLOGY

CONSULTING EDITORS:

## CHARLES D. SPIELBERGER and IRWIN G. SARASON

| | |
|---|---|
| Averill | • Patterns of Psychological Thought: Readings in Historical and Contemporary Texts |
| Becker | • Depression: Theory and Research |
| Brehm | • The Application of Social Psychology to Clinical Practice |
| Cattell and Dreger | • Handbook of Modern Personality Theory |
| Endler and Magnusson | • Interactional Psychology and Personality |
| Friedman and Katz | • The Psychology of Depression: Contemporary Theory and Research |
| Kissen | • From Group Dynamics to Group Psychoanalysis: Therapeutic Applications of Group Dynamic Understanding |
| Klopfer and Reed | • Problems in Psychotherapy: An Eclectic Approach |
| Reitan and Davison | • Clinical Neuropsychology: Current Status and Applications |
| Spielberger and Diaz-Guerrero | • Cross-Cultural Anxiety |
| Spielberger and Sarason | • Stress and Anxiety, volume 1 |
| Sarason and Spielberger | • Stress and Anxiety, volume 2 |
| Sarason and Spielberger | • Stress and Anxiety, volume 3 |
| Spielberger and Sarason | • Stress and Anxiety, volume 4 |
| Ulmer | • On the Development of a Token Economy Mental Hospital Treatment Program |

## IN PREPARATION

| | |
|---|---|
| Bermant, Kelman, and Warwick | • The Ethics of Social Intervention |
| Cohen and Mirsky | • Biology and Psychopathology |
| Iscoe, Bloom, and Spielberger | • Community Psychology in Transition |
| Janisse | • A Psychological Survey of Pupillometry |
| London | • Strategies of Personality Research |
| Manschreck and Kleinman | • Critical Rationality in Psychiatry: Quests and Inquiries |
| Olweus | • Aggression in the Schools |

# Handbook of Modern Personality Theory

EDITED BY

**Raymond B. Cattell**

*Professor Emeritus, Department of Psychology*
*University of Illinois*
*and*
*Resident, Department of Psychology*
*University of Hawaii, Honolulu*

**Ralph Mason Dreger**

*Professor, Department of Psychology*
*Louisiana State University*

HEMISPHERE PUBLISHING
CORPORATION

Washington     London

A HALSTED PRESS BOOK

JOHN WILEY & SONS

New York     London     Sydney     Toronto

Hemisphere Publishing Corporation
1025 Vermont Ave., N.W., Washington, D.C. 20005

Distributed solely by Halsted Press, a Division of John Wiley & Sons, Inc., New York.

1 2 3 4 5 6 7 8 9 0    M A M A    7 8 3 2 1 0 9 8 7

**Library of Congress Cataloging in Publication Data**

Main entry under title:

Handbook of modern personality theory.

   (The Series in clinical and community psychology)
   Bibliography: p.
   Includes index.
   1. Personality.  I. Cattell, Raymond Bernard,
1905–    II. Dreger, Ralph Mason.
BF698.H334      155.2      76-22764
ISBN 0–470–15201–X

Printed in the United States of America

# Contents

# Contributors

Thomas W. Bartsch
*Iowa State University, Ames*

Gordon G. Bechtel
*University of Florida, Gainesville*

Charles R. Bolz
*University of Texas, Austin*

P. L. Broadhurst
*University of Birmingham, England*

Donn Byrne
*Purdue University, West Lafayette, Indiana*

Raymond B. Cattell
*University of Hawaii, Honolulu, and Professor Emeritus, University of Illinois, Urbana*

Gerald L. Clore, Jr.
*University of Illinois, Urbana*

Karl H. Delhees
*St. Gall Graduate School of Economics, Business, and Public Administration, St. Gall, Switzerland*

T. E. Dielman
*University of Michigan, Ann Arbor*

Ralph Mason Dreger
*Louisiana State University, Baton Rouge*

Robert F. Drewett
*University of Durham, England*

Jochen Fahrenberg
*Universitaet Freiburg i Br., West Germany*

Richard L. Gorsuch
*University of Texas, Arlington*

Larry R. Goulet
*University of Illinois, Urbana*

Jeffrey A. Gray
*University of Oxford, England*

Wilson H. Guertin
*University of Florida, Gainesville*

S. B. Hammond
*University of Melbourne, Parkville, Victoria, Australia*

Theo Herrmann
*University of Marburg, Germany*

John L. Horn
*University of Denver, Colorado*

Akira Ishikawa
*Kansai University, Osaka, Japan*

Carroll E. Izard
*University of Delaware, Newark*

J. L. Jinks
*University of Birmingham, England*

S. E. Krug
*University of Illinois, Urbana*

John C. Loehlin
*University of Texas, Austin*

Robert E. Lushene
*Veterans Administration Hospital, Bay Pines, Florida*

K. B. Madsen
*Royal Danish School of Educational Studies, Copenhagen, Denmark*

W. George McAdoo
*Indiana University Medical Center, Indianapolis*

John R. Nesselroade
*Pennsylvania State University, University Park*

**Gerald R. Patterson**
*Oregon Research Institute, Eugene*

**K. Warner Schaie**
*University of Southern California,*
*University Park, Los Angeles*

**Klaus R. Schneewind**
*University of Trier, Schneidershof,*
*West Germany*

**Charles D. Spielberger**
*University of South Florida, Tampa*

**Arthur W. Staats**
*University of Hawaii, Honolulu*

**Aiga Stapf**
*University of Marburg, Germany*

**David C. Thompson**
*Consulting Psychologist, Philadelphia,*
*Pennsylvania*

**Lawrence F. Van Egeren**
*Michigan State University, East Lansing*

**Graham M. Vaughan**
*University of Auckland, New Zealand*

**Fredric Weizmann**
*York University, Toronto, Ontario,*
*Canada*

**G. J. S. Wilde**
*Queen's University, Kingston, Ontario,*
*Canada*

# Preface

Fully titled, this book might correctly be described as an *International Handbook of Modern Personality Theory*. It is international because we deliberately sought top authorities wherever they might be and, additionally, aimed at some balance among countries. The regretted omission of the Soviet Union is due in part to the lesser concern with individual-difference psychology there, but more tragically, to the death in an airplane accident of V. C. Nebylitsin, whose brilliant work had led to an agreement for his participation. Professor Gray of Oxford, whose authorship on Russian psychology is substantial, happily reinstates some of the flavor of what we have lost. Otherwise, our sampling indicates the development of psychology in the countries concerned, in Australia, Canada, Denmark, England, Germany, Japan, New Zealand, Switzerland, and the United States, and has the intended international quality.

The justification of the term *modern* requires reference to the historical trends elaborated in Chapter 1, to the effect that personality study has gone through three phases: a few thousand years of acute literary observation; a century or so of deeper but still nonexperimental and rarely quantitative clinical observation; and, roughly in the last 50 years, a phase of truly experimental research. The present *Handbook* has treated the concepts of the clinical phase of psychology as ideas to be checked by experiment or controlled quantitative observation. No chapters will be found of the unsubstantiated wordy kind such as emanate from a speculative basis in many symposia on personality.

At the same time, the experimental quantitative approach is not kept in the straight-jacket of classical, bivariate experiment. Intelligent strategy has long enjoyed the perception that multivariate experimental methods, especially those of flexibly integrated factor analyses, are necessary in handling the total patterns on which conceptions of personality must be based. It is recognized here that there is a time for emphasis on multivariate and a time for emphasis on bivariate experimental methods, the latter often becoming more appropriate when the former has isolated the significant entities—traits, states, processes, etc.—with which bivariate experiment can fruitfully operate. It is to be hoped that the experimental bases and operational definitions of the theoretical concepts in this *Handbook* will suggest, far more richly than usual, those more fertile further experiments to which graduate students and experienced researchers aim to devote themselves.

This volume was planned to be unusual, and possibly unique, in another respect, besides its international quality and strong experimental emphasis. It actually brought virtually all the contributors together, at a 3-day conference at the University of Illinois, to bring about some integration, some communality at least of language, and some attempts at cross reference among those with different viewpoints. It has been a justified reproach against many volumes of symposia that the contributions are held together by nothing but the cardboard binding. Obviously, in such an enterprise as this work, there must be complete freedom on the part of each contributor for the development of ideas. But this freedom is no excuse for private worlds in science. The absence of any fruitful interaction is often dismissed with a shrug as an inevitable feature of the lowly development of our science, compared with, say, chemistry or physics. This false liberalism is no longer tenable in the light of all the careful work that has been done in methodology in psychology in the last 30 years. There *are* applicable standards of experimental design and statistical inference; and to say that insistence on them is a holier-than-thou attitude is a sly evasion of hard work and self-discipline in meeting them. We as editors have tried, in both the original conference and subsequent editing, to strike a reasonably happy balance between the contributor's complete freedom of conclusion and editorial upholding of methodological standards and response to different conclusions by other contributors. We do not claim to have succeeded, but only to have tried. Incidentally, the situation regarding such matters is neatly illustrated in miniature by the recent articles of De Young and Vaughan on standards in factor analysis, wherein it is shown that failure to meet technical standards on which all would agree in a given model is often passed off as a more legitimate choice among alternative models.

The attempts made here to integrate methods and viewpoints is tied up with the training of students. It is unreasonable, as in some symposia, to expect students to resolve total differences of viewpoint and methodological standards that the experienced psychologists concerned have done nothing to resolve. The dearth of sincere attempts to explain the somewhat different methodological judgments involved may be partly responsible for the few students who are prepared, mathematically and statisti-

cally, to pursue higher integrations—despite the great promise for psychology from good technical integrations at the present juncture in our science. We are well aware that the fission of psychologists into a strictly scientific group, as instanced in the Psychonomic Society and the Society for Multivariate Experimental Psychology, and a humanistic group is not entirely a result of the lack of integrations of the sort we have endeavored to achieve. After all, remuneration often is greater in clinical or industrial practice than in academic fields. But this fission exists partly because integrations have not been as frequent as they could be. While not sacrificing scientific rigor, this volume offers something that should appeal to both groups. Aside from a few ultra-behaviorists who want to know nothing about what is in the *black box,* psychologists in both the scientific and humanistic traditions seek to study personality. Even though humanists—and, to be truthful, some experimentalists—may have difficulty with some mathematical concepts and formulas in this book, our authors have written clearly and logically so that their basic methods and contents can be understood by those whose mathematical sophistication does not match the authors'. At the same time, we do not apologize for the mathematical rigor represented herein, for modern personality theory requires it.

The cognoscenti who knew of the undertaking attempted in this volume, and have enquired with some persistence over several years as to when it would appear, could be told an interesting saga of publication problems encountered by the editors. Indeed, Raymond Cattell, who worked on the editing for the first 2 years and was let down by the bankruptcy of one publisher and the fear of bankruptcy by another when he saw the monumental size of the undertaking, came near to giving up and returning chapters to the so-carefully-chosen and diligently working authors. At that point, Ralph Dreger appeared, with fresh spirit, and has carried the project to completion in the face of still-renewed difficulties and the justifiable unrest of the authors. Actually, we would venture to say that the delays forced on the contributing authors and the consequent requirement that they rewrite their chapters to bring them up to date has brought a real gain in the maturation of the theoretical integrations presented. Nevertheless, the choice of authors to meet the catholicity of viewpoint desired, the producing of interaction among them, and the publication problems encountered have frankly made this a decidedly more exacting undertaking than the editors have previously experienced. Fortunately, we can finally thank Hemisphere Publishing Corporation; its consulting editor in psychology, Dr. Charles D. Spielberger; its president, William Begell; its managing editor and assistant editor, Evelyn Walters Pettit and Martha M. Mahuran, for superb cooperation in the final production. And above all, we can thank our authors who have produced and produced again out of the wealth of their expert knowledge a volume that we have reason to hope will stimulate and guide all serious students of psychology for years to come, justifying the vast labors that have gone into the production of the *Handbook of Modern Personality Theory.*

The reader may be guided in the use of this volume by its division into seven sections. The order of the sections implies some designed dependence of later chapters on earlier ones; and the first section particularly, on *Conceptions in Structured Measurement of Personality and Situations,* is probably necessary reading for most students before tackling any of the later sections. Professors in charge of personality, social, and clinical teaching will recognize that some chapters can be assigned to undergraduate reading whereas others belong more to the graduate level. As will be seen, we felt it would be for the readers' greater convenience if the separately provided bibliographies by the various authors were gathered together at the end of the book.

September 1, 1976

**Raymond B. Cattell**
*Honolulu, Hawaii*
**Ralph Mason Dreger**
*Baton Rouge, Louisiana*

# Section 1

## Conceptions in Structured Measurement of Personality and Situations

# 1

# The Grammar of Science and the Evolution of Personality Theory

**Raymond B. Cattell**
*University of Hawaii, Honolulu*

## 1 HISTORICAL TURNING POINT IN PERSONALITY THEORY CONSTRUCTION

For those engaged in research on that most challenging of all scientific problems—the human personality—these are stirring times. Until the turn of the century, personality in any real sense proved too elusive a quarry for our scientific, methodological resources. The inspired clinicians brought some order, but it is only in the last decade that we have begun to see the first dim emergence of genuine structural and functional laws, and the beginning of dependable prediction and control.

There has never been any lack of theories. Indeed, during the earlier casual climate in which exact meaningful measurement and calculation in behavioral science were not available, the exasperating condition prevailed in which a small growth of precise hypotheses tended to be completely lost in a jungle of rank, untestable, grandiose theories. These theories—still taught as academic exercises in many universities, possibly to hide the nakedness of the teachers' minds with respect to methodological muscle or logical elegance—were not necessarily wrong. Freud's original theories, for example, had good scientific syntax and much honesty of empirical reference. The trouble was that in any metric sense, and with respect to any mathematical model, one could not even begin to say whether they were right or wrong. And, as H. J. Eysenck (1960b) well pointed out, the alternative *pragmatic proof* of clinical or other application in regard to most of these theories is so loose as to have no real power.

The clinicians, as well as those acute behavioral observers in the style of W. James (1890) or McDougall (1932), and the innumerable armchair theorists could neither reach consistent conclusions nor make better behavioral predictions than could the man in the street. If an intelligent and sincere psychologist looked anywhere for a firm foundation in that half-century, he probably turned to theorists such as S. Freud (1949), McDougall (1932), or H. A. Murray (1938), who had played the game of theory construction with integrity and with more reverence than most for sheer faithfulness of observation. But the experimentalist recognized that what these theorists offered were makeshift structures, awaiting more precise and sophisticated methodology in research.

3

The experimentalist might well feel, with B. F. Skinner (1950), that it would be better, for both the students' education and the research advance of the subject, not to teach these theories at all. From this unsatisfactory state of affairs, the progressive student naturally began to turn to the canons of experiment. Unfortunately the only kind of experiment that *most* psychologists were aware of 30 years ago or more was classical, brass-instrument experimentation, borrowed without adaptation from the physical sciences by Wundt. It was essentially bivariate, that is, having one dependent and one independent variable. But personality and society are organizations, and the important concepts in organisms and organic wholes are only to be grasped, measured, and manipulated as *whole patterns* of variables. Multivariate experimental design (Cattell, 1966e) was the indispensable new tool developed to get past triviality in many areas of psychology, physiology, and sociology, as is documented here. While this lesson was being learned, journals were filled *ad nauseam* with experiments with highly particular and narrow variables, innumerable as the sands of the sea, which no one ever used again in the same way. Consequently, these studies offered no architectonic growth. This vast output was never digested.

Had the experimenters first used such a multivariate method as factor analysis to reach the underlying functional unities as, say, in fluid and crystallized intelligence, or the primary ergs, or anxiety, or the seven varieties of depression, subsequent manipulative and bivariate approaches using these factors could have moved ahead on a manageable number of variables to integratable results. Closely allied to this lack of perspective—this drowning of vistaed personality theory in preoccupation with in-numerable trivial and arbitrary operations—there persisted a naive ignoring of the scientific principle that taxonomy—description and measurement—must precede search for kinetic or dynamic laws (just as the single well-focused photograph frame must precede any attempt at a meaningful movie). The result was—and alas in many journals still is—a desolate scene consisting of an endless horizon of abandoned one-story shacks, where good training in multivariate experiments might by now, through programmatic research, have yielded the architectonic growth of a tall city of coherent theory. The beginning of that city can be seen in the work of many contributors to this volume—but, alas, quite a number of the theoretical links here remain unestablished because of this lag. They are frankly checks drawn on the future growth of such empirical research.

With the aspiration of stimulating more research that will maintain perspective, vision, and a methodology consistent with developing integration, this opening chapter grapples with basic problems of method and theory. It sets out (a) to define the nature of theory, (b) to ask how the inevitable scientific path of trial and error can be shortened by methods more quickly capable of revealing the potential *fit* of hypotheses, (c) to develop a working model—the vector-id-analysis (VIDA) model—which promises to offer broad-purpose approximation toward specific theories of closer fit (at least, it may prove a useful first vehicle in the pursuit of much personality research), (d) to show how personality theory can be kept in fruitful orientation to learning theory and to physiological and social psychology on its other frontiers and (e) to point briefly to contributions in this volume that illustrate progress along these lines.

## 2  NATURE OF THEORIES AND MODELS

It used to be said that the moment a scientist mentioned his favorite theory, in a company of pure philosophers of science, he was in dialectical trouble. Some of the greatest investigators in history intuitively decided to ignore the philosophers. Fortunately, for the rest, the excesses of pedantry passed in the early part of the century, and most psychologists now have a reasonable schooling in the logic and principles of method. Consequently, the long digression on the meaning of theory construction, which only a few years ago would have been necessary at this point, can be cut to one brief section.

A *theory* may be defined as an integrated set of explicit definitions and explanations. It satisfies the conditions of (a) maintaining internal, syntactical, and logical consistency; (b) bringing about external consistency, in that it bridges more than one set of data, introducing a single coherent explanatory framework; and (c) permitting deduction and extrapolation to several new testable hypotheses, applicable to as yet uninvestigated phenomena. Clause (b) is the chief means of differentiating a theory from a hypothesis, the latter being in one sense, a *little* theory, offering an explanation or mechanism for connections observed in a limited, special area and with only limited penetration to roots in postulates. A *postulate* is an assumption defining some basic element of a theory, and since it is considered self-evident, is not to be put on trial by experiment. Yet a postulate can ultimately fail and be dismissed if enough theories that contain it fail so that it is not fundamentally, but only in degree and temporary status, different from a hypothesis. The relation of *laws* to theory is that they constitute the external consistencies referred to previously, in (b) and in the predictions in (c). However, laws, which begin by being descriptive (e.g., mathematical laws), often come to involve causal "explanation." Nevertheless, as description, they usually come into existence before the theory and are likely to last after it is demolished.

Even in the preceding framework of definition, quite genuine theories may yet show considerable diversity. In the *Handbook of Multivariate Experimental Psychology,* I attempted to set out the dimensions along which a taxonomy for classifying theories could be begun (Cattell, 1966e). These are reproduced with some development in the following list:

1. Precise model vs. purely verbal formulation.
2. Local *construct* properties vs. imported metaphorical properties.
3. Few areas connected vs. many areas integrated.
4. Low complexity vs. high intricacy of formulation.
5. Mathematical starkness vs. physical enrichment of model.
6. Few deductions possible vs. many deductions possible.
7. High consistency achieved vs. poor consistency achieved.

Discussion of the first of these dimensions immediately requires one to distinguish between a theory and a model. A *theory* may have nothing but verbal elements, but a *model* must have some form of algebraic, geometric, mechanical, or familiar organic representation. Although there is currently much discussion of mathematical models, this should not mislead anyone into assuming that all models are mathematical. It suffices that a model is a pattern in part or in whole imported from some other area of scientific observation where it is already more fully understood and known to work reliably as a correct logical representation and explanation. For example, a theory of light borrows from wave motion known in water; a model of the atom, from our solar system; a model of intelligence (Spearman, 1927), from the physicist's concept of energy; a model of trial and error learning, from the digital computer; and a model of human motivation (the dynamic lattice), from a hydraulic system or from conductivity in electrical networks.

In each case an analogy or metaphor is used, implying thereby various degrees of importation from another area. This brings us to discussion of the second dimension of theory in the preceding list. Always some degree of *stripping down* naturally takes place in the process of borrowing. Thus, the wave theory of light has no use for the tang of salt water, or even for recognizing surface-tension phenomena; Spearman's *g* as energy did not propose to use the second law of thermodynamics; the use of the digital computer model in learning may not be tied to the usual binary computer system; and the hydrodynamic model in the dynamic lattice has no use for the density of the fluid. Any such stripping down is apt to be in the direction of mathematization of the model, because mathematics is the most universal of abstractive systems. But at some point it is always possible that a nonmathematical feature of an organic model, that is, a model of *organs* or *elements* from some natural source, carries an indispensable local meaning and should not be trimmed to utter abstractness.

Any theory has two main points: (a) Its *internal logic* or syntax is rooted in definitions by which its internal consistency is to be judged. The judgment of consistency can be made on a purely logical basis, in terms of the system of words or symbols. (b) Its *representational* or *semantic part* has to do with the translation of its symbols into phenomenal objects and processes through which its empirical fit is checked (Woodger, 1939). Incidentally, in this analysis of a theory, one might question the need for the seventh dimension in the list, *consistency achieved*, on the ground that the "degree of internal, syntactical consistency" at least should be assumed *always* to be adequate—as the following of algebraic rules in our formulae is always taken for granted. However, though one might thus argue that without this property it is not seriously worth considering a proposition as a theory, the existing theories can be ranked on the degree to which consistency is attained.

Consideration of the second aspect of consistency—the *semantic step*, from symbols to phenomena—should remind us that the pure mathematical model (necessarily sound in syntax) is likely to omit some features of any model that are important in testing against a full-bodied *reality* and are more likely to be retained in the organic model. For example, there is no such thing as causality in mathematics—only dependent and independent variables, disregarding any time sequence. To all this particular kind of extra *body* to a mathematical model (which most scientists intuitively desire), it is necessary to bring in a special analysis with respect to a time variable. (A good discussion of causality for psychologists is offered by Krause, M. S., 1971.) Similarly we may have to say, in some mathematical models (e.g., in psychophysics), that a certain variable in an electromagnetic wavelength (angstrom units) means color—and there is no color per se in mathematics. Thus, the model is commonly (and to a high degree if mathematical) lacking in complete sufficiency, but requires an appreciable subsystem of *semantic enlargements*. Similarly, when the schoolboy finishes his high school algebra example, he must remember whether $n$ is cows or apples, or whether the process of division meant sharing or scaling; the same holds more complexly for most models. When a philosopher of method like Lachman (1960) describes a model as (a) representational, (b) inferential, (c) interpretive, or (d) pictorial, we are reminded of the degrees to which these various uses are served by the *importation* in our second dimension.

Reverting for a moment to the first dimension of a theory—the extent to which it is represented to a precise model—let us note that the application of this yardstick is one of the quickest ways of detecting bogus theorizing. Not that a merely, and purely, *verbal* theory need be a sham. But that profuse growth of theories of personality that, as previously argued, proved a great obstacle to real theory development during the first half of this century, certainly contained hundreds of specious and merely literary products bankrupt in syntactical consistency and quantitative prediction.

Dimension 2—from *local construct* to *imported metaphor* properties—has already been briefly introduced, but is so important as to deserve expansion. The degree of dependence on imported as opposed to locally generated properties has to do with the continuum from empirical constructs (or intervening variables, in terms of MacCorquodale and Meehl,[1] 1948), to theoreti-

[1] Parenthetically, what they and several other writers apparently mean by "fact finding" is what actually should strictly be called the finding of *relations* and empirical laws, and even the development of *empirical constructs*. Here we have sought to contrast those constructs with facts as *fundaments*.

cal concepts. It can be noted as an aside that this is also a component in the transition from description to explanation. Description involves property concepts close to the data. Explanation, which is either (a) *causal* (having to do with a process) or (b) *structural* (explaining by reference to wider structural concepts), explains the concrete in terms of more broadly applicable causal and structural laws.

Since the use of *construct* and *concept* is currently in some confusion, their specific use to define a necessary continuum here requires a pause for definition. A *construct* is definable in the *immediate* relations given in the data phenomena, by inductive reasoning. A construct of two *types* of dots—round dots and oval dots—might arise from looking at a page of dots. A construct of *fuse* might arise from seeing several explosions, each preceded by a sputtering cord. A concept is on the same continuum with a construct, but they lie at opposite ends. It is an abstraction—which may be illustrated by *energy, capitalism, evolution,* or *electron*—bringing together and integrating constructs from several fields, and resting on the reliability of several logical processes used in its formation.

Oversimplified references to the construct-concept dimension grossly as a *dichotomy,* in which constructs have been described as complexes of relationships *immediately given* have evoked protests from the philosophers that even in saying A is above B, or C is a longer sort of thing than D, *some* importation (Herbart's apperception masses) occurs as in every human perception (i.e., inductive derivation of a construct always involves some extrainductive elements carried over by human habits of thought). This is true; but the degree of importation is important. The construct-concept issue also gets tied up with the realism-idealism question of whether regularities—laws—exist in nature or only in the scientist's head. Many a scientist believes the former (.e.g, Hogben, L. 1937), "The world view of science is not a by-product of human cerebration. The mountains and the valleys remain, regardless or whether we use (on our map) a new color scale to paint in the altitudes." Laws and models are admittedly in the mind of man; but unless we swallow Berkeley whole and unmodified, the relationships to which our law is an approximation exist as predictors in the real world.

The meaning of the *construct-concept* dimension may be illustrated in psychology by the progress which a construct makes— with added experiment and reasoning— toward a concept. In personality description, the experimentally obtained simple structure factor indexed as $C$ in $Q$ data (e.g., in the 16 Personality Factor [16 PF] or High School Personality Questionnaire [HSPQ] scales) leads to a description of $C$ as an *empirical construct*. This is done by abstracting inductively what is common to the highly loaded variables (and absent from the unloaded). The resultant source trait has behavioral features matching such notions as emotional stability or frustration tolerance. However, we now have a scale of definite validity for $C$, and with this a variety of relations can be sought in quite different fields. Thus from the relations to such criteria as neuroticism, delinquency, response to drug action, and so forth, one proceeds to the concept of *ego strength,* enriched further in terms of the dynamic lattice (see Gorsuch and Cattell, chapter 29). At that point, one reaches the full-fledged *theoretical concept* level, with such imported meanings as go with the general notions of inhibition, maximization of erotic satisfaction, subsidiation of motives, and the *hydraulic analogy* in the dynamic lattice. The meaning is enriched and becomes capable of leading to more

deductive checks in experiment. But, at the same time, there is a risk of misleading speculativeness, if, in broadening it, we have unfortunately imported not *extra meaning* but *surplus meaning*, that is, meanings not checked or checkable empirically in the areas from which they are derived (e.g., the trailing clouds of vague implication that came with the clinical notion of ego strength). Such importation of surplus meaning, along with the importation of checked and definite meanings (like scorpions in a shipload of bananas) is a danger to be set against the increasing *interest* of the enriched concept. The present writer's claim (Cattell, 1973a) that the term *construct validity* is better called *concept validity* should be seen in the light of the preceding.

Elsewhere (Cattell, 1966e, chapter 1), I have made, the point that the prestige and luxury of living on imported intellectual goods has led many psychologists (but not disciplined thinkers such as Burt, Hull, Skinner, and Thurstone) to speculative and even grandiose explanatory models where a modest empirical construct, close to the data, would have served steady scientific advance better. The latter has been particularly evident in the good levels of shrewdness shown by factorists in the interpretation of many new empirical personality factors. It shows again in the use of Cortertia, and of Activation (in relation to sentiment-structure factors) in preference to Arousal. The psychologist is reminded of the kind of increasing *distance* likely to occur in borrowing by the schematization in Fig. 1. If the importation succeeds, it may well enrich the developing concept, but the chances of failure of fit are certainly greater and more insidious than when using an empirical construct.

The next major dimension among theories concerns their breadth, that is, the number of data areas each attempts to

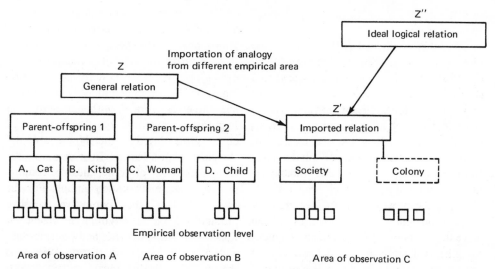

**FIG. 1.** Distance of importation in relation to the continuum from empirical construct to theoretical concept.

interconnect. This needs no explanation, though it would demand some discussion to advance its precise operational definition. Often this is referred to as the *importance* of a theory in the sense that in a theory like Einstein's, the tying together of such seemingly remote observations as those in the Michelson-Morley experiment, in the behavior of the planet Mercury, and in the energy developed by an atom bomb, is more *important* than one dealing solely with, say, the structure of chromosomes or the viscosity of fluids. Another way of defining this is in terms of the *negotiability* of a model, that is, How far are its terms and concepts acceptable as possible formulations across fields that were formerly sustained by local theories only? The multivariate character in the main theoretical framework suggested for personality in the present chapter is an illustration of an attempt at high breadth.

Dimension 4, *intricacy* or *complexity*, is self-explanatory. Although both by *Occam's razor* and Newton's *Natura est simplex*, a simpler theory is always preferred, we must

never forget that what we are after is the minimum complexity necessary to fit the facts—and in this necessary complexity, theories will vary appreciable. For example, the trait-view theory, the scale-vulnerability concept, and the instrument-factor concept introduced to explain questionnaire distortion (chapter 7, this book) are perhaps more difficult in their abstractness than is the simple *patching* of questionnaire interpretation by addition of notions of acquiescence, response styles, or social-desirability sets; but its wider negotiability, for example, simultaneously to ratings and questionnaires, and the goodness of fit to calculations recommend it over the coarser local models.

The last among the dimensions of theory that we need to consider is the dimension of *starkness*, diminishing as one goes from purely mathematical models toward more enriched organic models with features not definable in mathematics alone. This should never be confused with Dimension 1, from *precision* to *vagueness*, for a model at the *enriched* pole of Dimension 5 can be quite precise despite its not being stripped down to mathematics.

The inherent characteristics or structural basis of a theory or model analyzed (a) by the taxonomy of theories just studied and (b) by its functional or historical status, are two different things. Its potency and survival value in terms of inherent adequacy of fit, parsimony in handling the events studied, power of predicting remote phenomena, fruitfulness in producing new testable influences and guiding research, and even its plain popularity with students, depend only in part on the essential qualities in the preceding taxonomy. What actually happens to a theory historically, as Meissner (1961) and others pointed out, depends also on (a) its relation to historical environment, (b) the relative emphases by particular researchers with respect to use as a summarizing device, or as a philosophical formalizing of concepts, or as a heuristic stimulant and aid to research. And, in small communities, one must add (c) the emotional prejudices of established individuals! The fate of a theory is in the end related not only to its inherent characteristics, but the relation is complex and greatly determined in transit by socio-historical circumstances.

## 3 FUNCTIONS OF THEORY

After the general character of theory has been focused, there still remains the different problem of understanding how it actually gets used in research. How does any theory function in the strategy of research and in the climate of science as a social activity? Between the schemata of ideal steps as seen by the analytical philosopher of method, and the actual maelstrom of scientific trends as examined later by the social psychologist or historian, there are discrepancies that strain one's credulity.

Before examining those discrepancies, let us squarely accept the conclusion of a philosopher of method, Camilleri (1962): "The primary function of the scientist is to develop verified systematic theory." Surveying facts, performing crucial experiments, trial-and-error forays with concepts and hypotheses—these are but the craftsman's chores either loved or merely tolerated, by the participant scientist. Their aim is finally the production of a dependable comprehensive scheme for understanding. For the true scientist, the impressive finished product (as far as anything in science is finished) is the systematic body of smoothly and potently operating theory. Science *is* theory. The theory must contain a systematic *understanding*, permitting both prediction and dependable manipulation, and producing for society rewarding social technological application. (History may decide if the phrase "Science is theory" is sufficiently explained as an extreme manifestation in the infant science of psychology of a tendency [recognized at all times and in all sciences by the experienced more than the young], for those who find they have no flair for the tasks of actual research to write books on method and philosophy. It is certainly not the great figures in literature who set up academies offering the secrets of how to write successful novels and plays; in science, as a great discoverer has recently said, the procedures of successful research seldom follow the respectable textbook accounts given by the sideline philosophers of scientific method. The student who rightly feels that it is nevertheless important to appreciate the role of theory in the research process must thus be warned that among many genuine hints by experienced researchers on theory construction and experimental design, he will find much by scholarly sophists and pundits who are more concerned with sporting the socially approved livery of theory than with serving actual discovery.)

Between this true vision of theory as the queen of science, and the view of theory entertained by the contemporary social academic jet set, there is often sharp discord. Currently in psychology, for instance, several serious, outstanding psychologists (e.g., B. F. Skinner) have become critics of theory per se. The critics of too much self-conscious attention to methodology and philosophy of science point to degeneration of active research into scholarly posturing, humbug, and the prostitution of true scholarly aims to sophistry. The result has been that—except for those looking for material to occupy courses—courses on pure theory have come to be mistrusted.

Where is the touchstone by which a beginner can distinguish the gold from the pretentious pinchbeck of overelaborate theoretical systems? One brutal and academically disliked test is to ask to be shown the effective body of *technological* application corresponding to the theory. For men can agree on potency and economic usefulness, even when they cannot always discern theoretical truth in the abstract. The inescapable fact is that a true theory, as opposed to humbug, has technological potency, though it stay only potential for many years. At the close of the 19th century the volumes of psychological theory occupied at least as many feet of library shelf as those of chemical theory; but the technological gifts to society of our own science, in, say, the clinical control of mental disease, in substantially increasing the efficiency of years spent in school, and in eliminating such social diseases as war and crime, were practically invisible, compared with the useful products from the study of chemistry. Even a decade ago, if one examined what learning theory and personality theory had given to, say, school and clinic (that was new

and effective relative to what had been practiced in their absence), the only decent reaction was to blush at having discussed *theory* in the presence of other scientists.

Any oversimplified and heavily touted theory not only blocks alternative formulations in thought (more than if there were no theory at all), but it also strongly biases us in favor of selective, limited perception. For this reason it has been found a good laboratory pragmatic rule that any relation a researcher finds when *not* looking for it, as a prop to a theory, is likely to be more powerful and significant in the long run than one which he quotes as statistically supporting (at the $P < .05$ level) the theory he is interested in.

A special problem—not in *theory* itself but in *theorists*—arises from the fact that much science has to live in competitive socioacademic climates, whereby discussion of theory falls into what might be called the *jousting paradigm*. By this is meant that a tremendous investment of time and energy becomes funneled—when the socioscientific situation is simply that of two opposed theories—into a direct dialectic between these alternatives. Meanwhile, truth is often lying neglected on the ground, as a third and quite different alternative. The process of scientific investigation has features, on the one hand, of a detective in a court of law and, on the other, of the lonely explorer. When two theories battle in the courtroom, the ancient legalistic game of *guilty* versus *not guilty* prevails over the more tentative and sensitive spirit of exploration. Admittedly, there *is* a time, quite late in the process of a scientific investigation (once the mysterious influence has been caught and put in the dock by the detective), for such legalistic right-or-wrong examination. But the detective and the explorer, deftly balancing in their imaginations many alternative hypotheses, and free of the straitjacket of one pair of alternatives, offer, in general, better ideals of performance for the scientist than does the lawyer.

While seeking to look at the total situation of theories in science with an experienced eye, let us beware of the academic tendency to take the discussion of theory construction too far away from concrete, living research interests. There occurs epidemically in psychology departments, when naiveties of research design are previously exposed, a plan to correct this tendency by special courses on method and the philosophy of science. This does not get done in close association with the real problems of students, but as an abstract philosophy course. It has well been said that one cannot legislate morality; similarly, the philosophy and laws of method, remote from the concrete problems and opportunities of a scientific area, are no substitute for natural intelligence and scientific flair in the individual investigator. Such academic approaches are wasteful, probably for just the same reason that the alienation of statistical courses for psychologists, agriculturists, and economists from the special needs of their own departments has been, mainly, a loss (although, in this example, the existence of a common abstract basis in mathematics is at least sound and certain, which cannot be said of many abstract treatments of the so-called scientific *process*).

The preceding apparent digression into disorders of theory is surely justified by the infant vulnerability existing in the demonstrably immature phase of psychological theorizing in which we live. Some analysis of this problem has at any rate, been voted salutary and prophylactic by many of my students during their exposure to what purports to be theory. A remaining aspect of the theory problem—a possible intoxication

with models, even genuine models, for the sake of models—is discussed in section 5 of this chapter. Meanwhile, these appeals for a more sophisticated and even suspicious approach to the role of theory ought not to detract one iota from the recognition of sound theory construction as the heart of science.

## 4  NATURE OF EXPERIMENTAL DESIGNS

With these forewarnings and historical perspectives, let us now proceed to a brief résumé of the essential relations of theory to experiment, in the total research process—and, ultimately, as it concerns our topic, personality.

The topic of a taxonomy of experiment itself has been treated more fully elsewhere (Cattell, 1966e; Marx & Hillix, 1963), but with the help of a few diagrams and tables, the main issues can be clarified here. *Theory* has already been defined. An *experiment*—to which theory now needs relating—may in turn be defined as *a recording of observations (quantitative or qualitative) made by defined and reported operations, and in defined conditions, followed by an analytical examination of the data, by appropriate mathematical and statistical rules, for the existence of significant relations* (Cattell, 1966e).

Experiment so defined will have the dimensions shown in Table 1. It will be noted that the classical bivariate *brass instrument* experiment covers only one-quarter of the possible types of experiment, namely, those that are *bivariate* rather than *multivariate* (Dimension 1), and that are also interfering or *manipulative* rather than *freely occurring* (Dimension 2). As shown elsewhere (Cattell, 1966e) these dimensions

**TABLE 1** Six basic dimensions of experimental design

| No. | Symbol for dimension | Parameter title | Polar dichotomy | Polar notation |
|-----|-----|-----|-----|-----|
| 1. | N | Number of variables | Multivariate to bivariate | m–b |
| 2. | M | Manipulation | Interfered with (manipulated) to freely occurring | i–f |
| 3. | T | Time relation | Dated to simultaneous observation | d–s |
| 4. | C | Situational control | Controlled (held constant) to uncontrolled | c–u |
| 5. | R | Representativeness of relatives (choice of variables) | Abstractive to representative | a–r |
| 6. | D | Distribution of referees (population sampling) | Keyed to a biased sample (selected or "unrepresentative") to normal or true | k–n |

lead, by possible combinations, to a taxonomy of 29 viable distinct *types* of experiment (dropping some nonviable combinations), each with its appropriate advantages and fitnesses. In terms of theory building, an important difference in experimental designs lies in their relative potency for (a) theory (or hypothesis) *creation* as distinguished from (b) theory (or hypothesis) *testing*. In regard to creation, the advantage lies undoubtedly with multivariate designs, because of their capacity to present comprehensively total *patterns* of covariation, richer and more suggestive of well-born theories than is a mere difference of means on one or two variables. In regard to other aspects, such as testing hypotheses, the advantages are more evenly distributed. To these issues we can return in a moment when discussing the forms of mathematical-statistical analysis to be applied to the data gathered.

If the relation of theory to experiment is to be seen in true perspective, it is important that we abandon what is a misleading philosophy-of-science term for scientific investigation: namely, the *hypothetic-deductive method*. Admittedly we are being radical in asserting that a term more accurately descriptive of the essentials of what actually occurs is the *inductive-hypothetico-deductive* (IHD) method. For the former wrongly suggests that the hypothesis magically springs from nowhere, whereas in fact—unless we are dealing with psychotic illusions—it is reached by more or less intensive and organized induction from experience of data (or by borrowing from someone else's experience). The process of research is actually a *spiral* of experimental observation (or observations leaning upon experience), followed by analysis, followed by exploratory thinking (deductive in character), and followed by planned experiment, as summarized in Fig. 2.

Much debate usually ensues among philosophers around the IHD generation of theory. In the cause of brevity, we must bypass it to consider the next aspect of taxonomy: analysis of data. Analysis and data-gathering designs are, of course, closely mutually linked, and both are guided by the theory. Nevertheless, there are degrees of

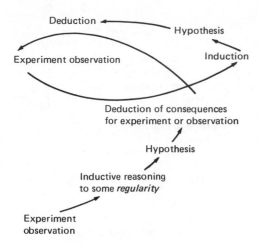

**FIG. 2.** The inductive-hypothetico-deductive spiral in theory building.

*B* Built-in complexity of model; *j*, jejune, to *h*, high-structuring.

*S* Number of simultaneous relationships; *o*, one only, to *g*, general or group.

*I* Information utilization; *p*, plenary, to *l*, limited.

Next are presented the types that can be formed by combining the poles from a dichotomizing of those dimensions.

| | |
|---|---|
| 1. *ejop* | 9. *vjop* |
| 2. *ejol* | 10. *vjol* |
| 3. *ejgp* | 11. *vjgp* |
| 4. *ejgl* | 12. *vjgl* |
| 5. *ehop* | 13. *vhop* |
| 6. *ehol* | 14. *vhol* |
| 7. *ehgp* | 15. *vhgp* |
| 8. *ehgl* | 16. *vhgl* |

The dimension of *built in complexity of model directly statistically examined* is an important one, separating for example, the results of a significance test by analysis of variance (ANOVA), dealing with an hypothesized simple *difference of means*, from a statistical test by factor analysis of a hypothesis that (a) a certain number of factors exist, (b) each is defined by a certain loading pattern, (c) that mutual correlations exist among them according to a defined matrix, and (d) that a certain superstructure of higher strata factors exists. The remaining analysis dimensions must be followed up elsewhere (Cattell, 1966e).

Having defined these parts of an overall investigation—the *theory* (with its expression in a relational system) followed by the *experiment* and the *analysis*—we can indicate in Fig. 3 how they are commonly brought together in the total research process.

One must not forget, in fitting Fig. 3 to any known investigation, that the term *theory* has the wide range of reference previously listed. At one extreme it could be

independence. For example, much data gathered for investigation by correlation of the significance of some predefined relation can be alternatively reexamined by analysis of variance. (One often prefers the correlational approach because it conveys more readily the *magnitude* of the relation, over and above its statistical *significance*.) Incidentally, the beginning student should be warned that through some narrow parochialism of thought, books are occasionally titled *The Design of Experiment* when, in fact, they are restricted entirely to designs using analysis of variance. Experiment in the comprehensive sense defined earlier is susceptible—whether it be bivariate or multivariate, manipulative or noninterfering—to analysis by either mean difference or correlational methods.

There are 16 main types of mathematico-statistical methods of data treatment. First, dimensions of analysis are set out here in four major dimensions.

*E* Extent of measurement, property assumptions (*power*); *e*, extended, to *v*, vacant.

nothing more than the scientist's assumption that "significant, lawful relations exist in this data," together, perhaps, with a hunch about which relations to analyze first. In this sense it may be true that "one *always* has a theory," but often the theory is scarcely more than "this is a curious bit of Nature in which I expect any explorations to reveal some order." The remaining feature, that is, other than the self-evident ones, to be explained in Fig. 3 is that of the *relational system*.

This concerns simply the kinds of relations that could exist among data, and concerning which evidence is to be collected. These relations must suffice to cover what is asked about in the theory, but otherwise they are free to be examined by whatever experimental design and analysis methods one has chosen to use. The act of defining the relational system aims only to set out systematically the possible relations which, as it were, exist passively in the data, waiting to be examined, as the planes of cleavage exist in a crystalline mass, to be opened up if desired. As Fig. 3 shows, any theory points

to the relationships in data which need to be selected from among the totality of possible relations, to express and test that particular theory. Concerning these choices of relations and the possible total of relationships for which they can be taken, some further comments are offered in the next section.

## 5 CHOICE OF VIABLE MODELS

From psychological theory in general, now that certain essentials have been defined, let us focus on personality theory. If there is any region on which the general advance of theory in all branches of psychology depends, more than on any other, it is surely the concept of personality. The undeniable fact is that human behavior—response in any form from perception to learning or decision making—is made by a *person*, that is, by the total organism. Any of those processes which we sometimes prefer to study in the abstract, such as perception, memory, learning, or conflict, is, in fact, bound to be in some degree also a

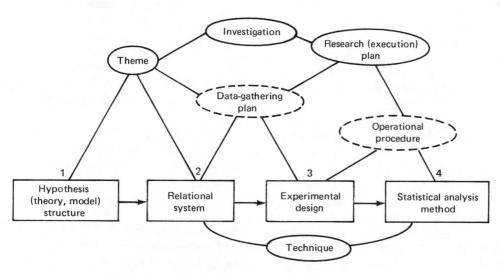

**FIG. 3.** Analysis of parts and aspects of a total investigation.

manifestation of personality. It is surely likely that these isolated forms of behavior are ultimately to be understood only in terms of laws governing the action of organisms as a whole.

Consequently, it is extremely important that theory in personality should have the best properties of theory as such, and be couched in exact models. But this is precisely what the vague, pretentious, but debilitated stuff called *personality theory* over the first half of this century has lacked and why good students have preferred to avoid it for such areas as perception, physiological psychology, learning, or psychometrics. Let us reconsider the three main historical phases of personality theory (Cattell, 1964b). In Phase One, extending from the beginnings of culture into the 18th and 19th centuries, formulation was permeated by a style of observation and generalization about human nature which may best be described as the *folklore and literary* phase. The accompanying insights, at their best, in, say, Shakespeare, Goethe, Voltaire, or Dostoyevsky, were extremely penetrating, but such study obviously never met the requirements of a science.

Following and overlapping with this phase, there developed a more self-conscious and scientifically organized *clinical* phase, with roots in ancient Greece, but beginning experimentally with Renaissance medicine. In medicine, clinical psychology did not grow to the limits of its powers as a research method until as late as the 19th century, with the work of Kraepelin, Charcot, Janet, and Freud. This was scientific in intent, deterministic in philosophy, and conceptually disciplined. But quantitative assessment and controlled experiment—even in the broader sense—were foreign to it. Personality data inevitably were biased toward the pathological, while statistical analysis and mathematical models to handle data were virtually unknown in its methodological treatments.

Somewhere between 1920 and 1940, the momentum of the clinical methodological phase passed its peak, and we entered on the third stage of theory development, now in its early and vigorous youth. Therein experiment and quantification are central requirements, and ever more sophisticated mathematico-statistical analyses and models are being introduced for theoretical explanation. Our concern in this book is definitely with this third phase, and our immediate questions here concern the ways in which the creation and use of models can best be pursued therein.

Now, although these pages have urged the handling of theory by precise models, let us heed the old saying that it is possible to have too much of a good thing. An excess of fertility is, indeed, the disease one most quickly encounters in models. The number of combinatory variations on the theme of even a minor model, considered merely as a set of fundaments and relations applicable to data in even a narrow field, is immense. Models are, indeed, potentially infinite; for those who like intellectual parlor games, model making need never stop. It can and does easily become an addiction, and it offers an ivory tower of escape from the vicissitudes and stubborn intractability of fitting theory into actual research. It is little wonder that there are many young psychologists eager to hang out the shingle of a theoretician and professional model maker. But what offers a prospect of perpetual employment to the methodologist and philosopher of science constitutes a nightmare of distraction to the genuinely active research scientist.

The abuses and diseases that might afflict model making are already familiar to anyone who has witnessed three or four decades of students let loose in the more abstract courses of mathematico-statistical methods—a field similar to but smaller than models. Psychology as a science desperately needs capable statisticians, but it seems an especially difficult integrative task for a student to learn to combine statistical know-how with a real liking for the developing ideas in psychology itself. Quite frequently a teacher has the painful experience of coaxing the student to climb the high ridge of psychologically based statistics only to see him slide down the other side, into pure mathematical statistics.

But more disturbing in its total effect on psychology than the loss of those able students who go over the hill is the loss of balance among those students who stay precariously on the hilltop. Every year many statistically ingenious papers appear that, from a *psychological* standpoint, can only be regarded as marvels of perverted ingenuity. Comparisons are odious; but as a concrete illustration, one may question how far some applications of canonical correlations and multiple discriminant functions are useful to theory development as distinct from calculations in applied psychology. Another loss of balance is seen in the compulsive statistician who does not realize that research there is a time for quick approximate procedures and another time for the highest accuracy.

One thing is certain: Out of this potentially infinite flock of models, only an extremely small minority will eventually survive as offering a fit to facts, whereas most will only have distracted theory with wild-goose chases. The problem is thus one of controlling the population explosion of diverse mutations by seeking to evaluate somehow in advance which of them has a reasonable chance of being applicable. Although the principle is undeniable that no psychologist should be restrained from arguing for any invented model whatever that takes his fancy, we are concerned to get the most fruitful results for man-hours of effort and the community's precious dollars of expenditure for research. And this can perhaps only be assured by the investigator's being steeped in the data. Thus if no miraculous new process for anticipating success gets created, we must depend on the old standbys of science: (a) The model must first have internal consistency and (b) it will probably be more viable if created by a scientist with a previously demonstrated flair for intuiting successful models, and on a basis of deep experience in the given area.

Although one may seem to belabor this last point, the importance of what I have elsewhere called "love of the data" or "attachment to the field" can scarcely be overemphasized. It means a dedicated and reverential attachment to what nature is offering to teach, as opposed to a roughshod attempt at exploitation for applied purposes, or an infatuation with one's subjective notions of how things ought to be. There is a tremendous range of individual difference among those in research with respect to this dimension, and one would hope that its effects will soon be better studied in the psychology of research and applied in the selection of researchers. There are undoubtedly some investigators who sensitively and penetratingly watch and listen to nature, to see what she is trying to tell them; and there are others who meet her, as it were, with arbitrary legal documents that she is requested immediately to sign. Darwin is a fine example of the first and perhaps Metchnikoff (and many lesser men such as Watson) of the second. In psychology, I think Thurstone, though he would give way to no man in interest in clear models, was a good example of the first. If I must choose an example from Thurstone's field of something that is dangerously close to the second, I would point to the subjectivity of *facet theory*. A grander but less perceived example, because it is so familiar a part of the scenery, is the classical learning theorists' determination to apply the rigid model of reflexology to forms of emotional integration learning which require other concepts.

One has the hunch that the willingness to listen to nature and learn comes basically from love and wonder about the natural phenomena themselves, such as the astronomer shows in his delights in the universe before his telescope, the botanist in his living plants, the geologist in his rocks, and so on. In any case, there seems little doubt that it is this appreciation and respect for the data that is fundamentally what leads to an early and sensitive adaptation of models to the indications in the data rather than to an endless mechanical trial-and-error substitution of profusely subjectively manufactured models. But there is probably also some indefinable flair that enables one man to anticipate that some cherished mathematical model will never do, while his more heavy-handed colleague persists without intuition of a misfit.

A history of psychology could aptly illustrate these two different philosophies within the domain of, for example, factor analysis, which actually was developed by psychologists in response to the crying needs of their data. This development occurred independently of its—partly prior, partly subsequent—development by mathematicians. Although one is happy to recognize ways in which it has benefited from being put in order by the mathematician, one is also painfully aware that what the mathematician considers the central features and character of the model are quite different from the forms that the psychologist finds vitally important. Indeed, among those psychologists who were more eager for the prestige of the mathematicians than the elucidation of psychological structure, the model has at times been subject to barbarous "simplifications," such as the substitution of components for factors, of orthogonal for oblique factors, and of image analysis in place of a due respect for a naturalistic (personality scheme) concept of a population of variables. What the mathematician considers elegant and what the psychologist sees as a beautiful fit to the nature of personality are certainly two different things.

However, over and above these subtle value systems that sometimes belong almost to the personality of the researcher (though also acquired by particular apprenticeships and experience), there must surely be some instantly cognitively applicable acquired principles that will help select models. The most logical of these would be to reduce the infinity of models by some objective *taxonomy* to a manageable dozen or so alternatives. Then, in any field of research, one could quickly give a trial to each of the dozen types of types, ultimately going to further elaboration in the most promising category. Such a taxonomic survey is considered in essence in Madsen's chapter at the end of this book and is discussed a little further here.

Meanwhile, one must not forget the first proposition of all—that a model should have the outer properties and the internal consistencies of a good model as such. Several criteria have been suggested for improving the sheer quality of models as models, by such leading writers as Feigl and Brodbeck (1953), Cohen and Nagel (1934), Marx and Hillix (1963), Woodger (1939), and many others. Notably, one thinks of Woodger's requirement of eliminating disunity by attention to syntax. This alone would enormously reduce the existing plethora of models. Perhaps one could insist also on certain further restrictive standards such as restricting only to *quantitative* models, or models that suggest from the beginning that they will intrinsically be applicable simultaneously across all areas of personality study.

A point often overlooked is that substantial gains, both in new ideas and in eliminating undesirables, are obtainable from considering, before theory construction, the *actual relations* available to express the theory in the Data Box itself (appendix 1, Fig. 4). That is to say, one looks at the totality of relations possible among persons, responses, background conditions, and so forth, in the domain of data collection. As Fig. 3 reminds us, any theory has to be translated, before the design of relevant experiment, into a statement of *expected relationships*. Now although the potential *models* are stubbornly innumerable, the kinds of data relationship by which they can be tested are relatively few and easily encompassed in a systematic treatment. The Data Box (Cattell, 1946, 1966e) or basic data relation matrix (BDRM) (appendix 1, Fig. 4) has basically five sets of entities—persons, situations, responses, environmental conditions, and observers. These, plus five corresponding sets of variants on each, giving 10 Cartesian coordinates (or with time added, 11 coordinates), are sufficient to describe any psychological event. Consequently, the *relations among behavioral events*, which is what constitutes the anchor of all psychological theories, can always be represented in a 10-dimensional Cartesian Coordinate system, but most commonly in 5 and sometimes in 1 facet of it. Hereafter we shall stick to 5 facets, though recognizing that with state variants

one could, less essentially, deal with 10.

The theory and theme of an investigation, regardless of whether the BDRM has been previously consulted for perspective, thus, ultimately, leads to a choice, within the relational system of the Data Box, of a particular set of relations among real objects or events. These are the relations to be empirically investigated. And this choice decides the experimental design of data gathering, which, in turn, indicates in what manner the observations are to be recorded. For example, if someone has a theoretical model about the way mood states affect behavior, of the kind Nesselroade and Bartsch discussed in chapter 8, he will need to investigate a succession of response measurements, variously measured, to each of several stimuli, under a series of different conditions, upon one person.

Incidentally, this systematic referral of research plans to the Data Box leads readily to a taxonomy of both theoretical models and data-gathering plans (Fig. 3).

## 6   STRATEGIC AIDS IN THEORY CONSTRUCTION

From the preceding first tussle with the problem the inexorable fact is surely evident that there is no royal road to choosing mechanically at the outset, by any simple set of rules, the most successful models, that is, those possessing greatest eventual survival value. In the last resort, if we are to preserve the indispensable condition of the investigator's freedom of choice, as he sits at the ever-bubbling spring of potentially effective theoretical models, we have to recognize that research shares—with sociopolitical reform, war, and racial evolution—the human bondage to trial and error; and we must be prepared to pay the tremendous price of a thousand mistaken mutations of theory to gain one that fits the demands of reality better than anything which has gone before.

Nevertheless, some escapes from waste and heartbreak may be summarized as follows:

1. One must acquire a flair for theory construction from laboratory experience oriented to an intimate acquaintance with the data, rather than play the game of model construction for its own sake.

2. At the same time, the scientist should be versed in the necessity of good syntactical and precise representational qualities in models.

3. In many fields, it would be desirable and possible to put further restrictions on the model, for example, that it be quantitative, or that it be intrinsically generalizable with consistency of syntax, across a defined, wider field, from the beginning.

4. A taxonomy of models may be developed that would facilitate economical trial and error of a few central representatives of each type in lieu of exhaustive searching in a limitless field.

5. A moderate saving might be made by constructing theory with a constant eye on the psychologist's *basic data relation matrix* —the relational system in Fig. 3. This helps to bring out the necessary parts and implications of a model in a way that might permit rejection of many false proposals at an early stage.

A few concluding comments on these summarizing points seems desirable. "Keeping close to the data" in the first instance is sometimes mistaken for an "atheoretical" stance. Such psychologists as Burt, French, Goldberg, Humphreys, Skinner, Thurstone, and Wrigley have in various public comments been accused of lack of interest in theory.

Wrigley (1960) in *Theory Construction or Fact Finding in a Computer Age*? explicitly says, "Theory is getting less important than (relation finding)," meaning apparently much the same as we have meant by "proceeding with *empirical constructs* and models close to the data," rather than *imported*, remote, theoretical metaphors. Some of the best modern uses of the empirical-construct approach are illustrated in the chapters of Byrne and Clore, Hammond, Herrmann, Horn, Ishikawa, Izard, Nesselroade and Bartsch, and Van Egeren in this book. By contrast, the completely finished metaphor or model imported from afar has the beguiling elegance of poetry or mathematics, which can so easily intoxicate the imagination.

Of course, if the long shot of borrowing some intricate theoretical construction from a neighboring more developed science—as Lewin did, for example, where he tried to borrow topology—actually succeeds, as it occasionally does, the result is striking and enlightening. The important point, as in the case cited, is that it *usually* does not succeed. However, one must keep a sense of aptness in relation to the history of psychology. Such success is surely more likely in a historically well-developed and precise science like chemistry or physics, with a broad supportive foundation of exact, empirically established laws, than in the present condition of psychology. Generally, the temptation, intellectually and socially, is to introduce the grand theory too soon.

Gains from the fourth strategy mentioned—that of employing a taxonomy permitting comprehensive trial of each of the chief types of theory in a systematic and economical way—cannot be quoted, because no taxonomy has yet been discussed enough to be accepted. Earlier, I suggested seven dimensions of theoretical models, but it must be confessed that they tell us no more about certain important differences of models than measures of height, length, and breadth tell us about the difference between a telescope and an internal combustion engine. The more important dimensions, in terms of our present needs, have still to be found.

Yet some hope of reaching a taxonomy perhaps lies in paying attention to the fifth dimension, that is, from *mathematical stark- ness to organic enrichment* of the model. What this dimension means should perhaps first be exemplified more fully. At the one pole stand purely mathematical models and, at the other, models with enriched or even surplus meaning borrowed, for instance, from other sciences. For example, from physics the psychologist might take a model from the behavior of gases, magnetism, entropy, heat transfer and radiation, or electrical rectification; from economics, the principle of diminishing returns, Gresham's law, the theory of marginal utility; from aeronautics, of supersonic flow, airfoils, jets in ideal fluids; from biology and physiology, homeostasis, and so on.

These enriched *organic* models have a high esthetic appeal, and sometimes contain features that are peculiarly apt. For example, the models from hydraulics and electrical networks that have been *imported* into the dynamic calculus and lattice, for motivation concepts (chapter 5), have, relative to, say, the pure theory of branching processes and the mathematics of path coefficients, some extra meaning beyond the purely mathematical. This meaning resides in such physical concepts as electrical potential, or fluid pressure gradients, and even viscosity. These can and do have some extra value in fitting the phenomena covered in what I have called the dynamic lattice (chapter 7).

Or again, computer models of personal- ity, as discussed by Tompkins and Messick (1963), have some structural digital com- puter properties that go beyond any mathe- matical model in the ordinary sense. Never- theless, the sheer probability of something closely developed to the needs of one field or domain of data being applicable in *all* respects to another is surely low. The poet may compare the sunset to a rose, and the elegant theorist refer to information as entropy, but the former does not expect the sunset to distil perfume, nor does the latter expect to warm his hands on information. Somewhere the elaborate metaphor shatters into its component fragments, each perhaps usefully applicable but only in a restricted part of the model.

A classical instance is the attempt to handle the behavior of radiant energy by a model, on the one hand, from wave trans- mission and on the other, in terms of projected corpuscles. At each stage of in- coming data one of the models broke down; for example, the interference phenomena were not well explained by corpuscles, and the absence of other evidence for an *ether of space* left no medium for the waves. In psychology theorists repeatedly return to an attempt to borrow the model of *energy* from physics (Freud, Spearman, and McDougall, each in his own terms), but the attempt to relate the concept to *operations,* like those in defining and measuring kinetic, potential, electrical, or chemical energy in physical science breaks down quite soon. Here again, it might be better to define operationally certain *empircal* constructs in a model, which seem absolutely necessary at some point in describing psychodynamics, rather than to import the *theoretical* construct of energy from the physical sciences.

In short, as we approach that aspect of the model that is likely to have the widest utility, we find in our hands only what is increasingly bare and mathematical.[2] Consequently, provided we are prepared to restrict our attempts at taxonomy to models at this *stripped* end of Dimension 5—the luxuriance of the other end being hopeless of further classification—it seems that the categorization of models in a taxonomy *could* receive guidance from the accepted divisions of mathematics. At least we could begin with a generic classification into algebraic models (including number theory and probability), geometrical (including topological) models, models employing analysis (including calculus, complex variables, and functional equations) and so on.

On this basis one can see that the statistical learning theory of Estes (1954); Bush and Mosteller (1955); Estes, Burke, Atkinson, and Frankmann (1957); Crisswell, Solomon, and Suppes (1962); and others belong in a class of probability models; that the theory of psychological states, from its crude form in Wundt, to the more developed and operational form in chapter 9 here, belongs in geometrical models; that games theory and decision theory are again algebraic probability models; that the factor-analytic source trait model is algebraic linear

additive, and that the theory of typing people as segregates (chapter 11) is a combination of algebraic, probability, and topological models.

By the indication of a possibility of classifying theoretical models in personality according to the branch of mathematics involved, we have perhaps not gained much. However, it is encouraging to note, as an aside on this, that psychologists are adventurously picking up their models from quite diverse areas of mathematics. It is interesting, also, to be forced to recognize that a theoretical model, as in the instance of topology, may have to use combinations of mathematical branches, as is true, for example, also in the design of an airplane. But unless and until a more developed and functional taxonomy of models is produced, taxonomical reference alone is perhaps not going to give us much help in generating a diversity of models for a particular psychological area, or in deciding ahead of time which type is going to be more viable.

## 7  THE VIDA MODEL

It is to be hoped that the preceding analyses of theory in its most general aspects will seem worthwhile to the psychologist despite his immediate interest being perhaps in some quite specific psychological theory only. At the very least, this explicit exercise in method and theory may save the personality theorist from blind alleys; at best, it will equip him for more potent construction. But there comes a point when even well armed with techniques, a psychologist must launch himself upon a sea of intuition[3] and, guided by whatever experience and flair he can

---

[2] When Bertrand Russell defines mathematics as "the class of all propositions of the form p implies q, where p and q are propositions containing one or more variables, the same in the two propositions, and neither p nor q contains any constants except logical constants," he is indicating a generality of the higher order. Nevertheless—or should we rather say because of this—mathematics does not give all that a scientist wants in his models. In particular, causality, absent from mathematics, must have physical time introduced for its definition, as an irreversible variable; and the *determinism* of science is something more than the *dependence* of mathematics. But there are many other instances of complex properties being more readily indicated by a physical model; for example, Freud's fixation and regression concepts might gain prediction from the physical notions of inertia and viscosity.

[3] Like that fine old theorist and mathematician Omar Khayyam, he may decide to "Divorce old barren Reason from (his) bed," and take the daughter of Imagination to spouse.

muster, set sail on a particular compass course to which he fully commits his fate.

In the 31 chapters of this book, concerned with personality structure, its origin in genetic and development processes, its diverse areas of expression, its relation to culture and group dynamics, its interaction with physiology, and its pathological breakdown, there are at least as many theories and points of view as there are authors. Nevertheless, as Madsen points out in the concluding chapter, there is much that these modern authors have in common. Indeed, they have in common, by deliberate agreement, the development of theories rooted in flexible application of quantitative observation, and experimental designs that are both multivariate and bivariate, both manipulative and noninterfering. Further, they agree to express theory in definite models.

The question therefore arises, Is there any explicit common model or framework on which personality theory can proceed at this point? Obviously no elaborate theory of an *enriched* as opposed to a *stark* kind is possible, because sufficient enrichment of many well-fitting models in the local research areas does not yet exist. Although the model we are about to suggest can indeed encompass the themes of all the chapters, it cannot, in the proper sense, integrate them; it can only supply a necessary basis for integration.

As one surveys the underlying models in the different chapters one conclusion quickly appears: *Vector representation* is an indispensable feature of all theories in this book. A multivariate approach necessarily leads to a multiplicity of dimensions for describing each personality, stimulus situation, response, and so on. A multiplicity of dimensions requires that a string of quantities for various calculations be arranged in an ordered sequence, which is called a *vector*. Now, in addition, we have adopted the convenient generic term *id* to cover each and all of the entities, which as *sets* form coordinates bounding the Data Box. A person, a stimulus, a response or an occasion is an id. It follows logically that in the self-contained and all-sufficient Data Box (or basic data relation matrix) the properties assigned to any one type of id must derive from relations to the other ids. The use of ANOVA or FACTAN (as we may abbreviate *factor analysis*) upon persons as relatives and the other four Cartesian coordinates as referees, necessarily leads to defining persons in terms of responses, stimuli, occasions, and so forth.

The most general framework for personality theory (and, for that matter, learning theory and other theories) may therefore be called *vector-id-analysis*, the VIDA model. What the ultimate nature of the laws and concepts that operate within it will be, we do not yet know. We know, however, that we are dealing with a theory which respects the need for concepts derived from this totality and expressible in vector terms wherever the properties of an id are involved.

The first, and most consistently recurring element in the VIDA model, is the behavioral specification equation (familiar in its bare bones to the factor analyst) as shown in Equation (3) in appendix 2. Here $a_{hij}$ is an act (response or performance) of the individual $i$ measured on a response $j$ for which the stimulus is traditionally indicated by $h$. (Frequently $h$ and $j$ are not independently variable, but are tied together in a single *test*, as in the usual psychometrist's usage.) The nature of $h$ and $j$ are considered held constant over all people. The $T$s are traits (here traditionally, scored for individual $i$ as $T_{xi}$ on a source trait or simple structure rotated factor $x$). The $b$s are *behavioral indexes* (algebraically, coefficients; statistically, factor-analytic *loadings*) expressing (geometrically as tangents to the partial curves for one source trait plotted on one variable, if one wishes so to treat them) *the rate of change of the response magnitude with change in trait magnitude at the given stimulus strength*, h.

In appendix 2, equations 1–5, the evolution of this specification equation from the simpler but emptier stimulus-response (S–R) paradigm of all behavioristic psychology is shown. Most early use of the S–R element by the *reflexologists*, from Pavlov through Watson, omitted completely any term for the organism and its properties. In due course the emphases of such *personologists* and physiological psychologists as Freud, McDougall, Woodworth, Murray, Beach, Miller, the present writer (1950), and others brought the organism $O$ into its obvious place in the equation, as in Equation 2, the second phase in appendix 2. Finally, the new model and the intensive factor-analytic experiments on personality realistically expanded this $O$ into a vector (of $T$s); and the stimulus situation, into a vector of $b$s. In due course, with the appearance of modulation theory (Cattell, 1963c), a fourth stage of development was added as shown by the appearance of the modular index $s_k$, which adds the effect of the ambient (background) stimulus conditions to those of the focal stimulus (chapters 7 and 18).

The development from the reflexological S–R to the relatively complex specification equation (appendix 2) is typical of the VIDA model in that the ids—the person and the situation—have each been developed into a vector quantity. In form, at least as far as equation (3) in appendix 2, this would be described by the statistical psychometrist simply as a *regression equation*, but here it has more psychological meaning as the term *specification equation* implies. It now specifies that the *predictors* are characteristics of the person stated in terms of factorial source traits and that the *weights* are behavioral indexes with implications about the properties of the stimulus and the response.

So far we have moved to the prediction of behavior from the interaction of a dimensionalized organism with a dimensionalized situation; but we have stayed with the simplest possibility within the VIDA conditions, namely, a linear additive equation from the two vectors. This is not a necessary restriction, but most of the possible exemplification of the VIDA model at present is in this simplest form. As the model progresses to describe processes as well as acts, more complex equations may be necessary.

Actually, the accommodating simplicity of this *stark* VIDA model permits it already to embrace in principle a variety of theories, from computer simulation to psychoanalysis. For example, if we grant psychoanalysis the benefit of the doubt that ego strength, anxiety, degree of instinctual regression, and so forth are unitary concepts, they can be substituted for the $T$s. It has sometimes been objected to such a fitting of psychoanalysis to this model that the Freudian sees ego, superego, and so forth, as elements of *machinery*, not as static dimensions of individual difference. But the $T$s are also functional elements of *machinery*. When $P$ technique and $dR$ technique are studied in chapter 8, by Nesselroade and Bartsch, it is evident that factor analysis establishes a dynamic functional unity as well as an individual *static trait* unity. Indeed, there is now evidence (Cattell, 1973a) that every individual-difference trait pattern shows functional unity, in that its parts vary together (by modulation) from occasion to occasion.

The further objection is sometimes raised that these unitary influences might not operate in the linear and additive form of our VIDA equation. This is quite a different argument. Our response to it is that if relations are curvilinear and multiplicative, the present model is a close enough approximation over initial small ranges to permit a rough initial identification of such trait structures. Experimentally, we can handle curvilinearity by determining the $b$s over short ranges of variation and combining them. That is to say, if they change from one range to another, a curve can then be established from the succession of short straight tangents.

## 8 EXTENSIONS OF THE VIDA MODEL IN PERSONALITY DYNAMICS

The rest of this chapter asks what integrations the VIDA model can offer in personality theory in relation to perception, learning, computer simulation, games theory, process theory, and so forth. The present section expands on the more central contribution to personality dynamics as such. This includes (a) the role of *states in modulation theory* and (b) the developments in handling motivation called the *dynamic calculus*. Personality learning as *structured learning theory* (in adjustment process analysis) is tackled in the next section, as also is the incorporation of observed and instrument factor effects in perturbation theory (chapter 7).

Regarding the first, every practical psychologist recognizes that for good prediction it is as necessary to know what mood state a person is in so as to know the traits of the person. The temporary, reversible states in which a man finds himself can be covered by the concepts of (a) moods or emotional states, (b) adoptions of roles, and (c) the stimulation of mental sets. It should be understood that (a) includes both *dynamic* states (e.g., hunger, lust, loneliness), and *general* states (e.g., arousal, depression, anxiety). However, all three concepts can be isolated, identified, and measured through $P$ and $dR$ techniques; and all have the same form in relation to modulator action, which powerfully affects them. The last of these—the *temporary operator* we call a *set*—has not yet been as clearly experimentally demonstrated as have roles and states (chapters 7-10).

Before examining the meaning and form of the model for modulation that enters into all three of these, let us stake out the expansion of the specification equation with which we deal when we make this extension. To give now full *body* to the specification equation (see Equations 1-5 in appendix 2), we shall let the $T$s become all three modalities of traits: $A$, abilities; $P$, general personality traits; and $D$, dynamic traits, and we shall introduce states, $S$s, and roles, $R$s (but not mental sets, as yet).

$$a_{hijk} = \sum_{a=1}^{a=\alpha} b_{hjka} A_{ai} + \sum_{p=1}^{p=\beta} b_{hjkp} P_{pi}$$

$$+ \sum_{d=1}^{d=\gamma} b_{hjkd} D_{di} + \sum_{s=1}^{s=\zeta} b_{hjks} S_{sik}$$

$$+ \sum_{r=1}^{r=\epsilon} b_{hjkr} R_{rik} + \text{specifics.} \tag{6}$$

Note that (a) the $b$s have subscripts for both stimulus $h$ and response $j$ (as well as for the specificity to the trait—ability, dynamic, personality, etc.); (b) the summation assumes several traits of each modality: a total of $\alpha$ abilities, $\beta$ personality traits, $\gamma$ dynamic traits, and so on; (c) the state and role terms have a $k$ under them, to indicate that they stand as measured at a particular time and situation $k$.

Now it is in dealing with change (state, perception process, learning, etc.) that the multivariate experiment first shows how it can build a bridge to the typical bivariate and process-oriented psychologist's experiment and its formulation. He typically measures the *mean j* response, $\bar{a}_{hjk}$ of a group of people under stimulus $h$, in condition $k$, and again after a manipulated or naturally occurring change he measures $a_{h_2jk_2}$. His interest is to relate, by some equation, as in Equation 7, the change in $a_j$ to the change in the stimulus $h$ or the situation $k$.

$$a_{h_2jk_2} - a_{h_1jk_1} = (f)(h_2k_2 - h_1k_1). \quad (7)$$

The difficulty in integrating the multivariate and bivariate experimental domains is not entirely due to the limitations of the bivariate design. There has also been a limitation to the multivariate design, at least in factor analysis, namely that in shifting from raw scores to standard scores, that is, to unit variance variables and factors, it precludes the examination of shifts in mean scores and changes in factor levels. By this artifact of the statistics, the change in Equation 7 from what would be called an *effect* in ANOVA is lost. When the $a_{hjk}$s are put in standard scores,

$$\sum_{}^{N} a_{h_1ijk_1} = \sum_{}^{N} a_{h_2ijk_2} = 0. \quad (8)$$

In ordinary, standard factor analysis, the rationale for standard scores is that the various variables, $a_1, a_2, \ldots a_j \ldots a_n$ are in raw-score scales having units of no particular meaning; and the only way to get rid of their meaningless peculiarities of metric is to bring them all to standard scores as in Equation 8. However, when as in the factor analytic design called $P$ technique or $dR$ technique we *repeat* $a_j$ in different situations, we have comparable units, or, at least, we can throw $a_{j_1}$, $a_{j_2}$, and so forth into a single distribution and obtain standard scores that respect the fact that the mean of $j$ on the occasion

when stimulus $h_2$ or situation $k_2$ is used is different from the mean of $j$ when $h_1$ is the stimulus or $k_1$ the situation. However, ordinary $R$-technique factor analysis can take care of the changes in mean of a whole group, expressing it in terms of factor contributions, just as it does the differences of individuals in the ordinary specification equation, provided it switches to what has recently been developed as *real-base, true-zero* factor analysis (Cattell, 1972d).

To show the extensibility of the VIDA model to other domains of manipulation or natural change with situation it is necessary here to glance ahead to the *modulation* development in chapters 7, 18, and others. No model is adequate that does not recognize that the organism not only responds to the stimulus but is changed by the situation. Thus, anxiety may cause a person to respond more rapidly to a focal danger signal, but a dangerous situation will also raise the level to the anxiety that so acts.

The need to recognize this complication has been met by *modulation theory*, which recognizes (a) that the environment can be split into a focal stimulus $h$ and an ambient situation $k$, which latter comprises the conditions that affect the state of the organism; and (b) that the coefficient to a trait (which is a factor loading when the linear additive VIDA equation happens to come from factor analyses) *must in consequence be split into two coefficients,* one a modulator index $s_{kx}$, which says how much the ambient situation $k$ characteristically changes the given state or trait level, and one $v_{hj}$, the *behavioral relevance* of the trait to the response $j$ to the focal stimulus $h$.

The concept of modulation was first introduced in regard to states, but experiment soon demonstrated that traits also modulate. The ambient situation can be either a general background condition as such or reverberating conditions from preceding actions that alter the individual's state condition and therefore change his response to the focal stimulus. For example, $k$ might be something like a high ambient temperature and humidity that make a person tired. Or it might operate by his meeting the focal stimulus, his wife, when he has just been made angry by something at the office. Again, $s_k$ can operate as the evoker of a role, as when he finds that the man he speaks to at the gas station is actually a student in his class.

An ambient stimulus will not work unless the person already possesses an innate or acquired tendency to react to it, such as hypothalamic mechanism for experiencing the anger pattern, or as teacher education, which has built in a readiness to assume the teacher role. These specific capacities to enter a state, role, or set we shall call a *proneness* or *liability* and represent by $L_x$ for the state or role $x$. Obviously, though this is concerned with bringing about a state, it is actually a true trait, or endowment, on which people differ, so that for any individual $i$, we write $L_{xi}$.

Initially, modulation theory supposes that a given ambient situation will have the same *meaning* for everyone; for example, being in a house on fire will provoke fear in all people more than being in a bus. Thus the basic formulation for describing the rise of a state $x$ from a state liability $L_x$ is written as follows:

$$S_{xik} = s_{xk}L_{xi}, \qquad (9)$$

where $S_{xik}$ is $i$'s level on state $x$ on the occasion $k$ and where $s_{xk}$ is the modulator giving the usual effect of the situation $k$ on the state response liability $L_x$; that is, it is the modulator term. (Incidentally, this is adequate only so long as we neglect the difference of means between situations, as we do in the usual factor-analytic specification equations.) To handle the whole change it is necessary to add a constant, specific to the group and the situation, $C_{xg}$, such that $S_{xik} = s_{xk}(L_{xi} + C_{xg})$. This means that in a strongly stimulating situation there will be a mean response rise as well as an increase in the dispersion of individuals.

If we now bring the relevance index $v$ into action, showing how the state will affect behavior, it will be seen that we have made the substitution (considering, for simplicity, the behavior to be all predicted by this state):

$$a_{hijk} = v_{hjx}S_{xik} = v_{hjx}s_{kx}L_{xi}. \qquad (10)$$

(Note: Hitherto we have dealt with $b$, the loading or behavioral index. With this more refined treatment the observed $b$'s are broken down into $v$s and $s$s; thus, $b = vs$.)

The technical experimental issues of how the modulators, $s$s, and behavioral indexes, $v$s, are to be separately evaluated, and the statistical issues of handling—in real-base factor analysis—the expression simultaneously of individual and group mean changes, must be left to chapter 7 and space elsewhere (Cattell, 1972a).

Initially we must take the approximation that $s_{xk}$ has a common value, the same for everyone; but later it may need to be adjusted to individuals. It is certain that the modulating values—which essentially state how much the average man is *emotionally involved* or affected by $k$ and other standard situations—in the last resort will differ according to individual experiences.

The breakdown of the initially given $b$ index can proceed further than to $v$ and $s$, for by manipulating the situation to remove any individual difference due to motor effectiveness, a purely perceptual term $p$ can be isolated. The full breakdown of each term in the linear model can then become

$$b_{hjkx} T_{xi} = p_{hx} e_{hjx} s_{kx} T_{xi}, \qquad (11)$$

where $p_{hx}$ is the relevance of $T_x$ to *perceiving* $h$, $e_{hjx}$ is its relevance to *effecting* the response $j$, and $s_{kx}$ is the *modulating* effect of $k$. Although this is here expressed as a product of coefficients, the alternative additive model $(p_{hx} + e_{hjx} + s_{kx}) T_{xi}$ can be tested for fit (Cattell, 1977).

It will be recognized (see chapter 18) that the vector of $T$s ($A$s, $P$s, etc.) in the specification equation (Equation 6) represents the *person*. If the terms in Equation 6 are now expanded as in Equation 11, it will be recognized that we have an expanded description of his *environment* in the vectors $p$, $e$, and $s$. These vectors describe the environment in psychological, not physical terms. For example, if $s_k$ is large on the fear erg $E_f$, then the situation has been described as a terrifying one. The relationships between these $p$, $e$, and $s$ vectors and the physical description of situations open up a broader science of which psychophysics is a special branch. It was suggested (Sells, 1963) that this area of study be called *econetics,* from *eco* (house or environment), signifying that its concern is relating the actual ecology to human reactions. At least, as a descriptive science of the psychological values attached to various indexed aspects of environment, econetics would be valuable, especially in social psychology.

These concrete illustrations are introduced to show that the VIDA model indeed has many applications in existing research data analyses. It has long shown good fit in regard to ability and general personality traits and, more recently, has proved apt to the opening up of the quantitative approach to psychodynamics, in the dynamic calculus (chapter 18) where we see (a) the recognition of ergs ($E$s) and sentiments (acquired aggregates of attitudes, $M$s) as distinct kinds of $D$s, (b) the concept of degree of conflict in a course of action being evaluated through the ratio of negative to positive $b$ loading values, (c) the discovery that strength of motivation needs to be measured through two distinct components, integrated and unintegrated, and (d) the concept of courses of action subsidiating to one another in a chain to a final ergic goal reward. This leads to the dynamic lattice and to methods of tracing it for purposes of prediction of dynamic readjustment, as in clinical work.

In defining the VIDA model here as *one* model of high generality of application, it was not intended to imply any unique universality, but only to show that attention to a good model can simultaneously advance many research areas. Obviously, it touches frontiers in systems theory, in social psychological application of games theory, and even in such closer areas as Estes' stochastic model for learning, where a complete change of model seems to be demanded. (Conceivably, even these will ultimately admit of some bridging.) But what is certain is that a multivariate attack on both personality and that social psychology that treats groups as organisms lends itself quite naturally to a multivariate representation of the organism and the various aspects of its environment. It lends itself further to a model expressing the interaction in products of the vector terms, which are most simply handled in additive fashion. In short, the VIDA model deserves to be exploited as far as it proves able to go in current research, and offers an important basis for theory integration in personality.

## 9   INTEGRATION OF PERSONALITY THEORY WITH PERCEPTION AND LEARNING

It has been an embarrassing, standard reproach to psychology for half a century that personality theory on the one hand, and learning theory and perception on the other, have not been united or even brought into much mutual contact. The unhappy rift has been partly due to personality theorists' (old style) treating their subject with limited vision as *individual differences* and to researchers in learning and perception reciprocally omitting the *person set* coordinate of the Data Box, and seeking complete *process* laws ignoring the characteristics of the organism. Some unstrategic and vague essays toward linking perception with personality were made with the new look at perception in the 1950s, which at least enlarged perception from cognitive into dynamic determiners. This concentrated on the study of projection and dynamic misperception (Anderson, H. H., & Anderson, 1950; Bruner, 1951; Cattell, 1957a; Cattell, Radcliffe & Sweney, 1963; Cattell & Wenig, 1952; Murray, H. A., 1938) and by expressions of personality factors in perception (Cattell, 1957a; Thurstone, 1938a). Similarly, there have been local bridges into the learning field, as in H. J. Eysenck's (1960b) concern with extraversion and reactive inhibition, the relating of conditioning rates to anxiety (Cattell & Scheier, 1961; Sarason, I. G., 1957; Taylor, J. A., 1951) and school learning to personality factors (Cattell & Butcher, 1968). But generalized interaction in a broad model common to learning and personality has hitherto not occurred.

The detailed development of an integration in structured learning theory needs a whole chapter (chapter 18). But as with states and dynamics, a relatively brief global picture can be given here. The first novelty is obviously that the **VIDA** model calls for formulation of learning in multivariate terms and is thus a complete break away from the reflexological model. All factors of personality enter into determining the rapidity of learning, and all dynamic structure factors (ergs and sentiments) have to be taken into defining and evaluating the rewards operating in reinforcement.

The most radical contrast of structured learning theory from classical reflexological theory occurs immediately at the descriptive level. Whereas the latter measures the dependent variable as an increment in frequency or intensity of a particular response, structured learning theory asks not only about this increment but about how it may be expressed in changes of three vectors of the specification equation as follows:

*Tri-Vector learning evaluation*

1. Trait Learning Change Vector: $T_{1i}$, $T_{2i}, \ldots T_{ni}$.

2. Behavioral Relevance Index Change Vector: $v_{j1}, v_{j2}, \ldots v_{jn}$.

3. Modulator Index Change Vector: $s_{k1}, s_{k2}, \ldots s_{kn}$.

That is to say, one assumes that only the most artificial laboratory learning will lead to change restricted to only one trait and that, in general, in the life experiences and clinical therapy with which the personality theorist is concerned, change will occur over most traits in the vector, though perhaps largely on one.

The changes in the second vector—the behavioral indexes—represent a change definable in the learning group as a whole in the way in which they perform the behavior. Theoretically it is possible for no gain in average score on $a_i$ to occur, but for the whole pattern of $v$s and $s$s to alter, so that an *inner learning* has taken place whereby people bring different traits to bear on the same performance.

Last and least studied in the tri-vector measurement of learning are the changes in the modulation vector—the $s$s. These represent another aspect of emotional learning in that people are now reacting to ambient situations with state changes and role adoptions not present before.

The tri-vector measurement of learning change is of course an integral elaboration of the VIDA model. Structured learning theory, however, is concerned with description only as a first step and proceeds to lawful explanation as a second. Here the advances reside first in being able, through objective measurement of specific ergic tensions in man, to write a quantitative statement of a vector of rewards. Second, it augments a statement of hypothesis about learning determinants, still essentially in accord with Hull or Tolman, by hypotheses that general state levels at the time of learning, such as arousal or regression, help determine the learning rate. Third, it seeks to account for the observed patterns in personality—the acquired source traits—by exploring the environment for reward schedules that operate simultaneously on several elements of behavior. Here, structured learning theory reaches over and integrates with the dynamic lattice and the dynamic calculus: the sentiment structures from learning schedules, and the plexuses in the dynamic lattice are different representations of the same thing.

Turning last to the VIDA model in its implications for the psychology of perception, we recognize two new possibilities: (a) the expression of the meaning of a perception in relation to personality; (b) the econetic relationships of psychological meaning, as in psychophysics, to features of the object itself. Two aspects of perception that scarcely concern us here are (a) the cognitive and brain function aspects, which are substantial but not immediately personality oriented, and (b) learning in relation to perception, since learning has been discussed previously.

As already pointed out, there are two distinct objectives in studying the perception of the environment: (a) to assign psychological parameters to a perception, and (b) the econetic problem of relating the psychological parameters to physico-social parameters, of which psychophysics is a subdivision with special conditions. Our concern here will be with the first, still little achieved.

In a broad sense, the meaning—at least the *common* meaning—of a perception resides in the $v$s and the $s$s of Equations 6 and 10 or the $p$s, $e$s and $s$s of Equation 11. If the $p$ value of a given perceptual response for, say, the factor of intelligence is large, the individual is dealing with a complex perception, for example, a geometric puzzle; and if the $s$ for the escape erg is large, he is contemplating some fearful thing. If the $s$ for the sex erg is large, it is something that stimulates amorousness, and so on. Some psychologists might wish to argue that the meaning lies in all the $s$s, not just those of the $D$ (dynamic) traits. All of these give the pattern of the emotional and dynamic changes which the ambient situation produces. This is true, and it is also true that any broad sense of "meaning" surely connotes what one *does* in response to the presentation, and this is settled by the $e$s too. All these vectors are thus essential to common meaning, at least if we are describing the *global* situation, that is, both the ambient situation and the focal stimulus to which the response is being made.

So much for the *common* perception, for, except in $P$ technique, the $p$s, $e$s, and $s$s are the same for all people. For the *individual* meaning, however, the $T$s also must come in. If Jane is more timid than Sally (lower on the $H$ factor), then the same somewhat dangerous situation seems much more dangerous to her. The first vector of meaning (focal stimulus) is therefore the set of products, $p_{hx}T_{xi}$; the second vector, $e_{hjx}T_{xi}$; and the third, $s_{kx}T_{xi}$. The importance of the $T$s becomes especially evident when we study the effect of defense mechanisms on perception, as in the work of Cattell and Wenig (1952) or of Cattell, Radcliffe, and Sweney (1963). Defense mechanisms are part of personality, and they affect considerably the perception by different people of the same presentation.

An important practical and taxonomic gain from the VIDA treatment of perception is the creation of an objective scheme for the classification of the psychological meaning of various environments. This would be a branch of what we have called *econetics*. It must be confessed that with a few exceptions, such as Barker, Kounin, and Wright (1943), Bellows (1962), M. Sherif and Sherif (1956), J. D. Singer (1965), and Sells (1963), psychologists have grievously neglected such a need for taxonomy and measurement of the environment. Lip service is paid to it (particularly by personologists who by emphasizing specific environments try to claim complete unstructuredness and specificity of personality) but neither solid research nor a suitable model have hitherto been developed. The use of the pattern similarity coefficient $r_p$, upon a representative array of $b$, $e$, and $s$ vectors as earlier, and application of the taxonome program (Cattell & Coulter, 1966) offer a basis for an objective classification of environmental objects by psychological meaning. Of course, the various actions about an object would have to be vector summed for its total meaning.

Finally, the present model has something to offer in defining what Herbart called apperception masses, and what in more recent work has been called perceptual sets. The hypothesis is put forward here—and it is purely a hypothesis—that the factoring of attitudes that yields sentiments, if made to include as variables more limited and temporary sets than measured in attitudes, will yield lower order, narrow factors within roles and within other sentiments, which represent *perceptual sets*.

The whole matter is examined in more detail in chapter 22; but the acceptance of these more limited variables means that our model would have to accept, in the language of factor analysis, the notion of the existence of a *debris* of small factors, approaching *specifics* in narrowness. For example, getting behind the wheel of a car calls into existence a host of particular skill and perception factors never operative outside a car. Such perceptual sets, like lower order factors, generally will be at the disposal of several distinct higher strata factors. This is sketched in Equation 12, where only two higher order factors appear, $A$ and $D$, and the cores or stubs of the $k$ small perceptual sets $m_1$ to $m_k$:

$$a_{hij} = b_{hjx}A_{xi} + b_{hjy}D_{yi} + b_{hjk_1}m_{1i}$$
$$+ \cdots + b_{hjk_p}m_{ki}. \qquad (12)$$

A bridge might conceivably be built from this notion of an ultimate fractionating of what begins as dynamic structure in sentiments into a *large* number of small sets, as just discussed, to the statistical learning theory model of Estes (1954) and of Bush and Mosteller (1951). However, the higher order structure would require common elements between one domain of learning and another, a proposition that seems so far not to have been experimentally investigated in learning models.

## 10  RELATION OF THE VIDA MODEL TO MORE REMOTE MODELS

The main model for personality is one that can readily be seen to be compatible, at least, with most prequantitative, clinical theories in the field and at the same time with the last 40 years of advance in psychometrics. As to the former, most psychoanalytic, Adlerian, and Jungian theories, as well as the concepts of Murray and McDougall and many others, can be raised to testable precision in the notions of *trait functional unities, summation of trait effects, conflict dynamic integration,* etc., set out previously. If there is any uncertainty on this point, it is because these preexperimental theories do not spell out their postulates, or offer evidence for the unitary character of their concepts or proceed themselves to any exact models by which the goodness of their predictions could be evaluated.

## 10.1  Games Theory

Turning to more recent theories, more explicit as to their models, we find three approaches mentioned at the opening of this chapter to which we must now return. Games theory on the face of things, presents a totally different type of model from the scheme of interacting structures. It typically sets out certain relatively simple rules for a game and asks what strategy of one or both *players* will lead to certain results, such as a consistent winning for one, a drawn game, the minimal time or number of steps for a game, and so on. Without detracting from the general importance of what Von Neumann and Morgenstern (1944) began, one must conclude that it has limited applicability to personality theory until these behaviors can be related to parameters of the players, too.

The analysis of strategy in games is aimed always at finding and defining an *ideal* play. Presumably, except in extremely simple matters, personality interactions, either with people or the physical world, normally follow an actual pattern that is far from any ideal play. Nevertheless, the dynamic lattice

is an excellent example of an adjustment problem in which a person is presented with a number of real-life opportunities and obstacles and asked to find the paths of behavior that will maximize his total ergic satisfaction. It is an excellent problem for a special development of games theory. The result moreover, would be expected to integrate well with the VIDA model because it enriches information about the way in which the sentiment type of source trait is brought about. It suggests that simultaneous reinforcement of the elements in a sentiment by a social institution is not the whole story. It directs us to consider the learning acquisition of such structures by the use of Bayesian statistical approaches, with conditional probabilities. It thus offers a submodel for analyzing the organic rise of the source trait unit itself.

## 10.2  Computer Simulation

Regarding the second of the more remote types of theory—those implied or expressed in the computer simulation of personality—perhaps we should, regardless of their apparent merit, be on guard against intoxication by the Zeitgeist. For example, in Tomkins' charming phrase for this use of the computer, as "a psychic wind tunnel," and the rest of his discussion, there is much that strikes one as at present more lyrical than operational. Apart from certain temporary risks of distracting or maiming the main direction of personality growth theory by the contemporary epidemic of enthusiasm for the computer, there appears to be the possible danger of a more persistent confusion. To clear it, we need to ask the question: When we talk of a computer model of personality, are we implying that the computer, as a machine, as we now know it, is a new kind of model in itself, or are we simply saying that the computer is a convenient way of trying out by constructed programs the basic varieties of mathematical models in personality theory with which we are already familiar? I believe the sober answer must be the second: It is mainly nothing but a sort of *fluoroscope* to watch mathematical models working, that this procedure brings gains in the understanding of the implications of particular mathematical models that are not only quantitative, but also qualitative, in comparison with any construction and try out of mathematical models that does not go through computer programs. There may be more than this, but there is at least this.

As to just what these gains will ultimately be, the scantiness of present experience admits only a rough estimate. Accordingly, only some statements of probability are risked here. Inasmuch as the computer possesses the particular set of four organs which we call an *input*, an arithmetic *processing organ,* a storage or *memory,* and an *output* unit, a set of parameters for the effectiveness of these parts can be considered as necessarily built into the VIDA mathematical model we already use. Granted this restriction to existing mathematical models, we are nevertheless permitted by experiment on the performance of various computers to obtain information on an empirical basis about the dynamic relation of these organs. That is to say, if we put essentially the same series of programs, for a series of performances, in a *population sample* of computers and factor the resulting performances we ought to obtain factors giving the parameters by which the four organs are *bounded* and evaluated. Possibly, there would just be one factor for each organ.

The principle asserted here is that wherever we set up a machine of any kind that operates according to a program of acts we have specified, observations on the actual running of the machine can still supply new information beyond what may have been written into the model. (Even today the horsepower of an internal combustion engine of prescribed bore, stroke, mixture, spark advancement, etc., or the braking power for prescribed drums and friction materials in cars are still determined empirically for various speeds.) This access of new information is partly due to the computer model's not being a pure mathematical model, but projecting itself some distance toward the concrete, along the abstract—the concrete dimension of model construction (appearing as Dimension 4 earlier). (It reminds us that in any borrowing of a metaphor from a neighboring science we also borrow some of the *dirt*—the error and incompleteness of understanding of its existing use.)

Although the computer may in a sense thus fall interestingly short of a fully specified mathematical mode, it may also demand, on the opposite side of the ledger, as Loehlin (1963) and Tomkins and Messick (1963) pointed out, a rigor and an order of objectification in stating a theory that is not *fully* guaranteed even in the ordinary statement of a model in purely mathematical symbols. Actually, this amounts to saying that the mathematician himself can be inadequate or inconsistent in writing down a system of equations for what he hopes to represent. In that connection, it is not unrealistic to recognize that laziness often overcomes the mathematician if the number of submodels he has to follow through becomes too large. The awkward refusal of the computer to work out *details* on its own initiative challenges the tendency of the mathematician at some points merely to sketch in the required complexity. It does so by its unanswerable rejoinder to error or nonsense—a hang up. If since the beginning of this century only those personality theories had been published that are capable of looking a computer squarely in the disc, the lives of students and everyone else would have been more honest, more leisured, and more fertile.

But there is a second way—over and above this invocation that it act as a mechanical superego—in which computer expression surpasses the mathematical model, and this I will call the *heuristic gain*. Again, it results from avoiding the weaknesses of human nature and is a gain of degree rather than a categorical one. A researcher with an abacus—granted infallible precision and infinite patience—could achieve the same result. However, these heuristic gains include (a) a rapidity of demonstration of the potentiality of a model, which keeps better pace with the freshness of the researcher's creative thinking; (b) a practical encouragement to play with a far wider array of combinations of parameters and algebraic submodels than the worker with a mathematical model alone could envisage handling at his desk in a lifetime (in short, it permits handling complexities and variances which the exigencies of life would rule out if we were restricted to older conventional means; see Colby's or Abelson's models in Tomkins & Messick, 1963); (c) a possibility of continuing experiment with a successful model *beyond the ranges* of the naturally available data.

The second of the heuristic gains might perhaps be illustrated by a personality learning experiment in which the computer is set to make $n$ different responses to each of $k$ different stimuli and is *rewarded* by being given an increased probability, for the next run, of making those responses that were signaled to be successful on the preceding. By plugging in different weights for the rewards, conceivably some radically different results would emerge, especially in effects that depended on ratios between the

speed of this process and some other ongoing process. The constructor of a primary mathematical model would be unwilling to face the staggering task of trying these variants on his model by personal calculation and would probably try out the model only with one set of constants. Almost certainly some very surprising and informative insights would be gained from a plan of systematically varying the mutual relation of these constants, and a similar play of variants on other models would illuminate hypothesis formation.[4]

It will be realized, of course, that the preceding play with varieties of program on the computer is referred to here not as the usual empirical checking, *for degree of fit to data* in any *precise* statistical sense. It is a means of getting a feeling for how the model works and what special machinery might need to be added before one is satisfied with the form in which it should be put subsequently to an experimental data check. In principle, what is being proposed is the same as what some great and candid mathematicians like Poincaré have admitted to be the origins of their abstract discoveries, namely, seeing relations in concrete examples before presenting the world with a finished abstract theorem.

Beyond these two heuristic gains, a third is sometimes claimed provocatively and persuasively, for example, by Colby (1963) and by Tomkins and Messick (1963). Tomkins and Messick stated: "A computer simulation might provide an experimental subject for whom conditions could be manipulated

---

[4] Some writers have described this sort of gain from the computer as a facilitation of dealing with greater *complexity* in a model, but this does not seem quite right unless complexity is understood as meaning simply the *number of variables*. It is better considered an opening of the door to permit far more variants of design in a mathematical model of any given degree of essential complexity.

that were too extreme, time consuming, difficult, dangerous or unethical to attempt with human subjects" (p. 316). This is a gift however, that needs to be looked at cautiously, for, as in a factor pattern, a change of range often seems to call up a change of mechanism and factor number.

Apart from the dangers just discussed, the computer simulation models have only a shortcoming which they share with a mathematical model per se, namely, that their use largely rules out those nonmathematical models that lie at the opposite end of the *starkness* dimension described previously. Since we have all along demanded the precision of mathematical models, this criticism may seem inconsistent. But we have asked for starkness as a final condition, and along the way the *surplus meaning* of other models may help provoke new mathematical models.

A minor issue in computer models is that of the critic who says that they are all right for cognitive models, but that one cannot put motivation and affect into computers. Such a critic tries to say that the computer is a passive *tabula rasa*, which can do nothing spontaneously without a human somehow putting his heart inside it. If this were not true, he says, nightmarish things might happen, such as going to the computer on Monday morning to give it a job and getting a printout saying "Not in the mood, and am going to spend the day writing poetry." Without going into detail, we can refer the reader to Loehlin's (1963) experiment—an experiment as yet insufficiently studied, and indeed, insufficiently appreciated. This illustrates by a clear demonstration that recognition, memory-affect and volition or dynamic need to act can be built into a computer. Analogues for *desire* can be set up and will function as long as the ampères last—and, after all, a human is equally tied to the supply of calories.

Granted this we can return to the basic question as to how far the computer simulation models of personality can be encompassed—or, at least, subsumed in essentials—under the general VIDA model. As W. Holtzmann has pointed out, Loehlin's "Aldous"—his computer mannikin—can be said to have recognizable *traits*, corresponding in magnitude to variance parameters built into the program; and we can add to these, as above, the parameters of the machine itself. The addition by Loehlin of the *dynamic* set of parameters is an important one, and has proved illuminating and provocative of new ability hypotheses in, for example, Cattell's triadic theory of ability structure (1971a), as contrasted to J. P. Guilford's (1967) model.

In closing this discussion specifically on computer models of personality, it should not be overlooked that in principle we need one computer to represent the personality and another the environment. Loehlin, for example, built his situations into the same machine, but it might more clearly underline the independence to have two machines, interacting. Along these lines it would be interesting to explore how the dimensions of situations in the model correspond to parameters put into such a program for the environment.

## 10.3  Value and Culture Dynamics Theories

Finally, any review of extant personality models, and their relation to the generic VIDA model, would not be complete without a wider sweep into the theories of personality as they are implicit in sociology, anthropology, and even in the *economic man*. Essentially these areas have personality without its genetics and much of its physiology; indeed, personality functions here, essentially, as a mere point of intersection of historical movements and cultural patterns. For the clinical psychologist, with his strong emphasis on individual motivation, and the physiological psychologist, with his constant referral to the gut, the cultural views (most pervasive, for example, in Marxian views of history) seem remote and disembodied. Nevertheless, in regard to mass effects, it is possible (without going the whole way with Hegel) to speak as if cultural movements have a dynamic of their own.

To handle such designs in any real, modern, and quantitative sense, it is necessary to resort to the dimensionalizing of culture patterns (Cattell, Breul, & Hartman, 1952; Cattell & Gorsuch, 1965; Jonassen & Peres, 1960; Rummel, 1963), and to models concerning the interaction of personality with group synergy and group syntality (Cattell, 1966e). Indeed, for those who want seriously to explore this direction of theory, there are now both actual empirically determined definitions of cultural dimensions and a systematic development of social models (syntality, synergy) such as will permit the observation and emphasis of social scientists to be positively integrated with the VIDA model. There is no need to consider the opposite poles of clinical and cultural dynamics—the *gut* and the *globe* theories, as we may call them—as mutually exclusive or unintegratable. Indeed, cultural dynamics can be derived from the basic needs of the individual, as illustrated, for example, in discussions of the *cultural pressure* dimension (Cattell, 1950c). Relations in personality-group culture interaction necessarily present a high level of complexity—representable by the transformations between two sets of dimensions, those of the group and those of the individual—but this problem gets ample discussion as the substance and theoretical theme of section 4 in this book, "The Sociological Domain of Personality."

## 11  SUMMARY

At this point, a summary is given concerning the evolution of theory and the VIDA concepts.

1. To understand the evolution of personality theory it is necessary to study both scientific theory construction per se and the sociohistorical flow of scientific discussion in which it is embedded. Our task is to understand and respect the former, though we must recognize the latter, but with no obligation to sustain historical trends that for social reasons (e.g., popularity based on easy assimilation) have long persisted, despite being erroneous or irrelevant. The stand taken here is that a requisite refinement of theory can proceed only on checks against quantitative observations and on a broad concept of experiment, embracing multivariate as well as bivariate, and noninterfering as well as manipulative, designs. The present theoretical development in personality is thus historically that of a third, *experimental* phase of personality study, superseding the remote *general literary* and more recent *clinical* method phases.

2. The general design of a theory-generating-and-checking investigation includes the succession of (a) an initial theory and hypothesis, (b) its projection into the possible *relational systems* defined by the Data Box, (c) the setting up of an experimental design to involve those relations in testable form, and (d) the examination of the results by a statistical evaluative design appropriate for the model.

3. It is stressed that the method of science is not the hypothetico-deductive but the inductive-hypothetico-deductive (IHD) method, which, in systematic investigations, becomes a spiral (Fig. 2).

4. To say that any theory should ideally be capable of statement in a clear model or

set of models is not to say that all models are mathematical. However, they must all have an internal logical, syntactical structure and an external reference or semantic code of proper reference to data. Theoretical models that are sound in this respect, nevertheless, may vary in position along some seven dimensions; their patterns in this framework present a basis for an objective taxonomy of theory construction.

5. Apart from intrinsic merits, theories and theory building are subject to distortions and disorders arising from the human and social setting of science. In personality, there was an altogether excessive growth of rather grandiose, uncheckable theories in the first half of this century, largely verbal and nonquantitative. More recently, many *tight* models have appeared, in response to demands for rigor. But preoccupation with models also has its dangers, in the form of a possible rash of abstract model making divorced from experiment. Meanwhile, perennially, human nature causes a sag toward subjectivity, that is, a forcing of *imported* subjective schemata on nature without adequate observational and experimental sensitivity to the regularities in the data (Fig. 1).

6. Since an infinite variety of models can be manufactured, of which extremely few will eventually achieve a really useful fit, effectiveness and economy in evolving theory by research faces the same problem as attempts at eugenic economy in biological evolution, namely, the need to acquire skill in anticipating which of the innumerable mutations is likely to have the rare quality of viability and significant advantage. Four ways of reducing waste are proposed: (a) attention to inherent correctness in model construction as such, that is, a well-worked-out syntax and semantics; (b) development of a taxonomy of models, whereby one of each type could be given a trial, representa-

tively; (c) regard for the principle of appropriate stages in IHD procedures. This means concentrating in the early stages on suggestions of laws and empirical constructs through intense study of the data. Larger imports of metaphorical models belong to a later stage, to which present-day psychology can aspire only rarely. (d) A receptivity of psychologists to models that are *stark* but of potentially larger breadth of applicability—as in the VIDA model—even at the cost of some initial approximation of fit. An understanding of the basic dimensions of research design (Fig. 3), experiment (Table 1), and data analysis (section 4) helps in effective model testing.

7. With these standards and aims, a survey of existing theoretical developments (e.g., the main clinical theories, reflexological learning theory, source trait theory, games theory, computer simulation, statistical learning theories, and cultural dynamics theory) shows that considerable resourcefulness and variety has been demonstrated in approaches to personality theory—at least since quantitative research began. More as an illustration of a model with real breadth of application than as an attempt to claim undue universality, the VIDA model has been described in some detail here. It begins with a two-term, first-degree polynominal, familiar in multiple regression and factor analysis as the *specification equation,* in which there is one vector describing the organism and one defining the properties of the environment. By bringing such a general behavior response specification equation into relation with the Data Box, which has, basically, five coordinates coresponding to five sets of ids—stimuli, responses, persons, conditions (occasions), and observers—we develop the specification equation to five vectors. These are capable of expressing the relations of organism and environment in behavior; in internal conflict; in learning; in

emotional change; in perception; and, indeed, in most psychological fields of analysis. As a brief acronym for vector-id-analysis the term *VIDA* is used to describe this model.

8. Although the linear specification equation is cited as a familiar expression of this model, the VIDA theory can extend well beyond this additive, linear interaction framework and is concerned with an array of further concepts that have received initial support from empirical data. They are (a) the source trait as a special, invariant species of factor; (b) the psychological state; (c) the conception of loadings, $b$s, as behavioral indexes; (d) the concept of liability to a state, as a personal sensitivity trait, $L_x$, specific to a state; (e) the introduction of modulation indexes, $s$s, expressing the stimulus effect in determining personal states; (f) the recognition of several distinct species of trait and state by modalities—$A$s, $P$s, $D$s, $L$s, $E$s, and $M$s; (g) the conception of mental sets and percepts as lower order dynamic traits, fractionated as fragments of role factors and sentiments; (h) the formulation of the environmental stimulus and its meaning as a pair of vectors, $b$s and $s$s or, alternatively, $p$s, $e$s and $s$s. With this goes the possibility of an objective taxonomy of the psychological environment and a development of psychophysics called *econetics*.

9. These define the VIDA model as a prototheory, on which further findings can build enriched concepts. Among the extensions of the prototheory now under investigation are (i) the formulation of maturation and learning as multidimensional change (by experience and time) in a multidimensional situation. This begins with the tri-vector theory for describing learning change and proceeds to explanatory laws of learning based on measurement of specific ergic rewards and coordinated reinforcement schedules produced by social institutions. (j)

The concepts of the dynamic calculus and the dynamic lattice may lead to higher levels of concepts of total energy and total integration and (k) the analysis of response *processes*, as distinct from single acts, in adjustment process analysis.

## 12  ORGANIZATION OF AREAS IN THE PRESENT BOOK

From the general theoretical basis of personality research just discussed, we now turn to the plan of the book. Insofar as the numerous contributors to this book were brought together by the common conviction that personality theory must grow from experimental and especially multivariate experimental foundations, the framework of the VIDA model is to some extent implicit in all. But for the rest, the developments are as diverse as the demands of particular areas and the cultural background of scientists from several countries might produce. Even in these individual theoretical positions, however, as those informed of the development of this book must realize, there is a degree of mutual interaction not found in books that merely put between the same covers the chapters of many contributors. For the contributors to this book were first brought together in a 3-day conference on the project, and they have sharpened their appreciation of common goals and conceptual standards since that initial meeting in other conferences and research exchanges.

Recognizing the logically and experimentally necessary *priority of meaningful measurement* and *clarity on taxonomic structure* to all genetic, developmental, and applied (criterion) work later, section 1 concerns itself with the foundation of structure. It begins with traits (Hammond, Wilde, Ishikawa, Dielman and Krug, and Horn), and proceeds to dynamic states and moods (Nesselroade and Bartsch, Spielberger,

Lushene, and McAdoo) to specifics relating situations to state and trait (Patterson and Bechtel), and so to the recognition of distributions and types (Bolz). In so doing, it also considers measurement and typing of *stimulus* situations, and the relativity of concepts to the observer and the mode of observation, that is, consideration of spurious instrument factors and the principles of *perturbation* theory.

The basis of meaningful measurement, sophisticated as to observer effects, being thus assured, sections 2 and 3 proceed to modern findings regarding the genesis and development of personality. It is an axiom for creation of promising developmental theory that nature-nurture research should first be done to determine whether the explanation for a given trait is best sought in the genetic or the learning domain. Section 2 presents chapters by leading authorities in behavior genetics, human and animal (Broadhurst and Jinks, Loehlin, and Gray and Drewett). Section 3 attempts to bring some organization into the most disordered area of all—that concerned with learning theory, in relation to personality. The approaches of Weizmann, Staats, Dreger, and Cattell represent the poles of reflexological, social, and clinical treatments of personality change, and the editors attempt integration—Dreger in terms of the real data of child development, and Cattell in terms of the radically new treatment through structured learning theory. H. J. Eysenck attempted elsewhere to bridge from structured personality concepts to classical reflexology, but the argument here is that reconciliation is possible only through the new concepts in structured learning principles (Cattell, 1977).

Since personality without an environment is meaningless, and the most important part of the environment that helps define structure is social, the next logical step, constituted by section 4, is a review of environ-ment, beginning with the family and its effects (Herrmann), proceeding through personality interaction in the immediate group (Byrne and Clore, and Vaughan) and the interaction with culture (Izard). These as yet cannot be handled on so tight a model as the earlier chapters. There follow in section 5 some aspects of personality that all students would consider vital—personality and perception (Schneewind), verbal learning (Schaie and Goulet), and physiology (Fahrenberg). These are in a classification sense *miscellaneous*, yet any one is important enough for a separate volume, as, indeed, the physiological aspects have become in such a book as H. J. Eysenck's *Biological Basis of Personality* and Nebylitsin and Gray's *Biological Bases of Individual Behavior.*

Although it is nowadays a common criticism of psychoanalysis that it formed its conclusions *wholly* from abnormal samples, yet it is also true that an adequate personality theory should *encompass* the pathological manifestations. This is the task of the Delhees, Guertin, and Van Egeren in section 6. Their excellent treatment achieves close integration with quantitative work on normal controls.

Finally, section 7 turns to integrations in three senses. First, in terms of a technological integration, Thompson asks how modern theory meets the needs of applied psychology; Cattell and Gorsuch turn to the problem that has long taxed psychology—the integration of the self, expressed in the superego and in life values; and Madsen asks how the whole theoretical approach in this book integrates with the philosophy of science. This book is an attempt to apply what is a necessary minimum of quantitative, experimental, and statistical standards as will make the beginnings of integration in personality research a sincere ideal. Critics can certainly point to instances where the editors might well have been less permissive, and demanded that differences of standard in accepting experimental significances or logical inferences be ironed out in the interest of greater consistency and architectonic growth. But a new type of common effort, with an unusual degree of effective interaction from leading contributors, from different countries and different specialties, has at least hopefully been inaugurated by this book.

## APPENDIX 1   THE DATA BOX AND FACTOR ANALYSIS

In Fig. 4, only three coordinates of the Data Box are presented, as the edges of a cube visible in perspective; the remaining two, beyond pictorial representation, are simply suggested by two interrupted lines (Observers and Background). In the full Data Box (Cattell, 1966e) each kind of id—person, stimulus, and so forth—is represented by two sets, one for the central mean

stable state of that entity, and the other for some immediate deviant state of the entity. Thus, there are alternately $5 \times 2 = 10$ sets of coordinates. (The term $C$, for background *condition* in Fig. 4, is more commonly represented by the symbol $E$ (to avoid confusion with covariance.) At the intersection (Cartesian product) defining the unique event of a given person, stimulus, response, and so forth coming together, the actual quantitative entry is commonly (in psychology) a magnitude of response.

It is not intended here to discuss factor analysis completely. But a general reference to both factor analysis and ANOVA is necessary if one is to perceive how the complete set of possible relations in the BDRM determines the expression of a theory. The terms $R$, $P$, and $Q$ *technique* (and several others; see Cattell, 1966e) have come into use to define ways of correlating and factoring the various id sets. For example, $R$ technique correlates responses (each tied to a particular stimulus) across people. But correlation is

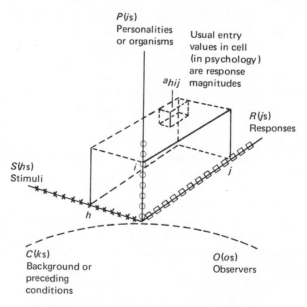

**FIG. 4.** The basic data relation matrix (Data Box).

only one method of analysis and the same $R$, $P$, and $Q$ modes of analysis could be set up for ANOVA instead (see Burt, 1966a). One would then be examining differences of means, to test significance of relationship in the same kind of data previously tested by correlations.

Factoring aims to elucidate the dimensions of any one set of ids, and thereby to make it possible to express any individual id in that set as a particular vector quantity (or profile). It should be noted that different domains of dimensions will be obtained according to which of the techniques is used, and, of course, according to which id set constitutes the relations (Cattell, 1966e).

The ways of dimensionalizing $C$, $S$, $O$, and $R$ are actually fairly numerous; to avoid later confusion, the reader should have some explicit overview of their relative aptness and significance. The discussions of possible Data Box analyses elsewhere (Cattell, 1966e) show that the dimensions we obtain from correlating a set of variables, called *relatives*, will depend, as just implied in contrasting results from $R$, $P$, and $Q$ techniques, on the nature of the population of *referees* over which they are completed. So far, in psychology, the referees from which the vector dimensions of stimuli, conditions, and responses were derived have been organisms (*people* or animals, to personality theorists). However, one could factor physical dimensions of stimuli across stimuli and simply get the salient physical characteristics by which to describe stimuli, and so on for other sets. But imagine next that we took some single response, say writing an essay in response to a teacher's request, and scored it in 20 different ways (e.g., length, number of $I$s, spelling, etc.) across people. We should then obtain the dimensions of this response (writing an essay) in terms of person variations, and it is likely that these would turn out to be possible expressions of people's dimen-

sions, as located when different variables are factored, each measured in one way. In other words, the dimensions that emanate from any correlational analysis, and that are the terms in the vector or profile, always apply to one particular class of referees—people, stimuli, responses, and so forth.

## APPENDIX 2   FIVE LEVELS OF DEVELOPMENT OF THE STIMULUS-RESPONSE MODEL

1. *The reflexological formulation*: $R =$ response; $f =$ any function; $S =$ stimulus.

$$R = f(S). \tag{1}$$

2. *The* personality theory *emendation*: Introducing $O$ for properties of the organism.

$$R = f(O.S). \tag{2}$$

3. *The multivariate experimental development of organism and situation parameters.* Here the $T$s are a vector of dimensions for $O$ and the $b$s (loadings) for $S$. The term $a$ is now written for an act or performance rather than a single reflex response; $h$ is the focal stimulus; $i$, the individual; $j$, the defined response act (performance). The $T$s are broad common traits (1 through $q$), and the $b$s are behavioral indexes (obtained as factor loadings), tied to stimulus, response, and trait. While $U$ is a unique trait including also an error of observation factor.

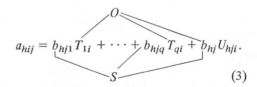

$$a_{hij} = b_{hj1}T_{1i} + \cdots + b_{hjq}T_{qi} + b_{hj}U_{hji}. \tag{3}$$

4. *The addition of modulation and analytic separation of action effects and modulation changes*: Here the originally obtained

loading has been split up into a $v$ term, which expresses the effect on performance of the modulated endowment $sT$ and an $s$ term, which says how much the ambient situation $k$ affects the trait or state-proneness endowment. The total situation has been split into a focal stimulus $h$ and an ambient situation $k$. The unique term $U$ is split into a specific term $T_j$ and error $E_j$.

$$a_{hijk} = v_{hj1} s_{k1} T_{1i} + \cdots + v_{hjq} s_{kq} T_{qi}$$
$$+ v_{hj} s_{kj} T_{ji} + E_{ji} \qquad (4)$$

5. *The complete analysis into four vectors corresponding to the sets of the Data Box*: Here $b$ has been further broken down, by experimental separation of perception and action behavior, into $ps$ (the perception vector) and $es$ (the execution vector), while the involvement vector of $ss$ remains the same. (The observer vector is not included to give the full five possible vectors).

$$a_{hijk} = p_{hj1} e_{hj1} s_{hk1} T_{1i}$$
$$+ \cdots + p_{hjq} e_{hjq} s_{hkq} T_{qi}$$
$$+ p_{hj} e_{hj} s_{hk} T_{hjk} + E_{ij} \qquad (5)$$

It will be observed that although, ideally, $p$ could be restricted to $h$, $e$ to $j$, and $s$ to $k$, the formula respects the possibility that the action $j$ also helps define the perception $p$; that the focal stimulus $h$ may be involved in the definition of the performance $j$; and that the modulation effect may spring from the total situation ($h + k$).

The product relation of $p$, $e$, and $s$ has been used here, but the psychological sense would allow as an alternative that they be additively treated.

# 2

# Personality Studied by the Method of Rating in the Life Situation

## S. B. Hammond
### *University of Melbourne, Parkville, Victoria, Australia*

## 1 THE NATURE OF $L(R)$ AND $L(BR)$ DATA

The sum total of ways in which we can make observations—the basis of all theory —on human personality has been divided by Cattell into three *media*, $L$ data (life record), $Q$ data (questionnaire and self-observation), and $T$ data (objective, laboratory-type behavioral measures). This division is not only convenient, but also a reminder of quite distinct properties and methods, initially needing separate study. These properties and their overlap were dealt with systematically by Cattell (1957a). Their essential congruence, which does not appear in the initial phases of comparisons, was shown by Cattell and his colleagues (Cattell et al., in press; Cattell, Pierson, Finkbeiner, Willes, Brina, & Robertson, 1976).[1] A spate of articles in the

1960's in which it was made to appear that ratings of personality are not much better than chance ratings prompted a number of

$Q$, for the hypothesized identical source traits in fact come out on the same factors.

Failure to reach such matching has often been due to crude rating procedures. In this case each person was rated by ten peers on behavioral variables observed in close contact over a long period, and the mean was taken. The theory tested in this study was that there exist real trait patterns in people which can be clearly isolated in factor analysis only if *instrument factors*, due to media, are first partialled out. This recent research showed not only that the primaries in $L$ and $Q$ data matched, but that the correlations among them also fitted the identity hypothesis, since they yielded the same standard second order factors.

The exception to these *instrument-transcending personality factors* were two factors which appeared in the questionnaire data but not in the ratings, and which seem to be the "desirability" *factors*—not *a* desirability factor as in Edwards— hypothesized by Cattell (the "respectability" and the "good fellow" desirability). So long as research distortion covered only the questionnaire medium debate could rage indefinitely over which factors are "distortions." It was the bringing of this issue into relation with the *observer behavior rating medium* of factoring, as studied in this chapter, which at length permitted evaluation of the patterns of self-distortion in the questionnaire medium.

[1] The vexed question of whether the personality factors found in *ratings by observers*, such as $A$, affectia, $B$, intelligence, $C$, ego strength, $D$, excitability, $E$, dominance, etc., are the same as those similarly indexed and named (by their essential meaning) as $A$, $B$, $C$, etc., in questionnaire data, after being untouched for 25 years, has recently received a definitive answer. Scoring the same 164 subjects on the 32 main marker variables for the rating ($I$ data) factors and the 32 scales for the 16 P.F. factors, Cattell, Pierson, and Finkbeiner (1976) demonstrated that at the unique simple structure rotational resolution the markers, $L$ and

responses including Cattell's (1973a), in which he points out that methodological inadequacies do not allow for the dismissal of ratings so easily, and especially that the investigators have extracted too few factors, fewer than the number detailed below as fairly solid findings in the $L(R)$ realm. However, there is no doubt that difficulties exist in obtaining $L$ data, for together with $Q$ data, the $L$-type assesses the field of everyday action and filters observations through human observers.

To maintain proper perspective it is extremely important to remember that the primary character of $L$ data is that they deal with *actual, everyday life behavior in the cultural setting, recorded independently of the subject's perception*. Within that definition, however, there are two subdivisions. The first, $L(R)$ data, is that in which the behavior is simply *recorded*, in specific behavioral categories, perhaps by an IBM counter: for example, number of days absent from work, number of car accidents, mean time late for appointments, number of fights with other children in the playground, etc. $L(R)$ data are the substance of what is commonly called "time sampling."

$L(BR)$ data, on the other hand are the same data observed and remembered by a human observer, which commonly involves some error and localism of observation (Cattell, chapter 7) and also, perhaps more vitally, some abstraction from the actual specific behavior of trait concepts, or at least, sub-trait concepts. As Cattell, Digman, Norman and others have shown, this last introduces a world of problems. Yet, most unfortunately, the vast bulk of $L$ data is of type two, that is $L(BR)$ data, with all of its distortions. Nevertheless, in the strategy of dimensional research in personality, it made good sense for Cattell to rely on this method of rating to get a first general conspectus of the whole field, and to use this map as a guide for gathering $Q$ and $T$ data. The present chapter is thus essentially on $L(BR)$ methodology and results, and it covers largely the more sophisticated period since Cattell defined such concepts as the personality sphere, the coordinated pursuit of structure in three media, and other major guides for $L$ data thereby contributing substantially to current personality theories.

## 2 SOME MAJOR METHODOLOGICAL PROBLEMS

### 2.1 The Design of Rating Studies and Some Results

Let us now consider more closely some main requirements for designing a study of ratings. (Cattell's "Nine methodological points for good rating" can be consulted here: [Cattell, 1957a].) When one person judges the attributes of another according to one or more rating scales we can expect that only some part of his judgments will correspond with the "true" attributes of the person being judged. Other parts of the judgments will correspond with, for example, his own tendencies to be hard or easy in judgment, his relation with the other person, including any shared group membership, the way the rating scale is worded, and so on. (See Guilford, J. P., 1954, for a good discussion of rating scale characteristics.) An adequate research design for rating studies is one which, at the very least, minimizes the effect of these extraneous influences and maximizes the correspondence between the true attributes and the judgments about the attributes. These problems are more intensively dealt with in chapter 7, particularly in *trait-view* theory.

A second main aim in research design in this field is that they should provide a rational basis for selecting a set of rating scales both for sampling the personality sphere and for constructing clear scales.

The first research designs that satisfied these two conditions were those introduced by R. B. Cattell (1945a). Their features may be taken as a model of essentials in this kind of work, in that the following four points were observed:

1. Maximizing the true variance by maximizing areas of behavior observations by taking groups of 16 individuals who had shared the same fraternity (or sorority) house, the same experience in the tank corps in action, etc., for at least 6 months.

2. Controlling the individual differences between judges (and therefore between groups) on leniency by requiring each judge to assign the 15 cases being rated into a fixed set of frequencies along a 5-point rating scale.

3. Controlling the idiosyncratic parts of the judgments of each judge by giving each subject a score on each scale based upon *the sum of the judgments made by the other 15 judges* about him on each scale in turn.

4. Providing a rational basis for selecting rating scales by treating some 6,000 adjectives listed in a dictionary of the English language as representing what Cattell called a complete personality sphere. By various empirical and mathematical means, he reduced the 6,000 adjectives to 35 rating scales, this being the greatest number of scales that he thought could be used in those precomputer days "as a matter of unhappy necessity" (Cattell, 1945a).

Cattell's research design has remained unchallenged, but also altogether insufficiently unexamined, as the only adequate research design for work in this field. In 1957 in *Personality and Motivation Structure and Measurement*, Cattell updated the design by improving the selection and wording of the rating scales, by extending the number to 42, and by setting out a more extensive list

of practical rules for making studies of ratings. Fortunately, a sufficient core of serious researches has used this common basis of broadly sampled marker variables as Cattell proposed, building up interlocking studies in which it is a fairly simple matter to compare one study with another.

Given an adequate research design and factor analysis for source-traits pursued at a sound technical level, a research worker might entertain four reasonable expectations:

1. The attainment of invariant solutions. After his preliminary studies (1945a, 1946) Cattell applied the research design to groups of men in fraternity houses and to groups of girls in sorority houses (1947a, 1948). He expected that the solutions he found in factoring and rotating the results for the girls would be closely similar to the results for the men even though the analyses were made independently and the rotations carried out blindly for simple structure, that is, without theoretical preconceptions acting as biases.

2. Production of theories of personality structure for testing in other media. The dimensions defined in rating studies should indicate the dimensions that might be expected to arise in studies of self-ratings (the $Q$ modality) and in studies of objective tests (the $T$ modality). Thus they give clues as to what tests and questionnaires should be included to test the existence of such traits.

3. Intermedium validity. If a single study leads to a set of personality dimensions based on ratings, and to a corresponding or similar set based on another modality, then it might be expected that, for example, the person who is rated as being highly intelligent will perform well on intelligence tests and will give corresponding self-reports. This original expectation of complete immediate agreement of the patterns and scores from different media was modified by Cattell's

discovery of *instrument factors* (or, alternatively, Fiske and Campbell's multimethod emphasis) into the hypothesis that matching will appear only when instrument factors in the different media are accurately located and set aside in extraction.

4. The production of external validities. If rating studies lead to personality dimensions in a group for whom there is also evidence of success in various everyday life criteria, for example, in some training course, then it can be expected that what are conceived   by virtue of the personality sphere as the main dimensions of personality is useful in predicting this criterion.

These four expectations, particularly the first three, might be said to comprise the grand prospectus of dimensional research in personality. Work is directed towards the production, in each modality, of corresponding and cross-validating sets of dimensions. In this enterprise it was hoped that the study of ratings would provide the starting point.

If these expectations had been satisfied, then the present chapter could have devoted itself to a straightforward account of the main personality dimensions and their meanings. But, except for a coherence of findings in the main factors found by consistent methods among Cattell and his co-workers, it must be admitted that many apparently incompatible or, at least, blurred and vague pictures have turned up. Since science must consider all published results, the present chapter must examine first the rating procedures and factoring methods employed in order to understand why this should be so, and how the procedures may be improved. A brief summary of results follows.

## 2.2  External Validity?

Tupes (1957) showed that this method led to ratings, some of which predicted an independent criterion of success made some years later. The prediction was at a level which was comparable with the reliability of the criterion.

## 2.3  A Standard Set of Factors?

There are now two "standard" solutions to the results of studies using Cattell's design.

### 2.3.1.  *The 12-factor Solution*

Cattell analyzed his two sets of results and in each case he arrived at about a dozen oblique factors. The two studies showed substantial agreement by the salient variable similarity index which he developed on six of the factors, moderate agreement on three, and a rather low significance of agreement on the last three of the factors. These factors show a fair degree of resemblance to the factors derived from an earlier rating study of Cattell's, and they show a surprisingly high degree of conceptual correspondence with factors derived from analyses of questionnaire material. They also show a fair level of conceptual correspondence with factors derived from the judgments of individual teachers about their pupils.

For all these reasons Cattell and his co-workers asserted that there is good reason to assume that there are at least 12 traits defined by rating studies, even though detailed correspondence is lacking in particular instances.

In discussing Cattell's research strategy, it must be noted that he has consistently held to the principle that personality research should aim to be comprehensive and that a factor or trait should not be discarded because it happens to be small in one particular study. This principle implies that he is bound to deal with some factors that are small, do not replicate well, and are hard to validate. In comparing his work with that of workers who stop short earlier in the factor extraction, as most have done, emphasis therefore must be placed on the larger, earlier traits that carry a large part of the variance rather than on the minor factors.

### 2.3.2. The 5-factor Solution

Tupes and Christal (1958) have shown that it is possible to select 30 of the 35 from Cattell's rating scales in such a way that 5 or 6 massive and pervasive factors invariably occur under orthogonal Varimax rotations and that they match Cattell's first 5 or 6 very well.

In later years Norman and Harshbarger (1965) had some success in building questionnaires aimed at the rating factors (as Cattell's 16 Personality Factor Questionnaire was aimed originally), and Norman also applied a 20-scale method to further groups of students at the University of Michigan, using 4 scales to define each of 5 factors.

It is important to note that this 5-factor solution has been shown to occur in many samples with the 30-scale set of ratings, but that it has had to be imposed on the full set of 35 scales. It should also be noted that each of the 5 factors defined in this way is pervasive—with substantial factor loadings on about half the rating scales. Cattell's criticism of this work and some others stopping short at 4, 5, or 6 factors are (a) that any sound test of number of factors shows decidedly more factors (commonly 11–13); (b) that one must remember that Varimax (being hobbled to orthogonality) cannot reach the best simple structure position, especially without support from all 12 factors; and (c) that in ratings, if only 6 or so factors (the number of second orders) are rotated, the result may miss the primaries altogether and go to a rough distorted picture of the second orders. A final objection to the 5-factor solution as pointed out by the present writer, is that it appears to leave a fair amount of the intercorrelation of

rating scales unaccounted for (which agrees with the independent Scree test indication).

### 2.3.3 Higher Order, Nesting, or Hierarchical Solutions

The present writer, in addition to rechecking Cattell's primaries on his own data by independent factoring and rotation, pursued the higher order or hierarchical patterns (see Cattell, 1957a). Cattell defines 6 second-order factors in rating data. That these are not the primaries of Tupes and Norman was agreed on by both Tupes and Cattell. However, the present writer reworked Cattell's data extracting and rotating only 4 factors, and it then happens that a rotation can be obtained that apparently goes directly to the second-order position. Thus one obtains factors which correspond to the groupings found by Cattell for primaries in terms of the secondaries under which they "hierarchically" fall, except that the loadings of the secondaries are directly on the variables (the 36 or 45 markers) instead of on the primaries.

Whether a psychologist chooses in practice to use 5 or more second-stratum factors, or the larger number of primaries which Cattell advocates, depends on his available time and the degree of accuracy of criterion prediction desired. As to the conceptual distinction, at present all we have to go on is Cattell's "influence" model which supposes that the secondaries act upon groups of primaries, partly determining their level. Thus anxiety (second stratum No. II) acts on the primary $C$ ego-strength, to reduce it, and upon ergic tension ($Q_4$) to increase it.

## 3 METHODOLOGICAL ISSUES IN RATING PERCEPTIONS OF JUDGES: TRAIT VIEW AND STEREOTYPE THEORIES

A review of ratings studies, orthogonal and oblique in resolution, shows that there can apparently still be arguments over how many rating primaries there are, anywhere from 5 to 13 or 14; and as regards the conclusions in the second-order realm, it is obvious that a much firmer determination of the correlations among primaries is necessary before the studies can begin to approach the certainties of those in the questionnaire domain.

This section and the one following set out methodological and conceptual questions vital to the pursuit of effective checking studies. Cattell (1957a) stated conditions governing rating requirements; others have proposed additional requirements regarding the number of variables and the conditions of good factor analysis. These we shall review and extend, asking "What features of some current designs have led to confusion over factor results?" and "What experimental evidence exists about rating reliability, etc.?" Let us begin with the judges and the rating situation.

### 3.1  Judges

In his review of this topic in *Personality and Motivation Structure and Measurement*, Cattell (1957a) offered several rules that should be satisfied by the sets of judges. These are as follows:

1. The period of observation should be at least 2 or 3 months, preferably a year.
2. Rating by peers is to be preferred, and rating by individuals in special role relations with the ratees is to be avoided.
3. The raters should be discouraged from discussing together the ratees since independent evaluation rather than reputation is required.

These three rules are intended to insure that the judges have a sound basis in experience on which to judge the complex true attributes of the ratees. The rules should maximize agreement between judges or "conspect reliability" so far as they depend upon valid grounds. The third rule is intended to avoid getting agreement on spurious grounds.

Cronbach (1955) suggested that each person deals with the problem of perceiving and interpreting the behavior of other persons by developing an "implicit personality theory." For the judge, this theory implies a notion of the relative frequencies of joint occurrences of various personality attributes. Passini and Norman (1966) suggested that judges of similar background might share certain core sets of assumptions about attributes that go together. They said,

We are assuming that a sizable proportion of persons tend to believe in common, for whatever reasons, that certain clusters of attributes occur jointly in other persons with probability, greater than .5, and that attributes in one such cluster are believed to occur more or less independently of those which form other such clusters.

And we assume finally that certain phenotypic aspects of dress, demeanor, physical size, movement, and the like are incorporated into these syndromal stereotypes.

The clearest example of the phenomena to which Passini and Norman referred is the notion of a "stereotype" of personality such that if a judge is told the skin color, or the race, or the occupation of a ratee then he applies a ready-made set of personality attributes to that person. Norman and Passini did not speculate about the way in which implicit personality theories are built up. Cultural conventions, for example, proverbs, and stereotypes offer probabilistic associations. It is likely that the common language also provides certain strong associations between pairs of adjectives, for example, "frank" with "open." The experiments of Asch (1946) in studying the effect of combinations of adjectives is relevant here, as also is the work on the association of words with high "social desirabilty," or which have similar values on Osgood's semantic differential factors. However, both Cattell (1957a) and Norman (1966a) pointed out that these latter principles would lead one to expect a general "halo" factor in ratings and this certainly does not occur. In Cattell's terms, "social desirability" comes from the factor itself.

It should be recognized that if a person builds up an implicit personality theory, then he does so because it is useful and leads to the best possible predictions from the evidence available at the time. An implicit personality theory is likely to be one that admits inferences based on minimal cues such as photographs, or occupational titles, up to the apperceptive mass that results from long-term acquaintance. At all stages it will serve to give the judge a simple coherent view of the ratee.

The author has suggested (Hammond, S., 1965) that the experimental basis of the judge making ratings, and of the ratee building up sets of personality competences, are likely, on social-psychological grounds, to build them in subsets corresponding to interpersonal, task, and intrapersonal objects because these are the common elements of all role relations throughout his life.

In the light of these considerations, it will not surprise the reader to learn that ratings' studies made on the basis of long acquaintance (Cattell, 1947a; Tupes, 1957); or studies based on only 3 days' acquaintance (Tupes and Christal, 1958); or studies based on 1 week's acquaintance (Fiske, 1949); or studies based on seeing a stranger at the time of rating (Norman and Goldberg 1966); or studies based on the photographs of ratees (Passini and Norman 1966) all yield a similar

factor structure when only 5 factors are extracted. These studies have not been analyzed by Cattell's methods; therefore, it is impossible to say whether the same invariance would occur by these methods. Digman (1963, 1965a), however, showed that the ratings made by individual teachers, or by pairs of teachers, usually yield a factor structure similar to those found by Cattell on the basis of the pooled judgments of many raters.

Certainly such a replication of the "true" personality structure by the "experiential map" in the rater's mind would be expected —at any rate up to a point—from the comprehensive handling of the findings in Cattell and Digman's (1964) perturbation theory, and Cattell's subdevelopment in trait-view theory (see chapter 7).

This theory would lead one to expect, first, that ratings based upon close and long experience will yield factor structures similar to those based upon minimal experiential ones. It is not known whether a massive basis of experience leads to a minimizing of semantic extrapolations and therefore to a more accurate definition of the factors involved, but Passini and Norman (1966) showed that studies based on longer experience do lead to stronger correlations of the factors with external questionnaire criteria. Second, although the factor patterns from the stereotype would be the same as those from the given data, yet the agreement between judges on the level of particular factors in particular individuals would be poorer, and poorer with any ulterior evidence of the true values, as the acquaintance with the subjects grows less.

Some evidence on this last point may be gained from Tupes and Christal's report of one sample of U.S. Air Force officers who rated one another after 3 days' acquaintance, and then, in entirely different groups, produced a new set of ratings after 6 months' acquaintance. If we treat the communality of rating scales as a reflection of the level of agreement of judges, then these two studies show, first, that there was substantial agreement between the judges at 3 days on ratings of assertive, talkative, energetic, adventurous, and frank. These are all descriptive scales referring to more or less directly observable social behavior, and no increase in agreement was noted on them after 6 months. However, on other rating scales there was a substanial increase in communality up to this same level of agreement by the end of this period. Among items referring to social behavior, for example, there were great increases in goodnatured, adaptable, and attentive. It appears, therefore, that judges agree more because their judgments are more veridical after longer acquaintance. Second, the initial work in rating can be regarded as a way of inducing an evaluative set on the part of the judges. The communalities of this group at 6 months are higher than those in any other study reported. This suggests that some such initial training might be useful in increasing the sensitivity of judges to the relations between behavior and rating scales.

The preceding discussions involve complex issues of both validity and reliability, but it is possible to consider reliability as such in a comparatively tight operational framework. The reliability of pooled judgments depends in part on the adequacy of the wording of the rating scales, which will be considered later. Reliability also depends upon both the number of judges involved and the level of agreement between them, which is our concern here. Cattell suggested (1957a) that more intelligent raters are likely because of the better "fit" of their stereotypes to data intrinsically abstract and complex, to give more valid and, therefore, more reliable ratings. He also noted that female judges agree better than do com-

parable male judges, a result he attributed to a greater and shrewder interest in people. It appears that the average intercorrelation between pairs of judges in good studies may be as low as .25 and rarely will exceed .45. Under circumstances where all judges may be taken to be about equally competent, we may treat an increase in the number of judges as increasing the reliability of the pooled judgments according to the Spearman-Brown prophecy formula. Table 1 sets out the reliabilities of pooled ratings to be expected on this basis for different numbers of judges and different levels of average interjudge or conspective reliability.

In designing a research study we are free to treat the number of judges and the average intercorrelation of judges as alternative ways of increasing the reliability of the final pooled ratings. If, by training and selecting judges and by wording rating scales, the average interjudge correlation between judges can be raised to .45, then eight judges will do better than 16 judges starting at .25 and almost as well as 24 judges starting at .25. This realization opens up the possibility of using a set of judges so that each of them makes judgments on only one-half or one-third of the rating scales.

This technique has been used by Tupes and Kaplan (1961) in a study of the wording of questions, and by Schaie (1963) so as to avoid having any pair of individuals judge

**TABLE 1**  Expected reliabilities of pooled ratings

| Number of judges | Average intercorrelation of pairs of judges | | |
|---|---|---|---|
| | .25 | .35 | .45 |
| 2 | .39 | .52 | .62 |
| 4 | .57 | .69 | .77 |
| 8 | .73 | .81 | .87 |
| 16 | .84 | .90 | .93 |
| 24 | .89 | .93 | .96 |

each other; but it has not been used, to the author's knowledge, as a way of doubling or tripling the number of rating scales used in a particular study without increasing the workload of a particular judge. It is not suggested that the judges be divided into two or three sets but rather that each judge be given his "book" of ratings, which is made up of some unique set of scales drawn under the restriction that each scale occurs in a specified number of rating books. This innovation appears to offer the best hope of extending the research design to the scope of 60–80 rating scales, which appear to be needed to test whether 12 important factors or more can be defined and found invariantly.

Parenthetically, it may be noted that in carrying out ratings Cattell offered the rule (to reduce what used to be called "halo" but is more broadly defined as "stereotype and cliché contamination") that each rating scale should be dealt with on an occasion that is different from that of others. Cross-contamination between scales would be further reduced if each rater dealt with his scales in a different order from anybody else. This is a second good reason for giving each judge a unique book of rating scales.

## 4  METHODOLOGICAL ISSUES CONCERNING CHOICE OF VARIABLES AND SUBJECTS

Dealing with purely statistical issues, first one turns to the number of subjects. The smallest rating study of any consequence used 124 subjects and the largest 790. There seems to be no particularly clear ground for choosing one number rather than another except that there is an increase in the size of the early latent roots with the larger samples. It is the author's prejudice that a sample of at least 200 cases is needed if 10

factors or more are likely to be found because correlation coefficients with small error terms are required. It is quite likely that rules for the number of subjects will be stated in time in terms of some minimum number of groups of subjects. Cattell's study of 15 sorority groups of 16 girls each seems adequate in size; however, because of withdrawals the male study had only eight fraternity houses, which seems to be an insufficient number to average out the effects of fraternity houses.

In practice it appears to be difficult to obtain widely representative populations who satisfy the requirements of long-term mutual acquaintance. Almost all the samples studied by Cattell, Tupes, Fiske and Norman were university students or had at least 2 years of university background, and the groups were studied while they were undergoing a demanding program of training. It is highly desirable to find out whether these common circumstances led to some factors being small because of selection—such as intellectuals ones—and to others being large but related to success or failure in course work. The author recently studied a group with secondary education who were undergoing a crash training program of 21 weeks and noted that the factors of intrapsychic tension became increasingly and strongly related to success in the course as ratings progressed from Week 4 to Week 12 to Week 16. In other words, anxiety manifestations had clear situational causes.

Some problems next arise—since no judge can know well a truly large sample of people—concerning the arrangements. If each judge uses a standard rating distribution, then the mean of each group of ratees on each rating scale will be the same. The standard deviations ($SD$) of each group need not be the same since they depend upon the conspective reliability. The judges are, however, forced to use the same initial $SD$.

Would these procedures do violence to reality? It is convenient to start the enquiry by assuming that the groups are drawn randomly from a population. In this case "real" or "true" variance is lost to the degree that there is the expected random variance of the means and *SD*s of the groups. If the groups are small, we might expect a considerable variation of their means; this variation would be less if the groups are large. Applying ordinary standard error formulae, it is fairly easy to show that about 9% of true variance is taken up between group means when groups are 12 cases each, about 7% for groups of 16 cases, and about 4% for groups of 24. Adding a smaller loss for the standard deviation we have a figure of about 10% of true variance lost between groups of 16 cases taken at random.

This loss is one source of attenuation for correlations between ratings and tests, since these losses do not affect tests. It may be presumed that the U.S. Air Force studies were made on randomly drawn groups and would suffer this loss of true variance. Because of random drawing we would not expect the restriction on one rating scale to be systematically related to the restriction on another.

The situation is quite different in rating studies which use students in fraternity houses. Roger Brown (1965), in reporting studies of the repute of different fraternity houses in the early 1950s, had this to say:

I used to ask the students in the undergraduate social psychology course to characterize the members of each House by selecting from a list of adjectives. In those days Lowell House, was thought to be predominantly "intellectual," Adams was for artists and musicians, Winthrop for athletes.

It seems likely that the differences between fraternity houses are as follows:

1. The differences are greater in size than those between randomly assigned groups.

2. The differences involve residence in group conditions that demand conformity to special differential codes of behavior; and

3. The differences involve systematic co-trait variation between groups. The "intellectual" will differ from the athlete on several dimensions.

There are no studies which indicate the size of these effects, but it is not unreasonable to guess that about 30%–40%[2] of the true variance between individuals on many traits is not only lost between groups but, in fact, acts to generate artifactual relations between factors due to the third characterization of differences. Effects of this kind fall under Category 3 of the perturbation influences discussed by Cattell and Digman (1964) and in chapter 7. They would become really serious in producing instrument factors and the attenuation of the correlations between ratings and tests or questionnaires in the same battery. Certainly there would be difficulties in reaching a good simple structure in orthogonal factors or properly estimating correlations among oblique factors when groups are not drawn randomly to start with.

Cattell suggested that this problem might be met in part by asking the judges to include ratings of some "artificial standardizing population," such as persons in a story or a movie presented to all judges. By this method the mean and *SD* of their individual

[2] *Editors' Note*: These estimates seem to us somewhat excessive. However, the main issue is whether the nature of the intergroup covariance is the same as that within groups, i.e., if it yields the same factors. In general it would, and there would be no problem except attenuation. However, the interesting effect with groups of special character brought out here by Dr. Hammond needs to be watched.

rating tendencies can be adjusted to a uniform standard. This would be a useful study to define the extent of the problem; but a simpler research strategy is first to get randomly assigned groups, if our objective is to define factors, and we can stand the attenuation from loss of intergroup effects.

Next we should consider the effects of some properties of the variables and the scales as such. Except for Fiske (1949) studies generally have used fixed distributions for ratings. Cattell asked his judges to rank the subjects (15 of them) and then converted the ranks to five categories placing one case in the top category, then four, five, four, and one in the other four. These are coarse categories; 8.4% of true variance is lost within the classes if we assume that the true distributions are continuous and normal. Tupes and Norman asked their judges to put one-third of the cases in each of three categories. Here the percentage of true variance lost within classes is much greater, 20.6.

The effect of using coarse categories on the intercorrelation of two judges is simply to attenuate it. If the correlation between the true scores of two judges is 0.45, then the expected attenuated correlation in Cattell's five-category cases is $.450 \times .916 \times .916 = .378$. In the three-category case of Tupes it shrinks still further to .284.

Table 2 sets out the consequent effects of this shrinkage for different numbers of judges.

It can be seen that Cattell, who used groups of 16, and Tupes, who used groups of up to 24 cases, were, in contrast to other investigators, losing little true variance because of coarse categories.

We may question whether it is necessary to rely on completely fixed distributions. It is possible to say to a judge, "The expected distribution *for an average group* is 1:4:5:4:1," but he may vary these numbers

**TABLE 2** Reliabilities based on a true inter-judge correlation of 0.45, which is attenuated by using coarse categories

| Number of judges | Ideal case | 5-category case | 3-category case |
|---|---|---|---|
| 8 | .87 | .82 | .76 |
| 16 | .93 | .91 | .86 |
| 24 | .96 | .94 | .91 |

up or down by one case in each category if he thinks that the group differs from average. Such a rule would retain the advantages of fixed distribution but would make the raters' task much easier and this method would allow the consensus of a group of judges to shift the mean and *SD* of a group by about as much as random variations would call for. In fact, a loosening of the rules in this way might make it reasonable to ask the judges to use a 7-point scale such as 1:2:3:3:3:2:1 with a slight gain in true variance. Cattell (1957a) recommended another design (all subjects be ranked by the judge, these ranks being converted on a normal curve by the experiment), evidently feeling that it invokes error to leave the decision to the judge as to how deviant the average and distribution of his group might be. Unfortunately, this method has not been used in any study subsequent to that book.

We come again to what we encountered first: The question of selection of variables, in which spanning the personality sphere is of primary importance. One of the most original and valuable aspects of Cattell's design was his attempt to represent systematically the whole range of personality attributes by successive reduction from the Allport and Odbert (1936) list of common adjectives in Webster's dictionary. One suspects that if Cattell had had a current computing facility in 1946 he would not have made the final reduction to 35 rating scales but would have used his intermediate stopping point at 67 or at 128 variable scales. In his 1957 review he increased the number of scales from 35 to 42 and considerably simplified the wording of many of the scales to the point where the descriptive sentences that go with the scales are elaborations of the key defining words. This simplification is likely to lead to increased rater reliability and to clearer divisions between the factors. These changes are in line with Cattell's rule that "the segment of behavior in question should be clearly defined, discussed and connotatively delimited by a list of actual behaviors."

Three different approaches can be adopted in this matter of the range and number of rating scales. One can, with Cattell, profess to be satisfied with minor extensions. One can, like Norman, assert that the proof of any factors beyond the first 5 requires a return to the original word lists, or one can suggest that new terms are needed which will define more clearly the boundaries of the 12 factors Cattell postulates.

Norman (1963a) selected 2,800 personality-trait words and defined their normative operating characteristics for a university population. For each word, he defined whether a student group knew the meaning of the word; obtained an average social desirability level for the word; and studied whether the word is applied to the self, a named friend, a neutral, or an individual who is disliked. Norman had not as of this writing taken the further step of setting up a new and extended list of trait terms, but his new word list makes this task easier.

A question that often arises in rating discussions is the advantage of bipolar over unipolar definitions. An enquiry which deserves mention here is that of Tupes and Kaplan (1961), who asked whether the positive pole (the socially desirable end) of a rating scale measures the same factors as the negative pole. He divided the judges in each group into three sets of four. One set used the positive pole, one the negative, and the third the usual bipolar form. Inevitably, he found a reasonable but not complete degree of agreement between the poles in each scale. This is the kind of research study that can be used to test the compatability of the poles in any new scales. For example, his study showed that the poles in one case—those of the scale conventional-unconventional—split between two factors. Conventional was treated as a lack of surgency, and unconventional-eccentric as a lack of the persistence factor.

It may be convenient for the reader to have some of the outcomes of this discussion duly summarized for practical methodological steps.

1. While retaining most of the 35 original markers to permit exact cross reference, the list should be considerably extended to permit better definition of later factors and that more exact tests (Scree, Tucker, Kaiser–Guttman [K–G], Lawley) be applied regularly to fix the number.

2. Since groups must be small, for acquaintance, they should be selected on the basis of random assignment and highly selective groups should be avoided.

3. Any study should have at least 15 groups to minimize the effect of deviant groups.

4. Rating scales should be on a 5- or 7-point basis of a "loosely fixed" kind.

5. Each group should contain about 20 people who are both judges and subjects, to allow for each judge to rate a unique selection of, say, half the rating scales.

6. Ranking and rating should be on one trait at a time and the internal consistency of these terms should be tested by reliability procedures before use.

7. Judges should stand in no highly specific role in relation to the subjects and

should see them through a large fraction of the day.

8. These studies should be analyzed to determine whether a dozen factors or more can be separately and strongly defined and whether, at the best simple structure position, these are oblique.

Given these eight conditions it might be possible not only to identify a "best set" of factors, but also to define the factor scores of individuals accurately, strongly, and without group artifacts. This is the essential precondition for cross-modality validation.

Now that we have taken up methodological and practical problems of ratings, we can proceed to assess the results of factor solutions of rating scale intercorrelations for both adults and children.

## 5 THE ORTHOGONAL APPROACH TO STRUCTURE IN L(BR) DATA

In terms of trying independent reanalysis of Cattell's rating data, it seemed desirable to analyze also in orthogonal terms.

Admittedly the normalized Varimax procedure leads to large conglomerate factors failing to spread the larger principal components, and thus yields pseudo-second-order factors. It seemed it might be an improvement therefore to use the Equamax method, which is intended to deal with this kind of problem. The study made in this section used the 240 sample of undergraduate girls as well as Cattell's parallel sample of 124 men. We hoped to arrive at a best solution under the requirement of the best agreement we could reach by this method between the two studies. The results were as follows:

1. Good agreement between the two studies at the level of 4 Equamax factors. These were closely similar to the extra-version, surgency and emotional control factors of Tupes, Norman, etc., plus a 4th factor that combined their other 2 "task-oriented" factors of persistence and culture.

2. Moderately good agreement between the two studies when 12 factors were taken, 9 of the 12 pairs of factors having substantial coefficients of similarity of direction although no pairs were really close.

3. Poor agreement between the studies when between 5 and 11 factors were extracted.

4. The 12-factor solutions were related to the 4-factor solutions in the sense that each of the 4 large factors was a bundle of several of the 12 factors.[3]

5. The distinction between the 12 factors, within any one such set or bundle, often rested upon the loadings on only one or two rating scales.

A brief discussion of the meaning of the factors follows.

*Factor 1* This factor has very high factor loadings (.5 or higher) on 9 rating scales, all of which are concerned with a good-natured, mild, trustful, and cooperative approach to interpersonal relations. It has been labeled by French (1953) the Agreeableness factor although its strongest loadings are on rating scales expressing good nature and undemanding and mild interpersonal relations. It could thus be considered a match for Cattell's Affectothymia versus Sizothymia, or alternatively for his Exvia.

*Factor 2* The eight rating scales with loadings above .50 are concerned with sociability, openness, talkativeness, and energetic assertiveness. Cattell coined the term

---

[3] No calculation has been made by the Cattell-White formula obtaining the projection of Cattell's second-order factors directly on the 35 variables, to permit an exact comparison with the broader factors here.

*surgency* for such a combination of energetic, confident sociable behavior; and this term has been adopted by J. W. French (1953) and others such as Tupes and Norman. However, the present factor is more general than Cattell's Factor *F*, Surgency, and could be his second-order Exvia or H. J. Eysenck's Extraversion factor.

These two factors divide up the items that refer to interpersonal relations into two sets, one concerning sociability in general, and the other the more fundamental attributes of trust, maturity, and cooperation which are necessary in close interpersonal relations.

*Factor 3* The four rating scales which have high loadings on this factor are concerned with emotional integration and the lack of neurotic manifestations. Since the rating scales for emotionally stable and emotionally mature have weaker loadings on this factor, however, than do jealousy, suspicion and dependence, it is surprising that this factor is referred to by Tupes and Norman as Emotional Stability, unless this is merely a euphemism for the Eysenckian term *Neuroticism*. Its obvious resemblances are to Cattell's *C* factor of Ego-Strength or, at the second order to his general Anxiety (inverted).

*Factor 4* This factor has five large factor loadings and four more substantial ones. The main ratings concerned are orderly, responsible, persevering, conscientious, and cautious—all of which imply a deliberate and persistent application to the carrying out of tasks. The next four loadings in order of size are conventional, self-contained, cooperative, and mild.

This factor is labeled by Tupes and Christal (1961) as Persistent, which brings out the task aspect. J. W. French (1953) used the label Dependability and Fiske (1949), Conformity. For two factors in this area, Cattell used Superego (*G*) and Self-

sentiment $(Q_3)$. It invites the speculation that several factors, all concerned with performance of hard tasks, may be mixed up here.

*Factor 5* This factor has high loadings on intellectual, independent-minded, and polished. The moderately loading scales include persevering, orderly, energetic. This set of scales has been given the label Culture by French, and this is followed by Tupes and Norman. It can be seen that this set of items is also concerned with task activities, but whereas the previous factor was concerned with the means for carrying out tasks, this one is more concerned with the person who is trained to make sophisticated, independent judgments about the means and the ends involved. It will be noted that the moderately loaded scales in this factor are the same as some in Factor 4, and it is clear that there is a considerable overlap between these two factors.

## 6 THE SUBSTANTIVE AND METHODOLOGICAL BASES OF THE OBLIQUE SOLUTION

The objection to such orthogonal programs as Equamax and Varimax, quite apart from their orthogonality, is that by reason of this analytical function they do not maximize what one needs to maximize, namely, the hyperplane count. They also fail to spread out the first large principal components. The ease of programing them has nevertheless led to an enormous use. Even the attempt by White to attach a last-minute switch in these programs from an orthogonal to an oblique final outcome still does not escape the poor distribution of variance from the large factors. The more radical solution of going to a topological program, Maxplane, though slightly more expensive, has been shown by Eber (1966) to produce clearer and more replicable results. However,

Cattell asserted that the results obtained by a skilled analyst using the Rotoplot program improves on the hyperplane count of any known automatic program 99 times out of 100. (In the Rotoplot program the analyst is given a photographic image of every pair of factors; he then decides the rotation each time by eye.) By this means the typical end count of a good resolution is 60%–80% in the ±.10 hyperplane.

Any analysis carried to an oblique solution yields (Harman, 1967; Thurstone, 1947) both a set of factor correlations with the variables (factor structure) and of loadings on the variables (factor pattern) (see Cattell, 1966h, for a discussion of these and other dimension-variable matrices), as well as a matrix giving the intercorrelations among the factors (from which the second and higher strata factors can later be derived).

Despite the fact that the command of methodology for maximum simple structure factors has reached the same high level in both $Q$ and $L$ data applications, it is unfortunately true that the available life record substantive data is far less adequate today than it is in $Q$ data. Three studies by Cattell in the 1940's still present virtually the only data meeting the six required conditions Cattell suggested for a sound and well-sampled basis of variables, though the Tupes and Warren data meet four of the conditions and some being processed for children by Digman and Dielman (section 8) also meet four.

The three Cattell researches were designed to interlock, one on 208 mature adult men, one on 133 undergraduate male students, and one on 240 female students, thus being close enough to cross check but able to give preliminary indications on possible age and sex differences of structure. In more detail they are described as follows.

*Study 1* This was the earliest, planned in 1940 and completed 4 years later (Cattell, 1945a) on 208 men, 128 of whom were soldiers in eight groups of 16 and the remainder were groups of businessmen, artists, and artisans. In this study the intercorrelations of 35 variables were calculated within equal-sized common-acquaintance subgroups by rank-order methods and then averaged for the whole study. Factors were extracted by the multiple group method of factor extraction and resulted, as is usual, in an oblique solution. By hand rotation a 12-factor solution was reached, which provided the initial definition of Cattell's Factors $A$ to $L$. Three of these, Factors $B$, $D$, and $K$, were poorly defined by the simple structure method used. Thurstone carried out an independent oblique rotation of these data and was satisfied to define 8 factors. Cattell noted that each of these 8 was included in his set of 12 and decided to retain the other 4 in case they could be found again in later studies. The multiple group approach has some tendency, possibly not destroyed in subsequent rotation, to put factors through clusters.

*Study 2* His second study of 133 fraternity men was based on 8 complete groups of 16 and one incomplete group on essentially the same 35 variables (Cattell, 1947a). The author, on Professor Cattell's initiative, and using Cattell's new programs, recalculated the correlations in this study, and it is clear that many of Cattell's difficulties in rotating the results of this study simply arose from clerical errors in 4 of the 595 correlation coefficients. It is perhaps a mark of the coarseness of grain of the 5-factor solution that Tupes had no difficulty in fitting this erroneous data with it.

*Study 3* A comparable study of 240 sorority women was based on 15 groups of 16. It is notable that twice as many groups of women as of men managed to cope with the heavy demands for time made on them by Cattell's research, and this indicates that the "survivors" among the men's group may have been a very select set. Consequently, we are bound to place much more weight on the results from the study of women. In addition, Cattell comments that the women seemed to put far more care into their ratings. In all studies, Tucker's criterion for the number of factors was used and gave the 11 or 12 factors actually extracted, not the 5, 6, or 8 that other investigators have "conservatively" taken from this data.

The two later studies were intended to build upon the first study, taking the hypotheses suggested by the first analysis and reshaping some of the definitions of variables more crucially to test the hypotheses, as follows:

1. To provide a clearer definition of each of Factors *A-L*.

2. To strengthen the definition of weak Factors *H-L*.

3. To redefine each rating scale from its original, "cluster"-based set to an "organic trait" form that took into account the correlates revealed in the first study.

4. To differentiate between factors that seemed rather closely related, for example, the two "schizoid" factors *A* and *K* and the three character factors *C*, *G*, and *J*.

Thus the later studies are only conceptually comparable with the first study. It is a great pity that a few errors in the second study impeded Cattell's strategy of finally defining the factors by getting independent matched solutions from the two later studies. In effect, Cattell's study of the women stands alone as the best example of an oblique solution. It seems to be defective in one minor respect only. Cattell notes that variables 7, Cool-Aloof, and 21, Polished, which define a new factor *N*, have communality estimates greater than 1.0. It seems that the sign of their intercorrelation −.367, was reversed; it should have been +.367. If

this were done, then Factor *N* would probably disappear from this study.

In the two later studies the factors were extracted by a centroid method. The women's study was hand rotated through 54 complete cycles, taking 18 months of calculation. It is interesting to note that after 23 cycles, only 7 factors had attained simple structure. These included (a) one factor defined by an intelligence test, (b) one psychologically undefined factor, and (c) five factors *A*, *C*, *F*, *G*, *K* which correspond closely to the five factors in the Tupes' type of solution. Other results similarly show *A*, *B*, *C*, *F*, *G*, *H*, and *T* as the "hardiest" factors, surviving a certain amount of clumsiness of factor-extraction procedures. When the other factors in the final solution are examined, we find, leaving aside Factor *N*, that none has a loading above .34 in this particular study, but this is true also of *T* studies.

Table 3 summarizes the occasions on which the psychological factors, designated

**TABLE 3**  Replication of rating factors

|         |      | Stu  | dy   |       |
|---------|------|------|------|-------|
| Factor[a] | 1945 | 1947 | 1949 | Tupes |
| *A*       | x    | x    | x    | x     |
| *C*       | x    | x    | x    | . x   |
| *F*       | x    | x    | x    | x     |
| *G*       | x    | x    | x    | x     |
| *K*       | x    | x    | x    | x     |
| *H*       | x    | x    | x    |       |
| *E*       | x    | x    | ?    |       |
| *D*       | x    |      | x    |       |
| *I*       | x    | x    |      |       |
| *M*       |      | x    | x    |       |
| *J*       | x    |      |      |       |
| *L*       | x    |      |      |       |
| *N*       |      |      | ?    |       |
| *B*[b]    |      |      |      |       |

[a]The letters *A, C, F*, etc., were used by Cattell (1957a) to represent personality rating factors.
[b]Based on intelligence test and its correlates.

by Cattell's letters, have appeared in the studies discussed here. Thus we note that $J$, $L$, and $N$, as of 1949, had failed to replicate. It is perhaps additional proof of the parallelism of $L$- and $Q$-data results that it is precisely these factors that also have smallest variance in $Q$ data. (In fact, $M$, $N$, and $O$ have the smallest variance in the more recent 16 PF factor check, Cattell, Eber, & Delhees, 1968.) In general, the original order of size variance of factors in these three earliest studies, which gave them their order $A$ through $N$, has been supported by later work, though with children (Cattell, 1963e; Digman, 1963) some change in magnitude order apparently occurs.

## 7  CATTELL'S CATALOGUE OF RATING FACTORS $A$ TO $N$

It has been pointed out that Cattell's research strategy of introducing the personality sphere concept of sampling all variables aims to "block in" all the main factors. Thus they may have the word "primary" attached to them in both senses. Having located the primaries (by then both in ratings and questionnaire data) he set out in 1957 to present a theory of the nature and origin of each factor to guide further research. For this latter purpose, as well as for completeness in this *Handbook* and for purposes of comparison with the realm of children's rating factors as given by Dielman in the following section, a brief catalog of Cattell's adult-derived rating factors is in order here.

### 7.1  The Primary Factors

*Factor L*(1). *A. Affectothymia versus Schizothymia* (formerly Cyclothymia vs. Schizothymia) named by J. W. French "cooperative"

| $A+$ Positively loaded | $A-$ Negatively loaded |
|---|---|
| Easy-going | Obstructive |
| Adaptable | Rigid, inflexible |
| Warmhearted, attentive to people | Cool, indifferent |
| Frank, placid | Secretive |
| Emotional, expressive | Reserved |
| Trustful | Suspicious |
| Impulsive, generous | Cautious |
| Cooperative | Hostile |

Cattell noted the strong resemblance to the similarly largest dimension in clinical observations by Kraepelin and Bleuler, Cyclothymia versus Schizothymia. Because of the persisting pathological associations these were later altered to the present (*sizo* means "flat" or "dry" emotionality). The resemblance of the "cooperative" factor to this in Tupes' analysis is clear. The corresponding factor in the Cattell oblique analysis had six scales with loadings between .42 and .55.

Cattell pointed out that Factor $A$ has certain similarities of loading patterns to Factors $F$, Surgency; $H$, Adventurousness; and $L$, Trusting, which may account for their having been confused earlier in the vague conglomerate of Extraversion ($A$, $F$, and $H$ are the main factors contributing to the second-order factor of Extraversion).

*Factor L*(2). *B Intelligent*

In Cattell's adult studies this rating factor was defined by the rather weak personality expression correlates of an intelligence test. For example, in the women's study the factor was defined by the following:

| | |
|---|---|
| Intelligence (by test) | .60 |
| Persevering versus quitting | .26 |
| Tough, poised versus easily upset | .23 |

*Factor L(3). C. Ego-Strength versus Proneness to Neuroticism*

| C+ | C− |
|---|---|
| Emotionally stable | Emotional |
| Free of neurotic symptoms, not hypochondriacal | Hypochondriacal |
| Realistic | Immature |
| Unworried | Worrying, anxious |
| Self-controlled | Changeable |
| Calm | Excitable |
| Persevering | Quitting, careless |
| Dependable | Undependable |

Cattell defined this as "the capacity to express available emotional energy along integrated as opposed to impulsive channels," and frustration tolerance and linked it with clinically defined studies of growth, under fortunate environmental conditions, of the self. It has since proved to have the widest association with clinical pathology of any factor. He noted that this factor sometimes becomes confused with *G*, superego strength, and that it is, along with Factor *L*, Trust, a major component in the second-order Anxiety factor.

This factor was named "Emotionality" by J. W. French. The corresponding of the Tupes' factor with this pattern is good. In Cattell's analysis of the women's study this was the largest of all the factors, having six scales with loadings above .46.

*Factor L(4). D. Excitability-insecurity*

| D+ | D− |
|---|---|
| Demanding, impatient | Emotionally mature |
| Attention getting | Self-sufficient |
| Excitable | Deliberate |
| Jealous | Not jealous |
| Self-assertive | Self-effacing |

This factor has rarely appeared clear in adult studies, and when it does, it tends to be highly correlated with *A*, *F*, and *C*. This factor of general excitement, however, is repeatedly found in studies of children.

*Factor L(5). E. Dominance-Submissiveness*

| E+ | E− |
|---|---|
| Self-assertive | Submissive |
| Energetic | Passive |
| Adventurous | Timid |
| Unconventional | Conventional |
| Willful | Obedient |

Cattell speculated that this factor rests upon a general temperamental forcefulness. In the women's study this factor appeared in a form that was better described in terms of self-assurance with no suggestion of dominant behavior, and had three loadings above .35.

*Factor L(6). F. Surgency-Desurgency*

| F+ | F− |
|---|---|
| Cheerful | Depressed |
| Sociable, responsive | Retiring |
| Energetic | Languid |
| Talkative | Not talkative |
| Placid | Worrying |
| Adaptable | Rigid |

This in one of the main factors in adult-rating studies and is the largest in child studies. Surgency is interpreted as being confident sociability based on experiences of success in social activities, while Desurgency is associated with a history of punishment, deprivation, and inhibition. This is one of the factors used in Tupes' analysis. In Cattell's analysis of the women's data it is a relatively strong factor with four loadings above .34.

*Factor L(7). G. Superego Strength*

| G+ | G– |
|---|---|
| Persevering, determined | Quitting, fickle |
| Responsible | Frivolous, immature |
| Insistently orderly | Relaxed, indolent |
| Conscientious | Unscrupulous |
| Attentive to people | Not attentive to people |
| Emotionally stable | Changeable |

French and Tupes called this factor "Conscientiousness" though Cattell prefers to call it superego strength on the grounds that it implies injunctions against sins of omission and commisssion, and therefore has the moral connotations of Freud's superego. However, he notes that (a) there is no reference here to guilt (which later appeared separately in Factor *O*), and (b) that the set of items might be interpreted as a rather obsessive collection of attributes associated with strong parental discipline.

*Factor L(8). H. Parmia versus Threat Reactivity (Threctia)*

| H+ | H– |
|---|---|
| Adventurous, likes meeting people | Shy, timid, withdrawn |
| Strong interest in opposite sex | Little interest in opposite sex |
| Gregarious, responsive | Aloof, self-contained |
| Kindly, friendly | Hard, hostile |
| Frank | Secretive |
| Impulsive | Inhibited |
| Self-confident | Lacks confidence |
| Carefree | Careful |

French named this factor "sociability." Cattell's interpretation was that this is a temperamental trait of high inheritance associated with high sympathetic reactivity to threat, at the negative pole (hence Threctia), and with high parasympathetic resistance to sympatheticotonia (hence Parmia), at the positive pole. This theoretical basis helps distinguish the "thick-skinned" sociability of *H* from the "warm amiability" sociability of *A*, and the "uninhibited behavior" sociability of *F*, despite the initial cooperativeness of their loading patterns on the original set of 35 common variables.

*Factor L(9). I. Premsia (acronym from Protected Emotional Sensitivity) versus Harria*

| I+ | I– |
|---|---|
| Demanding, impatient | Emotionally mature |
| Dependent, immature | Independent minded |
| Kindly, gentle | Hard |
| Aesthetically fastidious | Lacks artistic feeling |
| Imaginative | Realistic |
| Hypochondriacal | Not hypochondriacal |

This factor was not well defined in the initial adult rating studies though is has been better defined since. It is sometimes confused with Factor *D* because *D*+ and *I*+ share the "infantile, demanding, impatient" character. Cattell relates this factor to William James' "tender minded-tough minded" dimension and notes correlational evidence that persons high on this scale come from protective—indeed overprotected—family environments.

*Factor L(10). J. Coasthenia (or Coasindia) versus Zeppia*

| J+ | J– |
|---|---|
| Acts individualistically | Goes with the group |
| Passively obstructive | Cooperative |
| Inactive, meek | Active, assertive |
| Self-sufficient | Attention getting |

This factor is not well replicated or well defined in the adult studies. Descriptively it presents a circumspect individualism as opposed to a vigorous "going with the group." Coasindia is proposed as an acronym for "covert, asthenic, individualism."

*Factor L(11). K. Cultivation (or Comention) versus Abcultion*

| K+ | K— |
|---|---|
| Intellectual interests | Unreflective, narrow |
| Polished, poised | Awkward, socially clumsy |
| Independent minded | Easily embarrassed |
| Conscientious | Unscrupulous |
| Aesthetic tastes | Lacks aesthetic interests |

This is one of the five factors in Tupes' set and has occurred clearly in all of Cattell's adult studies. He interprets it as a "readiness to accept the culture pattern through good parent identification." It has only quite recently been found also in $Q$ data.

*Factor L(12). L. Protension*

| L+ | L— |
|---|---|
| Suspicious | Trustful |
| Jealous | Not jealous |
| Self-sufficient, withdrawn | Composed |

This is a small factor, somewhat difficult to distinguish from $A$, but well marked in $Q$ data and hypothesized to represent predominance of the use of projection as a defense mechanism.

*Factor L(13). M. Autia*
French calls this "unconventionality."

| M+ | M— |
|---|---|
| Unconventional, eccentric | Conventional |
| Aesthetically fastidious | Not aesthetically fastidious |
| Imaginative | Realistic |
| Placid, absorbed | Worrying, anxious |
| Intellectual interests | Narrower interests |

Cattell suggests that the essential feature of this set is not unconventionality but the strong inner life, and the capacity to be absorbed in thought, as defined clinically in autistic characteristics.

*Factor L(14). N. Shrewdness versus Naivete*

| N+ | N— |
|---|---|
| Polished | Socially clumsy |
| Cool, aloof | Attentive to people |
| Aesthetically fastidious | Not aesthetically fastidious |

A poorly established factor, $N$, is more than shrewdness, for it has empathy in its defining variables.

This is a very reduced account of the intensive discussion (Cattell, 1957a; Cattell, Eber & Tatsuoka, 1970) of the general nature of these factors, the theory that includes evidence concerning child studies, studies of biographical data related to these scales, research into nature-nurture effects, and a multitude of criterion associations.

## 7.2  The Second–Order Factors

It was only in 1957 that Cattell published a second-order analysis of his rating studies; for maximum dependability he based this analysis on the *average* intercorrelation of each pair of factors in the three studies. This approach has the added convenience of enabling him to include all 14 of the Factors *A–N,* regardless of whether they appeared once, twice, or three times. It can be argued that this procedure can give confidence only to the extent that there is obvious agreement in the three *R* matrices. Such agreement seems evident in the two male studies, but the present writer would argue that with the females the balance of agreement and disagreement of signs is even. The other justification offered for pooling the results of the studies is that second-order factors are extremely sensitive to sampling effects, and a truly general solution should be based on a wide range of cases.

There were six rather large second-order factors defined in this way. For indexing these Cattell has used roman numerals which have been preserved also for the *Q*-data second-orders, which match very well.

### *(L(BR)) I. Exvia versus Invia*[4]

| | |
|---|---|
| *F*, Surgency | .70 |
| *M*, Autia | .54 |
| *E*, Dominance | .54 |
| *A*, Affectothymia | .38 |

### *(L(BR)) II. Anxiety versus integration or adjustment*

| | |
|---|---|
| *C*(–), Lack of ego strength | .50 |
| *L*(–), Protension | .47 |
| *E*(–), Submissiveness | .32 |
| *K*(–), Abcultion | .54 |
| *B*(–), Low intelligence | .58 |

[4] Cattell adheres to this terminology for the exact patterns obtained for the second-order *Q*- and *L*-data factors, arguing that extraversion-introversion are now such popular and battered terms that precise work needs a precise verbal referent.

The pole has been inverted here because of an originally negative correlation sign.

### *(L(BR)) III. Cortertia versus Pathemia*

| | |
|---|---|
| *L*(–), Low protension | .72 |
| *I*(–), Harria | .68 |
| *A*(–), Sizothymia | .43 |
| *N*, Shrewdness | .34 |

This factor contains the key markers (*A*–, *I*–, *N*+) found in the *Q*-data second-order, which has been labeled Cortertia because of its correlation with the *T*-data *U.I.* 22, Cortertia (see chapter 4).

### *(L(BR)) IV. Independence*

| | |
|---|---|
| *N*, shrewdness | .46 |
| *G*(–), Low superego | .46 |
| *E*, Dominance | .33 |
| *D*, Excitability | .43 |
| *F*, Surgency | .27 |

This is in excellent agreement with the four chief markers found for the *Q*-data factor, which shows evidence of correlation with *T*-data *U.I.* 19, Independence, and has the same meaning.

These four factors correspond quite well with second-order factors from *Q* data; Eysenck's first-order approaches to the second-order, which he names "Extraversion" and "Neuroticism," are also clearly adumbrations of the first two factors here.

The other two second-order factors based on this composite study need further research and as yet permit no interpretation by matches with *Q* data or child studies. The interested reader will find them in Cattell (1957a, p. 321).

## 8  RATING FACTORS
## AT THE CHILD LEVEL
### (By Dr. T. Dielman)[5]

There has appeared in the literature a rather widespread "argument by analogy" (presumably from rough generalizations about the early embryo) that personality factor structure in children *should* be simpler, and have fewer factors, than that found in adults. This may well be so when one gets to the finer factors in dynamic and attitude data where one perceives that interests (sentiment structures) branch more finely with experience. But there is no reason to expect this where psychologists are now mainly working in ratings—with broad temperament and personality factors—and the empirical evidence in fact definitely does not support this "proliferation" notion. It shows essentially the same number and kind of broad personality factors—Affectothymia, Ego-strength, Intelligence, Surgency, Dominance, etc., at the primary level, and Anxiety and Extraversion at the secondary level—as have appeared consistently in adults. This issue and others are among those to which answers have been sought, and largely found, by the systematically planned cross-sectional structural studies at progressive age levels by Cattell and his coworkers. These have been carried out thoroughly with questionnaires, but, so far, adequate studies have appeared at only two or three levels in the rating domain, that is, with the main factor markers and thorough factor-analytic techniques.

Because of the technical unevenness of studies, appreciable space for discussion would be needed to explain the selective emphasis underlying the inferences made here about integration of findings. Apart from obvious technical weaknesses in some studies, notably in applying no precise test for number of factors, and in aborted searches for simple structure (see, e.g., Becker & Krug, 1964), ending in far too low a hyperplane count for significance, there has been a systematic weakness in the rating procedures themselves.

The rating defect shows itself first in a neglect in about a third of the reported studies of the need to include marker variables to recognize the theoretically well established source-traits, and in a roughness of definition of variables. Even when these easily remediable defects are avoided in future researches, there will still remain the systematic problem in child ratings of getting good nonrole ratings by peers over the total area of life behavior. One is almost forced to follow one of two not entirely desirable courses of action to get either (a) precise and refined variables and observations by teachers, and therefore from a special role relation and limited behavior area, or (b) ratings by peers, well averaged across several judges, but suffering from the inability of young children to conceptualize what the variables are. There are some ways (Cattell & Gruen, 1953) of beating some of the difficulties in the latter; but perhaps time sampling of actual behavior without trait concepts (Cattell & Peterson, 1958) or scales of actual *behavior* ratings (Dreger & Dreger, 1962) is finally the only satisfactory answer.

To date the preponderance of the child studies have followed the former course of action, with the exception of one as yet unpublished study at the adolescent level by Dielman and Digman and the Cattell and

Gruen (1953) study at the 9–14-year-old level. Table 4 presents in summary form the relevant information on each of the factor-analytic studies of child ratings. These studies and the results of each will be considered in turn. Although space prohibits consideration of the variables marking the factors in each of the studies, investigators' identification of the factors emerging from their studies is discussed briefly. The interested reader may refer to the original articles to satisfy himself that the factors exhibited suffieient degrees of congruence to share the same identification. Table 5 provides a summary of the factors that were identified, with the exception of Factor $N$, in two or more of the studies. In Table 5 the factors bear only the identifying letters which have been presented in section 7. The columns represent the various investigations and are

identified by the number associated with them in Table 4. Wherever new unidentified factors emerged in a study they are marked by an asterisk in Table 5 and the label applied by the original author on the basis of the marker variables listed. Some liberties have been taken by the current author in assigning factors in Digman's (1963, 1965 a,b) studies to the nomenclature proposed by Cattell. The difference is one of preference on the parts of the original authors for popular terms rather than one of substance, as determined by the marker variables.

As early as 1946, Cattell regarded his task in the area of child personality as one of investigating the results of adult investigations at the child level, in all three data domains. The pioneering effort in the $L(BR)$ domain was that of Cattell and Gruen (1953), who analyzed the ratings on 30

TABLE 4  Summary of factor-analytic studies of child ratings

| Investigator | Data source | Age of children | Analytic technique | No. of subjects | No. of variables | No. of factors extracted |
|---|---|---|---|---|---|---|
| Cattell & Gruen (1953) | Peer ratings | 9–14 | C–OB | 173 | 30 | 6 |
| Cattell & Coan (1957a) | Teacher ratings | 6–10 | C–OB | 198 | 39 | 13 |
| Cattell & Coan (1957b) | Parent ratings | 6–10 | C–OB | 145 | 61 | 16 |
| Cattell & Peterson (1958) | Free play (time sampling) (trained observers) | 4–6 | C–OB | 80 | 76 | 16 |
| Peterson & Cattell (1958) | Parent ratings | 4–6 | C–OB | 80 | 44 | 14 |
| Peterson & Cattell (1959) | Teacher ratings | 4–6 | C–OB | 80 | 36 | 9 |
| Digman (1963) | Teacher ratings | 6–10 | PA–OB | 102 | 39 | 11 |
| Cattell (1963e)[a] | Teacher ratings | 6–10 | PA–OB | 102 | 39 | 12 |
| Digman (1965a)[b] | Teacher ratings | 4–6 | PA–OB | 80 | 36 | 9 |
| Digman (1965b) | Teacher ratings | 9–14 | C–OB | 162 | 63 | 10 |
| Emmerich (1964) | Free play (time sampling) (trained observers) | 4–6 | PA–O | 38 | 31 | 6 |
| Emmerich (1966) | Teacher ratings | 4–6 | PA–OB | 53 | 24 | 3 |
| Becker & Krug (1964) | Parent and teacher ratings | 4–6 | C–O | 72 | 71 | 5 |

*Note.* In analytic technique column, C refers to centroid extraction, O to orthogonal rotation, OB to oblique rotation, and PA to principal axis extraction.

[a] Reanalysis of Digman's (1963) data.

[b] Reanalysis of Peterson and Cattell's (1959) data.

variables by peers of 173 children 9–14 years of age. Six factors were extracted and identified, on the basis of marker variables in common with factors previously identified at the adult level, as Surgency-Desurgency, Dominance-Submissiveness, Superego Strength-Unintegrated Weak Character, Ego-Strength-Proneness to Neuroticism, a factor tentatively identified as Protension, and an unidentified factor which shared markers with several of the factors identified in adult studies. This latter factor does not appear in Table 5 as it has not been replicated in subsequent investigations.

Cattell and Coan (1957 a,b) conducted a pair of investigations at the 6–10 age range utilizing ratings by teachers and parents. The details of these investigations are presented in Table 4, and it will be seen that 12 factors

previously identified in the Cattell and Gruen (1953) investigation (with the exception of the one unidentified factor) also appeared in these two studies. Also emerging were factors identified as A (Affectothymia vs. Sizothymia), H (Parmia vs. Threat Reactivity, or Threctia), I (Premsia, or Protective Emotional Security vs. Harria), and the O, (Anxious-Depression, or Superego Proneness) factor.

Peterson and Cattell (1958, 1959) and Cattell and Peterson (1958) studied 80 Chicago nursery school children via parental ratings, teacher ratings, and time-sampling records made by graduate students observers who had been trained to watch the specific behaviors in a playground situation. A glance at Table 5 reveals that agreement was reached again on Factors A, C, F, and G,

**TABLE 5**  Summary of replicated factor identifications across investigations

| Factor[a] | Investigation | | | | | | | | | |
|---|---|---|---|---|---|---|---|---|---|---|
| | 1 | 2 | 3 | 4 | 5 | 6 | 7 | 8 | 9 | 10 |
| A | | x | x | x | x | x | x | x | x | x |
| B | | x | | | | | x | x | | |
| C | x | x | x | x | x | x | x | x | x | x |
| D | | x | | | x | | | x | x | x |
| E | x | x | x | | x | x | | x | x | x |
| F | x | x | x | x | x | x | x | x | | |
| G | x | x | x | x | x | x | x | x | x | x |
| H | | x | x | | x | x | x | x | x | x |
| I | | x | x | | x | x | x | x | x | x |
| J | | x | | | x | | | x | | |
| K | | x | | | x | x | | | x | x |
| L | x | x | x | | x | x | | | | x |
| M | | x | x | x | x | | x | x | | |
| N | | x | | | | | | | | |
| O or Superego proneness | | x | x | x | x | | | x | | |
| Unidentified: associates with opposite sex more* | | x | | | | | x | | | |
| Oldest child: Parental training pattern* | | | x | x | x | | | | | |

*Note.* Asterisks indicate labels applied by the original author on the basis of the marker variable listed.
[a]The letters A–O were used by Cattell (1957) to represent personality rating factors.

which appeared most vividly on the earlier studies as well, with agreement in two of the three studies on half a dozen more. The time-sampling study presented no real basis for examination of congruences since all the variables were specific behaviors rather than traits. It stands alone (though four factors are tentatively identified) awaiting more time samplings with the same identical variables.

Digman (1963) and Cattell (1963e) conducted independent analyses of the same teacher-rating data collected by Digman on a sample of 102 elementary school children in the University of Hawaii Elementary School. The teachers rated 102 children on each of 39 behaviors by a rating system devised by Digman (and described in the 1963 publication). The two independent analyses agreed on 8 of the 11 extracted factors, as is discernible from Table 5. Two additional factors in Digman's investigation were most highly loaded by parental attitude variables on the one hand and sex of the child on the other. Cattell extracted a 12th factor which he regarded as the Superego-Proneness factor, $G$, which had emerged in earlier investigations.

Digman conducted two additional analyses of teacher-rating data (1965 a,b), the first of which was a reanalysis of the Peterson and Cattell (1959) data. Nine factors were extracted, as in the Peterson and Cattell (1959) analysis. Substantial agreement was reached on 7 of the 9 factors, Digman's analysis failing to replicate Factors $F$ (Surgency-Desurgency) and $L$ (Protension). Digman's (1965b) investigation of 162 children in the Hawaii public school system resulted in the identification of 10 factors, replicating the 9 that emerged from his reanalysis of the Peterson and Cattell (1959) data and resulting in an additional factor which was in agreement with Peterson and Cattell's $L$ (Protension). In second-order analyses pursued in Digman's (1963, 1965

a,b) investigations, 3 factors have consistently emerged, which he has termed Successful versus Unsuccessful Socialization, Freedom of Movement versus Restraint, and Emotionality, which correspond fairly well, respectively, with Cattell's Exvia-Invia, Independence, and Anxiety-adjustment. The second-order Socialization or Exvia factor is marked by high friendliness, competence, compliance, ego strength, and low tension. The second-order Freedom of movement or Independence factor is marked by high activity, dominance, and social confidence. The second-order Emotionality or Anxiety factor is marked by high hostility, tension, relational insecurity, and low ego-strength.

Emmerich conducted two investigations in the child rating area, one (1964) utilizing the time-sampling technique, and the second (1966) based on teachers' ratings. Both of Emmerich's studies were in the 4–6-year-old, nursery school range. Six factors were extracted in the 1964 investigation, in which the ratio of subjects to variables approaches unity; and Emmerich grouped the factors in terms of ratings by psychology students along three major dimensions of Interpersonal versus Impersonal Orientation, Active versus Passive Mode, and Positive versus Negative Attitude. In the analysis of teachers' ratings, Emmerich (1966) identified three factors, which he termed Aggression Dominance, Dependency, and Autonomy. Although it is impossible to determine with any degree of certainty due to a lack of overlap of the teacher-rating variables with earlier investigations, these three factors at least carry the flavor of the three second-order factors identified by Digman (1963, 1965 a,b).

A final study worthy of note is that of Becker and Krug (1964). Although the subjects-to-variables ratio is small, the rating results are quite congruent with the several analyses made by Cattell and Digman if one examines the grouping of the variables around the perimeter of the circumplex model preferred by Becker and Krug. The two large factors about which Becker and Krug have ordered their Varimax factors were termed Emotional Stability-Instability and Extraversion-Introversion, again corresponding to two of the second-order factors identified by earlier investigators and to Eysenck's two main factors.

In summary, many years of research have resulted in the identification of 14 primary factors in the child-rating domain which have been replicated across three or more investigations, and which fit the patterns designated *A, B, C, D*, etc. by Cattell and his co-workers operating at the adult level. The investigator interested in this domain now has much experience to guide him, a set of ground rules that have been laid out for the conduct of an adequate investigation in the rating domain, and a generally agreed "personality sphere" of approximately 40 rating variables which have been and can continue to be employed as common markers to permit calculation of congruence (though there is also an extended variable pool utilized across fewer studies). Criterion studies using these markers will be able to proceed with a sound knowledge of which personality factors have been identified by assessing the congruence of the resultant factors with those that have resulted in the past. It is important also to avoid the confusion of first-order, primary factors (at least 14) with second-strata factors (about 4) which should strictly emerge from factoring the primaries but can appear in mixed primaries and secondaries, in rough form, if only half a dozen factors are extracted.

# 3

# Trait Description and Measurement by Personality Questionnaires

## G. J. S. Wilde
*Queen's University, Kingston, Ontario, Canada*

## 1 SCOPE OF THE FIELD AND CHAPTER OUTLINE

Verbal measurements in the form of personality questionnaires have traditionally been among the most favored procedures for the identification and assessment of individual differences and personality characteristics. Hundreds of personality questionnaires have been made available and many of them are standard constituents of test batteries in psychological research and applied investigations. Yet, they have met with serious criticisms, especially in regard to validity. It is the purpose of this chapter to evaluate critically verbal measurements as a means to discover and assess personality traits, and to compare and integrate some of the major findings in the framework of personality theory.[1]

The chapter has been divided in eight sections. First, a definition of personality is presented in the form of a postulate, and it is shown how personality questionnaires may help in providing empirical support for this postulate. In section 3, a comparison is

made between verbal measures on the one hand and different measuring procedures such as behavioral and physiological on the other, especially from the point of view of factorial validity. The results of this evaluation demonstrate the usefulness of personality questionnaires quite convincingly. To highlight some significant features of the nature of personality questionnaires, a short history of the questionnaire method of personality measurement is presented in section 4. The various criticisms, as presented in section 5, have been categorized and the applicability of each is evaluated on theoretical and empirical grounds. Remedial procedures for some method weaknesses are also discussed here, but section 6 is devoted to problems of questionnaire subtlety and the implications of test-taking attitudes, such as social desirability set. One of the more salient conclusions drawn in this section is that the operation of such test-taking attitudes in the process of questionnaire responding is not necessarily detrimental to questionnaire validity. The possible reasons for this seeming paradox have been worked out in section 7. The importance of focusing on individual differences in item desirability opinions between subjects is stressed and empirical investigations are presented showing that this particular point of view

[1] This work was done with financial support from the Canada Council under grant GS0159. We also wish to express our thanks to Dr. W. R. Thompson for his many valuable suggestions regarding this chapter.

promises both more sophisticated measuring instruments as well as a more profound understanding of the nature of the personality traits being measured. It is argued, however, that these mechanisms also help to explain the effectiveness of present personality questionnaires, which deserve considerable confidence despite the many objections raised against them. Consequently, in section 8, some major findings of the verbal measurement of personality traits are presented. More specifically, the works of Guilford, Eysenck, and Cattell are compared and an attempt has been made to integrate their findings.

## 2  PERSONALITY AND SELF–REPORT

Personality can be and has been defined in many ways. The nature of the concept of personality may be demonstrated in the form of a postulate based upon the general psychological premise, $B = f(O,S)$: Behavior is a function of organism and situation. There are variations in $B$ which are not determined by $S$ but by $O$; there are variations in $O$ that are not transient like psychological states (e.g., pain, hunger, anxiety). There are nontransient (semipermanent) variations in $O$, which determine variations in $B$, but they are *not* action tendencies with regard *only to specific psychological objects* as is the case with interests and attitudes. There are nontransient variations in $O$, which do *not* determine variations of behavior in *specific situations only*, as is the case with roles. Postulating generality across objects and transituational consistency indicates that the study of personality has a wider scope than has the study of individual differences. Individual differences can be investigated one at a time, but the above elaboration by necessity specifies personality as a multi-

variate concept. Groups of variates showing functional unity (e.g., high intercorrelations) are considered to reflect constructs of personality differences, called *traits*; and demonstrating that such groups of interrelated variates exist provides empirical evidence for the postulate of personality. It has been customary in psychology not to focus on cognitive and intellectual variates in the study of personality traits. Personality traits are usually associated with orectic, temperamental, modal, affective, conative, or value-oriented aspects of behavior.

One of the first references to empirical procedures of identification, description, and measurement of personality traits was made by Galton (1884):

Character ought to be measured by carefully recorded acts, representative of the usual conduct. . . . We want lists of facts, every one of which may be separately verified, valued and revalued, and the whole accurately summed. It is the statistics of each man's conduct in small every-day affairs, that will probably be found to give the simplest and most precise measure of his character.

These statements indicate the original rationale behind the oldest—and still vigorous—methods of personality measurement: self-report and behavior rating, especially self-report, as this procedure may cover a wider domain of "small every-day affairs."

Despite their long standing, these procedures do not seem to be respected by everyone. On the contrary, they have a reputation of being superficial, transparent, fakable, and unsophisticated. And yet, even before 1960 more than 500 different self-report instruments were commercially available in the United States (Watson, 1959), and since, many more have been published. It is the purpose of this chapter, therefore, to analyze self-report procedures critically and to present material that may contribute to an objective evaluation.

The self-report techniques (personality questionnaires, inventories, personal data blanks, etc.) consist of a number of written questions provided with a limited number of precoded response options (agree-disagree, yes-no, etc.). Thus, they belong to the so-called *structured* assessment procedures. All individuals answer the same questions in the same order. The answers given by the subjects are valued according to a fixed numerical scoring procedure, which gives rise to one (single-trait) or several (multitrait) questionnaire scores located on an at least ordinal scale, which is supposed to reflect the personality trait(s) involved. The items usually have aspects of "usual conduct in small every-day affairs" as content, but some personality questionnaires comprise items regarding values, opinions of others, annoyances, proverbs, or still other contents. Inventories are usually easy to administer, as they can be taken in groups under the supervision of clerical assistants. Although the construction of questionnaires can be a time-consuming and complicated job, their ease of administration enhances their utility considerably. However, besides utility, other requirements should be considered: objectivity, reliability, validity, sensitivity, and comparability.

Reliability and sensitivity do not present a major problem. In the case of shortcomings, they can be improved by increasing the number of items, or by applying certain item-analytic results. Nevertheless, the frequently observed systematic retest effects (like increased or decreased average scores, Windle, 1954) have serious implications. The amount of objectivity is defined as the rigor of the scoring procedures, provided that one does not consider the subjective interpretation of the items by the subject as incompatible with objectivity. It seems, however, that such an altered concept of objectivity is confused with the concept of validity. Moreover, in section 5 it will be argued that there is no essential distinction in either sense of objectivity between questionnaire responses ($Q$ data) and performance tests ($T$ data). Several problems are associated with the requirement of comparability, which is fulfilled if a particular questionnaire score has the same meaning independent of the nature (sex, age, socioeconomic status, education, nationality, native language, and so forth) of the person obtaining this score, and furthermore if this independence exists across different testing situations (e.g. job application, medical examination, research setting, and anonymous test administration). If correlations exist between inventory scores and age or sex, for example, separate norms can be offered or some correction formula introduced; but this does not really answer the question whether the instrument measures the same attribute in men as in women, in the young as in the old, and so forth. Some of the problems associated with the use of questionnaires for cross-cultural comparisons are discussed in section 4 of this book.

## 3 FACTORIAL VALIDITY: A COMPARISON ACROSS MEASUREMENT MEDIA

Unfortunately, the literature does not abound with studies comparing the validity of personality inventories with that of other assessment procedures for personality traits such as morphological, physiological, expressive, projective and perceptual methods; performance tests; observation and rating; measurements of interests and attitudes; and other clinical procedures such as $Q$ sorts (Stephenson, 1953), "personal constructs" (Kelly, 1963), and clinical uses of the "semantic differential" (Osgood, Suci, & Tannenbaum, 1957). There is especially little evidence regarding the question of how these various methods compare regarding their use as instruments in the identification, description, and measurement of personality traits.

It appears, however, that ratings and self-report measures lend themselves better to trait identification than performance tests, probably because of the generally greater psychological insightfulness and possibly also because $Q$ data can cover a larger behavior domain than any single or combination of performance tests. The riches of rating and self-rating as mining grounds for the uncovering of personality traits seem to be real despite the accompanying unwanted rocks and dust. Personality traits of the observees can be identified despite general evaluative set, halo effects, refraction factors, and other biases on the part of the rater and despite social desirability set, response styles, and other sources of perturbation on the part of the person reporting on himself (Cattell, 1968b; Cattell & Digman, 1964). To find empirical support for this position, we may consider factor analyses involving variables from at least two of the measurement modes $L$, (life data, e.g., case histories and behavior ratings), $Q$, and $T$ at the same time.

Six performance tests, 15 physiological variables and 3 questionnaires were subjected to a factor analysis by Wassenaar (1956) in South Africa. The first and most definite factor was identified by him as Autonomic Lability or Neuroticism. All 3 $Q$ variables had significant loadings on this factor ranging from .40 to .72 with a median of .55, but only one of the six performance tests (to the extent of .35) and nine of the physiological variables (loadings ranging from .35 to .59 with median .50) had such loadings.

H. J. Eysenck (1952b) reported three factor-analytic studies, the results of which contain some information with regard to the present issue. In the first study 28 variables were analyzed, 19 performance tests, 8 questionnaire scores, and age. Subjects were over 300 normal and neurotic soldiers. Only one factor was interpreted in detail (Neuroticism), which showed loadings ranging between .02 to .48 with a median of .18. The questionnaires showed a median loading of .31 (range between .07 and .56). The second study, conducted by Markowe, Heron, and Barker, showed results which favored the $Q$ variables even more. The first factor in 25 variables was again identified as Neuroticism and showed loadings .43, .44, and .47 on self-report scales of annoyances, worries, and interests. Loadings of performance tests ranged between .00 and .45 with a median of .09. The study was conducted with 80 unskilled factory laborers; incidentally, it also provides an opportunity for a comparison across modes of variables for rating data. Psychiatric rating of mental health had a loading of .24 on the Neuroticism factor; and supervisors' ratings of job adjustment, of .36. These results showed factorial validities for the three types of data to rank $Q > L > T$. Results showing considerably smaller factorial validities for $Q$ data, however, were found in a third study of 100 adolescent twins. Besides Neuroticism and Intelligence, no other factors were carefully identified. Fourteen performance measures were factored together with three verbal variables: a scale for word dislikes, an adapted version of Brown's Personality Inventory, and a version of the Minnesota Multiphasic Personality Inventory (MMPI) lie scale. These variables correlated with the Neuroticism factor .25, .06, and −.08, respectively, whereas the performance variables varied in their correlation with Neuroticism between .01 and .66 (for static ataxia) with a median of .31.

Another study showing rather low factor

loadings of a neuroticism questionnaire was reported by H. J. Eysenck (1950). The Maudsley Medical Questionnaire (MMQ) and 15 performance tests, all designed to measure neuroticism, were applied to 105 ex-prisoners of war who, after returning from their camps in Germany, suffered from difficulties in adjustment, and to a normal group of 93 surgical cases. Static ataxia and body sway suggestibility showed high loadings, whereas the one loading of the MMQ was very small.

In the light of these contradictory findings, it is important to make a clear distinction between degree of neuroticism (which is an organismic variable) as an underlying disposition on the one hand, and degree of neurosis as the number and severity of manifest neurotic behaviors (which is a behavioral variable) on the other. A similar distinction is usually made between intelligence as a disposition and intellectual performance or productivity as a manifest behavior. In the case just mentioned, the great difference in experienced stress between the two subject groups could certainly explain the difference in manifest neurotic behaviors (case Vb, Fig. 1), even though the neurotic disposition might well have been the same in the two groups, unless it is assumed that soldiers high on neuroticism were more likely to be captured or to survive the treatment by the Germans. In other words, if the MMQ measured disposition rather than neurotic behavior, it would not necessarily have to discriminate between the two groups. The generality of the present issue pervades all personality trait assessment and certainly deserves a more detailed discussion than can be given in this context. This generality has a counterpart in the domain of intelligence. Culture-fair tests (Cattell & Butcher, 1968) have been developed to reduce the contamination with environmental stimulation, education, and

so forth in tests that did not properly distinguish between ability to learn (i.e., intelligence; measurement along the horizontal axis in Fig. 1) and amount of knowledge learned (measurement approximately along vector Va, i.e., inside the quadrant).

Turning back to the evidence regarding relative factorial validity of questionnaire scores, one would be inclined to infer from this limited information that questionnaire scores are certainly not inferior to other types of data and perhaps even better as a means of identifying unitary traits. That they might be better is strongly suggested by two studies (Claridge, 1960; Hildebrand, 1958) in which, in addition to Neuroticism factors, clear Extraversion factors were extracted showing very high loadings for the questionnaire variables compared with objective tests.

One might object that the evidence referred to is limited to neuroticism and extraversion. Regarding neuroticism, however, questionnaire scores could be expected to have strong competition with regards to factorial validity especially from physiological variables. One might argue that the rather high factorial validities of $Q$ scores are due to some spurious factors shared by all such variables (e.g., susceptibility to "tendency to complain" or "social desirability set"). The likelihood of such spurious method variance does not seem very great, however, as the $Q$ variables were in a definite minority in all the reported studies. Moreover, there is no reason to assume that such method variance does not play a part in the intercorrelations of performance tests.

In a comparative discussion of self-report validity, a reference to external criteria, of course, would seem to be in order. Here again, there is a paucity of relevant studies, but it is questionable if such investigations would lead to an evaluation different from the one based on factorial evidence. On a

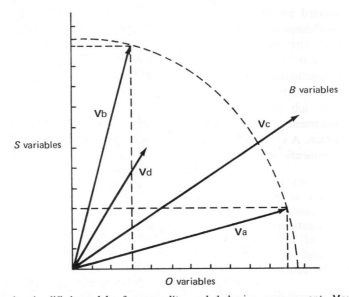

**FIG. 1** A greatly simplified model of personality and behavior measurement. Manifest behavior (*B*) is represented in the quadrant as the result (vectors a and b) of the subject's position on a trait (*O*) and differential environmental stimulation (*S*). The length of the vector **V** indicates the height of the subjects' score on the (manifest) behavioral variable. In addition to this phenotypic characteristic, the direction of the vector reflects the genotypic composition of manifest behavior, i.e., the relative contributions of *O* and *S*. Note that vectors **V**a and **V**b are of the same length, but different in direction. They would indicate two people equal in their amount of manifest neurosis, for instance; but in the case of subject "a" this is due more to his disposition, whereas the neurosis of subject "b" is predominantly determined by environmental stress. This model does not necessarily assume that dispositions and traits are inherited; they may well be due to past experience (differential exposure to earlier *S* variables: Environmental stimulations). Measurements of intelligence and personality traits should ideally take place along the horizontal axis and not inside the quadrant. Culture-fair intelligence tests fulfill this requirement better than education-sensitive ones.

practical level the predictability of external behavior is undoubtedly important, but its relevance to the present problem is limited to the adequacy of these nontest behaviors as criteria for the personality traits involved. Unless the factorial composition of the criterion behavior is known, little information useful to the present evaluation can be added. If one were to validate an anxiety questionnaire against physiological anxiety responses when the subject is expecting to receive an electric shock, we would first of all want to be sure that this kind of manifest anxiety is indeed of the same nature as the

dispositional anxiety purportedly measured by the questionnaire (Spielberger, 1966). Knowing that scholastic achievement is to a large extent determined by motivational factors (Cattell & Butcher, 1968), one would certainly not accept school grades as a satisfactory external criterion for the validation of intelligence tests. This argument, naturally, does not hold for the validation of questionnaires that were specifically designed to predict an external criterion. The classical studies by E. L. Kelly and Fiske (1951), by W. H. Hunt and Stephenson (1946), by Miles (1946), and by Shipley and

Graham (reported by Bray, 1948) demonstrated the usefulness of inventories beyond any doubt in such situations. Kelly and Fiske showed that "superficial" techniques, involving a questionnaire sent by mail to people for a few cents yielded better predictions of later job performance than an extensive assessment procedure at a cost of $300 per person. A comment by Hathaway (1959) may be mentioned in this context:

One rarely sees any mention of the cost in professional time as part of the validity or other value discussion of new or old tests. Some psychologists even seem to feel that the processes of testing should be kept complicated and that the psychologist should base his professional standing upon them.

## 4  SOME HISTORICAL AND METHODOLOGICAL ASPECTS

### 4.1  Historical Aspects

The first truly extensive investigation of "character" in line with Galton's suggestions was carried out by Heymans and Wiersma (1906). In 1905 they obtained behavior ratings by physicians on 90 items of some 2,500 subjects (later followed by teachers' ratings of some 3,800 adolescents). Unaided by factor-analytic routines or computers, they analyzed the ratings by physicians of fathers, mothers, and adult children in 450 Dutch families with remarkably modern purposes in mind: Which basic traits underlie the patterns of observed behavior, and to what extent are they inherited and related to sex? Three conceptually independent dimensions were identified: activity, emotionality and primary versus secondary function. Much later *activity* would emerge again in Guilford's factor analyses (1959), *emotionality* would be equated with Neuroticism, and *primary function* with Extraversion (*secondary function* with Intraversion).

After this work was introduced and continued by Wells (1915) in the United States, it was adapted by Woodworth and Poffenberger (House, 1926) for the development of their Personal Data Sheet. Woodworth had been asked by the National Research Council in 1917 to head a committee for the development of a group measure of adjustment that could be used to screen soldiers. The numbers of subjects to be psychologically examined was so unusually large that Woodworth looked for a more economic procedure than behavior ratings: "I was unable to incorporate directly any of the questions ... of Heymans and Wiersma, because their questions were designed to be answered not by the subject but by some acquaintance, whereas what I needed was a list of questions to be answered by the subject himself" (Woodworth quoted by Bell, 1939). Questions were derived from many different sources and provided with "yes" and "no" as response options. Some 200 questions, thought to be symptomatic of neurotic tendencies, were first applied to various samples of normal students and draftees. Items to which more than 25% of the subjects gave the "psychoneurotic" answer were rejected, as Woodworth assumed that such items could not be considered as to indicate real maladjustment. The final selection of 116 items constitute the first major self-report technique ever used. The Personal Data Sheet had a phenomenal impact on later developments. Now, more than 50 years later, few personality questionnaires do not contain items very similar to Woodworth's.

Yet, in view of the nature of the item analysis applied and the pragmatic purpose of the inventory, one may question whether Woodworth was indeed aiming at the identification and measurement of a more or less unitary trait as his predecessors Heymans and Wiersma did. Laird's Colgate Mental Hygiene Test (1925) was the first to contain a scale for intraversion-extraversion in addition to questions about psychoneurotic tendencies. However, his item analysis was also limited to endorsement statistics. An innovation to the logic of item analysis was made by Allport and Allport (1928). In the construction of the Ascendance-Submission Reaction Study, response weights in this self-report measure were determined by the average of the ratings *by others* on the characteristic involved. Although this presented an interesting rapproachment of behavior rating and self-report procedures, a more important methodological advancement was made in the development of the Personality Schedule of Thurstone and Thurstone (1930). Items had been selected and provided with a priori scoring weights, 1 for Neurotic answers and 0 for the alternatives. Total scores were calculated, the discriminating power of each item against this "criterion" was investigated, and the result led to either rejection or retention of the item in the scale. The principle of *internal consistency* in the construction of questionnaires was hereby introduced, and it was there to stay—at least in the development of *rationally* derived scales (Table 1). This trend in personality measurement was paralleled by that in attitude assessment, which shifted from procedures such as paired comparisons and equal appearing intervals to the method of summated ratings (Likert, 1932). Item analytic techniques were used by Bernreuter (1933b), Adams (1941), Darley and McNemara (1941), H. M. Bell (1939), and others in the development of a considerable number of personality inventories.

In roughly the same period, factor analysis was first applied to various personality inventories comprising more than one scale. Flanagan (1935) criticized the Bernreuter personality inventory for the high intercorrelations of its parts and factored the six scales into only two factors: Self-confidence and Sociability. Five factors were found to operate in the 13 scales of the Minnesota Personality Scale (Darley & McNemara, 1941). These and other factor analyses, however, were conducted ex post facto, that is, on already existing personality scales. As a logical next step in the application of item analysis to the development of inventories, J. P. Guilford (1934) calculated intercorrelations of *all items in the original item pool* and developed his questionnaire scales on the basis of selections of items with high loadings on the identified factors. In this way, he made theoretical and inductive contributions to personality theory in the process of designing empirical procedures for personality measurement. Guilford and his co-workers published several questionnaires and completed the development from endorsement analysis via item analysis into factor analysis as test-construction techniques.

## 4.2 Methodological Aspects

The history of personality questionnaires has shown important changes along dimensions other than that of types of item analysis. More than 20 years after Woodworth's Personal Data Sheet, an inventory was published that, according to Buros (1970), has attracted more attention than any other self-report technique. For the development of the Minnesota Multiphasic Personality Inventory, Hathaway and McKinley wrote a large number of statements with Kraepelin's psychiatric textbook as one of the main sources (Welsh & Dahlstrom, 1956). The scoring keys of the MMPI,

TABLE 1  Characteristics of rational and empirical techniques of personality test construction

| Construct-oriented | Criterion-oriented |
| --- | --- |
| Items are written on the basis of at least a "working theory" about the trait in question, which is supposed to reflect itself in the items. | The nature of the original item pool is relatively arbitrary. No specific requirements regarding content area, phrasing, or format can be stated. |
| Items are analyzed in terms of item-test correlation or item-item correlation to increase internal consistency. Item homogeneity indexes are used to retain or reject items and at the same time provide feedback on the "working theory." | Items are analyzed in terms of item-criterion correlations. Nondiscriminating items are rejected. Item homogeneity and internal consistency of the scale are of secondary importance. |
| Split-half and retest reliabilities are equally important. | Retest reliability is more important than split-half. |
| The trait or traits to be measured are usually unidimensional. | The factorial composition of the criterion used is usually not questioned, but taken for granted. |
| More oriented on variations in $O$ than in $B$. (See Fig. 1.) | More oriented on variations in $B$ than in $O$. |
| Validation is carried out along the lines of construct validation. | Validation takes the form of cross-validation on fresh samples of subjects divided into "known groups." |
| After completion of item analysis the test usually adds insight into nature of the trait. | Yields little feedback for theory. |
| Sensitive to personal opinions of the author regarding nature of the trait, number, and labels of factors to be extracted, preferences for orthogonal versus oblique solutions, etc. | Risk of capitalizing on chance factors; sensitive to systematic but irrelevant sources of variance, dependent on implicit or explicit theory underlying allocation of subjects in criterion groups. Criteria applied often very intermediate or indirect in nature and of questionable relevance. |
| Examples of inventories: Cattell's 16 PF (Cattell, Eber, & Tatsuoka, 1970); A. L. Edward's EPPS (1953); those discussed in the historical section, H. J. Eysenck's MPI and EPI (1959, 1963); Heron's TPPM (1956b); Kuder's Preference Record (1956); J. A. Taylor's MAS (1953). | Examples of inventories: MMPI, Gough's California Psychological Inventory (1956); E. K. Strong's Vocational Interest Blank (1943); Terman-Miles MF-test (1936). |

however, were not directly developed from either psychiatric theory or the usual item-analytic procedures discussed previously. Instead, the items were administered to different groups of patients characterized by certain psychiatric diagnoses (e.g., hysteria, schizophrenia, hypomania) and to normals, and each item was checked for showing response patterns discriminating between these "known groups." Nine empirically derived, clinical scoring keys were developed, and three other scales were added for the detection of motivational distortion. This test-construction technique is usually labeled *empirical* (or criterion-oriented) in contradistinction to the *rational* (construct-oriented) technique. An attempt to typify both approaches by stressing their differences is presented in Table 1. Rather than being alternatives, the two methods could play complementary roles in test construction. An integration of both procedures on a factor-analytic level may be attempted by making use of H. J. Eysenck's (1950) "criterion analysis." In this technique the external criterion is factorially analyzed, and at the same time some external anchorage is provided for the identification of the factors in the questionnaire. In studies by Butt and Fiske (1968), Hase and Goldberg (1967) and Goldberg (1972), empirical evidence is presented regarding the efficacy of the alternative strategies of questionnaire scale construction for both theory and practice.

When the criterion-oriented method is used, situations may occur in which the test has predictive validity, but one does not know what traits it actually measures. Travers (1951) reported on a biographical data blank predicting probability of making promotion in a particular industry. Through later analysis it was learned that the discriminating items were mainly pertinent to racial qualities of the employees. Thus, the predictive power of the test could be explained on the basis of racial prejudices of management.

The rational method, however, suffers from a certain amount of inevitable circularity that characterizes factor analytic discoveries. Peculiarities in input (item writing, item sampling, etc.) and extraction techniques, rotation, and so forth color the final results. This circularity is present even if *blind* analysis into some simple structure is carried out. The composition of the input variables will co-determine the number and nature of factors extracted. This condition implies a strong argument for a conceptual rather than a "realistic" interpretation of factors.

An interesting attempt to escape from arbitrariness was made by Cattell (1946) at the beginning of his factorial description of the personality sphere. Allport and Odbert compiled a list of some 4,500 terms used in the English language to describe differences between individuals. Cattell sorted these terms in 171 categories of approximate synonyms, added some elements from the typical psychological vocabulary (e.g., "aspiration level"), collected ratings of all terms on normal subjects, intercorrelated the ratings, and determined the clusters among them. Some 36 such clusters were considered to describe the *standard reduced personality sphere*, which, according to Cattell, is a concise but practically exhaustive description of personality traits. This approach, however, raises two major comments. First, one wonders if the sphere of personality and personality traits can be considered finite. It seems that there are as many differences between people as one is willing to distinguish. As the concept of "total personality" has no boundaries, it cannot be completely charted. Second, the dimensions of existing language do not necessarily describe the dimensions of some physical reality to be studied. It would seem rather unlikely, for instance, that a factor analysis of ratings of chemical compounds by means of descriptive terms, at the end of the last century, would have revealed the qualities of chemical elements as expressed in Mendeleev's Periodic Law.

## 5   CRITICAL ASPECTS OF SELF–REPORT TECHNIQUES

As mentioned in the beginning of this chapter, the questionnaire measurement of personality has met with many severe criticisms. They may be categorized under the following seven headings.

## 5.1  First Criticism

*People do not know themselves well enough to be able to give truthful answers.* Numerous authors stressed this point (Allan, 1958; Cattell, 1957a; Cronbach, 1949b; Vernon, 1964). Sometimes errors of memory are blamed, sometimes lack of experience. An item such as: "Do you think that you would be afraid to dive from a springboard?" is difficult to answer, according to Drake (1949), if one has never tried diving. Cattell stressed that "we are dealing with persons of varying degrees of self-knowledge." Nunnally (1959) argued that congruent validity of questionnaires is meaningless, as it may only imply that people are consistent in expressing illusory opinions of themselves.

## 5.2  Second Criticism

*The questionnaire technique suffers from problems of communication.* Questions may mean different things to different people (Allport, 1937; Anastasi, 1954; Freeman, 1955; Hutt, 1945; Rotter, 1954; Taylor, 1953). Cattell (1957a, p. 57) commented that "we are operating with persons of . . . different perceptions of the verbally defined stimulus situation." An item such as: "Do you often feel unhappy for no good reason?" is certainly ambiguous since many interpretations of "often," "feel unhappy," and "good reason" are possible. An additional difficulty is located in logical misinterpretations, due to negative phrasing such as: "Familiarity does not breed contempt."

## 5.3  Third Criticism

*Many real-life situations cannot be represented in verbal questionnaire items.* Examples were given by Allan (1958) of life situations too involved for an adequate description in a few lines.

## 5.4  Fourth Criticism

*People are capable of falsifying their responses.* Even if they are capable of giving a truthful answer, they may lie and give a response that is more desirable in their own opinion or to the experimenter's opinion as they see it.

Before taking up the last three criticisms, let us examine the first four. It is easy to refute the first three objections. They seem to be directed against the imperfections of what may be called the *inventory premise*, that is, the assumption that people are capable and willing to describe their behavior correctly. If one accepts the inventory premise, questionnaire items are indeed verbally defined stimulus situations, that is, verbal surrogates for behavior samples. It has certainly been one of the working assumptions in the development of the early questionnaires, hence the word *inventory*, but the premise was explicitly and vehemently rejected by Meehl (1945): "That the majority of questions seem by inspection to require self-ratings has been a source of theoretical misunderstanding, since the stimulus situation seems to request a self-rating, whereas *the scoring does not assume a valid self-rating to have been given*" (italics by Meehl). Despite their obsolescence, criticisms of the inventory premise continue obstinately to appear in the test reviews in the various Mental Measurement Yearbooks. Cattell (1957a) warned against the identification of factors and the establishment of psychological laws on the basis of item contents, yet he called these items "verbally defined stimulus situations." Meehl, however, came to an "explicit denial that we accept self-rating as a feeble surrogate for a behavior sample and (we should) substitute the assertion that a 'self-rating' constitutes an intrinsically interesting bit of verbal behavior, the nontest correlates of which must be discovered by empirical means."

As a means of assessing the utility of self-reports, Meehl referred especially to empirical (concurrent or predictive) validity, but his view may be properly extended to a more *construct oriented concept of validity*, which also seems implied in a comment by Guilford (1959). To a question such as "Did you ever hate your father or your mother?" a subject may say "No." Incorrect, in a veridical sense, as this reply may be, so Guilford says, it may reveal something about the subject's traits—lack of self-insight or tendency toward repression. The so-called lie scales that appear in many personality questionnaires may be mentioned as a characteristic example of this approach. In other words, it is possible to write items rationally on the basis of a working theory about what a person who is high on a particular trait is likely to say about himself.

Studies by Elias (1951), Gordon (1953), and the theoretical deductions by Broen (1960) clearly demonstrated that interpretive ambiguity is an advantage rather than a disadvantage. The advantage is based on the relationship between the trait of the person and the way in which he interprets the item. A quantitative index of item ambiguity has since been developed by L. R. Goldberg (1963).

H. J. Eysenck (1953b, 1964b) explained his standpoint by means of an example "Do you have frequent headaches?" Despite ambiguities of "frequent" and "headache" it is found that the item statistically discriminates between normals and neurotics. This may be due to more frequent actual headaches in neurotics, to their tendency to complain, to errors of memory, or to their perception of frequency of headaches in normals. "We are not interested in the causes of the observed difference, but only in the fact that our subjects can be diagnosed on the basis of their answers with greater accuracy than can be explained by chance" (Eysenck, H. J., 1953b; writer's translation). Eysenck's remarkable lack of interest in the causes of the observed differences may be attributable to a less intrinsic interest in questionnaire responses than was expressed by Meehl. Eysenck's position might have been somewhat undecided between retention and rejection of the inventory premise, which could also explain his use of terms like *truthful answering* and *falsification of the questionnaire*. These notions clearly pertain to the relationship between item response and actual fact, that is, veridical truth, a relationship that was characterized by him as being irrelevant. Ideally then, terms such as *lying, lie scale* and *deceit* should be removed from questionnaire terminology, although they may have some substance with regard to the state of mind of the subject as viewed by the person himself when he is taking a test.

Although the complete rejection of what we have called the inventory premise takes all the ground away from under the first three criticisms, the fact remains that people generally show more "adjusted scores" under nonanonymous test administration, or when instructed to make a good impression, when applying for a job, etc. In other words, the fourth criticism certainly applies but it needs a slight rewording: *Questionnaire responses are susceptible to test-taking attitudes.* These motivational states can take many forms, such as tendencies to complain; to make a good or bad impression; to appear progressive or conservative, fit for a particular job, unfit for military service; and to deserve medical attention, but the set to make a socially desirable impression is certainly the most prominent source of motivational distortion of self-report responses.

Another implication of rejecting the inventory premise is the denial of the fundamental difference that many see between objective test data and questionnaire scores. Responses to both kinds of instruments are of the same order and can be studied in the same way. If the term *self-report* is understood in this way, then its literal meaning is limited to the way people perceive questionnaires as different from performance tests; the usual distinction between $Q$ data and $T$ data makes sense only in this respect.

## 5.5 Fifth Criticism

*People give different answers to the same items after some time.* Benton and Stone (1937) found 8% of all answers in the Bernreuter Personality Inventory changed at immediate retest, 20% of all responses after 1 year, and 35% after 2 years and, likewise, 35% after 3 years, but he also noticed that 80% of the changes compensated one another in terms of total scores. This type of criticism may be understandable on the basis of the inventory premise, but it is not essential since reliabilities are usually assessed on total scores and not on individual items. According to Nunnally (1959), however, they are usually too low (between .75 and .85). Questionnaires are not all alike in this respect, and not always is a high reliability one of the purposes of test construction (e.g., the Gulliksen type of key: Gulliksen, 1950).

## 5.6 Sixth Criticism

*Questionnaires show little validity against external criteria.* Ellis (1946) and Ellis and Conrad (1948) analyzed hundreds of investigations in which external validities of questionnaires in military and civilian settings

had been studied. The general adverse conclusions of Ellis and Conrad were often quoted by later critics. It is not without importance to note, however, that validity coefficients between zero and .39 were called "negative," coefficients between .40 and .69 were labeled "questionable positive," and only those above .70 were considered "positive." J. P. Guilford (1959b) was certainly right when he called the general conclusions misleading. Moreover, we have seen that the relevance of the nontest behavior should be carefully considered before it is taken as a criterion in validity studies. More specifically with regard to diagnostic categories, it was emphasized by Hathaway (1959) that these categories are usually a result of cultural and historical trends and not of fundamental research. A dimensional analysis of abnormal behavior, such as proposed by H. J. Eysenck (1961a), seems indeed indispensable for a proper evaluation of the questionnaire method as a means of identifying and describing personality traits relevant to both normal and abnormal behavior.

## 5.7 Seventh Criticism

*Questionnaire responses are susceptible to response sets.* First noticed by Rundquist and Sletto (1936) and later reported by various other investigators (Lentz, 1938; Lorge, 1937; Thorndike, 1938; Thurstone, 1938b; Whisler, 1938) response sets were extensively discussed by Cronbach (1946, 1950). His definition of response set reads: "Any tendency causing a person consistently to give different responses to test items than he would when the same content is presented in a different form." Form and content cannot easily be defined independently, however, especially as "literal content" cannot be considered a useful concept when the inventory premise is rejected. Moreover, the semantic analyses by a linguist such as Bloomfield (1933) and psychologists such as Osgood, Suci, and Tannenbaum (1957) would lead to a definition of content or meaning of items in terms of the responses elicited by these items; and a description of response sets by means of notions such as "different responses" and "the same content" becomes logically inconsistent.

Response sets may be described as unintended sources of questionnaire (method) variance associated with the particular response options offered to the subjects. Avoiding explicit reference to "content," the between-subjects questionnaire variance can be considered to comprise of (a) variance reflecting the trait elicited by the verbal phrasing of the item; (b) variance elicited by response formats; (c) variance associated with states or traits other than intended; (d) variance due to test-taking attitudes; (e) variance due to other factors such as instructions (individual differences in understanding and interpretation), length (individual differences in fatigue and motivation), human interest and pleasantness of the task involved, face validity (individual differences in beliefs regarding the purpose of the test), and so forth; and, finally, (f) error. This is purely conceptual differentiation, as in particular cases the various kinds of variances may correlate considerably. One would have an example of this correlation if it were true that authoritarian personalities tend to have the beliefs expressed in $F$ items (e.g., "Obedience and respect for authority are the most important virtues children should learn"; type a variance); if they tend to agree with slanting generalizations and have the tendency to give extreme responses (type b variance); if they have the tendency to put themselves in a favorable light (type d variance); if they perceive the $F$ scale (Adorno, Frenkel-Brunswick, Levinson, &

Sanford, 1950) as a measure of say Moral Intransigence (type e variance) on which they would very much like to score high. Any of these sources of variances alone or in combination may determine the validity of a questionnaire or invalidate it.

A considerable number of response sets has been identified. The most prominent are listed in appendix 1, which also provides some selected references.

The tendency to give socially desirable responses is sometimes called a response set. If elicited at all by the characteristics of the questionnaire—rather than the test situation in general—it is certainly more a function of "content" than of response format. Moreover, a person wanting to make a good impression will endorse some items, reject some, evade still others, and so forth, and show little "rigidity of responsiveness." This particular tendency is better described as a test-taking attitude.

The operation of response sets—taking acquiescence as an example—in particular tests is usually detected by calculating the split-half reliability of the number of "yes" responses; or by comparing the correlation between subscores obtained on the yes-keyed items in a questionnaire and the no-scored items with the correlation expected on the basis of the internal consistency of the test; or by correlating the questionnaire score with a test that was specifically devised to measure response set only; or by demonstrating that the size of the correlations between the questionnaire and other tests is a direct function of the similarity in the proportion of yes-keyed items.

Most response sets show some amount of split-half reliability. If they are stable over time and show some consistency across different tests, they are sometimes called response *styles* rather than sets (Jackson, D. N., & Messick, 1962), to indicate that they are not just ephemeral. If they are not stable, they can only add error variance to the questionnaire scores. If they are stable and negatively correlated with the criterion or construct, they lower the validity of the questionnaire, and if they are positively related to the construct they contribute additional valid variance to the questionnaire. Thus sensitivity to response sets is not necessarily a bad thing. In a critical review of the literature on response sets, Rorer (1965) pointed out, however, that there is little convincing evidence that response sets actually play a large part in questionnaire scores.

Various corrective and preventive methods regarding response sets have been developed. Separate scores can be obtained on yes-keyed and no-keyed items and be used as in multiple correlation. Helmstadter (1957) devised a mathematical model for separate set and content components of a test score. Chance profiles have been calculated in order to detect random responding (Marks & Seeman, 1963). Forced-choice and multiple-choice items instead of "single stimulus" items are commonly suggested as a means of preventing the operation of response sets (as well as to reduce test-taking attitude variance) in questionnaire scores.

Another method is "balancing," that is, placing equal numbers of yes-keyed and no-keyed items in the questionnaire. Often, however, the erroneous belief is expressed (e.g., Messick & Jackson, 1958) that balancing eliminates acquiescence variance from total scores. This is certainly not the case even if the yes- and no-keyed items show matched distributions of $p$ values. Suppose a person should obtain a score of zero on a balanced neuroticism questionnaire because he is extremely stable. If he is acquiescent, he will say "yes" to some questions when he should have answered "no." His actual score, therefore, will be greater than zero. The

same holds for a subject with a strong "nay-saying" tendency; he will say "no" to some items to which he should have answered "yes" because of his stability. Scores that should be below average are heightened by yes- and no-saying tendencies; scores that should be above average are lowered by these tendencies. In other words, a regression toward the mean will occur, the amount of which depends upon the strength of the response set. The difference between balanced and unbalanced inventories is that the correlation between acquiescence and scores on a balanced scale will be zero when calculated over a random sample and differ from zero if the scale is predominantly yes-keyed or predominantly no-keyed. This circumstance favors the use of the former.

A third method for the prevention of response set is by warning the subjects against them in the instructions. Goodfellow (1940) obtained satisfactory results after telling his subjects in a psychophysical experiment: "Remember that in approximately one half of the trials the correct answer will be yes." In view of the particular nature of personality schedules, it does not seem likely that special instructions provide a useful means for suppressing response sets.

A completely different approach toward the problem of response sets has been suggested by various authors who reasoned that response sets might not be undesirable sources of variation in personality measures at all, but reveal intrinsically interesting aspects of personality. As early as 1948, Cattell found that acquiescence, extreme response set, and the tendency to shift responses in relation to indications of social desirability are systematically embedded in general personality factors. Only several years later, however, did a more general realization of such relationships arise.

Lewis and Taylor (1955) found a positive relation between extreme response set and anxiety as measured by J. A. Taylor's Manifest Anxiety Scale (1953). This was also observed by Berg and Collier (1953), who, in addition, found a relation between this set and body sway suggestibility. Atypical yes answers were found to relate to the Psychoticism factor in the MMPI, and atypical no responses to the Neuroticism factor (Barnes, 1956). An interesting interaction effect of intelligence and anxiety upon extreme responses has been observed in the Semantic Differential (Osgood, Suci, & Tannenbaum, 1957). H. J. Eysenck (1947) found Speed versus Accuracy related to Extraversion-Introversion. Soueif (1958) related extreme response set to intolerance of ambiguity, and many studies have investigated the role of acquiescence in authoritarianism. The tendency to give evasive responses to particular questionnaire items was related to self-defensiveness in a study of Wilde (1966b) in an effort to explore the construct validity of a validating scale (lie scale). Similar results were found by A. L. Edwards and Diers (1963).

These and many other similar findings have given rise to a reevaluation of response sets. Instead of attempts to repress them, new scales have been developed in an effort to maximize response set variance and minimize "content" variance. Berg (1959), Cattell (1957a), Couch and Keniston (1960) and Nunnally and Husek (1958) offered examples of such procedures. According to Berg, comparisons between his Perceptual Reaction Test (which attempts to measure response sets only) and "content-oriented" measures are quite favorable to the former. Stressing the relative unimportance of item content, Berg developed the Deviation Hypothesis, which maintains that "deviant response patterns tend to be general, hence those deviant behavior patterns which are significant for abnormality, thus regarded as symptoms (earmarks or signs), are associated with other deviant response patterns which are in noncritical areas of behavior and which are not regarded as symptoms of 'personality aberration.'"

In actual practice, any test response (on any type of test) that is marked by a minority of subjects can be entered in the scoring key of a deviant response scale. Wilde and Tellegen (1965) found that a deviant response scale developed on Neuroticism and Extraversion and some other items was at least as effective in discriminating between various psychiatric criterion groups as more traditional factor-analytic questionnaire scores. Studies by Norman (1963b) and Sechrest and Jackson (1962), however, cast doubt on the generality of what has been called "deviant response set," since the validity of the scales for the measurement of deviant response set seems to depend on the content of the items used for its assessment. In other words, as the content of the items does seem to play an important part, it may be questioned that deviant response set is a true set indeed. The dimensionality of deviation is still another problem.

Of major importance in the present context is the question of how much the measurement of response tendencies can contribute to the identification and description of personality traits. The previously mentioned studies have a markedly "empirical" or atheoretical orientation (Table 1). They may therefore throw only little light on the nature of important personality trait constructs. Many a psychologist would argue that personality traits should first be conceived as a product of inductive reasoning stimulated by empirical observation, but that measurement variables should be logically deduced from the believed nature of the construct.

## 6 THE SEARCH FOR QUESTIONNAIRE SUBTLETY: CORRECTIVE AND PREVENTATIVE MEASURES AGAINST THE INFLUENCE OF TEST-TAKING ATTITUDES

We now turn to the most serious objection raised against personality inventories, that is, their susceptibility to test-taking attitudes. There are a number of more or less standard procedures that are used to test questionnaire scores on sensitivity for motivational distortion. They have been listed in appendix 2. The instruction effects in investigations of the first type are usually found to be significant. However, not every person produces "better" scores, in comparison to standard instructions. Kimber (1947), for instance, found shifts between .3 and .8 sigma units on the California Test of Personality. Forty-one percent of his male subjects and 26% of his female subjects obtained the same or a better score under standard instructions. Bernreuter (1933b) found a correlation close to zero between scores obtained under standard and "best foot forward" instructions. He interpreted this—perhaps sophistically—as an indication of the limited importance of test-taking attitudes under naïve conditions.

The importance of realistic instructions in such experiments was emphasized by Rusmore (1956), who found correlations ranging between .64 and .79 between the two instructional situations, the average shift being approximately 9 centile points. This shift was, however, considerably greater when he used more suggestive instructions. He administered the Gordon Personal Profile to 121 students, informing them that the scores would be used for future vocational counseling. Three months later the test was administered again, but now with the added information given to the students that the scores would be used for allocating them in various summer jobs. The scores correlated at least to the extent of .74 and the average shift was 10 centile points on "emotional stability" and 9 centile points on "responsibility." These results were interpreted as proof for the fakability of the inventory involved; but Rusmore failed to correct for retest effects, which commonly amount to somewhat better scores at a repeated test administration (Sinha, 1964; Windle, 1954) and these might have explained his results.

The second method also usually shows significant differences in obtained scores, but here again are important exceptions. Sheldon (1959) did not find "better" average scores on the Minnesota Teacher Attitude Inventory when it was applied to actual applicants for teaching jobs. Heron (1956a) found a difference of approximately .25 sigma units in "emotional maladjustment" between applicants for the job of bus conductor who took the questionnaire as a part of the selection procedure and others who took it as volunteers in a research project. There is no evidence in Heron's report, however, that the two groups were properly matched, which also holds for an earlier similar investigation by Green (1951), comparing applicants with employees.

In later years fakability investigations have been carried out on the item level. "The relationship between the judged social desirability of a trait (i.e., item) and the probability that the trait will be endorsed" was demonstrated first by A. L. Edwards (1953). He had judges rate questionnaire items on a 9-point scale ranging from "highly socially undesirable" to "highly socially desirable." Average scale values of these items, obtained with the method of successive intervals, were then correlated with the $p$ values of the same items as observed in a sample of subjects. A positive correlation .87 was observed. Along similar lines, others found correlations consistently above .80. Gordon (1953) observed a correlation of .96 and also demonstrated that "social acceptability," "preference in others," and "preference for hearing said about oneself" are all highly related ($r \geq .94$). Although the size of this correlation was shown to be positively related to the average $p$ value of the self-report items involved (Wiggins, 1962a), it seems fair to conclude that the probability that an item will be endorsed can be rather accurately predicted if one knows the average social desirability attached to the item. The *causal* nature of this relationship, however, is not well understood; but data of this kind are usually interpreted as a demonstration of the fakability of the questionnaire involved.

After obtaining average social desirability ratings of 150 MMPI items, Edwards selected 79 that showed perfect interjudge agreement that either the "yes" or "no" response was the socially desirable one. These items were given to a number of persons who were scored for the number of socially desirable responses they gave. His Social Desirability Scale (SD scale) was subsequently reduced to the 39 most discriminating items with item-test correlations as the criterion. Numerous questionnaire scales have been correlated with this SD scale (which is an example of type-4 method in appendix 2); and the correlations have been usually found to be of such magnitude that—according to Edwards—after subtraction of SD variance, little variation is left in diagnostic or construct categories for which these questionnaires had been designed (Edwards, A. L., 1957, 1959b, 1962).

D. N. Jackson and Messick (1962) were particularly interested in the influence of SD set and acquiescence (as well as their interaction) in the MMPI and conducted a number of factor-analytic studies of these response determinants of MMPI scales. For this purpose they developed five different SD-set measures and factored them together with other MMPI scales. Their demonstration of a pervasive SD factor (Method 5 in appendix 2) is, however, considerably weakened by the way they sampled their variables. Even apart from the problems that arise from the extreme item overlap in these variables, one has to guard against oversampling of a particular type of scales relative to the others, as oversampling will almost inevitably give rise to a strong and salient factor having high loadings in these scales. If anywhere, the dangers inherent to the circular nature of factor-analytic approaches will come home to roost, it is in a case like this.

It seems evident, from the studies presented, that personality questionnaires *can* be faked. However, whether they *are* faked in actual fact and whether their fakability is detrimental to their validity, is an entirely different matter. A shift in scores—identical in amount or different for different subjects—under certain conditions does not necessarily imply a loss in validity, although it is definitely a serious inconvenience for test score standardization and comparisons across different test-taking situations.

Many attempts have been made to remedy the fakability of verbal personality measures in a quest for more subtle procedures. *Subtlety* can be defined as the characteristic of questionnaires that can be interpreted with validity, regardless of the nature, direction, and extent of the test-taking attitudes of the subjects. Space does not permit detailed description of the nature and merits of these "Subtilization procedures," which have been listed in appendix 3.

There is unfortunately only limited evidence regarding the effect of many of the measures mentioned in appendix 3. A positive influence of these procedures on questionnaire validity has generally more often been assumed than actually demonstrated. And those studies in which empirical comparisons of validity were made frequently do not favor the modifications suggested for subtilizing questionnaires. Ellis (1947) compared self-report and "projective" formats of a questionnaire in regard to their efficiency in identifying 40 "behavior problem boys" in 461 schoolboys (see 4a in appendix 3). The direct, self-report format showed superior validity.[2] A very careful investigation of similar nature was carried out in Sweden by Jonsson (1957). He administered a self-report and a "projective" version of 80 questionnaire items to some 200 summer school students. Validation criteria were obtained in the form of average ratings on the items by peers. The projective questions yielded validity coefficients with an average of .06 and sigma .30, but the direct method produced an average item validity of .30 with sigma .30. Rundquist (1940) and Gordon (1953) also used behavior ratings as validation criteria; both found that undesirable items were more valid than desirable items. Gordon observed a correlation —.36 between item desirability and item validity in undesirable items. Thus, an *increase* in validity could be expected for unacceptable items with a *decrease* in social acceptability. Actual validity gains due to Method 4 (a) through (g) have not been clearly demonstrated empirically, and they do not seem very likely in view of Gordon's findings.

Few investigations throw a light on the usefulness of "innocuous" item content in an effort to disguise the true (or at least intended) psychological meaning of the test.

[2] Editors' note: This finding is in keeping with results of administering questionnaires to young children. Although social desirability sets operate even among preschool children, direct self-reports appear to be more valid than with adults (cf.: Dreger's chapter, this *Handbook*).

H. J. Eysenck (1953b) compared six disguised tests with two straightforward self-report measures of neuroticism that involved direct questioning about neurotic symptoms. He concluded that the straightforward tests of neurotic tendency indicated this personality trait much better than the indirect tests. The most direct test discriminated better than all other tests combined.

An interesting possibility for disguised measurement of adjustment is suggested by the results of a study of "empathy" items by Van Zelst (1953). Each person was required to rank a number of types of music, magazines, and annoyances according to their (un)popularity in a specified population. The scoring key consisted of the actual order of popularity. Discrepancy scores between scoring key and subjects' ranks correlated .59 with "interpersonal desirability" in 124 industrial employees. Comparisons between this procedure and direct personality questionnaires have not been carried out, however. A comparative study of a self-report questionnaire and an inventory consisting of the same items in "error-choice" format with an external adjustment criterion has been conducted by Wilde (1966b), Wilde and Fortuin (1969), and Wilde and De Wit (1970). The error-choice technique, developed in social psychology (Hammond, 1948; Kubany, 1953; Weschler, 1950b), forces a person to choose between two alternative responses, each of which is equally wrong, but in opposite direction from the correct answer. All 150 subjects first completed a standardized personality questionnaire with scales for neuroticism, extraversion, masculinity-femininity, social desirability, deviant response set, and a lie scale. An hour later they were given an error-choice version of the same items. This version was presented to them as a "test of insight into people." Following each item, two percentages appeared, both equally distant from the true endorsement percentage in the general population (e.g., "Are your feelings rather easily hurt?" (63%–73%). The subject had to mark the percentage he believed to be correct for the general population.

None of the subjects reported any suspicion regarding the nature of this procedure which appeared to them as a test of information or ability to judge others and that does not seem to invite the person to put himself in a favorable light. Positive correlations were found between endorsement (in the self-report format) and overestimation of the population percentage (in the error-choice format) in 90 of the 91 items involved. Subsequently personality scores were calculated on the error-choice form (overestimations taken as if they were yes responses and underestimations scored as no responses). The resulting scores were correlated with the corresponding self-report scores and both with the external criterion, which consisted of diagnosed neurosis versus normality. For all personality scales in the questionnaire, positive and significant correlations were found between the self-report and error-choice versions; and with the exception of the lie scale, each of both types of scales was significantly related to the external criterion used. It was concluded, therefore, that the error-choice technique can produce valid measures of personality. The external validities of the error-choice scales were slightly lower than those of the corresponding self-report scales.

In a later investigation by Philipp and Wilde (1968, 1970) with special reference to extraversion, an error-choice version of the Eysenck Personality Inventory (Eysenck, H. J., 1963) was prepared and factored together with Cattell's Extraversion score of the 16 PF, Geidt and Downing's (1961) Extraversion scale in MMPI items, and two other Extraversion measures. As an external criterion a behavioral measure for extra-

version (stimulation-seeking behavior during isolation) had been included in this study. The results showed quite satisfactory factorial validity of the error-choice procedure for the measurement of extraversion. Like the empathy-type items mentioned previously, error-choice formats of personality questionnaires seem to hold an interesting promise for subtle measurement of personality traits.

The forced-choice type questionnaire is also expected to minimize test-taking attitude variance, as the response options are matched for social desirability (or endorsement frequency, Bartlett, 1960). Several authors investigated the relative validity of the straightforward and the forced-choice method with regards to external criteria (Gordon, 1951; Graham, 1958; Osburn, Lubin, Loeffler, & Tye, 1954; Perry, 1955; Zuckerman, 1952). Of these investigations only Gordon's is in favor of the forced-choice methods. Two of them favored the direct method. Perry and Osburn, Lubin, et al. concluded that forced-choice items have lower validities per item than straightforward questions and that the former show lower intercorrelations. They contend that the eventual test validity will therefore depend on the number of items and there is no universally superior method of constructing inventories. Graham's study is of special importance because it encompassed comparisons of a large number of questionnaire characteristics against an external validity criterion. In the present context the most relevant of his comparisons were between self-rating versus forced-choice, an empirical key derived under standard instructions and an empirical key derived under "fake good" instructions, a key on "obvious" items and one on items of which the psychological meaning was not obvious to the subjects. The questionnaire format consisting of direct questions, the key of which was derived under standard instructions, yielded the best validity of all combinations tested.

If a questionnaire is susceptible to social desirability set, one would expect it to show a lower validity in "threatening" situations (e.g., application for a job or employee screening for promotion) than in less binding situations. Wilde (1963, 1964) administered a personality inventory with two neuroticism scales to 10 groups of employees in industry. Six groups were tested anonymously and the remaining 4 groups had to fill in names and other personal data on the inventory booklet. Correlations with absenteeism in the previous year were calculated as measures of validity. The rather striking result was that the anonymous scores were slightly *less* valid than the nonanonymous scores. The same inventory was administered in two separate studies (unpublished reports, cited in Wilde & DeWit, 1970) to groups of subjects in a selection situation. The items were factor analyzed and the factor patterns and loadings were compared with factor analyses on questionnaire responses from comparable subjects who had been tested on a voluntary, inconsequential basis. If the SD susceptibility of the questionnaire has a negative effect on its validity, one should expect a distortion of the factorial composition in the selection situation (e.g., a confusion of the neuroticism and test-taking attitude factor). The investigators, however, concluded that there is no change in factorial validity of the inventory scores. The only difference found was a difference in mean scores, which is trivial and irrelevant to the present problem.

It can hardly be overemphasized that investigations of alleged validity loss of questionnaire scores due to sensitivity to test-taking attitudes should be carried out with some validity criterion as a yardstick. The shift in mean scores as a function of "fake good" or "fake bad" instructions or of

threatening situations do not provide necessary grounds, let alone sufficient ones, to conclude a detrimental effect upon validity. To push the argument a little further, one might just as well reason that the test scores under these instructional or situational conditions should be more valid because then the test-taking attitude of the subjects is relatively constant and will add less variance to the trait scores. Nevertheless, the repeated demonstration of these shifts in scores has induced some psychologists to put more confidence in projective tests. They are wrong for two reasons: in the first place because of the arguments as presented here, and, second, because of the evidence produced by Carp and Shavzin (1950), Weisskopf and Dieppa (1951), Meltzoff (1951), Cronbach (1949b) and Silverstein (1957) that projective tests like the Rorschach, Thematic Apperception Test (TAT), Sentence Completion, and Rosenzweig Picture-Frustration Test are no less sensitive to experimental instructions. Likewise, studies demonstrating the existence of similar effects of instructions on forced choice procedures (e.g., French, 1958, with regard to EPPS; Gordon & Stapleton, 1956; Longstaff & Jurgensen, 1953) do not invalidate these methods but do not provide indirect support for the use of straightforward "self-descriptive" personality inventories either.

In an effort to correct for test-taking attitudes post hoc, that is after the administration of a personality inventory, many scales have been developed. The consistency scale by Cady (1923) is one of the earliest. He repeated several items in his scale derived from the Woodworth Personal Data Sheet, in order to check upon self-contradictions of the subjects. Such validating scales are often presented as suppressor variables as they do not correlate with criteria but do correlate with trait scores, so that invalid variance can be subtracted from the latter. The *L* scale ("lie"-scale) in the MMPI consists of 15 items, derived from the work by Hartshorne, May and Shuttleworth (1928), and contains qualities which are either "desirable but improbable" or qualities which are "undesirable but probable" (e.g., "I do not always tell the truth"). This type of validating scale, which is encountered in many personality schedules, is constructed by means of the "rational" method (see Table 1), in contradistinction to the other types, the *K* scale and the *F* scale. The *F* scale (*F* stands for low frequency) consists of responses (either "true" or "false") which are very rarely given in samples of normal subjects and may pick up such things as inability to read, lack of understanding, gross abnormality or malingering.

In the Humm-Wadsworth Temperament Scale, 76% of all items indicate abnormality if answered "yes." The "no-count" (i.e. the number of items answered "no") was therefore considered as a measure for test-taking attitude (Humm & Humm, 1935). The *K* type of validating scale consists essentially of empirically selected items which discriminated between false negatives (patients with normal MMPI profiles) and true negatives (normals with normal MMPI scores). Other examples of *K* type test-taking attitudes scales were developed on the Bernreuter Personality Inventory by Ruch (1942), Cofer, Chance, and Hudson (1949), and Wiggins (1962). These investigators, however, used "fake good" role-playing instructions in order to develop empirical criteria for item selection. In the Edwards' type of social desirability (SD) scale, a procedure as in attitude test construction involving judges is used. Meehl and Hathaway (1946) were not very optimistic about a substantial validity increase of MMPI interpretation with the help of "no-count," *L, K* or *F* scales. Results obtained by H. F. Hunt

(1948), H. O. Schmidt (1948), F. T. Tyler and Dimichaelis (1953) were likewise discouraging. Schlesser (1953), on the other hand, observed an improvement of validity in the Personal Values Inventory for predicting grades in 1,200 students when *L* as well as *K* corrections were carried out.

It is difficult to say what accounts for the generally limited success of test-taking attitude scales. It could be that these "validating scales" have little validity for what they purport to measure, or it may be that test-taking attitudes, as far as present at all, do not severely limit the validity of questionnaires scores, however "fakable" they may be. The latter interpretation seems to be implied in a comment by Comrey (1958): "The fact that an individual is prone to exhibit himself in a favourable light, does not necessarily mean that he is therefore more neurotic or psychotic than his uncorrected score would indicate."

On the basis of the generally high (negative) correlations between the various MMPI and other scales and his SD scale, A. L. Edwards (1957) made the following comment: "The correlations between SD and scores on various personality inventories are of such magnitude that the residual or deviation scores may represent little more than error variance." This conclusion is, of course, only correct when it can be assumed that SD is a mere disturbing factor, which is not correlated with the attribute that one tries to measure with the inventory variable concerned. This assumption does not seem to be justified, at least not with regard to neuroticism and anxiety. Bendig (1960) performed two factor analyses on several neuroticism and anxiety inventories, a short version of the MMPI scale, Cattell's Motivational Distortion Scale (Cattell, 1955b), and A. L. Edwards' SD scale (also in a short version). Among Bendig's conclusions, the following is of special importance here:

The presence of a Falsification or Honesty Factor in these Inventory scores, as was suggested by Edwards among others, was also strongly confirmed, but it is evident that Edwards' Social Desirability Scale is not the best measure of this factor. The factor loadings of the abbreviated social desirability scale appear quite similar to those of the Anxiety and Neuroticism Scales and indicate that *the SD scores are a better measure of Factor EM (emotionality) than they are of Factor F (falsification).* (Italics added.)

In a canonical variate analysis by Wilde and Tellegan (1965), it was found that an Edwards-type SD scale was equally efficient in discriminating between 159 neurotics and 112 psychotics, as well as between the neurotics and 197 normal controls on two different neuroticism scales. Also, Cattell and Scheier (1961) found that willingness to admit defects in oneself tends to be inherent to the syndrome of anxiety, regardless of the situation it is measured in. These findings seem to imply that SD sensitivity is not necessarily an unfavorable quality of a personality questionnaire. On the contrary, the elimination or minimization of SD sensitivity might well eliminate a source of valid variance in questionnaire scores. The reader is reminded of the evidence regarding factorial validity of questionnaire scores when compared with various performance tests (section 3), from which it was concluded that questionnaire scores show quite satisfactory (if not better) validity in comparison to these other tests despite the more "objective" nature of the latter. In passing we may note that the insensitivity of these performance tests to test-taking-attitude influence is more generally assumed than empirically demonstrated and it certainly does not hold for "faking bad." It is true for performance tests (*T* data) that the purpose and particular aspects of the scoring procedures are often concealed from the sub-ject, but this does not necessarily imply that various test-taking attitudes or perceptions of the demand characteristics of the test do not influence the person's behavior on the test.

Summing up, it seems reasonable to draw a conclusion regarding SD-set susceptibility of inventory measures of personality, similar to the one drawn with regards to response sets: Test-taking attitudes *may* partially or completely invalidate inventory scores, but whether this actually occurs remains to be investigated in the particular case involved.

# 7 INDIVIDUAL DIFFERENCES IN SOCIAL DESIRABILITY OPINIONS AND THEIR POSITIVE USE FOR PERSONALITY MEASUREMENT

As the endorsement percentage of an item is highly correlated with its desirability value, and as some people endorse many more of these items than others do, one might hypothesize that the former subjects have different (i.e., higher) desirability opinions of these items than the latter. To test this hypothesis, the person is given the inventory with the traditional self-report instructions and also in a format for desirability judgments. From each person, two scores are thus obtained, the inventory score and his average desirability rating of these items (for no-keyed items the reverse or *un*desirability ratings are obtained for each item and averaged with the desirability rating of the yes-keyed items). The two scores are then correlated across persons.

During the 1960s two studies of this kind were published that also involved an external criterion. Wilde (1964) administered a neuroticism (N) scale and a neuroticism desirability (ND) scale, derived along the method described, to two groups of 200 soldiers who were involved in a selection program for officers in the Dutch armed forces that consisted in psychological testing and independent psychiatric screening by means of a diagnostic interview in which the candidates were given points for emotional stability in military conditions. In both groups the N and ND scales intercorrelated $r = +.49$, thus explaining 25% of all variance in the N scores and supporting the preceding hypothesis. In an effort to determine whether this source of variance can be considered valid, both N and ND scales were correlated with the external criterion. The N scale showed considerable validity, but the ND scale had essentially zero validity. It was concluded that in this case the ND scale might at best be used as an effective suppressor variable. In the study by D. N. Jackson (1964), which was inspired by Messick's (1960) investigation of the dimensionality of social desirability ratings in a structure of different "points of view," an Independence-Conformity Inventory was used. Along with self-report responses, desirability ratings of the items were obtained; both correlated with a behavioral criterion for social conformity. Correlations between self-report and the desirability scales were found to range between $+.59$ and $+.70$ in 127 undergraduate students, and the external validity of the desirability scale was somewhat higher than of the self-report counterpart.

Studies of this kind seem to advocate a fundamental reorientation regarding the problems of socially desirable responding. Instead of attempting to remove this type of variance from personality questionnaires, efforts may be made to construct questionnaires which intentionally capitalize on individual differences in item desirability opinions. An example of this was offered by Fifer (see appendix 3, item 6), who constructed a rigidity questionnaire with forced-choice items, matched for *average* social desirability. The options were rationally derived from a working theory of what attributes would be considered more desirable in the opinion of people high in rigidity. Persons were required to mark which of two attributes they would prefer to have. No self-report was wanted, but a statement of preference—hence the term *preference items*. In the study by Philipp and Wilde (1968, 1970), five questionnaire measures of Extraversion were involved: the E scale in the Eysenck Personality Inventory (EPI); an Extraversion scale on MMPI items; the composite Extraversion score on Cattell's 16 PF; Zuckerman's Sensation Seeking Scale, an error-choice version of the EPI E scale; and, finally, an Extraversion Desirability Scale (ED) developed with the EPI E items, using 7-point rating scales for each item. As a nonquestionnaire measure for Extraversion, a behavioral measure was included that consisted in rates of lever pulling for light and music as reinforcements in a situation of sensory restriction. The questionnaire measures were factored, showing that the ED scale had the highest loading of all in the first unrotated centroid factor which predicted the lever pulling rates. The ED scale correlated $r = +.82$ with the E scale. Taking attenuation for unreliability into account, it may be inferred that self-report responses to Extraversion items can largely be understood as to be due to differences between people in their appreciation for extraverted characteristics. The high factorial validity of the ED scale, plus the fact that the Extraversion factor predicted an external criterion, leads to the interpretation that ED variance is valid variance (unlike ND variance in the case of Neuroticism reported previously). In other words, extraverts like extraverted attributes better than introverts do.

This situation might be tentatively interpreted as follows. Some personality scales, like the ones for Anxiety and Neuroticism, measure the readiness of the subject to develop a particular *drive* (or drive-related) state. Other personality inventory scales, like the ones for Extraversion and the Independence-Conformity Inventory (Jackson, D. N., 1964), essentially measure value systems of the subjects. If values (and attitudes) can be equated with *habits* in the Hullian sense of the word, an interesting possibility of integrating personality theory with a comprehensive learning theory of behavior is offered. In Hull's theory, it is postulated that the probability of a particular behavior depends on the product of the intensity of a drive state and the strength of the habit of the organism to reduce the drive in that particular way. It seems worthwhile to investigate personality inventory scales further along the principle underlying the "trait desirability scales."

The most radical approach to the whole problem of response sets and distortions in questionnaires, which we have studied in the present and previous section, is that presented in *trait-view theory*. Instead of dealing with particular influences of social desirability, acquiescence and the like, this approach proposes a single alternative in which all kinds of distortion themselves are considered an expression of personality. In so doing, it asks only (a) what is the personality of the person distorting? and (b) what is the role in which he is operating? A specification equation can then be written which specifies the distortion on a particular factor scale as a weighted outcome of the person's true scores on personality factors plus his score in role involvement. As Cattell (1965) and Krug and Cattell (1971) showed, the role involvement can itself be measured as a factor with a specific loading in a specific test-taking situation.

## 8 MAJOR FINDINGS OF THE QUESTIONNAIRE MEASUREMENT OF PERSONALITY TRAITS

In the foregoing sections, empirical material and theoretical considerations regarding the use of personality inventories have been presented to provide grounds for a more objective judgement of their use in personality research. Verbal measurements of personality are certainly not fatally affected by the criticisms that they have encountered. More research is needed to determine why particular people (having certain personality traits) give particular answers to particular questions (measuring these traits). As a result of this type of research, two things may be anticipated: first, a better understanding of the psychological nature of the traits involved and the verbal behavior of the individuals characterized by these traits and, second, the development of more advanced and more sophisticated questionnaire procedures (Rogers, T. B., 1971). But even at this time, there is a sufficiently firm empirical basis for their use as methods to identify, describe, and measure personality traits. Therefore, we now turn to some of the major recent achievements in this domain.

The number of personality questionnaires and the variety of different traits that have been subjected to inventory measurement are countless and preclude an attempt at an inclusive discussion in this chapter. Besides limitations of space, there are other good reasons for making a selection. A vast number of questionnaire studies have been conducted with essentially one or only a few variables at a time. However useful in their particular context, questionnaire investigations of this kind are not helpful if one wants to develop a more comprehensive exploration of the domain of personality differences. A truly comprehensive taxonomy of personality traits necessitates information regarding the relative importance of traits such as their intercorrelation or independence; their hierarchical order; and their approximate number needed to account for the most salient differences between individuals in matters of social, educational, occupational, and marital relevance. The work done by J. P. Guilford and by Cattell in the United States, and by H. J. Eysenck in England has been the most productive in this respect.

To complete this chapter, the differences and similarities between the personality descriptions offered by these three authors are outlined.

Guilford's studies resulted in a number of questionnaires, all designed to measure salient traits of personality (Guilford, J. P., 1934, 1943, 1954; Guilford, J. P., & Martin, 1943). Dissatisfied with the high intercorrelations between some of the scales in earlier questionnaires, and in an attempt to include more traits in a single instrument, J. P. Guilford and Zimmerman (1949, 1956) reanalyzed the items and published their Temperament Survey. This inventory consists of the scales as presented in appendix 4.

More than J. P. Guilford, H. J. Eysenck was particularly interested in the identification and measurement of personality traits underlying pathological types of behavior; the major emphasis of his work has been on the identification of second-order, orthogonal factors. His earlier inventory (the Maudsley Medical Questionnaire) was essentially a single-trait instrument (for neurotic tendency) but he reanalyzed several scales of Guilford's into two orthogonal (independent) dimensions which he identified as Neuroticism and Extraversion. These are measured in the MPI (Maudsley Personality Inventory, Eysenck, H. J., 1959) as well as the Eysenck Personality Inventory (Eysenck, H. J., & Eysenck, 1963).

More recently, Eysenck's work resulted in the identification of a third personality factor, called Psychoticism. Like Extraversion and Neuroticism, Psychoticism may be measured differentially by means of personality questionnaires, and inventory scores of psychoticism have been shown to relate to other variables in a predictable manner (Eysenck, H. J., & Eysenck, 1968, 1969, 1971, 1972).

Guilford's $S$ factor (Social Introversion or Shyness) has repeatedly been found to be highly correlated both with Neuroticism and Extraversion. H. J. Eysenck (1956b) and Eysenck and Eysenck (1969) explained this result in terms of a dual theory of social shyness, while they stresss the unitary nature of Extraversion. The social shyness of neurotics is viewed as fear of people, whereas introverts do not care much for the company of other people and prefer to be alone. The neurotic introvert however, wishes that he could be more sociable. In the framework of Fig. 2, Guilford's $S$ factor might be thought to be located as first-order Trait $C$ on the primary trait level. Eysenck might have subsumed some of the items (like $k$, $l$, and $m$) under Dimension I (Neuroticism) and some (like $r$ and $s$) under Dimension II (Introversion-Extraversion). Eysenck's Extraversion factor is very closely related to Guilford's $R$ (Rhathymia) and to a lesser extent to Guilford's $S$ (Social Shyness). Guilford's Factors $D$ (Depression) and especially $C$ (Cycloid Disposition) are practically equivalent to Eysenck's Neuroticism. In an investigation by Thurstone (1951) of the factorial composition of the various Guilford scales, $D$ and $C$ were also found to be closely related to each other they were subsumed by Thurstone under a single factor that he called Emotionality.

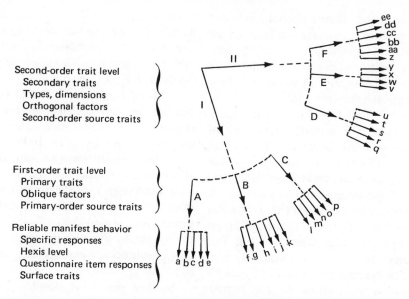

Second-order trait level
  Secondary traits
  Types, dimensions
  Orthogonal factors
  Second-order source traits

First-order trait level
  Primary traits
  Oblique factors
  Primary-order source traits

Reliable manifest behavior
  Specific responses
  Hexis level
  Questionnaire item responses
  Surface traits

FIG. 2 A simplified vector model of the hierarchial organization of personality, reduced to two dimensionality for graphic reasons. Three levels of abstraction are shown. The first level in the periphery comprises specific responses, which because of their reliability can be considered characteristic of the individual. Erratic, inconsistent responses are already discarded at this level. On the second level—closer to the origin of the space—the primary factors are found, indicating the functional unities (high inter-correlations) of the manifest specific behaviors. The angular separations of these points (a, b, c, etc.) with the origin of the space as reference indicate that they show higher correlations with one another within a cluster than with specific behaviors in other clusters. Abstracting from the primary (oblique) factors the secondary factors are found that show even greater angular separation. At an angle of 90° they would be orthogonal factors. (Vector lengths and locations have been distorted in this diagram; also, correlations between traits cannot be directly read off from the angles separating the vectors, as they are not necessarily located in the plan of the diagram, which is presented as a two-dimensional projection of the multidimensional personality sphere.)

Unlike Eysenck's, Cattell's preferred strategy for the description of personality usually was aimed at the identification of first-order or oblique, that is, correlated factors of personality differences. Whereas Eysenck developed his description of personality in view of the clinical relevance of the traits identified, Cattell concentrated his efforts largely upon the domain of individual differences within the boundaries of normal personality variation. Brevity compels us to refer the reader interested in a complete theoretical and technical description of the differences between the approaches taken by

Cattell on the one hand and Eysenck on the other, to books published by H. J. Eysenck and Eysenck (1969), by Cattell (1973a) and to Howarth's comparisons (Howarth, 1972a).

Taking trait descriptive words in the English language as a starting point (see section 4) Cattell made a large-scale attempt to identify personality traits by means of behavior rating, personality questionnaires, as well as other behavior modes. More than 30 factors (rubricised in the Universal Index: U.I.) have been identified, 16 of which can be effectively measured by personality inventory scales. Their technical labels and nature in terms of more familiar language are presented in appendix 5. Some of these primary traits are essentially uncorrelated (like $B$ and $F$ in Fig. 2) and others show sufficient intercorrelation (like $D$, $E$, and $F$ in Fig. 2) to load appreciably on secondary factors (Vector II in this figure). Two of those second-order factors are Anxiety and Introversion-Extraversion. Anxiety (or lack of it) can be measured as a weighted composite of the primary factors Ego-strength ($C$, see appendix 4), Parmia ($H$), Protension ($L$), Confidence ($O$), Self-sentiment Control ($Q_3$), and Low Ergic Tension ($Q_4$). This secondary factor can be equated with Eysenck's Neuroticism, whereas Eysenck's Extraversion corresponds to the second-order factor, constituted by the primaries Cyclothymia ($A$), Dominance ($E$), Surgency ($F$), Parmia ($H$) and Group Dependency ($Q_2$) in Cattell's factor-analytic description of personality.

The other major secondary factors operating in the primary source traits listed in appendix 4 are Tough Poise (Cool Rationality) and Independence, the meanings and associations of which are not yet fully understood, however.

The most comprehensive study of the second-order factors in the 16 primary personality traits was conducted by Gorsuch and Cattell (1967), and a detailed discussion of the taxonomic advantages of second-order versus first-order factors in the description of personality may be found in Cattell (1973a). Gorsuch and Cattell pooled the intercorrelation matrices obtained in seven heterogeneous samples, yielding a total sample size of 1,652 individuals. The results of this study are presented in Table 2, which lists the secondary factors in decreasing order of the amount of variance accounted for by each of them. Cattell (1955b, 1973a) presented evidence that the four largest

second-order factors in the questionnaire domain align with factors identified in objective tests, but this evidence has not always been replicated by other authors (e.g. Skinner, N. S. J. F., & Howarth, 1973).

To avoid confusion, it should be noted that Scheier and Cattell (1961) also constructed a neuroticism scale which is based on a number of scales in the 16 PF questionnaire. This neuroticism is not quite the same as Eysenck's Neuroticism factor (Cattell's Lack of Anxiety), as the authors included other scales that, in addition to those measuring the second-order anxiety factor, turned out to discriminate empirically between neurotics and normals (i.e., scales $I$, $F$, and $E$; see appendix 5).

Another source of possible confusion when comparing the results obtained with different self-report inventories is shown by the fact that response patterns such as Anxiety or Sociability may occur as transient states in people in reaction to particular stimulus situations, while these response patterns may not be characteristic for these persons across a large number of situations. The distinction between personality and mood, that is between *state* and *trait*, and the corresponding measurement techniques have been discussed in detail by Spielberger (1966c, 1972) and Cattell (1973a).

From Table 2 it can be seen that the two trait factors identified by Eysenck very clearly emerge as the prominent second-order factors in the more complex systems of both Guilford and Cattell. This is also the conclusion that Howarth (1972a) arrived at. These two factors can be theoretically understood and empirically approximated in terms of the more detailed factor categories of both Guilford and Cattell, and we must now turn to the question of correspondence between the personality-trait charts offered by the two latter investigators. Guilford and Cattell both attempted to cover a more

**TABLE 2** Second-order factors in the 16 Personality Factor Inventory, as obtained from pooled intercorrelation matrices

| First- and second-order factors | Second-order factors | | | | | | | |
|---|---|---|---|---|---|---|---|---|
| | I | II | III | IV | V | VI | VII | VIII |
| $A$   Sociable (vs. Cool, Aloof) | – | 46 | –54 | –23 | – | – | – | – |
| $B$   Intelligence | – | – | – | – | – | – | 87 | – |
| $C$   Ego-strength | –52 | – | – | – | – | – | – | – |
| $E$   Dominance | – | 44 | – | 36 | – | – | – | – |
| $F$   Surgency | – | 59 | – | – | – | – | – | – |
| $G$   Superego Strength | – | – | – | – | – | – | – | 85 |
| $H$   Adventurousness (vs. Timidity) | –42 | 62 | – | – | – | – | – | – |
| $I$   Sensitive (vs. Tough, Realistic) | – | – | –66 | – | – | –31 | – | – |
| $L$   Paranoid suspiciousness | 54 | – | – | – | – | – | – | – |
| $M$   Unconcerned (vs. Practical, Conventional) | – | – | – | 38 | – | 44 | – | – |
| $N$   Shrewdness (vs. Naïveté) | – | – | 27 | – | 49 | – | – | – |
| $O$   Guilt-proneness | 70 | – | – | – | – | – | – | – |
| $Q_1$   Radical (vs. Conservative) | – | – | – | 46 | 22 | – | – | – |
| $Q_2$   Self-sufficiency (vs. Group Dependency) | – | –34 | – | 41 | – | – | – | – |
| $Q_3$   Self-sentiment Control (vs. Lack of Integration) | –54 | – | – | – | 25 | – | – | – |
| $Q_4$   Ergic Tension | 76 | – | – | – | – | – | – | – |
| | | | | | | | | |
| I   Anxiety (vs. Integration) | 100 | | | | | | | |
| II   Exvia (vs. Invia) | –06 | 100 | | | | | | |
| III   Cool rationality (vs. Affectivity) | –15 | 32 | 100 | | | | | |
| IV   Independence (vs. Subduedness) | 26 | 06 | 03 | 100 | | | | |
| V   Cultured tact (vs. Spontaneity) | –16 | 14 | 10 | –06 | 100 | | | |
| VI   Untamedness (vs. Sensitive Practicality) | –01 | –16 | –23 | –17 | 06 | 100 | | |
| VII   $B$, Intelligence | –00 | –00 | 00 | 00 | 00 | 01 | 100 | |
| VIII   $G$, Superego Strength | –00 | 01 | 00 | –00 | –00 | –00 | –00 | 100 |

*Note.* $N = 1,652$. Only loadings above .20 are included; decimal points are omitted. The intercorrelations between the second-order factors are also included. From Gorsuch and Cattell, 1967.

comprehensive variety of personality traits by means of self-report techniques than Eysenck did, with the consequence that Eysenck's two major dimensions—Neuroticism and Extraversion—are more easily understood in either of the two other systems than vice versa.

Unfortunately, the literature does not abound with studies relating Guilford's and Cattell's systems with one another, but four studies were found pertinent to this problem. The 16 PF and the Guilford-Martin inventories were administered to 216 male and female college students by Becker (1961). Two estimates of each scale were obtained by separate scoring of split-halved scales. The resulting intercorrelation matrix was factored, and both orthogonal and oblique rotations were applied. Becker also reported intercorrelations between full-scale scores in both series of scales after correcting for attenuation, which is particularly helpful for our present purpose. The reason for the separate scoring of half-scales is to produce more variables and thereby to provide more information for the determination of the nature and number of factors. This particular provision was not made in a study by Michael, Barth, and Kaiser (1961), who intercorrelated the 16 PF scales and the 7 scales in Thurstone's Temperament Schedule (1951). The latter is a reduction of the Guilford scales. Thurstone had found only nine linearly independent factors in 13 Guilford scales, considered seven of them interpretable, and rotated those into oblique simple structure for psychological meaningfulness. The factors as obtained by Thurstone, however, show sufficiently high loadings in the original Guilford scales to allow an indirect comparison of Cattell's and Guilford's factors based on the material presented by Michael, Barth, and Kaiser (1961). The matrix of variables was factored and rotated according to Kaiser's Varimax method. The latter circumstance introduces another source of indirectness in the comparison in question, as it can only be based upon inspection of which of Cattell's factors and which of Guilford's factors load on the same Varimax factor in this study.

A considerably less speculative comparison of the two systems can be made on the basis of a study by Gibbons (1966), who applied selected items from the 16 PF and from the Guilford scales to 302 male and female undergraduate students. Forty groups of items were obtained to characterize 14 of the 16 Cattell factors, and the 15 Guilford factors were represented by 28 groups of

items. The resulting 68 questionnaire variables were intercorrelated, factored, and rotated twice in a way that is particularly relevant to the present question. First, the variables representing each of the 14 Cattell factors were each patterned towards that factor, and the Guilford factors were inspected for the extent to which they fit the Cattell factors. Subsequently, the procedure was reversed to see how well the Cattell factors would match with the pattern of the Guilford factors. A fourth investigation studied the conjoint factor structure of Guilford and Cattell trait markers in 600 personality questionnaire items (Sells, Demaree, & Will, 1970, 1971).

Table 3 attempts to summarize the evidence from the four studies. This table indicates what factor associations emerged in more than one of these studies and therefore seem to be consistent. Scales showing association between Guilford's and Cattell's factors in only one of the investigations, or not at all, have been omitted from Table 3. This

**TABLE 3**  Apparent associations between Guilford's and Cattell's personality scales

| Cattell scales[a] | Guilford scales[b] | | | | | |
|---|---|---|---|---|---|---|
| | S | R | D | C | N | M |
| C | | | x | x | | |
| F | | x | | | | |
| H | x | | x | | | |
| I | | | | | | x |
| O | | | x | x | | |
| $Q_4$ | | | | | x | |

*Note.* Associated scales are marked with an x.
[a] C is Ego-strength; F, Surgency; H, Adventurousness; I, Sensitivity; O, Guilt-proneness; and $Q_4$, Ergic Tension.
[b] S is Social Shyness; R, Restraint; D, Depression; C, Cycloid Disposition; N, Nervousness; M, Masculinity.

was considered to be the case in 10 Cattell scales and 8 Guilford scales, although an exception should perhaps have been made for the similarity observed by Becker between Cattell's factor $I$ (Premsia vs. Harria) and Guilford's $F$ (Friendliness) and $P$ (Personal Relations). The reader is moreover reminded of the tentative nature of this table, in view of the rather unorthodox way it was derived.

Be that as it may, Table 3 seems to give rise to two interesting observations. With the possible exception of scale $M$, all of the Guilford scales that lend themselves to matching with Cattell's factors are clearly related to either Neuroticism ($D, C, N,$ and $S$) or Extraversion ($S$ and $R$). Scale $M$ is similar to Cattell's scale $I$, which, however, appears in Cattell's Neuroticism scale. All of Cattell's scales corresponding to Guilford's factors appear in the second-order factors Anxiety (i.e., Eysenck's Neuroticism; scales $C, H, O,$ and $Q_4$) or Extraversion ($F$ and $H$), with the exception of scale $I$, which is, however, a measure of neurotic trend, as mentioned previously.

In other words, the correspondence between Guilford's and Cattell's systems can be economically described in terms of two dimensions of Eysenck's personality theory.

This also was demonstrated in a more traditional manner by Soueif, Eysenck, and White (1969). They factor analyzed the intercorrelations of 43 first-order personality scales, 13 derived from Eysenck, 16 from Cattell, and 14 from Guilford. Of the four common second-order factors that emerged, two had loadings in the scales of all three authors. These were interpreted as Neuroticism and Extraversion. Nearly all appreciable loadings of the remaining factors were observed in scales derived from Cattell.

Thus, it appears that there is greater agreement between the work of different investigators if one focuses on the constituents of independent, second-order factors rather than on primary traits that are not clearly parts of salient second-order factors. At first sight, it may appear somewhat surprising that there is greater agreement at a higher level of abstraction from specific responses (see Fig. 2) than at a lower, but it should be borne in mind that orthogonal factor extraction and rotation leads directly to a kind of pattern as exemplified by arrows I and II in Fig. 2. Specific responses are inferior to first-order factors in terms of stability; similarly, second-order factors show greater invariance than first-order factors across subjects of different sex, age, intelligence, social class, and nationality.

Summing up, it would seem reasonable to conclude that at least two personality dimensions have been clearly identified in independently conducted research. Both dimensions show satisfactory stability and saliency in groups of individuals of different nationalities. The two factors—Neuroticism and Extraversion—originally emerged more than 50 years ago in personality questionnaires which have since developed into effective procedures for the description and measurement of personality traits. Further research into the processes of responding to so-called self-report items in questionnaires and the mechanisms that are responsible for the fact that people of a specific personality make-up give the particular answers they give, will shed further light on the very nature of personality traits. By the same token, this research may be expected to produce further evidence that eliciting verbal behavior from subjects is scientifically legitimate as a means of studying personality and that personality questionnaires do not deserve many of the critical reactions they have received hitherto.

## APPENDIX 1   A LIST OF IDENTIFIED RESPONSE SETS

Response sets associated with specific item response formats:

1. *Acquiescence,* i.e., tendency to say "yes," "true," and "agree" rather than "no," "false," etc. (Couch & Keniston, 1960; Cronbach, 1946, 1950; Diers, 1964; Jackson & Messick, 1962; Messick & Jackson, 1958; Wiggins, 1962).

2. *Evasiveness,* i.e., tendency to say "undecided," "indifferent," "don't know," "both" to mark queries and median scale positions (Cattell, 1957a; Cronbach, 1946, 1950; Guilford, 1954; Nunnally & Husek, 1958; Osgood, Suci & Tannenbaum, 1957; Rosen, H., & Rosen, 1955).

3. *Extreme response set,* i.e., tendency to say "dislike much" rather than "dislike slightly," "strongly agree" rather than "slightly agree," to mark extreme scale positions (Berg & Collier, 1953; Frederiksen & Messick, 1959; Nunnally & Husek, 1958).

4. *Inclusiveness,* i.e., the tendency to give many rather than few answers on schedules where the number of responses is not specified (e.g., adjective checklists, worries checklists, some interest inventories; Cronbach, 1946, 1950; Frederiksen & Messick, 1959; Thorndike, 1938).

5. *Response sets in multiple-choice tests,* i.e., tendency to choose certain types of answers because of length, wording, serial position (Cronbach, 1950; Nunnally & Husek, 1958).

6. *Response position preferences,* i.e., tendency to mark left-hand rather than right-hand alternatives, to mark the higher rather than the lower percentage in error-choice items (Wilde, 1966b).

Other response sets, not associated with specific response options:

7. *Set to respond fast rather than accurately* (Cronbach, 1946, 1950; Eysenck, H. J., 1947, p. 144).

8. *Tendency to guess* (Cronbach, 1950; Graesser, 1958; Rubin, cited by Cronbach, 1950).

9. *Careless and haphazard, random responding* (Frederiksen & Messick, 1959; Marks & Seeman, 1963).

10. *Cognitive style, tendency to be consistent, criticalness* (Frederiksen & Messick, 1959; Gaier, Lee & McQuitty, 1953; Wallach, 1962).

11. *Deviant response set,* i.e., the tendency to mark the infrequently chosen (deviant) response options (Barnes, 1955, 1956a, 1956b; Berg & Collier, 1953; Norman, 1963b; Sechrest & Jackson, 1962).

## APPENDIX 2   STANDARD PROCEDURES FOR THE DETECTION OF THE EFFECT OF TEST-TAKING ATTITUDES ON QUESTIONNAIRE SCORES

1. The method of *experimental instructions.* The questionnaire is administered under standard instructions, and the scores obtained are compared with scores obtained under instructions "to make a good impression," "a bad impression," "to appear normal," to appear "fit for a particular job."

2. Comparing *"threatening" versus standard situations* of test administration (e.g., job applicants *vs.* employees).

3. *Item-analytic methods,* usually consisting of a demonstration that item endorsement probability is a function of average social desirability of the item.

4. *Correlating questionnaire scores with measures specifically designed to assess test-taking attitudes* (e.g., scales for social desirability (SD) set, lie scales, MMPI K and F scales).

5. *Factor analytic identification* of a social desirability set dimension in questionnaire responses.

## APPENDIX 3  A SURVEY OF PROCEDURES USED TO INCREASE QUESTIONNAIRE SUBTLETY

1. *Phrasing of instructions.* Emphasis of first impression, quick responding, efforts to motivate people to be frank (Bell, H. M., 1939). It has, however, been found that fast responding seems to increase the number of desirable answers (Hills, 1961).

2. *Method of administration.* Items on cards to be sorted, items to be sorted in boxes (in order to reduce awareness of answers already given), personal data (name, age, etc.) to be filled in afterwards; presenting questionnaire under innocuous title (e.g., "Biographical Inventory," Taylor, J. A., 1953).

3. Spreading *buffer items* between scored items, to distract the person from the true nature of the questionnaire. McCreary and Bendig (1954) however, found a correlation .96 between Taylor's MAS with and without buffer items.

4. *Phrasing of items.* (a) Items phrased in third person and people required to indicate whether they are "same" or "different." (b) "Projective" questions (e.g., "Do you think that many people often feel lonesome?" Ellis, 1947; Jonsson, 1957). (c) Item phrasing in past tense to mitigate their threatening character (Schlesser, 1953). (d) The use of items with obvious psychodynamic meaning versus covert diagnostic items (Seeman, 1953; Wiener, 1956). (e) Use of items with neutral average desirability values, or (f) desirable items for the measurement of undesirable traits and vice versa (Edwards, A. L., 1957); (g) balancing of socially desirable and socially undesirable items in the scale (Hand & Reynolds, 1961).

5. *"Innocuous topics"* as item content. Food aversion (Gough, 1946; Wallen, 1948); annoyances, proverbs (Bass, 1956, 1957; Baumgarten, 1952); "empathy" items (Kerr & Speroff, 1951; Van Zelst, 1953).

6. *Manipulation of response formats.* Forced-choice and multiple-choice self-report items blocks matched for social desirability (Edwards, A. L., 1953; Gordon, 1951; Shipley, Gray & Newbert, 1946); preference items (e.g., would you rather be (a) happy or (b) polite; (a) honest or (b) optimistic; blocks are matched for average social desirability (Fifer quoted by Barendregt, 1961); error-choice items (Hammond, 1948; Wilde & DeWit, 1970; "best" answer and "own" answer side by side (Voas, 1958). "Desirability scales," capitalizing on individual differences in desirability opinions, associated with personality traits (Jackson, D. N., 1964; Wilde, 1964).

7. *Validating scales,* consistency scale (Cady, 1923); SD scales (Crowne & Marlowe, 1964; Edwards, A. L., 1957); L-type, K-type and F-type scales as applied in the MMPI, SD scales empirically derived from role playing "fake good" instructions (Ruch, 1942; Wiggins, J. S., 1959).

## APPENDIX 4  PERSONALITY TRAITS MEASUREABLE BY QUESTIONNAIRES ACCORDING TO GUILFORD

Factor *G.* General Activity, strong drive, energy and activity, making the appearance of other attributes more pronounced.

Factor *R.* Restraint, opposite to Rhathymia, serious-mindedness, self-control as opposed to impulsivity.

Factor *A.* Ascendance, tendency to come to the fore in social situations, as opposed to inconspicuousness and submissiveness.

Factor *S.* Sociability, social extraversion, interest in company and quick intimate rapport.

Factor *E*. Emotional Stability, optimistic and cheerful, the opposite of depression, neurotic and cycloid tendencies.

Factor *O*. Objectivity, opposite to subjectivity, hypersensitivity and self-centeredness.

Factor *F*. Friendliness, agreeable, tendency to be liked, opposite to belligerent and hostile attitude.

Factor *T*. Thoughtfulness, thinking introversion, reflective, subtle and perceptive.

Factor *P*. Personal Relations, cooperativeness, tolerance versus fault-finding disposition.

Factor *M*. Masculinity, as opposed to femininity of interests and emotional reactions.

## APPENDIX 5 PRIMARY PERSONALITY TRAITS MEASURABLE BY QUESTIONNAIRES ACCORDING TO CATTELL

Factor *A, U.I.(L)*1. Cyclothymia versus Schizothymia (warm, sociable, good natured, cooperative, attentive to people, kindly, trustful vs. aloof, stiff, aggressive, obstructive, cool, hard, suspicious).

Factor *B, U.I.(L)*2. General Intelligence (bright, intellectual vs. dull, boorish).

Factor *C, U.I.(L)*3. Ego-strength (emotionally stable, mature, calm, realistic about life vs. emotionally unstable, immature, evasive, worrying).

Factor *E, U.I.(L)*5. Dominance versus Submission (ascendant, independent, stern, unconventional, tough vs. submissive, dependent, soft-hearted, conventional).

Factor *F, U.I.(L)*6. Surgency versus Desurgency (enthusiastic, talkative, cheerful, frank, expressive vs. silent, introspective, depressed, brooding, incommunicative).

Factor *G, U.I.(L)*7. Superego Strength (conscientious, persistent, determined, re-

sponsible, ordered, attentive to people vs. casual, undependable, quitting, frivolous, obstructive).

Factor *H, U.I.(L)*8. Parmia versus Threctia (adventurous, active, genial, impulsive, does not see danger signals vs. shy, timid, self-contained, apt to be embittered, restricted interests, quick to see dangers).

Factor *I, U.I.(L)*9. Premsia versus Harria (sensitive, effeminate, demanding, seeking help, affected, acts on sensitive intuition, hypochondriachal vs. tough, realistic, self-reliant, hard, acts on logical evidence, unaware of physical disabilities).

Factor *L, U.I.(L)*12. Protension versus Relaxed Security (suspecting, jealous, withdrawn, tyrannical, irritable vs. adaptable, accepting, outgoing, trustful, ready to take a chance, tolerant, permissive, composed).

Factor *M, U.I.(L)*13. Autia versus Praxernia (absent-minded, unconventional, interested in arts, imaginative, creative, immature in practical judgment vs. practical, concerned with facts, conventional, narrow interests, realistic).

Factor *N, U.I.(L)*14. Shrewdness versus Naivete (sophisticated, polished, exact, emotionally disciplined, esthetically fastidious, thoughtful of self and others, ambitious, expedient vs. simple, unpretentious, socially clumsy, sentimental, gregarious, simple tastes, no insight into self or others, trusts in accepted values).

Factor *O, U.I.(L)*15. Guilt Proneness versus Confidence (timid, insecure, worrying, depressed, easily upset, strong sense of duty, exacting, fussy, moody, phobic symptoms vs. self-secure, resilient, placid, expedient, no fears, given to simple action).

Factor $Q_1$, *U.I.(Q)*16. Radicalism versus Conservatism (inclination to experimentation, untraditional, interest in fundamental social issues vs. tendency to moralize, traditional, compliance to social rules).

Factor $Q_2$, *U.I.(Q)*17. Self-Sufficiency versus Group Dependency (resourceful, absorbed in creative work, no difficulty in making up his mind vs. conventional, fashionable, interested, and satisfied with group relations).

Factor $Q_3$, *U.I.(Q)*18. High versus Poor Self-sentiment Control (controlled, exacting will power, persistent, conscientious vs. uncontrolled, lax, nervous, distractible, easily hurt feelings).

Factor $Q_4$, *U.I.(Q)*19. High versus Low Ergic Tension (tense, excitable, disheartened by criticism, underachieving, frequent mood changes vs. phlegmatic, composed, overachieving, emotional balance).

# 4

# Trait Description and Measurement through Discovered Structure in Objective Tests (*T* Data)

Akira Ishikawa
*Kansai University, Osaka, Japan*

## 1. THE MAIN ORIGINAL EXPLORATIONS OF PERSONALITY THROUGH OBJECTIVE TESTS

As described in chapter 1, there are only three fundamental media through which measured or unmeasured data (e.g., *L* data, *Q* data, and *T* data) on personality can be collected, as a basis for research and theory. This chapter discusses the personality traits and their structural interactions revealed by *T* data or objective tests.

However, the tests and measures defined as *objective* in this chapter are somewhat different from the ones that have traditionally been named in works by Anastasi (1976) and Cronbach (1970), and older works on tests and test practices. By the crystallization of popular terms, tests have sometimes been classified broadly into four types: behavior rating scales, open-ended questionnaire procedures (e.g., interviews), objective-type questionnaires, and projective types of tests. This classification rests on superficial differences of the testing material. The essential meaning of "objective" in a more operational sense is discussed first, and then a precise definition of objective test is given.

The objective tests considered in this chapter are far more varied in type than the pencil and paper variety and include such tests as miniature situational tests, esthetic choices, stylistic tests (e.g., cognitive styles), projective tests, response sets, psychophysiological tests, and many others for which no terms yet exist as in the richly inventive work of Cattell and Warburton (1967). Furthermore, even some questionnaire (*Q* data) can come under the rubric of objective test if the questionnaire *response* is not accepted as a "description" of the subject himself (*Q* data), but is taken as his "behavior."

As seen in the *Mental Measurements Yearbook* (Buros, 1972), a tremendous number of studies have been conducted in the *T*-data domain but mainly on only a few kinds. However, the purpose of this chapter is neither to give a review for the findings on such various individual objective tests, nor to examine the "art" of inferring personality from such tests used as single indicators. For, as argued in this chapter, a univariative personality theory based on any individual test which measures only a narrow range of behavior is relatively fruitless. Rather it is the purpose of this chapter to introduce readers to the theories and principles used in the general construction of objective test batteries based on concepts of personality structure emerging from simultaneous analysis of many objective tests, and to give a summarized outline of the factors revealed by such a test battery.

The main pioneer work of creating objective tests in the light of multivariate experimental findings has been almost entirely the work of two laboratories—that of Professor Cattell (1948a) and his co-workers in the Laboratory of Personality and Group Analysis at the University of Illinois, and that of Professor H. J. Eysenck (1953c) and his co-workers at the Institute of Psychiatry, the Maudsley Hospital, London. More recently, systematic work in the Cattell and Eysenck traditions has begun under Howarth and Royce at the Center for Advanced Theoretical Psychology at the University of Alberta, under Fahrenberg, Pawlik and others in Germany, and under Tsujioka and the present writer in Japan. The greater part of our discussion therefore is centered necessarily on the fertile experimentation and theories of these two schools.

"Objective test" is just another name for "laboratory behavioral measurement," though personality tests are conceptually oriented to more complex theories than those guiding laboratory measurements on highly specialized topics such as perception or memorization. One has difficulty in understanding how this actual identity gets so frequently overlooked unless one reflects that the goals of these two groups of workers are so different in other respects (individual differences vs. common processes). They have also been separated in personnel by the fact that most "process" psychologists are bivariate in training whereas understanding of multivariate methods is indispensable for studying the global parameters of personality.

In this connection, if we include experiments to establish connections between single laboratory tests and single rated personality trait elements, the number of psychologists busy in the field is far greater than the half-dozen schools mentioned previously. However, the bivariate approach, as is argued in more detail elsewhere (e.g., Nesselroade & Delhees, 1966; Meredith, G., 1967) is an extremely inefficient means for discovering whole patterns of behavior. Except where it has operated to confirm particular relations already made meaningful in the context of larger patterns, for example, the role of low skin resistance in arousal, of steroid secretion in anxiety, of basal metabolic rate in the personality Factor *U.I.* 21, and of flicker fusion frequency in *U.I.* 22, the contribution to understanding personality structure has not been outstanding. These results can be utilized at a later stage, but the creative phase has been the emergence of a score of new personality dimension concepts from a programmatic use of multivariate experiment with objective tests.

## 2. A CLOSER LOOK AT OBJECTIVE TESTS THEMSELVES

Objective tests need to be seen in the perspective of tests and measurement devices generally, but, except for the proposal for a general taxonomy by Cattell and Warburton (1967), practically no text on psychological testing has attempted a comprehensive set of parameters.

Cattell and Warburton proposed the following parameters:

1. Objective versus self-evaluative.
2. Dealing with overt behavior versus physiological responses.
3. Continuous score in response versus classified categories.

4. Quantity of response versus extent of agreement with prescribed key.

5. Single, homogeneous versus evaluation as a score total pattern.

6. Normatively scored versus ipsatively scored.

However, another dimensionality reduces the preceding conveniently to three, as follows:

1. Objective versus self-appraising, defining the kind of stimulus-response situation and instrument given the subject (1 previously).

2. Selective versus inventive, defining the kind of response situation limitations (combining the preceding 3 and 4).

3. Conspective versus rative, defining the kind of scoring situation in which the examiner is placed. This defines the degree of objectivity of *scoring* (often mistaken for objectivity in the test as a whole).

Keeping the last in mind we can now move to define two degrees of objectivity in tests.

1. A test that requires something different from essay-type appraisal and involves an agreed key for selective (multiple-choice) or inventive (open-ended) responses, such that all psychologists scoring the test will get the same numerical result.

2. Objectivity is required not only for the scoring, but also the test stimulus situations and the whole mode of response must not permit any motivational distortion by the subject.

Finally, we may therefore reach a suitable definition of an objective test, as follows: An objective test is a defined situation with accepted instructions for response, in which a person's behavior is measured, for inferring

personality parameter levels, without his being aware of the ways his behavior is likely to affect the interpretation.

A constantly recurring problem in multivariate personality research for which an answer is vital is that concerned with matching the patterns of individual differences, or of state response patterns among various researches. Progress is negligible so long as different investigators use quite different variables; thus, the final requirement in the matching problem is programmatic research in which many of the same marker variables are deliberately used to correct and extend the researches of various laboratories. The particular few laboratories mentioned previously have been outstanding in the fruitfulness of their attacks on the personality structure problem partly because they have respected this scientific requirement. Indeed, despite differences of language and culture, it has been possible, as in the studies of child personality in objective tests at Kansai, Illinois, and Vienna, to translate the marker tests as found for certain factors by Cattell, and to obtain consistent results over the three cultures.

Marker variables cannot be conveniently located and reproduced with scientific identity of procedure, however, without a suitable indexing system. What has functioned effectively, since its original statement in the Japanese journal (Cattell, 1957b), sets out a universal index (*U.I.*) enumeration of factors and a double index for objective tests. The latter consists of a series of *T numbers* (now *T*1 to *T*445) for the actual test materials and procedures, and a series of response Master Index (M.I.) numbers (now *M.I.*1 to *M.I.* 2490) for the test scores. The scores are about five times as numerous as the tests because many tests are scored in half a dozen different ways or more.

By using these precise references to particular laboratory and other objective performances in experiments by many different investigators, it has been possible, in the integrations of adult researches by Hundleby, Pawlik, and Cattell (1965), and of child researches by Nesselroade, Schneewind, and Cattell (1970), to collate accurately patterns of factors and examine precisely the degree of replication of loading patterns under various conditions and on various populations. It is thus that the agreement of Cattell and Eysenck on the general Regression factor, *U.I.* 23, and of Brogden and Cattell on the general Anxiety factor, *U.I.* 24, was tested. Incidentally, among objective tests we must also include the objective motivation strength tests, of which over 100 devices have been tried that possess objectivity of miniature situational behavior (and conspection of scoring) precisely as for objective general personality tests. However, these and their outcomes are separately handled in chapter 5 by Dielman and Krug.

### 3  METHODOLOGY AND CONSTRUCTION PRINCIPLES IN THE O-A BATTERIES

A discussion of the roster of personality source traits as now known in objective tests follows in the next section. Before studying these, one must discuss some general methodological points encountered in reaching these patterns. In the first place, one must pay attention to at least half a dozen fine technical issues in factor analysis itself. These have been sufficiently handled in Cattell (1966e) and at various points in this book. Secondly, one must recognize the danger, brought out clearly in chapters 8 and 9, of mistaking a state pattern for a trait pattern. The great majority of trait-structure studies measure the subjects' performances only once—not several times, as would be

ideal—and a factor so formed can be a state. Both *U.I.* 24, Anxiety, and *U.I.* 22, Cortertia, might have proved to be states only, but later work indicates that each has a distinct trait and state pattern.

It has well been said, in all areas of psychology, that impressive as the step is that culminates in demonstrating distinct replicable factor patterns as such, it still has the onerous task of producing batteries of sufficient concept validity to be psychometrically satisfactory in experimental work. True, this second step has not proved overdifficult in the ability field; but in personality, all test and item loadings tend to be lower, alike in *L*, *Q*, and *T* media, and this situation has confronted test designers with a severe task.

One reason for the difficulty is the clinically obvious fact that personality behavior is comparatively complex, and when half a dozen factors enter into a given piece of behavior, not one of them can be well measured by it. Further, low loadings bring two more serious difficulties in their train: (a) Subtests in a personality factor battery must be more numerous than for an ability factor. An intelligence test may be adequate with as few as 4 diverse subtests; an objective personality factor battery often needs 10 per factor to reach measurable validity. (b) The lower loadings permit the loading pattern to change considerably from one population to another, and with it the $V_{fe}$ matrix—the weight of variables needed to give the best factor estimation.

As a result of the latter the ultimately necessary practice in personality measurement will be to use parallel, modified batteries, each adapted to a particular population—to university students, to high school students, to middle-aged persons, and perhaps even to men and women. Mainly through the work of perhaps a dozen psychologists, we are lucky to have objective test batteries measuring personality factors: (a) for adults—the AOA Adult Battery, (b) for high school age children—the HSOA (O-A standing for objective-analytic, or objective-factor analytic). From Cattell's initial battery (1955a) these have been brought to concept validities (that is, validities against the pure factor, of 0.85 to 0.95) by the work of Coan, Damarin, Dielman, Horn, Howarth, Hundleby, Meredith, Nesselroade, Pawlik, Schneewind, Schuerger, Tsujioka, Warburton, and others.

In this work the first step was to approach by strategically interconnected factorings over a global (personality sphere) span of variables; to "mark" factors by repeatedly using saliently loaded variables carried forward; to "move out" to occupy new areas, inventing new objective behavioral measurements in doing so; and to improve tests, aiming them at an ever clearer theoretical target, as the factor structure of the source traits emerged.

By 1965, as the landmark survey by Hundleby, Pawlik, and Cattell (1965) showed, some 21 factors, indexed *U.I.* 16 through *U.I.* 36 (*U.I.* 1 to *U.I.* 15 are the 15 confirmed ability factors of J. W. French, Ekstrom, & Price, 1963), had been replicated in 10-20 independent experiments and factorings reported in the journals of several countries. A "gear change" was then made, from wide exploration to intensive concentration on battery construction for the best replicated, most cross-cultural, most developmentally persistent, and most criterion-related factors. For the Adult Objective Analytic Battery (the AOA), Hundleby and Cattell chose *U.I.* 16, 17, 18, 19, 20, 21, 23, 24, 25, 26, 28, 30, and 32. For the High School Objective Analytic (HSOA), Schuerger, Dielman, and Cattell (1970) chose *U.I.* 16, 17, 19, 20, 21, 23, 24, 25, 26, 28, 32, and 33.

For each of the dozen or so factors 10 subtests were chosen, on the basis of mean loadings, hardiness to change of population, brevity (attempting to keep total testing within half an hour per factor) and objectivity of scoring, as well as low homogeneity (low mutual correlations to maximize validity for a given mean loading). No fewer than 8 of these subtests had to be group administrable, but 2 were always left as laboratory type, instrument-requiring, and individually administrable measures. Incidentally, one of the constant developmental aims in this battery production has been the ingenious transformation of original individually administrable tests to forms practicable in groups. Although the time of administration remains fairly long—about 3½ hours for 10 factors, not counting lost time for questions, etc.—it is short when one remembers that he is escaping the vulnerability to distortion of the questionnaire, and is covering 10 times as many dimensions as is covered by the usual intelligence test.

Much work in terms of broader standardization remains to be done with the O-A batteries, which were published in final practicable form in 1970, but acceptable reliabilities and validities—on a par with those of intelligence tests—have at last been reached in the personality measurement domain. At this stage the most interesting research begins for most people. There can be no doubt in the mind of any shrewd observer that a major cause of the surprising lag exhibited by general workers in personality in taking up the new developments in structured measurements has been the fear that they might be plunged into long and arduous studies in factor analysis. As Cattell pointed out, the clinician and the classical experimentalist do not need such knowledge to make effective use of the concepts and the source-trait batteries in their own researches.

The technical work in this area has been done, the dimensions located, and the batteries fitted together psychometrically. With a *logical* rather than a mathematical factor-analytic understanding, it is now possible for the experimenter employing, for example, analysis of variance designs, or the clinician interested in the dynamics of development, to use these batteries on a variety of theoretical problems.

In doing so, the user needs always to remember that the O–A is not just another test battery. It is the concrete expression of a widely based theory of personality structure, and as such presents the researcher with the operational means of working out further aspects of the theory. Without the thought on details of design, and the efforts of construction that have gone into these convenient batteries, the typical experimentalist would face an enormous labor of combing journals and reconstructing only briefly described test procedures whenever he wanted to get at one of these dimensions.

## 4 THE INTERPRETATION AND DEVELOPMENT OF SOURCE–TRAITS *U.I.* 16 THROUGH *U.I.* 36

As previously stated, it was the collating and evaluative surveys of the adult domain by Hundleby, Pawlik, and Cattell (1965), and of the child domain by Nesselroade, Schneewind, and Cattell (1970) that have made possible a high certainty of depiction of the principle source-trait patterns despite the vagaries of factor-analytic sampling and the slowness of mathematical statistics to develop the necessary significance tests for more complex parameters. These strategies have achieved by the convergence of a sufficiently large number of experiments what could be inferred with known significance from a single experiment. The initial studies

of Damarin, Peterson, Meredith, and others at the young child level may in time develop the consistency at that age now seen at older levels. Meanwhile, further progress is needed in methods of evaluating matches beyond that in the congruence coefficient (Burt, 1948; Tucker, 1951), the salient variable (Cattell, Balcar, Horn, & Nesselroade, 1969), and the configurative method (Kaiser, H. F., 1960; Cattell, 1965a).

In the present section there is space to list only a few of the actual tests for each factor; our aim will be to indicate in a phrase or two the general nature of the given source trait. Beginning with those of largest variance we have the following factors:[1]

*U.I.* 16 Assertiveness versus Submissiveness (ego-strength or ego-assertiveness)
Fast natural tempo and fast speed of motor and cognitive performances; carefulness; high self-assertion and frustration tolerance; upper-class tastes.

*U.I.* 17 Timidity versus Adventurousness (general inhibition; Thurstone's F–: slowness of perception)
High cautiousness and timidity, readiness to inhibit overt behavior under threat; less alert.

*U.I.* 18 Hypomanic Smartness
More rapid but superficial judgments; faster speed on motor tasks; personally less secure; more susceptible to social norms.

*U.I.* 19 Independence versus Subduedness (Thurstone's E+: suppressive manipulation of configurations)

[1] *U.I.* 1–15 correspond to the principal factors in ability tests as reviewed by J. W. French, Ekstrom, and Price (1963). Some changes may be required in terms of special populations (Cattell, Delhees, Tatro, & Nesselroade, 1971), but this list of *U.I.* 16-36 can be taken as fairly standard for a normal population.

Accuracy in Gottschaldt figures; greater severity of judgment; accuracy of picture memory; less criticism of self.

U.I. 20 Comention versus Individual Values
High acquiescence and tendency to conform with group norms; high sensitivity to punishment and disapproval.

U.I. 21 Exuberance versus Quietness
(H.J. Eysenck's Factor 2 in Cyclothymia-Schizothymia analysis)
Impervious to social suggestions; faster speed of social judgments; faster perceptual speed; high verbal and ideational fluency.

U.I. 22 Cortertia (Cortical Alertness) versus Pathemia
(Thurstone's C+: speed of reaction)
High immediate responsiveness, but low endurance, fast speed of reaction; tense restlessness and high level of activation; fast perceptual speed.

U.I. 23 Capacity to Mobilize versus Regression
(Eysenck identifies this factor with N, neuroticism)
Lack of rigidity; high ability to concentrate; high endurance of difficulty.

U.I. 24 High Anxiety versus Low Anxiety (general anxiety)
High manifest anxiety; increased susceptibility to annoyance and embarrassment; insecurity (feelings of guilt and self-depreciation); high drive tension level.

U.I. 25 Realism versus Tensidia
(close to Eysenck's psychoticism factor)
Low cognitive and perceptual imaginative power; high accuracy and speed on well-structured (conventional) tasks; reality-directed attitudes.

U.I. 26 Narcissism versus Noninvolvement
Pervasive efficiency and sophistication of response; high persistence; low self-evaluation but high sensitivity to threat; good immediate control.

U.I. 27 Grudgingness versus Trustingness

Low self-esteem; low aspiration level and test motivation.

U.I. 28 Asthenia versus Casualness
Low psychophysical momentum; lack of self-confidence and of steadfastness of opinion; increased negativistic criticism.

U.I. 29 Wholeheartedness versus Uncooperativeness
High speed and cooperativeness of response; little effect resulting from discomfort and threat; overreacting.

U.I. 30 Stolidness versus Tenseness
Stolid temperament (slow and less careful); little fluctuation of attitudes; restricted emotionality (aloof, dry).

U.I. 31 Wariness versus Slaphappiness
High stability of attitudes; high cautiousness; determined self-control; slow natural tempo.

U.I. 32 Exvia ("Extraversion") versus Invia ("Introversion")
"Extraversion;" optimistic self-confidence; high perceptual and cognitive fluency; social interests.

U.I. 33 Pessimism (Dourness) versus Optimism
Pervasive pessimism; depressed lack of self-confidence; conservative and anxious approach to environment.

U.I. 34 Autism versus Conventionality
Reasoning more "emotional" than "rational"; indifferent regarding social norms; high imaginative fluency; interest in the unusual rather than the usual.

U.I. 35 Laziness versus Enthusiasm
Low level of cognitive performance; sluggishness and torpor of behavior; lacking incisiveness; lack of fine motor control.

U.I. 36 Strong Self-Sentiment versus Lack of Foresightedness
High self-sentiment; foresighted restrictiveness.

In conclusion, it may be helpful to set forth briefly the steps in the formation of the factor concepts. Some of the steps have not been fully elaborated but ideally the investigator needs to do the following:

1. Examine the "goodness" in terms of the hyperplane count and statistical significance of the simple structure deduced by "blind" independent rotation in several related studies.

2. Check the significance of matching the agreement of the independently achieved factor patterns across studies by employing Cattell's index or other factor-matching coefficients.

3. Consider hypotheses, first, as suggested by the loading pattern itself, that is, as suggested by the nature of the variables that have high positive loadings, high negative loadings, and zero or near-zero loadings, though included in the study.

4. Analyze "extension" variables, that is, new hypotheses—suggested variables added to the markers, and their factor pattern, a pattern that serves as a powerful adjunct to the factor-interpretation problem. Variables that are correlated with the variables included are as crucial as the variables actually included in the factorization.

5. Determine the rank order of general variance of the factor among other factors and whether it is also found (with or without modification) at other ages and in other populations.

6. Inspect the correlations of the factor with questionnaire (*Q*) or life-rating (*L*) factors.

7. Examine the nature-nurture ratios between families and within families.

8. Examine age trends in the factor scores.

9. Look at the second-order structure among objective test factors in which the given factor might be involved.

10. Look for the evidence of state factors (*P* or incremental *R* technique) akin to the trait in pattern.

11. Examine correlations with (or group differences on) particular life criteria: for example, school success, clinical problems, and delinquency.

12. Seek evidence of effects of manipulative experiments on factor scores (i.e., applications to experimental contexts).

13. Study closely in a clinical sense the behavior of people known to be extremely high or low on the factor measurement.

## 5  DISCUSSION ON HIGHER STRATA STRUCTURE AND ALTERNATIVE THEORIES

As the main concepts in the primaries have emerged, attention has increasingly turned to the possible interactions among them, to the question of higher-strata factors, and to the relations of *T*-data patterns to *Q*-data factors.

The first exploration of higher-order structure in this domain by Cattell and Scheier (1961) revealed seven second-order patterns, which were soon confirmed by fresh samples (Cattell, Knapp, & Scheier, 1961) and showed excellent agreement with a later study by Pawlik (1961). The data in the last was taken to the third order by Pawlik and Cattell (1964), where three factors emerged surprisingly similar to the Freudian notion of ego, id, and superego. The theoretical interpretation of the seven second-strata factors arising out of the 21 primaries, and the three third-strata out of the seven secondaries is still wide open, but the foundation is factor-analytically unequivocal and ready for the crucial experiments that theoretical experience may suggest. A brief statement of the second- and third-order factors with first-order salients found in *T*-data research is shown in Fig. 1.

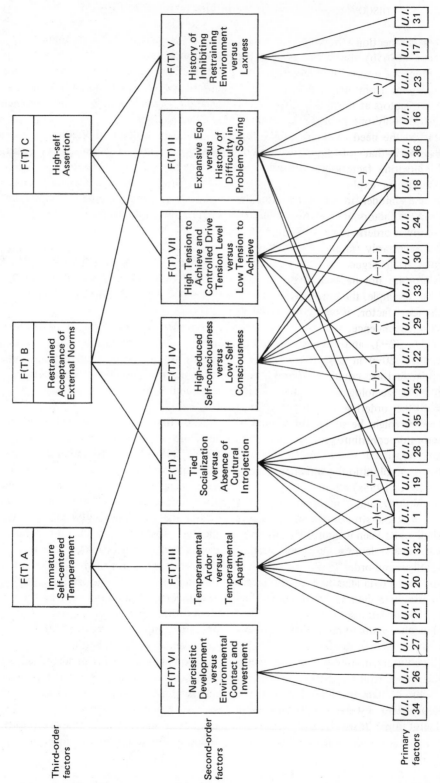

FIG. 1 Relationship among primary, second-order, and third-order factors extracted from the objective test (*T*-data) battery.

112

In this connection, however, Cattell pointed out (1965b) that the universally accepted model of a series of strata, permitting a hierarchy from many primaries to some master factors at the top of the pyramid, is not the only one or the most likely. He pointed to the need to explore also the *reticular model*—that of a network of causally interacting factors. Until more refined methods for exploring this are available, the *strata* model—in which the higher stratum (order) factors are hypothesized to act on the lower orders—is acceptable, but it does not necessarily imply a hierarchy. Moreover, Cattell argued that the higher strata factors are not necessarily more important. For example, the correlation, from a second-order factor, among intelligence (*U.I.* 1+), independence, (*U.I.* 19+), introversion (*U.I.* 32−), and responsible individuality (*U.I.* 20−) in the largest of the second-order factors, could be simply the intrusion of a sociological variable–social status—into the ordering of psychological factors. Others might be some basic physiological condition contributing to several personality primaries.

The early explorations by Cattell and Saunders (1950, 1955a) of the interrelation of factors in *L, Q,* and *T* media sufficed to show only that the situation was far more complex than had been imagined. It was not until the clear demonstration (Cattell, 1955b) that second-order factors in *Q* (and measurably in *L*) data aligned in some cases with primaries in *T* data, that a definite clue emerged. This relationship has been confirmed but still awaits extension to factors beyond *U.I.* 24, 32, 19, and perhaps 22.

By these connections light was thrown also on the chief rival alternative theory to that of Cattell, namely, Eysenck's three-factor theory. H. J. Eysenck (1953c) settled conceptually on three factors—general neuroticism, extroversion-introversion, and psychoticism—which he claimed to find equally in rating data (1953c), in objective test data, and later, in questionnaire data. Cattell's theory from the beginning had an altogether higher level of complexity and, incidentally, of precision of technical demonstration—though the simple trinity of Eysenck's account undoubtedly went over more easily with many psychologists and psychiatrists. As indicated, in *T* data Cattell found some 21 primaries, 7 secondaries, and 3 tertiaries. In *Q* data he found 16-24 primaries and found that among the 9 secondaries, 2-4 definitely matched primaries in the *T* data, namely, *U.I.* 24, Anxiety, *U.I.* 32, Extroversion, and possibly *U.I.* 19 and *U.I.* 22.

He argued that there are two faulty steps in Eysenck's procedure: (a) grossly underextracting—3 factors instead of 21 in both *Q* and *T* media—neglecting statistical indicators of number of factors, and (b) pursuing criterion rotations instead of simple structure or what he calls *confactor rotation*. It is a well-known characteristic of factor analysis that if there are, say, 10 primaries and 3 secondaries, one can get a *rough* approach to the patterns of the secondaries (directly on the variables) by stopping at 3 factors in the primary extraction. However, the emphasis is on the word *rough*, for with lost variance and vague rotation only the first of the three factors is an acceptable approximation, and the later factors are increasingly caricatures—finally reaching the point of losing all match—of the second orders properly located via the first order. Such a short cut tends to produce what Cattell aptly called *ersatz* second-order factors.

Further, criterion rotation makes the rough assumption that neurotics and psychotics differ from normals only on one factor, a position completely at variance with the significant six- and seven-factor differences found in the work of Cattell and

Scheier (1961), Cattell and Killian (1967), Cattell and Tatro (1966) and others. A number of workers have recently said that Cattell and Eysenck are converging on the same conceptual conclusions with such second-order $L$ medium and first-order $T$ medium factors as Anxiety, Extraversion, Psychoticism, etc. It is true that there is general conceptual convergence (if we accept that all the $Q$ and $L$ first orders are missing from the Eysenck formulation); but in the actual definition of the factors, and therefore in batteries and scales put out for clinicians to use, the *ersatz* factorings have given far rougher instruments and therefore less precise concepts.

Approximate rotations, and the taking out of *ersatz* second-order factors can easily lead to confusion of identifications and uncertainty as to how much variance remains to be explained. A case in point, which has caused much confusion to clinicians, is Eysenck's designation of one of his three main scales as neuroticism. This and his extraversion scale are just such first-order approximations to Cattell's second-order-defined scales of Anxiety (*U.I.* 24 in objective tests) and Exvia (*U.I.* 32). The present evidence (chapter 27) in any case is clear that Neuroticism is not a single factor, but a particular crucial combination of factors of which Anxiety is one of the largest. Eysenck also identified *U.I.* 23 as his Neuroticism (or $N$), though Cattell's second-order questionnaire factor, Anxiety, $Q$II, to which Eysenck's $N$ closely approximates, aligns with *U.I.* 24, the objective test (primary) Anxiety factor, and not with *U.I.* 23. Actually neurotics differ *significantly* from normals not only on *U.I.* 23 and *U.I.* 24, but also on *U.I.* 16, *U.I.* 22 and even on *U.I.* 25, the factor which Eysenck called *Psychoticism.*

There is thus considerable need at this juncture for an intensive, informed, independent investigation by other experimenters—of the kind that Sells gave to the points of difference in the Cattell and Guilford analyses in the $Q$ domain (Sells, Demaree, & Will, 1970, 1971)—of the personality concepts in the objective test domain. Such work requires unusual combinations of experimental and multivariate statistical skills, but it is vital now if the psychology of personality is to move onward to the full benefits of the experimental phase, which is now superseding the clinical and the literary phases. Much of the exploratory and creative work has been done; clear-cut theories have been laid out, and the laboratory and group measurement instruments with which they are operationally tied have been made available. An exciting vista of definite hypothesis testing across the whole frontier of personality research opens up to investigators.

## 6 NOTE ON THE METHODOLOGY OF MATCHING SOURCE-TRAIT FACTORS

The problem of matching results across studies is not a simple one, as remarked above, nor is it one yet resolved to everyone's satisfaction, although some advances (Cattell, Balcar, Horn, & Nesselroade, 1969; Schneewind & Cattell, 1970) should be noted. In general, assuming that the first step of accurately identifying variables themselves by actual inspection of tests and scoring procedures is accomplished, "similarity" (e.g., by eyeball inspection) is not good enough; more precise methods for factor matching are needed. The assumption now is that we are seeking to establish the identity of two source traits (causal sources) operating in different experimental samples and even populations, when unique solutions have first been obtained in each by simple structure (blindly reached) or simultaneously in both by confactor rotation.

The alternative possibilities of matching now depend on the following:

1. Direct statistical-mathematical comparison of *loading patterns* on the variables.

(a) By nonparametric, category methods: salient variable similarity index (*s* index) (Cattell, Balcar, et al., 1969), depending on dividing variables into salients and hyperplane variables on each factor.

(b) Parametric methods, considering size agreement of loadings:

(1) Congruence coefficient (Burt, 1948; Tucker, 1951).

(2) Profile Similarity Index ($r_p$) (Cattell, 1949).

2. Direct geometrical comparison by projecting both sets of factors into the same space:

(a) Procrustes transformation (Hurley & Cattell, 1962; Schoenemann, 1964), of which Ahmavaara's (1954) transformation analysis is a special case.

(b) The configurative method of Kaiser (1960) and Cattell (1965a).

3. Indirect methods or aids of factor matching:

(a) The size (mean variance contribution) of a factor.

(b) The occurrence of expected group differences and criterion associations.

(c) "Circumstantial validity," especially in the sense of having the expected correlations with other factors.

The *s* index and the congruence coefficient, both subjects of recent advances, notably in developing significant tests, have been widely used. The improvements in the *s* index have been noted (Cattell, Balcar, et al., 1969). For the congruence coefficient, the recent development has been the generation of significance levels (Schneewind & Cattell, 1970) for the application of the coefficient.

## 7. SUMMARY

1. Objective tests are not to be confused with merely objectively *scorable* tests—properly called *conspective*, that is, those in which two scorers will see the same score. They are definable as not resting on self-assessment (as in *Q* data), but as involving behavior that is scored in ways unknown to the subject.

2. Objective tests include laboratory, projective, cognitive style response set, etc., approaches, but principally they include a large domain of over 1,000 measures specifically invented by Cattell and his co-workers in relation to theoretical developments through source traits appearing as empirical constructs from factoring, in conjunction with *L*-, *Q*- and *T*-data variables. Six dimensions have been suggested, which the author has reduced to three, to aid taxonomic classification of the domain of objective tests (*T* data).

3. Bivariate experimental approaches to personality have labored under the systematic disability that personality concepts, which intrinsically demand attention to whole patterns, can never even be crudely represented by single behavioral variables.

4. Four main stages can be recognized in the development of findings and theory in this field: (a) The development of principles and findings as to a universe of variables (the personality sphere concept) whereby rather local (e.g., clinical), hunches can be transcended, and real meaning given to "broad" and "narrow," "first" and "second" strata traits; (b) the creation of actual behavior tests, which require fundamental inventive-

ness and vision, and their factoring in coordinated sets and ages; (c) the development of new technical devices in factor analysis to factor the experimental material with due regard to sample selection, extraction of the correct number of factors, improvement of simple structure and confactor rotation and tests of simple structure significance and of matching; and (d) the development of hypotheses and theories about the nature of first- and higher-stratum factors through further (often bivariate) research on their natural history, life-criterion relations, and manipulation.

5. Some 20 primary factors may now be considered reasonably well established, and 4 or 5 of them connect with patterns found in other media of observation. Among these, seven secondaries have been twice replicated, as well as tertiaries, which in Pawlik's analysis are likened to the psychoanalytic id, ego, and superego structures. Physiological, sociological, and genetic influences have been hypothesized as the origins of these structures.

6. A considerable stimulus to research in this area is now becoming available in the provision of 12-factor O-A (objective-analytic) personality trait batteries for children by Schuerger and for adults by Hundleby. Investigators who are not concerned or equipped to deal with factor analysis as such can nevertheless now measure these factors reliably in criterion and developmental researches. It seems to be an inherent characteristic of personality behavior that it is factorially complex, so that any one subtest commonly has only a .2 or .6 validity against the factor. Thus at least six to eight subtests (30–40 minutes of testing) are necessary per factor to reach validity equal to that customary in, say, intelligence tests.

7. Very brief theories have been offered regarding the nature of the principal factors. In some cases, for example, *U.I.* 17, General Inhibition, *U.I.* 22, Arousal (Cortertia); *U.I.* 23, Regression; and *U.I.* 24, Anxiety, there have been many checks and explorations, but in most cases the investigation of the theories still lags considerably.

8. A brief introduction is given to the extremely important technical problem of establishing factor identities across researches for which there are now several technical aids.

# 5

# Trait Description and Measurement in Motivation and Dynamic Structure

**T. E. Dielman**
*University of Michigan, Ann Arbor*

**S. E. Krug**
*University of Illinois, Urbana*

## 1 INTRODUCTION

The strategy of making section 1 of this book a study of the structures (and modes of measuring them) necessary for later points dealing with development, will be continued in the present chapter. But in the case of dynamic phenomena the treatment must be broader, more flexible, and also more subtle. Certainly structure here cannot be treated by the simple psychometric individual differences procedures which suffice—or almost suffice—for ratings and questionnaire variables.

Furthermore, we have the problem that the ideas and the very semantics of this area are entangled in a far more luxurious, historical growth of popular, clinical, and literary theories. In accordance with the aim of concentrating on modern theory, set out in chapter 1 and held in the title of this book, we shall, except for brief, historical references in this opening section, keep to theory derivable from experimental and quantitative methods. It is the custom of historians to maintain continuity, even at the cost of overlooking the sharp breaks that occur (probably in scientific thought more than in political and social habits), and also to attempt to explain the more developed in terms of the less developed. Yet only confusion is gained by considering Dalton's atoms to continue the idea of Democritus, or by saying that the experimental concept of ergs, discussed here, belongs to the tradition of hedonistic explanations.

Accordingly, our procedure here will be first to ask what concepts and theories are arising from that multivariate experimentation necessary to determine structure in so very complex a domain. Then we shall relate to these concepts the notions, no less modern in temporal terms that have arisen from bivariate methods over the past 25 years, and finally put the whole in a larger, historical perspective. The aim, even in this last phase, will not be historical as such, but will confine itself to bringing out the sharpest contrasts in the models propounded over the last 30 years, and to asking what crucial experiments and researches are now most needed.

Of course, even to delimit the area of discussion we must at least snatch a glance at history—at Plato's cognition, conation, and affection, for example, recognizing that we are here in the last two. Also, we might recognize, with Boring, Flugel, and other historians, three major lines of development in dynamic psychology, the first stemming from Freud, the second, derived from Leibnitz and Herbart, involving the notion of active ideas or motives in competition, and the third arising from the hedonistic philosophy of the early Greek philosophers. Nevertheless, for the present we must keep open the possibility that in this current multivariate theory of dynamic behavior we have hit on a maverick in the perspective of historical trends, a discontinuity in the curve of historical development.

## 2   THE COMMON FACTOR MODEL IN MOTIVATIONAL RESEARCH

With a statement of the aims of the present chapter now clearly in sight, we can proceed to examine fundamental concepts of motivation developed from extensive, multivariate analyses of dynamic, human behavior. Over a period of 25 years or more, these concepts were successively refined and integrated into what has become known as the "dynamic calculus" (Cattell, 1947b, 1950a, 1957a, 1958, 1959; Cattell & Baggaley, 1956, 1958; Cattell & Horn, 1963; Cattell, Horn, & Butcher, 1962; Cattell, Radcliffe, & Sweney, 1963; Cattell & Sweney, 1964; Cattell, Sweney, & Radcliffe, 1960; Sweney, 1961a, 1968; Sweney & Cattell, 1961, 1962). Cattell and Child (1975) have brought together those various findings and concepts into one volume.

The dynamic calculus took as its fundamental unit of measurement the attitude, defined by the following paradigm: "In

these circumstances, I want so much to do this with that." This statement is at once necessary and sufficient to provide an operational, behavioral specification for observations of motivational phenomena.

There are several important aspects of this paradigm on which we may focus. First, we may note the particular emphasis of each term. "In these circumstances" sets the stimulus situation in which the behavior takes place, acknowledges that behavior does not occur without antecedent conditions, and suggests that the situation itself contributes an independent source of variance to motivated behavior. One can easily imagine examples of stimulus moderating the strength and direction of motives. Hartshorne and May (1928) found strong evidence on this point in their initial studies of dishonesty and cheating. The researcher who works in the laboratory with infrahuman species realizes the effect on performance of deprivation levels and environmental conditions, to indicate only two possible elements of the stimulus situation. "I want so much" indicates the specific course of action selected from the organism's repertory of interests.

Secondly, we can distinguish in this paradigm two fundamental conceptions common to a number of motivational theories. "I want so much" suggests the force or energy of motivated behavior, while "to do this with that" indicates the direction of motivated behavior. These concepts have appeared, in one form or other, in drive reduction theories, instinct theories, and cognitive theories.

Next, we can see in the term "I want to do" the primacy of adaptation, as process, in motives over adaptation as outcome. That is, unlike personality structures, which we may consider primarily as outcomes of the adjustive process, motives are intimately concerned with the adjustment process itself.

Now that we have defined the primary unit of observation, we must realize that this observation cannot be made without employing vehicles or devices through which measurement can take place. Section 3, focuses more sharply on specific instruments. At this point in the discussion, however, it is necessary only to note that the measurement of an attitude is not independent of the choice of vehicle, whether it is an objective assessment of performance in a particular type of laboratory situation, or opinion preferences on a questionnaire. Rather, the measurement of motivation, as well as the measurement in any other content domain of behavior, is very intimately tied to the devices it uses. In section 5 this problem has been dealt with in somewhat greater detail. The interested reader may also wish to consult treatments of this issue in chapter 7 as well as J. L. Horn (1966c) and Cattell, Radcliffe, and Sweney (1963). The particular advantage of multivariate motivational theory is that it has not been overly parochial in its choice of devices, as has seemed to be the case in the work of other researchers (e.g. McClelland, Atkinson, Clark, & Lowell, 1953; Kuder, 1953). It has adopted the principle of "multiple manifestation" (Horn, 1966c) in contrast to the principle of "all our eggs in one basket." In this way, it has avoided to some extent the perturbations introduced by reliance on a specific test or a single technique.

With these preliminary notions clear, we can proceed to show the application of the model which has thus far proven most helpful in the analyses of these types of behavior. The specification equation of the common factor model is

$$a_{ijk} = \sum_j b_j S_{ji} + \sum_k c_k C_{ki}, \qquad (1)$$

where $a_{ijk}$ is the strength of attitude $j$ for individual $i$, as assessed by device $k$; the $S_{ji}$

terms represent the set of dynamic "structures" or traits discovered by factor analysis; the $C_{ki}$ terms represent dynamic "component" or energy (interest) types; and the $b_j$ and $c_k$ terms are behavioral indexes appropriate to the measured attitude and components respectively. More intensive discussion of these structures and components will follow in sections 3 and 4. Here we shall indicate their nature only briefly insofar as it pertains to a clear understanding of the attitude paradigm and the primary model for motivational research.

In our previous discussion, we have rather loosely employed such terms as *direction* and *force*. By invoking a mathematically refined model, we have increased our precision and enriched these same concepts. As it stands now, our statement about the nature of an attitude has been modified to read that an individual's measured attitude may be broken down into a linear combination of unitary influences, which may be identified empirically by a uniquely specified, invariant pattern of loadings across motivational variables.

The mathematical significance of the model has already been made clear in chapter 1. An example with specific reference to motivation may be of help in grasping the practical significance of the model as it is applied here to motivation strength. Thus, we may say that

I want very much to
go to the movies with
a friend of the opposite
sex
(as assessed by autistic
projection)

$$= \begin{array}{l} .7 \text{ (sex)} + .3 \text{ (narcism)} + .1 \text{ (assertiveness)} + .5 \text{ (unconscious interest)} + .1 \text{ (conscious interest)} - \\ .1 \text{ (imperative [moral] interest).} \end{array}$$

Here, we have substituted less abstract terms for $S$ and $C$ in the previous equation. It is, of course, to be taken as an example. The weights and terms used only approximate those which we would demand and find in a refined statistical analysis. It should be clear, though, even from this oversimplified example, that by application of the factor model, we have been able to reduce an extremely large set of attitudes and measurement principles into a more manageable and more reliable set of constructs to explain individual differences in interest strength.

## 3  MOTIVATIONAL COMPONENT RESEARCH

With the previous introduction to the basic terminology of the dynamic calculus or common factor model and an example of its potential resolving power in motivational research, we now move on to examine in more detail the basic constructs and research bearing upon the conceptual validity of the model. It will be recalled that the specification equation (equation 1) represents the strength of a particular attitude for a particular individual, as measured by a particular device, as a weighted sum of $j$ traits and $k$ components for individual $i$. It might be profitable at this point to descend to a lower level of abstraction and examine the operations by which the $j$ traits and $k$ components are measured.

Taking the attitude, as defined previously, as the basic unit of measurement, the researcher may arrive at a specification of the motivational components through an $R$-technique analysis (Cattell, 1966c) by holding the attitude constant, intercorrelating the responses of a number of individuals on a number of devices, and factoring and rotating to simple structure this matrix of intercorrelations. Alternatively, one may arrive at a specification of the components within an individual by $P$-technique analysis (Cattell, 1966c). In this approach the attitude strength of a single person would be measured on a variety of devices across occasions. The measures would then be intercorrelated and the resulting matrix factored. The number of discovered components in each case is determined by the number of factors extracted, which is commonly decided on the basis of such indexes as the Scree test (Cattell, 1966h), Tucker's Phi (Thurstone, 1938), or the Unit rule (Kaiser & Caffrey, 1965). The weights for the specification equation are those given in the rotated primary factor pattern matrix $V_{fp}$.

A list of the devices that have been employed in motivational component research is presented as Table 1. Although several earlier researches had been conducted employing some of these devices (Cattell, 1935, 1947b; Cattell, Maxwell, Light, & Unger, 1949), the first factor analysis of such devices was reported by Cattell and Baggaley (1956), on a large sample ($N = 374$) of adult males. Five major components were identified and labelled with the Greek letters alpha through epsilon. The first three appeared to be similar to Freud's concepts of id, ego, and superego. A later study by Tapp (1958) served to strengthen this implication. The fourth and fifth factors in the Cattell and Baggaley (1956) study (delta and epsilon) were respectively identified as a physiological reactivity factor and a memory aberration factor, similar to the sort which would be expected to be associated with the interference of repressed conflicts.

Cattell, Radcliffe, and Sweney (1963) investigated the replicability of these components in children with a large battery of individually and group administered devices. The subjects of the study were 167 sixth and seventh grade public school pupils. Two

**TABLE 1** Some principles of motivation measurement applied in device construction

| With increase in interest in a course of action expect increase in |
|---|

1. Preferences: Readiness to admit preference for a course of action.

2. Autism: Misperception, distorted perception of objects, noises, etc., in accordance with interest, e.g., Bruner coin perception study.

3. Autism: Misbelief, distorted belief that facts favor course of action.

4. Reasoning distortion: Means-ends, readiness to argue that doubtfully effective means to goal are really effective.

5. Reasoning distortion: Ends-means, readiness to argue that ends will be easily reached by inapt means.

6. Reasoning distortion: Inductive.

7. Reasoning distortion: Deductive.

8. Reasoning distortion: Eduction of relations in perception, e.g., analogies.

9. Utilities choice: Readiness to use land, labor, and capital for interest.

10. Machiavellism: Willingness to use reprehensible means to achieve ends favoring interest.

11. Fantasy choice: Readiness to choose interest-related topic to read about, write about, or explain.

12. Fantasy ruminations: Time spent ruminating on interest-related material.

13. Fantasy identification: Prefer to be like individuals who favor course of action.

14. Defensive reticence: Low fluency in listing bad consequences of course of action.

15. Defensive fluency: Fluency in listing good consequences of course of action.

16. Defensive fluency: Fluency listing justifications for actions.

17. Rationalization: Readiness to interpret information in a way to make interest appear more respectable, etc., than it is.

18. Naive projection: Misperception of others as having one's own interests.

19. True projection: Misperception of others as exhibiting one's own reprehensible behavior in connection with pursuit of interest.

20. Id projection: Misperception of others as having one's own primitive desire relating to interest.

21. Superego projection: Misperception of others as having one's own righteous beliefs relating to interest.

22. Guilt sensitivity: Expression of guilt feelings for nonparticipation in interest-related activities.

23. Conflict involvement: Time spent making decision under approach-approach conflict (both alternatives favor interest).

24. Conflict involvement: Time spent making decision under avoidance-avoidance conflict (both alternatives oppose interest).

25. Threat reactivity: Psychogalvanic resistance drop when interest threatened.

26. Threat reactivity: Increase cardiovascular output when interest threatened.

27. Physiological involvement: Increase cardiovascular output when interest aroused (threatened or not).

28. Physiological involvement: Finger temperature rise when interest aroused.

29. Physiological involvement: Increase muscle tension when interest aroused.

30. Perceptual integration: Organize unstructured material in accordance with interest.

*Note.* See footnote at end of table.

With increase in interest in a course of action expect increase in

31. Perceptual closure: Ability to see incomplete drawings as complete when material is related to interest.

32. Selective perception: Ease of finding interest-related material imbedded in complex field.

33. Sensory acuity: Tendency to sense lights as brighter, sounds as louder, etc., when interest is aroused.

34. Attentivity: Resistance to distractive lights, sounds, etc. when attending to interest-related material.

35. Spontaneous attention: Involuntary movements with respect to interest-related stimuli, e.g., eye movements.

36. Involvement: Apparent speed with which time passes when occupied with interest.

37. Persistence: Continuation in work for interest in face of difficulty.

38. Perseveration: Maladaptive continuation with behavior related to interest.

39. Distractivity: Inability to maintain attention when interest-related stimuli interfere.

40. Retroactive inhibition when interest-related task intervenes.

41. Proactive inhibition by interest-related task.

42. Eagerness, effort: Anticipation of expending much effort for course of action.

43. Activity, time: Time spent on course of action.

44. Eagerness, money: Anticipation of spending much money for course of action.

45. Activity, money: Money spent on course of action.

46. Eagerness, exploration: Readiness to undertake exploration to achieve interest-related ends.

47. Impulsiveness, decisions: Speed of decisions in favor of interest (low conflict).

48. Impulsiveness, agreements: Speed of agreeing with opinions favorable to interest.

49. Decision strength: Extremeness of certainty for position favoring course of action.

50. Warm-up speed, learning: Speed warming up to learning tasks related to interest.

51. Learning: Speed learning interest-related material.

52. Motors skills. Apt performance to affect interest.

53. Information: Knowledge affecting and related to course of action.

54. Resistance to extinction of responses related to interest.

55. Control: Ability to coordinate activities in pursuit of interest.

56. Availability, fluency: Fluency in writing on cues related to course of action.

57. Availability, free association: Readiness to associate to interest-related material when not oriented by cue.

58. Availability, speed of free association: Number of associations when interest aroused.

59. Availability, oriented association: Readiness to associate interest-related material with given cue.

60. Availability, memory: Free recall of interest-related material.

61. Memory for rewards: Immediate recall of rewards associated with interest.

62. Reminiscence, Ward-Hovland effect: Increased recall over short interval of interest-related material.

63. Reminiscence, Ballard-Williams effect: Increased recall over long intervals of interest-related material.

*Note.* See footnote at end of table.

TABLE 1 (*continued*) Some principles of motivation measurement applied in device construction

With increase in interest in a course of action expect increase in

64. Zeigarnik recall: Tendency to recall incompleted tasks associated with interest.

65. Zeigarnik perseveration: Readiness to return to incompleted task associated with interest.

66. Defensive forgetfulness: Inability to recall interest-related material if goal not achievable.

67. Reflex facilitation: Ease with which certain reflexes are evoked when interest aroused.

68. Reflex inhibition: Difficulty in evoking certain reflexes when interest aroused.

*Note.* After Cattell, 1959; Cattell & Horn, 1963; Cattell, Radcliffe, & Sweney, 1963.

analyses were conducted, aimed at two different attitudes, and each yielded seven highly similar factors. The first five factors in each case were close replications of the components discovered in adults by Cattell and Baggaley (1956). The additional two components were labelled *zeta* and *eta* and identified, respectively, as constitutional need and drive persistence.

Most of the devices which define the six components are identified in more detail in Table 1, principles of motivation measurement. The reader who wishes to familiarize himself in greater detail with the devices is referred to the original studies, and especially, to the Cattell and Warburton (1967) compendium for detailed description and administration instructions. A brief excursion into a description of these factors in terms other than measurement operations may be useful, however, in providing a "feel" for the concepts. First, to provide some explanatory framework, consider Cattell's (1965c) formulation of total ergic tension ($E$), which he regards as analyzable into six sources as follows:

$$E = (S + K) [C + H + P - aG - bG] , \quad (2)$$

where the $(S + K)$ term represents the stimulus situation; $C$ represents the constitutional endowment of a person with a particular source of ergic tension; $H$ represents the individual's learning history with respect to a particular erg; $P$ represents a momentary deviation of some aspect of the individual's chronic biochemical physiological level, as represented by the individual's $C + H$ combination, which might be taken together, as the individual's "expected" level of physiological gratification, and $aG$ and $bG$ represent the amount of goal satisfaction currently obtaining through physiological and psychological processes, respectively. Equation 2 is intended by Cattell (1959, 1965c) to express three distinct concepts to assist in the clarification of his research in the dynamic field. The $P - aG$ portion of the equation is regarded as the momentary level of "drive strength" (i.e., the deviation from the person's chronic physiological state less the amount of physiological gratification presently obtaining). When these two are equal, momentary, "drive strength," quite sensibly, drops to zero. The entire term in *brackets* $C + H + P - aG - bG$ is taken as the index of "need strength," i.e., the individual's constitutional and experiential components with respect to the gratification of a particular erg, in addition to the currently obtaining psychological gratification, summate with current drive strength to determine "need strength." When need strength interacts with a particular stimulus situation $(S + K)$ the total momentary "ergic tension level" $E$ results. (For example, a particular need may be amplified in one stimulus situation more than another, examples of which the reader can surely produce in abundance.)

Cattell, though reformulating the ergic tension equation later (Cattell & Child, 1975) into a more complex equation, had more simply taken the concepts of ergic *states* $Es$ as well as *traits* $Et$ into account. Suffice it to say here that ergic traits are conceived of as enduring motivational propensities, whereas ergic states are situation bound. The revised ergic tension equation, then is

$$E = Et + Es = (C + H) + (S + K)$$
$$(Ee - P - aG - bG), \qquad (3)$$

where all terms are the same in meaning as their counterparts in Equation 2, with $Ee$ representing the situationally modifiable excitability aspect of the ergic concept, and the $(Ee - P - aG - bG)$ set of terms interacting with the stimulus situation, while $C$ and $H$ are independent of the situation.

With this examination of the meaning of the terms in the ergic tension equation, a fuller discussion of the interpretation of the motivational components identified in the studies by Tapp (1958), Cattell and Baggaley (1956), and Cattell, Radcliffe, and Sweney (1963) can now be undertaken. For simplicity throughout the rest of this section, the Tapp study will be designated by the Roman numeral I, the Cattell and Baggaley study by II, and the Cattell, Radcliffe, and Sweney study by III. Table 2 summarizes the variables that have loaded the motivational component factors in the latter two studies.

*Factor alpha (Conscious id component)* This factor was the dominant one in

two of the three studies (II and III). Two hypotheses, which are cooperative to some extent, have been advanced with respect to interpretation of this component. One hypothesis is that alpha represents "conscious id," or the conscious expression, on the devices employed of the unconscious impulses resident within the person. This hypothesis was advanced due to the "wishful" nature of the devices which load this factor. For example, the "autism" measure (see Table 2) requires the person to complete sentences, identify ambiguous pictures, and indicate the extent to which he agrees with statements about the past, present, and future for which no objective answer is known. The extent to which his misperceptions or misbeliefs with respect to a given attitude are evidenced is taken as the autism measure of strength of interest in that topic. The other devices shown in Table 2 as loading the alpha factor are all of a similar "wishful" nature. A second hypothesis concerning the interpretation of alpha is that it represents the lack of currently achieved satisfaction, or more explicitly, the lack of currently perceived satisfaction, which would align it with the $bG$ term in the ergic tension equation.

*Factor beta (Reality directed component)* The second factor appearing in the three studies is marked primarily by the amount of information an individual has stored with respect to a given attitude (see Table 2). The possibility exists that this could represent an ability factor due to unsuccessful attempts to avoid such influences by ipsative scoring (Cattell, Radcliffe, & Sweney, 1963; Horn, J. L., 1966c). The authors of the studies felt, however, that ability has been sufficiently suppressed and have tentatively identified beta as "ego expression" or the realized interest which results from reality-oriented striving.

**TABLE 2** Loadings of motivational component factors alpha through eta on representative devices in three major studies

| Factor | Salient device variables | II | III(movies) | III(religion) |
|--------|--------------------------|-----|-------------|---------------|
| Alpha | Preference | 49 | 66 | 44 |
| | Choice to explain | 29 | 52 | – |
| | Id projection | (a) | 38 | – |
| | Visual attention | (a) | 31 | 42 |
| | Auditory attention | – | 39 | 43 |
| | Naive projection | 33 | 33 | 46 |
| | Autism | 64 | 14 | 29 |
| | Distortion of reasoning (ends) | 56 | (a) | 38 |
| Beta | Information | 33 | 20 | 31 |
| | Learning language | 23 | 56 | (a) |
| | Systolic pressure | −16 | −35 | −38 |
| | Diastolic pressure | −27 | −36 | −28 |
| Gamma | Information | −35 | 60 | 20 |
| | Word association | 50 | 50 | 49 |
| | Paired words | (a) | 20 | 27 |
| | Selective perception | (a) | 38 | 37 |
| | Superego projection | (a) | 28 | 02 |
| | Perceptual integration | −22 | −07 | −42 |
| Delta | Systolic pressure | −57 | −32 | −44 |
| | Diastolic pressure | −19 | −01 | −23 |
| | Psychogalvanic response (PGR) deflection | 15 | 53 | 48 |
| | Decision speed (opinions) | (a) | 45 | 39 |
| Epsilon | Memory of cues | 35 | 38 | 45 |
| | Reminiscence | −61 | −49 | −49 |
| | True projection | (a) | 08 | 23 |
| | Identification | (a) | −19 | −21 |
| Zeta | Speed (consensus) | (b) | 71 | – |
| | Decision strength preference box | (b) | 27 | 56 |
| | Impulsiveness on analogies | (b) | 25 | 30 |
| Eta | Superego strength | (b) | −31 | −56 |
| | Intelligence | (b) | −71 | −43 |
| | Maintained fluency | (b) | 42 | 23 |
| | Maintained perceptual task | (b) | 60 | 25 |
| | Maintained motor task | (b) | 06 | 26 |

*Note.* Study II is Cattell and Baggaley (1956). Study III is Cattell, Radcliffe, and Sweney (1963), the first part dealing with the movie attitude, the second with a religious attitude.

[a]Not used.

[b]Factor not identified in this study.

*Factor gamma (Superego component)* The gamma factor has been interpreted as "ideal self" or "superego" component due to the loadings by devices such as "information" and "oriented word association" which point to its integrated nature of the component such as one would expect with the acceptance of cultural dicta.

*Factor delta (Physiological reactivity component)* The delta factor has been marked by physiological measures as well as decision time. The possibility exists that this factor is a residual effect due to failure to completely remove the physiological device effect (Horn, J. L., 1966c). However, the tentative substantive interpretation of the delta component identifies it with the *P* term in the ergic tension equation, hypothesizing it to represent physiological need expression.

*Factor epsilon* The nature of this factor, although somewhat obscure, has been interpreted as motivation expression related to unconscious memories (i.e., arising from complexes). The loadings of opposite sign for "memory for cues" and "reminiscence" are the most consistent findings with respect to epsilon.

*Factor zeta (Constitutional need factor)* This factor was not identified in study II but appeared in skeleton form in study I, and with increased clarity in study III. It is marked by rapidity of consensus on the "movies" attitude, higher decision strength (the force with which a lever pull indicating a decision was made), and impulsiveness on analogies. Three hypotheses have been advanced concerning the nature of zeta. One is that it may be residual variance due to failure to fully remove speed of performance variance. While this hypothesis is not to be disregarded, the substantive interpretation of zeta has been that it represents either "unconscious id expression," due to the impulsive nature of the devices loading the factor, or "constitutional need expression," which identifies zeta with the *C* term in the ergic tension equation.

*Factor eta* To date this factor appeared in only one study (III) and has very tentatively been identified as the "stimulus excitation component," thereby linking it to the *S* term in the ergic tension equation. Cattell,

Radcliff, and Sweney (1963) pointed out that, although they considered it unlikely due to supporting evidence, eta could possibly represent a scoring artifact as all the tests loading the factor were normatively scored.

Second-order analysis in the motivational component realm yielded two factors in study II and five in study III. The fifth factor in the latter investigation was small and not interpreted. The first two large factors in each of the investigations (columns A and B in Table 3) have been labelled "integrated" (*I*) and "unintegrated (*U*) motivation," respectively.

The second-order component *I*, as can be seen in Table 3, receives high loadings from primary components beta "ego expression" and gamma "ideal self" in all analyses which distinguish it as a component of conscious, reality-oriented, integrated motivational investment. The primary Factor eta, "stimulus excitation," exhibited a high loading on the second-order *I* factor in the "religious attitude" analysis of study III, but not in the "movies attitude" analysis. Cattell, Radcliffe, and Sweney (1963) offered the hypothesis that this stimulus excitation effect is peculiar to the type of attitudinal structure being analyzed and that, in the case of religious attitudes, the stimulus is to self-sentiment, integrated structures. An alternative hypothesis forwarded in the interpretation of this second-order Factor *I* is that it represents the "engram" (*M*) component in Cattell's (1959) specification equation:

$$R_{ij} = \sum_j b_j E_{ij} + \sum_j b_j M_{ij}. \qquad (4)$$

This equation, which will be dealt with in more detail in section 4 of this chapter, represents response $R_j$ made by individual $i$ as a function of a weighted sum of the dynamic structure factors (see also section 6), the ergs

**TABLE 3** Second-order motivational components emerging from the Cattell and Baggaley (1956) and Cattell, Radcliffe, and Sweney (1963) analysis

| Motivation component | Cattell & Baggaley[a] | | Cattell, Radcliffe, & Sweney (religion) | | | | Cattell, Radcliffe, & Sweney (movies) | | | |
|---|---|---|---|---|---|---|---|---|---|---|
| | A | B | A | B | C | D | A | B | C | D |
| Alpha | 19 | 42 | −01 | .38 | .05 | −.02 | −.07 | .53 | .07 | −.26 |
| Beta | 75 | 18 | .39 | −.07 | −.07 | −.06 | .24 | −.07 | −.01 | .32 |
| Gamma | 35 | 18 | .22 | .02 | −.22 | −.52 | .51 | .06 | .03 | −.06 |
| Delta | 04 | 22 | −.04 | −.02 | .49 | .00 | −.08 | −.01 | .34 | −.05 |
| Epsilon | 06 | 12 | .03 | .41 | −.02 | .69 | .09 | .47 | −.06 | .52 |
| Zeta | − | − | −.03 | −.01 | .14 | .60 | .08 | −.01 | .35 | −.63 |
| Eta | − | − | .43 | .08 | .09 | .04 | .04 | −.64 | −.03 | .04 |

*Note.* Col. A = Integrated motivation; Col. B = Unintegrated motivation; Col. C = Physiological, autonomic reactivity to interest; Col. D = Appetitive, impulsive conflict.

[a] No factor extracted for C and D.

($E_j$s) and engrams ($M_j$s). The $E_j$s are primarily inherited, instinctual dynamic structure factors whereas the $M_j$s represent the "environmental mold dynamic source traits," which depend on the individual's experiences for their development.

The other large second-order factor emerging from the analyses (represented as column B, Table 3) was termed the "unintegrated" ($U$) motivational component factor as it received loadings from the primary components alpha (id) and epsilon (repressed complexes), in addition to smaller loadings from delta (physiological need expression) in one analysis. The hypothesis is that this second-order component represents the $E$ term in the specification Equation 4 being the unconscious, general unorganized id expression of motivational investment.

The third and fourth second-order components, represented as columns C and D, Table 3, have been labeled "physiological, autonomic reactivity to interest" and "appetitive, impulsive conflict," respectively. The former is composed of a large projection from the primary component delta, physiological need expression, and a smaller one from zeta, constitutional need expression.

As the primary component zeta did not emerge in the Cattell and Baggaley (1956) analysis, any possibility of the emergence of this second-order component of "physiological, autonomic reactivity to interest" was consequently obviated. The second-order component represented in column D, Table 3, "appetitve, impulsive conflict," behaved differently across the two attitudes, the only common high loading of like sign being received from epsilon, repressed complexes. The second-order component was also marked by a high loading from the primary component of zeta, constitutional need expression, but the loading was positive with respect to the religious attitude and negative with respect to the movie attitude. This opposite sign, in addition to the differential behavior of the "superego" component gamma, high negative loading on religious and low negative on movies, led Cattell, Radcliffe, and Sweney (1963) to hypothesize that, as these two attitudes are presumably quite opposite in the degree of moral encouragement in children, the second-order component is indicative of some appetitive, physiological, impulsive component involved in conflict and generating anxiety.

These first quantitative explorations of the domain of motivational components have succeeded, as is true of any scientific endeavor, particularly those which are exploratory in nature, in raising more questions than they have answered. The field is ripe for further exploration; the beginning, which was made by Cattell and his associates, offers the interested investigator a firm groundwork of measurement devices based on sound and quantitative study. But the delineation of components of motivation and their measurement comprises only the first step for the student of behavior dynamics, with the understanding of the interrelationships among the different dynamic structures being the next step to prediction and control. It is to these interrelationships that we now turn.

## 4  THE ORGANIZATION OF ATTITUDES: RESEARCH ON DYNAMIC STRUCTURES

Up to this point, our discussion has been concerned with the components of a measured attitude. In dynamic structure research, interest is centered upon the relationships among a diverse array of attitudes. Through $R$-technique analysis the procedure in such an investigation would be to measure a number of individuals on a number of attitudes (a number of devices may be used and their weighted sum assigned as a single score to an individual), intercorrelating these attitude scores, and subsequently factoring the matrix of intercorrelations. Typically, around 15 simple structure factors have resulted from such analyses with adult samples (Cattell, 1959). These factors were classified by Cattell (1959, 1965c) as "ergs" (genetically determined attitude structures common to all cultures, although the attitude objects and relative strength may vary across cultures, such as sex, fear, hunger,

etc.) and "engrams" (attitude aggregates that are culturally determined, such as religious beliefs, family attachments, etc.)[1] The "engrams" have been further subdivided into "sentiments" and "complexes,"[2] with the sentiments represented as the conscious, integrated attitude aggregates, whereas the "complexes" were defined by Cattell (1959) also as "object attachments of drives, though unconscious and less integrated." The operational distinction between the "complexes" and the "ergs" is not clear, although current research is aimed at such clarification (see section 7 of this chapter).

A number of studies providing evidence for the dynamic structure factors are available (Cattell, 1947b, 1950a; Cattell & Baggaley, 1956; Cattell, Butcher, Connor, Sweney, & Tsujioka, 1962; Cattell & Horn, 1963; Cattell, Radcliffe, & Sweney, 1963; Sweney & Cattell, 1962). J. L. Horn (1966c) provided a table of average loadings of the salient attitudes on each of the 11 most frequently replicated ergs and 5 most frequently replicated sentiments. These are reproduced as Table 4. (See also Cattell and Child, 1975.)

Sweney (1967) provided the first major review of the various dynamic structure studies. It should be apparent that the number of sentiments that research may discover as replicable, functionally-unitary, behavioral influences is potentially limitless. Since the development and expression of sentiments are directed by shared learning histories, we may expect great diversity among the sentiment structures of groups sharing a highly homogeneous environment, i.e., among several different cultures or subcultures. The major consideration then,

---

[1] See Equation 6 and associated discussion, section 6 of this chapter.

[2] See Equation 7 and associated discussion, section 6 of this chapter.

**TABLE 4** Summary of descriptions of some dynamic structure factors replicated in two or more studies with adults and/or children

| | | Average loadings | |
|---|---|---|---|
| Erg or sentiment | Major attitudes (begin each with "I want") | Adult | Children |
| 1. Security-fear erg | More protection from nuclear weapons | 48 | |
| | To reduce accidents and diseases | 33 | 22 |
| | To stop powers that threaten our nation | 38 | |
| | To go to mother when things go wrong | | 43 |
| | To be at home safe | | 38 |
| | To grow up normally | | |
| 2. Mating (sex) erg | To love a person I find attractive | 52 | |
| | To see movies, TV shows, etc. with love interest | 34 | |
| | To satisfy mating needs | 52 | |
| | To enjoy fine foods, desserts, drinks | 37 | |
| | To spend time with opposite sex | | 38 |
| | To dress to impress opposite sex | | 38 |
| | To go to parties where couples are invited | | 32 |
| 3. Assertive erg | To increase salary and status | 36 | |
| | To excel fellows in chosen pursuits | 40 | |
| | To dress smartly and command respect | 40 | |
| | To maintain good reputation | 33 | 20 |
| | To read more comics | | 34 |
| | To see that my team wins | | 39 |
| 4. Protective erg | Proud parents who do not lack needs | 47 | |
| | To insure that children get education | 40 | |
| | To help distressed adults and children | 40 | |
| | To help spouse avoid drudgeries | 33 | |
| | To take care of pet | | 38 |
| | Siblings to mind me | | 38 |
| 5. Sensuality erg | To enjoy drinking and smoking | 38 | |
| | To enjoy fine foods, desserts, delicacies | 41 | |
| | To sleep late, take it easy | 31 | |
| | To enjoy own company | 37 | |
| | To eat well | | 32 |
| | To have more holidays | | 41 |
| 6. Curiosity erg | To listen to music | 37 | |
| | To know more science | 29 | 37 |
| | To enjoy graphic arts and theater | 40 | |
| | To make my pictures beautiful | | 29 |
| 7. Gregarious erg (Sports sentiment) | To actively participate in sports | 30 | |
| | To follow team and be a rooter | 48 | |
| | To spend time in companionship with others | 23 | 28 |
| | To play games with friends | | 36 |
| | To go to parties where couples are invited | | 38 |
| 8. Pugnacity erg | To destroy powers that threaten our nation | 42 | 37 |
| | To see violence in movies and TV shows | 20 | |
| | To get even with others | | 37 |

*Note.* See footnote at end of table.

**TABLE 4**  *(continued)* Summary of descriptions of some dynamic structure factors replicated in two or more studies with adults and/or children

| Erg or sentiment | Major attitudes (begin each with "I want") | Average loadings | |
|---|---|---|---|
| | | Adult | Children |
| 9. Appeal erg (Parental-religious sentiment) | To heed parents and turn to them in need | 39 | |
| | To feel in touch with God or similar principle | 55 | |
| | Proud parents who do not lack needs | 47 | |
| | Influence of religion to increase | 60 | |
| 10. Construction erg | Take things apart, see how they work | | 38 |
| | To make projects in school | | 33 |
| 11. Narcism erg | To have attractive face and figure | | 32 |
| | Nice clothes to wear | | 31 |
| 12. Self-sentiment | To control impulses and mental processes | 40 | 32 |
| | Never to damage self-respect | 35 | 27 |
| | To excel in my line of work | 38 | |
| | To maintain good reputation | 37 | 34 |
| | Never to become insane | 39 | |
| | To be responsible, in charge of things | 31 | |
| | To know about science, art, literature | 31 | |
| | To know more about myself | 33 | |
| | To grow up normally | | 28 |
| 13. Superego sentiment | To satisfy sense of duty to church, parents, etc. | 41 | |
| | Never to be selfish in my acts | 41 | |
| | To avoid sinful expression of sex needs | 33 | |
| | To avoid drinking, gambling—i.e., vice | 21 | |
| | To maintain good self-control | 28 | 31 |
| | To admire and respect father | | 28 |
| 14. Religious sentiment | To worship God | | 34 |
| | To go to church | | 33 |
| 15. Career sentiment | To learn skills required for job | 34 | |
| | To continue with present career plans | 33 | |
| | To increase salary and status | 27 | |
| 16. Sweetheart sentiment | To bring gifts to sweetheart | 51 | |
| | To spend time with sweetheart | 41 | |

*Note.*  After J. L. Horn, 1966c.

becomes one of theoretic and practical significance of the various sentiment structures that have been uncovered. One approach which has thus far provided balance and direction in this research, though it may not be completely theoretically satisfying, is to sample broadly and extensively and to verify findings through independent replication.

The ergs, however, should have some theoretical limit. Cattell hypothesized as many as 21 ergs (see Sweney, 1967), of which those listed in Table 4 received the greatest degree of empirical support. Lest the reader link Cattell's approach with the now unpopular pastime of drive naming, let it be remembered that each erg hypothesized is, in theory, measurable; and such measurement and verification of each by multivariate experiment is a requirement. This linkage to operations and sound analytic techniques lends a "new look" to the dynamics of human behavior. Cattell's goal in this area has been to strike a reasonable compromise between the scientifically fruitless activity of listing drives which was indulged in by the armchair theorists and the rigid attitude fostered by the early behaviorists who would recognize a drive only when they "saw the stomach flapping" (Cattell, 1959).

The frequent replication of the dynamic structure factors provide the evidence concerning the construct validity of the Motivational Analysis Test (MAT; Cattell, Horn, Radcliffe, & Sweney, 1964; Sweney, Cattell, & Krug, 1970) which has been utilized in studies of the prediction of academic achievement (Cattell & Butcher, 1968; Cattell, Radcliffe, & Sweney, 1963; Pierson, Barton, & Hey, 1964).

An example of the relationship among ergs, sentiments, and attitudes and their respective roles in the complex matrix of human motives is represented in the "dynamic lattice," a device employed by Cattell as a "flow chart" of proximal and distal goals. A simple fragment of the dynamic lattice representation is presented as Fig. 1. H. A. Murray's (1938) notion of "subsidiation" is evident in the dynamic lattice, which shows each attitude in turn subsidiating to another, converging and redistributing from nodal points. For example, this hypothetical person's attitude concerning taxation is related to his attitudes concerning divorce reform, New York, and the President of the United States. It subsidiates, along with other attitudes, to attitude aggregates, or sentiments, concerning his bank account, political party, and country, which are in turn linked to various ergs shown at the right of Fig. 1.

# 5 MEASUREMENT AND APPLICATION OF THE DYNAMIC CALCULUS

In the previous section of this chapter we examined the primary model and the major concepts of the dynamic calculus. In this section we turn to somewhat more applied issues. First, we examine some measurement problems and their solutions that intervene between the levels of theoretical formulation and empirical observation. Then, we examine the application of the dynamic calculus to the investigation of an area of practical importance, the area of conflict.

## 5.1 The Measurement of Interests

It became apparent early in the history of motivational research that individual differences in ability were intruding into the scores on objective tests of motivation. It seemed that such objective test assessment avoided the frying pan of questionnaire distortion only to land in the potentially more dangerous inferno where ability factors warped and distorted the true attitudinal structure.

An example may help set the problem. Assume that we are interested in determining which of two persons shows greater strength of interest in a particular course of action. Both are given a series of test items, which require specific knowledge about a sample of interests and take this knowledge as an index of motive strength. Individual $X$ obtains a score of 5 on the attitude of interest; individual $Y$, a score of 10. Are we then justified in assuming that $Y$ is displaying greater motive strength? One other piece of information is available to us. We note that the total score of $X$ across all interests measured is 25, whereas $Y$'s total score is 50. A possible interpretation of these data is, of course, that the obtained scores do reflect the true state of affairs—$Y$

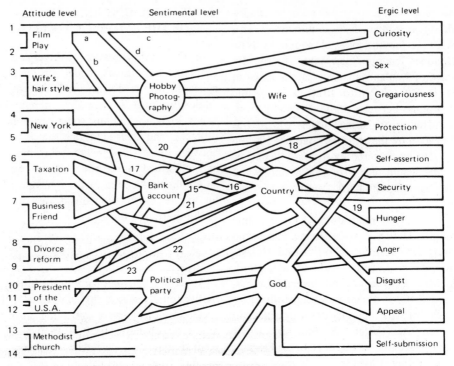

**FIG. 1** Fragment of a dynamic lattice, showing attitude subsidiation, sentiment structure, and ergic goals. From *The scientific analysis of personality* by R. B. Cattell, Harmondsworth, England: Penguin, 1965. Copyright 1965 by Penguin. Reprinted by permission.

is more highly motivated than $X$. An equally logical alternative, however, is that somehow our tests reflect general intelligence, memory capacity, or, more generally, abilities irrelevant to the measurement of motives. Whereas specific motives may direct the individual to acquire certain kinds of knowledge, his intelligence level may moderate the number of answers he knows, and his memory may moderate the number he can recall. Fortunately, this is not the type of question which must be decided a priori, but is one which can be put to an experimental test. When we give several tests of intelligence and memory, in which content is motive irrelevant, to these hypothetical people, we find in fact that $Y$ does somewhat better than $X$ on all such tests.

This simplified example serves to illustrate, rather grossly, the types of observations made in the early investigations of the dynamic calculus which led these investigators to rely on ipsative rather than normative measurement in the motivation area, that is, measures that were corrected for individual differences in ability.

There are potentially many levels in the measurement process at which such a correction may be introduced. Those most commonly used have been at the level of item presentation and the level of statistical correction. The first is relatively familiar because a number of psychological tests and questionnaires, measuring personality as well as motivation, have relied on some type of ipsative presentation format. Among the most popular would be the Edwards Personal Preference Schedule and the Allport-Vernon-Lindsey Study of Values, to mention only two. Typically, in this format, all positive combinations of choices are presented to the individual in counterbalanced fashion so that every person has the same total score on the tests. Individual differences in interests are reflected in the score level on each scale relative to all other scales. To continue our previous example, we may consider an information test in which items were made equivalent in difficulty level and presented to the subject in pairs. From each pair he is required to select only one of the two questions to answer.

This is, of course, a somewhat far-fetched example of an information test. Far more likely in this case is to attempt some form of statistical correction. The simplest correction to apply is to divide the score on each of the dynamic structures measured in the information format by the total number of items correct. A second alternative is to transform each individual's scores to a scale with a common mean and standard deviation. Or again, the investigator may apply a range correction and divide each score by the difference between the person's highest and lowest score. Regardless of which type of correction is chosen, the end result will be a score matrix in which each row, that is, each subject's set of scores, has been recentered about the subject's own mean. Individual differences in ability have been removed from the scores, and the dynamic structures can be precisely determined and accurately assessed free from the perturbating influences of ability.

The measurement instruments derived from the research of the dynamic calculus, MAT (for the adult age range) and SMAT (for high school students), have incorporated these principles into their design. Wherever feasible, fully ipsatized formats have been used in these tests. When such a presentation has proven either unwieldy or inappropriate, the handbooks have outlined statistical procedures for full ipsatization of scores.

## 5.2 The Calculus of Conflict

One of the most crucial issues within motivational research, in its theoretical ramifications to the researcher and in its practical implications to the clinician, is the topic of conflict.

The model chosen by the dynamic calculus permits a refined analysis of this phenomenon into several specific manifestations that may be individually investigated and clarified. The presentation of the fundamental model for motivational research in section 2 pointed to the primary distinction between dynamic structures as the goals or objects of motivated behavior, and the motivational components as the energies of motivated behavior. It should be immediately apparent that such a distinction suggests at least two sources of conflict: that arising from the strength of competing dynamic structures and that arising from the level of competing component energies. As an example of the first case, we may consider the case of a person who is simultaneously driven by loving attachment to his wife and family as well as a deep interest in enhancing his career. The two interests may conflict at a variety of points, such as when the person must work late at the office or make business trips which necessarily take him away from home.

As an example of the latter case, consider a person who has a strong unconscious interest (2nd stratum component, $U$) in seeing that his children receive the best education possible. His conscious interests ($I$), however, are less strong. As a consequence, he may not have taken the necessary steps, financial and otherwise, characteristic of integrated interest, to insure this education for this children. Such a preponderance of unintegrated over integrated interests is quite likely to increase the drive intensity level of his behavior without simultaneously affording the possibility of achieving the desired goal object.

Within the first case, conflict among the goals of motivated behavior, there is an extremely large number of possibilities open. We must acknowledge, however, that the situation is further complicated by the existence of moderate but significant correlations between the various dynamic structures. Table 5, which is taken from Cattell, Horn, Radcliffe, and Sweney (1964), shows the intercorrelations among the 10 dynamic structures measured by the MAT. It would seem, then, that in the case of the self-sentiment and the narcissism erg, which are correlated .20, that it would require proportionately greater interest in each to produce conflict, perhaps because they have shared in an overlapping set of behaviors, than in the case of the mating erg and superego sentiment ($r = -.35$), in which behaviors associated with each are mutually inconsistent.

In the case of conflict arising from the dynamic components, the same observations may be made. This situation may be somewhat less complex, however, if only because the components are fewer in number than the dynamic structures. Moreover, the rather clear 2-factor, second-stratum solution that has repeatedly been demonstrated limits, in some sense, the possible sources of conflict arising from competition among the components.

There is a third source of conflict, implicit in the dynamic calculus, but which has not yet received a great deal of experimental attention. This source of conflict may arise from interactions of the structures and components. As an example, we may conceive of a situation in which a person is simultaneously high on unintegrated fear and integrated self-sentiment. The unconscious fears may be inconsistent with his conscious attempts to present himself as personable, friendly, and open in his dealings with others. Numerous other examples can be conceived readily. Further experimentation is indicated in this important issue.

**TABLE 5** Intercorrelations of primary dynamic structure factors, as pure factors and as scale estimates on the Motivation Analysis Test (MAT)

| MAT scores | Fear | Mating | Assertiveness | Narcism | Pugnacity | Career | Sweetheart | Home-parental | Superego | Self-sentiment |
|---|---|---|---|---|---|---|---|---|---|---|
| | | | | Primary factor scores | | | | | | |
| Fear | | 22 | 01 | 14 | −04 | −08 | −08 | −24 | −13 | −01 |
| Mating | 08 | | 04 | 13 | 06 | −18 | −07 | −36 | −35 | 11 |
| Assertiveness | −01 | 14 | | 12 | 06 | −03 | −29 | −08 | 01 | −16 |
| Narcism | −02 | 12 | 06 | | −10 | 14 | −18 | −07 | −19 | 34 |
| Pugnacity | 02 | 00 | −12 | −10 | | −32 | 11 | −22 | −02 | −11 |
| Career | −12 | −02 | 00 | −09 | −02 | | −13 | −12 | −02 | −18 |
| Sweetheart | −01 | −14 | −18 | −28 | −10 | −16 | | 10 | −07 | 09 |
| Home-parental | −13 | −31 | −06 | −32 | −16 | 00 | 09 | | 02 | −06 |
| Superego | −23 | −35 | −17 | −32 | 06 | 06 | −06 | 20 | | −06 |
| Self-sentiment | −03 | 18 | −23 | 20 | 29 | −22 | 09 | −11 | −22 | |

*Note.* From *The Motivation Analysis Test, MAT* by R. B. Cattell, J. Horn, J. A. Radcliffe, and A. B. Sweney, Champaign, Ill., Institute for Personality and Ability Testing, 1964. Copyright 1964 by the Institute for Personality and Ability Testing. Reprinted by permission.

Before leaving the topic of conflict it may be helpful to indicate briefly the measurement principles that may be used to provide indexes of conflict, both for the individual and for the group.

We may first consider case 2, conflict among component levels, which has received the greatest attention to date. Instruments such as the MAT and the SMAT have been designed to employ several vehicles in measuring each dynamic structure. In both tests, several devices are known to load on the general unintegrated dynamic component $U$ and several to load on the general integrated $I$ component. For each dynamic structure, then the differences between the $U$ measure and the $I$ measure $(U - I)$ may be used to provide a practicable measure of conflict. Furthermore, a total index of conflict may be obtained by summing across the total number of dynamic structures measured $\Sigma_i(U_i - I_i)$. An index arising from considerations of the same source of conflict has been suggested by Delhees (1968a) and is based on the ratio of unintegrated interest to total motivational investment in a particular dynamic structure $U/(U + I)$. This latter index assumes that for equal differences between $U$ and $I$ measures, conflict will be less when integrated interest is high than when it is low. Whether one or the other of these two indexes has greater predictive value has yet to be shown. To date, the former index has been the more widely used.

Other indexes of individual conflict, appropriate to Cases 1 and 3 can be fairly easily constructed. For Case 1, conflict among structures, such an index might be:

$$\text{Conflict} = \sum \sum S_i - S_j$$
$$i, j = 1, 2, \ldots, N, i \neq j, \qquad (5)$$

where $S$s represent various dynamic structures. This would be an index of total

conflict. In most clinical situations, however, it is more probable that measurement of specific conflict areas would prove of greater value. For the third case, conflict arising from interaction among structures and components, we may consider an entire matrix of conflict $C$, the typical element of which, $c_{ij}$, would represent the difference between the unintegrated measure of dynamic structure $i$ and the integrated measure of dynamic structure $j$, that is, $S_{Ui} - S_{Ij}$. Again, the sum of all the elements in the matrix $\Sigma\Sigma C_{ij}$ would be formed to represent an index of total conflict within the organism. Such a matrix might also provide the basic data for a scaling of conflicts utilizing either the Thurstone methods or the techniques of multidimensional scaling (Torgerson, 1958). Either approach may prove quite helpful in ordering the elements of conflict.

Finally, Sweney (1968) suggested that conflict indexes may be summed across a set of individuals to provide an index of conflict for the group. Such an index may prove a welcome addition to other measures of group behavioral parameters.

## 6 THE DYNAMIC CALCULUS IN THE CONTEXT OF COMPREHENSIVE LEARNING THEORY AND ALTERNATE MODELS

In chapter 18 of this volume Cattell discusses comprehensive learning theory as applied to personality change. The purpose of this section is to consider the dynamic calculus concepts in the context of comprehensive learning theory and examine points of conceptual similarity and dissimilarity between Cattell's use of dynamic concepts and the dynamic concepts utilized by other theorists. The interested reader may find it profitable to return to this section subsequent to reading chapter 18; the presentation of the comprehensive learning theory concepts in the present chapter will of necessity be brief.

Recalling Cattell's basic specification equation (Cattell, 1959) the strength of some behavioral response $R_j$ for some individual $i$ is represented as a weighted sum of dynamic structure factors, ergs $E_k$s and engrams $M_l$s:

$$R_{ij} = \sum_k b_k E_{ik} + \sum_l b_l M_{il}, \qquad (6)$$

where the $b$'s are factor pattern coefficients obtained in the usual way. The engram factors $M_l$s are further resolved into sentiments $MS_l$s and complexes $MC_m$s and substituting these for the engram term the specification equation becomes

$$R_{ij} = \sum_k b_k E_{ik} + \sum_l b_l MS_{il} \\ + \sum_m b_m MC_{im}. \qquad (7)$$

In chapter 18 of this volume, Cattell represents an "act or response" which we will translate here into the $R_{ij}$ term used here, rather than the $a_{ij}$ employed in that chapter as a function of a weighted combination of ability source traits $A_a$s, personality-temperament source traits $P_p$s, and dynamic source traits $D_d$s. A further subscript $h$ is added to represent the situation in which the response occurs. Substituting the dynamic terms in Equation 7 above, for the $D_d$ terms in Cattell's equation results in

$$R_{hij} = \sum_a b_a A_{ia} + \sum_p b_p P_{ip} + \sum_k b_{hk} E_{ik} \\ + \sum_l b_{hl} MS_{il} + \sum_m b_{hm} MC_{im}. \qquad (8)$$

Having acknowledged the role of person-ality-temperament and ability source traits in Cattell's model, and as the $P$ and $A$ terms are unaffected by further development here, these terms will be dropped from further development of the model to render the

equations more manageable. The next step in Cattell's development of the model is the recognition of modulation by the situation $h$, discussed in chapters 1, 7, and 18 of this volume as well as by Cattell (1965c), Cattell and Digman (1964), Van Egeren (1963), Curran (1968), and Nesselroade (1967). Since traits are regarded as relatively stable, enduring aspects of the individual's person-ality, Cattell proposed that a given measured dynamic structure factor $D$ is composed of fixed trait $D_t$ variance in addition to state $D_s$ variance, which is sensitive to situational change. Consequently, splitting each of the dynamic terms in Equation 8 into state, represented by subscript $s$, and trait, represented by subscript $t$, terms yields the following (omitting the $A$ and $P$ terms):

$$R_{hij} = \sum_{ks} b_{hks} E_{sik} + \sum_{kt} b_{kt} E_{tik} \\ + \sum_{is} b_{his} MS_{sil} + \sum_{mt} b_{hmt} MS_{tim} \\ + \sum_{ms} b_{hms} MC_{sim} \\ + \sum_{mt} b_{hmt} MC_{tim}. \qquad (9)$$

Thus, in terms of the dynamic factors included in Cattell's model, a tendency to respond is, taking the first pair of terms on the right of equation 9, a function of the level of ergic traits $E_{tik}$s, which are regarded as hereditarily determined, as well as the ergic state levels $E_{sik}$s, induced by a particular stimulus situation. A simple example of the trait and state distinction here might be considered. Taking the sex erg as an example, individual $X$ might be innately higher in ergic tension with respect to the sex erg than individual $Y$; but if $X$ is placed in church and $Y$ in a brothel, $Y$'s sexual response is likely to be greater. It should be kept in mind that the motivational states are conceptually distinct from the general states such as elation-depression, anxiety, and arousal, which have been investigated by Van Egeren (1963), Curran (1968), and Nesselroade (1967) and discussed in detailed by Nesselroade in chapter 8 of this volume.

The previous model may strike the reader being introduced to multivariate research for the first time as unduly complex. Certainly it is of greater complexity than were earlier models that were based on simpler analytic techniques. It is the nature of the scientific endeavor, however, to improve on description and prediction as modern tools are developed; and the data analyses outlined in earlier sections of this chapter, based on modern analytic techniques, indicated the necessity for a model of at least the degree of complexity of the current specification equation. If the reader recalls the specification equation in Cattell's (1965c) text, he will notice that the complexity of the equation has increased during the past few years (compare with the current specification equation in section 3 of this chapter). This revision has been necessitated by the recent results yielded by the motivational state research. Indeed, the complexity of the current equation has surpassed Allport's (1954) conjecture that five distinct mechanisms are required to account for the various forms of "imitation" (dynamic traits and states in the glossary of the differential psychologist); but rather than dismaying of any one learning theory being able to account for these concepts, multivariate research has aimed at a learning theory sufficiently comprehensive to do so. Admittedly, that stage of development has not yet been reached, but subsequent interaction between theory and data will allow for increasing degrees of approximation to a prediction equation which minimizes error. In following this course, it was necessary to break with some of the traditional ap-

proaches to the study of motivation. The result of this break led to the ignoring of the multivariate research by most investigators in the area, as evidenced by a passing reference to such research, which has been of no small volume during the past 20 years, by objections raised in the volume by Cofer and Appley (1966), who claim to have done so due to a lack of arousal operations in the multivariate research designs. This claim reduces to the by now seemingly worn issue between the multivariate and bivariate approach. The bivariate investigator manipulates some independent variable and thereby defines his operations as "arousal producing," "drive incrementing," etc. The multivariate position is that sound measurement of necessity precedes such manipulative experimentation, for the manipulation of the independent variable $X$ may concommitantly vary $P$, $Q$, and $R$, unless the investigator is able to assert confidently and unashamedly that he has succeeded in "holding constant" all other variables; therefore, one has no idea of whether the change in the dependent variable $Y$ is due, wholly or in part, to the manipulation of $X$. Cattell as early as 1946 proposed that dynamic traits be defined as behavioral differences occurring when the tasks vary along an incentive dimension, but recognized that this definition assumed that the tasks psychologists require their subjects to perform can be classified by the psychologist as varying primarily in incentive value. Bivariate investigators tended to have faith in their classificatory powers, whereas multivariate investigators, rather than classify the tasks by inspection, rely on some quantitative method of classification, such as factor analysis of diverse sets of a priori measures. Results of such investigations can be found in Cattell (1957a), H. J. Eysenck (1953c), J. W. French (1951, 1953), J. P. Guilford

(1959a), Hundelby, Pawlik, and Cattell (1965), J. L. Horn (1966c), and Cattell and Warburton (1967).

As noted by J. L. Horn (1966c), however, an entirely successful separation of dynamic and temperament traits has not been fully achieved by factor analytic investigations, and correlations between dynamic and temperament traits (Cattell & Child, 1975) suggest that they cannot ever be fully separated. Until unambiguous results are forthcoming, the present writers will be content to reiterate J. L. Horn's (1966c) statement that the development of the dynamic calculus by Cattell stands as a significant advance in rendering distinct the operational definition of dynamic traits.

## 7　SUMMARY

1. The fundamental unit of motivation in the dynamic calculus model is the *attitude*, defined by the paradigm "In these circumstances, I want so much to do this with that," which takes account of the situation in which the behavior is to occur, the strength and direction of the motive, the specific course of action, and the attitude object. Several devices have been developed to measure a number of such attitudes.

2. Research that has held attitude constant and factored over a number of devices has typically yielded five primary and two secondary motivational component factors.

3. Research aimed at the dynamic structure holds the device constant (or sums over several) and analyzes the interrelationships among a number of attitudes. The factors resulting from such analyses have been classified as ergs, primarily genetically determined, and engrams, environmentally determined. The engrams are further subdivided into sentiments—conscious, learned attitude aggregates—and complexes—repressed attitude aggregates.

4. A currently important topic to both basic research and applied psychologists is that of conflict among motives. There are at least two sources of such conflict in terms of the dynamic calculus model: conflict among the components of motivation and conflict among dynamic structures. Several methods of deriving such indexes of conflict have been suggested, but the research necessary to evaluate the predictive efficiency of such indexes has not yet been conducted.

5. A further topic of interest to the researcher in the area of motivation is the elimination of individual differences of ability and personality from the assessment of motivational strength.

6. The inclusion of the dynamic concepts in Cattell's comprehensive learning theory provides the researcher with a model of human behavior that is at once richer and of greater complexity than any that precedes it. The possibilities for research aimed at testing the adequacy of the model are enormous, and the authors have attempted to outline a few directions future research should take.

# 6

# Personality and Ability Theory

**John L. Horn**
*University of Denver*
*Denver, Colorado*

## 1 ORIENTATION

### 1.1 Belief that Abilities are Important

Many books on personality theory do not contain a chapter on human abilities. This is an unfortunate omission. For if there is one side of personality that stands out more prominently than any other, it is the many faceted side on which the abilities are found. A citizen of any employment rarely gets through the course of a day without making at least several judgments about the abilities of his associates; such judgments are essential in many occupations. In psychological evaluations of personality, as in educational and industrial settings and in diagnoses of psychopathology, the abilities are as the *ground*, so to speak, against which the *figure* of the rest of the personality can best be seen. When one knows little about human abilities, one does not fully appreciate many other aspects of personality. Hence, it is important in studying personality to develop and maintain an apperceptive mass in which are embedded major regularities and viewpoints pertaining to human abilities.

The area of abilities is one of the oldest and most thoroughly researched in psychology. Today, it may well be true that more is known about human abilities than is known about any other aspect of personal-

ity. The meaning of an ability concept such as intelligence is based on an inductive-hypothetico-deductive chain of research that has coiled upward for over 70 years and in which literally thousands of hypotheses have been examined. Only a minuscule part of this research can be discussed in a single chapter of a book. Therefore, this chapter has been organized to provide an overview of some major findings and a summary of research trends that relate pointedly to efforts to understand the total person. At best, this presentation can provide only an introduction to topics the reader must study more intensively if he is to gain a really good understanding of human abilities.

### 1.2 Neglect of Some Kinds of Abilities

Emphasis in the chapter is placed on what, for lack of a better name, are called *intellectual abilities*, with the result that many important kinds of abilities—artistic, acting, musical, athletic, psychomotor, visual, auditory, and so forth—either are not considered at all or are given only passing mention. Such omissions may be justified (in part) on grounds that there are several recent, easily available reviews of relevant research on some of these other abilities (e.g., Cattell & Butcher, 1968; Fleishman, 1964, 1966; Guilford, J. P., 1959, 1967;

Horn, J. L., 1972a, 1973; Pawlik, 1966; Shuter, 1968; Staats, 1968a).

### 1.3  Abilities as Traits

Abilities are thought of as attributes that have many of the properties of *trait*, as this concept is used in general biology. That is, just as blue eye color indicates trait—defined as an enduring characteristic by means of which one person can be distinguished from another—so a magnitude $X$ of an ability is conceived of as indicating trait, in this case a more or less stable characterization of one person as distinct from another person for whom the magnitude of the ability is $Y$. This analogy is not accepted as perfect in all respects, of course. For example, it is not implied that individual differences in abilities are as stable as individual differences in eye color. Learning is important in the development of most abilities, but this is not true for eye color. There may be, and some recent evidence (Horn, J. L., 1972b) suggests that there is a small degree of reliable short period (hourly, daily) fluctuation in human abilities, whereas it is doubtful that any noteworthy amount of such change occurs in eye color. Although abilities are not precisely analogous to biological traits, they are similar enough to make the analogy useful.

Abilities are conceived of in terms of Cattell's attempts to specify logical, operational distinctions between different trait modalities (see Cattell, 1950c; Horn, J. L., 1972a). That is, the term *ability* is used to refer to consistent variations in behavior that accompany variations in the complexity of stimulus patterns to which subjects respond, whereas motivational traits are defined in terms of consistent behavior variations that accompany changes in the incentive values of stimulus patterns. Traits of temperament or style are indicated by the consistent variation that remains after variance (accounted for by motives and abilities) has been removed. Within this context of definition it is recognized that the concept of ability is an abstraction, that any measurement of an ability is based on observations of behaviors in which the ability is not manifested in pure form. This does not distinguish this kind of concept from any other; it merely serves to remind us that any theoretical formulation, however useful, is to some extent Procrustean.

### 1.4  Physiology and Heredity

It is common to refer to an ability such as intelligence as representing neurological potential. It may be implied in such usage that the purpose of research should be to explicate the concept using the terms of neurophysiology, biochemistry, or a similar discipline. Though this is a legitimate and useful way to define ability constructs, it is not the kind of definition developed here. The concept of intelligence will not be specified in terms of the number of neurons in the head or the ratio of grey matter in frontal as compared with lower sections of the brain or in any similar way. Instead, this chapter is based on definition in terms of behavior, not in terms of physiological or biochemical processes. Psychology is distinguished from other disciplines by the fact that the principal subject matter of study is overt behavior. It is necessary to define the major concepts of psychology in such terms in order to provide a basis for relating the phenomena of psychology to the phenomena of other disciplines. Thus, while there will be discussion in this chapter of some of the physiological underpinnings of human abilities, the purpose of such discussion is not to substitute physiological explanation for behavioral explanation, but merely to indicate links that may exist between physiological and psychological functions.

Most books and pedagogically oriented articles on abilities include discussion of what is called the *nature-nurture controversy*—basically a debate (with evidence in the better treatments) over whether manifested abilities, and particularly intelligence, are determined primarily by the influences of genetic endowment or the influences of the environment. Some treatments of this kind (most notably, in recent years, one by Jensen, 1969) even bring questions about racial differences into considerations of the nature-nurture issues. Here, however, these issues generally are ignored, not because they are not important or because they cannot be discussed in balanced and useful ways, but because space is limited and only a few matters can be considered. The issues have been rather fully discussed in a number of recent and easily obtained publications (see Burt, 1966b, 1972; Butcher, 1968; Butcher & Lomax, 1972; Hammond, S. B., 1975; Horn, 1974, 1976; Jensen, 1968, 1969), and the present author is best qualified to discuss other, perhaps equally important, issues.

The discussion here will center on description of the organization of abilities—evidence indicating the distinct kinds of intellectual capacities that people possess. Within this area of emphasis, most of the evidence to be considered is derived from studies of individual differences.

### 1.5  Divergent and Convergent Study

To gain perspective on the immense amount of research that has been done on human abilities, it is useful to recognize two broad categories of investigation. One may be referred to as *divergent*; the other may be said to be *convergent*.

Divergent research has been directed at demonstrating that particular kinds of behavior indicate intellectual functioning. The ambiguity of the term *intelligence* has been much increased by this kind of research. While one investigator has tried to demonstrate that memory—as measured by, for example, a paired-associates test—is integral to intelligence, another has aimed to show that analogic reasoning is essential to this function; still another has argued that intelligence is shown by an adaptive flexibility test; and other investigators have specified still other *essential* qualities of intellect. It reminds one of the blind men who were feeling different parts of an elephant and describing each part in some detail as if each part were the beast itself. The student who reads different accounts of what intelligence is, each account being based on a different set of measurement operations (a different test), is likely to come away with a belief that there is no such beast as intelligence.

Although the divergent kind of research has produced no small amount of confusion, it has had a salubrious effect, too; it has provided a large number of objective measuring devices with which to assess what are, according to the judgments of many insightful researchers, basic intellectual processes. Such devices have been developed to demonstrate a variety of thinking processes, such as those referred to as reasoning, abstracting, recognizing, recalling, encoding, decoding, problem solving, learning, and discriminating. Thus, divergent research has given us the means for obtaining operational definition of many of the ways people display abilities.

The confusion generated by this kind of research should not be underestimated, however. Integrative principles are needed to bring organization to the myriad of descriptions provided by divergent research and to give direction to further investigation. Convergent study answers this need.

Two basic approaches may be discerned in convergent study. These have been described in some detail in J. L. Horn (1972a) under the headings of a priori and behavioral theories. In essence, the former is characterized by common sense categories of classification, whereas the latter is based on classifications that derived from systematic analyses of substantial sets of data.

Cattell reminds us in the introductory chapter of this book that a priori classification, necessary as it is at many places in the development of theory, suffers from the fact that it is based most firmly on devotion to prior belief and what is called *logic*, rather than devotion to discovery of the novel regularities that can be found by careful study of data. When there are many complex elements to comprehend, as there are in the study of abilities, a priori classification can easily lead to arbitrary, conventional orderings that are virtually unrelated to actual functioning. When they can be used, empirical procedures are preferable for helping an investigator to become aware of the organizations that actually exist in a range of phenomena. Of such procedures, simple structure factor analysis is perhaps the most widely used in the study of abilities, although hierarchical factor analysis, as employed in the pioneering and insightful work of investigators such as Spearman (1904, 1927), Burt (1909, 1949) and Vernon (1950, 1961), also has been influential. In what follows, major emphasis is given to the implications of research based on simple structure analyses. In later sections, hierarchical models will be considered.

## 2 STRUCTURAL THEORY OF PRIMARY MENTAL ABILITIES

The many ability measurements obtainable with devices developed in divergent research may be said to constitute a domain

of intellectual processes.[1] A purpose of convergent research is to make this domain more comprehensible. In factor-analytic study, a sample of measurement devices (and consequent ability performances) is drawn from this domain and the analyses are directed at showing the number and nature of the basic processes operating over the observed performances. If the simple structure method of factor analysis is employed, an assumption of the analysis is that the basic processes will be indicated by about the same number of variables—that each will account for about as much of the total reliable (common) variability as any other. In contrast, hierarchical methods of factor analysis involve an implicit assumption that some abilities are broader (account for substantially more variability) than other abilities.

Replications of many simple structure studies, each based on overlapping but somewhat different samples from the variable domain (and based on quite different samples of subjects), have shown us that tasks which, a priori, might seem to be quite different have much in common and that seemingly similar tasks require rather different abilities. This research also has indicated that the multitude of tests developed in divergent research can be comprehended in terms of a relatively small number of basic abilities—what will be referred to as *primary abilities* (a name suggested by Thurstone, 1938b, in the pioneering investigation in this area).

The exact number of primary abilities is not presently known and, indeed, we should not imply that this number ever will be known with finality. The issue here is rather

---

[1] We might call this the *explored* domain by recognizing the likelihood that many basic processes of intellect have not yet to be described and measured.

similar to the one pertaining to the number of elements in chemistry: The number identified at a given time in history need not be the number needed to account for all observables studied (or to be studied) in the discipline. Shown in Table 1, however, are some of the better established of the primary abilities, as recorded by Cattell and Butcher (1968); J. W. French (1953); J. W. French, Ekstrom, and Price (1963); J. P. Guilford (1959, 1967); J. L. Horn (1965, 1970a, 1972a); and Pawlik (1966).

It is not possible in the confines of an overview chapter to provide the kind of detailed discussion that is needed to enable the reader to gain a good understanding of each factor listed in Table 1. Such discussion is provided in the references cited in the previous paragraph. The reader is well advised to consult these. Here, only some general points can be developed.

First, we may note that most factors listed in Table 1 are defined by several somewhat dissimilar tests—that is, tests which could be expected to involve different intellectual functions. The factors thus do not represent test specific behavior. They are not examples of the narrow meaning of operational definition in which a concept is defined in terms of the operations of a particular test. Instead, they can be said to represent operational definitions of functions which pervade performance on several kinds of tasks.

No single investigation has been large enough to allow for simultaneous identification of all of the factors listed in Table 1, and the factors are not equally well replicated. Some have been found in as few as three studies issuing from a single laboratory, whereas others have appeared in over 50 separate investigations conducted by almost as many researchers. Thus, questions remain as to whether particular factors are, in fact, distinct. According to the J. W.

French, Ekstrom, and Price (1963) summary, the evidence supports a claim that there are 24 separate primary abilities, whereas J. P. Guilford's (1967) report suggests that more than 60 distinct primaries can now be identified. The listing of Table 1 is a compromise of these two positions and is intended only to suggest the general nature of results in this area, not to provide the definitive summary. To understand the major implications for theory development, it is sufficient to recognize that at least several distinct abilities underlie what is commonly thought of as intelligence or, more broadly, intellectual functioning.

Not all the reliable variance of all the tests thus far considered in factor-analytic work can be accounted for by established primaries. Hence, it should not be assumed that the work of convergent research is by any means complete. On the other hand, it is true that the primaries account for the order of 70–80% of the reliable test variance in the studies in which they have been identified. It seems likely that in a truly comprehensive study, in which all established primaries could appear, the amount of reliable variance not accounted for by the primaries would be small.

The system of primary abilities is a considerable integrative simplification of the results from divergent research, although this might not seem to be true at first thought. But when it is realized that hundreds, perhaps thousands, of tests have been tried out in the hundreds of studies upon which Table 1 is based, one can see that even a system with as many as 120 primaries (as required in Guilford's 1967 theory) achieves a noteworthy degree of parsimony. Of course, further structuring of the data is desirable and is indicated by work that is discussed in subsequent sections; but much of this follows from development of the system of primary abilities. This develop-

TABLE 1  Primary mental ability factors

| Factors | J. W. French (1963) | J. W. French (1951) | J. P. Guilford (1960, 1967) |
|---|---|---|---|
| **A. Factors involving (primarily) figural content** | | | |
| 1. Visualization | *Vz* | *Vi* | CFT |
| 2. Flexibility of Closure, Gestalt Flexibility, Visual Cognition | *Cf* | *Gf* | NFT |
| 3. Speed of Closure, Gestalt Perception | *Cs* | *GP* | CFU |
| 4. Spatial Orientation, Spatial Relations | *S* | *SO* | CFS |
| 5. Perceptual Speed, Speed of Symbol Discrimination | *P* | *P* | ESU |
| 6. Figural Adaptive Flexibility | *Xa* | | DFT |
| 7. Semantic Redefinition | *Re* | | NMT |
| 8. Spatial Scanning, Perceptual Foresight | *Se* | | CFI |
| 9. Length Estimation | *Le* | *LE* | |
| 10. Figural Relations | | | CFR |
| 11. Figural Classification | | | CFC |
| 12. Speed of Alternating Reversals, Figural Spontaneous Flexibility | | *PA* | DFC |
| **B. Factors involving (primarily) symbolic content** | | | |
| 13. Induction, Symbolic Correlates | *I* | *I* | NSR |
| 14. Symbol Cognition | | | CSU |
| 15. Cognition of Symbolic Classes | | | CSC |
| 16. Symbolic Relations | | | CSR |
| 17. Convergent Production of Symbolic Systems | | | NSS |
| 18. Symbolic Identification | | | ESU |
| 19. Symbol Manipulation | | | ESR |
| **C. Factors involving (primarily) semantic content** | | | |
| 20. Verbal Comprehension | *V* | *V* | CMU |
| 21. Mechanical Knowledge, Mechanical Information | *Mk* | *ME* | |
| 22. General Reasoning, Deduction | *R* | *D* | CMS |
| 23. Syllogistic Reasoning, Logical Evaluation | *Rs* | *D* | |
| 24. Sensitivity to Problems | *SEP* | | EMI |
| 25. Judgment | | *J* | EMT |
| 26. Semantic Relations | | | CMR |
| 27. Experiential Evaluation | | | ESU |
| 28. Conceptual Classifications | | | CMC |
| 29. Penetration | | | CMI |
| 30. Conceptual Classifications | | | CMI |
| 31. Concept Naming | | | NMU |
| 32. Convergent Production of Semantic Classes | | | NMC |
| 33. Semantic Correlates | | | NMR |
| 34. Ordering | | | NMS |
| 35. Semantic Redefinition | | | NMT |
| **D. Semantic fluency factors** | | | |
| 36. Ideational Fluency | *Fi* | *IF* | DMU |
| 37. Word Fluency | *Fw* | *W* | DSU |
| 38. Associational Fluency | *Fa* | | DMR |
| 39. Expressional Fluency | *Fe* | *FE* | SSS |
| 40. Spontaneous Flexibility | *Xs* | | DMC |
| 41. Originality | *O* | | DMT |
| 42. Semantic Elaboration | | | DMT |

**TABLE 1** (*continued*) Primary mental ability factors

| Factors | Symbols used by | | |
|---|---|---|---|
| | J. W. French (1963) | J. W. French (1951) | J. P. Guilford (1960, 1967) |
| E. Memory factors | | | |
| 43. Associative Memory, Rote Memory | *Ma* | *N* | *MSR* |
| 44. Memory Span | *Ms* | *Sm* | *MSU* |
| 45. Meaningful Memory | | | *MMR* |
| 46. Memory for Ideas | | | *MMU* |
| 47. Visual Memory | | | *MFU* |
| 48. Memory for Spatial Order | | | *MFC* |
| 49. Memory for Temporal Order | | | *MMS* |
| F. Miscellaneous | | | |
| 50. Number Facility, Number | *N* | *N* | *NSI* |
| 51. Carefulness | | *C* | |
| 52. Schooling | | *Sc* | |
| 53. Perceptual (USES) | | | |

ment thus provides an important first step in the building of a comprehensive theory of human abilities.

The tests that define primary factors are representative of the tasks which are used to measure intelligence and general aptitude in well-known IQ tests, such as the Wechsler, Stanford-Binet, and Lorge-Thorndike. For example, the Information and Vocabulary subtests of the Wechsler scales are almost identical to tests which have been found to define the Verbal Comprehension primary ability factor, $V$, and the Arithmetic subtest of the Wechsler is almost the same as tests found to yield the General Reasoning primary factor, $R$. L. V. Jones (1949) has shown that the performance of 13-year-old children on the Stanford-Binet is predicted by the primaries $V, Rs, R, I, Ma, Ms, Vz,$ and $Cs$. Perhaps not all the thinking processes sampled in general IQ tests are represented by primary mental abilities, but the degree of overlap is much more impressive than the extent of uniqueness.

The overlap of primary mental abilities and IQ has several important implications.

For one thing, it means that research on and with primary abilities is, indirectly, research on intelligence. It means that the several distinct primary abilities are components of the intelligence that is measured by an IQ test. Since different IQ tests involve different collections of subtests and these measure different primary abilities, the intelligence that is measured with one IQ test may be comprised of different abilities than the intelligence measured by another such test. More specifically, this means that whether a person does well or poorly on what is called an intelligence test will depend on which of several primaries are well developed in the person. This is one reason why scores—that is, the IQs—obtained with popular intelligence tests may not agree. More important, this is one reason why there is disagreement in research results on development, or the effects of training: When studies involve different IQ tests, different primary mental abilities may be combined in the composite IQ score; thus, the different relations to independent variables can be found.

It is worth noting that a truly general

measure of *general intelligence* would need to be derived from tasks representing the established primary abilities that can be accepted as indicating some aspect of intelligence. No IQ test presently available is thus representative of what is known about human intellect.

The structure of primary abilities is surprisingly stable across a wide age span, from the first years in school until late maturity. That is to say that, although there is support for a differentiation hypothesis (Burt, 1954; Garrett, 1946; Reinert, 1970)—the idea that an undifferentiated intelligence in early childhood becomes differentiated into primary abilities during development—there is also substantial evidence indicating that the distinctions between different abilities can be seen both early and late in life and that, with rather obvious exceptions (no number ability until children have had opportunities to learn concepts of number), the kinds of primaries identified at different ages are quite similar (e.g., Balinsky, 1941; Cohen, J., 1957; Doppelt, 1950; Hundal, 1966; Osborne, R. T., & Lindsey, 1967; Quereshi, 1973; Reinert, 1970; Stott & Ball, 1965).

The evidence on the stability of factor structure over different age levels does not apply to the question of stability within the person. What evidence there is on this question suggests a simplex pattern; that is, test-retest correlations systematically decrease with increase in time between testings from about .8 over 1 year to perhaps as low as .3 over 5 years (Hoffstaetter & O'Connor, 1956; Humphreys, 1960; 1968).

## 3  THE SYSTEM OF PRIMARIES

### 3.1  Two Major Problems

Investigators who base their developments of theory about human abilities on factor analyses of test performances have become increasingly concerned about an increase in the number of factors identified at what is referred to as the *primary level*. Humphreys (1962a), expressing this concern, notes that "test behavior can almost endlessly be made more specific (and) factors can almost endlessly be fractionated or splintered." This problem is not unique to factor analysis, of course; it is a problem of all analysis. Spearman's (1927) criticism of the *oligarchic doctrine*—"that it leads to an endlessly growing list of faculties"—reminds us that the problem has been with us in the study of abilities for some time.

Factors need to be *over-determined*. Each factor should be represented in an analysis by a sufficient number of variables involving a single influence. The work of Humphreys, Ilgen, McGrath, and Montanelli (1969) suggests that no fewer than four variables per factor are required to give proper overdetermination to a factor solution. That is, if the system of primary abilities is to be regarded as a representative account of intellectual functions that characterize human ability performances, then in each study there should have been four tests indicating each function. Otherwise, the factor that could indicate the function is *underdetermined*. To a large extent, however, the sampling of variables for convergent research has fed on a disorderly growth of divergent research. The synthesis achieved with the system of primary abilities is, in part, merely a synthesis of the historical development of divergent study of mental processes, not a synthesis of an exhaustive and systematic sampling of all such processes. Moreover, some primary factors represent little more than the fact that what are virtually only parallel forms of the same test were included in the analyses.

To deal with the problems of splintering and underdetermination of factors, investigators have sought solutions in which a larger number of variables is required to define a factor than is the case in simple structure analyses. Such factors are said to be broad or more nearly general. There are two commonly used procedures for obtaining broad factors. In one procedure, the primary factors themselves are intercorrelated and factored. In a second kind of procedure, broad group factors are obtained at the level of factoring among tests. There is a variety of such factoring methods (see Burt, 1941; Harman, 1967; Vernon, 1950), but collectively they can be referred to as *hierarchical* procedures. These have been employed for years by British psychologists, perhaps most notably Spearman (1927, 1939), Burt (1941, 1949), and Vernon (1950, 1960). Here, we take a brief glimpse at some of the results that have derived from hierarchical factoring procedures and then examine some of the findings that have come from higher order factoring among primary abilities.

## 3.2 Hierarchical Solutions

The general nature of results obtained by British investigators with hierarchical factoring procedures is suggested by the findings summarized in Table 2. This summary is based on Vernon's work.

It can be seen that the first factor in each solution of Table 2 is *positive-general*; that is, every variable has a positive correlation with the factor. This kind of solution represents a persistent finding in research on abilities; that is, almost all tests designed to measure an aspect of intellect are positively correlated. This correlation is referred to as a finding of *positive manifold*.

In solutions such as those shown in Table 2, the first factor is determined by a procedure (centroid, principal-components) that tends to maximize the variance of a weighted linear composite of all the variables. The correlations of all variables with this composite will be positive to the extent that the positive manifold obtains. If some variables correlate negatively with others, some correlations with the general factor will be negative. Hence, a positive-general first factor represents positive intercorrelations among variables. The magnitude of the factor-variable correlations summarizes the magnitude of the variable-variable intercorrelations.

Table 3 shows positive-general factor results obtained over broad samples of ability variables in analyses that were chosen at random. In typical data based on tests that require persons to cope with complexities, investigators obtain internal consistency reliabilities of the order of .6–.8, test intercorrelations of the order of .2–.7, and positive-general first factor coefficients of the order of those shown in Table 3.

A positive-general first factor is often symbolized as $g$ or $G$. The facts that a $G$ factor summarizes (particularly the condition of positive manifold) are often interpreted as indicating individual differences in intelligence.

Just below $G$ in order of generality in hierarchical solutions are major group factors (of Table 2). Typically, one of these is identified as representing skills of the kind that are taught in the academic curriculum. The symbol $v{:}ed$, standing for verbal-educational, is used to label this factor. A second broad group factor, usually found to be characterized by spatial, symbolic tasks, is referred to as *mechanical-practical ability,* symbolized $k{:}m$.

Below these broad group factors in order of generality are *minor* group factors. The $v{:}ed$ dimension splits, as it were, into verbal and number factors similar to the $V$ and $N$ primary abilities; and $k{:}m$ splits into mechanical, spatial, and manual subfactors.

TABLE 2  Results summarized from Vernon's extensive work (1950, 1960, 1970)

| Test | G | k:m | v:ed | Gv | V | N | Mk |
|---|---|---|---|---|---|---|---|
| | | | Factors | | | | |
| Group-factor analysis on 1,000 Army recruits[a] | | | | | | | |
| Matrices | 79 | 17 | | | | | |
| Assembly | 24 | 89 | | | | | |
| Squares | 59 | 44 | | | | | |
| Bennett Mechanical | 66 | 31 | | | | | |
| Nonverbal Group Test | 78 | 13 | | | | | |
| Verbal | 79 | | 29 | | 45 | | |
| Dictation | 62 | | 54 | | 48 | | |
| Spelling | 68 | | 41 | | 43 | | |
| Instructions | 87 | | 23 | | 09 | | |
| Arithmetic 1 | 72 | | 49 | | | 39 | |
| Arithmetic 2 | 77 | | 36 | | | 32 | |
| Group-factor analysis on 500 ordinary seamen[b] | | | | | | | |
| Matrices | 71 | | | | | | 14 |
| Bennett Mechanical | 55 | 40 | | | | | 29 |
| Mechanical Information | 26 | 45 | | | | | 64 |
| Electrical Information | 50 | 31 | 14 | | | | 65 |
| Memory For Designs | 54 | 40 | | 40 | | | |
| Squares | 51 | 23 | | 40 | | | |
| Mathematics | 76 | | 32 | | | 34 | |
| Dictation | 49 | | 54 | | 30 | | |
| Abstraction | 79 | | 17 | | 30 | | |
| Group-factor analysis on Royal Air Force ground recruits[c] | | | | | | | |
| Matrices | 69 | 30 | 27 | | | | |
| Silhouettes | 59 | 30 | | 34 | | | |
| Spatial | 66 | 57 | | 11 | | | |
| Squares | 52 | 51 | | | | | |
| Group Spatial | 68 | 44 | | | | | |
| Electrical-Mechanical Information | 51 | 13 | 21 | | | | 55 |
| Practical Problems | 53 | 25 | | | | | 33 |
| Mechanical Diagrams | 70 | 12 | | | | | 42 |
| Mechanical Information | 67 | | 17 | 15 | | | 52 |
| Verbal | 67 | | 40 | | 40 | | |
| Spelling | 59 | | 31 | | 45 | | |
| Reading Comprehension | 59 | | 29 | | 38 | | |
| Clerical | 74 | | 35 | 22 | 25 | | |
| Calculations | 61 | | 70 | | | | |
| Arithmetic | 62 | | 67 | | | | |
| Scale and Graph Reading | 88 | | 33 | | | | |
| Dial Reading | 80 | | 32 | | | | |

[a] Gv and Mk not identified in this analysis.
[b] Gv not identified in this analysis.
[c] N not identified in this analysis.

**TABLE 3** Some typical positive-general first-factor results

| Variable no. | Study | | | | Variable no. | Study | | | |
|---|---|---|---|---|---|---|---|---|---|
| | A | B | C | D | | A | B | C | D |
| 1 | 57 | 53 | 56 | 60 | 20 | 09 | 21 | 51 | 62 |
| 2 | 53 | 46 | 48 | 37 | 21 | 56 | 44 | 32 | 60 |
| 3 | 54 | 46 | 62 | 43 | 22 | 62 | 50 | 69 | 60 |
| 4 | 54 | 53 | 34 | 50 | 23 | 51 | 46 | 68 | 69 |
| 5 | 64 | 42 | 40 | 70 | 24 | 53 | 20 | 50 | 64 |
| 6 | 53 | 45 | 53 | 68 | 25 | 57 | 36 | 47 | |
| 7 | 50 | 25 | 41 | 68 | 26 | 60 | 35 | 52 | |
| 8 | 49 | 54 | 40 | 68 | 27 | 50 | 30 | 41 | |
| 9 | 47 | 39 | 39 | 69 | 28 | 52 | 50 | 39 | |
| 10 | 57 | 42 | 58 | 46 | 29 | 36 | 41 | 46 | |
| 11 | 62 | 29 | 52 | 59 | 30 | 37 | 63 | 45 | |
| 12 | 57 | 46 | 34 | 45 | 31 | 53 | 43 | 38 | |
| 13 | 51 | 44 | 17 | 59 | 32 | 22 | 43 | 35 | |
| 14 | 41 | 36 | 27 | 44 | 33 | 40 | | -30 | |
| 15 | 58 | 54 | 37 | 39 | 34 | 62 | | | |
| 16 | 44 | 45 | 38 | 51 | 35 | 33 | | | |
| 17 | 60 | 32 | 20 | 47 | 36 | 65 | | | |
| 18 | 53 | 30 | 27 | 52 | 37 | 41 | | | |
| 19 | 41 | 62 | 39 | 45 | 38 | 48 | | | |
| | | | | | 39 | 13 | | | |

*Note.* Studies are as follows:

A, J. P. Guilford & Christensen, 1956, Centroid procedure; B, J. P. Guilford, Frick, Christensen, & Merrifield, 1957, Centroid procedure; C, Merrifield, Guilford, & Gershon, 1963, Principal-components procedure; D, Harman, 1967, p. 170, Principal-factor procedure.

The kind of theory associated with hierarchical factor solutions is well exemplified by the writings of Burt (1941, 1949). He (1949) expressed the following view:

(The) architecture of the central nervous system or "brain," as well as the events of developments, have a hierarchical form. . . . The mind is organized on what can be called a hierarchical basis . . . (in which) the processes of the lowest level are assumed to consist of simple sensations or simple movements, such as can be artifically isolated and measured by tests of sensory "thresholds" and by the timing of "simple reactions." The next level includes the more complex processes of perception and coordinated move-

ment, as in experiments on the apprehension of form and pattern or on "compound reactions." The third is the associative level— the level of memory and of habit formation. The fourth and highest of all involves the apprehension or application of relations. "Intelligence," as the "integrative capacity of the mind," is manifested at *every* level, but these manifestations differ not only in degree, but also (as introspection suggests) in their qualitative nature. (p. 53)

The empirical referent to the general factor at the fourth level in Burt's theory is the G factor of hierarchical analyses. This is fully discussed in theoretical terms by Spearman (1927).

One difficulty with the British results is that the solutions are not entirely objective (Horn, J. L., 1967a). The rotational criteria used to locate factors beyond the first in this work have not been entirely independent of substantive hypotheses. The first factor usually has been fixed objectively by a procedure that either maximizes, or approximately maximizes, the variance of the first positive-general factor, but in defining the second, third, and subsequent factors the investigator's judgments about the variables are allowed to determine which variables will be used to define a factor. A solution obtained by procedures that allow this kind of obtrusion of theory into findings can be said to be subjective. For a more detailed discussion of subjectivity in factor analysis and the kinds of problems this raises in scientific formulations see J. L. Horn (1967a, 1970b, 1976), J. L. Horn and Knapp (1973), and Humphreys, Ilgen, McGrath, and Montanelli (1969).

## 3.3 Correlation and Independence among Factors and Factor Domains

It should be realized that while the system of primary abilities is intended to provide description of independent attributes of personality, these attributes are not uncorrelated among themselves and are not uncorrelated with other attributes of personality. This is a provocative part of the general theory, one easily misunderstood by the student who is not well informed about the mathematical metatheory of vectors and spaces on which the substantive theory is based. However, the basic point can be illustrated with a simple analogy.

Consider the room in which (in all likelihood) you are sitting. The room is three dimensional. That is, one needs to think of measuring in three directions (vertical, horizontal depth, horizontal width) in order to

specify the locations of the objects in the room. Look into a corner of the room. The vertical line where two walls meet in this corner can be said to be one of the three dimensions, and the lines where the same two walls intersect the floor can be said to be the other two dimensions. All objects in the room—that is, all points on these objects—can be located by measuring along the three dimensions to get the three distances to the object (point). Thus, three dimensions are necessary to describe the objects (you could not get by with fewer), and three are sufficient (you do not need any more).[2]

The angles between dimensions in your room are probably very close to 90°. This respresents zero correlation between dimensions. But notice that the dimensions could be separated by less than or more than 90° (as in fun houses at some amusement parks), and three dimensions would still be necessary and sufficient to describe the locations of all objects in the room. One wall could be tipped in and another out, and you could still locate all objects in terms of their distances from the walls and the floor. An angle less than 90° corresponds to a positive (nonzero) correlation, whereas an angle larger than 90° represents negative correlation. Thus, the room dimensions could be correlated and still represent the fact that three independent dimensions are necessary and sufficient to describe the locations of all objects of a room. Such correlated room dimensions are analogous to correlated primary abilities.

If we can agree on a conventional way of naming the three dimensional measurements of any room (as, for example, "to ceiling," "along the north wall," "along the west

---

[2] This is not to say that all characteristics of the objects are thus described; only their locations are described.

wall") and if we will allow that the dimensional axes of rooms may themselves vary from room to room, then it is possible to identify higher order dimensions (or one such dimension) among the linear dimensions of rooms. Suppose, for example, that big rooms tend to have high ceilings, long north walls, and long west walls, whereas little rooms tend (on an average) to be small in all three of these dimensions. If this is true, then in measurements taken on samples of rooms, the three dimensions of floor, north wall, and west wall would be found to be positively intercorrelated and a general factor could be identified on the basis of these correlations. Such analyses would thus enable us to step up the abstraction ladder from the linear dimensions of space to a volume dimension. This kind of step can be made also in the realm of abilities by allowing primary ability dimensions to be correlated (if the data indicate this) and then factoring to define a second-order dimension or dimensions among the primaries.

One might suppose that the *personality* of a room would need to be understood not only in terms of size and the locations and shapes of objects (distance dimensions), but also in terms of the textures of objects—that is, whether objects are hard or soft, rough or smooth, and so forth. It is reasonable to suppose, too, that textures have dimensions independent of distance dimensions, independent in the sense that phenomena described in terms of one set of dimensions (distance) could not be adequately described in terms of the other set of dimensions (texture): One could not describe the hardness of objects in a room, for example, by use of distance dimensions. The distinction between distance and texture dimensions represents the concept of *independence of factor domains*. In the present context, it is a distinction between primary abilities and other attributes of personality.

Even when two dimensional *sets*—two factor domains—are independent, it is possible for a particular dimension of one set to be correlated with a dimension of the other set. For example, a dimension of hardness of objects in a room can be correlated with a dimension of vertical location of objects, if one finds that hard objects (e.g., light fixtures) are more commonly located in the upper part of a room. Similarly, a primary ability can be correlated with a nonintellectual dimension of personality even though the two dimensions are from dimensional systems that are quite independent.

It will be our purpose now to consider some implications of the fact that primary abilities are intercorrelated. In a subsequent section of this chapter we deal with the idea that ability dimensions are correlated with other aspects of personality.

## 3.4 Higher Order Factoring among Primary Abilities

When it was originally presented, Thurstone's (1935, 1938b, 1940b) simple structure model and theory of primary abilities (as outlined earlier) provided a distinct alternative to hierarchical theories of the kind mentioned in the last section. Rather than solving for a *G* factor and broad group factors, Thurstone solved for several separate, largely independent, and almost equally broad factors. It can be argued that if Thurstone required primary factors to be positively correlated,[3] then implicitly he accepted the need for a general factor. It appears, however, that initially he was open to persuasion by the data on this point. In

[3] In his early presentations of the simple structure model, Thurstone had orthogonal factors. Later, he argued that simple structure might not be achieved if factors were required to be orthogonal and that, therefore, the general model should be oblique.

1935 he wrote, "Even if the intercorrelations are positive or zero, it does not follow that the trait configuration can be inscribed in a positive manifold." Thus, he seemed to be saying that a positive manifold among test intercorrelations does not necessarily require a positive manifold among primary factors or a single factor at the top in a hierarchical factor solution.

In fact, Thurstone rotated to simple structure in a way that tended to maintain positive intercorrelations among the primary abilities. No doubt, too, repeated findings of positive manifold among intercorrelations of ability tests provided a persistent argument against acceptance of a one-level theory of primary abilities. Shortly after Thurstone's primary abilities studies appeared, H. J. Eysenck (1939), Spearman (1939) and Holzinger and Harman (1938) reanalyzed Thurstone's data to show that the correlations permitted a general factor in addition to some of the primaries Thurstone had found. It seemed, indeed, that the data required recognition of broader influences than were represented in the system of primary abilities. Then, in a widely cited study, Thurstone and Thurstone (1941), after carefully rotating $V$, $N$, $S$, $Fw$, $Ma$, and $I$ primary factors into a correlated positive manifold simple structure, reasoned:

If these six primary abilities are correlated because of some general intellective factor ... the rank of the correlation matrix (for the primaries) should be one.... Upon further examination, this actually proves to be the case.... Our findings ... support Spearman's claim for a general intellective factor.

This study was followed by several others showing a general factor among primary mental abilities (Blewett, 1954; Goodman, 1943; Mellone, 1944).

The first factor in a bifactor hierarchical solution is usually similar to the second-order factor derived from primary factor intercorrelations. The conclusion apparently following from this observation is that the $G$ factor isolated first in the British studies is equivalent to the second-order factor isolated last in the previously cited American studies. This seems to be the conclusion most investigators on both sides of the Atlantic have drawn. It seems, too, that it is often implicitly assumed that the ability factors regarded as *primary* in the United States (e.g., those listed in Table 1) are at least roughly equivalent to the factors just below *v:ed* and *k:m* in the British hierarchical solutions. There is a mild contradiction in these assumptions, however, for the last assumption implies that two factors (not one) should be found at the second order among primaries. Possibly, the $G$ factor would then be isolated at the third order.

According to the substantive theories of Spearman and Burt, the $G$ factor should have its highest correlations with tests that require high-level abstraction in the apprehension of complex relations, whereas perceptual, recall, and fluency tests should have relatively low correlations with $G$. In his review of several studies, however, Rimoldi (1951) found that the pattern of high and low coefficients in the general factor varied a great deal and was not consistently in accord with the theories of Spearman and Burt. It seemed that the pattern of loadings for the first factor defined in accordance with the procedures of hierarchical analysis mainly indicated the number of variables of a particular kind that were included in the analysis, rather than an ordering of variables in terms of the extent to which they required the eduction of relations.

In his own study, Rimoldi was especially careful to select variables in a way that properly represented the concepts of the theory of $G$. Considering the careful theorizing and design in Rimoldi's study, it is interesting that he found three factors, not one, in second-order analyses of the intercorrelations among primary abilities. His first factor was defined by the primaries known as Induction ($I$), Figural Classification ($CFC$), Evaluation ($Rs$), and Conceptual Classifications ($CMC$). This factor is thus similar to the broad group factor identified as $k:m$ in Vernon's system. The second factor in Rimoldi's results was defined primarily by Verbal Comprehension ($V$) and General Reasoning ($R$), but had a generous loading on Number Facility ($N$) as well. This is similar to the $v:ed$ factor of Vernon's system. The third factor involved only one unique primary, Cognition of Symbolic Classes ($CSC$). Rimoldi's results thus suggest that second-order analyses among primary abilities should lead to broad group factors of the kind that are identified second in hierarchical analyses, not to the $G$ factor that is identified first in these analyses.

There are now several studies in the literature which support the conclusion of the preceding paragraph (Botzum, 1951; Martin, L., & Adkins, 1954; and studies to be reviewed in some detail in the next section). It seems therefore that rapprochement between the results from hierarchical and primary ability factorings is possible. Indeed, it seems that we can think of human intellect as organized at one level of analysis in respect to a number of primary mental abilities that are themselves organized at a second level of analysis into clusterings representing a small number of broad abilities. These broad abilities may in turn be interrelated in ways that suggest an interlocking of influences at a general level in what is identified as $G$.

## 3.5 Analyses of the Wechsler Subscales

It is worth noting that the rapprochement of factoring work extends to a wider set of studies than those based on British hierarchical analyses and those designed to reveal primary abilities. In particular, there are a number of studies of the Wechsler subscales that show results that are compatible with the conclusions of the last paragraph. If the Wechsler subscales are regarded as markers for primary factors, the factors among the subscales may be regarded as indicative of the second-order structure of the primaries. With this assumption, the results from several studies can be seen to replicate a finding of two second-order factors which are similar to the $k:m$ and $v:ed$ factors found in hierarchical studies. A third factor is indicated with some consistency in some of these studies, as well as in the Botzum (1951) and Rimoldi (1951) investigations. This factor appears to represent a spatial-visualization function.

As a typical example of factor analyses of the Wechsler Adult Intelligence Scale (WAIS) subscales, we may take Birren's (1952) work. In this study, one broad factor was defined by Block Design, Digit Span, Arithmetic, and Digit-Symbols—a $k:m$ factor—whereas a second factor was defined by Vocabulary, Information, Similarities, and Comprehension—the $v:ed$ dimension. In several other studies on the Bellevue, WAIS, and the Wechsler Intelligence Scale for Children (WISC), there was good agreement in finding these two factors as well as another involving Object Assembly, Picture Completion, and Block Design (Balinsky, 1941; Burt, 1960; Cohen, J., 1957, 1959; Davis, P. C., 1956; Jackson, M. A., 1960; Saunders, 1958). Balinsky's (1941) and J. Cohen's (1959) results showed that the two main factors of the Wechsler scales appear consistently in separate analyses on different age groups in later childhood and adulthood, but the factor or factors beyond the first two are considerably more difficult to replicate using only the Wechsler subtests.

### 3.6 Data on Development and the Theory of Fluid and Crystallized Intelligence

As early as 1941, Cattell presented a theory that was intended to be consistent with findings of the kind reviewed in previous sections and also consistent with results, then emerging, pertaining to brain damage, aging in adulthood, and education experiences. Sixteen years later (Cattell, 1957a), the theory was extensively modified and several specific hypotheses were derived, at which time it was referred to as the theory of *fluid intelligence,* here symbolized *Gf* and *crystallized intelligence*, here represented by the symbol *Gc*. These two kinds of intelligence correspond to the two broad dimensions indicated in hierarchical and second-order primary factorings, *Gf* being similar to what was referred to as *k:m* in previous sections and *Gc* representing the findings indicated by what was referred to as *v:ed*.[4] There have been several tests of hypotheses derived from the theory—namely, in studies by Cattell (1963f, 1967b), J. L. Horn (1965,

1966b, 1972b), J. L. Horn and Bramble (1967), J. L. Horn and Cattell (1966a), Rossman and Horn (1972), Shucard and Horn (1972) on structure, and in the investigations of J. L. Horn and Cattell (1966b, 1967) on development. Several recent modifications of the theory were proposed to take account of results and theory pertaining to the acquisition of abilities (Cattell, 1963a, 1970a; Cattell & Butcher, 1968; Horn, J. L., 1965a, 1966b, 1967, 1968, 1972a, 1976). Only the barest of outlines of the theory can be given in what follows.

Perhaps the principal findings leading to the initial expression of the theory were those showing that if brain damage occurs in adulthood, some abilities are much more affected than are other abilities (see Crown, 1951; Hebb, 1949; Horn, J. L., 1965a, 1970a, 1972c; Payne, 1961; Willett, 1961). It appears that if intelligence is defined primarily in terms of the kinds of prudent judgment, sound inference, and clear expression that depend on knowledge of the culture and verbal facility—the abilities of *Gc*—then there may be relatively little permanent change in intelligence following brain injury, even that as severe as hemidecortication. But if intelligence is defined primarily in terms of performances on tasks demanding that people quickly perceive novel and complex relations or draw purely logical consequences—the abilities of *Gf*—then it seems there is loss of intelligence with brain injury, even when this occurs in areas other than the prefrontal lobes. These differences in patterns of effects appear only, or primarily, when brain injury is sustained in adulthood, or late childhood; if brain damage occurs at a young age, then all intellectual functions usually are found to be impaired, seemingly about equally.

The findings pertaining to aging in adulthood and performance on putative tests of

---

[4] To say that the *v:ed* and *k:m* factors are similar to the *Gc* and *Gf* dimensions respectively is not to say that they are identical or that the theories associated with the two sets of factors are in all cases congruent. Indeed, J. L. Horn and Cattell (1966a) pointed to notable differences between the two theories. Principal among these differences are the developmental concepts (there being several of these in *Gf-Gc* theory) and the fact that *Gf* is most closely linked with the Spearman concept of *G*, whereas in Vernon's theory *v:ed* is most closely related to *G* and *k:m* is said to be a kind of practical (as opposed to abstracting) ability.

intelligence are more extensive than those on brain damage and performance. But where the two sets intersect, they are in many ways complementary.

An overwhelming majority of cross-sectional studies relating aging in adulthood to performance on well-known IQ tests (e.g., WAIS, Stanford-Binet, and Army Alpha) have shown that the average of the scores for older adults is lower than the average for younger adults (for reviews, see Anastasi, 1961; Jones, H. E., 1959; Horn, J. L., 1970a; Tyler, L. E., 1960). In Horn's review, 15 of 16 studies supported this conclusion. In the study that provided the exception—a cross-sectional comparison of older and younger business executives—there was reason to believe that the circumstances of employment might have produced more stringent selection of the older persons on the criterion measure.

Findings frequently cited as contradicting the conclusion that IQ declines in adulthood can be seen on closer examination to be qualifications, not contradictions. For example, the results of many studies (Bayley, 1957; Shuey, 1948) showed that scores do not decline as early as some investigators had supposed; they suggested that the peak performance may be reached in the 20s rather than the teens, that decline is hardly detectable in the 20s and early 30s, and that over the span from age 30 to age 50 it is not noticeable if comparison periods are less than a decade. In some longitudinal studies (Jones, H. E., 1959), it can be seen that the first scores were obtained at an age (14–17 years) before peak performance would be attained and the follow-up scores were obtained at an age (29–33 years) before decline would be at all noticeable.

A few longitudinal studies (particularly Owens, 1953, 1966) and a large number of cross-sectional studies indicated that results which seem to contradict the findings show-ing decline of intelligence with aging in adulthood are mainly a consequence of different operational definitions of intelligence. Some studies used tests which measure $Gc$ primarily, while other studies involved tests in which there is emphasis on the measurement of $Gf$. When carefully evaluated, the results from these studies can be seen to be consistent with those pertaining to the effects of brain damage on abilities. In particular, when intelligence is operationally defined in terms of the kinds of abilities which are not much affected by brain damage, little or no aging decline is found; indeed, in several studies, increases were found. On the other hand, when intelligence is defined primarily in terms of the kinds of abilities affected by brain damage, then decline is clearly shown. In J. L. Horn's (1970a) review, no fewer than 20 studies indicated that with increasing age in adulthood, there was either no noticeable change or else improvement in performance on tests such as Esoteric-Word Analogies (the Concept Mastery test of the Bayley-Oden, 1955, study), Vocabulary, General Information, Similarities, Comprehension, Practical Judgment, Preplanning, Decisions, and Proverbs. These are the tests that characterize $Gc$. Horn found, however, that the evidence indicated notable decline with aging in performance on tests such as Common-Word Analogies, Matrices, Letter Series, Possible Classifications, Block Designs, and Digit Span, the tests characterizing the $Gf$ dimension. Since IQ tests are mixtures of the subtests for which decline is noted and the subtests for which no decline, or some improvement, is found, there tends to be a cancelling of the effects. Thus, depending on which kind of subtest provides the major portion of measurement variance in the IQ test, there can be aging decline or no such decline and apparent inconsistency in findings from one study to another.

Considering the fact that most of the studies on general IQ indicate decline in intelligence during adulthood, the suggestion is that these tests measure more of the functions of the *Gf* dimension than of the *Gc* dimension.

The evidence that J. L. Horn (1970a) reviewed suggests that, on the average, there is increase in brain damage with an increase in aging. This conclusion is reasonable because there are many factors that can produce brain damage (anoxia, blows to the head, monoxide poisoning, and a variety of intoxicants such as alcohol). These causes of brain damage can be expected to occur with chance-like frequency over time; thus the longer one lives, the more likely it is that some of these influences will have affected him. Most of the studies supporting this reasoning are cross sectional, but they indicate rather consistently that physiological differences in the brains of older, as compared with younger, adults parallel the differences in brains where damage is known to have occurred and brains for which there is no evidence of damage (for review, see Korenchevsky, 1962; Horn, J. L., 1970a; Gershon & Raskin, 1975). In particular, the evidence suggests that the average weight of brain neural tissue decreases from about 1,400 g in the late teens to about 1,350 g by age 55, while there is a complementary increase in "empty" space in the brain area.

The conclusion that seems to follow from these various findings is that the two broad factors which show up rather consistently in factor-analytic study may well represent, in one factor, clusterings of those abilities most affected by influences associated with brain damage and aging and, in the other factor, abilities not very much affected by these influences. It is instructive to consider how development might proceed to produce two such broad patterns of abilities.

Turning first to a consideration of development in childhood, it was found that the best predictor of achievement in school, university, and school-like training programs (e.g., in the armed forces) usually is previous achievement in similar situations. For example, the best predictors of school grades in 1 year are the school grades of the previous year (Humphreys, 1968). Moreover, the ability to predict a given year's achievement from the achievement of previous years increases with increase in grade level and with increase in the amount of previous achievement entering into the prediction.

Many factors are involved in producing achievement. Ferguson (1956) described how *transfer* can operate to produce achievement. Moreover, achievement at a given time in development can be seen to depend on the achievements of a previous period. Several studies (Duncanson, 1964; Fleishman, 1967; Humphreys, 1968) indicated that, as learning progresses in a particular area, it tends to consolidate in patterns of skills that are similar to the patterns represented by primary ability factors.

Cattell (1971a) and Hayes (1962) have emphasized the role of interests and sentiments in ability development. Skills are learned in the service of basic psychophysiological needs. Whether a particular ability is strongly developed can depend on the way needs are met at particular dynamic crossroads in development (Cattell, 1950c). In particular, relatively little progress in the development of some kinds of abilities (e.g., those of abstraction) may occur until after certain basic needs are satisified. Cattell's theory also involves the notion that motives become associated with institutions or particular persons—the home, mother, and particular teacher—and these then become instrumental in further development. For example, profound development of mathematical ability in a person may be attributed in large part to interactions one has with a mathematics teacher met in high school.

It is evident, too, that a variety of maladjustments contribute in complex ways to ability development. Indeed, neuroticism is sometimes mistaken for intelligence, particularly in childhood, although existing evidence suggests that the factors of Neuroticism exist in a variable domain that is independent of the domain of Abilities (Cattell & Scheier, 1961).

Other important influences in ability development include avoidance learning and inhibition, as emphasized by Jensen (1967), labeling and learning not to learn (Horn, J. L., 1967b), realism of aspirations (Hammond, S. B., 1976), and kind of reward (Bloom, 1965; Stolurow, 1964; Vernon, 1970).

Although achievements are conglomerates of many influences, there are reasons to expect that in broad terms school-like achievement is unitary. For one thing, the school is an institution with which are associated the satisfactions, and denials of satisfaction, of many motives; hence, the school is itself the core of a major sentiment. Children who learn to like school can be expected to achieve well in a broad spectrum of school subjects, whereas children who learn to dislike school will achieve less well in these subjects. Quite diverse achievements could be made unitary in the service of this sentiment. For another thing, there is genuine similarity (in the transfer sense) and interdependence in school achievements. In U.S. schools, one must learn to understand American English before he can learn mathematics in courses taught in this language; and learning the concept of addition has some transfer value in learning the concept of integration. Unitariness in achievement is produced also by the systems of prerequisites and time in service which operate in most educational institutions: A person who sits in a particular course and learns something there is allowed to go into another course and learn something there, even though there may be no transfer similarity or other interdependence between the two courses. Many influences can operate in this interdependent way to produce positive correlation in a wide variety of school-like achievements (see Horn, J. L., 1967b, 1968, 1970a). Collectively, these influences may be said to be those of acculturation.

Over the course of development, from infancy to old age, acculturational influences operate in a somewhat interdependent manner to produce a more or less unitary set of abilities that are commonly regarded as indicants of intelligence. To some extent, such influences operate independently of neural-physiological structural influences, which also affect intellectual development. Development of exceptionally favorable sentiment with respect to educational institutions, for example, can compensate for loss of capacity resulting from injury. Moreover, it appears that the abilities welded together by acculturational influences are also the abilities least affected by brain damage and aging in adulthood and are the abilities appearing in one of the broad second-level dimensions of factor-analytic research. Because these abilities appear to crystallize out of experience and yet also are abilities that people commonly refer to as indicating intelligence, Cattell labeled the factor of such abilities *Crystallized Intelligence.*

It has been noted that some tests that are said to indicate intelligence show that substantial decline in performance occurs when the neural-physiological structures are damaged. It has been noted, too, that the tests that most surely indicate this decline are those that most consistently appear in the second of two broad dimensions that have been identified in a variety of factor-analytic studies. It appears, therefore, that this second dimension represents a kind of intelligence, the functioning of which is rather immediately tied to the functioning of the neural-physiological structures. This kind of intelligence was said by Cattell to be *fluid* in the sense that it could be diverted into almost any activity calling for the exercise of intelligence. Whether or not this is a major characteristic of this form of intelligence, it has become known as *Fluid Intelligence*.

*Gf* is based on very basic intellectual capacities, which are here referred to as *anlages*; they seem to be little affected by acculturation influences. Such processes have been described in some detail in J. L. Horn (1970a). Here we might note simply that an ability like immediate memory (span of apprehension) is an example of an anlage function: The number of elements one can retain in immediate memory is affected by several factors (e.g., anxiety), but given a modicum of control over these, it would seem that a major portion of the variance in such memory reflects the ongoing function of an aspect of intelligence that is not very much affected by acculturation. Moreover, it seems that a number of reasoning tasks also involve this, or a similar, anlage function (Horn, J. L., 1968; 1970a).

What Horn referred to as *incidental learning* builds on the elementary anlage functions to develop in *Gf* a number of basic thinking capabilities called *aids*. Incidental learning occurs largely independently of the learning promoted by acculturation. For example, the evidence of several investigations based on the formulations of Piaget suggest that children learn such intellectual capabilities as conservation, reversibility, and nullifiability regardless of their nationality, language group, or culture, and whether or not they are raised by parents—and in schools—that urge them to acquire these skills. Yet the abilities acquired in this

manner are those involved in much concept attainment, reasoning, and abstracting—processes emphasized in the tests that define the *Gf* factor and show performance decline accompanying brain damage.

It follows from these various considerations that, at some order of analysis of the interrelationships among tests and consequent primary abilities, there should be found two broad factors representing two broad influences—that of acculturation and that of the neural-physiological structure. The factor representing the first kind of influence should be defined primarily by tests of acculturational achievement in the broad sense of this term. The factor representing the second kind of influence should be defined by tests in which the limits of the elementary relation-perceiving, correlate-educing capacities determine the limits of performance. The latter is the *Gf* factor, whereas the factor representing acculturation is *Gc*.

Table 4 provides a summary of the results from several recent studies showing the character of the *Gf* and *Gc* factors. This table shows that *Gf* is manifested in abilities involving reasoning (Figural-*CFR*, Symbolic-*I*, Semantic-*CMR*, *R*) and Memory (associative and span). Most noteworthy is the fact that the variables defining this factor are not of the kind that depend on advanced schooling or indicate learned occupations. The factor *Gc*, on the other hand, shows up most surely in abilities in which advanced acculturation is indicated, abilities such as Verbal Comprehension (*V*), Experiential Evaluation (*EMS*), Number (*N*), and Formal Reasoning (*Rs*).

Figure 1 presents a summary of results obtained on age differences in *Gf* and *Gc* in adulthood (Horn, J. L., & Cattell, 1966b, 1967). When relatively pure measures of these two factors are obtained by linear combination of the defining primaries and

**TABLE 4** Summary of some results from studies in which *Gf* and *Gc* factors have been identified

| Symbol | Behavioral indicant[a] | Approximate factor coefficient[b] | |
|---|---|---|---|
| | | *Gf* | *Gc* |
| *CFR* | Figural Relations. Eduction of a relation when this is shown among common figures, as in a matrices test. | .57 | .01 |
| *Ms* | Memory Span. Reproduction of several numbers or letters presented briefly either visually or orally. | .50 | .00 |
| *Ma* | Associative Memory. Given one part of materials previously together, reproduction of other parts. | .32 | .00 |
| *I* | Induction. Eduction of a correlate from relations shown in a series of letters, numbers or figures, as in a Letter Series test. | .41 | .06 |
| *R* | General Reasoning. Solving problems of area, rate, finance, etc., as in an Arithmetic Reasoning test. | .31 | .34 |
| *CMR* | Semantic Relations. Eduction of a relation when this is shown among words, as in an Analogies test. | .37 | .43 |
| *Rs* | Formal Reasoning. Arriving at a conclusion in accordance with a formal reasoning process, as in a Syllogistic Reasoning test. | .31 | .41 |
| *N* | Number Facility. Quick and accurate use of arithmetical operations, such as addition, subtraction, multiplication, etc. | .21 | .29 |
| *MMS* | Experiential Evaluation. Solving problems involving protocol and requiring diplomacy, as in a Social Relations test. | −.08 | .43 |
| *V* | Verbal Comprehension. Advanced understanding of language, as measured in a Vocabulary or Reading test. | .08 | .68 |

*Note.* After Cattell, 1963a, 1967b; J. L. Horn, 1965a, 1966b; J. L. Horn & Bramble, 1967; Horn & Cattell, 1967a.

[a]The referents here are primary factors, the names and symbols for which have been taken from J. W. French, 1951; J. W. French, Ekstrom, & Price, 1963; and J. P. Guilford, 1967.

[b]These are rough averages computed over the several studies in which the primary factor was used.

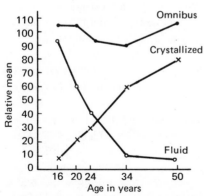

**FIG. 1** Performance as a function of age: omnibus, and fluid and crystallized intelligence. Based on results for *Gf*-pure, *Gc*-pure, and *G*-omnibus analyses in J. L. Horn and Cattell (1967).

when factors associated with gender, education, speediness, and visualization are controlled by analysis of covariance methods, *Gf* is found to decline monotonically from the late teens into the 50s, while *Gc* increases monotonically over this same period. When *Gf* and *Gc* are combined to give an omnibus measure of intelligence somewhat similar to the measure found in popular IQ tests, a curve of the kind shown at the top in Fig. 1 results. If *Gf* is entered as a control variable, the curve for the residual omnibus-*G* measure rises over the age range from the teens to the 50s, whereas if *Gc* is entered as a control variable, the curve drops, as for *Gf*.

This suggests that "general intelligence" measurements of the kind obtained in most IQ tests, and here represented in omnibus-$G$, are mixtures of two kinds of intelligence based on different kinds of developmental determinants.

In several expressions of $Gf$–$Gc$ theory, emphasis has been placed on the idea that $Gf$, more than $Gc$, reflects the potential of hereditary endowment, thus recognizing the evidence which indicates that a substantial proportion of the reliable individual differences recorded by IQ tests can be accounted for by variables representing heredity (Burt, 1958, 1966b, 1972; Jensen, 1969). It should be recognized, however, that this is only speculation; there are reasons to suppose that $Gf$ is no more closely associated with the influences of heredity than is $Gc$.

For example, although the anlage portion of $Gf$ would initially (before injuries to the central nervous system [CNS]) relate most closely to hereditary potential, injuries to the CNS may begin to occur immediately after conception and continue to occur throughout infancy, childhood, and adulthood (Horn, J. L., 1970a; Kawi & Pasamanick, 1968; Pasamanick & Knoblock, 1960); thus, anlage capacity at any stage in development can be as much a function of lack of CNS injury as of heredity. Moreover, as discussed earlier, much learning that builds the basic reasoning capacities of intelligence, and yet is not acculturation, can proceed somewhat independently of hereditary influences; the child born into an environment that encourages exploration, for example, need not be a child whose parents were exceptionally intelligent. Vernon (1970) found, for example, that Eskimo children raised away from the cities under conditions that greatly encourage independent exploration of the physical environment scored substantially higher in the abilities of Fluid Intelligence (and Broad Visualization) than did Eskimo children living in cities who, however, scored higher in the abilities of Crystallized Intelligence. On the other hand, some of the learning that is acculturation surely is promoted by recognition of hereditary potential. For example, the child who is admitted to an advanced school or put into the bright class is likely to be the child who is regarded as bright either because good heredity shows in his own achievements or in recognition that his parents are bright. In this respect, it should be recognized that the evidence showing a relationship between intelligence and the variables of heredity has been derived from studies in which, to a considerable extent, acculturation of the subjects has depended on the child's capacities (rather than on structuring by the society) and the tests have, partly for this reason, measured largely $Gc$ (although granted that they have measured $Gf$, too).

The study demonstrating that $Gf$ is more closely related to inherited potential than is $Gc$ has yet to be done. For several reasons, then, it would seem wise to hold in abeyance any strong assertions that $Gf$ is the inherited portion of intelligence, while $Gc$ is the learned portion. At present, it would appear that both $Gf$ and $Gc$ are, to some extent, products of heredity, perhaps about equally so.

In addition to the $Gf$ and $Gc$ factors, the work on the higher order structure of primary abilities indicates a broad visualization function, a broad auditory ability, and one involving the fluency primaries. The visualization function is manifested in primaries that involve "imagining the way objects may change as they move in space, maintaining orientation with respect to objects in space, keeping configurations in mind, finding the gestalt among disparate

parts in a visual field, and maintaining
flexibility concerning other possible struc-
turings of elements in space" (Horn, J. L., &
Cattell, 1966a, p. 268). Virtually every
variable that involves figures and pictures has
a significant correlation with this factor. The
broad Auditory factor is characterized by
ability to detect speech when distracting
sounds are superimposed and ability to
retain a sound percept and compare it with
other such percepts as they pass into awareness (Horn, J. L., 1973; Stankov & Horn,
1973). Recent evidence (Rossman & Horn,
1972) suggests that the broad Fluency factor
represents an important aspect of productive
creativity.

Several studies based on *Gf–Gc* theory are
now in progress. We might anticipate that in
the near future there will be improved
general purpose tests available to measure
these higher order factors and that several
further hypotheses of the general theory will
be put to the test.

### 3.7 Facet Theories

Several investigators have proposed a
priori systems of facets to organize information on human abilities and thereby cope
with the problems of proliferation and
underdetermination of factors (El-Koussy,
1955; Guilford, J. P., 1959b, 1967; Guttman, 1965; Humphreys, 1962a). These kinds
of theories and some of their limitations
have been reviewed recently in other readily
available publications (Carroll, 1972; Horn,
J. L., 1970b, 1972a; Horn, J. L., & Knapp,
1973) and so will be described only cursorily
here.

J. P. Guilford's (1967) structure of intellect model provides the best known example
of this kind of theory. This model is
represented in Fig. 2. A facet is represented
by a set of categories arranged along one

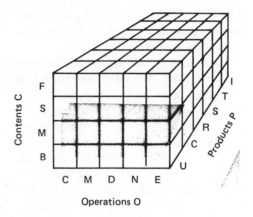

**FIG. 2** Guilford's structure of intellect model.

dimension of the parallelopiped in this diagram. One facet is Content (*C*), the categories of this facet being Figural (*F*), Symbolic (*S*), Semantic (*M*), and Behavioral (*B*).
A second facet is Operations (*O*), the categories of which are Cognition (*C*), Memory
(*M*), Divergent Production (*D*), Convergent
Production (*N*), and Evaluation (*E*). The
third facet is Products (*P*), represented by
Units (*U*), Classes (*C*), Relations (*R*), Systems (*S*), Transformations (*T*), and Implications (*I*). An ordered set of triples—a cell of
the parallelopiped—then defines what, in the
theory, is an ability. For example, a performance in which the product is a System
obtained by Evaluation of Semantic content
is expected to represent an ability. This
could be represented as *EMS* in the model. A
test designed to measure this ability is Word
Systems (Guilford, J. P., 1967, p. 197).
Because Guilford used the method of
orthogonal simple structure factor analysis
to test the implications of his theory, several
tests designed in this way are expected to
yield a factor.

Some facet theorists (notably, Humphreys) use this kind of system mainly only
as a guide for development of tests that are

likely to reveal interesting information about abilities. Evaluated relative to this purpose, facet theory has pragmatic value.

Other facet theorists, such as Guttman, are particularly interested in developing the system as a design for mathematical-statistical analyses that could reveal particular characteristics about the interrelationships among abilities. For example, Guttman (1958) showed that in a particular 90 cell facet design, there should be no more than 7 simple-structure factors. This kind of application of facet theory is in its infancy, but we may anticipate that noteworthy developments will occur in the next few decades.

The use of facet theory actually to account for observed interrelationships among measures of abilities is best represented by Guilford's theory. In this, there are serious limitations stemming particularly from the fact that the rotation methods in Guilford's work often have not been objective (Horn, J. L., 1967a; Horn, J. L., & Knapp, 1973; Humphreys, Ilgen, et al., 1969). The factors in this research were rotated to positions that maximize the agreement between the obtained factor coefficients and the pattern predicted on the basis of theory. The results of several studies indicate that this method of rotation can be used to support virtually any theory (Horn, J. L., 1967a; Horn, J. L., & Knaap, 1973). Thus, the support adduced with the method for any particular theory is not convincing. No one knows precisely the extent to which subjective rotation accounts for the support that was reported for Guilford's facet theory. It is evident from comparisons of the solutions obtained with objective and subjective methods of rotation, however, that the theory could not stand on the basis of evidence provided by objectively rotated factor-analytic studies.

## 4  SUGGESTIVE RELATIONSHIPS BETWEEN ABILITIES AND OTHER ASPECTS OF PERSONALITY

In developing a system of primary and broad second-order abilities, a foundation is laid for architectonic construction of a comprehensive theory of intellect. This work can also lead to a more systematic and enlightening explication of the interdependence of abilities and other influences in personality. At this stage in the development of personology, only the vaguest of outlines of the shape of this interdependence can be seen. It is worth paying some attention to these outlines, however, because there is promise that they represent shadows of some important facts about personality.

There is scattered but persistently recurring evidence (dating from Cattell, 1933a) showing that some of the tests that define primary abilities also help to define factors found among variables that do not directly (i.e., by the criterion of complexity) represent abilities (e.g., Cattell, 1945b, 1948a; Denton & Taylor, 1955; Guilford, J. P., Christensen, Frick, & Merrifield, 1957; Hundleby, Pawlik, & Cattell, 1965; Pemberton, 1952). The following examples seem to be particularly timely relative to contemporary emphases in personality research.

One example occurs with variables that define the Speed of Closure factor, $Cs$. Good markers for this factor, such as Street Gestalt Completion, have been found to be good markers, also, for the factor identified as $U.I.$ 17 (Universal Index, $U.I.$) and more descriptively defined by variables such as the following:

Questionable (e.g., risqué) reading preferences.
Small psychogalvanic response (PGR) depletion following presentation of stimuli.

Tendency to perceive suggested but non-existent shock.

Little reduction in finger-image activity when shocked.

Little involuntary muscle tension.

The most recent summary of the evidence on *U.I.* 17 interpreted it as indicating an absence of learned inhibition, the result being a kind of boldness and lack of caution (Hundleby, Pawlik, & Cattell, 1965). Earlier it was suggested that this may indicate low "reactivity of the sympathetic system to threat" (Cattell, 1957a; p. 240).

Perhaps a more provocative example of ability-temperament interaction is that given by evidence showing that the primary ability known as Flexibility of Closure, *Cf*, is related to the temperament dimension *U.I.* 19, labeled Promethean Will. A principal marker for *Cf* is also a principal marker for *U.I.* 19. This marker is a variable that has figured quite prominently in a wide range of research on personality. The variable is measured with a test that is variously known as Hidden Shapes (Getzels & Jackson, 1962), Embedded Figures (Witkin, 1959; Witkin, Dyk, Faterson, Goodenough, & Karp, 1962), Hidden Figures (French, J. W., Ekstrom, & Price, 1963; Guilford, J. P., 1959b), and Gottschaldt Figures (Thurstone, 1944).

Witkin and his co-workers found that Embedded Figures correlates as highly with the Rod-and-Frame, Tilting-Room, and Rotating-Room tests as these latter correlated among themselves (typical correlations being of the order of .3–.6). They interpreted the common function measured by the four tests as field independence: the tendency of a person "to separate some item—be it his own body, a rod, or a simple geometric figure—from its background or context; to 'break up' and deal analytically with a given situation; to maintain an active

'set' against the influence of the surrounding field" (Witkin, 1959). With this verbal definition and an operational definition given most frequently by the measurements obtained with the Embedded Figures test, Witkin and his co-workers have generated a large amount of research directed at showing that field independence represents a broad and important quality of personality. Although the conclusions of this research were based on analyses with small samples of subjects (particularly small relative to the number of variables analyzed) and even though double-blind or similar procedures to ensure operational independence of variables were not always employed, results were fairly consistent in suggesting that field independence related to such characteristics as the following:

1. Curious, active exploration of the environment and a history of this characteristic engendered by child-rearing.

2. Social autonomy or ability to hold oneself apart from the pressures of the social environment "sometimes even to the point of isolation from other people" (Witkin, 1959).

3. More fully developed awareness of self, of body concept, and of personal strengths and weaknesses.

Also, boys and men tended to score higher than girls and women. There were suggestions that the factor correlated with some indexes of maturity.

Standing alone, the results from Witkin's laboratory would not be compelling (partly for the reasons mentioned previously), but the evidence for the factor *U.I.* 19, found in 13 separate studies based on large samples of subjects, provides some confirmation of the pattern of relationships adumbrated in the Witkin research. The Hundleby, Pawlik, and Cattell (1965) summary indicated, for example, that in questionnaires the person high on *U.I.* 19 tends to be active, thoughtful, and free thinking; rather cold and distant in his relationships with other people; relatively critical of others; not overconfident; flexible in changing responses; unaffected by suggestions from others; and able to concentrate on problems in his head. The description of an aspect of personality provided in this factor is thus fairly similar to that provided in the work of Witkin and his co-workers. Whether we call this broad quality of personality *field independence* or Promethean Will is not too important; the interesting suggestion is that the ability, Flexibility of Closure, seems to be a part of this quality.

There is a considerable body of research suggesting that primaries that define *Gc* and are more or less direct products of school education—primaries such as *V* and *N*—are closely interrelated to variables indicating ego strength and superego development (Cattell & Butcher, 1968; Horn, J. L., 1961a). There are indications, also, that *Gv* and the visual primaries are associated with a quality of masculine reticence. In our culture, at least, males tend to score higher than do females in the visualization abilities. This occurs even when, in childhood, the males are of the same chronological age as the females; but, as is well known, most evidence of physical and psychological development indicates that at a particular chronological age, the female is at a more advanced developmental age than is the male (see Buffrey & Gray, 1973, for comprehensive review and, also, Vernon, 1972). Indeed, there is some suggestion that the observed male-female differences in broad visualization may be related to sex-linked capacities laid down in the germ plasma (see Bock & Kolakowski, 1973, and other work by Bock and his associates).

The trend for future research would appear to be in the direction of more fully exploring relationships of abilities to other variables of personality. A major point of this chapter is that personality must be seen to include the abilities if this exploration is to proceed most intelligently. In this spirit, we might hope that there will be a diminution in the common habit of referring to personality *and* abilities, implying that abilities are separate from personality, and that, instead, researchers, theorists, and practitioners will come to think of abilities simultaneously when they think about how to characterize personality in general or how better to understand a particular person.

## 5  SUMMARY

Abilities are traits of personality. They constitute an important part of the total personality and a part that has been studied more thoroughly than most other parts.

A large number of measurement instruments have been developed to assess aspects of intellect. The confusion occasioned by the number and diversity of devices for measuring abilities has been somewhat lessened by convergent research resulting in an open-ended system of primary abilities. These are not specific tests but, instead, represent functions involved in a variety of ability tests. They provide a flexible basis for studying the organization of abilities and the relationships between abilities and other aspects of personality.

Proliferation in the number of primary abilities has encouraged researchers to develop integrative systems to account for existing results. In hierarchical theories, the positivity of ability test intercorrelations is recognized more clearly than in most other theories. A general factor and two factors that are broader than the primary factors are indicated by research based on hierarchical systemizations.

In the theory of fluid and crystallized intelligence there is an attempt to integrate findings on structure with findings showing ability changes with development and CNS damage. The factor *Gf* is manifested in abilities that do not represent intensive acculturation. It is the more sensitive indicant of influences determined by physiological structure. The term *Gc* represents the individual's appropriation of the intelligence of a culture and, thus, is an indicant of the extent of acculturation. The two kinds of intelligence are indistinguishable early in life, become distinguishable as development proceeds, and in adulthood follow quite different paths of change with aging: *Gf* decreases monotonically throughout adulthood, whereas *Gc* seems to increase. Popular tests of intelligence involve mixtures of these two.

The sense modalities represent mediators of intelligence or particular enhancements of certain kinds of abilities. Broad factors indicating these kinds of influences have been identified only for the visual and auditory processes.

In facet theories, there is a backing off from observation of empirical relationships and an attempt to organize according to a priori principles such as kind of content (Semantic, Figural) and kind of output required (Units, Classes). It would seem that, at this time, facet theories are mainly of use for generating new ideas for test construction.

Several collections of findings suggest either that some of the primary abilities are particular manifestations of broad principles regulating temperamental or motivational aspects of personality or that they represent dynamic interaction between principles of intellect and principles of temperament.

# 7

## A More Sophisticated Look at Structure: Perturbation, Sampling, Role, and Observer Trait-View Theories

Raymond B. Cattell
*University of Hawaii, Honolulu*

## 1 MODERN DEVELOPMENTS IN GENERAL TAXONOMIC CONCEPTS

Traits and states have been discovered so far largely as factor patterns of covarying behavior, fixed in the first case, transient but recurring in the second. The behaviors are most of the time *potential*, their potentiality being confirmed when they actually appear through the advent of a situation. This model of a unified pattern fits cases such as Intelligence, Anxiety, and Exvia well enough for practical purposes, but the psychologist prepared for more sophisticated statistics and concepts realizes that the concept as it stands is only a coarse fit. Not only the simple acceptance of factor traits, but the even simpler-minded rejections of *trait theory* that crop up from time to time, lack the deeper perspective we now approach. Incidentally, the term *trait theory* is as superfluous as a *two-legged man* theory; for the alternative is a structureless theory of personality structure. Traits, states, role readinessess, sentiment processes, and other structures are all part of the development of trait theory (if one insists on so calling it), and the real questions concern mainly naive versus more sophisticated concepts for

recognizing, defining, and using these structures..

Taxonomy, as the list in chapter 1 will remind the reader, introduces a variety of concepts, but all are forms of trait theory. Rejection thereof springs either from that lack of perspective on the history of science that denies due concentration on taxonomy, or from aversion to clean mathematical models, or from early erroneous ideas of traits.

One may add that the rejection also arises from failing to perceive that anarchy, stagnation, and sterility are the alternatives to structural research. In the writings of Mischel (1968); Barker, Kounin, and Wright (1943); Moreno (1957); Fromm (1955); H. S. Sullivan (1953); and many lesser writers, one perceives an emphasis on the complete atomicity of behavior. The same is true of classical reflexological learning theory, which has hitherto prevented its development into structured learning principles. Elsewhere the rejection springs from a desire to deemphasize (rather, one hopes, than totally to deny) the importance of the *characteristics of the organism,* relative to the environment, as occurs in many sociological writings.

The assertion that there is some nontrait way of looking at personality is therefore left with the only possible shred of real meaning, that the critic is only objecting to the *particular* trait or attribute definition adopted. As to early possibly inadequate approaches to trait definition, some verbal definitions (see Allport, 1937) are so non-operational or syntactically paradoxical that one is entitled to object to discussing them. To demolish them as *trait theory* is to demolish a straw man. The question of whether traits exist in the meaning given here—that of a correlation cluster (*surface trait*) or unique, invariant factor (*source trait*) in behavior manifestations, as correlated over time or over people—is a matter for experiment and calculation, not *a priori* theories. The evidence is that distinctly more than 30% (and in most domains more than 60%) of the variance of most individual *bits* of behavior can, to our present knowledge, already be accounted for by a number of such repeatedly recognizable trait structures. These patterns of expression moreover, faithfully reappear, as shown by reliability coefficients, in responses to simuli. When one thus sets layers of philosophical or even methodological misunderstanding aside, the remnant of real disagreement among psychologists that remains is a limited one. One must conclude that the range of common and unique trait structure is important conceptually and worthy of scientific investigation.

As far as genuine theoretical attacks on the existence of personality structures are concerned, one expects and gets most from reflexologists, whose learning theories, as they stand, have been unable to cope with personality structure. To say, as some reflexologists do, that they are content with an atomistic description of personality, that is, with a *structure* consisting of a host of unrelated conditioned responses, devoid of real traits, arises partly from a low level of scientific aspiration. They do not ask and make no attempt to know how much of the organism's total behavior can be affected by the kinds of experiments they do. For example, the behavior therapist who sets out to extinguish a phobic reaction to a black cat—and may succeed in doing so—is apt to say that he is not concerned with such structural trait concepts as Ego-strength, Anxiety level, or such structural type concepts as Neuroticism. He does not ask if his treatment has produced change in such trait abstractions, but only whether the patient ceases to react with aversion to the black cat. Unfortunately, he has never demonstrated that the behavior change he brings about actually occurs in isolation, without affecting whole trait patterns. Paradoxically, in discussing his results theoretically, he uses verbal concepts implying that there is trait change, though he has made no provisions for recognizing and measuring traits. The fact is that the patient has ceased to react to Robinson's black cat when seen under bright electric light on the laboratory bench. But the description of this is apt to generalize to a conceptual statement that "the patient is cured of his fear of black cats," or even of a "phobic neurosis." Yet, *fear* and *neurosis* are, unquestionably, in our language, trait and type terms. Incidentally, this example is not a criticism of the potency of behavior therapy, but only points out that most users of atomistic, nontrait conceptualizations cannot support them by correlational evidence. Further, in theoretical discussions, they habitually slip out of the narrowness of their operational definitions, without noticing it when they come to summarize their findings. They are trait theorists who have built up no techniques for handling traits.

Our concern in this chapter, however, is not with whipping horses, but with outlining the important ways in which trait theory is now developing beyond the initial operational definitions in broad and specific, common and unique source traits (factors) and surface traits (clusters). By the illustrations of these in chapter 1 and elsewhere we realize that they will show themselves in correlations over people, that is in *R* technique, showing *common* traits, or over time in *P* technique, revealing *unique* traits. *States* are dimensions (common or unique) of patterns of *change* over time, dependent in turn on *liability proneness* traits. *Types* of people are patterns defined at the modal points in the distributions of people in the multidimensional trait space. *Processes* are individual or modal patterns in response and stimulus sequences in a behavior-dimensionalized space, as is shown later. The word *stimulus* should not be overlooked, for it reminds us that the great majority of processes involve constant interaction with the environment, requiring a dependable sequential appearance of events (stimuli) in the environment as well as readinesses in the organism. Consequently, a process cannot be defined by behavioral dimensions alone, but is an interweaving of psychological, behavioral, and physical and environmental dimensional description.

Because *type* receives extensive treatment later by Bolz and by Guertin, and *process* is examined comprehensively under learning, these have not received in the opening chapters the detailed precision of description offered for surface and source traits. However, this chapter must include precision in the basic concepts of *type* and *process per se*. As to the former, let us note that if a factor analysis is performed on variables common and apt to a large population, it will be possible to place each person afterwards *as a point in space* by his vector (profile) of scores on the trait dimensions obtained, as shown for two dimensions in

Fig. 1. In many kinds of data, especially skills, attitudes, and dynamic variables, it will then become evident that—even though there is approximate normal distribution on each variable separately, as is approximately true in Fig. 1—people will bunch, as shown. By adopting a suitable cutting limit on the profile-similarity coefficient, $r_p$ and employing the taxonome program (Cattell & Coulter, 1966), these natural condensations can be found objectively, and each *type* thus established defined by its modal profile. It is then likely to be found that new variables are apt for additionally defining any partic-

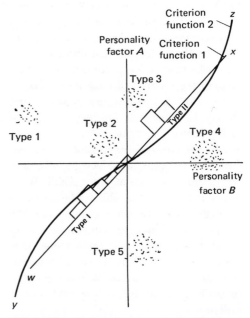

**FIG. 1** The relation of types to traits. Five types are represented, with respect to this two-factor profile. It will be noted that if some single criterion function is taken of these two factors (as in the SW-NE line) the number of recognizable types is reduced to two. This frequently happens with reduction of the dimensionality of the profile by taking some combination of the full dimensions for a *special purpose* measure. From *Handbook of Multivariate Experimental Psychology* by R. B. Cattell, Chicago, Rand McNally, 1966. Copyright 1966 by Rand McNally. Reprinted by permission.

ular type that one would not use for discrimination in the general population. For example, in a factoring inclusive of all classes in the animal kingdom one would then find that beak and wing length would not be used in the dimensions of a class but must be introduced among birds, number of fins among fish, and so on. Some persistent misconceptions in psychology, for example, as to the pattern of intelligence as a trait, arise from following the statistician's implication of an ideal population to which all humanity belongs, whereas the truth is that there are many types and that the structure of correlations is peculiar to each. This means that research should (a) locate the various types on population-wide, trans-type dimensions and then (b) place the individual by naming his type and giving his within-type trait dimension scores.

The notion of process has been regarded as central to the study of common processes (as in perception, learning, etc), which study has been contrasted to individual-difference studies. As such, it has virtually been left out of psychometry. But again, as in trait and type concepts, a more penetrating view shows that trait and process concepts also are interrelated. A single process on a single occasion may be defined in terms of a temporal pattern in the given set of variables. This defines some actual concrete process, but we need to go beyond that, because psychology is interested in processes that repeat themselves in the same individual or are common in the alternative sense of appearing in many people. To locate and define these for precision research it is necessary to improve on the "I behold a process" thinking of many learning theorists and to employ the same multivariate analysis techniques as are used in trait discovery. Briefly, these techniques (Cattell, 1966e) lead to a set of dimensions along the time dimension in which the process can be

uniquely defined as a thread, as shown in Fig. 2(b). Technical steps and conceptual implications can be read in more detail elsewhere (Cattell, 1966e).

Advances toward more sophisticated treatment of taxonomy than in the résumé of chapter 1 just given, take two main directions: (a) refining the concepts themselves and (b) introducing allowances for the perceptual difficulties of the observer in recording them. Just as in physics the Theory of Relativity and the Heisenberg indeterminacy principle have had to come to terms with the notion of inextricable involvement of the observer with the event, so in psychology a whole new research specialty has grown up around the way in which the structures are perceived, by persons and recording instruments. This is called *perturbation theory* and is concerned with the possibility of separating the truly existing structures from the perturbing influences associated with observers and instrument factors. As to the concepts of structure in and of themselves, the chief need is to go beyond the bald statement that "a trait is a factor," as it was meant when Spearman and Thurstone were making their first applications of factor analysis to find unitary traits in abilities. The variety of concepts and technical uses in factor analysis has moved forward since then through empirical findings and new models and statistical devices, to an altogether more refined and substantially enriched form. The contributions in this section by Hammond, Wilde, Ishikawa, Spielberger, and especially Dielman and Krug and Nesselroade and Bartsch provide us with stimulating ideas for the present integration, though their own necessary preoccupation with substantive findings has made it impossible for any one of them to show in his own chapter the full development of general concepts that is taking place.

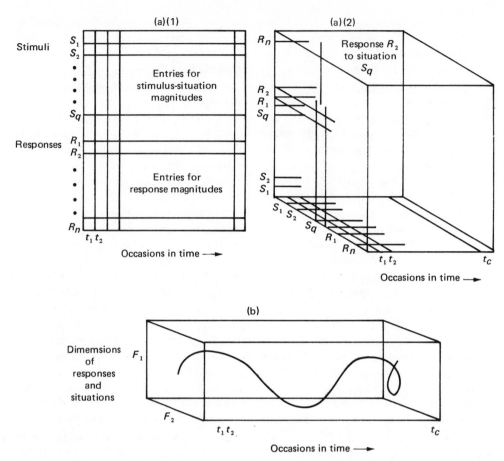

**FIG. 2** Model for representing a process. (a) Directly on variables as score sequence, [1] general case, [2] when responses can be tied reliably to particular stimuli; (b) in fewer dimensions from factoring variables and expressed (for two dimensions) graphically. From *Handbook of Multivariate Experimental Psychology* by R. B. Cattell, Chicago, Rand McNally, 1966. Copyright 1966 by Rand McNally. Reprinted by permission.

## 2  DEPENDENCE OF STRUCTURE ON THE SAMPLING AND CHOICE OF VARIABLES

Until the *personality sphere* concept was proposed, and its importance both for coverage and precision of simple structure was accepted, altogether too little attention was given in reaching trait concepts to the questions of (a) sampling of variables, (b) the ambient general stimulus situation at

times of testing, and (c) the sampling of persons.

In purely statistical terms, it is conceded by all who have checked Thurstone's proposition that simple structure is unaffected by addition or subtraction of variables, that within wide limits the factors found remain unaffected. By contrast, axes placed through homogeneous clusters will shift as one makes up items to construct new homogeneous clusters, that is, *source but not surface traits approach invariance.* Second, it is obvious that as we change the *modality*—ability, temperament, dynamic motivation—of the variables, we shall tend to get with largest variance the factors *corresponding* to the modality of our choice; for example, motivation factors will turn up with only small variance in ability variables. Third, we need not belabor the oft-encountered point that unless one begins with a *personality sphere*, that is, a strati-fied-stimulus-population-sampling principle, he is unlikely to have sampling-adequate representation of the necessary hyperplanes for rotation. Also, he lacks the necessary basis for distinguishing between broad and narrow (common and specific) factors, as well as any reasonable claim to having exhausted the main dimensions needed in the domain.

However, beyond these now commonly recognized desirables in variable sampling, there are other aspects of the actual variable and measurement situation to consider, some of which have been the object of critical discussion by Fiske (1971). We are familiar with the conception that all personality variables may be divided into $L$ (life record), $Q$ (questionnaire) and $T$ (objective test) data. But there are also certain cross classifications, one of the more important of which has to do with the *time duration* of the behavior observed. The psychiatrist, for example, who deals largely with $L$ data in the form of behavior rating will point out that many psychometrists, in education or laboratory experiment, deal with a score that represents only a *momentary* act, whereas his own crucial diagnoses often take *processes* as variables. For example, the insidiousness of onset, that is, the pattern of the onset process over an appreciable time, may be part of the diagnosis of one form of schizophrenia. Illustrating this problem, the findings by Cattell and Peter-

son (1958) show that time sampling of short bits of natural-situation behavior in nursery schoolchildren yielded factors that could not be easily aligned with those from questionnaires and ratings (which deal with patterns abstracted from more prolonged behavior).

Defining a total *personality sphere* of human behavior in a given culture from which a stratified sample can be taken for experiment may seem to some an academic exercise. But as these relevances illustrate, it is vitally important (to rotation; to separating broad and specific factors; to developing trait concepts transcending media of observation; to distinguishing ability, temperament, and dynamic modalities; to determining the strata to which factors belong; to linking rating with time-sampling observations, etc). It has been so recognized by various serious contributors to the field, notably in the approaches of Allport, Burt, Fiske, Goldberg, Horn, Nesselroade, Norman, Sells, Tupes, and Warburton. The advantages and disadvantages of basing the personality sphere on the semantic symbols for behavior built up in a culture were set out by the present writer (Cattell, 1946, 1957a) and an attempt was made (Cattell & Warburton, 1967) to supersede or, at least, supplement it by a more objective procedure. This begins with a survey-type *time sampling of behavior through 24 hours* of the typical member of our culture and recognizes that beyond the actual behavior there is an interface with *the ways of measuring behavior.* Any response can be measured in several ways, for example, time or error; and the contribution to defining the sphere by Cattell and Warburton consists of defining categories across which *measurement* can also be sampled. With the stimuli and responses given by the culture, and the modes of measuring response given by such a scheme, the foundation is provided for a nonarbitrary personality sphere of variables.

Except for the work of a few, such as Barker, Kounin, and Wright (1943) and Sells (1963) this exploration of an environmental taxonomy has been extremely slow.

In the stratified sampling principle from such a sphere, we have the basis for settling the question of *density of representation.* The discovery that whenever an alignment was found between personality factors in the *L* and *Q* media on the one hand, and the *T* data medium on the other, it was of *second* strata in the former with *first* strata (primaries) in the latter. The alignment suggested that somehow the density (closeness together in the personality sphere) of variables in the former is altogether greater than in the latter. A possible description of this density difference is that in the *L* and *Q* media we often make observations on many specific situations. For example, *Q* data may ask, "Are you nervous on heights?" "Are you afraid of the dark?" and so on, whereas in *T* data we may take a psychogalvanic response to a threatening stimulus in a single laboratory situation, which seems to stand as representative of response to many life situations, judging by the higher order at which *T*-data factors come out.

Properties of the *L*-, *Q*-, and *T*-media distinctions are discussed elsewhere (Nesselroade & Delhees, 1966). It is the structured issue of *process* that deserves one more comment, outside other discussions here. If the psychiatrist is inclined to criticize all tests as cross-sectional, *momentary behavior* and as *nonprocess* (in contrast to thought and behavior *processes* by which he recognizes his syndromes), it must be pointed out by reference to the compendium of Cattell and Warburton (1967) that this is not true of a goodly proportion of objective (*T*-data) measures. For many of the objective personality tests there devised, in the Cattell-Warburton index, express ratios, and other patterns, of behavior over

time (e.g., warming up and fatiguing on a task, *learning process* patterns, change of opinion when exposed to a succession of influences, and so on). It is indeed most important that the variables out of which source-trait structures and concepts are formed and recognized should include such longitudinal process behaviors as well as instantaneous act variables. In the rating domain, variables tend naturally to do so.[1]

For personality structure questions, perhaps the most vital use of the personality sphere concept is in deciding between broad and specific source traits. It is unfortunate that psychologists have not abandoned sooner the purely statistical jargon of *common* and *specific*,[2] referring to a mere ad hoc *matrix,* in favor of the more meaningful *broad* and *narrow* (or *specific*) trait. This old usage creates confusion, since *common* is

[1] It may seem paradoxical that in a formal sense, we have argued that a process is best defined as a sequence of positions measured with respect to dimensions found by cross-sectional analysis, whereas now we say, conversely, that elements in the cross-section analysis may often themselves first need to be recognized as processes. Actually it is not a paradox, but an expression of the subtle but basic *iterative* principle in all perception of structural form and process, which requires that one constantly cycle through the various possible directions of analysis. Structures are described partly in process elements; processes are defined in sectional elements, the conceptions in each being aided by some firm elements found in the other. A trait is thus a statement that various responses to various stimuli and various process behaviors go together.

[2] Specific factors in personality measures occupy the status of specific factors in any area of science. They may *really* in some sense be specific, or they merely represent the variance due to common factors yet undiscovered. Probably only very rarely are they, in the last resort, specifics in the former sense. Incidentally, we must remember that it is equally possible, by the model, that *a specific* is actually two or more specifics, present in any one test.

best used in trait taxonomy to oppose *unique*, meaning common to all people in a culture, versus individual or idiosyncratic. In short, *common to people* and *common to variables* is confused in our old terminology. If the statistician attempts escape from this confusion and suggests *general* for what is common to a number of variables, he lands us in difficulties, for the psychologist is scarcely concerned with the statistician's definition of what is merely something *general to a transient matrix* (which would, in any case, normally be evidence of a poor experimental design.) Consequently, the better terminology is (a) *broad-vs.-narrow* and *specific* (in declining order on a continuum) with respect to variables and (b) *common-vs.-unique* with respect to people.

Sampling breadth, as a basis for distinguishing broad, narrow, and specific (and one may still preserve the right to believe that scarcely anything in the human-behavior repertoire is entirely specific) can, in fact, have stable meaning only in relation to the *personality sphere concept* (Burt, 1937; Cattell, 1946; Guttman, 1959), or some equivalent thereto. However, it does not suffice to have the concept available if it is not used. Many smaller researches cannot cover the whole personality sphere domain, but they can attempt to recognize their locus and insure progressive, dependable advance in taxonomy by recognizing *marker variables* from past researches and incorporating them strategically. The advocacy of this strategy has had little effect on minor researches and on many PhD theses that started innocently in purely private worlds. But within the more sophisticated polity of systematic researchers, as in the work of Barton, Buss, Dielman, Digman, Dreger, Eysenck, Gorsuch, Guilford, Häcker, Hakstian, Horn, Karson, Nesselroade, Norman, Pawlik, Royce, Schmidt, Schumacher, Sells, Sweney, Thurstone, Tsujioka,

Warburton, and many others, it has paid great dividends in giving a sophisticated perspective of the relative breadth and essential interrelations of established source traits.

Some initial separation of domains of investigation is inevitable, as new investigators conceive new theoretical domains of interest and new operations of measurement. This happened, for example, when Radcliffe, Sweney, Adams, Cross, and the present writer left the general personality domain and set up operations for objective *interest and motivation* measurement. But within 15 years, a planned common factoring of old and new domains yielded effective checks. As Norman (1966) pointed out, such special areas of investigation inevitably create temporarily special paradigms—areas of new variables and conceptual discussion centering on a particular investigatory theme or domain. Obviously, as soon as some structure has developed in such paradigms, it is in the interest of science to link them deliberately and purposefully with other approaches. Thus, Guilford and the present writer, after some 15 years of refinement of two questionnaire foundations, were able to show that they occupied largely the same space, differing only as orthogonal and oblique rotations would be expected to differ.

There are still, after 35 years of strategic research, some riddles and dark areas in the domain of personality source traits. Even though investigation kicks off with a concept of a broad population of behaviors, the situation still remains, as in geographical exploration, that the domain is not fully known until every new direction of explorations fails to yield new territory. In the 30 years of exploration of $Q$ and $L$ data (now completed), on which the 16 PF questionnaire rests, the initial 18 factors were found (Cattell 1950a, Cattell &

Saunders, 1950), from which the best-replicated 16 were used. They were then extended to 23 factors in the normal domain, and the inclusion of pathological behavior, as in the Minnesota Multiphasic Personality Inventory (MMPI), extended it by 12 more. So far the factoring of these 35 primaries has not quite yielded secondaries equal in number to the number of primaries in $T$ data. It may well be, of course, that the tentative law that primaries in the latter are secondaries in the former does not hold over the whole spectrum, but the riddle also admits the guess that there exist some domains of behavior in one medium not touched by the other. Recent work (Cattell, Pierson, & Finkbeiner, 1976) suggests at least that $Q$ and $L$ data cover much the same domain, and factors like $Q_2$, $Q_3$, and $Q_4$, formerly given only $Q$ designation as *mental interiors*, now also have appeared in observer ratings. In evaluating present degrees of completeness of coverage, one must also consider the fact that both source traits measured in the $Q$ and $L$ data and those in the $T$ media, have proved able to give substantial predictions of general life criteria in clinic, school, and industry (see Thompson's chapter 30).

The dependence of factor-stratum decisions on choice of variables has been sufficiently indicated and the relevance to distinguishing modalities and separating true from instrument factors is discussed in sections 6 and 7 in this chapter. So we may complete this section by turning from sampling of variables to sampling of people. The word *sampling* is not used here in the usual statistical sense, but instead in the sense of *shopping around* among populations. The main misconception is that source-trait theory depends on demonstrating invariance of factor patterns. If the same influence, as a scientific, real-world *determiner,* is at work in different populations, and even different

samples, the appearance of *complete* invariance would be incompatible with the conclusion that it is the same source trait. Factor patterns alter with statistical selection, and with biosocial differences of population in age, sex, culture, and so forth. Proof that the same determiner is involved when such differences appear is a complex procedure (see Baltes, 1968; Buss, 1975; Cattell, 1977; Nesselroade, Schaie, & Baltes, 1972; Royce, 1973; Thurstone, 1938) unless a continuity can be shown through visible identity of pattern over small intermediate population changes. What we need especially to recognize in a more sophisticated view of traits (or states) as factors is that when a population is one of mixed types, the fit of the model and the mean size of loadings will be less than in a pure-type population. Thus, if we are to get measures of highest factor validity for men and women on intelligence tests or personality tests, the weights should be there from factoring men and women separately, not together. Indeed, one may conceive a continuum from the $R$-technique common trait on a very mixed group, through an intermediate common trait based on individuals all very much alike except in level, to the unique trait reached by $P$ technique on one of those individuals; only the last will give a really tight fit of model to psychological reality.

## 3  SCIENTIFIC CONCEPTUAL ORIGINS AMONG SOURCE TRAITS, TRAIT-CHANGE PATTERNS, AND STATES

There are three and only three ways in which the structural unitariness of a *response* pattern can be established, namely, by demonstrated covariation of response magnitudes across (a) different people, (b) different occasions in time, and (c) different stimuli. These have been called $R$, $P$, and $U$

techniques. (The last has only recently been considered and never experimented on. It yields factors in responses assigned as scores to variables. The argument is that if certain responses [for the average person] are simultaneously large, the reason must reside in psychological unity. Because the method is untried, it merely is mentioned here.) In more systematic Data Box language (Cattell, 1966e, p. 95), these would be indexed a *PS.a* design, an *ES.a* design, and an *SE.a* design.

In most personality investigation (other than some dynamic role patterns, in which *ER.a* technique is involved), if we keep to more familiar labelling, we are dealing with *PS.a* and *ES.a*, that is *R* and *P* techniques (the latter including *dR* technique). Now if, in *P* and differential *R* technique (*dR* technique) we factor *difference* scores from one time and situation to another, our model tells us that the patterns obtained will be of two kinds: (a) states and (b) trait change factors. Nesselroade and Bartsch (chapter 8) bring out clearly why this is so and illustrate the nature of the psychological states that are found. If we factor absolute scores, that is, over the individual differences of people on *R* technique, we shall obtain, as chapter 8 also brings out, both (a) traits and (b) states in the same matrix. This fact, that ordinary *R*-technique findings include states, as well as the desirability of performing *R* technique on scores averaged over several occasions, has not been sufficiently recognized.

Contrasting *R*-, *dR*-, and *P*-technique results gives us a firm operational basis for separately recognizing these patterns: For those patterns that are common to *T* and *dR* (or *P*) techniques are *states*; those that appear in both *dR*- (or *P*-) and averaged *R*-technique studies are *trait change*; and those that appear in *R*-technique studies alone are *traits*. This was illustrated in the area of Anxiety and Neuroticism (Cattell,

1972b; Nesselroade & Cattell, 1976). In the separation of state from trait-change factors, there are additional aids such as the recognition that (with the assumption that a trait grows as a tree does [uniform growth] rather than as does a house [phasic growth]), trait and trait-change patterns will be similar (Cattell, 1966e, 1973a) (already used in the second criterion). It will also be recognized that states fluctuate rapidly, whereas trait-change patterns tend to move steadily, and that trait variance increases and state variance decreases, as we average persons' scores across more occasions. In fact, the separation of state and trait is not based on a single operation (contrast of *dR* and *P* with *R*) but depends on further abstractions made from the results of these various procedures (see Cattell, 1971c).

The theory in *P* and *dR* techniques is, of course, that a state response pattern, such as anxiety, arousal, and so forth, is a neurophysiologically built-in and largely unlearned response (though it can, by learning, be attached to new stimuli). Nevertheless, we must recognize that it might vary (a) according to the time period over which it rises, requiring us to check short-period with long-period *P* and *dR* experiments, and (b) in the waxing period from the waning period. The homeostatic nature might act in a different order on the constituent variables from the stimulation patterns, that is, the up pattern could be different from the down. The question has been raised (and the Laceys claim [Lacey & Lacey, 1958] to have answered it affirmatively) that perhaps state response patterns might change with the nature of the stimulus and the individual. Doubtless some such effects exist, but the evidence has not yet proved it, for what seem to be two *surface state* different patterns of, for example, Anxiety in response to stimuli *A* and *B* may, in one case, be Anxiety plus Depression (each of which, when properly factored, retains its characteristic, stimulus-independent pattern), and, in another, Anxiety plus Stress. That is to say, the apparent observed variations could be due to different mixtures of *factors* in the correlation *cluster* (surface state or trait). To entertain the Lacey theory, it must be disproved that this is sufficient to account for alleged occasional idiosyncrasy, before looking further afield. A person's uniqueness certainly exists, on the other hand, though putting *P*-technique results side by side (Cattell, 1957a) has so far failed to show significant differences.

A real suspicion that state patterns might be nothing more than trait-change patterns or even artefacts from unreliability was voiced by the present writer. Although investigation indicated (see Cattell, 1966e) that differences in reliability or variance of the same variables between Occasions 1 and 2 in *dR* technique may artefactually produce patterns *similar* to the trait patterns, these defects were shown not to exist in the experiments. Nesselroade and Bartsch (chapter 8) systematically examined this question. The now extensive array of *dR* studies certainly yields as an empirical law (Nesselroade & Cattell, 1976) that every *R*-technique pattern is matched by a similar factor pattern in *dR* technique. This is seen, for example, in the second-order Anxiety and Exvia traits in the 16 Personality Factor Questionnaire (16 PF) (Wilde, and Nesselroade and Bartsch), the depression factors of Curran (1968) and Delhees (1968), and the *T*-data (objective test) factors (Cattell & Schmidt, 1972). This is proof only that trait-change factors are the same as the traits, which would be expected. But the fact that *state* factors also exist is shown beyond cavil by their appearance in *P* technique, which could not be susceptible to the artefact. (See Nesselroade and Reese, 1973.)

Writers in personality not sufficiently conversant with the nature and effectiveness of the multivariate model (and here one must, reluctantly, place Allport, 1937; Fromm, 1955; Horney, 1950; Rogers, C. R., 1951; Sullivan, H. S., 1953; and many clinical psychologists) have frequently attacked source-trait and state concepts, implicitly or explicitly, on the grounds that they do insufficient credit to the *uniqueness* of the individual. Without sufficient examination of the capacity of the structural, common-attribute, dimension approach to handle uniqueness, they seek to give scholarship to the criticism by involving the philosophical pedantry of the *nomothetic* and the *idiographic* antithesis.

The unwary may be tempted to believe that there is some idiographic branch of science, over and above the normal nomothetic form, whereas in fact idiographic is a supposed form of understanding outside science. *Nomothetic* means *understanding particulars in terms of universal laws,* and *idiographic* means *representing a notion or idea without reference to the name given to it, [the name] implying some general laws* (as in some squiggle on a piece of paper that apparently cannot be described by naming any geometrical figure concepts).

Actually these writers have created a problem from nothing. Idiographic understanding requires understanding of a particular event without reference to other cases and the nomothetic importation of classes and dimensions. One must leave to the philosophers whether knowledge can exist without comparisons, relations, and the concepts of general parameters. (How much do you know about red if you have seen no other color and no other objects colored red?) But certainly in science, with its general laws, there must be some *population* (people, occasions, variables—and, in the last resort, all of them) as the basis of the *laws*. There is no such entity, therefore, in science, as a truly idiographic approach, in the unscholarly meaning recently given the term. Such a sense of *idiographic* might conceivably belong to the emotional *understanding* of art or religion, though even at the emotional and sensory experience level, it is probable that meaning cannot exist without comparison.

Contrary to criticism of trait-state concepts, we see that the trait model respects uniqueness in two ways: (a) the individual profile is a unique combination of common trait measures, and (b) by switching to *P* technique, we can actually get the trait structures themselves in unique form. In the latter, the problem lies in comparing one person with another in terms of measures of *unique* traits. A solution of a philosophical kind is obtainable by classifying all unique patterns of, say, anxiety response, together by some pattern-similarity measure and considering scores on them (in standard scores over time) to be equivalent in meaning. This also must be considered as a solution to the problem of comparing source-trait scores and properties across ages and cultures to which the same exact pattern is *not* common, as was discussed earlier (see also section 4 of this chapter).

Most discussion and model building in current psychology, however, concern common trait systems. With this definition and within this system we nevertheless need to take a more sophisticated view than is generally understood from our (chapter 1) operational definition of a source trait as a simple structure (or confactor rotated) factor. We recognize that there must be further evidence. It must be replicated with good, but not normally perfect (+1.0), congruence coefficients. It must show unity in growth and decline and must do so under experimental manipulations. Beyond this, however, source traits will diversify according to various taxonomic characters. Al-

though some traits will be the simultaneous product of heredity and environment, others—called, respectively, *genetic* and *environmental mold traits*—may be wholly the effect of one kind of determiner or the other. The clearest instances are in the dynamic field, in the factor patterns of ergs and sentiments (chapter 18). As W. R. Thompson (1966), Burt (1960), Vandenberg (1962), and the present writer pointed out, a single powerful gene, with pleiotropic effects, could itself account for a correlation of several genetic maturational effects. Another dichotomy in the taxonomy is that between *present* influences, which are, as in fluid intelligence, probably an expression of current cortical efficiency, and *past* influences, which are no longer active but leave a deposit producing a present correlation. An example of the latter is the crystallized intelligence pattern of correlations found in, say, 40-year-olds, between verbal and numerical skills, partly due to these skills having been learned with equal intensity (unequal in different people) back in the high school period.

The brief glance given in this section and, still better, the chapter by Hammond, suffice to show that there are enough well-replicated source-trait patterns to justify research seeking next a diversity of psychological, sociological, and physiological influences in considering their origins. There are abilities such as fluid intelligence that represent some psychological *power* of relation eduction. There are others, such as Thurstone's *N* that represent a *unitary learning* influence. There are personality factors, like Protension (*L* in the 16 PF) that seem to be a *generalization of a habit of defense* by projection, and others, like Exuberance (*U. I.* 21), that suggest a root in some physiological pacemaker in the cortex. There are clear-cut sentiment factors, such as those to job, religion, and home, which are the impress of conditioning in the cultural mold of a particular social institution, and so on. The tracing of source traits to these and other classes of origin is in terms of research design, a matter for experimental hypothesis testing that can now extend beyond the original factor-analytic demonstration of unity.

## 4  PROBLEMS IN IDENTIFYING AND SCORING SOURCE TRAITS ACROSS CULTURE AND AGE GROUPS

It is sometimes remarked with astonishment that factor-analytic research may go on for 20 years in a certain area without a factor score useful to the practitioner ever being obtained and used. A case in point is the appearance of the *O-A Personality Battery* in 1976, though *T*-data research replicated the factors nearly 20 years ago. And when the phase of actually scoring and using factors begins, everyone concerned encounters unsuspected problems, revealing that the concepts are not always what they had been imagined to be.

Assigning reliable and valid factor scores, of course, is not just a concern of applied psychology. The process of interpreting factors, after adequate replication, begins with attempts to abstract some common determiner from the nature of the salient and nonsalient variables, and proceeds by refactoring with new variables chosen to test the best hypothesis. But a second phase deals with scoring the factor and, with the aid of that score, plotting age curves and other natural history as well as trying effects of manipulation. It is hard to say whether the 20-year delay psychology has experienced in regard to serious attempts at specific source-trait theories is to be credited more to scientific ideals of caution or ascribed to

sheer lack of enterprise and scientific perspective. But let us look at the scoring procedures per se.

In matrix terms, the weights for estimating a factor are obtained from the factor analysis, in the general oblique case, by:

$$V_{fe} = R_v^{-1} V_{fs}, \tag{1}$$

where $V_{fe}$ is the matrix of factor estimation weights applying to the variables, $R_v$ is the (unreduced) variable correlation matrix, and $V_{fs}$ is the factor structure matrix. Applying this to the test standard scores we obtain the *attenuated standard scores* for factors, $Z_f$, by:

$$\hat{Z}_f = Z_v V_{fe}, \tag{2}$$

(where $Z_v$ is the test standard scores) whence by a diagonal matrix stretching the attenuated scores by the inverse of the multiple $R$s we reach factor standard scores, thus:

$$Z_f = \hat{Z}_f D. \tag{3}$$

The first empirical finding that thrusts itself on the investigator is that $V_{fe}$ quite sensitively changes with sample and population, as pointed out in the previous section. The conceptual truth this reiterates to us is that a source trait is not to be defined as something *within* the individual. It is a complex relation of an individual, a population, an environment, a set of specific stimuli, and a set of specific responses. However, a particular score on it does belong to a specific individual. Nevertheless, one cannot file away the full definition of a factor by putting the battery for it in a folder. To preserve the full definition for

future replications, one would need to preserve the people and their environment also
in the folder.

From what has been said about changing
factor patterns with change and population,
it is recognized that the estimation weights
in $V_{fe}$ (Equation 1) must be adjusted. It is
true that even in a mixed group, we are still
statistically on perfectly firm ground in
using the $V_{fp}$ and $V_{fe}$ for that mixed group,
but it will not yield such a high multiple $R$
between the estimate from tests and the
pure factors, that is, the factor score
estimate will have lower validity. More
important to the theorist, it will not yield
him as definite an expression of the factor
(in the $V_{fp}$ loadings) on which to base his
theoretical interpretations of the source trait.
Certainly as a practical measure it would be
most desirable to have different batteries (or
different weights for the same battery) in
scoring people belonging to different subgroups. This point has been amply illustrated
by the present writer in *Personality and
Mood by Questionnaire*, notably in regard to
Howarth and Browne's (1971) assertion that
particular items in the 16 PF are not *valid*
simply because they do not load on Howarth
and Browne's particular (non-American)
population.

The score comparison problems that
arise, when batteries are thus adjusted in
content or weights, pitchfork us into a brief
systematic consideration of the problem of
comparisons of persons' scores across ages
and across cultures to which we have referred briefly in mentioning the equipotent
and isopodic methods. For it is when
patterns change, for example, in plotting an
age curve, that any obscurity in our concepts
can call the whole procedure in question.
Let us, therefore, face the issue of how we
can speak of source traits in different cultures and at different ages as being *the*

*same*—and how we can compare scores thereon.[3]

There are four kinds of situations in
which one may be called on to demonstrate
identity of traits across two studies, or to
compare factor scores:

1. Same variables, same population of
people (two occasions or samples).
2. Same variables, different population.
3. Different variables, same population.
4. Different variables, different population.

The first—examining goodness of matching of a hypothesized identical source trait
from two factorings on the same people—
requires only that we obtain the correlation
of the factor scores found in the two cases,
for we may carry the correlations across the
same people. The second—which is the situation of greatest frequency and importance,
and the one we are approaching—requires
regard for sampling laws within a population
and a different treatment when they actually
constitute two different populations. Since
scoring comparisons must be preceded by

[3] At a *patching* level, the problem of cross-
cultural score comparisons can be handled by
either (a) retaining only items which in an independent translation translate back accurately into the
original, or (b) standardizing on a subgroup which
shares both cultures, which generally means one
that is at least bilingual. At a level of more general
principles we can argue (a) that the items or
subtests, though different, are a random subset of
those by which the trait is expressed (as chosen by
loadings, say, above .4) in each culture and (b)
that difficulty (score) equivalences can be assigned
to them by having the two sets given in common to
a sufficient sample of other cultures. The problem
cannot be considered solved; but it is at least not
entirely a wild-goose chase, if, after identifying
source traits across cultures and subcultures, we
aim to compare levels across different populations
(see Cattell, 1969, 1970a).

demonstrations of factor matching, we must give attention to the three major pattern-matching devices: (a) the congruence coefficient (Burt, 1948c), (b) the salient variable similarity index (Cattell, Balcar, Horn, & Nesselroade, 1969), and (c) the configurative method (Cattell, 1964a; Kaiser, Hunka, & Bianchini, 1971). The third again lends itself to a correlation test, as does the first. The fourth offers well-nigh insuperable difficulties, but elsewhere (Cattell, 1969, 1970a), three solutions have been proposed: (a) the *person common-reference group* device (finding a group of people belonging to both cultures) which restores the problem to Situation 1; (b) the *test common-reference group,* which reduces it to Situation 2; and (c) the *common-variable population principle,* which assumes the two factors can be shown to sample equally well from a common population of salients. These may be studied in detail elsewhere (Cattell, 1969, 1970a).

A special approach possible in Situation 2, if one has available the actual raw scores of the persons in the two groups, is *joint factor analysis* in a single matrix, whereby a single factor system necessarily emerges on which the individuals of both groups can be scored. One must, however, note some possible distortion of meaning here because the within- and between-group variance-covariance is thrown together. If, for example, where two greatly different age groups are combined, the distortion from this source can be serious.

With raw scores available, two other approaches are possible. One approach is to bring each set of people to standard scores in their own group and then throw them together and factor. This *group mean equating* method, as we call it, cuts out the intrusion of between-group into within-group variance-covariance, but unfortunately it also cuts out any subsequent compar- ison of the two groups as to their mean scores. The reciprocal approach to this is to cut out the within-group variance-covariance and use only the between-group. This approach, which permits comparisons of group profiles, has been used by the present writer in cross-cultural comparisons and has consequently received the name (Cattell, 1957a) of the *transcultural factor* method. It takes, say, the correlations of the mean scores of, perhaps, 100 cultural groups on maybe 30 variables. It necessarily neglects the within-group variance, but develops a pattern common to all groups, and permits a score on the same factor to be given to all groups and all individuals. It will be seen that the *transcultural* and the *group equating* methods are reciprocal extractions from the *joint factoring* method.

The transcultural or joint group approach can be and has been used when it was necessary to plot age score changes on a factor. By lumping all ages together, or working with mean scores for each year group over a 50-year range, for example, a $V_{fe}$ matrix of weights can be obtained that is the same for people of all ages and therefore permits scoring all ages on the same weighting pattern, which makes the statistician happy. However, in stretching so far, it becomes a sort of coarse average of what should be distinct patterns. From the standpoint of the scientific model, what we need is something different from this simple statistical solution. A solution was set out in detail (Cattell, 1969, 1970a) as the *isopodic* and *equipotent* methods, which recognize that in making age and other compar-isons on factor scores we need continuously adjusted weighting patterns. On these we can do such things as integrate cumulatively over age spans. The complexity of the methods requires that they be left to reading in the sources indicated.

Across cultures, on the other hand, there

is no possibility, as a rule, of establishing identity and permitting score comparisons through the continuity of intermediate groups (except when the common membership device is possible). In that case, unless calculation of a transcultural factor pattern is possible (when there happen to be enough *groups* for correlation), one must fall back on the notion that all examples of factor patterns that form a closely cohering *species* of pattern, different from any other species of pattern, can be considered to have the same essential meaning. For example, the factor patterns for intelligence in, say, a dozen countries may be shown to belong to the same class, because the pattern-similarity coefficients among them are higher than any that one encounters between them for what are hypothesized to be *other species* of patterns, for example, Ego-strength, Surgency, Anxiety, and so forth. This approach rests logically on our capacity to sort factor patterns objectively into discrete types, just as profiles of individuals (section 1 of this chapter) are sorted by taxonomy into types. If this can be achieved successfully, then all in one class are said to represent the same comparable concept, (e.g., Intelligence, Anxiety) despite some differences of pattern of factor expression among members of that one species. These interpopulation differences in the pattern, say, of Anxiety, of course, will exceed the merely *statistical* differences of pattern among samples from the same population.

Among source traits thus reached by objective taxonomic treatment of loading profiles, there will, consequently, be two classes—which we may call *identity source traits* and *homologue source traits.* Let us suppose that in some cases the similar factor patterns in various populations finally can be traced as an influence to some one source, such as the concentration level of thyroxin in the blood. In this case our estimates of

the factor scores from the diverse manifestation, in different populations, of this *rapid neural response pattern* are attempts at measures (with some error) of literally the same thing. In other cases—to make an extreme case, the Intelligence factor in primates and in man—the factor cannot be referred to an identical influence, but only the same *class* of influence, identified as just discussed. This amounts to a logical and taxonomic equivalence, not an exact identity. This imperfection of having to refer to a homologue concept rather than an identity is not peculiar to behavioral science. Wherever there are complex derivatives of the identical basic elements of physics and chemistry—as in *intensity of sunlight, concentration of erythrocytes,* and so forth, the meaning will vary somewhat from place to place or species to species, because the composition of sunlight will vary with latitude and the nature of erythrocytes will vary with racial groups.

Finally, the estimation of factor scores sometimes brings us face to face with the extent of the approximation we commonly make in working with a linear and additive model. In the last resort, we realize that the source traits we find in nature do not fit exactly the simplified model of having linear relations to one another and to the variables they influence. These deviations, whenever they have been exactly investigated, have been found in 9 cases out of 10 to be much smaller than speculative critics imply. The linear model has proved to be a a hardy one in giving a reasonable fit under diverse conditions. In initial discovery of source traits, where we wish to find the nature and number of factors with minimum obscuration through these departures from the model, the tactic is for experiment *to take small ranges of variation,* thus using the virtually straight small sections (tangents) of a curve, (an approximation which is, of course, better when the whole plot is not very curved). But after identifying the factor, with appropriate weightings to measure it at various levels, we can, in bivariate experiment relating the factor to various variables, reach out for whatever polynomial equation best describes the nature of the interrelations of factor and variables and interactions of factors.

Factor analysis is thus the groundwork—the beginning, not the end—of the model for the final *behavioral equation*. Success in forming the initial foundation of concepts in ability, temperament, and motivational modalities of personality has demanded a truly flexible, sophisticated use of the factor model over a wide range of strategically planned situations. Reliable reproducibility of factor patterns has had to be the first requirement, before any elaborate theoretical developments could become appropriate. In strategic research in this area, with these goals, one must stress that random and isolated factor-analytic forays—alas, now perhaps two-thirds of what goes into the literature—have been relatively powerless compared with long-term programmatic research with repeated marker variables. Real progress requires a steadily explored extension in a jigsaw puzzle of variables and factors, reaching toward a complete picture.

## 5   THE MEANING OF ALTERNATIVE RESOLUTIONS OF SOURCE TRAITS IN RETICULAR AND STRATA MODELS

At several points in the chapters by Hammond, Wilde, Ishikawa, Dielman and Krug, Nesselroade and Bartsch, and especially in that by Horn, the full interpretation of structure has been sought by reference to *higher strata* (second- and third-order) factors. A second-order factor is, operationally, a factor found by correlating and factoring first-order factors. It is rotated to simple structure on the primaries; the correlations thus found among the secondaries may, in turn, yield tertiaries, and so on. Since clear conceptions of factor strata and related models are essential to a sophisticated grasp of trait structure, we now turn to this domain.

A distinction needs to be drawn between a second- or third-*order* factor and a second- or third-*stratum* source trait. The former gets its meaning from a single statistical operation; the latter requires additional checks as part of a scientific model. The main practical point of difference arises from the fact that investigators may unknowingly begin with a *mixture* of strata in their variables, for example, some being specific variables and some primary factors; thus, a *collation* of several experiments will be required, each experiment proceeding from one order to another to establish the true relations in terms of strata. Primary, secondary, and tertiary, and so forth, are strictly terms to apply to strata. For example, General Intelligence is placed as Factor *B* among the primaries in the 16 PF test; that is, it stands as a second order alone among primaries, but on factoring the 16 PF, this character of *B* is shown by the fact that at the second order it *continues* to stand alone among such secondaries (each loading *several* primary factors) as Anxiety and Exvia. Thus, it shows its true rank to be that of a second-*stratum* factor. This type of situation is illustrated in Fig. 3. As pointed out earlier, there is accumulating evidence that primary personality factors in *T* data (objective tests) align with secondaries in *Q* data, and this instance of Intelligence (a primary in *T* data that uses Thurstone's *N*, *V*, etc., subprimaries as variables) is one more illustration of that alignment. (This implies that Thurstone primaries and 16 PF primaries are at the same stratum level.)

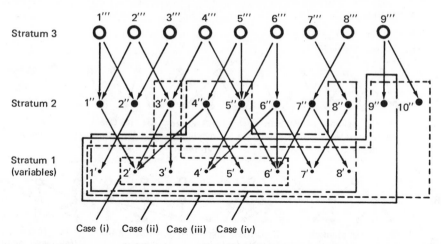

Stratum 3

Stratum 2

Stratum 1
(variables)

Case (i)   Case (ii)  Case (iii)  Case (iv)

**FIG. 3** Sorting out factor strata from factor orders. Possibilities of mistaking the stratum level of a factor. Case (i): 2 primary factor from Stratum 2 is accidentally included with variables from Stratum 1, and it has psychological representation in the other first-stratum variables. No problem arises. Case (ii): One primary factor from 2 is included in 1, and it has no psychological representation in Stratum-1 variables. Case (iii): Two or more primaries from 1 are accidentally included in 2, with no psychological representation in first-stratum variables. Case (iv): Two or more primaries from 1 are included in 2, and they have psychological representation in first-stratum variables. For fuller discussion, see Cattell, p. 245, in Banks and Broadhurst (1965).

However, the possibility also exists that the true model is not one of clear strata (as shown in Fig. 3) but of the more complex relations in the *reticular model* (Cattell, 1965b), as shown in the bottom left corner of Fig. 4, in which influences operate on one another in no simple design, and sometimes even with circular feedbacks. Figure 4 actually illustrates virtually all possibilities of factor variable interaction. Circular, feedback action, positive or negative, almost certainly occurs in the formation, developmentally, of personality structure; at present, the evidence suggests that the strata model is a tolerably good fit to the main findings. The research procedures necessary to trace out a reticular system have been only roughly worked out. They are certainly going to need supplementation of straight factor analysis by other experimental designs, notably path coefficient analysis

(see Cattell, 1977, for expansion of this section).

Incidentally, to accept a *stratum* model is not the same thing as accepting a *hierarchical* model, which involves special, narrower assumptions beyond those of strata. Primarily the hierarchy supposes that the strata also *pyramid*. The present writer gave reasons in more detail elsewhere (Cattell, 1968) for doubting whether, except in special cases such as the Fluid Intelligence factor, hierarchies are at all common. An *apparent* hierarchy is certainly common, for it appears *inevitably* as an artefact from the mathematical-statistical process—factor analysis having to take out fewer factors than there are variables at each stratum. If one broadens the base of the pyramid, as shown in Fig. 5, the factor previously supposed to be the keystone and monarch of the system ceases to be so.

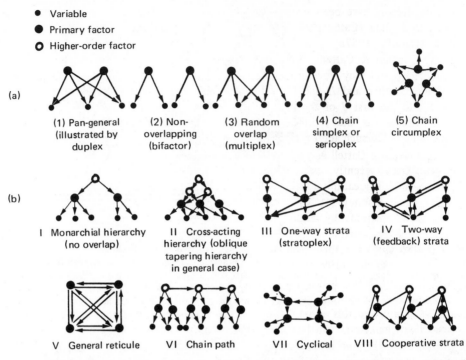

- ● Variable
- ● Primary factor
- ○ Higher-order factor

(a)

(1) Pan-general (illustrated by duplex)    (2) Non-overlapping (bifactor)    (3) Random overlap (multiplex)    (4) Chain simplex or serioplex    (5) Chain circumplex

(b)

I  Monarchial hierarchy (no overlap)    II  Cross-acting hierarchy (oblique tapering hierarchy in general case)    III  One-way strata (stratoplex)    IV  Two-way (feedback) strata

V  General reticule    VI  Chain path    VII  Cyclical    VIII  Cooperative strata

**FIG. 4** Principal possible models for operation of factors as influences. (a) Patterns or variables; (b) patterns of mutual interaction. The commonly assumed model in taking out higher-order factors is the multiplex, in which the loadings of the higher order on the lower order are free to assume any pattern of overlap (unlike for example, the pan-general (a)(1), where every first order is loaded by every second order) or the Holzinger bifactor type of nonoverlapping loadings (a)(2). With an additional stratum, this becomes the stratoplex (III). Contrasted to the pan-general and stratoplex models are a variety of special condition models; the general-reticule model (V) is the major contrast to the stratoplex model. Therein, as illustrated by four factors, causal action—independent contribution to the variance—can run in all directions. As yet, no analytic method can discover directly such a structure. At best, a series of manipulative multivariate experiments is required (from Cattell, p. 238, in Banks & Broadhurst, 1965).

The theory of strata needs to be understood for, among other things, a good sorting out of the issues in dispute about the true personality structure (at any rate in the $L$ and $Q$ data domains) among Guilford, Eysenck, Sells, the present writer, and others (as considered, for instance, in the chapters of Hammond and Wilde) depends thereon. The finding of partly different primaries by Guilford and the present writer can be resolved quickly. The former keeps to orthogonal factors, which permits only partial simple structure (reaches only a lower hyper-plane count). The two would not be expected to give the same structure; as recent work shows (Cattell & Gibbons, 1968), however, much the same personality *space* is occupied, and a simple matrix transformation can be made from one set of scores to the other. H. J. Eysenck and Eysenck (1967) (and, to some extent, Sells, Demaree, & Will, 1968), on the other hand, employ extractions and rotations that lead at the first order to a rough approach to second-stratum factors or to a mixture of first- and second-stratum factors (Cattell, 1973a). The second-stratum factors have been known for some years in $L$ data (Cattell, 1957a) and in $Q$ data (Cattell, 1957a; Cattell & Scheier, 1961; Gorsuch & Cattell, 1966; Karson & Pool, 1958) and they agree quite well across different studies and $L$ and $Q$ media with respect to the first 7 of the 8 or 9 factors demonstrable (as the recent surveys and collations of Gorsuch and Cattell, 1967; Cattell, 1973a; and Cattell and Nichols, 1972b show). Until recently, various other researches in this area, notably H. J. Eysenck (1964c) and Comrey (1970) have tried to find these positions by taking out fewer primaries from variables than an objective test for number of factors shows to exist. As DeYoung & Cattell (1974) showed conclusively, underfactoring leads to rotations that move directly to approximate second-order factors. However, this short cut leads to increasing distortion, after the first 2 or 3 factors, from the true projection patterns of the second orders (as legitimately reached through primaries), calculated directly upon variables. This error in Eysenck's *second order* patterns probably accounts for his confusing the Anxiety second order with the more composite Neuroticism concept, in that neurotics differ from normals significantly on several factors, beyond Anxiety. Lately, proceeding with better agreement to our designated 9 or 10 second orders, by taking out more factors, Eysenck has nevertheless (a) continued to label anxiety as Neuroticism, consistent with his earlier but blurred view of the factors, and (b) claimed that the second orders are the only discoverable constant factor patterns, that is, that there are no primaries, such as have been indexed in the $Q$ medium $A$–$Q_4$.

Since Eysenck has given wide publicity to this view, it is necessary to point out the following:

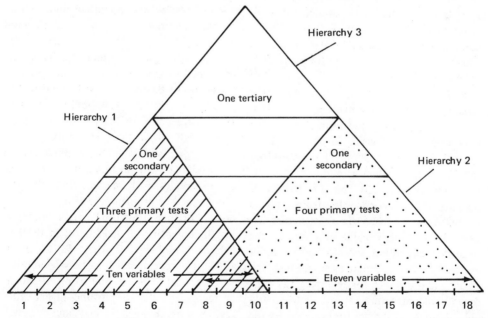

**FIG. 5** Hierarchies as artefacts; the relativity of hierarchies to the base of chosen variables: pyramids versus strata.

1. The number of factors at the primary level by any consensus of *objective statistical tests for factor number* continues to be close to our original 16-22 (the 16 PF plus 2 or 3 factors in the High School Personality Questionnaire [HSPQ], plus the *missing factors* [Cattell & Delhees, 1973], etc.).

2. Application of the Oblimax and Rotoplot rotation programs to his own data from the 16 PF items gives the recognized primary—not the secondary—structure, and with an improved hyperplane count to that offered by his second-order position.

3. The same result is obtained with Sells data on 2,000 cases.

4. Primaries parallel in meaning to those in *Q* data are obtained in *L* data (Cattell, 1957a; Hammond, this book; Tupes & Christal, 1961; Norman, 1963a).

5. If there were nothing but secondaries and specifies in the 16-PF scales we should expect the variance of the primary scales to be almost wholly accounted for by the secondaries. Actually an average of only about 60%-70% (Gorsuch & Cattell, 1967; Cattell, Eber, & Delhees, 1968) across all the known primaries is accounted for by second-order variance.

6. If the Cattell first orders were mere *variables,* that is, scales made up at random or arbitrary cluster positions (as in the California Psychological Inventory [CPI] and other nonfactorial scales) and therefore variable in nature, they would not retain—as they very definitely do—the same pattern of loadings on the second orders from study to study. Actually, when simple structure has been blindly, maximally reached at the primary level, with different variables (scales and items) and different ages (through the 16 PF and the HSPQ, for example), the same second-order structure appears with remarkable accuracy, as shown, for example, by the recent superbly executed study of Sells (1963; Sells, Demaree, & Will, 1970). Crit-

ical evaluations of methods in contending studies were made recently by D. S. Vaughan (1973) and DeYoung (1972). In short, the constancy of pattern of the primaries on the secondaries, when the primaries are measured by different actual scales and in different samples, attests to their own unique reality. An attempt to show what conditions cause rotational solutions to flip over between the primary and secondary simple structure positions (see Equations 4 and 7) was offered by Cattell (1969).

7. Additional support for the present primaries *A* through $Q_1$ comes from their constancy of rotation in *progressive rectification* (Cattell, 1973a) studies.

The issue with which psychologists could be most profitably occupied at this stage is not that of whether primaries or secondaries exist—they both undoubtedly do—but the question of what the meaning of secondaries may be. To be consistent with our basic *influence model* we should conclude logically that a secondary is an influence common in operation to a set of primaries. For example, it might be something that in the past aided in the formation of each primary (as seems to be the case with Fluid Intelligence and the primary abilities, Cattell, 1969) or a common mechanism of expression which all of them can utilize at the present time, and so on. Some concrete help can be looked for on this issue by recourse to plasmodes, where we find, in the Thurstone *box* problem, the *general size* of a box (Thurstone, 1938) to be second order to length, breadth, and height, or, in the *ball* behavior problem (Cattell & Dickman, 1962), the cost of a ball to be second order to weight and volume, and so on. It should be recognized that in pursuing higher order factors in psychology, we may land ourselves *outside* the strictly psychological domain. For example, the possibility has already been encountered that they may refer to genes, in the science of genetics, or to the structure of social institutions, as studied by sociologists. Some second-stratum factors in personality primaries might be physiological influences. For example, it has been hypothesized that Cortertia ($F$III in $Q$-data second orders) represents some physiological determiner of general activation level, and one can imagine some general energy level that would simultaneously favor the development of such personality primaries as Surgency, Dominance, and Excitability in Exvia-Invia.

Despite the fact that higher strata factors can thus be most logically considered as influences operating on lower strata, and contributing to their development or effective action, two well-known second-stratum factors, Anxiety and Exvia, suggest a quite different, complex conception of an influence. They suggest, in fact, that the influence is some sort of *mutual interaction* effect among the primaries. For example, in Exvia, covering Factors *A, E, F, H,* and so forth, Affectothymia (*A*), which involves liking people, brings the individual more frequently into company; Dominance (*E*), gives him competitive satisfactions therein; Parmia (*H*), relieves him of the burden of shyness; and Surgency (*F*), gives social skills that are reinforcing of social interaction. Thus the gains of each are dependent on another of this set of factors, and a *spiral* of mutually aided increments could ensue in which they tend to advance together. Possibly other models of influence than (a) the simple, direct action of common, underlying influence and (b) the interactive spiral, can be found to account for the phenomena of second and higher strata factors, but these are presently the most promising.

It is in respect to such possible alternative models for generating factors and factor structures that the "more sophisticated look" at personality structure in the present chapter particularly needs to be pursued. But in summary of strata models we should at least proceed to explicit formulae. Equation 4 first sets out the familiar resolution of a variable, for example, a stimulus response or a questionnaire item, into primary factors. In the following equations, $k + 1$ primary traits are represented by $T$s with Arabic subscripts; secondaries, by $T$s with Roman subscripts:

$$a_{ij} = b_{j1} T_{1i} + \ldots + b_{jk} T_{ki} + b_j T_{ji}. \qquad (4)$$

The corresponding action of a series of secondaries on any primary $T_p$ can be stated by:

$$T_{pi} = b_{pI} T_{Ii} + \ldots + b_{pK} T_{Ki}$$
$$+ b_p T_{Pi}. \qquad (5)$$

Here we may refer to the specific, $T_p$, left over as the *stub* or *core* of the primary source trait. It is the part which preserves its action as a primary when the rest has been absorbed as a product of the secondaries.

Now it is possible to obtain the loading of a secondary *directly on a variable v* by the calculation (sometimes called the Cattell-White formula, in contrast to the Schmid-Leiman formula) as follows:

$$V_{fp1Iv} = V_{fp1v} V_{fpII} \qquad (6)$$

where $1v$ refers to weights of primaries on variables and II to secondaries on primaries, while $Iv$ is a matrix of loadings of secondaries on variables. Then, if for simplicity of representation we illustrate with only one secondary, the score on a variable can be estimated as in Equation 7, from the weights of this secondary directly on the variable and also of the stubs of the primaries directly on the variable. The loadings of the stubs on the variables are the original weights proportionately reduced for the loss of variance in each primary stub due to removing the secondary variance. The resulting $b$s are shown with one secondary and $k + 1$ primary stubs, as

$$a_{ij} = \bar{b}_{j1}T_{1i} + \bar{b}_{j1}\bar{T}_{1i} + \ldots \bar{b}_{jk}\bar{T}_{ki}$$
$$+ \, b_j T_{ji}, \tag{7}$$

modified and distinguished from the earlier ones by a bar. The details of this calculation (known as the Schmid-Leiman [S–L] transformation) can be followed elsewhere, where the present writer (Cattell, 1977) presented a model closely related to this as the most promising for final representation of personality structure. It is called the *stratified independent determiners* (SID) model because it suggests that originally the ultimate determiners are uncorrelated, and that the primaries become correlated only through sharing contributions by higher strata factors. Nevertheless, and though the Schmid-Leiman formula is used to calculate ultimate influence directly on the variables, the S–L is only an *as if* convenience. Unlike the Schmid-Leiman, the SID does not suppose that higher orders act directly on the variables, but that factors in each stratum really act only on the stratum immediately below them.

The choice between the S–L and the SID model is sometimes difficult. It could be that if the second-order $T$s have simple structure directly on the variables, as Sells, Eysenck, and the present writer undoubtedly sometimes find in the case of questionnaire items, the correct inference is that they are *presently operative* influences directly on variables, as the S–L formula may suppose. On the other hand, if the secondaries demonstrate (as they normally do) simple structure on the primaries but not on the variables, the

inference is that they were influences operating in the formation of the primaries but do not exist as currently acting determiners directly on variables. With this small glimpse into the essential possibilities and methodological problems regarding higher strata factors in personality structure and trait meaning, we must be content with this brief survey.

# 6  ROLE TRAITS AND THE DEFINITION OF THE GLOBAL SITUATION BY FOCAL AND AMBIENT STIMULI

Progress in personality-structure concepts must march hand in hand with progress in representing environmental structure and action. We have already shown how the *behavioral indexes*—$b$s—and *modulators*—$c$s—in the behavior specification equation give a precise definition in *vectors* of the psychological meaning of the environment. We have also shown how the definition of a trait or state, as a factor pattern, is embedded in a racial population and a culture, needing to be defined in the trait or state definition. In recognizing modulators, we have also split the global situation into a *focal stimulus* and an *ambient situation*, recognizing that they are independent and can be combined in innumerable ways. We propose now to pursue this analysis further, particularly by introducing an operational definition of a role, and recognizing it as the major instance, over and above the provocation of states, of environmental modification, and of personality trait action.

Sociology and cultural anthropology have made much of roles and status obligations and can define much about differences of cultures in those terms. This fact, (e.g., that virtually all drivers will stop at a red traffic light and most men let a lady through a door first) has tempted the sociologist, on the one hand, to deny the importance of personality, and psychologists, on the other, to take the framework of roles for granted. But people differ in the extent to which they adopt roles and the degree to which their traits overrule them. The basic thinking required is still that of the Analysis of Variance (ANOVA) model, where role effects distinguish groups but personality gives within-group variance, or that of our typological analysis, where both within-type and between-type dimensions are generally equally important in a final behavioral measure.

A *role* can be defined with emphasis on any one of several aspects of its action; some definitions neglect all but one. A cultural anthropologist or a social psychologist concerned with, say, business administration may define a given role by its function in terms of group needs (Parsons, T., 1938); a group dynamics psychologist may define role structure by the set of actions a person has to perform (Oeser & Hammond, 1954); a sociologist may define it by the picture of expectations that all citizens have regarding persons in that role (Linton, 1956; Stogdill, 1950); and a student of perception may define it by the changes in perception of a situation that adoption of a role produces in the incumbent (Hake, 1966). Here we shall take for granted the anthropological and sociopsychological emphases, namely, that a role is socially useful and also the sociologist's map of how group members respond in various ways to the role holder. Our concern is with the effect of the role on the person, and the fact that a role incumbent is moved to perform certain actions that would not occur in a personality identical with his own outside the role. We recognize also that certain changes in his perceptions of situations naturally accompany this adoption of a role.

However, unlike others who also have defined role structures by sets of actions, we do not assume that these often subtle behaviors can be written down simply by qualitative inspection. The role pattern has to be empirically quantitatively detected, as a factor pattern—as a degree of doing this or that—just as in any trait pattern. Needless, perhaps, to add that this role structure, covering an array of special response tendencies, is considered an acquired trait. It belongs in the class of dynamic traits ($D$ terms in the behavior specification equation) and specifically among the $M$s (engrams, sentiments) expressed in a pattern of attitudes and associated perceptual and motor skills. In more detailed statements of the behavioral equation, we shall typically represent it by $M_R$ or as $R$ (with another subscript for each particular role). This is true regardless of whether the person is virtually always in the role, as a child is in relation to the mother, or whether it is intermittent, as when a judge puts on robes and sits on the bench.

Since much discussion at the introspective level has connected role adoption with changes (in the way the person perceives the situation), let it be clear that the present formulation fully embraces the perceptual aspect. Elsewhere (Sells, 1968, and in chapter 1) we have already formulated an equation for the meaning of a perception to include (a) a term typical of all people who perceive that situation, expressed in the specification equation by the behavioral indexes and modulation indexes ($b$s and $s$s) common to all people in that situation, and (b) the trait scores of the person, which define the specific contribution of his own personality to the meaning. Additionally, that model includes, beyond the major personality factor determiners, special perception terms corresponding to transitory cognitive activities, included as lower-level factors—mental sets—among the sentiment factors.

The Vector-id-analysis (VIDA) model (see Chapter 1) for role action includes both (a) a comparatively sudden access in magnitude of a behavioral index $b$, and of a modulator index $s$, on a term $R$ as the person steps into the role situation, and (b) the existence of a role term $R$, having a specific score for each individual, and representing the extent to which he has the skills and interests for assuming that role. The score on such a role-trait term will naturally be larger for a person capable of entering the role. These $R$, $b$, and $s$ terms, as shown in a matrix in Table 1, express two essential characteristics of role phenomena: (a) that one and the same person responds *differently* to one and the *same* focal stimulus when he is in the role situation and when he is not in it (ambient situation); and (b) that different people, despite having much the same general personality, will respond differently even in the same ambient, role-provoking situation, because one is more endowed in the role factor $R$ than others are, for example, when he is a father, when the others are not. The greater action of role behavior relative to personality behavior in a given person in a given situation may thus be due to a larger endowment of the person in $R$, or a larger endowment of the situation in $s$.

Earlier (chapter 1), it was suggested that the most developed form of the specification equation breaks down the observed $v$s (a fraction of the $b$ loading) into $p$ (perception) and $e$ (execution) terms, so that the typical entry has four terms, $p$, $e$, $s$, and $T$, in which the ordinary loading $b$ has first been broken into $v$ and $s$; then, by experimental manipulation, $v$ has been divided into $p$ and $e$. It would offer an attractively neat operational relationship if we could say that $p$ expresses variation of trait action over focal stimuli—the $h$s—$e$ over the variety of responses—the $j$s—and $s$ over the ambient situations—the $k$s. A psychologist, however, would ask whether this cleanness of separations means what it seems to mean. Does not the ambient situation, for example, alter the meaning of the focal stimulus in some more complex way than an additive effect? And although the ambient situation is given the role of modulating the factor itself, that is, altering momentarily the individual's level thereon, does not the focal stimulus also produce some modulation? Reflexological learning theory certainly has given drive-evoking powers to a focal stimulus.

That the focal stimulus perception $p_h$ does not account for the whole of perception is no problem: $s_{kx}$, $T_{xi}$ and even $e_j$ have been given roles in that, too. But it may well be that $s$ will need to be considered a function of *both* the ambient situation $k$ and the focal stimulus $h$. There will then be more to determining these values than the initially

**TABLE 1**  Role definition matrix for $T_{Ri}$

| Stimulus situations and responses | Involvement index | | | Modulator value | | | Change in mean | | |
|---|---|---|---|---|---|---|---|---|---|
| | $P_1$ | $\ldots$ $P_q$ $\ldots$ | $M_R$ | $P_1$ | $\ldots$ $P_q$ $\ldots$ | $M_R$ | $P_1$ | $\ldots$ $P_q$ $\ldots$ | $M_R$ |
| $j_1 h_1 k_1$ | $v_{11}$ | $v_{1q}$ | $v_1 R$ | $s_{11}$ | $s_{1q}$ | $s_1 R$ | $c_{11}$ | $c_{1q}$ | $c_1 R$ |
| $j_1 h_1 k_2$ | $v_{21}$ | $v_{2q}$ | $v_2 R$ | $s_{21}$ | $s_{2q}$ | $s_2 R$ | $c_{21}$ | $c_{2q}$ | $c_2 R$ |
| Etc. | | | | | | | | | |

*Note.* This analysis supposes $q$ personality factors and one role factor. The $v$s represents fractions of $b$ indexes.

proposed factoring over all four sets of the Data Box in a grid (Cattell, 1966e, 1977) design. The latter supposes we have variables that represent all possible combinations of focal stimuli, types of response, and ambient situations, and correlate these composite variables over people. The $p$ value for a given focal stimulus is the mean loading over all combinations of that stimulus with the series of responses and the series of ambient situations. The $s$ value is the mean loading for all combinations of that ambient situation with other sets, and so on. It will be noted that a form of score must be used, for example, time, that is applicable to all kinds of responses. Conceivably one will find fairly frequently that there are correlations between certain stimulus and certain response values, as part of the old problem that only some responses are appropriate to some stimuli. There are thus difficulties to be straightened out empirically, but the VIDA model offers the psychologist a beginning of splitting loadings so as to assign further indexes to personality factor source-trait expressions related to the situation and to response characters of the behavioral event.

Within this framework, it is now proposed to represent a role factor by a special term $M_R$, implying that it is a form of acquired sentiment, and to place it in the general specification equation along with Ability, $A$, Temperament, $P$, Ergic, $E$ and other sentiments, $M$, thus:

$$a_{hijk} = \sum_{w=a} pesA_{wi} + \sum_{x=q} pesP_{xi}$$
$$+ \sum_{y=m} pesE_{yi} + \sum_{z=o} pesM_{zi}$$
$$+ \sum_{R=t} pesM_{Ri} \qquad (8)$$

The subscripts of $p_{hw}$ (etc.), $e_{jw}$ (etc.), $s_{hkw}$ (etc.), are omitted to avoid cluttering

and we will leave the reader to set them in appropriately in this lengthy equation. What Equation 8 is saying is simply that $t$ role factors are operative along with $(a+q+m+o)$ general personality factors, and it implies that a person can be acting simultaneously in several roles. Our assertion is that the modulator action $s_{hkR}$ in a role trait generally is considerable, as in a dynamic state, so that a person moves in and out of a role strongly modifying his behavior according to the role cues in the ambient situation $k$. Indeed, unlike other $ss$, these modulators may prove to be all-or-nothing in their effects; that is, in general, a person is either in a role or out of it. As an ordinary driver, a person stops at a red light and does not expect other cars to stop as he passes; the same person as an ambulance driver behaves quite differently—and there is no halfway position to being *in* the ambulance-driver role.

What appears first as one factor among many will have its role character recognized by the loading properties shown and others. Like any other trait it will have its loadings irregularly scattered over the markers for personality factors; that is, all kinds of personality factors may experience expression in the role. However, it is likely to have fewer expressions and a more extensive hyperplane than most personality and ability factors, because a role generally operates in a limited number of situations. Finally, its separation will be assisted by noting that its loading will tend to align with a number of ambient situations recognizable as role cues, whereas a personality factor is unlikely to be so tied down in expression. This sort of pattern is illustrated in Table 2.

It should be noted, in passing, that the principles of choosing variables to recognize and separate role factors are close to those involved in separating the three modalities—abilities, temperament, and dynamic factors—though the specific properties to be

**TABLE 2** Experimental differentiation of role factor traits ($M_R$s) from general personality traits ($P$s) by pattern of loadings on variables

| Pre-planned combinations of focal ($h$) and ambient ($k$) stimulus situations and responses ($j$s) | Factors isolated | | | | |
|---|---|---|---|---|---|
| | $P_1$ | $P_2$ | $M_{R1}$ | $M_{R2}$ | $M_{R3}$ |
| $j_1 h_1 k_1$ | .6 | | .5 | | |
| $j_1 h_1 k_2$ | .7 | | | .6 | |
| $j_1 h_1 k_3$ | .5 | | | | .3 |
| $j_2 h_2 k_1$ | | .5 | .7 | | |
| $j_2 h_2 k_2$ | | .8 | | .6 | |
| $j_2 h_2 k_3$ | | .7 | | | .7 |
| . | | | | | |
| . | | | | | |
| . | | | | | |
| $j_m h_m k_1$ | .4 | .5 | .4 | | |
| $j_m h_m k_2$ | .7 | .4 | | .5 | |
| $j_m h_m k_3$ | .5 | .6 | | | .6 |

*Note.* A particular focal stimulus, $h$, is here in each case linked with a particular response, $j$. But the ambient stimuli, $k$, are paired with focal stimuli in all possible ways. The personality factors, $P$s, are loaded on stimulus response variables in no particular way that can be foreseen. But the role factors, $M_R$s, are loaded in regular relation to the presence of particular ambient stimuli, being thereby recognizable.

chosen, in variables for the latter, are more subtle (Cattell & Warburton, 1967, chapter 5).

An alternative form of the role models deserves brief mention. This model hypothesizes that the role will be a second-order factor, which, as such, would favor the expression of several particular first-order personality factors and sentiments. Of course, it would modulate, and as such, would modulate also the primaries affected. This model, which remains to be investigated, has the psychological appeal of explaining the dynamics of certain roles in terms of their giving expression to particular dynamic and other personality traits, and thus having appeal to particular personalities. In addition to the other characteristics, a role trait would have the property of a sentiment of activating various appropriate

sets within the $M$ hierarchy. One would anticipate, furthermore, some special relations of role traits to the Self-sentiment, with which they would have to be consistent. The clearest checks on role-trait structure so far have been those of Sweney (1969) and Krug (1968) (see also Krug & Cattell, 1971). In assigning scores on a defined role trait, it is obviously important to spread the choice of sample of variables with high weights as equally as possible over several different personality source traits expressions, to reduce spurious correlations of estimates with personality factor scores.

## 7 FOUR MAIN SOURCES OF PATTERN AND MEASUREMENT DISTORTION, AS COVERED BY PERTURBATION THEORY

A more sophisticated look at personality structure requires not only greater clarity on the conceptual and metric nature of the structures themselves, but also regard for effects due to distortion by observer and measuring instrument. Some debates seemingly about personality structure (e.g., Becker, 1964; Comrey & Duffy, 1968; Eysenck, H. J., & Eysenck, 1967; Guilford, J. P., 1976; Peterson & Cattell, 1959; Wiggins, J. S., 1973) could be resolved better nowadays (with the advance of perturbation theory), as belonging to the study of distortion.

Phenomena of perturbation, that is, of systematic effects showing internal inconsistency of observations not unlike those previously encountered in other sciences, such as astronomy and physics,[4] have been reacted to in the past in psychology by bringing in various ad hoc *excuses* for the discrepancy. Thus in psychology there is a considerable literature invoking stylistic and halo effects (see Wiggins, J. S., 1962), lie scales (Cofer, Chanee, & Hudson, 1949), acquiescence response sets (Dahlstrom, 1962), and especially by concepts of social desirability distortions (Edwards, A. L., 1957), to mention just a few approaches. Just as other sciences were led to some of their most important discoveries and new areas of systematization by explicit concentration on perturbations clarifying whether they were due to measurement or require real change of theory, so *perturbation theory* is offered in psychology. It aims to bring into a comprehensive, orderly, and predictively effective frame of reference much that practitioner-oriented researches

have attempted to handle by rather narrowly conceived notions such as that of a *social desirability factor*. There are, of course, in any case, *desirabilities* rather than *desirability* and, as J. S. Wiggins (1973) showed, the empirical evidence itself is incompatible with a single desirability factor.

Error in psychological conclusions is of two kinds: (a) sampling error, that is, making a wrong inference from what happens in a sample about what happens in the population, and (b) observation or measurement error. Our concern here is with the latter, which in turn has two forms: (a) the effect of error on some single measurement (e.g., a mean), and (b) the effect on a relationship, such as the pattern of a factor. It is with this latter form that the personality structure theorist is mainly concerned. Scientific advance consists of establishing new relations in existing data, but also *in cutting into the error variance*, that is, in finding relations in what previously was set aside as random error. What for some years we have called *perturbation theory* (Cattell & Digman, 1964) is a system for ordering, understanding, and conducting research on those obscurities in existing theoretical concepts that arise from perturbation by the observation and measuring processes. In terms of the Data Box, all of these effects arise from the fifth coordinate, which is called the *observer set* but includes the observer's instruments along with the observer. So far the measures in our theoretical models have been considered error free, and have been written $a_{hijk}$. To embrace measurement error, they would be written $a_{hijko}$, $o$ being the source of variance in the observer.

The branch of perturbation theory dealing with what *social desirability*, *acquiescence*, and other patchwork approaches have worked on is called *trait-view theory*, in which the observer is either another person

---

[4] The acceptance of elaborate epicycles in the pre-Copernican (Ptolemaic) models of the solar system is an example of failure to recognize properly the relativity to the observer, whereas the study of the poor fit mysteriously shown by the orbit of Uranus—considered as perturbation to be explained—is an example of the fruitfulness of precisely recognizing perturbations.

(*L* data) or the person observing himself (*Q* data). But to understand this particular theory, it is necessary first to describe general perturbation theory. This section, 7, presents a general taxonomy and verbal discussion of *perturbation theory*. Section 8 turns to the operational, experimental designs by which *instrument factors* and other perturbation factors are to be pinned down. Section 9 deals solely with *trait-view theory*—the special perturbation in *Q* and *L* data—because, in psychological practice, it is the most important segment of perturbation theory.

In the present limited space, the scope and divisions of perturbation theory can most readily be presented by a *map*, as in Fig. 6, the discussions underlying which will be found in Cattell and Digman (1964) and Cattell (1968b). Although the effects there classified affect both single measures and patterns, it is the effect on patterns that must be the theoretician's main concern.

The substantive and random-error factors at the top of Fig. 6 need no explanations; thus, discussion will begin with the first three forms of systematic perturbation. The fourth is elaborated in section 9.

## 7.1  Immediate Data and Data-Treatment Artefacts

These arise from correlations due to (a) shared scaling effects, for example, similar skewedness or coarseness of interval, on subsets of variables; (b) scoring systems that inadvertently create algebraic dependencies among variables; (c) the types of covariance index used, for example, correlation coefficient; and (d) the steps that lead to particular types of further analysis, for example, effects issuing as by-products of the model by which data are analyzed. Diverse concrete illustrations of the three

are, respectively, a scaling that produces a similar distortion on all members of a subset of variables—a scaling that tends to exaggerate whatever correlations exist among them and thus creates an apparent but actually nonexistent factor over the set; the use of the tetrachoric correlation instead of a Pearson coefficient, which tends to eliminate extremity (difficulty) factors; and the use of an orthogonal simple structure (contradiction in terms) rotation program, such as Quartimax or Varimax, which typically fails to disperse the first principal axis factor and thus creates a quasi-general factor where none exists (or makes a second-order factor more general than it should be).

Some of the Class 1 effects may be matrix-specific effects, that is, not occurring in other experiments with the same variables. These we would relegate to the upper left of Fig. 6, since our concern is with distortions repeating themselves across experiments. As to the magnitude of the spurious factors in II($b$)1, those from scaling effects and particular correlation coefficients are in general small; but those from defective rotational principles and resolution programs affect theories as wide as all psychology. In sheer magnitude of total contribution to confusion of concepts, nothing exceeds that from casual or hurried, last minute, purely automatic rotational resolutions. Rotation is actually the most important part of any factor-analytic research and, when properly completed, takes nine-tenths of the time and effort required for the total undertaking. There is one case, however, where the particular *index of association* used also produces large effects—when cross products are used instead of correlations or covariances. Another almost equally gross perturbation is seen where use of *Q* technique or ipsative scoring wipes out a whole factor, and distorts others (Cattell, 1950c, 1966e; Clemans, 1966).

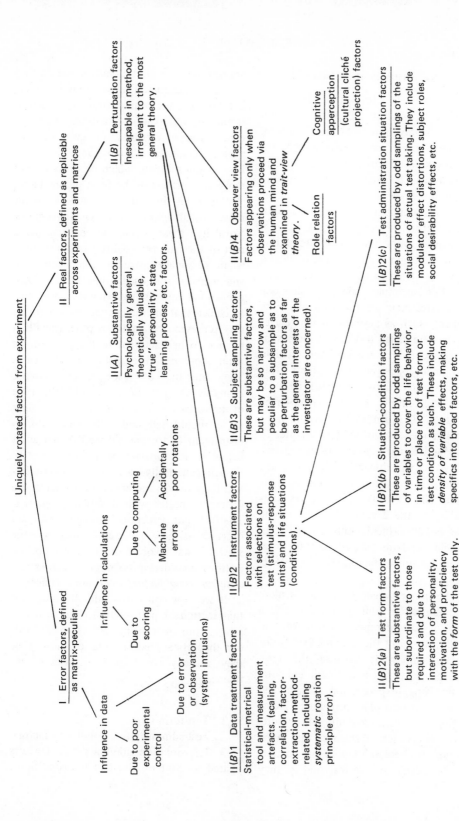

Uniquely rotated factors from experiment

I  Error factors, defined as matrix-peculiar

II  Real factors, defined as replicable across experiments and matrices

Influence in data

Influence in calculations

Due to poor experimental control

Due to scoring

Due to computing

Machine errors

Accidentally poor rotations

Due to error or observation (system intrusions)

II(A)  Substantive factors
Psychologically general, theoretically valuable, "true" personality, state, learning process, etc. factors.

II(B)  Perturbation factors
Inescapable in method, irrelevant to the most general theory.

II(B)1  Data treatment factors
Statistical-metrical tool and measurement artefacts. (scaling, correlation, factor-extraction-method-related, including *systematic* rotation principle error).

II(B)2  Instrument factors
Factors associated with selections on test (stimulus-response units) and life situations (conditions).

II(B)3  Subject sampling factors
These are substantive factors, but may be so narrow and peculiar to a subsample as to be perturbation factors as far as the general interests of the investigator are concerned).

II(B)4  Observer view factors
Factors appearing only when observations proceed via the human mind and examined in *trait-view theory*.

II(B)2(a)  Test form factors
These are substantive factors, but subordinate to those required and due to interaction of personality, motivation, and proficiency with the *form* of the test only.

II(B)2(b)  Situation-condition factors
These are produced by odd samplings of variables to cover the life behavior, in time or place not of test form or test conditon as such. These include *density of variable* effects, making specifics into broad factors, etc.

II(B)2(c)  Test administration situation factors
These are produced by odd samplings of the situations of actual test taking. They include modulator effect distortions, subject roles, social desirability effects, etc.

Role relation factors

Cognitive apperception (cultural cliché projection) factors

**FIG. 6**  Classification of obtainable factors and of the sources of perturbation obscuring substantive factors.

## 7.2  Instrument Factors

Instrument factors (see Fig. 6) constitute the second main class of perturbers, and probably a highly important one. The term has hitherto been used rather loosely for almost any kind of artificial factor structure that clearly can be seen to arise from common, uniform features of certain sets of the variables—features that are of a superficial or irrelevant nature. It seems desirable here, in more intensive work devoted to discounting artefacts, to separate a true sense of *instrument factor* from some broader, looser usages. For example, some effects due purely to treatment of the data after the experiment, such as algebraic dependencies in scores, were called instrument factors, as well as some (which we have separated in Fig. 6) under *observer view* effects (role relations, apperceptions). A typical instance of the latter would be if one observes strengths of 10 attitudes first by memory effects and then by autism (see chapter 5, Dielman and Krug) manifestations. Factoring will give 5 true dynamic structures (each a doublet)—if 2 attitudes are markers for each—but also 2 instrument factors, corresponding to the 2 vehicles, each running over 10 variables. Incidentally, special techniques and standards are necessary for rotating such instrument factors (Cattell, 1968b, 1977).

The term *instrument factor* needs more exact definition at this point, for it is a concept of considerable importance. Incidentally, we reject the term *method factor* sometimes employed, because the term method properly has a different connotation, involving experimental design and methods of analysis. The instrument factor arises from the instrumentality of measurement or observation, influences that come into action in a research before any posttest scoring or calculation begins, that is, they are not due to analytic *method* nor do they include *artefactors*. They are thus defined as due to shared characteristics in the actual testing or observation situations extending across several variables, or even to temporary, accidental stimulus conditions in the lives of the subjects, which produce local or temporary effects in the form of new factor structures in the data, over and above the more broadly replicable personality factors. Normally, these would not be considered part of the true personality factor structure, when personality structures are conceived and chosen for widest negotiability and conceptual universality. However, we must recognize that instrument factors sometimes may represent real ability or other traits that happen to be irrelevant to the goals of the main structural investigation at the time. They are out of place in the variance primarily being studied. The only other type of perturbation influence that one might argue should fall under the rubric of an instrument factor is what we have set apart below as an *observer view* influence. Although generically close to instrument factors these distortions are best considered as a different species with different properties. The fact that perception through the *human* observer is here involved, guided by the special laws involved in such perception, justifies considering *instrument factors* and *observer view factors* as separate concepts.

If we now concentrate the discussion on that section of perturbation (Fig. 6) which arises from instrument factors so defined, our theoretical analysis (Fig. 6) shows that they actually cover three varieties of influence:

1. Test-form factors.
2. Test-administration-condition factors.
3. Life-situation sampling factors (factors related to content area and life condition).

The word *test* here includes any form of observation or measurement, that is, *T, Q,* or *L* data. Distortion specific to ratings (*L* data) only and self-ratings (*Q* data) only are considered separately under *observer view effects*. A brief analysis of these subdivisions is required.

### 7.2.1 Test-Form Factors

These factors, II*B*2(*a*) in Fig. 6, are patterns due to interaction of real characteristics of the individual with the test form. However, the characteristics are so irrelevant, incidental, and unwanted in the main research that they are best set aside as instrument factors. An extreme instance would be a personality test with a reading vocabulary so high that part of the variance—appearing as a distinct factor—is due to reading ability, or one with, say, a 7-point scale of response where a response set to *extremity of response* could affect the results. Incidentally, much *response set* work has been obscure through lack of reference to perturbation theory principles. For in the *response sets* approach, effects demonstrated in objective-test personality research to be partly due to the action of real personality factors (Cattell, 1954) were not distinguished from the purely local intrusions that instrument-factor theory rightly recognizes as different and would set aside as spurious. Only by experiment with different forms of tests for the same recognizable personality factors can one find what patterns represent instrument-factor variance. An arbitrary, grossly literal, and a priori designation of a certain part of a test contribution as response set or distortion effect (as in the multimethod-multitrait formulation) simply will not do.

Test-form instrument factors, representing (as they ultimately do) real traits of people, can extend all the way from the matrix-specific, narrow, unimportant, and impertinent traits they typically are, to broad traits extending across whole domains of data, for example, all rating data. At the latter extreme, they are like a radio comedy broadcast leading into an intergalactic radio-telescope reception, that is, they are something interesting and comprehensible that merely happen to be quite out of place. A well-known instance of a quite meaningful instrument-factor intrusion appears in the ability *device* factors that contribute appreciably to test variance in objective motivation-strength measures as in the Motivational Analysis Test (MAT) and the School Motivational Analysis Test (SMAT) measures (see Dielman and Krug, this book) of Ergic Tension and Sentiment-strength, and which need to be systematically allowed for. It needed these findings concerning the systematic instrument-factor intrusion of ability into motivation measures to awaken conventional test users to the fact that for years they have failed to allow for the reciprocal but more subtle distortion—that of motivation instrument factors' leaking into intelligence tests.

### 7.2.2 Test-Administration-Condition Factors

These instrument factors, II(*B*)2(*c*) in Fig. 6, are similar in magnitude and fairly similar in form to test-form instrument factors, but are due to special conditions in the administration conditions. If a test requiring fine visual discrimination is given in a situation where some people have poor lighting, a factor of *light intensity at the given desk* would be expected to emerge. (And, if not recognized as an instrument factor in the subsequent analysis, it could be counted on to blur both personality structure conceptions and individual true scores.) The category of administrative conditions extends, however, from such gross physical effects to motivation conditions allied to *social desirability* (yet distinguishable from what Edwards specifically designates as *s.d.* in self-rating and which we consider here under observer view phenomena). Such a factor can appear over tests in one condition of administration, for example, by people trying unusually hard in an objective (*T*-data) performance under competitive as opposed to noncompetitive situations. To this general administrative-condition class belong also the state modulator effects and role effects, cued by some general ambient stimulus. It is true that according to the definitions of role in the last section, we might be inclined to consider these as instances of a role factor and therefore a real dynamic trait. Even if it were so, it would still be, from the standpoint of some re-search objectives and designs, an unfortu-nately intruding instrument factor. However, although arising from a role cue, the test-instrument-administration factor may not have the full breadth and meaning of a role cue, for it may arise from repeating just one specific, narrow form of a role cue across all tests and is really an expression of the role only through what is specific to a narrow expression of it.

Administration instrument factors are particularly likely to bedevil the results of analyses where the same tests have been given in, say, several different classrooms. With the several different attitudes to teachers and testing, along with dimensions as morale, relative staleness in testing, and so forth, which prevail in different classrooms, and from the personalities of several differ-ent experimenters, fairly large fractions of subject variance may be eaten up by such instrument factors.

### 7.2.3 Situation-condition or Life-situation Sampling Factors

These factors are shown as II(*B*)2(*b*) in Fig. 6. The effect of situation sampling

refers to two distinct subdivisions among effects: (a) those due to biased sampling of content (in regard to some symbolic *life space* population of behaviors) in the test-response variables themselves, and (b) those due to sampling of life situations in which the subjects are actually living, quite apart from the test. An example of the former would be taking variables in a personality test only from observed classroom behavior, for example, teacher rating. An example of the latter would be testing children during vacation time as contrasted to testing them (anywhere) during the school year.

In the former instance, all the sampled expressions of a trait such as, say, Domi-nance or Surgency, will be in the school situation; a child whose sentiment toward school authority happens to be strong may have all manifestations of these two traits, and perhaps of some others, proportionately reduce. The result will be that a school environment instrument factor will spread across these traits, and will either be located as such or will be rotated (by an investigator not too precise as to number of factors or rotation) into *refraction factors* (as discussed later). Note, for future generalization, that such an instrument factor need not spread across *all* variables measured in school, as the so-called multimethod-multitrait formula-tion—which is an alternative to the instru-ment-factor model—would fallaciously set out to analyze it. An instrument factor need not extend across the kinds of variables that in the *multimethod model* (Campbell & Fiske, 1959) are designated as common in *method*. Instead it would occur only in those behaviors in which the school calls for inhibition of Dominance and Surgency.

In this domain of odd test sampling of life situations, oddity can arise in two main senses: (a) by an imbalance between areas (in an extreme case through all tests being taken from only one type of life situation) and (b) by having an extreme high or extreme low density of representation in all areas (when each area is duly represented). The former is illustratable, as just indicated, by restriction to particular situational-response areas such as school, home, Sundays only, military life, club only, and so on. The second is more subtle, since it involves the new concept of *density*. In one area of behavior—say on the athletic field—one could take 1,000 different specific bits of behavior or perhaps 10 abstracted concepts, each supposed to cover 100 bits of such behavior. The shift along this dimension has been called a shift in density of representation. One would expect—and one actually finds—that if the investigator starts with a low density of representation—say 10 variables instead of 100 in the same behavior area—he will tend to go directly to second-stratum factors if the factors found from the 100 are designated first-stratum factors. Experiment indicates that $Q$-data items are likely to be much denser than are $T$-data items (a single startle-response measure in the latter may be the subject, implicitly, of 10 questionnaire items in the former). It is this effect of unintended differences of density of test sampling of situations that seemingly accounts for the second-stratum $Q$ data factors $Q$I (Exvia-Invia) and $Q$II (Anxiety), for example, appearing as the first-order $T$-data factors, as *U.I.* 32 and *U.I.* 24 (Hundleby, Pawlik & Cattell, 1965), respectively. Thus the effect of the second type of situation sampling in the stimulus-response units is to give us factors at different strata, whereas that of the first type—an imbalance of life-expression areas—is to give biased—and, commonly, systematically biased—estimates of personality factors, because some people express certain types of behavior in one situation more than others do in that situation. A good deal of this effect can be described as confounding of personal-

ity factors with role factors. Other effects, for example, specialized expression of sociability in school or dominance in the home, are due to differences in the area of reward and inhibition experience.

When we turn from the effect of sampling of test variables (in regard to their area of behavioral reference in life) to the sampling of the actual situations (implicitly, ambient stimulus situations) in which people live at the time of measurement, we encounter the interesting and little-discussed problem of how far a factoring of behavior reflects—and brings into our patterns of personality concepts—structures actually representing the structure of the environment. In a wider, abstract sense it may be said that since we have agreed that a trait structure is inherent in both persons and environment, it would be inconsistent to argue that there can be any concept of a *true* environment-free trait from which each local situation might depart to a stated degree. However, both statistically and theoretically, it is possible to conceive, designate, and measure a generalized trait as an abstraction from several local variable factorings and thus to recognize the effect of local situations in each of the more local patterns. For example, we can say the particular factor pattern of Intelligence or Ego-strength in U.S. culture is such and such, but we agree it will have some real modification in Georgia or New York.

Thus, anything but the most generalized, worldwide mean pattern must be recognized as actually reflecting systematically the pattern of the environment. This is true, at least, of ability and dynamic modalities in that mechanical-aptitude factor patterns grow up only in a mechanical culture, and interest in sports only where there are sports. If toward the end of a maze, rats encounter a bar press followed immediately by a paper hoop, those who complete the maze more frequently will get higher scores on both performances. The factor of *maze skill* will show both of these variables to be part of its patterns. Similarly, in human sentiment structures, say, in the source trait for the pattern of religious interests (see chapter 5, this *Handbook*), we find interests and attitudes bound together as they are bound in the opportunities of exercise existing in the social-institution pattern itself, that is, in the church. Or, in human abilities, the form of the Crystallized Intelligence factor ($g_c$, Cattell & Horn, 1967) will copy the school curriculum of the period.

These patterns are not instrument factors; they are the substance of real traits, which take their common form from the learning effects of a common environment. Some effects of this kind, however, can be viewed as instrument factors when they are highly local in place and time and when our main concern is actually with trait concepts and measurements that transcend such extreme degrees of parochialism. If we factor a mixed group of, say, rural and city folk on some general personality trait, such as Affectia (sociability), we have the possibility of taking out a common trait pattern and setting aside the rural-urban difference either as a bipolar instrument factor or as two instrument factors. This is discussed operationally in the next section of this chapter. But more typically, within the instrument-factor concept is the effect of including groups under two different *temporary* conditions, as when some are tested on an average day and others on a day of stress.

A special case of the intrusion of environment into obtained structure arises wherever a time or space limit is imposed—and a 24-hour limit is always present in human affairs. Suppose, for example, we present a rat with a limited life space consisting of a home cage, an open field, and an activity wheel and score his performance in each over a day (or an hour) by the time the rat

accords to each. Then there is bound to be a negative correlation, typically holding among all three scores. This falls in the same pattern as applying *ipsative scoring* to human interests, for in ipsative scoring the total circle of interest must reach the same score for everyone. The issue is a complex one, pursued elsewhere (Cattell, 1966e; 1969b; Clemans, 1966; Gorsuch, 1974), but the imposition of ipsatizing conditions most typically result in one large, negatively loaded instrument factor covering all fields, or in negative correlations among the first-order traits that results in a bipolar second order.

## 7.3 Subject Sampling Factors

These factors appear as II($B$)3 in Fig. 6. It is questionable whether extremes of sampling or compounding a population heterogeneous as to subpopulations should be considered a source of real perturbation factors. Typically, such extremes merely change the variance of true substantive factors already present. But reference to these effects is included here because, at least, they may exaggerate to serious proportions distortions from other sources that might otherwise be trivial. Changes in sheer range of subjects in samples from a homogeneous parent population will distort factor patterns and correlations according to well-known principles propounded by Thurstone (1938), G. M. Meredith (1967b), and others. These perturbations need to be recognized, but they are perturbations in a more limited sense—changes of degree rather than kind—compared with the generation of *false* factors as here studied. In general, with larger and, therefore (other things being equal), more heterogeneous samples, *apparently* new factors are more likely to appear, which are factors of too small variance to have been seen before.

Before considering the fourth main source of perturbation factors, we take up pragmatic problems of separating substantive from instrument factors.

## 8 PROBLEMS IN THE OPERATIONAL, EXPERIMENTAL SEPARATION OF SUBSTANTIVE AND INSTRUMENT FACTORS

Our concern previously has been with the necessary prior qualitative, conceptual analysis of the types of instrument factor, by source. In this section, we propose to describe the formal experimental operations connected with recognizing perturbation factors, as discussed earlier (and to some extent under trait-view effects, as discussed in section 9). For, as usual, it is one thing to recognize conceptually and define some effect, and quite another to bring it effectively to operational separation and measurement.

The operational issues are these: (a) How do we recognize the appearance of perturbation effects, particularly of instrument factors? (b) How can experimental design, notably in regard to selection of variables and conditions, be so set up as to avoid them, to reduce them, or to allow for them in dealing with substantive factors? The operational anwers are, in part, different according to the variety of instrument factors (II($B$)2 in Fig. 6), respectively, as to (a) test form, (b) administration, and (c) life-situation sampling. (The remedies for II($B$)1, data treatment, and II($B$)3, subject sampling, are too obvious to need discussion, while II($B$)4, observer view effect, is deferred for special discussion in section 9.)

The main points to keep in mind for avoiding or reducing instrument factor effects are that choice of variables and conditions should be such as to (a) provide the experimenter with the known highest loaded marker variables for the personality structures the existence and form of which he is concerned to test and that he will later want to measure, (b) arrange the expected overlaps of loading patterns in the ensuing factor pattern matrix so that each factor's pattern is randomized or balanced[5] with regard to the set of variables loaded by every other substantive factor and the instrument factors, and (c) choose variables so as to result in at least two (and preferably several) instrument factors to be present in any matrix. This avoids the situation of having one instrument factor covering all variables—which makes rotation of the true factor from the instrument factor virtually impossible. The rule for dependable recognition of factors is the same as that for reduced bias in factor-score estimation, namely, to spread one personality factor over variables covering several instrument factors and one instrument factor over several personality factors.

It will be noticed that this last practical step is reached both by perturbation theory (instrument-factor section) and by Campbell and Fiske's multimethod-multitrait (MMMT) approach. Apart from this important agreement, however, the MMMT and *convergent*

---

[5] Because most instrument factors are positive in all loadings it is not possible to balance positive and negative loadings in a *suppressor action* for the instrument factor (Guilford, J. P., 1959; Cattell, 1961a), but only to trivialize the instrumentation in the sense that a true factor estimate is not contaminated with just *one* of them more than various others. (This is Campbell and Fiske's *multimethod.*) With substantive traits, on the other hand (except abilities and motivation modalities), where loadings are just as frequently positive as negative, suppressor balancing of positive and negative loadings for an unwanted factor is commonly possible. At some future stage of psychology it may be possible, through finding instrument factors that load both positively and negatively or correlate negatively with one another, to make choices of variables calculated to get pure source-trait measurements.

and *divergent* validity approaches (Campbell & Fiske, 1959; Fiske, 1971; Jackson, D. N., (1975) are less comprehensive in conception than perturbation theory and, in the opinion of many who have studied both, less elegant as a model. In practice the chief difference is that MMMT defines *methods*, that is, instrument areas a priori, whereas perturbation theory *finds* instrument factors, recognizing both their natural boundaries and their natural varieties. This recognition of the true extent, variety, and size leads to something more than a gross statistical treatment by averaging methods. It *plans* with expectations, but it allows the test for the number of factors, and the natural position given by simple structure or confactor rotation to tell us where each instrument factor begins and ends. For example, it will also permit a certain instrumentality (*method*) to yield more than one factor if in fact that is the nature of the latter. The weakness of the MMMT and the convergent and divergent validity approaches is that even the best psychologist cannot say that because he uses, for example, a forced-choice presentation in a set of items, or, perhaps, a scoring by time in some performances and by errors in others, that the instrument factors correspond one-to-one to his a priori divisions. The accumulating evidence is that where the instrument-factor approach is followed, one can actually, by setting aside the various factors that appear in instruments, reach instrument-transcending general personality trait structure. The estimation of scores on such real personality factors has to proceed, however, through an assembly of diversely instrument-contaminated actual scores; and that requires an understanding of the proper weighting and balancing of the instrument factors, that is, knowledge of instrument structure per se.

Any insightful and accurate factor score estimation in general calls, therefore, for clear separation, recognition, and assessment of all kinds of factors—trait, state, role, instrument, or trait-view—involved in the variables. The important thing in locating and allowing for perturbing instrument factor patterns is that as research advances, we deliberately approach the instrument-free personality factor by putting in types of measures likely to mark as many different known instrument factors as possible. This involves regard for the list of instrument factors found in ways of scaling, or methods of administration, or kinds of life situations behind different sets of variables.

Since it still happens that books on psychometrics—especially when written by *itemetric* psychologists—argue that increases in scale homogeneity are always desirable, one must point out that the result of a good design in the preceding sense, in regard to assisting factor batteries to give unbiased (pure source trait) score estimation (ie., unbiased with respect to instruments) will be to *reduce* the homogeneity of the battery. Whereas allowing one or more substantial instrument factors to overlap entirely with the trait factor will increase the homogeneity correlations among items, the insightful design of an instrument-transcending trait battery will definitely reduce homogeneity indexes.

As pointed out by Cattell and Tsujioka (1964), traditional psychometrics has valued high homogeneity to a quite irrational extent and, indeed, has not hesitated to be naively critical in the applied field of batteries or scales that do not manifest positive homogeneity. But provided the factor-concept validity is as high as can be reached with available items, high homogeneity is actually to be avoided. For high homogeneity is commonly achieved, as just pointed out, by introducing among the items already well loaded on the real, required factor, an additional sharing of what aptly has been called a *bloated specific*. A bloated specific is what is actually psychologically a narrow, specific kind of behavior, as created by an instrument; it normally appears as a narrow instrument factor. However, when blown up into a broad factor by using the same contaminating specificity (instrumental or other) to cover all items for one important personality factor, it becomes a false *broad factor*. This effect is shown in Fig. 7 as a general case. Several specific instances thereof were exposed by Ishikawa in highly homogeneous questionnaires that, incidentally, were evaluated highly by reviewers who innocently worship high homogeneity as a goal (see Comrey, 1970; Howarth & Browne, 1971). It is somewhat

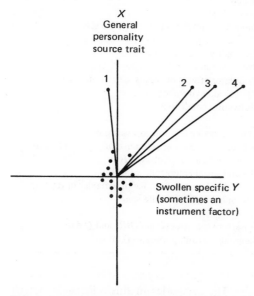

X
General
personality
source trait

1    2, 3, 4

Swollen specific Y
(sometimes an
instrument factor)

**FIG. 7** Bloated specific masquerading as a general factor. Increased homogeneity is normally brought about by adding common variance on *Y* to the existing common variance on *X*; e.g., the correlation of Variable 2 with 3 or 4 is much higher than that of 1 with 2. In a well-designed questionnaire scale, only items 1 and 2 (or 1 and 3, etc.) would be included. But in a scale put together on a criterion of high homogeneity, items 2, 3, and 4 would be chosen and would yield an *X* measure contaminated with much *Y*.

surprising to see how long it has taken for these newer concepts in test design (despite the writings of Campbell, Fiske, Horn, Humphreys, Nesselroade, and the present author) to bring these considerations to the general mass of test users. Thus, it is still not unusual to find the neophyte confusing a low homogeneity coefficient with low reliability or low validity, unaware that the low homogeneity is, in a good test, the deliberate effect of a design undertaken to randomize instrument-factor (method) influences, and to produce suppressor action (Cattell & Radcliffe, 1961; Guilford, J. P., & Michaels, 1960) with respect to other, unwanted substantive factors.

Exploration and classification of the domain of instrument factors and proper allowance for them in drawing conclusions about personality structure are some of the most important tasks facing personality research in the next decade or so. The perspective should be kept in mind that all instrument factors are real, in the sense of being organized individual differences within people, but that some are (a) trivial, irrelevant aspects of test performance, when personality factors are the aim, and others are (b) parts of personality factors, but sampling only some quite narrow situational or observational domain.

To complete this more sophisticated look at personality factors we need (a) to systematize the taxonomy of instrument factors, following the earlier discussion, and (b) to ask what misconceptions in our present theories of personality may have arisen from inadequate treatment of the instrument-factor problem.

Table 3 focuses on the instrument-factor section of Fig. 6 and gives a finer taxonomy and more detailed illustration of six kinds of instrument factor, classified under four main types of source. These indicate sources of *irrelevant*, unitary instrument-factor covari-

**TABLE 3**  Schema of covariation sources for exploring the map of instrument factors

| Source | Description |
|---|---|
| Behavioral (test) form:<br>  Classes of stimuli | Concrete<br>Symbolic<br>Life-purpose related<br>Experimentally detached<br>Familiar or unfamiliar |
| Classes of response and response<br>  instruction | To react always vs. to react only sometimes<br>Restricted vs. unrestricted, unprescribed<br>Inventive vs. selective, in prescribed area<br>Single response vs. repetitive, process response<br>Ordered prescribed sequence vs. unordered<br>Homogeneous vs. patterned response<br>Natural pace vs. maximum, limiting performance |
| Scaling and scoring | Raw score<br>Scaled<br>Normalized<br>Subject, or not, to simple response sets |
| Administrative conditioning | Personality of experimenter<br>Role relation to task<br>Modulator effects on states, e.g., from weather,<br>  physical environment, etc.<br>Motivation conditions |
| Life situation effects | Time of day or relation to vacations<br>Subculture and other reference population effects<br>On job, in school, or elsewhere<br>General social emergency conditions<br>Particular density of choice of variables in relation<br>  to individuals' total life space |
| Outside simple instrument factor effects,<br>  but contaminating, as perturbation factors | Observer view effects, in $L(BR)$ and $Q$ data<br>Sampling (within population) effects |

ance to which an experimenter should be alert and that he should deliberately seek to introduce and balance, to reduce the bias of any one. At the same time, there should be no assumption as in designs conceived in multitrait-multimethod ideas, that each technique (method) corresponds to one instrument factor, but balance sought should, instead, be calculated after the location of instrument factors.

The categories in this schema for search for instrument factors are initially those of $II(B)2(a)$, $2(b)$, and $2(c)$ in the perturbation-factor-analysis scheme (Fig. 6) but with some bearing on categories outside $II(B)2-$ the instrument-factor subsection. A more detailed development has been added within the parameters of *test form* from Cattell and Warburton's (1967, chapter 6) taxonomy of tests, since the stimulus-response features there categorized offer an initial systematic basis for instrument-factor search.

It is only recently, however, that personality research designs have heeded the principles mentioned in the last paragraph, and much of the original data from which Hammond, Wilde, Fiske, Goldberg, Horn, Ishikawa, Norman, Dielman, Krug, Wiggins, and other trait structure analysts writing in this book and this area have drawn their inferences have definitely fallen short of ideal designs. Consequently, they fell back on intuitive judgments in making allowances. Principally, they depended on analyses all in one medium, or all by one type of item, or even by a single rater—standing in one special role to the ratee—and so on. Indeed, it is astonishing to record that virtually all of the decade of research and discussing on instrument factors, for example, Desirability and Acquiescence, in questionnaires was based on factoring in the questionnaire instrumentality only. As far as the present writer knows, in 20 years of research, the only study designed on technically adequate ratings that factored ratings and questionnaires together was the study of Cattell, Pierson, and Finkbeiner (1976). Schaie's (1962) otherwise excellent study with the Child Personality Questionnaire (CPQ) used ratings of children by teachers who had insufficient knowledge of the children. The Cattell, Pierson, and Finkbeiner (1976) study showed for the first time clearly two desirability instrument factors in questionnaire data (Respectability and Good Fellow factors), with no corresponding factors in the observer ratings.

This case calls attention to the methodological problem of deciding what factors one has when, willy-nilly, one must work with data that are all from one instrumentality of observation. There are undoubtedly cases where instrument factors run across the whole matrix, the factors or factor not even being suspected, and certainly not set aside.

One must recognize in these cases of inadequate attention to choice of variables that if there is a general factor, an investigator of only average care and experience is likely to miss it. He can miss it through not anticipating it, as requiring an unusual methodology in rotation, or through having a poor test for number of factors. If he does miss it, and underfactors by one factor, it is likely that he will have trouble in getting good simple-structure rotation, and his best rotation will put the personality factors in correlated positions that will yield a false second order, corresponding to the missing instrument factor.

This situation is illustrated in the concrete example in Table 4. The true structure put into the plasmode is shown in Analysis (a), where it can be seen that the first seven tests show two personality factors in rating data alone and one that is picked up both in L and Q data. The first seven tests are shown to have a single rating instrument factor running across them. If the correlation matrix for these seven alone is factored, one obtains the results shown in (b1) or (b2). In the latter, the structure shown to be present in (a) is pretty well reproduced, but the underfactoring of (b1), leaving no space for the actual instrument factor, throws some of its variance into what should be the hyperplanes of the true personality factors. A repetition of this trial by taking the questionnaire data (variables 8–15) similarly results, despite prolonged and careful search for simple structure, in the comparatively poor reproduction of patterns in (b3). The probability is, therefore, that many substantive factor patterns, as we are now accustomed to recognize them, are actually distorted from their true form by a thick, uneven incrustation of instrument-factor variance.

**TABLE 4** Plasmode showing effect of factoring with and without awareness of all instrument factors

First-order factors operating in various degrees across 3 media

| Variable | Primary factor traits 1 | 2 | 3 | 4 | 5 | 6 | 7 | Instrument factors $L$ | $Q$ | $T$ |
|---|---|---|---|---|---|---|---|---|---|---|
| | | | Analysis (a): All media; all factors (the plasmode as originally constructed) | | | | | | | |
| $L$ Data | | | | | | | | | | |
| 1 | .6 | | | | | | | .3 | | |
| 2 | −.4 | | | | | | | .4 | | |
| 3 | .3 | .6 | | | | | | .5 | | |
| 4 | | −.5 | | | | | | .3 | | |
| 5 | | −.4 | .6 ⎫ | | | | | .4 | | |
| 6 | | | −.7 ⎬ 3′ | | | | | .5 | | |
| 7 | | | .5 ⎭ | | | | | .3 | | |
| $Q$ Data | | | | | | | | | | |
| 8 | | | .7 ⎫ 3″ | | | | | | .3 | |
| 9 | | | −.7 ⎭ | | | | | | .4 | |
| 10 | | | | −.3 | | | | | .5 | |
| 11 | | | | .5 | −.5 | | | | .3 | |
| 12 | | | | .6 | .6 | | | | .4 | |
| 13 | | | | | −.3 | .6 ⎫ | | | .5 | |
| 14 | | | | | | .5 ⎬ 6″ | | | .3 | |
| 15 | | | | | | −.4 ⎭ | | | .4 | |
| $T$ Data | | | | | | | | | | |
| 16 | | | | | | −.7 ⎫ 6‴ | | | | .3 |
| 17 | | | | | | .5 ⎭ | | | | .4 |
| 18 | | | | | | | .6 | | | .5 |
| 19 | | | | | | | −.7 | | | .3 |
| 20 | | | | | | | −.3 | | | .4 |

Second-order factors (implying $R$s among first orders)

| Primaries (including instrument) | Second-order factors I | II | III |
|---|---|---|---|
| 1 | .50 | | |
| 2 | −.60 | | |
| 3 | .70 | −.40 | |
| 4 | | .80 | |
| 5 | | −.60 | .75 |
| 6 | | | −.55 |
| 7 | | | .90 |
| $L$ | .15 | −.10 | .10 |
| $Q$ | −.10 | .10 | .10 |
| $T$ | .10 | .10 | −.10 |

| Second-order factors | $C_F$ correlations among second-order factors I | II | III |
|---|---|---|---|
| I | 1.00 | .20 | −.25 |
| II | .20 | 1.00 | .30 |
| III | .25 | .30 | 1.00 |

Analysis (b1) ($L$ data only, reduced to 3 factors)[a]

| | 1 | 2 | 3′ |
|---|---|---|---|
| 1 | 53 | −18 | −12 |
| 2 | −45 | −36 | −23 |
| 3 | 27 | 01 | −57 |
| 4 | 00 | −57 | 18 |
| 5 | −03 | −82 | 50 |
| 6 | −01 | 11 | −63 |
| 7 | 00 | −64 | 22 |

| | 1 | 2 | 3′ |
|---|---|---|---|
| 1 | 100 | | |
| 2 | −38 | 100 | |
| 3′ | 11 | 19 | 100 |

Analysis (b2) (Same correlation matrix as [b1], but 4 factors)[b]

| | 1 | 2 | 3′ | $L$ |
|---|---|---|---|---|
| 1 | 53 | −13 | 17 | −03 |
| 2 | −37 | 01 | 01 | 57 |
| 3 | 38 | 28 | 01 | 39 |
| 4 | −02 | −65 | 01 | 13 |
| 5 | −13 | −34 | 72 | −08 |
| 6 | 14 | −05 | −57 | 56 |
| 7 | −06 | −04 | 67 | 08 |

| | 1 | 2 | 3′ | $L$ |
|---|---|---|---|---|
| 1 | 100 | | | |
| 2 | −32 | 100 | | |
| 3′ | 08 | 22 | 100 | |
| $L$ | −09 | −11 | −06 | 100 |

**TABLE 4**  (*continued*) Plasmode showing effect of factoring with and without awareness of all instrument factors

| | First-order factors operating in various degrees across 3 media | | | | | | | | | | Second-order factors (implying *R*s among first orders) | | | |
|---|---|---|---|---|---|---|---|---|---|---|---|---|---|---|
| | Primary factor traits | | | | | | | Instrument factors | | | Primaries (including instrument) | Second-order factors | | |
| Variable | 1 | 2 | 3 | 4 | 5 | 6 | 7 | *L* | *Q* | *T* | | I | II | III |
| | Analysis (b3) (*Q* data only; no room for instrument factor)[c] | | | | | | | | | | | | | |
| | 3″ | 4 | 5 | 6 | | 3″ | 4 | 5 | 6 | | | | | |
| 8 | 64 | −04 | 03 | 13 | 3″ | 100 | | | | | | | | |
| 9 | −63 | −07 | 47 | 16 | 4 | −22 | 100 | | | | | | | |
| 10 | 00 | −49 | 45 | 07 | 5 | −02 | 26 | 100 | | | | | | |
| 11 | 02 | 54 | 06 | 60 | 6 | 03 | −44 | −02 | 100 | | | | | |
| 12 | −07 | 10 | 55 | 02 | | | | | | | | | | |
| 13 | −01 | 06 | −07 | 83 | | | | | | | | | | |
| 14 | 02 | −08 | 01 | 58 | | | | | | | | | | |
| 15 | 05 | −02 | 60 | −10 | | | | | | | | | | |

*Note.* All loadings except those enclosed by boxes should be near zero if the known factor structure has been reproduced properly. Data abstracted from Cattell (1961a).

[a]*L*-data variables from analysis (a): analysis without separation or extraction of an instrument factor. Only one factor interpretable; instrument variance blurs solution.

[b]*L*-data variables from analysis (a): analysis with allowance for instrument factor. Clear, correct outcome except for some spread of instrument factor.

[c]*Q*-data variables from analysis (a): lack of extraction and rotation of instrument factor leaves poor solution.

Unfortunately, even if sufficient dimensionality is included in the single medium analysis to permit emergence of the instrument factor, there will still be serious doubts about its rotational resolution, as with any general factor. For rotation, a general factor must be avoided, by having enough *hyperplane stuff* planned, by introducing *Q*, *L*, and *T* variables together as in Analysis (a), to be factored and rotated together. Otherwise, provided there is only one general factor, the attainment of the best structural position is best guessed at by putting that factor orthogonal to the rest. This has essentially been done in the matrix in Table 4, but even so, *L* in (b2) is a rather poor reproduction of *L* in (a). With the design in which hyperplane stuff is provided in the form of only one class (two in all) of instrumentality variables, as would be if the first 22 variables (*L* and *Q* media) in Table 4 were factored together, the rotational guidance is better, though the prevalent habit of stopping only with automatic program rotations might still run into trouble.

If only two nonoverlapping instrument factors are planned (as far as one can foresee them) in an experimental design, the fact that these will reach only 50% in their hyperplanes makes a correct outcome a bit questionable with anyone but a skilled factorist. Certainly one must recognize that a variety of alternative and degenerative solutions are possible, notably (a) bipolar factors, as in Burt's model (1940) in which (though the simple structure vanishes) one common positive instrument factor runs over all, and one bipolar is positive on $L$ and negative on $Q$; (b) the appearance of what have been called *refraction factors* (Cattell, 1968b, p. 170—the expression refers to seeing the same object twice, as when looking through a suitably cut prism). In the latter, which has instanced itself in several attempts at simple structure in a set of personality factors measured simultaneously in two media, each personality factor appears twice, once as a questionnaire form and once as a rating form, as shown for $G_Q$ and $G_L$ in Table 5. The factors are substantially correlated within pairs, but have tolerable hyperplanes. Actual instances are given for ratings and

**TABLE 5**  Alternative resolution into traits expressed simultaneously in two media and into refraction factors

| Factor | $C$ | $D$ | $F$ | $H$ | $G_L$ | $G_Q$ | Factor | $C$ | $D$ | $F$ | $H$ | $G_L$ | $G_Q$ |
|---|---|---|---|---|---|---|---|---|---|---|---|---|---|
| | First set of rating variables (L data) | | | | | | | First form of questionnaire scales (Q data) | | | | | |
| $A$ | +20 | −03 | +05 | +06 | −07 | −16 | $A$ | −03 | +06 | −19 | +06 | −04 | +07 |
| $C$ | +45 | −13 | −15 | −03 | −04 | +05 | $C$ | +36 | +28 | +07 | +20 | +07 | +03 |
| $D$ | +07 | +45 | +00 | −12 | −10 | −03 | $D$ | +01 | +65 | +00 | +20 | −04 | +36 |
| $E$ | +13 | −31 | −08 | +30 | −10 | +01 | $E$ | −27 | +14 | +00 | −03 | −18 | −51 |
| $F$ | +39 | −05 | −09 | +06 | +06 | +07 | $F$ | +00 | +10 | +49 | −03 | −06 | +04 |
| $G$ | −19 | −09 | +01 | +08 | +66 | +00 | $G$ | −16 | −01 | −03 | +03 | −04 | +58 |
| $H$ | +10 | −03 | −07 | +48 | +50 | +08 | $H$ | −10 | −06 | −09 | +36 | +10 | +01 |
| $I$ | −14 | +10 | −01 | +05 | −13 | −11 | $I$ | −17 | −13 | −07 | +02 | +00 | +08 |
| $J$ | −04 | +31 | −20 | +09 | −04 | +00 | $J$ | −12 | +10 | −05 | +05 | +01 | +05 |
| $L$ | +00 | +19 | +00 | +14 | −03 | +09 | $N$ | +19 | −09 | −27 | −17 | −25 | +05 |
| $M$ | +10 | −08 | −07 | −17 | +70 | +01 | $O$ | −04 | +04 | +03 | +09 | +04 | −08 |
| $O$ | −19 | −09 | +07 | −44 | −38 | +12 | $Q_4$ | −29 | +06 | −01 | +09 | −03 | +04 |
| | Second set of rating variables (L data) | | | | | | | Second (equivalent) form of questionnaire scales (Q data) | | | | | |
| $A$ | +03 | −28 | +15 | +53 | +00 | +11 | $A$ | +14 | +06 | −35 | −08 | +04 | −08 |
| $C$ | +49 | −12 | +19 | +19 | +07 | −01 | $C$ | +55 | +06 | −01 | −05 | −04 | −05 |
| $D$ | +00 | +20 | +00 | −14 | −10 | +09 | $D$ | +12 | +60 | +04 | −05 | +09 | +44 |
| $E$ | +00 | +05 | +01 | +48 | +19 | +03 | $E$ | +04 | +40 | −04 | −14 | −16 | +00 |
| $F$ | −13 | +03 | +46 | +27 | −65 | −04 | $F$ | −07 | +15 | +39 | −25 | +03 | −07 |
| $G$ | +12 | +12 | +07 | +25 | +76 | −04 | $G$ | +09 | +17 | −03 | −11 | −06 | +80 |
| $H$ | −07 | −09 | +04 | +55 | +22 | +07 | $H$ | −06 | +08 | +11 | +69 | −09 | +01 |
| $I$ | +32 | −01 | −07 | +09 | −22 | +03 | $I$ | −06 | −01 | +01 | +06 | +13 | +49 |
| $J$ | −06 | +12 | −04 | −41 | +07 | +01 | $J$ | +12 | +09 | +01 | +05 | −06 | −03 |
| $L$ | +10 | +06 | −11 | +00 | +10 | +00 | $N$ | +13 | +04 | +07 | +06 | −03 | +16 |
| $M$ | +12 | +01 | −07 | +44 | +37 | +04 | $O$ | −17 | +03 | −08 | +03 | −01 | +13 |
| $O$ | −03 | −22 | +07 | −48 | +13 | +07 | $Q_4$ | −06 | +00 | +04 | +03 | −06 | +11 |

*Note.* Source traits $C$, $D$, $F$, and $H$ have come to a simple structure position (with slight exceptions) which brings both $L$ and both $Q$ markers on the same factor, whereas a similar blind rotation to simple structure has resulted in the markers for $G$ (Superego) splitting into 2 positively correlated refraction factors. Data abstracted from Cattell (1961a).

**TABLE 6**  Increased clarity of structure from separating instrument factors

| Measure | Substantive factors | | | | | | | | | | Instrument factors | |
|---|---|---|---|---|---|---|---|---|---|---|---|---|
| | Assertiveness | Sex | Fear | Narcism | Pugnacity | Protectiveness | Self-sentiment | Superego sentiment | School sentiment | Home sentiment | Information | Autism |
| Autism measures | | | | | | | | | | | | |
| Assertiveness | 34 | | | | | | | | | | | 43 |
| Sex | | 15 | | | | | | | | | | 47 |
| Fear | | | 56 | | | | | | | | | 49 |
| Narcism | | | | 47 | | | | | | | | 53 |
| Pugnacity | | | | | 84 | | | | | | | 29 |
| Protectiveness | | | | | | 22 | | | | | | 36 |
| Self-sentiment | | | | | | | 41 | | | | | 56 |
| Superego sentiment | | | | | | | | 62 | | | | 24 |
| School sentiment | | | | | | | | | 18 | | | 40 |
| Home sentiment | | | | | | | | | | 37 | | 39 |
| Information measures | | | | | | | | | | | | |
| Assertiveness | 28 | | | | | | | | | | 47 | |
| Sex | | 56 | | | | | | | | | 37 | |
| Fear | | | 31 | | | | | | | | 44 | |
| Narcism | | | | 08 | | | | | | | 49 | |
| Pugnacity | | | | | 06 | | | | | | 48 | |
| Protectiveness | | | | | | 52 | | | | | 21 | |
| Self-sentiment | | | | | | | 41 | | | | 57 | |
| Superego sentiment | | | | | | | | 62 | | | 38 | |
| School sentiment | | | | | | | | | 18 | | 59 | |
| Home sentiment | | | | | | | | | | 37 | 49 | |

*Note.* Data for this table were taken from an ongoing research conducted at the Laboratory of Personality Analysis meant to determine the factor structure of the School Motivation Analysis Test. The matrix is a subsection of the 1 used in the analysis (60 variables; 23 factors; $N = 190$). In earlier analyses of this same type of data, failure to allow for the emergence of instrument factors resulted in a good deal of distortion of the substantive factors. In 1 analysis, for example, an insufficient number of factors was extracted. Quite unexpectedly during rotation, 1 factor that had shown a substantive interpretation in the early stages of analysis began to appear more and more certainly as an instrument factor. Moreover, it was impossible, either through analytic or visual rotation, to move the factor from this position.

questionnaires in Cattell (1969, p. 170), and are reproduced in shortened form in Table 5. It is clear that the variance of one instrument factor has gone into half of the true factor in one case and into the other half in the other case. However, Table 6 shows that a better alternative is possible if underfactoring is avoided, in which there are one personality factor and two instrument factors. That this is the meaningful solution is shown by a case permitting fuller insight, namely, that in which the instrument factors are well-known special capacities—autism and general information—as shown in Table 6. In this domain of dynamic structure factors based on objective measures of interest strength (autism and general information in this case), the alternative possible structures are well known and have been checked through the repeated factorings on the Motivation Analysis Test (MAT) by Krug, Laughlin, Sweney, Horn, and others. The alternatives are two only: (a) to have 10 substantive (dynamic structure) and 2 instrument factors, as shown in Table 5, or (b) to stop at the extraction of 10 factors and absorb the instrument-factor variance into the substantives. As would be expected from the previous discussion, the former better fits the Scree test for number of factors and gives a somewhat better simple structure. The latter has its use, however, in giving estimation corresponding to the actual 10 scales.

As is pointed out in section 9, there is good reason to believe that the rating medium—too often accepted as a criterion to test the suspect questionnaire—has at least as much instrument-factor variance in it as the questionnaire. However, most of it is apparently the *personal equation* of raters and is tied to their personality profiles; when we shift from single raters to a pool of *several*, as in the Finkbeiner-Pierson study, no definite evidence of instrument factors (as factors in *L* data not present in *Q* data) remains.

Nevertheless, so long as we deal with single observers there is probably more than one instrument factor in *L* or *Q* data. Apart from the test form, there are differences in *Q* data of administration situation, as we have called it. On the other hand, a questionnaire samples behavior around the clock, whereas rating is almost always of a limited and special situational sample or fraction of a person's behavior, for example, the hours in school. But granted that the variance common to the instrument—single or multifactor—is shunted off in a definite instrument factor, then trait-view theory says that the remaining variance-covariance will structure itself more clearly in *true* personality factors. The effect of several instrument factors, and the increased clarity resulting from separating them, is shown particularly in motivation data (Cattell, Radcliffe, & Sweney, 1963) and in the example from Krug shown in Table 5.

## 9   TRAIT VIEW: PERSONAL EQUATION, AND CLICHÉ THEORIES OF DISTORTION

Three broad sources of distortion of concepts and measures were glanced at under perturbation theory, and one of those sources—instrument factors—was intensively analyzed under three subdivisions. It remains to study the fourth main distortion in perturbation theory—that of *observer view effects*—which constitutes the most serious of all perturbations in *L* and *Q* data.

That the personality of the observer—rather than any mechanical instrumentality of ratings or questionnaires as such—is a major source of rating and questionnaire distortion has long been recognized. But as mentioned, the problem was tackled by local and uncoordinated concepts in contrast to the comprehensive trait-view theory we here propose. The issue of self-perception and perception of others has been discussed since antiquity by philosophers and novelists. Psychologists first reacted to it, as noticed in the rather obvious and gross effects in observer ratings, under the simple concept of a *general halo* effect (Johnson, D. M., 1948). After that came the suspicions about *response sets* in questionnaires (Cattell, 1950c, 1968b; Cronbach, 1950; Messick & Jackson, 1957; Wiggins, J. S., 1962) and of *projection* by clinicians. As we recognized, one formulation that has been popular is that of faking for general *social desirability* (Edwards, A. L., 1957; Cattell, 1964a). In practice there have been attempts to combat these distortions (in *Q* data) by lie scales (Dahlstrom, 1962) and motivation distortion scales (Cattell, 1960b); in addition, there have been examinations in terms of intrusion of *projection* effects, in pencil and paper tests of various kinds (Cattell & Wenig, 1952).

Perturbation theory (Cattell & Digman, 1964, and Fig. 6) as a whole actually began as an attempt to bring these diverse phenomena, together with the rapidly growing evidence on instrument-factor effects, into a single formulation. Probably instrument-factor theory and trait-view theory are its two most important branches. Trait-view theory ($II(B)4$ in Fig. 6) embraces all those perturbations, (originally starting with the idea of the halo effect) that have to do with the intrusion of the mentality of the observer, into the data from which analysis is expected to yield personality structure concepts. By definition, trait view must include both $L(BR)$—behavior rating of life-situation behavior—and $Q$ data (where the observer views himself). Here one would expect phenomena, principles, and laws to be substantially different from those having to do with the sheer instrument-factor effects just discussed. Also within trait-view theory we may expect to find emphases on two different effects, one having to do with general sociocultural effects, notably by *trait-view stereotypes,* operating on everyone's observations, and the other relating to the individual personality effects of the observer, which we may call *trait-view personal equation* principles.

Stated without some ultimately necessary cautions and elaborations, the essential principle in trait-view theory is that whatever misperception occurs may be predicted just like any other behavior by an individual by (a) certain cognitive furniture common to all people and (b) the particular personality factors (personality here including ability and dynamic traits, i.e., $A$, $P$ and $D$ terms) of the observing individual operating in the given environment. If these broad concepts are properly applied, it is unnecessary to bring in special ad hoc concepts such as tendency to extreme response, halo, acquiescence set, vulnerability to social desirability pressures, test faking, and so forth, which have hitherto been treated under the purely

ad hoc attacks on the problem. Perception is part of total behavior.

The phenomena under trait-view theory have thus been defined as different from the other three sources of perturbation; one may add that they are also different from deliberate sabotage, as when a person being rated acts a part (like a spy) or, in the questionnaire, deliberately gives random answers. Techniques for recognizing sabotage can be developed, but positive corrections, as in trait-view theory, are then not possible. Within trait-view theory, we must consider (a) the effect of *stereotypes,* that is, cognitive maps of what goes with what, which may be correct or incorrect, for example, that people who steal will be more likely to lie; that children who have more than average difficulty learning grammar will have more than average difficulty with mathematics, and other such common beliefs; (b) the effects on perception of the personality trait profile of the observer, including his role traits, and so forth, in a defined environmental situation; (c) the effect of ignorance in the observer concerning the observed person.

It will help in bringing out the nature of the clean break from *response set, desirability*, and *lie-scale* formulations if the new principles are first illustrated in trait-view theory in the aspect dealing with the *personal equation effects* rather than the stereotypes. That is to say, let us assume stereotype effects held constant while we consider how the actual nature of the traits in the observed person interact with the personality of the observer (which traits belong to the *same* person in $Q$ data but belong to a different person in $L$ data).

The model requires that we consider a concretely recorded score, $F_j$, ($j = 1$ to $k$) on each of $k$ factor scales (we keep to factor scales rather than odd variables, for the sake of closeness of theory to likely test practice). Corresponding to the rated score $F_{ji}$ (the score for individual $i$) is a *true* source-trait score $T_{ji}$. In the following behavioral equations the $b$s as usual will be behavior indexes (factor loadings), the $F$s the recorded, observed trait scores, and the $T$s the true trait scores. We shall suppose that any person's perception of traits, in himself or anyone else, is affected by his total personality, through projection and countless other mechanisms, which can be discussed later. This is the core of the *trait-view personal equation* theory: The distortion of perception (like any other behavioral act) is itself a direct and calculable expression of the observer's true personality (operating in the given appraisal situation).

In the behavioral equation here, as anywhere else, we have to remember that the ordinary factorial specification equation for an act tells only part of the story, statistically, namely the individual's deviation from the group mean. The distortion effects studied, however, should really include a change in the average level of the dependent variable, $F_j$, as well as in the relative position of individuals. It will be recognized in what follows that a constant needs to be added to the specification equation to express this shift in mean; the general meaning of the equation can be better conveyed in a less cumbersome form, however, by considering that constant as something to be added later.

The effects of the observer's personality traits in the given rating situation are therefore expressed by the ordinary behavioral equation, which is presented, summed, in the second term of Equation 9. (Equation 9a is first stated as a *general* function, the additive-linear property not being specified, but Equation 9b is the particular additive form from which we are, at present, compelled to proceed). This equation says that the distortion in the given trait perception, $F_{d.jiok}$ (where $d$ is for distortion, $j$ is the

particular trait rating being made, $i$ is the individual observed, $k$ is the ambient situation, and $o$ is the observer who is making the rating) is a function of the traits of the individual $i$ being observed (hopefully strongly so for the trait in question), of those of the observer $o$ and of certain constants $c_x$, to express effects on the mean (in standard score units) for everyone.

$$F_{d.jiok} = f\left[ \sum_{x=1}^{x=p} b_{ijkx}T_{xi}, \ \sum_{y=1}^{y=p} b_{ijyk}T_{yo}, \ \sum_{x=1}^{x=p} c_{ijkox} \right] \tag{9a}$$

In the linear-additive form this function can be stated as

$$F_{d.jiok} = \sum_{x=1}^{x=k} b_{ijkx}T_{xi} + \sum_{y=1}^{y=k} b_{ijky}T_{yo} + \sum_{x=1}^{x=k} c_{hijkxo}. \tag{9b}$$

This equation has some unusual features that need explaining. First, it is assumed that observer and subject are of the same species, so that they can both be described by the same $p$ source traits (in observation of animals or objects by humans this would be modified). The subscripts in Equation 9, however, are written $x$ for the subject and $y$ for the observer, because $b_{ijx}$ and $b_{ijy}$ are normally different values, and $T_{xi}$ and $T_{yo}$ certainly are. The coefficient $b$ is allowed to absorb what is usually $b$ and $s$, for simplicity here, and needs, therefore, the subscripts of both, $j$ and $k$. The predicted term $F_{d.j}$ is taken as the amount of distortion in the perception of trait $T_j$. The meaning of the subscripts is held the same as that of the usual order, but one must note the peculiarity that new referent terms are now needed. The peculiarity is that the stimulus, usually $h$, is here $i$, the individual seen; meanwhile the *actor*, usually $i$, is here the observer $o$, and the situation, $k$ is that of the observer not that of $i$. The particular rating being made—the response—remains $j$ as usual.

Equation 9 states the essence of things: The total distortion $F_{d.j}$ is a function of the *context effect* of the traits of the individual $i$ being observed, and of the traits of the observer $o$ in the observer *personal equation*. But how do we pull apart and estimate the values in the two parts? The simplest way is to do it by experimental control. If we wish to determine part 1, we wipe out the observer term by averaging over a large number of observers. That is to say, $n_1$ (subject) individuals are brought before $n_2$ (observers) and a score matrix constructed for each subject on each trait distortion, the entries being the mean values for $n_2$ (observers). If we knew the distortion directly, through having some *true* score for the individual $i$, the $b$ values could then be obtained as correlations and transformed to weights. But what we actually have is an observer estimate $F_{jiok}$, which is the sum of true and distortion value, thus:

$$F_{jiok} = T_{ji} + F_{d.jiok}, \qquad (10)$$

where $T_{ji}$ is true score on factor $j$. In these circumstances, obtaining the underlying true values is a matter for factor analysis. To do this we must get more variables than factors and we may therefore suppose the trait rating to be obtained in two different ambient situations, $k$s, so that with, say, 16 traits we have 32 variables. A typical row from the factoring of $F_{ji\bar{o}k}$s ($\bar{o}$ indicating averaged over observers) will then be

$$F_{ji\bar{o}k} = b_{ijk1} T_{1i} + \ldots + b_{ikj} T_{ji}$$
$$+ \ldots + b_{ikp} T_{pi}. \qquad (11)$$

(Note: an $i$ is added to the subscripts of the $b$s here to show the difference from $b_{ojk}$—

observer equation values—in Equation 12. It does not mean peculiar to a particular $i$. The term **i** is in boldface showing that **i**s are the referees.) By Equation 10, and the estimate of $T_{ji}$ from factoring variables like $F_{ji\bar{o}k}$ in Equation 11, the distortion $F_{d.j}$ can be obtained.

Next, from the same complete $n_1$ (subjects) and $n_2$ (observer) score matrix, we can eliminate the subject variance, starting with a score matrix of $n_2$ (observers) over $2p$ (performances), those performances ($F_{\bar{i}jok}$ estimates) being now averaged across *subjects*. A factoring of this will yield the distortion estimation due to observer, in the same way, as in Equation 12.

$$F_{j\bar{i}ok} = b_{ojk1} T_{1o} + \ldots + b_{ojkp} T_{po}. \qquad (12)$$

(The term **o** is in boldface to indicate that **o**s are the referees—and the variables constituted by the $i$s averaged score the relatives.) A new problem arises here, however, in that the factoring gives the observer's traits not those of the subject, so that no subtraction such as in Equation 10 is possible. However, we may take the *average* rating of the trait $F_j$ by all observers as the true value—and what firmer operational verdict could one get?—and obtain $F_d$s for observers as deviations therefrom. The correlations and weights for $F_{d.jiok}$s as distinct from $F_{jiok}$s will in both cases need to be worked out with the $F_d$s. We then have:

$$T_{ji} = (F_{jiok} - F_{d.jiok})$$
$$+ (F_{jiok} - F_{d.jiok}) \qquad (13)$$

The boldface **i** is in the first parentheses and **o**s in the second indicate the source of the two distortion measures (context and personal equation). If we take the two means—across subjects and across observers—as zero reference values, then we have a single observed value from which the two-part distortions are taken to estimate the true score. From a factor-analytic standpoint, some may argue for factoring the two score matrices ($n_1$ and $n_2$) on the same variables (say, $4p$ in number) together, that is, without averaging on each separately. But there is perhaps insufficient experience as yet in factoring matrices to give factors that belong to two different sets of referees to recommend this at this time.

Although there is virtually no psychological theory around the context effect (an illustration of such theory might be that the intelligence score of a person high in Surgency will be overestimated), there is plenty about the roots of misperception when observing others, in *projection*, and so forth. This has been oversimplified in psychoanalytic terms; Cattell and Wenig (1952) produced evidence for two distinct forms of projection, *dynamic* (true projection as known by the analyst) and *naive* projection (distortion positively correlated with the same traits in the observer). It is supposed in trait-view theory that *all* traits of the observer enter, to some degree, into the distortion. Indeed we have the interesting conclusion from Equation 12 that the trait scores of observers can be estimated simply from their ratings of the traits of others.

An attractive feature of trait-view theory is that it embraces both questionnaire and rating in the same model. The fact that the subject is his own observer in the questionnaire actually simplifies the solution to Equation 9; not only are the factor patterns the same (as we previously assumed), but even the factor scores are the same. If, furthermore, we are not interested in the analysis of the distortion as such, but only in the practical translation from gross scale scores to true scores, the solution becomes simple. One factors the observed scale scores, say on equivalent *A, B,* and *C* forms,

together to give thrice as many variables as factors and reaches a weighted sum of all scales (48 in the case of the 16 PF) to give a self-undistorted score for each trait. Parenthetically, the model for this turns out to be so similar to what has been called *variance reallocation* or *computer synthesis*, in which all scale scores are searched for possible variance contributions to the score on any one (Cattell, Eber, & Tatsuoka, 1970) trait, that a word is called for on the distinction. The difference is that the trait-view equation applies to a particular *ambient situation,* that is, the weights are calculated for a particular administration and test-taking role situation and are concerned with distortion by the subject. The computer synthesis values are averaged over many situations and represent the reallocation of misplaced variance arising from the structure of the test itself. Although only one $b$ value is obtained from factoring the questionnaire scales, in principle, one can consider it as made up of three parts: (a) $x$s due to the *context* effect, (b) $y$s due to the *personal equation* effect, and (c) $z$s due to misplaced (nonsuppressed) trait variance in the scales, thus:

$$F_{jik} = (x_1 + y_1 + z_1)_{ijk} T_{1i} + \cdots$$

$$+ (x_p + y_p + z_p)_{ijk} T_{pi}. \qquad (14)$$

The separation of $x$, $y$, and $z$ weights cannot be pursued here. The reader must be referred to the practical example by Krug and Cattell (1971c) for illustration. One needs to get a decent variable-to-factor ratio to recognize instrument factors and, also, to allow for the potentially large influence of *role factors* defining the subject's accepted role in the test-taking situation. (If $R$ is a role factor, the last $T$ in Equation 14 would be an $R$). In the case investigated by Krug, the weights on the role factors happened not to be as large as those on personality factors, but considering the different roles in which questionnaires are taken in clinics, industry, and so forth, the measurement and inclusion of role factors along with other general personality factors is surely important.

Some further interesting possibilities are opened up by trait-view theory. As implied, it offers an objective basis for discovering what kinds of test-taking situations exist, thus leading to an objective taxonomic classification. Types of psychometric situations can be located by applying the pattern similarity coefficient $r_p$ to the series of indexes $d_{hj}$s and $b_{hj}$s over different $h$s; as well as to the $c_{jk}$s. When this is done, it may be possible to point to, and expend sufficient effort on, developing distortion indexes for a reduced and practicable number of recognizable *types of distortion situations*. The practitioner will then be equipped to handle them more effectively than is now possible with lie scales or simple motivation-distortion scales.

Second, we have in the $x$s and $y$s of Equation 14, as found in various situations, the empirical basis for a whole array of psychological laws about naive and true projection, as well as most other defense mechanisms, and most temperament and ability traits, in their effects on perception of human beings.

Third, we have in trait-view theory a firm foundation for making also a *taxonomy of stereotypes and clichés* that arise from the cognitive equipment usually possessed by observers of various intelligence and social backgrounds. It is clearly evident from the striking findings of Passini and Norman (1966) in the rating of human personality, as well as from some findings of Cliff (1966), and the experiment of Cattell and Dickman (1962) in rating the *behavior* of inanimate objects, that we habitually fill in parts of any person or object perception—regardless of whether the direct data is available to us or is missing—by use of *stereotypes*. This has

been understood in principle in general perception, since the time of Herbart, at least, but hitherto we have had little evidence about the magnitude of its roles in rating and self-rating. Indeed, the error is widespread, largely due to the sociologist's preoccupation with prejudice, of overlooking the indubitable fact that the central tendency in most stereotypes is an effectively accurate map and guide to the average, *usual real* world. Stereotypes set us awry mainly in conjuring tricks.

To pursue stereotypes in more detail we must recognize (a) implicit or explicit beliefs about *both* correlations and distributions of traits, for example, the stereotype that a Scottish accent goes with a cautious and economical disposition; or that Communists and Fascists share an extreme high score on the trait of dogmatism, relative to the general population. If these stereotypes are correct, they produce no more distortion on observation and behavior than the expectation that a swing door will move when pushed or that a lowering gray sky is likely to lead to rain. But if, instead, the concept is a cliché, that is, as uncritically accepted as a stereotype, but wrong, then trait ratings will be distorted. Also, we must recognize (b) gestalt effects, whereby the perception of a part cannot scarcely be made in independence of the whole; (c) moderator, interactive effects *on perception,* for example, perceived Dominance ($E$ factor) is apt to be raised in level, in terms of the usual responses to cue levels, when Surgency ($F$ factor) is also high; and (d) semantic effects from definitions of traits (supplied for rating) that spill over into connoting levels on other traits. The form of designs of experiment for checking these four basic theories of origins through empirically obtaining weights in different circumstances, will be evident from the preceding. A detailed account is not possible here of certain alternative ways in which a cliché (or stereo-type if need be) can be incorporated in the perception—trait-view—equation as here advocated. It will be our assumption, from such work as that of Passini and Norman (1966), that stereotypes are far more frequently *true maps* from hard-earned experience than false clichés from social or emotional importations, and the weights will, therefore, usually act to reinforce and stabilize the true factor estimate $T_j$ in Equations 10, 11 and 12. Although a common cliché, or a stereotype, is a cognitive entity, unlike the ability, temperament, and dynamic traits we have hitherto considered factors to be, yet an important cognitive concept should appear as a broad factor, especially across judgment and rating behaviors. Its peculiarity would be, like that of a role or state factor, that it is highly subject to situational modulation, appearing only in certain ambient situations, with an unusual degree of transience. The magnitude of a stereotype factor, however, would be the observer's *estimate* of the magnitude of some element from the evidence he has from all other behaviors than that being scored at the time for the element. It should, in fact, appear as a second $T_j$ factor closely paralleling in pattern the first but present in the observer profile, not the subject profile. Similarly a cliché is a factor (a mental set, perception factor as discussed earlier) in the observer's profile (Term 2 in Equation 9b etc.), but systematically erroneous in its effects. Thus, if the observer believes that fluid intelligence is correlated with years of education, his ratings of these two variables across $n$ subjects will tend to be correlated, because his cliché factor loads both positively.

The appreciable role of stereotypes in rating is due to the fact that the exigencies of inadequate time and energy cause most observers to use only a fragment of the available empirical data, and to fill in the rest by stereotype. The closeness of this stereotype to reality in the Cattell and Dickman physical world study shows that no one can afford to have wrong stereotypes about the physical world, and the same is true in principle about the social and psychological domains, though no one has evaluated the relative accuracies of such stereotypes, and their relation to the age, intelligence, and social background of the rater. (It has been done in a qualitative way, but not in a systematic way permitting quantitative comparisons of physical and social-world stereotypes.)

Let us distinguish a *cliché* (in the meaning of its French root) from a *stereotype,* as a stereotype that is grossly inaccurate. This inaccuracy often is associated with its being peculiar to one individual or caught in some hurricane of fashion. Since individuals will possess in the latter case, common clichés to varying degrees, producing correlations among their parts, it should be possible, once they are located as factors, to treat them (even though they are cognitive entities, rather than traits) as if they are additional factors in the perception equation. Like any broad factor, they will spread across a variety of specific perceptions, with different weights in each and in principle can be handled by a specification equation of the usual form, thus,

$$F_{d.jiok} = \sum_{z=p}^{x=p} b_{ijkx}T_{xc} + \sum^{x=p} b_{ijky}T_{yo}$$
$$+ \sum b_{ykz}C_z + \text{constant (as}$$
$$\text{in Equation 9b)}$$

where the $T_x$s are the subjects' traits, the $T_y$s are the observers, and the $C_z$s are the cognitive clichés possessed by the observer.

A method of allowing for distortion in a factor score through observer distortion, which does not involve using an omnibus set of scales as in trait-view theory, has been proposed as *scale vulnerability theory*. It is actually a supplement as well as an alternative, for it takes into account a new variable in the estimation, namely the *susceptibility* of a particular questionnaire scale or observer rating to distortion. The reader must be referred elsewhere (Cattell, 1977) for the detailed solutions. A brief outline will be given here, to show how the concept works out with questionnaire scales. If $D_{ki}$ is $i$'s need to distort (from *dynamic and general personality* reasons) in situation $k$, and $V_{aj}$ is the vulnerability of scale $T_{aj}$ (which is test form $a$ for trait $j$), then

$$d_{aijk} = V_{aj}D_{ki}. \qquad (15)$$

If we take it that $d_{aijk}$ adds with the true score to give the observed score, which we will call $T_{aijk}$, then a factoring of many scores like $T_{aijk}$, for forms $b$, $c$, $d$, and so forth, would yield a specification for each like the following:

$$T_{aijk} = W_{akj}T_{ji} + V_{akj}D_{ki}$$

$$+ W_{ajku}U_{ajki}, \qquad (16)$$

where we assume only a specific factor, $U_{ajk}$, remains over when the true factor and the distortion are taken out.

Now the practical utility and aim of vulnerability theory is to allow a true score to be assessed simply from giving two scales for $T_j$ at the same time, which are of different known vulnerabilities. The second scale would be $T_{bjk}$, and it would have a similar equation to Equation 16. Knowing from the factoring of several scales in several situations the values $W_{akj}$, $V_{akj}$, $V_{bkj}$, and $W_{ajku}$, and the same for $T_{bjk}$, we can solve for $T_{ji}$ if we are willing to assume $i$'s endowment in the small specific $U_{ajk}$ is an average value (0). Then

$$T_{ji} = \frac{(V_{bkj}T_{aijk} - V_{akj}T_{bijk})}{V_{akj}W_{akj} - V_{bkj}W_{bkj}}$$

$$- \frac{(V_{akj}W_{akj} - V_{bkj}W_{bkj})}{V_{akj}W_{akj} - V_{bkj}W_{bkj}} \qquad (17)$$

Thus one does not need to know the strength of the individual's desire to distort, $D_{ki}$, but only that it is the same for the two test forms administered at the same time. With the observed $a$ and $b$ form scores, and the known values of the $V$s and $W$s from previous factorings, a solution is possible. An empirical study by De Voogd (see Cattell, 1977) tested the possibility that one could use the model without a unique factor at all, but this proved not to be possible, so the assumption of $i$'s equality in the two specifics at an average value must be made.

The sense in which trait-view and vulnerability theories are supplementary is that the former examines the distorting force in detail as to personality origins, whereas the latter leaves it as a single total, all in $D_{ki1}$. On the other hand, the vulnerability model includes regard for the specific vulnerabilities of the scales, whereas trait view leaves these values unanalyzed, absorbing them into the coefficients for the trait influences.

By whichever approach–trait view or vulnerability–one handles the impact of the personality in distortion, one must remember that the incorrect cognitive cliché will also play a part in the departure of the perception from precision, both as a pattern and as an individual measurement.

## 10  SUMMARY

1. Present operational concepts for handling the primary entities in taxonomy–trait, state, type, and process–are now effective and yield theoretically and practically valuable findings, as shown in the chapters of section 1 of this book. Nevertheless, there

is still need to develop certain more sophisticated models, concepts, and operations, especially concerning the effects of selection of persons and variables, different cultural populations, and the relativity of findings to observer, situation, and mode of observation.

2. Some of the failures to reach firm conclusions about personality structure arise from investigators' not recognizing the need for (a) a *personality sphere* defining a total population of variables, (b) systematic linkage of programmatic researches by marker variables, and (c) adjusting contingent generalizations to the special domains and settings of variables used. The typical structure obtained in behavior depends, in the first place, on the choice of variables. It is affected by such principles as (a) in the obvious sense that areas not represented or poorly represented cannot yield their structures or will yield rather distorted structures; (b) in the sense that instrument factors and other sources of perturbation cannot be cleanly separated and set aside with poor choice of (insufficiently diverse) instrument variables; and (c) in the sense that density of representation, relative to a conception of a total population of variables (personality sphere), will determine at what stratum the factor structures initially emerge from a given research.

3. Other failures to attain coherent and predictive structural findings spring from roughness of various correlational models. Sophisticated models must distinguish (a) surface and source traits; (b) common and unique (idiosyncratic) structures; (c) broad, narrow, and specific traits in relation to a personality sphere; (d) trait, trait change, state, and state liability structures; (e) processes; and (f) species types, which yield different in-type and cross-type traits, both necessary for defining the individual. Such

concepts are brought to matrix patterns by different operations (cluster search, $R$, $dR$, and $P$ technique, taxonomic programs). Factors so found also represent diverse causal and developmental concepts according to their setting and auxiliary evidence. For example, some patterns are expressions of *present* influences, as states and traits (e.g., cognitive powers and dynamic energy sources), whereas others, as scientific concepts, represent *past* (learning or experience) influences, which have deposited crystallized habit systems the elements in which are no longer necessarily dynamically linked. Moreover, there are further subclasses possible, for example, according to innateness or environmental molding, as ergs and sentiments found within the dynamic modality.

4. As scientific concepts, the preceding structures have to demonstrate their replicable identity across diverse actual experiments by their empirical factor and type patterns. There are four experimental data situations in which the problem of (a) identifying (cross-matching) factor patterns and (b) subsequently comparing scores on cross-identified factors may arise. The appropriate solutions for these are discussed and special proposals are made for joint factor analysis, for transcultural factor matching, and for a design of *continuously adjusted weights* for plotting score changes across age (isopodic and equipotent principles of calculation). In the last resort, the concept of the determiner hypothesized to be present in two or more matched patterns is either (a) the same, *identical* influence or (b) a representative of a *homologous class* of influences. In the latter case, to use the same scientific term, a *species resemblance* must be statistically demonstrated. In neither case are the factor patterns expected to be completely identical, but when statistically significantly matched, can be regarded as an identity

appropriately transformed by selection, and so forth, according to the same transformation principles as are operative in confactor resolution. The isopodic and equipotent methods of comparing scores on factors in different populations use similar principles.

5. An area of increasing importance in more sophisticated understanding of structure is that concerning recognition of the nature of higher order factors. The *strata* and *reticular* models are discussed, and the alternation of the Schmid-Leiman and Cattell-White patterns of projections on variables are presented. The preferred model for representation when strata are definitely present is the stratified independent determiners (SID).

6. Roles can be represented in the behavioral equation as factors extraneous to personality and state factors, but showing the susceptibility of the latter to strong modulator action from the ambient stimulus. Roles probably are best represented by a model that allows both for a fixed trait and a modulable state component. Both states and roles thus rest on the preexistence in the personality of *liability traits*, that is, a proneness or capacity for excitation that is subject to *modulation* by a stimulus situation. They are affected by an *ambient* part of the global stimulus (to be contrasted with the *focal* part to which response is made). In addition to being estimated by a factor score, a role has its particular character properly represented as a *role matrix* of *v*s and *s*s, for a standard, *important* list of situations. Role factors can be distinguished from general personality factors in research matrices by combinations of certain characteristics here listed.

7. Perturbation theory seeks to comprehend changes from the true values of (a) patterns and (b) individual scores resulting from properties of the observer, his instruments, and his situation. Initially it defines four sources: (a) data treatment (scaling and correlation devices), (b) instrument factors arising from common peculiarities in the instrument and situations of experimental measurement, (c) subject-sampling factors, and (d) observer view factors, peculiar to the human mind as an instrument of observation. Instrument factors can again be broken down into three or four types, such as test-form factors, situation or area-of-expression factors, and test-administration-condition artefacts. The superiority of the perturbation theory and instrument-factor analysis is pointed out conceptually and by examples.

8. In the rating (*L*-data) and questionnaire (*Q*-data) media of personality observation, the largest perturbations probably arise from category (d) in item 7, the human observer. Two models, supplementary and adaptive to particular purposes rather than alternatives in principle, were proposed for unraveling these effects, namely, *trait-view* theory and *scale vulnerability* theory. It is claimed that they offer a more comprehensive and elegant solution than the patchwork of ad hoc corrections for social desirability, response set, and so forth, by lie scales, distortion scales, and other measures. Trait-view theory supposes that any single rating is distorted by (a) *context* effects from the other traits of the subject observed; (b) *personal equation* effects from projection, and so forth, operating from the traits of the observer; and (c) the effect of *clichés,* a cliché defined as a stereotype that happens to be erroneous (to some substantial degree). These effects are stated in a *trait-view equation,* which can be solved for the true scores. In the case of the questionnaire, the personal-equation influences include test-taking role terms.

Scale vulnerability aims at the eminently practical goal of being able, by administering two scales for the same trait (but of known and unequal vulnerabilities to distortion) in any distortion situation, to calculate a true estimate from the comparison. It throws all the context and personality-equation sources of distortion in trait view into a single term, unconcerned about isolating them, but introduces values for the vulnerability of the scales themselves, such as are not analyzed out in trait-view theory.

# 8

# Multivariate Perspectives on the Construct Validity of the Trait-State Distinction

**John R. Nesselroade**
*The Pennsylvania State University, University Park*

**Thomas W. Bartsch**
*Iowa State University, Ames*

## 1  THE IMPORTANCE OF CHANGE CONCEPTS IN PSYCHOLOGY

Terms such as state, mood, affect, and emotion currently abound in theoretical statements about human behavior. As do a number of conceptual labels, these terms create few problems and are seemingly very useful when wielded at a purely verbal level. But as soon as one attempts to lure them into a more rigorous framework, they may be found to be too elusive to permit the integration of theory and related observation into a coherent system. Such concepts tend to be unsuitably flexible when verbally transported from one context to another, unless they can also be tied to a set of explicit operations and procedures and handled with objectivity and rigor.

Our aim in this chapter[1] is to examine certain aspects of psychological change, paying special, though not exclusive, attention to a class of short term, more or less reversible, change phenomena manifested in human behavior. Although the writers are in sympathy with the notion that what is

needed eventually are formulations that locate these concepts in empirically based antecedent-process-consequent schemes, our emphasis here is on determining a structural framework to encompass simultaneous changes in a variety of responses rather than intensive examination of one (or a small number) of response variables in relative isolation.

The present approach emphasizes deriving concepts or constructs directly from data as the initial step in the process of technically advanced theory construction, although it is clear that one's starting point can seldom be considered as beginning purely from either (a) data and advancing to theory, or (b) theoretical considerations and proceeding to data. Perhaps Adam had a clear choice, but for obvious reasons contemporary psychology has been denied the possible benefits of his introspections.

In the study of human behavior, as much as in any other scientific discipline, concern for various aspects of substantive change has prompted a major portion of the total research effort. Almost all branches of psychology, including those dealing with development, learning, pathology, social interaction,

---

[1] Originally drafted while the authors were at West Virginia University.

motivation, physiology, and so forth, are engaged in attempts to establish lawful relationships among changeable events. Many concepts depending on change measurement for their definition—such as maturation, degenerative process, trait change, complex state change, learned defense mechanism—have been employed in these fields with an almost complete lack of necessary operational definition. We here examine some of these concepts—principally those of state and trait change—in the hope of putting them on firmer conceptual footing.

In choosing to investigate the behavior of living organisms, the researcher sets for himself an arduous task in which he will often be confronted with frustrating events and, occasionally, with minor triumphs. The villain in the piece frequently is change (Bereiter, 1963), which either occurs when it is unexpected or which fails to occur when it is anticipated. From conception to senescence, the organism undergoes countless chemical, physiological, anatomical, and psychological modifications. Some of these changes take place rather slowly, as in the gradual ossification of skeletal structures, the development of motor skills, and the elaboration of an adequate repertoire of socially acceptable responses. Others, such as amitosis and autonomically controlled adaptive responses, may occur at prodigious rates.

In addition to changes occurring in the organism, the environment surrounding it is also constantly altering in an endless panorama of stimulation. These two kinds of changes—organismic and environmental—are not independent; they influence, cause, and otherwise modify each other, sometimes simply, but often in complexly interwoven patterns. The environment, though no more stable in many respects than the organism, is the more durable. One result of this arrangement is that responsibility for survival, both

physical and social, eventually falls to the organism, which must adapt its behavior to meet environmental demands. Successful adaptation may require altering the environment, the organism, or both.

In contrast to changes in the organism, we may introduce briefly at this point another notion, stability. Distinguishing changes within the broader context of behavior implies at least one other classification which for present purposes we will simply refer to as stability. Personality theorists, for example, have long been concerned with the permanent characteristics and attributes of the organism. This stability has been sought largely in two main areas: (a) stability of endowment or levels on measured attributes, and (b) stable, recurrent patterns of, and relationships among, changeable events. Ability and temperament traits are examples of the former, and processes such as learning and maturation exemplify the latter.

Put simply, the idea emphasized here is that as one of its attributes the organism is capable of being, in some sense, a "different" organism from one occasion to another as it behaves over time. In what way or ways is it a different organism from one point in time to another? In what ways does it remain the same? How can we define and describe both dimensions of change and dimensions of stability for the organism? These and related questions are discussed in subsequent portions of this chapter. First, however, a brief digression is in order, to provide some orientation concerning the particular methodological approach around which later discussion centers.

## 2 USE OF MULTIVARIATE METHODS IN STRUCTURING CHANGE

If the complexities of psychological change are to be dealt with successfully, the establishment of lawful relationships should center on appropriately basic and unitary response dimensions. Multivariate methods offer tools for systematic examination of a large number of variables as they change, thus enabling a researcher to determine which variables in a set actually manifest a tendency to change together in a patterned, unitary fashion (Nesselroade, 1970, 1976). These composite variables and the constructs inferable from them would seem, in the long run, to offer the most potential information and theoretical utility if intraindividual variation is to be structured.

Any single observable variable that one might select for study is liable to be affected by a number of influences other than the particular phenomenon it is supposed to index, and almost certainly it is not the optimum observation in terms of which to seek some law. As Cattell (1946), Cronbach (1957), and others pointed out long ago, rarely can a single measured response adequately index a psychological construct. Using multivariate analysis procedures, the single, observable variables, each of which tends to be pulled and pushed about by numerous forces, are really mere stepping stones to the more stable patterns of intraindividual change.

The establishment of concepts by means of carefully done factor-analytic studies has the advantage initially of putting one in the position of knowing which manifestations do not belong to the concept as well as knowing which ones do belong. Such information is crucial in rigorously distinguishing among dimensions of response. For example, it was pointed out (Cattell & Nesselroade, 1976) that much confusion has arisen from using terms such as anxiety, fear, stress, and threat almost interchangeably. The argument is that anxiety, stress, and fear can be distinguished factor analytically as distinct response patterns, and that once the response patterns are uniquely identified the question as to what classes of stimulus situation elicit the given response can be systematically investigated.[2]

Since the advent of individual-differences quantitative methodology as an approach to the dissection of behavior, the search has been conducted for more or less stable dimensions of interindividual variability that permit the symbolic representation of a given person as a set of numbers. These numbers, in turn, can be conveniently utilized in functional expressions to predict that individual's performance on some relevant task or behavior. Historically, this approach has been most pronounced in the area of human abilities, which developed in intimate contact with the best known, perhaps, of multivariate methods—factor analysis. The ensuing dimensions (factors) of covariation among tasks presumed to reflect ability attributes tended to assume the status of relatively fixed characteristics of the individual, and the conceptual label *trait* was seemingly tied closely to a highly sophisticated and powerful quantitative procedure. Or as Horn and Little (1966) expressed it, "because it is sensible to suppose that abilities are stable, it has been assumed that factors found among ability test performances must represent traits."

It is perhaps a little curious that the trait concept became entrenched so firmly in this context, for factor analysis, in and of itself, as usually done on a cross section of subjects at one point in time (*R* technique, see chapter 1), logically cannot be claimed to yield only factors which are stable in terms of a person's implied endowments (scores) thereon. We shall make an important distinc-

[2] It is worth noting that the logic of the multivariate approach can be applied to the stimulus domain also. Frederiksen (1972) surveyed past attempts and suggested directions for further research along these lines.

tion here, and elaborate it later, between a stable pattern of factor loadings or one kind of factor *invariance* (Thurstone, 1947) and *stable* factor scores.

More than 50 years of factor-analytically-oriented research have not succeeding in yielding a set of traits, cognitive or otherwise, by which we can bring the prediction of behavior in general to the desired level of precision. Obviously, in a prediction scheme of the type mentioned previously in which a person's relevant endowments are specifiable as quantities, it is advantageous to deal in attributes that are stable to the point that, once measured, the obtained values can be used a week, a month, or a year later and still be appropriate. But if this type of information is not sufficient to the task, then clearly other information must be used.

An alternative kind of predictor information to which many theorists are now turning is provided by the situation in which the behavior will occur (see Patterson and Bechtel, chapter 10). Others, however, after many years of trying to get "inside the organism," are understandably reluctant to participate in an unceremonious exit back to the environment (at least not without taking along their more cherished discoveries). Our concern here, however, is not directly with these as mutually exclusive alternatives but rather with a possible point of overlap to the extent that situations and their effects can be tied to dimensions of interindividual and intraindividual response variability.

## 3  INTRAINDIVIDUAL DIFFERENCES AND *P* TECHNIQUE

We can further define the topic of interest here and at the same time discuss one of the techniques currently being employed to reveal structure in intraindividual variation by considering briefly the methodology ~vn as *P*-technique factor analysis (see

chapters 9 and 10). In *P* technique one person is used as a source of data. This individual is measured on a selected set of attributes on a large number of occasions.[3] Each occasion of measurement, which typically involves the complete set of measures, may be at regular or irregular intervals depending on the experimenter's objectives (Cattell, 1966e). For example, the person might be measured once a day for a period of 100 to 150 days. The extent to which his scores on a given measure vary from day to day across the testing period reflects the magnitude of intraindividual variation. Moreover, the observation that two or more variables tend to covary across time may be taken as evidence (Bereiter, 1963) supporting the notion that the variables are, to an extent reflected in the magnitude of the association, measures of the same thing.

It is important to note that the covariance among two or more variables over time may result from either a single underlying common source or multiple underlying sources. Or, alternatively phrased, more than one common factor may be contributing to the observed covariance. What and how many such dimensions (factors) are involved? In a *P*-technique study, one attempts to answer this question, not just for two variables but for many, by a factor analysis of the covariances among all the variables in the original battery of measures. That is to say, using data obtained from the repeated assessment of one person, the variables are intercorrelated over the total number of occasions, the results are arrayed into a correlation matrix, and the matrix is then factor analyzed. The resulting factors represent a set of dimensions of intraindividual variability. Note that the source of variability *ostensibly*

---

[3] Karen Cattell, in 1946, was the first recorded subject for a longitudinal factor analysis on this basis (Cattell, Cattell, & Rhymer, 1947).

chanics of difference score factoring starting with the factor-analytic-specification equation (chapter 1) defined in such a way, it seems, as to be agreeable to both positions. First, consider a form of the basic specification equation:

$$a_{ji} = v_{j1}S_{1i} + \cdots + v_{jk}S_{ki} + u_{ji}. \tag{1}$$

Equation 1 simply states that response $a_j$ (Act $j$) of individual $i$ is a weighted sum of his factor scores. The $v_j$s are the weights (factor loadings) indicating the contribution of a particular factor to performance $a_j$, the $S$s are individual $i$'s factor scores, and $u_j$ is a factor that is unique to performance of $a_j$ (the variance of $u_j$ includes both specific and error variance).

A general expression for a set of specification equations for $N$ individuals on $n$ behaviors using matrix notation can be written as[5]

$$A' = V_{fp}S'_f, \tag{2}$$

where $A$ (prime denotes transposition of matrix) is an $N \times n$ matrix of scores for $N$ individuals on $n$ variables, $V_{fp}$ is an $n \times k$ matrix of factor loadings, and $S_f$ is an $N \times k$ matrix of factor scores. For simplicity we have omitted the specific factors, but relevant comments concerning them will be made at appropriate places in the subsequent discussion. We further specify that the columns of both $A$ and $S_f$ (rows of $A'$ and $S'_f$ contain deviation scores; that is, each column of $A$ and $S_f$ has its mean equal to zero.

Next a set of specification equations is defined for each of two occasions involving the same subjects ($N$) and variables ($n$) as

[5] The notation used here conforms as closely as possible to that suggested by Cattell (1966e). Where no confusion is likely to arise, various subscripts have been dropped for the convenience of all involved.

$$A'_1 = V_{fp1}S'_{f1} \tag{3}$$

and

$$A'_2 = V_{fp2}S'_{f2} \tag{4}$$

such that

$A'_1$ and $A'_2$ are of order $n \times N$,

$S'_{f1}$ is of order $k_1 \times N$,

$S'_{f2}$ is of order $k_2 \times N$,

$V_{fp1}$ is of order $n \times k_1$,

$V_{fp2}$ is of order $n \times k_2$, and

$k_1$ may or may not be equal to $k_2$

Thus far, we have simply stated that the scores on the variables for a given occasion are weighted sums of the individual's factor endowments on that occasion. Nothing has been said about the nature of the factors, i.e., whether they are the same (in some sense) from one occasion to the other.

Next, consider the following $2 \times 2$ table:

| Factor loading pattern | Factor scores | |
|---|---|---|
| | Stable | Fluctuant |
| Invariant | $a$ | $b$ |
| Not invariant | $c$ | $d$ |

One can conceive of a given factor falling in one of the four cells. For example, cell $a$ factors would not only show the same loading pattern on both occasions, but people would also tend to maintain their level of endowment from Time 1 to Time 2.[6] Cell $b$

[6] As is well known to those working in the field, the problems of finding and evaluating factor invariance are by no means solved. The theoretical presentation in this section obviously benefits from our avoidance of real data and consequent freedom to deal with strict numerical invariance of loading pattern.

factors would also have the same loading pattern across occasions, but scores could vary differentially from Occasion 1 to Occasion 2. Cell c factors would show different loading patterns from one occasion to the next, but scores on such factors would tend to remain stable. This might also be taken as evidence for identifying two factors as the same, in one sense, from Time 1 to Time 2. Cell d factors in this frame of reference would be the most erratic of the lot and do not offer any firm basis, in themselves, for cross-occasion matching. Nevertheless, Case d is needed for completion, and the pessimist is apt to insist that empirical data are most likely to fill this cell. To simplify the presentation, the case of constant changes for all persons on a factor will be treated as either Case a or Case c (stable factor scores) although this need not be done. Elsewhere (Nesselroade, 1967, 1973), the alternative of identifying such factors as change dimensions has been dealt with in detail. For the present treatment consider that, if all persons' scores changed by some constant amount from Time 1 to Time 2, the interoccasion correlation would be unity, thus implying perfectly stable factor scores by that mode of assessing stability.

We will take the position that a necessary, though perhaps not sufficient, condition for interpreting a given factor as a trait dimension is that the individuals' scores thereon tend to remain stable.[7] For various reasons it is desirable also to have factors with invariant loading patterns, but in the case of

traits (in this context) it is not taken to be a necessity. In some cases, one might reasonably expect to identify two trait dimensions even though the loading pattern is not invariant from one occasion to another. Such, in fact, is the position taken by Harris (1963a) in an analysis of ability data in which the factor scores are forced to remain stable, thereby accounting for observed changes as changes in factor structure.

Patterson and Betchel's examination of states and traits (see chapter 10) employs a quite different operational definition of the trait concept than the one being implied in the present discussion. For their developments, trait is a derived parameter for the person based upon his average state level measured over many different situations. By way of contrast, both trait and state dimensions in the present discussion are conceptualized as factors (dimensions of individual differences) potentially operating at any given point in time. Separation of these two types of hypothesized factors is to be made on the basis of temporal characteristics of the factor loading pattern and the individuals' factor scores.

Baltes and Nesselroade (1973) discussed the implications of the 2 X 2 table presented earlier for the study of personality and ability trait development in a life-span context. They paid considerable attention to issues of factor change and stability within a process framework but extensive comment here is not possible.

---

[7] This statement, as it stands, requires some qualification. Humphreys in 1960 and in subsequent communication strongly argued for researchers to be alert to the possibility of simplex-like relationships among repeated measures on what is ostensibly the same variable. He maintained that the same may be true for test-retest correlations based on factor scores. If so then, by the previous definition of trait, there can be no traits. Given adequate resources, this proposition of simplices for factor scores can be put to an empirical test, and it may turn out to hold for factors in certain substantive areas (e.g., developmental and growth data) and not for others (e.g., factors related to short term, reversible phenomena such as diurnal fatigue, the estrous cycle, and emotional responses in general). How stable the factor scores should remain and over what time period in order to retain the conceptual label *trait* is discussed subsequently.

Using the fourfold table as a reference point, let us now consider some of its implications for difference score factoring and, more generally, for the distinction between the concepts of psychological traits and states. First, we accommodate two kinds of factors: (a) a set of traits with invariant loading patterns and perfectly stable scores (cell $a$ factors) and (b) a set of factors upon which we initially place neither restriction (cell $d$ factors). Using these definitions, we may partition the separate-occasion factor-loading patterns $(V_{fp})$ and factor score matrices $(S_f)$ as follows:

$$V_{fp1} = [V_t \vdots V_{s1}], S'_{fl} = \begin{bmatrix} S'_{ft} \\ \cdots \\ S'_{fs1} \end{bmatrix} \qquad (5)$$

and

$$V_{fp2} = [V_t \vdots V_{s2}], S'_{f2} = \begin{bmatrix} S'_{ft} \\ \cdots \\ S'_{fs2} \end{bmatrix} \qquad (6)$$

where

$V_t$ = the factor pattern of $t$-trait factors,
$V_{s1}$ = the factor pattern of $k_1 - t$ Occasion 1 nontrait factors,
$V_{s2}$ = the factor pattern of $k_2 - t$ Occasion 2 nontrait factors,
$S'_{ft}$ = the factor scores for $N$ people on $t$-trait factors,
$S'_{fs1}$ = the factor scores for $N$ people on $k_1 - t$ Occasion 1 nontrait factors, and
$S'_{fs2}$ = the factor scores for $N$ people on $k_2 - t$ Occasion 2 nontrait factors.

Previously, appropriate matrices were defined as containing deviation scores; thus we can write an expression for the variance-covariance matrix of the difference scores as

$$C_d = \frac{1}{N} [(A'_2 - A'_1)(A'_2 - A'_1)'], \qquad (7)$$

where $C_d$ represents the variance-covariance matrix of difference scores and the other symbols are as defined above. For the sake of additional simplicity here, and in later discussion, let us also assume that the standard deviation of each variable remains the same from Occasion 1 to Occasion 2. Such an assumption, which may or may not be empirically justifiable, is not critical for the line of argument we are developing at this point. It should be noted, however, that changes in standard deviation from one testing to the next will exert an influence on the results which, depending on one's method of factoring, will be to some extent predictable. The more mathematically sophisticated student is encouraged to follow through on this (e.g., Kaiser & Caffrey, 1965; Meredith, W., 1964). Substituting the appropriate factor matrix equivalents for $A'_1$ and $A'_2$ we have

$$C_d = \frac{1}{N} \left\{ \left[ (V_t \vdots V_{s2}) \begin{pmatrix} S'_{ft} \\ \cdots \\ S'_{fs2} \end{pmatrix} \right. \right.$$

$$- (V_t \vdots V_{s1}) \begin{pmatrix} S'_{ft} \\ \cdots \\ S'_{fs1} \end{pmatrix} \left. \right]$$

$$\cdot \left[ (V_t \vdots V_{s2}) \begin{pmatrix} S'_{ft} \\ \cdots \\ S'_{fs2} \end{pmatrix} \right.$$

$$\left. \left. - (V_t \vdots V_{s1}) \begin{pmatrix} S'_{ft} \\ \cdots \\ S'_{fs1} \end{pmatrix} \right]' \right\} \qquad (8)$$

When the expression on the right-hand side of Equation 8 is expanded and the terms collected and cancelled, the result can be written as

$$C_d = \left[ V_{s2} \left( \frac{1}{N} S'_{fs2} S_{fs2} \right) V'_{s2} \right]$$

$$- \left[ V_{s2} \left( \frac{1}{N} S'_{fs2} S_{fs1} \right) V'_{s1} \right]$$

$$- \left[ V_{s1} \left( \frac{1}{N} S'_{fs1} S_{fs2} \right) V'_{s2} \right]$$

$$+ \left[ V_{s1} \left( \frac{1}{N} S'_{fs1} S_{fs1} \right) V'_{s1} \right] \qquad (9)$$

Now the first and fourth terms in parenthesis in Equation 9 represent within-occasion factor covariance matrices, and the other two terms represent between-occasion factor covariance matrices. These are signified by

$$C_{ij} = \frac{1}{N} S'_{fi} S_{fj} . \qquad (10)$$

Equation 9 may then be written as follows:

$$C_d = V_{s2} C_{s2s2} V'_{s2} - V_{s2} C_{s2s1} V'_{s1}$$

$$- V_{s1} C_{s1s2} V'_{s2} + V_{s1} C_{s1s1} V'_{s1} . \qquad (11)$$

At this point all terms involving traits (cell *a* factors) have vanished for algebraic reasons, leaving only the other dimensions as defined previously (cell *d* factors). In obtaining Equation 11 we have assumed, aside from the usual assumptions of the factor-analytic model, that (a) the specific factor of a given variable on one occasion does not covary with the specific factors of the remaining $n-1$ variables on the other occasion, and (b) the specific factor of a given variable on one occasion does not covary with any of the common factors on the other occasion.

The factor analysis of a covariance matrix (Tucker, 1951) leads to a general solution of the type

$$C = V_{fp} C_{ff} V'_{fp}. \qquad (12)$$

*C* is the variance-covariance matrix of the observed scores (whether difference scores, or otherwise) with the exception that each diagonal element of *C* represents that portion of the variance of an observed variable due to the common factors only, rather than the total variance of that variable. $C_{ff}$ is the factor variance-covariance matrix and $V_{fp}$ the matrix of factor loadings.

Using partitioned matrices we may write Equation 11 as either

$$C_d = [V_{s2} \vdots - V_{s1}]$$

$$\cdot \begin{bmatrix} C_{s2s2} & \vdots & C_{s2s1} \\ \cdots & \vdots & \cdots \\ C_{s1s2} & \vdots & C_{s1s1} \end{bmatrix} \cdot \begin{bmatrix} V'_{s2} \\ \cdots \\ -V'_{s1} \end{bmatrix} \qquad (13)$$

or

$$C_d = [V_{s2} \vdots V_{s1}]$$

$$\cdot \begin{bmatrix} C_{s2s2} & \vdots & -C_{s2s1} \\ \cdots & \vdots & \cdots \\ -C_{s1s2} & \vdots & C_{s1s1} \end{bmatrix} \cdot \begin{bmatrix} V'_{s2} \\ \cdots \\ V'_{s1} \end{bmatrix} \qquad (14)$$

Both Equations 13 and 14 are of the form $C = V_{fp} C_{ff} V'_{fp}$ (Equation 12). Note, however, that, as a function of subtracting the Occasion 1 observed scores from the Occasion 2 observed scores, either the factor loadings for Occasion 1 or the cross-occasion factor covariances are reflected (multiplied by $-1.0$). We may pause here to consider that

1. The difference score covariance matrix does yield a factor solution.

2. *Traits*, as ideally defined previously, necessarily vanish from the solution when differences are taken.

3. No factors are represented in the differences which are not present on the separate occasions.

One of the pertinent implications of the third point is that, although one may factor analyze an $n \times n$ matrix of covariances, he can expect $k_1 + k_2$ factors, given they are all of the cell $d$ type.

Next we can derive the expected differential-$R$ solution for cell $b$ factors (invariant patterns but fluctuant factor scores) by letting $k_1 = k_2$ and $V_{s1} = V_{s2} = V_s$ and writing Equation 11 as

$$C_d = (V_s C_{s2s2} V_s') - (V_s C_{s2s1} V_s')$$
$$- (V_s C_{s1s2} V_s') + (V_s C_{s1s1} V_s') \quad (15)$$

$$= V_s(C_{s2s2} - C_{s2s1}$$
$$- C_{s1s2} + C_{s1s1}) V_s'. \quad (16)$$

Denoting the expression in parentheses as $C_{ss}$ we have

$$C_d = V_s C_{ss} V_s'. \quad (17)$$

Thus again we have a solution of the type $C = V_{fp} C_{ff} V_{fp}'$. Now, however, each element in the factor variance-covariance matrix is a composite of either four covariance, or two covariance and two variance, terms. Thus, even though the loading pattern of a factor may be invariant over occasions, it can still emerge in the difference analysis, given differential changes in individual's scores on that factor from Time 1 to Time 2. These cell $b$ factors are of primary interest since, of the four types, they best represent our current ideas about psychological states.

The fact that cell $b$ (state) factors will emerge in a $dR$ factor analysis as well as in an $R$-technique analysis is one plausible explanation for the similarity of factor patterns noted by Cattell and Scheier (1961) and by Hundleby, Pawlik, and Cattell (1965) in comparing $dR$ and regular $R$-technique factor-analysis results. One interesting ques-

tion for which we have no answer at this point is this: Given that invariant factor loading patterns can be demonstrated, how much instability (function fluctuation) of factor scores will the conceptual label *trait* tolerate? As Cattell (1966e) pointed out in discussing this issue, even a person's height tends to vary systematically over a 24-hour period, yet we tend to think of stature as one of the more permanent attributes of the mature organism. The use of differential-$R$ analysis might provide an operational answer here in that, if intraindividual variation on a factor is sufficient to permit its emergence in a $dR$ analysis, then the label trait is inappropriate for that factor. Before we can say more about this, however, several other points should be considered.

Cell $c$ factors (stable factor scores without invariant patterns) may be examined in a manner consistent with the preceding developments by defining the following expressions:

$$A_1' = V_{t1} S_{ft}' \text{ and } A_2' = V_{t2} S_{ft}'. \quad (18)$$

(Here $S_{ft}'$ is used on both occasions since stable factor scores are specified.)

$$C_d = \frac{1}{N} [(A_2' - A_1')(A_2' - A_1')']$$

$$= \frac{1}{N} [(V_{t2} S_{ft}' - V_{t1} S_{ft}')$$

$$\cdot (V_{t2} S_{ft}' - V_{t1} S_{ft}')']$$

$$= \frac{1}{N} (V_{t2} - V_{t1})(S_{ft}' S_{ft})(V_{t2}' - V_{t1}')$$

$$= (V_{t2} - V_{t1})\left(\frac{1}{N} S_{ft}' S_{ft}\right)(V_{t2}' - V_{t1}')$$
$$\quad (19)$$

Letting $(1/N \, S_{ft}' S_{ft}) = C_{tt}$, we have

$$C_d = (V_{t2} - V_{t1})(C_{tt})(V_{t2}' - V_{t1}'), \quad (20)$$

which is of the form $C = V_{fp}C_{ff}V'_{fp}$.

In marked contrast to the outcome for cell $d$ factors, the present factor loadings are the *differences* between each loading on Occasion 2 and the corresponding loading on Occasion 1. The last statement, of course, depends on the one-to-one matching of factors across occasions; but that condition was stipulated by the stated restriction of stable factor scores. Thus, in this case (cf. Harris, 1963a) what might be regarded as a kind of trait factor (because of the stability of the individuals' endowments thereon) would still emerge in a difference score factoring although in somewhat mutilated form. Being confronted with a vector of loadings, which, unknown to the analyst, actually consisted of differences between Occasion 2 and Occasion 1 loadings, could make the practice of factor interpretation a most unsavory and indeed frustrating task.

About cell $d$ factors we will say little else except that at this point they do not seem as useful as the others from a taxonomic standpoint, although they may become so when one begins to consider how Occasion 1 differs from Occasion 2 in relation to variables external to the factor analysis, and that the algebraic expectation, as mentioned earlier, is that both Occasion 1 and Occasion 2 factors would emerge in a $dR$ analysis, the totality of which might be greater in number than one would be willing to extract from $n$ variables. This dismissal of case $d$ does not imply that such factors are unlikely to crop up. Baltes and Nesselroade (1973) and A. R. Buss (1974) discussed a potential role for such factors in the study of developmental transitions. Also, for example, in experimentation with drugs the effect may not be to shift subjects on replicable dimensions but rather to alter significantly the factor structure of response variables. This could lead to either Case $c$ or Case $d$ or to some marginally recognizable mixture of both.

This, then, is a brief account of the algebraic relationships between differential-$R$ and $R$-technique factor analyses. Admittedly, the well-known problem areas of factor analysis (communality estimation, number of factors, metric invariance, and rotation) have been avoided, but each of these is worth a chapter or more in itself. It has been shown here that the familiar linear model or factor specification equation can accommodate both dimensions of intra-individual change and dimensions of stable individual differences. In the course of the discussion it became apparent that the use of $dR$ and $R$ technique for isolating and studying these two kinds of dimensions does not, in itself, lead to unequivocal resolutions. On the one hand, differential-$R$ technique analysis, as indicated, may yield cell $b$, cell $d$, or "differenced" cell $c$ factors described previously. $R$-technique analysis, on the other hand, permits factors representing all four cells potentially to emerge.

It should be clear, therefore, that the investigation of change and stability in psychological measures requires more refined techniques and that these techniques must provide for the simultaneous consideration of structural invariance and temporal stability. Only then can a given factor, with confidence, be properly understood in a trait-state kind of framework and be integrated into a broader theoretical scheme. In the next section, brief discussion is given to a selected set of factor-analytic designs that provide for the simultaneous consideration of invariance and stability issues.

## 6  LEADS ON SEPARATING TRAIT AND STATE DIMENSIONS

The conceptual scheme embodied in the fourfold table presented earlier has served as a focal point for the preceding discussion concerning the relationships between $dR$-

and *R*-technique factor analysis. Before abandoning that scheme to turn to a discussion of substantive findings, we consider some of its more general implications for research.

One major issue concerns the taxonomic objective of isolating and identifying the different types of factors discussed in section 5. The trait-state distinction appears to be bearing fruit (Singer, J. L., & Singer, 1972), especially in the domain of self-reported anxiety. Methods and procedures for analyzing multivariate change data are being developed; indeed, the area is blossoming into one of exciting methodological innovation and substantive findings. Here we can but hint at some of these although it is clear that the need for a systematic appraisal is beginning to be felt.

In attempting to organize factors (as response patterns) into some classificatory scheme such as the fourfold table, are we to analyze data simply to discover what kinds of factors emerge, or should we proceed by constructing factors with certain features to more carefully explore their other characteristics? Some readers may recognize aspects of the naive-realism-versus-nominalism debate here but we shall refrain from making other than illustrative remarks. In any case, many procedures for analyzing multivariate change data can be ordered with respect to the degree to which constraints on either factor loading patterns or factor scores are specified (Nesselroade, 1976).

Consider, for example, data from two occasion multivariate studies of the type discussed in section 5. We briefly describe here three general approaches to analyzing such data which bear directly on the classification issue. Each one can be elaborated and refined into many particular applications, some of which accommodate more than two occasions of measurement.

First, one might proceed by separately factoring the data from each occasion of measurement. The two solutions could then be independently rotated to some criterion such as simple structure and the resulting factors evaluated in terms of temporal invariance of loading patterns and stability of factor scores.

Second, a slightly stronger approach would be to employ transformation techniques (e.g., factor matching procedures) deliberately to maximize factor loading pattern invariance, factor score stability, and so forth. The resulting factors could then be studied to see which niche they occupy in the scheme. For instance, one might rotate both sets to maximize invariance of loading pattern and then examine the degree of stability of the implied factor scores. Alternatively, the longitudinal factor analysis model of Corballis and Traub (1970) provides a rotational solution which has been shown (Nesselroade, 1972) to maximize factor score stability coefficients. If either of the two characteristics (invariance or stability) is maximized, the nature of the other is an empirically answerable question.

Third, a still stronger approach is to initially pool data across occasions and factor so as to build in either perfect invariance of pattern or stability of factor scores. The procedure of Harris (1963a), mentioned earlier, constructs factor solutions that exhibit perfectly stable factor scores. Rozeboom (1976) presented an elaborate model for the study of change in multivariate data which constrains the factor-loading patterns to be perfectly invariant across occasions. Hakstian (1971) offered a systematic treatment of procedures for components analysis which parallel closely our Cases *a, b, c,* and *d*.

These techniques by no means exhaust the possibilities. Cattell's (1966e) grid analyses, J. L. Horn and Little's (1966) discriminant function approach, Tucker's (1963) three mode factor analysis, and the maximum likelihood methods (Jöreskog & Sörbom, 1975) bring multioccasion data into the confines of a single analysis. In short, many data analysis procedures are now available and are waiting to be evaluated by empirically oriented researchers willing to invest their resources in collecting the necessary, technically demanding, but substantively crucial data.

A second major issue concerns the utilization of factor analytic methods in more traditional manipulative experimental designs. Although the practice of estimating and subsequently analyzing factor scores is abhorred by many, significant theoretical advances in the trait-state domain await the outcomes of studies in which attempts are made to manipulate factor pattern invariance, factor score stabilities, factor score mean differences, etc.

Proper manipulative work, in fact, may free us from the trait-state distinction as such by disclosing that the stability of factor scores, for example, is more fruitfully regarded as a continuum of values, the antecedents of which need to be explored, rather than a loose dichotomy. Explicating the antecedents for various degrees of invariance and stability of response patterns is a promising endeavor not only for the study of personality states, moods, etc., but for the study of personality development and change across the entire life span.

## 7  SUBSTANTIVE FINDINGS RELATED TO TRAIT–STATE ISSUES

To provide some additional perspective on the trait-state distinction from a factor-analytic viewpoint, the model will be considered in the context of substantive research. Our purpose here is not to be comprehensive but to consider selected research activity as it relates to issues outlined previously. Two areas seem to be among the most relevant.

One issue concerns the numerous and enthusiastic criticisms that have been leveled against personality traits in general. The other issue concerns the empirical investigation of affect or mood states.

Mischel (1968), probably the most cited spokesman in what has been called the situationalism controversy, argued that insufficient evidence exists to support either the temporal stability of trait measures or the situational generality of behaviors supposedly under the control of these traits. There is not room here to summarize the voluminous literature dealing with these issues, but comprehensive reviews are available elsewhere (e.g., Bowers, 1973; Mischel, 1973). We focus on only one outcome of the protracted discussion here. At the same time, we concentrate on the notion of temporal stability, for we believe it to be the more basic of the two issues.

The situationalism debate has led, not to an abandonment of interest in individual differences, but to a wider recognition of the need to modify the way personality research is conceptualized and executed. Currently, a major theme of this remodeling effort has focused on providing room for the influence of situational factors as they interact with personality characteristics to determine behavior (Mischel, 1973). Three activities which seem central to the interactionist position are the following: (a) isolating important attributes of persons and situations; (b) discovering how the attributes are organized within persons and situations, respectively; and (c) generating a theoretical account of how such configurations of attributes interact in determining behavioral outcomes. One implication is that the development of a reliable and parsimonious taxonomy of human attributes, and one of situations, remains the first task of the day. Success in generating a more complete account of behavior will, of logical necessity, rest on the quality of the components in the respective taxonomies. Whether the factor-analytic model is a fruitful way to generate these taxonomies is an empirical question. There is no reason to believe, however, that it should be excluded from what should undoubtedly be a multifaceted attack on an obdurate problem.

Perhaps the reader is asking why some researchers believe that factor analysis, in the past, contributed more to the problem than to its solution. Part of the answer to this question was provided by J. L. Horn and Little (1966) who noted that, primarily as a historical accident, trait theorists tended to assume rather than study the temporal stability of their measures. In other words, influential researchers who used factor-analytic methods placed unwarranted confidence in $R$-technique analysis as a means for isolating trait dimensions. Realizing that either trait or state factors can emerge from such an analysis, it is reasonable to suspect that existing measuring instruments possibly confound these two sources of variance. Although it is indirect and was mentioned earlier, some empirical support for this speculation may be found in the work of Hundleby, Pawlik, and Cattell (1965) who, in summarizing some 25 years' research, called attention to a general parallelism between the loading patterns produced by $R$ technique and those produced by $dR$ analyses. Such cross-technique matching of loading patterns is open to a number of interpretations (e.g., all resulting factors could be of the cell $b$ variety) and carefully designed investigations are needed to resolve the ambiguity. Perhaps for some dimensions the investigatory process might result in a disentanglement of trait and state factors. Trait dimensions thus refined might provide the basis for developing the taxonomies mentioned above.

A disentanglement of trait and state has

been proceeding in the area of anxiety for some time and merits brief attention here. Stimulated by the earlier work of Cattell and Scheier (1961), Spielberger (1966) suggested that much of the conceptual confusion and equivocal research findings that characterize the field stem from the failure to distinguish between trait and state anxiety and the use of measures that confound these two concepts. Subsequent work in this area was concerned with empirically showing a distinction between trait and state anxiety and with establishing their construct validity. Two studies reported here provide examples of how the factor-analytic techniques advocated in this chapter have been used to discriminate state from trait dimensions in the area of anxiety.

To demonstrate that trait and state anxiety exist as measurably distinct concepts, Cable (1972; Nesselroade & Cable, 1974) administered a questionnaire battery on two occasions, separated by a brief interval, to a group of college students. The measures included items from a trait-state anxiety battery under development and a similar instrument constructed by Spielberger, Gorsuch, and Lushene (1969). A single analysis was performed on the product moment correlations derived from data pooled over both occasions of measurement. This procedure forces the factor-loading pattern to be invariant (see section 6) and permits an inspection of factor score stabilities under that constraint. Final loading patterns of the two factors that were extracted and rotated to an oblique simple structure solution are presented in Table 1. In relation to the trait-state distinction, the variables show a strikingly consistent and supportive cleavage onto two factors. The theoretical distinction required that these dimensions also manifest differential levels of stability. When test-retest stability coefficients were calculated, using estimated factor scores,

**TABLE 1** Loading pattern of trait and state anxiety measures

| Variable[b] | Factor[a] | |
|---|---|---|
| | I (State anxiety) | II (Trait anxiety) |
| 1. State anxiety (S) | .93 | −.05 |
| 2. State anxiety (S) | .99 | −.13 |
| 3. State anxiety (CN) | .76 | .13 |
| 4. State anxiety (CN) | .77 | .06 |
| 5. Trait anxiety (CN) | −.01 | .74 |
| 6. Trait anxiety (CN) | −.13 | .86 |
| 7. Trait anxiety (S) | .08 | .84 |
| 8. Trait anxiety (S) | .10 | .81 |

*Note.* After Cable, 1972.

[a]Factor intercorrelation = .70.

[b]S signifies that a variable is a subset of items from the State-Trait Anxiety Inventory (Spielberger, Gorsuch, & Luschene, 1969); CN that a variable is a subset of items from an experimental state-trait battery under development by Cattell and Nesselroade.

they were found to be .68 for the state and .93 for the trait. An examination of average internal consistency reliability coefficients of the scales (about .81 for the state and .72 for the trait) indicated that the theoretically correct, discrepant stabilities of the two factors were not due to differential reliabilities of the measures.

To investigate the effect of various instructions both on the invariance of factor loadings and on the stability of factor scores, Bartsch (1976) used a design similar to that of Cable (1972) and incorporated manipulations hypothesized to alter the level of self-reported anxiety state but to leave unaltered that of self-reported trait anxiety. Factoring each occasion of data separately, Bartsch found a similarly consistent division of trait and state measures onto separate factors and, moreover, that whereas state factor scores were appropriately modulated, the trait factor scores were as appropriately impervious to the experimental manipulations. Bartsch (1976) included in his analysis measures of height, weight, and sex of subjects to define a third factor that would

permit comparisons between physical and psychological dimensions on both factor-loading pattern invariance and temporal stability of factor scores. The comparisons, summarized in Table 2, showed that all factors exhibited high temporal invariance but differential stabilities, as demanded by the theoretical expectations.

Investigations such as those of Bartsch (1976) and Cable (1972) demonstrate in a concrete fashion how the proposed techniques vastly extend the scope of factor analytic research. In addition, the studies reveal how information gained by the employment

**TABLE 2** Comparison of temporal invariance (by congruence coefficient) and stability levels between three *R*-technique factors

| Factor | Coefficient | |
|---|---|---|
| | Congruence | Stability |
| State anxiety | .971 | .709 |
| Trait anxiety | .958 | .862 |
| Sex, body size | .931 | .982 |

*Note.* After Bartsch, 1972.

of these methods may lead to a more accurate definition of personality trait and state dimensions. The Bartsch study especially, shows how functional relationships may be examined through the inclusion of experimentally manipulated variables. Such precise definition and the provision for situational manipulations seems vital to any subsequent attempt to articulate further the interactionist model.

The study of rapid and reversible changes such as emotional responses is an area that could benefit significantly from improved multivariate methodology. Cattell (1973a) pointed out that several major attempts to construct scales (Gottschalk & Gleser, 1969; Zuckerman, 1960) relied on clinical or rational criteria, with the result that too little is known about the structural composition of the measures. Other researchers (McNair & Lorr, 1964; Nowlis & Green, 1965) made use of factor-analytic procedures but tended to rely on single-occasion, R-technique strategies which, as was pointed out earlier, do not yield any information on the temporal stability of the resulting dimensions.

One desirable step in light of the critical review of Luborsky and Mintz (1972)—the assessment simultaneously of invariance and stability in the mood domain—was undertaken by Lebo (1972). P-technique data from five pregnant subjects were factor analyzed; and Lebo, with the help of various factor rotation procedures, defined several general patterns of mood change during prepartum and postpartum intervals.

One of the most systematic and comprehensive attempts to structure intraindividual variability by multivariate procedures has been the series of P- and dR-technique studies conducted over a period of many years by Cattell and various co-workers. The work has been summarized (Cattell, 1973a; Cattell & Scheier, 1961) and numerous implications of the research findings for prediction models, measurement procedures, and personality theory in general have been discussed. Researchers interested in trying to embrace personality in the broad sense can no longer afford to ignore the substantive and methodological issues that work on states has called to our attention.

## 8  SUMMARY

1. Concepts of change are of central importance to the study of behavior. Change concepts must be tied to explicit, rigorous measurement and analysis operations if they are to make a significant contribution to the integration of data and theory in this area.

2. In deriving a set of change constructs from empirical data, multivariate analysis procedures permit the investigation of a multitude of variables, all changing simultaneously, rather than the study of one or two variables in relative isolation. Determination of invariant, replicable dimensions of change underlying observed intraindividual variation may well account for some of the gaps now current in essentially trait-oriented systems.

3. Various writers argued that the covariance of two or more measures on a given entity over occasions is a necessary and sufficient condition for inferring that they are measures of the same thing. P-technique factor analysis, one method of structuring intraindividual variability, takes this inference as a starting point and then proceeds to determine the number and nature of such underlying sources of variation. It precludes sources of interindividual variation by using only one person as a data source.

4. Two major problem areas encountered in dealing with change are (a) questions of measuring and scaling change data per se and (b) the development and use of models by which to explore change structure. Many of the current procedures attempting to deal with the second problem involve variations

of one kind or another on the basic factor-analytic concepts. These are proving invaluable aids in bringing order into a complex, chaotic domain.

5. The linear specification equation of factor analysis can be defined to include both dimensions of interindividual and intraindividual variation. Thus the two may be brought into a common framework, and the useful information of both may be used to predict behavior. By various analytical techniques it may be possible to split up these two kinds of factors for further study and experimentation.

6. Substantive researchers can use the powerful factor-analytic model in a variety of ways to study the distinction between personality states and traits. Focusing on two major characteristics of factors—invariance of loading patterns and stability of factor scores—an investigator may proceed to establish parametric values for different substantive dimensions of interest, or he may introduce invariance or stability directly to defining characteristics of a factor. In many situations, factor models and manipulative experimentation can and should be combined to provide potentially fruitful research designs.

7. The ultimate usefulness of personality traits as a basis for developing a science of behavior has been seriously questioned by numerous psychologists. Alternative formulations include situationalism which, vis-a-vis trait theory, seems to miss the mark as widely on the other side, and a more temperate person-by-situation interactionist position. Further elaboration of the latter depends to a large extent on one's ability to dimensionalize precisely and exhaustively both person and situation characteristics. Refined application of various factor-analytic research designs and multivariate concepts such as the distinction between traits and states potentially offers valuable help in more carefully exploring the general theoretical worth of the interactionist approach.

# 9

# Theory and Measurement of Anxiety States

**Charles D. Spielberger**
*University of South Florida, Tampa*

**Robert E. Lushene**
*Veterans Administration Hospital*
*Bay Pines, Florida*

**W. George McAdoo**
*Indiana University Medical Center, Indianapolis*

The English language abounds with terms that are descriptive of emotions, and such terms serve to communicate nuances of feeling with clarity and power. Common sense and personal experience tell us that "feeling angry" and "being afraid" reflect different states or conditions of the organism which, more often than not, lead to different courses of action. Although emotional states cannot be directly observed, they may be reliably inferred from other observations. For example, Izard, in chapter 20 of this volume, provides impressive evidence that children can recognize and correctly classify nine different emotional states from photographs of facial expressions. He also demonstrates that this ability to identify emotions in others increases with age and is found in many different cultures.

Our goals in this chapter are to present a conceptualization of anxiety as an emotional state, and to discuss theoretical and methodological issues that arise in the measurement of anxiety states. The chapter is arranged in three sections. First, a conception of anxiety as an emotional state is proposed, and important methodological and terminological

issues and problems that arise in research on anxiety are discussed. In section 2, several general approaches to the measurement of feelings and emotions are considered, and five different self-report measures of anxiety as an emotional state are described. In the final section, two distinct anxiety concepts, state and trait anxiety, are defined; and a theory of anxiety is outlined which specifies interrelationships among the circumstances and conditions that evoke anxiety states in persons differentially disposed to experience such states.

## 1 THE EXPRESSION OF ANXIETY AS AN EMOTIONAL STATE

Contemporary interest in anxiety has its historical roots in the 17th-century philosophical views of Pascal and Spinoza, and many of the current conceptions of anxiety were anticipated by Kierkegaard over a century ago (May, R., 1950). It was Freud, however, who first attempted to explicate the meaning of anxiety within the context of psychological theory. He regarded anxiety as "something felt," an unpleasant affective state or condition of the human organism. This unpleasant state consisted of feelings of apprehension, dread, or anxious expectation and seemed "to possess a particular note of its own" (Freud, S., 1936, p. 69). Physiological and behavioral discharge phenomena associated with anxiety—for example, heart palpitation (transitory arrhythmia, tachycardia), disturbances in respiration, sweating, restlessness, tremor and shuddering, vertigo, and the like—were considered by Freud to be essential components of anxiety states, but were of little theoretical interest to him.

Objective anxiety was regarded by Freud as synonymous with fear. It involved a complex internal reaction to anticipated injury or harm from some external danger that was consciously perceived as threatening. The intensity of the anxiety reaction was proportional to the magnitude of the external danger that evoked it; the greater the external danger and the stronger the perceived threat, the more intense the resulting anxiety reaction. Neurotic anxiety differed from objective anxiety in that the source of the danger was the individual's own repressed sexual and aggressive impulses rather than some external circumstance. When a partial breakdown in repression resulted in "derivatives" of repressed impulses erupting into awareness, neurotic anxiety was evoked. Since most of the cues associated with these impulses remained repressed, neurotic anxiety was experienced as "objectless," or, as in the case of phobias, the relationship between the feared object and the original situation was not recognized.

In contemporary psychology, the term *anxiety* is perhaps most commonly used to denote a palpable but transitory emotional state or condition characterized by feelings of tension and apprehension and heightened autonomic nervous system activity. Research on transitory anxiety has focused on delineating the general properties of anxiety states

and identifying the specific conditions that evoke them. On the basis of an extensive review of the literature, Krause (1961) concluded that transitory anxiety is typically inferred from six different types of evidence:

1. Introspective verbal reports.
2. Physiological signs.
3. "Molar" behavior (e.g., body posture, restlessness, distortions in speech).
4. Task performance.
5. Clinical intuition.
6. The response to stress.

According to Krause's interpretation of conventional usage, introspective verbal reports provide the most widely accepted basis for defining transitory anxiety.

Basowitz, Persky, Korchin, and Grinker (1955) defined anxiety as "the conscious and reportable experience of intense dread and foreboding, conceptualized as internally derived and unrelated to external threat" (p. 3). This definition is consistent with the prevailing convention of inferring transitory anxiety from introspective reports, and with Freud's conception of anxiety as an emotional state. In addition to emphasizing the specific phenomenological qualities associated with anxiety states, Basowitz, Persky, Korchin, and Grinker (1955) also posited, as did Freud, that these qualities are consciously experienced. Thus, it is assumed that a person who is "anxious" can observe and describe his own unpleasant feelings and can report the intensity of these feelings. By this definition the notion of "unconscious anxiety" is rendered meaningless, but anxiety states may be evoked by consciously perceived derivatives of repressed impulses.

B. Martin (1961) proposed that anxiety reactions be viewed as complex neurophysiological responses that must be distinguished, conceptually and operationally, from the external or internal stimuli that evoke these responses. Thus, Martin dispensed with the traditional distinction between fear or objective anxiety as a response to real or external danger, and neurotic anxiety as a reaction to some unknown threat. Instead, he emphasized the importance of identifying and measuring the observable physiological and behavioral response patterns associated with states of fear or anxiety, and of differentiating anxiety states from other emotional reactions. Martin also made clear the need to distinguish between anxiety reactions and "defenses" against anxiety, i.e., responses that have been learned in order to reduce the intensity of anxiety states.

## 1.1 State Anxiety

Cattell and Scheier (1961) pioneered in the application of multivariate techniques to the definition and measurement of anxiety states. In their research, both phenomenological and physiological variables presumed to be related to anxiety have been studied with factor analytic procedures, notably such methods as $P$ technique, $dR$ (differential $R$) technique, and chain-$P$ technique (Cattell, 1966g). In this multivariate approach, which permits investigation of the covariation of a number of different measures over time, "state anxiety" has consistently emerged as one of the principal personality state factors.

Many of the variables that load Cattell and Scheier's state-anxiety factor also have high loadings on their trait anxiety factor. Since the pattern of these loadings is quite different, Cattell hypothesized that it should be possible to assess both state and trait anxiety from a single personality questionnaire by applying different weights to each scale item according to its unique contribution to the state and trait factors. In chapter 8 of this volume, Nesselroade presents the theoretical rationale and supporting mathematical formulation to justify obtaining state and trait anxiety measures from a single test instrument. But, as Nesselroade points out, a number of problems relating to factor-pattern matching and factor-score stability must be resolved before such procedures will have pragmatic utility in the measurement of anxiety as an emotional state.

In summary, the clinical and research literature on anxiety suggests that transitory or state anxiety (A state) may be conceived of as a complex, relatively unique emotional condition or reaction that varies in intensity and fluctuates over time. More specifically, A states consist of unpleasant, consciously perceived feelings of tension and apprehension, with associated activation or arousal of the autonomic nervous sytem. It may be noted that this conception is comparable in many respects to the definition of anxiety as an emotional state suggested by Freud (1936) and elaborated upon by Basowitz, Persky, Korchin, and Grinker (1955). It is also apparent that anxiety states must be conceptually distinguished from the stimulus conditions that arouse them and from the cognitive and behavioral maneuvers that are learned because they lead to anxiety reduction.

The presence of anxiety states in humans can be most meaningfully and unambiguously defined in terms of some combination of introspective verbal reports and physiological-behavioral signs. In essence, if an individual reports that he feels anxious (frightened or apprehensive), this introspective verbal report defines an anxiety state. The use of introspective reports in the measurement of anxiety states assumes, of course, that people are capable of distinguishing between different feeling states, and that they are motivated to report accurately and honestly. To establish the construct validity of measures of A state based on introspective verbal reports, experimental procedures must be employed to determine the relationship between these self-report measures and physiological and behavioral indicants of anxiety.

At this point, it may be helpful to introduce several important terminological distinctions that will facilitate further discussion of anxiety phenomena (Spielberger, 1972a, 1972b, 1975).

## 1.2   Stress, Threat, and Anxiety

The words *stress, threat,* and *anxiety* are often used interchangeably by those who research anxiety phenomena. We propose to employ these terms to denote different aspects of a temporal sequence of events that results in the evocation of an anxiety state. *Stress* refers to variations in environmental conditions or circumstances that occur naturally or that are introduced or manipulated by an experimenter. In essence, stress denotes external stimulus conditions or situations that are characterized by some degree of objective danger as defined by an experimenter or consensually validated by a number of observers.

While situations that are objectively stressful are likely to be perceived as dangerous by most persons, whether or not such situations are regarded as threatening by a particular individual will depend upon his own subjective appraisal. Moreover, objectively nonstressful situations may be appraised as threatening by persons who, for some reason, perceive them as dangerous. Thus, whereas stress denotes the objective stimulus properties of a situation, threat refers to the subjective (phenomenological) appraisal of a situation as physically or psychologically frightening or dangerous. The appraisal of a situation as dangerous or

threatening will be determined by individual differences in aptitudes, skills, and personality dispositions (traits), and by personal experience with similar situations in the past.

The term *state anxiety* (A state) refers to the emotional reaction or response that is evoked in a person who perceives a particular situation as personally dangerous or frightening for him, irrespective of the presence or absence of a real (objective) danger. If an individual appraises a specific situation as threatening, it is assumed that he will respond to it with an elevation in A state; i.e., he will experience an immediate increase in the intensity of an unpleasant emotional state characterized by consciously experienced feelings of tension, apprehension, and heightened autonomic nervous system activity (e.g., increased heart rate, blood pressure, and galvanic skin response). The intensity and duration of this transitory anxiety reaction will be determined by the amount of threat that is perceived, and by the persistence of the individual's appraisal of the situation as dangerous.

## 2   THE MEASUREMENT OF ANXIETY STATES

Cattell and Scheier (1961) noted that contemporary personality theory is founded on brilliant observation and intuitive clinical reasoning, but that it is largely devoid of objective measurement techniques and replicable experimental findings. Although there has been notable progress in the assessment of personality characteristics in the past two decades, most of the advances have occurred in the measurement of personality traits rather than in the evaluation of psychological states. Since personality traits and states reflect different types of psychological constructs, the conceptual differences between them must be clarified to make more meaningful our discussion of the measurement of anxiety as an emotional state.

## 2.1 Personality States and Traits

Personality states may be regarded as temporal cross-sections in the stream of life of a person; a personality state exists at a given moment in time, and at a particular level of intensity (Thorne, F. C., 1966). Although personality states are often transitory, they can recur when evoked by appropriate stimuli, and they may endure over time when the evoking conditions persist. Emotional reactions may be viewed as expressions of personality states.

In contrast to the transitory nature of personality states, personality traits may be conceptualized as relatively enduring individual differences in objectively specifiable tendencies to perceive the world in a certain way and in the disposition to react or behave in a consistent manner with predictable regularity. Personality traits have the characteristics of a class of constructs that Atkinson (1964) called "motives" and that Campbell (1963) referred to as "acquired behavioral dispositions." Atkinson defined motives as dispositional tendencies acquired in childhood that are latent until the cues of a situation activate them. Acquired dispositional concepts, according to Campbell, involve residues of past experience that dispose a person to view the world in a particular way and to manifest "object-consistent" response tendencies.

Personality traits may also be regarded as reflecting individual differences in the frequency and the intensity that certain emotional states have been manifested in the past, and in the probability that such states will be experienced in the future. The stronger a particular personality trait, the more probable an individual will experience the emotional state that corresponds to this trait, and the greater the probability that behaviors associated with the trait will be manifested in a variety of situations. Furthermore, the stronger the personality trait, the more likely these emotional states and associated behaviors will be characterized by high levels of intensity. But whether or not a particular personality trait will be expressed in overt behavior at a given moment in time will depend on the presence of appropriate evoking stimuli. In persons strongly disposed to experience anxiety, A-state reactions will be more readily evoked by threatening situations, or by internal processes such as the thought that one has done poorly on a task. Under happy or pleasant circumstances, in which anxiety-provoking stimuli are absent, even a person highly disposed to experience feelings of anxiety is not likely to do so.

## 2.2 The Measurement of Moods and Feelings

F. C. Thorne (1966) cogently argued that psychological states are the basic units for a study of human behavior, especially for the clinical psychologist. But transitory states have been largely ignored in psychological research, and attempts to develop instruments for the quantitative measurement of personality states have been infrequent because objective research methodology could not deal effectively with these constantly changing, subjective inner experiences. In this section, we briefly describe several approaches to the use of verbal self-report procedures in the measurement of moods and feelings. We then consider, in somewhat greater detail, five self-report instruments that have been developed in recent years to measure anxiety as an emotional state.

Responses to self-report scales are subject to falsification, and many different response sets operate to distort the results obtained with verbal report measures. Consequently, the use of verbal self-report scales to measure personality states rests on what G. J. S. Wilde, in chapter 3 of this volume, calls the "inventory premise"—the assumption that people are willing, and able, to correctly describe their own behavior. A discussion of the methodological factors that influence self-report measures is beyond the scope of the present chapter, but Wilde provides an excellent critical analysis of the assumptions that underlie the use of these techniques. The two most important assumptions are the following:

1. Questionnaires and self-report scales may be regarded as verbal surrogates for behavior samples.
2. The construct validity of self-report measures must be determined empirically within a theoretical context in the same manner that the validity of any other performance measure or personality scale is evaluated.

Hildreth (1946) was the first psychologist to develop a comprehensive battery of self-report scales for the assessment of feelings. From the verbal reports of military patients, he derived 175 phrases that typified moods and attitudes. These phrases were first classified into six categories. Each category was then scaled on the basis of the judgmental responses of psychiatric patients and hospital staff, using a modified Thurstone technique. The result was the Hildreth (1946) Feeling and Attitude Battery, a set of scales that measured various moods and affect states.

Each of the Hildreth scales consists of 8-10 items that define a particular mood-intensity dimension. The subject is instructed to read through the list of items for each scale category, and then to select the single item that most closely approximates the intensity of his subjective feelings "at the present time." The following items represent 5 of the 10 categories for Hildreth's Feeling Scale $F$, the depression-elation dimension: "Wish I were dead," "Pretty lousy," "Just fair," "Swell," and "On top of the world." Although validational evidence is limited, Hildreth noted that the results obtained with his scales were consistent with clinical observations.

A set of self-report scales designed to measure different affects or moods also was reported by Wessman and co-workers (Wessman, Ricks, & Tyl, 1960; Wessman & Ricks, 1966). These investigators used rational and clinical criteria to develop a number of Personal Feeling Scales that define affect dimensions such as tranquility versus anxiety, elation versus depression, social respect versus social contempt, personal freedom versus constraint, harmony versus anger, and energy versus fatigue.

The Wessman-Ricks and Hildreth scales are *cumulative scales* (Stouffer, Guttman, Suchman, Lazarsfeld, Star, & Clausen, 1950) in that the items are ordered to present increasing intensities of a particular feeling state. A rather different approach to the measurement of affective states was taken by Nowlis and Green (Green, 1964; Green & Nowlis, 1957; Nowlis, 1965; Nowlis & Green, 1965). They collected a large number of adjectives descriptive of mood states that could be used to complete the sentence, "I feel ____," and had subjects respond to sentences containing these adjectives by rating themselves on a mood-intensity dimension. On the basis of factor analytic procedures, Nowlis and Green derived scales for measuring 12 different mood dimensions. Nowlis (1961) discussed the conceptual framework for this research and provided one of the best general introductions to the methods and problems associated with the measurement of affective states. This approach has been subsequently extended by others, such as Borgatta (1961a); Clyde (1963); Lorr, Daston, and Smith (1967); McNair and Lorr (1964); and McNair, Lorr, and Droppleman (1974).

The range and reliability of the mood scales developed by Nowlis and Green is, unfortunately, quite limited. Many dimensions are defined by as few as three adjectives, and one dimension, nonchalance, is assessed by only two adjectives. Zuckerman and his colleagues developed an adjective checklist with better psychometric properties for assessing affective states (Zuckerman, 1960; Zuckerman & Lubin, 1965; Zuckerman, Lubin, Vogel, & Valerius, 1964). Zuckerman's Multiple Affect Adjective Check List (MAACL) differs from the adjective rating-scales developed by Nowlis and Green in at least two important respects. First, the subject is required to check only those words that describe how he feels, rather than to indicate the intensity of specific feelings. Second, the adjectives that define the three affective dimensions measured by the MAACL—anxiety, hostility, and depression—were selected rationally rather than by factor-analytic procedures. The resulting scales were empirically validated by contrasting high and low groups on the three personality dimensions.

Of the 132 adjectives that comprise the MAACL, 21 are scoreable on the anxiety key, 28 on the hostility key, and 40 on the depression key. The remaining items serve as buffer items from which additional scales may be eventually derived. Evidence of the validity of the MAACL as a measure of state anxiety is impressive; the hostility and depression measures were introduced too recently to permit an evaluation of them.

An additional feature of the MAACL is that the same set of adjectives can be used to measure traits as well as states. In the assessment of personality states, the subject is instructed to respond on the basis of how he feels "today"; in the assessment of personality traits, the subject is asked to respond according to how he generally feels.

## 2.3 The Measurement of State Anxiety

Wessman and Ricks (1966) measure state anxiety (tranquility vs. anxiety) by a single, 10-item cumulative scale. Subjects are required to indicate "how calm or troubled you feel" by checking one of the 10 items. The item that defines the lowest point on the tranquility-anxiety scale is "Perfect and complete tranquility. Unshakably secure." The item representing the highest point on this scale is "Completely beside myself with dread, worry, fear. Overwhelmingly distraught and apprehensive. Obsessed or terrified by insoluble problems and fears" (Wessman & Ricks, 1966, p. 271). The other 8 scale points reflect intermediate levels along an inferred dimension of increasing anxiety. Since Wessman and Ricks were primarily concerned with the elation-depression dimension, they reported only limited information about their anxiety scale.

The Anxiety factor that emerged as one of the basic mood dimensions in the research of Nowlis and Green (1965) was defined by the adjectives "clutched up," "fearful," and "jittery" (1965, pp. 45–46). Other adjectives that were also found to have loadings on the Anxiety factor were "apprehensive," "uncertain," "helpless," and "weak." However, for these latter adjectives, the findings were not entirely consistent. Consequently, in subsequent research, the Nowlis-Green measure of state anxiety consisted of only three adjectives—clutched up, fearful, and jittery—each of which is rated on a 4-point scale.

Cattell and Scheier (1960; 1961) used factor-analytic procedures to measure both personality traits and emotional states. As previously noted, their approach assumed that a single response to an appropriate stimulus item may reveal both trait and state characteristics, which may be determined by the differential weighting of the response. The Institute for Personality and Ability Testing (IPAT) 8-Parallel Form Anxiety Battery was developed by Scheier and Cattell (1960) for the "repeated measurement of changes in anxiety level over time." Each of the eight forms of this battery consists of subtests for which high loadings on a State-anxiety factor were demonstrated in differential-*R* and *P*-technique factor analysis. Although only limited validity data have been reported for this test as a measure of state anxiety, some encouraging results apparently were obtained in drug research (e.g., Barrett & DiMascio, 1966; DiMascio, Meyer & Stifler, 1968).

Several of the subtests in the 8-Parallel Form Anxiety Battery were taken from the Objective-Analytic (O–A) Anxiety Battery (Cattell & Sheier, 1960), which measures trait anxiety as defined by Factor *U.I.* 24 (Cattell & Scheier, 1961). These subtests ("Susceptibility to Common Annoyances," "Lack of Confidence in Untried Skills," "Honesty in Admitting Common Frailties," and "Susceptibility to Embarrassment") appear to reflect behavioral dispositions that are associated with anxiety, rather than anxiety states as we have defined them. Another subtest ("Questions") requires subjects to report the frequency with which a given symptom has been experienced in the past ("often," "sometimes," "never"), rather than the intensity of the experience in the present. Thus, it seems to us that the 8-Parallel Form Anxiety Battery is more closely related to trait anxiety than to state anxiety.

Zuckerman and his associates (Zuckerman, 1960; Zuckerman & Biase, 1962) developed the Affect Adjective Check List

(AACL) to measure both state and trait anxiety. The AACL was subsequently extended to include measures of hostility and depression, and renamed the Multiple Affect Adjective Check List (MAACL), described previously. State anxiety is measured with the "Today" version of the AACL and the MAACL, which requires persons to check adjectives that describe how they feel on the particular day the test is administered. The instructions may be modified, however, to require the subject to indicate how he feels at a certain time.

Zuckerman and Lubin (1968) published an extensive bibliography of studies in which the AACL and the MAACL were used to evaluate changes in anxiety states as a function of a variety of stress-producing and stress-reducing conditions. In these studies the usefulness of the AACL as a measure of day-to-day fluctuations in state anxiety was demonstrated clearly. Evidence for the validity of the Today Form of the AACL as a measure of state anxiety is impressive. However, the General Form of the AACL shows lower correlations with other standard measures of trait anxiety, such as the J. A. Taylor (1953) Manifest Anxiety Scale and the IPAT Anxiety Scale (Cattell & Scheier, 1963), than these measures typically correlate with one another (Spielberger, Gorsuch, & Lushene, 1970).

## 2.4  The State-Trait Anxiety Inventory

The State-Trait Anxiety Inventory (STAI) was developed to provide reliable, relatively brief self-report measures of both state (A state) and trait (A trait) anxiety. Item selection and validation procedures for the STAI are described in detail by Spielberger and Gorsuch (1966) and by Spielberger, Gorsuch, and Lushene (1970).

The STAI A-trait scale consists of 20

statements that ask people to describe how they *generally* feel. Subjects respond to each scale item (e.g., "I lack self confidence") by checking one of the following: "Almost never," "Sometimes," "often," "Almost always." Correlations between scores on the STAI A-trait scale and measures of trait anxiety such as the MAS and the IPAT Anxiety Scale range between .75 and .80 for college students, and are above .80 for neuropsychiatric patients (Spielberger, Gorsuch, & Lushene, 1970).

The STAI A-state scale consists of 20 statements that ask people to describe how they feel at a particular moment in time; subjects respond to each A-state item by rating themselves on the following 4-point scale: (a) Not at all, (b) Somewhat, (c) Moderately so, and (d) Very much so. Three important characteristics determined the test construction strategy for the development of the STAI A-state scale:

1. To maximize usefulness in psychological research, ease and brevity of administration were considered to be desirable qualities in a measure of state anxiety. A long involved scale would be unsuitable, for example, in studies of the effects of A-state on learning because taking the test might interfere with performance on the learning task. Furthermore, since rapid fluctuations in A-state may occur in a changing environment, a long test would be less sensitive to such variations.

2. A second characteristic that was sought in the development of the STAI A-state scale was high reliability. In evaluating reactions to various kinds of stress, the major interest is in differences in state anxiety that are obtained on two or more occasions of measurement. Because difference scores between any two occasions contain the error components of both the initial and final scores, the resulting difference

score will itself be low in reliability if these scores are only moderately reliable.

3. Only those items were retained for the final scale that showed higher means in a priori stressful situations than in nonstressful or nonthreatening situations. Thus, when the scale was given with instructions that required the person to report his present feelings ("Indicate how you feel *right now*"), each item was expected to reflect the subject's level of anxiety (A-state) at that particular moment in time.

The essential qualities evaluated by the STAI A-state scale involve feelings of tension, nervousness, worry, and apprehension. In developing the A-state scale, it was discovered empirically that such feelings were highly correlated with the absence of feelings of calmness, security, contentedness, and the like. Therefore, items such as "I feel calm" and "I feel content" were included to produce a balanced A-state scale; half the items pertain to the presence of feelings of apprehension, worry or tension, and the remaining items reflect the absence of such states. Thus, the STAI A-state scale defines a continuum of increasing levels of A-state intensity, with low scores indicating states of calmness and serenity, intermediate scores indicating moderate levels of tension and apprehensiveness, and high scores reflecting states of intense apprehension and fearfulness that approach panic. Sample items from the STAI A-state scale are as follows:

| | | | | |
|---|---|---|---|---|
| 1. I feel calm | 1 | 2 | 3 | 4 |
| 3. I am tense | 1 | 2 | 3 | 4 |
| 6. I feel upset | 1 | 2 | 3 | 4 |
| 12. I feel nervous | 1 | 2 | 3 | 4 |

When administered for research purposes, the STAI A-state scale should be given with instructions that focus on a particular time period. A person may be instructed to respond, for example, according to how he felt while performing on an experimental task that he has just completed. If the task is a long one, he may be instructed to respond according to how he felt early in the task, or while working on the final portion of the task. In clinical research, a patient may be asked to report the feelings he experiences in therapy interviews or how he felt while he visualized a specific stimulus situation in a behavior therapy session.

To measure changes in the intensity of transitory anxiety over time, the STAI A-state scale may be given on each occasion for which an A-state measure is needed. In research in which measurement of changes in A state during performance on an experimental task are desired, brief scales consisting of as few as four or five STAI A-state items provide valid measures (Spielberger, Anton, & Bedell, 1976; Spielberger, O'Neil, & Hansen, 1972). Multiple repeated measures of A state may be obtained either with the same or with different instructions as to the time period for which the subject's reports are desired. The subject may be asked to report how he feels immediately before he begins to work on an experimental task, and then, after he completes the task, he may be asked to indicate how he felt while he was working on it.

Correlations with other measures of A-state, such as the Zuckerman AACL (Today Form) provide evidence of the concurrent validity of the STAI A-state scale (Spielberger, Gorsuch, & Lushene, 1970). It also was demonstrated that scores on the STAI A-state scale increase in response to various kinds of stress and decrease as a result of relaxation training (Spielberger, Gorsuch, & Lushene, 1970). Additional evidence of the construct validity of the STAI A-state scale may be found in recent studies by Auerbach

(1971); Edwards (1969); B. Hall (1969); Hodges (1967); Hodges and Felling (1970); Lamb (1969); Lushene (1970); McAdoo (1969); O'Neil (1969); O'Neil, Spielberger, and Hansen (1969); Parrino (1969); Spielberger, O'Neil, and Hansen (1972); Spielberger, Auerbach, Wadsworth, Dunn, and Taulbee (1973); and D. A. Taylor, Wheeler, and Altman (1968).

Self-report measures such as the STAI may be criticized on many grounds. It may be argued, for example, that the items are ambiguous and mean different things to different people, or that people do not know themselves well enough to give truthful answers, or that many people are unwilling to admit negative things about themselves. Administration of the STAI A-state scale for clinical and research purposes has shown, however, that adolescents and adults with at least dull-normal intelligence are capable of describing how they feel at a particular moment in time. Most people are also willing to reveal how they feel during a therapy hour, or while performing on an experimental task, provided they are asked specific questions about their feelings, and the feelings were recently experienced. Of course, the clinician or experimenter who uses self-report scales to measure anxiety, or any other emotional state, must endeavor to motivate his patients or subjects to provide accurate information about themselves.

## 3  TRAIT–STATE ANXIETY THEORY

Research findings suggest that an adequate theory of anxiety must distinguish conceptually and operationally between anxiety as a transitory state and as a relatively stable personality trait. A comprehensive theory of anxiety must also differentiate between anxiety states, the stimulus conditions that evoke these states, and the defenses that serve to avoid or ameliorate them (Spielberger, 1966a; 1972a). In this section, state and trait anxiety will be defined, and a trait-state theory of anxiety will be proposed in which the relationship between these concepts is clarified. In setting forth this theory, we will attempt to describe some of the circumstances and conditions that appear to evoke different levels of A-state intensity in persons who are differentially disposed to experience A states.

### 3.1 The Concepts of State and Trait Anxiety

State anxiety (A state) may be conceptualized as a transitory emotional state or condition of the human organism that varies in intensity and fluctuates over time. A states are characterized by subjective, consciously perceived feelings of tension and apprehension, and activation of the autonomic nervous system. Level of A state is high in circumstances that are perceived by an individual to be threatening, irrespective of the objective danger; A-state intensity is relatively low in nonstressful situations, or in circumstances in which an existing danger is not perceived as threatening (Spielberger, 1976).

Trait anxiety (A trait) refers to relatively stable individual differences in anxiety proneness—that is, to differences in the disposition to perceive a wide range of stimulus situations as dangerous or threatening, and in the tendency to respond to such threats with A-state reactions. A trait may also be regarded as reflecting individual differences in the frequency and the intensity with which A states have been manifested in the past, and in the probability that such states will be experienced in the future. Persons who are high in A trait tend to perceive a larger number of situations as dangerous or threatening than do people who are low in A trait. They also respond to threatening situations with A-state elevations of greater intensity.

### 3.2 Anxiety and Stress

A major task for a trait-state theory of anxiety is to identify the characteristics of stressor stimuli that evoke differential levels of A state in persons who differ in A trait. Atkinson (1964) suggests that a "fear of failure" motive is reflected in measures of A trait, while I. G. Sarason (1960, 1972, 1975) notes the special significance for high A-trait individuals of factors in situations that arouse self-depreciating tendencies. On the basis of a review of the research findings obtained with various anxiety scales, I. G. Sarason (1960, pp. 401–402) concludes:

The bulk of the available findings suggest that high anxious Ss are affected more detrimentally by motivating conditions or failure reports than are Ss lower in the anxiety score distribution. . . . It is interesting to note that high anxious Ss have been found to be more self-deprecatory, more self-preoccupied and generally less content with themselves than Ss lower in the distribution of anxiety. . . . It may well be that highly motivating or ego-involving instructions serve the function of arousing these self-oriented tendencies.

In general, the experimental literature on anxiety is consistent with the hypothesis that situations that pose direct or implied threats to self-esteem produce differential levels of A state in persons who differ in A trait. Differences in the performance of high and low A-trait persons on learning tasks, for example, are most often found under conditions that involve failure experiences or "ego-involving" instructions (Spence, J. & Spence, 1966). Furthermore, circumstances that involve the risk of failure, such as academic achievement situations (Mandler & Sarason, 1952; Spielberger, 1962), or those in which an individual's personal adequacy is evaluated, e.g., taking an "intelligence test" or performing on a concept attainment task, appear to be especially threatening to persons with high A trait (Denny, 1966; Spielberger, 1966b; Spielberger & Smith, 1966).

Experimental investigations of anxiety phenomena have produced findings that are generally consistent with Atkinson's suggestion that fear of failure is a major characteristic of high A-trait people, and with Sarason's conclusion that ego-involving instructions are more detrimental to the performance of high A-trait subjects than low A-trait subjects. Apparently, failure or ego-involving instructions evoke higher levels of A-state intensity in high A-trait subjects than in low A-trait subjects. But whether a particular high A-trait person will show a corresponding elevation in A state will depend on the extent to which he perceives a specific situation as dangerous or threatening, and this will be greatly influenced by his past experience (Spielberger, 1976).

While the requirement to perform on different tasks may evoke high levels of A state in most people with high A trait, such tasks are not likely to be regarded as threatening by high A-trait persons who have the requisite skills and experience to do well on them. Conversely, a task or situation that most people would find nonthreatening might be regarded as extremely dangerous by a particular low A-trait individual for whom it had special traumatic significance. Thus, while measures of A trait provide useful information regarding the probability that high levels of A state will be aroused, the impact of any given situation on the intensity of A state can only be ascertained

by taking actual measurements of A state in that situation.

On the basis of intensive investigations of soldiers undergoing paratroop training, Basowitz, Persky, Korchin, and Grinker (1955) report that two different types of anxiety can be distinguished, which they called *shame anxiety* and *harm anxiety*. They based this distinction on the observation that higher levels of A state were evoked by the anticipation of failure than by fear of serious injury or death. Basowitz, Persky, Korchin, and Grinker (1955, p. 93) state:

Despite our prior conception that the primary source of anxiety would be related to the real or fantasied dangers of jumping, we found that feelings related to shame were often of greater importance. Trainees were often apprehensive not so much about the severe threat of bodily injury or death, but about the possibility of not measuring up to the task undertaken. This anxiety was expressed in a fear of failure; should one not "win his wings" he would be humbled before his peers and in the eyes of idealized older figures whom he was seeking to emulate.

Basowitz, and his co-workers theorized that "the distinction between the two different loci of anxieties is primarily a conceptual one. For the experiencer himself there may be only the unitary state of emotional distress" (pp. 272–73). The effects of psychological threats and physical danger on level of A state apparently depend on an individual's disposition to interpret these types of stressors as personally threatening. High A-trait individuals are sensitive to evaluation because they fear failure. Consequently, they manifest higher levels of A state than do low A-trait persons in situations that involve psychological threats to self-esteem.

There is evidence that persons with high A trait do *not* perceive physical dangers as any more threatening than low A-trait individuals. It has been observed, for example, that while threat of electric shock produces significant increases in self-report and physiological measures of A state (Hodges & Spielberger, 1966; Katkin, 1965), the magnitude of the increments in A-state intensity produced by shock threat is unrelated to level of A trait as measured by the J. A. Taylor (1953) Manifest Anxiety Scale (MAS).

### 3.3 A Trait-State Theory of Anxiety

The trait-state conception of anxiety presented in Fig. 1 assumes that the arousal of an anxiety state involves a process or sequence of temporally ordered events. This process may be initiated by an external stimulus that is appraised by an individual as dangerous, such as the imminent threat of injury or death faced by a soldier in combat; or the process may be cued off by situations that involve psychological stress, such as the threat to self-esteem that is encountered in performing on competitive tasks. Internal stimuli that cause a person to anticipate danger may also evoke higher levels of state anxiety. For example, a student who suddenly recalls that a test for which he has not prepared will be administered during the next class period is likely to experience an increase in level of A-state intensity. We have previously noted that situations or circumstances in which personal adequacy is evaluated are likely to be perceived as more threatening by high A-trait individuals than by persons who are low in A trait. However, the appraisal of a particular stimulus or situation as threatening may be influenced more by idiosyncratic skills and past experience than by either the objective danger that is inherent in the situation or the individual's level of A trait.

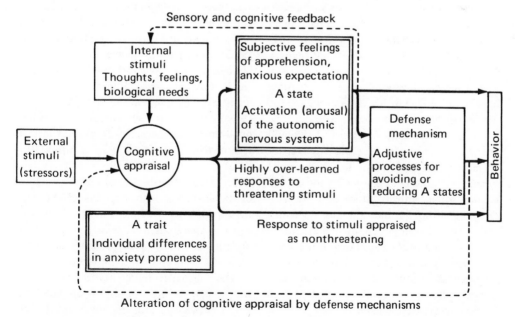

**FIG. 1** A trait-state conception of anxiety. From *Anxiety and Behavior,* edited by C. D. Spielberger, New York, Academic Press, 1966. Copyright by Academic Press. Reprinted by permission.

252 C. D. SPIELBERGER, R. E. LUSHENE, AND W. G. McADOO

Once a stimulus situation is appraised as threatening it is assumed that first, an A-state reaction will be evoked, and, second, the *intensity* of this reaction will be proportional to the amount of threat the situation poses for the individual. It is further assumed that the *duration* of the A-state reaction will depend on the persistence of the evoking stimuli and the person's previous experience in dealing with similar circumstances. Stressful situations that are encountered frequently may lead an individual to develop effective coping responses that quickly alleviate or minimize the danger and thereby immediately reduce level of A-state intensity. A person may also respond to threatening situations with defensive processes that serve to reduce the intensity of A-state reactions.

Through sensory and cognitive feedback mechanisms, high levels of A-state intensity are experienced as unpleasant and serve to initiate cognitive or motoric processes that have effectively reduced A states in the past. For example, an undergraduate subject in an experiment that involved the threat of electric shock initially appraised this experimental situation as dangerous and responded with a marked increase in heart rate. After briefly reflecting on his circumstances, the person reasoned that either he would not be shocked, or that if he was shocked it would not be very painful "because university officials would not permit this." Since the subject had no way of knowing if the experimenter would actually shock him, he used denial and intellectualization as defenses against the danger posed by the situation. Corresponding to his reappraisal of the situation, there was a decline in level of A-state intensity as measured by changes in heart rate and the subject's self-report of feelings of apprehension and tension.

It was noted previously that two important classes of stressor situations can be identified that appear to have different implications for the evocation of A state in persons who differ in A-Trait:

1. Individuals with high A trait appear to interpret circumstances in which their personal adequacy is evaluated as more threatening than do low A-trait people.

2. Situations that are characterized by physical danger are *not* interpreted as differentially threatening by high and low A-trait subjects.

Accordingly, differential elevations in A state would be expected for persons who differ in A trait under circumstances that are characterized by some threat to self-esteem, but not in situations that involve physical danger unless the individual's personal adequacy is also threatened.

With regard to the etiology of individual differences in A trait, it is assumed that residues of past experience dispose high A-trait persons to appraise situations that involve some form of personal evaluation as more threatening than do individuals who are low in A trait. We may speculate that biological and constitutional factors and childhood experiences influence the development of individual differences in A trait. Parent-child relationships centering around punishment are especially important in this regard. The fact that self-depreciating attitudes are aroused in high A-trait persons under circumstances characterized by failure or ego-involving instructions suggests that these people received excessive criticism and negative appraisals from their parents which undermined their self-confidence and adversely influenced their self-concept.

The schematic representation of a trait-state theory of anxiety that is presented in Fig. 1 provides a cross-sectional analysis of anxiety phenomena. Two different anxiety constructs, A state and A trait, are posited and distinguished from the stimulus conditions which evoke A-state reactions and the defenses that help individuals avoid or reduce A states. Figure 1 also provides a conceptual framework for classifying the major variables that should be considered in research on anxiety phenomena and suggests some of the possible interrelationships among them. In addition to the constructs of A state and A trait, the classes of variables that we believe to be most significant in anxiety research are the following:

1. The qualities of the external and internal stimuli that evoke anxiety states.

2. The cognitive processes that are involved in appraising various stimuli as threatening.

3. The defense mechanisms that are employed to avoid anxiety states, or to reduce the intensity of these states once they are experienced.

## 4  SUMMARY

In this chapter, we examined a number of theoretical, methodological, and terminological issues that arise in the investigation of anxiety as an emotional state. Several general approaches to the measurement of feelings and emotions were considered and a number of specific self-report procedures for measuring anxiety as an emotional state were described. Two distinct anxiety concepts, state anxiety (A state) and trait anxiety (A trait) were defined, and a trait-state theory of anxiety was outlined. The following general conclusions were reached:

1. The subjective quality of the feelings experienced in emotional states seems to be their most unique and distinctive feature. Emotional states also vary in intensity and fluctuate over time.

2. Anxiety may be viewed as an emotional state that consists of unpleasant, consciously perceived feelings of nervousness, tension, and apprehension, with associated activation or arousal of the autonomic nervous system. This conception of anxiety is comparable in many respects to the conception originally proposed by Freud.

3. Several different measures of state anxiety were discussed, and the development of the State-Trait Anxiety Inventory was described in some detail. The STAI is a new test that provides self-report measures of both state and trait anxiety.

4. A trait-state theory of anxiety was described in which the concepts of A state and A trait were defined and distinguished from the stimulus conditions that evoke A-state reactions and the defense mechanisms that help people avoid or reduce A states.

# 10

# Formulating the Situational Environment in Relation to States and Traits

**Gerald R. Patterson**[1]
*Oregon Research Institute, Eugene*

**Gordon G. Bechtel**
*University of Florida, Gainesville*

## 1 STATES, TRAITS, AND SITUATIONS

A complete understanding of personality would require detailed explanations of two different processes, namely, the process by which units of behavior are acquired, and the process through which these units come under the control of relevant social and nonsocial stimuli. Some perspectives would probably explore such additional content areas as the specification of the relations among these behavioral units, situations, feelings, and thoughts. However, whether one wishes to proceed at the level of the observable, or in terms of covert internal processes, it seems that a necessary first step involves an investigation of the effect of social and nonsocial stimuli upon ongoing social behaviors.

[1] Patterson also has a half-time position in the School of Education, University of Oregon. Computing assistance was obtained from Health Sciences Computing Facility, UCLA, sponsored by National Institutes of Health Grant FR-3. Both writers gratefully acknowledge the financial assistance provided by MH 12972, MH 10822, and MH 15985-01.

In observing the social behavior of deviant and normal children, it becomes apparent that the two groups do not differ so much in the kinds of response classes emitted. Rather they differ in the relative rates with which the presumed "deviant" behaviors occur; they also differ in the *stimuli* controlling these behaviors. By and large, a deviant response is one that occurs at too high a rate and in the wrong setting.

Most of the stimuli controlling behavior probably consist of the behavior of another person. Minor disruptions found in the give-and-take of everyday social interactions can have rather serious consequences. For example, if a complaint about the pain of an operation, which ordinarily produces a sympathetic response from the listener, produced instead a chuckle and a wry grin, we would say that the response was not matched to a socially "appropriate stimulus." A number of labels might be introduced to describe such behavior, but the consensus would be that if similar episodes occurred, this individual is not under ordinary stimulus control and, by implication, may be someone for society to be concerned about.

The purpose of the present chapter is to outline some procedures for investigating several dimensions of stimulus control. We use field data on social interaction as the basis for the analysis and a social-learning framework as a structure from which to generate hypotheses about the general process. Some attention is also given to the problem of defining *response units.*

The emphasis on social interaction in providing the basic units for constructing a theory of personality is, of course, not new. Contemporary workers in social psychology (Barker, 1963; Sherif, M., 1967) and psychiatry (Berne, 1961) have their historical counterparts among sociological theorists such as G. H. Meade (Strauss, 1964). In the present approach, actual observations were made of the moment-by-moment interchanges between people in a social setting such as the home or the classroom (Jones, R. R., Reid, & Patterson, 1975). Observations within these settings were replicated over a series of days to obtain stable estimates of interactional events. In these complex interactions each person served a dual role of "stimulus" for the behavior of the other person with whom he interacted *and* "responder" to the stimulation provided by the behavior of the other. In examining these interactions, there are several features of the data that immediately stand out. On the one hand, it seems clear that there are continuous moment-by-moment changes in the behaviors of a given person. However, when his behavior is sampled over extended periods, it is also apparent that there are repetitive patterns in his responses. We refer to the moment-by-moment changes in the rate of occurrence of these social behaviors as alterations in "state"; the summary term expressing the rate for a behavioral event as it is averaged *across* settings would represent a statement about "trait."

In a classroom setting, if the behavior of a person is sampled repeatedly over time, a plot of these events usually displays one overwhelming characteristic. There are enormous moment-by-moment fluctuations in the rate of occurrence of most social behaviors. As illustrated in Fig. 1 and in the careful observational studies of Ebner (1967) and D. Anderson (1964), these fluctuations in rate occur even if the time interval is as large as a day or a week. We hypothesized that these variations are not random occurrences, but rather are produced by the presence or absence of the relevant discriminative stimuli that control these behaviors (Patterson, 1974; Patterson & Cobb, 1973). The presence of a substitute teacher would be a case in point; the social stimuli emanating from the behavior of the peer group during the days immediately preceding the Christmas holidays would be another. As these and other less dramatic stimuli are presented to the child, they produce responses that have been conditioned to these stimuli. If the behaviors being investigated are conditioned to one of these discriminative stimuli, then the observation data will display a perceptible increase in rate. By the same token, if the behavior was not previously conditioned to any of the social and nonsocial stimuli presented, then the behavior will not occur.

We hypothesized that short term variations in rate, as they occur in the social environment, are usually produced by alterations in the discriminative stimuli and, to a lesser degree, by changes in the reinforcement schedules contingent on these behaviors. Explorations of these parameters as they relate to fluctuations in the rate of responding would constitute a contribution to our understanding of "state" variables. The present report outlines some procedures for carrying out such

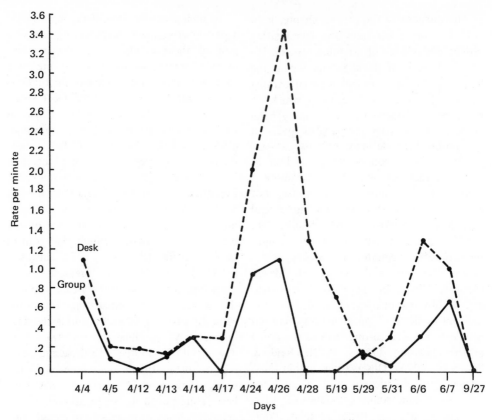

**FIG. 1**  Rate of movement about room (Mo) during "work at desk" and "work in group."

investigations. Data are presented which underline the impact of subtle changes in setting variables on the rate of responding. A new statistical model is presented that provides for tests of differences among members of a system in their mutual capacities as "discriminative stimuli" and as "responders." Some preliminary attention is also given to the problem of response units.

## 2  RECENT PROGRESS IN FORMULATING SITUATIONAL-STATE CHANGES

### 2.1  Taxonomic Considerations

Although in exploring the problem of stimulus control it would be convenient to have a taxonomy of situations, and though many writers wish for such a system (Sells, 1963), it is also true that there are a variety of ways of dimensionalizing the social matrix. At a theoretical level, Cattell's scheme to represent the meaning of each situation by a vector of behavior indexes (chapter 7, this *Handbook*) could lead to a systematic taxonomy of situations as soon as a sufficient number of specification equations are accumulated. His proposal for a specific branch of psychology, to be called "econetics," relates such values to physical and social measures of the situation per se (including psychophysics). Meanwhile, though other workers have not so comprehensively handled the environmental terms, discussion in this area is beginning to stimulate research, e.g., that of Dielman and Krug (chapter 5).

At this juncture each investigator will have to arbitrarily select what he hopes will be relevant stimuli and empirically establish what behaviors, if any, are controlled by their presentation. He must also determine empirically the "validity" of his selection. Certainly, the pioneering efforts of Roger Barker and the Kansas group have made great strides in carefully observing, at a gross level, the effects settings have on the social behaviors of children and adults (Barker, 1963; Barker & Wright, 1955). In Barker, et al. (1962) one finds what amounts to one of the first catalogues of social settings. It contains a list of social settings, such as "the schoolyard" and "the drugstore," together with observation data on the amount of time spent by adults and children in these settings. This study is an impressive empirical beginning in the analysis of the impact of settings (stimuli) on social behavior. Recently, other investigators have begun to sample specific features of other kinds of social settings (Gewirtz & Gewirtz, 1967; see also Rheingold, 1960). A comprehensive theory of the effect of situations on social behaviors will of necessity await the completion of more studies of this type.

## 2.2 Settings Analyses

Although the social-learning paradigm does not preclude the use of an across-subjects design, many current studies make use of single-subject analysis, akin to the $P$ technique. Such a technique lends itself particularly well to the investigation of the effect of settings upon behavior. For example, the data in Fig. 1 describe the day-by-day variations in the rate of occur-

rence for "hyperactivity" in the classroom.[2] The data were collected in a classroom setting for a "hyperactive" 7-year-old boy and consisted of the rate at which the child left his desk and moved about the room (Patterson, Jones, Whittier, & Wright, 1965). The occurrence of these responses was recorded at 15-sec. intervals. Each observation session lasted from 20 to 40 min. The observer also gave a brief description of each change in the classroom setting that occurred during an observation session. These descriptions suggested that within the gross classroom setting two subsettings reoccurred with sufficient frequency to provide a basis for analyzing their impact on the response events. These two settings were working alone at desk" and "working as a member of a group."

It is undoubtedly true that most classes of social behaviors are under the control of many different sets of discriminative stimuli. To determine which stimuli are relevant in controlling a response such as "movement around the room" (Mo), one could begin by examining the rate of occurrence for this behavior in each of the two settings, "working at desk" and "working as member of a group." If the

---

[2] The term *hyperactivity* was first brought into prominence in the writings of Strauss and Lehtinen (1947). Empirical investigations have shown that parents' descriptions provided, among other things, a common factor (Dreger & Dreger, 1962) that was appropriately labelled *Hyperactivity*. Factor analysis of observations of child behaviors plus parent report data also produced a similar Hyperactivity factor in a study of deviant children (Patterson, 1964).

The data from observation studies showed that the child labelled as hyperactive was not *qualitatively* different from other, nonhyperactive children; rather, he seemed to be engaged in turning out a few classes of "normal" responses at extraordinarily high rates (Ebner, 1967).

analysis demonstrated differential rates for these two setting units, then it would be possible to search for even more subtle classes of social stimuli within these settings which contribute to these differential rates. Presumably such a progression would produce increasing evidence of stimulus control.

In Fig. 1 only data from those days in which both settings occurred were used in the analysis. The graph illustrates the differential effect of the two settings on the rate of occurrence of Mo. Over the 15 days of observation, the Mo rates for the hyperactive child were consistently higher during those intervals when he worked alone at his desk. During the "desk" period his mean rate was .89 responses per minute, while during the "group" period it was .34; the difference between these means was significant beyond the .01 level (two-tailed test). However, it is also of interest to note the enormous variations in rate from one day to the next within either of these settings. Although the "group" and "desk" setting variables account for some variation, it is clear that other stimuli also have an important effect on these short-term fluctuations.

Patterson (1974) developed procedures for identifying the more molecular social stimuli within settings that control behavior. It assumes that these intraindividual covariations in rate of response are, in turn, a function of concomitant variations in the discriminative stimuli that control both of them. It is entirely possible that both responses are initiated by the same stimuli. Investigations currently underway will put this hypothesis to the test.

At the molar level, it would seem that many settings are more or less preprogramed for certain kinds of interaction processes, for example, cocktail parties, committee meetings, or a ride on the city bus. But to make predictions within settings and over time requires a more molecular analysis of the social stimuli to be found within settings. Here each person is both a responder and a discriminative stimulus in any transaction. That is, some of the changes in his responding arise from the particular reactions by the other person to his immediately prior social behavior. This reaction sets the occasion for the next response, which again may produce a consequence, which produces still further alterations in the ongoing behavior. It seems that at one level we must develop modes that describe these sequential chains. One such attempt is exemplified by the Markovian analysis of Rausch (1965). It is likely that further explorations will provide the basis for constructing the personality theories of the future. Such theories would be based on an analysis of observations made during interpersonal transactions. The sequential analysis of these chains of behavior would represent a fine-grained study of the effect of social stimuli on social behaviors. Preliminary studies suggest that such data can be used to make powerful predictions for single individuals within a setting (Patterson, 1974).

## 2.3 Status Analysis

At a less molecular level it is also possible to conceptualize the person as having some general status within his group as a "stimulus dispenser for others" and as a "responder to stimuli dispensed by others." Different persons become stimuli that repeatedly set the occasion for differential reinforcement of broad classes of social behaviors. In situation after situation, the mother may become a discriminative stimulus for the whining dependent behaviors of the young child, while the father either ignores or punishes these behaviors. The presence or absence of either one of these persons would produce fluctuations in the rate of occurrence of dependent responses. Thus the person serves a dual function, as a discriminative stimulus producing certain behaviors, and as a dispenser who provides reinforcing contingencies that maintain their occurrence. Presumably, the reinforcing contingencies maintain the person's status as a discriminative stimulus. If, for example, the mother seldom, or never, reinforced dependent behavior, then these behaviors would tend not to occur in her presence.

An effective method for estimating the stimulus status of people is provided by using observation data as a basis for sociometric analysis of small groups. By making repeated observations on the same dyad, we can collect data that reveal the discriminative stimulus value of every member for every other group member. In adapting this pairwise transactional approach to our present purposes, we shall conceptualize an individual as a "miniature situation" containing stimulus and reinforcement value for another person. For example, in studying individual $j$ we observe certain behavior rates which $k$ manifests in the presence of $j$, *and* we observe $j$'s behavior in the presence of $k$. Moreover, if we record $j$'s transactions with every other member of the group as well, we will be able to demonstrate "situational" differences affecting $j$'s emission rate for this response class. Each person constitutes a different set of discriminative stimuli for $j$'s behaviors.

In the next section we present an experimental design and illustrative analysis for these pairwise transactions within small groups. One component of our model reflects the differential status that the $n$ group members have as *discriminative*

*stimuli*, and another component of the model reflects the general level at which each group member emits certain social behaviors. The latter component provides an individual-difference scale of the $n$ group members for the *trait* tapped by these behaviors. Finally, the following analysis contains dyadic representations of each *pair* of group members. This makes it possible to test the fit of the stimulus and trait parameters, as well as to assess pairwise imbalance in these social transactions.

## 3  A SMALL GROUP ANALYSIS OF TRAIT SCORES

### 3.1  Experimental Design

Table 1 illustrates the $6 \times 6$ layout of pairwise observations for a family of six persons. The mother and her children were observed in the home over a period of 10 hours using a coding procedure described in detail by Patterson, Ray, Shaw, and Cobb (1969). The data summarize the frequency with which each person in the family displayed any one of a class of aversive behaviors toward each of the other members of the family. The behaviors in this

TABLE 1  Frequency of aversive reactions within the Ro family

| Givers | Receivers | | | | | |
|--------|-----|-----|-----|-----|-----|-----|
|        | Mo  | L   | E   | W   | Ch  | J   |
| Mo     |     | 28  | 5   | 12  | 17  | 10  |
| L      | 17  |     | 7   | 4   | 10  | 6   |
| E      | 4   | 5   |     | 9   | 2   | 6   |
| W      | 16  | 9   | 21  |     | 3   | 3   |
| Ch     | 10  | 6   | 6   | 3   |     | 1   |
| J      | 17  | 10  | 2   | 3   | 4   |     |

*Note.* Codes are described in detail by Patterson, Ray, Shaw, & Cobb (1969).

particular response class were: humiliate, ignore, threaten, noncomply, and physically punish.

In Table 1 a typical numerical entry $s_{jk}$ is the state score exhibited by individual $j$ in the presence of $k$; for example, the deviant child (W) dispensed 16 aversive consequences to the mother. The experimentally independent observation $s_{kj}$ is $k$'s state score in miniature situation $j$; for example, mother dispensed 12 of these behaviors to W.

The $j$th row in this design contains the observations $s_{j1}, s_{j2}, \ldots, s_{jn}$, which are the state scores observed for individual $j$ in the presence of the $n-1$ other group members. The differences in individual $j$'s score over these $n-1$ miniature situations (or individuals) are similar to the differences among settings reported for the hyperactive student described earlier. However, the hyperactive behaviors in Fig. 1 were plotted over classroom situations occurring *sequentially* in time, whereas the state scores in row $j$ of Table 1 were observed over a class of situations that are not time bound. For example, the state score $s_{jk}$ represents a frequency count over the *scattered* time periods during which $j$ interacts in miniature situation $k$.

### 3.2  Linear Model

Our parameterization of state score $s_{jk}$ is given by

$$s_{jk} = \alpha_j + \theta_k + \gamma_{jk} + e_{jk}, \qquad (1)$$

where  $\alpha_j = j$'s trait value, and $\Sigma_j \, \alpha_j = 0$,
   $\theta_k = k$'s  discriminative  stimulus value,
   $\gamma_{jk} = \gamma_{kj}$ = interaction between $j$ and $k$, and $\Sigma_{k \neq j} \, \gamma_{jk} = 0$ for $j = 1, \ldots, n$, and

$e_{jk}$ = random error, which is normally distributed with zero mean and variance $\sigma^2$.

Since $s_{jk}$ is an additive function in attributes $\alpha$ and $\theta$, Equation 1 provides a dual representation of the $n$ group members. The row parameters scale the individuals on trait $\alpha$, whereas the column parameters scale them on a complementary stimulus dimension $\theta$. For example, if $s_{jk}$ is the rate of $j$'s negativism toward $k$, then $\alpha_j$ represents $j$'s disposition to *exhibit* this state, and $\theta_k$ represents $k$'s discriminative stimulus value for eliciting aversive responses. The disposition $\alpha$ of Equation 1 captures the trait (or elevation) property of a profile of state measures, since the main effect $\alpha_j$ takes a fixed value within row $j$ of Table 1. Fluctuations in this profile are attributed to the varying values taken by stimulus attribute $\theta$, interaction $\gamma$, and random error $e$ in the $j$th row.

In Equation 1 the parameters $\gamma_{jk}$ reflect the departure of the pairwise layout from additivity in the main effects $\alpha$ and $\theta$. Conversely, if all the $\gamma_{jk} = 0$, then these main effects completely account for the nonrandom (or errorless) portion of the observations $s_{jk}$.

The final term in Equation 1 is $e_{jk}$, which is a random component (or error) contributing to the observed state score $s_{jk}$. Our assumption is that these errors are independently and normally distributed with zero mean and common variance $\sigma^2$. If the assumption of independence is violated, the significance tests deriving from Equation 1 will be inexact. However, the estimates of the parameters in this equation (see Tables 2 and 3) remain valid in the presence of correlations among the errors.

We complete our presentation of Equation 1 with a definition of imbalance for each pair $\{j,k\}$ of group members. In the

**TABLE 2** Estimates of the model parameters for the Ro family

| Family members | Mo | L | E | W | Ch | J | $\hat{\alpha}_j$ |
|---|---|---|---|---|---|---|---|
| Mo | | 5.55 | −8.08 | − .58 | 1.55 | 1.55 | 7.00 |
| L | | | −2.33 | −3.83 | .30 | .30 | .92 |
| E | | | | 9.05 | .68 | .68 | −3.54 |
| W | | $\hat{\gamma}_{jk}$ | | | −2.33 | −2.33 | 1.46 |
| Ch | | | | | | − .20 | −3.75 |
| J | | | | | | | −2.08 |
| $\hat{\theta}_j$ | 14.20 | 11.78 | 7.49 | 6.49 | 6.45 | 4.78 | |

*Note.* Codes are described in detail by Patterson, Ray, Shaw, & Cobb (1969).

**TABLE 3** Estimates of the dyadic imbalance parameters for the Ro family

| Family members | Mo | L | E | W | Ch | J |
|---|---|---|---|---|---|---|
| Mo | | 3.66 | 3.83 | −2.17 | 3.00 | − .34 |
| L | | | .17 | −5.83 | − .66 | −4.00 |
| E | | | | −6.00 | − .83 | −4.17 |
| W | | $\hat{\beta}_{jk}$ | | | 5.17 | 1.83 |
| Ch | | | | | | −3.34 |
| J | | | | | | |

*Note.* Codes are described in detail by Patterson, Ray, Shaw, & Cobb (1969).

layout of Table 1, this imbalance is manifested by a disparity between the transposed state scores $s_{jk}$ and $s_{kj}$, for example, when $j$ displays more negativism toward $k$ than $k$ returns to $j$. Therefore, dyadic imbalance $\beta_{jk}$ may be defined as the following parametric function, which is the difference between the expected (E) (or true) transposed scores:

$$\beta_{jk} = -\beta_{kj} = E(s_{jk}) - E(s_{kj})$$
$$= (\alpha_j + \theta_k + \gamma_{jk}) - (\alpha_k + \theta_j + \gamma_{kj})$$
$$= (\alpha_j + \theta_k) - (\alpha_k + \theta_j)$$
$$= (\alpha_j - \theta_j) - (\alpha_k - \theta_k)$$
$$= (\alpha_j - \alpha_k) - (\theta_j - \theta_k). \qquad (2)$$

Since $\gamma_{jk} = \gamma_{kj}$, the interaction terms are removed from this expression for $\beta_{jk}$, which is thus a parametric function in the corresponding row and column effects.

### 3.3 Estimates of the Model Parameters

The formula for the least squares estimate of $\beta_{jk}$ is given by Bechtel (1968), who also presents the formulas for estimating $\alpha_j$, $\theta_k$, and $\gamma_{jk}$ from the observations $s_{jk}$. These formulas provide the estimates given in Tables 2 and 3 for our family of six, whose pairwise negativism scores appear in Table 1. Table 2 includes the six negativism-trait (or $\alpha$) values and the six discriminative-stimulus (or $\theta$) values for the family members, along with the $\binom{6}{2} = 15$ interaction (or $\gamma$) estimates for the 15 pairs of members. Table 3 presents the 15 estimates $\hat{\beta}_{jk}$, which reflect the dyadic imbalances for this particular family.

### 3.4 Significance Tests of Hypotheses on the Model

Tables 2 and 3 include the dual scaling of our group members on the $\alpha$ and $\beta$ continua, as well as a dual scaling of the *pairs* of members on the $\gamma$ and $\beta$ continua. Although in many applications these measurements will be the primary goal of the analysis, we may supplement our measurement procedures with significance tests of hypotheses about the parameters estimated in Tables 2 and 3. The first hypothesis of interest is that the true pairwise layout (underlying Table 1) is symmetric. Since group symmetry means that $E(s_{jk}) = E(s_{kj})$ for all pairs $(j,k)$ of individuals, this hypothesis may be written as

$$H_\beta: \text{ all } \beta_{jk} = 0. \tag{3}$$

For Equation 1 this hypothesis is equivalent to

$$H_{\alpha,\theta}: \alpha_j = \theta_j + c \quad (j = 1, \ldots, n), \tag{4}$$

which is the hypothesis that the spacing among the $\alpha$ scale values is identical to that among the $\theta$ scale values. Hence, by means of Equation 1 it is possible to estimate the imbalance for each pair $(j,k)$ of individuals (see Table 3), and to test the overall hypothesis that the $n$-member group is symmetric (or balanced). Moreover, this hypothesis of group symmetry is the hypothesis that the individual-difference scales, $\alpha$ and $\theta$, are identical, except perhaps for a constant displacement. The acceptance of this hypothesis would indicate that none of the estimates $\hat{\beta}_{jk}$, such as those in Table 3, depart significantly from zero.

The "standard" hypotheses of Equation 1, which are similar to those of the two-way analysis of variance, are given by

$$H_\alpha: \alpha_1 = \alpha_2 = \ldots = \alpha_n,$$

$$H_\theta: \theta_1 = \theta_2 = \ldots = \theta_n, \quad \text{and} \tag{5}$$

$$H_\gamma: \text{ all } \gamma_{jk} = 0.$$

$H_\alpha$ is the hypothesis of the equality of the row effects, and $H_\theta$ asserts that there are no differences among the column effects. Final-

ly, the hypothesis $H_\gamma$ asserts that the true layout (underlying the observed values in Table 1) is additive or scalable in these row and column effects, i.e., that

$$E(s_{jk}) = \alpha_j + \theta_k \text{ for all } (j,k).$$

If all $\gamma_{jk} = 0$, then, except for random error, any state score may be represented as the sum of the $\alpha$ and $\theta$ values of the two transacting individuals. A group with an additive pairwise structure has, of course, a simpler parametric representation than one for which interaction effects are present.

The analysis of variance for Equation 1 is presented in detail by Bechtel (1971), who gives the $F$ tests of the four hypotheses for the equation. We use these formulas next in illustrating this variance analysis for the negativism data in Table 1.

Table 4 summarizes the results of the variance analysis for the four hypotheses, each of which is tested against the error term in the final line of the table. The first two tests evaluate the significance of the differences among persons upon the $\alpha$ and $\theta$ scales. The test associated with the $\alpha$ scale is a test of significance for the mean level, or trait, corresponding to these aversive behaviors. The test for the $\theta$ effect assesses the significance of the differences among family

**TABLE 4** Analysis of giving and receiving, interaction, and system symmetry for the Ro family

| Variable | df | SS | MS | F |
|---|---|---|---|---|
| Trait values ($\alpha$) | 5 | 397.8 | 79.6 | 5.41* |
| Stimulus values ($\theta$) | 5 | 318.4 | 63.7 | 4.33* |
| Interaction ($\gamma$) | 9 | 430.1 | 47.8 | 3.25* |
| Asymmetry ($\beta$) | 5 | 93.8 | 18.8 | 1.28 |
| Error ($e$) | 10 | 147.2 | 14.7 | |

*Note.* Ro is described in detail by Patterson, Ray, Shaw, & Cobb (1969).
*$p < .05$.

members with regard to their status as discriminative stimuli eliciting these aversive behaviors from others. The result of the interaction test indicates whether or not the estimated scale values in Table 2 fit the state scores in Table 1, that is, whether the estimated interaction effects in Table 2 depart significantly from zero. The final test evaluates the significance of the deviations from symmetry or balance for the total system. If all of the dyads in the Ro family (see Patterson, Ray et al., 1969) were equitable in their giving and receiving of aversive behaviors, then the data would indicate the acceptance of this hypothesis. However, if certain dyads $(j,k)$ display significant differences between $s_{jk}$ and $s_{kj}$, then the system itself would be characterized as nonreciprocal.

The first $F$ value ($\alpha$) indicates that the members of the family differed significantly in their dispositions to dispense aversive consequences for the behavior of other members. The mother and W dispensed these behaviors at the highest frequencies, which are revealed by the $\alpha$ scale values in Table 2. The second $F$ value ($\theta$) shows that there were also significant differences among family members in their status as discriminative stimuli for "pulling" these behaviors from other members. The presence of the mother seemed to set the occasion for the occurrence (and presumably for the reinforcement) of these behaviors. The older sister (L) also had high stimulus status, which suggests that these responses might be adult-oriented modes of controlling child behavior. Again, this situation is reflected in the $\theta$ scale values in Table 2.

The third $F$ value in Table 4 indicates that the scores describing the transactional data indicate a significant departure from additivity. The remaining $F$ value indicates that the family system is symmetric in the sense that the family members tended to

receive deviant behaviors at rates commensurate with the tendencies to dispense them. The person who gave the highest frequency of negative behaviors to other family members also received the most; conversely, family members who gave little, received little.

Perhaps we have belabored the obvious by illustrating in such detail the procedures for testing assumptions about the impact of stimuli on behavior. While the notion of stimulus control is both obvious and fundamental, it is sad that it has been so little explored within the framework of social interaction.[3] However, as important as such considerations may be, a parallel problem must also be considered before it will be possible to construct useful theories of social interaction. This problem is the specification of the units of behavior which are under stimulus control. Some preliminary aspects of the problem, which involve the definition of state scores such as those just analyzed, are considered in the next section.

## 4 UNITS OF BEHAVIOR FOR DEFINING STATE SCORES

At present, there is neither a theory of response structure nor even a readily agreed on means of defining classes of responses. It seems obvious that *any* classification scheme represents an arbitrary chunking of the stream of behavior. Indeed, there are a great variety of response classes that could be derived from even relatively simple chunks of behavior. For example, the rat presses the bar, which in turn activates the counter; the

---

[3] It is true, of course, that the extensive studies on "perception of others" represents an exploration of the individual's *perception* of social stimuli. However, the person's reports about, or descriptions of, social stimuli do not necessarily provide information relevant to the control these stimuli actually have on behavior.

behavior is recorded as "one unit." However, a closer examination of the actual behavior suggests that such a unit is not only a gross summary term but is entirely arbitrary. Actually, the rat attended to the bar, approached it several times, sniffed it, raised up, turned away, and then returned to press the bar with both forepaws. From this chain, or flow, of responses one could derive many classes, any one of which could be observed and counted.

## 4.1  Response Similarity

One means of deriving units of behavior is on the basis of similarity in the topography of responses. Thus some arbitrary decisions about the essential feature of the response topography would lead to the categorization "lever press," whether the response was effected with one forepaw or two, or produced by agile movements of the derrière.

Another variation in this approach is based upon similarity in response ranks when making cross-subject comparisons. For example, if persons who have high rates of $X$ also have high rates of $Y$, then $X$ and $Y$ are said to be members of the same response class. Much of the work on taxonomies of pathological behaviors is of this kind. The procedures used to derive the across-subjects correlations actually range from subjective estimates, as reflected in the a priori procedures in the American Psychiatric Association classification system, to more empirical approaches using factor analysis.[4] The mean-

ing (or validity) of such classes of responses derived by either approach must be established by additional studies that demonstrate, for example, the relevance of class membership to the presence or absence of antecedent "causes" or to treatment outcomes. At present, such validation studies are not encouraging and suggest that the current procedures for across-subjects chunking of large units of behavior may either be too gross for most purposes or irrelevant to the questions clinicians ask of them.

## 4.2  Response Function

A more dynamic approach outlined by Ferster (1964) and Kanfer (1965) represents an alternative (and equally arbitrary) means of deriving response units. This functional approach will probably generate "smaller" units of behavior, since class membership is defined on the basis of one or more restrictive requirements. Responses are said to belong to the same class or unit if they are under the control of the same discriminative stimuli. Under certain circumstances we might add the further requirement that the behaviors be under the control of the same reinforcing contingencies as well.

Such an approach has an immediate appeal in terms of several practical clinical considerations. Membership in a class perforce means that the behaviors are likely to occur in similar settings or in similar social interactions. Since these behaviors are under the same stimulus control, this could mean

---

[4] It is of some interest to note that the taxonomies now in use for classifying units of deviant behavior are actually mixed models that combine some features of both response topography and functional approaches. For example, toxic psychosis is specified partly on the basis of the antecedent process and partially on response topography. In addition, some clinical behaviors such as aggression are classified partially on

response topography and partially in terms of antecedent stimuli (the intent of the aggressor to injure) and partially on the basis of the victim's reaction. In the latter instance, if the victim laughed, the coder might class the response as "play" or "accident," rather than "aggression." However, in such systems the functional relations are not spelled out systematically for each class.

greater precision for intervention procedures. For example, a reduction in the frequency with which some discriminative stimuli are presented could reduce the rate of not just one, but several deviant behaviors. Altering the reinforcing contingencies for one member of the class might generalize to produce lower rates for other class members. Thus the definition of the class would at the same time provide the outlines of an intervention program. What is being proposed here is that a functional approach to the problem of response units will provide classes of behavior that relate to a variety of social and clinical phenomena. The material that follows outlines some procedures for empirically deriving such classes.

The data, which were collected in the classroom setting for the "hyperactive" 7-year-old boy described earlier, consisted not only of the response "moving about the room" (Mo), but also the following responses: "making noise" (Au); "wiggling feet, body, arms while seated in chair" (Ch); "hitting, pinching, threatening" (Ag); "not attending" (Na); and "talking to neighbor" (Tn). The occurrence of these responses was recorded at 15-sec intervals, and each observation session lasted from 20 to 40 min. The data were collected in 17 sessions over a 3-month period. Table 5 contains the rank order correlations (over occasions) among these responses.

The correlations suggest that Au (making noise), Ag (hitting, pinching, pushing), and Tn (talking to neighbor) covary "naturally." Since only Ag correlates significantly with Mo, this latter response is excluded from our behavior unit. On the days the person displayed high rates of Au, he also tended to display high rates of Ag and Tn. This covariation would suggest that in some gross sense these behaviors were under the same stimulus control, for example, that some

**TABLE 5** Summary of intrasubject correlations for six responses

| Response[a] | Au | Tn | Ag | Mo | Ch | Na |
|---|---|---|---|---|---|---|
| Au | | .48** | .46** | −.01 | .11 | .31 |
| Tn | | | .42 | .38 | .25 | .34 |
| Ag | | | | .43* | .17 | .12 |
| Mo | | | | | .24 | .12 |
| Ch | | | | | | −.18 |
| Na | | | | | | |

[a]Au = making noise; Tn = talking to neighbor; Ag = hitting, pinching, threatening; Mo = movement around room; Ch = wiggling feet, body, and arms while seated in chair; and Na = not attending.
*$p < .05$.
**$p < .01$.

discriminative stimuli occurring on these days tended to pull high rates for all three behaviors, but not for Mo. The cluster analysis identifies a subset of behaviors to be studied but does not, of course, identify the specific discriminative stimuli producing the behaviors Au, Tn, and Ag. That is, the correlational analysis represents only a first step, which tells us where to look, whereas the next step, the identification of the specific classes of discriminative stimuli controlling the behavior, requires another set of data.

The data were not originally collected with this second question in mind; therefore, no provision was made for intensive sampling of all the possible discriminative stimuli present on the various occasions. However, during the ad hoc analysis, the very gross settings "work at desk" and "work in group" had shown differential effects for the variable Mo. If the present analysis is correct, then comparable differences will *not* be obtained for rates of the behaviors in the cluster (Au, Tn, Ag). The data in Fig. 2 summarize the effect of the changes in stimulus conditions on this response class for the hyperactive child.

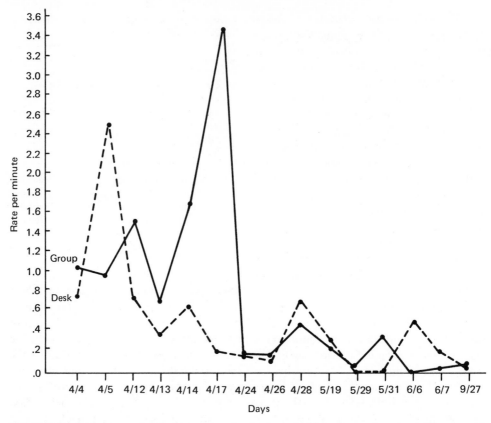

**FIG. 2** Rate of the composite (making noise, Au; hitting, pinching, threatening, Ag; talking to neighbor, Tn) during "work at desk" and "work in group."

Again, there were enormous variations in rate from one day to the next. While the "group" and "desk" stimulus variables account for some of this variation, it is clear that other setting variables also have an important effect on these short term fluctuations. However, here the effect of stimulus setting was the *reverse* of that displayed earlier in Fig. 1 for Mo. That is, for the composite class (Au, Ag, Tn) group work is associated with the higher rates of activity. At a crude level, then, we might say that the setting "group work" is a more effective discriminative stimulus for the composite class (Au, Ag, Tn), while the setting desk work is a more effective discriminative stimulus for the response Mo. Thus the outcome of the intrasubject correlational analysis is supported by the results of our primitive attempts to search for relevant discriminative stimuli.

While the graph indicates that the *composite* data do indeed support the prediction, this should also hold for each individual variable. The data in Table 6 summarize the median rates of occurrence of these variables in both of the stimulus settings. With one exception, the data support the hypothesis. While Mo displays a median decrease in rate when the child is in the "group work" setting, the variables Au and Tn show increases in rate of occurrence.

This analysis suggests that the setting variable had a different effect on the composite (Au, Tn, Ag) than upon the response Mo; that is, these two behavior units were under different stimulus control.

Additional support for the meaningfulness of the response class (Au, Tn, Ag) as distinct from Mo, is provided by the differential effect of manipulation on these two behavior units. The hyperactive child, whose behavior provided the data already described, underwent a set of classroom intervention procedures designed to alter his output of "hyperactivity." The details of this 1-day marathon intervention were reported by Patterson, Shaw, and Ebner (1969). These procedures produced better than 70% reduction in the rate of the deviant classroom behaviors that were used to define "hyperactivity" operationally, and the results persisted for at least a 6-month follow-up period. Previous research with the procedure had shown that different categories of responses were differentially affected by the intervention (Ebner, 1967). For example, in one study the category Mo was unaffected by the procedure (Patterson, Jones, Whittier, & Wright, 1965). In the present context, it was predicted that the composite class (Au, Tn, Ag) would display a "reaction" to the classroom intervention

TABLE 7   The effect of intervention on response categories

| Response | Baseline | Intervention |
|---|---|---|
| Auditory (Au) | .17 | .03 |
| Aggression (Ag) | .10 | .00 |
| Talking to neighbor (Tn) | .40 | .08 |
| Movement about room (Mo) | .29 | .28 |

program which would be both homogeneous within class and also different from that displayed by the category Mo. Specifically, it was predicted that there would be a reduction in the rate of occurrence for (Au, Tn, Ag) but not for Mo.

As a test of this hypothesis, the mean rates for all the behaviors were calculated, both for the baseline period and for conditioning. The data are summarized in Table 7. Again, the data show that class membership implies homogeneous reactions. All three members of the composite class display marked decreases in rate of responding following the intervention period. This result is in contrast to the rates for Mo which remain essentially unaltered in the presence of manipulation.

Generalization of intervention effects occurs in members of a response class, as was shown by Patterson (1974). In the latter the members of the response class were identified by a functional analysis of controlling stimuli rather than the correlational procedure. These findings lead to the hypothesis that significant $P$ correlation would identify responses that share a common set of controlling stimuli.

TABLE 6   The effect of change in setting on behavior rates

|  | Median rate per minute | |
|---|---|---|
| Response | Individual activity | Group activity |
| Intrasubject class responses |  |  |
| Au (noisy) | .11 | .17 |
| Ag (aggression) | .06 | .00 |
| Tn (talk to neighbor) | .05 | .15 |
| Nonclass response |  |  |
| Mo (move about room) | .35 | .25 |

## 5   SUMMARY

It was hypothesized that relevant discriminative stimuli are the primary determinants of short term changes in the rates of occurrence of social behaviors. Within this context, the analysis of social behavior and the antecedent stimuli that control its occurrence constitute an investigation of fluctuating states. The term *trait* is then defined as the average, across situations, of the rate for a given class of social behaviors.

Two different analyses were made to illustrate the application of a social-learning paradigm to field data. The purpose of these analyses was to functionally relate behavior to the stimulus setting. In the first analysis the rate of occurrence for one set of responses occurring in the classroom was shown to vary as a function of the classroom situation. In the second analysis a linear model was used with members of a disturbed family to test for differences in their rates of giving and receiving negative consequences. This latter analysis provides an estimate of the discriminative stimulus value of each member for receiving these behaviors, along with an estimate of each person's disposition, or trait, for dispensing them. Moreover, the model may be used to test for symmetry in giving and receiving for the entire family.

A brief discussion was also presented outlining some of the problems associated with specifying the units of behavior controlled by social stimuli. It was suggested that a functional analytic approach to the problem might provide a more efficient means of delineating classes of responses. In such an approach all elements of a given response class must be under the control of the same discriminative stimuli and the same reinforcers. Some data recorded in a classroom setting were analyzed to illustrate this method of "chunking" behavior.

# 11

# Typological Theory and Research

**Charles R. Bolz**
*University of Texas at Austin*

## 1 INTRODUCTION

This chapter concerns itself with the often-ignored and undeveloped theoretical issues of type and cluster analysis. Important questions have gone unanswered despite the many people who have worked in this area. These questions range from "What is a type?" to "How do we know when we have a cluster?" These are the kinds of basic issues that must be settled if the stagnation that has beset this area is to be overcome.

Those seeking information concerning the wide range of personality typologies, clustering methods, and their mathematics are advised to refer to Bolz (1972b). Neither methods nor mathematics are introduced in this chapter except those that are clearly necessary for the development of type theory and cluster-analytic theory. The time has indeed come for theoretical exploration and development.

This chapter considers some of the reasons for the decline of interest in classic typological theories of personality and examines the various potentials of an empirical typology. The mistakes and pitfalls of past work are reviewed so that we may avoid them and if possible develop a theory that not only incorporates these observations, but also allows us even greater insights. A well-known typological system, the clinical classification scheme, is then analyzed briefly in terms of the concepts that are developed within the chapter.

## 2 THE DECLINE OF CLASSIC TYPOLOGIES

The classic personality typologies that once dominated much of psychological theory have been quietly forgotten. Their demise was not a consequence of better typologies taking their place; instead, these typologies were ill-suited to their purpose. In the last two decades, the overwhelming attack from research studies armed with measurement scales, multivariate statistical procedures, and experimental manipulations signaled the death of classic theories of personality and personality types. Contemporary personologists tend to look with scorn on fellow researchers who entertain the concept of personality types. However, the cause of the decline of these personality typologies was not necessarily the weakness of the concept itself but rather the weaknesses of the particular typologies.

The paramount reason for the decline of classic personality typologies lies in their scientific inadequacy. These schemes had been overambitiously applied in an attempt at global coverage (Schreider, 1966), over-simplified in an effort to encompass human behavior diversity in a handful of gross categories (Chein, 1943), and overextended to presume to be exhaustive and cover every personality configuration. Simply too much was expected of and claimed for these kinds of personality theories. Most often the reason for the inadequacy was that many of these schemes were armchair inventions without empirical foundation. When empirical utility was then expected, only disappointment resulted. Others, derived from empirical research, suffered from statistical naiveté. W. H. Sheldon's (1942) theory of physique-personality types was developed through the use of ipsative scales in such a manner that the three basic variables presumed to be employed in the scheme turned out to be only two sources of variance (Humphreys, 1957). Many personality types such as C. G. Jung's (1953) introverts-extroverts turned out to be only the extremes of a population normally distributed along a single trait. Other typologies simply failed to identify segregates of people with distinct or commonly shared characteristics. The reason for this failure is due almost entirely to insufficient or total lack of statistical sophistication.

Another reason for this decline is that many personologists failed to realize the difference between a multidimensional approach to the exploration and definition of personality and the typological approach. S. Diamond (1957, p. 151) reflects this misunderstanding in his work on personality and temperament: "Actually ... the factorial approach ... is the modern counterpart of 'type' theory." Both approaches are based on a wide selection of diverse behaviors. Indeed, both select particular attributes of this behavior that can be specified reliably and in turn allow the prediction of the original behaviors. Both seek the regular patterns of these behaviors. However, as statistical methods and personality theories, the two approaches yield vastly different results. The dimensional approach, (usually) relying on correlational techniques, seeks to uncover the linear relationships of the behaviors across the population. The general expectation is that sources of behavior will be revealed. The typological approach, on the other hand, seeks the patterns of similarity or dissimilarity of behaviors among the population. The general expectation is therefore that homogeneous groups of people will be revealed.

Finally, the old problem of definition has severely hampered the development of personality type theories. The very ambiguity of the concept of type has led to the loss of respect for and interest in classical typologies. Cattell (1957a) compiled a museum of outrageous uses of the concept of type in psychology, beginning with William James and Carl Jung. One recurrent use or misuse is that of referring to individuals at the polar extremes of a normally distributed attribute as "two types." If a concept of type is to contribute something beyond simply high and low scores on a single dimension, it must encompass considerations of distribution.

Many writers have also noted the moral judgment that an effort to type people does an injustice to the humanity of the people so classified. Many of the attitudes toward typologies can be understood as arising from either an abhorrence of such segregation or the lack of respect in the possible viability of personality types. It is unfortunate that such social conceptions have become so identified with a scientific construct that even the abstract form of the construct loses its scientific respectability.

## 3  THE POTENTIAL OF TYPOLOGIES

Typological theory does, however, have a potential. If a reliable typology could be developed, if one could group people (or any objects) into meaningful, distinct, and homogeneous groups, the potential fruits to be enjoyed are many. There are three main categories of typologies that reflect both the nature of their assumptions and the amount of information to be derived from any given typology. At this point, the word *typology* is being used in the sense of a scheme whereby people or objects are placed into mutually exclusive groups, regardless of the nature of the derivation of the scheme. (It should be noted that even this minimal restriction excludes a number of well-known typologies and in this sense not all existing typologies will find themselves included in any of the three categories. Indeed, those typologies that cannot be included in any of the three can be considered to be without utility.)

The first category of typologies includes those in which the groups at least can be assumed to be homogeneous and distinct. *Homogeneous* means that all members of a group are similar to one another on the basis of the measures used. *Distinct* means that the distributions of the groups on the measures do not overlap. This classification would be useful in the field of education. Theorists have long maintained that the educational system would encounter fewer problems if the teacher were asked to teach a group of highly similar people rather than a heterogeneous group of individuals. With such a grouping, the teacher would not have to divide his attention among the diverse problems of the many different people. Confronted with students with similar problems, the teacher could proceed more rapidly and productively. In this setting, however, it is not presumed that the typology has a global nature; instead the typology of this example refers to a specific set of classrooms of students containing a homogeneous and distinct group of students. No attempt is made to extend the typology to behaviors or attributes other than those originally considered. No attempt is made in this example to extend the typology to other students or to the population of students.

The second category includes those typologies that make the additional assumption that the grouping scheme would be valid over the entire population on the basis of the measures considered. This kind of typology can remove some of the disorder from the relationship of variables. Some of what is classified as error may be accounted for by the fact that variables may have different relationships within different subgroups of a sample. The discovery of a set of subgroupings among research subjects may increase greatly the orderliness and reproducibility of the relationships among variables. D. G. MacDonald, Johnson, and Hord (1964) found greater linearity in the relationship between physiological reactions (heart rate and vasomotor responses) to an auditory stimulus in habituation over trials by dividing the subjects into drowsy and alert subjects. Stein's (1963, 1966) findings of Peace Corps volunteers' effectiveness also demonstrated this potential. The ratings of future effectiveness by the final selection board of the Peace Corps as the volunteers finished their training and their rated effectiveness after working in Columbian villages were correlated .31 but ranged from −.85 to +.89 within various groupings in Stein's type system. In this typology category, not only are the groups presumed to be homogeneous and distinct from each other, they must also be reproducible. These subgroups, while allowing the researcher to view the relationship among variables with greater clarity, also change the meaning of these relationships. If these relationships are to be understood, they must not be an artifact of the sample. Therefore, the subgrouping must bear generalization to the entire population when measured on these variables.

The third category includes those typologies which make the further assumption that the typology represents homogeneous and distinct groups that exist in the population when any of a number of possible attributes are being considered. Typologies that can be included in this category offer the scientist great power in terms of the tremendous increase in the efficient use of information. If types do exist and if they are accurately delineated, the efficiency in the use of information would be far greater. In terms of measurement, the scientist would need to conduct the measurement of individuals representative of a type only a limited number of times. For example, considering a group composed of dogs, we would make the same measurements on the dogs only until we were satisfied that we had accurately measured those variables. Then if we had to decide whether an object was a dog or not, we would not have to repeat all the measurements, but only the few it took to answer the question satisfactorily. Therefore, with only a small amount of data we could infer a great many things. In the example of the dogs, upon visually determining that an object is a dog on the basis of a few observations, we would infer quite comfortably a great deal more about the object without bothering to make the related observations. In terms of prediction, the scientist would have far greater insight because not only the direct measurements, but also the inferred measurements can be used.

Furthermore, the behaviors to be predicted should be likewise characteristic of the group. Once a prediction of behavior has been verified and found to be generalizable to members of the group, the power of prediction becomes more than a statistical guess. Likewise, treatment procedures, or the prediction of behaviors resulting from treatment procedures, would be far easier to develop. In terms of etiology and theory building, a "natural" type should provide the basis for stable advancement. All of this, however, depends upon the assumptions that our groups are homogeneous, are generalizable to other samples of the population, and are generalizable to other measurements and behaviors. Only in this case may we conclude that the statistical occurrence of segregation is based on "natural" types. The potential of any of these three levels should not be discarded as impossible, unscientific, or inhuman.

In recent years, there has been a broad renewed interest in the theory of cluster analysis. Literally scores of researchers have attempted to solve the methodological problems in the measurement of similarity and the locating of types. One has the feeling of being in a dark room with hundreds of other people, all of them fumbling around hoping to find the light switch. (To carry the analogy further, one also feels that there are thousands of people standing outside, saying that there is no light switch.) The potential in at least reducing data, if not also making it far more efficient, continues to drive many on.

Researchers in the area of scaling, in particular, view type and cluster analytic efforts as a possible solution to some of their problems. The development of stimulus scales is directly hampered by the sometimes gross differences in individuals.

Scaling theorists have resorted to various cluster analytic methods to clean up the data before attempting to scale it. Probably more than in any other area, the problem of individual differences is most severe. For example, if one were to ask a sample of people to rate their preferences for a variety of dog breeds for the purpose of developing a dog-preference scale, one would hope that the resulting scale would indeed reflect people's dog preferences. However, if some people in the sample loved Irish setters, and if others loved St. Bernards and Labrador retrievers but hated small dogs, and if still others loved Chihuahuas but hated large dogs, the resultant scale would be quite erroneous. In such a case, the need for homogeneous groups is paramount for the scale or scales to have any realistic meaning. This author conducted an exploratory study of dog-preference data (supplied by L. Jones, University of Illinois). The entire sample was first scaled. Then the raters were clustered and the groups then scaled. Clusters representing Irish setter, Collie lovers-Pekinese haters; Afghan lovers-Chihuahua haters; German shepherd lovers; Poodle, Pekinese, Chihuahua lovers-Bulldog, Great Dane, German shepherd haters; and Old English sheep dog, St. Bernard, Labrador retriever lovers were among the groups found. More important to the scaling theorists was that the differences in the scales was dramatic, as expected. The concept of stable individual differences is becoming increasingly important. Concurrently, the development of typological theory is becoming important.

## 4 PAST MISTAKES

Part of any theoretical development is the careful consideration of the mistakes and insights of past researchers. Progress has been slow in the area of type theory, but some very important observations can be made about past work.

As has been pointed out already, the theoretical approach to deriving a taxonomy of personality has proved to be a most useless endeavor. One can only be disappointed when one expects empirical rigor from these armchair inventions. This is not to say that they do not contain any thread of truth—for they might. An empirically derived taxonomy may prove to be similar to one or more of the classic taxonomies. It should be clear to the modern reader that for a taxonomy to have any repute in a modern science, it is essential that it be derived by some empirical and/or statistical means.

One of the more fruitful alternatives that many recent researchers have tried is to base a taxonomy on the groups derived by one of the number of cluster-analytic methods. This seems to be the wisest and most promising approach. It is a strictly empirical approach in that what is generalized is taken directly from the data. The taxonomies so generated often meet the assumptions of at least one of the three categories of useful taxonomies. Furthermore, the groups or clusters within a taxonomy often represent modal points in the frequency distribution. In this manner, there is an intuitive understanding of the statistical and measurement meaning of these taxonomies. For these reasons, it is assumed that the best approach to the development of typological theory is to pursue and develop cluster-analytic theory. Once we have the technology of an adequate cluster-analytic theory, we may attempt to answer the question, "Is the concept of type viable in the science of psychology?"

## 4.1  The Definition and Interpretation of
## a Cluster

If a cluster analysis is to be used, great care must be taken in how any particular method is interpreted and evaluated. The manner of interpretation, indeed the definition of a cluster, is of ultimate importance. It is this problem of definition and interpretation that, to a large extent, has stymied any real progress in cluster-analytic theory.

One approach to the definition of the concept of clusters or types is hierarchical clustering as represented in McQuitty's (1962, 1967) work. This notion is parallel to the taxonomic ventures of zoologists who classify objects into a system of species, phyla, and kingdoms. The basic assumption is that it is appropriate to analyze the data by forming sets and subsets of the objects in ever-increasing levels of generality and decreasing levels of individuality. There is the implicit, though not so often respected, assumption that types within a given level are of the same generality and that objects within a type share a common characteristic of a generality similar to that shared by objects in other types of the same hierarchical level. In the hierarchical clustering of people, this has not necessarily been true.

A second assumption of hierarchical clustering is that this kind of analysis is appropriate to the data. However, with some kinds of data, indeed most psychological data, this assumption is not valid. The situation for which this assumption approaches validity is one in which the density function of a particular cluster is severely nonmonotonic, as in Fig. 1. In such a case, it would be appropriate to speak of clusters of a lower order within a larger cluster. Within a biological framework, it is legitimate to categorize animals

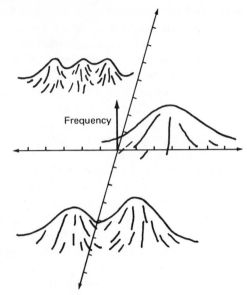

FIG. 1  A distributional interpretation of hierarchical clusters.

into narrow groups based on certain structural similarities. These categories also may be grouped in terms of some broader but commonly shared structural attribute. It is appropriate to such data to continue to generate ever more general or individualistic clusters. For example, we may group organisms on the basis that they have feathers and wings, or hair and four limbs. We may then group these two groups together on the basis that all members of both groups have vertebrae. However, most psychological data cannot be analyzed in such a manner. If a sample of individuals were to be compared with each other on the basis of scores on a battery of tests, it does not follow that ever more general hierarchical levels can be generated on the basis of lessening statistical restrictions of between-individual similarity.

It is reasoned by advocates of hierarchical clustering that it is valid to group clusters on the basis of their mutual proximity or similarity. This author does not believe this to be a supportable rationale. If, in using a statistical approach, one finds distinct clusters, there is little logic to grouping the clusters again.

A second concept of type worth noting is the polar type. Past researchers have used bipolared types that represented the extremes of one continuous distribution. Extraversion-introversion is an example. This definition, however, fails to meet the requirement of separation between types. It is equivalent to arbitrarily dividing a frequency distribution. For example, using the polar model, one would, upon viewing a population distribution of IQ scores, conclude that there are two types of people, dumb ones and smart ones. The meaninglessness of this approach is clearly evident.

A more direct approach to the definition problem is the spatial model in which each object to be clustered or typed is viewed in a spatial distribution. In the case where only one variable is being used, the space would be the univariate frequency distribution. In the case where two or more variables are being used, each variable is considered a dimension of a multivariate frequency distribution. The univariate situation is merely a special case of the more general multivariate situation. People, for example, can be assessed on many variables. Age, race, height, intelligence, attitudes, and the numerous personality and motivation factors are but a few. If people were viewed in a coordinate space where each axis is thought to be an important variable, then people types could be thought of as the differential density or clustering of people in the coordinate space.

If the spatial distribution of a population sample is normal or at least unimodal, then one can only conclude that there are no distinguishable subtypes within a joint distribution of the variables considered. If there are several modes, however, then each mode can be interpreted as representing a cluster or type of people. This conceptualization assures that all objects placed into a group will have statistically similar attributes. Such a definition appears to be appropriate to the data likely to be used in isolating people types. The fact can be demonstrated easily that multiple modal points can exist in a multivariate distribution even when the distribution projected on any one of the dimensions is normal (Cattell, 1968a).

Although the modal approach will clearly define the center of a group or type, it can present difficulty when defining the boundaries of groups. First, if a person is plotted between two modes, as if he were in a rowboat between two islands, does he belong to either group, and if so, which one? This problem obviously becomes difficult when there are a number of people in rowboats. However, a second and more serious problem is, How does one establish the boundaries of two (or more) modal groups when their distributions overlap? The situation can be seen best in Fig. 2. The answer to this problem is obviously not an easy one.

Cattell (1968a) modified the modality definition, which may solve the problem of overlapping groups, by pointing out that a significant mode may have a varying density or may have modes within itself. This would be like the peaks on the island in the ocean. Cattell called these peaks *homostats*, "operationally defined as 'standing in a similar (or same) position'" (Cattell, 1968a, p. 101). The term *segregate* was used for the islands, with the

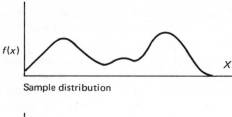

Sample distribution

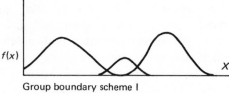

Group boundary scheme I

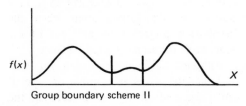

Group boundary scheme II

**FIG. 2** Possible methods of defining group boundaries.

usual meaning denoting an isolated group. The problems that occur with this refinement are that the homostats may often be spurious to the sample. Exploratory research has indicated that multivariate clusters appear to trail into each other. Instead of being a scatter of mounds, it appears that the multivariate distributions of people are more like bumps on a large mass. The researcher must be cautious of such a reality. Cattell's refinement should be taken seriously in that it is quite possible that some modal groups may form a chain or a more general group. Such a recognition would be wise when formulating a taxonomy of people. (It is interesting to note that in this situation the modal and hierarchal definitions are similar). In any case, when the spatial interpretation is used, the evaluation of a cluster method depends on the extent to

which the clusters the method locates represent modal points in the frequency distribution.

Another way to approach the problem of finding groups of similar people is that of profile analysis. Using this method, each person or object has a set of scores based on the variables being used. Each person then has his own profile of scores. One common profile system is the Minnesota Multiphasic Personality Inventory (MMPI) in which certain MMPI profiles or sets of scores are associated with various clinical diagnostic groups. If the data are analyzed as a collection of profiles, then Cronbach and Gleser's (1953) remarks are appropriate. There are three sources of variation among profiles: (a) elevation, the mean of all scores in a profile for a given object; (b) scatter, the square root of the sum of the squares of the object's deviation scores about its own mean; and (c) shape, the residual information in the score set after equating profiles for both elevation and scatter. A method could be evaluated in terms of how well it reflects these three sources of variance of between-individual similarity. When the profile-analysis interpretation is used, the evaluation of a cluster method depends on the extent to which the data are not distorted and on the extent to which the groups are composed of highly similar components. This delineation has greatly aided the understanding of some of the problems that must be solved in cluster-analytic theory. Even though the spatial and profile-analysis interpretations appear to be quite different, their resultant evaluations of cluster methods are essentially the same. If a cluster procedure distorts the data within the profile-analysis interpretation, there will be a parallel inadequacy within the spatial interpretation. Indeed, if an evaluation using one interpretation is confusing, often the other clearly specifies the situation. This can be seen as various mistakes and insights are considered.

In developing a clustering method, the theorist is faced with two major problems. The first of these is assessing the similarity between any two people or objects. In every method, even in the theoretically derived taxonomies, there is some assessment procedure to determine the similarity or dissimilarity of people. Obviously, the more modern methods are explicit about the similarity-assessment procedure. The evaluation of such procedures depends on the extent to which the resultant measures accurately reflect the between-individual similarity. The second major problem is interpreting the similarities to (a) determine the number of clusters, (b) locate the clusters, and (c) determine the membership of the clusters in a reliable and valid manner, so that the clusters are homogeneous and distinct.

## 4.2 Between-Individual Similarity

With regard to the problems of assessing similarity, one of the most deceptive pitfalls that have plagued cluster theorists is the use of correlational methods to assess between-object similarity. The Pearson product-moment correlation, for example, demonstrated considerable utility in the task of assessing covariation among measures. It was an obvious temptation to correlate objects, including people, on the basis of several measures. Correlational procedures, however, were designed to assess the covariation of measures, often equating means and variances. In this way, the predictive potency of one variable for another would be independent of any particular metric characteristics. However, an object's mean and variance of mea-

surements are of crucial importance when it is to be compared with another object. In a graphic geometric example, two profiles may have exactly the same shape, thus yielding a perfect correlational similarity, yet the elevation may be drastically different. When plotted in an object space, the distance between these two objects would be directly a function of the difference of the elevation of their profiles. Other procedures such as Spearman's rank order correlation, Kendall's (1948) tau, and Gengerelli and Butler's (1955) combination of subtraction of profiles resulted in similar distortions.

The simple distance between two objects, calculated as the square root of the sum of the squared differences of two objects on the measures used, is the most direct and accurate approach to assessing similarity among objects. Mahalanobis' (1936) $D^2$ was an improvement upon the simple distance function. Most of the statistics based on the distance between two objects provide extremely accurate assessments in terms of both the spatial and profile analysis interpretations (Bolz, 1972b). However, even in this direct approach there are hazards. The characteristics of the measures used, such as the means, variances, and intercorrelations, greatly affect distance statistics. In addition, a Euclidean distance is often assumed, but this is not a necessary assumption. Because such characteristics are quite often superficial and of no essential meaning or vary from experiment to experiment, the meaning of the interpoint distances is sometimes severely jeopardized. An often-used solution is to standardize the means and variances and orthogonalize the measures. Though this does allow some universality of interpretation of the interpoint distance, it does indeed alter the distribution of the objects. This alteration can be considered arbitrary and without significance to the real world.

Probably the most important insight was the development of the similarity statistic $r_p$, by Cattell (1949): $r_p$ is a distance measure that accurately reflects the distance-similarity between objects but avoids the restrictions of cruder distance measures. It is independent of the number of variables used and has a known expected distribution so that significance tests (Horn, J. L., 1961b) are possible. The values of $r_p$ range from $-1$ to $1$ with zero being a random probability of similarity based on the chi-square distribution. Although a revised version of $r_p$ was developed (Cattell, Coulter, & Tsujioka, 1966) for correlated variables, investigations by this author indicated that $r_p$ is sufficiently rigorous to justify its use with even moderately oblique factors without the severe distortions that result in a simpler distance measure.

One possibility that should be considered is the use of psychological similarity or distance. In multidimensional scaling experiments, for example, people are often asked how similar or how close two objects are. This kind of similarity measure is appropriate to both cluster and type theory concerns. Indeed, such a cluster model may well be useful in research on cognitive functioning and decision making. The interpretation would be that the subject's evaluative or decision-making processes, rather than being dimensional, are categorical.

## 4.3 Clustering Methods

With regard to the second major problem, that of evaluating the similarities, the use or misuse of factor analytic methods to locate clusters in a multivariate space is the most controversial and deceptive of mistakes.

Factor analysis in its many forms is undoubtedly one of the most powerful of statistical techniques available to the researcher. Researchers have used it to reduce a myriad of measures to a few concise factors and to put in order the overwhelming complexities of multivariate data. So impressive has been its productivity and potential that investigators like Stephenson (1936) were eager to turn its penetrating light upon the murky waters of personality typology. Its use, though, for this purpose has been severely and rightly criticized (Burt, 1937; Cattell, 1952a). The invalidity of the use of factoring the object or person space to locate clusters lies in the fact that the factor-analytic model seeks the dimensionality of the space rather than the clusters contained within the space. This simple fact is reflected in the observation that the number of clusters contained in a space may far exceed the number of dimensions of the space (Bolz, 1972b).

One of the more pervasive mistakes made by cluster theorists has been the development of clustering methods with varying degrees of subjectivity incorporated into the procedural steps. The complexity of the multivariate data used (and presumably required) is so great that any degree of subjectivity will decrease the probability of reliable and replicable solutions. Sawrey's (Sawrey, Keller, & Conger, 1960) clustering method is a popular method that is severely limited by its subjectivity. A person-by-person matrix of between-person $D^2$s is formed. A maximum $D^2$ limit is chosen for two people to be considered similar. A potential nucleus group of two or more similar people is selected. The order of selection proceeds from the individual who has the largest number of people within the limit of similarity. When a person is paired with another, he is eliminated from the matrix to prevent the potential nucleus groups from overlapping. After all similar people have been eliminated, the person with the next highest number of people within the similarity limit is selected. This procedure is repeated until only people with similarities less than the limit remain. A minimum $D^2$ of dissimilarity between nucleus groups is then chosen. Starting with the first person of the first nucleus group, any other person having $D^2$ with the first greater than the dissimilarity criterion is eliminated from the group. This procedure for selecting dissimilar groups and groups of similar people is continued until the two solutions converge. The obvious flaw with this and other similar methods is the choice of the $D^2$ criterion cutoff for similarity and dissimilarity. This kind of subjectivity and uncertainty has yielded results that are at best difficult to interpret.

The solution to the problem of subjective criteria led cluster researchers into yet another problem. Clustering methods were developed that incorporated a system of generating the criterion for such things as minimum similarity for group membership. It quickly became evident that this was not satisfactory because each clustering method then yielded only those clusters that matched its definitions. In other words, the solutions were not independent of the design of the methods. Having set rigid criteria for the size and shape of clusters, the methods were powerless to handle data in which clusters of varying sizes, shapes, and densities existed. In most cases, the methods searched only for circular clusters and accordingly found them. If, for example, a long, elongated

cluster existed in the data, these methods at best would find a series of small tangential circular clusters.

Another methodological problem has been the unrealistic prohibition of overlapping clusters. In many methods, such as Sawrey's, all the members of a cluster would be removed before they could be considered in some overlapping cluster. In this manner all successive clusters were cumulatively distorted.

Probably the least realized mistake originated from Tryon's (1938) cluster analysis, which attempted to generate clusters that maximized within-cluster similarity and minimized between-cluster similarity. While on the surface this appears to be a good notion, it may erroneously exclude or distort clusters. The within-cluster difference may conceivably be greater than the between-cluster differences. Fig. 3 portrays such a possible situation.

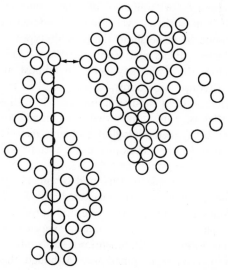

FIG. 3 Illustration of definitional problem of nearest neighbor.

All these mistakes testify to the fact that there are difficult inherent methodological problems involved in the task of locating clusters. While all these problems have been known to the more alert researchers, no one has yet solved them. Every method to date suffers from one or more of these mistakes.

There is yet another criticism that this author wishes to make. Bolz (1972b) considers no fewer than 41 major taxonomic methods. All but two or maybe three of these fail to locate homogeneous and distinct clusters. Even these two or three have proven to be insufficient. Far too often researchers have been satisfied to develop a method that appears to find clusters, when all that results is a "pretty picture." Nothing of any statistical bearing can be said about the clusters that may or may not exist in the data. Nothing of any statistical bearing can be said about the cluster solution generated. These "pretty pictures" are derived from models and procedures that do not evaluate the accuracy or validity of the solution. Without such an evaluation, no inferences should be made about the possible types or clusters. Fleiss and Zubin (1969, p. 235) stated that "the key defec' in almost all clustering procedures seems to be the absence of a statistical model." It is the belief of this author that the answers to the other methodological problems may be found in the development of a statistical model of clusters.

One example of this kind of mistake is the popular method suggested by S. C. Johnson (1967). This method produces graphic results that almost appear to transform a multidimensional distribution into a unidimensional one. Although this method has attracted a considerable number of believers, it has been justly criticized (Bolz, 1972b; Tatsuoka, 1971). Besides

methodological problems, it allows no objective manner for establishing cutting points for its cluster. More importantly, it does not allow any kind of statistical evaluation, despite its graphic results. For cluster theory to advance, it is absolutely essential that theories, models, and methods be developed that allow some kind of inferential evaluation of the data. If we are seriously to attempt to answer questions such as "Are there personality types?" we must develop a viable data-analysis procedure based on a statistical model.

It is clear that in our extreme concern about developing methods that avoid various methodological weaknesses, we failed to see the necessity of developing methods derived from models based on assumptions. If we wish to make some kind of statistical statement, we have to give up something in return; some essential assumptions will have to be made. If a data-analysis procedure is to be developed, a model of clusters must be developed in which certain assumptions are made and explicitly set forth, and the logical conclusions then pursued. Only then can statistical inferences be made. In this manner, a model of clusters may be tested in terms of the defensibility of its conclusions and of the power it has in terms of the degree to which its assumptions may be violated and still yield valid conclusions.

Having discussed the foregoing issues, this chapter now concerns itself with such a possible statistical model of clusters. This model illustrates the direction cluster and type theory could and probably should take. This model, presented originally by Bolz (1972b), has gone through several major changes. The particular form presented here is not necessarily the final one, but it represents the most advanced stage of cluster-analytic theory.

## 5 TYPE ANALYSIS: A STATISTICAL CLUSTER–ANALYTIC MODEL

Type analysis is a statistical model of clusters in which each object or person is considered to be a random sampling of a cluster drawn from a population of clusters. The type analysis model is based upon the fundamental hypothesis that the characteristics of an object may be viewed as a combination of (a) the characteristics specific to the type or cluster of which an object is a member, (b) the general characteristics of the population, and (c) the characteristics unique to the object:

Characteristics of Object
= Characteristics of Type
+ Characteristics of Population
+ Uniqueness.

The characteristics that can be attributed to, or accounted for, by the cluster may be restated in terms of the characteristics that are common between the object and cluster. It is then the degree of commonness or similarity that is of concern. This degree of commonness shall be termed *resemblance* (Res).

Likewise the attributes of an object not accounted for by the cluster that can be attributed to the population may be expressed in terms of the resemblance of the object to the population. This may be interpreted as the summed resemblance of the object with all other types or clusters in the population. In such a case, the type of which the object is a member shall be termed that object's *primary type*, whereas all other types shall be termed *secondary types* with respect to the particular object.

The characteristics unique to the object then may be interpreted as that resemblance (Res) of an object to itself that is due to uniqueness, or sampling error, or variance of the primary type, or error of measurement. Therefore the fundamental hypothesis becomes

Res(object) = Res(primary type)
+ Res(secondary types) + Res(unique).

A method using this model consequently would attempt to express the total resemblance of each object so that Res(primary type) approached unity and Res(secondary types) and Res(unique) approached zero.

At this point a method of assessing resemblance must be developed. It would be advantageous if resemblance had a known theoretical distribution that would permit the partialing of resemblance and a statistical interpretation of various values. Past research has demonstrated the desirability of assessing similarity among objects as a function of their interpoint distances. Under certain conditions these squared distances are distributed as a $\chi^2$. The necessary conditions are that each variable used in the calculation of $D^2$ is normally distributed with a zero mean and unit variance, and that the variables are independent of one another. In such a situation, the median $D^2$ is equal to twice the median $\chi^2$ with $M$ degrees of freedom, where $M$ is equal to the number of variables.

Before a formula for resemblance using $D^2$ is decided on, some theoretical aspects of resemblance should be considered. The smaller the $D^2$, the larger the value of Res should be. The resemblance of an object with itself (when $D^2 = 0$) should be unity. The lower bound of resemblance between two objects should be zero. Negative resemblance would have no theoretical meaning. The resemblance between objects $X$ and $Y$ can therefore be defined:

$$Res(X, Y) = \frac{K}{K + D^2},$$

where

$$D^2 = \sum_{j=1}^{M} (X_j - Y_j)^2,$$

$$K = 2\chi^2_{(M)}$$

and $M$ = number of variables. (The reader should note the parallel between Res and Cattell's $r_p$.) Res meets all the theoretical considerations, and probabilities can be associated to its values.

The next stage in the development of the type analysis model is the derivation of a partialing formula whereby the resemblance that can be accounted for by a particular type or cluster can be extracted. The concept of partialing implies a regression model. Such a regression foundation has already been implied in the type analysis model in which primary types are sought to account for the resemblance of objects. The linear regression model seeks a line that will best fit or account for the covariance of two variables on the basis of

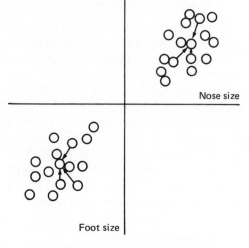

FIG. 5   Illustration of regression to points.

a sample of observations. When such a regression-to-a-line model is applied to objects, the limitations become obvious. For example, if people's noses and feet were measured, a cluster of people with big noses and big feet might exist, and a cluster of people with small noses and small feet might also exist. If a linear regression model were used to account for the similarity or covariance among the people, the solution of a line going through both clusters would result (Fig. 4). The inadequacy is obvious. However, if a model based on regression to points were used, a much more desirable solution would result (Fig. 5). These points then can be interpreted as cluster or primary type centroids. Once a regression point is determined, its effect or resemblance needs to be extracted so that the other regression points also may be determined. There are, however, mathematical difficulties inherent to the regression-to-points concept that are not part of the linear regression concept. The formal derivation of the partialing

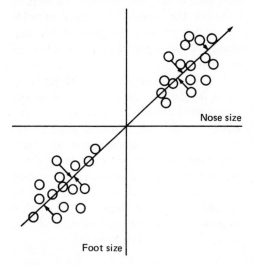

FIG. 4   Illustration of regression to a line.

formula remains to be developed. A formula has been developed, however, that does meet most of the necessary requirements. If $\mathrm{Res}(X,Y.Z)$ denotes the resemblance between the objects $X$ and $Y$ when the resemblance to type $Z$ has been extracted from both, then an extraction formula should satisfy the following conditions:

$$\mathrm{Res}(X,X.X) = 0$$

$$\mathrm{Res}(X,Y.Y) = 0$$

$$\mathrm{Res}(X,Y.Z) = \mathrm{Res}(Y,X.Z)$$

$$\mathrm{Res}(X,Y.Z,W) = \mathrm{Res}(X,Y.W,Z)$$

$$\mathrm{Res}(X,X) = \mathrm{Res}(X,Z) + \mathrm{Res}(X,X.Z).$$

The formula

$$\mathrm{Res}(X,Y.Z)$$

$$= \mathrm{Res}(X,Y) - \frac{\mathrm{Res}(X,Z)\,\mathrm{Res}(Y,Z)}{\mathrm{Res}(Z,Z)}$$

meets all but the last of these conditions. The first four conditions are necessary if the partialing formula is to be internally consistent. The last condition, however, is necessary for the model to be algebraically additive, so that Res(object) = Res(primary type) + Res(secondary types) + Res(unique). The formula can be used as a sufficient approximation of some future more complete formula for partialing in a regression-to-points model.

We now have a model based on a fundamental hypothesis, a definition of resemblance, and a formula for partialing resemblance. If the model is also to allow a statistical inference about the sampled population of clusters or types, one must accept some necessary assumptions. These assumptions may appear to be unduly restrictive, but it is only on the basis of

such assumptions that statistical tests can be made on the data.

The first set of assumptions concerns the population of clusters. It is assumed that there is a finite but unknown number of clusters. The centroid of each cluster has a significant resemblance to each member of the cluster. A significant resemblance may be defined as any value of resemblance that has an associated probability less than or equal to a specified level. None of the multivariate distributions of the clusters or types overlap with one another. The variables within each cluster are independent and have variances equal to $1/T$, where $T$ equals the number of types, clusters, or points being regressed to.

The second set of assumptions concerns the population of objects. The observed objects represent independent random samples of a set of clusters. The joint population of the set of clusters has some assumed characteristics. The measures of the attributes used to establish the resemblance among objects are independent. Furthermore, the measures have a mean of zero and a variance of one.

The methodological consequences of the assumptions permit some meaningful advances in cluster-analytic theory. The most important of these is the observation that the centermost object in a cluster is the one with the highest total resemblance to all other objects in the cluster. Since resemblance is an inverse function of $D^2$, to demonstrate that the total Res reaches a maximum, it is sufficient only to demonstrate that the total $D^2$ has reached a minimum. If the centermost object had the same attribute values as the cluster centroid, the object would have the smallest possible total $D^2$ with all other objects in the cluster. Given objects $X$ and $Y$ and a centermost object $Z$, then

$$D_{XZ}{}^2 + D_{YZ}{}^2 = \sum_{j=1}^{M} (X_j - Z_j)^2$$

$$+ \sum_{j=1}^{M} (Y_j - Z_j)^2$$

approaches a minimum as $Z$ approaches $(X + Y)/2$. This is easily proved by assuming that $Z = (X + Y)/2$ represents a minimum. Any shift toward either $X$ or $Y$ results in a higher summed $D^2$.

$$D^2 = \Sigma(X_j - Z_j)^2 + \Sigma(Y_j - Z_j)^2. \tag{1}$$

If

$$Z = (X_j + Y_j)/2, \tag{2}$$

then

$$D^2 = \Sigma\left(X_j - \frac{X_j + Y_j}{2}\right)^2 + \Sigma\left(Y_j - \frac{X_j + Y_j}{2}\right)^2 \tag{3}$$

$$= \Sigma\left(\frac{X_j - Y_j}{2}\right)^2 + \Sigma\left(\frac{Y_j - X_j}{2}\right)^2 \tag{4}$$

$$= \frac{1}{2\Sigma(X_j{}^2 + 2X_jY_j + Y_j{}^2)}. \tag{5}$$

If

$$Z_j = \frac{X_j + Y_j + e}{2} \quad \text{for any } e > 0 \tag{6}$$

and

$$X_j - Y_j \leqslant 0$$

then

$$D^{2'} = \Sigma\left(X_j - \frac{X_j + Y_j - e}{2}\right)^2$$

$$+ \Sigma\left(Y_j - \frac{X_j + Y_j - e}{2}\right)^2 \tag{7}$$

$$= \Sigma\left(\frac{X_j - Y_j - e}{2}\right)^2 + \Sigma\left(\frac{Y_j - X_j - e}{2}\right)^2 \tag{8}$$

$$= 1/2 \Sigma(X_j{}^2 - 2X_jY_j + Y_j{}^2 + e^2). \tag{9}$$

Therefore

$$D^2 = \Sigma(X_j - Z_j)^2 + \Sigma(Y_j - Z_j)^2 \rightarrow \text{Min.} \tag{10}$$

if

$$Z_j \rightarrow (X_j + Y_j)/2. \tag{11}$$

This centermost object is defined as the *ideal object* of its cluster within the particular sample. The expected values of the measures of the attributes of the ideal object are equal to those of the cluster centroid. The ideal object of a cluster is therefore identified as being the object with the highest total resemblance with all other objects in the cluster. Using the ideal object and the objects with which it has a significant resemblance as a starting configuration, a sample centroid may be computed. This would alleviate the problem of sampling error affecting the hypothesized cluster centroid because the sample centroid would be a better estimate of the population cluster centroid than the ideal object in any given sample. The sample centroid may be recomputed by using the configuration of the sample centroid and all the objects with which it has a significant resemblance, and then a revised sample cluster centroid could be computed. This can be reiterated until the difference between two consecutive centroids reached a desired minimum.

It follows that if only significant resemblance values were considered, then the object with the highest summed resemblance with all other objects would be an ideal object of its own cluster. It also follows that if the resemblance to this first ideal object or to the first cluster centroid was partialed out of the resemblance matrix, one could again use this procedure to locate a second potential ideal object. Given $N$ objects, up to $N$ potential ideal objects could be located. If a graph were made of the ideal objects or cluster centroids in their order of being located and their summed significant resemblances with all other objects, then it also follows that a sudden break in this monotonically decreasing graph would indicate the number of clusters that are represented in the data in a manner similar to the method used to determine the number of factors in a principal axes factor solution when one plots the amount of variance accounted for by each successive factor.

Once the number of clusters has been determined, objects may be assigned to a cluster on the basis of the centroid (or centroids) with which they have a significant resemblance.

The statistical consequences of the assumptions of the type analysis model permit equally important advances. It is assumed that a population of an unknown number of clusters has been sampled. Any particular sample of $N$ objects is obviously limited to representing at most, $N$ clusters. Since the objects are randomly drawn, the representation of any cluster is independent of the representation of other clusters. Furthermore, since there is an expected distribution of each cluster, there is a consequent expected summed $D^2$ between the cluster centroids and the cluster members. Therefore, a test of null hypothesis for a particular solution can be made on the basis of the probability of the observed summed $D^2$. For a one-cluster solution of $N$ individuals measured on $M$ variables, the summed $D^2$ would equal

$$\sum_{j=1}^{M} \sum_{i=1}^{N} \frac{(X_{1ij} - \overline{X}_{1j})^2}{1}$$

and would be distributed as a $\chi^2$ with $M(N-1)$ degrees of freedom.

The two-cluster solution summed $D^2$ would equal

$$\sum_{j=1}^{M} \sum_{i=1}^{N} \frac{(X_{1ij} - \overline{X}_{1j})^2}{1/2}$$

$$+ \sum_{j=1}^{M} \sum_{i=1}^{N} \frac{(X_{2ij} - \overline{X}_{2j})^2}{1/2}$$

and would be distributed as a $\chi^2$ with $M(N-2)$ degrees of freedom. Solutions of three or more clusters would follow the same format. As the $Q$th cluster centroid is located, a statistical test of the null hypothesis that there are $Q$ clusters may be made. Because of the assumptions, if too few or too many clusters have been located, a significant $\chi^2$ should result and allow the rejection of the null hypothesis. However, if the assumptions hold, there will be one (and only one) solution with a nonsignificant $\chi^2$ such that the null hypothesis cannot be rejected.

Another approach to the statistical evaluation of any given solution involves resemblance. Since resemblance has an expected distribution, a probability could be associated with a given resemblance. The difficulty is that the resemblances associated with a sample of objects are not independent of one another. If, however, the assumption was made that every time a resemblance was computed, the objects represented independent samplings from their respective clusters, $\chi^2$ distribution could be assumed. For example, when the resemblance between objects $A$ and $B$ was computed, the measures of objects $A$ and $B$ could be considered independent observations of objects $A$ and $B$. When the resemblance of objects $A$ and $C$ was computed, the measures of $A$ and $C$ would be considered repeated, but independent, observations of objects $A$ and $C$. In a sense, each object would have its associated sample of independent observations. This would allow a probability to be associated with a matrix of resemblances. However, when resemblances are partialed out of the resemblance matrix, the distribution of residual resemblances is again unknown. If and when this problem is solved, it will be possible statistically to infer from the residual resemblance matrix how good a solution is. Furthermore, as more resemblance is accounted for, it will be possible to infer how much better a solution is in a stepwise fashion. Presently, how much resemblance is being accounted for and how much more resemblance is being accounted for by each successive solution

can be computed, but without an associated probability.

Yet another statistical test, one that is independent of the type analysis model, is the multivariate test of differences of the clusters. Wilk's (1932) $\Lambda$ may be used for testing the significance of the overall difference among several sample centroids. Hotelling's $T^2$ statistic (1931) is the multivariate analogue of the familiar $t$ ratio for testing the significance of the difference between two independent means. This may be used in a pair-wise comparison of the clusters, though the lack of independence of multiple tests partially invalidates the use of this statistic.

To review briefly, type analysis is a model of types (or clusters) that allows a statistical analysis of the types that are represented in data that meets certain assumptions. The number and location of clusters and the cluster members are determined in an objective manner. In addition, the cluster solution can be evaluated statistically.

To demonstrate the effectiveness of the model, a sample of random normal deviates

**TABLE 1**  Resemblance matrix of Example 1

| Object | 1 | 2 | 3 | 4 | 5 | 6 | 7 | 8 | 9 | 10 | 11 | 12 | 13 | 14 | 15 |
|---|---|---|---|---|---|---|---|---|---|---|---|---|---|---|---|
| 1 | 1.0 | .93 | .96 | .90 | .99 | .12 | .17 | .15 | .13 | .15 | .17 | .17 | .15 | .18 | .17 |
| 2 | .93 | 1.0 | .98 | .97 | .92 | .12 | .17 | .15 | .13 | .15 | .16 | .15 | .14 | .16 | .15 |
| 3 | .96 | .98 | 1.0 | .86 | .94 | .13 | .18 | .16 | .13 | .16 | .17 | .16 | .15 | .17 | .16 |
| 4 | .90 | .97 | .96 | 1.0 | .87 | .13 | .19 | .17 | .14 | .17 | .17 | .16 | .15 | .17 | .16 |
| 5 | .99 | .92 | .94 | .87 | 1.0 | .12 | .17 | .14 | .12 | .15 | .17 | .16 | .15 | .17 | .16 |
| 6 | .12 | .12 | .13 | .13 | .12 | 1.0 | .74 | .73 | .95 | .87 | .15 | .14 | .14 | .14 | .13 |
| 7 | .17 | .17 | .18 | .19 | .17 | .74 | 1.0 | .77 | .71 | .86 | .16 | .16 | .15 | .15 | .15 |
| 8 | .15 | .15 | .16 | .17 | .14 | .73 | .77 | 1.0 | .76 | .94 | .16 | .16 | .15 | .16 | .14 |
| 9 | .13 | .13 | .13 | .14 | .12 | .95 | .71 | .76 | 1.0 | .89 | .17 | .16 | .16 | .16 | .15 |
| 10 | .15 | .15 | .17 | .17 | .15 | .87 | .86 | .94 | .89 | 1.0 | .17 | .16 | .16 | .16 | .15 |
| 11 | .17 | .16 | .17 | .17 | .17 | .15 | .16 | .16 | .17 | .17 | 1.0 | .88 | .96 | .91 | .96 |
| 12 | .17 | .15 | .16 | .16 | .16 | .14 | .16 | .16 | .16 | .16 | .88 | 1.0 | .92 | .92 | .92 |
| 13 | .15 | .14 | .14 | .15 | .15 | .14 | .15 | .15 | .16 | .16 | .96 | .92 | 1.0 | .88 | .97 |
| 14 | .18 | .16 | .17 | .17 | .17 | .14 | .15 | .16 | .16 | .16 | .91 | .92 | .88 | 1.0 | .89 |
| 15 | .17 | .15 | .16 | .16 | .16 | .13 | .15 | .14 | .15 | .15 | .96 | .92 | .97 | .89 | 1.0 |

**TABLE 2** First residual matrix of Example 1

| Object | 1 | 2 | 3 | 4 | 5 | 6 | 7 | 8 | 9 | 10 | 11 | 12 | 13 | 14 | 15 |
|---|---|---|---|---|---|---|---|---|---|---|---|---|---|---|---|
| 1 | .05 | .00 | .00 | .00 | .05 | .00 | .00 | .00 | .00 | .00 | .01 | .01 | .01 | .01 | .01 |
| 2 | .00 | .03 | .00 | .03 | .00 | .00 | .00 | .00 | .00 | .00 | .00 | .00 | .00 | .00 | .00 |
| 3 | .00 | .00 | .02 | .01 | .00 | .00 | .00 | .00 | .00 | .00 | .00 | .00 | .00 | .00 | .00 |
| 4 | .00 | .03 | .01 | .08 | .00 | .01 | .02 | .02 | .01 | .02 | .01 | .01 | .01 | .01 | .01 |
| 5 | .05 | .00 | .00 | .00 | .07 | .00 | .00 | .00 | .00 | .00 | .01 | .01 | .01 | .01 | .01 |
| 6 | .00 | .00 | .00 | .01 | .00 | 1.0 | .74 | .73 | .95 | .87 | .15 | .14 | .14 | .14 | .13 |
| 7 | .00 | .00 | .00 | .02 | .00 | .74 | 1.0 | .77 | .71 | .86 | .16 | .16 | .15 | .15 | .15 |
| 8 | .00 | .00 | .00 | .02 | .00 | .73 | .77 | 1.0 | .76 | .94 | .16 | .16 | .15 | .16 | .14 |
| 9 | .00 | .00 | .00 | .01 | .00 | .95 | .71 | .76 | 1.0 | .98 | .17 | .16 | .16 | .16 | .15 |
| 10 | .00 | .00 | .00 | .02 | .00 | .87 | .86 | .94 | .89 | 1.0 | .17 | .16 | .16 | .16 | .15 |
| 11 | .01 | .00 | .00 | .01 | .01 | .15 | .16 | .16 | .17 | .17 | 1.0 | .88 | .96 | .91 | .96 |
| 12 | .01 | .00 | .00 | .01 | .01 | .14 | .16 | .16 | .16 | .16 | .88 | 1.0 | .92 | .92 | .92 |
| 13 | .01 | .00 | .00 | .01 | .01 | .14 | .15 | .15 | .16 | .16 | .96 | .92 | 1.0 | .88 | .97 |
| 14 | .01 | .00 | .00 | .01 | .01 | .14 | .15 | .16 | .16 | .16 | .91 | .92 | .88 | 1.0 | .89 |
| 15 | .01 | .00 | .00 | .01 | .01 | .13 | .15 | .14 | .15 | .15 | .96 | .92 | .97 | .89 | 1.0 |

was generated. The sample contained 15 objects and 3 clusters such that there were 5 objects to a cluster. Four uncorrelated dimensions were used and the variance of the parent population from which the normal deviates were drawn was 1. The resemblance matrix is presented in Table 1. Object 3 proved to be the first ideal object. The residual resemblance after the first cluster centroid was partialed out is presented in Table 2. The procedure was continued until 12 ideal objects had been located. The resulting values for the resemblance extracted, total resemblance extracted, $\chi^2$, degrees of freedom, and the associated probability of each iteration are presented in Table 3. All these measures clearly indicate that three clusters are represented in the data. All of the objects were correctly clustered. This is admittedly

**TABLE 3** Solution statistics of Example 1

| Cluster | Ideal object | Resemblance extracted | Multiple resemblance | Chi square | df | Probability |
|---|---|---|---|---|---|---|
| 1 | 3 | .372 | .372 | 1487.9 | 56 | .000 |
| 2 | 15 | .323 | .645 | 1449.0 | 52 | .000 |
| 3 | 10 | .213 | .908 | 60.9 | 48 | .100 |
| 4 | 1 | .023 | .930 | 75.9 | 44 | .002 |
| 5 | 2 | .000 | .930 | 90.9 | 40 | .000 |
| 6 | 4 | .000 | .930 | 107.6 | 36 | .000 |
| 7 | 5 | .000 | .930 | 120.6 | 32 | .000 |
| 8 | 6 | .000 | .930 | 135.8 | 28 | .000 |
| 9 | 7 | .028 | .958 | 123.1 | 24 | .000 |
| 10 | 8 | .011 | .969 | 96.0 | 20 | .000 |
| 11 | 9 | .008 | .977 | 70.9 | 16 | .000 |
| 12 | 11 | .000 | .977 | 58.8 | 12 | .000 |

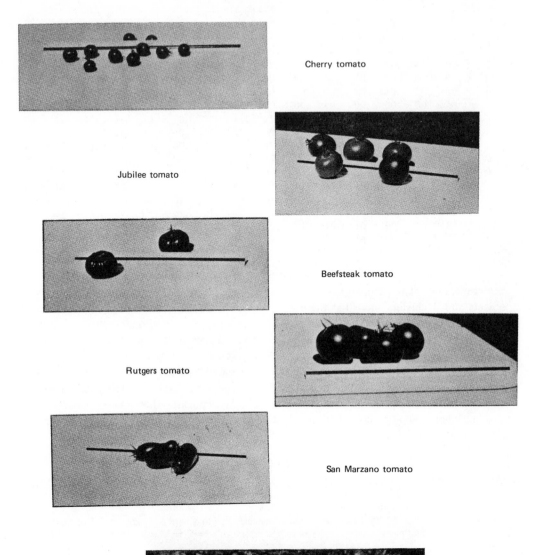

Cherry tomato

Jubilee tomato

Beefsteak tomato

Rutgers tomato

San Marzano tomato

**FIG. 6** Test of type analysis model in study of tomato varieties. From Bolz, 1972a.

**TABLE 4**  Measurements used in the tomato plasmode

| Item | Measurement | Item | Measurement |
|------|-------------|------|-------------|
| 1. | Date fruit formed | 20. | Splash–distance |
| 2. | Fresh weight | 21. | Deflection under 1 lb. weight |
| 3. | Length of stem | 22. | Deflection under 2 lb. weight |
| 4. | Diameter of stem | 23. | Puncture resistance |
| 5. | Number of leaflets | 24. | Squash resistance |
| 6. | Number of cracks | 25. | Length of leaflet |
| 7. | Rating of redness | 26. | Rolling distance |
| 8. | Rating of color uniformity | 27. | Skin thickness |
| 9. | Minimum diameter | 28. | Number of seeds in top half |
| 10. | Maximum diameter | 29. | Number of seeds in bottom half |
| 11. | Minimum height | 30. | Average width of ribs |
| 12. | Maximum height | 31. | Number of ribs |
| 13. | Convolution depth | 32. | Minimum core diameter |
| 14. | Circumference | 33. | Maximum core diameter |
| 15. | Area of top imprint | 34. | Acidity of juice |
| 16. | Area of bottom imprint | 35. | Rating of sweetness |
| 17. | Displacement | 36. | Rating of goodness |
| 18. | Volume | 37. | Solid weight |
| 19. | Splash–volume | | |

artificial data but the power of the model is evident. The true test is, How much power will the model have with real data that does not conform strictly to the stated assumptions?

A second test of the type analysis model has been made in a study of five varieties of tomatoes (Bolz, 1972a). One hundred tomatoes from five varieties (Cherry, Jubilee, Beefsteak, Rutgers, and San Marzano) were measured on 37 variables (Fig. 6 and Table 4). A factor analysis of these variables produced 6 factors. The type analysis of the 100 tomatoes on the 6 factors is presented in Table 5. Clearly, the analysis indicates the presence of 5 types.

**TABLE 5**  Type analysis solution statistics for the tomato plasmode

| Cluster | Resemblance extracted | Multiple resemblance | Chi square | df | Probability |
|---------|----------------------|----------------------|------------|-----|-------------|
| 1 | .316 | .316 | 1687 | 594 | .000 |
| 2 | .243 | .559 | 2435 | 588 | .000 |
| 3 | .179 | .738 | 2429 | 582 | .000 |
| 4 | .145 | .882 | 1783 | 576 | .000 |
| 5 | .086 | .968 | 618 | 570 | .085 |
| 6 | .007 | .975 | 654 | 564 | .006 |
| 7 | .003 | .977 | 715 | 558 | .000 |
| 8 | .003 | .980 | 782 | 552 | .000 |
| 9 | .002 | .983 | 835 | 546 | .000 |
| 10 | .008 | .991 | 890 | 540 | .000 |
| 11 | .000 | .991 | 925 | 534 | .000 |
| 12 | .002 | .993 | 892 | 528 | .000 |

The model correctly categorized all 100 of the tomatoes.

## 6  THE TYPOLOGY OF PSYCHOPATHOLOGY

Having developed the typological theory thus far, it would be interesting and beneficial now to review briefly a contemporary approach to personality typology. The American Psychiatric Association's diagnostic scheme of mental disorders is probably the most widely known and widely used typology in modern psychology. Numerous theories, notions, measurement techniques, and therapies have been developed around the categories that are denoted by such well-known labels as psychosis, neurosis, schizophrenia, and paranoia. The typology is loosely based on the disease model used in physical medicine, in which the physician, in order to alleviate a patient's set of symptoms, must discover the disease that is causing them. However, the weaknesses of the use of the disease model to interpret psychological behavior disorders are many and appear to outweigh the advantages.

The inadequacies of the current formulation of psychiatric diagnosis have been noted frequently in the last few decades (Ash, 1949; Foulds, 1955; Harrower, 1950; Hoch & Zubin, 1953; Jellinek, 1939; Mehlman, 1952; Roe, 1941; Rogers, C. R., 1951; Rotter, 1954; Scott, W., 1958; Thorne, 1953; Zigler & Phillips, 1961). The response to this imposing body of criticism has been varied, ranging from a position that the system needs further refinement and purification (Caveny, Wittson, Hunt, & Herman, 1955; Foulds, 1955), through steps toward major revisions (Cattell, 1957a; Eysenck, H. J., 1952b; Leary & Coffey, 1955; Phillips, L., & Rabinovitch, 1958; Wittman & Sheldon, 1948), to condemnation of all labeling approaches, (Menninger, 1955; Noyes, 1953; Rogers, C. R., 1951). For a deeper analysis of these criticisms the reader should refer to Wilson Guertin's chapter 25: "Classification in Psychopathology" in this text.

A major criticism put forth regarding the conventional diagnostic system is that its categories lack homogeneity; that is, its classes encompass people who vary widely in respect to symptomatology, test scores, prognosis, and so forth (King, 1954; Phillips, L., & Rabinovitch, 1958; Rotter, 1954; Wittenborn, 1952; Wittenborn & Bailey, 1952; Wittenborn & Weiss, 1952; and Zigler & Phillips, 1961). Empirical support for this argument came from a study by Zigler and Phillips (1961) in which the presence or absence of 35 representative pathological symptoms was rated by psychiatric judges. Of these, 30 were rated as present in a sample of manic-depressives, 34 in a character disorder sample, and all 35 in both neurotic and schizophrenic groups.

The purpose of this section is not to evaluate the appropriateness of the disease model, but to discuss the adequacy of this diagnostic system of psychopathology as a typology. Such a discussion would be concerned with the evidence that the diagnostic categories represent types of pathology. The concept of type is not part of the disease model and thus this kind of discussion may seem pointless (to the clinician). However, it also appears reasonable to expect that if a disease is causing the symptoms such that the disease has a sufficient degree of uniqueness for a diagnostician to recognize it, then indeed this uniqueness also should give rise to statistical types. If perhaps such types do not form, then maybe not only is the typology weak, but also the disease model inappropriate.

In regards to the previously described three categories of typologies, the clinical typology appears to make the assumptions used in the third category. Clinical diagnostic groups are assumed to be homogeneous and distinct; the grouping scheme is generalized to the entire population of mental patients; and these groups are regarded as being natural in that there are expected differences between groups on a wide variety of measures. If a cluster analysis were conducted on the appropriate data, then the resulting clusters should represent the various diagnostic categories.

This author has conducted cluster analyses using three cluster procedures on each of three different clinical samples. The data collected on the three clinical samples represented different kinds of variables. A sample of 114 persons—including psychotics, neurotic depressives, schizophrenics, manics, and normals—measured on 24 objective tests (Cattell & Schmidt, 1972) was analyzed. Another sample of 314 people—including institutionalized patients representing paranoia, schizophrenia, psychoneuroticism, personality disorders, manic-depressive depression, and normals—measured on 20 objective tests (Tatro, 1966) was also analyzed. Another sample of 300 subjects—including people representing paranoia, chronic schizophrenia, personality disorders, organic brain syndromes, neurosis, and affective psychosis—measured on 28 questionnaire scales was analyzed. In none of the three samples were there any clusters found that were comprised mostly of people diagnosed as being from one clinical category. Instead, the clusters were a senseless collection of persons representing vastly different clinical pathologies. A typical example is a cluster that was composed of two paranoids, two chronic schizophrenics, one personality-disorder patient, and three organic-brain-damaged patients. Simply, this author has yet to find any indication that the clinical diagnostic scheme represents what one would consider to be types of psychopathologic disorders.

Besides the more traditional, theoretical approach to clinical diagnosis, there has been considerable interest in a more empirical assessment of traits of psychopathology and trait patterns or types of psychopathology. Gilberstadt and Duker (1965), Marks and Seeman (1963), and R. D. Fowler (1965) present typologies of MMPI profile types. Gilberstadt and Duker (1965) portray MMPI profile types as empirically observed sets of traits that serve to sort persons into meaningful diagnostic groups. Their approach "reflects a clinical-statistical investigation of the empirically derived hypothesis that certain frequently recurring MMPI profile patterns are associated with certain trait clusters that are significant and specifiable" (Gilberstadt & Duker, 1965, p. 8). MMPI profile types have been empirically isolated on the basis that each type "seemed to represent (a) cardinal type or . . . occurred with high frequency" (Gilberstadt, 1969, p. 57).

The procedures used to isolate the MMPI profile types do not make any empirical or statistical use of the multivariate distribution of MMPI scale scores. The authors present no evidence (a) of the statistical significance of the profile types; (b) of the validity of their typologies (i.e., how profile types represent functional clusters of patients in the clinical population rather than arbitrary diagnostic categories); and (c) of the accuracy of their model (i.e., consideration of the magnitude of the residual error in their solutions, and how well their solutions represent the data). The evidence that has the closest bearing on the sufficiency of the profile typologies comes from the observations of

Briggs, Taylor, and Tellegen (1966), B. C. Glueck (1966), Pauker (1966), and Sines (1966). These observations were that the classification rates of the typologies vary from 20%–80%. From the point of view of the typological theory presented earlier, it is at least premature to accept any of these typologies of MMPI profiles as being valid. More importantly, there is reason to reject these typologies without further research or discussion because the methods by which they were derived almost totally ignored the distributional nature of MMPI profiles. To the extent that such cardinal MMPI profile types are perceived as being useful to the clinician, these schemes of categorizing clinical patients might be productive. However, one should clearly recognize that there is little empirical evidence that these schemes represent a typology of psychopathology.

## 7  SUMMARY

The field of type and cluster analysis has many historical roots for the behavioral scientist. The field yet may yield substantial insights. Much of the progress in the field has been in terms of the development of measures of similarity and procedures for analyzing the similarities. The approaches to these two problems that have been proposed are many and varied. However, these developments have failed to realize the potentials of the field because there has not been a parallel development of a theory or theories of types and clusters.

A theoretical approach, termed Type Analysis, is presented. It is argued that a clustering procedure should allow (a) an objective determination of the number of clusters, (b) an objective determination of the characteristics of each cluster, (c) an objective determination of the membership of each cluster, and (d) a statistical evaluation of the validity of a cluster solution. The type analysis model represents the attributes of an object as a function of the attributes of the type of which the object is a member, plus the attributes of the general population, plus the attributes specific to the object. A procedure has been derived from the model that meets the preceding four criteria.

The typology of psychopathology is discussed as an example of an applied typology. The validity of this and other typological solutions is quite limited. The development of fruitful typologies is dependent upon the development of typological models and theories appropriate to the variables used to describe the population being typed. A distributional model of clusters appears to be most appropriate for the majority of psychological variables. The type analysis model is offered as a next step toward developing valid typologies.

# Section 2

## The Genetic Bases of Personality

# 12

# Psychological Genetics, from the Study of Animal Behavior

**P. L. Broadhurst**
**J. L. Jinks**
*University of Birmingham, England*

## 1 INTRODUCTION

### 1.1 Individual Differences in Psychology

#### 1.1.1 Previous Lack of Progress

Individual differences are a salient fact of any behavioral analysis, but the techniques for dealing with them are incommensurate with their importance. Nowhere is this relative failure more evident than in the field of psychological genetics, where a whole range of determinants of behavior, often new to the psychologist and attributable to heritable variation, must be recognized as a major factor.

Those psychologists, like J. B. Watson, who took an extreme environmentalist position may be blamed for this disappointing progress. Watson's influence on American psychology, based on the commanding position he rightly enjoyed as the culminator of the methodological revolution of behaviorism, meant that his erroneous doctrines came to be accepted along with his beneficial ones. Thus, earlier contributions of those, such as Francis Galton in England, who perceived the importance of the heritable determinants of individual differences, were not developed, and psychological genetics stagnated in the decades before World War II. A little was done in twin study with humans and in

selection experiments with rats, such as Tryon's (1940) work in establishing the justly famous "maze-bright" and "maze-dull" strains.

Another reason for the lack of progress was the absence of a definitive method of analysis applicable to behavior. This problem was not exclusive to psychology. Genetics itself was concerned with the challenge of the analysis of continuous variation for which Mendelian analysis had proved to be unsuitable. Despite Fisher's (1918) brilliant insight—largely unheeded for three decades—little was done here either until the postwar period.

However, the last 20 years have seen a remarkable development in the methods of analysis of quantitative inheritance. Biometrical genetics as developed by Mather and his school at Birmingham, England, is perhaps the most important and promising for the psychologist; what follows is based on this approach. However, the potential importance of other approaches to quantitative genetics (Falconer, 1960; Thoday, 1966) should not be overlooked.

#### 1.1.2 Multiple Causation

*Phenotype* is a term used in genetics to denote the totality of the properties of an organism, or their measurable potential, and no judgment regarding their causation

295

is implied. Thus behavior is a phenotypic property of an individual just as much as skin or eye color or height. A consequence flowing directly from regarding behavior as a phenotypic property—or phenotype, shortly but less correctly—of an organism is the adoption of the fundamental genetical equation that

Phenotype = genotype + environment,

and a broadly based, essentially biological view of behavioral analysis ensues. This is because the genotype, the conglomeration of hereditary potential, fixed at the moment of fertilization, is now known to have a real basis in terms of cellular composition. Its effects are mediated via the chromosomes carried in the nuclei of the two cells, one from each parent, which fuse on fertilization, and the elucidation of the processes involved is one of the most fascinating success stories in contemporary biology.

But the equation also stresses the joint determination of behavior, on the one hand, by inherent causes—ascribable to heredity, that is, the genotype and, on the other, by external agencies—the environment. These are, respectively, the "nature" and the "nurture" of Shakespeare's description of Caliban (in *The Tempest*), and adapted by Galton for his formulation of the fundamental problems in this area long before there existed analytical methods for their solution. Thus, although individual differences in behavior are both environmental and genetic in origin in varying proportions, we cannot assess the relative contributions of these two classes of causal agencies merely by measuring the individual differences at the phenotypic level. Breeding to compare two or more generations is essential, since only in reproduction can chromosomal inheritance operate and its effects be assessed.

We do not refer solely to experimental mating in the laboratory. The study of parents and offspring, for example, and even fraternal (dizygotic) twins, implies differences in the genotypes being studied. The single exception to this generalization, long familiar to psychologists, is identical twins, reared apart. Their monozygosity allows the identity of genotype to be presumed, and the effects on it of enforced environmental differences evaluated (see chapter 13 by Loehlin, this *Handbook*).

The other term in the genetic equation, the environment, deserves equal emphasis, but needs it less. Psychologists have long been aware of the important part played by environmental agencies at all levels in the determination of individual differences. From patterns of child rearing to subtle nuances of instruction-generated set in the experimental situation, the effects of environmental stimuli of all kinds have been recognized.

### 1.1.3 Special Nature of the Phenotype

The problem of the quantitative variation typical of behavior already touched on, was only recognized as a problem in its own right when psychologists realized the futility of applying Mendelian genetics in its simplest form, using expansions of Mendelian ratios of a complexity that eventually became self-defeating. No longer could the heritable contribution to phenotypic variation be ascribed to the action of a few major genes of large effect. Some major effects resulting in individual differences in behavior can be detected, however. If a major difference in behavior can be traced through a lineage or is inherited as an all-or-none effect leading to discontinuous segregation, the separation of genotypic and environmental effects can be achieved using relatively simple classical Mendelian methods. Examples in man are amaurotic familial idiocy and phenyl-ketonuria, which also usually leads to severe retardation. The latter, however, highlights the environment even in a pathology determined by major gene effects, since some relief from phenyl-ketonuria results from feeding alanine-free diets once the metabolic defect is detected.

But few behavioral differences encountered in man and those animals studied in any detail are of the simple, all-or-none kind. Typically they show small, continuously varying differences requiring careful psychometric methods for their measurement. This is not to say that the extremes of such distributions do not differ in a major way. A familiar example is the distribution of measured intelligence in man. There are arguments about its precise shape—the effect of major genes causing severe retardation necessarily distorts the lower tail—but there is no gainsaying, first, the quantitative nature of the variable, and second, the large range it spans.

### 1.1.4  Special Difficulties in Analysis of Quantitative Variation

The absence of discrete phenotypes representing the observable expression of the effect of major genes, largely uncomplicated by the overlay of environmental variation, necessitates a special methodology. It aims, first, to allow the separation of the phenotypic differences into components attributable to environmental and to heritable variation respectively and, second, to allow the further partitioning of those major divisions. Thus, environmental variation may subsume effects attributable to the life history of the individual, including, among mammals, maternal effects, as well as stimuli associated with the measurement of the phenotype. Heritable variation can be further subdivided into the fixable and the non-fixable—the former representing the additive genetic component and the latter dominance variation, subject to change by segregation in subsequent generations. Assumptions about the genetic model upon which partitioning is based are discussed later. The methodology has a third aim, highly relevant to quantitative variation, to allow the assessment not only of the relative importance of the genetic and environmental contributions to phenotypic variation but also the extent and nature of their interaction. Genotype-environment interaction is fundamental in understanding the genetic bases of personality and cannot be encompassed without recourse to the analyses afforded by the biometrical method.

### 1.2  Previous Methods of Analysis in Psychogenetics

#### 1.2.1  Human Phenotypes

The two methods most widely employed have been used ever since a genuinely scientific interest was taken in the possibility of behavioral inheritance in man, paralleling the interest in morphologic features aroused by the Darwinian revolution in biology of 100 years ago and due largely to Francis Galton, who employed both methods. The first is that of familial correlation, parents with offspring, between siblings, and so forth, of which his early technique of tracing sustained eminence in families is but a variant, and the other is the method of twin study which Galton also pioneered. The combination of these two in Cattell's Multiple Abstract Variance Analysis (MAVA) (1953) initiated a breakthrough in the biometrical analysis of human behavioral phenotypes. Nevertheless, such analysis presents special problems consequent not on the mechanism of heredity in man, shared with all other sexually reproducing species, but rather on the cultural embargo on experimental intervention in the reproductive process which makes the mating of humans for experimental purposes unthinkable in our society which regards any limitation on choice of mate as undesirable, even for overtly eugenic purposes, except insofar as the avoidance of incest is involved. With this limitation is coupled a less severe but equally restrictive one on experimental manipulation of the environment to any degree beyond the trivial.

### 1.2.2  Animal Phenotypes

Most psychological work in the animal field has used selective breeding as the major technique. Selection is essentially assortative mating imposed on a population. The genotypic effect is achieved via the phenotype by mating like with like, so that phenotypes more extreme than those found in the original population are often achieved, usually after many generations of selection. Selection may be bidirectional, creating pairs of strains. Several such strains of rats have been widely used in animal psychology: In addition to the Tryon strains, there are C. S. Hall's (1938) emotional and nonemotional strains and the Maudsley (Broadhurst, 1960) and Roman strains (Bignami, 1965), selected for emotional reactivity and for conditioned avoidance-response acquisition, respectively. Some selection has also been done with mice (e.g., Lagerspetz & Lagerspetz, 1971) and with *Drosophila* (e.g., Manning, 1963). But selection is not a technique well adapted for partitioning of environmental and heritable variation in the way described. Whereas selected strains provide biological material of extreme behavioral interest, little can be derived regarding gene action beyond estimates of heritability.

Such estimates merely indicate the value of the proportion of the genetic variation to the total variation observed: the dynamics of the genes involved, their interaction with each other, and the environment need a subtler approach.

Such an approach is the standard genetic technique of the crossing of purebred strains in the way pioneered by Mendel. However, only recently were there reports of any volume of behavioral work employing this powerful methodology. This is partly because of the emphasis on selection of the few psychologists concerned with psychogenetics in the United States in the 1920s and 1930s, as in genetics itself at the time; but also partly because of the paucity of purebred strains of rats, the subject of choice of the animal psychologist, which contrasts with the greater availability of purebred strains of mice, a species only recently finding favor as a subject for behavioral work of this kind (Lindzey & Thiessen, 1970). The use of *Drosophila* has been limited despite the advantage presented by the numerous strains, many of them well-documented mutants. Moreover, the four (only) chromosomes of this genus make possible chromosomal assays of behavioral phenotypes, though few have been reported (e.g., Hirsch & Erlenmeyer-Kimling, 1962).

### 1.2.3  Plant Phenotypes

The analysis of plant phenotypes has seen the greatest development of quantitative methods. This chapter is largely concerned with the transfer of these methods to the superficially unpromisingly different area of behavioral phenotypes. The success achieved in this translation is probably attributable to the fundamental similarity of the problems encountered in agricultural genetics to those in psychogenetics. The debt psychologists already owe to statistical methods developed primarily for plant experimentation—we still use such terms as "missing plot"—is widely recognized and is similarly dependent on the utility of those methods in the analysis of characteristics as complexly determined as those for which they were originally designed.

## 1.3  Advantages of Nonprimates

The advantages for the analysis of behavioral phenotypes that follow from the use of nonhumans are many, though nonhuman primates share with man difficulties over the extent of the control of the mating systems without offering corresponding benefits to be had from other species. This absence of control over the genotype in monkeys and apes stems not from cultural inhibitions but rather from the relatively long developmental period of the principal laboratory species of primate, their small "litter" size (no larger than that of man) and the absence of stability of sexual pairs, so that unlike human families, siblings that can constitute replicates may be lacking. Though such multiple matings, under certain circumstances, can prove advantageous (see section 5.2.3 on diallels of individuals), the instability of the non-human primate "family" renders comparison with the human difficult. These developmental considerations have meant that no pure or even relatively uniform strains of ape or monkey have been established. While this state of affairs, which obtains in many other nonprimate and nonlaboratory species, persists, the conceptual advantage of studying species more closely akin to our own than the rodents typically used is outweighed by the lack of genetic control.

The principal benefit of the complete control that can be exerted over the genotypic composition of the population or sample studied lies in the simplifying assumptions in the analysis. Thus the purebred strains of rat, mouse, and *Drosophila* that are homozygous, or nearly so, at most important gene loci, make it possible to ascribe variation among litter mates to environmental origin, just as the common genotype of monozygotic twins enables us to assess the contribution of environmental variation in human personality measurement. Crossing and back-crossing such strains will create populations whose genotype can be precisely predicted, with analytical consequences for the partitioning of heritable variation into its different kinds.

Selection can also exert a powerful, if indirect effect on the genotype to create strains, differences in whose genotype, operating against a uniform environmental background, may largely contribute to phenotypic differences observed between them.

Other advantages of laboratory animals, especially, hardly need stressing: Large families, short gestation, and short developmental periods are all obvious. Again, the use of certain genera or species for special characteristics of importance, such as sensory function, may be desirable, but there are other reproductive features of potential interest that do not appear to have been exploited in its service. Examples are the unusual developmental modes of the marsupials, and the regular production of monozygotic quadruplets by the nine-banded armadillo (Broadhurst, 1963).

The control possible over environmental effects achieved by the use of laboratory animals is yet another advantage. The use of rewards and punishments of a type or intensity not acceptable to human subjects is a relatively trivial example; the control which may be exerted over the total environment from birth is not. Such control is of paramount importance in psychogenetics, not only to insure its uniformity the better to display genetical determinants, but also to vary it systematically in genotype-environment interaction. Maternal effects are an environmental feature of special importance in psychogenetics and may be studied in their own right and as a complicating element in the analysis. Thus we regard the environment as operative from the moment of conception onwards, so that intrauterine effects in mammals, as well as those attributable to postnatal maternal behavior, are properly regarded as environmental in origin. Here again, these effects can be manipulated in laboratory animals by a diversity of techniques in ways not possible with humans (see section 2.4.2 on maternal effects).

## 2  THE BIOMETRICAL APPROACH

### 2.1  Basic Tenets

The essential feature of the biometrical approach is that variation is multifactorial, both genetically and environmentally. The genetic contribution is governed by genes inherited in Mendelian fashion and having effects similar to one another, supplementing each other, and being small in relation to the total variation. Smooth, continuous variation of the phenotype arises from discontinuous, quantal variations of both genotype and environment. Generally, effects of single genetic and environmental factors will be too small to follow individually.

### 2.2  Properties of Polygenic Systems

Consequent upon multiple gene control is the balancing effect of many genes, some having a positive, increasing effect and others a negative, decreasing effect in determining the genotypic contribution to the phenotype. Hence different combinations of genes may make the same contribution. Indeed, the more genes in the polygenic system controlling a particular trait, the greater the number of possible combinations likely to make exactly the same contribution. A further consequence of multiple control is that genotypes producing identical phenotypes may differ by as many genes as genotypes producing widely different phenotypes. Thus, even in a uniform environment we cannot infer genetic identity from phenotypic identity, nor can we equate degree of phenotypic divergence with genotypic divergence in any meaningful way. Only a genetic analysis can tell whether phenotypic similarity is due to genetic similarity or to a similar balance being achieved by different gene combinations.

Another consequence of multiple gene control is that the relationship between $F_1$ (the first filial cross) and the pair of inbred strains from which it derives ceases to show dominance relationships in the way possible when the genes involved are few in number. Thus, an $F_1$ lying halfway between its parents on the metric on which the phenotype is measured need not thereby indicate the absence of dominance. Indeed, such a position is compatible with complete dominance at all gene loci but with the increasing allele being dominant at half the loci and the decreasing allele dominant at the other half, that is, ambidirectional dominance. Equally, an $F_1$ that falls outside the parental range does not necessarily indicate a high level of dominance or even overdominance. On the contrary, it is compatible with a low level of unidirectional dominance of genes distributed more or less equally between parental strains. Because of these balancing effects of increasing and decreasing genes and of dominant increasers and dominant decreasers, only a fraction of the potential genetic variation is visible at any time between inbred strains and between them and the $F_1$s to which they give rise. The rest is hidden by internal balancing, but can be released by segregation or fixed by inbreeding and selection. In the absence of a simple relationship between $F_1$ performance and dominance, to avoid ambiguity it is usual to refer to the deviation of the $F_1$ from the midparent performance as potence rather than dominance.

## 2.3  Heritable Variation

In setting up models of the genetic contribution to continuously varying phenotypes, we must allow for the following kinds of gene action and interaction.

1. Additive variation, arising from differences between homozygous combinations of the genes. For a single locus it is one-half the difference between AA and aa genotypes and is usually denoted by the symbol $d_a$.

2. Dominance variation, arising from the deviation between the value of the heterozygote Aa (obtained by crossing the parental homozygotes AA and aa) and the midparental mean of these two parental homozygotes. This deviation is denoted by the symbol $h_a$.

3. Nonallelic interactions, the variation arising from the modification of the contribution of AA, Aa, and aa to the phenotype in the presence of different genes at another locus (B–b). Three types may be recognized: interaction between homozygous combinations at both loci (e.g., AA or aa with BB or bb), usually symbolized by $i_{ab}$; interaction between a homozygous combination at one locus and a heterozygous combination at the other (e.g., Aa with BB or bb and Bb with AA or aa), symbolized by $j_{ab}$; and interaction between heterozygous combinations at both loci (e.g., Aa with Bb), symbolized by $l_{ab}$.

## 2.4  Environmental Variation

### 2.4.1  Nature of Environmental Variation

Environmental variation, defined by exclusion in that all variation that occurs in the absence of a known heritable cause is attributed to the environment, is regarded as operative only after the moment of conception—the point in time at which the genotype is fixed by virtue of the fusion of parental gametes. Two possible exceptions may be noted. The first results from mutagenic treatments, such as ionizing radiation, of the gametes before fusion giving rise to chromosomal and other detectable effects on the offspring. Such an effect is regarded as environmental even though antedating conception, but its expression could be recognized only via genetic mechanisms which are adequately understood. The second exception is environmental effects mediated via the mother and probably hormonal in action, such as premating stress (see section 4.1.1). While some effects on behavioral phenotypes have been detected (see Joffe, 1969, for review), none has been analyzed in biometrical genetical terms to allow the heritable and the environmental components to be distinguished in a way that renders the distinction now being made of practical consequence.

Psychologists and geneticists traditionally have had different views of the contribution of the environmental to the total variation. For psychologists, interest in environmental variation has been paramount. To manipulate the stimulus conditions of an organism in any way is to change its environment, be it ever so slightly. And the more major treatments, even when limited to the course of an experiment, such as food deprivation with animals or sensory deprivation with humans, are environmental in origin. When the total life history of the organism is manipulated, then, clearly, environmental variation is both massive and powerful in its effects. Coupled with such interest has been too often an insensitivity to the importance of heritable variation, with the result that environmentalists have been led into erroneous conclusions sometimes of considerable theoretical consequence. The neglect of differences in the strains of rats used in their experimentation, for example, led learning theorists of the late 1930s and 1940s into controversy that might have been resolved earlier, as H. J. Eysenck (1967) and M. B. Jones and Fennell (1965) pointed out.

Paradoxically, one genetic difference of concern to psychologists is often not recognized as such. This is the sex difference. The exploration of sex differences in human behavior has hardly received the attention it deserves, despite the intrinsic interest of the problem and the wealth of evidence available, for example, on emotional differences (Gray, J. A., 1971). Certainly there has been little work seeking to differentiate the effect of this most important of genetic differences from environmental effects. Perhaps the obviously major involvement of environmental, especially cultural, determinants has deterred workers from making the attempt. At the animal level, the reasons have been different. Sex-associated behavior, such as the reported increase in activity during the estrus of female rats, has often been invoked as reason for limiting choice of subjects to one sex—usually males—only, often with little apparent justification for so doing. But in psychogenetical work, sex perforce has been recognized as a variable, though the exploitation of its potential as a genetic variable has not always been as complete as the experimental designs employed would permit or even demand (see sections 4.1.2 and 5.3).

Geneticists have been less cavalier in their attitude to the contribution of environmental variables. The primacy of their interest in heritable variation is rarely expressed in the total neglect of the component of lesser interest, but rather in an absence of comparable sophistication in handling it. Thus, although the environmental component may also be subdivided into many categories, these subdivisions have usually depended solely on the exigencies of the experimental design. Nevertheless, the rather simple treatment of environmental variation adopted by geneticists can be generalized to cover any degree of complexity desired, as may be seen in the work of Penrose (1954) and others relating to birth weight, which is especially sensitive to environmental influences during pregnancy. Consequently, analysis, based on the study of familial correlations, has been pushed farther than is usually the case. Figure 1 shows the partitioning of the total variation of birth weight of the human infant into the various components. Note how small is the proportion of the variation ascribable to the infant's own genotype, which involves, of course, the father as well as the mother, since the first three segments, reading counterclockwise, total only 18%. All the rest, 82%, is environmental. Whereas much of it (53%) is concerned with identifiable maternal variables, a large proportion (30%) relates to

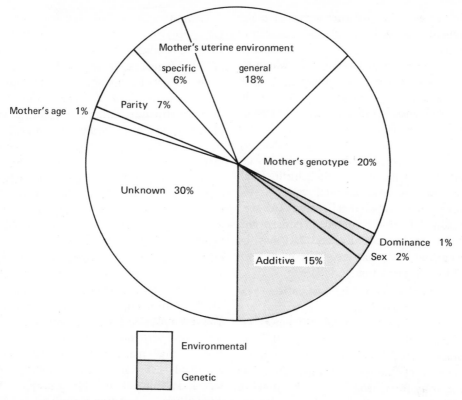

**FIG. 1** The partitioning of variation in human birth weight (from Falconer, 1960; Penrose, 1954). The total phenotypic variation may be divided into various components, each represented as an approximate percentage of the total (see text for further explanation).

unknown causes in the uterine environment. Of the half of the total variation identified, 20% is due to the mother's genotype—the genetic variation, mostly additive, between mothers, in the birth weight of all their children. The remaining 33% of the maternal variation originates in differences in uterine environment, the first segment being general to all the mother's offspring and the remainder specific to particular infants. The mother's age and parity have an identifiable, though relatively small influence (1% and 7%, respectively).

Work with animals (Jinks & Broadhurst, 1963), shows a similar situation with respect to birth weights, though the picture changes if body weight is studied developmentally. Thus, this phenotype shows a genotype-environment interaction that changes with age.

### 2.4.2 Major Classes of Environmental Variation

*Within and between families* One class of variation, recognized and explored by geneticists, is the distinction between variation occurring *within* as opposed to *between* families. While heritable components may also contribute largely to this difference in variation, the contributions of differences in familial environment are also explicitly allowed for in the biometrical model. They are expressed as a subdivision of the environmental variance $E$, where $E_1$ is the variation within families, and $E_2$ is the variation between families. In animals, this difference is often within and between litter difference; thus, the $E_1$ is not complicated by problems generated by differences between individuals of the same parentage in the time of their birth. In all the cases of environmental variation expressed in the biometrical analysis (see e.g., section 5.1 on noninbred material), this distinction between $E_1$ and $E_2$ may be recognized, either as an effect in its own right or in interaction.

*Maternal effects* Maternal effects exemplify correlated environments that can lead to the environmental differences occurring between members of different families being larger than those between members of the same family. They can take many forms ranging from the effect of nutrients contained in the egg, to the effects of maternal behavior in the preweaning period, all of which can be affected by maternal age and parity. This consideration accounts for the superiority, for experimental work in psychogenetics, of organisms having family sizes larger than one, and partly for the interest in twin study in humans. Twins, even if dizygotic, parallel laboratory animals in sharing the same maternal environment since they are born simultaneously (see chapter 13 by Loehlin, this *Handbook*).

Paternal effects can also sometimes assume importance in behavioral work, and considerations related to maternal care will naturally apply in some species. Whereas such is rarely the case in laboratory animals, it is sometimes found in other species, including man, though much subject to cultural determination.

*Cultural effects* The influence of the cultural environment is clearly a variable of some consequence contributing to individual differences. It does not assume the same importance in animal as in human psychogenetics, however, since differences in social structure having environmental implications are not usually encountered. If they are, they result from experimental manipulation of social variables, though something akin to spontaneously arising differences in social structure were observed in experiments involving a "behavioral sink" (Calhoun, 1962). Thus, Southwick (1955) showed that the fate of different colonies of mice depended on the social climate, traceable in one case to the influence of an individual mouse's behavior, which in turn implicates genetic variables. This example illustrates the importance of genotype-environment interaction, and it is evident that many environmental forces identified here are characteristically observed in interaction with genotype. To discuss them in isolation is artificial.

Other aspects of cultural determinants that we may identify in experimental animals relate to social behavior in the context of familial—usually intralitter—relationships. Most siblings interact through the mother, though there is the possibility of direct interaction not maternally mediated. It is dubious that we should identify such effects, if observed, as cultural. But conceptualize an interaction of members of the same litter, having (a) an effect on behavior, which is (b) transmitted socially from one generation to the next. No indubitable examples are at present extant, though Japanese macaques are reported as developing a "cultural" habit of washing food provided for them (Tateishi, 1958). Probably the learning is from parents, however, rather than siblings.

*Treatments* Phenotypic differences resulting from deliberately imposed treatments are familiar in psychology and constitute environmental variation under explicit control. Such treatments can be arbitrarily classified into the long and the short term. The former involve manipulations of the subjects' life history after conception by, for example, direct stimulation of the infantile organism or by treatments of the mother (or father) or of more remote ancestors which occasion differences mediated via the mother (Denenberg & Whimbey, 1963). Such effects may be prenatal or postnatal and are special cases of maternal effects under experimental control. While the treatment may be of limited duration, it occurs at a crucial time in the development of the organism and thus has long-term effects to be detected in adulthood. A single treatment with a steroid hormone given in infancy may modify sexual development profoundly. Analysis of data from one such experiment is given in section 7.2. Variations in husbandry, diet, and so on may be similarly effective.

Treatments characterized as short term are those imposed for the duration of an experiment. They include the whole range of psychological stimuli. Specifically, drugs, both in kind and dosage; conditions of practice; test experience; motivation; and so forth can all be recognized within the framework of a biometrical analysis. Examples are given later.

*Random variation* A final class of environmental variation we must recognize is that attributable to random, uncontrolled, or uncontrollable variation, familiar in ANOVA terms as *residual error variation.* The reliability of the measurement of the behavioral phenotype may be included here, though it is better to recognize psychometric variables as a separate category and treat them accordingly, since such

effects may be strain limited, providing yet further evidence of genotype-environment interaction.

## 2.5 Genotype-environment Interaction

Not all environmentally produced variation is additive in that it affects all individuals in the same way and extent, regardless of their genotypes. Thus we can recognize a source of variation that is neither genotypic nor environmental in origin but results from the specific interaction of both. This contribution is usually symbolized by $g_{ij}$, the interaction of the $i$th genotype with the $j$th environment.

## 2.6 Extrachromosomal Variation

Techniques of detection and analysis have made it increasingly clear that non-chromosomal hereditary factors contribute to continuous variation as much as to discontinuous variation. Formally, this source of variation is indistinguishable from maternal inheritance in some aspects; indeed, it may be one major cause. No specification other than that available for the analysis of maternal effects has yet been developed, and no convincing behavioral examples have yet been reported.

## 3 MODELS AND STRATEGIES OF ANALYSIS

### 3.1 Preliminary Considerations

A comprehensive model for all the genetic and environmental contributions to the phenotype would require considerably more parameters than we could estimate from the information in any one investigation. It is necessary, therefore, either to minimize or discount some components to concentrate on those remaining. Which components we choose depends on such considerations as the aim of the investigation, the subjects, the degree of control, and previous results using similar subjects and environments. If fortunate or perspicacious enough to be working with inbred strains of animals maintained in controlled environments, we can achieve much.

Let us be quite clear, however, that there is no theoretical limit to the complexity of the biometrical model. Indeed, models allowing for situations considerably more complex than those that arise in practice are already available. Hence, where the data are extensive and the investigations suitably designed, methods are available for estimating all the parameters without assumptions. The limitations are practical only and are dictated by the nature of the subjects and facilities available.

## 3.2   Scales and Scaling Tests

A suitable scale on which to measure individual differences is important in the biometrical approach. An adequate scale is one that maximizes the predictive value of the estimates of the parameters obtained. Of necessity, complex effects such as nonallelic and genotype-environment interactions are minimized; we can rarely allow for their effects in the models fitted because of paucity of data. Hence we must usually assume them unimportant and insure this by choosing a scale on which their contributions are minimized. Doing so involves no new principle: The scale on which we measure behavior is arbitrary since it is not based on prior knowledge of how the genotypic and environmental causes act and interact. Transformation of data from one such arbitrary scale to another to improve the validity and precision of tests of significance is an

accepted statistical procedure. A logical and valuable extension is a scalar change that removes interactions and hence improves the predictive power of a biometrical analysis assuming their absence.

It has been amply shown, both with data and models, that scalar changes can achieve the desired result. The number of components to consider when partitioning the phenotypic variation can then be reduced to four: additive, dominance, environmental, and maternal plus extrachromosomal. But certain types of interactions arise that are not readily removed by scalar changes without thereby obliterating the phenotypic differences we seek to analyze. We therefore approach each case empirically.

Since an adequate scale has minimal interactions, we require *scaling tests* to decide whether the criterion is satisfied by detecting interactions present in the data. Unfortunately, tests to decide the adequacy of the scale can be applied only to crosses between inbred strains and the generations that can be derived from them by sib- or back-crossing. We can consider three situations.

### 3.2.1  Mendelian Cross

In the first, we have measured the two inbred parental strains ($P_1$ and $P_2$) and $F_1$, $F_2$ and back-cross generations derived from them. The various methods of detecting nonallelic interactions can be illustrated by reference to the expected generation means on the full model (Broadhurst & Jinks, 1961). These expectations can be given in terms of six parameters: $m$, $[d]$, $[h]$, $[i]$, $[j]$, and $[l]$ [1] which are the sum or

―――――――――

[1] It should be noted that the definition of the interactive parameters $[i]$, $[j]$, and $[l]$ was improved from that given in the reference cited previously. Details are given in Mather and Jinks (1971).

**TABLE 1** The expected generation means in terms of the additive $[d]$ and dominance $[h]$ components and the interactions between pairs of homozygous genes $[i]$, pairs of heterozygous genes $[l]$, and between pairs of genes, one of each pair being in the homozygous and the other in the heterozygous state $[j]$

| Generation[a] | Designation | Parameters[b] | | | | | |
|---|---|---|---|---|---|---|---|
| | | $m$ | $[d]$ | $[h]$ | $[i]$ | $[j]$ | $[l]$ |
| Mean of larger inbred parental strain | $\bar{P}_1$ | 1 | $+1$ | | $+1$ | | |
| Mean of smaller inbred parental strain | $\bar{P}_2$ | 1 | $-1$ | | $+1$ | | |
| Mean of cross between $P_1$ and $P_2$ | $\bar{F}_1$ | 1 | | $+1$ | | | $+1$ |
| Mean of cross between sibs of $F_1$ | $\bar{F}_2$ | 1 | | $+\frac{1}{2}$ | | | $+\frac{1}{4}$ |
| Mean of back-cross of $F_1$ to $P_1$ | $\bar{B}_1$ | 1 | $+\frac{1}{2}$ | $+\frac{1}{2}$ | $+\frac{1}{4}$ | $+\frac{1}{4}$ | $+\frac{1}{4}$ |
| Mean of back-cross of $F_1$ to $P_2$ | $\bar{B}_2$ | 1 | $-\frac{1}{2}$ | $+\frac{1}{2}$ | $+\frac{1}{4}$ | $-\frac{1}{4}$ | $+\frac{1}{4}$ |

[a]Further generations means can be derived in similar fashion, but they are unlikely to be of use in behavioral work using mammals as subjects.

[b]Thus, for example,

$$\bar{P}_1 = m + [d] + [i]$$

and

$$\bar{B}_2 = m - \tfrac{1}{2}[d] + \tfrac{1}{2}[h] + \tfrac{1}{4}[i] - \tfrac{1}{4}[j] + \tfrac{1}{4}[l].$$

balances of the effects over many genes of the kinds of gene action and interaction shown in Table 1.

One method of detecting nonallelic interactions is to derive relationships between the generation means which hold— within the sampling errors of these means— only if interactions are absent, that is, $[i] = [j] = [l] = 0$. For example, in the absence of nonallelic interactions

$$\bar{F}_2 = \tfrac{1}{2}\bar{F}_1 + \tfrac{1}{4}\bar{P}_1 + \tfrac{1}{4}\bar{P}_2.$$

We therefore have the expectation

$$\bar{P}_1 + \bar{P}_2 + 2\bar{F}_1 - 4\bar{F}_2 = C,$$

where $C = 0$ within the sampling error of $C$, which is

$$\sqrt{V_{\bar{P}_1} + V_{\bar{P}_2} + 4V_{\bar{F}_1} + 16V_{\bar{F}_2}}$$

for the sum of the degrees of freedom of the four sampling errors $(SE^2)$ of the means in this expression. A list of similar relationships applicable to mammals that hold only in the absence of nonallelic interactions is given in Table 2.

An alternative method of detecting nonallelic interactions is to estimate $[i]$,

**TABLE 2** Scaling tests and relationships

| Scaling test | Relationship | |
|---|---|---|
| A | $\bar{P}_1 + \bar{F}_1 - 2\bar{B}_1$ | $= 0$ |
| B | $\bar{P}_2 + \bar{F}_1 - 2\bar{B}_2$ | $= 0$ |
| C | $\bar{P}_1 + \bar{P}_2 + 2\bar{F}_1 - 4\bar{F}_2$ | $= 0$ |
| D | $\bar{B}_1 + \bar{B}_2 - 2\bar{F}_2$ | $= 0$ |

*Note.* These are relationships between generation means that hold in the absence of nonallelic interaction, the failure of which provides scaling tests for detecting the presence of interactions.

**TABLE 3**  Estimates of the interaction parameters and their sampling errors

| Parameter | Estimate of parameter | Sampling variance |
|---|---|---|
| $[i]$ | $2\bar{B}_1 + 2\bar{B}_2 - 4\bar{F}_2$ | $4V_{\bar{B}_1} + 4V_{\bar{B}_2} + 16V_{\bar{F}_2}$ |
| $[j]$ | $\bar{P}_2 - \bar{P}_1 + 2\bar{B}_1 - 2\bar{B}_2$ | $V_{\bar{P}_2} + V_{\bar{P}_1} + 4V_{\bar{B}_1} + 4V_{\bar{B}_2}$ |
| $[l]$ | $\bar{P}_1 + \bar{P}_2 + 2\bar{F}_1 + 4\bar{F}_2 - 4\bar{B}_1 - 4\bar{B}_2$ | $V_{\bar{P}_1} + V_{\bar{P}_2} + 4V_{\bar{F}_1} + 16V_{\bar{F}_2} + 16V_{\bar{B}_1} + 16V_{\bar{B}_2}$ |

$[j]$, and $[l]$, as in Table 3. The standard errors of the components can thus be obtained and tests of their significance by the customary methods applied. In the absence of nonallelic interactions, the estimates of $[i]$, $[j]$, and $[l]$ will not differ significantly from zero.

A third test for nonallelic interactions is the joint scaling test (Cavalli, 1952; Mather & Jinks, 1971). Here we estimate weighted least square values for $m$, $[d]$, and $[h]$ from the generation means, assuming the absence of nonallelic interactions. The weights used are the reciprocals of the squared standard errors of the generation means, that is, $1/V_{\bar{P}_1}$, $1/V_{\bar{P}_2}$, and so forth. The weighted squared deviations of the expected and

observed generation means are then a $\chi^2$ with $(n-3)$ degrees of freedom, with $n$ the number of observed generations means. With $\chi^2$ nonsignificant the $m$, $[d]$, $[h]$ model is adequate; hence,

$$[i] = [j] = [l] = 0.$$

The application of these tests to behavioral data is illustrated by the data of McClearn (1961) relating to mouse activity. Table 4 shows the outcome of the scaling tests to McClearn's data, in their original form and after a square root transformation, which McClearn found the most suitable of the ones he tried. The final column shows the extent to which it

**TABLE 4**  The A, B, and C scaling tests applied to mouse activity on the original and on a transformed (square root) scale

| | Test | Deviation | Standard error | Significance |
|---|---|---|---|---|
| | | Original scale | | |
| A: | $\bar{P}_1 + \bar{F}_1 - 2\bar{B}_1$ | 12.40 | 17.78 | NS |
| B: | $\bar{P}_2 + \bar{F}_1 - 2\bar{B}_2$ | 53.00 | 13.38 | $p < .001$ |
| C: | $\bar{P}_1 + \bar{P}_2 + 2\bar{F}_1 - 4\bar{F}_2$ | 84.00 | 36.06 | $p < .05$ |
| D: | $\bar{B}_1 + \bar{B}_2 - 2\bar{F}_2$ | 9.30 | 17.60 | NS |
| | | Square root transformation | | |
| A: | $\bar{P}_1 + \bar{F}_1 - 2\bar{B}_1$ | .40 | .88 | NS |
| B: | $\bar{P}_2 + \bar{F}_1 - 2\bar{B}_1$ | 3.10 | 1.06 | $p < .01$ |
| C: | $\bar{P}_1 + \bar{P}_2 + 2\bar{F}_1 - 4\bar{F}_2$ | 3.70 | 2.30 | NS |
| D: | $\bar{B}_1 + \bar{B}_2 - 2\bar{F}_2$ | .10 | .91 | NS |

*Note.* The units in this and Tables 5–7 and 9 are the number of 5-in. squares entered by 50-day-old mice of 2 inbred strains (C57 black and a standard albino) when placed for 3 min. in a cabinet. From McClearn (1961).

**TABLE 5**  Estimates of the parameters in the interaction model for activity in mice on the original scale

| Parameter | Estimate | Standard error | Significance |
|-----------|----------|----------------|--------------|
| $\hat{m}$ | 58.8 | 35.35 | NS |
| $[\hat{d}]$ | 67.6 | 3.21 | $p < .001$ |
| $[\hat{h}]$ | −8.6 | 81.33 | NS |
| $[\hat{\imath}]$ | 18.6 | 35.21 | NS |
| $[\hat{\jmath}]$ | 40.6 | 18.39 | $p < .05$ |
| $[\hat{l}]$ | 46.8 | 49.88 | NS |

*Note.* From McClearn (1961).

reduces the significance of the deviations from zero, minimizing the effects of the nonallelic interactions.

The alternative approach of Table 3, applied to these data, gives the results in Table 5, which shows the interaction parameters with those for the mean, additive, and dominance components. Only $[j]$ reaches marginal significance on the original scale.

Finally, the joint scaling test yields Table 6. The highly significant deviation from the additive-dominance model on the original scale confirms the need for the square root transformation used by McClearn in evaluating the gene action

governing activity by the strains of mice used. He showed, for example, clear evidence of dominance for genes governing higher, rather than lower, activity.

With no genotype-environment interaction the contribution of the environment to phenotypic variation will be the same for all genotypes. Thus, we can measure the magnitude of this contribution in inbred lines and their $F_1$ crosses since it is responsible for all the observable variation within them. Thus, if the parental and $F_1$ generations are equally exposed to the environmental causes of variation, as in an adequately designed experiment, departures from equality in variation within each parental strain and the $F_1$ will indicate genotype-environment interactions.

McClearn's data provide an example of this effect and the extent to which it can be countered by transforming the original scale. The values shown in Table 7 are drawn from his Table 1. As he notes, "It may be seen that the parental-strain variances have been essentially equated by the transformation although the $F_1$ variance is still greater than the parent-strain variances" (p. 675). Where, as here, the highest variance (the $F_1$) is associated with an intermediate mean, it is difficult if not

**TABLE 6**  Joint scaling test applied to activity in mice on the original scale

| Generation | Generation means | | Estimates of parameters in additive-dominance model | Goodness of fit of model |
|------------|------------------|--------------------------------------|--------------------------------------------------|--------------------------|
|            | Observed | Expected on additive-dominance model | | |
| $P_1$ | 145.0 | 145.68 | | |
| $P_2$ | 9.8 | 8.75 | | |
| $F_1$ | 97.0 | 72.89 | $\hat{m} = 77.216$ | |
| $F_2$ | 66.2 | 75.05 | $[\hat{d}] = 68.463$ | $\chi^2_{(3)} = 17.58$ |
| $B_1$ | 114.8 | 109.28 | $[\hat{h}] = -4.330$ | $p < .001$ |
| $B_2$ | 26.9 | 40.82 | | |

*Note.* Joint scaling test from Cavalli (1952). Application to mouse activity from McClearn (1961).

**TABLE 7** Transformation of scale to reduce genotype-environment interaction applied to activity in mice

| Generation | $n$ | Original scale Variance | Square root transformation Variance |
|---|---|---|---|
| $P_1$ | 19 | 723.7 | 1.3 |
| $P_2$ | 18 | 58.4 | 1.6 |
| $F_1$ | 21 | 1660.6 | 5.4 |

*Note.* From McClearn (1961).

impossible, to find a transformation to equalize the variances. McClearn's square root transformation, while not entirely satisfactory, is probably as good as can be achieved.

### 3.2.2 Diallel Cross

By using a set of crosses known as a diallel cross (see Broadhurst, 1969), we can detect both nonallelic interactions and genotype-environmental interactions using parental and $F_1$ generations only. The test for nonallelic interaction involves grouping the parental and $F_1$ families into arrays, an array being a set of $F_1$ and parental families that have one parent in common and are hence related as half-sibs. Two statistics are obtained from each array, $V_r$ (the variance of family means in an array) and $W_r$ (the covariance of the family means in an array on their noncommon parent). With no nonallelic interactions, $(W_r - V_r)$ is a constant over all arrays. The first of two problems associated with this test is a purely statistical one involving the testing of the constancy of $(W_r - V_r)$ over arrays. Two methods have been used, both of which fall short of perfection. One is to test the variation of $(W_r - V_r)$ over arrays against its own error obtained from replicate estimates of $(W_r - V_r)$ for each array. The other is to test the regression of $W_r$ on

$V_r$ which is expected to be linear and of unit slope, if $(W_r - V_r)$ is constant. Both can be tested in the usual way. The second problem arises because the failure of another assumption, unique to diallel analysis, namely, random distribution of the genes among the inbred parental strains, also leads to the failure of the $W_r/V_r$ relationship, although failures from this cause have rarely been demonstrated in practice.

Since every family in a diallel set is either an inbred parent or an $F_1$ cross, all within-family variation will be environmental in origin. In a properly designed experiment, therefore, we detect genotype-environment interaction by the heterogeneity of within-family variances.

An example of these techniques is found in emotional reactivity in the open-field test, which was analyzed in a replicated diallel cross of six strains of rats (Broadhurst, 1959, 1960). Application of the test of the variation of $(W_r - V_r)$ over the six arrays gave nonsignificant results for both the defecation and the ambulation scores. Similarly, the regression of $W_r$ on $V_r$ did not depart from linearity in either case. Thus the indications did not point to significant nonallelic interactions. The situation with respect to genotype-environment interaction, however, was less satisfactory. Whereas the ambulation scores showed no significant inhomogeneity of the within-family variances, the defecation scores did. A square-root transformation reduced this inhomogeneity to nonsignificant proportions without affecting the linearity of the $W_r$, $V_r$ regression, and the analysis proceeded on this basis (Broadhurst & Jinks, 1966).

### 3.2.3 Triple-test Cross

A more widely applicable test for nonallelic interactions, which has been described by Kearsey and Jinks (1968); Jinks, Perkins, and Breese (1969); and Jinks and Perkins (1970), is an extension of the $F_2$ back-cross design of Comstock and Robinson (1952). No example of this approach is yet available in the psycho- genetical literature but its efficiency has been demonstrated for morphological traits in insects and plants (Jinks, Perkins & Breese, 1969), and a partial reanalysis of some of Broadhurst's (1960) data along these lines has been attempted (Fulker, 1972).

### 3.3 Alternatives in Scaling

Two situations arise. In the first, the scaling criteria are met on the original or transformed scale and a simple model of gene and environmental action is adequate. In the second, no adequate scale can be found; we must either proceed to an approximate analysis making unjustified assumptions about interaction, or fit more complex models that allow for it.

#### 3.3.1 Model Fitting on an Adequate Scale

*First-degree statistics* When the scale is adequate, weighted least squares estimates of $m$, $[d]$, and $[h]$ components of the generation means are obtained as part of the joint scaling test along with their standard errors (see section 3.2.1). These estimates are sufficient to predict the means for any generation that can be derived from an initial cross between two inbred strains. For reasons given earlier, the ratio $[h]/[d]$ is a potence, rather than a dominance, ratio whose value depends as much on the distribution of genes and the direction of dominance as it does on the level of dominance.

*Second-degree statistics* On an adequate scale there are only three sources of variation (if we ignore maternal effects,

etc., see section 4), namely $D = \Sigma d^2$, $H = \Sigma h^2$, and $E$, the additive environ- mental variation. The expected contribu- tions of these three components to the commoner generations encountered in animal-breeding studies are given in Table 8. The square root ratio $(H/D)^{1/2}$ measures the true dominance level.

We illustrate these formulae by the experiment of McClearn (1961) on activity in mice, described earlier. Table 9 shows the components of variation, calculated both on the original and the transformed, square root scale. The value for $H$ is shown as zero because the estimates as calculated proved negative, which is impossible for a second-degree statistic. Consequently, the $(H/D)^{1/2}$ ratio measuring true dominance cannot be calculated, and no differentiation made between "narrow" and "broad" heritability ratios (see section 6 below). Those given in Table 9 are somewhat lower than the values for broad heritability given by McClearn for the two scales (60% and 69%, respectively), based on less exhaustive analyses.

The present analysis, though broadly unsatisfactory, illustrates the difficulties occasionally encountered in biometrical genetics. In this case no scalar transfor- mation can be effective in removing the large nonallelic interactions and genotype- environment interactions that cause the difficulty. Therefore, we conclude from our analyses that an additive, dominance model is inappropriate, but that more data—for example, from second back-cross and sib- mated $F_2$ generations—are needed to de- termine the correct model and to investi- gate more fully the nature of the undoubtedly complex gene action involved.

Next, we must consider second-degree statistics in the case of diallel sets of crosses. On an adequate scale, four genetic parameters are required to account for the

**TABLE 8** The contribution of the additive ($D$), dominance ($H$), and environmental ($E$) components of the variation in the generations specified measured on an adequate scale

| Generation and component of variation | Designation | Expectation |
|---|---|---|
| Variation within a family of an inbred line | $V_{P_1}$, $V_{P_2}$, etc. | $E_1$ |
| Variation between family means of an inbred line | $V_{\bar{P}_1}$, $V_{\bar{P}_2}$, etc. | $E_2$ |
| Variation within an $F_1$ family | $V_{F_1}$ | $E_1$ |
| Variation between family means of an $F_1$ | $V_{\bar{F}_1}$ | $E_2$ |
| Variation within an $F_2$ family | $V_{1F_2}$ | $\frac{1}{2}D + \frac{1}{4}H + E_1$ |
| Variation within a $B_1$ family | $V_{1B_1}$ ⎫ summed | $\frac{1}{2}D + \frac{1}{2}H + 2E_1$ |
| Variation within a $B_2$ family | $V_{1B_2}$ ⎭ | |

heritable component of variation in all the statistics obtainable. The parameters are

$$D = \Sigma 4uvd^2,$$

$$H_1 = \Sigma 4uvh^2,$$

$$H_2 = \Sigma 16u^2v^2h^2,$$

and

$$F = \Sigma 8uv(u - v)\, dh,$$

where $u$ is the frequency of increaser genes and $v$ of decreaser genes. These frequencies are simply relatable to the random mating parameters $D_R$ and $H_R$ (section 5.2.2).

**TABLE 9** Estimates of the components of variation assuming an additive, dominance model for activity in mice, in which dominance is taken as zero

| Component | Estimates of component | |
|---|---|---|
| | Original scale | Square root transformation |
| $D$ | 972.925 | 6.925 |
| $H$ | 0 | 0 |
| $E_1$ | 1025.825 | 3.425 |
| Heritability | 32% | 50% |
| $\dfrac{\frac{1}{2}D + \frac{1}{4}H}{\frac{1}{2}D + \frac{1}{4}H + E_1}$ | | |

*Note.* From McClearn (1961).

When $u = v = \frac{1}{2}$, as it does in a cross between a pair of inbred lines, $D$, $H_1$, $H_2$, and $F$, as well as $D_R$ and $H_R$, reduce to the $D$ and $H$ described earlier.

The contributions of these parameters to the variances and covariances obtainable from a diallel set of crosses are given in Table 10. Application of these expectations can be found in the diallel cross of rats for emotionality referred to earlier. Table 11 shows the components of variation calculated, in this case, for each of the 4 successive days on which the test was administered, allowing a sensitive estimate to be made of the interaction of genotype with changes in environment resulting from the subjects' experience of the situation. The authors (Broadhurst & Jinks, 1966) conclude that for defecation, the test situation increases the expression of genes responsible for low scores, and that for ambulation, genes responsible for intermediate scoring emerge as dominant.

On an adequate scale we can also use the $W_r/V_r$ relationship to infer dominance properties of the genes. For example:

1. The mean value of $(W_r - V_r)$ over all arrays $= \frac{1}{4}(D - H_1)$ after correction for environmental components, hence we can test whether $D$ is greater than, equal to, or less than $H_1$.

**TABLE 10** The contribution of $D$, $H_1$, $H_2$, $F$, and $E$ to the statistics obtained from a full diallel set of crosses, including reciprocals, between $n$ lines measured on an adequate scale

| Statistic | Designation | Expectation |
|---|---|---|
| Variation between inbred parents | $V_{OLO}$ ($V_p$) | $D + E$ |
| Mean variation within an array | $V_{OLI}$ ($\bar{V}_r$) | $\frac{1}{4}D + \frac{1}{4}H_1 - \frac{1}{4}F + E(n+1)/2n$ |
| Mean covariation within an array | $W_{OLOI}$ ($\bar{W}_r$) | $\frac{1}{2}D - \frac{1}{4}F + (1/n)E$ |
| Variation between array means | $V_{ILI}$ ($V_{\bar{r}}$) | $\frac{1}{4}D + \frac{1}{4}H_1 - \frac{1}{4}H_2 - \frac{1}{4}F + E(n+1)/2n^2$ |

2. Arrays with the smallest values of $W_r$ and $V_r$ contain most dominant genes, those with the largest value most recessive genes.

3. By examining the ranking of the arrays for their mean performances and their proportion of dominant to recessive genes, we can see if dominance is associated with a high, low, or intermediate performance and hence infer the direction of dominance.

### 3.3.2 Model Fitting in the Presence of Nonallelic Interactions

*First-degree statistics* Fitting the full interaction model to the generation means needs data from at least six different generations. The simplest set comprises the two parents, $P_1$, $P_2$, and $F_1$, $F_2$ and back-crosses of the $F_1$ to each parent, $B_1$ and $B_2$. These allow a perfect fit solution of the six parameters $m$, $[d]$, $[h]$, $[i]$, $[j]$, and $[l]$, though testing the adequacy of this model requires more than six generations. With fewer than six generations we can estimate only various combinations of the parameters (Broadhurst & Jinks, 1961).

In addition to obtaining an estimate of the potence ratio from $[h]$ and $[d]$, we can classify the predominant type of interaction present from the relative sign of $[h]$ and $[l]$, (Jinks & Jones, 1958; Mather & Jinks, 1971). If $[h]$ and $[l]$ are both significant and have the same sign, the interaction is mainly of a complementary type, that is the pairs of interacting genes have a greater effect when associated than is expected from their individual effects when separate, while if they have opposite signs it is mainly of a duplicate type, that is, the pairs have a smaller effect when associated than expected. This distinction is important when considering the genetic

**TABLE 11** Estimates of the random-mating components of variation from a diallel cross for emotionality in rats

| Day | $D_R$ | $H_R$ | $E$ | Heritability (Narrow), (%) |
|---|---|---|---|---|
| Defecation (square root transformation) | | | | |
| 1 | .24** | .09 | .20 | 41 |
| 2 | .13 | −.05 | .27 | 20 |
| 3 | .06 | −.04 | .22 | 13 |
| 4 | .07 | .05 | .17 | 16 |
| Ambulation | | | | |
| 1 | 3.4*** | .2 | 1.0 | 62 |
| 2 | 3.1*** | 1.4 * | 2.5 | 30 |
| 3 | 4.6*** | 1.8 * | 2.3 | 45 |
| 4 | 4.1*** | 3.7 * | 2.5 | 38 |

*Note.* Units are, for defecation, number of fecal boluses deposited per day, and, for ambulation, number of floor units traversed per day in the open-field test given when adult. From Broadhurst and Jinks (1966).

  *Significantly different from zero at $p < .05$.
 **Significantly different from zero at $p < .01$.
***Significantly different from zero at $p < .001$.
It is impossible to assess the significance of the $E$ component in this way since the interblock difference itself defines the error variance.

basis of heterosis and the genetic architecture of a character, (see section 7).

*Second-degree statistics* Second-degree statistics have not been used to estimate the contribution of nonallelic interactions to the variances and covariances obtained from generations derived from crosses between inbred lines, but they have been used to detect and classify interactions. In particular, the $W_r/V_r$ relationship has been used to distinguish between interactions which are mainly of the complementary type from those that are mainly of the duplicate type (Mather & Jinks, 1971).

## 4  MATERNAL EFFECTS AND SEX LINKAGE

Two phenomena lead to a failure of models assuming that reciprocal crosses have identical phenotypes. These two phenomena are maternal effects and sex linkage. Both can lead to differences between reciprocal crosses.

### 4.1  Crosses between Pairs of Inbred Lines

#### 4.1.1  Maternal Effects

If we make all possible reciprocal crosses between strains 1 and 2, there are two possible $F_1$s: $1♀ × 2♂$ and $1♂ × 2♀$. Producing the $F_1$s by mating sibs of opposite sex in each $F_1$ yields two $F_2$s corresponding with the two sorts of $F_1$ parent, namely $♀(1♀ × 2♂) × ♂(1♀ × 2♂)$ and $♀(1♂ × 2♀) × ♂(1♂ × 2♀)$. Two further $F_2$s are infrequently reared which involve reciprocal crosses between animals from the two *different* reciprocal $F_1$s. The two back-crosses $B_1$ and $B_2$ can be generated in the various ways shown in Table 12. In each generation we can test the means of reciprocal crosses for significant differences without expectations as to the direction or

**TABLE 12**  The various ways in which the two back-crosses, $B_1$ and $B_2$, to two parental (P) strains, 1 and 2, can be generated

| $B_1$ | | | $B_2$ | | |
|---|---|---|---|---|---|
| $P_1$ | | $F_1$ | $P_2$ | | $F_1$ |
| $1♀$ | $×$ | $♂(1♀ × 2♂)$ | $2♀$ | $×$ | $♂(1♀ × 2♂)$ |
| $1♂$ | $×$ | $♀(1♀ × 2♂)$ | $2♂$ | $×$ | $♀(1♀ × 2♂)$ |
| $1♀$ | $×$ | $♂(1♂ × 2♀)$ | $2♀$ | $×$ | $♂(1♂ × 2♀)$ |
| $1♂$ | $×$ | $♀(1♂ × 2♀)$ | $2♂$ | $×$ | $♀(1♀ × 2♀)$ |

consistency of these differences from one generation to another. Alternatively, we can construct models, all having a common basis: the assumption that the heritable contribution to the offspring phenotype has two major components. First, the offspring genotype contributes $[d_o]$, $[h_o]$, $[i_o]$, $[j_o]$, $[l_o]$, and so forth; second, the maternal genotype contributes $[d_m]$, $[h_m]$, and so forth (Barnes, B. W., 1968).

On an adequate scale we have, therefore, five parameters $m$, $[d_o]$, $[h_o]$, $[d_m]$, and $[h_m]$. If no adequate scale can be found, there are various possibilities: interaction among the genes of the offspring genotype; or interaction among the genes of the maternal contribution or both; or, further, interaction between the offspring and the maternal genotype, that is, $[i_{om}]$, $[j_{om}]$, and $[l_{om}]$. However, we proceed on the assumption that such complexities of interaction are unimportant until we are forced to accept otherwise.

An example of this approach as applied to behavior may be found in Fulker's (1970) partial reanalysis of Joffe's data (1965) on the open-field ambulation of adult rats whose mothers had been stressed prior to mating. Table 13 shows the results for these Maudsley strains and their $F_1$ crosses, both for the rats bred from stressed mothers and controls with mothers not treated in this way. We can observe an

**TABLE 13** Estimates of components of the maternal effect on ambulation of rats whose mothers had been stressed prior to mating

| Generation | Means | | |
|---|---|---|---|
| | Controls | Stressed | |
| $P_1$ (MNR) | 44.97 | 35.33 | |
| $P_2$ (MR) | 27.25 | 36.53 | |
| $F_1$ { MNR♀ × MR♂ | 33.45 | 37.40 | |
| { MNR♂ × MR♀ | 28.77 | 24.95 | |

| Parameter | Estimates | | Standard errors |
|---|---|---|---|
| $[\hat{d}_o]$ | 6.53 | −6.83 | $[d_o], [h_o] = 3.60$ |
| $[\hat{d}_m]$ | 2.34 | 6.23 | $[d_m] = 2.55$ |
| $[\hat{h}_o]$ | −5.00 | −4.75 | |

*Note.* From Joffe (1965). The 2 Maudsley strains used were selectively bred for high (MR) and low (MNR) emotional elimination in the open-field test. Units are number of floor units traversed per day in the open field when adult; from Fulker (1970).

interaction of genotype and environment, the latter mediated, in this case, via the maternal effect on the offspring. The maternal effect $[\hat{d}_m]$ is significant only in the case of the offspring of stressed mothers, as judged by the value of its standard error, and not for the controls. The additive genetic effect for the offspring borders on significance for both groups, though the maternal stress has reversed its direction. Thus it acts in opposition to the additive genetic effect, suggesting a maternal buffering, moderating the phenotypic expression of the offspring genotype. The potence effect is consistent in magnitude, though negative for both groups, indicating that genes governing lower rather than higher ambulation in the open field tend to be dominant, a finding generally supported by other experiments using these Maudsley strains.

### 4.1.2 Sex Linkage

Sex linkage expresses itself by a reciprocal $F_1$ difference, usually confined to progeny of one sex only in each genera-tion. In a cross between two inbred strains, a sex linkage leads to a reciprocal difference between the heterogametic (XY) but not between the homogametic (XX) sex in the $F_1$ generation (males and females respectively in mammals). In the $F_2$s raised by sib-mating within each of the two types of reciprocal $F_1$s, it is the homogametic sex which shows a difference between reciprocal crosses. As a result the expectation (Table 2) that $\bar{P}_1 + \bar{P}_2 + 2\bar{F}_1 - 4\bar{F}_2 = 0$ no longer holds even in the absence of nonallelic interactions if the test is made for each sex separately for each reciprocal cross. It does hold, however, if averaged over reciprocal crosses in each generation. Hence rearing reciprocal crosses separates sex linkage from the effects of nonallelic interactions.

Sex linkage also affects second-degree statistics obtained from segregating generations. For example, a single autosomal gene contributes $\frac{1}{2}d^2 + \frac{1}{4}h^2$ to the variance of the $F_2$ generation in both reciprocal crosses in both sexes. Each sex-linked gene, on the other hand, makes a different contribution,

**TABLE 14** The contribution of a single sex-linked gene to the variation of the $F_2$ generation according to direction of crossing Strains 1 and 2, and the sex of progeny, illustrated for a mammal

| Cross | | Sex of progeny | $F_2$ variation |
|---|---|---|---|
| Mother | Father | | |
| $(1♀ \times 2♂) \times (1♀ \times 2♂)$ | | Female | $\frac{1}{4}(d_x - h_x)^2$ |
| | | Male | $d_x^2$ |
| $(2♀ \times 1♂) \times (2♀ \times 1♂)$ | | Female | $\frac{1}{4}(d_x + h_x)^2$ |
| | | Male | $d_x^2$ |

as shown in Table 14. The effect of sex-linked genes on the second-degree statistics is seen by the failure of a model that assumes only autosomal gene contributions, providing that other causes of failure are eliminated by appropriate scaling tests.

## 4.2 Diallel Sets of Crosses

In a diallel set of crosses between inbred lines, each cross must be reciprocal to detect maternal effects and sex linkage. Their contributions to the differences between pairs of reciprocal crosses will be identical to those just described, and hence we detect and estimate their contributions. A number of standard analyses of variance of diallel sets of crosses contain items, for example, the $c$ and $d$ items of the Hayman (1954) analysis, which specifically test for maternal effects. This analysis is readily extended to test for maternal effects that arise from sex linkage and are confined to the heterogametic sex.

## 5  ANALYSES WITHOUT INBRED STRAINS

### 5.1  Problems

Where the subjects are unrelated individuals or prospectively unique members of a population, then the individual rather than a strain or population becomes the unit of any mating program to investigate the cause of variation. Such a situation, common in human psychogenetics, has the following analytical consequences:

1. There is no method of testing if nonallelic interactions and genotype-environment interactions are present on the chosen scale; therefore, there are no criteria for adequacy of scale.

2. The complexity of the mating program is limited by the number of matings in which a single individual can participate, a limitation usually more severe for females, since the additional problems potentially created by maternal age and parity on the behavior of progeny reduce the advantages of repeated matings with the same mother.

3. Since each male and female in the population is prospectively unique, reciprocal mating cannot detect maternal effects and sex linkage.

4. We cannot obtain estimates of the environmental component of variation from variation observed within inbred lines and $F_1$s.

### 5.2  Solutions

Considerable ingenuity of design and analysis, therefore, must be exercized to achieve biometrical analysis within the given limitations.

### 5.2.1  Twin Study

Many limitations are removed, however, in species showing the natural genetic experiment of twinning, the possibilities of which psychologists and geneticists have long exploited (see chapter 13 by Loehlin, this *Handbook*). Not only do comparisons of monozygotic and dizygotic twins raised together and apart allow us to estimate genetic and environmental components of variation and to gain insight into the gene action and the mating structure of the population, but they also allow us to detect genotype-environment interactions and correlations (Jinks & Fulker, 1970). In general, we approach the problem without these special advantages.

### 5.2.2  Analysis of Variance

The simplest design, applicable to all experimental animals, is to pair off males and females in the population at random and to rear families—a biparental design (Mather, 1949). The total variation ($\sigma_T^2$) can then be partitioned into the variation between-family means ($\sigma_B^2$) and the mean variation within families ($\sigma_W^2$), with the expected values:

$$\sigma_B^2 = \tfrac{1}{4}(1+f)D_R + \tfrac{1}{16}(1+f)^2 H_R + E_2$$

$$= \text{full-sib covariance}$$

and

$$\sigma_W^2 = \tfrac{1}{4}(1+f)D_R + \tfrac{1}{16}(1-f)(3+f)H_R$$
$$+ E_1,$$

where $D_R = \Sigma 4uv[d + (v-u)h]^2 \ (= D + H_1 - H_2 - F$ of the diallel mating components) and $H_R = \Sigma 16u^2 v^2 h^2 \ (=H_2)$; $E_1$, $E_2$, $u$, $v$, $d$, and $h$ are as previously defined; and $f$ is the coefficient of inbreeding (Wright, 1921). With the original population itself mating at random, then $f = 0$; if inbreeding to some extent, then $0 < f > 1$; and if completely inbred, $f = 1$.

These expectations assume all interactions absent. Even so, this simple model is too complex for a solution from the two statistics available ($\sigma_B^2$ and $\sigma_W^2$) without further simplifying assumptions, as follows, in order.

1. That the population is mating at random, i.e., $f = 0$, in which case

$$\sigma_B^2 = \tfrac{1}{4}D_R + \tfrac{1}{16}H_R + E_2$$
$$\sigma_W^2 = \tfrac{1}{4}D_R + \tfrac{3}{16}H_R + E_1$$
$$\overline{\sigma_T^2 = \tfrac{1}{2}D_R + \tfrac{1}{4}H_R + E_1 + E_2}$$

leaving four unknowns to be estimated from the two statistics.

2. That of the four unknowns, $H_R$ generally makes a smaller contribution to the total variation than $D_R$ because of its smaller coefficient ($\tfrac{1}{4}$). Where the family size is generally large, $E_2$ will be smaller than $E_1$ because it is based on the variance of family means rather than of individuals. Hence, if we wish an approximate a solution, it is preferable to minimize $H_R$ and $E_2$ by putting $H_R = 0$, and $E_2 = 0$ and estimating $D_R$ and $E_1$ rather than the reverse.

Sometimes we can obtain an estimate of $f$ from the past history of the population, or minimize $E_2$ by breaking up family groups and either rearing all individuals together or each individual in isolation. Raising a second, replicate family from each mating will estimate $E_2$; but problems of maternal age and parity cause this procedure to be rarely used (section 5.1, item 2 in the listing of problems).

Clearly, though this mating design is widely applicable, the information it provides is of limited value.

### 5.2.3  Parent-offspring Correlation

Another simple analysis applicable to the same experimental design is to estimate the parent/offspring covariance. It is estimated as the covariance between the mean scores of the two parents and the mean of their family. This covariance has the general expectation:

$$\mathrm{cov}_{\bar{p}.\bar{o}} = \tfrac{1}{4}(1+f)D$$
$$+ \tfrac{1}{4}(1-f)H_1 - \tfrac{1}{4}(1-f)H_2 - \tfrac{1}{4}F$$
$$+ cE_2,$$

where $c$ (correlation of environments) is the only new term. Again in the absence of simplifying assumptions this statistic provides little insight into the control of the variation, since we cannot estimate the relative contributions of the eight unknowns. Two assumptions, however, help considerably. Thus with random mating ($f = 0$) the covariance becomes $\tfrac{1}{4}D_R + cE_2$; and if we assume that the family environments of parents and offspring are uncorrelated (i.e., $c = 0$), $cE_2$ disappears from the expectation.

The covariance can then be used in one of two ways. First, it can be combined with the estimates of $\sigma_B{}^2$ and $\sigma_W{}^2$, obtainable from the progeny families, thus providing three statistics without adding to the number of unknown parameters.

Second,

$$\frac{2\mathrm{cov}_{\bar{p}.\bar{o}}}{\sigma_T{}^2} = \frac{\tfrac{1}{2}D_R}{\tfrac{1}{2}D_R + \tfrac{1}{4}H_R + E_1 + E_2},$$

which is the proportion of the total variation among the progeny accounted for by $D_R$ (see section 6).

For further information, more complex mating designs may be used, of which the most useful for laboratory animals is the so-called *nested design*. A random sample of males is crossed to a larger random sample of females from the population so that each male is crossed at random to a number of females, whereas each female is only mated once.

We now have three types of relationship among the progeny families, namely, members of the same family or full siblings, members of families with the same father but different mothers (half-sibs), and members of unrelated families with different fathers and different mothers. The total variation is subdivided into three:

$$\sigma_F{}^2 \text{ (between fathers)} = \tfrac{1}{8}(1+f)D_R = \text{half-sib covariance}$$

$$\sigma_{MF}{}^2 \text{ (between mothers, within fathers)} = \tfrac{1}{8}(1+f)D_R + \tfrac{1}{16}(1+f)^2 H_R + E_2$$
$$= \text{full-sib-half-sib covariance}$$

$$\sigma_W{}^2 = \tfrac{1}{4}(1-f)D_R + \tfrac{1}{16}(1-f)(3+f)H_R + E_1$$

$$\overline{\sigma_T{}^2 \qquad\qquad = \tfrac{1}{2}D_R + \tfrac{1}{4}H_R + E_1 + E_2.}$$

Again we add the further statistic, $\mathrm{cov}_{\bar{p}.\bar{o}}$.

By assuming $f = 0$, or alternatively estimating its value, we can separate the effects of $D_R$ and $E_1$, but we cannot separate $H_R$ and $E_2$. We must therefore assume that either $H_R$ or $E_2$ is zero to estimate the other. Making all the assumptions discussed, we can also estimate the

proportion of variation due to $D_R$ as either

$$\frac{2\mathrm{cov}_{\bar{p}.\bar{o}}}{\sigma_T{}^2} \quad \text{or} \quad \frac{4\sigma_F{}^2}{\sigma_T{}^2}.$$

Despite obvious advantages, this design still falls short of a complete solution of the simplest model.

One further complexity of design, though not achieving a complete solution, does provide additional information. This is to rear half-sibs related through common mothers as well as through common fathers. The easiest method of producing both is to mate a sample of males with a sample of females in all possible combinations—a diallel cross of individuals, in fact. Unfortunately, the inevitable problems arise—the limitation on the number of times the same female can be used for mating and of maternal age, parity, and so forth. Limiting the number of matings per female limits the size of the male sample to the same extent since every male must be crossed to each female, and small samples lead to unreliable results. A compromise is to carry out this mating design on small samples but to replicate it on independent samples drawn from the population. The separate estimates of the various statistics from each sample can then be averaged before equating them to the biometrical expectations, in which the total variation can be divided into four parts:

$$\sigma_F^2 \text{(between fathers)} = \tfrac{1}{8}(1+f)D_R$$

$$\sigma_M^2 \text{(between mothers)} = \tfrac{1}{8}(1+f)D_R$$

$$\sigma_{F \times M}^2 \text{(interaction between fathers and mothers)} = \tfrac{1}{16}(1+f)^2 H_R + E_2$$

$$\sigma_W^2 = \tfrac{1}{4}(1-f)D_R + \tfrac{1}{16}(1-f)(3+f)H_R + E_1$$

$$\sigma_T^2 = \tfrac{1}{2}D_R + \tfrac{1}{4}H_R + E_1 + E_2 .$$

Despite the additional statistic, our ability to estimate the parameters is unaffected, because $\sigma_F^2$ and $\sigma_M^2$ share the same expectation. But a comparison of $\sigma_M^2$ and $\sigma_F^2$ will detect maternal effects that inflate $\sigma_M^2$ but not $\sigma_F^2$.

A comparison of these alternative analyses was given by Jinks and Broadhurst (1965), from which the illustrations, again relating to the emotional elimination of rats in the open-field test and shown in Table 15, are drawn. Additional estimates of heritabilities were presented by Broadhurst (1969).

## 5.3 Sex Differences

In the absence of sex differences, we can pool sexes to obtain family means and within-family variances. If sexes differ, one likely cause is sex linkage, which can be identified. Thus, assuming $f = 0$, the full-sibling correlation $(\sigma_B^2/\sigma_T^2)$, estimated from any of the mating designs described previously, differs in magnitude according to the sexes of the siblings compared in the presence of sex linkage (Mather & Jinks, 1963). For example, if we assume $f = 0$, the relative sizes of the correlations $r$ when sex linkage is present are

$$r_{SS} > r_{BB} > r_{SB},$$

where

SS = full sibs of homogametic sex (i.e., sisters, in mammals),

BB = full sibs of heterogametic sex (i.e., brothers, in mammals), and

SB = full sibs of one of each sex.

Furthermore, $r_{SS}$ can be greater than .5—the theoretical maximum—when sex linkage is absent. (See chapter 14 by Gray and Drewett, this *Handbook*.)

We can also use the correlation between parent and offspring similarly. For exam-

**TABLE 15** Comparison of structures and outcomes for various alternative mating designs for noninbred populations of individuals, illustrated with data on emotional elimination in female rats

| | Mating design | | |
|---|---|---|---|
| Item | Biparental $(MS^a)$ | Nested $(MS)$ | Diallel (individuals) $(MS)$ |
| A   Between families | 20.34 | | |
| A { A₁   Between fathers | | 1.858 | 1.5114 |
| A₂   Between mothers, within fathers | | .834 | |
| A₂ { A₂ₐ   Between mothers | | | 2.1338 |
| A₂ᵦ   Interaction fathers × mothers | | | 1.0289 |
| B   Within families | .39 | .171 | .1707 |

| Component | | Expectation | $MS$ | $MS$ | $MS$ |
|---|---|---|---|---|---|
| A | $\sigma_B^2$ | $=\frac{1}{4}(1+f)D_R + \frac{1}{16}(1+f)H_R + E_2$ | 5.40 | | |
| A { A₁ | $\sigma_F^2$ | $=\frac{1}{8}(1+f)D_R$ | | .082 | .0787 |
| A₂ | $\sigma_{MF}^2$ | $=\frac{1}{8}(1+f)D_R + \frac{1}{16}(1+f)^2 H_R + E_2$ | | 0.181 | |
| A₂ { A₂ₐ | $\sigma_M^2$ | $=\frac{1}{8}(1+f)D_R$ | | | .2085 |
| A₂ᵦ | $\sigma_{F \times M}^2$ | $=\frac{1}{16}(1+f)^2 H_R + E_2$ | | | .3239 |
| B | $\sigma_W^2$ | $=\frac{1}{4}(1-f)D_R + \frac{1}{16}(1-f)(3+f)$ $\times H_R + E_1$ | .39 | .171 | .1707 |
| A + B | $\sigma_T^2$ | $=\frac{1}{2}D_R + \frac{1}{4}H_R + E_1 + E_2$ | | | |

| Heritabilities$^a$ | % | % | % |
|---|---|---|---|
| **Broad$^b$** | | | |
| [A/(A + B)] × 100 | 93.3 | | |
| [(A₁ + A₂)/(A + B)] × 100 | | 61.0 | |
| [(A₁ + A₂ₐ + A₂ᵦ)/(A + B)] × 100 | | | 78.2 |
| **Narrow** | | | |
| [2A₁/(A + B)] × 100 | | 19.0 | |
| [(A₁ + A₂ₐ)/(A + B)] × 100 | | | 36.7 |

*Note.* Units are number of fecal boluses deposited per day in the open-field test. Adapted from Jinks and Broadhurst (1965).

$^a$These formulae are only applicable if $f = 1$, as in the present case. For other $f$ values, alternative ratios can be derived, for example, if $f = 0$ (randomly mating populations) the ratios shown for narrow heritability should be multiplied by 2 to correct the estimate, as may be seen from the expectation of the components in this table. .

$^b$Assumes $E_2 = 0$.

ple, with $f = 0$, the correlations between mothers and sons and between fathers and daughters will be equal and both will be greater than that between fathers and sons (Mather & Jinks, 1963).

## 6   HERITABILITY

Biometrical analyses are often summarized in the form of heritabilities. There are two kinds, "narrow" and "broad." In general, the narrow is the proportion of the total variation that is additive, whereas the broad is the proportion of the total variation that is genetic in origin. In terms of the simple additive, dominance model, the narrow form is

$$\text{ht}_n = \frac{\frac{1}{2}D_R}{\frac{1}{2}D_R + \frac{1}{4}H_R + E_1 + E_2}$$

and the broad

$$\text{ht}_b = \frac{(\frac{1}{2}D_R + \frac{1}{4}H_R)}{\frac{1}{2}D_R + \frac{1}{4}H_R + E_1 + E_2}$$

for a random-mating population. Heritabilities, a convenient means of portraying the proportion of the variation ascribable to various causes, also have a predictive value for short term selection experiments. Over a few generations of selection, the expected response is the product of the narrow heritability of the population under selection and the selection differential, the deviation of the selected sample mean from the generation mean (Falconer, 1960). Hence, the expected response is proportional to the heritability for the same selection differential; the higher the heritability the greater the response, and vice versa.

It is possible to estimate the heritability without first partitioning total variation into components $D$, $H$, $E_1$, and $E_2$, as already noted. For example, narrow heritability $\text{ht}_n$ can be obtained as

$$\frac{2\text{cov}_{\bar{p}.\bar{o}}}{\sigma_T^2}, \frac{4\sigma_M^2}{\sigma_T^2}, \frac{4\sigma_F^2}{\sigma_T^2}, \quad \text{or} \quad \frac{2(\sigma_M^2 + \sigma_F^2)}{\sigma_T^2}$$

from the appropriate designs (section 5.2.3). Examples of heritabilities are summarized in Table 15. The results of a selection experiment can also be used to estimate the so-called *realized heritability* by rearranging the expression used to predict the outcome of selection; that is, the realized heritability is the ratio of the observed response to selection and the selection differential.

An estimate of heritability strictly applies only to the circumstances in which it is obtained, although it is frequently used in a looser sense. Thus the values of $D$ and $H$ or $D_R$ and $H_R$ are characteristic of the inbred or random-mating population investigated, respectively. They will not apply to another population or to the same population if changed by selection. Equally, the values of $E_1$ and $E_2$ will be characteristic of the environment in which the subjects are reared, and they will be inappropriate if the environment changes. Hence, heritability is a property of the population and not of the trait. It is, therefore, incorrect to refer to *the* heritability of a trait as if established for all time and all circumstances.

## 7   OTHER CONSIDERATIONS

### 7.1   Heterosis

Heterosis is the extent to which an $F_1$ produced by crossing two inbred strains exceeds the parent which is better, that is, fitter in an adaptive sense. It is an important phenomenon in commercial breeding and it also has evolutionary significance (see section 9).

The expected magnitude of heterosis was given by Jinks and Jones (1958). If the heterosis results from the $F_1$ exceeding the score of the higher scoring parent $P_1$, it is defined as $\bar{F}_1 - \bar{P}_1 = ([h] + [l]) - ([d] + [i]) = $ positive value. If it results from an $F_1$ scoring lower than the lower scoring parent $P_2$, heterosis is defined as $\bar{F}_1 - \bar{P}_2 = ([h] + [l]) - (- [d] + [i]) = $ negative value.

If the appropriate tests show nonallelic interactions are absent, then these expectations reduce to:

$$\bar{F}_1 - \bar{P}_1 = [h] - [d]$$

and

$$\bar{F}_1 - \bar{P}_2 = [h] + [d].$$

In either case, there is heterosis when $[h] > \pm[d]$. Directional dominance, positive or negative, can exceed the additive component, given (a) overdominance or (b) dispersion of dominant genes.

These alternative interpretations differ in having important theoretical and practical consequences that can be illustrated by a two-gene model.

The two crosses of interest are those having parents differing in respect of both differences. These are the following:

1. AABB × aabb
2. AAbb × aaBB

both of which give $F_1$s AaBb.

In Cross 1, where the genes in the parents are *associated* (increaser with increaser and decreaser with decreaser),

$$\bar{F}_1 - \bar{P}_1 = (h_a + h_b) - (d_a + d_b)$$

and

$$\bar{F}_1 - \bar{P}_2 = (h_a + h_b) + (d_a + d_b).$$

For heterosis to be observed in this cross, $\pm h_a$ must be greater than $d_a$ and/or $\pm h_b$ must be greater than $d_b$. The heterozygous state must be superior to either homozygous state at one or both loci; that is, there must be overdominance for heterosis to occur.

But in Cross 2, where the genes are *dispersed* in the parents (increaser with decreaser),

$$\bar{F}_1 - \bar{P}_1 = (h_a + h_b) - (d_a - d_b)$$

and

$$\bar{F}_1 - \bar{P}_2 = (h_a + h_b) - (-d_a + d_b).$$

Therefore, heterosis may arise when $h_a \leqslant d_a$ and $h_b \leqslant d_b$ when the genes are dispersed in the parents, if $h_a$ and $h_b$ have the same sign. Thus, heterosis can arise without the heterozygous state at any locus being superior to the homozygous.

When tests indicate nonallelic interactions present, the expectations for heterosis given earlier in this section show that many combinations of additive, dominance, and interactive effects can lead to heterosis. However, heterosis appears most strikingly when $[h]$ and $[l]$ have the same sign, $[d]$ is small, and $[i]$ is small or negative. These are the conditions in which we have a complementary type of gene interaction (see section 3.3.2, first subsection) and dispersed genes.

To investigate the cause of heterosis we need, as a minimum, the parents $P_1$, $P_2$, the $F_1$, $F_2$, and back-crosses $B_1$ and $B_2$ to provide sufficient statistics to decide if nonallelic interactions are contributing to the generation means and estimates of all components of heterosis with interactions present (section 3.3.2). Although parents and $F_1$s have been used to investigate heterosis (Bruell, 1964; Parsons, P. A., 1967), they are insufficient, unless they are analyzed as a complete diallel, to determine its cause; they can only detect its presence.

## 7.2 Genotype-environment Interactions

The expected generation means for inbred parents and the generations derived by crosses between them in the presence of genotype-environment interactions were given by R. M. Jones and Mather (1958); Bucio Alanis (1966); Bucio Alanis and Hill (1966); and Bucio Alanis, Perkins, and Jinks (1969) and were extended to many inbred lines and a diallel set of crosses by Perkins and Jinks (1968). Assuming a simple additive and dominance model for the heritable contribution, the phenotype of an inbred line $P_i$ reared in environment $e_j$ can be written as

$$\bar{P}_{ij} = \mu + [d]_i + e_j + g_{dij},$$

where

$\mu$ = the mean averaged over $i$ lines and $j$ environments,
$[d]_i$ = the additive genetic contribution to the $i$th line,
$e_j$ = the additive environmental contribution of the $j$th environment, and
$g_{dij}$ = the genotype-environment interaction of the $i$th inbred line with the $j$th environment.

As defined,

$$\sum_j \hat{e}_j = 0 \quad \text{and} \quad \sum_{ij} g_{dij} = 0.$$

In the case of a pair of inbred lines, $P_1$ and $P_2$, reared in each of $j$ environments,

$$\mu = \sum_j (\bar{P}_{1j} + \bar{P}_{2j})/2j,$$

$$[d] = \sum_j (\bar{P}_{1j} - \bar{P}_{2j})/2j,$$

$$e_j = (\bar{P}_{1j} + \bar{P}_{2j})/2 - \mu,$$

and

$$g_{dj} = (\bar{P}_{1j} - \bar{P}_{2j})/2 - [d],$$

where $\bar{P}_{1j}$ is the mean of $P_1$ in environment $j$, and so forth.

Similarly the $F_1$ obtained from a cross between them when reared in the same $j$ environments has the expectation

$$\bar{F}_{ij} = \mu + [h] + e_j + g_{hj},$$

where $\mu$ and $e_j$ are defined as previously and $[h]$ is the dominance genetic contribution and $g_{hj}$ is the genotype-environment interaction of the $F_1$ with the $j$th environment:

$$[h] = \sum_j [\bar{F}_{1j} - \tfrac{1}{2}(\bar{P}_{1j} + \bar{P}_{2j})]/j$$

and

$$g_{hj} = \bar{F}_{1j} - \tfrac{1}{2}(\bar{P}_{1j} + \bar{P}_{2j}) - [h].$$

The expectations of other generations of general interest are summarized in Table 16. These expectations can readily be extended in three ways: first, by adding $g_{dij}$ and $g_{hij}$ to the expectations, with the same sign and coefficient as $[d]_i$ and $[h]_i$, respectively; second, by including nonallelic

**TABLE 16** The expected generation means in the presence of genotype-environment interactions for the commoner generations

| Generation | | Expectation | |
|---|---|---|---|
| Description | Symbol | General | Special case ($g_{ij} = \beta_i e_j$) |
| Inbred parents | $\bar{P}_{ij}$ | $\mu + [d]_i + e_j + g_{dij}$ | $\mu + [d]_i + (1 + \beta_{di})e_j$ |
| $F_1$ hybrid | $\bar{F}_{1j}$ | $\mu + [h]_i + e_j + g_{hij}$ | $\mu + [h]_i + (1 + \beta_{hi})e_j$ |
| $F_2$ ($F_1 \times F_1$) | $\bar{F}_{2j}$ | $\mu + \frac{1}{2}[h]_i + e_j + \frac{1}{2}g_{hij}$ | $\mu + \frac{1}{2}[h]_i + (1 + \frac{1}{2}\beta_{hi})e_j$ |
| $B_1$ ($F_1 \times P_1$) | $\bar{B}_{1j}$ | $\mu + \frac{1}{2}[d]_i + \frac{1}{2}[h]_i + e_j + \frac{1}{2}g_{dij} + \frac{1}{2}g_{hij}$ | $\mu + \frac{1}{2}[d]_i + \frac{1}{2}[h]_i + (1 + \frac{1}{2}\beta_{di} + \frac{1}{2}\beta_{hi})e_j$ |
| $B_2$ ($F_1 \times P_2$) | $\bar{B}_{2j}$ | $\mu - \frac{1}{2}[d]_i + \frac{1}{2}[h]_i + e_j - \frac{1}{2}g_{dij} + \frac{1}{2}g_{hij}$ | $\mu - \frac{1}{2}[d]_i + \frac{1}{2}[h]_i + (1 - \frac{1}{2}\beta_{di} + \frac{1}{2}\beta_{hi})e_j$ |

*Note.* See text for definitions of the symbols used.

interactions; and third, by including interactions of these nonallelic interactions with the environment by introducing gs corresponding with $[i]$, $[j]$, and $[l]$. If we estimate the genetic components from the observed generation means in any one environment $j$, using the formulae in section 3.2.1, the estimate of $[d]$ is in fact $[d] + g_{dj}$, the estimate of $[h]$ becomes $[h] + g_{hj}$, and so on. Hence, the estimates of $[d]$ and $[h]$ will differ from one environment to another depending on the magnitudes and signs of the $g_j$s for each environment.

It was established empirically (Bucio Alanis, 1966; Perkins & Jinks, 1968) that the estimates of the $g_{dj}$s and $g_{hj}$s are often a linear function of the corresponding $e_j$s, that is,

$$g_{ij} = \beta_i e_j + \delta_{ij},$$

where $\beta_i$ is the linear regression of $g_{ij}$ on $e_j$ for the $i$th line and $\delta_{ij}$ is the deviation from the linear regression line for the $i$th line. We can therefore write

$$\bar{P}_{ij} = \mu + [d]_i + (1 + \beta_i)e_j + \delta_{ij}$$

and so on for the other generations.

Where this model fits, that is, the $\delta$s are zero, each strain can be characterized by two parameters: $[d]_i$, its relative mean performance over all environments, and $\beta_i$, the rate of change in the performance with changes in the environment. If $\beta_i$ is positive, the strain has above-average sensitivity to the environment among the strains studied, that is, a greater rate of change, whereas if $\beta_i$ is negative it has a below-average sensitivity, that is, a lower rate of change.

This approach may be illustrated with a reanalysis of data presented by J. A. Gray, Levine, and Broadhurst (1965), again using the Maudsley strains (MR and MNR) and the $F_1$ between them. Table 17 shows the estimates of the various components of the means and their interactions, for the defecation scores observed in the adult rats, separately for the two sexes. The additive environmental components ($e_j$) attributable to the three treatments are larger than their control value in both sexes. Furthermore, the genotype-environment interaction components ($g_{dj}$) are linearly related to the corresponding environmental components with highly significant regression slopes ($\beta$). Hence the performances of the two strains under the different treatments can be described by the simple relationships given in Table 17, which show the MR strain to be more sensitive to environmental effects than the MNR, having a larger coefficient of $e_j$.

A comparable analysis of the less complete $F_1$ data (omitting estrogen) provided by J. A. Gray, Levine, and Broadhurst (1965) shows that the $F_1$ is intermediate in sensitivity to the remaining environmental effects, having a value not significantly different from the average $\beta$ for the two parental strains.

Although similar models can be developed for second-degree statistics and for random-mating populations (Jones, R. M., & Mather, 1958), the only practical application of this approach to noninbred populations was given by Jinks and Fulker (1970), who showed how the special properties of twins can be used to detect genotype-environment interactions in human populations.

## 7.3 Number of Genes

Methods of estimating the number of genes or groups of genes acting together are among the least satisfactory procedures in biometrical genetics. The reason is that they assume that all genes are equal in

**TABLE 17** Estimates of the genotypic, environmental, and genotype-environment interaction components of the emotional elimination of rats of the MR and MNR strains

| Component | Environmental treatments ($j$) | | | | |
|---|---|---|---|---|---|
| | Control | Estrogen | Androgen | Placebo | Overall |
| | | | Females | | |
| $\hat{\mu}$ | | | | | 1.981 |
| $[\hat{d}]$ | | | | | 1.969 |
| $e_j$ | −.794 | −.306 | .506 | .594 | 0 |
| $\hat{g}_{dj}$ | −.781 | −.294 | .494 | .581 | 0 |
| $\beta$ | | | | | .979* |
| $\bar{P}_{MRj} = 3.950 + 1.979\, e_j$ | | | | | |
| $\bar{P}_{MNRj} = 3.950 + .021\, e_j$ | | | | | |
| | | | Males | | |
| $\hat{\mu}$ | | | | | 2.153 |
| $[\hat{d}]$ | | | | | 2.103 |
| $\hat{e}_j$ | −.316 | −.091 | −.003 | .409 | 0 |
| $\hat{g}_{dj}$ | −.365 | −.065 | −.028 | .459 | 0 |
| $\beta$ | | | | | 1.124* |
| $\bar{P}_{MRj} = .426 + 2.124\, e_j$ | | | | | |
| $\bar{P}_{MNRj} = .426 − .124\, e_j$ | | | | | |

*Note.* See Table 13. Rats were exposed at 5 days of age to different environmental treatments, comprising injections of both male and female hormones (androgen and estrogen) to both sexes as well as a group given a placebo (oil) and a noninjected control group (Gray, J. A., Levine, & Broadhurst, 1965). Units are number of fecal boluses deposited per day in the open-field test given when adult.

*Both βs are significantly different from zero but not from one another.

their effects, and the failure of this assumption leads to an underestimate of the number involved. Furthermore, the simplest methods—the only ones applicable to data from animal-breeding experiments— make the additional assumption that all the increasing alleles are present in one parent and all the decreasers in the other, a situation likely to arise only in extreme selections. Failure of this assumption leads to further underestimation of the number of genes. Better methods of estimating the number of genes, each subject to their own limitations, were described by Cooke and Mather (1962). In general their complexity renders them beyond the scope of most experiments of interest in psychogenetics.

Examples of the estimation of the number of genes for behavioral data were given by Broadhurst and Jinks (1961) and by J. P. Scott and Fuller (1965). The latter, however, are subject to considerable objections (Broadhurst & Jinks, 1967).

## 8  FURTHER ELABORATIONS OF THE MODEL

Mather (1949) and Mather and Jinks (1971) showed how models can be constructed that allow for the effects of linkage between the genes controlling a metrical trait and they have been elaborated to cover all situations that are likely to arise in an animal-breeding program (e.g., Jones, R. M., 1960; Van der Veen, 1959). These models suggested methods for detecting the presence of linkage; determining its phase, that is, coupling or repulsion; and estimating the number of linked genes. In practice, however, an experimental breeding program beyond the scope of any laboratory at present except for an organism such as *Drosophila melanogaster* (Cooke & Mather, 1962) is required. Such is the case with procedures described

by Thoday and his colleagues (see Thoday, 1966, for review) for determining the number of genes controlling a metrical trait and locating their positions on the linkage maps.

## 9  IMPLICATIONS

It has only been possible to hint at the implications to be drawn from the application of the biometrical approach in the examples of behavioral analyses cited in this chapter. In several cases no behavioral examples are yet available, though plant data sometimes exist. This situation reflects the tendency for theory to outstrip practice, so that analytical techniques and methods lie fallow while researchers come gradually to learn of their existence. The long flirtation of psychologists with quantitative genetics is a case in point, but the banns have now been posted and there is every hope that a fertile union may be consummated.

One aspect of the methods of analysis of behavioral data described in this chapter is their generality. It cannot be overstressed that they can be applied to each aspect of the phenotype of the organism it is desired to study, given that the characteristic is subject to mensuration. Adequacy of the scale of that measurement can be examined in ways familiar to the psychometrically inclined psychologist, as can the assumptions required by the analysis. The genetic relationships among the groups or individuals involved are to some extent irrelevant, since their consequences are now largely understood and appropriate allowances can be made in the analyses outlined. It is sufficient that the extent to which a greater degree of imprecision of outcome must be accepted, as a consequence of the use of less-than-optimal data, should be understood.

The implications for the study of personality theory are clear. Especially with respect to animal analogues of relevant human characteristics, the way is now open to mount investigations that seek to measure in relatively precise fashion, genetic, environmental and interactive determinants. The implications for theories of personality, especially those postulating an important or indeed crucial environmental involvement, are open to test in a way hardly possible previously, when a major proportion of the observable variation was denied a place in the causal analysis or crudely subsumed under error variance. Moreover, such recognition has other fall-out benefits: Emphasis on the measurement of interaction between heredity and environment forces a consideration of the interactive effects of each within itself. Such a view has long been familiar to the developmental psychologist, concerned with environmental forces interacting sequentially with maturational ones, but it is perhaps less familiar to experimental psychologists who, until relatively recently, often eschewed the antecedents of their experimental material. Essentially we are stressing the freedom that the potentialities of the biometrical analysis of behavioral phenotypes gives the psychologist interested in considering the impact such variables may have on the behavior being measured. The generality of the analyses allows effects to be evaluated in as great a detail as the excellence of his data and his persistence warrant.

The uses to which these relatively new methods of analysis have as yet been put are limited. Examples given have mainly been derived from experimental work with inbred strains of laboratory animals. Applications to human data promise future advances. Perhaps it is premature to suggest the utility of biometrical genetics in psychology, but there are two general lines that can be discerned—one more clearly than the other.

The first is the illumination that findings in this area may bring to discussions of the evolution of behavior. Already, data from work on animals, such as the interaction of heritable components with the experience of the test can bear on hypotheses about the way the behavior evolved—that is, in reconstructing how certain aspects came to be selectively advantageous to the species because of the dominance of the genes governing them. Broadhurst (1968) and Broadhurst and Jinks (1974) explored this theme more fully elsewhere.

The second area in which the biometrical approach may contribute is at once less theoretical but more remote. Its application to human data promises increased understanding of the limits heredity and environment place on each other's expression, so that a time may come in which quantitative characteristics may share with some major gene defects the possibility of being manipulated in their expression by deliberately manipulating environmental influences. For example, environments may be experimentally identified which reduce the stress or provide the necessary arousal an individual's genetic make-up needs for the optimal expression of his inherited potential. Implied here is a considerable program of research to identify the environmentally sensitive and resistant aspects of the relevant behavioral phenotypes in a way more precise than the current, largely speculative ideas we entertain today of what is a good environment for rearing children of various personality types. By the same token, we shall need to determine the extent to which heredity imposes a limit on environmental manipulation. Clearly, these are major tasks, but the social implications are immense, important, and challenging; and the main outlines of the way such a program might be attempted are now, in our view, discernible.

## 10  SUMMARY

1. Individual differences are multi-determined, and an adequate analysis includes consideration of both heritable and nonheritable sources of variation. The techniques of biometrical genetics, though largely derived from plant investigations, can be applied to behavioral phenotypes.

2. The biometrical approach recognizes heritable (genetic) causation; nonheritable (environmental) causation; and the interaction, both between and within these two major classes, as contributing to the observed, phenotypic variation.

3. Analysis involves a concern with the adequacy of the scale of measurement so that interactions between genotype and environment can be detected and, if necessary, minimized, enabling the parameters of the biometrical model to be fitted, using both first- and second-degree statistics.

4. Techniques of proven applicability in the analysis of behavioral phenotypes include the classical crossing of inbred strains and rearing first- and second-filial and back-cross generations and the diallel cross—the method of complete intercrossing of several strains. The triple-test cross also shows considerable promise.

5. Environmental maternal effects and sex linkage of genes are perturbations to be reckoned with but they can be accommodated within the biometrical model and their effects assessed.

6. Analysis using subjects from species for which inbred lines of a high degree of genetic uniformity are not available is possible, but precision of outcome suffers.

7. Heritability is a convenient index expressing the ratio of the genetic to the total variation of a personality trait in a given population.

8. Heterosis ("hybrid vigor") is a complex phenomenon primarily due to genetic interactions whose effect can be assessed. The analysis of genotype-environment interaction can proceed if various environmental treatments to be investigated can be adequately defined. The minimum number of genes involved in determining a given phenotype can be estimated.

9. The biometrical model can be further elaborated to analyze situations of a greater degree of complexity than yet required in psychology: Its application appears to lie primarily in understanding the evolution of behavior and in assessing the extent to which genetic potential can be maximized by optimalizing the environment.

# 13

## Psychological Genetics, from the Study of Human Behavior

**John C. Loehlin**
*University of Texas at Austin*

## 1 INTRODUCTION

If we extrapolate from research with lower animals (see chapter 12, this *Handbook*), it is plausible to assume that the genes contribute in some measure to the variations of human personality and temperament which we observe about us. Furthermore, on the basis of animal, clinical, and cross-cultural evidence, we must assume that environmental influences also contribute substantially to the observed diversity of human personality and temperament. To anyone who is curious about the origin of human personality differences, the question then naturally arises: to what extent are these observed personality differences genetic in origin, and to what extent environmental? At least two qualifications to this question must be made immediately. First, the question might have different answers for different human populations: In some populations greater or less genetic diversity may exist with respect to a trait, or greater or less environmental pressure may be brought to bear upon it. Second, any answer may be complicated by the fact that the genetic and enviromental influences on a personality trait may be positively or negatively correlated, or may interact with one another in various ways. These last possi-

bilities are explored further in a later section of this chapter.[1]

The question of the relative influence of heredity and environment, of course, is only the first of many interesting questions that may be asked, including the following:

1. Can we say something specific about what the genetic and environmental influences *are*, and how they are interrelated? Or can we at least classify them roughly—for instance, into those operating within and those operating between families?

2. What are the detailed mechanisms by which particular genetic or environmental influences have their effects? (In the case of the genes, this leads us into biochemistry and neurophysiology and endocrine physiology—see chapter 25, this *Handbook*—in the case of the enviroment, into conditioning and learning—see chapters 14–18).

---

[1] Some of the ideas presented in this chapter were developed in association with R. C. Nichols at the National Merit Scholarship Corporation during the summer of 1967. I would also like to acknowledge helpful comments on a preliminary version of the present chapter from I. I. Gottesman, R. C. Nichols, S. G. Vandenberg, and S. Seitz. Because of lengthy publication delays, this chapter has undergone several revisions after reaching what was presumed to be its final form. Thus earlier versions that have been cited by the author and others as "in press" differ in some significant ways from the present version.

3. What is the biological or cultural evolutionary history that has led to the operation of these particular genetic and environmental influences at this time in this population?

4. What consequences might be expected if specified genetic or environmental changes were to be introduced?

Questions such as the preceding, of course, are easier to ask than to answer. The available data on human personality do not permit us to proceed very far down the list. Most of the discussion in this chapter is in terms of the simple question of estimating relative genetic and environmental influences on personality traits, although some attention is given to interrelationships within and between the genetic and environmental influences.

Our discussion is restricted in other, somewhat arbitrary ways. We confine ourselves largely to the normal personality, although psychiatric genetics offers many fascinating byways (Rosenthal, D., 1970). The examples we present are chiefly restricted to data obtained with personality questionnaires and inventories, mostly because there is more of it. With certain groups, such as children, ratings have often been used (for example, Brown, A. M., Stafford, & Vandenberg, 1967; Scarr, 1968; Willerman & Plomin, 1973). For samples of the rather fragmentary and inconsistent data from objective and projective tests of personality, the reader is referred to reviews by J. L. Fuller and Thompson (1960, chap. 8), Vandenberg (1966), and Mittler (1971, chap. 6). However, the methods of analysis we discuss may be applied to data gathered by any instrument—there is nothing magical about the use of personality inventories for research into the genetics of personality. By and large, we ignore the technical problems of trait measurement (see chapters 2–8, this *Handbook*) and such methodological matters as sampling biases, age corrections, and twin diagnoses. These are important practical issues in conducting and evaluating human behavior genetics research, but space does not permit covering everything, so we focus mainly on the theoretical models, with some limited account of the results of their application to data. The reader will find many additional matters covered in the texts of J. L. Fuller and Thompson (1960), Mittler (1971), and McClearn and Defries (1973) and in volumes edited by Ehrman, Omenn, and Caspari (1972); Glass (1968); Hirsch (1967); Manosevitz, Lindzey, and Thiessen (1969); Schaie, Anderson, McClearn, and Money (1975); Spuhler (1967); and Vandenberg (1965b, 1968b). Reviews with extensive literature references include W. R. Thompson and Wilde (1973); *Annual Review* chapters by McClearn and Meredith (1966); Lindzey, Loehlin, Manosevitz, and Thiessen (1971); and Broadhurst, Fulker, and Wilcock (1974).

## 2 METHODS IN PSYCHOLOGICAL GENETICS

We may distinguish at least two approaches to the study of genetic influences on behavior; we may call these approaches *gene centered* and *trait centered*, respectively. The first approach takes a known genetic condition and asks: What are its behavioral consequences? The second approach takes some behavioral variable of interest and asks: What are the genetic influences on this variable? (Parallel approaches may be taken in studying environmental influences: One may ask either, What are the consequences of this kind of treatment? or, What treatments affect this sort of behavior?)

The gene-centered approach seems not to have been very extensively explored with personality variables, although one finds occasional remarks in the clinical literature about the behavior of sufferers from various genetically-based anomalies. Systematic personality study of people with known genetic defects would seem to be an approach meriting substantial investigation (Anderson & Siegal, 1968). This line of attack may have better possibilities than some of offering clues to the detailed mechanisms whereby the genes affect personality. Another possibility is to start from genetically based traits with no social stigma attached to them, such as blood groups. An example of a study with this design is that of Cattell, Young, and Hundleby (1964), who administered the High School Personality Questionnaire (HSPQ) to 481 boys in the United States and Italy for whom blood group data were also available. An association with blood grouping was found for only one of the HSPQ scales, Factor I (sensitivity-toughness). Such an association should, of course, be replicated before much effort is spent on its interpretation.

Most of the research to date on genetic influences on human personality has followed a trait-centered approach. Personality characteristics are measured, and an attempt is made to assign the observed variation to genetic and environmental sources. The methods used are essentially those of quantitative or biometrical genetics (Falconer, 1960; Jinks & Fulker, 1970), which has had its principal development in plant and animal research, although a classic paper (Fisher, 1918) used data on human stature.

A basic goal of quantitative genetics is to apportion the observed variation of a trait into various theoretical components. The measure of variation ordinarily used is the variance. The notion of dividing variance into additive components is familiar to psychologists in connection with the analysis of variance and multiple regression, and the methods to be discussed are closely related to these.

In the psychological and genetic literature, the extent to which the genes influence a trait is often expressed by a *heritability coefficient,* which is a ratio of genetic to total variance; i.e., the heritability is the proportion of the population variance that is genetic in origin. Two such coefficients are commonly distinguished, the so-called *broad* and *narrow* heritabilities. The former, sometimes called the coefficient of genetic determination, refers to the total proportion of the trait variance that is genetic in origin. The "narrow" heritability, on the other hand, includes only that portion of the genetic variance that contributes to the average resemblance between parents and their children, the so-called "additive" part (which excludes effects due to genetic dominance and epistasis).

In most behavior genetic literature on humans, the term *heritability* is used in the broad sense; it is in this sense that it will be used in the present chapter, unless noted otherwise.

To partition the variance of a trait into genetic and environmental components, one begins by observing the correlation among persons who differ in their degree of genetic relatedness or enviromental similarity. In animal research, this is relatively straightforward, since it is possible to manipulate matings and to assign animals randomly to well-controlled environments. In research with humans, on the other hand, not only is experimental control generally impracticable, but under natural conditions people relatively similar in genetic endowment (for example, siblings) tend also to be subject to relatively similar environments (for example, the same parents).

However, in some cases (twins, adopted children) these naturally occurring correlations are disrupted to some extent, permitting inferences to be made about the relative impact of genetic and enviromental factors on the traits under investigation.

Methods have been developed based on *resemblances* among individuals and on *differences* among individuals. The measure of resemblance most often used is the intraclass correlation coefficient. The commonest measure of difference is the within-group (or within-pair) variance. These are simply related:

$$r_{\text{intraclass}} = \frac{V_B}{V_B + V_W},$$

where $V_W$ and $V_B$ are the within- and between-groups components of variance, respectively. For estimating these components from family data, the methods of Jinks and Fulker (1970) or Elston and Gottesman (1968) may be used. In the present chapter we symbolyze the intraclass correlation coefficient based on a particular group by $r$ plus a suitable subscript: Thus $r_{\text{IT}}$ is used for identical twins reared together in their natural families, $r_{\text{SA}}$ for genetic siblings reared apart in separate families, $r_{\text{UT}}$ for unrelated children reared together (by adoption), and so on. The intraclass correlation expresses the extent to which individuals in the specified relationship are more alike on the trait in question than are unselected individuals: Thus $r_{\text{IT}}$ expresses the extent to which members of identical twin pairs are more alike on some trait than individuals from the population paired at random.

First we present formulas for apportioning variance using the intraclass correlations of identical and fraternal twins, and then methods based on adopted children. Finally, we consider the advantages of com-

bining different groups into a single design, as proposed by Cattell (1953b, 1960a). Each set of formulas yields estimates of the proportions of genetic and enviromental variance within and between families, which we symbolize by $V_{\text{WG}}$, $V_{\text{WE}}$, $V_{\text{BG}}$, and $V_{\text{BE}}$. For simplicity, we assume that any appropriate adjustments for age differences, restriction of range, or test unreliability have already been made to the correlations.

## 3 TWIN DESIGNS

In the case of twins, we may use the following formulas:

$$V_{\text{WE}} = (1 - k_1 k_2 r_{\text{IT}}) + (1 - k_2) r_{\text{FT}},$$
$$V_{\text{WG}} = (1 - k_2 r_{\text{FT}}) - V_{\text{WE}},$$
$$V_{\text{BG}} = k_3 V_{\text{WG}}, \text{ and}$$
$$V_{\text{BE}} = k_2 r_{\text{FT}} - V_{\text{BG}}.$$

The intraclass correlations $r_{\text{IT}}$ and $r_{\text{FT}}$ are obtained from the data. The parameters $k_1$, $k_2$, and $k_3$ represent assumptions that must be made, explicitly or implicitly, in obtaining the theoretical variance proportions. These parameters may be (and often are) assumed to be unity, in which case they may be dropped from the equations; however, there are obvious advantages in making this process explicit.

The first parameter, $k_1$, reflects the possibility that identical twins may systematically be treated more alike with respect to the trait in question than are fraternal twins. This parameter is discussed in more detail shortly.

The second parameter, $k_2$, adjusts for a possible difference in environmental similarity between fraternal twins and ordinary siblings. This parameter can be estimated empirically, if data from both twin and sibling pairs are available. Or, given sib data, one could simply substitute $r_{ST}$ for $k_2 r_{FT}$ in the equations for $V_{WE}$, $V_{WG}$, and $V_{BG}$. Most available evidence does not suggest very large differences between $r_{FT}$ and $r_{ST}$ for personality traits. Crook (1937), in summarizing a number of earlier studies, gave an average correlation of .22 for fraternal twins and .19 for siblings. Comparable average correlations calculated from the data of Cattell, Blewett, and Beloff (1955) are .20 and .23, respectively. Fraternal twin correlations of about this magnitude remain typical—the median $r_{FT}$ for assorted personality scales was .19 in the studies surveyed by Vandenberg (1967b); corresponding recent sibling data seem to be scanty. On the whole, then, $k_2 = 1.0$ is probably defensible as a first approximation in the personality domain, although one might wish to question this for particular traits.

The third parameter, $k_3$, permits allowance to be made for assortative mating and genetic dominance or epistasis. This parameter equals $r_{gs}/(1 - r_{gs})$, where $r_{gs}$ is the genetic correlation between siblings; thus $k_3$ is 1.0 when $r_{gs}$ is .50—the value expected if all genetic variance is additive and mating is random. The presence of positive assortative mating (the tendency of like to marry like) in the parental generation tends to raise $r_{gs}$ and $k_3$, and the presence of negative assortative mating or nonadditive genetic variance tends to depress both.

In quantitative terms,

$$r_{gs} = 1/4 \, (1 + c_2 + 2c_1 c_2{}^2 m),$$

where $m$ is the phenotypic (observed) correlation between spouses on the trait in question, $c_1$ is the proportion of the variance that is genetic, and $c_2$ is the proportion of the genetic variance that is additive. (The equation derives from Fisher, 1918—see also Crow & Felsenstein, 1968, or Jinks & Fulker, 1970).

Low positive assortative mating probably prevails in the personality domain. Spouse correlations appear to average around .15 for personality traits (Anastasi, 1958, p. 280). The extent to which nonadditive genetic variance is present is less clear. There is no reason to suspect a very close association of most personality traits with reproductive fitness, and thus the genetic variance present might be expected to be mostly additive in character. On the other hand, patterns of electrical activity in the brain are not very closely associated with reproductive fitness either, so far as anyone knows, yet their correlations in identical and fraternal twins rather strongly suggest marked genetic nonadditivity (see, e.g., Buchsbaum, 1974; Lykken, Tellegen & Thorkelson, 1974).

Thus $k_3$ conceivably could be appreciably less than 1.0 for personality traits; however, it is unlikely that it would be much greater than 1.0.

Let us return to the parameter $k_1$. Is it reasonable to assume that the environments affecting the development of personality are as different for members of identical as for members of fraternal twin pairs? If so, we may set $k_1 = 1.0$. Most users of twin data have explicitly or implicitly made this equal-environment assumption. On the face of it, it seems implausible. Identical twins tend to spend more time together than fraternal twins, and have more common close associates (Jones, H. E., 1955; Koch, H. L., 1966; Smith, R. T., 1965). Peers and teachers respond to them more similarly (Sells & Roff, 1967). In addition, the other twin presumably constitutes an important part of the environment affecting personality development: insofar as identical twins are more alike than fraternals, they have more similar environments in this respect as well. Parental beliefs about the twins' zygosity might also play a role, although Scarr (1968) presented some contrary evidence. All this suggests that the value of $k_1$ should be less than 1.0.

However, there is another line of argument holding that twins' environments may be, in an important sense, more dissimilar than those of nontwins. The environment in question here is the dynamic interpersonal one created by the twins' and others' efforts to differentiate the twins from each other. Thus one twin may come to be identified as the extrovert and one as the introvert, one as the leader and one as the follower, and so on. This negative correlation built into the social pressures on the twins might require that $k_1$ (and perhaps $k_2$) be given values *greater* than 1.0. Such a "contrast effect" has been proposed as fitting the data for personality traits in the extroversion-introversion domain by Shields (1962), Jinks and Fulker (1970), and Elston and Gottesman (1968). The similarity of appearance of twins may also be a factor—the pressure for behavioral differentiation may be greater when it is difficult to distinguish the twins physically (Plomin, Willerman, & Loehlin, in press).

A third possibility exists: that any greater (or lesser) similarity of twins' environments may not, in fact, be relevant to the personality trait under consideration. This is subject to empirical test: Given an appropriate measure of environmental similarity, one can correlate it with personality trait differences over pairs *within* the two twin groups. In one study (Bloch, 1969), while a greater similarity of identical twin environments was demonstrated, it proved to be independent of the variable of interest; hence the equal-environment assumption could appropriately be made. A similar lack of association between a number of environmental differences and personality trait differences has been reported from the extensive data of the National Merit Twin Study (Loehlin & Nichols, in press).

In short, the traditional assumptions of the twin method, that $k_1$ and $k_3$ are equal to unity, are not lightly to be made, for personality traits. Can these parameters be estimated empirically? One possible approach to doing this is outlined in an appendix to the present chapter.

The design for twin data analysis just described can be related to several other methods proposed for estimating heritability from twin data. Three such formulas are Holzinger's (Newman, Freeman, & Holzinger, 1937), Nichols' (1965), and Jensen's (1967b), which are, in our symbolism, respectively:

$$\frac{r_{IT} - r_{FT}}{1 - r_{FT}}, \frac{2(r_{IT} - r_{FT})}{r_{IT}}, \text{ and } \frac{r_{IT} - r_{FT}}{1 - r_{gs}}$$

For all the formulas (except Nichols', where correction is automatic), one may or may not elect to correct for unreliability of measurement (by dividing the computed $r$ by the reliability coefficient of the test). If uncorrected, the coefficient expresses the genetic variance as a proportion of the total variance; if corrected, as a proportion of the reliable variance. If good estimates of reliability are available, the latter is perhaps the more meaningful, but the correction can lead to bizarre results if reliabilities are low and poorly estimated.

The numerators of all three heritability formulas are based on the subtraction ($r_{IT} - r_{FT}$), but their denominators differ. Jensen's formula is equivalent to heritability as estimated via the twin design presented in this chapter, if $k_1$ and $k_2$ are assumed equal to unity. Holzinger's formula gives the proportion of genetic variance within twin pairs, under the assumption $k_1 = 1$; this will equal the proportion of genetic variance within families if $k_2 = 1$ and will be an estimate of overall heritability if the ratio of genetic to environmental variance is the same within as between families, an assumption that may be difficult to justify. Nichols' formula is an estimate of the ratio $(V_{WG} + V_{BG}) / (V_{WG} + V_{BG} + V_{BE})$, under the assumptions $k_1 = k_2 = k_3 = 1$. The formula has the practical advantage of an automatic adjustment for error of measurement, but this also subjects it to some hazards if the intraclass correlations are low (Nichols, 1969). In any case, it does not estimate the same quantity as the others, unless $V_{WE}$ is zero.

Note that all three formulas make the equal-environments assumption $k_1 = 1$.

# 4 RESULTS OF TWIN STUDIES

Estimates of genetic effects from twin studies are usually based on the difference in correlation between identical and same-sex fraternal twins. Typical intraclass correlations obtained on personality inventory scales in a number of different twin studies in the United States and Europe are shown in Table 1. The values given are the medians over the set of personality scales used in each study. These values range from .26 to .60 for the identical twins, with a median of .48, and from .00 to .37 for the fraternals, with a median of .24. The correlations for many of the individual studies are subject to large sampling errors (see next section), but the total numbers of twins involved in the table are fairly substantial, 2,028 identical and 1,428 fraternal pairs, so the overall medians ought to be reasonably dependable.

The implications that these average values of .48 and .24 have for estimates of the heritability of typical personality traits depend on the assumptions made about $k_1$, $k_2$, and $k_3$, and the reliability of the scales. If all three parameters are assumed equal to 1.0 and .75 is taken as the typical scale reliability, the estimate of $V_G$ is .64, with

$V_{WE}$ and $V_{BE}$ equal to .36 and .00, respectively.

However, in 6 of the 16 samples, the median values obtained are inconsistent with a model that assumes purely additive genetic variance plus common environmental variance equal for both identicals and fraternals $(k_1 = k_3 = 1)$ unless sampling error is invoked to save the model. In these studies the difference between the typical $r_I$ and $r_F$ exceeds $r_F$, and twice that difference exceeds $r_I$—outcomes impossible under the model. If $k_1$ is taken as .9 and $k_3$ as .65 (see Appendix), five of the six discrepant studies yield acceptable average values. These assumptions lead to estimates of $V_G = .42$, $V_{WE} = .42$, and $V_{BE} = .15$, for the overall median intraclass correlations of Table 1. As we shall see, studies of identical twins reared apart suggest a bit higher heritabilities than this, although the data in that case are much more limited.

Table 1 shows only typical values for identical and fraternal twin correlations on personality inventory scales. Obviously, in any particular study some range of correlations, and of differences between identical and fraternal twin correlations, will be found for different traits. Are these differences dependable, in the sense that certain traits will tend to show consistently higher heritabilities than others? In principle, one can hardly doubt that this must be the case, to some degree at least. But in practice it has proven remarkably difficult to demonstrate consistent differences in heritability among personality traits. In their review, W. R. Thompson and Wilde (1973) noted a failure of such consistent differences to emerge when the two sexes are compared. Loehlin and Nichols (in press) examined the general question in some detail in the National Merit Twin Study data and in the literature and observed a surprising lack of consistent high or low heritabilities among traits in the

**TABLE 1** Median identical (I) and fraternal (F) intraclass correlations on personality inventory scales in various twin studies

| Study | Number of pairs | | Median correlation | | No. of scales | Inventory[a] |
|---|---|---|---|---|---|---|
| | I | F | I | F | | |
| Carter (1935) | 40 | 43 | .60 | .33 | 4 | Bernreuter |
| Newman, Freeman, & Holzinger (1937) | 50 | 50 | .56 | .37 | 1 | Woodworth |
| Vandenberg (1962) | 45 | 35 | .55 | .00[b] | 7 | Thurstone |
| Gottesman (1963) | 34 | 34 | .45 | .21[b] | 31 | HSPQ, MMPI |
| Wilde (1964a) | 88 | 42 | .50 | .34 | 4 | Amsterdam BV |
| Gottesman (1966)[c] | 79 | 68 | .48 | .31 | 18 | CPI |
| Partanen, Bruun, & Markkanen (1966) | 157 | 189 | .26 | .18 | 4 | Special |
| Nichols (1965)[d] | | | | | | |
| Males | 207 | 126 | .53 | .25[b] | 24 | CPI |
| Females | 291 | 193 | .50 | .35 | 24 | CPI |
| Vandenberg et al. (1967) | 111 | 92 | .47 | .24 | 12 | Comrey |
| Schoenfeldt (1968) | | | | | | |
| Males | 150 | 53 | .40 | .36 | 7 | Factors |
| Females | 187 | 103 | .49 | .33 | 7 | Factors |
| Canter | 39 | 44 | .37 | .15[b] | 31 | EPI, Foulds, 16PF |
| Eaves & Eysenck (1975) | | | | | | |
| Males | 120 | 59 | .42 | .21 | 2 | PEN |
| Females | 331 | 198 | .42 | .15[b] | 2 | PEN |
| Horn, Plomin, & Rosenman (1976) | 99 | 99 | .46 | .18[b] | 18 | CPI |
| Median | | | .48 | .24 | | |

*Note.* Studies with less than 30 pairs of each kind not included. The Wilde, Partanen, Canter, Horn, and Eaves studies used adult twins, remaining studies used adolescent twins. Partanen and Horn sampled all males; other sexes combined unless indicated. All fraternal pairs like-sexed.

[a]HSPQ = High School Personality Questionnaire; CPI = California Psychological Inventory; MMPI = Minnesota Multiphasic Personality Inventory, BV = Biographical Questionnaire; EPI = Eysenck Personality Inventory; PF = Personality Factor; PEN = Psychoticism, Extraversion, Neuroticism.

[b]Correlations inconsistent with $k_1 = k_3 = 1$ (see text).

[c]Data reported in another form in source cited, intraclass correlations courtesy the author.

[d]See Nichols (1969).

personality, interest, and even ability domains. Political, social, and religious attitudes, however, do show evidence of consistently lower heritabilities than personality traits in their data. Not everyone agrees with this assessment of the evidence concerning differential personality trait heritability. For instance, J. M. Horn, Plomin, and Rosenman (in press) expressed a more optimistic view.

## 5  SAMPLING ERRORS

If one is interested in estimating the relative influence of genes and environment upon behavioral traits (in contrast to demonstrating merely that some nonzero degree of genetic—or environmental—influence exists) fairly sizable samples are required, substantially larger than those typically reported in the literature.

An approximate standard error for a heritability coefficient based on twin data may be obtained from the following expression (Loehlin, Lindzey, & Spuhler, 1975, p. 288):

$$\sigma_{h^2} = 2 \sqrt{\frac{(1 - r_{\mathrm{IT}}{}^2)^2}{N_{\mathrm{IT}}} + \frac{(1 - r_{\mathrm{FT}}{}^2)^2}{N_{\mathrm{FT}}}}$$

where the $N$s are the number of pairs in the two twin groups, and the $r$s are the intraclass correlations. Jensen's formula or its equivalent is assumed, with $r_{gs} = .5$ ($k_3 = 1$).

For illustrative purposes, Table 2 shows the approximate sampling errors if the two $N$s are equal and the identical twin and fraternal twin correlations are .5 and .3 respectively.

It should be clear from Table 2 that if one wishes dependably to distinguish, say, heritability coefficients of .40 from heritability coefficients of .60, one needs to use large samples of twins. The many inconsistencies in the twin-study literature are all

TABLE 2  Sample size and approximate standard errors of heritability coefficients from twin designs

| $N^a$ | Approximate standard error |
|---|---|
| 25 | .47 |
| 50 | .33 |
| 100 | .24 |
| 200 | .17 |
| 400 | .12 |
| 800 | .08 |
| 1,600 | .06 |

[a]Number of pairs in each of the 2 twin groups.

too intelligible: Until recent years the typical such study has used on the order of 40 or 50 pairs of each kind. Fortunately, large-scale twin studies are becoming increasingly feasible, by identifying twins in mass testings carried out for other purposes (Husén, 1959; Nichols, 1965; Schoenfeldt, 1968).

## 6  FOSTER SIBLING DESIGNS

Comparison of natural and adopted siblings provides an alternative way of making inferences about heredity and environment, although this approach has been little used, compared with the twin method. Two designs may be employed, one starting from genetically unrelated children reared together by adoption, the other based on siblings adopted into separate homes. Equations for each design are given as follows:

$$V_{\mathrm{BE}} = k_4 r_{\mathrm{UT}},$$

$$V_{\mathrm{BG}} = r_{\mathrm{ST}} - V_{\mathrm{BE}},$$

$$V_{\mathrm{WG}} = V_{\mathrm{BG}}/k_3,$$

$$V_{\mathrm{WE}} = (1 - r_{\mathrm{ST}}) - V_{\mathrm{WG}},$$

$$V_{BG} = k_5 r_{SA},$$

$$V_{BE} = r_{ST} - V_{BG}, \text{ and}$$

$$\left.\begin{array}{l} V_{WG} \\ V_{WE} \end{array}\right\} \text{same as above.}$$

The $V$s represent proportions of variance, as before. The $r$s represent intraclass correlations within sets of siblings reared together or apart, or unrelated children reared together in the same family. The parameter $k_3$ is the same as that used in the twin design, and represents the assumptions made concerning assortative mating and nonadditive genetic variance. The parameters $k_4$ and $k_5$ represent the particular assumptions made about adoption.

The parameter $k_4$ allows for the fact that the correlation between genetically unrelated children reared together by adoption may underestimate or overestimate the normal effects of common family environment. Genetically, it makes no difference whether these children are adopted and natural children in a family or unrelated adopted children: A comparison of such families could shed light on some of the environmental assumptions. In any case, if families containing adopted children treat their children more differentially, $r_{UT}$ will be too low. Selective placement will also affect $r_{UT}$. Restriction in the range of infants available for adoption, or the placing of infants into homes systematically like (or systematically unlike) the homes from which they came, will tend to result in the two infants placed in a given home being more alike than if placement were purely random. If such selection is related to the trait in question, $r_{UT}$ will be too high.

In the second set of equations, the parameter $k_5$ allows for the fact that siblings adopted into separate families may be more (or less) alike than their genetic relatedness

would suggest. Within-family differentiation of treatment should play a lesser role here than in the first design, since the two persons are in different families. However, any culturally standardized "adopted child" treatment would tend to inflate $r_{SA}$. Selective placement would presumably tend to operate in the same direction: the homes into which two sibs were placed would be less different than under random placement.

The effect of selective placement on the variance estimates is opposite in the two designs—in the one case leading to an underestimate of $V_{BG}$ and in the other to an overestimate. Thus the simultaneous execution of both designs would permit an evaluation of this factor.

The situation with regard to sampling error is somewhat more favorable for the foster sib designs than for the twin designs, especially for the second design, where the heritability estimate is obtained from only one intraclass correlation. This means that the standard error will be smaller by a factor of about $\sqrt{2}$, and the number of pairs required for a given level of accuracy is approximately halved. Use of large samples of the more readily available ordinary sib pairs will have beneficial effects on sampling error in both foster sib designs.

## 7 IDENTICAL TWINS REARED APART

Another often-discussed design, involving both twins and adoption, compares identical twins reared apart in separate families with those reared together (Juel-Nielsen, 1965; Newman, Freeman, & Holzinger, 1937; Shields, 1962). This design permits the following analysis:

$$V_G = k_6 r_{IA},$$

$$V_E = 1 - V_G,$$

$$V_{WE} = 1 - k_1 r_{IT},$$

$$V_{BE} = V_E - V_{WE},$$

$$V_{WG} = V_G/(1 + k_3), \text{ and}$$

$$V_{BG} = V_G - V_{WG}.$$

The parameters $k_1$ and $k_3$ have the same meanings as in the ordinary twin design ($k_2 = 1$ is implicitly assumed in the third equation). The parameter $k_6$ is analogous to $k_5$, and adjusts for any tendency of separated twins to be placed in homes more similar than those of the population at large (surely a likely occurrence, although see Burt, 1966b). This design, then, is not necessarily more powerful or free from assumptions than the other foster sib designs, and is inherently plagued by small sample size. It gives a more immediate division into total genetic and environmental variance, however, than the other designs we have discussed.

Newman, Freeman and Holzinger (1937) reported a correlation of .58 on the Woodworth-Mathews neuroticism scale for their 19 separated identical pairs. And Shields (1962), with 42 such pairs, obtained correlations of .61 and .53 on scales of Extraversion and Neuroticism. While the numbers of pairs are small, with correspondingly large sampling errors, the studies are in fairly good agreement, and for plausible values of $k_6$ tend to suggest that some two-thirds of the reliable variance of these traits may be genetic in origin. Given the rather lower values of $V_G$ obtained earlier via identical-fraternal comparisons, this result should be taken cautiously.

## 8 OTHER FAMILY CONFIGURATIONS

In addition to twin, sibling, and foster-sib groups, other correlations such as those between parent and child, half-siblings, cousins, or other relatives, may under some circumstances yield valuable information. Unfortunately, in human populations genetic and environmental correlations tend to run parallel in most such cases, making differential inference difficult. Some exceptions, however, may be worth noting:

1. The adoption situation may yield other unconfounded family correlations, such as parent-child, in addition to the sibling correlations mentioned earlier.

2. If the environmental influences on a trait can be assumed to be unrelated to family membership (i.e., all the environmental variance is $V_{WE}$), then correlations among parents and children, cousins, half-sibs, etc., may be used to estimate heritability or to test hypotheses about the genetic transmission of the trait, using any of the regression methods of the animal geneticist (see Falconer, 1960, chap. 10).

3. If observed correlations depart markedly from those predictable on genetic grounds, this may provide evidence of environmental influence. If one's environmental hypothesis holds that stubborn parents should have stubborn children, genes and environment are confounded, and a positive parent-child correlation conveys little information. But if one's environmental hypothesis holds that stubborn parents should have compliant children, then evidence to this effect is clear-cut support for the hypothesis, since the genetic prediction is stubborn children.

4. Correspondingly, if the observed correlations fit a genetic hypothesis, but depart markedly from expectations based on environmental similarity, legitimate genetic inferences may be drawn. One case is where sex linkage is involved: if observed father-daughter and mother-son correlations are substantially in excess of like-sex parent-child correlations, under conditions where

one would expect experiential factors to produce the opposite pattern, this would strongly suggest that the trait in question was influenced by genes, and that these genes were on the X chromosome. (For a possible example from the ability realm, see Bock & Kolakowski, 1973).

## 9  HEREDITY AND ENVIRONMENT CORRELATION AND INTERACTION

Interpretation of the various heritability coefficients and variance components described in preceding sections of this chapter is straightforward if genetic and environmental influences are uncorrelated and combine additively in their effects on the trait in question. Some complexities are introduced by departures from these conditions.

First, let us be clear as to what we mean by the assertion that heredity and environment are correlated, or that they interact. While sometimes confused, these are not the same assertion. Heredity-environment correlation implies that different genotypes are selectively *subjected* to different environmental treatments. Heredity-environment interaction implies that different genotypes *respond* differently to environment.

For example, consider the offspring of emotionally stable parents. These children may tend to receive genes predisposing them to emotional stability, and they may also tend to be treated in ways conducive to the development of emotional stability. This is a heredity-environment *correlation*. Nothing is said about how the genetic and environmental influences combine—just that certain ones tend to occur together.

On the other hand, consider the assertion that people of certain genotypes will thrive in stressful environments of a sort that tend to incapacitate lesser souls. This is an asser-

tion of a heredity-environment *interaction*. Nothing is said about whether such individuals are more or less frequently subjected to such environments, just that when they are, they respond differently.

How will the presence of heredity-environment interaction or correlation affect the interpretation of variance components and heritabilities derived from designs such as those we have been discussing in this chapter?

A precise answer depends, of course, on the exact form of the hypothesized interaction or correlation. We did not pursue the matter into its finer ramifications, but merely indicated the direction of effects to be expected in some particular cases of interest. This information is presented in Tables 3 and 4. Table 3 indicates the effects of the hypothesized conditions on intraclass correlations for the various groups, and Table 4 translates these into effects on variance components and heritability coefficients. The cells in Table 4 marked "small effect" (S) represent cases where opposing tendencies are involved, so that the net effect of the condition will tend to be small, with its direction depending on the details of the quantitative relationships.

As indicated in Table 3, the effect of heredity-environment *interaction* will in general be to lower intraclass correlations. In the limit, if every distinct combination of genotype and environment is completely unique and unpredictable from any other, the intraclass correlations in all groups will be zero. As Table 4 suggests, the most pronounced effect of interaction is to inflate estimates of within-family environmental variance—at the expense of genetic or between-family environmental variance, depending on the design.

Three cases of heredity-environment *correlation* are considered. In the first two

**TABLE 3**  Effects of heredity-environment interaction and correlation on intraclass correlations

| Condition | $r_{IT}$ | $r_{FT}$ | $r_{ST}$ | $r_{IA}$ | $r_{FA}$ | $r_{SA}$ | $r_{UT}$ | $r_{UA}$ |
|---|---|---|---|---|---|---|---|---|
| Interaction | L | L | L | L | L | L | L | E |
| Correlation: | | | | | | | | |
| Type A (−) | E | H | H | L | L | L | H | E |
| Type B (−) | L | L | L | L | L | L | L | E |
| Type C (+) | H | H | H | E | E | L | E | E |

*Note.* L = lower, H = higher; and E = approximately equal (compared with correlation when heredity and environment are additive and independent). For explanation of correlation types, see text. The term $r_{IT}$, for example, represents the correlation for identical twins reared together in their natural families.

cases, labeled Type A and Type B in Tables 3 and 4, a correlation between heredity and environment arises because a gene-produced difference on the trait in question or a related trait leads to the subjection of individuals to different environments. In particular, we have illustrated cases where the environmental feedback is negative: that is, where environmental pressures are brought to bear against behavioral deviations (cf. Cattell's "Law of coercion to the biosocial mean"—Cattell, 1975a). The effects of such a negative feedback process on intraclass correlations will differ depending on whether it operates within families (Type A), or across families (Type B); that is, whether the pressure is for conformity to a family standard, such as parental expectations, which may differ in different families, or whether the pressure is for conformity to society-wide norms. If the environmental pressures on a trait should be toward diversity rather than conformity—i.e., if heredity-environment correlation is positive—the effects will simply be the reverse of those shown in the tables. Such positive feedback may be more common in the ability realm: Specialization of talent may be encouraged by family or society even when eccentricity of temperament is not.

**TABLE 4**  Effects of changes in Table 3 on variance components and heritability coefficients

| Condition | Twin $V_{WE}$ $V_G$ $V_{BE}$ | Foster I $V_{WG}$ $V_G$ $V_{BE}$ | Foster II $V_{WG}$ $V_G$ $V_{BE}$ | Identical twin $V_{WE}$ $V_G$ $V_{BE}$ | Heritability coefficients Ho Ni Je |
|---|---|---|---|---|---|
| Interaction correlation: | H  S  L | H  S  L | H  L  S | H  L  S | L  H  S |
| Type A (−) | S  L  H | L  S  H | S  L  H | S  L  H | L  L  L |
| Type B (−) | H  S  L | H  S  L | H  L  S | H  L  S | L  H  S |
| Type C (+) | L  S  H | L  H  S | L  S  H | L  S  H | H  L  S |

*Note.* H = higher, L = lower, S = small effect (due to compensating changes). Coefficients: Ho = Holzinger's, Ni = Nichols's, Je = Jensen's. For explanation of correlation types, see text. The term $V_{WE}$, for example represents the enviromental variance within families.

The two kinds of correlations just mentioned are produced by heredity-environment relationships that develop during the life of the individual. Some between-family heredity-environment correlations (Type C in the tables) may have origins antecedent to the individual. For instance, the children of some families may tend to receive both genes and treatment predisposing them to emotional difficulties. The sign of such a correlation may conceivably be either positive or negative. Stable parents may provide both genes and environment conducive to stable children, but dominant parents might provide genes conducive to dominance and environmental pressures conducive to submission. The effects of a positive correlation are shown in the tables; the effects of a negative correlation would be just the opposite. (For a more formal treatment of gene-environment correlation, see Meredith, W., 1973.)

In interpreting variance estimates, it is important to note that some of them are less sensitive than others to the effects of interactions and correlations of the sorts described. In particular, Table 4 suggests that estimates of genetic variance based on the twin and first foster sib designs are fairly resistant to such distorting influences, while estimates of the division of environmental variances within and between families are fairly sensitive to them.

## 10  CATTELL'S MULTIPLE ABSTRACT VARIANCE ANALYSIS

The Multiple Abstract Variance Analysis (MAVA) proposed by Cattell (1953b, 1960a) is a design which, in a sense, combines the various designs presented separately earlier in this chapter. Cattell's "limited resources" version of MAVA uses the groups of the twin and foster sib designs; his full version

adds identical twins reared apart and half-siblings. The MAVA design aims to solve for the four basic variance components $V_{WE}$, $V_{WG}$, $V_{BE}$, and $V_{BG}$, plus the correlations (covariances) among these. An extension of the design to solve for non-additive heredity-environment interactions has been proposed by Cattell (1963b), but not yet developed in detail.

We may illustrate some features of the basic design in a simplified version. The symbolism has been modified slightly for consistency with the other designs presented in this chapter. The variances to the left of the equals signs are the observed within-group variances; those to the right are the theoretical variances and covariances to be solved for:

$$V_{WIT} = V_{WE'},$$

$$V_{WFT} = V_{WG} + V_{WE'} + 2\text{Cov}_{WGWE'},$$

$$V_{WST} = V_{WG} + V_{WE} + 2\text{Cov}_{WGWE},$$

$$\begin{aligned} V_{WSA} = V_{WG} + V_{WE'} + V_{BE'} \\ + 2\text{Cov}_{WGWE'} + 2\text{Cov}_{WGBE'} \\ + 2\text{Cov}_{WEBE'}, \end{aligned}$$

$$\begin{aligned} V_{WUT} = V_{WG} + V_{WE'} + V_{BG} \\ + 2\text{Cov}_{WGWE'} + 2\text{Cov}_{BGWE'}, \text{and} \end{aligned}$$

$$\begin{aligned} V_{WUA} = V_{WG} + V_{WE} + V_{BG} + V_{BE} \\ + 2\text{Cov}_{WGWE} + 2\text{Cov}_{BGBE}. \end{aligned}$$

Covariances that on theoretical grounds should be zero have been omitted (for example, $\text{Cov}_{WGBG}$). Variances and covariances which may differ from the values given elsewhere in the set of equations are marked with primes. For instance, the variance within pairs of identical twins reared together may estimate a quantity different from the normal within-family environmental variance—hence the prime on $V_{WE}$ in the first equation. As given, the equations cannot be solved, since they contain too many unknowns. If, however, we assume (a) that the variances $V_{WE'}$ have some particular relations to $V_{WE}$ (i.e., that $k_1$ and $k_2$ have some particular values) and (b) that there is no selection, selective placement, or selective treatment of adopted children (corresponding to $k_4 = k_5 = 1$), then the last two covariance terms of the equation for $V_{WSA}$ become zero, the primes disappear from this equation and the equation for $V_{WUT}$, and a partial solution of the equations becomes possible. $V_{WG}$ and $2\text{Cov}_{WGWE}$ will remain confounded (Loehlin, 1965a).

The sampling-error situation for the MAVA design is somewhat difficult to assess. Presumably, if the equations are solved in an efficient manner, it should be possible to estimate some of the variances with samples on the order of those required for comparable accuracy in the twin and foster sib designs. However, quantities requiring more indirect solutions would presumably call for very large samples.

## 11 MULTIVARIATE HEREDITY-ENVIRONMENT ANALYSIS

The discussion so far has focused on ways of analyzing components of variance of single traits. The extension to the multivariate case is immediate. Covariances (including correlations) can be partitioned in exactly the same fashion as variances (Kempthorne & Osborne, 1961). One simply uses cross-correlations (trait $a$ in individual 1 vs. trait $b$ in individual 2) in place of intraclass correlations (trait $a$ in individual 1 vs. trait $a$ in individual 2). Any of the designs for partitioning variance, including MAVA, may be adapted to partitioning covariances,

keeping in mind that the components now sum to the total covariance rather than to unity, and that they may be negative.

Starting with intercorrelation and cross-correlation matrices for a set of traits, one may obtain in this manner matrices representing each of the various components: within-family environment, within-family heredity, and so on. These matrices may be interpreted directly, factor analyzed, or subjected to other multivariate analyses. (Bock & Vandenberg, 1968; Eaves, 1973; Eaves & Gate, 1974; Loehlin & Vandenberg, 1968).

How are the factors obtained by such procedures to be interpreted? In principle, this is straightforward. The factors from the environmental components should reflect the effects of common environmental influences on trait development or definition (cf. the "environmental mold" source traits of Cattell, 1946). The factors from the genetic components could on occasion reflect the multiple (pleiotropic) effects of single genes, but probably more often would represent major nodes further along in the complex network of pathways that mediate between genes and behavioral events: hormone levels, physiological reactivity, physical attractiveness, intelligence, physique—any confluence of genetic effects which in turn has ramifying influences on behavior (cf. Cattell's "constitutional" source traits). In practice, however, things are not likely to be so clear cut. For example, the "same" source trait might easily show up in both domains, if, for example, the cultural definition of a certain trait depends in part on its biological configuration, or if item overlap or other method-related factors are involved.

As an alternative to first partitioning the covariances of the observed variables and then factoring, one may factor the observed covariance matrices first, and then estimate the variance components of the resulting factors (cf. Roudabush, 1968). This approach is less likely to detect structural differences between genetic and environmental influences.

Vandenberg (1965a) proposed a multivariate method that assumes a multiplicative, rather than an additive, relation between heredity and environment. The within-pair variance-covariance matrix of identical twins is taken as providing an estimate of environmental influences, and a rotation matrix is sought that will transform it into the corresponding matrix for fraternal twins. Such a transformation matrix is then interpreted as representing the influence of heredity. It appears that this method will not be able to locate genetic influences not already represented to some degree in the environmental covariance. Indeed, if there are more underlying dimensions in the fraternal twin matrix than in the identical twin matrix, a solution is impossible; a matrix does not exist that will make the desired transformation. However, in at least one instance, similar results were obtained by multiplicative and additive approaches to the same data (Loehlin & Vandenberg, 1968).

Another possible strategy is to screen variables from a given domain (say, personality inventory items) into sets of relatively high and low heritability, using univariate methods, and then to factor analyze these sets separately. Factors that emerge from one factoring but not the other, or are much stronger in one than in the other, may be interpretable as representing genetic or environmental influences. In one application of this approach to personality data, there appeared to be more similarities than differences between factors obtained from personality item clusters of high and low heritability (Loehlin, 1965b). The heritability estimates were based on twin samples of around 40 pairs, however, so the study should only be regarded as illustrative.

Two applications of this method to the item pool of the California Psychological Inventory (CPI) yielded somewhat conflicting results. J. M. Horn, Plomin and Rosenman (1976), with samples of around 100 pairs, obtained some evidence of different factors from low and high heritability items. Loehlin and Nichols (in press), with larger samples of about 500 and 350 pairs, were unable dependably to classify CPI items descriptive of personality into high and low heritability categories, thus raising at least a question about the reproducibility of the Horn results.

Still another approach, a nonmetric multivariate analysis, based on a Guttman-style facet design, was suggested by Lingoes and Vandenberg (1966) and applied for demonstration purposes to some personality and ability data from a small twin sample.

Finally, Eaves (1973) suggested a multivariate analysis that can be carried out with only identical twin data. Essentially, this method, like the others, analyzes the covariance structure of the differences within identical twin pairs to study the structure of environmental influences. It then seeks composite dimensions along which between-pair effects are maximum relative to within-pair effects, and rotates the resulting "genetic factors" to simple structure. As Eaves noted, these are genetic factors only if one assumes the absence of any important effects of common environments of the twins. Eaves demonstrated his technique by an application to data from 101 identical twin pairs' responses to the 80 items of the Eysenck Personality Inventory. Given the limited sample size, the difficulties of working with dichotomously scored and often unreliable single items, and the problematical assumptions required, it is probably wisest to consider this study, too, as essentially illustrative of a method rather than substantive.

We thus have a variety of proposals for multivariate attacks on the heredity-environment problem, but so far none of these has been applied on a scale that will allow us to draw solid conclusions concerning the structure of the genetic and environmental influences on personality.

The theoretical merit of a multivariate approach to psychological genetics, as compared to a trait-by-trait univariate approach, can hardly be overstressed. It may often be useful to know that 40% of the variance of a given personality trait in a given population is genetic and 60% is environmental. If one knows with which other traits the genetic portion of the variance is shared, and with which other traits the environmental portion is shared, however, one is in a vastly better position to generate useful hypotheses about what is going on. Such knowledge is obtainable from—and only from—a multivariate approach. But, clearly, large samples will be required for research of this kind.

## 12   SUMMARY

1. A variety of methods exist for assessing the influence of genes and environment on the personality traits of normal humans.

2. One may study the effect of certain genes on personality (a gene-centered approach), or one may investigate genetic and environmental influences on given personality traits (a trait-centered approach). The latter approach is much commoner; it often results in a heritability coefficient expressing the proportion of variance of a trait that is genetic in origin. A more refined method divides the variance of a trait into the within- and between-family variance components $V_{WG}$, $V_{WE}$, $V_{BG}$, and $V_{BE}$.

3. Identical and fraternal twin correlations permit solving for the variance components, if assumptions are made about the similarity of identical and fraternal twin environments, the similarity of fraternal twin and sibling correlations, and the effect of assortative mating and nonadditive genetic variance.

4. A survey of twin studies employing personality inventories suggests moderate heritabilities for traits in the personality domain, but inconsistencies are common.

5. Sampling error considerations suggest that quite large samples are needed for estimating heritabilities dependably from twin data, samples much larger than those used in most existing studies.

6. Correlations between siblings reared apart in separate families, or between unrelated children reared together by adoption, provide alternative ways of estimating variance components. In these designs, assumptions must be made concerning selective placement and possible differential treatment of adopted children.

7. Correlations between identical twins reared together and apart provide still another means of estimating variance components, requiring assumptions similar to those of the twin and foster sib designs. Two such studies tend to suggest somewhat higher estimates of $V_G$ than do the ordinary twin studies reviewed.

8. Correlations between other relatives usually confound genetic and environmental effects, but under certain conditions may permit useful inferences.

9. Genetic and environmental influences may sometimes be correlated or may interact. The effect of such correlations and interactions on the variance components can be evaluated in simple cases.

10. Cattell's Multiple Abstract Variance Anslysis can be considered a combination of the simple designs described earlier. It permits some inferences about heredity-environment covariances, but may require very large samples.

11. A number of multivariate approaches to heredity-environment analysis have been proposed. Covariances (including correlations) may be partitioned into components by methods similar to those used with variances. Analysis of such matrices should yield valuable information about genetic and environmental effects on the development of human personality.

## APPENDIX   AN APPROACH TO SELECTING PLAUSIBLE VALUES OF THE TWIN METHOD PARAMETERS $k_1$ AND $k_3$

If one is willing to assume that $k_1$ and $k_3$ have values that remain constant over a set of traits that vary in their genetic and environmental components, it may be possible to set some limits on plausible values of these parameters. Table 5 illustrates this approach with some twin data from the California Psychological Inventory (Nichols, 1969). It will be observed that when the assumptions $k_1 = k_2 = k_3 = 1$ are made (in the set of columns in the middle of the table), several negative values for $V_{BE}$ are obtained. One can eliminate these by lowering either $k_1$ or $k_3$, but if the former is done alone it produces negative values of $V_{BG}$ (at $k_1 = .82$) before it eliminates the negative values of $V_{BE}$. Lowering $k_3$ alone can produce all positive variances, but this require going down to $k_3 = .58$, which assumes a rather marked degree of genetic

**TABLE 5** Variance components of California Personality Inventory scales under two assumptions concerning parameters $k_1$ and $k_3$

| Scale | Correlations | | Reliabilities[a] | $k_1 = k_3 = 1.0$ | | | $k_1 = .9, k_3 = .65$ | | |
| | $r_{IT}$ | $r_{FT}$ | | $V_{WE}$ | $V_G$ | $V_{BE}$ | $V_{WE}$ | $V_G$ | $V_{BE}$ |
|---|---|---|---|---|---|---|---|---|---|
| Do | 54 | 27 | 80 | 32 | 68 | 00 | 39 | 45 | 16 |
| Cs | 58 | 48 | 79 | 27 | 26 | 48 | 34 | 08 | 57 |
| Sy | 53 | 30 | 77 | 31 | 60 | 09 | 38 | 38 | 24 |
| Sp | 54 | 25 | 76 | 29 | 76 | −05 | 36 | 51 | 13 |
| Sa | 50 | 29 | 70 | 29 | 60 | 11 | 36 | 38 | 26 |
| Wb | 49 | 30 | 86 | 43 | 44 | 13 | 49 | 27 | 24 |
| Re | 49 | 36 | 82 | 40 | 32 | 28 | 46 | 16 | 38 |
| So | 54 | 36 | 83 | 35 | 42 | 22 | 41 | 25 | 34 |
| Sc | 56 | 32 | 87 | 36 | 56 | 09 | 42 | 35 | 23 |
| To | 53 | 36 | 86 | 38 | 40 | 22 | 45 | 23 | 33 |
| Gi | 47 | 30 | 79 | 40 | 44 | 16 | 46 | 26 | 28 |
| Cm | 36 | 17 | 63 | 43 | 60 | −03 | 49 | 40 | 11 |
| Ac | 46 | 17 | 79 | 42 | 74 | −15 | 48 | 51 | 01 |
| Ai | 55 | 40 | 75 | 27 | 40 | 33 | 34 | 21 | 45 |
| Ie | 52 | 34 | 81 | 36 | 44 | 20 | 42 | 26 | 32 |
| Py | 41 | 22 | 62 | 34 | 62 | 05 | 40 | 40 | 20 |
| Fx | 48 | 21 | 71 | 32 | 76 | −08 | 39 | 51 | 09 |
| Fe | 36 | 19 | 73 | 51 | 46 | 03 | 56 | 30 | 14 |
| Median | 51 | 30 | 79 | $36^b$ | 53 | 12 | 42 | 33 | 25 |

*Note.* Data from Nichols (1969), sexes combined—498 identical and 319 fraternal pairs. Decimal points omitted throughout the table.

[a]Corrected split-half reliabilities based on 500 men and women, from Megargee (1972, p 31).

[b]Components calculated from medians.

nonadditivity. However, if $k_1$ is set slightly below unity, say at .9, one can eliminate negative variances at a somewhat more moderate level of genetic nonadditivity ($k_3$ of around .65). The values of the variance components under these assumptions are shown in the right-hand portion of Table 5.

Naturally, the appropriateness of these parameter estimates depends on one's willingness to make the necessary rather strong assumption of constancy of the parameters across traits. It is also implicitly assumed that the negative estimates of $V_{BE}$ are invalid—that they do not, for example, reflect mere sampling fluctuation around population values near zero, or genuine contrast effects. Thus Table 5 should probably be taken mainly as illustrative of an approach, rather than as establishing dependable values of $k_1$ and $k_3$ for the personality domain.

# 14

# The Genetics
# and Development
# of Sex Differences

**Jeffrey A. Gray**
*Oxford University, England*

**Robert F. Drewett**
*University of Durham, England*

The study of personality is the attempt to describe and account for consistent patterns of individual differences. Any causal account of personality must describe both (a) the enduring structural and functional neuro-endocrine basis of the observed patterns of individual differences and (b) the developmental pathways by which this basis is produced (Gray, J. A., 1968). The study of behavioral sex differences offers unique advantages in the analysis of the second of these two problems; consequently, it also contributes substantially to the solution of the former. In this chapter, we concentrate on only a few of the many sex differences in behavior in an attempt to justify these claims. Our choice of sexual and emotional behavior was dictated by a decision to emphasize the developmental aspects of sex differences and the desire to highlight the potentialities and the pitfalls arising from arguments that extrapolate from animal experiments to man in this field. Much of the detailed experimental work describes the neuroendocrine control of such behavior in the rat and other rodents. We believe that without such a detailed consideration, the pitfalls of comparative psychology will loom

larger than its potentialities. The behavioral differences between the sexes are pronounced, and there is ample evidence of their existence in the literature (Broverman, Klaiber, Kobayashi, & Vogel, 1968; Garai & Scheinfeld, 1968; Gray, J. A., 1971a; Gray, J. A. & Buffery, 1971; Maccoby, 1966; Maccoby & Jacklin, 1975; Ounsted & Taylor, 1972a). These differences are not confined to sexual and reproductive behavior. In man they include differences in sensory thresholds; sensory preferences; perceptual, motor, and linguistic skills; the patterning and variance of performance on IQ tests; emotional behavior, mental illness, and antisocial behavior; and questionnaire measures of numerous major factors of personality. In other mammals sex differences are no less extensive. The complexity of the behavioral differences between the sexes allows us to regard *gender* as a major dimension of personality that is analogous to that studied under the name of *introversion-extraversion* or *neuroticism*. However, such a gender continuum is unlike any other personality continuum in that (a) scores on it are bimodally distributed (although not without variance around the modes); (b) its modes may be precisely identified in terms of a set of nonbehavioral criteria (chromosomal, morphological, and endocrinological); (c) these criteria may be applied with certainty to man and other mammals and, in this way, one can match male with male and female with female across different species (in contrast, how often would one be sure that introverts and extraverts had been identified among rats, monkeys, and men?); and (d) these criteria may be treated as independent variables either in human clinical material or in appropriate animal experiments.

This last point requires amplification. Usually, the formation of hypotheses concerning a structural basis in the brain for a personality factor, or concerning the developmental pathways by which this basis is produced, is a shot in the dark; and the testing of such hypotheses is equally difficult. Most commonly, they are derived from the data they seek to explain and can be linked to animal experimentation only by an extended chain of argument (Gray, J. A., 1973). Examples would be H. J. Eysenck's (1957) excitation-inhibition-balance theory of extraversion, or J. A. Gray's (1964) treatment of Russian data on the strength of the nervous system in terms of level of arousal. One advantage of a study of sex differences is that it provides an immediate source of likely hypotheses concerning the physiological basis of the observed behavior. The source of these hypotheses is our knowledge of the basic mechanisms of sexual differentiation in the mammal; this knowledge has greatly increased in the last two decades. These mechanisms are essentially the same in a number of mammalian species, including, probably, primates. Furthermore, the same mechanisms appear to control the development of sex differences in nonreproductive behavior as those that control the differentiation of sex-specific reproductive physi-

ology. Thus, given a sex difference in human behavior, whether this is directly concerned with reproduction or not, plausible hypotheses to account for the development of this sex difference may be derived in a way that is independent of the data they seek to explain. Of course, such hypotheses require independent verification in humans; but, at the very least, the animal studies clearly indicate the sort of data that could provide such verification.

This approach is limited, however, to the *development* of the physiological basis of observed sex differences. It does not necessarily tell us anything about the structural basis in the brain that is responsible for such sex differences. To tackle the latter problem, it is necessary to establish an experimental analogue of the behavior to be studied in an animal whose brain can subsequently be investigated. Even here the study of sex differences can lead one onto solid ground. This is not usually true when it is necessary to argue that a certain form of behavior in man and some other form of behavior in an experimental animal are the same (Gray, J. A., 1973).

For example, consider the sex difference in aggressiveness. As reviewed by J. A. Gray (1971a), it is virtually a universal feature of mammalian (and, indeed, of vertebrate) species that the male is more aggressive than the female, and that this sex difference is expressed principally, or only, in intraspecific competitive activities concerned with establishing social dominance (Gray, J. A., & Buffery, 1971). Of the various mammalian species studied, ranging from mice to chimpanzees, the observations are sufficiently similar (tallying of aggressive encounters involving actual physical assault, display of submissive or dominant gestures, withdrawal of one animal from the path of another, etc.) that one has no qualms in relating them to *intraspecific aggressiveness*.

Furthermore, the universality of direction of the sex difference observed in these studies greatly increases one's confidence that similar processes of behavioral control and evolutionary adaptation are at work in all cases of intraspecific aggressiveness studied. Turning one's attention to man, one finds the word *aggression* applied to a different range of behavioral observations than those made in the animal cases; yet one thing remains constant—males engage in these forms of behavior much more than do females (Gray, J. A., 1971a; Maccoby & Jacklin, 1975). This could be coincidence. Parsimony bids us conclude, however, (a) that we are again dealing with a fundamentally similar form of behavior that displays essentially the same difference between the sexes already observed in related species and (b) that both the behavior and the sex difference are likely, therefore, to be controlled by essentially the same factors in both man and the other species studied. Such a conclusion is more plausible if (as is true with aggressive behavior) the comparative data are sufficient to allow one to assert that there is a constant trend throughout the mammalian class, including the primate species most closely related to ourselves.

If, in this way, one is able to establish a plausible hypothesis that a sex difference in human behavior is matched by a sex difference in a similar form of behavior in rat or monkey, it is possible to go on to study the controlling systems in the brain and endocrine system of the experimental animal. This analysis is closely linked with an analysis of the developmental pathways by which sex difference is attained. For, as we shall see, important clues regarding the neuroendocrine control of behavior that shows a sex difference can be derived from studies of the sexual differentiation of the brain during early development. Moreover, if the analysis is successful, it offers useful hypotheses concerning control of the behavior in question, and the sex difference in this behavior in man.

# 1  GENETICS OF SEX: Y CHROMOSOME

Sex differences, of course, must start with the genotype of the gamete. As is well known, the normal mammalian pattern is for the female to have two so-called X chromosomes, whereas the male normally possesses an X and a Y chromosome. These chromosomes are named according to their appearance under the microscope (Fig. 1), the X chromosome being characteristically considerably longer than the Y. It should be noted, however, that the association between sex and these chromosomal patterns is not immutable. In birds, the reverse correlation is the rule, with XX constituting the male and XY the female. Additionally, in a number of different mammalian species, including man, individuals have been described that are phenotypically normal, or almost normal, males, but that possess an XX genotype (Cattanach, Pollard, & Hawkes, 1971). In the mice studied by Cattanach, Pollard, and Hawkes (1971), it appears that this condition is the result of a dominant gene mutation on an autosome (i.e., a chromosome other than the X and Y, or sex, chromosomes). However, if such rare anomalies are ignored, it is clear that since there are no differences between the sexes in their autosomal constitution, observed phenotypic sex differences must derive from the X and Y chromosomes. That is, they must derive either from the fact that the male has a Y chromosome and the female does not, or from the fact that the female possesses two X chromosomes and the male only one.

Whereas major chromosomal abnormalities (such as the addition or deletion of a chromosome to or from a normal pair) are usually incompatible with life in the case of

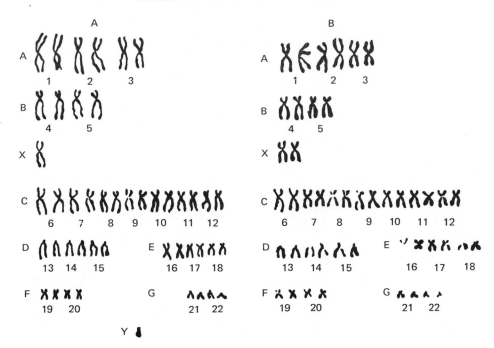

**FIG. 1** A: The chromosomes of a male, arranged in pairs according to their size, indicating the seven groups that are conventionally distinguished. B: The chromosomes of a female, arranged in the same way. The chromosomes are often referred to by their numbers, assigned by decreasing size as indicated underneath the groups. From *The Genetics of Human Populations* by L. L. Cavalli-Sforza and W. F. Bodmer, San Francisco, Freeman, 1971. Copyright 1971 by Freeman. Reprinted by permission. Photographs by L. Razari.

autosomes, many abnormalities of the sex-chromosomal constitution have been described in man. The majority of these are either XXY (Klinefelter's syndrome), XO (i.e., one X chromosome only—Turner's syndrome), or XYY. From studies of these and other abnormal cases, it is clear that the presence of a single Y chromosome is normally both necessary and sufficient for the phenotypic sex to be essentially male. The number of X chromosomes present does not affect the outcome, provided there is at least one; a single Y chromosome on its own is apparently incompatible with survival, since no such individuals have been described. In the absence of a Y chromosome, the phenotypic sex is essentially female, no matter how many X chromosomes are present.

Thus, genetically speaking (given that there is one X chromosome to sustain life), the critical factor determining sex is the presence or absence of a Y chromosome.

The critical developmental function of the Y chromosome appears to be that of specifying the formation of a testis from the primitive ovotestis. In the presence of a Y chromosome, the medulla of the ovotestis develops into a testis at the expense of the cortex. In the absence of the Y chromosome, the reverse happens—the cortex develops into an ovary at the expense of the medulla. Thereafter, the normal development of a male phenotype is largely under the control of a hormone, or hormones (especially testosterone), secreted by the testis. These principles were first clear-

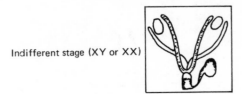

Indifferent stage (XY or XX)

Normal XX

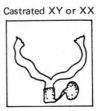

Castrated XY or XX

Castrated XY or XX
+ testosterone

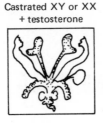

Normal XY

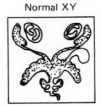

XY + testicular feminization

**FIG. 2** The role of testosterone and the effect of the *Tfm* mutation on the embryonic development of the Wolffian duct (shaded), Müllerian duct (outlined), and urogenital sinus (solid black). The pair of bean-shaped bodies at the top of each square signify gonads: Indifferent gonad (outlined), ovary (filled with small circles), and testes containing two tubules. From "Simplicity of Mammalian Regulatory Systems Inferred by Single Gene Determination of Sex Phenotypes" by S. Ohno, *Nature*, 1971, **234**, 134–137. Copyright 1971 by *Nature*. Reprinted by permission.

ly established in a series of embryological experiments on rabbits and rats (Jost, 1971). The embryo is initially equipped with primitive ducts that can develop into the female internal genitalia (the Müllerian ducts) and into the male internal genitalia (the Wolffian ducts). In the normal genotypic female, the Müllerian ducts automatically differentiate to Fallopian tubes and uterus, and the Wolffian ducts regress. In the normal genotypic male, the Müllerian ducts regress and the Wolffian ducts differentiate into the vas deferens, seminal vesicles, and epididymis. If a male embryo is castrated sufficiently early, the pathway of development proceeds as it would in the normal female, in the same way as if the ovaries are removed from the female embryo (Fig. 2). The exogenous administration of testosterone to a genotypic female embryo or to a castrated male causes the Wolffian ducts to differentiate as in a normal male, but the Müllerian ducts fail to regress (Jost, 1953). From these results Jost (1961) concluded that in the absence of any hormonal influence from the testis, the embryo (whether genotypically male or female) differentiates into a female. Differentiation into a male requires testosterone (to stimulate differentiation of the Wolffian ducts into the male internal genitalia) and Factor X, also normally secreted by the testis, to cause regression of the Müllerian ducts.

These principles have been shown to

apply to numerous endocrinological and behavioral sex differences, some of which we examine later. In these, testosterone continues to be an important factor. The way this hormone exerts its effects during sexual differentiation was recently clarified by a series of studies of the *testicular-feminizing* mouse.

The syndrome of testicular feminization, originally described in man and subsequently found in cattle, rats, and mice (Ohno, 1971), occurs in individuals with an XY karyotype who possess testes but otherwise differen-

tiate primarily as phenotypic females (except that they lack female internal genitalia). As pointed out by Ohno (1971) (see Fig. 2), this syndrome could be explained if testosterone fails to have its normal effects but Factor $X$ continues to perform its function of destroying the Müllerian ducts. In a series of studies Ohno offered substantial experimental support for this view and developed a theory concerning the normal action of testosterone that is potentially of great significance. Ohno's (1971) theory is illustrated in Fig. 3. He proposed that in the

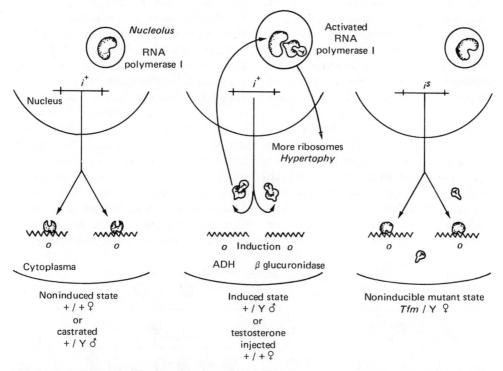

**FIG. 3** Single-gene control of mammalian sexual phenotypes. The term $i^+$ represents the wild-type allele of the X-linked *Tfm* locus. Its product (☺) serves as a translational repressor of alcohol dehydrogenase (ADH) and β-glucuronidase in the cytoplasm until the arrival of testosterone (♀). When it becomes bound to testosterone or its metabolites (such as DHT), it moves into the nucleus and activates RNA polymerase I in the nucleolar region, thus causing increased production of ribosomes and hypertrophy. $i^s$ represents a mutant *Tfm* allele; its product (☺) has lost the binding affinity to testosterone. The o (operator) region in each RNA (wavy line) signifies a homologous base sequence shared by ADH and β-glucuronidase mRNAs which is recognized by the product of i gene. From "Simplicity of Mammalian Regulatory Systems Inferred by Single Gene Determination of Sex Phenotypes" by S. Ohno, *Nature*, 1971, **234**, 134–137. Copyright 1971 by *Nature*. Reprinted by permission.

normal male a gene (symbolized by $i^+$) produces a protein that binds to certain operator regions shared by those messenger RNAs normally activated by testosterone. In this way, the product of gene $i^+$ blocks the activation of these messenger RNAs. Testosterone (or, more accurately, an intracellular metabolite of testosterone, perhaps 5-$\alpha$-dihydrotestosterone) binds this gene product to itself, and thus releases the block on the translation of the RNA into the appropriate enzyme. (Other details of Ohno's theory are presented in Fig. 3.) In this way testosterone is able to activate its target cells. In the syndrome of testicular feminization, there is (Ohno proposed) a mutation of the $i^+$ locus to a gene, $i^s$, so that its product continues to bind to the same operator regions of the messenger RNAs and represses translation, but loses its binding affinity to testosterone. Therefore, the process of masculinization that normally proceeds from the XY karyotype stops after the formation of the testis itself, since testosterone is unable to perform its usual functions. In support of this hypothesis, it has been shown in both mice (Attardi & Ohno, 1974; Gehring, Tomkins, & Ohno, 1971) and men (Keenan, Meyer, Hadjian, Jones, & Migeon, 1974) that tes-

ticular feminizing individuals lack a specific binding protein for 5-$\alpha$-dihydrotestosterone.

In man, cattle, and rats, the mode of inheritance of testicular feminization is compatible with either autosomal dominant mutation with male limitation or with X-linked mutation (see Fig. 4). However, linkage studies in the mouse by Lyon and Hawkes (1970) demonstrated that X-linked inheritance is more likely. According to Ohno (1969), a gene that is X linked in one mammalian species is almost always X linked in others (an important point to bear in mind later when we consider X linkage). Therefore, it seems probable that the locus of the gene (as postulated by Ohno) that regulates testosterone-induced differentiation is on the X chromosome in man as well.

Ohno's theory accounts for the otherwise strange fact that mutation at a single locus (as in the testicular-feminization syndrome) is able to block the unfolding of the complex series of events that, in the normal animal and at the instigation of testosterone, constitute the process of sexual differentiation. As we shall see, since this process involves many features that are of an essentially psychological character, his theory is potentially applicable to the development of

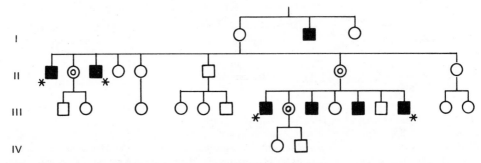

FIG. 4  Pedigree of the testicular feminization syndrome. Note that autosomal dominant inheritance with male limitation or X-linked recessive inheritance explains the prima facie pedigree evidence. Circles with dots centered in them indicate women who are hairless (by examination). Black squares indicate men who have the testicular feminization syndrome. Asterisks mark cases of the syndrome that have been confirmed surgically. From *The Genetics of Human Populations* by L. L. Cavalli-Sforza and W. F. Bodmer, San Francisco, Freeman, 1971. Copyright 1971 by Freeman. Reprinted by permission.

the relevant aspects of the adult personality. Furthermore, there is evidence that other hormones—especially thyroxine (Balázs, 1971) and, perhaps, corticosterone (Levine & Mullins, 1966)—have a profound influence on the development of the central nervous system and subsequent adult patterns of behavior. Thus, it is conceivable that a full understanding of the developmental pathways by which testosterone—and so the Y chromosome—affects adult mammalian behavior may be an important step in the creation of a general developmental theory of personality. For this reason, later in the chapter we devote considerable attention to the evidence that the developmental effects of testosterone include a number of important aspects of behavior.

## 2  GENETICS OF SEX: X CHROMOSOME

The specification of a testis and the ensuing widespread effects caused by the secretion of testosterone, which are attributable to the activity of the Y chromosome, are important in the development of the organism. However, this is virtually all the Y chromosome does; it appears to carry no other genetic information. According to Cavalli-Sforza and Bodmer (1971), only one genetic character, hairy ears, is "reasonably well substantiated" as being Y linked in man. An interesting view (Ounsted & Taylor, 1972b) is that one function of the Y chromosome is to slow down the rate at which genetically controlled development takes place. In this way, the strikingly slower maturation of the male, which is consistently expressed in a wide diversity of the physiological and behavioral measures, could be accounted for. However, although Ounsted and Taylor marshalled a number of plausible arguments defending their position, at present there is no direct evidence in its favor.

In constrast, Cavalli-Sforza and Bodmer (1971) state: "Up to sixty genetic differences in Man have been identified as being X-linked, and important progress has been made towards the construction of a linkage map of the human X chromosome." The imbalance between the amount of genetic information carried by the X and Y chromosomes probably reflects the much greater length of the X chromosome. Consequently, in a male the majority of genes carried on the X chromosome are not matched by a gene on a paired chromosome. This is one reason that genetic mapping of the X chromosome has proceeded so fast: the fact that the male is effectively haploid (single chromosomed) for the X means that his phenotype reflects his genotype directly for this chromosome. The normal female, of course, is diploid (double chromosomed) for the X chromosomes, as for the autosomes. This difference in the number of X chromosomes between normal males and females has important consequences for the expression of a character determined by X-linked genes in the two sexes.

Consider the case of a single X-linked recessive gene, with frequency in the population $q$, the dominant allele having frequency $1 - q = p$. Since the males in the population are effectively haploid for the X chromosome, they will express the dominant and recessive phenotypes with the same frequencies, $p$ and $q$, as the dominant and recessive alleles occur in the gene pool. The females, on the other hand, will express the recessive phenotype only with frequency $q^2$, since they must receive the recessive allele from both parents. Assuming complete dominance, they will express the dominant phenotype with frequency $p^2 + 2pq$, the first term in this expression representing the individuals homozygous for the dominant allele and the second representing the heterozygotes. If the character involved is a metric one, it can be shown that various statistical consequences follow. In particular, certain patterns of correlations between parents and offspring, depending on sex, would be expected to occur (Buffery & Gray, 1972). A son receives his single X chromosome from his mother. A daughter receives two X chromosomes, one from her mother and one from her father. Using our simple assumptions, the expected pattern of correlations arising from these facts is as follows: The mother-son correlation = the father-daughter correlation = $\sqrt{q/(q+1)}$; the mother-daughter correlation = $q/(q+1)$, that is, the square of the former two correlations; and the father-son correlation is zero. These correlations, and the sibling-sibling correlations, which can be similarly derived (Mather & Jinks, 1963), are plotted as a function of the dominant gene frequency in Fig. 5. (A complete discussion of the statistical expectations derivable from X linkage is given by Mather & Jinks, 1971.)

These expectations, derived from simple Mendelian theory, are of more than academic interest to psychologists. The data obtained in four studies of visuospatial ability (reviewed by Buffery & Gray, 1972; see also Bock & Kolakowski, 1973) agree with the predictions concerning the parent-offspring correlations. In fact they agree so well that the most reasonable hypothesis consistent with the data is that visuospatial ability is substantially determined by a single recessive gene, carried on the X chromosome, that determines superior performance with a frequency between approximately $q = 0.2$ and $q = 0.5$ (Buffery & Gray, 1972; Bock & Kolakowski, 1973). Table 1 shows the relevant correlations found in the four studies. The general supriority of males over females on tests of visuospatial ability (Buffery & Gray, 1972; Maccoby & Jacklin, 1975) can also be predicted on this model. Since the postulated recessive gene is for superior

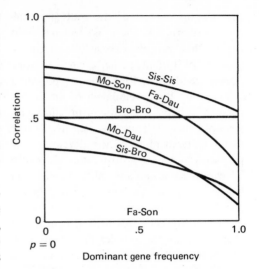

FIG. 5 Familial correlations as a function of dominant gene frequency in the case of X-linked inheritance. Sis = sister; Mo = mother; Fa = father; Dau = daughter; Bro = brother. From "Further Evidence of Major-gene Influence on Human Spatial Visualizing Ability" by R. D. Bock and D. Kolakowski, *American Journal of Human Genetics*, 1973, **25**, 1–14. Copyright 1973 by *American Journal of Human Genetics*. Reprinted by permission.

performance, such performance will occur in a proportion $q$ of males, but only $q^2$ of females. Detailed data concerning this deduction are presented by Bock and Kolakowski (1973).

There are difficulties with this view, however. As pointed out by Garron (1970), the fact that individuals with Turner's syndrome (Money & Ehrhardt, 1968) and individuals with the testicular-feminization syndrome (Masica, Money, Ehrhardt, & Lewis, 1969) do not display male levels of visuospatial ability (indeed, they do significantly worse than normal females) is inconsistent with a simple sex-linked inheritance model. Since these individuals carry one X chromosome, as do normal males, their distribution of visuospatial scores should, if X linkage is the only factor in play, be the

TABLE 1   Parent-offspring correlations in four studies of visuo-spatial IQ

| Family relationship | Stafford, 1961 | Corah, 1965 | Hartlage, 1970 | Bock and Kolakowski, 1973 |
|---|---|---|---|---|
| Mother-son | .31 | .31 | .39 | .20 |
| Father-daughter | .31 | .28 | .34 | .25 |
| Mother-daughter | .14 | .02 | .25 | .12 |
| Father-son | .02 | .18 | .18 | .15 |

same as that of normal males. This is true, for example, for color blindness, which is known to be determined by an X-linked recessive gene (Cavalli-Sforza & Bodmer, 1971). To circumvent this difficulty Bock and Kolakowski (1973) suggested that in addition to being X linked, visuospatial ability is, to some extent, also dependent on testosterone activation. Of course, this is lacking in Turner's syndrome and is ineffective in testicular feminization. Stewart, Skvarenina and Pottier (1975) studied spatial ability in the rat and reported evidence to support this suggestion. Rats show a sex difference in learning spatially complex mazes but not in other learning tests; further, as in the analogous human case, males normally perform better than do females (Buffery & Gray, 1972). Stewart, Skvarenina, and Pottier (1975) found that the administration of testosterone propionate to neonatal female rats elevated their scores on a test of maze-learning ability in adulthood to a level indistinguishable from that of males. This result indicates that the spatial superiority of the male rat depends on the action of endogenous testosterone in early infancy.

Only further research can determine whether testosterone has this effect in man. However, there is one interesting observation consistent with it: During development, if testosterone is needed for full expression of the genome, it would be expected that the heritability of visuospatial ability would be greater in males than in females. Bock and

Vandenberg (1968) obtained this result in a study of monozygotic and dizygotic twin pairs tested with the Differential Aptitude Test battery. Of the eight separate sections contained in this battery (spatial, numerical, abstract reasoning, verbal, mechanical, clerical, spelling, and detection of grammatical errors), only in spatial ability did the heritability for boys exceed that for girls. In boys, heritability was demonstrated at the .00001 level; the ratio of the variance within dizygotic twin pairs to that within monozygotic twin pairs reached 4.05. In girls, heritability was significant at only the $p = 0.07$ level, and this ratio was only 1.48.

So far, we have considered the consequences of only one X chromosome in the male and two X chromosomes in the female. However, now there is substantial evidence in support of Lyon's (1961) hypothesis that one of the X chromosomes is usually rendered inactive early in the development of the normal female. This inactivation appears to occur randomly with respect to which of the two X chromosomes is affected in a particular cell. Once such inactivation has occurred, however, multiplication of the cell maintains the inactivated X in the resulting clone of cells. Thus, the female appears to develop as a mosaic of populations of cells, some with one X chromosome inactivated, some with the other (Lyon, 1970). One estimate of when X inactivation occurs in the mouse is 3.5 days from conception (Gardner & Lyon, 1971). During this very early period, it appears that two sex chromosomes are needed for normal development, because in Turner's syndrome (in which there is only one X chromosome), there are a number of morphological abnormalities, including a characteristic webbing of the neck. Thus, even though it appears that a single functional X chromosome is sufficient for most purposes, it is possible that the specific deficit in visuospatial performance, displayed by individuals with Turner's syndrome (Money & Ehrhardt, 1968), may represent a developmental deficiency arising from the absence of a second sex chromosome during this early period.

Although Lyon's (1961) X-inactivation hypothesis has received considerable support, it should not be thought that the inactivated X chromosomes are totally without effect on development. On the contrary, studies of the IQ of persons with abnormal sex-chromosome complements (Moor, 1967) have shown a consistent decline in intelligence as the number of inactivated Xs increases. In such persons, the rule appears to be that only one X chromosome is functional in any cell: All X chromosomes except one are inactivated. Indeed, this is how abnormal sex chromosome constitutions are detected; the *Barr bodies* that are seen in microscopic investigations of cell samples from individuals under investigation, and that are used to determine the karyotype, are probably the inactivated X chromosomes (Lyon, 1970). Moor's (1967) data are shown in Fig. 6. This figure also shows similar data for the number of ridges in fingerprints (Penrose, 1968; Polani, 1969). There is a striking similarity in the results obtained: Both IQ and finger-ridge counts decline monotonically with added superfluous X or Y chromosomes, and the effects of additional X chromosome on IQ apparently outweigh those of additional Ys.

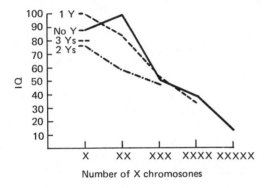

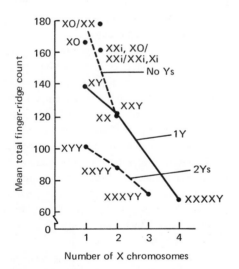

FIG. 6 Mean IQ (top) and total finger-ridge count (bottom) as related to number of X and Y chromosomes. From "What do we know today about the inheritance of intelligence and how do we know it?" by S. G. Vandenberg, in R. Cancro (Ed.), *Intelligence: Genetic and environmental influences,* New York: Grune & Stratton, 1971. Copyright 1971 by Grune & Stratton. Reprinted by permission.

## 3 TESTOSTERONE–INDUCED DIFFERENTIATION: OVARIAN CYCLE IN RODENTS

As we have seen, the masculinizing activity of the Y chromosome is chiefly effected by testis specification and subsequent testosterone release. We now consider how this process affects, in known instances, the differentiation of sexually dimorphic behavioral characteristics.

It is necessary to begin this section with a detailed consideration of gonadal endocrinology (Everett, 1961). First, the initial experiments in this field concerned the sexual differentiation of the ovarian cycle. The principles established in these experiments have been extended, both experimentally and inferentially, to sexually dimorphic behavior. Second, one of the main principles resulting from these experiments is that testosterone exposure during infancy often alters the sensitivity of the adult brain to hormones. Third, although gonadal endocrinology follows essentially the same pattern throughout the mammalian class, there are important differences between species, particularly in the female. Therefore, it is necessary to ensure that homologous endocrine states of different species are properly identified, if valid extrapolation to man is to be made from the animal experiments, which provide the bulk of data.

The endocrinology of the male is much simpler than that of the female. There is one male sex hormone (androgen) that is, testosterone, and in an unchanging environment it is secreted by the testis without major spontaneous fluctuations in level. By contrast, in the female there are two classes of sex hormones—estrogens (principally estradiol) and progestagens (principally progesterone)—secreted by the ovary, and these may have both synergistic and antagonistic interactions (Courrier, 1950). Both hormones display regular cycles, even in an unchanging environment. In addition, the female undergoes major changes in the hormonal state during pregnancy, lactation, and menopause.

The female hormonal cycles vary in different species. The fundamentals of the mammalian cycle however, may be illustrated by the guinea pig (Fig. 7). The first phase of the cycle, leading to ovulation, involves the growth of the ovarian follicle and is known as the *follicular phase*. At the end of this phase, a burst of estrogen secretion precipitates a burst of luteinizing hormone from the anterior pituitary that causes ovulation. After ovulation, the ovarian follicle is transformed into an endocrine organ that is specific to mammals and known as the corpus luteum. This organ secretes progesterone throughout the second phase of the cycle, which is the *luteal phase*. Variants on this fundamental cycle occur in different species. One major variant is found in man, the great apes, and the Old World (but not the New World) monkeys, in which the uterine wall breaks down when the corpus luteum regresses at the end of the luteal phase. This is menstruation; hence, the cycle in these species is called *menstrual*. In a second variant, the corpus luteum does not become functional and secrete progesterone unless the animal mates during the follicular phase. If mating does not occur, the follicular phase recommences immediately after ovulation. This is the cycle in many rodents, including rats, mice, and hamsters. If mating does occur, and conception does not ensue, there follows a luteal phase that is essentially like that in the guinea pig; in this species, however, this is termed *pseudopregnancy*. In the third major variant, ovulation is a reflex response to mating. Species showing this pattern (including rabbits and cats) are known as *reflex ovulators*. Once ovulation has occurred, however, the luteal phase follows spontaneously. If ovulation does not occur, estrogen secretion is prolonged until the active ovarian follicles regress. (We shall ignore the additional complications introduced by pregnancy and lactation, since there are few data available on the behavior of laboratory animals in these states.)

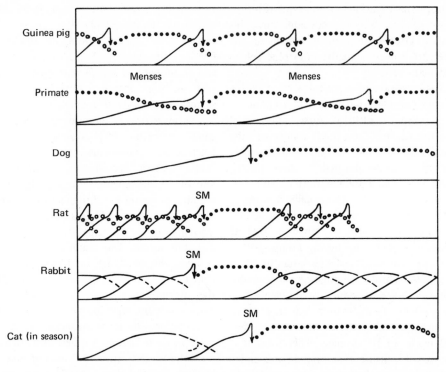

**FIG. 7** Cycles of representative, familiar mammals. Solid line, the follicular phase, highly schematized and inaccurate in detail; dashed line, atresia; arrow, ovulation; solid circle, fully active corpora lutea; open circle, corpora lutea regressing or otherwise not fully active. When sterile mating or equivalent stimulation (SM) is introduced, the cycles of the rat, rabbit, and cat become directly comparable with those of other species. From "The Mammalian Female Reproductive Cycle and Its Controlling Mechanisms" by J. W. Everett, in *Sex and Internal Secretions* (Vol. 1), edited by W. C. Young, Baltimore, Williams and Wilkins, 1961. Copyright 1961 by Williams and Wilkins. Reprinted by permission.

Clearly, any extrapolation to man, from animal data on the sex-hormonal control of behavior in females, is more difficult than similar extrapolation to males. Care must be taken to respect the different variants of the fundamental female mammalian cycle; to match similar portions of the cycle between species; and, in concluding to a difference between the sexes, to sample all appropriate portions of the female cycle. As an example of this last point, consider J. A. Gray's (1971a) conclusion that, in the rat, the male is more fearful than the female, whereas in man this sex difference is reversed. It is

possible that, rather than representing a true species difference, this arises because all the rat data are obtained from females that are in the nonluteal phase, whereas the human data average luteal and nonluteal phases together. Studies of the behavioral effects of pseudopregnancy in the rat would help to resolve these issues. We know of only one such study (Banerjee, 1971).

We have confined our attention here to levels of gonadal steroids. It is well known, however, that both the testis and the ovary are controlled by protein hormones secreted from the anterior pituitary. In the female, the hormones involved—generically known as gonadotropins—are the follicle-stimulating hormone (FSH), which causes the follicles to grow and secrete estrogen; the luteinizing hormone (LH), which causes ovulation; and the luteo-tropic hormone (LTH), which maintains the corpus luteum and stimulates it to secrete progesterone. In the male, interstitial-cell-stimulating hormone (ICSH), which is probably identical to LH chemically, causes testosterone secretion. The ICSH levels usually remain constant, giving rise to the constant testosterone levels, whereas the three gonadotropins in the female vary cyclically and produce the ovarian cycle shown in Fig. 7. The cyclicity, however, does not reside in the pituitary itself, since it is known (Harris & Jacobsohn, 1952) that cross transplanting pituitaries between adult male and female animals leaves the female cycle intact and does not produce a cycle in the male. There is evidence that the cyclicity is, in fact, produced by hormones (releasing factors) that are secreted by cells in the hypothalamus and travel by way of the portal stalk to the anterior pituitary (Harris & Campbell, 1966). The critical area within the hypothalamus has been shown, by experiments involving lesions and various kinds of stimulation applied to the brain, to lie in the preoptic area (Barraclough, 1967). The hypothalamus is, of course, under the modulating control of higher nervous structures, of which the most important appear to lie in the limbic system, especially the amygdala and the hippocampus (Donovan, 1971).

It appears from the foregoing that, as far as sexual endocrinology is concerned, an adult male mammal differs from a female in that (a) he possesses a testis, not an ovary; and (b) he possesses a brain (probably a preoptic area) that is incapable of sustaining cycles of gonadotropin release from the pituitary. Therefore, there is the question of how this difference between the sexes develops: that is, given the existence of male-determining chromosomal material in the genotype, how does this actually determine the differentiation of male gonadal endocrinology?

Much of the relevant experimental work has been done on the rat and guinea pig (Neumann, Steinbeck, & Hahn, 1970). In both species, it has been shown that there is a critical period during which testosterone, whether secreted endogenously by the testis or administered experimentally, produces irreversible changes in the control of the ovarian cycle. In the rat the critical period occurs immediately after birth (until about 10 days), a period during which high levels of testosterone are present in the blood, as shown by Resko, Feder, and Goy (1968). In the guinea pig, which at birth is more mature neurologically than the rat, the critical period occurs prenatally. A summary of experimental findings in the rat follows: If the testis is surgically removed from a 1-day-old male, in adulthood this animal is capable of sustaining typical ovarian cycles in an implanted ovary; conversely, if the infant (up to about 5 days) female rat is injected with a small quantity of testosterone, then in adulthood she is incapable of sustaining such cycles. In view of the evidence that the ovarian cycle is controlled by neurons in the preoptic area (Barraclough, 1967), it might be expected that this would be the critical site of action of testosterone. This expectation is supported by the observations of Raisman and Field (1972; 1973) that there are characteristic differences between the sexes in the disposition of synapses along neurons in the preoptic area and that these differences respond to the same infant treatments that affect the control of ovulation: The synaptic pattern characteristic of the male rat was changed to that characteristic of the female by neonatal castration, and the female pattern was changed to the one characteristic of the male by injections of testosterone. Thus, it appears probable that one action of testosterone on the developing brain is to alter the growth and pattern of connections of specific neurons.

## 4 TESTOSTERONE-INDUCED DIFFERENTIATION: SEXUAL BEHAVIOR

So far, we have been concerned with sex differences in gonadal endocrinology and their development in rodents, since the basic principles of sexual differentiation are both simple in this field and well worked out. Before we consider how these principles might apply to behavioral sex differences in man, we should first see how well they apply to sex differences in the behavior of animals.

The most obvious behavior to study is sexual behavior, and this has been thoroughly studied. The main measures used have been certain motor patterns that form part of normal male and female mating behavior in rats and guinea pigs. These have been lordosis in the female and mounting, intromission, and ejaculation in the male. *Lordosis* consists of raising the haunches and moving the tail aside. The term *mounting* is used to describe a motor pattern in which the male places his front paws on the female's haunches. *Intromission* describes a mount from which penile insertion actually ensues, this being followed by a backward spring by the male, who then licks his penis. *Ejaculation* involves actual seminal emission; following this, the male falls off the female without the spring characteristic of intromission. At the end of a completed sequence of this kind, the male is refractory to further sexual stimulation for a period. The motor patterns characterizing each of the behaviors in the sequence can be identified even in an animal in which literal intromission and ejaculation are not possible, due to genital inadequacy or any other cause.

Lordosis is a response to the male and, in the normal female, is dependent on the ovarian hormones, estrogen and progesterone. Hence, it is elicited with maximum ease at about the time of ovulation and is usually impossible to elicit at other times. Thus, lordosis defines the estrus cycle, estrus being the period of maximum sexual behavior. An ovariectomized female fails to show the response to an adequate stimulus, but the exogenous administration of estrogen and progesterone in an appropriate dosage and sequence restores the response. Lordosis is not normally shown by a male, and administration of these hormones to one, whether intact or castrated in adulthood, facilitates it only minimally. Thus, for lordosis to occur, the requirements appear to be (besides an adequate stimulus) a female animal and an appropriate hormonal status.

For this purpose, a female animal may be produced either by taking a normal genotypic female or by castrating a genotypic male in infancy; conversely, a genotypic female may be reduced to showing the level of lordosis displayed by the normal male if she is injected with testosterone in infancy. Thus lordosis appears to undergo sexual differentiation the same way as the ovarian cycle; that is, testosterone administered in infancy suppresses the normal female patterns. Although it is by no means established, it seems likely that this effect of testosterone is mediated by an action on hypothalamic neurons. Both lesions studies and studies employing intracerebral hormone implants implicate the anterior and ventromedial hypothalamus in the control of lordosis (Dörner, Döcke, & Moustafa, 1968; Kennedy, 1964; Lisk, 1962; Singer, J.J. 1968). Furthermore, Nadler (1971) showed that implants of testosterone in the diencephalon of infant female rats also suppress adult lordosis.

The three male motor patterns are dependent on testosterone, since they eventually disappear after castration in adulthood and may be restored by exogenous administration of the hormone. The normal female responds with a respectable degree of mounting if an adequate stimulus is present, i.e., optimally, another female in estrus. Furthermore, mounting is increased in females by exogenous testosterone in the same dose range as that required to restore mounting in the castrated male (Beach, 1968). Thus, unlike lordosis, neither mounting nor its hormonal control appears to be sexually dimorphic. The intromission pattern is infrequently observed in normal females, and the ejaculatory pattern is rarely observed. However, intromission rates rise when exogenous testosterone is administered to the adult, though not be a level comparable to that shown by a normal male. Studies using the neonatal treatments have shown that castration of the infant male does not reduce mounting in the adult: on the contrary, if anything, this activity is increased (Beach & Holz, 1946; Gerall, Hendricks, Johnson, & Bounds, 1967). Intromission and ejaculation are much reduced (Beach & Holz, 1946; Gerall, Hendricks, et al., 1967).

There is controversy as to whether this failure of ejaculation results from peripheral or central changes in animals castrated in early life, since such animals have less well developed penes (small and with fewer penile papillae) than normal rats. Hart (1972), in an elaborate series of experiments, demonstrated that peripheral factors cannot account for the failure of ejaculation in these animals. Hart castrated rats on the 4th day of life and injected some with testosterone and others with fluoxymesterone, a synthetic androgen that maintains peripheral

androgen sensitive tissues but has no central nervous system effects. The fluoxymesterone produced peripheral phallic development equal to that found after treatment with testosterone; but the animals so treated, unlike the testosterone treated animals, were still incapable of ejaculation. After transection of the spinal cord, there were no difficulties in local penile reflexes between the two groups, indicating that the difference was due to sexual differentiation within the brain.

In addition to these differences of organization, the areas of the hypothalamus controlling male sexual behavior are different from those controlling female sexual behavior: The latter, as we have seen, are in the anterior and ventromedial hypothalamus and the former include the medial forebrain bundle (Hitt, Hendricks, Ginsberg, & Lewis, 1970). A lesion in the medial forebrain bundle disrupts male-type sexual behavior in both sexes, but does not disrupt female-type sexual behavior. Thus, the normal female seems to possess two separate and functional systems, with separate anatomical locations in the brain, one for female-type sexual behavior and one for male-type mounting. Apparently, in the normal male the former mechanism is suppressed by testosterone in infancy, which also completes the organization of the male-type sexual response system. However, it is important to note that occasionally untreated males will display levels of female-type sexual behavior comparable to that shown by a normal female (Beach, 1971), as well as normal male-type behavior. Such an animal may be produced experimentally by castrating a genotypic male on the first day of life and injecting it with androstenodione, which is an androgen secreted with testosterone by the fetal testis (Goldfoot, Feder, & Goy, 1969). Thus, in genotypic females and genotypic males (infrequently in males), both male-type and female-type sexual behavior may be expressed. Of course, such bisexuality is not possible for the ovarian cycle, or the emotional behavior we consider later, in which there is a single continuum.

In primates, including man, the first thing to consider is whether genital morphology and the ovarian cycle are subject to the same testosterone-induced differentiation as in rodents. It has been established that high plasma levels of testosterone occur prenatally in the male rhesus monkey (Resko, 1970). In the human male such an analysis has been carried out only in umbilical cord blood at delivery, and testosterone levels were not higher in males than in females (Mizuno, Lobotsky, Lloyd, Kobayashi, & Murasawa, 1968; Rivarola, Forest, & Migeon, 1968). This does not, of course, rule out the possibility that testosterone levels are higher in the male than in the female at an earlier critical state of gestation. Exogenous testosterone administered to pregnant rhesus monkeys masculinize the external genitalia of genotypic females (Young, Goy, & Phoenix, 1964), as would be expected from the studies on subprimate mammals. In the human, a similar androgen-induced hermaphroditism is seen in genotypic girls born to mothers treated with progestins (which have androgenic effects), or girls suffering from hyperadrenocorticalism (a disorder in which the adrenal cortex produces an excess of androgenic hormones), also known as the adrenogenital syndrome (Erhardt & Money, 1967; Money & Erhardt, 1968). Thus, as far as genital morphology is concerned, the effects of androgenic hormones appear to be the same in man and the rhesus monkey as in rodents.

Regarding the ovarian cycle, there is now firm evidence that the sexual differentiation found in rodents does not occur in primates. Peretz, Goy, Phoenix, and Resko (1971), for example, failed to affect the ovarian cycle

by large, prolonged injections of testosterone to pregnant mothers even though these injections affected genital morphology and (as we shall see) certain features of play behavior. The study by Karsch, Dierschke, and Knobil (1973) is even more convincing. They showed that normal male rhesus monkeys subjected to gonadectomy in adulthood responded to estradiol with a release of luteinizing hormone just as normal females do. This result is unequivocal, since, obviously, if the normal male has not sexually differentiated, then no further investigation of pseudohermaphrodites is needed.

It is also clear that in adult humans the dependence of sexual behavior on gonadal hormones differs in important respects from the picture we described for rodents.

In males there is suggestive evidence (Money, 1961) for androgenic control of coital frequency. The effects of castration, however, are difficult to evaluate, because with age there is a gradual decline in coital frequency (Kinsey, Pomeroy, & Martin, 1948). There are data that show an increase in sexual interest following androgen administration to castrated males (Money, 1961). There is also an elegant single case study of a male castrate and the effects of androgen administration on objective measures of sexual arousal. This study again indicates androgenic control (Beumont, Bancroft, Beardwood, & Russell, 1972). However, there are numerous reports of continued sexual activity for many years after castration (Kinsey, Pomeroy, Martin, & Gobhard, 1953). In view of the data on adrenal androgen control of sexual behavior in the human female, the possibility cannot be excluded that androgenic hormones from this source are able to substitute for absent testicular hormones in the male of our species, too. However, it is known that such adrenal control does not contribute to the maintenance of sexual behavior in male rats

(Bloch & Davidson, 1968), hamsters (Warren & Aronson, 1956), cats (Cooper & Aronson, 1958), or dogs (Schwartz, M., & Beach, 1954) after gonadectomy. Thus, it appears that sexual behavior in the human male is dependent on testicular hormones, though perhaps to a lesser extent than in rodents. The picture in other male primates (Michael, R. P., & Wilson, 1974; Phoenix, Slob, & Goy, 1973; Young, W. C. 1961) appears similar to that in human males.

On the other hand, the available evidence does not suggest that the ovary controls the sexual behavior of women the way it controls the behavior of rats. W. H. James (1971) analyzed information collected from daily coital diaries, including data from McCance, Luff, and Widdowson (1973); Kinsey, Pomeroy, et al. (1953); Udry and Morris (1968); and his own study, and showed that the most striking phenomenon found in them is a postmenstrual increase in coitus. He pointed out that pooling data from cycles of different length produces a misleading impression that this postmenstrual increase is a more general increase during the follicular phase. A slight increase in coital frequency occurred toward the middle of the cycle; however, James noted that its occurrence 9–11 days after the end of menstruation remained constant across cycles of different lengths (23–31 days); therefore, its relationship to the pre-ovulatory rise in estrogen secretion remains ambiguous. James attributed the post-menstrual rise in coital frequency to a release from deprivation incurred during the menstrual period.

The lack of any clear effect of ovarian estrogens during the menstrual cycle is echoed in the general finding that ovari-ectomy and the menopause do not reduce coital frequency, except through purely local effects on the vaginal wall (Kinsey, Pomeroy, et al., 1953; Money, 1961). This appears to indicate a change in hormonal control, rather than a lack of it, since adrenal androgens probably do enhance sexual responsiveness in women (Waxenberg, Drellic, & Sutherland, 1959). These authors found that, in women treated by both adrenalectomy and ovariectomy for breast cancer, loss of sexual responsiveness was associated specifically with adrenalectomy. This was so whether the adrenalectomy was performed before or after the ovariectomy and occurred in women in whom the adrenalectomy resulted in a clear mitigation of symptoms and improvement in general health. Thus, in women, there appears to be a shift to control of sexual behavior by adrenal androgens.

This shift, however, is not specific to humans. At any rate, similar findings have been reported in rhesus monkeys. Male-female monkey pairs show rhythmic changes in sexual activity; coitus is reduced during the luteal phase and increases at about the time of ovulation. However, it is not certain that these rhythms should be attributed to behavioral changes in the female. One factor that is definitely involved is a change in the attractiveness of the female for the male, this being partly due to the maximal emission of pheromones of vaginal origin at the time of ovulation (Michael, R. P. 1968). The published data on sexual behavior actually initiated by the female, as distinct from the behavior she elicits from her consort, do not show any consistent and systematic cycles over the menstrual period (Michael, R. P., 1968). Thus, although R. P. Michael (1968) argued that in the female rhesus monkey sexual motivation is under some control by ovarian hormones, there is no unequivocal evidence supporting this argument. In contrast, there is evidence that, in female rhesus monkeys as in women, sexual behavior is controlled by androgens of adrenal origin. Everitt, Herbert, and Hamer (1972) and

Everitt and Herbert (1971) showed that rhesus female sexual behavior declines dramatically after adrenalectomy, or after chemical blockade of the adrenal cortex by dexamethasone injections. Injection of adrenal androgens, but not of glucocorticoids, restored sexual behavior in these animals.

It seems, then, that sexual behavior in primates, including man, may differ in at least two important ways from the behavior among rodents. First, the behavior of the female appears to be controlled by adrenal androgens, rather than ovarian estrogens. Second, it appears that the ovarian cycle is not subject to testosterone-induced suppression in the developing male. There are not direct studies of the differentiation of sex-typical sexual behavior in the adult primate; however, such studies likely will be available when the rhesus monkeys masculinized by prenatal injections of testosterone in Young's laboratory reach maturity. We know of no relevant data from our own species. Thus, the only arguments that can be made regarding the differentiation of sexual behavior in man must depend on extrapolation from the rodent experiments.

In view of the differences between primates and rodents, such extrapolation is hazardous. Nonetheless, far-reaching extrapolations have been made, especially concerning the etiology of human homosexuality. Tentative suggestions that the principles of testosterone-based sexual differentiation *might* account for this condition (e.g., Levine, 1966; Loraine, Ismail, Adamopoulos, & Dove, 1970; Young, Goy, & Phoenix, 1964) have been outdone by more explicit claims that they *do,* and that they might even serve as the rationale for prophylactic treatment in infancy with androgens or antiandrogens (Dörner, 1969; Dörner & Hinz, 1968). As far as we know, the only experimental evidence from human studies cited as support for these claims is the observation

that male homosexuals have lower levels of circulating testosterone than do heterosexuals (Loraine, Ismail, et al., 1970). However, apart from the impossibility of using this finding retrospectively to estimate prenatal testosterone levels, it is always possible that it is a consequence, rather than a cause, of homosexuality or of factors associated with homosexuality. In view of the lack of experimental support for these claims, we must carefully scrutinize the legitimacy of extrapolation from the animal studies.

The behavior that needs special explanation is that of the exclusive homosexual, that is, in the case of the male, one who engages in sexual activity only with other males. The mixed behavior, in which an individual engages in sexual activity both with members of the same sex and with members of the opposite sex, is less surprising, since such behavior is frequently reported in other species (Beach, 1948). In contrast, under normal conditions exclusive homosexuality appears to be a prerogative of our own species. Furthermore, the incidence of such behavior is quite high: According to the Kinsey reports, as many as 4% of males and 1–3% of females fall in this category (Kinsey, Pomeroy, & Martin, 1948; Kinsey, Pomeroy, et al. 1953). To account for exclusive homosexuality, it was suggested (Dörner, 1969; Dörner & Hinz, 1968) that in males there has been some failure of early androgenic differentiation of the brain sites controlling sexual behavior, and in females, there has been some unusual exposure to androgens that have masculinized these sites. (There are no chromosomal abnormalities found exclusively among homosexuals: The females remain XX and the males XY.)

Human homosexual behavior is defined by the choice of the sex of the partner. Any sexual behavior, no matter what form it takes, is by definition homosexual if it occurs with a partner of the same sex. In contrast, in animal studies sex-typical sexual behavior is defined in terms of motor patterns. Tests of lordosis, for example, may involve stimulation from a male, another female, or, quite commonly, an experimenter's hand. Conversely, there do not seem to be any special motor patterns that characterize the sexual behavior of one or the other sex in man (Masters & Johnson, 1967). Thus, the phenomenon of homosexuality in humans is not the same as the phenomena associated with alterations in sexual differentiation in rodents.

The second point we must make is that the failure of sexual behavior in the infant castrate male rat is specifically associated with a failure of the ejaculatory reflex (and not, as we have seen, with a failure to approach or mount the stimulus animal). There is no evidence of this anomaly in human homosexual males.

Third, the androgenization of the female rat produces a specific insensitivity to estrogens, shown both by a lack of sexual activity and by a lack of LH release. There is no evidence that estrogens control sexual behavior, even in the normal human female; and evidence indicates that the LH response to estradiol does not differentiate at all in primates, even in normal males.

There is also direct evidence that those researchers with the sexual-differentiation view of homosexuality must find difficult to accommodate. In particular, the genotypic females with the adrenogenital syndrome (Ehrhardt, Epstein, & Money, 1968), who had been exposed to sufficiently high levels of perinatal androgens to affect their external genitalia, play behavior, and IQ, did not become lesbians, as they would if high levels of androgen (insufficient, however, to produce physical stigmata) were the usual cause of female homosexuality. Money (1970), one of the leading investigators in this field,

reviewed similar material, and his conclusions essentially agree with ours: It is unlikely that abnormalities in the process of sexual differentiation account for the incidence of homosexual behavior in chromosomally and morphologically normal individuals.

# 5 TESTOSTERONE-INDUCED DIFFERENTIATION: AGGRESSIVE BEHAVIOR

As we have seen, one way in which testosterone-induced differentiation of sexual behavior works is by suppressing the sensitivity of the central nervous system structures to ovarian hormones in adulthood (the ovarian cycle and lordosis in female rodents). In the case of a second form of behavior that is (a) sexually dimorphic and (b) differentiated during early development by the action of testosterone—aggression—the principle appears to be different. In this case, testosterone seems to sensitize the central nervous system structures that mediate aggressive behavior to the action of testosterone in adulthood.

As reviewed by J. A. Gray (1971a), in most mammals, males are more aggressive than females (the hamster is an exception: Payne, A. P., & Swanson, 1970; Vandenbergh, J. G. 1971). Moreover, in those species in which adequate studies have been done, the sex difference is noted to be specific to certain kinds of aggression only: those termed *defensive* or *intraspecific* in contrast to *interspecific* or *predatory* aggression. Thus, sex differences in aggressive responses have been observed when rats or mice are caged together after a period of prior isolation, when they are exposed to social crowding, or when two animals are simultaneously given footshock. No sex differences are observed, however, in mice fighting for possession of food, nor in the rat's mouse-killing response. The distinction between defensive and predatory aggression is particularly clear in the cat, which adopts two quite different motor patterns in the two situations. When stalking its prey (e.g., a mouse), the cat is silent, its back is low, its hair is smoothed down, and its ears are normally raised; in contrast, during an agonistic encounter with another cat or with a dog, the cat hisses or growls, its back is arched, its hair is raised on end, and its ears are flattened back (Nakao, 1971). The distinction between defensive and predatory aggression is supported by studies in which the brain has been lesioned or stimulated electrically. The studies reveal that different brain structures control the two kinds of behavior. Both the cat's rat-killing response and the rat's mouse-killing response depend, in part, on activity in the lateral hypothalamus (Hutchinson & Renfrew, 1966; Karli, Vergnes, & Didiergeorges, 1969), an area that is also of critical importance in the control of food-seeking behavior (Grossman, S. P., 1967). Defensive aggression, on the other hand, depends on structures in the corticomedial amygdala, the ventromedial hypothalamus, and the central grey matter of the midbrain (Kaada, 1972; de Molina & Hunsperger, 1962; Nakao, 1971).

Greater male aggressiveness has also been observed in a number of primate species, including the stumptail macaque, the Japanese macaque, the rhesus monkey, and the chimpanzee (see Gray, J. A., 1971a). The relevant data are mainly concerned with agonistic interactions that are probably homologous to the cat's defensive aggression. Thus, among most mammalian species, it seems reasonable to generalize that males are predisposed to a greater degree, or intensity, of display of intraspecific aggressive behavior than are females. In human males, there have been numerous experimental demonstrations of greater aggressive-

ness (Maccoby & Jacklin, 1975, Table 7.1) to reinforce the cross-cultural unanimity that males are far more likely than females to be convicted of criminal acts involving violence (Sutherland & Cressey, 1955); therefore, the most parsimonious view is that this tendency continues in our own species. There is also a sex difference in agonistic encounters during play in juvenile primates: Males display a greater tendency than do females toward rough-and-tumble play, chasing play, and threatening behavior in the rhesus monkey (Goy, 1968; Harlow, H. F., & Harlow, 1965), and the squirrel monkey (Baldwin, 1969), as well as in our own species (Blurton-Jones, 1967). That essentially the same neural structures are involved in primate aggression as in the rat and cat seems to be shown by the evidence that structures in the amygdala control aggression in both rhesus monkey (Kling, 1972) and man (Mark, Ervin, & Sweet, 1972).

Regarding hormonal control of defensive aggression in rats and mice, it was shown that castration of males in adulthood reduces the level of aggression, and administration of testosterone restores it. However, administration of testosterone to adult females has no effect, and estrogen does not affect aggression in either sex (Gray, J. A., 1971a). Neonatal castration of the male rat or mouse reduces the level of aggression seen in adulthood to that of the normal female, and such an animal no longer responds to exogenous testosterone with an increase in aggressive behavior. Conversely, neonatal injection of testosterone to genotypic females, combined with adult injection of testosterone, produces levels of aggression comparable to that of the normal male (Gray, J. A., 1971a). Thus, for high levels of defensive aggression, the requirements appear to be a male animal, whether genotypic or as a consequence of neonatal androgenization of a genotypic female, and sufficient levels of testosterone.[1] It seems that the effect of the administration of testosterone to infant animals is to sensitize the brain structures, which control defensive aggression, to the action of testosterone in adulthood. As we have seen, the most likely structures involved are in the corticomedial amygdala, the ventromedial hypothalamus, and the midbrain. At least one of the relevant sites was shown to respond to neonatal manipulations of testicular hormones. Mattock and MacKinnon (1975; personal communication, 1976) presented evidence that in female pubertal rats, the incorporation of labeled amino acids into protein is accelerated in the medial amygdala as compared with males; and that neonatal testosterone treatment alters the normal female rate of incorporation into a rate characteristic of normal males. It is likely that these biochemical changes in the amygdala relate to a functional sex difference, but there is no evidence that the relevant sex difference is in aggressive behavior; they could relate, for example, to the marked sex differences in the feeding behavior of rats (Valenstein, 1968; Valenstein, Cox, & Kakolewski, 1970), since the corticomedial nuclei of the amygdala are known to be part of the systems that control food intake (Grossman, 1967; Kaada, 1972), or to sex differences in the control of puberty (Mattock & MacKinnon; personal communication, 1976).

Regarding primates, it is more difficult to find evidence either for control of aggression by testosterone in the adult animal, or for testosterone-induced differentiation of aggressive behavior into the male type. However, existing evidence is consistent with the view that the patterns found in rodent studies have persisted among primates, and we know of no contrary evidence.

Beach (1948) summarized a number of admittedly anecdotal or clinical observations in man that castration of the adult male leads to a reduction in pugnacity, which may be restored by testosterone injections. In a group of young male prisoners, Kreuz and Rose (1972) found that plasma testosterone levels were significantly higher in those persons who had committed more aggressive or physically violent crimes than among those whose offences had been larceny or burglary. However, there was no correlation between plasma testosterone levels and the incidence of fighting while in prison. In the rhesus monkey a correlation was found between plasma testosterone levels and both aggressive behavior and rank in the dominance hierarchy formed among a group of free-living males (Rose, R. M., Holaday, & Bernstein, 1971). The direction of causation, of course, cannot be inferred from such a correlation; it could mean that high social dominance allows testosterone levels to rise (Rose, R. M., Gordon, & Bernstein, 1972), that high testosterone levels lead to high social dominance, or that both are caused by a third variable. A study by Joslyn (1973), however, offers evidence for a causal role of testosterone in the control of aggressive behavior: exogenous administration of the hormone to female rhesus monkeys in a mixed-sex juvenile group increased their level of aggression and caused them to become dominant over the initially dominant males. This result suggests that testosterone facilitates aggressive behavior in primates but that, unlike rodents, female primates are also responsive to the hormone. This may be related to the existence of androgenic control over sexual behavior in female primates, which we discussed previously.

---

[1] Recent work on the golden hamster makes it clear that this species constitutes a considerable exception to these rules at a number of points (e.g., Drickamer & Vandenbergh, 1973; Payne, A. P., 1974; Payne, A. P., & Swanson, 1970, 1971, 1972; Vandenbergh, J. G., 1971).

With regard to the developmental basis of the sex difference in aggressiveness, there are two relevant studies, one on rhesus monkeys and one with humans. Female rhesus monkeys masculinized by prenatal injection of testosterone to the mother display greater amounts of rough-and-tumble play than do normal females during childhood and approach the levels displayed by normal males (Goy, 1968). Money and Ehrhardt (1968), reporting on their interviews both with the patients and with their parents, stated that genotypic girls masculinized by exposure to prenatal androgens (progestin-induced hermaphrodites and cases of hyper-adrenocorticalism) show unusually high degrees of tomboyishness: They have "intense outdoor physical and athletic interests"; they are "known to self and others as a tomboy"; and they have a strong interest in boys' rather than girls' toys. It should be noted that these are the same patients in whom sexual interest and orientation showed no effect of early androgen exposure. Thus, prenatal exposure to androgens appears, in our species as in the rhesus monkey, to have masculinizing effects on aggressive behavior, but not on sexual behavior. An interesting feature of the sexual differentiation of rough-and-tumble-play is that, in the juvenile rhesus monkey, this is apparently not under the control of current androgen levels (Goy, 1968). Thus, sexual differentiation of this behavior cannot be produced by sensitizing brain structures to the later effects of testosterone, as occurs in adult rodent aggression.

## 6 TESTOSTERONE–INDUCED DIFFERENTIATION: FEARFUL BEHAVIOR

We have concentrated on sexual and aggressive behavior, since we wished to emphasize the major principles in the physiological control of sex differences. There are, however, a number of other behavioral sex differences that are subject to testosterone-induced differentiation; and likely there will soon be further progress in this area.

One particularly interesting set of testosterone-induced sex differences in rodents involves behavioral measures that, as concluded by J. A. Gray (1971a, b), may relate to a general trait of fearfulness (though this conclusion was questioned by Archer, 1971). These include defecation and ambulation in the open field, emergence tests and tests of exploratory behavior, and shuttle-box-avoidance learning. On all these tests, males obtain scores indicative of higher fearfulness. (The reverse sex difference, however, appears to hold at the human level: Gray, J. A., 1971a; Gray, J. A., & Buffery, 1971.) These sex differences all seem to be subject to testosterone-induced differentiation. This has been shown for open field behavior in at least seven studies (Blizard & Denef, 1973; Drach, Cox, Kakolewski, & Valenstein, cited by Valenstein, 1968; Gray, J. A., Lean, & Keynes, 1969; Gray, J. A., Levine, & Broadhurst, 1965; Pfatt & Zigmond, 1971; Stewart, Skavenina, & Pottier, 1975; Swanson, 1967), for emergence times by Pfaff and Zigmond (1971) and Swanson (1967), and for shuttlebox avoidance by Beatty and Beatty (1970).

We have also concentrated on the genetic and developmental factors that give rise to the behavioral differences between the sexes. However, there is evidence that these factors may also affect individual differences within the sexes, so that an understanding of them may have wide implications for a general theory of the physiological basis of personality.

Generally, within a sex, it does not appear that individual differences in the display of hormone-dependent behavior result from differences in the amounts of circulating hormones at the time of behavior testing. In a group of male guinea pigs, for example, Grunt and Young (1952) measured the vigor of sexual behavior, then castrated them, injected all animals with a standard dose of testosterone, and remeasured sexual behavior. The rank ordering of the animals was essentially unchanged in the second test, as compared with the precastration measures. Thus, the differences between individual males did not reside in the levels of circulating hormones, but were due to the sensitivity of the target organs (whether in the brain or in the periphery) to testosterone. Similar observations were made in rats by Larsson (1966).

In an extension of this design, using rats, Pfaff and Zigmond (1971) rank ordered the animals according to their performance in tests of sexual behavior and on an emergence test. The rats had been exposed to appropriate treatments (testosterone injections or castration) in infancy and were given standard doses of exogenous gonadal hormones at the time of behavior testing in adulthood. Pfaff and Zigmond's (1971) findings indicated that the rank orders on the two tests were essentially the same: Those rats responding to gonadal hormones with high levels of female sexual behavior, whether genetic males or females, tended to emerge most frequently; that is, their behavior was characteristic of normal females. Similarly, males showing the most frequent intromissions were least likely to emerge in the emergence test. Thus, these results suggest that in infancy, testosterone alters the reactivity of a number of different brain mechanisms to a similar extent, in a way that spans more than one kind of behavior. Thus, at least some part of the individual differences within sexes, in sex-hormone-dependent behavior, may result from dif-

ferences in the effects of testosterone on the infant's brain. These differences fall short of the pathological sex reversals with which this chapter has largely been concerned.

Other evidence suggests the same conclusion. J. A. Gray (1971b) pointed out that many of the behavioral and physiological differences that Broadhurst (1960, 1975) produced in the Maudsley Reactive (MR) and Maudsley Nonreactive (MNR) strains of rats (selectively bred from an original Wistar stock for high and low levels of defecation, respectively, in the open field) conform to the pattern: As male is to female, so MR is to MNR. We recently obtained a striking confirmation of this generalization in experiments on the septal control of the hippocampal theta rhythm.

J. A. Gray (1970a) proposed that the brain system (Fig. 8) that mediates fearful behavior in the rat involves a hippocampal theta rhythm in the frequency band 7.5–8.5 Hz that is controlled by pacemaker cells in the medial septal area (Stumpf, 1965). Fear-reducing drugs, such as sodium amobarbital,

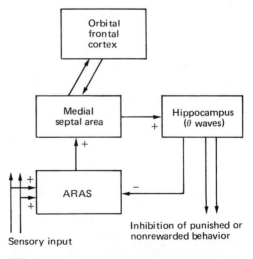

FIG. 8 Negative feedback loop whose activity is presumed to underlie the inhibition of punished or nonrewarded behavior (i.e., fear and frustration) in the rat (see Gray, 1970a).

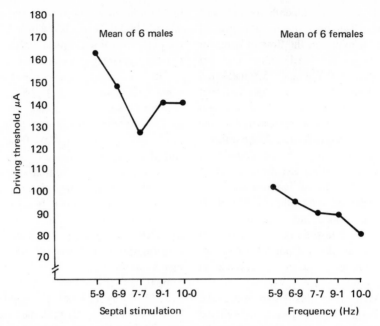

**FIG. 9** Mean thresholds for septal driving of hippocampal theta rhythm as a function of driving frequency in male and female rats (from Drewett & Gray, in preparation).

alcohol, and the benzodiazepines, raise the threshold for production of a theta rhythm by electrical stimulation of the medial septal area, selectively, in this frequency band (Gray, J. A., 1976; Gray, J. A., & Ball, 1970; Gray, J. A., McNaughton, James, & Kelly, 1975). This effect is probably due to an action on the dorsal ascending noradrenergic bundle (Gray, J. A., McNaughton, et al., 1975), though serotonergic mechanisms are probably involved also (Gray, J. A., 1976). Drewett and Gray (1976, in preparation; see Gray, J. A., 1972) investigated sex differences in the threshold for elicitation of the theta rhythm as a function of frequency of septal stimulation in unselected Wistar and Sprague-Dawley rats. Their findings are presented in Fig. 9. Whereas there is a characteristic dip in the resulting *theta-driving* curve at 7.7 Hz in the male, this dip is absent in the curve obtained from the female. Accordingly, we also took theta-driving curves from MR and MNR males rats: whereas the MR curve resembles that previously obtained from other males, the MNR curve is like that previously obtained only from females (Fig. 9). These results, combined with our findings (Drewett & Gray, 1976, in preparation) that in the adult the dip in the unselected male theta-driving curve is dependent on testosterone (while the female curve is independent of current ovarian hormones), raise the possibility that in the low-fearful MNR males Broadhurst's (1960) selective-breeding experiment involved a reduction in the sensitivity of the septo-hippocampal system to testosterone.[2] This change in sensitivity to testosterone is likely to involve serotonergic pathways (as previously indicated by Sudak & Maas's

[2] So far, we have been unable to demonstrate the expected behavioral effects of testosterone (increased fear or increased susceptibility to frustration) in normal rats (unpublished experiments).

(1964) study of the Maudsley strains), or noradrenergic pathways (Gray, J. A., McNaughton, et al., 1975), or both.

There is other evidence that supports the hypothesis that breeding experiments such as those Broadhurst (1960) conducted may involve alterations in the physiological control of sexually dimorphic behavior. Inbreeding (which was a feature of Broadhurst's selective-breeding program) reduces sex differences in open-field defecation in the mouse (Bruell, 1969); Sines' (1961) experiment on selective breeding (again combined with inbreeding) of rats for high and low susceptibility to ulceration also had this effect, as did Broadhurst's experiments (Broadhurst, 1960; Gray, J. A., Levine, & Broadhurst, 1965). Some data from this laboratory (Gray, J. A., Drewett, & Lalljee, 1975) indicate that such a reduction in the size of the sex difference in open-field behavior may sometimes be due to an alteration in the processes of sexual differentiation. An unsystematically inbred strain of hooded rats was found (Gray, J. A., & Lalljee, 1974) in which the sex difference in open-field defecation was the reverse of that usually seen: The females obtained higher scores. A series of experiments in this strain in which testosterone was administered to the infant female and infant males were castrated revealed defecation to be consistently unaffected by the neonatal treatments in either sex. This result contrasts sharply with the positive findings (Blizard & Denef, 1973; Gray, J. A., Lean, & Keynes, 1969; Gray, J. A., Levine, & Broadhurst, 1965; Pfaff & Zigmond, 1971; Stewart, Skvarenina, & Pottier, 1975; Valenstein, 1968) reported for these treatments when the sex difference in open-field defecation takes the usual direction (males defecating more).

Therefore, it is possible that selective breeding for relative fearfulness or inbreeding in rodents involves a reduction in the effectiveness with which testosterone in infancy masculinizes the neural structures responsible for the control of fearful behavior. This process might take place in one of two ways. Either the events controlled by the Y chromosome—specification of a testis and of the levels of testosterone to which the developing brain is thus exposed—could be altered; or the genes in which expression is altered by the inductive effects of testosterone could become relatively refractory to its effects. This happens on a massive scale in the syndrome of testicular feminization. Only further research can indicate whether either of these proposals has any merit or whether anything similar takes place in man.

## 7 SUMMARY

The potentialities and pitfalls of the comparative study of sex differences in behavior in mammalian species are discussed. Used carefully, such data can make a unique contribution to a theory of the physiological basis of personality. Major principles of the genetics and development of sex differences, as established by studies of morphological and behavioral development in rodents, are described; and their possible applications to personality differences, both between and within the sexes in man, are discussed. Special emphasis is placed on sexual (including homosexual), aggressive and fearful behavior, and on the control of such behavior by hormones acting on the brain. The effects on behavior of the X and Y chromosomes, in both normal and abnormal karyotypes, are also discussed.

# Section
## 3

## Personality Change and Development

# 15

## Learning Theory, Personality, and the S-R Paradigm

**Fredric Weizmann**
*York University*
*Toronto, Ontario, Canada*

### 1 TRAIT THEORIES AND LEARNING THEORIES

There is general agreement that much of what we call personality is learned, but the question of how much relevance personality and learning theory have for one another has always been a moot one. An even more appropriate question is why these two approaches were not developed along more complementary lines. That is, personality is usually described in terms of what G. S. Klein (1967, p. 464) called "integrative consistencies in behavior," whereas learning usually is defined as changes in behavior (or a major subset of such changes) due to experience. In short, both personality and learning theory are concerned with two aspects of the same problem: the general problem of behavioral consistency and change. Since both areas are concerned with similar problems, the question of why they did not evolve a common approach is a highly pertinent one.

One reason is that personality theorists (and correlational psychologists generally), have emphasized the person as the unit of consistency and couched their explanations in terms of *traits* (Cattell, 1950c; Guilford, J. P., 1959), or types. At the risk of oversimplifying, it is probably fair to say

that personologists have been more interested in characterizing people across situations and have been less interested in situational variables per se. Learning theorists, on the other hand, generally have been concerned with predicting the effects of environmental variables across people.

K. W. Spence's (1944) somewhat invidious distinction between stimulus-response (S-R) and response-response (R-R) laws helped to formalize this difference. Response-response laws, while considered useful, were not genuinely scientific because they only related responses to one another (i.e., were correlational) rather than to objective stimulus conditions, as did S-R laws. This distinction was lamented by some (e.g., Cronbach, 1957) and challenged by others; Jessor (1956), for example, pointed out that stimuli, far from being unrelated to responses, are, in fact, inferred from them. The logical independence of a stimulus from a response in a given experiment is due to the fact that it is defined prior to and independent of the relevant responses in that particular experiment. Response-response relationships can be investigated in the same way, and need not be treated as ad hoc and nonpredictive.

Despite these and other objections (e.g., Dulany, 1968), the dichotomy continues to be an influential one, as exemplified by attempts to extend S-R theory to complex human behavior (e.g., Skinner, B. F., 1964; Staats, 1968). Indeed, one important current thrust in personality theory and research is the search for the situational antecedents of personality variables, although this is probably inspired more by disillusionment with trait theories (Mischel, 1968; Peterson, 1968) than by Spence's arguments.

Campbell (1963) pointed out an additional difference between the learning and personality traditions stemming from their sources of data. Learning theory was erected largely around the study of mute infrahuman organisms. Thus, the stimulus determinants of responding must be inferred from nonverbal behavior. Insofar as the stimulus (as opposed to the observable response) is inferential, it is also somewhat *ghostly*; and its identification, problematic. These experimental situations are usually kept as simple as possible to reduce the complexity of the inferential chain and the risk of error. Further, the explanatory thrust of learning theory since J. B. Watson (1914) and Hull (1930, 1943) was toward the elucidation of response determinants, since they are more observable than covert perceptual and central processes. Attempts to deal with such covert processes typically proceeded by interpreting them as the consequences of response mechanisms (e.g., Berlyne, 1965; Osgood, 1957; Skinner, B. F., 1964; Staats, 1963).

For personologists, as well as for perceptual and cognitive psychologists, observations typically begin with humans in situations in which verbal reports constitute the primary source of data. As Campbell (1963, p. 127) noted, explanations derived from people about their behavior are unlikely to be couched in the form "I made Response B to Stimulus A," but rather in terms of feelings, phenomenal states, intentions, and so forth. William James (1890), in fact, argued that there is no consciousness of willing motor responses at all. Thus, explanations built around such subjective reports are apt to be generalizations of phenomenal states and to deemphasize the importance of the response.

These differences in approach led to marked differences in the kinds of theories that have been offered to explain behavior. For most nonlearning personality theorists, those aspects of the situation to which the person responds were determined by personality traits, needs, defenses, and values. Thus, concepts such as set, expectancy, and hypotheses were at least tacitly implied as bridges between personality and cognitive variables, on the one hand, and the situation, on the other. Further, to employ a distinction made by Schroder, Driver, and Streuffert (1967), many of these theorists were concerned with structural as well as content variables. That is, they were not only interested in what is learned but how it is learned and how it will be used for subsequent adaptive purposes. As structural variables, the characteristic manner in which a person pays attention, forms and uses hypotheses, and generally approaches situations can be studied in its own right, as adaptive style.

Until relatively recently, however, most experimental psychologists were critical of attentional concepts. In an influential article, Gibson (1941) argued that the concept of *set* was confusing because it was unclear as to whether it referred to a tendency to respond or to perceive in a given way. Further, although not logically necessary, such concepts were often applied in an ad hoc manner. C. W. Eriksen (1954) perhaps most aptly summarized prevailing attitudes when he noted that the "concept of set has shown itself in the history of psychology to be both broad and ambiguous enough to hide many important problems" (p. 180).

In terms of classical learning theory, of course, attentional concepts appeared mysterious. If, in an effort to keep theory close to observation, one begins one's conceptual unit (as opposed to a unit of experimental convenience) with a stimulus and terminates it with a response, then the central attentional processes that precede the stimulus will remain obscure. Insofar as stimulus selection and attentional processes were considered at all, they were seen as residues of previous conditioning or reinforceable responses in their own right (Hull, 1943; Wyckoff, 1952).

It has become apparent that such variables play a major role in the experiment. The work of Orne (Orne, 1962; Orne & Evans, 1964; Orne & Scheib, 1964) and others (e.g., Friedman, N., 1967) suggests that people's behavior is extremely dependent on their expectancies and attitudes regarding the experiment. Similarly, Dulany (1962, 1968) adduced much evidence attesting to the importance of knowing people's hypotheses and intentions in predicting their behavior. In other areas, too, attentional variables have attained a good deal of prominence (e.g., Kagan & Kogan, 1970).

Although the problems raised by set, hypotheses, or general adaptive strategies do not arise to the same extent if one uses infrahuman organisms as experimental subjects, not all these difficulties are avoided. One gets a different picture of the capacity of such organisms, depending on their manner of rearing and their previous experiential history. Usually, sophisticated

animals give a much more cognitive performance than do naive ones (e.g., Birch, 1945; Harlow H. F., 1949; Thompson, W. R., & Heron, 1954).

With humans, however, one does not have the option of using naive subjects. Even in the case of infants, evidence is accumulating that there are large and meaningful individual differences in patterns of attending (e.g., Lewis, M., 1969; Greenberg & Weizmann, 1971). As Schroder, Driver, and Streuffert (1967) noted, the most frequent way of dealing with individual differences and adaptive strategies in experiments is by simplifying the situation. As suggested earlier, such simplification ostensibly minimizes the problem by reducing the number of ways the person can respond and so helps insure that he will respond in terms of the way the experimenter has defined the situation. N. E. Miller (1959, p. 242) pointed out that such simplicity also avoids questions concerning the nature of the stimulus or the response; calling a level press a response is unlikely to raise general issues about the response as a unit of behavior.

Statistically, this simplification has the effect of tightening up the experiment. That is, since reducing individual differences maximizes treatment effects, any constraints placed on the way people may respond reduce experimental error variance. As Orne's work (1962) suggests, such effects are not completely successful. Indeed, Mischel (1973) noted that people often respond to stimuli other than those intended by the experimenter; this observation is now accepted as a commonplace.

Insofar as experimental constraints standardize such factors, they restrict the range of adaptive strategies that can be brought to bear in the situation. It is doubtful that much of what we call *personality* is manifested when the situation is greatly restricted, since such constraints prohibit the adaptive organization that defines what we mean by personality. Even when these strategies are not totally restricted, they are effectively obscured.

One kind of experimental constraint can be produced by arousing *preemptive* universal motives relating to states of physiological deprivation or pain avoidance. A second sort of constraint is typified by social norms. Still a third kind of constraint, one quite typical of psychological experiments, consists of attempting to limit what a person may do to one particular level of *molecularity*, which prohibits the organization of the response at other levels. Let us take memory span as a hypothetical example. Without coding, this span will cluster around seven (Miller, G. A., 1956) or, as Mandler (1968) suggested, five. If, however, we allow people to use whatever strategies are available to them in a memorization task, we would probably obtain different results, notably a large increase in the variability and range of scores. At the same time, however, individual styles of responding in the freer situation would probably correlate more highly with complex molar personality variables than would responses in the more controlled situation.

Given the assumption that the ongoing processes already mentioned are merely historical residues of earlier associative relationships, then it would follow that these processes merely obscure more *basic* S–R mechanisms, and their effects should be reduced statistically or experimentally. If, however, complex molar organism-environment interactions are ubiquitous, then attempts to disregard them can result in a highly limited and artificial perspective.

This point may be illustrated by Staats' (1963) comments on a paper by W. A. Russell (1963). Russell criticized learning mediational models that consider only situations where one source of stimulus input is operative on the grounds that they do not specify what would happen when several such sources are available. Staats' reply was that the "difficulty lies more with the complexity of the events under question rather than the attempt to deal with these events with behavior principles." His point was, of course, that there is a difference between explanatory principles derived from the laboratory and constructed around an ideal case and the application of these principles in more complex situations. It is not the distinction between the *ideal case* and *real life* that is objectionable, nor is it the fact that the explanations of real-life phenomena are often circular and difficult (and sometimes impossible) to disprove. One can almost always posit a hypothetical reinforcement history to explain some real-life bit of behavior. Such a distinction and such circularity are probably characteristic of any extension of a theory beyond the laboratory. The point at issue is the narrowness of the circle. How an organism responds to a situation in which there are multiple inputs represents the norm in even the best controlled experiment. Thus it may be necessary to understand this more molar process before we can understand fully how an organism comes to respond to a single input. We may be settling for too little in the way of possible explanation.

It is interesting to compare the preceding approach with traditional trait or typological theories of personality. Such theories define personality as a stable unitary entity that may be manifested in a variety of ways, including test performance. This approach was criticized (e.g., Mischel, 1968; Rotter, 1954), for positing more individual consistency than one can actually find, and failing adequately to conceptualize the interface between person and situation. (Mischel, 1976, however, found more consistency in his later work than in his earlier studies.) Even granting the profitability of conceptualizing personality as being composed of a number of independent traits or invariant interpersonal needs, how is one to know which trait will emerge in what situation?

What is interesting about the comparing of trait theories vis-a-vis learning theories is that each approach appears to fill gaps left by the other. One emphasizes person consistency; the other environmental consistency; and both have difficulty dealing with the interface between person and situation. In a sense, the two are complementary rather than competitive. Such approaches as these probably continue to exist side by side because each supplies what the other lacks.

The last 15 years, of course, have seen a reemergence of concepts dealing with central processes. This revival of interest in more complex processes probably results from a number of influences, including that of Piaget (1950); Russian work on the orienting reflex (Sokolov, 1960, 1963); evidence concerning the neurophysiological bases of attention and expectancy (Pribram, 1967); new developments in psycholinguistics (Chomsky, 1965); and the growing awareness of the importance of cognitive variables (Neisser, 1967), computer models of information processing (e.g., Newell & Simon, 1963; Reitman, 1965), and new emphases on nonhomeostatic sources of motivation (Berlyne, 1966; Hunt, J. McV., 1971). Though some investigators in these areas have attempted to remain in the S-R tradition (Berlyne, 1965; Maltzman, 1968; Osgood, 1968), it is probably fair to say that these develop-

ments, in part, were inspired by, and in turn led to, a dissatisfaction with traditional formulations of *complex processes* and to a relaxation of behavioristic strictures regarding research and theory building (e.g., Deese, 1969; Hebb, 1960; Koch, 1959). Even those theorists who have remained within a learning framework have attempted to broaden learning theory in various ways.

Despite these developments, however, with the important exception of Mischel (see following discussion) there have been relatively few attempts to apply them to personality. Even some prominent social-learning approaches that emphasize observational learning and modeling (e.g., Bandura, 1969) leave the nature of the cognitive processes that underlie symbolic and observational learning rather vague.

Further, aside from the attempted Hullian-Freudian synthesis (Dollard & Miller, 1950) of the 1940s and 1950s, there has been little attention given to the conceptualization of individual differences. Even where such differences are acknowledged, it is often for the rather narrow purpose of accounting for the nonuniform effect of an experimental treatment, as when K. W. Spence (e.g., 1958, 1964) employed individual differences in drive level (as inferred from questionnaire indexes of anxiety) to explain differential performances in conditioning. At most, such differences may be raised to the level of personality traits, as H. J. Eysenck (1964) proposed with regard to differences in conditionability.

Typically, one conceives of individual differences in terms of the differences in what people have learned as a consequence of their divergent learning histories. Yet there is evidence that such differences exist even in early infancy and that infants are not simply passive recipients of stimuli, but through their activity help create their own environment (e.g., Bell, R. Q., 1968, 1971).[1] Nonetheless, the view that individual differences are reducible to past learning which, in turn, is due solely to external factors, is by no means restricted to operant-learning approaches.

The problems in dealing with the sorts of variables discussed here within learning theory were perhaps inevitable given the nature of the classical learning paradigm. This paradigm leads one to think of a prototypical organism (e.g., the treatment of individual differences as error) making a prototypical response (e.g., the restriction of a response to a single level of organization) in a prototypical situation (e.g., the use of a single situation of short duration with little concern for its representativeness or *ecological validity*, in Brunswik's terms). The approach one uses to deal with each of these three problems is of course related to the way one deals with the other two. The consequences of this strategy are that one has difficulty in dealing with organismic differences, structural and organizational processes, and complex processes.

The following section examines some issues that arise when one attempts to deal with these complexities while remaining, at least in part, within a social-learning-theory framework.

---

[1] Bowers (1973) and Wachtel (1973) took this point one step further and suggested that people, by their behavior, tend to generate situations that are typical of them. Thus, as Wachtel (1973) notes, the situations in which people find themselves may be described, in an important sense, as a characteristic of one's respective personality. Both these authors, in the articles cited in this note, have provided critiques of *situationist* theory and method that overlap and are highly consonant with many of the points made above.

## 2 INTERACTIONISM, SOCIAL-LEARNING THEORY, AND PERSONALITY

One of the most important spokesmen for the application of social learning models to personality is Walter Mischel (1968, 1969, 1971, 1976); his critiques of trait theory have been highly influential largely because of the persistent failure of investigators to find evidence for transsituational consistency in behavior.

Mischel (1973, 1976) states that one must reconceptualize personality from the standpoint of recent advances in cognitive psychology and social-learning theories and examine the interaction between person and situation from the perspective of the resultant cognitive social-learning framework.

Several of Mischel's critics (e.g., Bowers, 1973; Staats, this volume), while welcoming the emphasis on cognition, have noted that Mischel's later work represents a considerable change from his earlier views (Mischel, 1968, 1969, 1971) in this regard. Similarly, Endler (1976), in a report on interactionist approaches to personality, implicitly recognized the change in Mischel's position by classifying his early writings as representing a situationist point of view and characterizing his later position as interactionist. This is important since, as Ekehammar (1974) noted, interactionism probably represents the dominant trend in current personality theory and research, one that embodies most of the considerations advanced previously in this chapter.

Specifically, Endler's (1976) description of interactionism not only emphasizes the continuous dialectical interactive nature of behavior, but cognitive factors and psychological meanings as the primary determinants of behavior. Viewed from this perspective, most of the criticisms of learning theory may be summarized by saying that learning theory has not shown itself able to incorporate these considerations, which we have argued are essential for an adequate theory of personality (or behavior generally). Mischel's later attempts to do so, therefore, deserve close attention.

The relevant question that needs to be asked with regard to learning theory (as with the modifications of trait theories represented by state-trait theories, e.g., Spielberger, 1966, 1972, which have moved closer to an interactionist position) is whether it can provide the basis for an interactionist psychology without violating the assumptions of the underlying theory.

In attempting to answer this question, however, Mischel leaves contradictions between cognitive and social-learning theory unresolved. For Mischel, social-learning and cognitive theories are complementary ways of viewing behavior. Thus, if one is concerned with changing behavior, Mischel suggests that a focus on the conditions necessary to achieve such changes is appropriate, and with it the utility of a language that employs concepts dealing with reinforcement, conditioning, modeling, and so forth. On the other hand, the theorist interested in how these operations produce their effect may find it more useful to employ a cognitive language, making use of concepts concerned with information processing, rules, constructs, expectancies, and so on.

The point that one's viewpoint influences the language one employs and the way events are constructed is not in dispute; in fact, a similar point was made earlier in this chapter. What is disputable is whether and in what sense an amalgamation of social-learning and cognitive theory is possible.

On the weakest level, it is possible simply to characterize learning terminology as a theoretically neutral technical language (Kendler, 1968) that can be employed as a language of convenience. Alternatively, this author argued previously, as have others (e.g., Dulany, 1968), that learning concepts have theoretical implications that go beyond those of a neutral descriptive language. In any case, the kind of amalgamation Mischel appeared to suggest is somewhat broader than this. The basic issue that renders such an integration problematic has to do with the extent to which and the way in which cognitions are linked to the concrete situations from which they emerge. Cognitive theory has always stressed that the *rules* or inferences that people make considerably transcend the situations from which they have been derived.

By contrast, learning-theory explanations, even liberalized S–R models (e.g., Osgood, 1957, 1968), intended to account for the generality of thought and cognition, emphasize the specificity and situation-bound nature of the information gained from the person's commerce with the environment. One suspects that such an emphasis exists not least because of the amenability to experimental control a situational model implies, together with a putative gain in objectivity and precision.

The traditional way learning-theory models have attempted to account for the apparent generality and freedom from immediate environmental circumstances exhibited by behavior has been to postulate chains of implicit covert stimuli and responses, governed by the same principles applicable to overt S–R chains, which mediate between the environment and the final overt response. Such a strategy is by no means restricted to *multistage* or *mediated* S–R theories. Jakobovits (1966) noted that even a *single-stage* learning theorist such as B. F. Skinner (1957) makes use of such mediated S–R chains. In fact, the employment of such chains is closer to early behaviorist usage than is commonly supposed (Goss, 1961).

There are several advantages such a conception provides. It can account for the fact that a *sign* can represent a stimulus without thereby evoking the same response; i.e., a sign evokes only that part of the chain that is implicit and mediative. Further, by postulating complex inter-actions among covert S-R chains, one can offer S-R explanations of thinking and symbolic activity (e.g., Berlyne, 1965; Osgood, 1968).

Cognitive theorists have been extremely critical of learning theorists for their assumption of environmental specificity and *control* vis-a-vis cognitive processes (e.g., Chomsky, 1959). Impressed by the apparent rule-governed nature of symbolic activity and human behavior generally, cognitive theorists (e.g., Arbib, 1969; Chomsky, 1957; Dulany, 1968) have sug-gested that the indefinite extension and application of such rules cannot be ac-counted for by theories that view learning as the acquisition of specific bits of knowl-edge (whether construed in terms of re-sponses or not).

Fodor (1965, 1966) argued that multi-stage learning theories offer no significant advantage over single-stage theories in this respect. The central problem these theories face, according to Fodor, is that the mediating response, which is a fractional derivative of the overt response, is either part of several overt responses, correspond-ing to a number of quite distinct stimuli, or it is part of a single overt response. In the former case, the linkage between the mediator and what it is supposed to signify will be indefinite and ambiguous. In the latter case, there will be a one-to-one relationship between the mediator and the response, in which case the multistage model reduces to a single-stage model, with

each separate S-R association needing to be established separately. Hence, according to Fodor, one cannot achieve the dual aim of accounting for generality while maintaining the specificity and precision of single-stage learning theory.

Certainly, none of these contentions have gone unchallenged (e.g., Berlyne, 1966; Osgood, 1966; Suppes, 1969) and any attempt at resolving them would require far more extensive treatment than can be given here. The point, however, is that the integration of learning theory and cognition is exceedingly problematic and raises issues that are among the most far reaching of any in psychology.

Adding observational and vicarious learn-ing mechanisms, even with the added specification that learning involves the acquisition of relatively large units of knowledge, and not just small discrete responses, does not obviate the issue of specificity between social learning and cognitive theory.[2] (One important instance

---

[2] In speaking of situational specificity as an issue that divides learning and cognitive theorists, one must not confuse it with the separate issue of situational specificity as it occurs in the debate between learning and trait theorists. In the latter context, the issue involves the existence or nonexistence of behavioral consistency; in the former, the emphasis given is on the person's active construction of a model of the world, which extends well beyond any situational given. This distinction does not necessarily prejudge the question of whether cognitivists are interactionists or not: some, of a more rationalist persuasion (e.g., Chomsky, 1965) are not, since for them the basic cognitive structures are prefigured and the environment simply provides opportunities where-by these structures can be made manifest. Others, especially those who are developmentally ori-ented, (e.g., Piaget, 1950) are interactionists, since despite the emphasis given to the internal cognitive system qua system, it is ultimately the interaction between child and environment that propels cognitive growth.

of the divisive nature of this issue can be found in the conflict between Piagetian and social-learning-theory views of moral development. See Bandura & McDonald, 1963; Turiel, 1966.)

In fairness to Mischel, it should be noted that he states that it is difficult to know how to conceptualize the nature of what people learn; further, he grapples with the issue dividing cognitive and social-learning approaches (Mischel, 1976). It is uncertain at this point if he answers the larger question of whether, and on what basis, an integration between the two is possible. Certainly serious conceptual obstacles exist to such a union; and although it is easy to suggest the possibility of a cognitive social learning approach to personality, it is by no means clear that such a possibility has been realized. If these issues cannot be resolved, it is doubtful whether a learning approach can provide a theoretical basis on which to build an interactionist psychology.

## 3 ON COGNITIVE APPROACHES TO PERSONALITY: SOME SUGGESTIONS

The previous sections of this chapter explored a number of proposals, both past and present, regarding the application of learning theory to personality, and suggested some of their limitations, especially with regard to their inability to encompass attentional and structural variables in a satisfactory way. This final section examines some attempts to deal with such variables stemming from cognitive-personality formulations that stress *stylistic* consistencies within people, as well as individual differences in approaching situations. Thus, for G. A. Kelly (1955), people organize their knowledge about themselves and the world into what he called "personal constructs," which are employed

to understand events and guide behavior. The primary motivational goal, according to Kelly, is the expansion and validation of one's construction system. Harvey, Hunt, and Schroder's (1961) "conceptual systems" approach is somewhat similar to Kelly's, but more formally stresses different organizational modes of processing and combining information from the environment and their developmental precursors.

Other personality theorists, working in different traditions (notably, Gardner, Holzman, Klein, Linton, & Spence, 1959; Kagan & Moss, 1962; Witkin, Dyk, Faterson, Goodenough, & Karp, 1962), also have been concerned with consistencies in cognitive functioning. Although these systems are all somewhat different, they all involve a common contrast between, in Wallach's (1962) words, "active, analytical, articulated, specific, critical cognitive functioning [and] cognitive functioning that is passive, global, vague, diffuse, uncritical" (p. 200).

These theories encounter difficulties in linking people to specific situations. Wallach (1962) provided an excellent illustration of this point. As mentioned earlier, Witkin, Dyk, et al. (1962) and Kagan and Moss (1962) both proposed an analytical-global distinction. Although the former stressed perceptual, and the latter verbal-intellectual functioning, the respective descriptions of the two kinds of functioning parallel each other highly. In describing some differences between these two kinds of functioning, Faterson (1962) reported that her analytic (or field-independent) group had greater success on the Block Design, Picture Completion, and Object Assembly subtests of the Wechsler Adult Intelligence Scale (WAIS) than did the global (i.e., field-dependent) group. There was no difference between the two groups, however, on the verbal subtests of the WAIS. She interpreted this result to indicate that the former group of subtests require a person to analyze wholes into parts and then reintegrate them—critical analytic ability—whereas the latter group makes no such demands.

Kagan and Moss, on the other hand, found that their analytical subjects did better on the verbal (Vocabulary and Information) subtests than did the global subjects. They interpreted this finding to be consistent with their analytic-global distinction inasmuch as the verbal subtests required critical analytic functioning.

Wallach's point, of course, is that the analytic-global distinction is indeed slippery if it can so blithely absorb conflicting evidence. One reason for this difficulty is that personality constructs are high-order abstractions that need to be linked to specific situations by lower order constructs. In the preceding example, it would appear that lower order constructs, which would specify how different cognitive styles would interact with different kinds of stimulus materials, are missing or are only supplied in a post hoc manner.

The problem is one characteristic of *moderator variable* strategies, in which one searches for variables (analytic-global functioning in the previous examples) that modify the effects of other variables. The utility of such strategies for personality research came under criticism (see Endler, 1973, for a summary of these criticisms) since, as in the present case, they frequently do not increase the accuracy of prediction. The problem appears to be that such variables are not chosen theoretically; hence, their role in relating abstract personality and cognitive variables to concrete behavior is not well articulated.

Similar problems exist in much of the research relating to Kelly's theory. Here the difficulties stem from the fact that the primary dimension employed to charac-

terize and compare individual construct systems is *cognitive complexity*, which refers solely to the number of dimensions available for construing a given dimension. However, cognitive complexity is essentially a frequency measure (Weizmann & Protter, in press), and is dependent on a number of nonpersonality factors, such as the opportunity to be exposed to a given domain and the existence of conventionalized and hence directly teachable ways of construing events in an area. Thus cognitive complexity may bear only a minimal relationship to higher level cognitive and organizational variables.

Indeed, the evidence to date (Crockett, 1965; Epting, 1967) suggests that only modest relationships exist among cognitive complexity scores obtained in different domains of thinking, or between cognitive complexity measures and other indexes of cognitive functioning (Vannoy, 1965).

If the problem with the analytic-global formulation lies in going from abstract cognitive personality variables directly to overt behavior, the problem with cognitive-complexity-type measures lies in relating simple behavioral frequencies to higher level cognitive-processing variables. In both cases the problem is in linking overt behavior to inferred modes of organization.

Some concepts derived from information-processing models (e.g., Miller, Galanter, & Pribram, 1960; Newell & Simon, 1963; Reitman, 1965), and in particular the feedback loop model, popularized in psychology by Miller, Galanter, and Pribram (1960), together with their concept of "plans" may help provide an initial solution to this problem. There are two key features of this model: first, that goals and the activities that satisfy them are hierarchically arranged, with tasks broken down into subtasks and subgoals, which in turn may be further subdivided as far as necessary; second, that a goal or subgoal is satisfied when feedback from environment-altering responses indicates a match between the environment and an internal standard, thus signifying the attainment of a desired outcome.

Of key importance for personality theory is the fact that styles of attending and processing environmental information, whether engaged in simply to gain information or to guide action, can be translated into this model. The advantage of such a translation is that the linkage between overt behavior and abstract processing variables must be made explicit. If one translates the analytic-global distinction into such a language, for example, one would need to specify at each point in the hierarchy the different sorts of internal standards involved, the characteristics of the informational and perceptual units employed, and how the resulting information is transformed. The result would be a distinction elaborated in terms of varying processes, not an overly global, static one.

This concentration on cognitive and stylistic consistencies does not rule out other more traditional personality consistencies, such as social needs and motives. It does imply, however, that insofar as they manifest themselves behaviorally, they do so through a cognitive medium that likely involves judgments as to the relevance of that motive and the appropriateness of behavior guided by it to the situation. A man described as *dominant*, for example, may not appear so in talking to his boss. This *trait*, however, might appear in more molar interactional patterns. Thus, one may find this hypothetical man becoming involved in many situations in which he can be dominant rather than finding him dominant in all situations (see also Footnote 1). The point is that this *macrotrait* is connected to the situation by a complex

hierarchical process and is not automatically reflected in the situational microcosm.

This way of looking at personality actually bears a great deal of resemblance to much current work in personality theory. In Kelly's theory, for example, not only is behavior guided by the discrepancy between organized standards (constructs), but the constructs themselves are hierarchically organized in that some constructs are broader than and include (i.e., are superordinate to) other constructs. Hinkle (1965), in fact, reported some provocative work investigating the logical implication of constructs depending on their location in the hierarchy; i.e., it is more difficult to change a superordinate construct than a subordinate one.

Gardner, Holzman, et al. (1959) also argued for such a hierarchical model, although their work focused more on styles of attending and thinking rather than on the contents (elements or constructs) of the network and their interrelationships (see also Wachtel, 1967). They suggested a distinction between cognitive controls and cognitive styles: The former refer to lower level organizing principles, such as the degree of field articulation, whereas the latter refer to a constellation of such controls.

G. S. Klein (1967), writing from a psychoanalytic viewpoint, suggested construing motivation discrepancies from standards rather than in energic-libidinal terms. Similarly, Simon (1967) offered some specific suggestions on how an information-processing model could account for the interlocking of cognition with emotion and motivation.

Although such attempts as those sketched here may point in the direction of developing the kind of cognitive-organization model of personality discussed here, their promise has not, in general, been exploited. With the exception of Hinkle (1965), for example, little work has been done in emphasizing the organization aspect of Kelly's system or in providing methods for measuring such organization. Similarly, as Kagan and Kogan (1970) noted, the hierarchical distinction between control and style has not been consistently maintained by the cognitive-style theorists.

An additional problem lies in the integration of conceptions of cognition that focus on individual styles with those that emphasize universal processes, leaving little room for individual variation in cognitive growth and functioning. This is true even for interactionists, including Piaget. (For further discussion and some suggestions regarding this problem within a developmental context, see Fowler, W., 1976.)

Despite these difficulties, a cognitive organizational approach to personality would have a number of advantages, a point in which there appears to be a growing consensus among otherwise disparate thinkers (e.g., Schroder & Suedfeld, 1971). The conjoining of cognitive and personality theory would bring about a union in which personality theorists, with their appreciation of individual differences, might have much to offer, as well as much to gain.

# 16

## Social Behaviorism: Unified Theory in Learning and Personality

**Arthur W. Staats**
*University of Hawaii, Honolulu*

Behaviorism was begun self-consciously by John Watson as a revolt against a tradition that considered the determinants of human behavior to be within the person. The traditional view involved a consequent decrease in interest in the behavior and the environmental events that determine it. Moreover, the traditional view inferred a host of internal mental processes or structures as the causes of human behavior. Watson suggested that such concepts were inappropriate. Rather, the actual behavior of humans should be studied, as well as the manner in which the behavior was learned.

Watson considered personality to be a person's behaviors. This is a simple schema. It suggests two realms of study when one is interested in behavior change. The first realm concerns the basic learning (conditioning) principles, and the second realm is the application of these principles to problems of dealing with human behavior. As is indicated later, this paradigm is too simple. However, Watson's behaviorism included significant knowledge of learning principles, and he also demonstrated the manner in which conditioning could affect human behavior (Watson, J. B., & Raynor, 1920). Serious elaboration on the use of condition-

ing principles in dealing with problems of human behavior did not occur until the 1950s.

In 1950 Dollard and Miller and also Mowrer published books about combining learning theory (of a Hullian variety) and psychoanalytic theory. In Dollard and Miller's account, psychoanalytic theory provided the basic personality theory and clinical treatment methods, with learning theory serving a supporting role.

Several years later, in American psychology, also, there were efforts to use Skinner's operant-conditioning apparatus and procedure with human subjects. O. R. Lindsley (1956) demonstrated the effects of reinforcement with psychotic patients, and Bijou (1955) did the same with mentally retarded children. Although these were valuable demonstrations that reinforcement principles apply to human subjects, these early studies did not make analyses of the behavior problems of their subjects in terms of conditioning principles, or attempt to use conditioning to treat these problems. No concept of abnormal behavior or personality was derived from these studies. After demonstrating that these special populations were subject to instrumental conditioning,

389

neither these studies nor the operant conditioning theory indicated an avenue of continued progress in working with behavior problems. Other studies were conducted showing that verbal behavior could be increased through reinforcement (Greenspoon, 1950; Kanfer, 1958; Krasner, 1958), but again without analyses of human behavior, or personality, or treatment of behavior problems.

## 1  BEHAVIOR THERAPY: CLASSICAL-CONDITIONING METHODS

In the 1950s, however, there was a direct extension of learning principles to the treatment of human behavior problems with an analysis of abnormal behavior. Both developments began within Hullian, or modified Hullian, learning-theory frameworks. Joseph Wolpe developed procedures for the treatment of anxiety using the concept of conditioned inhibition. According to this concept, each time a stimulus is presented and a response is elicited, an inhibitory process builds up (to some maximal strength). The principle suggests that repetition of a response will lead to an inhibitory process for the response, some of which is conditioned and becomes permanent. A person required to repeat an undesirable behavior—stuttering, for example—would learn inhibition for the behavior.

Wolpe also formulated a method to eliminate inappropriate anxiety. Procedurally, if a response incompatible with anxiety was made to occur in the presence of the stimulus situation that elicited the anxiety, the incompatible response would be conditioned to the stimulus. Wolpe primarily employed relaxation as the response incompatible with anxiety. Practical considerations also led him to have a person imagine the anxiety-producing stimulus (although the behavioral justification for this cognitive

procedure had not yet been made). In addition, Wolpe had the person list different situations that elicited anxiety, ranging them in a hierarchy from the most intense to the least intense. In therapy, the patient would go through the list, beginning with the situation producing the least anxiety, imagining each situation, until this could be done without anxiety and with relaxation (Wolpe, 1958).

Wolpe and others applied this *systematic desensitization* method to various cases involving anxiety. He did the pioneering clinical research necessary to verify the procedures as a therapy and, thereby, provided a basis for extensive research and clinical practice. This careful work and the use of specified procedures were important elements in his contribution. Wolpe assiduously recorded the results he obtained in his clinical practice. The basic data consisted of patient self-reports of anxiety reactions to the anxiety-producing stimuli for which they had been treated, and he used as a criterion of success an 80% reduction in anxiety. According to Paul (1969, p. 73) Wolpe's data showed a 92% success rate.

Since the first clinical studies of systematic desensitization, there has been much extension and corroboration of the methods, some involving controlled laboratory studies, comparisons of the effectiveness to other methods, and measures of success other than self-reports of patients. For example, Lang and Lazovik (1963) worked with patients with snake phobias, using an objective measure of how closely the patients would approach a live snake. Experimental subjects receiving systematic desensitization improved more than the control subjects. A 6-month follow up revealed that the experimental group had retained their advantage.

Paul (1966) conducted the first large-scale factorial study of systematic desensitization, using people who were phobic about interpersonal situations, such as public speaking, and rotating the therapists through the different treatment methods employed. Physiological measures of anxiety and trained observers were used to rate anxiety during a speech before an audience. Both measures were taken before and after treatment; in long-term follow-up data, desensitized persons showed less anxiety than did those treated by insight-oriented methods or those treated in the several types of control conditions. Desensitization had 85% success, versus 50% for insight therapy, 50% for a nonspecific attention-placebo treatment, and 22% for untreated controls. Franks (1969) provided an excellent compendium of the various behavior therapy findings and procedures that now exist.

Although Wolpe did not deeply analyze his methods in terms of the principles involved, it is thought that systematic desensitization involves classical conditioning procedures. The phobic stimulus may be considered to be the conditioned stimulus that elicits an anxiety response in a person. When this stimulus (actually a class of stimuli) is repeatedly presented while the person relaxes, the anxiety response is unlearned (that is, the previous anxiety conditioning extinguishes).

Classical-conditioning principles also have been employed in the opposite direction where a person has learned an inappropriately positive emotional response to a stimulus. For example, the positive value of alcohol for alcoholics has been reduced by pairing the stimulus of alcohol with some other stimulus that elicits a negative emotional response (see *aversion therapy* in Franks, 1969). As another example, fetish objects have also been paired with negative emotion-eliciting stimuli in classical conditioning procedures. For example, Raymond (1956) described a patient who had a baby carriage fetish. This investigator paired pictures of baby carriages with electric shock, and the patient was thereby relieved of his fetish.

## 2 BEHAVIOR MODIFICATION: CLINICAL AND EDUCATIONAL USE OF REINFORCEMENT

The developmental path using reinforcement principles in the analysis and treatment of clinical problems is not as well known as that for systematic desensitization. Behavior modification has been attributed to Skinner's theory, but it actually began in the context of the general use of reinforcement principles. The informality of the first work and of its dissemination tended to obscure its derivations.

The first analysis of abnormal behavior with suggestions for treatment using reinforcement principles concerned a schizophrenic patient with confused speech, characterized by responses that were the opposite of those considered appropriate. For example, the patient would reverse the use of *yes* and *no*. At that time, this abnormal behavior was considered important for what it was thought to tell about the patient's psychodynamic motivation (Laffal, Lenkoski, & Ameen, 1956). The present author, however, considered the patient's opposite speech important in and of itself. Speech is a central type of human behavior, and any abnormal speech can be considered a severe problem. Rather than wondering what psychic problem the opposite speech indicated, his learning analysis was concerned with what conditions and principles could bring about and maintain such abnormal behavior (Staats, A. W., 1957).

The verbal conditioning studies had shown that social attention made contingent on the utterance of certain words would increase the frequency of such utterances.

For example, Greenspoon (1950) demonstrated that if the experimenter said "mmm-hmm" when a person said plural nouns (in a task of simply saying any words aloud), the person would be conditioned to say plural noun words more frequently. Other studies suggested that various kinds of social attention would act as a reinforcer in social interaction. Made contingent on a type of speech, the attention given would result in the increase in frequency of that type of speech (Talbot, 1954; Verplanck, 1955).

In this first behavior analysis of abnormal behavior, this author (Staats, A. W., 1957) suggested that the schizophrenic's opposite speech is an example of psychotic behavior that is learned and maintained by reinforcement. This author had seen similar cases in psychiatric wards where mental health workers socially reinforced psychotic language (and other behaviors), because the symptoms were interesting in terms of what the unconscious motivations might be that produced the symptom. Psychoanalytic theory suggested that the abnormal symptom was not in itself important, but what it might indicate about the patient's underlying motivations and conflicts was interesting. Extensive protocols of interviews with the patient with opposite speech provided evidence suggesting that this process was at work. It was clear that the patient's normal speech was of little interest to the clinicians involved; however, when the patient uttered one of his unusual statements, the doctors became interested. They would ask him why he said what he did, and so on. The clinicians were interested in exploring the abnormal speech, because they thought it would reveal something about the inner nature of the patient and his underlying need to express hostility. In their interest in exploring the symptom, the clinicians also gave the patient material

reinforcement contingent on the abnormal behavior. For example, when the patient responded "No" when asked if he wanted a cigarette, he was given the cigarette anyway, and he smoked it. This author's behavior analysis stated that this was a case of positively reinforcing an abnormal behavior, and, like the clinician's use of social reinforcement, would train the patient to speak in his confused manner. This author then indicated how an analysis of an abnormal behavior, in terms of learning principles, provides a basis for suggesting treatment.

Reinforcements such as these [social and material reinforcers for the abnormal behavior], without concomitant admonition, would be unlikely to occur in the normal person's social environment.

Certain implications are derivable from this interpretation. If the opposite speech is maintained by positive reinforcement, then lack of such reinforcement should lead to extinction of such behavior. For example, withholding the cigaret should weaken the strength of opposite speech and giving the cigaret to correct speech should strengthen that type of response (Staats, A. W., 1957, pp. 268–269).

In this behavior analysis, the author suggested that there are other sources of reinforcement for opposite speech. Moreover, it was suggested that the principles of reinforcement apply generally to other types of abnormal behaviors. It may be added that prior to this time the author had made other behavior analyses and had conducted behavior-modification procedures in the naturalistic situation. In two of these behavior-modification procedures, Jack Michael participated; and the behavior analysis of the opposite speech was also conveyed to him. Two years later, J. Michael and Teodoro Ayllon completed their study that provided empirical support of the principles

(Ayllon & Michael, 1959). They showed how abnormal behaviors could be learned and unlearned by manipulating such things as social reinforcement.

For some years following this inauguration of behavioral analysis, behavior-modification studies depended on two elements. One element was the behavior analysis, using the principles that had been advanced in this author's analysis of opposite speech; that is, abnormal instrumental behaviors are learned through reinforcement principles, and they can be treated by using reinforcement principles. The other was the research method extended by Ayllon and Michael (1959)—the use of clinical cases that recorded the patient's response while reinforcement variables were manipulated. Many later studies were conducted using these two elements (see Ashem & Poser, 1973; O'Leary & O'Leary, 1972).

## 3 TOKEN-REINFORCER (ECONOMY) METHODS

Though it was an important step to begin to consider human behaviors that are symptomatic of psychopathology in terms of reinforcement principles, it was necessary to move to more complex, functional repertoires of human behavior. Having verified the behavior-modification principles with simple behaviors, in 1958 this author chose to extend the general methods to the complex area of language development. One focus of this work was on reading and reading problems and the design and testing of the first token reinforcement system for use with clinical and educational problems. The token-reinforcer system employed poker chips of different colors as token reinforcers of different values. This system was tried with junior high school children who had reading problems. The children selected the back-up reinforcers that they

could obtain when they accrued a sufficient number of tokens. Each child received the tokens for reading responses; the more desirable or more effortful responses were reinforced with the more valuable tokens. The children, who were problems in the classroom, became vigorous, attentive workers in the token-reinforcer program, and they learned well.[1]

This author communicated the efficacy of the token-reinforcer system, and its general implications, to Jack Michael in the summer of 1959. He and his associates and students began using the system and disseminating the methods. Also, this author described the token-reinforcer system to Ayllon just before the latter went to Anna State Hospital. It was suggested that the system could be used for training hospitalized patients in functional behaviors, rather than in just the symptomatic behaviors. Ayllon and Azrin then introduced the token-reinforcement system in an entire psychiatric ward at Anna State Hospital (1965).

While the dissemination of the token-reinforcer system and the behavior-modification principles was beginning, the author went on to conduct further studies in the efficacy of the methods in working with the complex behaviors of reading, both original reading and remedial reading (Staats, Finley, Minke, & Wolf, 1964; Staats, Staats, Schutz, & Wolf, 1962). The young children in these studies received marbles as tokens that they could exchange for edibles or toys of varying values. It was suggested that the methods and principles could be extended to treat various problems and populations of children.

[1] Judson R. Finley and Karl A. Minke, as undergraduate research assistants, administered the behavior-modification procedures. Richard E. Schutz also participated in the conduct of the study.

These developments may be extended to the study of a number of types of significant behavior acquisitions, e.g., speech learning, arithmetic learning, etc., and to various special populations, such as deaf children, mutes, mental retardates, etc. . . . This could also involve work which had remedial objectives, e.g., remedial reading problems, the training of autistic children, general reading problems in children resulting from deficient "motivation" (Staats, A. W., Finley, et al., 1964, pp. 146–147).

The author wrote this in 1962. The next year Montrose Wolf, who had been a graduate assistant in this work, began extensive behavior-modification work with young children at the University of Washington. For example, Wolf, Risely, and Mees (1964) undertook treatment of an autistic boy who had self-destructive temper tantrums and would not wear glasses necessary to retain his vision. Lovaas extended this work with autistic children (Lovaas, Berberich, Perloff, & Schaeffer, 1966). Many additional treatments of behavior problems in children also were conducted within this context (Allen, K. E., Hart, Buell, Harris, & Wolf, 1964; Bijou, Birnbrauer, Kidder, & Tague, 1967; Harris, F. R., Johnston, Kelley, & Wolf, 1964; see also Fargo, Behrns, & Nolen, 1970; Krasner & Ullmann, 1965; O'Leary & O'Leary, 1972).

The suggestion for the general use of a token economy was first presented in the following passage, addressed to the school situation.

As an example, consider the nursery school or kindergarten situation. Some of the reinforcers present in these school situations have been described—games, recesses, toys, snacks, rest periods, television, desirable activities of various kinds, and social approval. These are potent reinforcers but for the most part they are not made con-

tingent upon the individual behaviors to be strengthened. Since most of these reinforcers occur only infrequently in the school day, however, very few could be provided and thus only a few behaviors reinforced.

These reinforcers might prove to be very effective, however, if they were incorporated into a procedure involving a token system. For example, a recess could be exchanged for 100 tokens, and the tokens could be made contingent upon 100 appropriate responses. Through employment of such a token system effective use could be made of many reinforcers that are a natural part of school training.

The development of such a system of reinforcers might necessitate some changes in school organization. For example, one way to use a token system might be to have a "work" room for the learning activities and other rooms for dispensing the "primary" reinforcers. . . . The child would stay in the work room until he accrued a given number of tokens and then go to one of the "reinforcer" rooms to receive his primary reinforcer . . . (Staats, A. W., 1963, pp. 457–458).

This analysis described the use of the token-reinforcer system in an institutional setting. In the 13 years since publication, many studies have been conducted using the token system and other aspects of this analysis. For example, Ayllon and Azrin (1968) set up a token system in a psychiatric ward in which patients received tokens for self-care behaviors, making beds, working in a laboratory or a laundry, cleaning the kitchen, and so on. Atthowe and Krasner (1968) extended the token-reinforcer procedures to another mental hospital ward, giving tokens contingent on the performance of desirable behaviors, such as attending to assignments, self-care, or going out on pass, as well as avoidance of undesirable behaviors, such as bed wetting. There was a before-and-after comparison of the efficacy of the program, and significant increases were noted in the various desirable behaviors and in the number of men discharged when the token program was in operation. There have been many other clinical applications of the token-reinforcer system.

The same is true of uses of the system in educational institutions. The author's 1963 analysis of token-reinforcer methods for the schools suggested that natural reinforcers, such as activities and entertainments, could be used, in addition to material things. Later behavior-modification studies began to employ a diversity of back-up reinforcers, including the concept of the natural reinforcer. For example, Bushell, Wrobel, and Michaelis (1968) included a special-event ticket that children could use to attend a brief movie, a theater group rehearsal, a story-telling episode, an art or gym class, a trip to a park, and similar activities. The 1963 analysis also suggested the use of a workroom and a reinforcer room. B. L. Hopkins, Schutte, and Garton (1971) showed that in first- and second-grade children the rate and quality of printing and writing could be reliably increased using these procedures. As another example, J. G. Osborne (1969) employed free time as a reinforcer, as did Lovitt, Guppy, and Blattner (1969), in training fourth-grade children in spelling accuracy. In a remedial class, Wolf, Giles, and Hall (1968) used backup reinforcers similar to those originally outlined.

## 4  ELEMENTAL BEHAVIORISM AND THE REJECTION OF THE CONCEPT OF PERSONALITY

Up to this point, the works that have been described fit into the paradigm that was set forth by J. B. Watson. Elementary principles of learning—classical conditioning and instrumental conditioning—have been applied directly to human behavior and to problems of behavior change. In the present work it is unnecessary to include the concept of personality, other than Watson's suggestion that personality is behavior. The various analyses and studies in behavior therapy and behavior modification demonstrate that learning principles are important in understanding human behavior. Many behaviors can be analyzed in a straightforward manner into learning principles, and such analyses will suggest treatment procedures. It is important to demonstrate these learning principles because they validate and show the generality of the principles.

But does this paradigm, which is in agreement with Watson's early behaviorism, yield all the power that a concept of learning could offer? Behaviorists, such as Skinner, have accepted this elemental or radical behaviorism paradigm. This is a paradigm that includes two elements: (a) the basic study of animal learning principles and (b) the application of these principles to human behavior. This author suggests that the paradigm is incomplete, is simplistic, is in error, and must be replaced by a third-generation behaviorism. Some of the ways that the radical behaviorism approach is an obstacle to further progress are outlined here, providing a basis for describing a third-generation behaviorism that appears to have greater potential for meeting the demands.

To begin, Watson's behaviorism was a revolt against prevalent approaches to the study of human behavior. A strong element of his behaviorism was thus a criticism and rejection of nonbehavioristic concepts, principles, and methods of study. Skinner's second-generation behaviorism continued these characteristics. Thus, in Skinner's writings there is hardly any reference to any source of knowledge other than that deriving from work that used his principles of learning, his apparatus, and his methodology of research. In addition, Skinner criticized other sources of knowledge that did not employ operant theory and methodology, examples of which are given here.

Personality is an important traditional-versus-radical-behaviorism issue. The traditional concept of personality is that some process or structure within the person is a cause or determinant of his behavior. Watson's statement that personality is behavior treats personality as an effect. This theory was followed by second-generation behaviorists (see Keller & Schoenfeld, 1950), as well as more recent operantly oriented theorists (Lundin, 1961) and social-learning theorists (Mischel, 1968, 1971). That is, personality considered as behavior is thought to be a consequence of learning conditions, not a cause of what the individual does or what he experiences. This radical behavioristic concept has caused a separation from approaches using the traditional concept of personality as a cause. Thus, radical behaviorism had the effect of suggesting that there is no need for special concern with personality—that is, concern with such things as the continuity in behavioral characteristics demonstrated by people over their life spans, or the general and characteristic nature of the person's behavior over various situations, or the uniqueness of individual behavior, or the central fact that there is a causative role of personality.

To continue, the traditional concept of personality provided a foundation for an interest in personality measurement. That is, consideration of personality as causal in determining behavior suggests that it would be important to measure personality; and rejection of the concept of personality, including its causal properties, provides a basis for rejection of personality measurement. Thus, in general, radical behaviorists have rejected psychometrics. In contemporary times, Skinner's general approach provided the basis for this rejection, as did his specific statements, as shown in the following statement eschewing self-reports and verbal tests.

Instead of observing behavior, the experimenter records and studies a subject's statement of what he would do under a given set of circumstances, or his estimate of his chances of success, or his impression of a prevailing set of contingencies of reinforcement, or his evaluation of the magnitude of current variables. The observation of behavior cannot be circumvented in this way, because a subject cannot correctly describe either the probability that he will respond or the variables affecting such a probability. If he could, he could draw a cumulative record appropriate to a given set of circumstances, but this appears to be out of the question (Skinner, B. F., 1969, pp. 77–78).

This orientation tended to restrict contemporary behaviorists in several ways. For example, it was suggested that operant conditioning apparatus should be used for measurement purposes and thereby establish the stimuli that will serve as reinforcers (rewards) for the person (Patterson, 1967; Weiss, 1969). Kanfer and Phillips stated: "Behavioral assessment in the future is likely to depend upon elaboration and extension of laboratory analogue or response sampling techniques" (1970, p. 518). Others limited the potential scope and methods of psychometrics, based on the behavioristic rejection of personality. Mischel (1972), for example, stated that the psychological test should measure the same behaviors it is intended to predict, thereby ruling out the use of verbal tests of traditional psychometrics.

Again, a related development is the atomism and oversimplicity that tends to characterize most current practitioners of a behavior-modification approach. It should be emphasized that this author values the specificity of the early behavior modification works, some of which already have been described. But this does not suggest that all human behavior or behavior problems can be cast in simple terms. Whereas it is important to select straightforward problems that can be simply depicted and can be shown to be amenable to treatment using reinforcement, this does not mean that everything will fall into this paradigm. Nevertheless, almost all work in behavior modification is of this nature. Concepts based on this work, for example, the concept of abnormal behavior (Ullmann & Krasner, 1969), have necessarily been atomistic, not general or unifying. Also, personality theories based on the radical behavioristic concept have shown the same characteristics. For example, Mischel (1968, 1971) was atomistic in the sense of being concerned with relatively specific behaviors and environmental circumstances and in focusing on present rather than past conditions of learning. Moreover, he was criticized (Alkers, 1972; Bowers, 1972) for suggesting that "people show no consistencies, that individual differences are unimportant, and that situations are the main determinants of behavior" (Mischel, 1973, p. 254). Mischel seems to have modified his position, however, to the idea that "*some* of the people show *some* consistency *some* of the time" (Mischel, 1976). In this later work Mischel departed from his earlier radical behaviorism, explicitly indicating his opposition to radical behaviorism. These developments (see also Mischel, 1973) represent changes that bring his work into greater congruence with the present behavioral-interaction view of personality (Staats, A. W., 1971, 1975).

There is one remaining area that needs to be mentioned, and that is the behaviorist revolution that included the rejection of concepts of internal, mental processes or structures. This orientation continues, even in cases where there is objective justification for the concepts. For example, although Skinner's learning theory nominally recognized the principle of classical conditioning and the fact that emotional responses (in his terms, respondents) are classically conditioned, he rejected the importance of classical conditioning and the importance of emotional responding. Operant conditioners, as the name implies, concern themselves with the principles of reinforcement. In this orientation, almost nothing has been done—in animal research, or with human subjects, or in behavior-modification studies—with emotional change through classical conditioning. Moreover, Skinner reemphasized that emotions have no causative role in the determination of human behavior (1975). He outlined the misguided ways that people think that their *feelings* (*loves, fears, anger,* and so on) have some effect on their behavior. He suggested that concern with emotions is an attraction "along the path of dalliance." He stated: "In short, the bodily conditions we feel are *collateral products* of our genetic and environmental histories. They have no explanatory force" (1975, p. 43).

This view springs from Skinner's basic learning theory, where the classical conditioning of emotions and the instrumental conditioning of overt behavior are considered to involve separate principles of learning—the former involving an interesting but unimportant type of behavior, and the latter involving the central aspect of human behavior.

Although this chapter cannot deal with the various elements that must enter into a third-generation behaviorism, an outline is given of a basic learning theory that recognizes the related nature of classical and instrumental conditioning. With this basic learning theory, it is possible to consider the human emotional-motivational system and thereby to introduce the concept of personality in a way that provides a basis for resolving the schism between personality theory and behaviorism. Moreover, the other weaknesses of radical behaviorism that have been described can be corrected in the social behaviorism outlined here.

## 5 THREE–FUNCTION LEARNING THEORY

To begin, let us recognize that various stimuli elicit an emotional response based on the organism's biological structure. Food elicited salivation in Pavlov's dogs, but also would elicit other responses indicating an emotional response; for example, a change in heart rate, a change in blood flow to bodily organs, and changes in the central nervous system. It is generally recognized, following Pavlov, that if another stimulus is presented with food a number of times, the new stimulus will eventually elicit the emotional responses that the food elicits. This is the principle of classical conditioning.

It is also recognized, following Thorndike (and later Hull and Skinner), that if the animal performs some instrumental (skeletal muscular) response and if it receives a bit of food, the animal will make the response more frequently in that situation. In a particular situation, animals will be instrumentally conditioned to certain behaviors if those behaviors are followed by reinforcement.

Skinner considers that these two types of conditioning are separate. In contrast, however, it is suggested that they are closely related. This can be seen when the focus of the learning theory is on the *functions* that a stimulus can have. For example, it can be seen that one stimulus was involved in the examples of each type of conditioning. Food serves as an unconditioned stimulus (UCS)

to elicit an emotional response in classical conditioning. But food also serves as a reinforcing stimulus (RS) to strengthen the instrumental responses the food follows. Thus, food, as a stimulus, is both a UCS and an RS. Moreover, in the process of classical conditioning, any stimulus paired with food will eventually have both functions. It will become a conditional stimulus (CS) having the power to elicit an emotional response, and the stimulus will become a reinforcing stimulus. It will have the power of strengthening the instrumental behavior it follows (see Zimmerman, 1957).

To exemplify this, let us say that the animal is reinforced (with a bit of food) for making a bar-pressing response in a Skinner box. With repeated trials, the animal will make the response more frequently. Let us consider the box as the stimulus that elicits the response. This stimulus may be called the directive stimulus (DS), because it directs or brings on instrumental behaviors. But is this all that the stimulus situation becomes? After all, the food is paired with the stimulus situation, which meets the criterion for classical conditioning. It is suggested that through the classical conditioning process, the directive stimulus will also become a conditioned stimulus and a reinforcing stimulus–it will be a C-R-DS (Staats, A. W., 1968b, 1975).

This is called a three-function learning theory because it states that there are three related functions of such stimuli. In the process of instrumental conditioning, the directive stimulus elicits the instrumental response, it elicits an emotional response, and hence it has reinforcing properties. Classical conditioning and the emotional response, far from being corollary, become central. Further developments of this learning theory (Staats, A. W., 1968b, 1975) demonstrated that as a stimulus comes to elicit an emotional response in the mature organism, it comes as a consequence to elicit a whole class of instrumental responses (in addition to having reinforcing properties). That is, the elaboration of the theory states that stimuli that elicit a positive emotional response will thereby tend to elicit a large class of *approach* or *striving-for* behaviors. Conversely, because of this, stimuli that elicit a negative emotional response will tend to elicit a large class of *escape, avoidance,* or *striving-against-or-away-from* instrumental responses.

It is through this mechanism that instrumental behaviors can be changed by classical conditioning—a phenomenon that was completely overlooked by Skinner. That is, there are clear experimental results showing that classical-conditioning procedures can be conducted that would be expected to make a stimulus elicit an emotional response. As a consequence, however, the animal will now approach the stimulus in a way that he has not done before (e.g., Staats, A. W., & Warren, 1974; Trapold & Winokur, 1967). In terms of behavior change, of course, it is because changing emotional responses change overt, instrumental behavior that behavior therapy is important in clinical psychology. When a phobia (fear), or an emotional response, to a stimulus is changed, the individual behaves differently in an overt, instrumental way toward the stimulus. Usually, it is the change in instrumental behavior that is central. Changing the emotional response is the means to an end. There are many important implications that result from this difference in basic learning theory. The three-function learning theory has significant indications for change in every area in which learning theory is relevant. These cannot be covered here. However, the implications for the personality level of the theory are discussed.

## 6 THE EMOTIONAL–MOTIVATIONAL PERSONALITY SYSTEM

Whereas there are methods for changing emotional responses in behavioral work, these are concerned with changing specific emotional responses that create problems for the person. As previously indicated, there was no concept of personality in a causative role in behavioristic approaches. The manner in which this concept can be introduced is exemplified in describing the person's emotional-motivational personality system (Staats, A. W., 1963, 1968b, 1971, 1975; Staats, A. W., Gross, Guay, & Carlson, 1973).

The importance of the three-function learning theory for understanding human behavior cannot be seen clearly until one considers (a) the complexity of the learning that is involved with emotional learning; (b) the complexity of the emotional-motivational system a person learns; and (c) the effect this has on what a person experiences, what he learns, and what he becomes.

A person has innumerable emotional-conditioning trials in his lifetime. He has the biological basis for emotionally responding to various stimuli, ranging from food to sex on the positive side, as well as various negative emotion-eliciting stimuli. Through pairing with these emotion-eliciting stimuli, various other stimuli come to elicit emotional responses. For example, various *social* stimuli—such as specific people, voices, physical features of people, dress, customs, behaviors, gestures, and so on—elicit positive or negative emotional responses. Various activities do this also, such as reading, sports, television, selling things, and working in various ways. Various *material* and physical things acquire emotional qualities, such as cars, houses, jewelry, climate, and geographic features. Different *cognitive* objects and events will acquire positive and negative emotional value, such as ideas, opinions, religious concepts and rituals, political principles, types of magazines, and newspapers. Central in this latter area is that a person's language—hence his thought and reasoning, and so on—contains a multitude of emotion-eliciting stimuli. There are thousands of words that elicit a positive or negative emotional response in people. And these words can be combined in an infinity of ways to be emotion eliciting.

It is suggested that most of a person's emotional-motivational system is learned, according to the principles of classical conditioning. This does not mean that each of these emotion-eliciting stimuli has been paired with food, or some other primary emotion-eliciting stimulus. This is not necessary, because once a stimulus elicits an emotional response in a person through conditioning, that stimulus may be effective in producing emotional conditioning to new stimuli in further conditioning.

An understanding of how a person acquires his complex emotional-motivational system requires an analysis of the manner in which his conditioning experiences are constituted and how his experiences may differ. It is suggested that a person's conditioning history is infinitely complex and extends over his lifetime. His conditioning differs as a consequence of his primary social experiences, especially in his family. He has conditioning experiences as a function of his peer group, social class, culture, educational institution, and so on.

Other aspects and principles of the emotional-motivational system have been described (Staats, A. W., 1975). For example, the absolute and relative strengths of the emotional-reinforcing-directive stimuli in a person's system would be affected by deprivation. For example, it was shown (more strongly for food-deprived subjects than for nondeprived subjects) that food words elicit the physiological emotional response of salivation (Staats & Hammond, 1972), serve as reinforcers (Harms & Staats, 1976), and serve as directive stimuli for an approach response (Staats & Warren, 1974). It was also suggested that the person's emotional-motivational system has a hierarchical structure and that certain classes of emotional stimuli have greater strength than others. The studies of the effects of deprivation-satiation indicate the manner in which shifts in the hierarchies can occur through deprivation.

Although deriving from a different theoretical context and employing different principles, the present concept of the emotional-motivational system provides an integrating framework for traditional concepts of motivation, such as Maslow's (1943) notion of hierarchical levels of motivation; H. A. Murray's (1938) classification of needs, including his notion of viscerogenic and psychogenic needs; Freud's (1935) notions of cathexis and sublimation; and Cattell's (Cattell & Child, 1975) psychometrically based concept of motivation as a dynamic trait system.

## 7  EMOTIONAL–MOTIVATIONAL SYSTEM AS A PERSONALITY TRAIT

It was stated previously that radical behaviorism did not include the concept of personality in its theory of human behavior in a manner that meets the traditional demands of personality theory. The concept of personality is one of the central elements of the social behaviorism that has been proposed Staats, A. W., 1968b, 1971, 1975). It has been suggested that a child begins very early to learn repertoires of behavioral skills. It is necessary to describe these behavioral skills and indicate the principles and conditions by which they are learned. In addition, these repertoires of behavioral skills are important, because they have causative functions, which may be summarized as follows.

The personality repertoires play their role in (1) directly determining future behaviors, (2) making it possible to respond and learn in new situations, and (3) altering the individual's social and physical environment in other ways that affect his development. . . .

What the individual is at the beginning depends upon what has happened to him. But what he *is* then determines what will happen to him, and therefore what he will further become. The individual's behavior is determined. But his behavior determines what he becomes . . . (Staats, A. W., 1971, pp. 335–336).

While this concept cannot be fully elaborated here, the concept of the personality repertoire, or system, can be characterized by reference to the emotional-motivational system (with emphasis on the manner in which the emotional-motivational system functions according to the three-function learning principles) in determining what the person experiences, what he will learn, and how he will behave.

The concept of the emotional-motivational system is that a person, in his extensive conditioning history, learns to respond emotionally to a unique and complex set of stimuli. This means that the nature of his emotional-motivational system will determine what stimuli will provide an emotional experience for him—and this will differ in different persons. Moreover, the person's emotional-motivational system will determine what stimuli will serve as rewards and punishments in learning new instrumental behaviors. Two people in the same learning situation may learn different instrumental skills, depending on their emotional-motivational systems. Finally, the person's emotional-motivational system will deter-

mine, by directing his instrumental behavior, what he will approach, and thus experience, and what he will avoid, and thus not experience.

Laboratory verification of these causative aspects of the emotional-motivational system began with three experiments. People were given Strong Vocational Interest Blanks, one of the various personality tests that measure aspects of the person's emotional-motivational system. Then persons were selected who had interests similar to the interests of music teachers or performers, and dissimilar to those of chemists. Other persons were selected who had the opposite interests. It was expected that the labels *music* or *chemistry* would have different emotional-motivational characteristics for these two groups and would differentially attract their approach behaviors. Thus, they were introduced to an experimental situation that involved approaching and selecting an article to read from one of two different stacks labeled *music* or *chemistry*. The approach and selecting behaviors of the persons was determined by their emotional-motivational systems, as measured by the Strong Interest Inventory (Staats, A. W., et al., Gross, 1973). It was concluded that the emotional-motivational system of a person will help determine what he approaches and, thus, what he experiences, what he learns, and what he further becomes.

In another experiment, the Strong test was used to select items that were positive (like) or negative (dislike) interests for each person. Later, these people participated in a concept-learning task that involved using the interest items as rewards or punishment. Persons were conditioned to select a concept stimulus when a response to the stimulus was followed by the presentation of a positive interest item; they were not conditioned to select a concept when it was followed by a negative interest item (Staats,

A. W., et al., Gross, 1973). It may be suggested that, what a person learns in terms of instrumental behaviors will depend on his emotional-motivational system. It would be expected that if two people could be selected who would have different emotional responses to the same items, these two people would learn the opposite behavior when subjected to the same conditioning circumstances involving presentation of the items.

In addition, another study showed that a new stimulus paired with positive interest items will have a positive emotion-eliciting value for people. Another stimulus that was paired with negative interest items had negative emotional value (Staats, A. W., Gross, et al., 1973). Since different people have different interests, this suggests that what the person experiences emotionally in a situation and, thus, the way he is conditioned emotionally to new stimuli in that situation will be determined by his interests (an aspect of his emotional-motivational system).

## 7.1  Emotional-Motivational System and Social Behavior

It is suggested that a person's emotional-motivational system affects the way he behaves toward the various stimuli he encounters in life, according to the three-function learning principles. A central class of life's stimuli is social and the effects of this emotional-motivational personality trait on social behavior should be mentioned.

Originally, it was suggested (Staats, A. W., 1964, 1968b) that the emotional-motivational functions of a social stimulus would help determine the ways that the social stimulus affects a person's behavior. Thus, a person who elicits a positive emotional response in another should be capable of conditioning the person to a positive emotional response to any other stimulus with which the indi-

vidual pairs himself. For example, Sigall and Landy (1973) found that the male partner of an attractive female is evaluated more highly than the partner of an unattractive female. Moreover, the positive-emotional individual should be capable of acting as a reinforcing stimulus for the person. Sopolsky (1960) first showed that people similar to the person (and hence positive) are more effective reinforcing agents. Byrne and co-workers (Byrne & Clore, 1966; Byrne & Nelson, 1965; Golightly & Byrne, 1964) presented an approach to attraction based on this model. Byrne and Clore added other aspects of the three-function learning principles to this model (Byrne & Clore, 1970; chapter 22, this volume), so presently there is little difference in principles. The research of Bryne and his associates derives from the same principles and provides strong support for the three-function learning-theory approach to social interaction (Staats, 1975).

In addition, a person who elicits a positive emotional response in another person should elicit a broad class of approach behaviors. Early (1968) showed that if children were conditioned to a positive emotional response to isolates in their classroom, the children would approach and play with the isolates more frequently. Berkowitz and Knurek (1969) showed that the same principle operates in a negative way by first conditioning the subjects to a negative emotional response.

These are but examples of the manner in which the concept of the emotional-motivational system and the three-function learning principles can be employed to account for social behaviors. It is suggested that these principles are involved in broad classes of behavior in social psychology, such as attraction, aggression, conformity, impression formation, imitation, and leadership (see Staats, A. W., 1975, for a complete presentation). These findings are relevant whenever a personality change involves social stimuli.

## 7.2 Emotional-Motivational System and Abnormal Behavior

Radical behaviorism, including our behavior-therapy and behavior-modification studies, has not served as a basis for an abnormal psychology, other than enumerating the behavior problems that have been treated using those methods. It is suggested that an abnormal psychology must be based on a concept that includes a personality theory.

The emotional-motivational system is not the only personality trait that must be considered in the context of abnormal behavior (see Staats, A. W., 1975, for a description of other personality systems), but it is an important one. It was suggested that various diagnostic categories refer to disturbances in the emotional-motivational system. For example, the "waning of interests, loss of ambition, emotional indifference" (Coleman, 1950, p. 245) of the simple schizophrenic may be considered as deficits in the emotional-motivational system. Deficits or inappropriate aspects in the emotional-motivational system typify other diagnostic categories, such as childhood autism, neurasthenia, homosexuality, and psychopathic personality.

The social behavioristic approach suggests that a full abnormal psychology is necessary for a soundly based, comprehensive behavioral-treatment field. It is necessary to have detailed descriptions of the personality systems relevant to the different abnormal categories, because it is suggested that the personality systems cut across the categories and are more basic descriptions than are the categories. It is also necessary to detail how the personality systems are learned and maintained in abnormal psychology; how

the personality systems affect a person's social interactions and social and physical environment and, thus, the person himself; and how the acquisition of abnormal personality repertoires will prevent the acquisition of normal personality repertoires. A first step in providing this foundation has been attempted (see Staats, A. W., 1975, chapter 8), but this area requires concentrated effort if the piecemeal nature of behavior therapy and behavior modification is to change. That is, many problems will involve personality change, not just the change of simple instrumental responses or specific emotional responses.

## 8 SOCIAL BEHAVIORISM AND PSYCHOMETRICS

In 1962 this author designed a study to show that factor-analytic sets of personality-test item responses constitute classes that can be instrumentally conditioned according to reinforcement principles (Staats, A. W., Staats, Heard, & Finley, 1962). The study corroborated the analysis and suggested that such personality traits as sociability and general activity may be learned. In the article based on the study, this author also indicated that in the field of psychometrics (see Cattell, 1946) there were notions compatible with the learning analysis. The author also suggested that learning analysis and psychometrics should be integrated. Further behavior analyses of psychometric instruments and concepts were made (Staats, A. W., 1963), including an extensive analysis of intelligence (Staats, A. W., 1971). A program for the integration of psychometrics and the social behavioristic approach has been outlined (Staats, A. W., 1975, chapter 12). An addendum to this suggests, as an example, that theories of motivation that derive from psychometric methods (Cattell & Child, 1975) should be considered in social behavioristic terms, and that the social behavioristic concept of the emotional-motivational personality system should be elaborated through the use of psychometric methods.[2]

This integration is made possible by the development of a learning theory that includes a concept of personality with specification of personality systems. One necessary ingredient is the elaboration of the learning principles to include the description of a person's language-cognitive system. To understand how it is possible to use verbal items on personality tests to provide indications about nonverbal aspects of the individual's personality, one must understand how language derives from basic learning principles, as well as how the individual's language is a major personality system that is related to the other personality systems. It is suggested that a successful behavioral approach to problems of behavior change in clinical psychology, child psychology, and education is impossible without the parallel development of a psychometrics deriving from and integrated with, the behavioral analysis (Staats, A. W., 1975).

## 9  SOCIAL BEHAVIORISM, BEHAVIOR THERAPY, AND BEHAVIOR MODIFICATION

As indicated, our behavior therapy and modification procedures and principles are valuable tools in behavior change. While they are appropriate primarily for specific and relatively simple behaviors, often the central problem is of that type. Nevertheless, Watson's paradigm of radical behaviorism, which is the foundation of most of this work, can only produce a piecemeal body of knowl-

edge. The paradigm of moving directly from the elementary principles of animal learning to the human level does not include much that is essential for a general theory of human behavior.

In contrast, social behaviorism is a multilevel paradigm that recognizes various levels of knowledge. (a) At the base of the paradigm is the basic learning theory (which must be related to biological study, at an even higher level). (b) The next level of study involves specification of human-learning and social-interaction principles—those that must be considered because of the human's uniquely long and complex learning history, and the fact that humans serve as stimuli for each other and for themselves. The various social interactions important in social psychology are relevant in the paradigm. (c) Social behaviorism includes a personality level of study—a level concerned with the behavioral analysis and description of the personality repertoires, how they are learned, and how they function to affect a person's own behavior, what he learns, what he experiences, and what he becomes. (d) Closely related to this level is an abnormal psychology, which concerns the use of the personality concept and principles, and the description of personality repertoires, such as the emotional-motivational system, in constituting a theory of abnormal personality. (e) Again, closely related, the social behaviorism paradigm includes the need for a psychometric level that will join and use the products of previous levels in conjunction with the methods and concepts of the field of psychometrics. (f) Clinical treatment in clinical psychology, education, and so on, will then rest on the preceding levels of study. For example, we would expect the abnormal-psychology level (see Staats, A. W., 1975) to provide a basis for clinical treatment. As another example, personality-test instruments derived from or based on

---

[2] It may be noted that Raymond B. Cattell is working on the integration of his theory of personality and learning theory (see chapter 18, this *Handbook*).

learning analysis and research would be expected to yield treatment prescriptions in the clinical and educational situation.

Even at present the paradigm has a strong experimental and clinical foundation, at least to the fourth and fifth levels. The approach, however, provides analyses, suggestions, and principles for a richer potential, which is in character with Kuhn's (1962) description of the term *paradigm* as a programmatic framework.

## 10  SUMMARY

J. B. Watson's first-generation behaviorism was a revolt against traditional concepts and methods in psychology. It rejected these methods and concepts, and this characteristic continued in second-generation behaviorisms, such as B. F. Skinner's. It is suggested that these parochial, simplistic features of radical behaviorism are now anachronistic. The third-generation social behaviorism is founded on a new basic learning theory, and it suggests a unification of relevant behavioral and nonbehavioral sources of knowledge of human behavior in the study of personality and personality change.

Today the next level of the revolution, the new horizon, is rapprochement of the new order with the old. This involves the development from the insular approach of elemental behaviorism to one that is general in the principles and concepts it incorporates, in the observations it makes, in the methodologies that it utilizes, and in the problems with which it attempts to deal. . . . The time has come to make the next advance, the incorporation of the various sources of knowledge of man (Staats, A. W., 1972, p. 6).

# 17

# Developmental Structural Changes in the Child's Personality

Ralph Mason Dreger
*Louisiana State University, Baton Rouge*

What are little girls made of?
   Sugar and spice and everything nice.
And what are little boys made of?
   Snips and snails and puppy dogs' tails.

## 1  A THEORETICAL AND METHODOLOGICAL POSITION

Every personality theorist constructs a model of personality. What follows in this chapter is molded by the eclectic theory expounded in *Fundamentals of Personality* (Dreger, 1962, 1966, 1972). In turn, this position has been greatly influenced by a considerably modified psychoanalytic theory, by the theories of one of the editors of this *Handbook* (Cattell, 1946, 1957a); by those of H. J. Eysenck (1970) and J. P. Guilford (1959); by the extensive clinical practice of the author, based on Ginott's (1961) practical formulations; and by the many years of teaching in which the author has engaged. Basically, this model of personality is structurally related to Freud's, though with the important addition of role functions. It is expressible in terms of the functions and trait structures found by multivariate experimentalists, and the model is hospitable to whatever research has been done in child personality.

There are several limitations to the approach to children's personality set forth in this chapter. Profoundly thought-out theories of development are not summarized here or incorporated except obliquely, theories such as Adler's (1935; Ansbacher & Ansbacher, 1956), Bowlby's (1969, 1973), Dabrowski's (1967; Piechowski, 1975), E. H. Erikson's (1963), Mahler's (1975), Piaget's (Flavell, 1963; Piaget & Inhelder, 1969), or H. Werner's (1948). Nor are the findings of Harlow and his associates (e.g., Suomi, Collings, & Harlow, 1973) directly cited in the following pages. In a single chapter an amalgamation of all these often-divergent theories would be beyond the limits necessary in even a chapter of a handbook, and indeed beyond the capacities of this writer, given unlimited space. That these theorists have influenced the writer in many ways, however, should be evident.

Another fundamental restriction that limits this chapter is the use of the literature of the West and primarily that of Great Britain and America with only scant attention to other cultures. Cross-cultural comparisons such as those of Rosenblatt and Skoogberg (1974) on birth order would be extremely valuable, but beyond the scope of this chapter. This limitation is also that of the literature in the scientific journals for the most part, yet it is a limitation on the generalizability of the findings reported here.

Still another grave shortcoming of the chapter is found in the acceptance of many studies that are sometimes defective in research methodology. Some of these defects are the use of data from unreliable sources, the apparently reckless (but often unavoidable) exclusion of subjects from experiments with young children, the sometimes disconcerting changes in response patterns that may not reflect personality changes at all (Sutton-smith, Rosenberg, & Morgan, 1961) but may merely be regression effects (Baltes, Nesselroade, Schaie & LaBouvie, 1972), and in factor-analytic studies, grossly disagreeing conclusions concerning the number and identification of factors. It is simply impossible in the space allotted to examine critically all the contradictory findings. To try to synthesize the vast literature and theories (Santostefano & Baker, 1970) is a task that often must be approached intuitively since multivariate, bivariate, and clinical studies are intermingled somewhat indiscriminately.

On the positive side, the general model for this chapter does take into account the insight growing among personality theorists that parts of the environment must be systematically incorporated in the study of personality, not merely as influences on the personality but as parts of the personality. Hints of this concept are found in several of the chapters of this book, but also stem from H. S. Sullivan's (1953), Mullahy's, (1970), and Laing's (Laing, Phillipson, & Lee, 1966) work in psychiatry, Barker's (1968) and Caldwell's (1969) explorations in ecological psychology, Proshansky's (Proshansky, Ittelson, & Rivlin, 1970) and other's environmental psychological approach, and even in the predictions of child-behavior problems from mother's child-rearing practices (Dielman, Barton, &

Cattell, 1974; Dielman & Cattell, 1972). Only a few have begun to use open-systems concepts (von Bertalanffy, 1968) in child or adult research. And few indeed have recognized the logical necessity of regarding portions of the environment as integral to the personality, but the number is growing (Angyal, 1941; Dreger, 1962; Mullahy, 1970; Murphy, G., 1947; Parr, 1970; Studer, 1970; Sullivan, H. S. 1953).

Other positive developments could also be stated, but these will have to speak for themselves. With the preceding limitations in mind, we can pursue the research on children's temperament, ability, and general personality structure and what changes take place in infancy, early childhood, and later childhood.

## 2  GENETIC, CONSTITUTIONAL, PRENATAL, AND PERINATAL INFLUENCES ON STRUCTURE AND CHANGE IN CHILDREN'S PERSONALITY

First, we consider genetic components in the development of children's personality structure. Approaching the substantive aspects here requires the new look in terms of both the "new genetics" and behavior genetics. These two seem to present contrary indications for understanding the behavior of children. On the one hand, as Callaway (1970) demonstrated in a review of our knowledge of gene action, the experience of the organism modifies the DNA–RNA protein (enzyme) level, so that even myelinization of the nervous system is altered by such experience. The Central Nervous System (CNS), through which temperament, abilities, and other higher order functions of the personality are mediated, is modified cybernetically not just in function but in morphology. This nongenetic control of gene action must certainly be given recognition in the determination of children's personality structure and its components. (For example, innate mental capacity or fixed temperament may be more in the eye of the beholder than in the nervous system of the individual.)

On the other hand, behavior-genetic analysis has tended to show clear genetic components in language, in ability, in temperament traits, and possibly even in interest patterns (cf. Freedman & Keller, 1963; Lenneberg, 1969; Scarr-Salapatek, 1975; Thompson, W. R., 1968; Vandenberg, 1967b, 1968a; Wilson, R. S., 1975). Accordingly, we may recognize some behavior patterns that are gene determined, even when they appear almost exclusively products of the environment, and others that are experience determined but in reality have possibly unrecognized genetic foundations. Perhaps separation of the components into their respective parts, as, for example, by Cattell's (1970b) Multiple-Abstract Variance Analysis (MAVA), may clarify the picture; but in line with much of the thinking in genetics today, it may be found that the nature of the transaction, not merely the interaction, of genes and environment is difficult to convey in this type of analysis (i.e., when independent variables exert influence on dependent variables but alter one another as well). These dynamic feedback arrangements are underscored by the several essays and research reports in Glass (1968); Jeffrey (1969); Proshansky, Ittelson, and Rivlin (1970); and Reaser (1972) and in the classical experiments of Sontag and Wallace (1935a, b, 1936). For many years R. Q. Bell, R. R. Sears, and L. H. Stott have been suggesting the feedback situation represented in the concept of transaction. This type of dynamic interaction was given concretely in the work of M. R. Yarrow, Waxler, and Scott (1971), who observed the conditioning of adult behavior by preschool

youngsters (and anecdotally in the reports of mothers concerning toilet training, "He wasn't trained, I was.").

In particular, then, we can note genetic and environmental determinants relating to sex differences and age and, somewhat more fully, those relating to abilities and temperament. Garai and Scheinfeld (1968) justly (at times) complained that not enough attention is paid in personality research to fundamental sex differences, although developmental psychologists are probably less inclined to ignore such differences than investigators using adult subjects. Many of the differences, however, that are attributed to genetic factors can be shown to be culturally produced, as Mead (1949) so eloquently demonstrated in her studies of primitive societies. And even some primary characteristics may come from prenatal rather than genetic predisposition (Young, W. C., Gray, & Phoenix, 1964). In respect to age, it is fairly well agreed that maturational age is largely under genetic determination but only within gross limits. The stage type of a theorist like Piaget is opposed by the continuous development theorist, who points out that the so-called stages so overlap that it is difficult to tell in which stage a child may be. And yet, nowhere has this writer found denial that certain functions such as walking, talking, and abstract reasoning must be preceded by some almost certainly genetically-controlled morphologic developments. So rapid is maturation in infancy that the Russian Papousek (1967) calls into question studies that make comparisons of young infants differing by more than 3 months of age. From a personality standpoint, considering maturation, we should expect differences in the infant's and child's personalities to arise merely from a difference in age. It is still being debated how much difference there is, for instance, in the intellectual structure of children of differing ages; but it would be remarkable indeed to find no difference in such structure from age to age, though whether the alterations that are found result more from maturation or experience is not settled.

More specifically, we can learn from Vandenberg (1967b) who, after reviewing genetic components in anthropometric characteristics, pointed out that hereditary factors are known to exist in motor skills, in autonomic nervous system functioning, in color vision and visual acuity, in audition, in perception of certain tastes, and possibly in smell and pain perception. Such tests as Kohs' Blocks and the Gottschaldt Figures reveal differences in visual perception between monozygous and heterozygous twins. In intellectual functioning, Vandenberg's analyses suggest that there are factors of intellect that do not follow the pattern of familial resemblance shown by the IQ. Specifically, of six Thurstone factors, Number, Verbal (Comprehension), Space, and Word Fluency appear to be significantly under genetic control, while Reasoning and Memory do not. So, too, though with less certainty (possibly on account of the factorial complexity), the individual subtests of the Weschler Intelligence Scale for Children may differ in heritability.

A few temperament characteristics beginning with Introversion-Extraversion (Scarr, 1969) are shown to have hereditary components, that is, identifiable variance can be attributed to heredity in comparison with the general situation in which we must acknowledge that nothing human could exist without some combination of heredity and environment. Gottesman (1963) used the Minnesota Multiphasic Personality Inventory (MMPI) (a mixture of clinical syndromes and temperament trait scales) and Cattell's High School Personality Questionnaire (HSPQ) to show hereditary components in the characteristics of twins. As in other studies, Social

Introversion on the MMPI indicated the most influence of heredity. Depression and (whatever makes up) Pyschopathic Deviate revealed about equal hereditary and environmental influences; Psychasthenia and Schizophrenia have some smaller hereditary components. Gottesman differs somewhat from Cattell in respect to the HSPQ, but both regard the following factors as having appreciable hereditary determination: B, General Intelligence; E, Submissiveness versus Dominance: H, Shy, Sensitive versus Adventurous (or Parmia in Cattell's neological system); and J, Liking Group Action versus Fastidiously Individualistic (Asthenia). It must be recognized that the preceding reports are not of direct investigation of children for the most part; only by extrapolation can we conclude that infants and young children would possess these same heredity-environment ratios. One may argue that it denies the influence of heredity to call into question results from older ages as applicable to younger children. But it is not, for different phenotypic manifestations may present themselves at different ages. At least, a considerable body of research, some of which is cited in the latter portion of this chapter, suggests that temperament patterns may change from one period of life to another. Thus, certain patterns may show up at only certain times in life even though they are under the control of gene action. A clear parallel here is the trait of baldness, which has been adequately identified as hereditary but which usually does not manifest itself until later in life.

There are undoubtedly some temperament characteristics (Scarr, 1966) other than those mentioned that will prove to be directly genetically determined (not just indirectly as all characteristics are). The suggestion that Cattell makes is a sound one; that is, in assessing hereditary components in children's personality structures and changes in them, it is necessary to do so with known structures of traits such as Cattell's, rather than merely acquiescing in the banal judgment that, heredity and environment interact in producing such-and-such a chance characteristic.

Closely related to genetic factors in children's personality structures are those classified as constitutional—somatic and physiological characteristics present after environment has had some impact on the genetically given. Rather fundamental here is the person's body build. L. Murphy (1967) pointed out that body build, usually presumed to be a constitutional constant, instead fluctuates in childhood. However, body build probably levels off into one of Sheldon's categories later on, indicating among other things the delayed activity of genes. At any one time in childhood, though, some relations may hold. Kagan and Garn (1963) found that large-chested children tend to be more intelligent than children with smaller chests. R. N. Walker (1963) discovered from mothers' ratings the sex-differentiated body type-temperament relations seen in the table below.

After considering genetic and constitutional components of children's personalities far too briefly, we turn to prenatal and perinatal influences. Whatever genetic factors operate in the production of personality structure in the child, it is now fairly well established that prenatal experiences may markedly affect the establishment of any particular personality or group of personalities. A vast amount of evidence was accumulated by Ashley Montagu (1962) on prenatal influences affecting embryo and fetus. Jordan (1971) provided a valuable, more recent, supplement. Although now there is no doubt that just about anything in appropriate form can pass through the placenta, interchanges also take place before the placenta itself is formed.

Sufficient behavioral correlates have not been studied yet to make definitive judgments in many cases, yet the relations established between certain prenatal or perinatal experiences and certain types of mental deficiencies suggest that other functions of the personality may well be affected by various chemical or physical agents, particularly at critical periods in the develop-

|            | Boys                                      | Girls                                    |
|------------|-------------------------------------------|------------------------------------------|
| Endomorph  | Bossy, quarrelsome, poorly coordinated    | "Good girls"                             |
| Mesomorph  | Good appetite, not orderly, do not tire easily | Good appetite, love exercise, energetic |
| Ectomorph  | Well-coordinated, not easily discouraged  | "Bad girls"                              |

ment of the unborn child or neonate. By analogy with some of the results reported by R. D. Young (1967), at least gross motor activity level could be so affected. Some rather fundamental temperament differences in personality structure likely may arise

from prenatal or perinatal experiences (Young, W. C., Gray, & Phoenix, 1964) rather than from genetic factors or postnatal experience. Later changes in personality structure, likewise, may take place as the child reacts to the reactions of others to his prenatally or perinatally determined behavior (Stott, 1962).

A facet of determination of child personality structure falling in the penumbrae of heredity and environment is that of birth order (Rees, A. H., & Palmer, 1970). Students of Alfred Adler know of his contentions that the older child (son, according to Adler's masculine chauvinism) is more conservative, responsible, and authority oriented, the youngest more radical and rebellious, while the middle child is "as if he were in a race . . . and trains continually to surpass his older brother and conquer him." As is often true, the picture is more complicated than at first supposed. (Schooler, 1972, said there is no picture; Breland, 1973, said there is.)

Reviews by Bradley (1968) and Warren (1966) indicated that first-born children are more susceptible to social pressure than later-born children, thus supporting Adler's position to a degree. But, also, the evidence is strong that first borns are overrepresented in college populations, which could mean that they are more striving than later borns, this time in contradiction to Adler. A sex difference shows up here. External locus of control, one indicator of authority orientation, is higher in first-born males, but not in females, while social responsibility and rigidity are higher in first borns of both sexes (MacDonald, A. P., Jr., 1971), again a mixed bag for Adler. Postulated higher authoritarianism among first borns has not materialized in controlled investigations (Eisenman & Cherry, 1970; Greenberg, Guerino, Lashen, Mayer, & Piskowski, 1963; Stotland & Dunn, 1962). Also contrary to hypothesis, divergent thinking in school children is more pronounced among first-born than among later-born children (Lichtenwalner & Maxwell, 1969). In fact, intellectual performance in general (at least $g$ type derived from

Raven's Progressive Matrices) almost certainly is superior in first-born children (Belmont & Marulla, 1973; Breland, 1974). Early studies (Thurstone & Jenkins, 1929; Willis, 1924), as Zajonc and Markus (1975) pointed out, came to a different conclusion, but most of the more recent investigations support the first-born superiority. What the reasons are for these demonstrated differences in intellectual functioning, aside from their probably not arising from social status factors, are yet to be discovered. Zajonc and Markus (1975) offered a confluence model that takes into account family size and spacing between children, as well as birth order, a model that holds considerable promise of explaining both the general findings of first-born superiority in intelligence and the apparently anomalous results of Thurstone and others earlier and the equally anomalous discovery of an increase in intellectual level in later-born children of large families (Belmont & Marulla, 1973).

Birth order and its concomitants may be involved in temperament functioning in a differential way, depending on external conditions. Experimental confirmation is found in several places (Rhine, 1968; Rosenfeld, 1966; Suedfeld, 1969). Low achievement arousal, for example, brings greater conformity behavior in first-born girls, but high arousal brings less conformity. Need achievement and need affiliation, presumed characteristic of first-borns, may be affected by neutral or stressful conditions. The lower level of anxiety that has been found in first-borns may be raised under anxiety-provoking conditions.

The various influences which we have mentioned in this section, derived from hereditary and experiential sources, must be recognized in both the structure and changes in children's personalities. Again, we must stress that these influences operate not merely in an interactive manner, but in a feedback manner, whereby gene action affects environment which in turn returns messages to alter gene action, and temperament and intellect patterns affect environments which in turn affect temperament and intelligence patterns.

## 3 BASIC STRUCTURAL PROPERTIES OF TEMPERAMENT IN NEONATES AND INFANTS

Mothers often report about their children, "He was that way ever since he was born. He was aggressive [or withdrawing or hyperactive or whatever] the first day I saw him." These reports of an infant's basic temperament patterns may be exaggerated. Yet there appear to be marked differences among infants of a fairly fundamental nature in basic reaction patterns. Russian psychologists have spoken of types of nervous systems that differentiate children from one another (Chudnovskii, 1963; Govallo, 1961/1962; Vasilev, 1962). Whether one uses logical classification, or higher order factor analysis, or clustering procedures, types of youngsters can be delineated, yet there are no absolute types so far discernible. Even psychoanalysis does not claim that its types have been formed at this stage (Fenichel, 1945). As has been discovered in recent years, types may be found by matching profiles of scores on a number of dimensions (Bolz, 1972b), but this procedure is clearly not an absolutist typology.

Infants, therefore, are considered to vary along several dimensions, either logically or factor-analytically derived. Old timers in the child development field will perhaps think of Gesell and his colleagues' "behavior patterns" (Gesell & Amatruda, 1947; Gesell & Ilg, 1943; Gesell, Ilg, Ames, & Rodell, 1974). The only dimensions one can deduce from Gesell's work are the twin ones of

self-activity and sociality, which in proper balance lead to self-containment. Adding another dimension to Gesell's (logically, though not necessarily intentionally), Escalona (1963) studied 28-week-old children and came up with the dimensions of pleasure-unpleasure, behavioral autonomy, and responsiveness to external stimuli, the latter two seeming to match Gesell's. Birch and his associates (Birch, 1962) enumerated 9 reaction patterns that characterized 22 children, ages 2–24 months: activity level, rhythmicity, approach-withdrawal, adaptability, intensity of reaction, threshold of responsiveness, quality of mood (corresponding to Cattell's Desurgency-Surgency), distractibility, and attention span and persistence. In factor-analytic terms, these are what might be primary dimensions, in contrast to Gesell's and Escalona's second- or third-order dimensions.

Factor analyses of infants' behaviors parallel logically derived dimensions to a degree, but, as might be expected, not completely. From sound and color motion pictures and also demographic data of 32 first-born infants, Bell (1960) found from a centroid analysis and Varimax rotation five factors, which were named Arousal, Depth of Sleep, Tactile Sensitivity-Strength, Oral Integration, and Fetal Position. Bell's conclusion is that there are a number of well-organized but not yet well-related systems in the infant. (The correlations among the factors, however, suggest more relation than Bell finds.) A factor analysis on so few children probably horrifies factor analysts, who are accustomed to hundreds of cases, but they need to know how difficult it is to get any sizable sample of infants, at least, for intensive study. Further, as Rummel (1970) reports, often the results of analyses with fewer subjects than is statistically and mathematically sound are quite comparable with those from larger numbers of subjects (in Rummel's cases subjects are nations, but in this author's experience they have been children). The names of Bell's factors may not be satisfactory, but the dimensions to which they refer seem entirely realistic.

One other factor study of infant behavior demonstrates similarity of dimensions to Bell's, insofar as comparable variables enter into them. G. Schmidt (1967) used nurses' ratings on 31 characteristics of infants and children, arriving at primary factors that were designated Lively Activity, Tension versus Relaxation, Excitability, and Social Orientation. Second-order factors were reported as Extraversion and Emotional Lability.

After reviewing a number of studies of social and emotional behavior in infants, Ricciuti (1968) recognized three major dimensions: (a) Approach and Withdrawal, which he considers to be among the most fundamental of phylogenetic and ontogenetic processes; (b) Exploratory Behavior, Curiosity, "Intrinsic Motivation"; and (c) Arousal or Activation, Orienting and Alerting Responses. More is said later about major dimensions.

One trend in the latter half of the 20th century has emphasized the active nature of the infant and young child in his or her[1] responses to the world. This trend has been most evident in discussion and research on competence (Stone, J. L., Murphy, & Smith, 1973; White, R. W., 1959).

In comparison with the "theoretically constructed" infant who was passive, helpless, and shaped primarily by experiences, . . . the "real world" infant has come to be viewed as skilled, active, and socially influential. In short, he or she is competent

[1] Elsewhere in this chapter, the masculine pronouns are used, for the sake of sentence clarity.

(Appleton, Clifton, & Goldberg, 1975, p. 103).

Murphy and her associates (Murphy, L. B., 1962) distinguished competence from coping, which they referred to skill achieved rather than to processes leading to a level of competence. Hirsch (1972) and J. McV. Hunt (1972b) limited the concept of competence to intellectual functioning. Neither the distinction nor the limitation seems satisfactory. The first seems like a semantic distinction that is no difference, unless one identifies competence solely with performance. The second does not take account of the fact that competence is a gross infant function that can be analyzed for special purposes into separate functions, sensorimotor, intellectual, social, etc. but in the intact infant is a synthesis. Appleton and her colleagues (1975) suggested that though the infant is low in competence, relatively speaking, given the type of environment in which he is found, the newborn is very effective in controlling the environment by crying and other actions and can even control some of his own bodily activities. In the first 2 years of life, competence develops greatly in influencing caretakers, maintaining attention, manipulating objects, and engaging in bodily position changes in space. From the personality-structure standpoint, we may regard competence as a higher order dimension or as a secondary process phenomenon relating to ego strength (Zern, 1973). There are wide theoretical differences between the two positions represented here, but they are not immediately relevant to the descriptive approach we are making to competence in behavioral manifestations, which imply something within.

True to the orientation of this chapter, we cannot leave this section on the structure of temperament without pointing out the fact that it is nearly impossible to speak of any temperament trait or characteristic *in vacuo*: Virtually all have external reference of some sort. In the light of role and small-group research and even in view of modern psychoanalytic concepts of symbiosis and individuation (Mahler, Pine, & Bergman, 1975) and of attachment and loss (Bowlby, 1969, 1973), the dimensions of infant temperament cannot be limited to "within the skin" domains. Where does temperament leave off and role begin in the dyadic relation of mother and infant (Stern, C. S., & Caldwell, 1969), or in polyadic relations in the family (Walters, J., & Stinnett, 1971)? For convenience we may speak of temperament structure as if it were entirely within the skin of the infant; for more adequate analysis, such dimensions as Approach-Withdrawal can scarcely be considered apart from a social matrix the boundaries of whose elements are fuzzy (in the modern mathematical sense of fuzzy sets).

From the data available it is impossible to say, "There are thus and thus many dimensions of infant temperament." Ricciuti's (1968) reduction of all dimensions to three is satisfactory for some purposes, but so is the inclusion of nine factors (logically, not factorially derived) by Birch (1962) for some purposes. This is the same argument that has held Eysenck and Cattell apart for many years (not by any means the only argument that has). Eysenck's neat scheme serves many research purposes quite well; and so has Cattell's. As a clinician the writer has found Cattell's more extensive system of factors more useful than he has Eysenck's rather thin system. But he recalls that Eysenck's system was born out of a clinical setting, and presumably the British clinicians who have worked with him have found his system satisfactory. The issue might be settled by fixing on either a primary level or some higher level of factors, and agreeing

that these factors, at whatever level, are *the* factors of infancy and early childhood; but such agreement cannot be found among factor authorities, so it is hardly expected that child development investigators should do much better. An agreed-upon taxonomy of infant temperament and in general personality, including role functions, would be highly desirable; at present there is none. We venture to suggest that the dimensions of temperament most likely to emerge in such an accepted set would include at least the following: Activity or Arousal Level (including Rhythmicity), Approach-Withdrawal, Pleasure-Unpleasure, Attention Span or Persistence (possibly involving Distractibility and Exploratory Behavior), Competence (including Behavioral Autonomy), and, what has not been emphasized in the literature, Hostility-Compliance.[2]

## 4 THE STRUCTURE OF INTELLECT IN INFANTS AND YOUNG CHILDREN

When we turn to the dimensions of intellect in infancy and childhood, we face most of the issues confronting intelligence research in general (Butcher, 1968; Butcher & Lomax, 1972; Cancro, 1971; Cattell, 1963a, 1964b, 1971; J. P. Guilford, 1967; Guilford & Hoepfner, 1971; Horn, J. L., 1976; Horn, J. L., & Cattell, 1966a, 1967; Humphreys, 1967; Hunt, J. McV., 1972b; Jensen, 1970; Vernon, 1961, 1972; Wiseman, 1967), and likewise those arising from vastly divergent theories of the devel-

[2] Although the writer has been able to find only one set of authorities who mention Hostility (Stern, G. S., Caldwell, Hersher, Lipton, & Richmond, 1969), certainly some account has to be taken of the infant who does not cooperate in feeding, cries so as to be viewed as angry by others, stiffens his body, and so forth. In Horney's terms, such an infant moves "against the world."

opment of intelligence and/or learning abilities (Bandura & Walters, 1963; Fenichel, 1945; Garrett, 1946; Hunt, J. McV., 1961; Inhelder & Piaget, 1958; Isaacs, 1930; Kay, 1972; Piaget & Inhelder, 1969; Staats, 1971; Vygotsky, 1962; Werner, H., 1948; Wolman, 1972b). Inasmuch as it is almost impossible at present to reconcile these theories, only a few major attempts to determine the structure of intellect in infants and young children are presented here. One of these (Stott & Ball, 1965) is, however, a massive and significant attempt.

After reviewing and evaluating research on intelligence tests of infants and preschool children, Stott and Ball detailed the results of their own extensive study. They used 5 infant tests and 11 preschool or school-age tests of both verbal and performance varieties. Altogether 1,926 children from 14 age levels between 3 months and 5 years were examined. The factor analysis done on the data by the principal axes method was followed by Varimax and graphic orthogonal rotations with a parallel biquartimin rotation. Factors thus derived were compared directly with Guilford's Structure of Intellect Model, plus additions such as Gross Psychomotor and Hand Dexterity appropriate to the motor nature of some of the tasks. Table 1 gives a partial picture of the factors that appeared at the different age levels, as Stott and Ball identified these factors from the major tests.

Stott and Ball pointed out that cognitive and convergent abilities are overrepresented and other abilities are underrepresented. Divergent production, related (some think) to creative abilities, is present in the infant scales, but not in the preschool scales. One striking fact, if the analysis is correct, is that the infant tests cover a wider range of intellectual functions than do the preschool tests, a result probably rather surprising to some students of intelligence. The investiga-

tors also remarked about the fact that at two levels of the same scale the factor structures are somewhat different, one reason no doubt why so often there is little or no relation between tests at an early age and later, even though presumably a child is tested with the same test. There is no evidence that infant tests are less valid measures of abilities at the age level than are tests of older children.

Charlesworth (1968) commented on the parallels between Stott and Ball's factors in infancy and Piaget's concepts of sensorimotor abilities. Another aspect to which he called attention is that infant tests involve affective components related to the development of cognitive processes as Hurst also found with the Merrill-Palmer tests (Hurst, 1960, 1963). Charlesworth argued for a cognitive, perceptual learning theory, suggesting that all cognition in the infant is not the result of motor feedback, that the infant perceives and cognizes more than the immediate motor response indicates, and thus that the lag between perception and performance found in older children is also present in the infant.

Although limited to 4-year-olds, the work of Sitkei and Meyers (1969) follows in the same Guilford tradition. Lower and middle-class white and black children were tested, and six factors were extracted and rotated by Varimax. These with their Guilford letter designations are: Verbal Comprehension (*CMU*), Ideational Fluency (*DMU*), Perceptual Speed (*EFU*), Figural Reasoning (*NF*),[3] Memory Span (*MSS*), and Picture Memory (*MMU*). Most likely other factors could be produced given more tests (and hopefully more subjects). One side result of interest to both developmental students and factorists is that the Knox Cubes test, which would seem to be purely a performance test,

[3] Probably *NFR*, cf. J. P. Guilford (1967, p. 460).

**TABLE 1** Summary of factor interpretations, allowing comparisons of tests, and age levels for interpreted factor content

| Intelligence factor[a] | Age level (months) | | | | | | | | | | | | | | Total |
|---|---|---|---|---|---|---|---|---|---|---|---|---|---|---|---|
| | Cattell | | California | | Gesell | | Merrill-Palmer | | | | | Stanford-Binet (L) | | | |
| | 3 | 6 | 6 | 12 | 6 | 12 | 24 | 30 | 36 | 48 | 54 | 36 | 48 | 60 | |
| Cognitive: | | | | | | | | | | | | | | | |
| CFU | X | X | X | | | | | | X | | | X | | X | 6 |
| CFR | | | | X | | | | | | | X | | | | 2 |
| CFS | | | | | | | X | X | X | X | | | | | 4 |
| CFT | | | | | | | | X | | X | X | | | X | 4 |
| CFI | X | | | | | | | | | | | | | | 1 |
| CMU | | | | | | | X | | | | | | | | 1 |
| CMR | | | | | | | | | | X | | | X | | 2 |
| CMS | | | | | | | | | | | X | | | | 1 |
| CBU | | | X | X | | X | | | | | | | | | 3 |
| Total | | | | | | | | | | | | | | | 24 |
| Memory: | | | | | | | | | | | | | | | |
| MFU | | | | | | | | | | | | | | X | 1 |
| MFR | | | | X | | | | | | X | | | | | 2 |
| MFS | | | | | | | | | X | | | | | | 1 |
| MSS | | | | | | | | | | | | | | X | 1 |
| MMU | | | | | | | | | | | | | X | | 1 |
| MMR | | | | | X | | | | | | | X | X | | 3 |
| MBR | | | | X | | X | | | | | | | | | 2 |
| Total | | | | | | | | | | | | | | | 11 |
| Divergent products: | | | | | | | | | | | | | | | |
| DFU | X | | | | | X | | | | | | | | | 2 |
| DFR | | | X | | X | | | | | | | | | | 2 |
| DFT | | X | | | | | | | | | | | | | 1 |
| DBR | | | | | | X | | | | | | | | | 1 |
| Total | | | | | | | | | | | | | | | 6 |
| Convergent products: | | | | | | | | | | | | | | | |
| NFU | | X | X | | | | | | | | | | | | 2 |
| NFR | X | | | | X | | | | X | X | | | | | 4 |
| NFS | | | | | | | | X | X | | X | | | | 3 |
| NMU | | | | | | X | | | | | | | | | 1 |
| NMI | | | | X | | | | | | | | | | | 1 |
| NBR | | | | | | X | | X | | | | | | | 2 |
| Total | | | | | | | | | | | | | | | 13 |
| Evaluation: | | | | | | | | | | | | | | | |
| EFU | | | | | | | X | | | | | | | | 1 |
| EFS | | | | | X | | | | | | | X | | | 2 |
| EMR | | | X | | | | | | | | | | | | 1 |
| EMS | | X | X | | X | | | | | | | | | | 3 |
| EMT | | | | | | | | | | | | | X | | 1 |
| Total | | | | | | | | | | | | | | | 8 |
| Others: | | | | | | | | | | | | | | | |
| Hand dexterity | | | | | | | X | X | X | | X | | | | 4 |
| Gross Psychomotor | | | | | X | X | | | | | | | | | 2 |

**TABLE 1** (*continued*)  Summary of factor interpretations, allowing comparisons of tests, and age levels for interpreted factor content

| Intelligence factor[a] | Cattell | | California | | Gesell | | Merrill-Palmer | | | | | Stanford-Binet (L) | | | Total |
|---|---|---|---|---|---|---|---|---|---|---|---|---|---|---|---|
| | 3 | 6 | 6 | 12 | 6 | 12 | 24 | 30 | 36 | 48 | 54 | 36 | 48 | 60 | Total |
| Whole body | | | | | X | | | | | | | | | | 1 |
| Locomotor | | | | | X | | | | | | | | | | 1 |
| Reflex | | | | | X | | | | | | | | | | 1 |
| Total | | | | | | | | | | | | | | | 9 |
| Total | | | | | | | | | | | | | | | 71 |

*Note.* From "Infant and Preschool Mental Tests: Review and Evaluation" by L. H. Stott and R. S. Ball, *Monographs of the Society for Research in Child Development*, 1965, *30*, 151 pp. Copyright 1965 by *Monographs of the Society for Research in Child Development*. Reprinted by permission.

[a]Letter designations refer to J. P. Guilford's (1967) factors. For example, *CMU* is Verbal Comprehension; *EFU* is Perceptual Speed; *NFR* is Figural Reasoning; *MSS* is Memory Span; and *MMU* is Picture Memory.

loaded highest on the Verbal Comprehension factor. Either the factor is misnamed (but since it has been so long identified, probably not), or we have another indication that so-called performance tests are highly saturated with verbal components.

The work of Stott and Ball, Hurst, and Sitkei and Meyers bears on the long-continuing controversy over whether intellectual functions grow out of a single general ability, the *differentiation hypothesis* (Garrett, 1946), or begin as complex and multidimensional (Cohen, J., 1957, 1959). Although the evidence cited previously and other studies (McCartin & Meyers, 1966; Orpet & Meyers, 1966; Quereshi, 1973; Wallborn, Blaha, & Wherry, 1973) tend to support the latter position, other evidence (Osborne, R. T., Anderson, & Bashaw, 1967; Osborne, R. T. & Lindsay, 1967) is interpreted to support Garrett's developmental theory. It is at this point that methodological problems enter in, involving the number of tests or variables, the number of factors, matrix diagonal values, rotation methods, and possibly levels of factors.

To this writer, multidimensionality rather than unidimensionality appears to be the case with infants and young children. Although we do not discuss adolescents or older children here, some light can be thrown on the situation by considering the case with them at this time. Although Guilford rejected the Garrett hypothesis, his evidence is only contrary to that hypothesis through early school age. Evidence for the high school ages was given by Fitzgerald, Nesselroade, and Baltes (1973), who concluded that adult mental structure emerges before adolescence. On the other hand, Very and his associates (Dye & Very, 1968; Very, 1967; Very & Iacono, 1970) presented contradictory data indicating that the number of factors decreases from college level to 11th grade to 9th grade and 7th grade. This is definitely a situation where further research is necessary, not only to settle the conflict about adolescence but also to establish continuities into middle and early childhood.

## 5  THE STRUCTURE OF TEMPERAMENT IN PRESCHOOL AND SCHOOL AGE CHILDREN

The child of 4 and 5 years of age has been studied and factors of temperament derived by a number of investigators who tend to come up with different factors (cf. Dielman and Krug, chapter 5, this volume; Emmerich, 1964, 1966; Grossman & Levy, 1974). Though by some kind of congruence process these factors might be equated, only rough attempts have been made to do so. In addition to the studies mentioned by Dielman and Krug, only a few outstanding investigations are given attention here. Some of these have used rating scales by important others in the child's life and some questionnaire responses of children themselves. Possibly this is as good a place as any to recognize that what are definitely temperament differences among children (or adults) may nevertheless reflect cultural and ethnic differences as much as individual differences (Gynther, 1971; Haney, 1967; Williams, W. S., 1971).

Using a combination of McQuitty's linkage analysis and factor analysis, Stott (1962) found 14 factors emerging from the matrix derived from 63 4-year-olds. Examples of these factors are Sociocentricity versus Egocentricity, Independence versus Dependence, Social Ease versus Shy Unfriendliness, and Personal Instability versus Stability and Inner Control. Names of factors can be misleading, especially when, as in the last one, inference is made to what is going on inside the youngster. Nevertheless, if these factors are anywhere nearly appropriately named, they and others Stott set forth are very much like dimensions others have found in young children.

As part of a longitudinal study of young children, factors of nursery school behavior were derived by Emmerich (1964, 1966)

from observations and teacher ratings. Three relatively independent factors, out of six initially extracted, are Aggression-Dominance, Dependency, and Autonomy. Claiming that Emmerich's choice of variables was limited and weighted in the Freudian psychosexual model, Grossman and Levy (1974) enlarged their range of variables to include coping or competence items suggested by Erikson's and White's theoretical formulations. Their factoring of teachers' ratings yielded five factors: Social Confidence, which they compare with Emmerich's Dominance; Cooperation, a passivity factor rather like Emmerich's Dependency; Task Persistence, possibly related to Emmerich's Autonomy; Mobility, corresponding to nothing of Emmerich's since the latter had no pertinent variables; and Aggression, much like Emmerich's factor. As with many studies with children, both of these suffer from small samples; but once again, the results are not out of keeping with what astute observers might expect or what others similarly situated have found. One judgment that may be made about Grossman and Levy's scales is that to name them Behavior Rating Scales for Children is to misname them, for such characteristics as social orientation, leadership, ability to abstract, or empathy can scarcely be called behavior.

A somewhat more extensive assessment of preschool temperament (personality) structure by Damarin and Cattell (1968) yielded 18 principal axis factors, 5 second-order factors, and 2 third-order factors. Because these were derived from miniature situations personality tests, their names tend to reflect test format, for example, Absorption in Creative Play, Pride in Achieving Standards, and Interest in Dramatic Play. But some of the factors sound familiar to those who have used factored tests with older children or adults: Commentive Superego or Fear of Punishment, Reflective versus

Impulsive Closure, and Anxiety. Second-order factors were named Control of Associative Processes, Alert Enthusiasm, Crystalized Ability, Crystalized Perceptual-Motor Skills, and Inhibition of Expressiveness. Finally, the third-order factors appear to relate largely to ability and achievement: Fluid Ability and Self-confidence, and Crystalized Achievement. That names may be misleading is underscored by the fact that the second-order factor, Crystalized Ability, has nearly as high a loading on· the third-order factor, Fluid Ability, as on Crystalized Achievement.

As part of the downward extension of the Cattell series of personality questionnaires (16 Personality Factor Questionnaire [16PF], High School Personality Questionnaire [HSPQ], Children's Personality Questionnaire [CPQ], Early School Personality Questionnaire [ESPQ]), an endeavor has been underway for several years to establish a Preschool Personality Questionnaire (PSPQ) (Cattell & Dreger, 1974). Following several initial factorizations (e.g., Cattell & Peterson, 1959), a number of studies using altogether approximately 2,000 children have been carried out, with reliability checks and social desirability scales, utilizing analyses by principal components, Varimax, and Promax primarily, though there are some Maxplane rotations now in process for clearing up structure. From one of the studies on 616 first grade children, 26 factors appeared reasonable by several indexes; among these are the following, which indicate both dimensions recognizable from other investigations and more specific dimensions in keeping with the greater coverage of the "personality sphere" in the PSPQ:

Homebound, Feminine Passiveness versus Adventurous, Masculine Aggressiveness

Secure, Affectionate Affiliativeness versus Insecure Rejection of Affection

Cyclothymia versus Schizothymia

Surgency versus Desurgency

Egocentricity versus Allocentricity

Passivity versus Activity

Adventurous Maturity versus Cautious Immaturity

Trustful Optimism versus Misanthropic Pessimism

Secure Sleep versus Troubled Sleep

Capable Fastidiousness versus Messiness

Socialized Satisfaction versus Nonconforming Dissatisfaction

Dominant Independence versus Timid Dependence

Those who know preschool children will recognize the dimensions of real children represented by the names of the factors. The consistency of these factors has been determined in part by the reliability studies, but in part also by the judgment of child experts. It takes no expert, however, to recognize the consistency of the first factor from its highest loaded items (see Table 2).

After many years of experience testing preschool youngsters, the writer and his colleagues are convinced that preschool children provide as valid and reliable reports of their own feelings, attitudes, and interests as older children and adults, and often probably more so. It is generally easier to detect when they are not reporting reliably by their position responses, random responses, and omissions.

Although it must be admitted that no definitive structure of preschool personality has been achieved, the approaches reported above and others are suggestive of certain basic dimensions which include Egocentricity versus Allocentricity, Independence versus Dependence, Aggressiveness or Dominance versus Submissiveness, Stability versus Instability, Activity versus Passivity, Surgency or Optimism versus Desurgency or Depression, Affiliativeness versus Rejection of Affection, Affectionateness or Love versus Hostility and possibly Maturity versus

**TABLE 2**  Personality test items

| Item no. | Loading | Item content |
|----------|---------|--------------|
| 6 | .550 | Would you rather (A) color a book, or (B) climb a tree? |
| 40 | .481 | Would you rather (A) go out and pick some flowers, or (B) play ball? |
| 50 | .423 | Would you rather (A) watch people dancing to music, or (B) hear a story about airplanes? |
| 23 | .418 | Would you rather (A) listen to pretty music, or (B) watch two dogs have a fight? |
| 197 | .396 | Which toy animal would you rather have: (A) a sheep, or (B) a crocodile? |
| 26 | .369 | Would you rather (A) look at some new books, or (B) play a noisy game where you pretend to be a wild animal? |
| 198 | −.432 | Would you rather be (A) a soldier, or (B) a farmer? |
| 11 | −.441 | Do people every say you get too excited? (A) Yes, or (B) No. |
| 190 | −.474 | Would you rather have (A) a tricycle, or (B) a doll? |
| 193 | −.568 | When you're playing, would you rather be (A) a cowboy, or (B) a doctor? |
| 65 | −.662 | Do you like to shoot a gun? (A) Yes, or (B) No. |
| 191 | −.697 | Would you rather have (A) a gun, or (B) crayons? |

*Note.* The fact that 5 of these items cluster in the last decade of items has no significance; the order of items was determined by a table of random numbers.

Immaturity and Nonanxiousness versus Anxiousness.

What is the situation with school age children? Reference to chapter 5 by Dielman and Krug in this volume will give a partial answer in respect to ratings. Hundleby, Pawlik, and Cattell (1965) summarized the results from seven studies employing objective tests for children from preschool to 13 years of age. By *objective*, these authors mean tests that not only can be administered and scored objectively, but also cannot be faked because the subject cannot discern the purpose of the test (Cattell & Warburton, 1967). Hundleby and Cattell (1968) extended this research with an extensive study reported here later. In the questionnaire realm, Cattell and Coan (1958), Furneaux and Gibson (1961), E. W. Labouvie and Schaie (1974), and Rachman (1969) offered research that throws light on the subject or darkness, depending on one's viewpoint.

To the uninitiated it may be surprising that we have to divide research reports into those that use rating scales, those that use questionnaires, and those that use objective tests. However, there are discrepancies among studies not only within modality but also between modalities.

Ratings of children have reported differing numbers of factors (e.g., Digman, 1972; Schaie, 1966; Tobias & Michael, 1963). Digman, in a review of his own large-scale rating investigations with young schoolchildren, concluded that only seven factors can be found: Industry (persevering, planful, self-reliant, as opposed to lethargic, fickle, irresponsible); Creativity (original, imaginative, curious, socially confident, eccentric); Ego-strength ([−] rigid, [−] emotionally unstable, [+] adaptable); Unnamed, but much like Egocentricity versus Allocentricity (jealous, self-centered, assertive, rude, complaining, suspicious, touchy as opposed to self-minimizing, submissive, considerate); Unnamed but like Cattell's Schizothymia versus Cyclothymia (gregarious, energetic, happy as opposed to thoughtful, seclusive); Compliance (neat, mannerly, considerate, careful, esthetically sensitive, obedient as opposed to spiteful, careless); and Tension (tense, nervous, fearful).

Fewer factors are reported by a number of investigators using the rating modality. For example, Black (1965) found only three, General Adjustment, Introversion-Extraversion, and an Ego-strength factor of a sort. In Great Britain, Hallworth (1965) could find only two temperament-type factors, Extraversion and Emotional Stability, and one factor of Situational Anxiety. In the United States, Peterson (1960) reexamined the Cattell and Peterson (1959) study and two others that Dielman and Krug report in this volume. Peterson concluded, first, that matchings of factors from age to age (4, 7, and 11 years) are not clear and, second, that only two factors are really firm and definite: those that correspond with Cattell's second-order Exvia and Anxiety (Eysenck's $E$[xtraversion] and $N$[euroticism]).

Before commenting on those discrepancies, we should consider the evidence for temperament factors in school-age children from questionnaires and objective test data. Since the late 1950s (Cattell & Coan, 1958), one major branch of developmental psychology has continued to work with at least a dozen primary factors in the questionnaire realm, basing the research on the Early School Personality Questionnaire (though E. W. Labouvie and Schaie, 1974, by reducing the number of items from the ESPQ, also reduced the number of factors). For nearly the same length of time another major developmental tradition (Furneaux & Gibson, 1961) has concentrated on only two factors, $E$ and $N$, as related primarily to the Junior Eysenck Personality Inventory. The Eysencks summarized work up to the time (Eysenck, H. J., & Eysenck, 1969) for ages 7-16 years. As with the adult Eysenck inventories, item factoring generates two major components that are identified with $E$ and $N$

(plus a lie factor). However, further analyses with Promax rotations yield at least seven interpretable factors, named to correspond with their adult counterparts (though the Eysencks warned about the dangers of labeling factors): Psychosomatic (dizziness, nervousness, tummy aches, worries); Moods (needs cheering, mood swings, pessimism); Sleeplessness (worries, loss of sleep); Sociability (liking excitement, preferring group activity); Impulsiveness (acting without thinking, sudden decisions); Jocularity (accepting dares, liking joking, ready answers); and Shyness (shyness with strangers, quietness). Second-order factors are, as in the case of adults, uninterpretable. Third-order factors come out nearly the same as the principal components $E$ and $N$.

Presumably, the differences between the findings on children's personality structure from Great Britain to the United States are not national or cultural, but primarily methodological. Some of the same factors derived from questionnaires appear to be emerging at the primary level. At secondary or higher levels, agreement on $E$ and $N$ appears to be or could be reached (Rachman, 1969), though by analogy with the adult situation Cattell and his cohorts might find more factors than Eysenck and his followers.

In the objective testing of children by far the most extensive work has been done by Cattell's colleagues. And among the most extensive investigations is that reported by Hundleby and Cattell (1968). Seventeen rotated factors were obtained for responses from sixth-grade children. The reference-vector structure, either computed directly or estimated by Dwyer's extension method, was compared with an averaged reference-vector structure from previous objective test studies with children. Examples of the factors, identified by what the authors considered to be the match with Cattell's Universal Index factors and by several test variables suggesting their substance, are: Promethean Will (greater accuracy with Gottschaldt figures, higher ratio of final to initial novel performance, better memory for designs); Exuberance or Ideational Fluency (higher total verbal fluency on topics, greater number of objects seen in unstructured drawings); and Comention or readiness to accept cultural demands (greater pessimism about doing good, greater tendency to agree). The general impression one gets from the attempts to match the obtained factors with previous ones is that there are few that really match well. However that may be, Hundleby and Cattell appear to be firmly convinced that there are far more than six or seven factors derivable from objective test data.

As one reviews the research on children's temperament structure as reflected in the different measurement modalities, and recognizing the wide disparity from the acceptance of 2 basic dimensions to 26 dimensions, it becomes evident that there will have to be greater agreement on instruments to be used for assessment and on methods of analysis (number of factors and rotation methods particularly) before any real agreement can be reached on the number and kinds of factors found in the school-age child's temperament structure. In the meanwhile, some practical problems confront those who work with children; a few words need to be said in this respect.

Perhaps all patterns of child temperament can be reduced to two; the writer does not see how they can be, given the amazing variety and complexity of children's behaviors, but he is willing to admit his judgment may be wrong. Nevertheless, for most practicing educators and clinicians, it would seem more needs to be known specifically about a child than his relative scores on, say, $E$ or $N$. Take just one area of temperament, for example, that which has generally been designated *rigidity*. It does give more information for tailoring a program for any one child to have his scores on five factors (Graziano, 1962), Set, Proactive Inhibition, Perseveration, Intolerance of Ambiguity, and Stimulus-Binding, than to have a score on some general rigidity factor, even if the latter can be achieved mathematically. The same can be said for Peterson's (1960, 1961) reduction of children's problems to two factors, Conduct Problems and Personality Problems, compared with Dreger's 25–30 problem factors (Dreger, 1970). Further, even the statistical analyses from Eysenck's laboratory do not always come out all $E$ or $N$. Sybil Eysenck's first analysis did yield only two factors, plus the lie factor (Eysenck, 1969), but her second one gave 20 factors (Eysenck & Eysenck, 1969). Of these 20, accepted on the basis of statistical criteria, S. Eysenck accepted only 7 and rejected 13 on the basis of lack of "psychological meaningfulness." Possibly more than seven are justified even if at present they make no psychological sense. At least, from a practical standpoint more rather than fewer are called for and from a theoretical standpoint, more rather than fewer cannot necessarily be gainsaid. Most likely, the ordinary life-temperament structure of school-age children probably contains somewhere between 2 and 26; the writer's judgment would make the number closer to 26 at the primary level, and perhaps between 2 and 5 at the secondary or higher level.

## 6  CREATIVE ABILITIES IN THE STRUCTURE OF CHILDREN'S PERSONALITY

Only a small amount of the vast literature on creativity can be assessed in this brief section. The names and work of Galton, Lombroso, Lange-Eichbaum, Kretschmer,

Terman, Hollingworth, Witty, J. P. Guilford, Getzels and Jackson, Barron, Taylor, Butcher, Cattell, Torrance, Wallach, and Kogan, among many others, should be invoked here. Witty's (1951) review and those of J. P. Guilford (1967), Cattell and Butcher (1968), Butcher (1972), and J. P. Guilford (1968) offer some overview of the research in creativity in general. What is meant by creativity has not been clearly delineated at times. Arasteh (1968), in reviewing creativity and related processes in children, stated that the concept has been conceived as a complex, involving at least imagination, fantasy, originality, giftedness of divergent thinking, and curiosity. Likewise, in Guilford's long-term research on abilities, the multifactorial nature of creativity has been stressed (Guilford, J. P. & Hoepfner, 1971; Hetrick, Lilly, & Merrifield, 1968), with all types of intellectual contents, operations, and some transformation products represented. At least the factors of Ideational Fluency (*DMU*), Spontaneous Flexibility (*DMC*), Associational Fluency (*DMR*), and Originality (*DMT*) were found by Guilford at the sixth-grade level.

Two of the general issues in creativity have been found in the literature of research on creativity in children, that concerning the identification of divergent abilities with creativity, and that pertaining to the relation between creativity and IQ. In the first instance, Guilford's distinction between convergent and divergent abilities has been found to be blurred sometimes, if one regards the latter as synonymous with creativity. W. C. Ward (1968), for example, tested a concept put forth by Mednick (1962) in connection with his Remote Associations Test to the effect that formation of associative elements into new combinations, which is largely a convergent process, is the basis of the creative process as well. In fourth and sixth graders Ward found

that there was little shared variance between the divergent and convergent measures, but creativity was present in the association process, a result raising the question whether in children convergent processes are also creative ones, as we may suppose that they are in adults at times.

The second major issue relating to the assumed distinctiveness of IQ intelligence and giftedness or creative abilities was put in bold relief by Getzels and Jackson (1962), who claimed that their studies had shown some but not a great deal of correlation between the two. We cannot enter into the extensive controversy over this contention. About the same time as the former authors were making their claim, Torrance (1962), whose work on creativity has engaged him for many years, was also asserting that his studies showed that IQ intelligence and divergent thinking are not by any means the same. However, Wallach and Kogan (1965) maintained that their work gave only partial support to the distinction between intelligence and giftedness and in fact in large part contradicted Getzels and Jackson. Certain context effects (Elkind, Deblinger, & Adler, 1970) or other artifacts, including age differences, may suggest reasons for differences among the studies. As is often the case, it may be that the answer in this issue is both yes and no; that is, yes, there is some distinction, but no, it is not absolute.

Of considerable interest to students of personality who recognize the interactions and transactions among different functions of the personality is the relation some investigators have found between temperament factors and creative ones. Cattell and Butcher (1968), who reject as virtual specifics many of Guilford's factors that purport to be creative factors, find that personality (temperament) factors like Cattell's *A*−, Schizothymia, *E*+, Dominance, *M*+, Autia, and $Q_2$, Self-sufficiency, predict creativity better than IQ intelligence predicts it. W. C. Ward (1969) also found temperament variables more important. Children with similar IQ's, when assessed for creativity, are distinguished from one another by temperament variables, according to Arasteh (1968). Creative children are described as having sensitivity to the environment, as well as nonconformity, freedom of expression, playfulness, curiosity, and manipulating ability. Some sex differences appear in Arasteh's work but it is not entirely clear what they are or what they mean.

In comparison to adults, in whom impulse control appears to be related to creativity (Barron, 1968), children very well may not show the same relation, for Wallach and Kogan (1965) discovered reflectivity to be associated with higher intellectual performance but not necessarily with creativity. And W. C. Ward (1968b) found no relation between the reflectivity/impulsivity dimension and creativity. Also contrary to findings in adults, in whom introversive tendencies are associated with highly creative abilities, creative children have been described at the preschool level as more sociable than others, and creative early school children show more interest in the environment than do their peers (Greenberger, O'Connor, & Sorensen, 1971). There then seems to be a change, for later school years and adulthood do not show the same relation; at least, eminent creative persons express the sense of isolation they felt as children.

Through the preschool years there appears to be an increase in creative capacities, at any rate in those segments of society that value such qualities. It is probably true that other large segments do not reinforce creativity even in the preschool years (Busse, 1969; Gray, J. A., 1964; Hess, R. D., 1964). But the majority of middle-class families seem to foster independence and originality in these years, as do many preschools. Then,

both peer and authority figure pressures may inhibit creative urges. Torrance (1962) suggests that peer sanctions, rising to hostility, and rejection in the later grammar school years operate to isolate the creative youngster. And teachers may like what Torrance calls the "competent plodder." The isolative feelings that eminent individuals report of their childhood may well be felt by many other creative children who do not later become eminent, since they may lack the combination of temperament qualities that determine in good part the achievement of eminence. They just retire, as it were. Yet W. C. Ward's (1968a, 1969) manner of teasing out creative responses from young children suggests that given the right conditions those youngsters could be encouraged to make outstanding contributions to the world just as well as the ones whose other qualities make them rise despite a society partly structured to discourage creative achievement.

# 7  PERMANENCE AND CHANGE IN THE STRUCTURE OF CHILDREN'S PERSONALITY

Coan (1972) discussed continuities and changes in personality at different ages, the types of changes that are possible, and methodological problems involved in assessing continuity and change. Problems and procedures relating to measuring change were also covered in C. W. Harris (1963b). Here we consider substantive aspects of personality permanence and change in childhood.

## 7.1  Effects of Natural External Conditions, Family Influence, and Intrapersonality Transaction

Even in periods when the public and some authorities on childhood have regarded childhood, especially infancy, as the time of change, and adulthood as the time of permanence, there are those who conclude that external conditions may not have such important effects as sometimes assumed. They pick out infancy in particular (Caldwell, 1964; Stevenson, 1957), but do not limit their conclusions to infancy (Yarrow, L. J. & Yarrow, 1964). On the one hand, we are reminded that "the more things change, the more they remain the same" because of hereditary influences (Lenneberg, 1969; Vandenberg, 1967b, 1968a). Yet, on the other hand, we cannot escape the fact that changes do occur in personality structure because of role changes as the person moves from infancy to childhood. That role changes in themselves constitute personality changes was argued (convincingly, we think) by Dreger (1962, 1966).

Germane to what changes in role and other behaviors is the question of who changes whom. R. Q. Bell (1968, 1971), Harper (1971), Kohn (1966), Osofsky (1971), and Waldrop and Bell (1964, 1966) are among the increasing number of those who have found that the child influences the behavior of others as much as others influence him, not only with family but with peers and caretakers other than parents. Hereditary, congenital, or later acquired factors may generate behaviors in others which to the infant or child signal, "Change!" or "Remain the same!" (Clapp, 1967). It is not a one-way street, as it sometimes appears (Honzik, 1967). We would not by any means minimize the influence of parents, siblings (e.g., Longstreth, Longstreth, Ramirez, & Fernandez, 1975) or others; it is only that the transactional nature of the child's relations to important others has often been neglected.

Thus, the child's personality structure may remain the same because he influences the environment to treat him in a manner that reinforces the same behaviors; or the child may change because he requires the external world to reinforce changes in role behaviors (Lichtenberg & Norton, 1970). External conditions may initiate changes in the child's personality which in turn force changes in the external world; or these child-induced external world changes may suppress changes in the child. In all cases the use of the concept of transaction is more appropriate than that of interaction.

To illustrate permanence and change related to external conditions and family influence, we turn to one of the relatively few longterm studies of personality development from childhood to adulthood, the FELS Longitudinal Study (Kagan & Moss, 1962; Moss & Kagan, 1964). Thirty-six male and 35 female infants were enrolled in this project and followed into adult life with periodic assessments of intellect, temperament, and social role behaviors. If the difficulties in measuring change (Harris, C. W., 1963b) do not negate the conclusions the FELS researchers drew, we have good evidence as to what changes and what remains the same in the child's personality. Ratings for aggressiveness, passive-dependency, and achievement behaviors correlated with similar ratings in adulthood present the following picture. For aggressiveness, males but not females exhibit similar patterns from childhood to adulthood. For passive-dependency, the opposite holds. For achievement behaviors, both males and females show the same patterns from relatively early childhood to young adulthood. The FELS investigators proposed a reasonable explanation for these findings: Cultural reinforcements are stronger for aggressiveness in males at all ages, and for passive-dependency in females, whereas such reinforcements operate non-differentially for achievement. (Achievement behaviors in males and females in young adulthood must be different, for it is obvious that females generally are not given the opportunity to engage in the same achievement behaviors as males.)

What part, one may ask, does heredity play in determining the continuities the FELS study revealed? The research was predicated on and was interpreted in the framework of a social role model, so the place of hereditary aspects was not assessed. Is there room for what authorities in behavioral genetics insist are real genetic effects on behavior? I think so. In the first place, the correlations between ratings at different ages are far from perfect, leaving considerable unexplained variance. Further, cultural reinforcements may alter role behaviors that do not coincide with temperament inclinations; ratings would not necessarily catch this distinction. The writer at one and the same time holds that roles are portions of the personality but that they are not the entirety of personality. Temperament as assessed by self-reports is not the same as role behaviors. Therefore, an assessment of role behaviors that can be explained by a role model does not negate some measure of hereditary determination of temperament. Accepting the explanation of the FELS study results does not preclude accepting also other explanations set forth by Vandenberg and others of the behavioral genetic school.

Supplementing and complementing the influence of external forces (and genes, if they can be considered external influences) are those intrapersonality transactions that generate changes or reinforce continuities in the child's personality structure. Many examples could be given, but a few will suffice. For one example, as suggested previously, Reflectivity-Impulsivity appears to be fairly stable in its manifestations in the child, as does general intellectual capacity (Kagan, 1965); but extremes of the tempera-

ment characteristic may have quite specific effects on intellectual functioning in the preschool years and later (Maccoby, Dowley, Hagan, & Degerman, 1965; Schwebel, 1966). Also, in a three-way transaction, learning ability in approval-dependent children may be differentially affected by Impulsivity (Crowne, Holland, & Conn, 1968).

Another related example is that of conscience or superego which has been a concern of philosophers and psychologists for many years (or rather, centuries) extending into the present (Aronfreed, 1968; Dreger & Barnert, 1969). In the first part of this century Hartshorne, May, and their colleagues (1928, 1929, 1930) in the Character Education Inquiry (CEI) determined that ethical conduct and ethical belief are relatively unrelated. There were challenges even then by Gordon Allport and Prescott Lecky, among others. In more recent years, Grinder (1964) concluded that, in line with the CEI findings, the behavioral and cognitive characteristics of a mature conscience actually develop relatively independently in younger children. This conclusion, however, was not allowed to stand unchallenged. Henshel (1971) did a rather neat study with French Canadian girls in the fourth through the seventh grades, paralleling the Hartshorne and May studies, by giving the girls value questions under one set of circumstances and an opportunity to cheat in another set. The correlation coefficients for the fourth through the seventh grades are $-.02$, $-.35$, $-.63$, and $-.78$; in other words, possession of stated values of ethical belief and acceptance of the opportunity to act contrary to those standards were unrelated in the youngest group but correlated negatively and progressively more so in the older girls. (One wry conclusion is forced on readers of studies like these: The adult experimenters engage in the boldest of deceit in trying to assess the honesty of children.)

Thus, though it may be true that ethical conduct and ethical belief are independent in the early years, the actual development may well tend toward a joining of the two in later years of childhood. However, even in younger children, some investigators have not found the independence Henshel discovered as complete as a —.02 correlation would indicate (Rubin & Schneider, 1973). Biaggio (1968) found rather complex relations among the behavioral, cognitive, and affective components of conscience: High ego strength coupled with high moral judgment (cognitive component) relates to internalized guilt (affective component) but not to a lower incidence of cheating (behavioral component). The other combinations of low or high ego strength and low or high moral judgment appear unrelated to either internalized or externalized guilt. Even greater complexity of relations among components was reported by Van Den Daele (1968). An increasing correlation from 6th through 12th grades is obtained between ego ideal (a superego component) and measured intelligence; extrapolation to early childhood suggests that no relation holds at all. In turn, although ego ideal and moral judgment are related in these later years of childhood and adolescence, intelligence is correlated with moral judgment for girls only.

Moral judgment itself and its relations to other functions of the personality have been studied extensively, especially under the influence of Piaget's and Kohlberg's stage formulations of development (e.g., Kohlberg, 1973; Piaget, 1932). Kohlberg's idea that role-taking ability is closely related to moral development is supported by some important but limited research by Moir (1974) in New Zealand, who found that at least for preadolescent girls a substantial proportion of variance in moral maturity is accounted for by measures of general, nonmoral role-taking ability.

What effects cultural shifts in moral values (Dreger, 1975; Schonberg, 1974) have on the development of superego functioning and its interrelations with other portions of the personality has not been adequately assessed. Greater tolerance for what had been regarded as wrongs in prior generations is too evident to need scientific documentation, though Schonberg (1974) provided it. Changes to other ideas of what constitutes wrong, such as pollution, racial and economic inequities, and the war system, are also widely recognized. But what these content changes have to do with the structure of the superego and its relations to other portions of the personality structure is another matter. A perusal of the *Psychoanalytic Study of the Child* and the *Handbook of Child Psychoanalysis* reveals that child psychoanalysts, who should be the most interested in the overall picture, as compared with their more hard-nosed colleagues in academic research disciplines with their more piecemeal approach to the ethical and conventional, are certainly aware of the vast cultural changes of this century, but are either not concerned about any structural personality changes wrought thereby, or more likely not convinced that such changes affect the superego structure. Research psychologists have yet to assess possible changes in structure by identified measures of conscience, like Cattell's Superego factor or J. S. Guilford's (1974) derived from her Values Inventory for Children. (Actually, several factors coming from this inventory can be considered superego factors.)

Other examples of transactions among variables within the personality could be adduced, but these are sufficient to show how one set of functions may alter another, which in turn alter the first, and they in turn may affect a third variable, which alters their functioning, and so on. Thus, changes or continuities result in the structure of the child's personality.

## 7.2  Effects of Experimental Interventions

Instrumental and classical conditioning techniques have been utilized extensively in collaboration or individually to modify behaviors. Especially in the form of behavior modification or behavior therapy the former has been used to make great strides in altering behaviors. For those who wish to follow the learning theory (yes, even Skinner's) bases of behavior modification, references too numerous to mention exist (*inter alia*, Ferster & Perrott, 1968; Holland & Skinner, 1961; Kanfer and Phillips, 1970; Keller, 1969; Krasner & Ullman, 1965; Skinner, B. F. 1938, 1953, 1969; Ullman & Krasner, 1965). As for practical applications, here too, are many volumes and articles (*inter alia*, Bandura, 1969; Barrett & Lindsley, 1962; Bijou & Baer, 1967; Cohen, D. J., 1962; Goldfried & Merbaum, 1973; Lazarus, A. A., 1972; Levis, 1970; Krumboltz & Thoresen, 1969; Lindsley, O. R., 1964; Midlarsky, 1967; Neuringer & Michael, 1970; Patterson, 1963; Patterson, Littman, & Bricker, 1967; Phillips, E. L., & Wiener, 1966; Schaeffer, H. H., & Martin, 1969; Timmons & Noblin, 1963; Wolpe, 1969; Woody, 1969). Thoughtful evaluations can also be found (e.g., Franks, 1969; Kopel & Arkowitz, 1975; London, 1969; Russell, E. W., 1974).

Changes arising from behavior modification principles fit comfortably into the model of personality undergirding this chapter; they basically constitute role changes in a large number of instances, and role changes are accepted as personality changes (Angyal, 1941; Dreger, 1962;

Murphy, G., 1947). Specific changes documented in the literature may or may not involve extensive role changes, but some undoubtedly do among the host reported in respect to stuttering and fluency, reading, writing, arithmetic, obstreperous behavior, autism, commanding behavior, cooperative behavior, tantrums, isolate play, left-right discrimination, modelling behavior, walking (in retardates), conceptualizing, lack of speech, social responsiveness, crying, self-destructive behaviors, aggressiveness, and altruism, to name only some of the behaviors purportedly modified by behavioral interventions.

Despite criticisms of behavior modification, undoubtedly many and significant have been the changes in behavior patterns from the application of learning principles. These changes have often been of quite important characteristics, and they are not ephemeral. However, it is notorious that many agencies can bring about fundamental changes in personality functioning. The caveman whose skull was trephined allowing the demon to escape most likely underwent a vast and long-lasting personality change. Foxhole conversions, visions of the Holy Grail, the sight of a child in distress, awakening to long-suffered injustices leading to rebellion (in Camus' sense), and perhaps even Grandma's "little lessons" to her grandchild no doubt have brought profound and extended changes to some personalities. Placing behavior modification among other forms of intervention (Russell, E. W., 1974) reveals that it is not much worse or much better than other forms.

The main objection the writer has to a number of research reports on behavior therapies is not that changes have not taken place, but that the investigator naively assumes that the mechanical application of behavioral techniques is the only major independent variable. Instead, the social reinforcer is often by far the most important one, or other variables not directly under manipulative control. "This is the problem of proof: the demonstration that the particular environmental manipulation applied was indeed responsible for producing whatever behavioral change was noted subsequently" (Sherman & Baer, 1969). (See also Heller & Marlatt, 1969, and Krasner & Ullman, 1965). There is little doubt that, whatever is responsible, alterations of a rather fundamental nature have sometimes occurred in children with the use of behavior modification.

Changes occurring with the use of other interventions, ordinarily not considered behavior modifications, like psychotherapy, drugs, hypnosis, computer-assisted instruction, and so on, can certainly be documented in many cases. If these alter ability, temperament, role, or motivation or interest pattern, they are, in the degree that they change the latter, to be regarded as personality changes. Examples of such changes can be found in many places, but they have been shown to take place in some fundamental functions that have sometimes been regarded as impervious to change: conservation (Feigenbaum, 1971; Kingsley & Hall, 1967; Sigel, Roeper, & Hooper, 1966); creative abilities (Khatena, 1971); IQ level (Levinson, 1971); aggressiveness (Bandura & Walters, 1963; Eron, 1963; Friedrich & Stein, 1973). Exception can be taken to some of the studies cited (as to almost any study done under the sun), but enough evidence has accumulated to suggest that intervention methods of various kinds can alter some fundamental personality functions.

The use of established primary personality dimensions to measure the general personality changes that undoubtedly take place would advance knowledge considerably in child psychology as it has with adults

(Cattell & Rickels, 1965; Hunt, J. McV., Ewing, La Forge, & Gilbert, 1959). Without the use of an established system like Eysenck's or Cattell's, research sometimes is methodologically unsound, in that the reported change or lack of change may arise from the unreliability of the instrument rather than the intervention technique.

## 7.3   What Changes and What Remains the Same?

Bits and pieces of the substance of changes and continuities have been brought out through this chapter. In some ways the present state of our knowledge can be given accurately: We know in part, and we prophesy in part. Only a partial picture can be painted at this time.

Earlier in this chapter we cited Black's reduction of personality dimensions to three, General Adjustment (Eysenck's Neuroticism), Introversion-Extraversion, and Ego-strength. Black believed that there was no evidence of any systematic change in the factor structure across seven grade levels, both elementary and high school. Others have tended to find more change than Black found. Anthony (1973) and Warburton (1972), while not denying that the factor structure does not change, nevertheless cited evidence that Introversion, at least for students, decreases relatively to about 13 or 14 years of age, then increases after that. In respect to Cattell's traits, Schaie (1966), using teacher ratings of 25 boys and 25 girls at each grade level from ages 6 through 18 years, reported age differences in 11 out of 15 traits and sex differences in 10 out of 15. Table 3 shows these remarkable results.

This table demonstrates several things if we accept the reliability of the measures and their validity as representing reality. Sex differences that have shown up here and elsewhere remind us that different patterns

**TABLE 3** Analyses of variance testing the hypotheses of age and sex differences for factors $A$ to $O$

| Factor | Age | | Sex | | Interaction | | Residual[a] |
|---|---|---|---|---|---|---|---|
| | MS | F | MS | F | MS | F | MS |
| $A$: Cyclothymia versus Schizothymia | 27.30 | 2.34** | 218.66 | 18.76** | 12.38 | | 11.65 |
| $B$: Intelligence | 4.92 | | 38.41 | 9.23** | 7.05 | | 4.16 |
| $C$: Ego-strength versus Proneness to Neuroticism | 55.93 | 3.21** | 443.65 | 25.44** | 18.26 | | 17.44 |
| $D$: Excitability versus Insecurity | 30.48 | 2.72** | 504.36 | 44.94** | 7.45 | | 11.20 |
| $E$: Dominance versus Submissiveness | 38.46 | 2.55** | 936.00 | 61.99** | 8.91 | | 15.10 |
| $F$: Surgency versus Desurgency | 38.30 | 2.68** | 164.50 | 11.51** | 16.05 | | 14.29 |
| $G$: Superego Strength | 17.45 | | 572.46 | 54.93** | 8.92 | | 10.42 |
| $H$: Parmia versus Threctia | 27.38 | 2.06* | 44.98 | | 14.04 | | 13.32 |
| $I$: Premsia versus Harria | 4.99 | | .01 | | 36.54 | 10.41** | 3.51 |
| $J$: Coasthenia | 13.06 | 2.15* | 10.10 | | 7.15 | | 6.07 |
| $K$: Comention versus Abcultion | 27.62 | 4.59** | 234.00 | 38.87** | 8.31 | | 6.02 |
| $L$: Protension versus Inner Relaxation | 7.67 | 2.07* | 44.46 | 12.02** | 4.34 | | 3.70 |
| $M$: Autia versus Praxernia | 7.37 | | .89 | | 1.88 | | 4.45 |
| $N$: Shrewdness versus Naivete | 28.58 | 5.44** | 164.51 | 31.33** | 7.38 | | 5.25 |
| $O$: Guilt Proneness versus Confidence | 9.91 | 3.25** | 9.85 | | 3.75 | | 3.05 |

*Note.* $N = 650$; 25 subjects per cell. From "Year-by-year Changes in Personality from Six to Eighteen Years" by K. W. Schaie, *Multivariate Behavioral Research*, 1966, **1**, 293–305. Copyright 1966 by *Multivariate Behavioral Research*. Reprinted by permission.

[a]Since the main variables are fixed constants, the residual variance becomes the appropriate error term. $F$ ratios are evaluated with 12 and 624 $df$ for age: 1 and 624 $df$ for sex; and 12 and 624 $df$ for the interaction term.

*Significant at or beyond the 5% level of confidence.

**Significant at or beyond the 1% level of confidence.

of the same basic structure may discriminate between boys and girls. Second, the urging of the investigator that narrower ranges of developmental level be used in describing children seems well taken; broad designations such as "middle childhood" may not be appropriate in many instances. And last, it must be remembered that the values represented are average values; considerably different patterns might emerge from individual longitudinal measures.

Other cross-sectional studies can just be mentioned: Dye (1968) on mental test

factors; Penk (1969) on perceptual responses; and E. V. Sullivan, McCullough, and Stager (1970), on conceptual level, moral judgment, and ego.

Longitudinal studies of personality development yield much more adequate information on what actually changes in any individual (Sontag, 1971). For all the usefulness of cross-sectional investigations, they refer in reality to an abstract being who never truly progresses from age to age. Yet so many methodological problems, as well as practical ones, beset such studies that it is no wonder they are numbered in the dozens in contrast to thousands of cross-sectional studies (cf. Baltes & Nesselroade, 1970; Cattell, 1970b; Emmerich, 1968; Freud, A., 1963; Kohlberg, 1968; Rutter, 1970; Skard, Inhelder, Noelting, Murphy, & Thomas, 1960; Schaie, 1965; Schaie & Strother, 1968; and Werner, H., 1948).

In the early part of the 1960s, Kagan (1964) listed 10 major longitudinal studies. Others have been reported since then: R. Q. Bell, Weller, & Waldrop (1971); Faterson & Witkin (1970); McCall, Appelbaum, & Hogarty (1973); Neimark (1975); A. H. Rees & Palmer (1970); Waldrop & Halverson (1975); and E. E. Werner (1973). Others are indicated in the following discussion. In the space allotted, no adequate review could be given to these studies. But we can draw some general lessons about personality change from them.

Sometimes there are sleeper effects operating, in that correlations between traits measured at widely separated times may be greater than with measurements in intervening periods, for example, expressiveness-reserve and placidity-explosiveness (Bronson, W. C., 1969); activity level (Walters, C. E., 1965); IQ intelligence (Hindley, 1965; Werner, E. C., Honzik, & Smith, 1968); modesty (Macfarlane, Allen, & Honzik, 1962); and effects of biological insult (Jordan, 1971). Another lesson suggests itself: Parents' education and occupation relate to mental test performance both early and late (Rees, A. H., & Palmer, 1970). In this connection, another sleeper effect shows up: Early maternal behavior may better predict a mother's and a child's behavior in childhood than her intermediate behavior does (Moss & Kagan, 1964). Still another lesson, not recognized sufficiently, is that different tests tap different functions, which may differ from age to age (Hopkins &

Bibelheimer, 1971), and the same test may only be semantically the same from age to age (Stott & Ball, 1965); in developmental terms, then, more or less consistency may be shown than is measured.

We may learn also that despite measurement problems, investigators insist that there are some psychological functions that show consistency over long periods of time. Without passing judgment on the validity of the claims, we can list them at least as hypotheses; possibly, in some cases the claims are entirely justified, such as: body concept (Faterson & Witkin, 1970); associative creativity (Kogan & Pankove, 1971); worries (Anderson, 1960); need achievement (Feld, 1967; Kagan & Moss, 1962); friendliness, cooperativeness, nondistractibility, attentiveness, being systematic, comprehension, accuracy in boys (Schaefer, E. S., & Bayley, 1963); passivity, dependency, aggression, sexuality, social interaction, compulsivity, impulsivity, nurturance (wanting to be of help), hyperkinesis, introspectiveness (Kagan & Moss, 1962; Waldrop & Halverson, 1975); withdrawal-expressiveness, reactivity-placidity, passivity-dominance (Bronson, W. C., 1966, 1967, 1969); IQ-type intelligence (Kangas & Bradway, 1971; though compare McCall, Appelbaum, & Hogarty, 1973). Complicating the results listed is the fact that sex differences are found in a number of studies. For example, Kagan and Moss (1960) reported that passive and dependent behavior in children correlates with young adult behavior for females but not for males. A number of behaviors consistent for boys do not show the same continuities for girls, and vice versa (Bell, R. G., Weller, & Waldrop, 1971; Kangas & Bradway, 1971; Schaeffer, E. S., & Bayley, 1963).

One final observation must be made about longitudinal studies. As far as this writer is concerned, the controversies over stage theories of development, as proposed by Piaget, will only be settled by long-term investigations, not by cross-sectional studies. Only one such study is known to the writer, and that is not a really long-term study at that. Neimark (1975) found that cognitive development is an orderly, sequential process, as postulated by Piaget. The major questions raised over a period of time will not be answered by just one, limited study (cf., for example, Ausubel, 1957; Hunt, J. McV., 1961; Sigel, 1966). One suspects on the basis of what is presently known that a general orderly sequence will be shown, but that stages are not clear cut, overlapping one another, and that regressions occur, not only in the cognitive realm but in others, as has been shown for the Freudian psychosexual stages.

Once more, it must be emphasized that, as in cross-sectional studies, an agreed-upon system of personality traits, in all realms from the biological, through the intellectual and temperamental, to role functions, is required to make meaningful the reality of continuity or change. This condition has not been met in most longitudinal studies.

## 8  SUMMARY

The model of personality utilized for the present chapter incorporates all functions from the basic biological to the social functions known as roles as portions of the personality. Physical, intellectual, temperament, and social roles, such as position in the family, can have heritable components. These are taken into account in descriptions of the infant's personality structure in its major manifestations of temperament and intellect. In the preschool and children's structure of personality, there seem to be more than just a few traits or characteristics, though the number is not known definitely. In the special realm in the personality structure, creativity, the issues of divergent thinking and its relation to creativity, and of IQ and creativity are not solved; but in any case it appears that temperament factors are important in creative expression. From both longitudinal and cross-sectional studies it may be concluded that even basic functions may be changed in part by both naturally occurring and experimentally produced conditions. To determine what changes and what remains the same the better method is the longitudinal one.

# 18

## Structured Learning Theory, Applied to Personality Change

### Raymond B. Cattell
*University of Hawaii, Honolulu*

### 1 THE HISTORICAL FIXATIONS OF LEARNING THEORY

Learning theory has two roots—reflexological conditioning (Pavlov to Skinner) and personality development observations (mainly by the clinicians). During the past 50 years most learning theory textbooks have built systematically largely on the former, because its closely controlled and simplified situations have permitted more precise formulations than have the gropings of clinicians and personality learning observers. Beginning with Pavlov, in the concept of classical conditioning, reflexological conditioning has, nevertheless, gone through some rather extreme acrobatics—notably in trying to retain the conditioning paradigm in *operant conditioning*, the dynamic nature of which is better indicated by a quite different title, *means-end learning*. It also has used bizarre oversimplification in attempting to reach out to the kind of learning with which the personality theorist is concerned. It is time that personality theory put its house in order as far as personality change and learning are concerned. This chapter hopes to show that in doing so it can contribute a whole new wing to the advancing army of learning theory concepts, a wing that best can be designated *structured learning theory*.

Learning theory that was centered on the *total human* organism, beginning with Thorndike's law of effect, became lost in a too facile and undisciplined psychoanalytic and clinical jungle of explanations. One cannot refrain from wryly commenting, in returning to a systematic attack on the problem 50 years later, that good mutual appreciation for each other's approaches existed between Pavlov and Thorndike, which, had it been continued, might have kept the *reflexological* and the *full organism* approaches integrated. Hull (1952), among others, extended one branch of his total theory to sketch in a structural and motivational approach. However, time never permitted him to concentrate on it; and the poor level of objective understanding of personality and motivation structure available in the 1940s precluded any decided development.

That the mutual isolation of learning theory and personality theory is a standing reproach to our science has been sadly recognized by learning psychologists for two generations—and with increasing perplexity and concern. In 1953 a determined attempt was made to find a bridge by calling together prominent researchers from both fields (Spence, Harlow, and Mowrer, for example, from learning) in the *Kentucky Symposium* (1954). It failed for reasons which the learning theorists may describe on their side, but which the present participant in those discussions can readily define from the personality side.

433

Although the clinicians were, at that time, lacking the clear-cut structural and measurement concepts discussed in the opening chapters of the present *Handbook* and though they had no clear model for the multivariate, holistic approach they intuitively always followed, their experience embraced a wealth of observations calling for explanation. The reflexologists, on the other hand, seemed never to have taken a real look at what—in personality change—had to be explained. Enamored of the neatness of their penny-in-the-slot model, they eagerly forced it on all fields, with a ludicrous poorness of fit which any real acquaintance with the field concerned would have prevented. My own emphasis at that meeting and again here is on looking first at *what has to be explained*. However, the personality theorists were at that time as unprepared as the reflexologists for the necessary marriage, for they had not formulated personality structure in measurable terms, nor developed a personality theory in quantitative models and equations. This lack of development is reported in more detail in the *Kentucky Symposium* (1954, p. 93) thus:

There is one simple respect in which it should be said initially that learning theory is more seriously disabled than clinical psychology, namely, that whereas clinical psychology has had extensive empirical contact with personality problems, learning theory has had virtually none. Since I have a strong predilection for laws that develop out of the phenomena to which they are supposed to be relevant, I cannot feel confidence, scientifically, in learning laws taken over ready-made from another area and transposed—unless and until they justify and enlarge themselves in relation to personality measures themselves.

The proposed ideal research strategy of first determining personality structure and then determining its laws is therefore embarrassed from the beginning by attitudes and conditions in the history of psychology and psychologists. (And in this case I favor Oscar Wilde's definition of history, namely, "an account of things that should never have happened.") However, if we may aim even now to institute a more ideal and effective sequence I suggest that we recognize five steps, or phases, and I propose to list these and devote 10 minutes' discussion to them. First there is a phase of precise, quantitative investigation of existing structure in the organism, in this case of human personality structure; second there is the step of producing reliable instruments for unitary measures of these meaningful structures and functions; third—and here I ask you to bear with my eccentricities—I would ask for an initial investigation of the part played by constitution and heredity in these measured patterns and structures, so that we do not waste our time trying to explain by learning theory what is really a maturational phenomenon. The fourth stage would be the application of the usual stimulus response learning experiment design involving sequential, causal, longitudinal analysis of what has been ascertained in cross section in 1 and 2. . . . Fifthly we can expect the laws of learning themselves to be enriched and modified . . . by a feedback of these augmented principles into laboratory [experimentation]. Perhaps ten years hence. . . .

But the issue goes deeper than a question of readiness of methodology at that time—important though a mature methodology is in shaping the right formulation of hypotheses and models. The story of attempts at integration is a sad reflection on the whole misleading slant given by the too facile and premature use of *reflex* and *conditioned*. The former, if it kept to what had actually been established, was operative only with regard to atomistic and commonly largely unconscious bits of behavior, such as an eye blink or a dog's leg twitch. The latter, one would think, would surely have had to admit many parameters, such as reward, that obviously enter into most learning, but these were not regarded by those who explained all by classical conditioning. Even the term *conditioned*, itself, was a mistranslation, as E. R. Hilgard and Bower (1966) and Barnette (1963) pointed out.[1]

Ultimately, as facts forced attention on the need to involve the total situation-motivational constellation, this oversimplified and inadequate model brought the more inbred reflexologists to the contortions of calling the new approach *operant conditioning*, where, but for the social accidents of schools of psychology being based on "the simplest explanation for the greatest number of students," a far more profitable multivariate analytic model could have entered the field earlier. Indeed, what we are proposing involves the principle that every learning experience is a *multidimensional change in the structure of the organism brought about by the interaction of a multidimensionally defined organism with a multidimensionally represented situation*. What this means in precise models is set out in section 3; meanwhile, in section 2 it is necessary to clear the ground by taxonomically setting aside changes that are *not* learning from changes that are the main concern of learning theory. In short, to answer "What is learning?"

## 2  TAXONOMIC CLASSES OF TRANSFORMATION AND LEARNING MECHANISMS

Since our initial departure from current practice is to turn attention to describing the

[1] Hilgard and Bower (1966) stated that the original term used by Pavlov should have been "conditional;" this, incidentally, might have sparked more curiosity as to what the conditions are.

changes, especially in personality, to be explained before offering devices, such as conditioning, to explain them, let us begin sorting out *learning, maturation,* and *transformation.*

By transformation one means a change due to experience, which is no more *learning* than is the rusting of iron or the improved fit of an old shoe. For the organism it might be a blow on the head, a vitamin deficiency, or an exposure to great stress. We have included maturation under the larger label of *endogenous modification,* or *volution* (maturation and involution). This is a "genetic clock" effect that includes aging trends, as well as changes of the same general nature that happen to be generated by inherent cycles rather than a trend. Rather than spend space in the text on matters probably already familiar to the reader let us use Fig. 1 as a logical summary, with extensions to what are essentially footnotes to the text. Note particularly the four distinct kinds of learning shown in Fig. 1—coexitation learning (CE), means-end learning (ME), integrative learning (IE), and ergic goal modification (GM). These are described in the following sections.

### 2.1  Classical Pavlovian Conditioning

This type of learning is little different, except in precision of instrumentation, from the English *associationism* of Locke and Mill and is stated in form undistinguished from Pavlov's (in definition, not experiment) by Lloyd Morgan. Therein *simultaneity* (usually, an overlap in immediate succession) *of experiences* binds them in future mutual recall or response.

It is not our purpose here to join the battle over the relative importance of classical conditioning (briefly designated as Skinner's CRI) and instrumental or operant conditioning (means-end learning, or Skin-

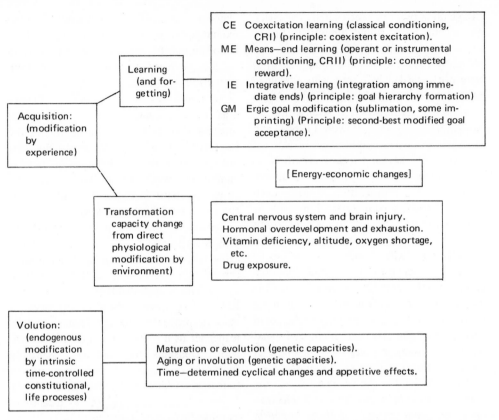

**FIG. 1** Sources of behavior change: acqusition and volution. *Learning* is defined as change in the response usually given to a particular stimulus; this change can be shown to be related to events specifically connected with the response. *Transformation* is defined as change simply through undergoing exposure to conditions. The term is thus proposed for specialization here as an environmentally determined change that is *not* learning and not acquired in a goal-directed learning experience, but through passive experience. *Volution*, covering evolution and involution, is change not dependent on experience, either passive or in active learning, but only on time and normal physiological process.

ner's CRII), but the nature of each deserves some brief analysis. That nature, we believe, is best designated, in the case of CRI, by the term *coexcitation learning*. Actually the conservative Hilgard and Bower treatment uses the happy phrase "coupled-excitation" but loses this sense again in relapsing to the old jargon. There is much to suggest that some degree of discharge of the common excitation from two stimuli or ideas is also necessary, and in that sense "common exit of two excitations" would be a fuller

definition. In any case, in referring to structured learning, here and elsewhere, we used the attractively brief expression *co-ex* learning, which reminds one of both features.

As to the common exit or response, a vital piece of evidence for incorporation is the well-known fact that the conditioned must precede the unconditioned in time. One may wonder, however, whether this has been mistakenly elevated from a merely correlated to an *essential* causal condition.

In word association and elsewhere, remembering is aided in some degree in both directions. It has been suggested by several investigators that the direction of association is primarily determined by the relative intensity (excitation level) of the two stimulus experiences. This would invoke a second principle beyond that of necessary sequence, namely, that a directional *leak* tends to be made from the lesser to the greater excitation, and perhaps a third principle that movement is from the excitation without a natural discharge to excitation that has one. The normal experimentation on classical conditioned reflexes (CRI) may be said to involve all three, for (a) the unconditioned stimulus must follow, (b) it possesses a path of discharge, and (c) it is normally the greater (natural and neurologically given) excitation.

Many parameters of the CRI paradigm remain to be investigated, but it has already been the subject of substantial critical research beyond the Pavlov-Watson concept. Of special interest to the concepts developed here is the work of Brogden (1939), Wynne and Brogden (1962), Hoffeld, Thompson, and Brogden (1958), and Rescorla and Solomon (1967), essentially supporting the conclusion that two *cognitive stimuli* can become associated by contiguous presentation without any evident dynamic, motor-discharge *response*. The findings on this S–S bond support the general evidence on word memorizing, and evidence going back to Mill's "association by contiguity," not only that two stimuli get functionally linked, (so that one thereafter will produce a response that has been learned for the other) but that the link, to some degree, exists in both directions. Although a particular temporal sequence in this type of learning determines the greater facility in the direction of remembering, the present writer's hypothesis would be that this sequence is not so much

inherent, as it is one of the three previously mentioned subprinciples, which produce a greater or lesser result from what is *fundamentally* a linking by coexcitation. The operation of these subprinciples may be of different levels of importance in different species, that is, in the effect of time lag (Bitterman, 1967).

The hypothesis would therefore be that the terms *coupled excitation* (Hilgard, E. R., & Bower, 1966), *coexcitation*, or *coexisting excitation* would be better, less misleading expressions, clearing the phenomenon of the false associations—especially the association with "instrumental conditioning" (means-end learning)—of the attempts to overgeneralize the "conditioning" gadget. By this position, the typical CRI would already be a mixture of the two really distinct principles at work—coexcitation and means-end learning. That is, it would be a hybrid of the pure coexcitation principle, and, by reason of the motor discharge, which is in a general sense a preordained reward (as in a sneeze), would involve also the means-end principle. The co-ex principle would then simply state that two stimuli producing two cognitive excitations (of course with previous cognitive engrams of their own) will become so associated that, after repetition of the contiguity, the stimulation of one will evoke the cognitive excitation also of the other. The definition of the cognitive excitation need not depend on introspective report or even on the Russian emphasis on neurological interpretation, but can be based on behavioral signs of excitation, such as we define in motivation component factor $\beta$ and $y$ in the dynamic calculus. The attempts of Osgood (1953) and Kimble (1961) to reduce CRI to reward learning may at first seem to be in opposition to the above and in favor of a monistic system, but to this writer they seem to show that CRI has reward properties, while leaving intact (but also

R. B. CATTELL

438

unconceived) the co-ex concept, which, after all, definitely stands outside traditional reflexological response concepts.

## 2.2  Means-end Learning

Personality theory has long been familiar, both in clinical work and in Thorndike's law of effect, with a principle that can be stated with most regard for economy and breadth of application as follows: When an organism is stimulated (internally and externally) to pursue a certain goal, any new act that turns out to provide a quicker or more reliable means to the end becomes favored as the response on future occasions. Hilgard called this *instrumental learning*, which accurately describes what it is; but the phrase risks confusion due to several other familiar associations of the word *instrument*. Skinner's *operant conditioning* has become a more widespread term for this kind of learning, probably because of the volume of work done by his students, as well as the reluctance of many learning psychologists to cut the umbilical cord to Pavlov's *conditioning* label. However, the more one considers this principle in wider contexts than laboratory experiment, and particularly when one considers application to the varied forms of behavior seen in personality learning, the more clearly he perceives the essential determiner of learning to be expressible as the tendency of the act to be successful as a means to an end. This phrase has the virtue of being more behavioral in connotation than the phrase *law of effect*, which required the hedonistic and, therefore, introspective meaning of "giving pleasure." Accordingly, we shall henceforth use *means-end learning* (ME learning) as the most apt, brief designation for reward learning or learning by reinforcement, it being understood that we can objectively define drive goals and their intermediate

subgoals as *ends*. Incidentally, one can recognize that some reluctance of conservative reflexologists to accept this label as more essential arises, not only from fear of the admittedly undesirable teleology of such use of *drive goals*, but also from classical conditioning being unable to get a goal or end into operational terms. So long as the definition of a goal remains nonobjective in its discovery and nonoperational in its definition, the reluctance is justified. Meanwhile, however, the advance of motivation research by multivariate, structuring methods has brought the specific recognition, and general definition, of ergic goals into a truly operational framework (see chapter 5, this *Handbook*, and Cattell & Warburton, 1967, chapter 5).

There have been many attempts to reduce CRI and CRII (co-ex and means-end learnings) to a monistic explanation. They have taken the form (cf. Morgan, Pavlov, Tolman; Staats & Staats, 1963; Staats, 1975) of saying that co-ex is sufficient, or conversely (Hull, 1943; Miller; Thorndike, 1932; Zener, 1937; and perhaps Mowrer), of explaining co-ex learning as a special form of ME learning. In the anti-monistic direction we have Skinner and many others (whom the present writer would initially follow) firmly stating there are two phenomena, at least; and the more extreme position of Gagné (1967) even calls for eight different varieties.

## 2.3  Integrative Learning

This type of learning, except in certain asides, has been omitted from the scheme of most learning theory statements made by present establishment textbooks. However, in personality research it can by no means be left out; indeed, it repeatedly challenges us as a central problem. We can define an integration of behavior as something occurring among several distinct means-end goal learnings such that, by inhibition and compromise, a new response is found that gives the *largest discoverable total satisfaction* to the collection of disparate and conflicting needs. This *confluence learning* (as it might also be called) is highly important.

To distinguish it from general ME learning, to which in a generic sense it belongs, we may call it IE (Integrated End) learning. Obviously, it can exist logically as a distinct category only if we suppose that the ultimate ends in various ME learning are categorically distinct, that is, that ergic needs exist which cannot further be subsidiated to some common goal but only balanced. If this were not the state of affairs, the give and take of mutual suppression of ergic goals would be only a matter of different routes (means) to some common end goal instead of adjusting a sum over several independent kinds of satisfaction. The factor-analytic evidence (chapter 5) so far points to several such distinct ergic goals in both man and animals that are categorically different in quality and mutually unsubstitutable. Nevertheless, the theory also requires that satisfactions, in some way, can be equated among them in terms of some rate of exchange.

Consequently, when we accept the existing evidence (chapter 5 by Dielman and Krug, chapter 12 by Broadhurst and Jinks, chapter 14 by Gray and Drewett, and chapter 25 by Fahrenberg) that these goals are innately given, whether viscerogenically or in the central nervous system, then it is incorrect under Principle 2 (section 2.2) to conclude without special demonstration that one erg can be substituted for another without modification of the reward law; that is, it is unsafe to assume a genus of "general drive" quality until the separate species of ergs are themselves understood.

The hedonistic generalization that all behavior is for pleasure has been understood since the time of Mill and McDougall to be a hollow and virtually circular verbalism. Research may in time show rates of exchange among the various distinct ergic satisfactions, or lead to operational recognition of some common factors or common coin. But meanwhile, and indeed as long as various ergic goals are conceived as dynamically distinct, any learning that involves *a pattern of mutual inhibition among the ergic goals*, that is, keeping to some prescribed response hierarchy among them, is in form and nature something new, beyond ordinary means-end learning. It *may* prove to have several principles and parameters in common, but it is surely likely to have—at least at an initial descriptive level—many features which are necessarily different from Principle 2. Of course, like most learning, it can be subsumed in a simple formal sense under operant conditioning; that is, course of action A is inhibited because course of action B is more strongly rewarded. But this is so abstractive a model that little is actually said about the complex pattern of learning— of inhibition, deferment, and alternation of different ergic satisfactions—which probably involves new and complex balancing principles, emergents no longer simply deducible from means-end learning laws as such.

Reasons for IE learning's being neglected in animal research (apart from early work on conflict by Warden, 1940, and others) reside in (a) uncertainties about the nature and number of biological drives (often dismissed with the gratuitous assumption that non-visceral drives, like curiosity, fear, and gregariousness, must be *secondary*) and (b) the petrification of experiment on ME learning in manipulative maze learning where a single goal valency (satisfaction) pursuit is deliberately imposed, in unnatural isolation from life's problems. Only in human learning—outside the laboratory and spread over several months of everyday life in a complex environment—can this type of learning be easily studied. Incidentally, a common direction of solution in integrative learning is *confluence learning* (Cattell, 1950b, chapter 8) that is, the finding of a solution through temporary postponements and inhibitory actions that avoids the need for any simple mutual suppression and discovers, instead, new modes of action that simultaneously give satisfaction to several drives.

## 2.4  Goal Modification Learning

Whereas sections 2.2 and 2.3 deal with modification on the way to some (ultimately) innately given goal, the clinicians have observed, in sublimation, regression, and perversion, a form of learning in which even the goal itself is changed. This modification of the form of satisfaction in the culminative consummatory activity of an essentially biological goal might be doubted, as a clinical misperception, were it not that experimenters have noted something close to it in some forms of imprinting. These interpretations need a more critical examination of data and their analysis than has yet been made. It is tentatively proposed here that a fourth descriptive category be kept open calling the attention of research to a possible basically different form of learning. In this type of learning, an ergic, biological goal is itself changed; it is no longer satisfied as genetically intended but undergoes some substitution. In some cases (e.g., hunger), any radical modification would mean the death of the organism, but in others (e.g., homosexuality), appreciable modification can occur by substitution of another end satisfaction. This we shall index as GM, for goal modification.

These four forms of learning, CE, ME, IE, and GM, are not mutually exclusive in any given learning situation. The possibility must be considered—as by Thorndike, Miller, and Mowrer and also by Leontiev (1966) and other Russian psychologists—that some supposed pure CE learning (classical conditioning) is often actually mixed with ME learning. This fourfold taxonomy does not ignore certain cross classification that may be made (e.g., into blindly varied behavior vs. intelligently insightfully changed learning). However, the whole parameter of *intelligent-insightful versus accidental connection* can be set aside as a comparatively irrelevant cognitive feature, in relation to the more fundamental dynamic-process laws concerning the formation of connections. Structured learning does not consider these the whole story but incorporates the effects of existing traits and states in the organism into the learning equation.

Whether these four forms of learning can ultimately be reduced in some sense, or require perhaps even an additional fifth extension in the form of an *energy-economics* principle, is a matter for perhaps a generation of further learning theory research. Under the possible concept of energy-economic changes, not actually discussed in Fig. 1, the possibility is contemplated that exercise of a particular drive can increase the general level of energy (a difficult term to define in psychology so far, yet meaningful) for the *whole drive*, not merely for some particular behavioral expression, as in the learning principles in sections 2.1, 2.2, and 2.3. Exactly what such an energy-level change means operationally must necessarily be left unspecified in this brief allusion, but such change would be conceptually very different from the first three learning forms, and possibly distinct from the fourth. The question also must still be considered whether reactive inhibition could not better be explained by an *energy-output reduction law*.

## 3  A HALF-WAY HOUSE TO STRUCTURED LEARNING: THE APA MODEL AND THE EPA MATRIX

Turning from a survey of what may be called contingently the *mechanisms of learning*, let us look systematically at the description of learning change, which these principles may explain. To many reflexologists what has to be explained is very simple: the appearance of a new response to an old stimulus, or a new stimulus to an old response. But to those who recognize the organismic truth that it is unlikely any part reaction can be explained adequately without incorporating the total organism in the explanation, this is inadequate. The change in viewpoint required might seem to be described as one from a microscopic to a macroscopic view, but that does not mean that we are content to lose sight of the specific stimulus-response (S-R) behavior. Since we know that at least two-thirds of the variance of specific bits of behavior in the adult human can be explained in broad source-trait and state organizations, however, we prefer to begin with the global change and then consider the relation of the specific bit of behavior to the global change of which it is part. Except for a lower animal in a highly artificial laboratory situation, no learning is confined to specific conditioning of narrow behavior; and even the laboratory animal is actually learning on many more fronts than the experimenter intends.

The central behavior-specification equation (Chapter 1) is

$$a_{hijk} = \sum_{x=1}^{x=l} b_{hjx}s_{kx}A_{xi} + \sum_{y=1}^{y=m} b_{hjy}s_{ky}P_{yi}$$
$$+ \sum_{z=1}^{z=n} b_{hjz}s_{kz}D_{zi} + \text{uniqueness}, \quad (1)$$

where $a$ is a defined kind of measure of the response $j$ by person $i$, to focal stimulus $h$ in situation (occasion, condition, ambient stimulus) $k$.

There are $l$ ability traits, like $A_x$; $m$ general personality traits, like $P_y$; and $n$ dynamic traits, like $D_z$. The $i$ subscript says how much of each of these individual $i$ has. The $s$s are modulator indexes saying how much the ambient situation $k$ (which may sometimes include $h$) changes the level of the trait. For example, if $D_z$ is proneness to anxiety (the situation in an examination), $s_{kz}$ will have a large value. The $b$s are behavioral indexes (perceptual and executive combined) saying how much an increment in a given trait causes an increment in the behavior $a_{hj}$. (See Chapter 1.)

The reflexologist and the experimenters with verbal memorizing have sought formulae for increments in $a_{hj}$ (the response to stimulus $h$) and have plotted learning curves for such. They may also say they are interested in a new stimulus supplanting $h$ or a new response supplanting $j$. However, these phenomena can be dealt with by the preceding comprehensive treatment, in that we may consider $a_{hjk}$ to start from zero in the special case when $j$ or $h$ is new.

However, here the approach of structured learning theory is entirely different from this concern with an increment alone. With such an approach, one is not content to know what the change is in $a_{hijk}$, on the left, but also wants to know what the change is in the values on the right. Naturally one uses the empirical values of $a_{hijk}$ in the population and individual to reach conclusions about the values on the right, but the understanding of what has happened lies in the scientific model on the right. That model deals with three vectors (series of numbers): (a) a behavioral or executive vector of $b$s, which says how traits affect the behavior; (b) a modulation vector of $s$s, which says how the situation evokes changes in the proneness traits; and (c) a vector of personality factor scores for the individual, which we symbolize as $Ts-T$ including all three trait modalities, $A, P,$ and $D$.

The meaning of the first two vectors will be explored more fully later, but the third is familiar to everyone, for example, in vocational guidance work as a personality (ability, temperament, motivation) profile. Therefore, in this introductory illustration of structural learning, we consider this familiar vector first. The experimental work of Barton, Cattell, and Vaughan (1973), Barton, Bartsch, and Cattell (1974), Cattell, Rickels, et al. (1966), Graffam (1967), J. McV. Hunt, Laforge, and Gilbert (1959), and others has shown that, in fact, life-learning experiences will significantly change levels on individual-factored source traits · and that, of course, this will be accompanied by *reflexological* changes in atomistic behaviors. We propose here to describe a first and rougher attempt (than later, below) to relate the describable, measurable change (the learning) to the environmental experience in a way that will lead to *first-order learning laws*, that is, laws largely at a statistico-mathematical level not resolved into deeper psychological laws.

What we shall call *Experience Path Analysis* (EPA) learning theory deals with paths of experience, the frequency of treading them, and the formulation of a vector showing what a particular path does to a whole series of personality factors. Admittedly, this first formulation is rough; yet it has the virtues of (a) being useful and effective on personality traits with which the psychologist is actually concerned in general practice and theory and (b) dealing with actual common life paths, such as getting married, going to college, suffering physical disablement, and succeeding in politics. Paths may be defined either in such concrete

experiences or with more psychological analysis in *adjustment-maladjustment sequences* possible in all areas, and therefore cutting across areas of experience as a second mode of classification. Such *Adjustment Process Analysis* (APA) is illustrated in Fig. 2; and the reader is referred to Cartwright and Cartwright (1971) and Cattell and Child (1975) for a fuller description.

Now the aim of the EPA is either (a) the applied one of estimating what will happen to a given person, knowing his path-experience frequencies and the general learning matrix, or, conversely, (b) a pure research, knowing a person's personality change and his experience, to deduce the general learning law matrix. These are represented in matrix Equations a and b in Fig. 3.

The essence of the EPA model is given in Equation 2 where $T_{ikc}$ is the change $c$ in trait $T_k$ for individual $i$. The coefficients $f_{i1}$ to $f_{iv}$ are the frequencies with which the subject has experienced paths 1 through $v$, and the values $e_{1k}$ to $e_{vk}$ are the *potencies*, for learning change, of the paths of experiences 1 to $v$ on personality trait $T_k$.

$$T_{ikc} = f_{i1}e_{1k} + f_{i2}e_{2k} + \cdots f_{iv}e_{vk}. \quad (2)$$

There are similar equations for changes in other traits, $T_1$, $T_m$, and so forth. It will be noted that the assumptions are (a) that the motivation and reward conditions are considered already fixed and defined in the experiences; (b) that effects are additive; (c) that over the range considered effects are linearly related to frequency of repetition; and (d) that the *prior* personality structure of the individual does not enter the prediction. (The later, more comprehensive models will not admit the exclusion of information in (d) but will assume, instead, that the make up of the person at the beginning is another determiner of his

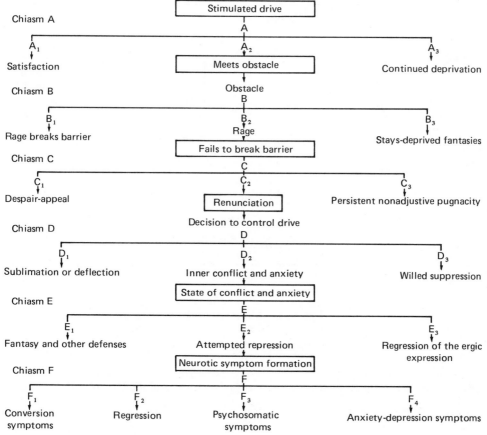

**FIG. 2** The adjustment process analysis chart (from R. B. Cattell & D. Child, *Motivation and Dynamic Structure,* New York: Wiley–Holt, 1975, p. 60).

personality learning, and that motivation and reward terms can be separately analyzed and weighted in the total path experience.)

For several people exposed differentially to several experiences, the total calculation can readily be arranged for matrix handling by computers, as shown in Fig. 3.

By multiplying a row of $L$ (which tells how much in general a trait change in the given trait is affected by *one* experience of each of the four paths of experience) by the given person's ($P_1$s) column of frequencies of experience of the given paths, we obtain an estimate of how much his trait $T_a$ will have changed.

The possibility may be considered that the matrix $L'L$ (from values entered as deviations from the mean, and which has the character of a $dR$ covariance matrix) when factored will indicate (either immediately or at the second order) the number of independent experiences necessary to account for the observed changes. A similar treatment of $FF'$ would yield experience dimensions in terms of common frequencies. This supposes, of course, that one enters with a sufficient number of experience variables and more people than experiences.

Although the EPA model does not give us all we eventually need in a comprehensive

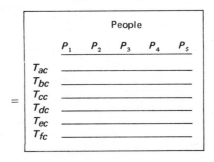

Trait learning law matrix **L**

Frequency of path-experience matrix **F**

Trait-change matrix **C**

**FIG. 3**  The adjustment process analysis model arranged for matrix calculation. To solve for $L$:

$$L \times F = C \tag{a}$$

$$L = CF'(FF')^{-1} \tag{b}$$

structural learning model, it has the virtue of recognizing that a situation must be considered to affect all traits and that one trait must be considered affected by all situations. For experimental work with humans, it also respects the important practical truth that since the laboratory cannot be used significantly to affect human traits, and since the situations in life that significantly affect traits do not get manipulated in isolation one by one, but can only be recorded as they jointly occur, a solution is possible only by more sophisticated mathematical-statistical designs. We cannot hold everything else constant in human life while we try the effect of one path, because each person is pursuing several paths at once. (Of course, one could average over many people, but that is costly and less adequate.) But by matrix algebra, as shown in Fig. 3, we can extract a statement about learning as "a multidimensional change in a multidimensional system." Hence, we use the vector model, with matrix calculations over several traits, people, and situations.

As a caution, one must point out that the gross change recorded in EPA need not always be learning only. Transformation—as opposed to learning—perhaps can be neglected in most brief laboratory or short-period life observation and measurement experiments. But, obviously, such factors could not be neglected in life changes over any appreciable interval of time, where such sophisticated analyses of changes in time-change curves must be considered, as are set out (see Baltes, 1968; Cattell, 1970b) in Equation 3:

$$T_c = T_{c_{e1}} + T_{c_{e2}} + T_{c_{e3}} + T_{c_{e4}}. \qquad (3)$$

Here the subscripts to the trait change refer, respectively, to endogenous change (volution) $e_1$, to *ecogenic* change normal to a culture across different historical moments $e_2$, to *epogenic* effects peculiar to a particular historical epoch (but shared by all persons) $e_3$, and to purely individual life-experience deviations $e_4$ from the average $e_2$ and $e_3$ experiences. It is not proposed here to ask how this breakdown can be effected (see preceding references), but only to emphasize the need for due regard, in any comprehensive long-term structural learning experiments with humans, for aspects commonly disregarded in animal experimentation.

## 4  A MORE COMPLETE DESCRIPTION OF STRUCTURAL LEARNING: TRI-VECTOR AND QUADRI-VECTOR CHANGE

The full model of structured learning theory involves the following:

1. The representation of change by several vectors, such as that we have just studied.
2. Inclusion of the existing traits of the individual in the learning equation.
3. Representation of the stimulus situation in a system of dimensions.
4. Calculation of reward (reinforcement) in terms of a known specific set of ergic tension (drive intensity) reductions.

5. Representing and explaining the sequences in a learnt process of persistence toward a goal with varied behavioral means, by sentiment process structures.

Our concern in this section is with the first.

In passing, let us repeat certain tenets and warn about some dangerous pseudodefinitions in use. Those tenets are as follows: (a) Any learning experience affects more than one response act. (b) "Stimulus" and "response" must not be made identical with the terms "cause" and "effect." (c) Multivariate concepts require multivariate experiment, since bivariate treatment is not capable of isolating the patterns involved. (d) The terminology of *internal stimulus* for drives and other states is best avoided. The latter—the internal thrusts to behavior—like stimuli, are specifics within the *generic* category of *causes*, but are a different species and deserve some such term as *impulsions*. (e) Note that there are diverse aspects, depending on *P–, Q–, R, S, T,* and so forth factor techniques, of the multivariate approach to learning. The approach taken here should not be confused with, for example, Tucker's analysis of individual learning curves. (Tucker, p. 479 in Cattell, 1966e). All these potential approaches (only Tucker, 1966, Fleishman & Hempel, 1955 have actually begun them) extend and are consistent with that developed here, but need to be differentiated.

The model for *personality in being*, as it accounts for present action, has been set out in Equation 1, which was fully discussed in chapter 7 in the concept of the VIDA model. In connection with states and state proneness or liability *L*, it has been pointed out that

$$S_{kxi} = s_{kx}L_{xi}, \qquad (4)$$

where $S_{kxi}$ is the state $x$ in situation $k$ as experienced by and scored for individual $i$.

What this modulation model recognizes is that the ambient situation and the person's proneness determine the level of the $S$ at the given occasion, and that the behavioral index $b_{hj}$ tells us how much the state assists (or, if $b$ is negative, inhibits) the behavior $a_{hijk}$, thus:

$$a_{hijk} = b_{hjx}s_{kx}L_{xi} + \text{other similar}$$

terms.                                                    (5)

Since we can suppose that all traits modulate slightly, though not so much as states, *the whole behavioral equation will consist of three vectors*—one of $b$s, one of $s$s, and one of $L$s, essentially $T$s. Hence the expression at the head of this section: tri-vector change. However, more refined experiment and analysis may well lead to $b$ being further split into a perception $p$ and an execution $e$ term so that the typical expression would be

$$a_{hijk} = p_{hx}e_{jx}s_{kx}T_{xi} + \text{similar terms}, \quad (6)$$

in which case the description and estimation of behavior would require a quadri-vector statement. (The procedures in breakdown of the loading to components are given in Cattell, 1971, and, more fully, 1977.)

For a description of how it is proposed to obtain the $p$, $e$, and $s$ terms from what is initially given in factor analysis—the ordinary loadings—the reader must be referred elsewhere (Cattell, 1971b, 1977). That the loadings do in fact change as learning occurs was shown most clearly in the ability-performance field by Fleishman and Hempel (1955), though the work of Hendriks (1971) and of Laughlin (1973) in regard to attitudes and dynamic traits also shows changing loadings of ergs on attitudes as emotional learning proceeds.

Although the separation of the crude factor loading into $p$, $e$, and $s$ components is, as indicated, a technicality to be read

elsewhere (Cattell, 1977), the reader should pick up here the general nature of their operations. The learning change is to be caught by refactoring the same group before and after the learning experience, on the same variables, on only one or two of which learning may have been introduced. *The comparison of two successive* R-*technique analyses can be expressed three different ways*, with varying completeness. These can yield "explanations" of learning change that involve one of the following: (a) changes in the person's trait scores ($T$s) without changes in behavioral indexes ($b$s) and modulators ($s$s); (b) changes in behavioral indexes and modulators without changes in trait levels; or (c) changes in both. They are briefly described as follows:

1. Distinct factoring. Here one factors variables $a_{11}$ through $a_{1n}$ (before learning) and $a_{21}$ through $a_{2n}$ (after learning) as two separate sets. (Here, and throughout Fig. 4, $a_{12}$ means variable $a_1$ measured on Occasion 2, whereas $a_{21}$ means Variable 2 on Occasion 1.) This will yield distinct $T$s, $b$s, and $s$s, which can be compared by the methods discussed later. It has the disadvantage, absent in items 2 and 3 following, that the factors are not identical and require some assumptions (Cattell, 1970a) about comparison of scores on them.

2. Common pre- and post-variable matrices. Here $a_{11}$ and $a_{12}$, and, similarly, for all variables to $n$, are put in the same correlation matrix and factored together. This is shown in Fig. 4, section 1(a), where the extra subscripts, $a$, $b$, and $c$ identify the scores of Adams, Brown, and Clark. When such a score matrix as that in section 1(a) is factored, it yields the factor matrix in 1(b), in which the loadings from a single factor column have been segregated into an $O_1$ (Occasion 1) and an $O_2$ column to show how the comparison of loadings would be

made. (Any estimation of the factor from the weights derived from these two weight columns would be estimates of the same factor, and the difference of the two estimates would scarcely be a real factor score-change estimate.)

3. The double subject method. Here one treats each subject as two people—the person before the learning and the person afterwards. This yields a single-factor pattern for before and after (missing the $b$ changes), but permits strictly comparable factor score estimates for the before and after person. Thus, here $a_1$ and $a_2$ are treated (each in its own distribution) as measures on a single conceptual $a_1$ variable, but entered twice, once for the person as he was on the first occasion, and once as he was on the second. The symmetrical relations of the second and third procedures can be illustrated by the forms of the brief score matrices and factor matrices set out in Fig. 4.

In the second method, Fig. 4, 1(a) and 1(b), there will be a problem of eliminating doublet factors (in $a_{11}$ and $a_{12}$), for which Tucker, in his combined matrix factoring (1966) suggested a solution.

Methods 2 and 3, despite the appeal of simplicity, do not give us both the vector changes—$T$s and $b$s—but one or the other; for a full analysis of structured learning, Method 1 is essential. However, it brings problems in comparing factor scores. These problems can be met only by *real base* factor analyses (Cattell, 1972d) or the isopodic and equipotent scoring methods (Cattell, 1970a).

## 5  NATURE OF THE LEARNING PROCESS

Let us ask what the changes in $p, e,$ and $s$ coefficients mean. (The changes on the $T$ traits are familiar.) A change in a $p$ loading on trait $T_x$ means that trait $T_x$ has become more important in making the perception. For example, Fleishman found a fall in the loading of general ability (essentially) as a manipulative skill was learned. Thus, decisions that, at first, had to be made with substantial aid from intelligence came to be relegated to various skilled habits. As to the executive vector of $e$s, one can see that the speed and accuracy of performance of a diplomatic interpreter might, at first, in shyness before important politicians, be regulated more by personality factors, such as $C$ (Ego-strength) and $H$ (Parmia), but later acquire a larger loading directly on his fluency and memory factors.

Changes on the third vector—the modulation vector—need more discussion. Where the modulator $s_{kx}$ on a certain trait (or state proneness) $T_x$ changes the variance, the level of the factor may also be considered to have altered. For example, a group of children riding a bus might be involved in a frightening accident. The modulation $s_{kx}$, where $k$ is "riding in a bus" and $x$ is the anxiety proneness trait, would then step up in that group between a pre- and post-accident factoring. Staats (1975) firmly took the position that such changes are brought about by classical conditioning (co-ex learning), the inside view of the bus now being associated with the unconditioned fear reaction to the accident.

This writer would agree that many $s$ changes are partly of this origin. However, a second mechanism that must be considered, especially with the $D$ (dynamic) traits in Equation 1, is that when a situation leads regularly to reward of a given drive, the experience is likely to step up the excitation of that drive. This would be a form of ME learning. However, exactly what is meant by "excitation" here, in relation to "ergic tension" as used in drive-reduction concepts, remains to be clarified.

1. (Method 2) Common pre- and post-variable matrices

| | Variable | | | | | |
|---|---|---|---|---|---|---|
| | $a_{11}$ | $a_{12}$ | $a_{21}$ | $a_{22}$ | $a_{31}$ | $a_{32}$ |
| Adams | $a_{a11}$ | $a_{a12}$ | $a_{a21}$ | $a_{a22}$ | etc. | |
| Brown | $a_{b11}$ | $a_{b12}$ | $a_{b21}$ | $a_{b22}$ | etc. | |
| Clark | $a_{c11}$ | $a_{c12}$ | $a_{c21}$ | $a_{c22}$ | etc. | |
| et al. | | | | | | |
| to | | | | | | |
| $N$ | | | | | | |
| cases | | | | | | |

| | $T$ | |
|---|---|---|
| | $O_1$ | $O_2$ |
| $a_{11}$ | $b_{11}$ | |
| $a_{12}$ | | $b_{12}$ |
| $a_{21}$ | $b_{21}$ | |
| $a_{22}$ | | $b_{22}$ |
| $a_{31}$ | $b_{31}$ | |
| $a_{32}$ | | $b_{32}$ |
| to | | |
| $2N$ | | |
| variables | | |

(a) Distinct index factoring: score matrix arrangement (2nd method)

(b) Factor pattern matrix showing behavior index change (2nd method)

2. Double subject method

| | $a_1$ | $a_2$ | $a_3$ |
|---|---|---|---|
| Adams 1 | $a_{a11}$ | $a_{a12}$ | $a_{a13}$ |
| Adams 2 | $a_{a21}$ | $a_{a22}$ | $a_{a23}$ |
| Brown 1 | $a_{b11}$ | $a_{b12}$ | $a_{b13}$ |
| Brown 2 | $a_{b21}$ | $a_{b22}$ | $a_{b23}$ |
| Clark 1 | $a_{c11}$ | $a_{c12}$ | $a_{c13}$ |
| Clark 2 | $a_{c21}$ | $a_{c22}$ | $a_{c23}$ |

| | $T$ | |
|---|---|---|
| | $O_1$ | $O_2$ |
| Adams 1 | $T_{1a}$ | |
| Adams 2 | | $T_{2a}$ |
| Brown 1 | $T_{1b}$ | |
| Brown 2 | | $T_{2b}$ |
| Clark 1 | $T_{1c}$ | |
| Clark 2 | | $T_{2c}$ |

(a) Distinct trait level factoring: score matrix arrangement (3rd method)

(b) Factor score matrix showing trait score change (3rd method)

FIG. 4 Contrast of trait change and behavior index change formulations, through different designs in factoring learning data.

An important corollary from the structural learning model, and one that reflexological learning is powerless to handle, is that *learning can occur without any increment taking place in the actual performance*. It is possible (as the following illustrates in simple arithmetic terms) for the *same* actual performance score to be accompanied by *changes* in the vectors:

$$a_{ji} = b_{ji} \times T_{11} + b_{j2} \times T_{21}$$

Prelearning  $24 = 3 \times 6 + 2 \times 3$

Postlearning  $24 = 2 \times 5 + 7 \times 2$

Structured theory is thus capable of telling us, when no measurable change has occurred in the performance, that learning has nevertheless taken place. Such absolute absence of performance may be uncommon; but large changes in the manner of doing something, or in motivation for doing, with relatively little overt change in behavior, are not uncommon in the complex field of human learning behavior. Of course, such changes will not be detectable from bivariate designs with a single dependent variable of performance. This is one of many instances where the multivariate, holistic approach alone is capable of explaining what happens in a controlled, restricted, neat bivariate experiment lacking the broader evidence necessary to understand the law that is actually operating.

At this juncture in developing structured learning theory, it is necessary to bring in the contribution of the dynamic calculus (chapter 5 and Cattell & Child, 1975). For although the co-ex (CRI) form of learning does not speak of reward, we shall argue that it is ultimately dynamic in nature and, since means-end learning (CRII) undoubtedly is, all learning is to be brought to a dynamic basis. Indeed, in a larger context, the dynamic calculus and structured learning may be seen as two growing pillars that promise support for an edifice of theory with utility in many areas of psychology.

Let the reader be reminded that the main elements in the dynamic calculus (chapter 5) are the following:

1. Evidence on the number and nature of human ergs.

2. Evidence on the number and nature of sentiment structures developed in our culture.

3. Validation of objective motivation-strength measurement principles and devices, showing two large secondaries across seven or eight primaries. These have interestingly different properties so that measurement of ergic tension level or sentiment strength in one has different predictive meaning from the other.

4. The representation of any given attitude strength by a specification equation on ergs and sentiments.

5. The representation of the learned satisfaction paths by the model of the *dynamic lattice* (Fig. 5) and the development of methods of mapping it.

6. The development of equations for predicting decision and expressing level of conflict and degrees of integration.

Although descriptions of these parameters and features are available in Dielman and Krug's chapter 5, the briefest summary of essential concepts in the calculus and the lattice might be convenient here. They include the following:

1. The concept of the *attitude*, as a stimulus situation and response course of action, with a given interest strength, the latter definable as a vector of loadings on ergic and sentiment factors. This is the operational building block in the experimental investigation of dynamic structure.

2. The notion of subsidiation (Murray, H. A., 1938) as a succession of attitudes from subgoal to subgoal to final ergic consummatory goal.

3. The inference, largely but not exclusively by factor analysis, concerning subsidiation connections in the dynamic lattice and the existence of dynamic trait structures: ergs (innate) and engrams (acquired)—the latter divisible into sentiments and complexes. A sentiment or subsentiment is a $D$ as it operates as a dynamic set in the description of process.

4. The concept of motivation component factors ($U$ and $I$) distinct from dynamic structures ($D$s), and presenting the touchstone by which the *validity* of any device for the objective measurement of motivation strength is calculated.

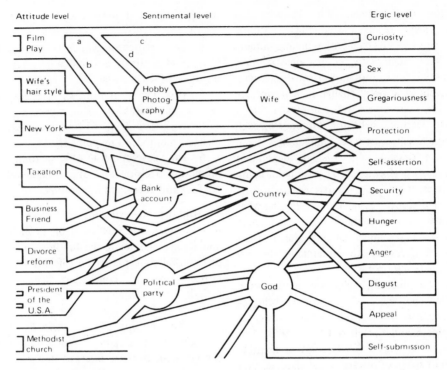

**FIG. 5** The dynamic lattice (from R. B. Cattell and D. Child, *Motivation and Dynamic Structure,* New York: Wiley-Holt, 1975, p. 60).

5. The calculus of dynamic summative and conflict effects by vector methods, and such findings as that the unintegrated (U) motivation component is typically higher than the integrated (I) in an area of conflict.

6. The observation that in the dynamic lattice the learning of new habits usually proceeds by additions to the distal end (the ergic goals being considered the proximal end). Thus, later habits have greater goal distance than do older ones.

A practical contribution of the calculus and the lattice is the measurement of ergic tension levels and reductions in man. Hitherto, as in animal experiments, strength of motive had to be inferred from environmental manipulations, for example, hours of deprivation and level of incentive (money in human experiments, etc.). Along with this goes the possibility of recognizing qualitative differences in different ergic motivations, for example, hunger, gregariousness, and fear, instead of resting on the possible fiction of undifferentiated drive, as in Hull's (1952) formulations.

Structured learning supposes that an increase of response potential occurs through reward of coexcitation. Parenthetically, let it be noted we use the word *reward*, since reinforcement is being used ambiguously—sometimes for a reward, sometimes for the increment of response occurring through whatever causes it.

It is proposed, for semantic clarity, to let *reinforcement* describe the change in a stimulus-response connection. To say it becomes reinforced is to say that it becomes stronger. To say that it is *rewarded*, however, is only to say that gratification of an erg occurred through the sequence. The terms *reinforcement* and *reward* frequently are used indiscriminately, to the confusion of discussion. Reinforcement could conceivably arise through influences other than reward, notably through coexcitation if classical conditioning is held not to be a reward phenomenon.

At this point, as we approach the central nature of structured learning, we have to account not only for the rise of structures but for the very nature of acquiring learning anywhere. As to the former we point, for the moment, to three processes that could generate acquired unitary trait structures such as are evidenced in sentiment factors: (a) variations in individual exposure to social institutions (church, school, athletes in peer groups) that simultaneously reward all response elements in the pattern; (b) a concept akin to stimulus generalization, but actually involving the discovery of an aid, which operates effectively over several situations (this has been developed primarily to explain unitary abilities [Cattell, 1971a] but it can be applied here too); and (c) the existence, in the behaviors being learned in the pattern, of common high loadings on some existing unitary sentiment. For example, if a man has a strong sentiment for psychology and perceives various mathematical skills as serving those interests, the weight of his main sentiment will load the specification equation for learning gain in *all* the new attitude and interest elements in the mathematical sentiment. The unity in the parent sentiment will thus tend to produce a unity in the offspring. The classical case is the development of crystallized intelligence $g_c$ from fluid $g_f$ intelligence (Horn, J. L., 1968), as seen in the investment theory.

A more detailed development of these mechanisms must be left until later, while we attack the more fundamental issue of how learning, in any shape or form, occurs. It may seem that in accepting CRI (coexcitation) and CRII (means-end, or reward) learning we already have sufficient answer. But both are more at a descriptive than an explanatory level. Analyses of co-ex learning must be brief, because of lack of evidence. Russian psychologists, for example, Leontieff and Luria, have sought explanations, at the psychological level, of some principle that two areas of excitation in the brain will almost tend to run together. There must be a physiological explanation, at least as epi-phenomena, but for the present let us deal in "concepts inferred from behavior," which need not be immediately tied down in neural terms. What we have is surely the tendency of a newly aroused excitement (the conditioned stimulus [CS]) to join up with a more powerful one, which also possesses an existing outlet (the unconditioned response [UCR]). Possibly, as various writers have attempted, a further or supplementary explanation can be found in CRII terms (means-end, reward) in that the conditioning stimulus is an anticipation of the unconditioned response, and its appearance leads to earlier satisfaction of that response. This assumes that the smallest reflex, such as an eyeblink, has a dynamic reward quality, but anyone who has responded with a scratch reflex will have no difficulty in this concept of a minidrive. On the other hand, there are initial difficulties in applying a dynamic reward explanation to the CRI phenomena when a stimulus is made to evoke an unpleasant emotion, such as fear or disgust.

In personality, at the descriptive level, measured learning seems almost universally involved, and we must give intensive attention to it. The finished structure, which we see in that acquired part of the personality which we call sentiments, attitudes (including the ego and the self-sentiment), etc., has the form of a lattice, as shown in Fig. 5.

Its characteristics are *ergic goals* (which have appeared as the factors loading consummatory behavior most highly); *attitude* courses of action *subsidiating* to one another and to various subgoals; and a distal (leftward) extension of the lattice as learning continues in a complex culture. Factoring yields specification equations showing how much each attitude course of action leads to the satisfaction of various ergs (final goals) and various sentiments (intermediate goals) thus:

$$a_{ijk} = b_{j1}s_{k1}E_{1i} + b_{jp}s_{kp}E_{pi}$$
$$+ b_{jm1}s_{km1}M_{11}$$
$$+ \cdots b_{jmq}s_{kmq}M_{qi}, \qquad (7)$$

where there are $p$ ergs ($E$s) and $q$ sentiments ($M$s).

To account for the learning of this lattice we have to account for the learning of a tract or complex chain, for a lattice is a criss-cross of chains. An analogue to this is the chain reflex, but an attitude chain is more molar. Some explanations for the former, for example, as a CRI series, need not necessarily work here. It was perceived early in reflexological learning developments that in a series of subgoals, stimuli $k_1$, $k_2, \ldots, k_{(n-1)}$, $k_n$, as in Fig. 5, a possible explanation, and one experimentally supported, was that if $a_n$ is the behavior at the consummatory ergic goal, then $a_{(n-1)}$, which brings the animal to $R_n$ (the possibility of $a_n$), itself acquires rewarding properties. Consequently (under such concepts as secondary reinforcement and Hull's [1952] "fractional anticipatory goal responses"), the rewarding property of the subgoals, each concluding one course and becoming a stimulus to the next, *could be passed on down the line.*

The basic feature hitherto used in dynamic reward explanations—*that reward is the reduction of an ergic tension*—unfortunately runs into difficulties, though its central tenet seems logically inescapable. For if it is drive strength that produces behavior then the familiar cessation of behaviors at ergic goals, or even intermediate goals, must surely mean that drive reduction is produced at those points. This would correspond to a sequence as shown in Curve 1 in Fig. 6, where a drop occurs as each subgoal is reached, with a large drop at the end. The present writer has criticized this model on the grounds that it does not fit a number of observations, both subjective and behavioral. One objection—that learning occurs most strongly at the goal end of a maze—may not be legitimately counted among them, since (a) in the normal course of learning, by distal extension that part is most repeated; and (b) it is drive reduction rather than drive strength that offers reward and thus might be greater toward the end (means of measuring it has been poor).

On the side of positive evidence, both of subjective excitement and of various learning phenomena (Blodgett, 1929; Mackintosh,

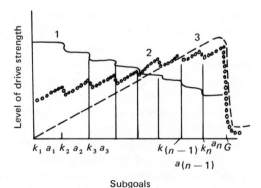

FIG. 6  The drive-reduction paradox. Curve 1 represents a drive reduction hypothesis; Curve 2 represents a compromise . . . drive tension by drive reduction at subgoals; Curve 3 represents inherent drive tension.

1974), however, there is much that points to rising drive tension throughout the run, as shown in Curve 3, followed by great reduction at the goal. In this case we encounter the major difficulty that the organism willingly undertakes a course of action resulting in continuously rising drive tension. By definition, this is "punishing," or more exactly, moving into a state of increasing dissatisfaction. Though this curve *might* explain learning, it will not fit ordinary behavior itself. An attempted compromise is shown in Curve 2, where there is sufficient drive reduction at each subgoal to account for its being learned, but the tension still rises throughout the run. To this it can be objected that the notion of moving toward an increasing tension is not made more tolerable by chopping it into bits.

The solution suggested here (and elsewhere, Cattell, 1977, in more detail) is what may be called a *multistate theory of learning dynamics*. It hypothesizes that "drive tension" is oversimplified and that, in fact, two or more distinct kinds of factors are involved. The introduction of this theory with any decent basis has become possible only through the multivariate experimental study of human states (by $P$ and $dR$ techniques). We know that for each of the located ergs there is a measurable *ergic tension state* (Cattell & Child, 1975) and that, in addition, there are what may be called *general states*, such as anxiety, excitement, regression, and depression (Barton and Cattell, 1976; Curran and Cattell, 1974). Third, it is clear, though surprising, that sentiments also change as unitary entities, involving some form of cognitive excitement or responsiveness coterminous with the boundaries of the sentiment.

In a learning experience in a new area, the sentiment structures do not exist. Though other factors may later prove to play a part

in the multifactor theory, we propose to begin with a theory resting on three factors: (a) The internally originating (viscerogenic, appetitive) drive strength, symbolized as $E_u$ and meaning the unintegrated motivational component measure in the erg, $E$. (b) An arousal state, which may or may not be wider than any given drive, though we shall suppose that within one drive it can be represented as $E_a$, the integrated motivation measure for the given erg. (Later research may show arousal, connected with hypothalamic stimulation, to appear as a broad second-order factor among drives.) (c) A generalized state of excitement, visible as a behavioral factor (Cattell, 1957a; Curran, 1968; Curran and Cattell, 1974) but also subjectively as a pleasurable excitement (in all but extreme exhaustion).

The state of general excitement, from overwhelming varieties of common observation, behaves as Curve 3 in Fig. 6. But there is no reason for the viscerogenic $E_u$ to so behave. Hunger, thirst, sex, and gregariousness may be considered to have their levels fixed by deprivation and internal process; and the latter would, in the course of an experiment, produce only a slight, steady rise as in Fig. 6. It is suggested that this is open to the same criticism—the paradox that the animal seeks a higher tension rather than the reward of tension reduction. One must point out that the rise has nothing to do with stimulation in the run. It occurs inexorably by an internal clock, running regardless of where the animal is. Consequently, refusing to pursue its run is no solution to this rising tension, and there is no objection to positing it. However, the increment we called *arousal*, due to the environmental stimulation, must be assumed by contrast to be pleasurable, that is, behavioristically and operationally conceived, to *lead the individual to seek further stimulation* of the drive.

One would expect that for this to be pleasurable, in biological operation, stimulus must have led previously to satisfaction. The apparent difficulty with this (e.g., that sources of sexual stimulation or the stimulation of curiosity that never in the past led to anything but frustration, are nevertheless sought) dissolves when we recognize that there are both learned and *innate* stimuli to a drive. The triggers in a genetic pattern have to be built into the average experience of the race, not of the individual. As noticed elsewhere, there is a remarkably close similarity of model between the trial and error of evolution and of learning. This similarity needs to be taken into account not only when the past million years and the present culture differ, producing an *irrational* persistence of unrewarded subgoal behavior, but also of the greater readiness with which certain responses are learned when they happen, in our culture, not to be so different from ancient stimuli (e.g., the arch smile of a coquette).

There are implications for modification of the ordinary action model in this two-factor model, which there is no point in pursuing here until there is more experimental checking. But there is a clear implication that the $E$ term has to be considered as consisting of two parts: the appetitive, viscerogenic *drive strength* component $E_u$, and the arousal part $E_a$, such that $E_a$ is an occasion-generated component of a different quality and role from $E_u$. This generation of ergic tension from a drive was formerly represented (Cattell, 1959) by

$$E = (s_k + y)[(C + H + (P - pG) + (B - bG)],  \quad (8)$$

where $s$ is stimulus (modulator) strength, $C$ and $H$ are, respectively, constitutional and personal historical determiners of strength of the drive and of no further concern here. The terms $P$ and $B$ are, respectively, physiological and behavioral *need strengths*, modified by current levels of gratification, $pG$ and $bG$. We are now compelled to modify this by making

$$E_u = [C + H + (P - pG) + (B - bG)]  \quad (9)$$

and $E_a$ equal to $(s_k + y_i - 1)E_u$, where $y$ is now to have a subscript for an individual $i$.

If it were not for $y_i$, the strengths of $E_u$ and $E_a$ would be perfectly correlated, which we suspect (Horn, J. L., 1966c) is not the case. So $y_i$ must be some individual proneness to arousal, apart from the strength of $s_k$. The model supposes, then, that except for this the strength of arousal is primarily a function of the need strength at the time and the strength of stimulation (due largely to past experiences). In other words, arousing stimuli produce greater effect when the internal drive level is higher. This degree of independence of $E_u$, need or drive strength, and $E_a$, arousal, solves the drive-reduction paradox and presents us with a new learning model. It solves the drive paradox since the individual will be willing to advance into higher stimulation; for the $E_u$ form of ergic tension that is *unpleasant* barely increases (Fig. 7), whereas the arousal component, $E_a$, which is pleasantly exciting and anticipatory, increases disproportionately.

This solves the problem of strength of goal-directed *existing* action at any subgoal, which is specified by an equation involving drive strength and the drive arousal, the latter in part derived from the former. But how does it fit learning? Learning, by the multivector structural theory involves (simplifying to two vectors) a change in the $b_j$s

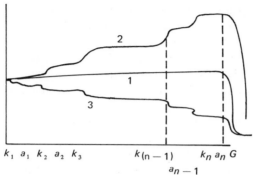

$$k_1 \quad a_1 \quad k_2 \quad a_2 \quad k_3 \qquad k_{(n-1)} \qquad k_n \quad a_n \quad G$$
$$a_{n-1}$$

**FIG. 7** Courses of drive strength and arousal in an attitude chain or maze run. Curve 1 represents slow, time-regulated growth of appetitive drive strength. Curve 2 represents arousal, as product of (1) and the subgoal–stimuli effects; Curve 3 represents a possible course in nonappetitive, nonviscerogenic drives where approach to goal brings reduction.

and in the $s_k$s. The stimulating value (the reinforcing value) of situation $k$ has increased, as shown by an increase in $s_k$; and the tendency of a given amount of ergic tension and arousal to lead to response $a_j$ has been augmented, as shown by the increase in $b_j$.

How are these increases brought about? Hull (1952), K. W. Spence (1968), and others replied that $s$ changes because the animal makes fractional anticipatory goal responses, or because reward is transferred leftwards in the dynamic lattice (Fig. 5) through secondary reinforcement. Staats (1975), using CRI only, said the individual is experiencing an emotional response (translate *drive arousal*) as he encounters each $k$ subgoal, so that they become conditional arousers. While admitting such coexcitation conditioning, it is not easy to see (unless constant repetition can do it) why $k$ should actually *augment* rather than merely reinstate a state of arousal. The dynamic calculus suggests rather that the amount of the subsequent reward is a major determiner of the increase in $s_k$. Similarly, the

augmentation of the behavioral index $b_j$, that is, the readiness to respond (frequency) with $a_j$ (or the strength or skill in $a_j$) is, by the vast evidence of instrumental conditioning experiments, a function of the reward at $G$, the final goal.

We have raised the possibility that the ergic satisfaction for different ergs may have different efficacy for committing to memory (engramming). The value $E$ would not actually be a scalar, that is, on a single dimension, but a vector involved (according to later experience) in leading up to the reward, which suggests a further refinement in the formulation. The behavioral equation for the original act will have behavioral indexes and modulators much larger for certain ergs than others. The model should therefore express the magnitude of reward as something taking place within the vector pattern of ergic tensions associated with the particular act, $a_j$, and applying to the particular Ms associated with it. Thus if the ergic part of the equation for the act were $.3E_1 + .8E_2 - .2E_3$, and an accidental ergic satisfaction, having nothing to do with act $j$ and other acts derived from $h$, occurred soon after the act, $j$, having the vector values $.1E_1 + .6E_2 + .3E_3 + .9E_4$, the model should not permit the $.3E_3$ and $.9E_4$ to operate, for they are inconsistent with sustaining dynamics of the act $j$.

Parenthetically, we have allowed in Fig. 7, Curve 3, that in nonappetitive ergs the possibility exists that the achievement of part-way goals will bring some actual drive-strength reduction, as when self-assertion lessens when the individual finds he has partly mastered some achievement, the fear drive diminishes as the person gets farther from the danger and nearer the goal of safety. If this is so—and no learning experiments currently deny it—a substantial array of secondary differences should appear between appetitive and nonappetitive innate drives. This, incidentally, would illustrate our earlier objection to learning models that posit "drive in the abstract" instead of respecting the known differences in natural history of the ergs. If a curve such as 3 is found, it would help answer the question that now faces us: What learning mechanism produces the leftward shift (distal in the dynamic lattice, from the proximal ergic goal rewards) both in arousal properties in Curve 2, and (if it exists) in ergic tension reduction in Curve 3?

When one is fully immersed in research on lower animals, in learning that is wholly by trial and error, it is easy to forget that the relation-perceiving capacity of human intelligence must, in a substantial proportion of learnings, mean that $k_{(n-1)}$ becomes pleasantly arousing because its connection with $k_n$ and the final goal is fully and insightfully perceived. And, in nonviscerogenic ergs, where the goal is not a comparatively sudden and complete physiological satisfaction, but a spread-out affair (since safety is rarely total and success in achievement is not always well defined), the subgoals at $k_2$, $k_3$, and so forth, can properly be said to give some satisfaction—not "anticipatory" but immediate—to the ergic tension ($E_u$) as such.

Nevertheless, the more difficult problem of how distal shifts, both in arousing properties, $s$s, and in acquisition of learned responses, $b$s, come about in trial-and-error learning must be attacked. At the same time we must also clarify the theory in terms of whether reward is wholly expressed by $E_u$ reduction or whether $E_a$ reduction also plays a part. Since there has been no application so far of the Motivation Analysis Tests (Cattell, Horn, Sweney and Radcliffe, 1964; Sweney, Cattell, and Krug, 1970), with their $U$ and $I$ component measures, to this aspect of human learning, any position adopted at the moment as to whether reward is the drop on Curve 1 at $G$ or also the drop on Curve 2 can be based only on common-sense observation. If the reader reflects on everyday incidents of learning, he may agree with the writer that the height of arousal per se (the $E_a$ component), as well as that of the inherent appetitive need strength $E_u$ at the time of détente by goal reward, combines to contribute to the amount of learning.

Another problem in drive-tension, reward-learning concepts has been that it apparently requires the impossible explanation of having causal action operate backwards in time. As far as learning of behavioral links (the acquisition of significant $b$s) is concerned, that has been handled (Cattell, 1973a) by accepting the unquestionable evidence (retroactive inhibition, reminiscence, etc.) that a cognitive event reverberates for minutes and hours. Consequently, if we suppose the reward acts on the diminishing remnant of that reverberation, as shown in Fig. 8, we explain both a basis for the action and the observed fact that learning declines with time lapse between the operant S-R and the reward. Just what goes on in what is broadly covered by reverberation, one must at present leave to the debates of students of memory phenomena (Kimble, D. P., 1967; Restle, 1975; Spence, K. W., & Spence, 1967–1968). But reorganization by relating to existing cognitive and dynamic structures is evidently central; and that would mean qualitative, discriminative effects, as well as simple decline of reverberation, which we need not pursue.

The more novel problem is to indicate a mechanism—if, as here, we take the position that an increase in arousal property $s_k$ is, in substantial part, not a CRI effect but a function of subsequent satisfaction after reaching the subgoal $k$. (It will be remembered we have ruled out cases of insightfully

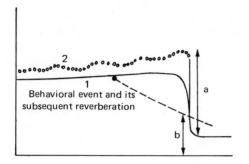

FIG. 8 The fixing of cognitive–behavioral link magnitude by reward. Learning = $f$(a.b.), i.e., a function of $a$ and $b$ as yet not further definable. Curve 1 shows the inherent time-bound rise in need strength; Curve 2 shows the subgoal-stimulated rise in arousal; $a$ = magnitude of reward; $b$ = cognitive-behavior link reverberation remnant at times of reward.

connecting subgoal and goal and are dealing with the numerous blind trial-and-error kinds of learning.) Only a law, with no depth of explanation, seems possible at the moment, by saying that reward properties (emotional meanings) can also be transferred backwards by reverberation of the memory of the subgoal until reward occurs; that is, the $s$s are subject to the same action as the $b$s, though what is augmented is now a pleasant-arousal quality coming at the subgoal rather than an increased executive response effectiveness.

This mechanism needs to be compared for general potency with Hull's "fractional anticipatory goal response" and "secondary conditioning" explanations of distal shift. The question must also be raised whether, as applied to subgoals, *arousal property* as defined here and *intermediate reward property* are conceptually quite the same. In Fig. 6 they are shown occurring at the same moment, at subgoals, but as being different; and we have there supposed that intermediate partial satisfaction, in Curve 3, is possible only in nonviscerogenic drives.

Contingently, we would argue that the attempt to explain (in viscerogenic drives) the goal-pursuit enhancement at subgoals by drive-reduction rewards is oversimplifed and that the newly operationally defined and measurable conception of *pleasant arousal* is needed. The implication of *pleasant* is, of course, that an increment is rewarding, but because we have a single word *reward* (or reinforing situation) does not mean that we are committed to a single factor—need reduction. We are hypothesizing here, instead, that every drive strength $E$ has two components, which may well be the $U$ and $I$ (Unintegrated and Integrated) components now experimentally well demonstrated (Cattell, Horn, Radcliffe, & Sweney, 1964). The extension of that aspect of the dynamic calculus which is brought about as it gets related to learning theory is that the $U$ and $I$ components of every unitary erg are, respectively, need, strength, and excitation (arousal) of a pleasant kind. The rewarding pleasure is a forepleasure of the goal, which, however, is a biologically built-in response capacity that evolved to get the animal over the difficulty of facing a mounting unpleasant biologically determined increase of need tension. If the unpleasantness of stimuli relating to a need increased with the increasing unpleasantness of the need tension, there would be increasing avoidance of any possibility of ultimate satisfaction. The arousal pleasure component, which we have tentatively identified with the (second-order) motivation component $E_I$, comes from a biologically generated response mechanism, the object of which is to drown the unpleasant ergic tension in arousal reward, which can be generated when stimuli and paths have been found that lead to the goal. That is to say, it is biologically given, but what it attaches to is a matter of specific learning.

## 6  CONTRIBUTION OF THE DYNAMIC CALCULUS TO STRUCTURED LEARNING THEORY

Let us relate the dynamic aspects of structured learning to wider issues and to certain formulations of K. W. Spence (1956), Berlyne (1960), S. B. Sarason (1966), and several others on the motivational aspect of learning. Initially, for simplicity, let us keep to a single ergic goal, as in a rat learning a maze under hunger. Let us also pay our respects to an aspect hitherto neglected here, namely, the difference between engramming (committing to memory) and recall. The inference from an operationally observed change in behavior to an engram will clarify as we proceed. For the moment consider an engram as $m$. The memory effect $m_{hj}$ operates in response $a_{hj}$, and shows itself in the behavioral index $b_{hj}$, (stimulus $h$, response $j$), defining the role of the given erg. Later we give $m$ further context as an attitude or set with the larger framework of a sentiment $M$. What has been said about reward to the remnant of a cognitive-executive reverberation can now be stated as

$$m_{hjy} - m_{hjx} = a_{hjx}[1 - C(t_2 - t_1)]$$
$$\cdot (aR_u + bR_a). \qquad (10)$$

On the left is the gain in memory engramming of the response $j$ to the stimulus $h$, which could be from zero (when $m_{hjy} = m_{hjx}$); $x$ and $y$ are the pre- and post-learnings; $t_1$ and $t_2$ are the times, respectively, of making the $j$ response to $h$, and of the final goal reward. $R_u$ and $R_a$ are the need and arousal rewards, respectively; and $a$ and $b$ are simply relative weightings. Parenthetically, the absolute level of $R_a$ at the time of reward to $R_u$ is probably the more appropriate score to use here. $C$ is the rate of decline of the reverberatory activity and is such that $[1 - C(t_2 - t_1)]$ would reduce to

zero after a period of, say, 1 hour (depending on subject species). Thus Equation 10 simply says the engramming effect is a function of the strength of response $a_{hj}$, an inverse function of the lapse of time between action and reward, and a function of need reduction and absolute level of arousal at the time, with different weights for each. Cumulative learning trials would introduce a term in Equation 10 for frequency of reptition, and it may be that the weighting would give *frequency* greater importance than *reward*.

An analogous expression would be used for the learning of arousal properties in the situation $(j + k)$, $k$ being the ambient situation and $j$ the focal stimulus. Here we write the arousal increment directly as $(s_{jktx} - s_{jkty})$ instead of some inferred structure from it, thus:

$$(s_{jky} - s_{jkx}) = s_{jkx}[1 - C(t_2 - t_1)]$$
$$\cdot (aE_u + bE_a). \qquad (11)$$

One would conjecture that the weight $b$, on the absolute level of arousal $E_a$, at the time of consummation, would be relatively large here.

Now a contribution of personality theory to learning theory that must not be lightly passed over is that it supposes the abilities ($A$s), dynamic traits ($D$s), and even the temperament traits, ($P$s), enter into the prediction of any learning. Thus Equation 10 must be regarded as true only when all these are held constant (an impossibility) and the proper, though more complex learning equation, is

$$m_{hjkyi} - m_{hjkxi} = \sum b_{hja}s_{hka}A_{ai}$$
$$+ \sum b_{hjp}s_{hkp}P_{pi}$$
$$+ \sum b_{hjd}s_{hkd}D_{di}$$
$$+ X_i \qquad (12)$$

where $X$ is the whole expression on the right of Equation 10 (with the $i$ subscript added, since here we are adding $i$ subscripts as we move in Equation 12 to values for a given individual).

In moving from an $m$ value to actual behavior $a$, let us first switch to the larger context of $M$s, sentiments, each made up of loadings on many $m$s. The integration of dynamic calculus concepts with learning theory brings about a clear resolution of the sometimes obscure relation of learning (engrams) and performance. For example, animal psychology was at one time perturbed by findings like those of Blodgett (1929) that a rat taught at a low level of incentive could, by switching to high incentive on the last occasion, perform as well as another rat run at high incentive throughout the learning. In Equation 11 we are (a) taking only the $D$ terms of Equation 12 and (b) dealing not with the learning as the dependent variable (on the left) but with actual behavior, after learning experience. The learning ($m_{hjkyi} - m_{hjkxi}$) has now been incorporated in a raised $M$ value on the right, since performance is both memory trace (engram) and present motivation, and we have

$$a_{hijky} = b_{hju}s_{hku}E_{ui} + b_{hja}s_{hka}E_{ai}$$
$$+ b_{hjm}s_{hkm}M_i. \qquad (13)$$

The performance is a sum (a product is also possible) of the need, strength, and arousal components with the engramming that has taken place, in what we know takes the form (in broad, common traits) of sentiments, $M$s. Thus, in the rat studies citied, $M$ is the learning; and it has been shown slightly responsive to drive rewards as in Equation 10, relative to frequency of repetitions. This engram deposit is *activated* by the modulator $s_k$.

The empirical evidence for both modulation of sentiments and for their arrangement in factor-order hierarchies is at present thin. Except for experiments by Cattell and Cross (1952), Shotwell, Hurley, and Cattell (1961), and J. R. Williams (1959), only peripherally aimed at these issues, there is no guidance in $P$ technique regarding process effects as such. Regarding the factor order (stratum) issue, there are some more developed and coordinated dynamic studies in $R$ technique. There (see chapter 5, this *Handbook*) the discovery of role factors distinct from general dynamic factors (Delhees, Cattell, & Sweney, 1970; Krug & Cattell, 1971) which are apparently responsive to ambient situations (having $ha$-tied patterns) gives some support to the idea that dynamic behaviors typically yield a hierarchical or fractionated pattern of factors. Thus the behaviors typically involved in a role-factor pattern are also determined by smaller factors, tied to narrow subsets of focal stimuli within the role. In view of the methodological problem that it is difficult in some factor analyses to decide between entirely independent (nonordered) factors loading the same variables in a hierarchical pattern, as distinct from an order hierarchy of factors themselves, it is premature to decide which of these the $R$ technique results better support (with implications of probability for the corresponding $P$ technique analysis).

What the $R$-technique factorings indicate for role action is, however, a helpful illustration at this point. Thus, if we take the teacher role, we recognize that persons who may otherwise have the same personality factors may have different endowments in the teacher-role factor, which we may call $D_1$, and which covers a set of $a$s also affected by personality factors. They will behave differently on being put in front of a class according to whether they possess endowment in teacher role attitudes and skills.

Within this role, however, the teacher's behavior can be modulated, according to whether ambient stimuli having to do with subject matter or class discipline appear in two subsets within the role, which we may call dynamic traits $D_{21}$ and $D_{22}$ (the first expressions are designated 2 because they follow $D_1$) and are equivalent. Next we note that within the area of behavioral problems, a modulating ambient stimulus "general poor order" ($ha_5$) or an outstanding nuisance ($ha_4$) may appear, raising the readiness, respectively, of one of several new subsentiments or sets, $D_{31}$, $D_{32}$, and so forth. The particular strengths of focal stimuli, $a_8$, $a_9$, and $a_{14}$, on that morning, combined with the stimulated (modulated) factor strengths, will decide the sequence of acts. (Note that $D_1$, however, is unlikely to have been strong enough in itself to have provoked, in conjunction with any focal stimulus at that phase, any of the responses now appearing.)

When one emphasizes the trait change (proneness) terms (which are modulable) rather than the fixed traits as we have previously, it is easy to recognize that in the active, modulated form they operate precisely as what, in psychology, have been widely called *mental sets*. Indeed, by the use of the term *dynamic sets*, we have adopted the view that sets are identical with the more fractionated factors found in the sentiment realm. In psychological terms, it is suggested that there may be no sharp line between the larger dynamic traits—at least the *M*s—as now commonly isolated (chapter 5) and a temporary mental set, such as causes us to press the brake pedal (when in the driving seat—the necessary *h*) at a red traffic light, or to wait expectantly for a partner's ace in a game of bridge. A dynamic trait, such as a sentiment to religion or to a career is, by this theory, of the same "stuff" as a mental set, neurologically in behavioral history, but is simply more permanently in action and broader in reference to stimuli. It is essentially a large set that is fractionable, through hierarchies, to many attendant smaller sets.

Even with the ability, temperament, dynamic, and learning experience terms resulting when the preceding equations are combined, we are not at the end of factors needing to be considered. In the domain of temporary states, two classes of unitary dimensions of change have been explored (chapter 5) by *dR* and *P* techniques, namely, *ergic tension states* corresponding one to one to the primary drives, and *general states*, of which anxiety, arousal, regression, elation-depression, fatigue, and alertness are the main instances. Since the latter have only recently been defined with sufficient rigor to lead to batteries constituting relatively pure measures, two important questions in the learning area remain largely unanswered, as follows: Since general states must have some role in learning and recall, over and above that of traits (including dynamic ones) plus reward, what is that role? What is the relation of general states to specific ergic states?

As to the latter, one can see in a general way that what happens to *any* ergic state is able to produce effects on the same general states. Thus, depression can spring from failure of satisfaction in any erg—gregariousness, sex, hunger, and so forth and anxiety from uncertainty of satisfaction (see the APA chart, Fig. 2). Probably, though the second-order factoring of ergic tensions is still inadequate to prove it, arousal or excitement is also a general state correlated with the rise of arousal (ergic tension) in any single erg.

These matters need clarification because important writings, for example, those of K.

W. Spence (1956) and S. B. Sarason (1966) consider anxiety an important general motive in learning, whereas Malmo (1959), Berlyne (1960), Duffy (1962), and others essentially raise arousal to the status of the only general motivator. As far as anxiety is concerned, this writer has developed elsewhere with some precision (in Spielberger, 1966, 1972) a model for anxiety as a derivative of primary ergs, with three main scores, as follows:

$$A = a_e + a_c + a_p. \qquad (14)$$

The component $a_e$ is the contribution from the ergic tension $E$ of the drives being excited, but its effect is augmented by the degree of uncertainty $U$ about the best course of action for satisfaction, as well as the individual's temperamental proneness to fear $F$, that is, his susceptibility to threat. Thus,

$$a_e = E \cdot U \cdot F. \qquad (15)$$

(This has constants and some elaborations in the Spielberger presentation, 1972.) The second component, $a_c$, is what Freud described as the threat to the ego, and which we may operationalize as fear of loss of control, with whatever painful consequences have come from that before. If we consider the personality factors $C$, Ego-strength, $G$, Superego, and $Q_3$, Self-sentiment, to represent the individual's sources of control, then

$$a_c = \frac{1}{(C + G + Q_3) - ka_e}, \qquad (16)$$

where $k$ is a scaling constant. This component of anxiety increases as the ergic tension source of anxiety climbs closer to the strength of the controlling forces.

The third component is theorized to be the threat of definitely known and expected loss or deprivation. One might argue that this is only disappointment or depression, not anxiety. If a man knows *for certain* that he will have a tooth removed tomorrow, it could be that he will experience no anxiety about it; if we argue that he is anxious because there is *always* an element of uncertainty in life, then this formula would merely return us to the $a_e$ component. Social psychology measures, however, tell us that anxiety is higher in people of lower economic resources, and it seems reasonable to add a term for low gratification as an effect of a *certain* loss of satisfaction (as in the case of the dentist), thus:

$$a_p = a_e - S, \qquad (17)$$

where $S$ is the amount of habitual gratification from a course of action. The resulting formulation from substituting in Equation 14 looks complex (though it is simpler than the earlier formulation it replaces in Spielberger):

$$A = 2E \cdot U \cdot F - S + \frac{1}{(C + G + Q_3) - k(E \cdot U \cdot F)}. \qquad (18)$$

In general terms, this is saying that anxiety is a function of the stimulated drive level, of the fear of deprivation, of the degree of cognitive uncertainty regarding suitable action, of certain personality traits that magnify any fear response, and of others that determine degree of control. Anxiety is related to motivation as a complex by-product and not as the whole of motivation. It would indeed be a dreary philosophy that all our acts are generated by anxiety.

Any beneficial role of anxiety, except in sympathetic system conditioning, in learning is questionable. This degradation product of ergic sources is substantially negatively related to school achievement (Cattell & Butcher, 1968). This at least shows that general states have some role as qualifying influences in learning and recall, but nothing can be done theoretically, at the moment, other than being sure to include them in the specification equations, for learning, and for performance after given engram gains. A hypothesis deserving investigation is that one influence of general states is to cause better recall when the profile of state scores in the individual at recall more closely resembles the profile of state scores existing at the time of learning.

If we carefully examine the accumulating evidence on the nature of state dimensions, in both questionnaire and objective (including physiological) test performance, we encounter what seem to be two factors in the area of general arousal and excitation, $U.I.(S)$I being the Universal Index ($U.I.$) number of the Excitation factor and $U.I.(S)5$ and $U.I.(S)6$ of the arousal pattern. The former seems to indicate a general cognitive alertness, shown in low electrical skin resistance, quick reaction time, and so forth, whereas the latter seems more like a hypothalamic and adrenal pattern. The work surveyed by Duffy (1962) and that carried out by Malmo (1959) and others since, seem to suggest a similar division in animal and physiological research into a cortical activation based on the rubrospinal, and a drive arousal based on stimulation of the hypothalamus. We see the first operation in the process of becoming awake, and in the latter, when various emotions are aroused. Though independent in nature, there is bound to be some correlation in action. For example, though activation (Cognitive Excitement, $U.I.(S)1$) is possible without arousal ($U.I.(S)6$), the converse is unlikely to occur (except perhaps under alcohol?).

Of the general states, the levels in arousal

and activation are the most deserving of experimental relation to learning. Although the latter is evidenced to be *general*, we consider the possibility in the next section that it is also possible for a single cognitive area to show a special activation level within a general activation. There is no evidence at present that would negate this possibility.

## 7  DYNAMIC MODEL FOR A PROCESS OR TRACT

Three mechanisms that might account for the rise of structures, such as are found in the sentiments, have been briefly set out. Granted the action of reward, producing changes in the $b$ vector (the linking of behavior with stimuli on the way to goals) and changes in the $s$ vector (the linkage of ergic arousal to subgoal situations), there is no real difficulty in accounting for the rise of such sentiment structures as those to church, school, hobbies, and home. The explanation of the collection of attitude action courses found loaded in the self-sentiment requires a more sophisticated look. But as argued elsewhere (Cattell, 1950c, 1977) a satisfactory explanation is possible under mechanism 5 (section 4 of this chapter), namely, that the preservation and maintenance in good condition of the physical, social, and emotional self is a prerequisite for virtually all other satisfactions. This common concern produces a general factor over the attitudes involved, to the extent that people vary in the perception and acceptance of this ultimate connection.

The personality structure that is more difficult for structured learning theory to account for is that governing persistence with varied means toward any major goal. Reflexological theory has boggled at the very idea. It can account for a chain reflex, but nothing more, and even in insects, as ethologists like McDougall (1932) have pointed out, we see some capacity to depart adjustively from the prescribed sequence.

Let us contrast with an attitude chain, (such as can be followed like a thread through the dynamic lattice, Fig. 5) what we will define as a *tract* of the dynamic lattice. A tract is a section lifted out of the dynamic lattice. Each subgoal situation can be reached (brought to satisfaction) by a combination of courses of action. For example, the subgoal of an adequate bank account can be reached by earning actions and saving actions, and it can be the springboard for several new courses of action (the bank account may lead to better eating or, alternatively, to a vacation).

An initial objection may be raised by some to the whole idea of a model in which there is an apparent predestined coordination of internal readinesses and external sequences. For since such coordination cannot come about by the environmental sequence's being determined by the internal one (as might happen, however, in dreams, or a Berkeleyan universe), one must suppose that the sequence in the animal is an imitation (genetically or by learning) of the external sequence. But surely this last is not difficult to assume, provided the cosmic, environmental sequences are themselves reasonably stable. Granted this tolerable stability and the animal's acquisition of an imitation of the most probable sequence, a rational enquirer, nevertheless, might still doubt that in fact they could mesh together often enough to give satisfaction or survival. The abundance of instances of such coordinations (genetically in the insect and plant world, and by learning in the mammalian world) is surely ample proof that the improbabilities are not so high that they can work together, despite some grief, to insure survival. The hunger in our example may often go supperless; but a model of successive sets, successively trig-

gered, seems capable of supplying sufficient reward.

On closer inspection of the nodes of the lattice (Fig. 5), in Fig. 9 one sees that description of a *subgoal* such as $k_{11}$ actually requires three parts: (a) the consummatory response in the course of action leading up to it, namely, $j_{11}$; (b) the situation created, $k_{11}$ which has a pleasurable arousing effect, by $s_{k11}$ (and in nonviscerogenic drives also some degree of reward, perhaps, other than the pleasurable excitement defined by $s_{k11}$; and (c) an array, of possibly several stimuli, $h_{11.1}$, $h_{11.2}$, etc., which will lead to action if the situational arousal, $s_{k11}E$, before their appearance has been sufficient. The choice among these actions, $h_{11.1}$, $h_{11.2}$, and so forth will depend on the strength of these stimuli. It is likely that this means simply that one or another, in the vicissitudes of the usual environment, will be absent altogether. But if we are to speak of the relative strengths of these stimuli, then we may have to lose the simplicity of supposing all motivation arousal to be $s_k$ and write it $s_{hk}$. That is, the focal stimulus $h$ in the factor model not only determines the response through $b_{hj}$, the executive loading, which represents the goodness of past learning, but also through *some* augmentation, by entering into $s_{hk}$ of the present arousal. Space forbids a digression on that here. We shall contingently consider the action at a node of the lattice as a clearly separated three-part action, (a) of consummatory $j$ experience, (b) drive arousal by the ambient situation $s_kE$, and (c) responsiveness to the $b_{hj}$ values of the newly encountered stimuli.

Now we are defining a tract not as any piece taken at random out of a lattice, but as a part connecting some major situation $K$ with an ultimate goal $G$, (which could be ergic or sentiment based), such that the behavioral alternatives are largely concerned with converging on that goal (Fig. 9). A few

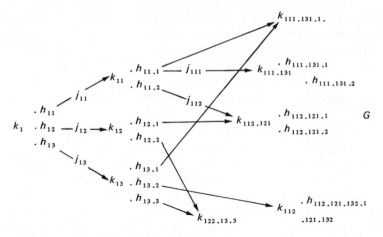

**FIG. 9** A typical tract structure with lattice notation, where $k$ is an ambient situation at a subgoal (as in $s_k$ in the behavioral equation); $h$ is a focal stimulus occurring at or immediately following that goal and provoking course of action $j$ (as in $s_k$ in the behavioral equation); and $j$ is a specific course of action, as in an attitude, test performance, etc. An individual's ($i$) performance is thus the usual score $a_{hijk}$. Not all $j$s have been labeled. Note that each ambient situation $k$ can harbor several stimuli, $h$s, for new courses of action, $j$s. Each $k$ carries the number subscript of the focal stimulus course of action ($h$ and $j$) that led to it. The new stimuli that lead on from it carry this number plus a new digit for the order of those stimuli as attached to the particular $k$. Thus $h_{112}$ means the second stimulus available at ambient situation $k_{11}$, which acquired its number from being the object of the course of action from stimulus $h_{11}$ attached to $k_1$.

subgoals, as in the interrupted lines at the top right and lower left of Fig. 5 may also subsidiate to goals outside the system. But what we mainly have in such a tract is an acquired learning system for going from $K$ to $G$, *despite moderate changes in the environment from time to time, such as would completely ruin any attempt to do so by a simple chain reflex learning*.

We are facing the problem of "persistence toward a goal with varied behavior" that most distinguishes mammalian from insect behavior (Bitterman, 1967; McDougall, 1932) and that simple reflexological learning principles have found baffling. In terms of Fig. 9 the organism can start from $k_1$ and be propelled to $j_{11}$, $j_{12}$, or $j_{13}$ action according to the presence or absence of one or two of these stimuli at the moment. Thereafter, there are again alternatives, but all typically lead to the goal $G$.

The task facing structured learning theory is (a) to describe a machinery that will account for such behavior and (b) to explain its acquisition by learning. Considering the former, one notes that the central problem is the existence at subgoals of an arousal that simultaneously enhances the response potential to several stimuli, $h_1$, $h_2$, and so forth. This means that, in the light of past learning, any one of the action responses from these has been found ultimately to lead to the desired goal. Here the circumstances (of the *presence* of $h_1$, or $h_2$, or $h_3$) are allowed to call the tune. But in the interaction of organism-structure and circumstances there is give and take; for in a second sense, it is the structure that decides the action. It does not, because it provides arousal that is operative only for the three stimuli and no others.

To consider what evidence we have, other

than that of observed actions such as were just described, for the existence of a fairly broad arousal, let us turn to the motivation-strength factorings across many attitudes in research on the dynamic calculus. There we find sufficiently solid evidence for the sentiment patterns—the $M$s in the behavioral equation—but less clear suggestions, mainly in children, for much more fragmentary structures, which appear as substructures within sentiments. If we may be permitted to join scattered clues, we would argue that with narrower attitude variables one would find a factor hierarchy within every sentiment, $M$, consisting of a few subsentiments. These might be labeled $m$s, and so on through attitudes to mental sets, which we will call $t$s, and which are brought in momentarily to meet this and that needed reaction within an attitude. Thus if we brought the behavioral equation from obliquity to a Schmid-Leiman model (Cattell, 1977, chapter 9), the response of, say, turning the steering wheel at a particular corner on the way to a party, would be

$$a_{hijk} = b_{hjx}s_{km}M_{xi} + b_{hjy}s_{ky}m_{yi}$$
$$+ b_{hjz}s_{kz}t_{zi} \qquad (19)$$

(though normally with more than one $M$ and $m$).

Here $M$ would be a general sentiment to enjoying parties, $m$ the concern with journeying to a particular place, and $t$ the set to a particular corner on the journey. (As noted elsewhere, the sets are multiply commanded by many sentiments, as smaller variables often are loaded on many factors.)

At this point, we should recognize the kinship of a tract, as defined previously, to a process. In both there is an overriding purpose guarding the subdevelopments and a prescribed sequence of subsidiated satisfactions. The difference is only one of time

relations, which are not as important as they seem. In a tract of a sentiment to a college education, for example, a person may buy books, attend lectures, and write papers. These are done repeatedly in almost chance order, though in subsidiation terms one buys books to study and perhaps studies to write papers. In a process, however, we have a particular kind of tract in which all action proceeds in a relatively short time and in the subsidiation sequence order. Thus, "driving to a party" requires that gasoline be put in the car before one starts, that the suburb be found before one looks for the particular road, and so on. However, the same pattern of alternative $h$s for a given $m$ prevails, since on reaching the river bridge and realizing with pleasant arousal that he is on the right track, the driver takes one of two available roads on the other side according to the stimulus of which road appears to have less traffic.

It is perhaps in this more simple instance of the process that one can more easily see the dynamics. Our hypothesis is that taking up the goal of a particular sentiment process (or, in an animal, being placed in a familiar start box) produces a rise in excitation level *of the whole aggregate of attitudes*, i.e., the sentiment ($M$), connected at any stage with the unfolding process or tract. If the condition of the initial set of stimuli ($h_{11}$, $h_{12}$, and $h_{13}$ in Fig. 9) sets off action course $j_{11}$ rather than $j_{13}$, then the $k_{11}$ (also $m_{11}$) reached by $j_{11}$, rather than the $k_{13}$ (also $m_{13}$) reached by $j_{13}$, comes to a state of arousal. The explanation of arousal here differs from the reflexological one in a chain reflex, for although we hypothesize that the performance of the act $j_{11}$ is one cause of arousal at $k_{11}$, we also suppose a major part of the arousal coefficient $s_{k11}$ to be due to the path's having previously led to reward.

Thus any action in the process has its strength determined, as Equation 19 shows, partly by the general level strength and arousal of the total acquired sentiment structure $M$, partly by the strength and arousal of a subsentiment, as at $k_{11}$, which we denote $m_{11}$, and partly by some quite specific set, $t_{11x}$, one of the $n$ sets within the course of action $j_{11}$ that is operative in the behavior measure. A general model for reducing the complex S–R data of a process by a meaningful analysis has been presented by this writer (1966e) as *component process analysis* (see Fig. 10).

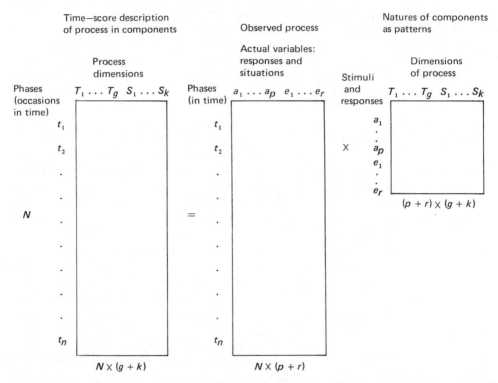

**FIG. 10** Component process analysis: the dimensional description of a process by a factor matrix of stimulus and response data (from $P$ technique). In matrix symbols:

$$S_{pf} = S_{pv} \cdot V_{p \cdot fe}$$

where $S_{pf}$ is the description of a process in terms of scores on factors over time; $S_{pv}$ is the process description in stimulus and response variables; and $V_{p \cdot fe}$ is the factor pattern describing the dimension of the process, that is, the pattern dimensions of change. In the matrices above,

$a_1 \ldots a_p$ = response magnitude measure,

$e_1 \ldots e_r$ = environmental situation magnitude measures, and

$Ts$ and $Ss$ = process component factors largely defined respectively by $a$s and $e$s.

Note, however, that in the $Ts$ (trait patterns of response) there will be some effects on situational stimuli $e$s. Conversely, the situational dimensions, $Ss$, will have some loadings on the responses, $a$s, for which they are partly responsible.

This type of analysis typically takes a group of $N$ people measured on $n$ variables on each of $v$ occasions (steps in a process or successive learning trials). However, it treats the organism as a single entry, either by averaging the $N$ or taking some one person. Variables are then correlated (as relatives) over trials (times, occasions—as referees), and a $P$-technique factoring is used to recognize the dimensions through which the process weaves its way over time. If one proceeds from dimensions to types of curves within these dimensions, as one would in $R$ technique from factor to types of people (in the taxonomy program), the process leads to *component process analysis.*

By contrast, the generalized-learning-curve approach takes only *one* variable (the learning effect that the psychologist decides is of special interest to him) and $N$ people (who are kept as $N$ people), and $v$ occasions (successive learning trials). The correlation is between trials (as relatives) and over people (as referees) and yields factors with a loading pattern extending itself over a series of trials. Component process analysis, on the other hand, has a loading pattern over variables. The confusion of the two has perhaps arisen because both present (in the *Handbook of Multivariate Experimental Psychology*) the analysis of a process into actual graphs of several component curves, each plotted over the same trials and capable of combining to some actual curve. But in the component process analysis, the curves are scores on a given factor for every point in the succession of trials for the average person (or some one person). They state how much that factor curve is dominant in the process at a particular phase of the learning. In Tucker's (1966) generalized-learning curves, on the other hand, a factor score is given to one person on a single variable, for a succession of time points, and it characterizes his performance from beginning to end in that

way. The generalized-learning-curve components thus explain how different people get their own peculiar learning curve forms on one variable. The *proto-processes* of component process analysis, on the other hand, explain how different forces come into effect at different phases of the learning curve, for the average person.

It is the stated aim of component process analysis initially to "discover, recognize and define elements in a process" (Cattell, 1966e, p. 393), but later to group many such proto-processes into natural taxonomic groupings by pattern-similarity coefficients to define the central tendencies in such typical processes as "the process of adolescence," "learning to swim," and "training to become an air pilot." When progress is made in such descriptive analysis, that is, in locating the component processes by component process analysis, we shall begin to be ready for experiments on learning laws. The present dynamic process analysis needs extra features.

## 8  LEARNING DYNAMICS OF A SENTIMENT OPERATING IN A TRACT

The concept of a set, and the variety of experiments thereon, goes back a long way (e.g., Ach, 1910; Aveling, 1926; Michotte). The innovation here is to consider a set as the final splinter factor when factor analyses of motivational measures are carried down to sufficiently small bits of behavior. Thereby what has been found out about sets can be used to illuminate the nature of a sentiment. This makes a sentiment a kind of "dynamic field" in which all perception and action are structured during the time it is in excitation.

The hypothesis is that when certain ambient and focal stimuli are presented, the sentiment $M$ is raised *as a whole*, in all its cognitive and potential action connections, to some enhanced level of excitation. The actual response potential of some action is, as Equation 19 states, a sum of the general sentiment excitation, plus that of the subsentiment $m$, determined by consummation of act $j_{11}$ and the presence of the new ambient situation $k_{11}$, plus the effect of a particular focal stimulus $h_{11.1}$. Parenthetically, if the psychologist wants to keep all the arousal in one term, he could reconstruct Equation 19 (omitting $t$ for simplicity):

$$a_{hijk} = b_{hj(xy)}(s_{kx}M_{xi} + s_{ky}m_{yi}) \qquad (20)$$

Herein the expression in parentheses would be the full motivation, and $b_{hj}$ would be the expression of what stimulus $h$ makes out of that motivation in producing course of action $j$.

The way Equation 20 would be reached factorially would need some statistical digression, but a more important statistical digression needs to be made at this point to ask how the *ordinary* formulation in Equation 19 is reached. There is an experimental difficulty here, obscure but not to be bypassed. By hypothesis, $j_{111}$ and $j_{112}$ in Fig. 9 have a common motivation from $m_{11}$, that is, ($s_{k11}m_{11}$ actually) but they are alternatives, determined by the relative strengths of $h_{111}$ and $h_{112}$ and incapable of occurring together. If we seek by factor-analytic methods to discover this structure, using frequencies or strengths of $j_{111}$ and $j_{112}$ as measures, we should find that both would be positively loaded on a factor due to $m_{11}$s being unitary, but loaded with the opposite sign on a second, situational factor $S$, which expresses the positive scoring relation of $j_{111}$ and $j_{112}$, as shown in Table 1. It is assumed that the correlations are obtained in the case of $R$ technique by repeated runs for each person, so that graded frequency scores can be

**TABLE 1** Factor pattern generated by two alternative behavioral expressions from a common arousal source, provoked by alternative stimuli

| Response | Factors | |
| --- | --- | --- |
| | $M_{11}$, strength of arousal | $S$, stimulus prevailing at the time |
| $a_{j_{111}}$ | .5 | −.5 |
| $a_{j_{112}}$ | .5 | .5 |

*Note.* Product of 2 rows = observed $r$ between responses $a_{j_{111}}$ and $a_{j_{112}}$ = 0.

obtained for the two expressions, and similarly if $P$ technique is used.

With such reasonable examples of loadings as are presented, it will be seen that the observed correlation could be negligible, and in this case is actually zero. Nevertheless a good factor analysis could reveal the $m$ structure, which is shown as a factor here. Alternatively, measures of the *latent*, rather than the actual, expression of $m$ could be taken, for example, galvanic skin responses to threats to the interests it covers.

Obviously, structured learning theory needs to check this hierarchical hypothesis of $t$s within $m$s within an $M$ as soon as possible, to discover how it is generated by learning. There is a little difficulty in accepting the distal creep in the lattice of both response magnitudes (expressed by $b$s and attached to specific stimuli) and arousal magnitudes (expressed by $s_k$s and attached to subgoal situations), as described in section 5, on the elemental learning processes. Regardless of whether $j_{111}$ or $j_{112}$ is used, the ambient situation of the subgoal $k_{11}$ has led to ultimate satisfaction and becomes endowed with the sum of the reward effects of $j_{111}$ and $j_{112}$. It thus has a unitary nature, in stimulating a subsentiment $m_{11}$, as shown by the factor $M_{11}$ in Table 1.

If the structure and nature of sentiment,

subsentiment, and set are the same, except for size, then we are saying that as the individual confronts $K_1$ (Fig. 5), the sentiment excitation of $M$ as a whole is brought into action. In humans there is no difficulty in conceiving this $K$ stimulus. A person says, "Today is a good day for my hobby of sailing, and I will take off" (or for working on my thesis, or whatever). The conceptual scope of the human symbolic thought processes activates forthwith (though perhaps with some warming up) the whole cognitive-emotional $M$ system having to do with sailing. An $m$ system concerned with choice of sails to hoist follows, and the $j$s are decided by such stimuli ($h$s) as the sails available in the locker and the forecast of wind. In the animal, a total $M$ excitation may be harder to demonstrate; but, by hypothesis, when the rat is put in the familiar starting box, some excitation of a cognitive system, covering all doors and turnings to be met, arises.

At this point the enquiring mind of the reader may turn to the important, but rarely discussed, question of the relation of unitary sentiments to unitary abilities. The gross fact revealed by research is that they factor out as distinct entities but, except for a study by Horn (1972b), there is no evidence that they modulate in a unitary way. The career, hobby, religion, home, and other sentiments factor out in dynamic trait measurements and the primary abilities—verbal, numerical, and so forth—factor out of ability performances. Yet, as brought out with more detailed illustration elsewhere (Cattell, 1971b) there must be systematic relations of the cognitive-ability unities constituted by sentiments and those ability unities we know through factor analysis. In the last resort, we must regard, say, numerical ability, as a dynamic set that can be turned on in the service of any sentiment. Reflections such as these cause us not to abandon the otherwise-unpromising notion of later sets being turned on (modulated) by an accumulating line of connections from earlier $s$s, rather than reverberations of $M$s per se. In any case, we are reminded that the stuff of abilities is not so different from that of dynamic traits and may indeed be close to what we measure through integrated motivation components.

A question concerning the excitation of a sentiment and its parts, which remains virtually untouched, experimentally, is whether a sentiment excitation and an ergic arousal are the same. Formerly we attached an $s_k$ to a sentiment just as we do to an erg, because experimental evidence (Cattell & Child, 1975; Horn & Sweney, 1970) clearly shows that the various part expressions of $M$ vary from occasion to occasion precisely in the same way as those of an erg, as *its* ergic tension level changes. (Incidentally, this discovery that a sentiment is not a fixed strength was a surprise, since the literature of dynamic structure and attitudes places these in a *fixed traits* category.) But we have claimed a distinction to exist between a discovered factor (in $R$ technique) which seems to be activation, as a sort of cognitive alertness and excitation, and another representing ergic arousal; and we have brought this distinction into line with neurological concepts.

An answer to this ventured elsewhere (Cattell & Child, 1975) is that arousal shows itself in the $U$ (unintegrated) component in objective motivation tests, and activation excitement in the $I$ (integrated) component. However, we have speculated alternatively in this chapter that $U$ and $I$, respectively, are the internal viscerogenic and the external, arousal components in ergic tension. However, the variety of factors found in motivation-component analysis—some seven primaries in all—is enough to provide both angles of analysis (within ergs and between ergs and sentiments) with an available empirical answer in terms of known factors, when the experiment gets around to using relatively pure batteries for the components.

The present writer (though not all of his colleagues in dynamic calculus research) favors the theory that ergs and ergic arousal are *both* expressed in the *U* component, and sentiment strength and activation in the *I* component measures. If this should be confirmed, the difference between the internal, appetitive tension of an erg, which rewards when reduced, and the arousal product thereof through external stimulation, may have to be sought in the general state of arousal, which can be pleasant. It would be measured in a general state (perhaps associated neurologically with the pleasure center of Olds, 1958, and others) which could be a derivative of *any* ergic tension, and perhaps definable as a second-order factor among the ergic primaries. Until these structures are clarified and rendered validly measurable as distinct factors, the dynamics of learning is bound to remain in a patchwork of unconfirmable and speculative models.

## 9  SUMMARY

This chapter has attempted to sketch the essentials of radically new concepts in learning theory. To do so in restricted space it has had, on the one hand, to leave some loose ends and, on the other, to assume perhaps somewhat more knowledge of multivariate techniques and results than the student in learning commonly has. (The latter difficulty is remediable, however, through other chapters in this book.) The main points follow:

1. A reorientation of thinking is necessary at the outset because of historical fixations of existing texts in assiduous application of the reflexological model, and in a disproportionate concentration on animal-learning problems. The reorientation involves (a) concern with explaining the personality structures as known in personality theory, (b) recognizing the new explanatory measures offered by the dynamic calculus, and (c) considering learning as a structural change in the behavior equation (tri-vector theory), rather than merely as performance gain.

2. To investigate learning per se it is necessary to begin with clearer taxonomic distinctions than have commonly been made between learning and other kinds of change, notably the changes defined as *transformation* and *volution*. Within learning the following varieties are recognized at the descriptive level: co-ex learning (coexcitation), means-end learning (operant conditioning, CRII), integration learning (a dynamic concept), and goal satisfaction transformation (sublimation). (CRI is regarded as a combination of co-ex and means-end learning.) The first two can be studied, as they have been, on single stimulus response variables, but the others, and eventually the first two, require multivariate approaches.

3. Structured learning may be comprehensively defined as concerned with relating multidimensional changes in an organism to a multidimensional learning situation. The dimensions are represented by values in vectors of (a) demonstrated unitary traits and states in the organism; (b) executive (behavioral index) *b* loadings in the behavior-specification equation; (c) modulator indexes, *s*s, in the specification equation representing environmental effects; and (d) ergic tensions, arousal and excitation (activation) measures, time, and frequency values in the learning experience.

4. The step to any dynamic or other explanation cannot be made until description of behavior in being is tolerably complete. The description of a single response is made by the behavioral equation involving three vectors described in item 3. The description of an ongoing process, or tract in the dynamic lattice, requires matrices of sequences of such specification *b*s and *s*s.

5. A halfway model to full structured learning, useful as a teaching device and in practical calculations restricted to evidence on the personality vector changes, is available in experience process analysis (EPA) matrices. It provides a comprehensive system for indexing paths in an adjustment process, and learning laws linking frequency of path transits to changes in an individual's *T* vector. As indicated, its restriction is omission of the *b* and *s* vectors.

6. The full structured learning model has to begin with the mechanisms of learning regardless of whether they apply to atomistic reflexes or the more structured developments in personality theory. Co-ex and CRI learning are accepted as *partly* responsible for *s* changes, but means-end (CRII) rewarded learning is considered major in *s, b,* and *T* changes. The classical conception of reward as drive reduction is found inadequate, because it is paradoxical. Instead, a distinction is made between internally generated appetitive *need*, disturbing in its rise and rewarding in its decline, and an *arousal state* that is a product of stimulation of need by subgoals, which previously led to drive reduction. A weighted composite of need and arousal emotion is hypothesized to account both for the response behavior and, with perhaps different weightings, for the amount of learning. Every experience has a declining cognitive reverberation, and the amount of engramming of the stimulus-response connection is a function of the residual reverberation at the time of reward and the magnitude of that reward.

7. Granted such mechanisms capable of explaining learning of *any* element of behavior, the special contribution of structured learning theory is accounting for the rest of the known personality structures, that is, for their unitary pattern character, as trait or process. The trait unity is explained by three principles active in diverse situations: (a) the impact of attachment to social institutions, each of which later provides a reinforcement schedule for a particular set of behaviors, and which, being greater in more attached people, develops a factor in individual-difference correlations; (b) the *agency* effect, as described in developing patterns of ability and corresponding approximately to the stimulus generalization concept in reflexological learning, and (c) the *investment* effect, understandable in terms of the tenet of structured learning that the learning equation must include the effect of existing traits in a person. A new unitary pattern can then arise by investment of a major existing unitary pattern, as in the case of crystallized intelligence arising from fluid intelligence. This question of the growth of structure was examined from some interesting angles by Baltes, Nesselroade, and Cornelius (1976).

8. As with traits, so with processes: Structure has to be described before it can be explained. A process and a tract out of the dynamic lattice are similar except for more rigid time sequence in the former, and they generally represent the functioning of what has been located in individual-difference factors as a sentiment, *M*. It is hypothesized that a sentiment is actually a factor hierarchy going down through subsentiment factors to attitudes and to sets.

Any action that is typically at a *set* level is to be estimated by a Schmid-Leiman type of behavioral equation, in which strengths of $M$, $m$ (subsentiment), and $t$ (set) make a combined contribution. In a *process* beginning with activation of the given sentiment, this structure is capable of explaining (as a chain reflex is not) persistence toward a goal with varied direction of effort. The excitation of different $m$s by different ambient situations (subgoals) and of responses by different stimuli produce a coordination suitable for the stimuli and ambient situations that happen to turn up.

9. The theory supposes that a situation which touches off one part of a sentiment tends to cause a rise in excitation of the whole: that recognized in the $s_{kx}M_x$ term. It occurs similarly for $m$s and $b$s. The acquisition of this capacity of a situation to evoke the whole sentiment excitation, through learning experiences, depends on a cognitive activation principle, spreading effects to the boundaries of the sentiment system; and this is not yet fully understood.

In learning, the engramming (committing to memory) is measured by the resulting $M$ terms, but the actual performance on any occasion is given by a behavior equation involving both $E$ (ergic tension) and $M$ terms. A correct assessment of the amount of learning ($bsM$ terms) is consequently impossible from immediately observed behavior unless the $E$s are independently known or assessed.

Since more than one course of action can subsidiate to one subgoal (ambient situation), the index numbering of that ambient situation $k$ must include both. The ancestry of subsidiating attitudes can thus lead by the third subgoal to as many subscripts as a child has great-grandparents—or more. The notation could therefore get cumbersome, but some complexity is realistically necessary, and when quantitative analyses of the dynamic lattice are made by path coefficients, these identifying numbers are part of the calculation procedures. They are also psychologically meaningful in tracing the learning sources of various behaviors.

# Section

# 4

# The Sociological Domain of Personality

## Personality and Culture:
### General Concepts and Methodological Problems

Since comparison is the great generator of scientific ideas, there can be little doubt that the study of personality could have been greatly enriched by the access of activity in cross-cultural research that began in the last decades. Incidentally, much of this research, notably that on attempts to quantify culture patterns as such (Cattell, 1950d; Cattell, Breul, & Hartmann, 1952; Cattell & Gorsuch, 1965; Gibb, 1956) is simultaneously a contribution also to social psychology, per se. However, the question of how much of the impressive volume of *personality* cross-cultural research will remain as a permanent contribution has been critically raised by several psychometrists, notably by Humphreys, by Cattell, and by J. Mc V. Hunt.

The criticism centers on the logical argument that when numerical comparisons are made between cultures—and all comparisons are implicitly numerical—there must be proof (a) that the concept measured is the same and (b) that the scale units are comparable. For example, one might ask, Is there a unitary concept of intelligence applicable to the inhabitants of the Congo and of New York City? If so, can one construct a test (or mode of observation) that is equally valid (or two tests that are equally valid) for these populations? Last, by what means can one cross calibrate or obtain common scale units by which comparisons could be evaluated validly?

Obtaining answers to these questions has seemed to many psychologists to offer such insuperable difficulties that they have shunned the whole area of cross-cultural research. Yet Section 4 of this *Handbook* has somehow to come to terms with this potentially rich area of insights into personality. Furthermore, it needs to be said that a psychology built up only in one culture is a travesty of science. The concepts of science, by the nature of science, must be international and universal. A generalization about anxiety or intelligence should apply to an identical, or exactly translatable concept, even though, as in any other science, one would expect a law of action to take into account the local data—in this case, the particular cultural setting.

Most psychological concepts are patterns, that is, complex multivariate relationships among observed elements; this is true regardless of whether we speak of traits or of processes. It is encouraging in cross-cultural comparisons of psychological concepts to reflect that the great majority of conceptual patterns, being patterns of covariation (over individual differences, over growth increments, or over rises and declines in a process pattern) can be examined and tied down as uniquely determined simple-structure factors. And, to date, it is in these terms that the most substantial logical and psychometric success has so far been reached by the psychologists (Baltes & Nesselroade, 1970; Cattell, 1957a, 1969; Nesselroade & Reese, 1973) who have attempted to answer the crucial questions posed by the critics of cross-cultural research. Parenthetically, the issues are not confined to cross-cultural research; they only become more apparent there. The problem of operational identity of concept and of scaling units actually arises in every comparison of social sub-groups, of groups at different ages (Nesselroade & Reese, 1973), and so on.

The answer suggested by the present writer (Cattell, 1957a, 1969) is that identity of concept must rest on either one of two bases: (a) an actual identity of factor, in the sense that an identical source of variance, for example, a source trait, can be shown to produce the two observed loading patterns, granted the two populations and situations; (b) an identity of class, as when we say that all hats are hats, because greater pattern resemblance can be found among the members, though not necesarily very high, than exists between any of them and members of another set of objects. It was on this second basis that Izard (see chapter 20) began his research on transcultural emotion concepts, though he has now begun to apply factor-analytic procedures. The particular set of statistical operations by which identities of either the factor or class type can be tested are not discussed here. They can be studied in a series of psychometric developments elsewhere (Ahmavaara, 1954; Cattell, 1944, 1945, 1966h; Cattell & Cattell, 1955; Fischer & Roppert, 1965; Meredith, G. M., 1967; Sixtl, R., 1964; Tucker, 1951).

Once an acceptable identity by the con-factor rotation and matching procedures has been reached, there remains the problem of achieving comparable score units. The principle proposed (Cattell, 1969) for handling this has been called the *isopodic principle* and has the aim (as the name denotes) of putting both the factor weights and the variable scores to which they apply *on an equal footing* in the two cultures. The equipotency of the weighting systems is easily achieved, but achieving comparability of scores on the variable scales is more difficult and requires recourse either to the *relational-simplex* or the *conormalization* principle (Cattell, 1970a) for obtaining equal interval scaling.

No actual research has yet observed these requirements, and the critic is entitled to doubt that any existing cross-cultural evidence offers more than an approximation to the statement of differences between cultures. Nevertheless, attempts to observe these principles have been made first, in the ability field, by such researches as Vandenberg's (1959) comparison of primary mental abilities between American and Chinese cultures, and McArthur and Elley's (1963), Rodd's (1958), Cattell's (1969), and Weiss' (1968) studies of the structure of general intelligence in culturally different groups. In the personality field, a check on the factor structure of personality in the questionnaire domain, with respect to the whole series of Factors $A$ through $Q_4$ has now been carried out over an impressive array of cultures— American, Australian, English, French, German, Indian, Italian, Japanese, Mexican, Portuguese-Brazilian, and so forth. (See Cattell, Eber, & Tatsuoka, 1970; Tsujioka &

Cattell, 1965a.) In some, only one study or only a second-order study has been made, and there is no doubt that sytematic follow ups are called for, with suitably refined matching techniques. But enough has been done to show the following at a high level of confidence: (a) The same number and nature of factors is present across most cultures, that is, "human nature is primarily the same"; (b) any one factor, nevertheless, has what appears to be a significant difference in some areas of expression, for example, in the Dominance, $E$ factor, loading pattern in Italy and the United States (see Cattell, Eber, & Tatsuoka, 1970; Lynn, 1971 on scores); (c) quite substantial and, by ordinary tests, significant differences of *level* on almost half the known factors exist between at least half of the cultures so far compared. These last have been incorporated in various theories of cultural dynamics.

More recently data have begun to appear from *objective* (nonquestionnaire; see chapter 4, this *Handbook*) measures of personality factors, notably from a comparison on about 80 identical behavioral subtests of American, German, and Japanese children (Cattell, Schmidt, & Pawlik, 1973). Here again the factor structure itself is surprisingly similar. For example, General Inhibition (*U.I.* 17), Anxiety (*U.I.* 24), Regression (*U.I.* 23), Exuberance (*U.I.* 21), and so forth, appear across the three studies with a high matching index significance (Schneewind & Cattell, 1970).

It would therefore seem only a matter of time and application before the means are available—in the form of comparable batteries in different countries with known loadings on the same source traits—for cross-cultural studies on primary personality factors and on such ergic (emotional) factors as in the Motivation Analysis Test and the School Motivation Analysis Test. (Tests at the school level are desirable because true samples of a population are hard to get at a later age). The possibilities of illumination of personality-dynamic, familial-developmental, and group-dynamic theories that arise once a soundly comparable measurement theory and practice exist, would be hard to overestimate.

# 19

# Personality and Culture: The Family

Theo Herrmann
Aiga Stapf
*University of Marburg, Germany*

## 1 INTRODUCTION: FAMILY AND PERSONALITY

Family influence is one of the most important environmental influences on personality. This fact can hardly be disputed. It seems all the more strange that the development of theories and models concerned with family influence have not progressed sufficiently. Older global theories have serious scientific weaknesses. Ogburn's defunctionalization theory (Ogburn, 1955), Freud's psychoanalytic concepts, and Zimmerman's cyclical theory (Zimmerman, 1949) are often profound but relatively sterile, insofar as testable hypotheses are concerned. A year's sampling, for example, of recent issues of the *Journal of Marriage and the Family* revealed only one reference to Freud, and that in an article on psychotherapy; none to Ogburn; and only two articles, one by Zimmerman, in which Zimmerman's theory is mentioned. On the other hand, Parson's theories of structure-function (Parson, T., & Bales, 1955) applied to the family have yielded research fruit, but leave much to be desired from a multivariate analysis standpoint.

While lacking valid theories and models for the most part, we are at the same time confronted with a vast amount of empirical data that cannot yet be integrated theoretically into the existing body of knowledge, as discussed by Herrmann, Stapf, and Deutsch (1975). Present research relating family influence on personality collects data unrelentingly, thus falsifying a good deal of the global theories of the first half of our century. But at the same time present research tries as well to save parts of those earlier theories by modifying them (e.g., Sears, R. R., Maccoby, & Levin, 1957, and Sears, R. R., Rau, & Alpert, 1965).

The newly created theories are still mainly descriptive; they result mostly in empirical constructs (see chapter 1). Thus, factor-analytical investigations show dimensions of parental style of socialization (Coan, 1966). Still no theory explains satisfactorily how parental style of socialization works, or respectively, how—*in concreto*—it forms certain personality traits in the child (Herrmann, 1966).

Family influence on personality has as yet not been integrated in a concrete form in Cattell's VIDA (Vector-Id-Analysis) Model (chapter 1). Research on this subject, for instance, could try to detect various dimensions of syntality of a child's family as environmental variables and the relations of these syntality dimensions to properties of the child and of the adult later on.

Present and future theories of family influences ought to consider at least two aspects: (a) theory formation has to keep up an optimal level of abstraction in respect to what is to be understood by family. A theory of family influence can neither be valid for all families without exception, nor only for some or a single family (e.g., the Jones family). Theories of family influence in relation to personality research should be restricted to the most common and ordinary (modal) type of family in our culture. Moreover, (b) theory formation in all cases has to consider family influence itself to be a highly complex multivariate system. (The two aspects are pointed out here.)

G. C. Homans (1950) concluded that marriage is the most successful of all human institutions. If so, the same applies to the family. For all we know, the family is universal—that is, the family exists in every known culture. However, Murdock (1949) pointed out that only 25% of all cultures known to us show that type of family common to western culture. The prevalent type of family in western culture is the kernel family (Parsons, "nuclear family"; Zimmerman, "atomistic family"). This type of family encompasses two generations: a man, his wife, and their mutual children. (There may be, of course more relatives belonging to the family, but the family is already "complete" without them.) The kernel family has developed out of the extended family, the "clan family" (see Zimmerman, 1949, "trustee family"). The clan family, as sometimes found in our culture, expecially in the rural regions, is of a complex construction; it consists in general of three generations: parents of one parent, parents, and children, together with a certain number of further relatives, the latter also being regular members of the

family (e.g., mother's brother). (Benedict, 1949; Myrdal, 1945).

The complete supersession of the clan family by the kernel family is not yet concluded. Many in-between stages exist. But in western culture, and especially in urban regions, the kernel family is the typical (modal) type of today's family (Cattell, 1950c; Parsons, T., & Bales, 1955; etc.). The kernel family as a rule lives in spatial isolation from the family of the parents (neolocism); selectivity in marriage is decreasing (gradual abolition of "marriage bars"); the family is economically independent of relatives; the dependency on neighborhood is also declining; there are almost no economic interactions between the members of the family (i.e., the family does not function as a production unit); the social status of the family depends extensively on the father's job; many former family functions have been delegated to institutions outside the family (e.g., food production, teaching of children); and family members have more opportunities for emotional satisfaction outside the family. Discussion of family influence in respect to personality research refers mostly to this modern type of family, the kernel family (e.g., Cattell, 1950c; Homans, 1950; Parsons, T., & Bales, 1953; Riesman, 1950).

According to T. Parsons (1955), the main task of the family in our culture is to be " 'factories' which produce human personalities." On the one hand, the human being usually receives his genetic constitution from the family in which he grows up; on the other hand, his family is his first environment. The family is the model of the culture and of the society he is growing into; it is the mediator between culture and individual.

Psychology describes the family primarily as that part of the environment in which the growing individual is being socialized. Socialization is a specific "interactional process whereby a person's behavior is modified to conform with expectations held by members of the group to which he belongs" (Secord & Backman, 1964). In his family the child learns the attitudes, opinions, and value orientations most important to him, which will become foundational for his life as an adult. Moreover, here he receives his physical care and education and training important to adjustment to his special culture (Parsons, T., 1955). A child will develop his self-concept in later life through the role (see chapter 17) he takes on in the family. (See, among others, Miller, D. R., & Swanson, 1958; Parsons, T., & Bales, 1955; Secord & Backman, 1964). These few cursory references demonstrate the complexity of the subject of family influence. We do not yet have a reliable psychological taxonomy of family influence. We therefore suggest a rough classification in the subsections following.

To begin with, since Galton we know of the existence of regular connections, as were suspected, between traits of an individual and traits of other members of his family, especially those of his parents, since the members of a family are bound by heredity. (For reference, see chapters 1, 12–14, 16, and 24). We know, for example, that the source-trait "general intelligence versus mental defect" ($B$) covaries with the intelligence of the parents. Part of the common variance of this trait of parent and child is due to heredity. But it is necessary to stress that not all "nonenvironmental" contributions to personality are identical with heredity. Cattell (1953b), Cattell, Blewett, and Beloff (1955), Cattell, Stice, and Kristy (1957), Anastasi and

Foley (1948). J. L. Fuller and Thompson (1960), and many others have pointed out the complex interactions between heredity, environment, and special "nonenvironmental" as well as "nonheredity" determinants. In this way the development of the individual is determined by mutations, by segregation of genes, by properties acquired in the uterus, by alteration of body state through life experience, and by stages of "structural development" (Anastasi, 1958), together with heredity and general environment. If, for example, the family atmosphere is favorable to the development of the individual's verbal intelligence, part of this atmosphere might be a direct result of a high verbal intelligence of the parents. It is, moreover, quite possible that a parent's educational effort is being reinforced by the child's rapid development. But this development may also be due to heredity. It becomes apparent at this point that parents and family do not function solely as pure environmental influence; we always have to consider the previously mentioned interactions as well.

Thus, if family influence is regarded as *environmental* influence, that is to say, if we do not consider the interactions with heredity and with some other determinants, the following classification seems appropriate.

## 1.1 Family Influence as Mediator of Social, Cultural, and Epochal Influences

The family determines the individual as mediator of social, cultural, and epochal influences (Leslie, 1967). If, for instance, a family belongs to the protestant middle class, the mere *belonging* of the child's family to this specific subculture (confession) and to this specific social class will influence the child in a specific way (Waters & Crandall, 1964). (Cultural influences on the individual are only of interest here insofar as they are mediated by the family.) This aspect of family influence is so important that the next major section is devoted to it.

## 1.2  Influence of "Family Character" (Syntality)

Families may be understood as "personalities" just as individuals can be described as personalities (Cattell, 1950c, Cattell & Stice, 1960; Cattell & Wispe, 1948; also chapter 1). In this case families are understood as unanalyzed units, without considering the single members and the relations between these family members. According to Cattell and Wispe (1948), syntality covers dynamic, temperamental, and ability traits of the group that influence the child. For instance, relations are found between differences of families on the syntality dimension "democratic-authoritarian" and specific properties of the children of these families.

## 1.3  Influence of Family Structure

Here, the family is not considered as an unanalyzed unit, but rather the influence of the family on the child is described by means of role-, rank-, and interaction-structure of the family (family as "unitas multiplex"). For instance, large and small families, or patriarchal, matriarchal, and equalitarian families differ with respect to their influence on the child's growing personality. This principle applies as well to the role and the ordinal position which the child takes in the family (oldest sister, youngest brother, etc.). Role and position determine, to a considerable extent, the

development of the child's personality. Section 3 takes up in detail the respective influences of family character and family structure.

## 1.4  Family Influence as Defined by the Personalities of Single Socialization Agents

Families and their influence on the socialization of the child can differ in respect to important personality traits of representative family members (as examples, families in which the father is excessively dependent, or the mother is emotionally immature and submissive, etc.).

## 1.5  Family Influence as Defined by Parental Attitudes and Child-rearing Techniques

A person's family background can be described in respect to dominant parental attitudes and specific child-rearing techniques. For instance, the parental style of socialization may be cold and rejecting, or warm and accepting; families with early and strict toilet- and modesty-training may differ in respect to their influence on the child from families with different techniques, etc. Section 4, the concluding portion of this chapter, details these family influences.

The interaction of the five modes of family influences (as environmental influences) on the shaping of personality is shown in Fig. 1. (Only a few of the important hypothetical interactions are symbolized by arrows.)

## 2  THE MEDIATION OF SOCIAL, CULTURAL, AND EPOCHAL INFLUENCES

At this point we elaborate on the first of the family influence factors. "Individuals

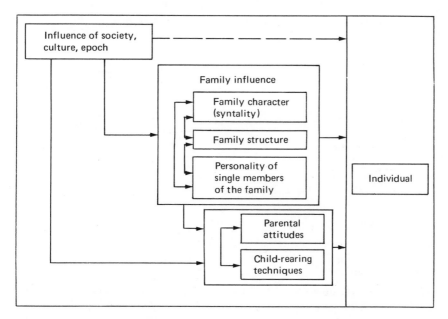

**FIG. 1** Modes of description of family influence.

who share a set of values, beliefs, practices, and information, and who pass these views from one generation to the next, constitute a culture." This definition given by R. C. Johnson and Medinnus (1965, p. 175) shows the functioning of the family as a mediator. According to T. Parsons and Bales (1955), who speak for authorities in the field, the "internalization of the culture of the society" takes place mainly in the family (see also Bronson, W. L., Kalten, & Livson, 1959; Lippitt & Radke, 1946; Rosen, B. C., & D'Andrade, 1959).

Using the example of achievement motive, McClelland, in *The Achieving Society* (1961), developed a theory of the relations of culture, family, and personality. According to the German sociologist Max Weber (1930) close connections exist between the ethics of Protestantism (especially of Calvinism) and the spirit of the modern capitalistic system of economics. Both Protestant faith and capitalistic ideology agree that the individual should trust

neither in God's nor man's mercy but instead rely only on himself. In our world it is important to achieve and succeed by one's own effort. Empirical investigations such as those of Marian R. Winterbottom (1958) find a strong achievement motive in sons of parents who stress early parental socialization for independence and individual initiative. McClelland and his co-workers found manifold evidence of these facts with Protestant parents (see the critique by Triandis, Malpass & Davidson, 1973). Weber's hypothesis and these empirical results are integrated by McClelland in a theory demonstrated in the accompanying simple diagram (Fig. 2).

Max Weber's hypothesis refers to the connection of two aspects of a culture: religious and economic ideology (A → D). For one thing, McClelland's theory refers to the familial and personal mediation between these two cultural aspects (A → B → C → D). For another, the theory describes at the same time how family

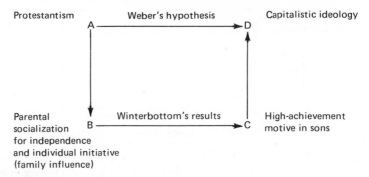

FIG. 2 McClelland's theory of the relations among Protestant ethic, capitalism, independence training, and achievement motivation.

influence (parental socialization) mediates between a cultural aspect (Protestantism) and an individual personality trait (need for achievement) $(A \rightarrow B \rightarrow C)$.

We must point out, however, that these connections are normally modified by several other variables. Thus, for example, Protestantism has different consequences in middle-class families than it has in working-class families. The vertical mobility of a family is also of importance: Catholic middle-class families with a tendency for social ascension act more "Protestant" (that is to say, they evoke more achievement motive in their children) than Protestant families of the working-class without social mobility (Rosen, B. C., & D'Andrade, 1959).

Since in western culture individuals are hardly at all "tradition-directed" and less and less "inner-directed" (Riesman, 1950), it will probably become more and more difficult to confirm interdependencies as described by McClelland's theory. Today's norms and values residing in "other-directed" persons are subject to quick change. Many families are on their way from one subculture (e.g., the subculture of social class) to another. Fewer and fewer cultural patterns of norms and fewer concrete behavioral patterns are constant

enough to be handed down from parents to children. We can hardly look on children as the "followers" of their parents. In most cases parents are only able—if at all—to send their children on their way with hazy principles and little concrete advice for behavior (as in the 19th century "The Good Boy's Soliloquy" and "The Good Girl's Soliloquy" [Arnold, 1969]). Thus, Riesman's "inner-directed" individual was developed, living and acting in accordance with abstract value orientations that were mediated in the family. But, as Riesman stressed, the transference of merely abstract normative patterns from parents to children is no longer possible in some social groups. Thus, for the "other-directed" individual, the family scarcely functions as mediator of general cultural norms. In his case, the family is merely able to start him off in life with trivial advice, expecting him only to be well-liked and well-adjusted. The "other-directed" individual no longer lives according to continuous and consistent social normative patterns. He tries, rather, many mercurial adjustments to the normative patterns of that specific social group to which he belongs temporarily. Ruth Benedict (1934) stressed the point of our living in a "discontinuous" culture": In their families children are learning a social role they hold only while they are children, one which they do not keep in later adult life.

The rapid changes of cultural normative patterns are made evident by a comparison between the ideology of the contemporary modal family in the United States and the former "frontier" ideology (Turner, 1921), or by comparing the contemporary German modal family with the German "post war family" (Schelsky, 1954). Looking farther back, the differences appear to be even greater: During the first half of the 16th century, European parents of higher social ranks gave their children a book to read by Erasmus of Rotterdam (his "Colloquia"), which contained among other things a dialogue between a young man and a prostitute and hints at venereal diseases (Muchow, 1962). This kind of reading was quite in agreement with normative patterns of child-rearing in those days. (Erasmus dedicated this book to a 6-year-old child, his godson).

The quick changing of norms may also be seen by the following results: A. Davis and Havighurst (1946) at the close of World War II found that middle-class families bring up their children more harshly and inhibit the child's impulses earlier than do lower-class families. Only a short time later Maccoby and Gibbs (1954) came to rather contrary conclusions. D. R. Miller and Swanson (1958), Bronfenbrenner (1961), Ewert (1966), and others believe that such diverse results may be accounted for partly by the rapid alterations of normative patterns in child rearing. Reasons for these quick alterations may be found in the influence of mass media and in the "scientific approach" to education, which is quite usual today. Diverse results might be interpreted as reflecting the fact that normative child-rearing patterns of the

typical middle-class family are being accepted by lower-class families and partly even exaggerated.

Research on the mediation of normative patterns in the family is being complicated not only by the quick changes of traditional normative patterns and value orientations, but by the leveling process between social strata, between town and country, between religious groups, and by the interactions of different attributes of social groups and epochal conditions. Nevertheless, it is still possible today to differentiate between many if not most families in respect to which group they belong, and which specific group norms and value orientations they mediate to their children's developing personality.

We mentioned the problem of religious orientation earlier in connection with the research of McClelland. D. R. Miller and Swanson (1958) also found—in the lower classes—more Protestants than Catholics who are so-called "entrepreneurial" parents (the opposite would be "bureaucratic" in this case). These parents prefer to rear their children to be self-reliant, independent, and risk-taking. However, the authors could not confirm these differences between religious orientations in the middle class. Herrmann (1966; Herrmann, Schwitajewski, & Ahrens, 1968) compared German Catholics and Protestants and found, through questionnaire data, more severe child-rearing practices in Catholic mothers. They give less support to their children and tend to inquisitorial behavior patterns. (A typical statement: "Parents must know their children's most secret thoughts.")

We have also stressed the point that research work on differences in family influences in respect to belonging to different social classes does not always lead to corresponding results (Ewert, 1966). Yet it may be expected according to work by Himmelweit (1955), Douvan (1956), R. R. Sears, Maccoby, and Levin, (1957), Bronfenbrenner (1958), Kohn (1959a, 1963), B. C. Rosen (1961), Herrmann, Schwitajewski, and Ahrens (1968), K. H. Stapf, Herrmann, Stapf, and Stäcker (1972), and others, that the following discriminations between middle-class and lower-class families are relatively stable: Middle-class families show less physical punishment; they rather tend to punish their children by withdrawal of love. Their punishments are more concerned with the child's intention of acting than the overt behavioral act and the effect of acting. They demand more conformity, they are more dogmatic in opinion, and they stress more abstract norms (that is to say, they stress less situation-centered norms). Middle-class families give their children more opportunities to interact verbally with adults; they are more child-centered and demand more inner control from their children, as well as more self-direction and the development of conscience. They also seem to tolerate more aggression and sexual play. It is to be expected that middle-class parents—compared with parents of the lower class—are less rejecting, less fearful, and less uncertain in their parental roles.

Insofar as these results may be generalized, "middle-class child-rearing practices" may be interpreted from the point of view that, if compared, these families, despite vast changes, still set forth solid and unquestionable value orientations. The stability of certain normative principles leads to an enhancement of certainty in parental behavior patterns. Middle-class parents hardly ever demonstrate the mere reinforcement of wanted overt behavior in their child-rearing techniques or the extinction of unwanted overt behavior. Almost every parental act of child-rearing

leads to an increase of introjection of parental norms and values. We might perhaps infer that Riesman's "inner-directed" individuals—as of mid-century Riesman thought they were still in the majority—probably originate from middle-class families rather than from lower-class families. It may also be inferred that middle-class families mediate more strongly than lower-class families what we would call the "official ideology" of our culture (cf. Milner, 1949: "Core culture").

## 3  FAMILY CHARACTER AND FAMILY STRUCTURE

According to Cattell (chapter 1) *syntality* is "a vector measurement of the organic behavioral dimensions of a group, analogous to personality." Syntality is a function of population qualities and group structure qualities:

$$\bar{G} = f(\bar{R}, \bar{P})$$

where $\bar{G}$ is syntality and $\bar{R}$ and $\bar{P}$ are structure and population (Cattell, 1948b, 1950c; Cattell & Stice, 1960; Cattell & Wispe, 1948). Population qualities are meant to be the mean and sigma of the group on all parameters of individuals (group members). The structure of the group implicates the roles and relationships, statuses, etc., which are in principle independent of the single group member.

Cattell and Stice (1960b) found relatively stable factorial syntality dimensions in "neonate" groups (newly formed face-to-face groups of about 10 male adult persons). One important syntality dimension is termed by Cattell, for example, "High Synergy through Leadership versus Disintegrative Low Morale." This factor marks high satisfaction with the group and with the leader, and high scores in objective performance tests (for instance on the dynamometer); it may be interpreted as "interest in the group's existence and purpose" (so-called "leadership synergy"). Another dimension is labeled "High immediate Synergy through Personalities versus Low Intrinsic Synergy." Here we find high loadings in motivation, we-feeling, and leadership arising in connection with low mean paranoid scores and higher mean intelligence, and emotional maturity in the members of the group.

A further dimension is denominated "Frustration through Temperamental Heterogeneity." Here we find high *variance* in several personality factors of members (*N, M, L, I*), and high mean of *M* associated with internal dislike of the group situation, need for leadership techniques, and rigidity of individual attitudes. Altogether about 13 syntality dimensions prove to be relatively stable.

Analogous to this system, setting up of a *taxonomy of families as unitary groups* seems certainly possible. However, the principal dimensions of family syntality are apt to appear different from those of "neonate" groups. It seems probable that family syntality depends on family members as well as on the group structure of the family. Moreover, it seems probable that family syntality is influenced strongly by the individual qualities of "central" or "leading" members of the family, particularly the main socialization agents (father and mother). So it is reasonable to suppose that "Democratic versus Autocratic Homes" may turn out to be a dimension of family syntality. Cattell and Wispe (1948) found with face-to-face groups of students a syntality dimension, "Friendly Urbanity and Savoir-faire versus Lack of Group Self-possession," which may be interpreted as "democratic versus autocratic atmosphere" (Cattell, 1950c, pp. 337, 371; see

also Bronfenbrenner, 1961; Ingersoll, 1949; Schelsky, 1954). The democratic (vs. autocratic) character of a family seems to depend on the family structure (Bronfenbrenner, 1961; Elder, 1961; Rosen, B. C., 1959; Strodtbeck, 1958; Wurzbacher, 1954), as well as on personality traits of family members (Harris, I. D., 1959; Rosen, B. C., & D'Andrade, 1959; Strodtbeck, 1954).

Among others the following characteristics determine how democratic (vs. autocratic) a family appears as a unitary group: size of family, division of parental control between father and mother (family structure; Bossard & Sanger, 1952; Ingersoll, 1949), the differences in age and educational level of parents (variance of scores of members), the mean level of anxiety of family members (mean score of all members), together with the professional status and job security of the husband, as well as the acceptance of role as a mother on the part of the wife (scores of single members). In reference to the study of Cattell and Wispe the following *dimensions of family syntality* are expected to be found besides the dimension "Democratic versus Autocratic Homes": "Indulgence versus Nonchalance," "Intellectuality versus Lack of Intellectuality," "Personal Adjustment versus Lack of Personal Adjustment," "Hustling versus Nonhustling," "Acceptance versus Rejection," "Severity versus Easy Casualness," and "Nagging versus Absence of Friction" (Cattell, 1950c, pp. 337f.).

If we know these or other basic dimensions of family syntality, we may investigate the connections of these dimensions to the personality development of children growing up in these families. Bronfenbrenner (1961), for instance, found (see also Strodtbeck, 1958) that a democratic family atmsophere may have negative influences on the child's growing personality: Sons from democratic homes often lack initiative and independence; they likewise tend to be highly conformist. However, Elder's (1961) results deviate here. Lippitt and Radke (1946) showed that children from democratic homes are more likely to quarrel and fight with other children, are more inconsiderate of others, and more insensitive to praise and blame (See also Peterson, Becker, Shoemaker, Luria, & Hellmer, 1961); one's frame of reference may make these positive or negative traits.

There are many studies on the effect of *family structure* on the child's personality. Besides family size (Rosen, B. C., 1959) and besides the differentiation of patriarchal, matriarchal, and equalitarian structures (Ewert, 1966), the influences of marital adjustment and divorce ("broken homes"), together with the effects of maternal employment, have been investigated (Cattell, 1950c; Glueck, S. & Glueck, 1957; Hoffmann, L. W., 1959; Landis, J. T., 1960; Leton, 1958; Nye, 1959; Stolz, 1960; Stroup, 1956). Results indicate, for example, that in many cases the long-lasting conflict situations ahead of the actual divorce are more traumatic to the child than the divorce itself. Further results show that the damage done by maternal employment was formerly overestimated. However, difficulties do occur in cases of employment of mothers with small infants. Effects depend probably more on maternal working motives than on the fact of the actual employment or nonemployment of mothers.

Studies by Cattell, Delhees and Sweney (as yet unpublished) show that psychological research on family structure should start from objective family data as well as from ratings of parents or external observers. It is also important, however, to know how family structure is *perceived by the children*. Ratings on how "patriarchal" a family is, differ quite often from one another when done by external observers, parents, or children. According to Emmerich (1961), children *perceive*—regardless of the "real" family structure—their fathers as more powerful, more competent, and as a major source of punishment. Kagan, Hosken, and Watson (1961) reported that children *rate* their mothers to be friendlier, less strict, and less punitive. Herrmann, Schwitajewski, and Ahrens (1968), on the other hand, discovered that the average 10 to 12-year-old child in Germany generally *perceives* his mother as more severe, but also as more supporting than his father, again apart from the objective role assessment in the family. According to the children's judgment, mothers possess a greater "intensity in child-rearing" than fathers.

The *perceived* family structure and the perceived qualities of the main socializing agents determine the child's personality development probably at least as much as the "real" characteristics of family and parents. Studies by S. W. Gray (1959) indicated that elementary school boys are better adjusted if they *perceive* themselves to be similar to their fathers. The more older children *perceive* themselves similar to their parents, the less they are being accepted by their peers. Much research work has been done with systematic behavior observation of parent-child interactions at home and in the laboratory (Lytton, 1971; Patterson, 1971; Stapf, A., 1973).

Close connections generally exist between the child's *perception* of the family and the "real" characteristics of that family. Consider, for instance, the results by Gray: According to psychoanalytic theory (Erikson, E. H., 1950; Freud, S.,

1924; Fromm, 1941; Hofstätter, 1964; Parsons, T. & Bales, 1955; Sears, R. R., Maccoby, & Levin, 1957; Sears, R. R., Rau, & Alpert, 1965; Sullivan, 1953; Toman, 1954; Wyss, 1961) these schoolboys are well adjusted and perceive themselves similar to their fathers because they have learned to identify themselves with their fathers' normative patterns and taboos. Identification of this kind is "defensive" or "reactive," respectively. The boy's successful identification leading both to good adjustment and to the judgement of similarity to father is identical with the solution of an inner conflict. This conflict is termed *Oedipal conflict* in psychoanalysis. In Freud's conception each boy has to experience this conflict. (For critique on this subject see Kardiner, Linton, DuBois, & West, 1945; Kohlberg, 1962; Maccoby, 1961; Malinowsky, 1927; Mead, 1928, 1930, 1935). The Oedipal conflict occurs when the little boy, during a special stage of his development (normally starting at the end of his third year), experiences a sexual attachment to his mother. He wants to show his love in a sexual manner to the person who is to him his most cherished and most important benefactress. He also tries to compete with his father in respect to his affection for his mother. Naturally, any sexual behavior directed toward his mother is rejected by her, and tensions arise between son and father. Thus, the boy has to fear losing the love of both parents. The son wants to maintain his father's love but, at the same time, hates him as a rival (Oedipal conflict). The normal solution of this conflict would be the son's identification with his father ("defensive identification;" Sears, R. R., Rau, & Alpert, 1965). Thus, he tries to be like him, and he models his behavior after his father's. After all this, psychoanalytical theory finds it easy to posit that boys are well adjusted after successful identification with fathers (Gray, S. W., 1959). (For further details, see also Bandura, 1962; Geer & Turteltaub, 1967; Johnson, R. C. & Medinnus, 1965).

The theory of Oedipal conflicts and especially its psychological implications in respect to sexuality have often been criticized. Hofstätter (1964) stressed the point that the Oedipal situation may be explained by using the social-psychological concept of *divergence of roles in leadership*. According to Bales and other scientists, social groups quite often form a role-differentiation of two leaders: a "task" leader and a "social-emotional" leader. The "task" leader usually ranks high on initiation, receiving, and guidance, but is not ranked high on liking. The "social-emotional" leader helps to boost group morale, releases tensions in difficult situations, and is usually the best liked. The steeper the rank gradient (or the greater the mean difference of positions of group members), the more distinct the role divergence will be.

Families may be described as groups whose members hold very diverse rank positions: In almost any case, parents hold positions much higher than their children. In these groups the development of great role divergence among leading group members arises. As a rule, father takes the role of the "task" leader, and mother the role of the "social-emotional" leader. This division implies—especially in a patriarchal family structure—that, in constrast to the mother, the father is perceived by the children as not well liked (since he is "task oriented"). The stronger and the more task-oriented the father happens to be, the sooner a feeling of hatred will arise in the children against him. Hofstätter believes this situation to be the source of Oedipal conflicts. Bronfenbrenner (1961) stresses the point that patriarchal family structures do not necessarily have to be a disadvantage, since sons from these families are nonconformist and at the same time responsible and full of initiative.

Hofstätter's theory does not explain why sons develop the Oedipal conflict and daughters do not. We find this to be an obvious weakness in his theory. Thus, Hofstätter's theoretical position is still unable to replace the psychoanalytical theory of Oedipal situation and of defensive identification with the father. Freud's Oedipal concept is rather speculative and up to this date by no means confirmed (Sears, R. R., Rau, & Alpert, 1965). But many empirical studies demonstrate the characteristically diverse way in which boys' and girls' personalities develop. Some of these differences at least do not contradict Freudian theory.

Compared with girls, boys perceive their parents as more severe and less supporting (Hawkes, Burchinal, & Gardner, 1957; Herrmann, Schwitajewski, & Ahrens, 1968). Boys feel less accepted by their parents; they then try more often to win their parents' attention by negative behavior (Sears, R. R., Rau, & Alpert, 1965). Boys are more aggressive, since parents tend to be more permissive toward the aggressive boy. Moreover, boys seem to develop less internal control in comparison to girls (Sears, R. R., Maccoby, & Levin, 1957). The sex role of boys seems to be determined earlier and more firmly than the sex role of girls (Johnson, R. C., & Medinnus, 1965; Rose, A. M., 1951; Sarason, S. B., Davidson, Lighthall, Waite, & Ruebush, 1960). Differences in the development of conscience and superego in boys and girls seem to depend probably on the interactions of sex of the children, family structure, and child-rearing techniques. A

great deal of research still remains to be done (Bronfenbrenner, 1961; Sears, R. R., Maccoby, & Levin, 1957; Sears, R. R., Rau, & Alpert, 1965).

The interacting influence of family character and structure on personality is evident in those studies which deal with the relations between sibling position (birth order) and personality characteristics of individuals. According to Alfred Adler, siblings are heavy competitors. In his opinion, adults possess personality characteristics which they have achieved during childhood in rivalry with their siblings. Adler believes *first-born children* hold a good starting position: The eldest child usually is bigger and stronger than his (or her) brothers and sisters, and he (or she) is asked and expected to be wiser than the younger siblings. Thus, these eldest children "carry the burden" of their parent's confidence. If they are able to live up to these role expectancies, they become "keepers of order." In later life they act conservatively, and they show a liking for power and its maintenance. First-born children risk running into severe difficulties when they fail to fulfill the hopes and anticipations which their families had expected of them. It is the eldest child's special problem that the affection and attention formerly given generously to him (or her) while he (or she) was the only child is transferred to the later-born children after their arrival. Thus, the first-born child feels "dethroned" and often reacts with depression and despair.

According to Adler, the *second-eldest child* experiences especially intense sibling rivalry. To these children life is a struggle against the more powerful older sibling, toward whom the second-born child feels resentment and jealousy. In Adler's opinion, the maintenance of power is the main problem of the eldest child; but jealousy becomes the major problem of the second-born child.

The *youngest child*, according to Adler, grows up in a warmer family atmosphere than his (or her) older brothers and sisters. Nevertheless, conflicts might arise easily if the youngest child is looked on as the smallest, weakest, and "dullest." Usually he (or she) reacts to this situation by developing strong ambitions, or, as often the case, by showing self-pity and cowardice. Frequently the child tries to solve the problem by giving excuses and by general laziness.

A great number of empirical studies have confirmed Adler's "theory of competition" in some parts, and have been able to modify and define it more exactly in others (Medinnus & Johnson, 1969). The FELS studies (Baldwin, 1946b; Lasko, 1954) and studies by R. R. Sears (1950), R. R. Sears, Maccoby, and Levin (1957), Vuyk (1959), H. L. Koch (1960), Thomas, Birch, Chess, and Robbins (1961), Hilton (1967), and other scientists demonstrate that *first-born children* tend to identify themselves more with their mothers, they act less openly aggressive but show more hidden aggression, and their general behavior toward adults is often ambiguous. First-born children experience frequent "fears of failure" and feelings of threat. They are more used to the company of grown-ups, their verbal abilities are developed earlier, and often they are better planners. However, they do not possess a wide range of interests. They receive more verbal stimuli from their mothers. The frequency of communication between first-born children and parents is remarkably high, but they nevertheless receive less indulgence and usually are subject to more parental restrictions. In respect to child-rearing

practices, mothers are more extreme, more interfering, and more inconsistent in their treatment of the first born.

*Single children* resemble the first-born children in many cases. Quite often they are overprotected, dominating, and egotistic. Here, too, we find a rapid development of verbal abilities and a high IQ. The single child is overrepresented among scientists (Sears, R. R., 1950; West, 1960).

Despite the fact that parents are less indulgent toward him, the first child is a wanted child, more often than the later-born children (Sears, R. R., Maccoby, & Levin, 1957). Therefore, in most cases he (or she) is born into an atmosphere of emotional warmth. He tends to become, consequently, all the more frustrated by the arrival of siblings. It is remarkable how many children react in a disturbed way when a sibling is born. They regress to more infantile behavior patterns or become aggressive (Thomas, Birch, Chess, & Robbins, 1961). However, it remains to be explained whether the traumatic experience of being "dethroned" causes long-term consequences in later life.

According to Schachter's (1959) results, eldest children show a strong need for affiliation when grown up. The author finds the following mediators between birth order and affiliation when studying first-born children: anxiety over losing parental love, a seeking for approval and support, and dependency (on this subject also see Harlow, H. & Harlow, M., 1962). Further studies report on interactions of birth order and sex of children, these results having reducing effects on Schachter's report (see Sampson, 1962). In this connection, it may be of interest that personality traits of younger siblings depend on the sex of older siblings to the extent to which younger children adjust to the specific sex characteristics of their older brothers and sisters (Brim, 1960; Koch, H. L., 1960). Rosen (1961) found interactions between sibling position, family size, and social status of the family. H. L. Koch (1960) stressed the importance of age differences between siblings.

According to Toman (1961), marriage prognosis will be favorable when both partners are able to maintain in matrimony the roles which they held as siblings in childhood. As an example, other things being equal, the elder brother of a younger sister ought to marry the younger sister of an elder brother. J. R. Hilgard (1951), however, believes it to be rather unfortunate when role attributes of former sibling positions are transferred to marriage.

Finally, we would like to point out that family syntality and its influence on the child's growing personality depends partly on the *personality of the main socialization agents* (especially on the mother). I. D. Harris (1959) noted that the child of a "rebellious mother" will become a rebel against any rule interfering with his needs for pleasure. The child of a "dependent mother" will search for interpersonal emotional warmth more than the average child. Emotional, immature mothers in conflict with their maternal roles tend to react rejectingly toward their children. As a result, such children tend to turn out to be aggressive and rebellious. They try to attract motherly attention by lying, stealing, and demonstrating antisocial behaviors (Sullivan, H. S., 1953; Symonds, 1949). We often find the "overprotective mother" rearing a self-centered, willful child, lacking self-control (Levy, D. M., 1943). Positive relations exist between overprotection and Premsia (*I*) (Cattell, 1965c). Children of extremely powerful and strict fathers possess little confidence that they will "get a grip on life," and show little desire for

achievement in adult life (Heilbrunn & McKinley 1962; Mussen & Kagan, 1958; Strodtbeck, 1958).

According to R. R. Sears, Rau and Alpert (1965) and other students of the problem, the connections between personality traits of mothers and the characteristics of their children are moderated by the children's sex. Thus, a negative correlation is found between mother's sex anxiety and the dependency (attention seeking, emotional upset after wrong-doing, etc.) of her daughters. But this result does not apply to sons. We may infer from such interactions and from other empirical data that a person's personality determination by his family background may not be regarded in a simplified manner. Syntality, influencing the growing personality of the child, implicates a rather large number of basic dimensions; and it is in itself a function of group structure and personality of group members. Leaving aside syntality, it is also important to investigate family structure, the personalities of socialization agents and their interactions, and the effects of these classes of determinants on the child's personality.

## 4 PARENTAL ATTITUDES, NORMS, AND CHILD–REARING PRACTICES

Parents differ in respect to their parental attitudes, in respect to norms they apply to judge the "rights" and "wrongs" of their parental behavior, and in respect to their "instrumental" parental behaviors and child-rearing practices and techniques. These attitudes, norms, and parental behaviors certainly depend on culture and society, on the global family syntality, on the family structure, and finally, on the personalities of mother and father (Cattell, 1950c). It may be expected, for example, that in a family possessing the syntality characteristics "Friendly Urbanity and Savoir-faire versus Lack of Group Self-possession," (syntality Factor 7, Cattell & Wispe, 1948), a relatively "democratic" family atmosphere dominates, and that parent-child attitudes will be rather warm and accepting instead of being cold and rejecting.

Before investigating the determinants of parental attitudes, norms, and behaviors by family characteristics for one thing, and their influence on the child's personality for another thing, the question of a *taxonomy of parental attitudes, norms, and behaviors* arises.

Present factorial studies show differing results (Coan, 1966; Eyferth, 1966; Herrmann, Schwitajewski, & Ahrens, 1968). However, the following two basic orthogonal dimensions appear in many reports: Autonomy versus Control, and Acceptance (Warmth, Love) versus Rejection (Hostility) (Baldwin, 1946a; Baldwin, Kalhorn, & Breese, 1945; Herrmann & A. Stapf, 1971; Johnson, R. C., & Medinnus, 1965; Milton, 1958; Schaefer, E. S., 1959; Sears, R. R., Maccoby, & Levin, 1957; Stapf, A., 1973; Stapf, K. H., Herrmann, Stapf, & Stäcker, 1972).

Aside from these two basic dimensions, the Factor "Permissiveness versus Restrictiveness" is found relatively frequently. Here "permissiveness" does not mean laissez-faire and a rejection of the parental role. "Permissiveness" in this case means that parents intentionally give the child the opportunity of engagement and independent acting (Johnson, R. C., & Medinnus, 1965). We still do not quite know how closely related the two factors of "Permissiveness versus Restrictiveness" and "Autonomy versus Control" are. Becker (1964) offered a *hypothetical model* of parental attitudes with three *orthogonal*

dimensions: Restrictiveness versus Permissiveness, Warmth versus Hostility, and Calm Detachment versus Anxious Emotional Involvement. According to Eyferth (1966) many factorial structures of parental attitudes may be rotated to allow an interpretation in the sense of Becker's model.

Factor analyses dealing not with parental attitudes but with instrumental parental behavior as perceived by the children yield in most cases two or three dimensions of *perceived parental behavior.* Siegelman (1965, 1966) extracted three factors: Loving, Punishment, and Demanding. Herrmann, Schwitajewski, and Ahrens (1968) found in a German sample the above-mentioned Factor "Punishment" and another factor, which was labeled "Parental Support," containing both "Loving" and "Demanding" items.

In respect to this we always must take into consideration which class of empirical data serve as a basis for factor analyses. In most cases we expect to find different factorial structures (different in number and meaning of factors, different clarified factor variances) when analyzing, for example, parental attitudes as expressed by parents, parental attitudes as perceived or expected by children, parental behaviors as observed by external observers, or parental behaviors as perceived or expected by children. According to results by Sewell, Mussen, and Harris (1955), the basic dimension "Autonomy versus Control" (or alternatively, "Control versus Permissiveness") breaks up into as many as 7 oblique factors when relatively heterogeneous data which concern specific parental behavior are factorized. The authors discovered, among others, the following separate factors: "Permissiveness in Early Feeding Situations," "Permissiveness in Toilet Training," "Nonpunitive Treatment of Misbehaviors," and "Practices Making for Early Independence" (Coan, 1966).

The two or three basic dimensions frequently found seem to have the character of *higher-order factors*. When factorizing Baldwin's FELS Parent Behavior Rating Scales (Baldwin, Kalhorn, & Breese, 1945), M. Roff (1949) found seven oblique simple-structure factors. Lorr and Jenkins (1953) in turn extracted three broad second-order factors from Roff's data (Coan, 1966): Dependence versus Encouragement, Democracy of Child Training, and Organization and Effectiveness of Control in the Home. Results show that psychology does not hold a satisfactory taxonomy of parental attitudes, norms, and behaviors. Some basic dimensions (sometimes labeled differently) are found in many studies, especially the dimension "Autonomy versus Control." There exist many empirical studies on the influence of important parental attitudes on the child's development. Some of these influences were already mentioned in connection with the personalities of main socialization agents (especially the mother).

Many authors have investigated the influence of rejection (Baldwin, 1946b; Cattell, 1950c; Heilbrun & McKinley, 1962; Hoffman, M. L., 1963; Lippitt & Radke, 1946; Mussen & Kagan, 1958; Schachter, 1959; Sears, R. R., Maccoby, & Levin, 1957; Sears, R. R., Rau, & Alpert, 1965; Symonds, 1949; Whiting & Child, 1953). Parent *compliance* and *overprotection* were examined by Symonds (1949), Levy (1943), Baldwin, Kalhorn, and Breese (1945), P. S. Sears (1953), and R. R. Sears, Maccoby, and Levin (1957). Children seem to suffer more long-term damage from rejection than from overprotection. Empirical studies deal increasingly with the effect of special child-rearing practices and with the interactions between child-rearing practices and general parental attitudes.

R. R. Sears, Maccoby and Levin (1957) reported that neither love, emotional warmth, and spoiling, nor emotional coldness, rejection, and withholding of love will lead to a satisfactory identification with parents, to internalization of parental norms and standards, or to formation of conscience. Rather, the most fruitful effects of identification, internalization of norms, and formation of conscience seem to be caused by a general nurturing, loving, and accepting attitude, together with some withdrawal of love (as intended punishment technique). (On the subject of formation of conscience see also Marke & Nyman, 1963; Mowrer, 1950, 1960b; Sears, P.S., 1953).

Examining the influences of parental attitudes, behaviors, and their interactions on the development of the child's personality, we have to consider—as in the case of family structure—how the child *perceives* these attitudes, behaviors, and child-rearing techniques. For example, children seem to develop expectations (cognitive schemata) of parental reinforcement schedules. Herrmann, Schwitajewski, and Ahrens (1968) demonstrated with the help of discriminant functions that different parental reinforcement schedules are expected by boys versus girls, children from middle-class families versus children from lower-class families, and Protestant versus Catholic children. Children who expect reward and support from their parents show relatively high verbal intelligence, scholastic aptitude, and creativity. They tend to perceive more positive reinforcement and have a broader perspective of their future prospects. They are accepted by their peers. Children who expect punishment and severity from their parents have high test anxiety scores. They are dependent on authority and acquiescent but also intolerant of minorities and persons of lower social status (Stapf, A., 1975; Stapf, K. H., et al., 1972).

According to Freud's psychoanalytical theory, special child-rearing techniques—such as weaning and toilet training—are decisive for the development of the child's personality (see Erikson, E. H., 1950; Toman, 1960; Whiting & Child, 1953; Wyss, 1961). In Freud's opinion serious frustrations may be caused by weaning a child too early and too strictly. In his theory this traumatic experience causes a general loss of trust and confidence in later adult life. So-called "orally frustrated" individuals are often believed to be apathetic, emotionally unstable, insecure, and anxious. This opinion has been confirmed empirically only for rather extreme cases (see also Klatskin, Jackson, & Wilkin, 1956; Sears, R. R., Maccoby, & Levin, 1957; Sewell & Mussen, 1952; Simsarian, 1947; Thomas, Chess, Birch, & Hertig, 1960; Traisman & Traisman, 1958). If valid results on long-term effects of maternal weaning practices and the personality of the grown-up exist at all, they are only able to confirm that the personality and general attitudes of the mother influence the child's personality and also influence her weaning practices. Thus the general attitudes and personality of the mother act as mediator between the child-rearing technique and the personality of the child. Tallman (1961) showed the importance of the mother's ability to *adjust* her actions to every specific child-rearing situation. This adaptibility is an important maternal personality trait and has remarkable influence on the child.

The timing and severity of toilet training seem to be connected more closely to the personality of the mother than to the development of the infant's personality. Mothers with high sex anxiety strongly value cleanliness and modesty. Thus, they try to force their children to an early sphincter control. Toilet training will only then prove to be disturbing to the child when early and strict training takes place in an atmosphere of maternal coldness and rejection (Sears, R. R., Maccoby, & Levin, 1957). Long-term consequences of toilet training, however, have only been confirmed in extreme cases. No stable connections have been proved between this kind of child-rearing practice and the child's personality for the large range of the average population.

The engraving of maternal influences on the personality development of the child has been treated under the subjects of *hospitalism* (Spitz, 1945) and *anaclitic depression* (Casler, 1961; Yarrow, L. J., 1961). M. A. Ribble (1943, 1944) and Spitz (1946) stressed the importance of skin-to-skin contact between mother and newborn child in respect to the baby's physical and psychic development. (See also Anastasi, 1958; Beach & Jaynes, 1954; Reisen, 1961.) It must be questioned if the absence of the mother (or mother substitute) is the main cause for the damages Ribble and Spitz report concerning "unmothered" infants. A number of empirical studies urge the alternative hypothesis that these fatal results are caused by the restriction of *sensory stimulation* during the infant's first year (Anastasi, 1958; Secord & Backman, 1964; Yarrow, L. J., 1964). Thus for the infant the presence of mother is so important because she represents the most important part of his environment and the source of most stimuli (see Ainsworth & Bell, 1970; Escalona, 1969; Schaffer, 1971).

Much speaks for the fact that damage is especially liable to occur when, during the first year, the infant is separated from its mother *after* having lived together with her for some time and after strong emotional bonds had already developed between mother and child. On the other hand, we must consider that damages may also be caused by unfavorable familial circumstances, leading to a separation from mother later on (Pinneau, 1955). Till today there exist no conforming results in respect to whether damages caused by maternal deprivation and/or restricted sensory stimulation actually do cause irreversible damages ( Dennis & Najarian, 1957; Goldfarb, 1945; Rabin, 1958; Yarrow, L. J., 1964). Above all, it has not been sufficiently clarified whether absence of the single mother figure really is the main cause for the fact that these early-deprived infants turn out to be less intelligent, retarded in social maturity, negativistic, passive, fearful, and apathetic in later life. We believe that Ribble's lack of "mothering" does not suffice to explain hospitalism and anaclitic depression.

Judging by the influences of different child-rearing practices such as weaning, toilet training, specific punishment techniques, and also by "mothering", etc., and in accordance with the present results on the subject, we stress that it is probably the emotional atmosphere of the home and the personalities of the parents (especially the mother) that influence the child's growing personality rather than the particular child-rearing techniques used (Johnson, R. C., & Medinnus, 1965). The importance of interactions of parental instrumental behaviors with general parental attitudes and norms has already been mentioned.

## 5  SUMMARY

Available theoretical concepts describing and explaining the interdependencies of family and personality (family influence on the growing personality of the child) are for the most part unsatisfactory. Earlier global theories have been largely modified by a great number of empirical studies. Future theoretical developments ought to consider family influence as a very complex multivariate matter. Theories of family and individual must act on a medium level of abstraction; that is to say, these theories will neither be valid for all families without exception nor for only a few concrete families. The type of family to which the present research work on family influence refers is the "kernel family."

Parents and children are bound by heredity. Influences of heredity interact with influences of environment depending on the family as well as with determinants that represent neither hereditary nor environmental influences (mutations, segregations of genes, stages of structural development of the child, etc.)

Family influence as environmental influence may be described under at least five different aspects:

1. Family influence as mediator of social, cultural, and epochal influences.
2. Influence of "family character" (syntality).
3. Influence of family structure.
4. Family influence as defined by the personalities of single socialization agents.
5. Family influence as defined by parental attitudes, norms, and child-rearing techniques.

Family influence as mediator between culture and individual seems to be decreasing. Reasons for this may be found in the leveling process between social strata, religious orientations, and town and country, together with rapid changes of traditional normative patterns and increasing social mobility, etc.

If we look on the family as an

unanalyzed unit, we are able to detect dimensions of family character similar to the basic personality dimensions of individuals (Cattell's "syntality"). These syntality dimensions may be related to personality traits of children growing up in these families. However, we still do not possess a sufficient taxonomy of family syntality. But important influences of family structure (for example, large vs. small families, patriarchal, matriarchal, equalitarian families, sibling position [birth order]) have been studied empirically with good success. Freud's theory of Oedipal conflicts and the boy's "defensive identification" with his father have not been sufficiently proved by empirical investigations, but neither have alternative theories.

Individual personality traits of the parents, parental attitudes of socialization, and concrete parental behavior are a strong influence on the growing personality of the child. Studies on the basic dimensions of parental attitudes and parental behavior show differing results. It is stressed that investigations into the effects of special child-rearing techniques (for example, weaning and toilet training) cannot be performed adequately without the consideration of interactions between child-rearing technique, personality of the mother, sex of child, and general emotional atmosphere of the family.

Present research on hospitalism and anaclitic depression is disputed. It remains to be clarified as to whether the defects which hospitalized or other separated children suffer are actually caused by the absence of the single mother figure.

# 20

# The Emotions
# and Emotion Concepts in
# Personality and Culture Research

Carroll E. Izard
*University of Delaware, Newark*

## 1  THE PROBLEM OF DEFINING
## EMOTION CONCEPTS

The term *emotion* is a chronic source of controversy and misunderstanding in science, art, and literature, as well as in everyday life. The confusion over emotion has led to attempts to throw it out of psychological science in favor of the more palpable phenomena of activation (Duffy, 1962), to subsume it under the more respected rubric of perceptual process (Leeper, 1965), and to redefine it as a combination of undifferentiated arousal and cognition (Mandler, 1975; Schachter, 1971).

Despite the seeming chaos regarding their nature and their rightful place under the sun, emotion concepts continue to be frequently used in descriptions of persons and interpersonal relations and as explanatory concepts in the behavioral and social sciences. It has been proposed that the emotions constitute the primary motivational system for human beings (Izard, 1971; Tomkins 1962, 1963). Perhaps the ubiquity of emotion concepts is one kind of evidence for their importance in human affairs. Yet the confusion about emotion and its role in personality and social systems is testimony to its complexity, flexibility, and relative invisibility, characteristics that make the problem of definition a formidable one.

One of the difficulties in defining and studying emotion has been the tendency to use the term as a global catchall for everything relating to affect, but difficulty has also arisen from efforts to distinguish a large number of emotions. I shall be concerned with nine fundamental emotions, though I do not mean to imply that there is anything final about the number 9 or that I am using the term *fundamental* in any special sense. By fundamental emotions I mean the unitary and relatively more simple emotions that constitute one type of motivation or one type of motivating, cue-producing experience. For example, interest, enjoyment, and anger are considered fundamental emotions, whereas concepts like anxiety or depression are considered as patterns or combinations of emotions involving two or more of the fundamental emotions. (See Izard, 1971, 1972, and Appendix to this chapter for a listing of the fundamental emotions and patterns of emotions.)

The central aims of this chapter are threefold. First, it delineates an operational definition for each of nine fundamental emotions. Second, it demonstrates the effectiveness of these emotion concepts as transcultural variables, as indicators of important similarities and differences among cultures. Third, after showing that these emotion concepts are transcultural, it presents evidence for their usefulness in studying developmental processes.

## 2   FACIAL EXPRESSION, EMOTION, AND BEHAVIOR

Before going further, some clarification of terminology is necessary. Historically the term *facial expression* has been most commonly thought to be the result of a particular emotion. That is, a pattern of muscle contractions in the face was thought of only as an expression of felt emotion, or as an effect of, or a response to, an emotion.

In the author's view the facial pattern of a given emotion is expressive mainly in the sense that it communicates something intrapsychically via feedback mechanisms and socially via interpersonal perceptual processes. However, it also plays a causal and regulatory role in emotion (Gellhorn, 1964; Izard, 1971; Peiper, 1963; Tomkins, 1962, 1963). For these reasons facial behavior is best thought of as a component of emotion rather than as an effect. The term *facial patterning* would perhaps be better, except where historical and contextual considerations require the older term. The term *facial expression* will continue to be used in this chapter, with the exception that its meaning has been modified by these additional assumptions.

There are sound theoretical grounds for turning to the face and facial expressions as a means for differentiating emotion constructs. Tomkins (1962) and Gellhorn (1964) pointed out how the highly differentiated neuromuscular mechanisms of the face, in contrast to the slow and undifferentiated viscera, make it quite possible for facial activity to be a part of the physiological processes of emotion. I define

emotion as a three-level concept, with the behavioral-expressive level consisting primarily of facial activity.

In his exhaustive work, *Cerebral Function in Infancy and Childhood*, Peiper (1963) also posited a strong relationship between facial expressions and emotions. He challenged investigators in this area to seek further understanding of the close correspondence, particularly in infants and young children, between facial expressions and the inner processes of emotion.

Gellhorn (1964) gave the most detailed neurophysiological formulation of the role of facial behavior in emotion. He marshaled experimental evidence to support his basic hypothesis that proprioceptive discharges stemming from the activity of the striated muscles contribute significantly to the physiological processes underlying the emotions. This contribution is accomplished in two ways: (a) by the effects of body posture on the setting of the hypothalamic balance and (b) "through *facial contraction patterns* which lead to afferent discharges via the hypothalamic-cortical system and interact with cultaneous facial impulses in the cortex" (Gellhorn, 1964, p. 457, italics added).

Concepts of direct and specific relations between the emotions and facial expressions date back to man's earliest recorded history. Classical Greek theater used facial masks to portray happy (comic) or sad (tragic) characters as early as 500 B.C. Literature is replete with reference to man's face as the window to his soul, his innermost experiences and feelings.

There are empirical grounds, too, for turning to facial expressions in the study of the emotions. Despite a long and controversial history, psychophysiological data (Schwartz, Fair, Greenburg, Friedman, & Klerman, 1973) and cross-cultural emotion recognition studies (Ekman, Friesen, &

Ellsworth, 1972; Izard, 1971) show that the study of facial expressions of the emotions provides a most convincing method for defining and assessing emotion constructs in personality and psychopathology. There are three aspects of the research on facial expressions that have some relevance to the problem of defining emotion constructs as useful psychological variables.

## 2.1 Facial Expression as a Source of Cues in Interpersonal Behavior

Our everyday experience tells us that facial expressions convey important cues and signals, sometimes rather specific information. Few of us have difficulty recognizing the unequivocally happy, sad, or angry face. No one would seriously doubt that a speech delivered with contempt for the audience would have a different effect if it were delivered with genuine interest in the audience.

Several empirical studies bear out these common-sense observations. Izard (1964) showed that role-played emotions in dyadic interactions had a significant effect on both intellectual performance and interpersonal perception. Izard, Cherry, Arnold, and Fox (1965, p. 62ff) showed that learning occurred more rapidly in a picture-trigram paired-associates learning task when the pictures (facial photographs) had positive-affect stimulus value than when the pictures had negative emotional value. Izard and Nunnally (1965) showed that facial photographs rated as expressive of positive affect in comparison with affectively negative photos were rated significantly higher on favorable personality characteristics (e.g., friendlier, more attractive, more intelligent). Ekman (1965) showed that cues from the face and head yield more information

regarding the emotional states aroused in stress interviews than is conveyed by body cues. He found that facial cues alone (with no other information) enabled people to make quite reliable and valid judgments about the interviewees' reactions to stress.

R. E. Miller, Murphy, and Mirsky (1959) used a conditioning paradigm to demonstrate that rhesus monkeys can differentiate between pictures of fearful and nonfearful monkeys. That is, the cues or information contained in one monkey's emotional expression in face and posture reliably evoked avoidance behavior in the observing animal.

Michotte's (1950) hypothesis that motion or motion pattern is more important than facial expression in determining observer judgments of interacting figures was disconfirmed in an interesting study by Thayer and Schiff (1967). They found that facial expression and motion pattern interacted and that judgments depended, in fact, on the congruence of facial expression and motion pattern. However, in considering the relative importance of the two, they thought that facial expression functioned as the critical stimulus information for the judgment of an encounter.

Savitsky and Sim (1974) standardized some videotape sequences in which different people told about "crimes" they had committed. The legal offenses were prejudged to be of equal seriousness, but the "actors" portrayed different emotion expressions as they related their stories. Preexperimental raters successfully categorized the expressions in terms of discrete emotions. The judges' (subjects') task was to indicate the severity of punishment that was appropriate for each actor. The results showed that the judges' selection of punishments was significantly influenced by the actors' expressions. For example, judges chose less severe punishments for actors expressing distress or sadness as they related their stories and more severe punishments for those who looked happy or angry.

Some, though not all, of the foregoing researches contribute directly to the definition of specific emotion constructs, but all are relevant here for two reasons. They show that facial expressions convey important and sometimes quite specific cues or information of real significance for interpersonal perception, substantially influencing judgments of personality traits and behavior in interpersonal encounters. Further, perception of emotion expressed by others can significantly alter rate of learning and performance.

## 2.2 Emotion Expressivity and Personality

A number of studies (Block, 1957; Buck, Savin, Miller, & Caul, 1969; Jones, H.E., 1935; Landis, C., 1932; Lanzetta & Kleck, 1970; Learmonth, Ackerly, & Kaplan, 1959; Prideaux, 1922) have found an inverse relationship between physiological (internal) arousal and overt expression under various stimulus conditions.

Lanzetta and Kleck reviewed several possible explanations for the observed inverse relationship between physiological arousal and overt expressivity. H. E. Jones (1950) suggested that autonomic arousal and overt behavior are substitutional modes of reducing tension. Thus, if one inhibits an overt display of affect it will be internalized and dissipated physiologically. Conversely, if a person expresses the affect externally, there will be a minimum of internal activity. Block (1957) argued against Jones' explanation and maintained that tension can be reduced by motor behavior or cognition, but not by autonomic activity. Schachter and Latané (1964) argued that a certain type of person (primary sociopath) fails to learn to

apply emotional labels to his states of internal arousal; thus, although physiologically extremely labile, he is overtly nonemotional.

Lanzetta and Kleck added another possible explanation. They held that some people during socialization were punished for affect expression and thus learned to inhibit expressivity. These persons come to experience response conflict between expressing and inhibiting expression in affect-arousing situations. The individual's physiological arousal level becomes a joint function of the arousal value of the stimulus situation and the conflict over expression or inhibiting expression. They explain the "internalizers' " better performance as perceivers of others' affective displays on the grounds that such people have become sensitized by virtue of their own conflict over affect display.

A study by Buck, Savin, Miller, and Caul (1969) used a different experimental paradigm and extended the analysis of differences between physiological responding and overt expressiveness. Instead of electric shock, they presented the subjects with a series of slides that had been prerated on a pleasantness-unpleasantness continuum. The judges' task was to determine whether the expressor was viewing a pleasant or unpleasant slide. They used both male and female subjects and found the females to be better expressors (senders) then males. They repeated the earlier finding of a negative correlation between facial expressiveness and physiological responsiveness (skin resistance and heart rate).

In their study of the personality characteristics of "internalizers" and "externalizers," Buck, Savin, Miller, and Caul (1969) showed that internalizers were more introverted and had lower self-esteem than externalizers. Internalizers were also more impersonal in their vocal descriptions of their emotions.

One finding which stands in apparent contradiction to the others showed that internalizers had higher scores on sensitization on the Byrne (1961b) Repression-Sensitization scale. The puzzle here is that previous studies have described sensitizers as persons who express their emotions freely rather than denying them. Further research will be required to elucidate the meaning of this finding.

Buck and co-workers had another possible explanation of the oft-repeated finding of a negative relationship between physiological responding (internal arousal) and overt expression. They suggested that experiences associated with learning to inhibit overt expression tend to be stressful and threatening and that the stress, and not the inhibition per se, produces the increased physiological responding.

In a later study Buck, Miller, and Caul (1974) attempted to validate the differences between good and poor expressors (nonverbal senders) in a nonlaboratory situation. They used an experimental situation to obtain scores on expressiveness (sending ability) and correlated this with teachers' ratings of a number of different observable responses. They found significant negative correlations between expressive (sending) ability and the following types of behavior: "is shy," "fears strangers," "is emotionally inhibited," "controls his emotions," "is quiet and reserved," "is cooperative," "is an introvert." They found sending ability positively correlated with the following types of behavior: "often shows aggression," "has high activity level," "has many friends," "expresses feelings openly," "is impulsive," "is often difficult to get along with," "expresses his hostilities directly," "tends to be rebellious and nonconforming," "is bossy," "often dominates other children," "is an extravert." Though their findings are interesting and have important implications, there are some difficulties with the study. The correlations were based on rather small samples (six girls, eight boys) and the types of behavior being rated by the teachers were often highly overlapping and even synonymous. Despite these limitations, the investigators have opened up a potentially fruitful line of investigation relating to the concept of overt expressiveness and autonomic arousal and between expressiveness and personality characteristics.

Studies of expressiveness should probably allow for the possibility that voluntariness and involuntariness of expression, though commonly accepted as categorically different in terms of conscious control, actually vary on a continuum of awareness. Some voluntary (or partially voluntary, intentional) expressions, such as those that occur when one wants to show sympathy, may be performed at a low level of awareness. The same may be true of the child who willfully increases its expression of genuine distress to elicit the desired or needed help.

## 2.3 Universality of Facial Expressions

Our everyday experience tells us that the facial expression of enjoyment, shame, or fear means something more than a temporary rearrangement of physiognomic features. It is commonly assumed that the frightened face signifies the experience of fear and that the experiencing person will think and act like a person afraid.

A variety of empirical studies supports the common-sense observation that facial expressions reliably signify the subjective experience of emotion and real inner events that have observable behavioral consequents. In the classical study of the conditioning of emotional reactions in "infant Albert," J. B. Watson and Raynor (1920) referred to the "puckered face" in response to the distressing stimulus. C. Landis' (1924) experiment showed a number of clear and logical relations between stimuli, facial expressions, and specific emotions reported in subjective experience. For example, photographs of people reporting feelings of disgust while viewing vivid illustrations of the "diseases of China" showed common facial expressive behavior—"vertical wrinkles of the forehead, partial closure of the eyes, the firm closure of the lips, the depression of the corners of the lips and a slight raising of the wings of the nose" (p. 331). Most elements of this description are common to the traditional descriptions of disgust.

Bridges' (1930, 1932) observations of involuntary expressions of emotions in infants point up the presence of facial activity at early ages. Of course, there is the puckering and crying response at birth; and the widened eyes and tense muscles of fear were observed at 7 months.

Goodenough (1933), J. Thompson (1941), and Fulcher reported studies with blind people which offer evidence that different facial expressions are reliably identifiable and that a particular expression signals a specific emotion. They interpreted their data as evidence for genetically based expressions that emerge in their final form through maturation. For blind persons, as with normal subjects, a facial expression of a given emotion (e.g., anger) had logical antecedents (a stimulus situation that could be seen as anger inducing) and logical consequents (aggressive behavior).

The findings of the foregoing empirical studies, together with our everyday experience, constitute a formidable argument for a direct relationship between a given emotion and a particular, relatively fixed pattern of facial activity. It follows from this contention that people in the course of normal development should become capable of easily recognizing facial expressions of the emotions and that it should be easy to demonstrate this recognition experimentally. However, psychologists investigating people's ability to classify facial expressions have met with partial success, at best, and often with outright failure (Buzby, 1924; Feleky, 1914; Frois-Wittmann, 1930; Landis, C., 1929; Langfeld, 1918; Munn, 1940; Ruckmick, 1921).

Schlosberg and his associates (e.g., Levy & Schlosberg, 1960) succeeded in showing that with a good series of posed expressions and sufficiently careful methods of experimentation, people can reach considerable agreement in classifying pictures into emotion categories. Yet, despite the use of caution and the attainment of relative success, a number of pictures in the final series was agreed on by less than 38% of the subjects.

Woodworth and Schlosberg (1956), Honkavaara (1961), Lévy-Schoen (1964), and Tomkins (1964) indicated that photographs of posed expressions of emotion afforded an effective means for studying the emotion components of personality. However, all the series of photographs and most of the methods of obtaining responses that have been used in the past suffer one or more serious deficiencies (cf. Honkavaara, 1961). These deficiencies, together with a remarkable lack of theory or even problem definition, probably account for the notorious inconsistencies among findings from research on facial expression.

Izard (1971) developed a series of photographs of facial expressions of the emotions; this series was designed to surmount the difficulties of the older sets. The photographs were first administered to 50 male American college students, who were asked to give *free response* descriptions of the expressions. The average percentage of free responses that were judged to be in the intended emotion categories for the 32 pictures was 62%.

Following the free response or expression labeling experiment the photos were projected again, one at a time, for classification into fundamental emotion categories. The results of this experiment were dramatically clear (Izard, 1971). The average percentage of responses classifying the 32 pictures in the appropriate emotion categories was 83%, whereas 12.5% agreement would be expected by chance.

The expression-labeling experiments and the classification experiments showed that there are facial expressions that are consistently described and classified in terms of specific emotion categories. That is, a great majority of the people successfully matched photographic and verbal symbols of the emotions. They agreed, for example, that certain photographs represented anger but not fear, while certain other photographs represented fear but not anger. It follows that the anger expression (facial pattern), as represented by the photograph, and the anger concept, as represented by the defining adjectives on the list of Fundamental Emotions, are indexes or symbols of the emotion of anger.

## 3  EMOTIONS AS TRANSCULTURAL PHENOMENA

Izard's (1971) expression-labeling and expression-classification experiments with American students yielded convincing evidence that within a given culture there exist both pictorial and verbal indexes for the different fundamental emotions. However, these findings are subject to the learning-theory criticism that we have merely discovered some cultural stereotypes. People simply learn certain labels for certain facial expressions, and hence neither facial expression nor label need have any referent in other physiological or behavioral processes.

This criticism leads to the hypothesis that different cultures and socialization practices should quite naturally lead to intercultural variations in both the expressions and their labels. The successful extension of the expression-labeling and expression-classification experiments (Izard, 1971) across eight widely separated national-cultural groups effectively refuted this criticism and argued strongly for the existence across cultures of a set of valid human states and processes that consistently give rise to a corresponding set of expressive behaviors and verbal concepts. Expression labeling, or free responses to the facial photographs, and the data from the expression-classification experiments demonstrated a consistently high degree of success with which the varied cultural groups matched facial expressions and verbal concepts, both of which are valid symbols or representations of the emotions.

Ekman, Sorenson, and Friesen (1969) extended the emotion (expression) classification research to preliterate cultures in New Guinea and Borneo. They sought isolated, nonwestern samples who had been least affected by modern technological, commercial, and ideological currents. They interpreted their results as essentially similar to those of the present author and as supporting the notion that there are pan-cultural elements in facial affect displays that have pan-cultural meanings.

These data support the hypothesis that certain facial expressions are genetically determined transcultural variables and suggest that the underlying states or processes that give rise to the facial expressions and to the consistency of their verbal labels are indeed the fundamental emotions. The empirical data indicate that the behaviors that constitute the facial expression and the verbal labeling are relatively fixed and specific for a given emotion. Of course, some variation in expression and labeling occurred within emotion categories, variations which in the main were still grouped and identified appropriately. Some interindividual and intercultural differences relating to the emotions would be expected on the basis of differences in family structure and dynamics, particularly differences in child rearing and socialization (see chapters 5 and 16).

In a theoretical treatment of the emotions and the emotion system, Izard (1971) defined emotion at three levels—neurophysiological, behavioral-expressive, and experiential. The studies presented in this section have focused first on demonstrating the transcultural nature of emotion at the behavioral-expressive level as represented by photographs of facial expressions. Second, these studies have shown that these behavioral expressions (facial patterns) were consistently defined and classified in verbally defined categories; this finding supports the proposition that the connotative properties and hence the experiential or phenomenological concomitants of the expressions are also transcultural. In sum, it seems quite reasonable to infer that underlying the empirically delineated facial patterns and the associated verbal symbols that signify experiential emotion are certain emotion-specific neurophysiological processes and that the separate fundamental emotions are part of the biological make-up of human beings.

These findings and conclusions suggest that the emotions may be among the most fundamental and universal phenomena in personality and culture. Two important questions are raised by this conclusion: (a) To what extent are these emotions important determinants of social systems and cultural processes? and (b) To what extent are the emotions we have identified as transcultural important determinants of personality processes? The emotions or the

emotion concepts as we have defined them have not been used as variables by many investigators in personality and culture studies. Nevertheless, it is possible to explore, in a general way, each of the two questions posed. With regard to the first, we can examine the place of the emotions in some of the traditional work done by the cultural anthropologist and the personality and social psychologists who have collaborated with them or used their data (section 4). Section 5 attends to the second question by examining some experimental studies that have investigated emotion concepts cross-culturally.

## 4 STUDIES OF EMOTION CONCEPTS BASED ON ANTHROPOLOGICAL OBSERVATIONS

The work of Benedict (1934), Mead (1937), Whiting and Child (1953), and of numerous other cultural anthropologists and social psychologists (e.g., see Kaplan, B., 1961) leaves little doubt that behaviors verbally tagged as emotion or emotional are transcultural phenomena. Concepts of joy, anger, disgust, contempt, distress, anxiety, fear, shame, and guilt are common in these and other cross-cultural research reports. Though the lack of a generally accepted and adequate theory of the emotions makes it difficult to assess the degree to which these researchers hold common conceptions of the phenomena involved, there are strong indications that common denominators exist.

Spiro's (1961) study of ethnological data led to his formulation of a functional relationship between personality and social systems in which he recognized the importance of what he termed *emotional needs* and of individual motivation, which is easily related to emotion. He began with the observation that from a comparative biological perspective human social systems are a functional requirement of human life. Human existence requires socially shared behavior patterns that satisfy "(1) biological needs, (2) those group needs that are an invariant concomitant of social life and (3) those emotional needs that develop in the interaction between biology and society" (p. 96).

Conversely, a social system can continue only if its members will perform the necessary and culturally prescribed roles. Since roles are functions of separate persons, the individual personality becomes a requirement for social system. The personality is ultimately responsible for motivating the role performances that give a society its form and order.

Since most major personality theories link motivation and emotion in one way or another, it is reasonable to say that the important role Spiro has assigned to motivation is at least shared by emotion.

Whereas emotion has not been explicitly recognized as an organizing or guiding principle in personality and culture studies, in one way or another cultural anthropologists and social psychologists are frequently led to emotion concepts to explain social and cultural phenomena. Fear or anxiety, as well as love, hostility, and contempt, have often been considered as prime motivators in the socialization process (Dollard & Miller, 1950). Shame and guilt have been used to explain individual conscience and social sanctions (Mead, 1956; Piers & Singer, 1953). Indeed cultures have been stereotyped as friendly, hostile, contemptuous, or fearful (Leeper & Madison, 1959, pp. 98-133), or as "shame cultures" or "guilt cultures" (Benedict, 1946).

One of the most significant psychological analyses of cultural anthropological data is that of Whiting and Child (1953). Their data were drawn from the Cross-Cultural File of the Institute of Human Relations at Yale and consisted of the accounts given by anthropologists of the customary behavior of members of 75 primitive societies. The emotion concepts of anxiety and guilt figured prominently in their analysis of custom and custom potential, the cultural counterparts of habit and habit potential as defined in general behavior theory. Their study focused on socialization or child-training customs or practices and their effects on adult personality. For each of several dimensions of behavior (e.g., anal, oral, sexual) judges were required to read anthropological documents for each of the 75 societies and make ratings as to the degree to which child-training practices resulted in the development of satisfactions (acquired rewards) or socialization anxiety (acquired drive).

Whiting and Child hypothesized that the greater the severity of socialization in a system of behavior the greater would be the anxiety associated with that system and the more that system would be the focus of concern and worry in adult life. This hypothesis was well supported by the data. They also hypothesized that the greater the initial indulgence (satisfaction) of a young child in a given system of behavior the more likely will performance of responses in that system be a source of security and satisfaction for the adult. General support for this hypothesis was clearly lacking. Whiting and Child speculated about the meaning of the difference in the two findings but were unable to come up with a satisfactory explanation.

A reasonable explanation may be found in terms of the different role played by the emotions in the practice of child indulgence on the one hand and in the practice of severe socialization on the other. First, consider the basis for the judges' ratings of child indulgence. In rating child indulgence, the judges were concerned with (a) duration of initial period of indulgence, (b) amount of freedom given the child to perform his initial habits in the given behavior system, and (c) encouragement of these habits. These behaviors relate primarily to what I would term *drive satisfaction* or *biological need satisfaction* as distinguished from emotion-related behavior. Now, consider the basis for the judges' ratings of severity of socialization. In rating socialization practices judges were concerned with (a) brevity of socialization, (b) severity of punishment, and (c) frequency of punishment. All these practices or behaviors are virtually certain to be emotion-activating or emotion-related behavior.

To the extent that emotion, as distinguished from biological drive, plays the key role in human motivation, there is a simple explanation of the different findings for the effects of indulgence (drive satisfaction) and for severity of socialization (development of patterns of emotional behavior). Severe socialization of the child alters the emotion or motivation system, the dynamics of personality; early indulgence in relation to biological drives does not.

Knapen (1958) used observational and interview techniques to study the influences of child-training practices on the development of personality in a Bacongo society. He found certain practices that were radically different from those of Western cultures. Up to the age of weaning the child is given almost complete indulgence. Moral sanctions are invoked only after highly undesirable behavior occurs, usually socially observable behavior that could cause grave embarrassment to the clan. Punishment is light or negligible when other members of the society do not learn of the offense. The same offense may provoke intense reprobation if it is generally talked about. Thus,

internalized values were purely social values rather than a coherent value system. He concluded that this led to observable effects in adult personality traits. One of the effects was that fear of others was stronger and more frequently observed than sense of guilt. This is opposite to the order of the frequency of these emotions in Western cultures.

The possibility that cultural customs or patterns of managing and responding to fundamental emotions play a significant role in personality and social processes is also supported by sociological evidence. An example is Siegel's (1955) study of the role of high anxiety level in cultural integration and societal cohesion. He defined cultural integration as the interrelatedness among elements of a social system. "A tightly integrated system is characterized by the strong centralization of values; that is, the tendency for broad sectors of the culture to be related to a few key values supported by a strong *emotional* reluctance to change" (p. 42, italics added). He defined anxiety as the anticipation of danger, pointing up that whole groups or societies may develop the habit of responding to certain cues with anticipation of danger or anxiety. Siegel analyzed three cultures—the Hopi, the East European Jewish Shtetel, and the Hutterites—where he found both a high level of anxiety and a high degree of cultural or social integration. He reasoned as follows:

Assuming that anxiety states are painful, especially when experienced intensely, it is expected that some opportunities are necessary to relieve tensions and to dispel them temporarily. The only universally approved mode of behavior which has this function is participation in communal life itself. Many of the real and supposed dangers of individuals are removed at least in part by the comfort of common participation in group-centered activities (Siegel, 1955, p. 43).

Though not made explicit by Siegel, the inference is quite clear. The cultural custom or pattern of responding to fear generated by cues perceived in common by the members of a society led to a decrease in individualism and an increase in group cohesion and the values, beliefs, and practices that maintain it.

A similar phenomenon of personality-culture interaction can be found in the cultural customs or patterns of response to the emotion of shame. Although the lack of adequate theoretical conception and definition of the emotions led to some errors in ethnological accounts of shame and shame-related behavior, it is still quite clear that there is similarity across cultures in the basic emotion that is experienced but also intercultural differences in social conditions that lead to the emotion. Whiting and Child (1953) suggested that guilt in some form and to some degree is present in all societies and that guilt typically results from deviation from cultural rules or idiosyncratic standards of behavior. The fact that cultures differ considerably in the extent to which the individual or the society is expected to monitor behavior and mete out punishment for deviation led Benedict (1946) to dichotomize cultures as shame cultures or guilt cultures. Ausubel (1955) criticized this dichotomy, reasoning as did Tomkins (1963) that guilt and shame basically are the same emotion though distinctions may be drawn in terms of emotion-activating conditions (Ausubel) or at the level of conscious experience (Tomkins). Izard (1972) showed that shame or shyness and guilt can be represented as relatively independent empirical factors.

## 5 EXPERIMENTAL STUDIES EXAMINING EMOTION CONCEPTS CROSS–CULTURALLY

Grinder and McMichaels (1963, 1964, 1966) showed that personal behaviors in relation to shame and guilt vary with cultural concepts and practices. In the first experiment they studied the relative effect of "a shame and a guilt culture" on resistance to temptation. Following Mead's (1956) observation that Samoans are guilt free since their behavior control depends entirely on external sanctions, Grinder and McMichael hypothesized that in a temptation situation where people could envision no social sanction for transgression, Samoan children (from a shame culture with behavior control by social sanction) would show less resistance to temptation than would American children (from a guilt culture with behavior control by own sanction). They measured resistance to temptation by a game in which children had to cheat to win the proffered prize or reward. The children did not know that the experimenter had a sure way of detecting those who falsified their scores in the target-shooting game. Two weeks after the target-shooting session, the children were administered a multiple-choice story-completion measure of guilt. The stories described a transgression wherein the transgressor could not be detected, and the children were required to check the response that best described what they would feel and do if they were the character in the story. They found, as predicted, that significantly more of the Samoan children (100%) yielded to temptation and falsified their scores on the target-shooting game. Further, the Samoans had significantly lower means on all three dimensions of the story-completion guilt measure—remorse, confession, restitution. However, the magnitude of the

**TABLE 1** Responses to the question: "Which emotion do you understand the least?

| Emotions most frequently chosen | Western cultures[a] (%) | Japanese[b] (%) |
|---|---|---|
| Distress-anguish | 10 | 5 |
| Disgust-contempt | 20 | 5 |
| Shame-humiliation | 21 | 68 |
| Fear-terror | 22 | 5 |
| Other | 27 | 17 |

[a]$N = 212$ males.
[b]$N = 42$ males.

Samoans' scores on the story-completion test showed they were far from free of guilt or the effects of conscience as Mead implied.

In a later study, using the same tests, McMichael and Grinder (1964) found no differences between Japanese-Americans and white Americans in Hawaii. It was the study of the Japanese that led Benedict (1946) to the same-culture concept, but it might be argued that there has been much cultural change since her study and that Hawaii may not provide an adequate testing ground for the hypothesis. In a third study McMichael and Grinder (1966) found some evidence that guilt development, as measured by their procedures, was weaker in Japanese-American children in Hawaii who had little exposure to American culture than in those with greater exposure.

Izard (1971) obtained evidence that some apparent intercultural differences in emotion-related behavior may be in attitudes toward the emotions rather than in the emotions themselves. Following the emotion-labeling and emotion-classification experiments, he administered a questionnaire designed to get at attitudes and personal experiences with the emotion. Subjects were instructed to answer the questions with one of the emotions on the list of fundamental emotions that had been provided for the classification experiment.

In answer to the question, "Which emotion do you understand the least?" the males from the eight western cultures divided the majority of their answers between three negative emotions, but 68% of the Japanese named shame-humiliation (see Table 1).

In answer to the question, "Which emotion do you dread the most?" there are even more dramatic differences (Table 2), with the Japanese having a much higher percentage of responses in the category of disgust-contempt.

Yet in answer to the question, "Which negative emotion do you experience most frequently?" the Japanese did not differ from those in western cultures on either shame-humiliation or disgust-contempt. However, the data suggest that westerners experience anger more frequently than do Japanese (see Table 3).

Izard's data (1971) not only point to a basic cross-cultural similarity in emotion at the behavioral-expressive and experiential levels but to possibly important intercultural differences in attitudes toward the emotions and possibly in the frequency of experiencing certain of the emotions. Generally consistent with this is the finding of McMichael and Grinder that though cultural differences in emphasis on internal control (Americans,

**TABLE 2** Response to the question: "Which emotion do you dread the most?"

| Emotions most frequently chosen | Western cultures[a] (%) | Japanese[b] (%) |
|---|---|---|
| Distress-anguish | 15 | 12 |
| Disgust-contempt | 10 | 69 |
| Shame-humiliation | 28 | 7 |
| Fear-terror | 31 | 12 |
| Other | 16 | 0 |

[a]$N = 212$ males.
[b]$N = 42$ males.

TABLE 3  Response to the question: "Which negative emotion do you experience most frequently?"

| Emotions most frequently chosen | Western cultures[a] (%) | Japanese[b] (%) |
|---|---|---|
| Distress-anguish | 37 | 48 |
| Disgust-contempt | 22 | 21 |
| Shame-humiliation | 11 | 14 |
| Fear-terror | 0 | 5 |
| Anger-rage | 30 | 12 |

[a]$N = 212$ males.
[b]$N = 42$ males.

Europeans) or external control (Samoans, Japanese) may lead to differences in the frequency of yielding to temptation or in the way guilt is depicted, there are feelings of guilt following transgression in both types of cultures.

Evidence reviewed by Munroe and Munroe (1975) supports the idea that emotion experiences in infancy and childhood influence personality development and social behavior. For example, they found the neglect of the emotional needs of the infant and young child tended to produce adult personality traits of fearfulness and suspicion.

## 6 THE EMOTIONS AND DEVELOPMENTAL PROCESSES: EVIDENCE FROM DIFFERENT CULTURES

Some exciting evidence regarding the role of emotion in early development was presented in a report from the Pediatrics Institute of the Academy of Medical Sciences of the USSR (Kistiakovskaia, 1965). The research was concerned with the "animation complex," defined as the infant's original positive expressive emotional reaction, consisting of three kinds of responses—the facial expression of smiling,

vocalization, and animated movements of arms and legs. Kistiakovskaia introduced this report with the following statement: "All of practical experience in child rearing shows that a timely appearance of these responses is of much significance to the neuromental and physical development of children" (p. 39). Her principal findings of relevance to the present chapter are the following:

1. The positive emotional expressive movements aid the infant in the basic matter of exploring his environment by sustaining visual concentration, increasing both its duration and stability.

2. Satisfaction of organic needs may reduce or eliminate some of the negative emotions, but such biological drive satisfaction does not lead to positive emotional reactions.

3. Affectionate communications with another person at close range is considered the most effective means to the development of positive emotional reactions.

The role of the face and facial expression in human development, particularly in the development of the positive emotions so important in social responsiveness and interpersonal ties, points to the importance of investigating the development of the ability to recognize and label the facial expressions of the fundamental human emotions. Ability to discriminate among the various expressions should furnish a direct index of an important kind of social perception, perception of nonverbal cues that denote the emotional state of the perceived.

Studies by European psychologists have shown that perception of expressions of emotion plays a significant role in certain cognitive processes of children (Honkavaara, 1961; Lévy-Schoen, 1964). The relative importance of emotion perception in the behavior measured in the experiments varied with the nature of the stimulus situations, the subsequent response alternatives, and the age of the subjects. Honkavaara concluded that "matter-of-fact" (palpable) perception preceded "expression" perception by several years. Lévy-Schoen, in presenting children the possibility of forming a concept of similarity (of persons) either on the basis of palpable objects ("accessories") they were wearing, or on the basis of facial expressions, found that responses were based on accessories until age 8–10 years, after which expression dominated.

In a modifed replication and extension of Lévy-Schoen's experiment, Savitsky and Izard (1970) showed that children could use emotion-expression cues in forming a concept of similarity as early as age 5 or 6 years, 3–4 years earlier than the age found by Lévy-Schoen. They attributed the great difference to better methodology and to clearer and stronger emotion expressions in their photographs.

In an earlier study by Gates (1923), children showed an increase in ability to interpret facial expressions with increasing age. She later found that this ability was substantially correlated with "estimated social or emotional maturity" (Gates, 1925).

Izard (1971) adapted his emotion-labeling and emotion-recognition experiments for children. He found that children of different cultures (American and French) showed a similar and steady progression in their ability to demonstrate (nonverbally) their recognition of nine fundamental emotions. Interestingly, American and French children differed significantly in the development of their ability to give appropriate free-response labels to the expressions, an ability that would be expected to be more influenced by sociocultural variables.

A study by Odom and Lemond (1972) used both emotion-recognition and emotion-expression techniques. They studied the relationship between childrens' ability to discriminate among emotion expressions and their ability to produce emotion expressions on request. They used two different tasks to measure emotion discrimination: a matching-discrimination task in which the child had to match one of the four photographs with a model held by the examiner and a situation-discrimination task in which the child had to point to the photograph that matched a situation verbally described by the examiner (e.g., "show me the one being chased by a mean dog"). They also used two means of obtaining voluntary expressions: an imitation-production task in which the child attempted to "make a face like you would if you felt like these people do," the stimuli being two photographs of different people showing the same expression. The second technique was a situation-production task in which the experimenter read the same situations as used in the imitation task and asked the child to make a face as if he were in that specific situation. The experimenters used the series of photographs developed by Izard (1971). Their subjects were 32 kindergarten and 32 fifth-grade children from schools in middle-class neighborhoods.

Their results showed that the older children made more correct responses on both tasks than the younger children and that more correct responses were made in the discrimination tasks than in the production tasks. Further, more correct responses were made to some expressions than to others. Children who had a discrimination task first made more correct responses across both tasks than did those who had a production task first. The results also showed that children obtained higher scores on the discrimination tasks than on the production tasks. The discrepancy between discrimination and production was significant $(p < .01)$ for all expressions except interest and joy. The authors thought that the improvement in production (voluntary expression) with age might reflect greater refinement in the stored representations of expressions (Gibson, D. C., 1969), but that the level of production accuracy might be lowered by the inhibiting effects of socialization factors as well as other unidentifiable influences (Izard, 1971).

## 7  SUMMARY

1. The problem of defining emotion concepts was seen as resulting from the oversimplification of these highly complex phenomena that have neurophysiological, behavioral-expressive, and subjective-experiential components.

2. The work of a number of theorists and researchers in psychology, neurophysiology, and ethology supported the hypothesis that facial behavior is an important component of emotion.

3. Empirical definitions consisting of photographic representations and corresponding verbal concepts were established for nine fundamental emotions. The definitions were validated in a number of cross-cultural experiments.

4. Evidence based on anthropological observations and from controlled experiments supported the proposition that the fundamental emotions as defined in this chapter may be viewed as transcultural variables that influence personality and interpersonal behavior.

5. Empirical data demonstrated that children's ability to recognize the nine fundamental emotions develops at a regular and similar rate in different cultures and that emotion expressivity may be related to physiological arousal and observable personality variables.

## APPENDIX: THE FUNDAMENTAL EMOTIONS

As indicated in the text, no agreed-upon classification of emotions has been accepted by the author or other authorities. Studies beginning with Wundt have resulted in the number of "fundamental emotions" being given as anything from two to ten. The following list of basic emotional patterns is reasonable on the basis of both factor analytic studies and logical analyses. It has proven useful in intracultural and cross-cultural research. Therefore, it is set forth as a useful categorization of emotions without any pretense as to its finality.

1. *Interest-Excitement*: concentrated, attending, attracted, curious.

2. *Enjoyment-Joy*: glad, merry, delighted, joyful.

3. *Surprise-Startle*: sudden reaction to something unexpected, astonished.

4. *Distress-Anguish*: sad, unhappy, miserable, feels like crying.

5. *Disgust-Revulsion*: repugnance, aversion, distaste, sickened.

6. *Anger-Rage*: angry, hostile, furious, enraged.

7. *Shame-Humiliation*: shy, embarrassed, ashamed, guilty.

8. *Fear-Terror*: scared, afraid, terrified, panicked.

9. *Contempt-Scorn*: disdainful, sneering, derisive, haughty.

# 21

## Personality and Small Group Behavior

**Graham M. Vaughan**
*University of Auckland, New Zealand*

## 1 THEORETICAL AND METHODOLOGICAL CONSIDERATIONS

In relating personality characteristics to group process, the focus of this chapter is restricted to small groups, to situations in which the individual can interact with all others. This task contains at least three problems: (a) clarifying the levels of discourse that can relate two conceptual systems, (b) making generalized (transsituational) statements about behavior, and (c) deciding which variables to consider. Each problem is considered here.

### 1.1 Levels of Discourse

The psychological significance of group studies lies in examining the effects that social interaction can have on individual behavior. The interest of the social psychologist is in the behavioral dependence one person has on another (cf. Zajonc, 1966), which derives in turn from interaction. Several meanings and consequent avenues of analysis can be attached to *interaction*: the individual's effect on a group, a group's effect on the individual, the individual's effect on other individuals, and a group's effect on the individual's orientation to other groups. This chapter deals with the first two meanings only. The chapters by Clore and Byrne and by Schneewind overlap with the third meaning, and the fourth

meaning (which emphasizes intergroup process) is outside the theme of this *Handbook*. In the instance of the second meaning, the connotation of *effect* excludes *change* or *development*. Such meanings could legitimately view the group as a therapeutic agent, or deal with cultural groups (cf. Izard's chapter) or with primary groups (cf. Hermann's chapter) insofar as they affect personality development.

Our view, then, takes in the two-way relations between the individual and the small group—in particular that kind of group in which a person has little or no control over member selection. This covers nearly all laboratory group studies in that they typically use ad hoc groups, but it extends to those real-life settings where most people's influence on other-member selection is curtailed, as in work groups.

### 1.2 Transsituational Behavior

#### 1.2.1 Personality

How consistently do people really behave? Personality theorists committed to a *trait* position believe that there are aspects of behavior relatively insensitive to change over time and through varying situations. Although some theorists, such as Cattell, also regard traits as dynamic (i.e., behavior-controlling structures), the present author believes that the recent broadsides delivered

511

at trait doctrines by social-learning theory (e.g., Mischel, 1968, 1973) can be handled at a lower level of conceptual inference. One simply asks whether a trait label is a useful descriptive term in classifying a differential tendency of people to generalize across a set of defined stimulus situations. Mischel posed the problem as follows:

It is widely assumed that traits are relatively stable and enduring predispositions that exert fairly generalized effects on behavior.... Support for the value of trait-state theories would require demonstrating, first, that people do behave consistently across many diverse situations.... It would also be necessary to show that inferences about an individual's traits and states permit important predictions about his behavior (1968, pp. 6, 9, 10).

The main thrust of Mischel's subsequent criticism of the trait concept was directed at the response consistency claim of its adherents. Janis, Mahl, Kagan and Holt (1969) took the view that a "trait ... is a descriptive, not an explanatory concept" (p. 578). Further, Levy (1970) argued that assigning a trait score to a person "is only to state the probability with which we expect him to behave in some fashion.... Explanation for his behavior does not reside in this statement; only its prediction" (p. 205). Even at this descriptive level, Mischel queried the utility of the trait concept, pointing to low correlations (in personality research) across situations. As Bem (1972) put it, we are asked "by Mischel's more radical implication that we change our initial premise and assume cross-situational correlations to be zero until proved (or explicitly constructed) to be otherwise."

Operating descriptively, and excluding dynamic considerations, three characteristics are assumed in research: (a) response consistency to a defined stimulus, (b) behavioral generality to a variety of stimuli, and (c) normality of distribution of derived trait scores. Trait assessment can be based on life records, questionnaire responses, or *actual* behavior; but in any instance, the trait score is built up by *aggregating* performances. On a questionnaire, a raw trait score consists of the number of times positively keyed items are checked or negatively keyed ones are rejected: The total score implies that consistently expressed behavior has been assessed through a number of contexts (items). This view of the function of items is similar to Horst's (1966) observation that tests consist of a collection of stimulus elements (items), "each one of which [items] can be regarded as a separate and distinct measuring device ... A test which has a hundred items in it is therefore a collection of devices for measuring each of a hundred variables" (p. 110). Ignoring the separate problem of item validity vis-à-vis *actual* behavior, the argument is that a trait score is a description of a person in transsituational terms.

If the assumption of trait score normality is thought through, something more can be added to the foregoing argument: Behavioral generality *increases* as the score becomes more extreme. Response predictability for any one situation, then, is a function of the extent to which the person's trait score varies from the population mean—the more it varies, the better the prediction. Continuing to assume that the trait in question is distributed normally in the population, then the average person gets an average score. As a consequence, predictability in any one situation for most (i.e., average) persons must suffer unless situation-specific characteristics are accounted for. This argument is, to an extent, in sympathy with Mischel's; but there is a caution not to discard what is of value. In his assessment of Mischel's stance, Bem (1972) advised us to proceed with the strategy that "inconsistency is the norm"; the present author sees this, ironically, as the essence of normally distributed scores on a trait dimension. Interestingly, though, Bem went on to discuss the role of moderator variables (interaction effect in an analysis of variance [ANOVA] design), and also the possibility that *traits* may operate for the person that have phenomenonological reality only for him;[1] in either instance, he stated, we might be able to predict: "(1) certain behaviors (2) across certain situations (3) for certain people." This is also the kind of conclusion offered in this section: The orthodox, psychometric meaning of *trait* implies behavioral consistency only with extreme scorers.

In all, low correlations are not the end of the road for the trait personologist. Cattell long argued that there are a finite set of behavioral dimensions that are likely to be of use in describing activity; and, as L. R. Goldberg (1971) put it:

Those individual differences which are of the most significance in the daily transactions of humans with each other will become encoded into the natural language as single-word trait-descriptors.

Low correlations with behavioral criteria may serve only to indicate that the descriptors are efficient predictors for only a few persons, and that situation-specific indexes are needed for most.

### 1.2.2 Social Behavior and Trait Correlates

The foregoing touches on issues within a framework of personality assessment. When test instruments are employed to provide correlates of behavior, problems arise and

[1] In later writings, Mischel (1973, 1976) goes some way toward admitting that individuals may construe the environment in a consistent way.

none more so than in the instance of predicting social (interactional) behavior. Consider the statement "leaders are extraverted." Extraversion is a trait descriptor; it implies response consistency for any one person to any one stimulus, and also behavioral consistency for some across situations. *Leadership* ought to imply the same, but social research rarely indulges in such explicit analysis. Consequently, the statement given probably has not been tested.

At this point, we must now ask what kind of research designs might be used for examining such an hypothesis, and more generally for relating trait descriptors to behavior in groups. A logical breakdown of potential designs is outlined in Fig. 1.

The designs are identical to the extent that a personality trait ($Y_N$) is assumed to have been measured. They differ in terms of the generality of the social behavior assessed ($X_N$, $X_n$, $X_1$) and, less importantly, by way of sampling procedures adopted. The subscripts for the variables $X$ and $Y$ indicate the following: $N$ means that many diverse behaviors (or items) have been sampled and that the derivation of a trait score (even for social behavior) is therefore possible; $n$, that sufficient behaviors have been sampled to test for behavioral generality; and 1, that only one behavior has been sampled.

Design A is one in which knowledge of a domain of social behaviors is sufficiently advanced and sampled ($X_N$) to permit the derivation of a trait score. The added availability of a personality trait score ($Y_N$) means that a set of bivariate scores are at hand, permitting a correlational analysis. Use of the design must indicate that response consistency, behavioral generality (differing across persons), and normality of score distribution have been clearly established in some dimension of social or group process, and that a search for personality correlates

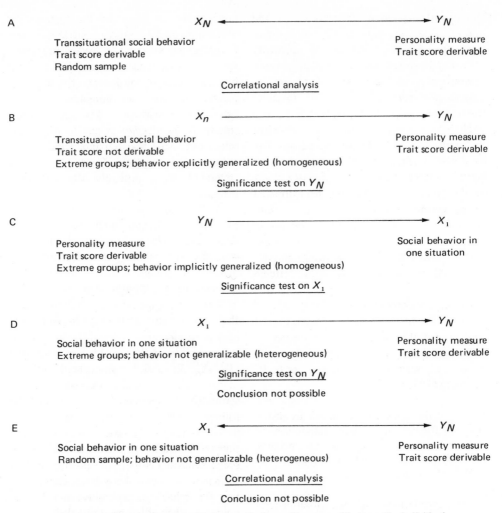

**FIG. 1** Sociopersonality research designs dealing with group effects on the individual.

has become worthwhile. The author is not aware of any investigation that has progressed to this point.

Design B is a fairly primitive substitute for Design A. The kind of study envisaged is one that samples just a few $(X_n)$ from a domain of social behaviors. The design assumes that these separate behaviors yield separate scores, but not that these scores can be aggregated directly to yield a trait score. Instead, use is made of groups of extreme scorers, persons who score either consis-

tently high or consistently low across the chosen situations. Attention is here restricted to those whose social behavior scores are relatively stable across situations, and who therefore constitute a *homogeneous set*. It is highly probable that these persons would be allocated either high or low trait scores, relative to the domain of behaviors in question, if such scores were calculable. The design could also solve certain practical problems inherent in Design A, in which the repeated testing of people could lead to decreased motivation or increased suspicion of deception. Statistical analysis would be effected on trait scores ($Y_N$) derived from a personality measure as the dependent variable.

Design C involves trait scores ($Y_N$) derived from a personality measure as the independent variable. The dependent variable $X_1$ bears its subscript to emphasize its solitary, situation-bound nature. This is true, despite the probability that within a given investigation multiple responses can be observed on the given measure. "It is important to recognize the distinction between a test as a measure of a single variable and a test as a collection of devices for measuring a number of variables" (Horst, 1966, p. 110). Consequently, the results of a study using this kind of design are limited to describing the relationship between two sets of scores: one set based on a specific behavioral variable, the other on scores each one of which measures a separate variable, so that the set as a whole is implicitly transsituational (i.e., trait-like). Without further experiments, generalizations from the observed relationship to other specific behaviors ($X_2$, $X_3$, etc.) are not possible.[2] The broader conclusions inherent in the nature of the results for Designs A and B are not available in C.

Design D uses a solitary measure of social behavior, $X_1$, as the independent variable. It is not known to what extent the responses of high-scoring and low-scoring people are specific to $X_1$ or are generalizable to other randomly selected measures ($X_2$, $X_3$, etc.). In terms of transsituational consistency,

[2] Argyle and Little (1972) believe that results at this level can still have meaning. An effect specific to a situation can be thought of as a situation-trait interaction. This, in turn, can lead to a debate as to how much *variance* is attributable to the person, the situation, and the interaction. Bowers (1973) has gone so far as to argue that an *interactionist* position is the only one tenable.

then, the persons constitute a *heterogeneous set*.

Design E suffers from a fault similar to that noted for Design D. No estimate is possible of the identity or otherwise between an individual's score on $X_1$ and $X_2$, $X_3$, and so forth. Although a correlational analysis of the results of an E-type study might look possible, an interpretation would carry no more meaning than it would following significance testing in a D-type study.

### 1.2.3 Conclusions

Although Mischel's (1968) criticism of the utility of the concept of trait carries much weight, crucial and truly relevant data are still lacking. The present author has put forward criteria of a trait none of which requires either a reification of the concept or a proposal of causal properties. At least five kinds of research designs are possible in the field of research (sociopersonality) in question, only some of which can offer meaningful results. Designs A, B, and C stand up to a logical analysis. Design A has probably never been used; B has been used very rarely; C has been employed quite commonly, but its limitations due to specificity remain largely unrecognized. The designs most often used are C, D, and E. The present author criticizes the usefulness of Designs D and E. Of course, it can be argued that meaning occasionally (if fortuitously) has emerged from studies within these categories, since investigations using different, single measures of social behavior sometimes yield comparable results. At the same time, conflict between studies might well be explained in part by the arguments advanced here.

### 1.3 Framework of Discussion

An orientation to sets of personality and group process variables is given here. It should be pointed out, however, that a review of the relationship between such sets could be scaled for describing arbitrariness depending on whether the variables examined derived from the reviewer's whim, from trends in univariate research, or from dimensions based on multivariate research.

### 1.3.1  Personality Variables

In an earlier review, Mann (1959) selected seven personality dimensions to relate to group process. Seven are also chosen here, though the list is not identical to Mann's. Although a multivariate approach such as Cattell's would have favored attending to source traits in this context, the adoption of such a tactic would result in a severe attrition of variables and of studies dealt with, since group research has rarely employed such units. Furthermore, some variables (e.g., authoritarianism) seem to have fascinated many group researchers, even though these might have been more efficiently presented as a composite of variables (cf. Bereiter, 1966).

The variables selected represent, rather simply, what investigators have chosen to focus on and, from a multivariate viewpoint, represent a mixture of primary factors, second-order factors, trait composites, and loosely aggregated variables:

*Adjustment*: Includes descriptions of stability, maturity, self-confidence; opposite meanings are anxiety, neuroticism, psychoticism. The attributes are often derived from observer ratings and sometimes from peer ratings, questionnaire devices such as Taylor Manifest Anxiety Scale (MAS), and the second-order factor in the 16 Personality Factor Questionnaire (16 PF).

*Extraversion*: Includes outgoing, surgent, cyclothyme, sociable. Most studies, however, use the global concept. Ratings are com-

monly employed, and sometimes a questionnaire measure such as the 16-PF second-order factor.

*Dominance*: Includes ascendance, and more obliquely, aggression. Ratings and questionnaires are used, the latter including the 16-PF primary Factor $E$.

*Intelligence*: Includes problem solving ability, and (less justifiably) creativity. The more global concept of intelligence is usually assessed by an IQ test, whereas the more specific referents given above are usually tapped by ratings.

*Interpersonal sensitivity*: Includes empathy, considerateness, social perceptiveness, concern for others; also friendliness, low suspiciousness. Reports often use the global term, even though it is almost certainly multidimensional. Ratings are usually employed, most often being estimates by self and peers.

*Authoritarianism*: Includes autocratic, respect for authority, authority submissive. Again, the global term is almost certainly multidimensional. Assessment is by both ratings and questionnaires, the latter especially in terms of the California $F$ scale.

*Needs*: A nonspecific aggregate, including need achievement, affiliation, approval, affection, social love. Both ratings and tests are employed. A popular test devised by McClelland uses Thematic Apperception Test (TAT) material.

The first five variables coincide with Mann's list, indicating continuing interest in them. Increasing mention in the literature of authoritarianism and various needs is at the expense of Mann's variables of Masculinity and Conservatism. The present list is not adhered to rigidly in the following review of studies, serving rather as a guide for discussion. Other personality measures are referred to occasionally, and a few broader based studies are examined individually.

### 1.3.2 Group Process Orientation

There are no currently agreed-upon means of insuring that a reviewer can select group behavioral dimensions that are both important and independent. Different categories can be found in source works (Hare, 1962; McGrath & Altman, 1966), which have been defended on grounds of utility but not in terms of measurement. Bereiter (1966) argued that the isolation of legitimate group structural properties must derive from interactive behavioral data and not from formal structural characteristics. However, a basic ordering of group properties sufficient to describe the major functions of the small group remains a research problem of major magnitude.

In this chapter, three aspects of group functioning are examined; no claim can be made for their independence or comprehensiveness, though they do incorporate most personality-oriented small group studies:

1. Member composition and the group process. The focus is on the effects of specified personality variables on the group process. Dependent variables include task activity, social-emotional activity, participation, productivity, and problem solving.
2. Role emergence. An individual's personality can affect the opportunity for acting out certain roles. Although this should apply to all possible roles in a group, most research has been with the particular role of leader.
3. Social stimulus and the individual. The emphasis here is on the person's response to the group as a unit. Studies in person perception, which could be thought of as dealing with "differentiated others," are excluded. Rather, the interest is in a group which has reached *clotting point* (cf. Brown, R., 1965, p. 673) and its effect on the individual. Conformity is one process especially considered here.

The functioning of personality in relation to each of the three aspects of group process are examined in the remaining sections of this chapter.

## 2  MEMBER COMPOSITION AND GROUP PROCESS

### 2.1  Multivariate Research

A major, if isolated, contribution to this field was a study by Cattell and Stice (1960). Cattell's conception of group structure and performance can be variously traced (Cattell, 1948b, 1962b; Cattell, Saunders, & Stice, 1953). His position is a dynamic one. He postulated that group goal achievement is instrumental in satisfying individual needs. Cattell's description of a group requires details from (a) *population* characteristics (the group mean and variance on individual parameters, e.g., personality dimensions, attitudes, and beliefs), (b) *structure* (specifying roles, statuses, and organization), and (c) *syntality* (group behavior acting in a unified fashion).

The Cattell and Stice study was an ambitious work, first reported in 1945, aimed at determining the principal syntality dimensions of neonate groups. From 80 10-man groups, intercorrelations were obtained on 93 variables (personality, sociometric, observer ratings, and performance). The groups met for three 3-hour sessions over a week.

The results were factor analyzed (multiple analysis, rotating to simple structure) to determine dimensions for each session. This revealed which factors were transient and which were stable through a group's life. Stability over at least two sessions was found for 14 dimensions, 9 of which were loaded strongly by personality factors. These 9 dimensions were found not to load in one-to-one fashion with Cattell's primary

16-PF factors, but rather with groups of such factors or even with factor variances. The authors felt that some of the dimensions were in fact second-order personality factors and others were *interactional emergence* factors. The first kind were envisaged as population rather than syntality factors, since they might be obtained independently of group interaction (see upper part of Table 1). The emergence factors derive from loadings on personality factors that are either uncorrelated primaries, not merging at

**TABLE 1**   Personality-syntality factors stable across group sessions

| Factor description | 16–PF factors | Effects on group performance |
|---|---|---|
| Syntality factors as second-order personality factors: | | |
| Surgent Democratic Communicativeness | $F, I-, N$ | Much verbal interaction, free discussion, planning by many, members like one another, little argument, accurate in tasks requiring cooperation. |
| Unsophisticated Suggestible Palaver | $F-, I, N-$ | Argumentation, long planning, high suggestibility (in jury task). |
| Garrulous Nervous Emotionality | $M, O, Q_4, (H-), (L)$ | Poor performance under stress, difficulty in making coordinated judgments, preference for nonverbal activities. |
| Syntality factors as interactional emergence factors: | | |
| High Immediate Synergy | $B, LO, (C), (O-), (Q_4 -)$ | High degree of leadership, motivation, we-feeling, organization, orderliness. |
| Adventurous Forcefulness | $C, E, F, G, H, Q_3$ | Preference for outgoing tasks, low individuality in discussions. |
| Intellectually Effective Cyclothyme Role | $A, E, L-, (B), (Q_1)$ | Accurate performance, though responsive to emotional appeals (jury task); intelligent mutual coordination. |
| Sophisticated Democratic Determination | $N, Q_3{}^v, (B-{}^v), (H), (L), (L^v)$ | Determined, decisive in action, good morale, motivation, lack of frustration, low suggestibility. |
| Frustration Through Temperamental Heterogeneity | $I^v, L^v, M^v, N^v$ | Need for leadership technique, internal dislike, rigidity of individual attitudes, dislike of discussion, poor performance generally. |
| Frustration of Group Through Dominance | $E, (O^v)$ | Group atmosphere free but general dislike of group life; poor performance on tasks demanding organization. |

*Note.* The listed 16-PF factors have average loadings of at least .30 and generally exceed .40. Those given in parentheses had relatively high loadings on 1 group session only and an average loading of less than .30. A negative sign indicates a negative loading. The superscript $v$ indicates a variance. From Cattell & Stice (1960).

a second-order level or factor variances (see low part of Table 1). Table 1 is a condensation by the present author of these extensive results.

The first two syntality factors in this table are both loaded by the primaries *F, I,* and *N* and may be polar opposites of a unitary dimension. Cattell and Scheier (1961) referred to this grouping as a second-order personality factor that is probably basic to Neuroticism. This might mean that when members are generally high on *I* (Premsia) and low on *F* (Desurgency) and on *N* (Naivete), the group as a unit is neurotic: The behavioral consequences include much arguing and slowness in starting tasks. The third upper factor possesses primary contributors to a second-order factor of anxiety (cf. Cattell & Scheier, 1961), with group behavioral consequences of nervous garrulousness, poor performance in facing shock, and so forth.

The emergence factors in the lower section of Table 1 include a series of uncorrelated primaries and several instances of heterogeneity (high variance) on a given characteristic among members. Many behavioral consequences are noted in the table.

In all, Cattell and Stice mount the argument that group performance can be considerably influenced, sometimes dramatically and sometimes subtly, by the personality characteristics of its members. Their experimental groups were randomly constituted, and it is regrettable that no studies since have attempted to replicate their findings by systematic group selection in terms of member characteristics.

## 2.2 Univariate Research

Nearly all research on personality effects on group performance shows little concern for testing the independence of chosen group process dimensions; and in most cases,

"Dimensions" reads singular rather than plural. Mann's (1959) review permits condensation of earlier findings.

### 2.2.1 Participation Rate

Mann noted a clear positive relation between participation rate and *intelligence,* a trend supported by later studies (Kiessling & Kalish, 1961; Stager, 1967). Mann pointed to a similar relationship for *adjustment,* and this has also been substantiated (Cleveland & Morton, 1962; Haythorn, 1953; Kiessling & Kalish, 1961). Cervin clouded the issue slightly by reporting a positive link with emotional stability (1955) and then with emotional responsivity (1957). A general positive relation with extraversion was recorded by Mann and with *dominance* by Evans (1960).

### 2.2.2 Task Activity

This measure overlaps with participation rate when the latter is defined as total activity rate (cf. Mann). In those studies where a distinction is possible, task activity can be assessed in the following ways: (a) the number of task contributions and (b) the number of contributions proportional to the total number of any participative acts. In these terms, *intelligence* is positively associated with (a) but negatively with (b). It seems that the intelligent person makes more task contributions in total, but that these are submerged in a great number of generally participative acts. *Adjustment* likewise relates positively to (a) but negatively to (b), and a similar interpretation is possible. Mann pointed out that task and participative acts are generally not distinguishable in studies of *extraversion.*

### 2.2.3 Productivity

The output of a group has been variously defined, for example, number of solutions, solution time required, and solution quality. In one sense it appears to be strictly a performance measure, but it can be argued that it is related to task activity. If a distinction is to be maintained, it would be that not all task activity is *successful* or productive. Further, productivity can occur at the expense of members' social-emotional needs. Hare (1962) developed these points further.

The variable has been widely researched in relation to members' characteristics. It has been related to high *adjustment* (Cervin, 1957; Greer, 1955; Haythorn, 1953; Kipnis & Wagner, 1967; League & Jackson, 1964; Mussen & Porter, 1959; Stotland, Thorley, Thomas, Cohen, & Zander, 1957). Similar associations have been reported with *interpersonal sensitivity* (Exline, 1960; Greer, Calanter, & Nordlie, 1954; Hall, R. L., 1956; Katz, Maccoby, & Morse, 1950), with *members' intelligence* (Nakamura, 1955; Stager, 1967; Tuckmann, 1964, 1967), and with *leader's intelligence* (Fiedler & Meuwise, 1963; Greer, Calanter, & Nordlie, 1954).

In relation to *needs*, Mussen and Porter (1959) reported that productivity was rated higher by members when *n* Aggression was low. In relation to *authoritarianism*, Haythorn, Couch, Haefner, Langham, and Carter (1956b) claimed no difference in performance between high and low scorers, though the latter discussed more intelligently. High authoritarians are apparently more efficient (Haythorn, Couch, et al., 1956a), but higher production goes with democratic supervisors (Katz, Maccoby, & Morse, 1950).

A plausible hypothesis, not well explored, is that productivity varies with the manner in which task requirements (and role demands) are congruent with available member characteristics. Attention is given later to this question of member heterogeneity.

### 2.2.4 Social-emotional Activity

Interpreted positively, this refers to agreement, solidarity, and tension release. This aspect of group process has received little attention. Mann (1959) referred to only two studies indicating that positive activity relates to higher *intelligence* and better *adjustment*.

Undoubtedly, the concept is complexly related to participation, task activity, and productivity. As mentioned, high productivity may depress positive social-emotional activity. Again, negative social-emotional activity, with associated frustration and tension, may follow from incompatibility of members' characteristics (as in Cattell & Stice, 1960); this in turn might adversely affect task activity and productivity.

Research in this field has implications for group therapy. One investigator found that members assessed as hostile or affectionate may project these feelings (Taylor, F. K., 1954, 1955). Inhibitory or facilitative outcomes in the group therapy process, therefore, could depend partly on the member characteristics of a given group.

### 2.3 Heterogeneity of Member Personality

Research on the effects of member heterogeneity on group process is suggestive though not extensive. Scodel and Mussen (1953) paired discussion dyads of high and low *F*-scale scorers, finding that the former rated the latter as authoritarian, suggesting a need to create an illusory in-group. Shaw (1960) argued that the extent to which homogeneity relates to group efficiency will depend on group structure and on the member characteristics in question. This has relevance for a study (Altman & McGinnies, 1960) in which group homogeneity varied in terms of California *E*-scale scores. The groups discussed ethnic conflict; those which were heterogeneous showed less spontaneity and more interpersonal conflict. This seems reasonable in that the independent variable was so closely related in kind to the discussion topic. Again, Shaw's point is relevant to Smelser's (1961) study in which Dominant (D) and Submissive (S) individuals were paired in combinations D-D, S-S, and D-S, and then assigned a dominant or submissive role. Productivity was maximal when the independent variable and the role were congruent (i.e., D-S persons in a D-S role combination), so that heterogeneity was effective in this specific way (cf. Fry, 1965). Heterogeneity in intelligence, however, may lead to higher interpersonal conflict (Stager, 1967).

On a broader front, L. R. Hoffmann and Maier's (1961) groups were selected to maximize Guilford-Zimmerman profile homogeneity or heterogeneity. Better problem solving occurred in heterogeneous groups. High variance on certain temperament factors gave a reverse result for Cattell and Stice (see Table 1). Schultz (1958) argued that heterogeneity can have good effects only when members differ in compatible ways, that is, when their differing characteristics are complementary.

The relationship between member heterogeneity and group process is obviously complicated. Cattell and Stice suggested that high variance on certain characteristics will prejudice good performance generally. However, where heterogeneity involves compatibility and is role relevant, the resulting congruence probably enhances satisfaction; the diverse orientation and skills should combine to facilitate productiveness.

## 2.4 Member Personality and Orientation

If personality in fact affects interaction, one might expect it to determine one's whole orientation in a social context: One might attend chiefly to self-interest, to the job at hand, or to the needs of others. Extensive research by Bass (1967) indicated substance in such a threeway division. Bass developed three scales reflecting differing individual orientations in group activity: self (one's own needs), interaction (fostering interpersonal relations), and task (obtaining group goals). Of interest here are data relating the orientation (Ori) scales to personality. Significant correlations with two personality instruments, the 16 PF and the Edwards Personal Preference Schedule (EPPS), are shown in Table 2.

A feature of the 16-PF and Self-Ori relations is evidence of anxiety. Although Bass did not discuss his material in these terms, it is clear that primary contributors to Cattell's second-order Anxiety are involved: $C(-)$, $L$, $O$, $Q_3(-)$, $Q_4$. It seems that anxious persons are concerned with their own needs, with consequent little interest in the objectives of other group members. EPPS $n$ Aggression and 16-PF Dominance ($E$) are also related to this scale. With the Interaction-Ori scale, sociable as distinct from assertive extraversion is detectable in the scale's relation with Cyclothymia ($A$) and Group Dependency, ($Q_2-$) being supported by EPPS $n$ Affiliation. With the Task-Ori scale, there are suggestions of aloofness, seriousness, and *drive* in the scale's association with Schizothymia ($A-$), Dominance ($E$), Desurgency ($F-$), Harria ($I-$), Self-sufficiency ($Q_2$), Self-sentiment Formation ($Q_3$), and EPPS $n$ Endurance. Bass describes the *types* as follows: The Self-Ori person asserts himself, competes, is visible, but is not interested in controlling. He is motivated to gain extrinsic rewards, but in so doing is irritable and has neurotic tendencies. The interaction-Ori person wants to belong, to affiliate, and to depend. The

**TABLE 2** Significant correlations between orientation scales and 16 Personality Factor Questionnaire (16-PF) and EPPS scales

| Orientation scale | 16-PF scales | | | | | | | | | | | EPPS needs |
|---|---|---|---|---|---|---|---|---|---|---|---|---|
| | A | C | E | F | I | L | M | O | Q₂ | Q₂ | Q₄ | |
| Self | − | + | | + | + | + | + | | | + | + | Aggression (+) Heterosexual (+) Change (−) |
| Interaction | + | | | | | | | | − | | | Affiliation (+) |
| Task | − | | + | − | − | | | + | + | | | Endurance (+) Heterosexual (−) |

*Note.* The algebraic sign indicates the direction of the observed relationship. The results are significant at the 5% level. From Bass (1967).

Task-Ori person is liberal, intelligent, intellectual, and open minded (and, it should be added, withdrawn).

Generally, Bass pointed to important ways in which personality characteristics bear on group process, and particularly on the mode in which a person addresses himself to the social setting.

## 3  ROLE EMERGENCE AND LEADERSHIP

Situational factors such as group survival and goal achievement are crucial in influencing the process of role differentiation (cf. Jones, E. E., & Gerard, 1967), and it might be tempting to conclude that personal characteristics have no effect on the way in which a group is constructed. The very range of population characteristics available, however, constrains the possibilities of role differentiation. Given that role differentiation is most noticeable in the early life of a group, personality ought to relate to individual suitability for certain roles. For maximum efficiency, "the better the fit of role and personality, the less need for elaborate organizational structures to ensure that everyone does his share" (Jones, E. E.,

& Gerard, 1967, p. 665). This point gathers strength from the earlier discussion of member heterogeneity in which role-personality congruence has some apparent effect on productivity.

Unfortunately, there are no data clarifying the relation between personality and role emergence in the general sense. Attention is therefore confined to one aspect of role differentiation, emergent leadership. Suffice it to say that research relevant to other possible roles is sorely needed.

Conflict concerning the relative weights attributable to personal and situational variables has characterized many leadership studies of the past few decades. According to one author, "not only do [reports] affirm that there are few characteristics in common among leaders but also that the differences far exceed the similarities" (Kemp, 1964, p. 197). Another (Steiner, 1964) asked that a global concept of leadership be replaced by several more unidimensional terms. A simplistic approach in which leaders possess attributes in an all-or-none fashion has long been abandoned (cf. Gouldner, 1950), and it has been argued (e.g., Burke, 1965) that reviews such as

Stogdill's (1948) rebuff a trait theory of leadership—despite those (e.g., Borgatta, Couch, & Bales, 1954; Jennings, 1960) who have pursued the *great man* hypothesis.

The issue can be restated in the terms adopted in Section 1 of this chapter: Is there any evidence for leadership-behavior consistency across situations, at least for some people? Trait-like behavior, at the lowest level of inference, is compatible with (a) low transsituational consistency for most, but high consistency for some persons; (b) predictive power increasing for most individuals by accounting for situational variables; (c) more predictive power for most people by restricting personality inferences to specific situations. Designs A, B, and C (Fig. 1) would provide pertinent data, but little research fits any of these categories. The findings reported here represent an attempt to pull available threads together.

### 3.1 Multivariate Research

Cattell and Stice (1960) defined a leader by his influence on group syntality; but their level of data, in fact, forced them to resort to structural definitions. Three criteria were used: observer ratings of highest degree of leadership, observer ratings of frequency of leadership acts, and the leader elected by other members. Significant differences on these criteria between leaders and members, on the 16 PF, are shown in Table 3.

Five factors differentiate on all criteria. Scores on $G$, $H$, $O$, $Q_3$, and $Q_4$ suggest that leaders have well-integrated character, adventurousness, emotional responsiveness, organizational precision, a capacity to see decisions through, and freedom from anxiety and worry that otherwise might sap confidence among members.

Other results in the table provide data of a situation-bound nature. Intelligence ($B$) relates only to leadership *acts*; this characteristic favors the technical leader with ready solutions. Emotional stability ($C$) characterizes the leader (principal) who actually leads and who (as Cattell and Stice thought) most influences syntality. Surgency ($F$) picks up two criteria, suggesting that the surgent person may catch the limelight and then hold it. Notable by its absence is Dominance ($E$); the authors view a tendency to identify authority with domination as misleading.

### 3.2 Other Findings

Despite a high proportion of studies of questionable design (Types D and E in Fig. 1) and a lack of systematic hypothesis

---

TABLE 3   Significant differences between leaders and nonleaders on 16 Personality Factor Questionnaire (16-PF) scales in terms of three leadership criteria

| Leadership criteria | 16-PF scales | | | | | | | | |
|---|---|---|---|---|---|---|---|---|---|
| | $B$ | $C$ | $F$ | $G$ | $H$ | $M$ | $O$ | $Q_3$ | $Q_4$ |
| Principal leader | | + | | (+) | + | | − | + | + |
| Frequent leadership acts | + | | + | + | + | | − | + | (−) |
| Elected leader | | | + | + | + | − | − | + | (−) |

*Note.* The algebraic sign indicates the direction of the observed relationship. The results are significant at the 5% (and 10%) level. From Cattell and Stice (1960).

construction, some pattern in the results from various sources survives.

High *adjustment* in leaders is a common finding (cf. Mann, 1959). Cattell and Stice (1960) pointed to emotional maturity and character integration. Self-orientation was noted by Bass and Dunteman (1963), self-confidence and emotional control by P. D. Nelson (1964), and self-reliance by R. C. Wilson, Beem, & Comrey (1953). Cattell and Stice (1960) also pointed to freedom from anxiety. Borg and Tupes (1958), however, related higher neuroticism ratings to leadership; but since these were peer ratings, the result may have been a person-perception effect deriving from the follower role. Differences in adjustment *between* leaders may occur. Student leaders may be less well adjusted than other kinds (Olmsted & Monachesi, 1955; Williamson & Hoyet, 1952); if so, the (undefined) characteristics of student organizations may place weight on some aspects of maladjustment.

Leaders are apparently more *extraverted* (cf. Mann, 1959). Borg and Tupes (1958) confirmed this trend, whereas Bass and Dunteman (1963) did not find leaders to be self-oriented, that is, they are at least looking out to the group and sometimes to the task. Cattell and Stice (1960) found only two factors ($F$ and $H$) out of six contributors to second-order Extraversion that distinguished leaders. This might suggest that sociable rather than assertive aspects of extraversion relate to leading.

Studies of *needs* are few. Leaders tend to be more job motivated (Nelson, P. D., 1964), and in groups requiring organizing they display achievement orientation (Rychlak, 1963). Burke's (1965) research is relevant, but is referred to later because of its emphasis on the leader-follower interaction.

*Intelligence* and leadership has been much investigated, and earlier studies point to a positive relationship (Mann, 1959). Borg and Tupes' (1958) finding can be added to the trend. Mann noted, however, that the median correlation was only .25. This kind of comment is noted here to drive home the fact that one-to-one relationships in the realm of personality study are a pipe dream (cf. the use of specification equations in Cattell's work). Allowance must also be made for the operation of situation-specific characteristics: Intelligence might be related to leadership acts rather than principal or elected leadership (Cattell & Stice, 1960), for example.

Although *dominance* is supposedly related to leadership, some reservations are in order. Mann's (1959) review and Borg and Tupes' (1958) findings support this trend, but Burke (1965) wrote of members *perceiving* leaders as autocratic, and only when a leader's social distance score was not congruent. Leaders have been typified as having *aggressive* needs, according to observer ratings (Nelson, P. D., 1964) and TAT responses (Rychlak, 1963). Cattell and Stice (1960), however, failed to relate dominance to any of their leadership criteria, though Surgency ($F$) and Parmia ($H$) were involved. This suggests that ratings of dominance confuse it with *outgoingness* and *adventurousness* (components of Cattell's Extraversion). Such a possibility warrants closer inspection.

Bass, McGehee, Hawkins, Young, and Gebel (1953) reported a negative relationship between *authoritarianism* and leadership, using observer-rated leadership behavior and $F$-scale scores. A similar effect was noted by Hollander (1954), using peer ratings of leadership.

*Interpersonal sensitivity* and leadership have been widely investigated. Mann (1959) inferred a positive link, but only a minority of reviewed studies produced significant results. Mann referred to Campbell's (1955) criticism that when a person's guess on his status is the measure of sensitivity, correlations with actual status may be spuriously high. In addition to studies noted by Mann, it has been found that leaders have a more "positive" attitude (Bass, McGehee, et al., 1953), show greater perceptiveness (Meyer, 1951), and are more considerate (Katz, 1950). The cluster of variables subsumed here seems to have lost appeal for researchers more recently.

### 3.3 Interaction of Variables

Cattell and Stice (1960) hypothesized that characteristics affecting group syntality might be not only second-order personality factors but also emergent interactional factors. In their findings, a number of first-order factors were associated with *specific* leadership criteria (cf. Table 3). This effect is interactional with respect to leader and situation. Interactions as such could be extended to include the leader-follower relationship. Borg and Tupes (1958) implied that different results obtain when observer and peer ratings are compared. Bass and Dunteman (1963), noted that member orientation interacts with leader orientation. Haythorn, Couch, et al. (1956b) reported an interaction for authoritarianism: Leaders showed this behavior for authoritarian followers but not for democratic followers, irrespective of the leaders' scores on the $F$ scale.

Burke (1965) related leader personality to both follower personality and the situation. There were four leader-follower combinations, varying on $n$ Achievement ($n$ Ach) and social distance (SD, on Fiedler's Assumed Similarity of Opposites—ASo—index). An interaction between SD and $n$ Ach was noted. There was lowered felt tension in followers when needs were met: High $n$ Ach followers felt this when their

leader was high in SD, while low $n$ Ach followers felt so when their leader was low in SD. Once again, a specific congruence is noted here, this time relating certain leader-follower characteristics; and it is interesting to note that Burke found 14 higher-order interactions using ANOVA, some of these relating to task variables as well.

Interactions, however, introduce some conceptual difficulty. Mischel (1973) rightly pointed out that the more *moderators* (interaction variables) are required to qualify trait prediction, the more situation-specific any generalization becomes.

## 4 SOCIAL STIMULUS AND THE INDIVIDUAL

In a sense, this section, more than any other, concerns the person. Up this point, we have stressed the interaction process and role emergence as functions of member characteristics. By contrast, the individual is now the figure, and the group is the ground. The special focus of researches has been on the individual's behavior as influenced by group consensus; by common usage, change has been referred to as *conformity*. This term has been variously interpreted (cf. Gerard & Miller, 1967). A conception of conformity as an end product, similar, say, to group problem solving, has led much research into a blind alley. Productive investigation defines it as a process of social influence involving a norm-regulated movement response (cf. Hollander & Willis, 1967), which, in turn, can be linked to communication, conflict, coping, attitude change, and the like. At a theory level, it is possible to discern in the literature the beginning of an integrative process moving to incorporate conformity within a larger body of knowledge.

The immediate interest concerns the extent to which the individual's personality relates to his tendency to conform, to be independent, or perhaps to resist a group norm. The remainder of the section deals with the present author's work on transsituationality and conformity, together with other studies that, on the whole, provide quite consistent information despite problems in both design and assessment.

## 4.1 Transsituational Conformity

The issue of establishing transsituational behavior, as discussed in the first section of this chapter, has been examined in the specific context of conformity (Vaughan, G. M., 1964). The background literature reflects diametrically opposed viewpoints: the assumption (rarely explicit) that conformity is an enduring individual characteristic and the argument that there is only room for situational determinants.

To test consistency in conformity, Vaughan exposed 64 females to four kinds of situations: simulated group pressure, written reports of a majority consensus, an injunction delivered by an authority figure, and a questionnaire index of acquiescence. Intercorrelations for these variables ranged from zero to .40, and only two of six were significant. At this point, the data were reanalyzed in terms of Design B in Fig. 1. Extreme groups ($N = 23$) were selected for consistent-high or consistent-low scores across the two variables correlating best, and it was found that the groups were now differentiable on a third variable. Finally, when the latter was incorporated as a third criterion, distilling the extreme groups still further ($N = 12$), the groups were differentiated on the remaining variable. The paradox of these results, derived from poor to moderately correlated variables for the full sample, is that they are consistent with the basic meaning of a trait descriptor. A more precise meaning is given to the situationist-personologist debate: Most persons are, in fact, inconsistent (average in the trait sense), and a few are consistent (high or low in the trait sense). The picture fits that of a normal distribution of trait behavior across diverse situations. For the few people who are consistent (i.e., relatively insensitive to contextual parameters), a search for other characteristics that might underly their behavior made some sense.

These high- (HC) and low-conforming (LC) subjects were compared on a large number of measures—16 PF, the Objective-Analytic Battery, an Australian Council for Educational Research (ACER) IQ test, Ascendance-Submission (A-S) Reaction, California Fascism ($F$) Scale, Rokeach Dogmatism ($D$) scale, and Eysenck Toughminded and Radicalism ($T-R$) scale. While corroborative, the Objective-Analytic results are omitted here. An independent experiment (White, K. D., & Vaughan, 1967) of 37 consistent male scorers from a pool of 240 was added to the study; and main results are summarized in Table 4.

These results show that both male and female high conformers score high on Authoritarianism as measured by the $F$ and $D$ scales; this effect survives even when $F$-scale scores are controlled for acquiescent set (Vaughan, G. M., & White, 1966). The HC males are high on $G$ (Superego Strength—"attentive to people" and "oriented to group goal"). The HC females are high on $I, L, O,$ and $Q_4$ (connotations include "sensitive," "dependent," "insecure," "inadequate," and "tense"). The LC males' and females' scores on $T-R, Q_1,$ $M,$ and $Q_2$ suggest "radicalism," "unconventionality," and "dissatisfaction with group integration"; both are also higher on IQ. Specific to LC females are indications of "ascendance," "maturity," and "exactness."

Generally, these results indicate broad differences between consistently high and

**TABLE 4**  Significant differences between high- and low-conforming persons on 16 Personality Factor Questionnaire scales and other selected measures

| Designation | Male | Female |
|---|---|---|
| High-conforming (HC) persons | Authoritarianism (Cal-*F, D*) <br> Superego Strength (*G*) | Authoritarianism (Cal-*F, D*) <br> Premsia (*I*) <br> Protension (*L*) <br> Guilt Proneness (*O*) <br> Ergic Tension ($Q_4$) |
| Low-conforming (LC) persons | Intelligence (*B*, ACER) <br> Radical ($Q_1$, T-R) <br> Autia (*M*) <br> Self-sufficiency ($Q_2$) | Intelligence (*B*, ACER) <br> Ascendant (*E*, A-S) <br> Ego-Strength (*C*) <br> Shrewdness (*N*) |

*Note.* The differences are within sex. Groupings take into account the direction of each difference; e.g., HC males are more authoritarian than are LC males and LC males are more intelligent than are HC males. Results are significant at the 5% level, most, in fact, at the 1% level. From Vaughan, G. M. (1964); White, K. B., and Vaughan (1967).

consistently low conformers and specific sex differences. The HC people as a whole were authority submissive. Additionally, males were conscientious and group-goal motivated to the exclusion of independent judgment (cf. Bass' Ori concept of interaction-orientation); females were sensitive, with some signs of anxiety (cf. Self-Ori). In contrast, LC subjects were generally more intelligent (cf. Task-Ori). Additionally, males were radical, unconventional, and implicitly lacking in group orientation; females were dominant, stable, and disciplined. To some extent, these results find support in independent research reported in the next section.

## 4.2  Other Findings

A complex relation appears to exist between *adjustment* and conformity. Self-rated adjustment has indicated a positive association, whereas other measures suggest it is negative (Mann, 1959). Either self-rating techniques are basically suspect, or HC subjects are people who respond in a socially desirable way by avoiding self-descriptions that appear damaging. The more reliable, negative association noted by Mann has generally been confirmed in other studies. HC subjects are low in self-esteem and self-confidence (Crowne & Liverant, 1963; Crutchfield, 1955; Hoffman, M. L., 1953; McDavid & Sistrunk, 1964; Schroder & Hunt, 1958; Smith, K. H., 1961) and, as might be expected by definition, lacking in independence (Back & Davis, 1965; Cleveland & Morton, 1962; Phelps & Meyer, 1966; Strickland & Crowne, 1962). When adjustment is defined as anxiety, a complication arises. Among male subjects, a negative relationship between anxiety and conformity has been observed in research using designs of Type *C*, as in Fig. 1 (Janis, 1954; Mangan, Quartermain, & Vaughan, 1959, 1960). Studies using the suspect Type E design are equivocal, a negative association in one instance (Goldberg, S. C., Hunt, Cohen, & Meadow, 1954) and no relationship in others (Steiner & Rogers, 1963; Tuddenham, 1959). Among female subjects, a positive association has been reported (Goldberg, S. C., Hunt, et al., 1954; Steiner & Rogers, 1963; Vaughan, G. M., 1964).

This sex difference was explored in a Type C study (Vaughan, G. M., & Taylor, 1966), and was clearly confirmed. The effect could indicate that the pressure situation could sharpen culturally expected sex-role behavior in anxious subjects that would include ascendant and submissive responses in males and females, respectively.

A negative relationship between *intelligence* and conformity has been noted several times (Crutchfield, 1955; Divesta & Cox, 1960; Nakamura, 1955; Vaughan, G. M., 1964; White, K. D. & Vaughan, 1967). Low conformity has been associated with creativity and individuality (Barron, 1952). An interaction with emotional responsiveness was observed in one case (Carment, Schwartz, & Miles, 1963), and a slight reverse trend was reported in an experimental condition where a group decision had to be reached (Rath & Misra, 1963). This was interpreted as showing that high-intelligent persons were more adaptable to group needs. A qualification attaching to most of this research is that samples are usually restricted to a student population and that a curvilinear relationship might be observed over an extended intelligence range. One finding already points in this direction (Crutchfield; 1951), which should serve as a reminder that nonmonotonic relationships could be common in the personality-conformity field (cf. McGuire, 1966).

The relation of *extraversion* to conformity is not clear. As with adjustment, a conflict in findings based on self-rating versus other measures is evident (Mann, 1959). Recent studies support a negative link characteristic of research employing other than self-ratings (Carment, Miles, & Cervin, 1965; Divesta & Cox, 1960; Stimpson & Bass, 1964).

To some extent, *needs* have been related to conformity. A positive association has been observed with *n* Approval (Crowne & Liverant, 1963; McDavid & Sistrunk, 1964; Moeller & Applezweig, 1957; Strickland & Crowne, 1962), and with *n* Affiliation (Hardy, 1957); a negative association has been noted with *n* Achievement (Divesta & Cox, 1960; McDavid, 1959; Stimpson & Bass, 1964).

At first inspection, *authoritarianism* was convincingly related to conformity, the association being positive (e.g., Canning & Baker, 1959; Crutchfield, 1955; Nadler, 1959; Solomon, 1963; Steiner & Johnson, 1963; Vaughan, G. M., 1964). There were no reports of a negative association, although some nonsignificant findings occurred (Gorfein, 1961; Hardy, 1957; Weiner & McGinnies, 1961). However, evidence exists that some of the variance in the commonly used $F$ scale is attributable to acquiescent response set, so that an observed relation between the scale and a measure of conformity might simply reflect a basic tendency to acquiesce (cf. Small & Campbell, 1960). G. M. Vaughan and White (1966) found a positive association of transsituational conformity with acquiescent-free $F$ scale scores. The net result seems sensible, in light of R. Brown's (1965) conclusion that the authoritarian is a person who agrees with authority opinion, assuming only that a peer majority, in fact, constitutes authority.

## 5  SUMMARY

1. Only two levels of discourse are utilized in this chapter, one concerning the individual's effect on the group, the other reversing this sequence.

2. Two central problems require close attention in the field of research in question. The first problem raises issues of transsituational behavior and the meaning of *trait*.

Unless these issues are adequately handled, the consequences at best are situation-specific results, and at worst conflict across studies and occasional uninterpretable results. The second problem relates to the adequacy of variables employed in research. There is a lack of investigation utilizing independent and unidimensional variables, both at the personality and group process level.

3. Multivariate research suggests that member composition relates meaningfully to total group performance (syntality), that there are two kinds of group process dimensions: second-order personality factors and interactional emergence factors. Univariate research has produced numerous findings, many of which are inconclusive or even in conflict. However, discernible trends indicate ways in which member composition affects participation rate, task activity, productivity, and social-emotional activity. Heterogeneity of member characteristics can facilitate performance where there is congruence of personality and role. Some evidence suggests that a person's characteristics can affect his general orientation in a social context.

4. Role emergence and personality have been substantially investigated only concerning the particular role of leadership. Both multivariate and univariate approaches indicate some individual characteristics associated with situation- or activity-specific leadership. Leadership behavior as a trait has found few supporters in the literature; but within the context of discussion adopted in the earlier part of this chapter, this problem has not been dealt with adequately. It is in no way contradictory to the meaning of a trait descriptor that situational variables play a major determining role.

5. The individual's reaction to the group as a social stimulus leads to the much-researched field of conformity. Individual characteristics have been found to relate meaningfully across situations; however, as with the topic of leadership, undoubted major emphasis is to be placed on the action of situational variables.

6. Proliferation of univariate studies will not advance the field significantly as it now stands, unless the problem of transsituationality is faced head on, and unless more leads are provided in establishing firm dimensions of group-process analysis.

# 22

# The Process
# of Personality Interaction

**Gerald L. Clore, Jr.**
*University of Illinois, Urbana*

**Donn Byrne**
*Purdue University, West Lafayette, Indiana*

If each human being represents a unique configuration of personality characteristics, the prediction of an individual's behavior would appear to be a difficult goal at best. To take an additional step and venture predictions about the effects of interactions among persons seems almost foolhardy. Nevertheless, by specifying necessary limits on the kinds of situations to be considered, a number of investigators have devised models that attempt to account for specific aspects of interpersonal behavior. Similarly, the present discussion is limited primarily to a consideration of formulations concerned with interpersonal attraction. Rather than a comprehensive but cursory survey of the field, we consider more fully a few specific contributions, ordering them with regard to three general problems: principles for the prediction of attraction, motivational bases of attraction, and processes of attraction development.[1]

[1] The writing of this chapter was supported by Grant MH 14510 from the National Institute of Mental Health, Gerald Clore, principal investigator, and by Grant GS–40329 from the National Science Foundation, Donn Byrne, principal investigator.

## 1 PRINCIPLES FOR THE PREDICTION OF ATTRACTION

### 1.1 Similarity of Spouses

Scientific interest in interpersonal attraction began with Sir Francis Galton in the mid-19th century. He was concerned with evolutionary processes and eugenics, and it is not surprising that marriage-partner selection became a focus of study. Galton (1870) and his student Karl Pearson (1903) concluded that their investigations showed assortative mating—a tendency of "like to like." Nearly 100 years later Galton's intellectual descendant, Raymond B. Cattell, revisited the problem. Cattell and Nesselroade (1967), using sophisticated extensions of Galton's mental tests and Pearson's correlational techniques, investigated the effects of personality similarity on mate selection and marital stability.

These investigators outlined three alternative principles of marriage partner selection: likeness or assortativeness, completion, and exchange. According to the likeness hypothesis, a given person will be most attracted to another like himself, and stably married partners will resemble each other more than those in unstable marriages. Furthermore, if the likeness hypothesis is exclusively valid so that similarity is the only basis for choice, characteristics that are desirable or have adjustment value should be evenly distributed in the married and unmarried populations. On the other hand, the completion hypothesis states that people tend to choose others who can augment their self-concept or life adjustment by bringing to the relationship characteristics that one person by himself lacks. For example, someone who is socially awkward might be attracted to another who is socially adroit. Though this illustration seems reasonable enough, the reciprocal attractiveness of the socially adroit person to one who is socially awkward seems less probable. Consequently, as a subprinciple of the completion notion, the exchange hypothesis has been proposed. Exchange would operate if each partner brought some characteristic with adjustment or survival value to the relationship. Thus a viable marriage might result from the union of an intelligent man with a wealthy woman. According to the completion and exchange principles, each person seeks desirable characteristics in the other so that the sum of the group's adjustment capacity exceeds that of either individual.

Using Cattell's Sixteen Personality Factor Questionnaire (16 PF), which includes measures of 15 personality dimensions and intelligence, the investigators compared the scores of 102 stable and 37 unstable married couples. Those classed as unstable were either separated or had requested marital counseling. Consistent with the likeness hypothesis, the scores of partners from stable marriages were significantly related in a positive direction on 8 of the 16 traits and in a negative direction on none, whereas unstably married partners yielded significant negative correlations on 3 traits and significant positive ones on only 2. In all, the stable couples were significantly more similar than the unstable on five variables. The prediction from the completion and exchange principles concerning stability is not unambiguously testable since no a priori designation of trait desirability exists. Some manner of exchange was, however, evident. Of all the off-diagonal intercorrelations of personality variables, 41 in the stable and 37 in the unstable group were significant against a chance expectation of 12. Evidently, a kind of exchange operates at least in the selection of partners, although apparently not differently for stable and unstable pairs, while likeness is the important variable for stability.

In the years between the investigations by Galton and by Cattell, factors related to marital selection have been the focus of active research interest. In general, highly consistent correlations indicate that marital partners are similar with respect to physical dimensions (Pearson, 1903), sociological characteristics (Hollingshead, 1950), personality variables (Burgess & Wallin, 1953), values (Kelly, E. L., 1937), and attitudes (Schooley, 1936). Some investigators compared the correlations for married couples with those for partners paired at random; the magnitude of the former coefficients consistently exceeds that of the latter (e.g., Byrne, Cherry, Lamberth, & Mitchell, 1973; Hunt, A. M., 1935; Murstein, 1961).

An exception to the generally reported homogamous selection has been suggested for need variables. Winch proposed a theory holding that the greatest mutual satisfaction would result from matches based on complementary rather than similar needs (Winch, Ktsanes, & Ktsanes, 1954). The complementarity notion is certainly intuitively compelling and has generated a sizable body of research but very little empirical support (Lindzey & Byrne, 1968). In a detailed review of marriage research, Tharp (1963, p. 107) concludes, "It is our judgement, in view of the foregoing discussion, that the complementary-need hypothesis as now stated is not tenable."

## 1.2 Role and Situational Variables

Levinger and Breedlove (1966) cited the importance of role and situational variables in marriage research, as follows:

We propose that there is a positive correlation between actual agreement and attraction, but only to the extent that such agreement promotes the achievement of the group's goals. The more that agreement is *instrumental* for furthering the goals of the marital relationship, the higher should be the correlations with marital satisfaction (p. 368).

Although their results provided only suggestive support for their proposition, they found it useful for explaining previously incompatible findings. Similarly Tharp (1963) stressed the necessity of dealing with the role expectations of husbands and wives in his review of research on marriage patterning. In this regard Wallin and Clark (1958) investigated desired frequency of coitus among married couples. They found that the greater the assumed similarity the higher subjects rated their marital satisfaction. This study is instructive because the investigators chose a class of behavior obviously relevant to the roles of husband and wife.

Also relevant to a consideration of role and situational factors in attraction is a study by Bermann and Miller (1967). In this instance a different kind of naturally occurring relationship was considered—pairs of student nurses who had chosen each other as roommates. As in the Cattell and Nesselroade study, stability of the partnerships was the critical dependent variable. Stable roommate relationships which the girls wanted to maintain were compared with unstable matches which either or both wanted to terminate. The investigators emphasize the utility of considering not only the compatibility of the partners' traits but also the compatibility between each girl's traits and her role as a student nurse. For example, on intuitive grounds the authors felt that a pair with one dominant and one deferent girl would ordinarily be an efficient working team. However, since high dominance was found to be incompatible with the role of student nurse, pairs with one dominant member tended toward instability, regardless of the partner's personality.

Bermann and Miller considered scores on nine personality traits; and the likeness hypothesis was again supported, five of the correlations being positive and significantly larger in the stable than in the unstable roommate pairs. Also, since a number of off-diagonal correlations were significant in the matrices for stable and unstable pairs, some kind of exchange was occurring in addition to the operation of the likeness principle.

In another analysis, stable roommate pairs were also found to be significantly more similar than unstable partners in interests as measured by *The Allport-Vernon-Lindzey Study of Values* (Allport, G. W., Vernon, & Lindzey, 1951). The authors pointed out that the interests characteristic of stable pairs were relevant to their roles as nurses, for example, religious and social service interests.

As an index of characteristics desirable for those in the nursing student role, the responses of sociometrically chosen students to the Edwards Personal Preference Schedule (EPPS; Edwards, A. L., 1959a) were compared with the responses of isolated and rejected girls. By this means, traits that differentiate socially and vocationally successful and unsuccessful students could be determined. This measure of trait acceptability agreed with independent ratings by four members of the nursing faculty instructed to indicate characteristics most and least likely to cause trouble on hospital wards. Girls who were social isolates shared the unacceptable traits of exhibition and autonomy, and rejected girls were dominant and aggressive. The least troublesome qualities and those characteristic of popular student nurses were abasement, deference, nurturance, order, and endurance. That sociometrically chosen girls were characterized by role-desirable traits demonstrates a relationship between attractiveness and role-relevant characteristics.

The foregoing sample of correlational research on naturally occurring relationships suggests that general principles of personality interaction, such as the likeness hypothesis, may need to be qualified in specific ways when investigating stability in real-life situations. Bermann and Miller found that role demands may alter otherwise compatible pairings, but it is also likely that role taking sometimes serves to make otherwise unstable relationships viable. Newcomb (1956) suggested that a relationship between two disagreeing people can be held together by agreeing to disagree; that is, by avoiding the issue. The division of labor within a marriage often seems to serve just such a function. To the extent that the partners are dissimilar in inclination, the traditional marital roles stave off conflict by minimizing areas of joint concern. This strategy probably reduces the proportion of mutual punishments; however, it also reduces the husband's and wife's similarity of experience and limits the opportunities for mutual rewards so that the affective character of the relationship tends toward neutrality or mutual indifference.

This reasoning suggests that the stability of a relationship may be due to factors other than high interpersonal attraction. For example, Bermann and Miller found that the readiness of a girl to dissolve an inadequate relationship with her roommate depended on her popularity and thus her chances of finding another acceptable roommate. Another such barrier to changing roommates existed because the girls saw such a change as a public denigration of the roommate. In marriage the belief that divorce is a sin would similarly act as a barrier to the dissolution of a couple even though the two people felt little attraction for each other. Thus, the effects of role and situational demands on both attraction and stability (and the less-than-perfect correspondence between attraction and stability) limit the relevance of research on preexisting relationships for understanding interpersonal attraction per se.

## 1.3  An Experimental Approach

One way to avoid role and situation-specific complications and to study interpersonal attraction isolated from such extraneous complications as stability is to adopt a laboratory approach. In this regard it has been pointed out that because of the obviously multidetermined nature of attraction, one must either use a multivariate methodology in the uncontrolled situation or move to an experimental situation where aspects of the complex relationships may be isolated (Byrne, Griffitt, & Stefaniak, 1967). Commenting on the state of research in the area of personality and attraction, Byrne,

Griffitt and Stefaniak suggest the following:

One reason for empirical inconsistency is the peculiar penchant of personality and social psychologists for methodological creativity such that almost every investigation represents an exploration in procedural novelty. That is, different investigators employ different independent and dependent variables in situations of varying complexity in which a seemingly limitless array of parameters is operative (p. 83).

One alternative to methodological and hence conceptual chaos is the consistent application of an easily replicable experimental paradigm. Although the research using this approach has been summarized in a series of chapters and books (Byrne, 1971; Clore, 1975; Clore & Byrne, 1974), several experiments that have manipulated similarity and dissimilarity of personality are mentioned here. Griffitt (1966), using a measure of self-ideal discrepancy, Byrne, Griffitt, & Stefaniak (1967), and Byrne & Griffitt (1969), using a measure of repression–sensitization, concluded that attraction to another person is a positive linear function of the proportion of similar personality characteristics presented. In one of the repression-sensitization studies two sources of variance were encountered. Not only were people attracted to strangers who answered specific items in the same way as they did, but also to those whose position on the repression-sensitization dimension was near their own, regardless of responses to individual items.

A closer look at the standard method used in these experimental studies may be helpful. Typically, the subject is asked to study another person's responses to a personality scale after taking the test himself. He is told that better-than-chance judgments can be made about another person on the basis of that person's answers to the test, and the person is instructed to try to form an impression of the stranger in order to rate him on an Interpersonal Judgment Scale (Byrne, 1971). The scale is composed of six 7-point items requiring estimations of the stranger's intelligence, adjustment, and other qualities. Also included are two items concerning how much the person believes he would like the stranger and how much he would enjoy working with him. These two items are summed to provide the measure of attraction (split-half reliability = .85). In this experimental paradigm the responses of the other person are actually supplied by the experimenter, thus giving him the ability to program the stimulus properties of the supposed stranger.

The method was initially developed for use with attitude stimuli; but within the same basic procedure, the type of presentation and kind of information about the bogus stranger was varied in successive studies. For example, the stranger's response to attitude scales was presented in mimeographed form (Byrne, 1961a), in a sound movie or tape recording (Byrne & Clore, 1966), in combination with information about race (Byrne & Wong, 1962) or in physical attractiveness (Byrne, London, & Reeves, 1968), and along with information concerning his economic status (Byrne, Clore, & Worchel, 1966). In all these situations, attraction is a function of the *proportion* of similar characteristics associated with the stranger. Typically the correlation between proportion of similarity and attraction is about .60, although if the race of the stranger, prejudice of the subject, and personally evaluative feedback about the subject are included along with similarity-dissimilarity of attitudes, a multiple $R$ of .84 has been reported across five experiments employing 553 subjects (Byrne & Erwin, 1969).

### 1.4  Similarity as Reinforcement

In addition to studies of attitude similarity, the same linear relation was found when the person received a stranger's evaluation of his creativity in making up stories (McDonald, 1962). To tie together the effects of such diverse conditions, it has been suggested that they be considered special instances of a more general class of positive and negative reinforcements. In this way, according to Byrne (1969), "A wide variety of seemingly different stimulus conditions can be conceptualized in terms of a single unifying construct rather than as an infinite array of unrelated conditions each requiring a new set of explanatory principles." According to this conception, the most important aspects of interpersonal events for predicting attraction are the rewarding and punishing messages they contain. Seen in this light, similarity would lead to attraction only when it was rewarding. Under conditions in which the role relationships were such that dissimilarity mediated reinforcement, one would expect a reversal of the similarity-attraction relationship. Grush, Clore, and Costin (1975) noted that most of the similarity research conerns peer-peer relations in which "attraction" refers to liking as a friend. When they investigated college students' attraction toward their instructors, they found that instructors were liked more by students who were dissimilar to them in personality than by those who were similar. The influence of role and situational factors were underlined by the fact that the dissimilarity effect held only for traits that were relevant to the teaching role. Students seem to have reasoned, "If teachers are to lead and direct me in the learning process, they ought to possess more of those traits instrumental for effective teaching than I do."

We have already discussed how role and situational factors influence the stability of roommate relationships among nursing students. Bermann and Miller, it will be recalled, found similarity of dominance to characterize unstable roommate pairs. Dominance was seen as maladaptive for the role of student nurse. They also found, however, that when choosing new roommates, the girls tended to choose on the basis of similarity even with regard to dominance. Consistent with this finding, the principle proposed earlier suggests that the perception of similarity in others is generally a rewarding state of affairs that leads to attraction. However, in the role of student nurse and in the practical situation of getting on with a roommate, similarity of dominance over time may produce conflict rather than rewards. If attraction is a function of positive reinforcement, it must change as the reinforcement contingencies change. Increased conflict presumably leads to lower attraction and, finally, efforts to find another roommate. Such a distinction between attraction before and after interaction suggests interesting research possibilities. For example, *exposure* to someone taking the dominant role would be expected to lead to attraction in the similarly dominant subject although *interaction* might eventually lead to dislike.

The most impressive evidence for the reinforcement function of attitude similarity comes from a study by Lombardo, Weiss, and Buchanan (1972). They designed an ingenious experiment in which people held a "conversation" via an intercom connecting two rooms. On each of 12 traits, a topic was announced over the intercom, and a person was confronted with a lighted sign saying "Throw switch if you wish to comment." Unknown to the subject, the purpose of this study was to see how quickly he would throw the switch as a function of whether the other person subsequently agreed or disagreed with his comment. Specifically, the first person commented on the issue for about 20 seconds and then heard agreeing or disagreeing comments from the other person (a confederate). There were 12 issues discussed, half of which had been rated "interesting" and half of which had been rated "uninteresting." All groups received 50% agreement, but the agree group received agreement on the interesting issues, and the disagree group received disagreement on the interesting issues. The yield group received an initial indication of disagreement on all issues but a shift to agreement on the interesting items after the person made his statement.

In two different experiments, strong conditioning effects were obtained for the two reinforced groups (yield and agree) compared with the punishment (disagree) group. The disagree persons were relatively slow to respond, while the agree subjects showed increasingly rapid responding, and the yield group displayed still more highly motivated performance. These experiments represent unambiguous evidence that attitude similarity is reinforcing by showing that the speed of responding increases when followed by agreement. The evidence is especially noteworthy because this experimental procedure eliminates explanations based on demand characteristics or on the person's interpretation of his behavior as correct or incorrect. The yield group demonstrates not only the reinforcing function of agreement but also that performance is further enhanced when agreement is preceded by disagreement on the same issues.

## 1.5  Small Groups

There are, of course, other possible conceptual gambits in a systematic treatment of attraction. Marriage partners, friends, and roommate pairs might be considered as examples of small groups. Such an option is compatible with a reinforcement approach and has the heuristic advantage of linking the problem to the considerable body of research on group dynamics. For example, Cattell (1962c) proposed a model of groups based on the definition of a group "as a set of persons such that the presence and action of all is necessary to certain conscious and unconscious positive satisfactions of each" (p. 209). According to Cattell's approach, the synergy of the group is divided into that used in the performance of tasks, effective synergy, and that used in keeping the groups functioning, maintenance synergy. A group is an instrument for the satisfaction of the needs of its individual members, and the group survives only as long as such satisfaction is obtained. The dynamic model of Cattell and the reinforcement model under consideration here, then, both hold that the coherence of a group, whether of two persons or more, depends on reinforcement. Such a position is not dissimilar to Tharp's conclusion: "Marital satisfaction is a function of the satisfaction of needs and/or expectations specific to husband and wife roles" (1963, p. 115). Insofar as he is concerned with need satisfaction, the previously mentioned theory of Winch's is similar. The only difference between Winch's position and that of the reinforcement model is that he has stressed complementarity, rather than similarity, of needs as satisfying.

In an extensive study of small groups, Cattell and Stice (1960a), consistent with the similarity hypothesis, found that heterogeneity of personality on the 16 PF led to a sense of conflict, dislike of discussion, long decision time, and poor performance. Further, A. J. Lott and Lott (1965) reviewed the literature on group cohesiveness. A general finding reported in this area is that intermember attraction is greater in successful than in unsuccessful groups. The Lotts, comparing theoretical explanations of such group cohesiveness, state:

There is a clear agreement among many contemporary theorists that attraction will follow if one individual either directly provides another with regard or need satisfaction, is perceived as potentially able to do so, or is otherwise associated with such a state of affairs. Furthermore, the specific antecedent variables which empirical research has shown to be related to interpersonal attraction can, for the most part, be interpreted in support of this general proposition (p. 287).

In respect to the foregoing, one might answer the question implicit in this section (What personalities are attracted to each other?) by saying that one person is attracted to another insofar as he is rewarded by the other person, and that merely being similar is frequently a rewarding state of affairs.

## 2 MOTIVATIONAL BASES OF ATTRACTION

We propose that the role of similarity and dissimilarity in interpersonal attractiveness can be subsumed under a more general relationship between attraction and reinforcement. In this section possible motivational bases for this assertion are explored. Theoretical analyses of attraction generally have centered around a hypothetical construct more or less motivational in nature. The best known of these constructs are Heider's concept of balance, Osgood and Tannenbaum's congruity principle, and Newcomb's strain toward symmetry.

The earliest systematic treatment of the similarity-attraction relationship was that of Heider (1946, 1958). From gestalt principles Heider postulated a tendency toward *balance* as an intrinsic characteristic of cognitive processes. A similar notion is embodied in Osgood and Tannenbaum's (1955) *principle of congruity*. They suggest that is is simpler to hold the same evaluation of both another person and his assertions than to hold different evaluations of them. From either of these points of view a person tends to like those that agree and dislike those that disagree, either relationship being balanced or congruent.

Newcomb (1953, 1956, 1971) deals, somewhat as Heider does, with states of equilibrium or symmetry. Newcomb's *strain toward symmetry* is a hypothetical state of tension occurring under conditions of discrepancy between one's own and another's attitude toward an object. Symmetry comes to be preferred because of its instrumental value in (a) making the behavior of another person more readily calculable, thereby minimizing failures in relations with other people; and (b) increasing confidence in one's own orientation toward the object, $X$. In discussing similar issues, Secord and Backman (1965) have invoked these same two advantages as a basis for the tendency toward *congruency* in interpersonal relationships.

For Newcomb and for Secord and Backman, symmetry or congruency is desirable because it is functional, one of these functions being to make the behavior of other people more predictable and understandable and the second being to validate the appropriateness of one's own opinions and behavior. We discuss these and other possible functions served by similarity one by one.

## 2.1 Understanding Function

A. Cohen, Stotland, and Wolfe (1955), using clearly and ambiguously written stories, found a relationship between ease of understanding and evaluation. They concluded that objects which are more clearly understood tend to be more positively evaluated than those only vaguely understood. It is relevant here that Cattell (1962c), in his model of group processes, stated that one of the basic motivations contributing to the coherence of groups is the gregarious satisfactions they afford. If other people are understood better by virtue of their similarity to oneself, then presumably the gregarious satisfaction of interacting with them would be greater. Such increased satisfaction might serve as the basis for the reinforcing character of similarity.

## 2.2 Validational Function

The validational function of similarity in determining attraction and maintaining congruency is most relevant with respect to Festinger's concept of *social reality*. According to Festinger:

Opinions, attitudes, and beliefs which people hold must have some basis upon which they rest for their validity. . . . Where there is a high degree of dependence upon physical reality for the subjective validity of one's beliefs and opinions, the dependence upon other people for the confidence one has in these opinions or beliefs is very low. At the other end of the continuum where the dependence upon physical reality is low . . . the dependence upon social reality is correspondingly high. An opinion, a belief, an attitude is "correct", "valid", and "proper" to the extent that it is anchored in a group of people with similar beliefs, opinions, and attitudes (1950, p. 272).

This concept was later incorporated into Festinger's (1954) theory of social comparison processes in which he postulated a drive to evaluate one's opinions and abilities. One relies on the social definition of reality; that is, he compares his opinions and abilities with others to the extent that physical or nonsocial means of validation are unavailable.

The importance of models and imitation in personality development was demonstrated in the work of Bandura and Walters (1963b). In view of the pervasive influence of models on behavior, it seems reasonable to suppose that the extensive training a child receives in imitating and the considerable instrumental value inherent in behaving like others would engender in the child active needs for social confirmation. Such confirmation or consensual validation insures that his or her reactions, feelings, and ideas are appropriate to the environmental situation. As Dollard and Miller pointed out, a child "is corrected for mistakes, and eventually learns to have anxiety about responding differently from other people" (1950, p. 119).

Although social comparison processes seem most clearly relevant to attitudinal data, in some respects attitudes, interests, emotions, and personality variables are more or less indistinguishable. For the psychologist, at least, all these characteristics are basically individual differences in behavior in response to certain stimulus situations. The previously mentioned study by Byrne, Griffitt, and Stefaniak (1967) illustrates the continuity of the behavioral continuum from attitudes to emotions and personality. In this experiment, people made true-false responses and studied another person's responses to the 127 items of the Repression-Sensitization Scale. Examples of these items are: "Once in a while I think of things too bad to talk about;" "I have very few quarrels with members of my family;" "I am happy most of the time;" and "At times I feel like picking a fist fight with someone." Presented in the true-false format, personality and attitude responses are obviously alike. Regardless of whether paper-and-pencil responses such as these or real-life behaviors are studied, similarity of personality or attitude refers to the performance of the same class of behavior in response to the same situation. Such considerations suggest that one could extend Festinger's concept of social comparison processes from attitudes and opinions to emotional states (Schachter, 1959) and to personality characteristics (Byrne, Griffitt, & Stefaniak, 1967). With regard to paper-and-pencil versus real-life personality behavior, Byrne, Griffitt, and Stefaniak (1967) pointed out that the relationship between scores on a personality test and specific extra-test behavior is for the most part imperfect or unknown. It is small wonder that some investigators of personality variables have found the similarity-attraction phenomenon somewhat elusive, since the characteristics being studied by the investigator are in an uncertain relationship to the stimulus a given person encounters and to which he reacts.

## 2.3 Effectance Function

Among the plethora of needs and motives hypothesized to explain psychological findings are a number which, though differently labeled and invoked in different situations, appear to refer to the same sort of process. Examples are the need for cognition or the need to experience an integrated and meaningful world (Cohen, A., Stotland, & Wolfe, 1955); the need to be able to know and predict the environment (Kelly, E. L., 1955; Pervin, 1963); the desire for certainty, which involves understanding the environment and making it predictable (Brim & Hoff, 1957); and the drive to evaluate one's own opinions and abilities (Festinger, 1954). It has been suggested that these various conceptions all fit within R. W. White's (1959) *effectance motive* since each involves a concern with effective interaction with the environment (Byrne & Clore, 1967). According to White the effectance motive is an intrinsic need to develop an effective familiarity with the environment, and the attainment of competence in this endeavor is characterized by feelings of efficacy. The previously mentioned functions of similarity may be seen as effectance satisfying. Thus, *understanding* other people's point of view and receiving *validation* for one's own view from others would both provide evidence of one's effectiveness.

White proposed effectance as a positive motivation to explain the exploratory and curiosity behavior of children and animals in novel or dissimilar situations, but some research suggests that exploratory behavior is accompanied by negative rather than positive affect. Presenting slides of nonsense syllables, Chinese characters, and male faces, Harrison (1968) reported that visual exploration was negatively related to liking of the stimuli. Alternatively, it does seem likely that people prefer an intermediate amount of stimulation between predictable sameness and frightening strangeness. It has been argued that the same motivational construct that accounts for curiosity or a preference for increased stimulation could also account for a negative response to stimuli that lie further along the continuum of unfamiliarity, unpredictability, and unexpectedness (Byrne & Clore, 1967). Does this suggest a curvilinear rather than a linear relationship between similarity and liking? Perhaps after continued exposure to highly similar others, dissimilarity rather than similarity would become attractive. Some data consistent with this assertion were reported by Fromkin (1972). Confronted by so much interpersonal diversity, however, it seems unlikely that such saturation is frequently experienced with regard to other people, so that similarity is generally more satisfying.

A number of investigators have specified arousal conditions for human and animal subjects in terms of stimuli that are unfamiliar or strange (Berlyne, 1955; Dollard & Miller, 1950; Welker, 1956; Zimbardo & Miller, 1958), ambiguous (Brim & Hoff, 1957; Cohen, A., Stotland, & Wolfe, 1955), variable (Munsinger & Kessen, 1964), uncertain (Gerard, 1963; Lanzetta & Driscoll, 1966), unexpected (Maddi, 1961), unpredictable (Elliott, 1966; Gergen & Jones, 1963), or a discrepancy from an expected outcome (Carlsmith & Aronson, 1963; Dember & Earl, 1957).

A rather elaborate test of the proposed motivational effects on attraction was reported by Byrne and Clore (1967). To generate effectance arousal, a color movie with sound was created that contained a series of scenes having no meaningful interrelationship and in which the sequence of events within a scene followed no logical scheme. The 10-minute film served as a standard, controlled stimulus situation which was ambiguous, unfamiliar, and unpredictable. A brief, self-report instrument was also constructed as an independent

measure of effectance motive arousal. The scale reliably discriminated the experimental film from both anxiety-arousing and neutral films. As a further check on the reliability of ambiguous, unpredictable stimuli in eliciting arousal, a second experimental movie was constructed that was indistinguishable in its effects from the first. In the major part of the experiment, people viewed the film and were then presented with the bogus responses of another person concerning attitudinal topics in some cases and his interpretation and reaction to the movie in others. High levels of self-reported arousal had disruptive effects, dampening the similarity-attraction relationship, but moderate arousal intensified positive and negative reactions to similar and dissimilar strangers. The findings were interpreted as the result of variation in effectance motivation.

## 2.4  Approval Function

In addition to the previously discussed functions of similarity, desire for acceptance has been proposed as the motivational link between similarity and attraction or affiliation. D. Nelson (1967) suggested that similarity provides the subject with cues of the stranger's approval. Also, Aronson and Worchel (1966) suggested that the agreement-attraction relationship may be due, at least in part, to an implicit assumption that people who hold attitudes similar to our own will like us. Because existing data (Byrne & Rhamey, 1965) were incompatible with that hypothesis, they proposed that if people were actually to meet in a face-to-face interaction, information concerning what one thought of the other would completely determine attraction, with similarity and dissimilarity of attitudes having a negligible effect. Although they interpreted their findings as confirming the hypothesis, a replication and reanalysis of the data (Byrne & Griffitt, 1966) indicated clearly that both variables were effective in a face-to-face situation. Thus, the similarity-attraction relationship does not depend on cues to a person that the similar other will like him.

## 2.5  Efficiency Function

For real-life relationships such as married couples or roommates, as opposed to experimentally produced attraction, a major source of reinforcement resulting from similarity is the greater efficiency of the partnership. Individual and group goals can be effectively attained when less effort is required to ameliorate differences and resolve conflicts. For example, numerous frustrations would be avoided in a marriage with someone of similar interests merely because fewer compromises would be required to decide on such things as the expenditure of time and money. Considered within Cattell's model of groups, if all of the group synergy in the relationship goes into maintenance, little effective synergy remains for the completion of tasks. Indeed, if differences are too great, the work of maintaining the relationship may exceed the satisfactions obtained from it, resulting in an unstable match. It seems likely, then, that the efficiency function of similarity is paramount when attraction in ongoing relationships is considered.

## 2.6  Other Functions

We have mentioned a few of the many functions that might be served by similarity and that could contribute to its effect on attraction. Among other possibilities are the following. Zajonc (1968) demonstrated that mere frequency of exposure leads to increased liking for a stimulus. Since similar characteristics are more familiar, they might also be more attractive purely for that reason. Alternatively, Fishbein and Ajzen (1972) argued that attraction depends solely on the extent to which one believes a stimulus person to have positive traits. They indicated that similarity leads to attraction because people assume that similar others have positive traits automatically, and that attraction is a logical and not a motivational phenomenon. Finally, S. C. Jones and Regan (1974), in experiments testing Festinger's social comparison theory, suggested that one might choose to affiliate with a similar person because of the predictive function of similarity. In one of their experiments, people had an opportunity to learn from similar others what would happen to persons like themselves in later portions of the study.

Of course to some extent the question of the primacy of motives between the similarity-attraction and similarity-affiliation relationships is an empty one. For example, it is not difficult to conceive of a situation in which the discovery of another person who is similar to oneself is rewarding due to increased confidence in the validity of one's beliefs, feelings, and behavior. Just as easily imagined are circumstances in which similar characteristics in another person are rewarding as cues to probable reciprocal liking. Given these conditions, the general question of motive primacy is not meaningful, although within a given experimental setting the extent of involvement of each motivation might be determined. The answer, of course, would be relevant only to the specific stimulus conditions under which it was obtained.

It might be noted that the utility of the several theoretical explanations for attraction phenomena lies in the pervasiveness of the generalization beyond the specific data at hand and in the fertility of the proposition in generating meaningful research. Contrary to the expectations of some, theories are not likely to be overthrown by a single devastating crucial experiment or even by a series of experiments (Theory A in the lead over Theory B by 14 $F$ ratios to 6). Rather, some propositions gradually are accepted as providing greater generality and fertility. The present authors have suggested a reinforcement interpretation couched in terms of stimuli and responses. Even if one is not instantaneously converted to such an approach, at least it may be seen that reinforcement theory is able to deal with relatively complex behavior performed by a relatively complex organism in a relatively complex situation. Somewhat too often, reinforcement approaches provide a straw man for cognitive theorists in terms of characterizations of an empty organism yielding muscle twitches in response to simple and sterile stimuli. In the following section, two compatible reinforcement approaches will be presented in somewhat greater detail.

## 3 PROCESSES OF ATTRACTION DEVELOPMENT

Most of the models previously discussed are only tangentially concerned with the process whereby interpersonal attraction develops. As a first step toward specifying the nature of that process, A. J. Lott and Lott (1968) suggested that attraction be defined as an attitude toward another person, a proposal that makes relevant the literature on attitude acquisition. In this regard D. Katz and Stotland (1959) present a theory of attitudes, as follows:

Affect is related to need satisfaction. Objects which satisfy a need or are associated with

need satisfaction acquire pleasant affect and are evaluated favorably. The individual will also behave positively toward such objects, since by doing so he assumes the continuance of his present need satisfaction or need satisfaction in the future. Need satisfaction leads both to positive affect and high evaluation and to positive behavior toward the object (pp. 444–445).

This statement embodies a conceptualization quite similar to that of the models to be presented in the present section.

As elaborations of a reinforcement approach to attraction, Byrne & Clore (1970) and the Lotts (Lott, B. E., & Lott, 1960; Lott, A. J., & Lott, 1968) present models for the development of attraction. Although the models are quite similar, the Lotts have primarily investigated attraction resulting from success in instrumental learning situations, whereas Byrne and Clore, drawing on somewhat different data, base their model on classical conditioning principles.

### 3.1 Lott and Lott Model

The foundation of the Lotts' model is Doob's (1947) definition of an attitude as an implicit response which anticpates and mediates patterns of overt response. In this view, attraction, or a positive attitude toward another person, consists essentially of learning to anticipate reinforcement in the presence of that person. The basic postulates of the model, drawn primarily from a Hull-Spence instrumental-learning framework, are as follows:

1. Persons are discriminable stimuli.

2. Reinforcement is accompanied by overt or covert goal responses ($R_g$ or $r_g$).

3. These responses to reinforcement

become conditioned to all discriminable stimuli present at the time.

4. A person present during reinforcement will come to elicit $R_g$ or $r_g - s_g$.

The general nature of the experimental situations used to test the model can be seen in an early study by the Lotts (Lott, B. E., & Lott, 1960). Sixteen same-sex groups were formed composed of three children who had not chosen each other on two previous sociometric tests. The groups played a noncompetitive game ("Rocket Ship") in which some were rewarded with plastic cars for success and others were not. An hour after playing the game for the second time, the classroom teacher administered a sociometric test in which each child chose two others for a vacation in space. The children who had received reinforcement during the game made significantly more choices from the other children in their play group than did those who had not experienced reinforcement. This finding was later replicated once using the game format but with nickels for rewards (James & Lott, 1964) and again in a classroom situation with eye contact and positive response by the teacher as a reward (Lott, A. J., & Lott, 1968).

In these experiments association in itself is all that is considered necessary for the development of attraction. It is sufficient for the formation of a positive attitude toward another person for him merely to be consistently present during receipt of reward; there need not be a perceived instrumental or other direct relationship between the person and the reward.

As predicted by the model, it has been shown that persons are better liked when associated with immediate than with delayed reward (Lott, A. J., Aponte, McGinley, & Lott, 1969) and that attraction can also be produced when the person experiences only vicarious reward (Lott, A. J., Lott, & Matthews, 1969). Concerning the latter finding, it was suggested that observing the goal responses of another person evokes an empathic $r_g - s_g$ in the subject: the likelihood of the empathic response being a positive function of the observer's attraction toward the person receiving reward. If the person is similar or described as similar to the subject or to others attractive to the subject, the authors propose that the empathic $r_g - s_g$ would be elicited through the operation of stimulus generalization. Supporting evidence is provided in a study by Jellison and Mills (1967), in which college women were exposed to the bogus responses of another student who described herself similarly or dissimilarly on items from the EPPS. After studying the stranger's responses, the students learned either that nothing unusual had happened to the other woman or that she had won a free trip to the Paris fashion showings. Contrary to a prediction from Heider's theory that envy would result, attraction toward a similar other increased when the other had good fortune. One of the interpretations the authors consider for this finding, which is consistent with the empathic $r_g - s_g$ hypothesis, is that "pleasure may have resulted from a tendency to empathize with the emotions of a similar other" (p. 462).

Additional deductions from the Lotts' model follow when it is considered that variables which affect $r_g - s_g$ should also influence the probability and speed of evocation of $r_g - s_g$ (attraction) by a previously neutral stimulus. For example, they suggest that the strength of $r_g - s_g$ should increase with the number of rewarded trials on which the person is present. Other variables including drive and incentive factors have also been shown to influence how much a person who happened to be present during reinforcement is liked

(Lott, A. J., Bright, Weinstein, & Lott, 1970).

Among the consequences of having developed attraction toward another person is the ability of that person to function as a secondary reinforcer, and as such to be able to strengthen, maintain, or shape the behavior of the liker by his presence. The $r_g - s_g$ mechanism has also been hypothesized by Doob and others to have drive properties. It follows, therefore, that in the presence of liked others, a person's behavior should reflect increases in drive level. As a test of this deduction A. J. Lott and Lott (1966) found that on a foreign-language learning task, fourth- and fifth-grade children performed better in the presence of classmates they liked than when neutral others were present. Similarly, in a laboratory study, Byrne, Krivonos, and Friedrich (1975) used three learning tasks and found that pairs of similar people performed better than dissimilar pairs on all three tasks.

The model proposed by the Lotts is primarily concerned with the development of positive attraction or liking, but, as they suggest, a logical extension of the approach is to consider disliking an anticipation of punishment or frustration. Presumably as a consequence of association with noxious experience, the fractional anticipatory component of the frustrative responses, $r_f - s_f$ (Amsel, 1962), will come to be evoked by a discriminable stimulus person. We will consider next a model somewhat similar to the model under discussion here, but which has been more concerned with the development of both positive and negative interpersonal attitudes.

### 3.2  Byrne and Clore Model

The first section of this chapter presented a reinforcement approach to the similarity-

attraction relationship. In the second it was suggested that satisfaction of the effectance motive by means of social comparison processes was the basis for the reinforcing function of perceived attitudinal, emotional, and personality similarity. Stemming from these concerns, an extended reinforcement-affect model has been proposed by Byrne (1971), Byrne and Clore (1970), Clore, (1966), and Clore and Byrne, (1974).[2] In this model, interpersonal attraction is seen as one of a broader class of evaluative responses, and perceived attitude and personality similarity are conceptualized simply as one of many possible kinds of reinforcement (Fig. 1). As in the Lotts' model, evaluative responses are evoked by a stimulus as a consequence of associated reinforcement. The model is a general one and holds that positive and negative evaluations of discriminable stimuli stem from classically conditioned affective responses. It is assumed that any stimulus that is reinforcing also serves as an unconditioned stimulus (UCS) for an implicit affective response. The experienced quality of the response varies along an affective dimension from pleasant to unpleasant. Although initially neutral, any discriminable stimulus (including a person), if consistently associated with reinforce-ment, becomes a conditioned stimulus (CS) evoking an implicit affective response. The rate of acquisition and the strength of the resulting conditioned response presumably varies with the duration of the interstimulus interval, the intensity of the stimuli employed, and other variables relevant to classical conditioning.

Overt evaluative responses to the CS are conceived to be mediated by the covert affective responses conditioned to it. These

[2] Thanks to Gene Byron Miles for his contribution to our understanding of the function of models in science.

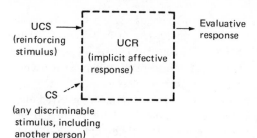

**FIGURE 1** Evaluative responses as a function of reinforcing stimuli associated with a conditioned stimulus. UCS = unconditional stimulus; CS = conditional stimulus; UCR = unconditional response. From "Effectance arousal and attraction" by D. Byrne and G. L. Clore, *Journal of Personality and Social Psychology Monograph*, 1967, 6(4, whole No. 638). Copyright 1967 by the *Journal of Personality and Social Psychology*. Reprinted by permission.

evaluative responses include self-report descriptions of one's feelings in the presence of the CS, verbal assessments and indications of attraction or dislike, sociometric choices or rejections, and any other approach or avoidance behavior toward the CS. The evaluation of the stimulus person is assumed to be dependent on and mediated by the implicit affective response associated with him or generalized to him. It should be recalled that the experimental situation out of which the model was developed requires the person to make judgments based on a stranger's responses to an attitude or personality scale. The perceived similarities and dissimilarities are assumed to be positively and negatively reinforcing and to produce pleasant and unpleasant implicit affective responses. The experienced quality of these implicit responses is reflected in the person's self-reported like or dislike of the stranger. An experiment reported by Byrne and Clore (1970) in which people recorded their feelings after exposure to similar and dissimilar attitudes provides evidence of the pleasant-unpleasant response

continuum. After hearing tape recordings of other students expressing their views, subjects responded on six of the evaluative scales of Osgood's Semantic Differential. There was a significant tendency for subjects to feel comfortable, good, happy, pleasant, and positive after hearing their own views corroborated and to feel uncomfortable, bad, unhappy, unpleasant, and negative after exposure to dissimilar opinions. This method has been extended by Sachs and Byrne (1970).

The function of the implicit affective response in determining overt responses is similar to the function proposed by K. W. Spence (1956) for the implicit emotional response, $r_e$, in his theory of aversive classical conditioning. These implicit responses, like the fractional anticipatory goal response mechanism used by Doob and the Lotts, serve as expectations of future reinforcement. Of course, outside the laboratory, the expectation associated with another person is rarely of a purely positive or negative nature. Probably no one experiences only univalent reinforcement even from the best-liked friend or the most-feared adversary. When both positive and negative reinforcements of varying magnitude are associated with a given CS, the resulting implicit affective response is some combination of the individual responses. Byrne and Rhamey (1965) suggested that the affective response is a function of the weighted proportion of positive reinforcements, or

$$AR = f\left(\frac{\Sigma(PR \times M)}{\Sigma\,(PR \times M) + \Sigma\,(NR \times M')}\right)$$

The expression states that the affective response is a function of the sum of the weighted positive reinforcements (Number × Magnitude) divided by the total number of weighted positive and negative reinforce-ments. The proportionality formula has been enormously useful to investigators of attraction by enabling them to make quantitative comparisons across different studies. Without such a general statement, a given experiment, no matter how elegant, stands alone except for whatever qualitative comparisons its directional results allow. A number of different formal models of stimulus combination have been proposed recently including averaging, adding, and category models (e.g., Anderson, N. H., 1971; Fishbein & Ajzen, 1975; Wyer, 1974). Though the models and the techniques for evaluating them have become more sophisticated in recent years, it is not clear that we are closer to agreement on the optimal form that such models should take. But before one concludes that such modeling is a waste of time, it should be remembered that confusion exists primarily because all of the contenders do a reasonably good job of accounting for the most common findings.

Of the multitude of predictions that can be derived from a reinforcement conception model, evidence consistent with several has been reported. It has been shown that autonomic responses follow exposure to attitudinal stimuli (Clore & Gormly, 1974; Gormly, 1971), that UCS magnitude in the form of variation in topic interest influences overt attraction responses (Clore & Bal-dridge, 1968), and that moderate increases in drive level intensify the similarity-attrac-tion relationship (Byrne & Clore, 1967). An experiment by Griffitt (1968) tested the prediction from the present model that attraction is a function of reinforcement associated with, but not directly attributable to, the stimulus person. As in the standard experimental method previously described, Griffitt's subjects made interpersonal judg-ments about bogus strangers who had expressed, on 12-item attitude scales, either 75% or 25% similar opinions. In addition to the direct reinforcement of similar attitudes from the other person, half of the participants in the experiment received the customary 1-point addition to their psychology grade while the other half received a bonus of 4 extra points. Besides the usual relationship between attraction and similarity, the additional reinforcement associated in time, but not attributable to the stimulus person, resulted, as predicted, in a significant elevation of attraction at both ends of the similarity-dissimilarity dimension.

According to the model, such reinforce-ments influence attraction to the extent that they elicit positive affective reactions. If the affect hypothesis is accurate, one should be able to change attraction directly by chang-ing the affective state of the perceiver. A number of ingenious studies have been re-ported that have done just that. Affect manipulations have included confining people in hot and crowded rooms (Griffitt & Veitch, 1971), showing them depressing or elating films (Gouaux, 1971), an having them overhear a radio broadcast of either good or bad news (Veitch & Griffit, 1975). In each case attraction was influenced as predicted by the nature of the affective state the perceiver associated with the stimulus person. Some additional studies using similar techniques have reported somewhat more complicated effects demon-strating individual differences in reactions to mood-inducing films (Bleda, Bell, & Byrne, 1973) and difficulties in predicting who will and will not be associated with the perceiver's affective state (Friedman, Rubin, Jacobson, & Clore, 1975).

Since direct comparison of predictions from alternative approaches to attraction is rarely available, one such experiment is of special interest (Stapert & Clore, 1969). The design contrasts predictions of the balance theories and the association model. Balance theories rest on a homeostatic model in which rejecting the source is one of the ways to reduce the arousal occasioned by disagreement, while in the conditioning model the source is disliked because of his *association* with the arousal, but not as a means of reducing it. The experiment showed that attraction toward an agreeing person was greater after prior disagreement then after prior agreement. These results are consistent with a conditioning model and contrary to a homeostasis model, because they indicate that the arousal from the first disagreer remained (even though he was rejected) to intensify attraction to the subsequent agreer.

Although we have concentrated on examples of the development of attraction toward other people, the process model presented here is intended to be general in scope covering evaluative responses to any discriminable stimulus. As such, the evaluation of groups, objects, words, and activities as well as other people is relevant. The linear relationship obtained between evaluation of another person and proportion of positive reinforcements associated with him has also been reported for attraction to a task and degree of task success (Locke, 1965). With children as subjects, a positive relationship has been found between evaluations of nonsense syllables and number of positively reinforced trials (Nunnally, Stevens, & Hall, 1965) and with rats between running speed and concentration of glucose in the reward (Young, P. T., & Shuford, 1955). Young's proposal that positive and negative affective states regulate the rat's behavior is similar to the present view that implicit affective responses regulate evaluative behavior in human subjects.

The present model and that of Lott and Lott are obviously very much alike, and much of the data presented in support of one can be considered relevant to the other. Despite the similarity of the two approaches, several differences in emphasis emerge upon comparison. For example, the Lotts have generally studied the intermember attraction or cohesiveness of groups, while Byrne, Clore, and their co-workers have typically dealt with the attraction of single subjects toward experimentally controlled stimulus persons. Furthermore, the Lotts have emphasized the desirability of using a variety of dependent measures with its attendant advantage of broadening the sample of measures from which inferences to extralaboratory behavior are made. The Byrne group has been concerned with response consistency, opting to use the same measure across experiments for the sake of generating findings which are numerically as well as conceptually comparable. Beyond the methodological differences, Griffitt,[3] in discussing the relevance of his findings for the two models, points out that the $r_g - s_g$ mechanism used by Lott and Lott is an incentive construct, while $r_e$ used by Byrne and Clore is a drive construct. If, as Black (1965) reasoned, the operations that affect drive also influence incentive, perhaps the two models are functionally one.

In conclusion, the general philosophy behind the models considered here has been succinctly stated by A. J. Lott (1966): "By defining attraction toward persons in S-R terms we are able to place this concept within a large nomological net in which other concepts have already been linked, theoretically and empirically, and which

---

[3] Personal communication, November 1968.

provides a basis for derivations specific to the investigation of social behavior." If such models do not fit the data, they must be discarded, but if they are worthwhile, one may expect them to play the role of midwife in the formulation of a genuine theory of attraction and in the generation of experimental situations that might not otherwise have been conceived.

The foregoing discussion has moved from a consideration of descriptive principles and motivational hypotheses to process models. Although we have dealt fully only with models based on learning theory, other analogues would probably serve the modeler's function as well. At the present state of research in interpersonal behavior a search for theoretical closure is premature. Of more immediate value is the stimulation of conceptually interrelated research efforts.

## SUMMARY

The foregoing discussion of interpersonal attraction considered principles for the prediction of attraction, motivational bases of attraction, and processes of attraction development. In the consideration of principles for predicting attraction, research was reviewed which indicated the following:

1. Marriages, and stable marriages in particular, are composed of people with similar personalities, attitudes, and other characteristics.

2. Role and situational factors influence the relationship between similarity of personality and stability in a relationship.

3. When the variety of conditions that influence attraction are conceptualized as reinforcements, attraction toward another person may be seen as a function of the relative number of positive reinforcements associated with him.

From a variety of theoretical formulations, motivational bases for the similarity-attraction relationship were proposed. A number of the postulated needs can be subsumed under the effectance motive, a need to develop an effective familiarity with one's environment. Thus, encountering similar attitudes, interests, emotions, and personality characteristics in others provides evidence for the appropriateness of one's own interpretation of the environment.

Finally, two more-or-less interchangeable models of the process of attraction development were considered. Attraction and other evaluative responses are seen as mediated by associated or conditioned affective responses. The degree of positive evaluation depends on the extent to which positive rather than negative reinforcement has been associated with the evaluated object. Data relevant to the models were reviewed.

# Section

# 5

## Special Expressions
of Personality

# 23

# Personality
# and Perception

Klaus A. Schneewind
*University of Trier*

## 1 A GENERAL MODEL OF TRAIT, STATE, AND SITUATION–PERCEPTION INDICATORS FOR THE ACT OF PERCEPTION

Let us begin our consideration of the relation of personality to perception with the simple statement that we are able to observe the particular behavior of a particular person in a particular situation at a particular time. Thereby we may presume that the person's behavior as well as the situation can be described objectively, that is, with an ideally maximum degree of interobserver reliability. What we do not know, however, is how the person perceives the specific situation in which his behavior occurs. This lack of knowledge is directly related to the question to what extent the particular behavior is due to determinants that have nothing or little to do with the actual situation, and to what extent the behavior is triggered by situational influences. Stating the problem in such a way means taking for granted that a specific behavioral expression that is observable here and now, in fact is determined by organismic and situational influences. The most general statement of such a conceptualization was presented in the form of an equation in R. S. Woodworth's (1958) stimulus-response model (Equation 1):

$$P_{ij} = f(O_i, S_j). \qquad (1)$$

This equation refers to a particular behavior $P_{ij}$, which is supposed to be a function of the organism $O_i$ and the situation $S_j$.

The model of stimulus, organism, and response (S-O-R) has been expressed in a multivariate form, one that works to an encouraging degree, by Cattell's specification equation

$$P_{ij} = b_{j1} T_{1i} + \cdots + b_{jk} T_{ki}, \qquad (2)$$

in which (see chapter 7) the $T$s are traits and the $b$s are behavioral indexes, both obtainable factor analytically. Already one approaches here a key to the relation of perception to personality in that every trait has conceivably its own expressions in perceptual behavior ($P_j$). Nowadays the problem is not so much to prove that there are organismic and situational influences but that there is, rather, some need to demonstrate the extent to which those different determinants are operating. Nevertheless the distinction between organismic and situational influences has an important bearing on the meaning of the two concepts *personality* and *perception*. The part of organismic determinants of actual behavior can be conceived as *dispositions* in the sense of W. Stern (1921),

Allport (1937), Symonds (1931), or Campbell (1963) or *traits* in the sense of Cattell (1946, 1957a) and J. P. Guilford (1959a), that is, behavioral correlates remaining relatively stable across different situations and occasions (Herrmann, 1969).

Since the term *trait*—or the more precisely operationally defined *source trait*—is usually referred to as a rather technical term by personality researchers who use the factor-analytic model, the term *disposition* is sometimes used in the sense of an action tendency that predisposes a person toward certain behaviors. This view has been put forward more recently by Hollander (1971) who stated that "dispositions are actuated as a result of the individual's perception of the situation" (p. 396). Those dispositions can be investigated, organized, and structured for every single person. The particular quality and structural arrangement of all those dispositions for one individual might be called *personality*. It should be noted that dispositions may be conceived as a composite of hereditary determinants and stable action and reaction patterns due to the individual's personal learning history. One part of those dispositions will certainly consist of a person's cross-situationally and cross-occasionally stable modes of perceiving his environment.

As equation 2 shows, however, traits or dispositions alone are not sufficient to account for a particular behavior in a particular situation. Assuming that to a larger or smaller extent actual behavior is also instigated by the specific properties of the situation, we might conclude that all changes in a person's environment that are accompanied by changes of his behavior must have been put in effect by some kind of input-processing mechanism. This mechanism may be called perception. Thus the term *perception* is operable with respect to actual behavioral events, and the dilemma of not

knowing how a particular person perceives a given situation can be solved by pointing at those behavioral changes which coincide with objectively describable changes of the situation.

Later it will be shown at greater length that situational changes do not necessarily account for all the behavioral changes that can be observed, since there are also oscillations in behavior that are due to particular physiological, motivational, and learning events. Those behavioral fluctuations tend to occur temporarily and are usually referred to as states and defined and recognized by $P$ and $dR$ techniques of multivariate experiment (Cattell, 1957a, 1966i; Nesselroade and Bartsch, chapter 8 of this *Handbook*). If one separates states from situational influences one might be interested only in those properties of a particular situation that contribute in a stable way to a particular behavior. The underlying assumption is that, except for behavioral fluctuations due to states, a person consistently perceives a particular situation in the same way. This does not necessarily mean that a person will never perceive the same situation differently on various occasions, but those changes will be attributed to what might be called *perceptual states*. Therefore, we might want to make a distinction between stable situation-specific behavioral changes which serve as indicators for the stable perception of a particular situation and those changes of behavior stemming from perceptual changes across occasions in an objectively unchanged situation.

Since we are talking about observable behaviors on the one side and about constructs referring to behavior patterns labeled, for example, as traits or states on the other side, it will be useful in any case to start out with actual observable behavior. Those behavioral manifestations or components of them are indicative for the constructs in question; therefore, we might refer to them as one might refer to all behavior as *construct indicators*. From the conceptual analysis previously given, three main types of perceptual constructs and construct indicators can be distinguished:

1. Perceptual trait indicators are stable across situations and occasions. They form part of an individual's system of trait dispositions and therefore belong to what has been called personality. As soon as some of those perceptual disposition indicators are tied together to patterns of behavior we might talk about perceptual disposition constructs.

2. Situation-perception indicators are those that remain stable across occasions for just one particular situation but not across different situations. Patterns of situation-perception indicators will be called situation-perception constructs.

3. Perceptual state indicators fluctuate from occasion to occasion even if the objective situation remains exactly the same. Patterns of perceptual state indicators will be referred to as perceptual state constructs.

The three classes of indicators and constructs appear to be important for any conceptual analysis of the terms *personality* and *perception*. We see, for example, that the phenomena covered by the term *personality* can be grouped so that they fall under perceptual disposition constructs and other dispositional constructs not primarily related to perceptual influences.

All behavioral expressions due to situational changes can at the same time be conceived to be expressions of the individual's perception. Thus, we may have only one class of situation-perception constructs. States, however, may be divided into perceptual and nonperceptual state constructs depending on whether cross-occasional behavioral changes are influenced by an altering perception of the same situation, or whether other nonperceptual influences like the present physiological state account for those changes in behavior. The three classes of constructs and their subdivision in perceptual and nonperceptual constructs may be studied in all their possible interrelations. At present we are far from knowing enough about those constructs and their relations to each other. However, in a later section of this chapter we try to evaluate some substantive research evidence according to the classification of relevant constructs and their interrelations.

In summary, it can be stated that in studying personality in relation to perception, we are dealing with three classes of constructs—personality, situation perception, and state constructs—that either fully or partly refer to perceptual phenomena and can be interrelated as far as dispositional and perceptual constructs are concerned. An empirical demonstration of the existence of those constructs has to be carried out by using multivariate rather than bivariate methodology. The actual behavioral expressions of those constructs reside in the realm of test behavior and real-life behavior, although the latter is much less frequently used in actual research. A manipulative and situationally controlled experimental design seems to be easier and more feasible for laboratory experiments although the generalizability of such a research strategy to more biotic situations in the person's life space should be kept in mind.

The following sections outline some models that have been developed to throw some light on individual differences in perception. All these models are based on a multivariate experimental methodology, and some of them have been tried out in illustrative examples of research.

## 2  CATTELL'S MODULATOR THEORY

Probably the most global approach to a comprehensive quantitative treatment of personality and perception was presented by Cattell (1963 a, c, 1966i). He employed the general S-O-R model of Equation 2 and adds (a) the theory of modulators (Cattell, 1963c), which integrates not only the concepts of personality and situation perception, but also concepts outside this area such as role and mood; and (b) the notion of a special perceptual instrument called a dynamic-cognitive set. A brief account of the essence of his theory, concentrating mainly on personality and perceptual influences, follows.

Cattell began with Woodworth's stimulus-response formula, which can be developed under the simplest assumptions, for example, linearity and additivity of the underlying model to a more articulated formula roughly indicated in Equation 2 and more fully in Equation 3.

$$P_{ji} = \sum_{x=1}^{x=k} b_{jx} A_{xi} + \sum_{y=1}^{y=l} b_{jy} T_{yi}$$

$$+ \sum_{z=1}^{z=m} b_{jz} D_{zi} + \sum_{z=1}^{w=n} b_{w} S_{wti}. \qquad (3)$$

In this formula $P_{ji}$ represents the perceptual response of an individual $i$ in a situation $j$. The $T$s of equation 2 are here developed into their specific modalities—$A$s for $k$ ability or cognitive factors, $T$s for temperamental source traits, and $D$s for $m$ dynamic structure traits. The $S$s refer to the states discussed in the general model, and of course, they will have a $t$ subscript for time as well as $i$ for individual, since unlike the trait dispositions they will change rapidly with time. The $b$s are factor loadings or, in more general terms, behavioral indexes specifically related to the particular situation when the individual's response has been recorded. The $b$s might here be named more specifically *perceptual situational indexes* since they reflect the person's perception of a particular situation. It is important to note here that the perceptual situational indexes already represent the psychological meaning of the situation rather than the physical situation itself. As Cattell pointed out in discussing "the meaning of a situation," these $b$s represent meaning only if we set up an experimental situation in which there is no motor difficulty in making the response (see Cattell, 1963a). These $b$s, moreover, will have different empirical values according to the total, for example, an instructional or role situation in which the behavior takes place. Cattell has shown (see chapter 7) how distinct behavioral index values can be obtained for (a) the focal stimulus, (b) the background or ambient stimulus, and (c) the global stimulus, which (a) and (b) together constitute.

Thus, at this point it seems useful to introduce a more differentiated view of what the term *situation* actually means. What Cattell calls the *global situation* comprises all the externally and internally given situational influences on a person, and divides, as indicated, into focal and background situations. Focal situations are mainly related to the external stimulus situation which the individual encompasses at a given moment with a relatively high degree of consciousness, whereas the ambient, or background situation, takes into account all those external influences that are not necessarily a vital part of the whole situation. Cattell also recognizes in the ambient situation (a) residual effects from preceding stimuli and (b) phenomena that can only partly be controlled by experiment, for example, specific instructions and particular attitudes in the individual. An example may illustrate what the difference between focal and background situations actually is. Suppose we are dealing with a reaction-time experiment. The apparatus whereby reaction time is measured may be called the focal stimulus, whereas the furniture of the laboratory, the temperature in the room, the number of experimenters present, a specifically motivating instruction, and the attitude the subject holds toward the experimenter, constitute the background situation. All of them together make up what has been called the global situation. Certain parallelisms should be noted here between Cattell's factor-analytically calculated and defined concepts, and certain concepts from Helson's (1948) adaptation level theory. Helson also uses the terms *focal, background,* and *residual stimuli* and employs them in a fairly similar ideational way. However, Cattell's concepts apply to operationally definable and measurable values in multivariate experiments which do not form a part of adaptation theory.

One important implication of Cattell's model as presented so far should be mentioned here. In Equation 2 a specification equation is written out that applies only to one response, $P_{ij}$. Specification equations such as the one in Equation 3 can easily be stated for virtually every response $P_{ik}$, $P_{il}$ ... $P_{in}$. This results in a set of equations that could be solved for their corresponding situational indexes. Those situational indexes could then be submitted to further analysis. Cattell (1963a) suggested that, in using the pattern similarity coefficient $r_p$ (Cattell, 1949), it could be found out "how much one situation resembles another psychologically" (Cattell, 1963a, p. 49). A matrix of $r_p$s could then be factor analyzed by ordinary $Q$ technique, thus resulting in an objective taxonomy of perceived situations.

Cattell's distinction of focal and background situations brings about some further

differentiation of the model. What happens if we leave the focal situation untouched while the background situation is changed experimentally? This of course, would result in a change of the situational indexes which in turn exactly reflects the impact of the altered global situation on the individual. Those differences of the situational indexes can be interpreted as perceptual changes due to a role (see also Cattell, chapter 7, this volume).

The following formula (Equation 4) summarizes this process:

$$P_{ij} - P_{ijr} = (b_{j1} - b_{j1r})T_{1i} + (b_{j2} - b_{j2r})T_{2i} + \cdots + (b_{jm} - b_{jmr})T_{mi}, \quad (4)$$

where $P_{ij}$ is the performance of individual $i$ in situation $j$; $P_{ijr}$ is the performance of individual $i$ in situation $j$ and role situation $r$; $b_{jm}$ is the situational index of situation $j$ with respect to trait $T_m$; $b_{jmr}$ is the situation index of situation $j$ and role situation $r$ with respect to trait $T_m$; and $T_{mi}$ is the trait $m$ of individual $i$.

It should be mentioned that in Equation 4 we took account also of states—$S$ terms. There is also a possibility that one or more particular role factors will show up when certain background conditions are given. Assuming that changes in the situational indexes reflect trait utilization in roles, it will be clear that a particular role will find its behavioral manifestations in a whole set of responses rather than just one response. Here, again, changes of the corresponding situational indexes can be submitted to a $Q$ analysis, thus yielding an objective taxonomy of the perception of a specific role. Furthermore, those responses can be elicited under different background conditions that are always associated with the same focal situation. Subsequent analysis of changes in the situational indexes under those conditions would finally result in an objective taxonomy of roles.

Besides traits, states, and roles, there might be one factor or more that reflect those mental sets specifically related to a particular situation. The full model then can be written as follows:

$$P_{ijkl} = \sum_{T=1}^{m} b_{jklt1} T_{1i} + \sum_{S=1}^{o} b_{jkls1} S_{1i}$$

$$+ \sum_{R=1}^{r} b_{jklr1} R_{1i}$$

$$+ \sum_{P=1}^{t} b_{jklp1} P_{1i}. \quad (5)$$

Equation 5 means that a particular response $P_j$ of an individual $i$ which has been performed in focal situation $k$ and in a background situation $l$ can be analyzed into the sum of all relevant trait factors $T$ multiplied by their corresponding situational indexes $b_{jt}$ plus the sum of the product of all state factors $S$ and their behavioral or situational indexes $b_{js}$, plus the sum of the role factors $R$ and their situational indexes $b_{jr}$ plus finally, the sum of specific mental set factors $P$ and their corresponding situational indexes $b_{jp}$.

The introduction of the last term, $P$, in Equation 5 brings us to the discussion of Cattell's second main innovation in perception theory, namely the *dynamic-cognitive set*. At first, in an earlier work by Cattell and Scheier (1961), an attempt was made to dispense with the concept of a perception altogether, as superfluous, since it appeared that the general behavioral specification Equation 3, predicting an act directly from trait and state terms, positively required intervening variables in the nature of a perception term. However, the pressure

toward accepting a special term actually came from empirical factor-analytic results, which pointed increasingly to a hierarchy descending to ever more narrow, temporary factors in the dynamic ($D$ trait) area. In particular, role factors ($D_R$ traits) seem to break down into perceptual sets specific to a situation. *Set* is an old and honored term in psychology, but hitherto has played little role in factor analysis. The concept here is that dynamic traits ($D$s) typically control, and, indeed, consist of, a hierarchy of dynamic sets with cognitive accompaniments. A specific percept term, $P$, thus finally appears at the bottom of the hierarchy. This notion, with its physiological substrate, is developed more fully elsewhere.

An interesting segment of Cattell's general theory of modulators is what he calls *trait-view theory* (Cattell, 1966e). Trait-view theory is designed to give an answer to a question that recently has become modern in social perception research: How do people perceive other personalities? For a more detailed treatment of problems arising from an interaction model of trait-view theory the reader is referred to Cattell (1968c).

## 3 TUCKER'S GENERAL MODEL FOR INDIVIDUAL DIFFERENCES IN THE DIMENSIONALITY OF PERCEPTIONS

In this section we turn to a multivariate method of determining the inter- and intra-individual multidimensionality of perceived stimuli. The essentials of this model were published in full detail by Tucker and Messick (1963). The essentials of Tucker's model are reviewed here in brief.

Tucker's reasoning rests on a theorem stated by Eckart and Young (1936). It was proved by R. M. Johnson (1963). The Eckart-Young theorem says that any fundamental data matrix (Horst, 1963) can be analyzed in a diagonal matrix pre- and postmultiplied by conforming orthonormal matrices. Equation 6 states this theorem in matrix notation:

$$X_{N \times n} = P_{N \times r} D_{r \times r}^{1/2} Q'_{r \times n},\qquad (6)$$

where $X_{N \times n}$ is the data matrix of order $N \times n$; $P_{N \times r}$ is the left orthonormal of order $N \times r$ and it also holds that $r < n$; $D_{r \times r}$ is the diagonal matrix of order $r$; and $Q'_{r \times n}$ is the right orthonormal of order $r \times n$.

The diagonal matrix of Equation 6 is a matrix of nonnegative eigenvalues, and both orthonormals are matrices with corresponding eigenvectors. It is important to note that this procedure reduces the original data matrix, which is of rank $n$, to one of lower rank just by cutting off those eigenvalues of the diagonal matrix that cause no substantial changes when the data matrix will be reconstructed. The left orthonormal $P$ represents the person space, whereas the right orthonormal $Q'$ is a matrix of eigenvectors of the variables. By simple matrix operations, Equation 6 can be transformed into Equation 7:

$$X_{N \times n} = F_{1_{N \times r}} D_{r \times r}^{-1/2} F'_{2_{r \times n}}.\qquad (7)$$

Equation 7 is the "basic structure" (Horst, 1963, 1965) of matrix $X$, which means that any data matrix can be analyzed in a factor matrix $F_1$ and the transpose of another factor matrix $F_2$. $F_1$ represents the factor space of persons and is equivalent to what usually is called $Q$-technique, whereas $F_2$ is the factor matrix of variables—in factor analysis known as $R$ technique. It can be shown that the diagonal matrix remains the same for the data matrix and the derived matrix of cross products or covariances. From that it can be concluded that each eigenvalue in the diagonal matrix has a corresponding person and variable vector,

each uniquely related to the other. This leads to the conclusion that persons and variables can be represented in the same $r$-dimensional space.

If we introduce similarity ratings of pairs of stimuli as variables in the data matrix then we would get a set of distance ratings for each individual in the rows of the data matrix. In case all persons hold the same "point of view" in perceiving the stimuli, which would be revealed by identical configurations of stimuli among rows, we would get just one interindividual dimension with its corresponding intraindividual structure of stimuli. If more than one interindividual dimension can be found, then there exist more "points of view" in perceiving the same set of stimuli. Each of these points of view will be associated with an interindividually differing intraindividual perceptual structure of stimuli. The corresponding intraindividual structure of stimuli is not necessarily one dimensional. The dimensionality of the configuration of distance ratings can be determined by ordinary multidimensional scaling methods (Torgerson, 1958).

Tucker's model of individual differences has been checked in a series of studies (for a review see Sixtl, 1967; Tucker, 1964b). In one research (Helm & Tucker, 1962), distance ratings of colored chips had to be made by a group of nine people with normal color vision and four with color deficiencies. All persons were thrown together in one data matrix, and the resulting matrix of cross products was analyzed according to the procedure described previously. Three simple structure-person factors could be isolated. Factor I proved to be a constant, whereas Factors II and III clearly represented a dimension of normal-sight people and color-blind people, respectively. It could also be shown that the structure of color stimuli was a clearcut two-dimensional one whereas color-deficient subjects came fairly close to a one-dimensional perception of colors.

The advantage of Tucker's model is that people can be sorted in typical categories of "points of view" without knowing in advance about the person's underlying determinants of perception. In another research this advantage has been used in uncovering the structure of "implicit personality theories" (Bruner & Tagiuri, 1954; Cronbach, 1958), as revealed in distinct structures of trait relationships. The most comprehensive study using Tucker's method was conducted by Pederson (1965), who analyzed similarity ratings of 50 trait names. The analysis yielded three distinct points of view, the first of which was interpreted as a response set factor. The second factor was believed to represent the conventional point of view, and the third factor led to the interpretation of an authoritarian point of view. The interpretation of these three factors was facilitated by inspecting the changes of the structure of trait relationships from viewpoint to viewpoint. The intraindividual structure of the conventional point of view had been determined by a subjective kind of qualitative factor analysis. This procedure become necessary since Pederson had only an incomplete matrix of trait similarity ratings. By his type of analysis Pederson arrived at seven factors which he believed to be oblique. These factors were labeled as Social Desirability, Mental Potency, Emotionality, Stability, Sociability, Sophistication, and Greediness. In more recent studies on perceptual, conceptual, and judgmental types in processing simple sensory and more complex clinical information, it has been shown that there are clear-cut personality correlates that make those types psychologically more meaningful in view of their corresponding perceptual structures (see, e.g., Messick & Kogan, 1966; Skager,

Schultz, & Klein, 1966; Walters & Jackson, 1966; Wiggins, N., & Fishbein, 1969; Wiggins, N., & Wiggins, 1969).

Tucker's model of individual differences in perception clearly demonstrates that people can be grouped in interindividually differing types of perceivers. Those interindividual differences go along with differing intraindividual structures of objectively describable stimuli. It is hard, however, to decide whether those homogenous perceptual types show an intraindividual structure which is due to perceptual disposition constructs, situation perception constructs or even perceptual state constructs. This can only be decided when an experimentally induced variation of situations and measurement occasions is introduced to pinpoint cross-situational and cross-occasional stability of the obtained structure.

## 4 BRUNSWIK'S MULTIPLE-CUE MODEL

In many cases the stimulus situation a person is responding to is composed of several different stimulus attributes, which will be used by the person to make a "correct" response. Those stimulus attributes or cues will be differentially weighted when they are used and, thus, will contribute to the correlation between the global stimulus situation and the individual's response. A model based on assumptions like those was first set forth by Brunswik (1955, 1956). The analysis of data obtained on the basis of this model was developed by D. R. Hammond (1955) and Hursch, Hammond, and Hursch (1964) in applying multiple-regression procedures. The model can be outlined as follows: A distal variable $Y_e$ is composed of $n$ cues $X_1$ through $X_n$. Each cue $X_i$ is correlated with the distal variable $Y_e$, which results in a set of correlations of the type $r_{e,i}$. Those correlations are called *ecological validities*. Moreover each cue is correlated with the person's response $Y_s$ to the distal variable $Y_e$. Those correlations $r_{s,1}$ are called utilization coefficients or *functional validities*. Finally there is the correlation $r_a$ between the distal variable $Y_e$ and the individuals' response $Y_s$. Brunswik maintained that the latter correlation can be expressed as a function of the ecological and functional validities provided by different cues of the distal variable.

The usefulness of Brunswik's multiple-cue model has been demonstrated, for instance, in applying multiple-regression equations to data gathered by Todd (1954). In Todd's study, 10 clinicians made judgments of IQ scores of 78 patients after inspecting the patients' scores on 19 Rorschach factors. The Rorschach factors were conceived as cues, whereas the distal variable was given by the patients' actual score on an objective intelligence test. Thus, the multiple correlations between the 19 Rorschach cues and the distal variable as well as the IQ estimate could be computed for each clinician separately. The correlation between distal variable (objective IQ score) and judgment (estimated IQ score) was determined next, and then the goodness of prediction could be checked.

Brunswik's model appears to be especially designed to uncover individual differences in the analysis of situation-perception constructs, since changing ecological validities would not only result in a different ecology but also in more or less drastic changes of a person's response system. Some evidence for this has been provided in a multiple-cue learning experiment as conducted by Summers (1962). In Summers' study, 17 people judged geometric forms (distal variable) with three different stimulus characteristics (cues) with known ecological weights to yield correct line-length judgments (response). During 4 blocks of 64 trials, each of Summers' subjects first had to give a judgment and then were presented with the correct line length. The results of this study indicated that the subjects changed their use of cue utilization during the learning session. It could also be shown that people differ markedly in their degree of cue utilization and their use of cue utilization relative to the ecological validities of the cues.

The findings of Summers' study seem to be of some importance for an objective analysis of perceptual state constructs, since the same set of cues might change its corresponding set of differential weightings within the response system of a person during a sequence of subsequent exposures to the same distal variable. Moreover the perceptual structure of underlying stimulus attributes might alter along with changes due to learning influences (Newton, 1965). Brunswik's multiple-cue model and various methodological improvements based on it have been extensively used in recent years, especially in the field of clinical judgment (for a review on this type of research see Goldberg, L. R., 1968). An interesting and promising combination of Tucker's individual-differences model and Brunswik's multiple-cue model has been tried out in a study by N. Wiggins, Hoffman, and Taber (1969). There it could be shown that different types of judges also differ in their weighting and combining of a set of behavioral cues presumably pertaining to the field of intelligence in order to arrive at complex intelligence judgments. In still another experiment, Slovic (1966) demonstrated that the consistency of cues in a study on social perception depends on the differential value and the specific configuration of the whole set of cues according to the kind of feedback information provided for the judges.

It seems that more recent extensions of the Brunswikian multiple-cue model using linear and configural techniques as well in analyzing perceptual data (see, e.g., Wiggins, N., & Hoffman, 1968) along with a factor-analytic typological approach will result in a fuller understanding of process and structure in the field of perception and, at the same time, make clear that personality and perception are intrinsically interrelated.

## 5  SOME FURTHER CONSIDERATION OF THE FACTOR-ANALYTIC MODEL OF PERCEPTUAL AND PERSONALITY CONSTRUCTS

In the first section of this chapter we referred to a conceptual framework of personality and perception research. Three types of perceptual constructs were distinguished there, labeled perceptual disposition constructs, situation perception constructs, and perceptual state constructs. It was postulated that each of those constructs should be operable with the help of corresponding construct indicators. We now try to fit these concepts into a multivariate model. The assumptions of this model are the most economic and simple to think of since it is taken for granted that all relationships among the data fed into this model are linear, additive, and noninteractive.

To demonstrate the essence of this model, let us start with an example. Suppose we are measuring the reaction time of a particular person $P_1$ in a representative sample of situations and furthermore, suppose that we have a representative sample of measurement occasions for each situation. Reaction time might be conceived as a construct indicator forming part of a hypothetical construct that might be called *physical alertness*. This construct indicator can be split into three components, which exactly correspond to those classes of constructs and construct indicators mentioned previously.

Let us first look at what we called *disposition construct indicators*. According to the definition of dispositions given earlier, we would say that the dispositional part of reaction time is what remains constant across different situations and occasions.

Next we must know whether different situations have an impact on $P_1$'s reaction time response, that is, whether $P_1$ perceives something different when presented with an objectively changed situation. If this holds true we would take only the stable situational component for further analysis, that is, only that part of a measured behavioral act that remains constant across different measurement occasions within a particular situation.

Finally, parts of the reaction time score vary within situations from occasion to occasion. Again, these fluctuations form part of the total score and belong to the class of state indicators. It is evident by now that any measured behavioral manifestation can be decomposed in three component scores, which then might serve as dispositional, situation perception, and state construct indicators.

The next step is to process those three types of component scores separately, to throw some light on the organization and structure of dispositional, situation perception, and state indicators, notably their contribution to their corresponding constructs. We outline briefly how this can be done with the help of factor-analytic techniques.

Let us look at the dispositional component scores. A multitude of variables could be decomposed in their corresponding components. Moreover, a whole set of individuals could be treated in the same way as $P_1$ in our example. Thus, we would finally get a data matrix of $N$ subjects and $n$ trait indicators if we took only the dispositional component scores. According to Equation 7, this data matrix could only be analyzed as follows:

$$_TX = {}_TF_1 {}_TD^{-1/2} {}_TF_2',  \qquad (8)$$

where $_TX$ is the data matrix of trait indicators; $_TF_1$ is the factor matrix of person space of trait indicators ($Q$ technique); $_TF_2'$ is the transpose of the factor matrix of trait indicator space ($R$ technique), and $_TD^{1/2}$ is the diagonal matrix of eigenvalues of trait indicators.

An analysis according to Equation 8 would result in a taxonomy of persons with respect to trait indicators; in addition, it would yield a taxonomy of trait indicators. The latter would give us the structure of dispositional constructs. Those dispositional constructs could then be grouped into a class of factors that are mainly loading those trait indicators requiring perceptual performance and into a class of other factors that might be categorized as nonperceptual disposition constructs.

Next we turn to the situation-perception component of a behavioral act. Here, again, we could analyze only that part of the total score responsible for measurable differences aligned with objective situational changes. For a whole set of people, variables, and situations we would get a grid of data matrices (Cattell, 1966e) rather than one data matrix. The analytic procedure, however, would remain the same as for the analysis of dispositional component scores. Equation 9 represents the factor-analytic treatment of situation-perception indicators:

$$_PX = {}_PF_1 {}_PD^{-1/2} {}_PF_2',  \qquad (9)$$

where $_PX$ is the grid of data matrixes of situation-perception indicators for a set of situations; $_PF_1$ is the factor matrix of person space of situation-perception indicators ($Q$ technique); $_PF_2'$ is the transpose of the factor matrix of situation-perception indicator space ($R$ technique), and $_PD^{-\frac{1}{2}}$ is the diagonal matrix of eigenvalues of situation-perception indicators.

Analyzing a data matrix of situation-perception indicators as given by Equation 9 would present us with a taxonomy of persons with similar points of view in perceiving situations. The same analysis would also yield a taxonomy of perceived situations for that particular group of individuals. The resulting factors would then be situation-perception constructs. (It also would be possible to determine the structure of objectively describable situations regardless of the persons' responses in making use of controlled manipulative experimentation [Cattell, 1966e]). The resulting taxonomy of objective situations could then be compared with the perceived structures of different perceptual points of view.

Finally, we deal with the last component score of global behavioral acts that remains to be considered, that is, perceptual and nonperceptual state indicators. Those, too, can be processed according to the factor-analytic treatment. Here, again, the data matrix would consist of a grid of component scores that take into account occasional variation of a set of variables. Equation 10 gives the corresponding formula for analysis:

$$_SX = {}_SF_1 {}_SD^{-1/2} {}_SF_2',  \qquad (10)$$

where $_SX$ is the grid of data matrices of state indicators for a set of situations and occasions; $_SF_1$ is the factor matrix of person space of state indicators ($Q$ technique); $_SF_2'$ is the transpose of the factor matrix of state indicator space; and $_SD^{-1/2}$ is the diagonal matrix of eigenvalues of state indicators.

Both factor matrices of Equation 10 isolate person and state factors, respectively. The person factors represent types of people with a similar state structure, and the state factors give the actual state structures of those types of people. Some of these factors are due to perceptual changes within a particular situation and, therefore, might be called *perceptual state constructs*.

So far we have outlined the bare essentials of a unifying factor-analytic model of perceptual and personality constructs. It becomes more evident, however, that this model is able to handle all the constructs of the conceptual analysis as outlined in the first section of this chapter within a factor-analytic framework.

## 6    PERSONALITY TRAITS AND PERCEPTUAL ABILITY FACTORS: SOME UNSOLVED ISSUES

That a substantial connection exists between personality and perception is clear at the empirical level from various researches already cited, and at the theoretical level from such models as those of Cattell and Tucker. The particular form of the connection in these two representative theories may seem different at first. In one case, the act of perception is given as a function of the individual's possession of traits of all modalities, but with particular emphasis on the endowments in dynamic modulated traits, which are the basis for the appearance of particular dynamic-cognitive sets. In the other, the personality expresses itself in the dimensionality evident in the perception.

These two theories and others that may appear like them are not intrinsically inconsistent and might later be bridged by common concepts. However, to the psychologist accustomed to think of perception as a cognitive process and personality as a set of trait structures, some awkward issues of definition present themselves. For example, he might want to know whether some of those dispositional constructs can be classified as strictly perceptual disposition con-

structs. This issue will be encountered in the contention of Witkin that field-independence is a perceptual concept, and of Cattell that it is more completely understood as a general personality trait of independence—the source trait *U.I.* 19—outcropping in the perceptual expressions. Actually, it is generally agreed that we decide the modality of a trait by inspecting the contents and processes of the defining variables of these constructs; that is, it has to be checked whether the construct indicators require responses that are predominantly of a perceptual kind, like tasks where the person is asked to distinguish details in a complex arrangement of stimuli, to compare patterns of stimuli with respect to their similarity, or to identify drawn objects where just a few lines or dots are given. In other words, if we assert that a structure is a purely *perceptual trait* it must be shown that all its manifestations (loadings) occur only on behaviors that are free of, say, motor ability, reasoning, manipulative aptitude, and so forth.

We begin by looking at factor trait structures that have appeared in variables produced with a wide inventiveness in designing perceptual tests. The pioneer study in this field was done by Thurstone (1944), and it remains one of the finest examples of inventive test construction and thorough experimentation. The total number of people involved in Thurstone's study was 194, although several of them did not take the complete test battery. The average number of people for the computation of correlation coefficients totaled 170. Forty-two variables were used for the final analysis although the whole battery of tests consisted of 60 variables.

The variables were intercorrelated, and the resulting correlation matrix was factor analyzed. Eleven factors were extracted and then rotated obliquely to simple structure.

Only 5 out of 11 factors appear to be broad perceptual factors, namely Speed and Strength of Closure (Factor *A*), Rate of Reversals in Perception (Factor *D*), Flexibility in Manipulation of Configurations (Factor *E*), Speed of Perception (Factor *F*) and Speed of Judgment (Factor *J*).

A second study deserving mention here (since it was based on a fairly large sample of variables, most of them in the perceptual area) is M. A. Roff's (1952) work in which 70 tests were administered to a medium sample size of 450 pre-aviation cadets ranging in age between 18 and 19 years. The variables were intercorrelated and factor analyzed. The factor extraction was stopped at 18 factors, which then were rotated to oblique simple structure. Roff came to the conclusion that "eight of the factors of this set may, because of their intercorrelations, be considered as forming a family of related perceptual factors" (Roff, M. A., 1952, p. 27). The central factor of this group of factors seems to be the one which has been named Perceptual Speed. This factor is similar to the Perceptual Speed Factor in Thurstone's study. The other factors belonging to that group of clear-cut perceptual factors were labeled as follows: Plotting Directional Thinking, Length Perception, Perceptual Closure, Sequential Perception, Complex Reaction Time, and Perception through Camouflage. Although there was some indication that perceptual factors correlate higher with each other than with nonperceptual factors, a second-order factor analysis that would have thrown some light on this was not carried out by Roff. From Thurstone's and Roff's study it can be concluded, however, that even on the level of primaries there exist a number of relatively independent perceptual factors that clearly can be distinguished from other nonperceptual factors like those measuring intellectual abilities.

The fact that there are distinct perceptual factors that, by means of their loading patterns, stand out against other nonperceptual factors does not necessarily imply that nonperceptual variables will not load on them at all. Having found in his earlier studies of temperament factors that they expressed themselves partly in perceptual performance, Cattell (1963c) raised the question, on the appearance of Thurstone's factors (1944), that the latter—or some of them—might strictly be temperament factors. This question had meaning only if Cattell could point to some principle of selection by which the variables for his temperament traits were chosen, but this had been explicitly put forward in his *personality sphere* concept (chapter 1, this *Handbook*). He and his co-workers then proceeded with the major undertaking of locating the main personality structures on a basis of objectively measurable behavioral acts (Cattell, 1946; Cattell & Warburton, 1967) in which, however, they deliberately incorporated "marker variables" for the chief perceptual-ability factors of Thurstone, and later of Roff (Cattell, 1957a).

It will suffice here to say that, so far, some 21 factors have been found by means of objective test devices and that virtually all of those factors have been matched across 10 independent experimental studies or more (Hundleby, Pawlik & Cattell, 1965). In almost all of this series of factors (*U.I.* 16 through *U.I.* 36), a perceptual component is represented to a larger or smaller extent. Eight factors, however, appear to be particularly related to perceptual tasks. This can be proved easily by inspecting the averaged (central tendency) loading patterns of each of these replicated personality factors (Hundleby, Pawlik, & Cattell, 1965). A list of those eight temperamental factors with considerable saturations of perceptual tasks is given in Table 1. This table also presents a

**TABLE 1**  Objective-analytic test personality factors loading perceptual tasks

| Universal Index (*U.I.*) | Factor title | Involvement of perceptual tasks |
|---|---|---|
| *U.I.* 17 | Timid Inhibitedness versus Lack of Inhibition (corresponds to Thurstone's Factor *F*) | Slow speed of perceptual tasks, high susceptibility to perception of threatening objects |
| *U.I.* 18 | Hypomanic Smartness versus Slow Thoroughness | High speed of perception in simple perceptual tasks, superficiality of perception |
| *U.I.* 19 | Promethean Will versus Subduedness (corresponds to Thurstone's Factor *E*) | High competence, flexibility, and accuracy in perceptual tasks |
| *U.I.* 21 | Exuberance versus Suppressibility | High speed and fluency of perceptual judgment, maintenance of perceptual competence under impoverished conditions |
| *U.I.* 22 | Cortertia versus Pathemia (corresponds to Thurstone's Factor *C*) | Fast speed of performance in perceptual and nonperceptual tasks |
| *U.I.* 25 | Less Imaginative, Task Oriented Realism versus Tense Inflexidia | Little competence in unstructured perceptual and cognitive tasks, but high speed and tempo in simple perceptions |
| *U.I.* 32 | Exvia versus Invia | Less accurate, more fluent perception and thinking |
| *U.I.* 34 | Inconautia versus Practicalness | High imaginative perceptual fluency, but little carefulness and accuracy in perception |

*Note.*  Abstracted from Hundleby, Pawlik, and Cattell (1965).

brief description as to how those factors are influenced by perceptual processes.

Since all these factors also load personality behavior of a kind having nothing to do with perception, and since they predict everyday-life criteria in a way that would be clinically expected of personality factors, there can be no question that the greater part of general perceptual behavior is predictable from personality factors in the broader personality-sphere sense (including ability and dynamic structure traits). Space

forbids running over all personality factors to explore the particular quality of each of their perceptual contributions, but we may take one already discussed above (*U.I.* 19, Independence) and the reader might be recommended to look at *U.I.* 21, which also aligns with one of Thurstone's purely perceptual *outcrop* factors (Cattell, 1957a).

*U.I.* 19, Independence versus Subduedness (as it has been called descriptively) has been found in as many as 14 independent studies. In Table 2 the loadings of the 12 most consistently and highest loading variables are averaged.

It should be noted, however, that the 12 variables in Table 2 are just half of the study of *U.I.* 19 since there are at least 76 more variables with substantial loadings on this factor. Nevertheless it can be seen that an important part of *U.I.* 19 is made up by generally competent performances, especially in the area of perceptual tasks. Exactness, controlled responses, independence of mind, and low error scores are the main

attributes of both the perceptual and the general performance measures. Clearly, *field independence* and capacity to separate parts in perceptual tasks is only one particular aspect of the behavior of a person who is scoring high on *U.I.* 19. Other variables indicate that determination, unaffectedness of distraction, adaptive flexibility, and social detachedness are also important aspects of this factor. Therefore the overall picture of a typical *U.I.* 19 person who is determined, accurate, and independent led to the inter-

**TABLE 2**   Mean loadings of 12 variables on *U.I.* 19 (Promethean Will versus Subduedness)

| Variable title | Mean loading | No. of studies |
|---|---|---|
| Higher proportion correct in perceptual closure | .35 | 6 |
| Higher accuracy in perceptual closure on Gottschaldt figures | .28 | 5 |
| Higher score: index of carefulness | .17 | 7 |
| Faster rate of alternating perspective | .18 | 7 |
| Less criticism of self relative to criticism of others | −.14 | 10 |
| Larger number correct in perceptual closure | .31 | 3 |
| Fewer erroneous reactions under complex instructions | −.20 | 7 |
| Lower motor (and motor-perceptual) rigidity | −.06 | 12 |
| Higher severity of judgment | .13 | 9 |
| Faster speed of perceptual closure | .13 | 8 |
| Fewer slanting lines crossed—CMS | −.13 | 10 |
| More correct movements in two-hand coordination | .23 | 7 |

*Note.* Abstracted from Hundleby, Pawlik, and Cattell (1965, p. 172).

pretation of this factor as general temperamental Independence, at one time more picturesquely—indeed, aptly described—as Promethean Will.

As one considers evidence of this kind, he may well begin to doubt that "perceptual" as a category has any major utility. It gained its momentum in the early days from introspective rather than behavioristic psychology. And although Cattell and Scheier (1961) have abandoned their extreme position that it suffices to proceed in prediction directly from personality traits to behavior, treating perception as a superfluous intermediate concept, the dynamic-cognitive set term that Cattell would now include in the behavioral equation derives strictly from behavior (not introspection) and—though truly a perceptual term—plays a small part, over and above the personality terms in predicting the response to a situation.

The present location and identity of a perceptual concept comes strictly from the demonstrable involvement of the senses, and of memory action determined by a factor-analytically recognizable dynamic-cognitive set. But this perceptual component itself seems to have an almost trivial role in determining the behavioral response to most stimuli, by comparison with the role of major personality factors. One is left wondering just why the particular part of the behavioral process that happens to employ the senses is artifically separated out for a special area of study.

Except for these hypothesized and as yet incompletely exemplified specific, narrow perceptual dynamic set factors, none of the usual broad personality factors influencing perception is nearly enough restricted to perceptual expressions to justify calling it a Perceptual factor. By the same token, one would also not think of calling such a personality factor a Motor factor or a Memory factor. The relation of personality to perception, analogous to its relation to motor expression or to the process of memory recall, is that it commands expression through perception and, in statistical terms, accounts for a major part of the variance in any sample of perceptual performances.

# 24

## Trait Theory and the Verbal-Learning Processes

**K. Warner Schaie**
*University of Southern California, Los Angeles*

**Larry R. Goulet**
*University of Illinois, Urbana*

### 1  INTRODUCTION

This chapter surveys the somewhat sparse literature on the relation between personality variables and verbal-learning processes. A number of paradigms are examined for the more important verbal-learning processes to permit speculation as to how the latter might relate to personality traits. Also, it will be shown how such processes may themselves be important in the development and maintenance of stable personality patterns.

Although many other definitions of personality may be in order, we shall here confine ourselves to the discussion of traits rather than states or their dynamic interaction. Such limitation seems necessary in discussing the relation between personality and verbal learning since the large amount of information available on processes subsumed under verbal learning has generally been gathered independent of the structures of dynamic behavior theories. Indeed, verbal-learning paradigms have been considered particularly relevant to test propositions about personality dynamisms or states because of this independence. It seems quite appropriate therefore to relate the basic processes involved in paired-associate learning, transfer of training, serial learning, etc.

to some of the known components implicit in a trait-theory approach to the description of personality structure.

If we are to relate personality structure to verbal-learning processes, we must be clear as to the level of equivalence of our data. Thus we may begin by exploring relationships with the major surface traits such as anxiety or introversion-extroversion. Needless to say, such surface traits in personality structure analysis appear as second-order factors and may indeed be pictured as the state equivalent of a series of other more basic source traits or primary personality factors. On the other hand, it is the behavioral equivalent of the surface trait—or in its simplest form the bi-polar adjective description denoting the criterion behaviors—that can be most directly related to processes of acquiring and maintaining behavior.

Explication of the formal relationships between a personality trait-oriented conceptual framework and the semantic scheme used by the worker interested in the specifics of response acquisition, maintenance, and extinction of learned behavior requires the formulation of satisfactory operational definitions. Several different approaches may be taken to this problem, but it seems obvious that verbal-learning paradigms are the most convenient laboratory tasks that may be used to relate personality variables to learning and performance. A variety of rather convincing reasons can be provided for this position.

First, theory and methodology involved in the study of verbal learning have been highly developed; and sufficient data exist to insure the reliability of obtaining either the phenomenon or the phenomena that are being related to specific dimensions of personality.

Second, verbal-learning tasks can be modified along several dimensions (e.g., length of list, intralist similarity, and response meaningfulness) and also each variable can be related to the same dependent measure and task difficulty. But each of these variables affects criterion performance in a different manner. Thus, the rate of paired-associate (PA) learning is directly related to response meaningfulness because of the differential degrees of extra-experimental learning for high and low meaningfulness items. High intralist similarity (especially high stimulus similarity) retards PA learning specifically because of associative interference.

Third, the tasks typically used for verbal-learning paradigms may be designed to control for the effects of pre-experimental (or extra-experimental) transfer of learning. (or extraexperimental) transfer of learning. For example, the PA task may be constructed such that the effects of language habits, acquired before the subject's appearance in the laboratory, are minimized. Such effects may be accomplished in a number of ways including minimizing intralist stimulus, intralist response, and stimulus-response similarity in a PA task consisting of, for example, paired adjectives. Or the PA list may be constructed to consist of items (e.g., trigrams) that have low frequency of occurrence in the printed language. Such lists minimize the degree to which the items are integrated (learned) before the initiation of practice on the PA task.

The detailed attention that must be given to the independent variables that are manipulated when using verbal learning paradigms cannot be overemphasized. Control of the independent variables becomes even more important in experiments where an attempt is made to relate personality attributes to performance on verbal learning tasks. To be sure, the relation between scores on personality variables (e.g., source traits) and on learning performance may be specified; however, the prediction derived from personality theory must be directly concerned with the exact conditions under which the expected relationship will occur. For example, to find a correlation between PA learning and anxiety is not as important as delimiting the boundary conditions under which this relationship holds. Although scores from two different source traits may each be positively correlated to the rate of PA learning, only one of these traits may be correlated to performance under conditions where meaningfulness of materials is high and intralist similarity is low. The second source trait, however, may relate to performance on a PA task involving high similarity. A statement relating each subject variable to task difficulty alone therefore does not identify the manner in which each variable affects criterion performance.

The attempt to formulate the relationships between the trait-theoretical approach to personality and the concepts of interest to the worker in verbal learning must be largely speculative since almost no work in the area of verbal learning has been conducted within a personality-trait framework. This state of affairs, however, is true in its entirety only with respect to traits and first-order personality factors. For the second-order factors such as anxiety and extroversion-introversion, we find a substantial body of literature, notably the work with the Taylor Manifest Anxiety Scale (MAS) and the work of the Maudsley group on the relation of performance and intro-version-extroversion. It is therefore both possible and profitable to examine in detail the work on verbal learning in relation to these second-order personality dimensions. Because of its close relation to work with the dimension of cyclothymia-schizothymia, we also attend briefly to the work on verbal learning in schizophrenics.

Many of the methodological issues and problems discussed for the second-order factors are also equally relevant to the source traits. Their discussion, however, is delayed until the section on the second-order factors because of the greater volume of pertinent research. Finally, consideration is given to the applications of modern multivariate approaches to a possible reconciliation of the divergent approaches in the work on verbal learning with the interests of the factor-analytically oriented personality researcher.

## 2  VERBAL LEARNING AND THE SOURCE TRAITS

Several of the basic personality factors (or source traits) identified by Cattell and his colleagues in the rating, questionnaire, and objective test domains (cf., Cattell, 1957a) lend themselves quite nicely to an investigation using a variety of verbal learning tasks. Whenever we attempt to draw inferences from the effects of specific subjects' attributes, we need to remember that this implies that we have attained precise control over the *task* or experimental variables known to affect performance independently of the interaction of the task and subject variables. But it is not enough to specify that performance in paired-associate

learning, for example, will vary directly with a subject variable unless it is possible to point to a specific reason for expecting this relation. Such specification implies that the component processes involved in the task (e.g., response learning, associative learning) can be identified and, in addition, that the variables affecting each of these components are known. Finally, it must be restated that direct comparisons of performance as a function of personality variables can be misleading. That is, equal rates of acquisition in a verbal-learning task for two or more groups of people differentiated on personality variables does not necessarily imply null effects of the variable being manipulated but may also be the effect of opposing facilitative and negative effects on different component processes involved in the task.

Implications connecting the personality dimension, affectothymia-schizothymia, better known as cyclothymia-schizothymia (Factor A), to verbal learning can be generated from two sources: the research relating to the identification of the factors responsible for psychological deficit in schizophrenia (e.g., Lang & Buss, 1965) and the verbal descriptors of the dimension itself. Cattell (1965c) described persons representing the negative end of the factor (schizothymic) as being rigid as well as critical, cool, aloof, precise, and suspicious. It is clear that both lines of research lead to the same conclusion, that schizothymic persons should be susceptible to associative interference. It is likely moreover that the performance of schizothymic people on tasks involving competing responses (e.g., high intralist similarity) would be inferior to that of affectothymic persons.

Similar predictions would be made for tasks involving sources of negative transfer. In fact, rigid behavior, whenever manifested, can be conceived as involving interference from earlier learned habits. It is important to mention that such competition from previously learned habits can be investigated directly in the laboratory by using the paired-associates A–B, A–C (stimuli identical, responses different on the two lists) transfer paradigm. In this case the source of competition is under direct experimental control. Alternatively, the source of associative interference can be attributed to extra-experimental (extralist) learning, i.e., to learning that has occurred before practice on the experimental task. In either case, negative transfer would not be expected unless the earlier learned habits relate to the new task in an A–B, A–C fashion. In addition, inferior performance for schizothymic persons would be expected only where some source of associative interference is available. Reference should also be made to the earlier and somewhat less controlled work on proactive and retroactive inhibition going back to the work of Spearman's students (Bernstein, 1924) and the more recent factor-analytic work on the dimensions of rigidity, most of which includes verbal-learning tasks (e.g., Dudek & Kleemeier, 1950; Schaie, 1955, 1958; Schaie & Parham, 1975; Scheier & Ferguson, 1952).

Other implications relating source traits to overt performance can be derived. Eysenck (1963, 1964a) and McLaughlin and Eysenck (1967) characterized the personality factor "ego strength vs. emotionality and neuroticism" (Factor C) as representing a measure of drive. Furthermore, Cattell described the behavior of persons scoring at the negative end of this factor as random and ineffective. It follows directly that such "ineffective behavior" can be attributed directly to high autonomic nervous system (ANS) arousal (cf. Eysenck, 1963, 1964a; Malmo, 1958; McLaughlin & Eysenck, 1967). It also follows that other source traits related to ANS arousal (e.g.,

introversion-extraversion, A; parmia-threctia, H; and high ergic tension-low ergic tension, Q4) would relate to performance in the same manner as that described by Malmo (1958) in discussing the relation between performance and level of arousal. However, it is important that empirical tests of this assumption with the verbal-learning task take full account of the opportunity to perform component analyses such as looking at the effects of response-learning, associative learning, etc. (cf. Goulet, 1968).

Personality Factor D has been described by Cattell as the "excitability factor." It is presumed to be predominant in children; however, Cattell had difficulty in defining it clearly in the questionnaire domain for adults. At the high school age level, this factor is described as representing the dimension "stodgy versus restrained," and it is also found in the rating of disturbed mental patients. The highly excitable person is described as irrepressive, positive, and assertive but at the same time is characterized by mind-wandering distractibility. Low-excitability persons, on the other hand, are described as placid, deliberate, constant, and not restless. It is likely that high-excitability persons are also subject to associative interference from earlier learned habits, accounting for greater distractibility. All the relationships postulated thus far are based on reasonable extrapolations of the research literature. With respect to the other major source traits, we must limit ourselves to rather superficial speculation. These speculative associations might be summarized as follows:

The adjectives generally describing Factor E (dominance vs. submissiveness) imply a dimension from assertive, egotistic leadership roles to the display of a dependent and conforming milquetoast personality. Consequently, a subject with a high score on this factor might be expected to experience difficulty in following the detailed and often trivial-appearing instructions that must be used with most laboratory learning exercises. A high score on Factor F (surgency vs. desurgency), on the other hand, is probably advantageous on tasks where response speed and the tendency to be willing to guess would be important. The desurgent individual, contrariwise, would be at an advantage in a situation where deliberate and cautious response is required.

Most of the remaining basic source traits would be expected to relate to the situational context of the learning experiment rather than to specific response paradigms. Thus, standing on Factor G (super-ego strength vs. lack of acceptance of moral standards) would seem to relate primarily as a contributor of error variance since a person with a low G score might perform less well simply because of his difficulty in attending to rules. Likewise, it might be expected that Factor J (fastidious individualism vs. liking group action) will relate to the social context within which learning occurs, although it might conceivably mediate fatigue and/or inhibition at the coasthenic trait end.

One remaining source trait (Factor I) deserves special attention because it may reflect a response style of relevance in complex learning tasks. "Premsia versus harria" (protected emotional sensitivity vs. hardness and realism) is Cattell's equivalent of James' tender-versus-tough continuum. In contrast to Factor H, it is supposed to be attributable entirely to acquired response processes and is thought to distinguish between the premsic (emotionally sensitive) and the harric (tough and realistic) person. It is argued further that the harric individual acts on logical evidence, whereas the premsic person acts on intuition and is quite a dependent person. Thus, the harric individual might pay more attention to structural cues, while the premsic person may be

less subject to sources of negative transfer since he is presumed to be less attentive to extrinsic matter.

# 3 VERBAL LEARNING AND THE SECOND–ORDER PERSONALITY FACTOR OF ANXIETY

## 3.1 Questionnaire-Defined Anxiety

Almost no work has as yet been done relating questionnaire or test anxiety as measured by the factored instruments now available (cf. Cattell & Scheier, 1961) with the verbal-learning paradigms. A great deal of work is available, however, measuring questionnaire anxiety with the Taylor Manifest Anxiety Scale (MAS) and other structured questionnaires. Although it is true that the MAS has been deemed variously to be an index either of chronic or situational anxiety (see Goulet, 1968, and Spielberger, 1971a, for reviews), it would still more properly be relevant to the trait-theoretical position than is the Test Anxiety Questionnaire developed by Mandler and Sarason (1952), which was identified specifically as a measure of situational anxiety (e.g., Pagano, 1970; Pagano & Katahn, 1967; Sarason, I. G., 1956, 1957a). This work is reviewed here in some detail, beginning with the relation between anxiety and some of the traditional verbal-learning paradigms.

### 3.1.1 Paired-associates Learning

This task has been found to be convenient in the study of basic learning processes. It has also been used to test various theoretical propositions related to the interaction of a number of personality variables and performance. The variable most often studied is that of anxiety where the major impetus for research has been a test of the Taylor-Spence theory (e.g., Spence, J. T., & Spence, 1966; Spence, K. W.,

1956, 1958; Taylor, J. A., 1953, 1956). The basic implications of the Taylor-Spence formulation are described in this section, followed by a detailed examination of the predictions concerning the interaction of anxiety and performance that may be derived from the theory.

J. A. Taylor (1953) originally developed the Manifest Anxiety Scale (MAS) as a measure of the general motivational (drive) level of human subjects. Taken from Hull's (1943) concept of drive as a general energizer, MAS-defined anxiety was considered to measure a hypothetical emotional response $(r_e)$ typically aroused by noxious or aversive stimulation. The MAS, then, was taken as a measure of a person's level of $r_e$ and therefore his level of drive. As in Hull's theory, drive involved general energizing or general arousal properties and thus was considered to be a multiplier of all habits elicited in the situation.

According to the Taylor-Spence theory, the performance of high-anxious (HA) persons would be expected to be superior to that of low-anxious (LA) persons throughout learning under conditions where the to-be-learned responses are dominant. Under conditions where incorrect responses are dominant, the performance of HA persons would be expected to be inferior initially to that of LA individuals, followed by superior performance of HA persons at the point in learning where correct responses attain dominance in the response hierarchy. In other words, anxiety was viewed as having deleterious effects on performance in tasks where one or more task-specific competing responses were dominant over the correct responses. Superior performance of HA persons was expected when correct responses were dominant. This is the case in paired-associate learning when all obvious sources of intralist similarity are minimized.

Further implications relating to the effects of MAS-defined anxiety may be derived when intralist similarity is high. For example, a PA list may be constructed which is characterized by high intralist response similarity and low intralist stimulus similarity; e.g., a low-sim/high-sim list. With this task, the interfering effects of high response similarity would be expected to be greater for HA persons. However, the immediately preceding statement does not necessarily imply superior performance for LA persons in PA learning either in the early or late stages of learning.

Analysis of PA learning into two functional stages highlights this apparent paradox. Underwood, Runquist, and Schulz (1959) suggested that PA learning involves two stages, response-learning and associative learning. The response-learning stage involves the integration (learning) of the specific responses as units available for recall, whereas the associative stage relates to the hooking up of the specific stimuli and responses. With analysis, the learning of a single PA pair may be considered to involve, at the very least, two separate habits, rather than one as Spence (e.g., 1956, 1958) previously assumed. This analysis into stages also leads to the implication that deleterious effects of anxiety must be localized in the associative stage (Underwood, Runquist, & Schulz, 1959) of PA learning.

The learning of a low-sim/high-sim list clearly defines a task where the correct response to each stimulus in the list is not dominant. However, the expectation of superior or inferior performance of HA and LA persons in learning the low-sim/high-sim list is dependent on the relative effects of high response sim on the two stages of PA learning. For example, high response sim facilitates response learning because the integration or learning of one response generalizes to the other responses in the list. In this case, the Taylor-Spence theory would imply superior performance of HA persons relative to that of LA persons. On the other hand, high response sim disrupts the associative stage of PA learning because of competition between similar responses. This latter effect implies inferior performance of HA persons. It is apparent that the prediction of superior (or inferior) performance of HA individuals in PA learning (which involves both the response-learning and associative stages) is dependent on the magnitude of the interfering effects of response sim on the associative stage relative to the facilitative effects of response sim on the response-learning stage.

The use of a PA task involving high stimulus similarity and low response similarity; i.e., a high-sim/low-sim list, involves an analysis that is much less complex. High stimulus similarity has deleterious effects on associative learning but no concomitant effects on response learning (Underwood, Runquist, & Schulz, 1959). Thus, the Taylor-Spence formulation relating to the interaction of anxiety and performance suggests that LA persons would be superior to HA persons up to the point in learning where the correct response to each stimulus attains dominance over competing responses.

It is apparent that the prediction of superior performance for LA persons, relative to HA persons, can be made only if the deleterious effects of high similarity on the associative stage outweigh the facilitative effect of high similarity on the response-learning stage. Happily, this prediction can be tested in a number of ways. As has already been mentioned, this source of confounding can be circumvented by varying stimulus similarity rather than response similarity. Second, the opposing effects of similarity on the response-learning and associative stages hold only when meaningful word responses are used, rather than, for example, nonsense-syllable response (Jung, J., 1965;

Mazzei, 1969). Presumably this disparity is evident because high-sim words can be grouped on the basis of some mutual associative or superordinate word category, whereas nonsense syllables (where similarity in terms of letter duplication is varied) cannot be grouped or recalled on this basis.

Finally, techniques have been devised to provide for the independent measurement of response availability and associative learning in the PA tasks. For example, response learning can be assessed by asking for response recall at various stages of PA learning without providing the stimuli as cues or requiring associative learning (e.g., Underwood, Runquist, & Schulz, 1959).

Similarly, associative learning can be studied in the absence of response learning by modifying the PA task to fit an associative matching situation (e.g., Jung, J., 1965; Mazzei, 1969), or a multiple-choice task (e.g., DeVoge, 1968; Horowitz, 1962). In effect, the associative-matching or multiple-choice tasks involve the measurement of a subject's accuracy when associating stimuli to responses where both stimuli and responses are available to him. It is clear that the study of associative learning for HA and LA persons under conditions of high stimulus (or response) similarity would yield valuable evidence concerning anxiety-performance interaction. Under these conditions the performance of HA individuals would be predicted to be inferior to that of LA persons at least for the early stages of practice. On the other hand, with an associative matching task involving low stimulus and response similarity, the performance of HA persons should exceed that of LA persons throughout the course of learning.

The single study involving the assessment of PA learning of HA and LA persons as a function of similarity yielded negative results (Levitt & Goss, 1961). In their Experiment I, Levitt and Goss found no interaction between stimulus similarity (high, low) and MAS-defined anxiety (high, low), whereas in Experiment II no interaction between response similarity and level of anxiety was found. In both experiments, HA and LA individuals learned the PA lists at comparable rates. This was true for both the high- and low-sim lists, even though the high-sim list was more difficult (indicating the existence of competing responses).

### 3.1.2 Transfer of Training

Paradigms for the study of transfer of training in PA learning have obvious utility in the study of the anxiety-performance interaction. As an example, the A–B, A–C paradigm provides a convenient and sensitive means of experimentally manipulating response competition on the second list (A–C). In this list, competition effects are attributed to interference from the first-list (A–B) association. Thus, early in second-list practice, the B responses may be assumed to be the dominant, but incorrect, responses to the second-list stimuli. In this situation, the Taylor-Spence formulation involves the prediction of inferior performance by HA persons early in practice, followed by superior performance at the point in practice where the correct (C) items are the dominant associative responses to the stimuli (A).

The preceding analysis, however, considers associative factors and does not consider the response-learning stage of A–C acquisition. As mentioned previously, the response-learning stage would be facilitated for HA persons relative to LA individuals. Thus, the opposing facilitative (response-learning) and interference (associative-competition) factors quite possibly confound the comparison of performance between HA and LA persons on the second list. Fortunately, the transformation of performance on the A–C list to an estimate of transfer circumvents the confounding.

The control paradigm used as a baseline against which to assess the direction and magnitude of transfer in PA paradigms is designated A–B, C–D (stimuli different, responses different on the two lists). Performance on the second list is not subject to specific interference from List 1 associations and therefore no differential response competition would be expected for HA and LA persons on this list. As with the A–C list, however, the response-learning stage would be differentially facilitated for HA persons with the expectation of equal facilitation for the two paradigms (A–B, A–C and A–B, C–D). It is apparent that the subtraction of the performance on the C–D (control) list from that of the A–C list for each level of anxiety would circumvent the confounding of response-learning and associative-interference effects. An additional reason for translating absolute performance in transfer paradigms to estimates of transfer is the circumventing of possible confounding of anxiety and nonspecific transfer effects (e.g., learning to learn, warm-up). Goulet (1968) discusses elsewhere further implications relating to anxiety and transfer of training.

There have been few studies concerned with anxiety-transfer comparisons. Standish and Champion (1960), using a modified A–B, A–C design, found results in accord with the Taylor-Spence theory even though the appropriate control treatment was not included as a baseline against which to evaluate transfer effects for HA and LA persons. Katahn (1964) and Katahn and Dean (1966), using a modified PA task analogous to an A–B, A–C transfer situation, also reported data generally in accord with the Taylor-Spence theory. Katahn and Lyda (1966) found that HA persons have significantly more errors on a transfer task even though HA and LA persons learned the second list at equal rates. Again the appropriate control treatment was not included, and an estimate of net specific transfer was unavailable.

### 3.1.3  Serial Learning

The serial learning task has been used quite often to compare the performance of HA and LA individuals. However, only one study has analyzed the data in a manner such that opposing facilitative and interfering effects were unconfounded (Spielberger & Smith, 1966). The utility in using a serial learning task to compare the performance of HA and LA persons is apparent only if it can be ascertained whether the task involves competing responses. That this is the case is not questioned in that differential competition effects for beginning and end versus middle items provide the primary explanation for the classical serial position curve (e.g., McCrary & Hunter, 1953). On the other hand, the theoretical explanations as to the locus of the competition differ (e.g., Young, R. K., 1962).

Spielberger and Smith (1966) compared the performance of HA and LA persons on a serial task as a function of stage of practice (early or late), a necessary requisite in testing the Taylor-Spence theory with tasks involving competing responses. In addition, Spielberger and Smith recognized that response competition was greater for the middle items than for the beginning or end items in a serial list. On this basis, they analyzed the data for the middle items (e.g., items at positions 6, 7, 8, and 9 in a 12-item list) separately from that for the beginning and end items (items 1, 2, 3, and 12). The performance of HA persons exceeded that of LA persons for the easy words throughout learning except for the first 5 trials. On the hard words, the performance of LA persons exceeded that of HA persons for the first 15 trials, after which the performance of HA persons was better. As may be seen, complete support for the Taylor-Spence theory

was found. It should be mentioned, however, that support for the theory was found only under conditions where people were given ego-stress instructions before practice on the task. No support was obtained when neutral (nonstress) instructions were used. The results of other studies comparing the performance of HA and LA persons in serial learning under nonstress instructions have also been equivocal (Deese, Lazarus, & Kennan, 1953; Kalish, Garmezy, Rodnick, & Bleke, 1958). However, the data in these studies were not analyzed with respect to serial position and/or stage of learning.

High intralist similarity has also been used to increase the degree of intralist competition in serial learning. The studies comparing LA and HA persons in high-sim serial tasks have also been equivocal, with results indicating inferior (Lucas, 1952; Montague, 1953; Nicholson, 1958) or equal (Deese, Lazarus, & Kennan, 1954; Saltz & Hoehn, 1957) rates of learning for HA individuals. However, with high intralist similarity, the possibility remains that facilitative (response-learning) and interfering (associative-learning) effects were confounded.

### 3.2  Task-defined Anxiety

It may be questioned whether the definition of anxiety by means of the MAS or other questionnaire-derived ordering may indeed be the most economical way to consider the construct of anxiety in a context where operations are largely in the nature of objective tests (see Saltz, E., 1970; Spielberger, 1966a). Consequently, it is of interest to consider the evidence of anxiety related to verbal learning where the construct is defined in terms of the characteristics of the situation rather than the typical response patterns of the subject. The theoretical formulations of Mandler and Sarason (1952) and I. G. Sarason (1956, 1958) also allow for specific predictions regarding the interaction of anxiety and performance. In general, Mandler and Sarason (1952) and I. G. Sarason (1956, 1958) suggest that performance of HA persons will occur only under experimental conditions where task-irrelevant responses are elicited. The latter are expected to occur when the subjects are ego-involved in the task or when performance is measured under stressful conditions. Both the degree of ego involvement and stress can be manipulated by instructions before practice on the experimental task. This assumption highlights the basic difference between the Taylor-Spence and Mandler-Sarason formulations. The Taylor-Spence position maintains that inferior performance of HA persons will be manifest only in tasks where task-specific competing responses are present. This prediction holds independently of the degree of stress elicited by instructions, etc., and even though the latest formulation of the Taylor-Spence position (Spence, J. T., & Spence, 1966) does assume deleterious effects of stress on performance for both HA and LA persons. On the other hand, the Mandler-Sarason position implies inferior performance of HA persons *only* when some degree of stress and/or ego involvement is present. This prediction holds both for tasks characterized by maximum or minimum degrees of response competition.

The experimental evidence related to the theories of Taylor and Spence and of Mandler and Sarason, for the most part, has used different anxiety scales to differentiate their subjects. The Test Anxiety Questionnaire (TAQ), developed by Mandler and Sarason (1952), was constructed to provide a measure of anxiety specific to test situations rather than of generalized drive, for which the MAS was developed. I. G. Sarason (1958) suggested that anxiety will be more related to performance if the anxiety scale is specific to situations similar to the experimental conditions.

The Taylor-Spence and Mandler-Sarason formulations both imply inferior performance of HA persons in PA learning when the list is characterized by high intralist similarity if the subjects are ego involved in the task. However, the two positions make differential predictions when the task is characterized by low similarity (low intratask competition). Unfortunately, the studies testing the Mandler-Sarason hypothesis have used serial learning tasks that involve task-specific competition. Data are needed to examine the generality of the Mandler-Sarason hypothesis where intralist competition is minimized.

The results of a study by Goulet and Mazzei (1969) are relevant here. In their experiment, the performances of HA and LA persons were compared in PA learning under conditions of low or high stimulus similarity. In addition, each group was divided at the median level of intelligence, defined in terms of the composite score on the ACT. The PA lists learned involved seven adjective-nonsense syllable pairs used by Feldman and Underwood (1957). The nonsense syllables ($\bar{X}$ association value = 11.4%) were identical in the two lists, whereas the adjectives were characterized by either low or high similarity. The lists were presented at a 2:2 sec. rate with a 4-sec. intertrial interval and were practiced to a criterion of one perfect repetition of the list. Before practice on the list, individuals were given ego-stress instructions, which involved a statement that mastery of the task was highly related to IQ and that college students mastered the task rapidly.

The results of the experiment are presented in Fig. 1. The data indicate the mean number of trials for persons in the four anxiety-IQ groups to reach a criterion of 1, 2, . . . , 7 correct responses.

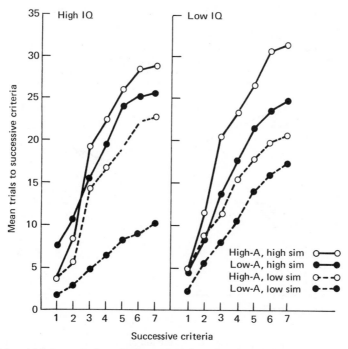

**FIG. 1** Mean trials to successive criteria as a function of anxiety, intelligence, and similarity.

As may be seen, the performance of HA persons was inferior to that of LA persons for each level of IQ and stimulus similarity. The effects of intelligence were related to performance only in interaction with anxiety and trials. This interaction was accounted for primarily by the rapid learning of the LA/low-IQ persons who learned the low-sim list.

The data provided complete support for the Mandler-Sarason hypothesis and the generality of the deleterious effects of anxiety to tasks characterized by either high or low intratask competition. In addition, a further analysis of the data provided suggestive evidence related to the nature of the effects of anxiety on performance. The measure involved the determination of the first trial at which each response was emitted during learning whether paired correctly or incorrectly with the appropriate stimulus. Postman (1962) suggested that this measure

reflects the person's confidence in the response to be attempted. Measures of the confidence threshold were determined for each pair for each person by counting the trial where the response was first given without concern whether it was paired appropriately, and the mean first-given scores for each person were determined. Summary data for the confidence threshold measure are presented in Fig. 2.

The main effects for anxiety and similarity were statistically significant. The effect for similarity supports Ekstrand's (1966) conclusion that people typically withhold responding until fairly confident of the correct pairing of stimulus and response. The performance of HA persons was inferior to that of LA persons under both levels of intelligence when learning the low-sim list. The same was true for the HA/low-IQ persons who learned the high-sim list. On the other hand, the performance of HA/high-IQ

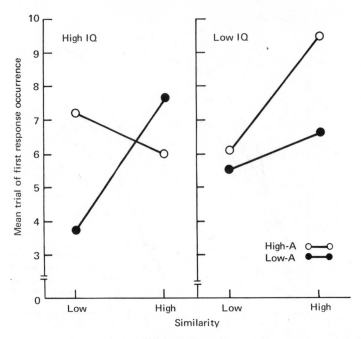

**FIG. 2** Mean confidence thresholds as a function of anxiety, intelligence, and similarity.

persons was superior to that of the LA/high-IQ persons who learned the high-sim list even though criterion performance on PA learning (Fig. 1) was inferior for the same people. The preceding differences for the first-given measure were reflected in a statistically significant Anxiety X Intelligence X Similarity interaction.

A possible explanation of the performance differences between HA and LA persons in PA learning is provided by the data relating to confidence thresholds. That is, under stress instructions, the HA persons may withhold responding until fairly confident of the stimulus-response pairings, whereas LA individuals may require a lower degree of confidence and thus respond earlier in practice where a lower degree of associative strength exists between stimuli and responses. The HA/high-IQ persons were not disrupted by associative interference (high-similarity), providing some insight into

the nature of the effects of intelligence on learning.

The data relating to confidence thresholds are important in a number of respects. First, they suggest an interpretation of the effects of anxiety in PA learning in terms of performance differences rather than learning differences. Furthermore, the deleterious effects of TAQ-defined anxiety on PA learning may be considered to be localized in the associative stage. In addition, the interpretation in terms of performance differences suggests that the confidence thresholds of HA persons can be modified. For example, people can be encouraged or instructed to guess, thereby reducing the confidence threshold. Such instructions may be particularly important with older people who may have a long reinforcement history that has discouraged guessing behavior (see Birkhill & Schaie, 1975). Since the reduction of the confidence threshold would be expected to be greater for HA than for LA persons, performance differences in PA learning as a function of anxiety might thereby be reduced or eliminated.

A final comment should be made regarding confidence thresholds, PA learning, and anxiety. As mentioned previously, the Mandler-Sarason hypothesis implies inferior performance of HA persons only under stress instructions or ego involvement. It is possible that the major effect of stress (or ego involvement) is to increase the confidence threshold, with the effect being more pronounced for HA persons.

The effects of stress have also been suggested as a factor differentially affecting the performances of HA and LA persons when the MAS was used as the measure of anxiety. For example, I. G. Sarason (1956, 1957a) and Spielberger and Smith (1966) found that stress instructions (induced by failure or ego-involving instructions) retard the performances of HA persons to a greater extent than they do those of LA people if tasks involving competing responses (e.g., serial learning) are used. On the other hand, J. A. Taylor (1958), using a low-sim (noncompetitional) task, found that performance of HA individuals was superior to that of LA persons even though the stress instructions had detrimental effects on the performance of both groups.

## 3.3  The Yerkes-Dodson Law, Verbal Learning, and Anxiety

Other investigators (e.g., Malmo, 1958) have suggested an alternative position relating to the interaction of anxiety and performance. Malmo's views are essentially based on assumptions relating to the Yerkes-Dodson law, which states that first, performance varies as an inverted-U function of physiological activation (drive, arousal); and, second, the level of arousal leading to optimal performance varies inversely with task difficulty. Thus, the level of performance is assumed to increase with increasing arousal up to some optimum point after which further increases in arousal hinder performance. The level of arousal leading to optimum performance is further assumed to be lower when people are performing difficult rather than easy tasks.

Certain aspects of Malmo's theorizing relate to both the Taylor-Spence and the Mandler-Sarason formulations. For example, tasks involving competing responses are implicitly more difficult than those where competition is minimized. As such, the Malmo position can explain the superiority of HA over LA persons in low-sim (easy) tasks and inferior performance of HA persons in high-sim (difficult) tasks if the assumption is made that HA individuals are performing at a more optimum level of performance than LA persons on the easy task but have surpassed this optimum level when learning the difficult task. Unfortunately, such reasoning tends to be circular unless some independent estimate of task difficulty is available. That is, whenever the performance of HA persons is found to exceed that of LA persons, it can be assumed that HA persons were learning under an optimal level of arousal; or, if the performance of LA individuals is found to exceed that of HA persons, the assumption that HA persons had surpassed the level of optimal arousal can be made. This type of confusion results because task difficulty is discussed in the literature both in terms of an independent and/or dependent variable.

Fortunately it is possible to define task difficulty quite independently of level of anxiety or level of arousal. For example, task difficulty can be defined by degree of intralist similarity (as already discussed) or by the degree of response meaningfulness (M) (e.g., low, high) in a PA task. High M responses are already fully or partially integrated (learned) before practice on the PA task, whereas low-M responses require substantial integration before completion of the response-learning stage (e.g., Underwood & Schulz, 1960).

It is apparent that Malmo's position predicts similar results in comparisons of performance between HA and LA persons whether task difficulty is defined by intralist similarity or response M. It is also important to note that high-sim tasks involve response competition where the manipulation of response M does not. The Taylor-Spence position implies inferior performance of HA persons only when intratask similarity is varied. The data that are available relating to the performance of HA and LA subjects (MAS-defined) where response M has been varied have yielded nonsignificant results (e.g., Harleston, 1963; Harleston & Cunningham, 1961; L'Abate, 1959; Levitt & Goss, 1961). However, there are results suggesting that performance of HA persons is inferior to that of LA persons if an extremely low level of meaningfulness is used (e.g., Saltz & Hoehn, 1957). Stress instructions through raising the level of arousal should also interact with level of task difficulty (defined either in terms of response M or intratask similarity), both alone or in combination with level of anxiety.

## 4  VERBAL LEARNING AND THE SECOND–ORDER TRAITS OF EXTRAVERSION AND NEUROTICISM

The variable of extraversion-introversion has also been found to relate to verbal learning. In general, current research in the area concerns hypotheses formulated by H. J. Eysenck (1963, 1964a), which suggest that introverts are characterized by higher states of arousal than extraverts. The relations between arousal and a generalized drive state have already been discussed, and it is clear that many similar predictions can be made concerning the interaction of verbal learning and extraversion-introversion of verbal-learning/MAS-defined anxiety.

Furthermore, McLaughlin and Eysenck (1967) have postulated that the personality dimension of neuroticism is analogous to a drive state. Again, clearly defined predictions, similar to those of Taylor-Spence relating to MAS-defined anxiety and performance, can be made for the interaction of stability and neuroticism and verbal learning. McLaughlin and Eysenck, however, also incorporate the basic assumptions concerning the Yerkes-Dodson law (e.g., Malmo, 1958) concerning the state of arousal/drive and performance.

As a test of this proposition, McLaughlin and Eysenck categorized people into four groups: stable extraverts, neurotic extraverts, stable introverts, and neurotic introverts. The assumption was made that the degree of arousal/drive would vary from low to high, in the preceding order, and, implicitly, that the person's arousal (related to the degree of extraversion) and his drive (related to the degree of neuroticism) would combine to determine the overall state of arousal. It was further assumed, in line with the implications relating to the Yerkes-Dodson law, that on easy tasks the stable extraverts would show suboptimal arousal, whereas the neurotic introverts would be characterized by a state of superoptimal arousal. On complex (difficult) tasks, improved performance was predicted for the stable extraverts, relative to the remaining three groups, because of the assumption that optimal level of arousal (and thus performance) varies directly with the complexity or difficulty of the task.

In PA learning involving a low-sim/low-sim list, superior performance of the neurotic extraverts was found followed by that of the stable introverts, stable extraverts, and neurotic introverts. With a low-sim/high-sim PA list the ordering of performance from good to poor for the four groups was stable extraverts, neurotic extraverts, stable introverts, and neurotic introverts. The ordering of performance in PA learning for the four groups can be explained for both the easy and difficult tasks. That is, for the easy (low-sim/low-sim) task, optimal performance favored persons characterized by an intermediate level of arousal (i.e., the neurotic extraverts), whereas for the difficult (low-sim/high-sim) task, the optimal level of performance was assumed to shift toward the low arousal group (i.e., the stable extraverts).

Jensen (1962) also compared the performance of extraverts and introverts on a serial learning task involving nine colored geometric forms. The rate of presentation of the items was either 2 sec. or 4 sec. No differences in rate of learning were found for the extraverts and introverts although the performance of extraverts was somewhat better than that of introverts under the fast (2-sec.) rate. In the same experiment Jensen (1962) found that subjects differentiated on the basis of neuroticism (high and low). No differences in rate of learning were found under the 4-sec. rate of presentation. However, the performance of the high-neuroticism persons was markedly below that of the low-neuroticism persons under the 2-sec. rate of presentation. Jensen also reasoned that the effects of neuroticism are similar to those of a drive state and that neuroticism affects performance in much the same manner as does MAS-defined anxiety. The fast rate of presentation was likened to a difficult task (relative to the slow rate of

presentation), with the similar prediction of disruption of performance for the high-neuroticism (high-drive) subjects under the fast rate.

It is clear that the recent theorizing concerned with the extraversion-performance and neuroticism-performance interactions shares points in common with the Taylor-Spence formulation relating to anxiety and performance. In fact, the formulations can be interchanged with only small modifications. Two small differences are apparent. The first concerns the conditions under which the formulations of Eysenck and Taylor-Spence expect the performance of high-drive subjects (as measured by the degree of introversion, neuroticism, or MAS-defined anxiety) to be inferior to that of low-drive persons. The Taylor-Spence position implies (e.g., J. T. Spence & Spence, 1966) inferior performance of high-drive subjects only when task-specific interfering responses are present, whereas the formulation of Eysenck (e.g., McLaughlin & Eysenck, 1967) implies inferior performance of high-drive persons under high degree task difficulty, independently of the manner in which task difficulty is defined (e.g., high similarity, low response meaningfulness, etc.). Second, the Taylor-Spence theory does not necessarily imply that performance of high-drive people will be inferior to that of low-drive persons throughout the course of learning, whereas Eysenck's formulation implicitly (because it is based on assumptions related to the Yerkes-Dodson law) leads to the prediction of inferior performance throughout the course of learning.

Verbal-learning paradigms have also been used in an attempt to identify the nature of the psychological deficit in schizophrenic subjects. For example, a rather impressive amount of research suggests that schizophrenics are more subject to associative interference than are normal controls. Lang and Luoto (1962) used a PA mediation paradigm where stimuli were identical and the response terms were word associates on the two lists. For half the PA pairs, the word associates on the two lists were paired with the identical stimulus, setting up a condition for mediated facilitation. For the remaining pairs, the sets of associated responses were paired with different stimuli on the two lists, a situation conducive to mediated (associative) interference. The results indicated equal degrees of mediated facilitation for the schizophrenics and normal controls. However, for the mediated interference pairs, the performance of schizophrenic subjects was much inferior to that of the controls.

Other direct evidence indicating greater susceptibility to associative interference has been collected by J. T. Spence and Lair (1964), Kausler, Lair, and Matsumoto (1964), and Mednick and DeVito (1958). Spence and Lair found a greater tendency toward intruding, inappropriate errors in PA learning. Kausler, Lair, and Matsumoto (1964), in comparing schizophrenic and control subjects under the A–B, A–C and A–B, A–Br stimuli found that negative transfer (where performance on the control A–B, C–D paradigm is subtracted from that of the experimental paradigm) was significantly greater for the schizophrenic group.

Indirect evidence regarding this contention relates to studies comparing schizophrenics and normals on tests of word association; on these tasks, the associations of schizophrenics show much more variability, both over time and between subjects. In addition, schizophrenics gave more uncommon associations (Johnson, R. C., Weiss, & Zelhart, 1965; Sommer, Dewar, & Osmond, 1960) especially when instructed to give the associations characteristic to most people (Wynne, 1963).

The basic problem is to determine whether the susceptibility to associative interference is a symptom of some underlying disorder or a predisposing cause. In this respect, Mednick (1958) extended the Hull-Spence theory and assumed that schizophrenics are characterized by intense anxiety and thus by heightened drive. With this assumption, the propositions relating to the Taylor-Spence theory concerning anxiety performance can be applied directly in predicting schizophrenic behavior in verbal-learning tasks. A somewhat related view concerns the level of somatic or ANS arousal with heightened arousal for schizophrenic subjects. Here, the assumptions relating to Malmo's (1958) propositions concerning Yerkes-Dodson law and performance can be applied. Lang and Buss (1965) provided an excellent review of the literature related to these two propositions, concluding that the evidence favoring either the Taylor-Spence or Malmo propositions is contradictory. However, a further conclusion reached by Lang and Buss is that a susceptibility to associative interference underlies much of the schizophrenic's behavior disturbance.

## 5  SOME FURTHER CONSIDERATIONS

We have gone to some pain to detail in what manner the phenomena observed in the experimental study of verbal learning in the laboratory may be related to second-order factors in the personality domain. It now remains for us to specify how such relationships might be capitalized upon by future personality researchers in a more programmatic manner. Two basic lines of inquiry become readily apparent. The first concerns the systematic exploration of differences in response acquisition as related to the basic personality source traits. It would be possible, of course, to examine criterion groups defined by low and high scores on the various questionnaire-defined traits similar to the manner in which verbal learning phenomena have been explained in relation to anxiety as defined by the MAS. Such an approach, however, would merely provide further descriptive information on subject variables related to verbal learning. Yet, it is the interaction between the learning process and the subject variables which is of primary interest. A much more promising line of inquiry, consequently, would be the application of recent advances in multivariate methodology to a direct exploration of the relation of known personality dimensions to learning-process variables. What we have in mind is the application of principles outlined by Cattell (1966c) in his discussion of data box principles as well as the utilization of Tucker's (1966) multimode factor anlysis techniques.

What are the strategies required to make maximal progress? Figure 3 illustrates an appropriate schematic. As may be noted from this schematic, we are concerned first of all with a multitrait-multimethod approach (Campbell & Fiske, 1959) with respect to the personality source trait. This is essential since we cannot be sure to what extent method variance will interfere with the clear definition of relations between personality parameters and learning processes (see also Schaie & Nesselroade, 1968). Next, it would seem highly desirable to study the interrelationships between different learning tasks at the same time that data are obtained on the subject variables in the population for which this information is gathered. Such an approach, of course, may be difficult due to the confounding effect of one task upon the other. But, there is no reason why a data box cannot be constructed by using canonical (respectively intraclass) correlations, which would eliminate the necessity of collecting all information on the one and same set of subjects.

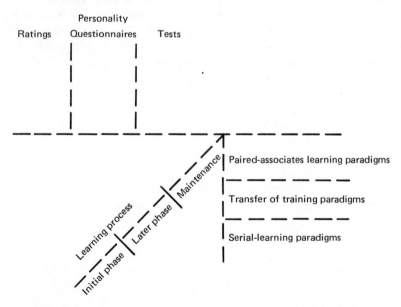

**FIG. 3** The three-way factor analysis of verbal learning and personality.

Similarly, recently developed methods of factor analysis for the determination of generalized learning curves (Tucker, L. R., 1966) make it possible to perform component analyses of, for example, PA learning throughout the course of learning the list. A low-sim/high-sim list provides the best example. As will be recalled, high similarity has differential effects on the response and associative stages of PA learning. It should be possible to identify two factors, one associated with each of the stages of PA learning. Furthermore, the incorporation of selected personality scores into the design makes it possible to ascertain the differential effects of the personality measures on the two stages. The preceding discussion relating to component analyses and the effects of MAS-defined anxiety are especially relevant here. It finally seems most profitable to pay close attention to verbal learning as a developmental process. That is, as has been stated previously, it is reasonable to assume that the early stage of the acquisition process will interact differently with a given personality variable (this clearly is known to be true for the second-order anxiety factor) than will be true for a later stage of learning; even further changes in interactions must be expected when retention is included in a design that, of necessity, must have a temporal axis.

No mention has been made thus far of the problem that learning processes, thought to be related to personality-trait formation, must of necessity occur over lengthy periods of time. Thus, in addition to the explication of learning parameters, it becomes important also to note the differential role of learning parameters depending on the developmental stage of the organism. The concerns with the generalizability of cross-sectional or single cohort longitudinal studies (cf. Schaie, 1965, 1973) extend consequently also to the explication of relations between verbal learning and personality developments. Again, multivariate studies extended over relatively short time segments, as well as covarying learning parameters, personality traits, and cohort membership are most likely to provide more satisfying answers.

The kind of programmatic approach outlined in brief summary here is likely to lead to significant advances in our understanding of the relationship between verbal-learning processes and the many facets of personality structure. It is hoped that the increasing methodological sophistication of young researchers entering the field will lead to early progress.

# 25

# Physiological Concepts in Personality Research

Jochen Fahrenberg
*Universitaet Freiburg i. Br., Germany*

## 1 INTRODUCTION

The biological basis of personality can be studied from four points of view: neurophysiology, psychophysiology, behavioral pharmacology, and behavior genetics. Following these four lines of approach, considerable progress has been made in recent years, but in respect to personality research, there seems to be some lack of integration.

Neurophysiology, profiting from advanced neuroanatomy and neurochemistry, has become significant for personality research; and neurophysiological concepts have aroused considerable interest among psychologists, for example, activating mechanisms in reticular and limbic systems, self-stimulation, and drug experiments. Neuro-"psychology" and physiological psychology or psychobiology (as it is understood by Gazzaniga & Blakemore, 1975; Grossman, S. P., 1967; Thompson, R. F., 1967; and others) are concerned with central nervous system (CNS) substrates of perception, motivation, and behavior, using typically neurological methods mainly in animal studies: ablation and lesion-producing techniques, electrical or chemical stimulation of cerebral structures, often in highly controlled univariate designs.

Certainly, we are far from being able to describe personality traits in neurophysiological or neuropsychological terms. Our hypotheses about physiological correlates of traits and states still rest considerably on physiological measures of peripheral, that is, effector organ functioning. This so-called *behavioral psychophysiology* can be understood as an extension of behavioral analysis to include "molecular" autonomic, endocrine, and motor functions, bearing in mind that effector organ functioning reflects CNS impulses as well as somatic conditions of the periphery. Behavioral psychophysiology is typically concerned with personality correlates of hormonal and other biochemical excretion patterns of autonomic lability, of sensory thresholds, of muscle tension, and so forth. Multivariate studies of humans are characteristic for this domain, using polygraph recordings; clinical tests of the autonomic nervous system (ANS); biochemical analysis of blood, saliva, and urine; telemetry of physiological behavior in everyday life.

The genetic basis of personality and embryological aspects have been discussed in chapters 12, 13, and 14. In a few instances, predominantly concerning metabolic errors or metabolic lesions, the causal connections have been clarified in detail; in most instances, however, it is still unknown how an established genetic determination of certain personality traits develops and how the genes express themselves through neuro-endocrine endowment, hormone balances, and enzyme systems. It may be presumed that the genetically determined individuality first of all appears in morphological traits of the organism, in internal structure, including endocrine glands and CNS, as well as in body configuration. Therefore it is useful to mention research contributions of constitutional psychology to our knowledge of somatic factors and personality.

Behavioral pharmacology has become a major research orientation in animal psychology as well as in personality research. Although relatively little is known yet about pharmacodynamics, (i.e., the mode of action in a biochemical sense), the method of stimulation by psychoactive drugs has some advantages over more direct neuro-physiological methods of stimulation and control. In particular the action of stimulant and depressant drugs has been investigated, linking the observed differential drug effects in some instances with personality dimensions and hypothetical constructs such as activation or excitation-inhibition-balance.

After a discussion of a few points of measurement and methodology, some physiological concepts are presented concerning (a) peripheral autonomic and motor processes, (b) hormonal and other biochemical processes, and (c) CNS processes. Subsequently, some contributions from behavioral pharmacology and from constitutional research are considered. Contributions from comparative physiological psychology, from ethology as well as clinical evidence concerning particular psychosomatic disorders, brain damage, and drug treatment, have been omitted completely.

Because of the extent and complexity of this domain, the presentation is restricted to giving a rough picture of those concepts and of those experimental results that—in the author's opinion—are the most important for personality research and that indicate its future course. This chapter concludes with a short discussion of multivariate psycho-physiological studies. Psychophysiology, through increased knowledge and awareness of the biological basis of personality, essentially contributes to the theory of psychological traits (chapter 4 by Ishikawa, this *Handbook*); psychological states (chapter 5 by Dielman and Krug, and chapter 8 by Nesselroade and Bartsch); and, in particular, anxiety, stress, and related motivation states (chapter 9 by Spielberger, Lushene, and McAdoo).

## 2 MEASUREMENT, METHODS, AND METHODOLOGY

Somatic data can be roughly classified as follows:

1. Morphological data shows the following: (a) gross body configuration, distribution, and relative development of tissue components, bones, muscles, and fat, providing an abundance of anthropometric variables; (b) configuration and relative development of inner organs, for obvious reasons rarely considered although biologically more important than bone structure; (c) fine structure variation of neurons and other cell bodies.

2. Physiological data shows the following: (a) CNS activity, that is, bioelectrical and biochemical processes in cortical, subcortical, and spinal structures, including central structures of the ANS and neuro-secretion of the pituitary gland—serving central integration and control of the organism; (b) activity of sensory systems, that is, threshold properties and activity of exteroceptors and proprioceptors—serving orienting, adaptive, and defensive reactions of the organism by supplying information

about environmental changes and bodily position; (c) activity of autonomic and endocrine systems, that is, efferent control of smooth muscles, glands, and the heart, and afferent information processing of visceral sensations (enteroception) serving metabolism, homeostasis, adaptation, growth, and reproduction; (d) activity of striated muscles, mediated by pyramidal and extrapyramidal pathways, that is, discrete action potentials of motor fibers or generalized innervation tonus (muscle tension defined by integration of discrete potentials); (e) motor reflexes, static and dynamic motor coordination, voluntary controlled movements, actions and speech—serving locomotion and communication.

This classification of data and somatic systems is meant to serve practical purposes only. The overlapping and functional connections are evident, since organismic activities imply integrated patterns of motor and autonomic functions, under the influence of afferent nervous impulses from receptor organs and under control of the CNS. There is a strong trend toward overcoming the rigid dichotomy of autonomic and sensomotor (animal) systems because it is untenable in a strict fashion, either on histological or on biochemical grounds regarding transmitter substances; it is also untenable on physiological grounds, because even in such elementary reflex actions as sucking, sneezing, and breathing there are integrated somatomotor-visceromotor patterns. Another dichotomy, voluntary versus involuntary somatic processes, has become less significant in this concern under the impact of demonstrated voluntary control of "autonomic" functions (Lassner, 1967; Luthe, 1969).

Physiological processes, that is, patterns or sets of elementary physiological func-

tions, show a marked intraindividual variability of "function fluctuation," which introduces serious sampling and measurement problems. Recorded physiological data are merely points or sections of multiple, complex time series. Morphological signs and body configuration, of course, can also be conceived as physiological processes with a slow speed of change. Moreover, physiological and morphological data manifest a considerable amount of interindividual variability.

Schreider (1966) argued that the relative interindividual variability in somatic data is not less than in behavioral (psychological) variables. Comparative biostatistics of sufficient extent, however, are still missing. The *milieu interne*, at least, appears to be much more unstable and specific for each person (cf. Childs, 1970; Masuda, 1969; Myrtek, 1975a; Sargent & Weinman, 1966; Williams, R. J., 1956) than it appeared to past researchers.

The foundation of differential physiology and the development of trait description of physiological data relations unfortunately appears to be of little interest to physiologists. If one had a univeral index of physiological traits and states to start with, one could look for covariation with established factors of temperament, motivation, and ability. But trait studies presuppose interest in individual differences, and in physiology the main concern is about *general* laws of functioning. The personality researcher in this field will encounter a wealth of univariate or oligovariate studies, some state descriptions and some pathophysiological syndromes, but, with a few exceptions, he will find neither standardized test batteries and elaborate norms for individual comparison nor operationally defined trait or state concepts. In physiology, dimensional analysis of surface data according to the latent trait concept, which seems to be essential for personality assessment, is an unusual line of approach.

The burden seems to be laid on psychophysiology and constitutional psychology to begin with trait and state studies in somatic data, and most of the pioneers in this field have done so. Trait or type description is necessary because it appears to be of little use to correlate somatic data in an isolated fashion, for example, circumference of the skull or respiration rate, with complex habits or even more complex temperament traits. Obviously, we have to recognize quite different levels of organization and various degrees of abstraction or complexity that require previous studies of somatic data relations and probably a hierarchical model. Only a few large-scale studies have been done conforming to this level of structured measurement by means of factor analysis or other advanced methods of data handling.

The data theory of physiological measures is still in its beginnings concerning (a) sampling procedures regarding variables, stimulus situations, and individuals; (b) control of error variance due to intake of food and fluid, drugs, alcohol, and nicotine, due to renal function, to minor somatic disturbances, and to diurnal and seasonal changes; (c) problems of parameter abstraction from recordings that represent multiple equilibria of physiological subsystems; (d) initial values and reactivity scaling; (e) specificities of physiological reactions (individual and stimulus-specific patterns); and (f) adequacy of the latent trait concept.

In the future, pattern analysis and taxometric procedures, auto- and cross-correlation methods, and auto-regressive models, as well as differential equations, must be used, examined, or developed to foster appropriate mathematical description of multiple time series and oscillatory action

of physiological subsystems (response systems).

Questions of methodology, of methods, and of measurement are not discussed in detail here since there are some reviews and reference books concerning instrumentation, recording techniques, and data analysis (Brown, C. C., 1966; Cattell & Warburton, 1967; Fahrenberg, 1967; Geddes, 1972; Greenfield & Sternbach, 1972; Levi, 1975; Lykken, 1968; Martin, I., 1973a; Mefferd, 1966; Myers, 1971; Myrtek, 1975a; Myrtek, Foerster, & Wittmann, 1976; Royce, 1966; Schoenpflug, 1969; Strong, P., 1970; Thompson, R. F., & Patterson, 1974; Van Egeren, 1973; Venables & Christie, 1975; Venables & Martin, 1967; Wilson, R. S., 1967). Three points, however, need a brief comment.

Selection of variables is questionable in nearly all psychophysiological studies; in many instances it is not satisfying from a physiological point of view since the validity or meaning of the somatic measures is unclear. Variable selection is affected by certain practical and technical difficulties, for example, by insufficient recording facilities, by problems of interference and serial correlation, and by degree of inflicted pain. Technical and economic considerations further limit the number and range of recorded functions. This is a crucial issue, particularly in factor-analytic research, which aims at fundamental dimensions and, therefore, should represent the universe of somatic data in an unbiased way.

Second, it is suggested that in physiological data nonlinear and nonadditive data relations are prominent—well illustrated by the compensatory regulation of blood pressure, involving stroke volume, heart rate, and peripheral resistance of the arterial system. Each parameter basically can vary in the opposite direction. A stimulation now may cause an increase in cardiac output (increase of minute volume), but this may happen without a resulting change in arterial pressure because of compensatory decrease in peripheral resistance. It is appropriate to think of recorded physiological data as vectors representing a multiple equilibrium. When isolated from other data, the mean value of a variable or a mean change is not easy to interpret.

Compensatory regulation and function fluctuation appear partly to be responsible when occasionally one must deal with quite contradictory elements within the same physiological pattern. On the other hand one must conclude that physiological data and factor loadings receive significance in most instances actually in the context of other physiological observations and on the basis of known functional relationships. In most investigations, there is no point in using only *one* physiological variable (PGR or heart rate); but there is a strong motive for the researcher to include as many relevant parameters as possible, to establish valid trait and state descriptions and to facilitate interpretation of the observed patterns. One-stimulus/one-channel recording procedures in behavioral psychophysiology are as obsolete as one-lesion/one-behavioral-measure designs in neurophysiology, at least where motivation and personality are concerned.

Finally there is a methodological issue implied when psychophysiological or psychosomatic correlates are discussed—the so-called *mind-body problem* (cf. Feigl, 1958). The mind-body problem as a metaphysical question is not a topic for psychology today. But sometimes in psychosomatic medicine one encounters a certain opinion on mind-body relationships, mainly in the case of "psychogenic" disorders, when emotions or "mental" events are supposed to "cause" a somatic disorder. Interaction models of this sort should be avoided since physical effects must have physical causes and psychosomatic disorders are not psychogenic but cerebrogenic. Somatic and behavioral processes on the one side, and inner experience and well-being on the other, are essentially different frames of reference and require different categories of cognition. Categories of the physical world and of the intrinsic world are incompatible, and only when combined can they make up the whole picture of psychosomatic phenomena.

From a methodological point of view, it is probably the best policy to adopt the principle of *complementarity*, which has been formulated by Niels Bohr to describe the two incompatible but necessary categories in the so-called wave-corpuscle dilemma in physics. Physiological categories, behavioral categories, and inner experience are to be viewed as complementary ways of describing psychosomatic phenomena (cf. Delius & Fahrenberg, 1966).

## 3 PHYSIOLOGICAL CONCEPTS – PERIPHERAL PROCESSES

The physiological trait concept best known among psychologists is probably that of Eppinger and Hess (1915), sympatheticotonia versus parasympatheticotonia (vagotonia). This polarity was considerably extended and modified by other authors, but still seems to be the dominating concept in describing autonomic system functioning.

Eppinger and Hess realized the morphological dichotomy of the ANS in a sympathetic and a parasympathetic branch and the antagonistic innervation of effector organs. They postulated that the tonus (activity level) of the branches could vary independently; thus, they extended the principle of antagonistic innervation to the regulation of the organism as a whole.

Wenger (1948) adopted the concept of sympatheticotonia-parasympatheticotonia. Although in the beginning he thought the differences in transmitter substances (adrenergic-sympathetic and cholinergic-parasympathetic systems) to be more important, he later returned to the original Eppinger and Hess concept, which primarily is based on morphological considerations (Wenger, Engel, & Clemens, 1957). In his extensive studies of individual differences in ANS function tests, Wenger followed this idea of functional antagonism: One of the two systems may show phasic or chronic dominance leading to a state of autonomic imbalance. From factor-analytic research, an Autonomic factor finally emerged, representing ANS functioning. The multiple-regression equation for the estimation of this factor in normal males ($T$ scores) reads (Wenger, 1948, Table 42):

$\overline{A}$ = 0.41 heart period + 0.30 sublingual temperature (reflected) + 0.18 diastolic blood pressure (refl.) + 0.17 log palmar conductance change + 0.14 salivary output + 0.09 forearm conductance (refl.) + 0.09 palmar conductance (refl.); low $\overline{A}$ indicating dominance of the sympathetic nervous system (SNS).

Although variable selection, factor-analytic technique, and extent of generalizations are questionable, this research is a pioneer work in multivariate psychophysiology, supplemented by many normative data on clinical and normal samples (Wenger, 1966; Wenger & Cullen, 1972).

By further studies, however, Wenger, Engel, and Clemens (1957) were forced to admit (a) that Autonomic factor estimates based on resting data are not necessarily related to autonomic reactivity under stimulation, and (b) that there are significant differences in autonomic resting patterns, even in people with the same factor estimate. The significance of patterns and the frequency of mixed patterns corresponds well with clinical data and with the principle of response specificity developed by Malmo, Lacey, Engel and other psychophysiologists (cf. Engel & Moos, 1967; Lacey, 1967; Sternbach, 1966). Wenger, in this respect, returned to functional and pattern analysis, which were suggested by clinicians and physiologists. It is noteworthy that Wenger's extensive and continuous work has failed to stimulate others to replicate and test further some of his findings.

Much earlier, W. R. Hess (1925, 1968) recognized that the principle of antagonistic innervation may be obvious when isolated effector organs are analyzed, but becomes inadequate for describing functional states of the organism as a whole. As Hess pointed out, we usually observe synergistic actions; for example, during physical work or during emotional tension, some organs show parasympathetic effects, and other organs show sympathetic effects. A synergistic pattern is defined as a set of functions that are coordinated and controlled by higher, mainly hypothalamic centers; the components of the synergistic pattern depend on the situational demands. In particular, Hess specified a so-called *functional polarity*, the ergotropic-trophotropic state dimension.

The ergotropic phase is defined by generalized sympathetic discharges, increased catabolic processes, cardiovascular adjustment (rise in blood pressure and heart rate), inhibition of the gastrointestinal tract, increased tone of the striated muscles, cortical desynchronization, and alertness. This syndrome in some respect corresponds to Cannon's (1929) emergency reaction and to Selye's (1950) alarm reaction of the pituitary-sympathetic-adrenocortical system;

however, the concept of ergotropic phase has a broader meaning because it includes cortical and gamma system activity. The trophotropic phase is defined by increased parasympathetic discharges, increased anabolic (restitution) processes and gastrointestinal functions, relaxation of the striated muscles, cortical synchronization, lessening of somatic responsiveness, and a state of drowsiness or sleep (Monnier, 1963; Sturm & Birkmayer, 1976).

Gellhorn (1967, 1970) adopted W. R. Hess' designations of ergotropic and trophotropic syndromes and discussed the relationships between these systems and their central neural controls in emotion, in sleep and waking, and in conditioning. He argued (a) that the systems are reciprocally related; (b) that ergotropic and trophotropic symptoms are separated under most physiological conditions; and (c) that an ergotropic/trophotropic quotient, that is, balance of both systems, is the chief factor determining alertness, mood, and emotion. Tonicity and reciprocity of ergotropic and trophotropic systems, in his opinion, will be basic concepts of psychophysiological research in the future.

Wezler, Thaver, and Grieven (1940) and Losse, Kretschmer, Kuban, and Boettger (1956) demonstrated in several thorough studies that humans vary in respect to their habitual resting level along this ergotropic-trophotropic dimension. But still the question remains whether it is useful to conceptualize one general dimension of autonomic functioning, either resting values or reactivity measures. This general factor hypothesis was presented by Eysenck (Eysenck, H. J., & Rachman, 1965, p. 31): "We may postulate that some people are innately predisposed to respond more strongly, more lastingly, and more quickly with their autonomic system to strong, painful or sudden stimuli impinging upon

the sense organs." But Eysenck conceded that this autonomic lability probably is shown more particularly in one or the other of the many parts of the ANS rather than by the system as a whole, although some people may show an exaggerated overall reactivity.

The unidimensional concept of autonomic regulation was criticised by other authors, among them Cattell, who differentiated among a general autonomic factor and two more specific, sympathetic-adrenergic and parasympathetic response patterns (cf. section 8, this chapter). Factor-analytic studies, indeed, have shown that there is quite a number of first-order factors in autonomic data (e.g., Carl-Zeep & Carl, 1969; Delius, Kottek, & Fahrenberg, 1968; Ismail, Falls, & Macleod, 1965; Wenger & Cullen, 1972; and extensive but still unpublished studies from our laboratory by Myrtek and others). Royce (1966) and Fahrenberg (1967) reviewed most of these studies. Royce included some "factors of emotionality" that have been isolated in animal studies.

Recent work in our laboratory by Myrtek and Kruse confirmed the relatively small proportion of common variance in a heterogenous set of autonomic variables which were obtained from 100 male students. Blood pressure, heart rate, pulse wave velocity, tidal volume, and other ventilation measures, oxygen utilization, and so forth, were measured during rest, during apnoea, hyperventilation, exercise (100 Watt), and orthostase-data from steady state as well as reactivity scores. The investigation included erythrocytes and leucocytes, electrolytes, catecholamines, blood sugar, lipids, and ratings of four autonomic lability symptoms, besides a number of psychological questionnaire data. Factor analyses were performed on 13 comparatively homogenous subsets of variables, for example, cardiovascular and respiratory measures during exercise or biochemical data. The average intercorrelations between subsets on factor score level were as low as on raw data level; that is, they were practically insignificant, although a few coefficients suggested functional relations that must be investigated further.

Many investigators have observed that intercorrelations of ANS measures generally are low, but perhaps not so low as to be incompatible with the assumption of trait-like functional unities. It is true that the interpretation of reported factors of ANS measures seems to be questionable in most instances. Altogether, there is some doubt whether factor-analytic investigations so far have proved to be the adequate procedure in this domain. Factor-analytic studies, admittedly, are handicapped because the selection of physiological measures still is far from being representative and because dependencies due to measurement and calculation are particularly obvious among physiological data.

There is need for large-scale surveys, which guarantee appropriate variable selection and reliable measurement. In addition to ANS reactivity, there are some other concepts, for example, individual differences in physical fitness and endurance, in muscle tension, sensory thresholds, conditionability, and habituation of autonomic reactions; it is worthwhile to include these aspects in psychophysiological personality research. Having established patterns of correlation characteristic for subsystems (e.g., cardiovascular functioning), one could look for complex dimensions or types describing the organism as a whole.

Hess and many physiologists do not conceive the observed synergistic patterns in terms of habitual traits, but as changing (and perhaps recurrent) patterns of functioning due to momentary situational demands, each representing a more or less complex intergrative effect of lower or higher levels of brainstem, diencephalic, or even higher centers. From a physiological point of view, therefore, one will learn more about physiological individuality by special study of these integrative processes (e.g., the coordination or dissociation of cardiovascular functions, metabolic processes, and work output during physical work). In some ways such studies and the analysis of transients and decrement of oscillatory responses, for example, of pupillary reflex or of cardiovascular response when the body is tilted, go deeper and are much more relevant than simple PGR or heart rate recordings. More sophisticated methods of functional analysis are desirable (Drischel, 1953, 1962; Oppelt & Vossius, 1970), as well as consideration of biological rhythms (Colquhoun, 1971; Lund, 1974; Sollberger, 1965).

## 4  PHYSIOLOGICAL CONCEPTS – HORMONAL AND BIOCHEMICAL PROCESSES

Hormones are important and more or less specific regulators of the internal environment, affecting motivation and manifest behavior as well as individual well-being. Endocrine systems are closely connected with neural systems and with autonomic functions, for example, by the mediating effect of the hypothalamus and the pituitary gland on other endocrine glands and by integration of autonomic and hormonal activity in the sympathetic-adrenergic-adrenocortical activation pattern. A full understanding of the endocrine adjustments and of hormonal correlates of personality, of course, must take into account all the possible interactions and multiple controls among various neural, neurohumoral, and endocrine systems (Bajusz, 1967; Gellhorn,

1967, 1970; Mason, 1972, 1975; Monnier, 1963).

Since Cannon (1929) and Beach (1948), there has been a growing interest in hormones and behavior, extending in recent years to other substances: enzymes, vitamins, and various metabolites. But the search for hormonal and biochemical correlates still is focused on a few substances. The most prominent are the catecholamines (adrenaline, noradrenaline) and the steroid hormones (cortisol, 17-hydroxycorticosteroids, 17-ketosteroids) in urine or plasma and, in the second place, plasma lipids (free fatty acids, triglycerides, cholesterol) and thyroid hormone, testosterone, and the estrogens.

Increase of catecholamine secretion, when not of pathological origin or influenced by extraneous stimuli (e.g., smoking, coffee, and alcohol), indicates ergotrophic phase and energy mobilization; adrenaline (epinephrine) reflects adrenomedullary activity; the transmitter substance noradrenaline (norepinephrine) reflects sympathetic-adrenergic system activity. Although selective catecholamine secretion, that is, dissociation between adrenaline and noradrenaline measures in relation to different emotional qualities, has been reported in some studies, as a whole both systems seem to respond rather unspecifically to a wide variety of common tasks and activities as well as to direct experience or to the anticipation of psychosocial stressors (Levi, 1972; Mason, 1972, 1975). There are large interindividual differences in habitual level of sympathetic-adrenomedullary activity under normal life conditions and in response (amplitude as well as temporal pattern of return to baseline) to psychosocial stimuli and life events. These seem to be associated in part with personality variables. Results from catecholamine-excretion studies indicate an interrelation between hormonal response measures and acute performance efficiency as well as enduring personality traits, for example, school performance and emotional adjustment (Fine & Sweeny, 1968; Frankenhaeuser, 1975a; Johansson, Frankenhaeuser, & Magnusson, 1973).

Increased adrenocortical activity, measured by the fractions of 17-OHCS and 17-KS, has been observed to follow exposure to a variety of psychosocial stimuli, but the pituitary-adrenocortical system seems to respond more slowly and at somewhat higher stimulus intensities than does the pituitary-adrenomedullary system (for review see Mason, 1972, 1975). Interactions among the stress-response systems may prove to be of considerable importance.

A high level of catecholamine or adrenocortical hormone excretion certainly may indicate intense alarm reaction as well as constitutional lability or hyperreactivity of neuroendocrine mechanisms; low excretion levels may indicate stability as well as exhaustion or torpidity of reactions—the interpretation depends on stimulus intensity and duration, consistency of repeated estimations, and other parameters. Thus the individual coping style and effectiveness of psychological defenses are likely to be responsible where a paradoxically decreased secretion during psychosocial stimulation is observed.

Thyroxin and the gonadal hormones, testosterone and the estrogens, have received less attention, partly because of the expenditure involved and the low reliabilities of all hormone assay methods compared to ANS measures. Laboratory requirements are still a severe handicap to psychoendocrine research, but considerable improvement can be anticipated by utilization of modern radio-immuno-assay procedures.

There is some evidence for the relationship between thyroid and gonadal activity and psychosocial stimuli (cf.

Alexander, Flagg, Foster, Clemens, & Blahd, 1961; Mason, 1972, 1975; Persky, Zuckerman, & Curtis, 1968; Whybrow, Prange, & Treadway, 1969). Mason (1975) strongly argued that not only the sympathetic-adrenomedullary and pituitary-adrenocortical systems, but also the pituitary-thyroidal, pituitary-gonadal, growth hormone, and insulin systems should be included in today's psychoendocrine research, to obtain profiles of multiple concurrent hormonal responses. These profiles provide the empirical basis for analyzing the multiple balance and the degree of nonspecificity or selectivity of endocrine regulation.

Concerning other biochemical data, some research reports—though still to be confirmed or elaborated—should be mentioned: for example, reports indicating a relationship between high uric-acid storage and achievement motivation (Dunn, 1963; Mueller & Beimann, 1969), reports concerning stressor-induced changes in plasma lipids (Gottschalk, 1969; Carlson, Levi, & Oroe, 1972), and reports concerning biochemical correlates of intelligence and ability factors (cf. Royce, 1966) or dealing with blood groups and personality traits (Cattell, Boutourline, & Hundleby, 1964; Maurer-Groeli, 1974). The speculative lactate theory of anxiety (Ackerman & Sachar, 1974; Grosz & Farmer, 1969; Levitt, E. E., 1972; Pitts & McClure, 1967) is an instructive example of how precarious a direct interpretation of biochemical data can be.

Basically, in psychoendocrine research a significant correlation has been established between certain hormonal measures and emotional states. However, the attempts to describe personality characteristics corresponding to profiles or types of endocrine dysfunction still rest on speculative grounds (cf. Bleuler, 1964; Mason, 1972; Sulman, 1960), but they invite multiple measurement and correlational analysis. Individual differ-

ences in neurosecretion, hypersecretion or hyposecretion of endocrine glands, metabolic deviations, and recognized biochemical and enzyme deficiencies have become a major subject of psychophysiological research. Again, as in autonomic and other physiological data, there is a need for representative and multivariate studies, because the meaning and validity of a single biochemical variable remains questionable.

## 5 PHYSIOLOGICAL CONCEPTS – CENTRAL NERVOUS SYSTEM PROCESSES

Neurophysiology is fundamental for the discussion of the biological basis of personality. Neurophysiological research has shown a remarkable progress; there is an abundance of experimental data demonstrating close dependence of motivation, emotional behavior, and learning on cerebral functions; and, in some instances, localizations of certain mechanisms are already given (Bykov & Kurzin, 1966; Eccles, 1966; Ehrhardt, 1975; Gellhorn, 1967; Gloor & Feindel, 1963; Hess, W. R., 1968; Jung, R., 1967; Ploog, 1964; Pribram & Luria, 1973; Rickles, 1972; Sigg, 1975; Stellar & Sprague, 1966; Teitelbaum, 1964).

In particular, the reticular system and the limbic system have attracted research interest. The reticular *formation* is a structure of the brainstem, but on physiological grounds the so-called reticular *system* additionally includes certain diencephalic structures. The reticular system relays sensory impulses to the cerebral cortex. It has been suggested (Moruzzi and Magoun, cf. Lindsley, D. B., 1970) that the arousal level of the CNS depends on the degree to which the cortex is bombarded by impulses from the nonspecific *ascending reticular activating system* (ARAS). The cortex in turn may arouse the reticular system and there is an ordered interaction of activating and deactivating processes, determining the state dimension of wakefulness (excitation, consciousness) and sleep. The reticular system furthermore is supposed to be a basic coordination system serving elementary reflex behavior (e.g., viscero-motor-somatomotor patterns of respiration and circulation).

Recent research has introduced more sophistication. We must acknowledge at least half-a-dozen distinct activating and deactivating neural complexes (Dell & Moruzzi); some of these exercise influence on coordination of certain cortical systems and modulate arousability of cortical regions; some exert a selecting action on central or peripheral parts of sensory organs, some on motor and autonomic pathways. These complexes facilitate some of these systems and inhibit others. The reticular system, therefore cannot be considered a *unit*.

The limbic system (as viewed by Broca, Papez, MacLean, Kluever & Bucy, Grastyan) is a morphologically complex system comprising the hypothalamus and certain other subcortical and neocortical structures, among others the hippocampus formation, the amygdaloid complex, the septal area, and the cingulate gyrus. The limbic system is of great importance as a complex regulating system for release, reinforcement, modulation, adaptation, and inhibition of drives, emotions and, generally speaking, of highly organized behavior patterns. Stimulation of certain neural structures will elicit the ergotropic or the trophotropic syndrome or distinct somatic activity patterns: rage, aggression, or escape behavior as well as—in humans—speech, laughing, or feelings of oppression and anxiety. Of particular interest are anatomical areas mediating "central reward and punishment" (Olds & Milner, 1954; Olds & Olds, 1965), certain "start" and "stop" systems respectively

(Lilly), found in self-stimulation experiments.

Neocortical structures, hippocampus and amygdaloid areas of the limbic system exert an influence on afferent stimulation of the hypothalamus and on the hypophyseal (pituitary)-adrenocortical system. Essentially it appears to be a modulatory effect to secure adaptation of those mechanisms, organized in various subcortical structures, to changing internal and environmental conditions.

In recent years the complex functions of the frontal lobes have been studied intensively, particularly the nonspecific reticulothalamo-cortical systems and efferent fronto-thalamic connections. Activation mechanisms, selective attention and integrated sensomotor information processing are essentially influenced by these systems (Homskaya, 1973; Lindsley, D. B., 1970; Nauta, 1971; Scheibel & Scheibel, 1967; Skinner, J. E., & Lindsley, 1973).

Neurophysiology has accumulated evidence that drives and emotions, pleasure and aversion, orienting reaction and habituation, and inborn and learned reactions have distinct morphological-physiological substrates with various levels of integration in brainstem, diencephalon, and cerebral cortex. Results, in most instances, have come from neurophysiological studies on rats, cats, and apes; but many fundamental results probably will be valid for humans, too. The most efficient methods for analysis of motivation have been a combination of cerebral stimulation and behavior observation, analyzing general behavior patterns (Hess, Holst) or conditioned reactions (Brady, Doty, Gastaut, Pribram, Konorski) or self-stimulation (Delgado, Lilly, Olds), and stimulation of patients during neurosurgery (Penfield, Sem-Jacobsen).

Now, how does personality research profit from modern neurophysiology? At least some reviewers (Jung, R., 1967; Ploog,

1964) seem to be rather reserved about its application in psychology or even in psychiatry. Stimulation experiments, macroelectrode and microelectrode tracings, and techniques of "evoked potentials" and "direct cortical responses" are incapable of delivering detailed information about the actual neural mechanism. Personality research, however, would be dependent on a specified, rather detailed inventory of neurophysiological processes, that is, data of neural activity measured separately for a number of reticular, limbic, and cortical subsystems, to describe neurophysiological correlates of individual differences and of trait and state concepts. Second, even the use of existing neurophysiological methods, with the exception of the electroencephalogram (EEG), is restricted where humans are concerned and, thus, imposes severe handicaps. Therefore, EEG tracings have attracted much attention in psychophysiological research.

Variation of EEG corresponding to variation in the wakefulness-sleep dimension is well documented, but there are still many doubts about relationships between individual differences in EEG measures and personality traits. Extraverts are possibly less aroused compared to introverts; fast alpha-rhythm perhaps will be found in alert and easily distracted people with good motor dexterity; theta waves perhaps are related to emotionality; abnormal EEG is found more often in children with behavior disorders and in psychopathic personalities than in normal persons. There are, however, many inconsistencies and experimental deficiencies, for example, inadequate sampling procedures of subjects, extraneous effects of experimental conditions and data handling, previous somatotherapy, and the problem of temporal instability of EEG pattern (Becker-Carus, 1971; Gale, 1973; Jung, R., 1967; Mundy-Castle, 1957; Roes-

ler, 1975; Shagass, 1972; Vogel, W., Broverman, & Klaiber, 1968; Wilson, W. D., 1965).

Progress in the neurosciences is obvious; however, we must ask how this information can be applied practically in personality research. Lacey (1967) argued that psychophysiological concepts are needed that are physiologically consistent with brain mechanisms, and Rickles (1972) tried to suggest examples of modular functioning in the CNS. But meanwhile, facing the lack of clear-cut neural mechanisms that might be measured separately and possibly matched with psychological traits and states, psychophysiologists often have preferred to use certain hypothetical constructs and peripheral tests of individual differences. Concepts of *behavioral activation, energy mobilization, arousability, strength of nervous system, excitation-inhibition-balance, vigilance,* and *satiation* (Berlyne, Duffy, Eysenck, Head, Hebb, Koehler, Lindsley, Malmo, Pavlov, Teplov) are certainly of heuristic value, although perhaps pseudophysiological.

The neuropsychological concept of activation (arousal) assumes a dimension of intensity (energy mobilization, general activity) of the organism as a whole. It has been shown that many data can be organized efficiently by use of this concept (Brady, 1975; Claridge, 1967; Duffy, 1962, 1972; Eason & Dudley, 1971; Malmo, 1959; Martin, I., 1973b). Serious problems of definition and measurement, however, must not be overlooked.

Many neurophysiological data contradict unifactorial concepts of activation and, thus, are in agreement with psychophysiological findings about different patterns of emotion and state change (cf. Gray and Drewett, chapter 14, in this *Handbook*; Claridge, 1967; Ehrhardt, 1975; Elliott, and Lacey & Lacey in Obrist, Black, Brener, & Dicara, 1974; Eysenck, H. J., 1967; Fahrenberg,

1967; Lacey, 1967; Martin, I., 1973b; Routtenberg, 1968). Lacey, among others, pointed out that low correlations obtained between central and peripheral indexes of activation, the dissociation of somatic and behavioral activation, somatic response patterning, and visceral afferent-inhibitory feedback from the cardiovascular system to the brain are contrary to a general factor of activation. The notion of a single dimension of nonspecific activation (arousal) probably has to be abandoned. There is a clear trend to return to more differentiated concepts— EEG-arousal, autonomic activation, and behavioral activation. These still need better operational definitions to determine the degree of their supposed partial independence. They will, after all, exceed a simple matching with reticular, limbic, or frontal cortex systems.

Of growing interest in neurophysiological personality research are concepts developed by Soviet researchers: the Pavlovian typology and a trichotomy of responses made to stimuli: orienting reaction, adaptive reaction, and defense reaction. Among these the orienting reaction (orienting reflex) is perhaps known best. This reaction consists of arousal symptoms (EEG changes), changes in skeletal musculature, optico-vestibulary orientation, increase in sensitivity of sense organs, and ergotropic activation. Intense stimulation will produce a defensive reaction (startle pattern) with aversion and overt motor and autonomic reactions, but with slow habituation compared to orienting reaction. The adaptive reaction, on the other hand, tends to preserve homeostasis, is localized in most instances, and does not show habituation (cf. Groves & Thompson, 1970; Horne & Hinde, 1970; Jung, R., 1967; Lader, 1967; Lynn, 1966; Peeke & Herz, 1973; Sokolov, 1963b; Uno & Grings, 1965; Van Olst, 1971).

Pavlov suggested three dimensions of higher nervous activity to explain observed individual differences in animal and human conditioning experiments. The basic properties are as follows: The first is (a) strength of excitatory and of inhibitory processes (strength of nervous system). High absolute thresholds, little response decrement at high stimulus intensities, and ability to maintain a conditioned response under intense or prolonged stimulation are considered to be characteristic of a strong nervous system. Next is (b) balance (equilibrium) of excitatory and of inhibitory processes. People with a predominance of excitatory processes will exhibit relatively little active internal inhibition, slow extinction, and slow habituation. The final property is (c) mobility of excitatory and of inhibitory processes, that is, differences in speed with which one process is replaced by another process. Pavlov's clinical speculations and personality types based on these fundamental properties seem to be of less interest today, but the suggested neuropsychological concepts, (hypothetical constructs, of course) have proved to be of considerable heuristic value, since Teplov, Nebylitsyn, Rozhdestvenskaya and others (cf. Gray, J. A., 1964; Lynn, 1966; Nebylitsyn & Gray, 1972) attempted to give better operational definitions.

Nebylitsyn (1972) proposed a modified system that introduces three notions of mobility—mobility proper, lability, and dynamism. Second, he proposed a different notion of balance. He postulated four basic nervous system properties: (a) *strength* (prolonged maintenance of characteristic levels of response, e.g., high thresholds and low reactivity vs. low thresholds and high sensitivity), (b) *mobility* (substitution of one nervous process for the other, e.g., rapid transformation of a positive into an inhibitory stimulus vs. slow transformation), (c) *lability* (high speed of initiation [chronaxie], irradiation, concentration, and termination of nervous processes vs. low speed of nervous processes), and (d) *dynamism* (rapid generation of conditioned reactions vs. slow generation of conditioned reactions).

The individual positions along these four dimensions must be measured separately for excitatory and for inhibitory processes; from each pair of measures, a derived score is calculated for balance between excitatory and inhibitory processes. A complete assessment of an individual should thus result in 12 scores, 8 primary and 4 secondary (balance) scores. The experimental methods to establish this individual status by means of the procedure worked out in Teplov's laboratory are rather complex, involving the measurement of sensory thresholds, threshold estimation of transmarginal inhibition, EEG analysis, several indicators of the orienting reaction, and a number of conditioning experiments under different qualifications, using caffeine as a stimulant in some instances. Since there are several qualitatively different procedures to assess strength, mobility, lability, and dynamism, problems of standardization and comparison arise.

Dimensionality and generality of the proposed measures of neo-Pavlovian personality measures are yet to be investigated, and the precise relationships between various indicator methods need to be worked out.

H. J. Eysenck (1957, 1967) and J. A. Gray (1964, 1967, and Gray and Drewett, chap. 14 of this *Handbook*) tried to identify neo-Pavlovian dimensions with some concepts of western psychology, with arousability, with conditionability, and with Eysenck's view of the excitation-inhibition balance. Introversion-Extraversion corresponds to strength of nervous system (sensitivity), but it also comes close to the notion of equilibrium in dynamism (conditionability). Meanwhile, experimental investigations, including marker variables of both research orientations, proved that the interrelationship of these dimensions is exceedingly complex (Mangan, 1967; Mangan & O'Gorman, 1969; Nebylitsyn & Gray, 1972).

Given the concept of strength of the nervous system, it can be deduced that threshold measures from different sensory qualities and modalities are correlated to a significant extent. The empirical data, so far, are not in favor of this trait-like concept of generally high versus low sensitivity. Ippolitov (1972) obtained absolute threshold values of vision (brightness), auditory (noise), and electrocutaneous (by electric pulse generator) perception. Intermodal correlations were positive but insignificant in the first study (27 healthy students) and, with exception of vision and auditory threshold, insignificant in the second study (34 persons). Recent work in our laboratory by Guenther included, among other data, six threshold measures: auditory (2,200 Hz pure tone), gustatory (sodium chloride), olfactory (Eugenol), cutaneous (Streeter's pressure method), electrocutaneous (Noterman's method), and vestibular (swivel-chair method). Absolute thresholds were estimated by discrete ascending procedure of the method of limits. The mean intercorrelation of $r = 0.13$ in a sample of 60 young adult males is insignificant although coefficients were mainly positive and significant in the case of gustatory/olfactory, gustatory/cutaneous pressure, and electrocutaneous/vestibular thresholds.

In Nebylitsyn's theory, ease and speed of forming both positive and inhibitory conditioned reactions depends on "dynamism," presumed to be unconnected with "strength" and "mobility" of the nervous system. Strictly speaking, he postulated two neurophysiological syndromes, dynamism of excitatory and dynamism of inhibitory processes; and he stated that the balance of both is the basic index related to development of a positive and inhibitory conditioned reflex (CR). From this point of view it is doubtful whether it is admissible to conceive a trait-like dimensional concept of "conditionability" to be assessed merely by acquisition of positive CRs. Nebylitsyn conceded interanalyzer differences, where conditioning parameters seem to be rather specific for various subsystems of the organism. Eysenck, however, from his notion of the excitation-inhibition balance, suggested a consistent CNS characteristic and many investigaters have tried to establish reliable measures of individual differences in conditionability and to prove generality of this concept by correlating measures from different conditioning procedures, (e.g., eyelid, galvanic skin response [GSR], salivation, verbal conditioning). The neo-Pavlovian work, on the other hand, primarily rests on the photochemical conditioned reflex and conditioned EEG reactions. The generality of conditionability is still unclear (Davidson, Payne & Sloane, 1968; Eysenck, H. J., 1967; Franks & Franks, 1966; Nebylitsyn, 1972) because representative studies with standardized methods are lacking. The serious methodological difficulties of stimulus conditions, schedules of reinforcement, and definition of criteria of what constitutes a "good" performance (speed, amplitude, duration, efficiency?) are discussed by I. Martin (1975). Recent work in our laboratory by Malotki and Lysko included various parameters of the eyelid CR and the GSR conditioned response and failed to confirm the supposed intersystem correlation; a significant negative relationship, however, was obtained between CR frequency in eyelid conditioning and unconditioned stimulus (UCS) threshold ($r = -.40$ in 82 male students). This result indicates that the individual's reflex sensitivity to the applied air puff cannot be disregarded; furthermore, interlaboratory comparison will require calibration of effective air pressure in millimeter water column at the cornea.

Habituation of the orienting reaction, that is, response decrement under repeated stimulation, is considered to be an elementary learning process and probably therefore indicative of basic brain processes. Several investigations have been concerned with individual differences in habituability in normal persons as well as in neurotic persons and in brain-damaged patients (Holloway & Parsons, 1971; Lader & Wing, 1966). Here, too, a standardized procedure or "habituation test" needs to be worked out for reliable interlaboratory comparison. Certainly, there are marked individual differences, as in GSR- or EEG-alphablock response habituation, but again empirical results are not in favor of a trait-like concept of general habituability, since the consistency of various measures of the orienting reaction has not been established sufficiently. Indexes of habituation rate seem to be rather specific for certain physiological response systems and highly dependent on experimental conditions and instructions (Koriat, Averill, & Malmstrom, 1973; McDonald, D. G., Johnson, & Hord, 1964; Orr & Stern. 1971; Van Olst, 1971).

Differential psychophysiology has thus elaborated several important concepts concerning individual differences in CNS processes, namely, arousability, sensitivity, conditionability, and habituability; these have attracted much empirical work as well as theoretical speculation. The consistency and generality of these concepts; their interrelation; and, basically, the reliability of measurement and refinement of operational definitions are currently the object of much study. As matters stand, adoption of these concepts by personality theory and research still requires special precautions.

Further study is required before reaching a satisfying answer to the question of whether the hypothesized properties of higher nervous sytem activity are leading parameters of the individual's psychophysiological organization and the question of whether these parameters could be matched with known personality dimensions. Mutual theoretical refinement and coordinated experimental work on the neo-Pavlovian dimensions and on the trichotomy of reactions to novel stimuli appear to be desirable in today's psychophysiological personality research.

## 6  SOME CONTRIBUTIONS FROM BEHAVIORAL PHARMACOLOGY

Compared with neurophysiological stimulation technique, the oral application of psychoactive drugs appears to have some advantages as a means of quantitatively controlled CNS stimulation without inflicting pain or lesions. Drugs could serve as tools for producing patterns of model behavior by reversible chemical lesions (Efron, 1968; Elkes, 1967; Essman, 1973; Trouton & Eysenck, 1960, Uhr & Miller, 1960). The site and the biochemical mode of action, however, are unknown in most instances; furthermore, probably a large part of observed variance is attributable to biochemical individuality, that is, to individual differences in enzyme activity, individual rates of metabolizing certain drugs, and specificities of the *milieu interne* (Masuda, 1969; Williams, R. J., 1956). The main difficulties of psychopharmacological personality research arise from the following

circularity: Before psychoactive drugs can be used as standardized tools in behavioral research their drug action profiles should be established objectively by referring to relevant psychophysiological dimensions; on the other hand drugs must be employed in validation of exactly these concepts.

Several ways of providing provisional classifications of psychopharmaca have been suggested—the trichotomy psycholeptica, psychoanaleptica, and psychodysleptica (Cornu, 1963)—or in a more detailed classificatory system (Essman, 1973; Stroebel, 1972). From different points of view and regarding different physiological systems, the following aspects have been considered by Jacobs (cf. Elkes, 1967):

1. Sedation–hyperactivity.
2. Arousal–partial blocking of arousal–blocking of arousal–practically no effect.
3. Anesthetic reaction–potentiation of anesthetics–antagonism to anesthetics.
4. Parkinsonism–Anti-Parkinsonism.
5. Sympatholytic effects–sympathomimetic effects–parasympatholytic effects–practically no effects.
6. Hallucinogenic–nonhallucinogenic.

Taxonomy is not at all satisfying; in some instances the classification of drugs will depend on dosage, and paradoxical effects on behavior are not unusual.

In fact, psychopharmacological personality research has focused on so-called stimulants and depressants, a stimulant drug being an agent that increases functional activity and a depressant drug being an agent that decreases functional activity. This terminology, of course, is an abbreviation that by no means comes up to the complexities of the previously mentioned dimensionality.

H. J. Eysenck (1967) recommended a more operational definition of the terms *stimulant* and *depressant* (a) by identifying the hypothetical dimension of drug action with arousal (excitation) and depressed arousal (inhibition) and (b) by pointing out typical representatives of each class. Stimulant drugs, according to Eysenck, have an arousing and therefore introverting effect, depressant drugs a dearousing and therefore extraverting effect. He underlines that stimulants sometimes may show paradoxical action. These phenomena perhaps are to be understood in terms of the inverse U relation between arousal and performance.

It is well documented that barbiturates depress reticular activity in a rather specific and selective way; thus, barbiturates have become a standard of comparison for the investigation of other drugs. Amphetamines, pipradrol, and caffeine are considered to be typical stimulants. Neuroleptica and tranquilizers, for example, phenothiazine, meprobamate, and reserpine, have a much more complex action, intermediate in some respects, but depending on dosage and on individual differences, partly dearousing, but different from sedation induced by barbiturates.

By incorporating drug effects in the theoretical frame of reference, Eysenck succeeded in deducing a number of predictions about the direction of drug effects on performance in objective behavior tests; these have been tested experimentally (c.f. Eysenck, H. J., 1963). Empirical results revealed several inconsistencies as well as favorable results (Eysenck, H. J., 1967; Legewie, 1968). Eysenck specifically referred to sedation-threshold measurements (Shagass' method), which have proved to be successful in behavioral pharmacology, using EEG measures and slur-of-speech criteria in the course of intravenous infusion of sodium amytal. A number of investigations proved—in accordance with the drug postulates—that hysterics and psychopaths have lower thresholds compared with those of anxiety neurotics and other dysthymic individuals.

An additional line of approach should be pursued whereby drugs affecting motor systems, sensory systems, or the ANS in an analogous manner are investigated with reference to hypothetical personality constructs. Wenger, Clemens, Darsie, Engel, Estess, and Sonnenschein (1960) tried to determine the action profiles of adrenaline and mecholyl compared with sodium chloride, anchoring in this way an ANS-reaction pattern, which could serve as a standard pattern of comparison (Chessick, 1966). Lader and Tyrer (1972), accordingly, studied the central and peripheral reaction profile of beta-blocking sympatholytic agents.

Behavioral pharmacology is now a major factor in determining the course of research, and many drugs have been tested for behavioral effects with reference to various behavioral measures and observations. Numerous suggestive studies have been done, extending, as an example, from strain and regression of intellectual functions (Lienert, 1963) to individual differences in drug effects between low-emotional and high-emotional subjects (Munkelt, 1965). Regarding personality research, the psychopharmacological concepts (drug postulates) by Eysenck appear to represent the first systematic appraisal of this subject, which will be of considerable importance for the biological basis of personality as soon as neurochemistry provides more information about site and mode of drug action.

## 7  SOME CONTRIBUTIONS FROM CONSTITUTIONAL RESEARCH AND BEHAVIOR GENETICS

The biological constitution is the basic morphological, physiological, and psychological structure of a person as determined by his genetic endowment and molded by environmental influences on growth processes and personality development. Constitutional research is concerned with individual differences in the relatively stable phenotype (physique and personality), with somatopsychic (in particular, psychomorphological) correlations and types and with their predictive value for somatic pathology and psychopathology.

There are some 60 typological systems of body build, most of them dealing with a few, selected anthropometric measures of height and circumference. Disagreement about number and definition of factors—apart from a length and a breadth factor—is evident (cf. Behnke, 1961; Rees, L., 1973; Royce, 1966). It is only fair to mention that Kretschmer (1967) considered about 200 scaled variables in somatotyping, compared with a maximum of 15–30 variables in most Anglo-American studies. In recent years, admittedly, there is a growing concern about skin-fold measurement, soft-tissue roentgenography, and body-composition analysis (Brozek, 1965; Cheek, 1968). Variable selection again appears to be a problematical aspect of most investigations in this field.

In his review, Tanner (1953) pointed out that little had been published on the relationship between body build and physiological function. The reason might be that most somatotypes represent a rather superficial anatomy (Schreider, 1966). After all, there has been some progress since 1953. A mass of data has accumulated around Kretschmer's typology, indicating, among other physiological correlates, a relationship between the pyknic body type and more ergotropic level of functioning, and between the leptomorph body type and more trophotropic level of functioning. This is still a working hypothesis since the empirical studies lack refined treatment. The main point seems to be that Kretschmer's somatotypes have a physiological and a psychological significance. From the beginning and more pronouncedly than other constitutionalists, Kretschmer thought somatotyping to be a bridge to autonomic-metabolic traits and to endocrine regulation. He pointed out that somatic features are a morphological representation of functions and reflect the results of genetically determined growth patterns and growth tendencies, more or less synchronized with each other (or desynchronized in some individuals during puberty).

Sheldon (1942), too, but less explicitly than Kretschmer or Conrad (1963), claimed a correspondence of somatotype factors with physiological traits and with temperament traits. Constitutional research by Lindegard and Nyman (1956) is of considerable importance: dimensions of body build (length, sturdiness, fat, and muscularity) were correlated with ketosteroid-excretion and with rated personality traits, following Sjoebring's system. Significant correlations were reported, for example, between muscularity, excretion rate of steroid substances, and "stability" ("emotional warmth and heaviness of expressive behavior vs. emotional coolness"). On the other hand, P. K. Bridges and Jones (1967) observed lower cortisol levels and higher neuroticism scores in students with physiques of primary muscularity. Rees and Eysenck pointed out that leptomorph body build is associated with effort syndrome and with dysthymic (emotional and introvert) personality syndrome. Low, but statistically significant correlations between threshold values of three sensory modalities and somatotype were reported by Rusalow (1972)—high total sensitivity of the partial pyknoid type and low sensitivity of the partial athletoid type. On the other hand, it is known that methodologically refined investigations in many instances have failed to confirm constitutional hypotheses, thus giving rise to serious criticism of the marked overrating of psychomorphological correlations (cf. Rees, L., 1973; Royce, 1966; Schick, 1964; Schreider, 1966; Zerssen, 1976).

From his review and statistical reanalysis of many data, Zerssen concluded that the main variations of gross body build can be assessed by means of three independent dimensions: (a) general skeletal size, (b) fat, and (c) robustness, that is, stoutness versus slenderness (leptopyknomorphy). The correlation coefficient $r = 0.20$ between factor scores of robustness and "mental vitality"—a questionnaire factor covering emotional stability and masculinity—proved to be low but significant in a sample of 115 young male adults. As a main conclusion, Zerssen suggested a rather unspecific psychomorphological relationship between physical robustness (muscularity and endomorphic mesomorphy) and broad temperamental characteristics (somatotonic extraversion, emotional stability, and autonomic balance).

Constitutional psychology, by its very aims, must lead to multivariate analysis including physiological as well as behavioral traits, and in consequence, of course, must lead to genetic research. Inheritance of ANS and EEG characteristics has been amply demonstrated by a number of twin studies (e.g. Claridge, Canter, & Hume, 1973; Fox, H. M., Gifford, Valentine, & Murawski, 1970; Kryshova, Beliaeva, Dmitrieva, & Zhilinskaya, 1963; Levene, Engel, & Schulkin, 1967; Lykken, Tellegen, & Thorkelson, 1974; Shapiro, A. P., Nicotero, Sapira, & Scheib, 1968; Vandenberg, Clark, & Samuels, 1965; Vogel, F., 1963). Hereditary effects are evident in many other physiological and neurological characteristics, to say nothing of genetically determined trait variance of ability and temperament (cf. chapters 12, 13 and 14).

Looking at summaries of behavior genetics (Fuller, J. L., & Thompson, 1960; Kaplan, A. R., 1976; Shields, 1973; Thompson, W. R., & Wilde, 1973; Vandenberg, 1965), we are still on speculative grounds when we try to bridge the gap between genes and physiological or psychological traits and when we try to discuss the genetical meaning of a trait factor (Royce, J. R., 1966, 1973; Thompson, W. R., 1968b), whether we assume congruence or noncongruence of gene and trait. Even from the 90 (about) inborn errors of metabolism discovered, in only a few instances do we know approximately the chain of causes. But what are the biochemical and embryological mechanisms whereby genetic information is translated into traits of psychophysiological significance, such as the Riley-Day syndrome of combined behavioral, autonomic, and motor dysfunction? Genetical endowment might express itself either by structural variation of the nervous system, or by hormones, or by enzymatic process, all of them in complex interaction. Because of this multiple-factor causation, we must avoid, as Fuller and Thompson underlined, a so-called biochemical phrenology, in which simple enzyme systems replace the bumps of the cranium.

More thorough analyses in this domain presuppose suitable units of description; taxometric procedures and factor analysis of representative data appear to be important for constitutional psychology, to overcome, perhaps, the growing disappointment about generally low and inconsistent correlation patterns.

# 8 PSYCHOPHYSIOLOGICAL TRAITS AND STATES

Personality, motivation, and ability, together with their individual differences, have a biological basis; therefore, each trait or state dimension must have a nonspecific or specific morphological-physiological aspect. At present, those traits and states are called *psychophysiological*, in which the physiological correlates are comparatively well-known and very prominent in central or peripheral functioning (anxiety, etc.). Naturally, this distinction is not fundamental but due to differences in accessibility, as in some instances physiological correlates are easier to observe. Psychophysiological traits and states are integrated patterns, for example, correlation or factor patterns, indicating substantial contributions of physiological and psychological variables.

An outstanding domain for complementary somatological-psychological observation and integration is the group of so-called *functional and psychosomatic disorders* (International Classification of Diseases [ICD] Nos. 300.5 and 305) in psychosomatic medicine (cf. Delius & Fahrenberg, 1966; Graham, D. T., 1972; Levi, 1971) and in the so-called *corticovisceral pathology* (Bykov & Kurzin, 1966). Psychophysiological personality research focusing on psychophysiological trait and state concepts appears to be a basic discipline for a number of related fields (Ax, 1964; Eysenck, H. J., 1973; Fahrenberg, 1967; Greenfield & Sternbach, 1972; Levi, 1971). In the present chapter neither research on psychosomatic disorders nor— paradigm of psychophysiological investigation—on emotion can be reviewed (cf. Levi, 1975; Venables & Christie, 1975) but the contributions of *differential physiology* to modern personality theory and research must be considered.

For the purposes of this chapter and to stimulate discussion, the physiological point of view has been stressed. Some useful concepts and some possible research orientations have been mentioned in this area, which still, in many aspects, is *terra*

*incognita*. Progress will come from more sophisticated physiological measures and concepts, from more reliable laboratory procedures, from more valid and representative variable selection, and from structured (dimensional or taxometric) measurement rather than from global or univariate studies. Interindividual trait studies and intraindividual state studies are equally important. For some physiological and biometric reasons, psychophysiological studies within individuals have some advances; but multiple time series of this kind include serious methodological problems not to be underestimated (Fahrenberg, Kuhn, Kulick, & Myrtek, 1976; Harris, C. W., 1963a; Mefford, 1975; Wieland & Mefford, 1970).

There have been, of course, many attempts to correlate physiological measures of all categories with personality variables (for summaries see Cattell, 1957a; Duffy, 1962; Eysenck, H. J., 1965, 1967; Fahrenberg, 1967; Royce, 1966), that cannot be reviewed here. Some investigators have used inadequate measures on the physiological side; some have used crude measures on the personality side; many have used doubtful measures on both sides and related arbitrary physiological or morphological variables with arbitrary personality data. Most of these studies are based upon a few autonomic functions, questionnaire scores, or psychiatric ratings. Motor functions and biochemical and neurophysiological variables are rarely included; on the other side, mainly temperament traits have been selected. There are only a few studies concerning physiological correlates of ability and intelligence (cf. Royce, 1966).

We must distinguish two basic models of psychophysiological investigation: (a) analyzing combined samples of physiological and psychological data in order to isolate psychophysiological patterns, and (b) establishing physiological patterns first and then, later on, looking for correlates or matches with known psychological patterns, dimensions, or types. Probably, the second approach is more promising, since it appears to correspond better to the assumption of different levels of biological organization.

Constitutional psychology, particularly the work of Kretschmer, and Pavlov's neuropsychology have encouraged psychophysiological trait studies; the main contributions, however, have come from Wenger, Eysenck, Cattell, and their associates.

Wenger (1948) described three physiological factors: Thyroid factor, Blood-sugar factor, and Autonomic factor; only the latter bore significant relationships to personality factors, measured by the Guilford-Martin questionnaire. High $\bar{A}$ score, indicating parasympathetic dominance, was positively correlated with factor scores of Depression, Cyclothymia, Lack of Cooperativeness, Subjectivity, and Nervousness. One point worth remembering is that Autonomic factor scores were more closely related to personality factors than any single physiological variable. H. J. Eysenck (1953a) noticed that this psychological factor pattern corresponds well to a second-order factor, Neuroticism, as he conceived it. But there is one serious contradiction in Wenger's results: On the one hand, parasympathetic dominance (high $\bar{A}$) is related to the Neuroticism syndrome in the questionnaire; on the other hand, Wenger observed that neurotic persons exhibit a sympathetic dominance of ANS. Cattell (1957a) in his discussion of these data, tried to solve these inconsistencies in terms of three Autonomic factors.

Eysenck's typology on the level of second-order factors, linking Neuroticism (emotionality) with Autonomic Reactivity and linking Introversion-Extraversion with Arousal (excitation-inhibition) is well known, so that it will be sufficient to summarize the main points of his theory (Eysenck, H. J., 1947, 1965, 1957, 1973; Eysenck, H. J., & Eysenck, 1969).

An individual high on Neuroticism (emotionality) when compared with an individual low on Neuroticism will (a) exhibit a hyperreactivity and lability of the ANS or parts thereof; (b) display a low stress tolerance towards physical or psychological stimulation, conflict, and frustrating situations; (c) behave under certain circumstances like an individual high on drive; a high level of drive particularly in avoidance situations is predicted. Emotional excitability may lead to facilitation of performance or to deterioration of performance, depending on the Yerkes-Dodson law and on complex interactions of drive, stress experience, and task difficulty.

The question of whether the hypothesized relationship between ANS reactivity and emotional lability has been confirmed empirically, will find different answers depending on the mode of observation used: $Q$ or $T$ data. In $Q$ data, Fahrenberg (1969, 1975) reported substantial correlation coefficients ($r = 0.63$, $N = 903$; and $r = 0.56$, $N = 330$) between a neuroticism scale equivalent to Eysenck's Maudsley Personality Inventory–Neuroticism ($MPI-N$) and a self-report scale developed to assess the frequency of subjectively experienced somatic symptoms and autonomic lability. From this study, from Eysenck's earlier work, and from several other investigations (e.g., Schalling, Cronholm, and Asberg, 1975), a consistent self-concept of generalized psychosomatic disregulation is evident. On the other hand, in $T$ data there is considerable doubt whether objectively determined individual differences in ANS-resting and ANS-reactivity measures will correlate to a significant and reproducible extent with $N$-scores derived from standard questionnaires, or whether factor-analytic investigations will result in a clear-cut dimension of autonomic lability, hyperreactivity, or autonomic lability-emotionality—even on the second-order level (cf. section 3 of this chapter; Fahrenberg, 1967; Myrtek, 1975a; Othmer, Netter-Munkelt, Golle, & Meyer, 1969). Recent work in our laboratory by Myrtek, Walschburger, Medert-Dornscheidt, and Kruse failed to confirm both these assumptions. The comprehensive study, important parts of which are still to be published, is based on two samples of male students ($N = 107$ and $N = 100$) and a sample of cardiac, mainly coronary patients ($N = 210$) and includes over a hundred biochemical and autonomic, resting, and reactivity measures as well as various $L$ data and $Q$ data. Psychophysiological research at present tends to support the view that there are a number of first-order factors, the common variance of which appears not to be sufficient to give rise to a prominent second-order factor of autonomic-emotional lability—in contrast to $Q$ data results. Data relations in this domain are complex; but Myrtek (1975a), in a pilot analysis which applied hierarchical cluster techniques to the data, observed four reproducible clusters: (a) high in sympatheticotonia, low in physical fitness, few somatic symptoms experienced, low emotional lability; (b) high in vagotonia, good physical fitness, average or less than average somatic symptoms experienced, comparatively low emotional lability; (c) high in vagotonia, good physical fitness, average somatic symptoms experienced, high in emotional lability, low blood pressure; (d) high in sympatheticotonia, low physical fitness, many somatic symptoms experienced, high in emotional lability. Simple correlational analysis or factor analysis of the psychophysiological patterns indicated here would obviously result in insignificant averaging.

Introversion-Extraversion in Eysenck's system is considered to be the second major dimension of personality and independent from Neuroticism. Eysenck postulates that differences in Introversion-Extraversion correspond to differences in respect to the speed and strength with which excitation and inhibition are produced and the speed with which inhibition is dissipated, excitation and inhibition being the overall resultants of all the excitatory and inhibitory potentials in cortical activity. A person high on Extraversion compared with a person with a low score will behave in a less aroused and more fatigued manner. (We are referring here to the individual's CNS, not to his manifest behavior.) Experimental personality research has elaborated a number of deductions that have been made from these postulates, with regard to sensory thresholds, perceptual phenomena, motor behavior, involuntary rest pauses, conditionability and learning, achievement, aspiration, and so forth.

From H. J. Eysenck's (1967) detailed summary, it can be concluded that there is considerable evidence in favor of some of these predictions, although in some respects certain specifications of the original concept appear to be necessary, mainly with regard to explicit consideration of the inverted-U relationship between arousal and performance and to the breaking up of excitatory and of inhibitory processes. So far, confirmation of behavioral and performance data seems to be somewhat more convincing compared with such CNS concepts as sensitivity, arousability, and conditionability (cf. Davies & Tune, 1970; Eysenck, H. J., 1971; Franks, 1963; Gale, 1973; Lovibond, 1964; Nebylitsyn, 1972; Nebylitsyn & Gray, 1972; Siddle, Morrish, White, & Mangan, 1969; Smith, S. T., 1968; Spence, K. W., 1964). Recent work in our laboratory, already mentioned in section 5 of this chapter, failed in some respects to support Eysenck's psychophysiological postulates. Guenther investigated the relationship between absolute sensory thresholds of six modalities and the extraversion score *FPI-E* (Freiburger Personlichkeitsinventar-Extraversions-Skala); the auditory threshold alone was significantly but negatively ($r = -0.36$, $N = 60$) related to *FPI-E*, but positively related in a second investigation by Lysko ($r = +0.22$, $N = 83$). In 51 males students. Schroeder observed insignificant correlations between *FPI-E* and several indexes of individual differences in habituality of heart rate, peripheral vasoconstriction, and four measures of EEG alpha block; the only exception was a correlation coefficient of $r = -0.30$ between *FPI-E* and a habituation index based on the Torres-criterion of alpha-block habituation (Torres, 1968); that is, introverts appeared to be higher in habituability in this investigation. Malotki and Lysko, in their evaluation of more than 50 parameters derived from speed, amplitude, duration, and efficiency of eyelid conditioning, obtained the predicted correlation with *FPI-E* in a single, relatively poor criterion of speed ($= -.22$, $N = 78$) but not in the essential CR-frequency value, although experimental conditions ought to have favored introverts (90% partial reinforcement, relatively weak UCS, 65-mm mercury column at air pipe outlet, and small International System of Units [SI] 440 msec); normal distribution of CR frequency as well as reliability estimates were satisfying. Problems in experimental method and measurement, however, are obvious, and definite statements will require further thorough investigation in this complex domain.

Eysenck proposed a neurophysiological basis of both hypothetical constructs: Difference in behavior related to Neuroticism (emotionality) and Autonomic Reactivity are identified with differential thresholds of arousal in the visceral brain (limbic system); differences in behavior related to Introversion (excitation, arousal)-Extraversion (inhibition) are identified with differential thresholds in various parts of the reticular activating system. Thus, Eysenck suggested a partial independence between cortical arousal and the generalized autonomic activation with strong skeletal-motor involvement. Although some Pavlovian concepts are incorporated in this theory, it seems to be at variance with neo-Pavlovian orientation (Nebylitsyn, 1972). In a theoretical modification of Eysenck's model, Gray replaced the ARAS by the feedback loop comprising ARAS, frontal cortex, septal area, and hippocampus. Next, he suggested that there are differences between introverts and extraverts, not in general conditionability, but in the introvert's higher susceptibility for punishment and frustrative nonreward (Gray, J. A., 1964, 1967, 1973; Nebylitsyn & Gray, 1972).

Even those psychophysiologists who appear to be critical of Eysenck's theory will have to agree that there is at least heuristic value in these concepts. Probably psychophysiological personality research will have to test such theories—though considered by physiologists, perhaps, as pseudophysiological—to attain a frame of reference and testable predictions about central and peripheral physiological correlates of behavior data.

The most elaborate studies leading to tentative trait and state indexings have come from Cattell and his co-workers. The great majority of these reported factor patterns include loadings on a number of physiological and biochemical variables, in some trait factor patterns, and even in somatotype variables. It should be acknowledged that these factor patterns demonstrate the result of extensive psychophysiological investigations, taking into account behavioral data and questionnaires, as well as ANS and CNS measures in an outstanding research program. A full review of these personality factors with physiological and somatotype associations is omitted here since they have been summarized in a number of books and recent articles on trait factors (Cattell, 1973; Cattell & Scheier, 1961; Howarth, 1972b; Hundleby, Pawlik, & Cattell, 1965; Nesselroade & Delhees, 1966), on state factors (Barton, Cattell, & Curran, 1973; Cattell, 1966b, 1972b; Luborsky & Mintz, 1972), and on motivation factors (Cattell & Child, 1975).

Among trait factors, *U.I.* 16, 21, 22, 24 are of particular interest; and State Universal Index (*S.U.I.*) 1, 4, 5, 9, among the state factors. The following abstract is based on the aforementioned reports (Universal Index, *U.I.*).

*U.I.* 16. Unbound, Assertive Ego versus Bound, Disciplined Ego. Fast speed of perception, judgment and psychomotor performance; high self-assertiveness in competitive situations; strong physique (longer and thicker bones, larger amount of muscle and fat, fast speed of physical movements); higher muscle tension; higher level of arousal (frontal EEG measures); higher blood pressure; less endurance in treadmill.

*U.I.* 21. Exuberance versus Suppressibility. Impervious to social suggestion; faster speed of social and perceptual judgment; high verbal and ideational fluency; sensitivity to threat and emotional stimulation; slight body build (lower weight, smaller shoulder width, smaller muscular index); high physiological resting level (basic metabolic rate [BMR], systolic blood pressure, hand tremor) and high reactivity (GSR, heart rate, metabolic rate); less muscle tension; more static ataxia.

*U.I.* 22. Cortertia versus Pathemia. High speed of performance; over-readiness to respond, but low endurance, higher level of arousal (occipital EEG measures, flicker fusion frequency); tenseness and restlessness

(muscle tension, fidgetometer frequency).

*U.I.* 24. High Unbound Anxiety versus Good Adjustment. High manifest anxiety and ergic tension; insecurity, guilt and self-depreciation; susceptibility to annoyance and embarassment; higher score on anxiety tension checklist; asthenic physique; low strength and endurance; high systolic blood pressure; high body sway suggestibility.

*S.U.I.* 1. Activation (excitement) versus Torpor (unreactiveness, parasympathetic dominance), corresponding to *U.I.* 35(−). Surgency and extraversion; low body sway suggestibility; low ratio emotional/nonemotional recall; better immediate memory for words; small GSR activity and low initial resistance; high blood sugar; high systolic blood pressure; high body temperature.

*S.U.I.* 4. Effort Stress. Low fluency and low rigidity; high level of anxiety (*Q* data); good memory, commit and recall; high 17-ketosteroids; faster heart rate.

*S.U.I.* 5. Sympathetic (adrenergic) Autonomic Response. Poor control of cognitive and other performances; high percent lymphocytes; small percent neutrophils; high erythrocyte count; high blood sugar; large GSR upward drift in relaxation; faster heart rate; high increase of heart rate after startle.

*S.U.I.* 9. High Anxiety versus Low Anxiety (general autonomic activation), corresponding to *U.I.* 24(+). High level of anxiety (*Q* and *L* data); lack of confidence; faster heart rate and respiration rate; high systolic pulse pressure; low initial skin resistance; low serum cholinesterase; high plasma 17-ketosteroids.

Additionally, somatotype associations are indicated for *U.I.* 28 and 32; higher muscle tension for *U.I.* 17, 23 (−), and 35; higher autonomic resting and reactivity for *U.I.* 20(−), 23(−), 29, 34, and 35.

Cattell was encouraged by these many salient loadings to give tentative interpretations of the physiological meaning of these patterns. These factors, of course, must have many more physiological correlates, though still unknown. The question is, whether those physiological variables, which are the most important from a physiological point of view, have already been included to a sufficient extent. Some characteristics of the ergotropic syndrome and some indicators of arousal can be found here in several factor patterns; the same can be said of muscle tension, psychomotor performance and biochemical data. On the other hand, there are comparatively few indexes of supposed dimensions of CNS functioning, for example, differential arousability, habituability, conditionability, and sensitivity. By analysis of combined samples of physiological and psychological raw data we probably will encounter a different situation compared to an alternative strategy that first tries to establish patterns, trait or state concepts of individual differences in physiological data—which are perhaps of lower order than $L, Q$ and nonphysiological $T$ data.

Cattell, like Eysenck, favors two distinct concepts of somatic activation: (a) cortical arousal, which corresponds mainly to Cortertia ($U.I.$ 22), (b) general autonomic-endocrine activation, which corresponds to Anxiety as a trait ($U.I.$ 24), and Anxiety as a state ($S.U.I.$ 9). The naming of $S.U.I.$ 1 as Parasympathetic Dominance and of $S.U.I.$ 5 as Sympathetic (adrenergic) Autonomic Response seems to be more hypothetical. Recently Cattell tried to identify Cortertia as a general level of stable activation with the Pavlovian dimension of Strength (Cattell 1972a; Cattell & Child, 1975).

In some instances more definite interpretation of physiological constituents of Cattellian factor patterns could be achieved by extension of physiological measurements to include further ANS and CNS variables as well as different stimulus conditions. Certain cardiovascular measures, (e.g., stroke volume and peripheral resistance), multiple record-

ings of autonomic reactions by polygraphs as well as additional biochemical and hormonal measures (e.g., catecholamines and thyroid hormone), would be of particular interest in this respect to settle problems of interpretation. However, factor differentiation and identification is made more easily by referring to loadings in behavioral variables instead of physiological or morphological variables. It would be a different starting position if we could include scores of complex physiological processes, for example, estimates for tonic level of the ergotropic system and of the trophotropic system, or in a different context, possibly, scores for the neo-Pavlovian dimensions. Research along these lines and development of suitable physiological test batteries for the assessment of complex physiological processes in humans seem to be most promising. For these reasons, a direct identification of $U.I.$ and $S.U.I.$ factor patterns with physiological concepts reviewed in sections 3–5 of this chapter appears to offer some difficulties although many interesting associations are given that may generate still more precise hypotheses for integrated psychophysiological research, as has been demonstrated by Pawlik and Cattell (1965).

Some of the important physiological factor loadings have been replicated by further studies, but the results are difficult to compare due to partially overlapping sets of variables and, particularly in state investigations, due to different techniques of factor analysis ($P$, chain-$P$, and $dR$ technique). Thus, issues of research strategies and preferences for hypotheses-generating or hypotheses-testing work with regard to psychophysiological trait studies have been discussed (Cattell, 1972a; Eysenck, H. J., 1972, Gray, J. A., 1973; Howarth, 1972b; Royce, 1973).

In drawing some conclusions: Physiological—and sometimes pseudophysiological—concepts are of growing importance in modern personality research, and application of psychophysiological techniques and findings is common practice in psychosomatic medicine. At present, a number of psychophysiological state and trait patterns have been delineated that give a frame of reference for future research programs. The biological basis of personality will become more obvious when individual differences can be described with reference to relevant physiological concepts instead of single or arbitrary measures. Most desirable in this respect are improved methods of functional analysis, advanced mathematical models, and thoroughly elaborated physiological concepts.

In physiology and in psychophysiology, much progress has been made in methods and measurement: by more sophisticated reactivity and function tests; by recording up to 16 functions simultaneously; by computer-assisted analysis of physiological variables; by biochemical assay procedures; and by integration techniques, frequency-analysis and time-series analysis. New physiological concepts have emerged, recognizing the importance of subsystems and of multiple equilibria, concerning the recognition of patterning and of response specificities and taking into account the importance of transients and oscillatory responses. Practicable models of psychophysiological personality research will have to make use of these developments.

## 9  SUMMARY

1. The biological basis of personality can be studied from four different angles: neurophysiology, psychophysiology, behavioral pharmacology, and behavior genetics. Psychophysiology essentially contributes to the theory of states and traits, and it is hoped that psychophysiology will help toward understanding the relationships between CNS processes and individual differences in behavior patterns.

2. Physiological data can be obtained from central processes as well as peripheral autonomic and endocrine, motor, and sensory processes. Physiological individuality recently has attracted research interest of physiologists, and the foundation and development of state and trait description have been accomplished mainly by psychologists. Meaningful variable selection and recognition of compensatory regulations and of functional content of data are fundamental for psychophysiological research. The data theory of physiological measures still is in its beginning. In some instances theoretical questions that are implied in mind-body relationships will be encountered. These can be managed best methodologically by assuming complementarity of physiological, of behavioral, and of introspective categories refering to psychosomatic phenomena.

3. Physiological concepts drawn from peripheral processes include, among others, sympatheticotonia-parasympatheticotonia, ergotropic-trophotropic state, autonomic imbalance, and muscle tension. Analysis of resting measures and reactivity measures of many functions, analysis of oscillatory response, intraindividual time series, pattern analysis, and other more sophisticated methods are desirable to establish state and trait description of certain subsystems and of the organism as a whole.

4. Physiological concepts drawn from hormonal and biochemical processes are closely connected with concepts of ANS functioning. Research interest has focused on catecholamines and on adrenocortical hormones; these are considered to be indicator variables of ergotropic-sympathetic phase and alarm reaction. In future,

differences in enzymatic activities and metabolic deficiencies as well as additional hormone measures will be likewise important.

5. Physiological concepts drawn from neurophysiology mainly refer to reticular system functioning, to limbic system functioning, and to cortical excitation-inhibition. Arousal according to EEG measures; behavioral activation; the neo-Pavlovian typology of higher nervous activity; and the trichotomy of orienting, defensive, and adaptive reaction to novel stimuli are remarkable themes in experimental research. Individual differences in arousability, sensitivity, conditionability, and habituability are of particular theoretical interest although consistency and generality of these concepts lack empirical evidence.

6. Contributions from behavioral psychopharmacology have come mainly from experiments using stimulant and depressant drugs, although stimulation-sedation is only one aspect of drug action on CNS. Many data can be organized following the "drug postulates" that stimulants have an introverting effect while depressants have an extraverting effect and that introverts will have higher sedation thresholds. Further dimensions of drug action and other categories of drugs (tranquilizers, drugs acting on ANS, etc.) will have to be studied in an analogous manner.

7. Contributions from constitutional research and behavior genetics have documented that there are inherited physiological patterns, expressing themselves in certain morphological signs (body build), in metabolism and autonomic regulation, and—perhaps—in temperament and psychomotor style.

8. Psychophysiological personality research is concerned with physiological correlates of personality traits and states. When the biological basis of personality is analyzed, all categories of physiological and morphological data and all the relevant physiological concepts must be included. More than others, the work of Wenger, Eysenck, Cattell and their associates has stimulated research on psychophysiological trait and state patterns. Psychophysiology still is in its beginnings, but considerable effort is being made to use more sophisticated physiological methods and advanced mathematical models.

# Section

# 6

## The Psychopathology of Personality

# 26

## Classification
## in Psychopathology

**Wilson H. Guertin**
*University of Florida, Gainesville*

### 1  INTRODUCTION

Psychiatric classification is supposed to be more than a parlor guessing game or a battleground wherein disagreeing psychiatrists work out their hostilities. Useful psychiatric classification must help the patient in some way. Since psychiatric classification is a complex process, with many disparate views on how to best establish a diagnostic system, we will postpone discussion of it and look first at the simple empirical approach to medicine.

Empirical medicine establishes a generalization of the form that when $X$ is present $Y$ will occur; e.g., when a particular treatment is employed, a normal physical condition in the patient is restored. A primitive practitioner of the healing arts may have found that the skin becomes normal after the application of a particular substance to a certain type of skin lesion. Establishing the generalization from one or two cases, he continues to use the treatment for all such cases. Of course, the omission of treatment may produce equally satisfactory results. The primitive practitioner's mind is closed to any alternative, however, once he is convinced of the value of the original treatment. Primitive witchcraft and superstitions that are accumulated through this process and persist in a scientific society can be debunked only through experimentation.

It is no surprise to find some areas of psychiatry and clinical psychology employing empirical relationships derived many years earlier which have never been adequately tested. Psychiatric diagnosis, developed in the setting of empirical medicine decades ago, remains essentially unchanged today. While the value of psychiatric diagnosis has been frequently challenged by clinicians and researchers, only minor modifications have been made in practice; and few workers have produced more sophisticated alternatives.

### 2  TYPES OF PATIENT VARIABLES

The number of patient variables that could enter into the predictive psychiatric model are too numerous to be manageable. The ones actually to be employed must be selected on the basis of the probability that they will contribute to the prescription of an effective therapy and predict outcome for the individual class. Some classification of the types of variables that might enter prediction will be helpful in discussing their promise.

Patient variables may be either current or historical. Current variables may be subgrouped as follows:

1. Physical-physiological. Results of medical examination and findings by special laboratory procedures.

2. Ability. Results of psychological testing for intellectual functioning and deficits in special abilities.

3. Personality. Results of psychological testing, observational rating, or questionnaire responses provide normative scores on a number of personality dimensions.

4. Psychodynamic idiosyncracies (symptoms). Results of psychological testing, observational rating, or questionnaire responses provide a picture of personality peculiarities in the areas of attitudes, interests, preferences, beliefs, habits, ego defenses, and body reactions. They are frequently reported in summary form in the order of presumed importance for establishing diagnosis, recommending therapy, as well as predicting outcome.

5. Mental status interview. Similar to item 4 but based largely on interview with the patient.

The historical type of patient variables are primarily obtained through questionnaires, interviews, and consultation of records. They may be subgrouped as follows:

1. Birth and early childhood. Largely a medical history overlapping with the next item.

2. Child-rearing practices.

3. Family and home. Includes family constellation and environment as well as interaction of patient and family members.

4. School. Social adjustment often more important than academic focus.

5. Community. Activities and adjustment.

6. Health. Includes previous hospitalization, diagnosis, and treatment.

7. Vocational. Includes armed service record.

8. Marital. Focus is on relation to opposite sex and living circumstances.

## 3 RELATIVE VALUE OF TYPES OF PATIENT VARIABLES

If we take the position that all things occurring in a patient's past will have affected his present psychiatric and psychological status, then theoretically we can dispense with the historical variables and employ current patient variables only. In actual practice this ignoring of antecedent conditions is unsatisfactory because a clearer picture of current status variables is obtained by reference to antecedents. It may be supposed that improved definition of current variables and techniques for measuring them quantitatively will decrease the practical need for dependence on historical-type variables.

Except in the case of organic brain damage or relevant physical disease, the medical history is seldom revealing. However, the medical history persists as an essential procedure because residual symptoms from important disorders may be missed in the current evaluation.

Psychological testing for abilities can be helpful in some cases and possesses the advantage of supplying objectively determined patient variables. Psychodynamic idiosyncracies and mental status interviews have proved to be, by far, the most singly important sources of data for making outcome predictions, despite the error introduced by using a fallible judge to evaluate the variables, which are seldom stated in quantitative form.

Personality and trait variables are valuable but overlap with psychodynamic idiosyncracies (symptoms). Personality questionnaires such as the Minnesota Multiphasic Personality Inventory (MMPI) often are helpful by disclosing an extreme deviation on a personality dimension that corresponds to a psychodynamic idiosyncracy.

## 4  PERSONALITY VARIABLES AND PSYCHOPATHOLOGY

Here we encounter a major theoretical problem. Are the symptoms of mental illness merely expressions of the extremes of personality traits or should they be regarded as psychopathological entities requiring a special type of measurement? For the sake of consistency within this chapter, we will assume the latter to be true. If a personality dimension represents a normal range of values characteristic of people, it does not follow that a very extreme value represents merely a statistically infrequent occurrence of a normal functioning. The psychopathological view would maintain that serious breakdowns of normal functions constitute conditions which are qualitatively different and need to be regarded in a pathology frame of reference. Whereas the heart with auricular fibrillation can be identified by recording its several hundred beats per minute, the condition is pathological; and there are associated symptoms ordinarily unrelated to heart rate variations within the normal range.

The excellent review and analysis of the literature given by Lorr, Klett, and McNair (1963) reveal that few investigators try to establish psychiatric classification by employing personality variables or traits. Most investigators use symptoms in classifying psychotics although such a bias is not nearly as evident in the classification of neurotic conditions.

There is considerable evidence to indicate that personality and cultural features (hereafter subsumed under the term *personality*) are important in establishing the nature of the particular patient's syndrome picture. Opler (1959) convincingly illustrated this in observed differences between Irish and Italian schizophrenics. A paranoid farmer believes that people are stealing his cattle, while his city counterpart believes that his enemies are destroying his business. A repressed, hostile person when drunk becomes quarrelsome, whereas the well-adjusted individual is much less likely to become offensive.

Two statements about the place of personality dimensions in a predictive system summarize this position. First, psychopathological symptoms often are reflected in extreme personality trait scores but not always, because the two are not necessarily correlates in a normal sample. Second, personality traits tend to modify symptom expression and must be brought into a highly predictive system. Whereas these traits may be regarded as troublesome and interfering, they must receive full cognizance in a successful system.

## 5  TECHNIQUES OF MEASURING PATIENT VARIABLES

There have been some major expressions of concern over the techniques used to measure current patient variables. Both Cattell (1952a) and Becker (1960) noted the discrepancies in factor-analytic dimensions of personality and symptoms when obtained from questionnaire data as compared with those derived from tests or ratings. Much of the discrepancy probably is related to response biases such as acquiescence and social desirability (faking normal) of subjects completing questionnaires, although Becker goes so far as to question the existence of traits. Measurement specialists have not been able to derive response bias-free scores; but Cattell and Schaie and others have been able to identify instrument factors, which, when put aside, permit viewing the personality trait itself. Lorr pointed out that ward observations lead to somewhat different factors than emerge from interview ratings.

Projective techniques set out to eliminate the usual questionnaire response biases by disguising the task so that the subject would not know what were conventionally desirable responses to give to the stimuli. Anybody knows you should reply "No" to the questionnaire item, "Are you afraid you might commit a crime of violence?" Yet, it is by no means obvious that a corresponding response on the Rorschach Ink Blot Test of perceiving "two bears fighting" is revealing important socially unacceptable information about relationships with others. Unfortunately, the usefulness of tests like the Szondi have not been affirmed in published studies; moreover, tests such as the Rorschach and the Thematic Apperception Test, which have proved more useful, provide results that are so poorly quantified that they are difficult, if not impossible, to work into a dependable predictive system. Tests like Cattell's 16 Personality Factor (PF) test show more promise in measuring personality dimensions and providing a quantified score. Scheier, Cattell, and Horn (1960) showed that their objective test factors (Universal index, $U.I$) $U.I.22$ and $U.I.23$ are closely related to anxiety and neuroticism.

Mental status variables (surface traits) have proved most valuable in exploring common variance in factor-analytic studies of psychotics, but the error introduced by examiner judgment and nonstandard interview situation places limits on this mode of data gathering. The objectivity and standard conditions possible only through the use of tests make it desirable that more effort be expended in developing and using objective tests for measuring patient variables. Until recently, despite theoretical promise, the use of tests in measuring patient variables has not been productive. Cattell and Tatro (1966) showed that objective test measures of patient variables (surface traits) do indeed have promise, and more work along these

lines should be valuable. Goals of high reliability and validity probably can be realized only with this type of measurement.

In the foregoing description of variables we have been viewing them cross-sectionally, that is, obtaining the measures at one point in time, say at the time of admission to a hospital. Some distinctions in a classification system for at least a few classes will have to examine change of a variable with the passage of time. For example, the change of state from mania to depression in the cyclic manic depressive would have to be evaluated through repeated measures over a period of time. Fortunately, the change aspect in the classification of psychopathology seems generally of little importance even though it can not be ignored for certain states.

The suggestions by Cattell (1952b) of bringing time into correlation and factor analysis have not been followed through by much actual research. However, Tucker's (1964a) expansion of the factor analytic model to three modes may encourage investigators to include the time dimension without having to exclude other variables in the conventional modes. Lorr (1966) brought the time dimension under scrutiny in two ways. The chapter by Rice and Mattsson reports on measures repeated over the course of the illness; and they found types different than those identified by Lorr. The chapter by Klett and Lorr reports on profile changes after treatment: "While the level of the profile has decreased, the profile shape or general configuration has remained the same" (Lorr, 1966, p. 117).

## 6  RELATIONSHIPS BETWEEN PATIENT AND OUTCOME VARIABLES

The simple empirical approach to medicine is encountered in the numerous investigations of the relationship between patient variables and outcome variables. Patients who have left the hospital are compared with those who have not to see if there is a relationship between outcome and the following: age, intelligence, sex, education, socioeconomic status, national origin, and many other variables too numerous to mention. Similarly, such patient variables have been studied in relation to the benefits (*outcome* after treatment) of such treatment as electroshock. These studies usually produce little of value when they ignore the critical variables associated with diagnosis. When patient variables are studied even within a single diagnostic category, the low degree of relationships found with outcome variables is far from satisfactory when compared with similar studies of nonpsychiatric patients with a uniform disease picture. The failure of psychiatry and psychology to produce an adequate predictive system points to the importance of establishing reliable and useful psychiatric classification.

One of the few benefits of studying patient variables within a diagnostic group, even through sampling with admittedly weak diagnostic groups, is the identification of patient variables that seem to bear a low but dependable relationship to outcome. Such findings help select the most promising patient variables for inclusion in the refined classification system. For example, patient statements revealed in mental status examinations as having "committed a terrible sin" or wishing he "was never born" are often related to imminent suicide attempts. Thus, the value of such mental status variables is established empirically; and these variables need to be included in data on the patients and should be permitted to enter the diagnostic scheme.

## 7 CONFIGURATIONS OF PATIENT VARIABLES

Single data variables by themselves can be misleading. A young male patient with a "wise-guy" attitude may acknowledge wishing he "was never born." Still, the likelihood of a suicide would be nil; and this would throw off the results from a simple predictive equation. The contingency (coexistence) of both the mental-status acknowledgment and some corresponding emotional evidence of dysphoria (sadness) will greatly improve prediction of suicide. This configuration, based on two variables, is only the beginning because the prediction can be improved further by adding the case-history variable of previous suicide attempts. As we add many variables to be looked at simultaneously, the possible combinations become overwhelming. Frequently encountered configurations associated with suicide may be obscured in the mass of data. When the complexity of data overwhelms the human mind, one should, these days, think about the application of analytic statistics that can be executed on electronic computers for the solution of such problems.

The basic difficulty with empirical medicine is that it is a simplification which often fails to work. For instance, the yellowing skin and sclerae can be relieved successfully by surgery, only if the disease is obstructive jaundice. Any relationship between the symptoms and outcome after treatment depends on a configuration of symptoms. This complex situation calls for the introduction of the more abstract concepts of disease and diagnosis. The abstract medical model is

Etiology → Pathology → Symptomatology
→ Disease → Outcome

Discussion of etiology and pathology is beyond the scope of this chapter, but this is no problem since many diseases were diagnosed and treated before etiology and pathology were known.

The position taken in this chapter, as elsewhere in this book, is that the complexities of constructing comprehensive theories and developing highly predictive systems in the behavioral science require the application of multivariate analytic techniques implemented by the high-speed electronic computer. Conferences of various clinicians of different backgrounds and beliefs are incapable of reaching agreement on which patient variables should enter into the process, let alone developing useful comprehensive psychiatric classification systems. No aggregate of minds will suffice to handle the complexity of the multitude of configural possibilities that need to be brought into consideration.

## 8  DIAGNOSIS

As Zubin, Sutton, Salzinger, Salzinger, Duvdock, and Peretz (1961) pointed out (see Zubin, 1967) there are at least 50 different types of psychiatric classifications around the world. Actual classifications with local hospital modifications in either nomenclature or application probably are nearly as numerous as the hospitals themselves.

Zubin (1967) reviewed the overall agreement in psychiatric diagnoses reported by various investigators and found it ranged from 64% to 84%. Kreitman's summary (Kreitman, Sainsbury, Morrissey, Towers, & Scrivener, 1960) showed 24%–89% agreements reported for gross categories; for subcategories it ranged from 12% to 74%. Guertin (1956) asked six skilled psychiatrists to designate symptom rating associated with five schizophrenic subclasses. Intercorrelations revealed agreement on subtypes ranged from 7% to 32% of the variance. Factor analysis disclosed some of the basis for disagreement in nomenclature.

Three rather similar studies explored the degree of homogeneity of symptomatology for diagnostic categories generally regarded as dependable. Factor analyses should show single type factors. Guertin (1958) found four type factors for paranoid schizophrenics, Wittenborn and Bailey (1952) found six type factors for involutional psychotics, and Wittenborn and Weiss (1952) found six type factors for manics.

Ward, C. H., Beck, Mendelson, Mock, and Erbangh (1962) analyzed sources of disagreement in psychiatric diagnoses and found almost two-thirds of the disagreement was attributable to inadequate nomenclature. Inconsistency for the diagnostician accounted for another third of the disagreement, with only 5% stemming from inconsistency of the patient.

W. G. Smith (1966) attempted to reduce the major sources of disagreement in diagnosis by asking clinicians to establish 38 stereotypes of mental disorders using 41 symptoms. Agreement on stereotypes was a high 86%, demonstrating the value of quantifying the patient variables. A computer program then matched the patient's symptom ratings to the stereotypes to provide the likely diagnosis. Such an approach is a concrete demonstration of the value of eliminating vagueness in nomenclature; further, this approach eliminates the personal errors in matching patient characteristics to the diagnostic pattern. Of course the procedure assumes reasonably valid evaluation of symptoms, which is not too hard to accept under carefully arranged conditions. However, a major weakness is the necessity to assume that existing stereotypes will be highly useful for predicting outcome and recommending valuable treatment.

There is considerable evidence that existing diagnostic schemes are not soundly based on symptomatology. Not only is diagnosis weakly tied to symptoms, but the nature of the prescribed treatment for each diagnosis seems even less closely tied to diagnosis. A study by Bannister, Salmon, and Lieberman (1964) looked at the 14 therapies prescribed for patients with gross diagnosis of neurosis, psychosis, or brain damage. Assuming that the most frequently prescribed therapy for a given diagnosis was the "correct" one, then 818 patients out of 1,000 had the "incorrect" therapy prescribed for them. When the gross diagnoses were broken down into subclasses, the number of "incorrect" prescriptions dropped to 671—still hardly satisfactory from the patient's point of view.

## 9 DIAGNOSIS AND OUTCOME

Of course, all the blame for the weak link between diagnosis and therapy cannot be placed on diagnosis since most psychiatrists have found their faith in the value of these treatments rather shaken. H. J. Eysenck (1952a) reviewed the reports of 19 investigators of improvement rates under psychotherapy and concluded that there is little evidence to support the view that psychotherapy facilitates recovery from neurotic disorder. Similarly, electroshock underwent such severe research attack that most shock boxes are now gathering dust on hospital shelves. Nor is pharmacological treatment entrenched strongly enough to be impervious to attack.

It is more encouraging to learn that diagnosis is related to case outcome. Norris' English sample (1959) showed a high release rate for manic depressives and neurotics, but low for schizophrenics and geriatric disorders. Zubin, Sutton, Salzinger, et al. (1961) reviewed reports about outcomes for subtypes of schizophrenia and found surprisingly high agreement between prognosis and diagnosis. Some caution in interpreting these results is necessary since history of previous hospitalization and long-term maladjustment, which are fairly good predictors of outcome, could cause symptomatically questionable cases to be assigned to the categories customarily associated with a poor prognosis.

## 10 PROBLEMS CONFRONTING PSYCHIATRY

The present state of psychiatry as a predictive system is highly inadequate. The reasons for inadequacy are many; therefore, we will summarize them here to bring them together.

Diagnosis must be ultimately based on patient variables or configural patterns of them. There is little uniformity in practice as to what types of patient variables should define diagnoses. Even the present description of a diagnosis includes a conglomeration of historic and current variables. There is no uniform way specified for measuring the variables, it being left to the psychiatrist whether to use test, questionnaire, or interview (rating) data, or any combination of these. Furthermore, the variables are not quantitatively stated, so it is left to the clinician's judgment (which is subject to his own personality) to decide whether a patient has a pathological degree of a trait. Unfortunately, the objectivity and quantification inherent in psychological testing has failed to offer the assistance it should. Too often psychometric researchers have been on wild goose chases developing projective instruments that can add nothing except confusion to what already can be obtained from the mental status interview.

With all the confusion about the patient variables to be used for establishing and employing a diagnostic system, it is not surprising that the definitional link between patient variables and diagnosis remains unclear. Nor does this situation in the present practice of psychiatry permit us to look clearly at the relationship between personality dimensions and diagnosis to help us decide whether to elaborate the definitional connections or to eliminate them.

The definition of diagnostic groups depends more on clinical experience and literature stored away in the psychiatrist's head than on any explicit statements about symptomatology and configurations. While the relationship between diagnosis and outcome is high enough to encourage the use of diagnostic classification, it is low in comparison to nonpsychiatric disease models.

Whereas one of the main purposes of diagnosis is to recommend the best treatment, the relationship between diagnosis and appropriate treatment is unbearably low. Some of the difficulty in establishing diagnosis-treatment links stem from the weak classification system that prevents identification of a homogeneous group of patients to be studied for the benefits from specific treatments.

Psychiatrists and psychologists have been trying to patch up the system for decades without much success. A radically new approach is called for; some suggested directions in the use of analytic statistics are discussed in the next section.

## 11  MULTIVARIATE APPROACHES: INTRODUCTION

In relating patient variables to outcome, the first decision to be made is whether to relate the data level variables directly to outcome or link them through theoretical constructs such as syndrome and diagnosis. The empirical approach has been rather unproductive, as seen in an earlier part of this chapter. The need for some form of configural view of patient variables has been illustrated, but these configurations are themselves theoretical constructs. Before we consider theoretical approaches, the suggestion first made in 1947 will be examined.

Ellson (1947) saw the possibility of cataloguing the scores a person obtained on a battery of tests (or test items) and noting the associated criterion value. With a large

catalogue or norm of such profiles and their known criterion values, it is necessary only to take a new profile and see which of the norm profiles it matches best and use the catalogued criterion value as the predicted value for the new subject. Such an approach becomes increasingly feasible with machine technology improvements in speed and storage capacity.

Such an approach almost eliminates the likelihood that a clinician can keep the norms in his head and match the new profile to them, thereby removing him from diagnostic decision making. If the clinician were to employ the norm tables like a computer, he should be fired for being inefficient and inaccurate. While that, in part, accounts for little attention being given to Ellson's approach, there is a more theoretical objection.

The use of a single person's catalogued profile and criterion score as the norm to judge a new profile and predict the criterion score is a very unreliable practice. Although it is possible to group similar norm profiles together into clusters by various methods to increase reliability, such a procedure constitutes typing people and as such introduces the theoretical construct of type. If the reader has been persuaded that the empirical approach holds little promise, he will be ready to follow along on the possibilities of employing theoretical constructs for relating patient variables to outcome.

Even though we have decided to go the route of theoretical constructs we are faced immediately with another important decision. Is a disease such as paranoid schizophrenia a designation of a *type* of pathological person or is it merely a description of a collection of symptoms covarying in a sample of pathological cases? The position in this chapter is that the term *mental disease* corresponds to the type (see chapter 11) rather than syndrome model for the following reasons:

1. Unique configurations found in a single diagnostic type frequently are composed of variables that do not covary in a general psychiatric sample. They are covariates for only that one type of individual. For example, while hostility and expressiveness are two important traits found together in paranoid schizophrenics, they are not highly correlated together in a sample of mixed schizophrenics.

2. Psychopathological disorders are generally viewed as whole-body dysfunctions rather than as encompassing only several traits or reactions. That is, the whole person is affected in a unique way so that he functions or looks like others in that type category, assuming personality traits are constant. (It will be recalled that personality traits were brought into our system to explain symptom differences in disease mates.)

3. Unlike many physical diseases, the major psychiatric diseases usually are mutually exclusive. That is, a person usually is not diagnosed as a paranoid schizophrenic and a neurotic at the same time.

4. Common word usage affirms that the psychiatric illness is a type label not a trait or syndrome deviation. For instance, usually we say "a person is a paranoid schizophrenic," rather than saying he has paranoid schizophrenia.

5. As Lorr (1966) has succinctly stated, "Types thrive on the presence of discontinuities." If there are a small number of rather discrete psychopathological disorders, as there appear to be, they will correspond to types of people rather than the numerous possible conbinations of degrees of syndrome presences.

It may be, as Lorr suggested, that the neurotic disorders may prove to be better classified by syndromes, and the psychoses by type classification. Though typing of psychoses has been tried and found satisfactory, there is little evidence to judge the value of typing neurotics. We must await further evidence before we can be sure it will prove equally valuable. Note well that while asserting the preference for a type of approach to psychopathology, we are not denying the superiority of the trait approach to establishing personality descriptions.

It seems likely that in addition to symptoms (patient data variables), syndrome factors, and type factors, another more abstract concept, *diagnosis,* must be introduced. The diagnosis, the ultimate classification, can then be established by reference to type, syndrome, and patient variables simultaneously to provide for the nuances that differentiate rather similar patients with different outcomes. Such theoretical complexity makes it impossible to set forth a useful, elaborated theory now; but it will keep before us the ultimate structure of a useful theory for the future.

Now it is appropriate to consider moving from the empirical model of Ellson to using clusters of people in the norm catalogue. Visual inspection of correspondences in profiles may be used as a basis for clustering people with a small number of cases. McQuitty (1961) set forth many techniques for clustering profiles on a more objective empirical basis. The more sophisticated reader will immediately think of the intercorrelations among profiles as a way of describing similarities so that clusters of people can be formed. Unfortunately, two profiles may be highly correlated because they have the same shape yet be very different in average level of the scores. For example, Matthews, Guertin, and Reitan (1962) found Rapaport's control group profile correlated .83 with their right-hemisphere brain-damaged group despite the fact that the brain-damaged profile showed marked deviations of subtests from one another and the overall intellectual level was much lower.

Many writers have proposed using some measure of the distance between pairs of scores on the two profiles as a measure of similarity. See Guertin (1971) and Guertin and Bailey (1970) for procedure and program for factor analyzing distances. It is usually contended that the distance measure matches profiles for level, shape, and average variance simultaneously. Making such an assumption about the value of the distance measure in psychopathology probably is a serious error. Profiles of low average variance and at the same average level can give relatively small distance scores, yet the shapes of the two profiles may be exact opposites. The configurations of symptoms and their severity (average deviation) are more critical features for classification of psychopathology than is average level. For this reason, the writer developed a procedure for successively analyzing profiles (Guertin, 1966). First, they are intercorrelated and analyzed into similar shape families; then each family is analyzed independently using a distance measure; thus, clusters within the shape family are identified as having similar level or similar average variance. The procedure employs successive factor analysis and is expensive to perform, even though it has been programed for computer analysis. Lorr (1966) used both distance and correlation as similarity measures for his grouping procedure, but not successively.

Other workers (Cattell & Coulter, 1966; McQuitty, 1961; Nunnally, 1962; Saunders & Schuman, 1962; Sawrey, Keller & Conger, 1960) have proposed procedures for identifying clusters or types of profiles (people) based primarily on distance functions. Their procedures are much more eco-

nomical, hence practical. However, the usefulness in classification problems of psychopathology may prove limited.

Despite the promise of the type approach to classification in psychopathology, the syndrome approach (clusters of symptoms instead of people) has been given much more attention. Perhaps this is not surprising since conventional factor analysis ($R$) has a longer history than the transposed form ($Q$) that leads to types of people. The syndrome is a theoretical construct based on the contingency of several symptoms found in a general sample of psychiatric cases.

The symptom data may be from mental status or ward behavior ratings, questionnaire responses or test responses for either $R$ or $Q$ factor analyses. The symptoms or test items all are intercorrelated, and clusters of symptoms or items emerge. The intercorrelation matrix usually is factor analyzed and the resulting matrix is rotated for meaningfulness to an approximation of simple structure (see Cattell, 1952a). The factors so identified constitute the syndromes, which are then regarded as the basis for classification. The corresponding operation, using personality items with average people, produces factors called *traits*. By analogy we could call the syndromes *symptom traits*, but the term *syndrome* is retained in this chapter.

## 12 MULTIVARIATE APPROACHES: FORMULATING SYNDROMES

T. V. Moore (1933) initiated research in this area by studying the interrelationships among 32 symptoms describing 367 schizophrenics and manic depressives. Degan (1952) reanalyzed the data with factor analysis. Dahlstrom (1949) performed a similar study but included a broader sample of patients.

The writer made a similar investigation (Guertin, 1952a) but restricted the sample to schizophrenics. Wittenborn (1950) and Wittenborn and Bailey (1951) reported two studies based on rather broad hospital samples. Lorr, O'Connor, and Stafford (1960) vigorously pursued answers to questions raised in the previous studies. The research of Lorr and his associates has shown the continuity needed to make sense out of the scattered studies using various samples of subjects with different types of patient variables.

Studies are reviewed by Lorr, Klett, and McNair (1963) and integrated with the earlier ones to confirm 10 interview syndromes and 3 ward syndromes. The interview syndromes are excitement, hostile belligerence, paranoid projection, grandiose expansiveness, perceptual distortion, anxious intropunitiveness, retardation and apathy, motor disturbances, disorientation, and conceptual disorganization. The three ward syndromes, which are less clearly established, are hostile belligerence, resistiveness, and overactivity. Lorr (1971) reported several cross-cultural confirmations of previously identified syndromes and suggested several additions.

Two other lines of investigation merit brief attention here. First is the concept of two types of schizophrenics called process and reactive, which has produced many research reports, yet holds little promise. Rather than constituting a type or syndrome classification, they appear to be two ends of a continuous dimension describing premorbid history and relating to prognosis.

The other area of investigation revolves around H. J. Eysenck, who has persisted in maintaining a view of psychopathology based on two independent dimensions, a psychotic and a neurotic factor. He attacked the multifactor approach and he and Lorr exchanged views in the Journal of Clinical Psychology in 1963. With data variables taken from a highly abstract level and appropriately manipulated statistically, a small number of factors can be observed. Lorr showed that he too can reduce factor complexity by successive factoring of lower order factor matrices to obtain higher order factors until he is left with only one general factor. Lorr's three second-order factors correspond somewhat with the schizophrenic categories: catatonic, paranoid, and hebephrenic.

The chief merit of exploring second and higher order factors would lie in studying etiology and physical aspects of the disease rather than providing classification. Distinctions between cases based on first-order factor scores seem important in indicating treatment and prognosis—the goal of psychiatric classification.

In the studies reviewed in this section there is a mixture of various types of patient variables. Cattell's classification into *surface traits* and *source traits*, depending on the nature of the variables entering the factor analysis, is discussed in the introductory chapters of this book. The number and nature of syndrome factors derived will depend on whether surface or source traits are employed. For example, the surface traits obtained from the scales of the MMPI present a different factor space than when source traits are obtained by analyzing the individual MMPI items. These source traits from the MMPI seem to correspond closely to those in the Cattell 16 Personality Factor battery. It would appear desirable to seek source trait factors to provide comparability between studies of syndrome factors.

## 13 MULTIVARIATE APPROACHES: FORMULATING TYPES

The writer was the first to employ transposed factor analysis in an attempt to identify types in a sample of schizophrenics (Guertin, 1952b). Only a few other factor-analytic studies appeared subsequently, and all contained shortcomings similar to the first until Lorr entered this area of activity.

A basic problem in this method lies in describing identified type factors in a communicable way. When a syndrome factor is presented, it can be described by the symptom items that are loaded on it (the factor matrix). However, when a type factor is presented, the corresponding factor loadings are for the subjects in the analysis. It is meaningless to the reader, who does not know them, to say that Frank, Sarah, and John loaded better than .50 on Type Factor I, and it is more misleading to name the factor than it is in the case of conventional factor analysis. One is forced to describe the symptoms of these heavily loaded subjects to get an idea of what the type factor represents, but the symptom data have been lost in the factor analysis. The writer (Guertin, 1961b) proposed the use of the duMas Manifest Structure Analysis as a way of relating the symptoms back to the obtained type factors. A simpler procedure was used by Stammeyer, who correlated each symptom with each type factor. There are objections, however, to both these techniques.

Lorr took two big strides in one by developing a sound set of syndromes before attacking the typing problem. His use of factor-analytically based syndromes as data variables instead of symptoms provides a more even control of variables entering the determination of the types; at the same time, his method reduces the number of variables needed to describe the types. If one assumes, as is often done, that the syndrome areas should be equally represented in the profiles being used for typing, he can weight each syndrome score inversely to the correlation of that syndrome with all other syndromes.

The second major problem in developing factor-analytically based types lies in devising a suitable statistic for expressing similarities of profiles or profile-pattern matches. The interested reader is referred to the theoretical and mathematical discussion of the general problem of typing given by Cattell and Coulter (1966). So far the emphasis has been on the use of distance measures, but there is considerable doubt as to the suitability of such measures. The writer's solution, mentioned earlier, consists of successively analyzing for shape families through correlations and then for other clustering of distance and average variance through a distance measure. As yet there has been little application of this procedure in typing. It would be premature to set forth research findings of types as serious proposals for psychiatric classification as long as results depended only on distance measures.

Lorr's more recent book (1966), on typing psychotics, is exploratory but most helpful. He and his colleagues analyzed profile similarity with both correlation and a distance measure and obtained similar, although not identical type structures. They found persistence of type (based on correlation similarity) even when there was case improvement after treatment. Whereas chronic patients revealed similar type structure to that of acute patients, two additional factors appeared. The value of typing was evidenced by their findings, which suggested that their identifiable types were related to "differences in background, clinical condition, and outcome."

The findings of types presented by Lorr are by sex, duration of illness, and type of variable employed. The reader is referred to the book for details, but the acute types found were as follows: excited, excited-hostile, hostile paranoid, hallucinated paranoid, intropunitive, grandiose paranoid, anxious-disorganized, retarded-disorganized (female), disoriented (male), retarded motor disturbed (male), and excited-disorganized (female).

Other attempts to derive types of psychiatric patients through linkage analysis have been reported. They will not be reviewed here because, while linkage analysis has merit as an empirical tool, it may be too empirical to resolve data into the minimum number of patterns required for a useful classification system.

## 14 MULTIVARIATE APPROACHES: PRAGMATIC CONSIDERATIONS

Almost all investigators who have contributed to the methodology of classifying psychopathology have had to deal with immediate problems first. The historical order has been first to contribute to the methodology, then to establish useful variables, then to develop a syndrome classification, and, finally to produce a type classification. Important problems still exist in the field because they have been postponed for consideration in later investigations.

The value of a proposed classification lies in the hope it will lead to prediction of outcome and provide recommended best treatment and management. It is possible to set up the classification through use of multivariate analysis of patient data while simultaneously inserting pragmatic tests of prediction as a criterion for retaining symptoms, syndromes, and types. In practice, this has been too imposing a task; therefore, the process has been divided. First, the classification is established and then nonpredictive syndromes and types can be eliminated. Such an approach probably will lead to classification that is not easily

modified later because the fault often will lie with the choice of type of patient variable and the particular variables utilized. Changing variables will necessitate modifying syndromes and then types as well.

Overall, Hollister, Johnson, and Pennington (1966) quantitatively derived three depressed subtype categories and were able to show that when two drugs were administered, the response was predictable from a knowledge of the subtype classification of the patient. M. M. Katz (1968), working with quantitatively derived subgroups of schizophrenics, also showed that with two drugs one can predict outcome from a knowledge of the subtype classification of the patient.

The term *diagnosis* should be used to indicate the application of a taxonomy that has proved predictive. The term *disease* should be reserved for the diagnostic label that not only has proved prognostically useful but implies a uniform etiology and pathology. We are still far from the level of development of disease reached in physical medicine, but good classification is helpful in establishing a disease. By homogeneous grouping of cases, the common etiology and pathology as well as the prognosis are likely to become more apparent.

Investigators employing factor analysis for establishing classification have studied either symptom factors or personality factors (traits), but seldom both simultaneously. If both are studied together, they are intermixed in determining factor structure. One of the next tasks is to retain the established type and symptom factors but study subfactors that develop within the factor when premorbid personality traits introduce their variance. So far, the broad sampling of heterogeneous subjects has prevented the subfactors from appearing in the results of the analyses. See Cattell (1970, p. 31) for another formulation of this problem.

Of course, a complete exploration leading to types such as Irish paranoids, Italian paranoids, etc. is impossible. However, a systematic study with the Cattell measures of personality traits seems clearly indicated. Studies of cultural differences may be subsumed under personality by bringing important cultural differentiae into additional trait dimensions, which in turn can be related systematically to the syndrome and types.

Classification also must take into account various stages of sickness, viz. course of illness. When shapes of profiles are used as a prime basis for comparison, different degrees of disturbance during course of the illness may appear as subclusters with different amount of disturbance reflected in lower or higher average variance and level. No doubt, Cattell's suggestions (1952b) of factor analyzing a single individual over time will be helpful in identifying which subclusters represent stages of the same illness.

## 15  SUMMARY

1. Types of patient variables that may contribute to classification were considered along with an evaluation of the relative value of each.

2. The relationship between personality and symptoms was discussed. While personality traits and symptoms may often be correlates, they are not necessarily so. At least for the classification of psychoses it would seem profitable to view personality traits as modifiers of symptoms and therefore necessary in a predictive system.

3. Problems in traditional ways of evaluating patient variables were discussed. The superiority of mental status symptoms as predictors of outcome was seen in a brief discussion of research findings.

4. The importance of configurations or patterns of variables, rather than depending on variables measured singly, was illustrated.

5. The meaning of the diagnostic process was discussed, and the inadequacies of present systems and current practices were presented.

6. Factor-analytic approaches to the problem of establishing a new classificatory system were explored.

7. Investigations aimed at developing syndrome factors were reviewed and discussed briefly.

8. Investigations aimed at improving methods of establishing type factors were reviewed briefly and discussed.

9. Concerns were expressed over the current theoretical approaches to classification and some suggestions were made for directing future effort.

# 27

## The Abnormal Personality: Neurosis and Delinquency

**Karl H. Delhees**
*St. Gall Graduate School of Economics,
Business and Public Administration,
Switzerland*

## 1 CLINICAL MEASUREMENT FUNCTIONALLY RELATED TO PERSONALITY STRUCTURE

A marked conceptual and experimental breakthrough has occurred in normal personality measurement by the application of refined, multivariate experimental-statistical techniques (Delhees, 1974). Precise measurements and new concepts have been introduced to the previously often cloudy discussions of deviant behavior patterns by placing them on a firm mathematico-statistical basis. It is in the framework of this development that the present chapter attempts to link the abnormal personality of the neurotic and the delinquent with the dynamics of the normal personality.

The core of what is presented here also serves as evidence that it is possible in the study of abnormal behavior to obtain a very close operational relationship between experiments and clinical concepts. In fact, the method of inquiry of the clinical and the multivariate experimentalist prove to be one. Both study the covariation of behaviors and attempt to reach the underlying concepts which account for them. Both study the variables that have shown themselves to recur in a combination of responses (Cattell, 1957b, 1967a; Cattell & Scheier, 1961;

Delhees, 1966a, b). Multivariate analysis, however, yields response patterns expressible in terms of a "specification equation" (see chapter 1).

Following this line of inquiry, we start with the assertion that neurosis and delinquency are to be located in terms of unitary response patterns, not by particular stimuli. The bulk of experimental data presented in this chapter shows that the concepts found by the multivariate experimentalist correspond to real functional unities in the organism which can be analytically separated from such patterns as anxiety, stress, depression, and introversion, with which they are frequently confused (Delhees & Cattell, 1971b). Only then can the study of therapeutic changes and experimental influences in the abnormal personality proceed.

## 2 THE PATTERN OF NEUROTICISM MEASURED BY QUESTIONNAIRE

Our discussion here is mostly concerned with measurement devices that are well founded on factor analytic research (Delhees & Cattell, 1970). We limit our description of the neurotic behavior pattern to the Sixteen Personality Factor Questionnaire, the 16 PF

(Cattell & Eber, 1966), because far more clinical profiles and specification equations have been collected on this test than on any other factored questionnaire. Truly distinctive profiles of such syndrome groups as anxiety hysterics, obsessionals, conversion hysterics, homosexuals, drug addicts, alcoholics, and criminal offense groupings have been systematically presented by Cattell (1957b, 1973), Cattell and Eber (1966), Cattell and Scheier (1961), Fuller (1966), Pierson (1964), Karson (1965), Phillips and Delhees (1967), and many others described in the *Handbook for the Sixteen Personality Factor Questionnaire* (Cattell, Eber, & Tatsuoka, 1970).

First, let us see how a group of diagnosed neurotics (all types) differs from well-adjusted members of the general adult population. As Fig. 1 shows, neurotics in the broader sense (neurotic subgroups will be discussed later) have in common low ego-strength ($C-$), low dominance ($E-$), low surgency ($F-$), low threctia ($H-$), high premsia ($I+$), high protension or projective defenses ($L+$), high autism ($M+$), high guilt-proneness ($O+$), and high ergic tension

($Q_4+$), i.e., more undischarged, unsatisfied drive. Thus the pattern of divergence on particular factors is quite selective and unique, for the clinically defined neurotic differs significantly from the normal on at least eight factors (Delhees & Cattell, 1971a). Added to these are suggestive differences, still in the maladjusted direction, of lower superego development ($G-$) and a less developed self-sentiment ($Q_3-$). If we obtain the score on the general (second-order) anxiety factor by abstracting it from $C, H, L, M, O, Q_3,$ and $Q_4$, we recognize that the neurotic is highly anxious. For example, among the components of the second-order anxiety factor, on ego-strength his average score on a 10–point scale is about 3.1, compared with 5.5 for the average (the sigma for the normal American adult population is 2.0 Stens on all factors, and the mean is 5.5), and on guilt-proneness it is about 8.3, again as compared with 5.5 for the general population average.

The appearance of low $C$, ego-weakness, in the neurotic will probably not surprise many clinicians. The low-$C$ person is easily upset, subject to moods and to neurotic

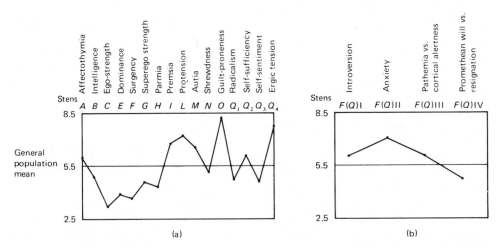

FIGURE 1 First order (a) and second order (b) differences of general neurotics and normals on the 16 Personality Factor (PF).

fatigue, and cannot achieve realistic expression of his drives and steady satisfaction for his needs. Low $C$ appears, among others, in drug addicts, in most psychotics, in alcoholics, in homosexuals, and in psychopaths (Delhees, 1966a). That ego-weakness is associated with anxiety is clearly shown by the consistent correlation of $C(-)$ and Universal Index 24 ($U.I.$ 24), the general anxiety factor in objective data to be discussed later.

A second important characteristic of the neuroticism[1] pattern is a low score on Factor $E$, dominance. This is not universally found in psychopathology; e.g., psychopaths are high on $E$. $E$ tends to be somewhat positively correlated with social status, best known from Allport's ascendance-submission reaction study (Allport & Allport, 1928). Low dominance ($E-$) occurs most markedly in neurotics, probably being a consequence of frequent failures and social disapproval and loss of self-confidence. The high $E$ person, on the other hand, has been found less prone to projection (Wenig, 1952), another characteristic of the neurotic behavior pattern (high $L$, protension or projective defenses). Submissiveness, $E(-)$, and desurgency, $F(-)$, are particularly useful in distinguishing between neurotics and psychopaths. The latter show a high endowment in both $E+$ and $F+$. Among the neurotic subcategories, the depressive neurotics are particularly low on $E$.

In addition to factors $C$, $E$, and $F$, which are highly hereditary in origin, premsia ($I$), guilt-proneness ($O$), and ergic tension ($Q_4$) are all prominent in distinguishing neurotics from normals. That the neurotic is higher on the $I$ factor, premsia, indicates an overprotected emotional sensitivity. Its generally

accepted psychological meaning (Cattell, 1957b) is that he is somewhat "spoiled." Factor $I$ has a high environmental determination, derived presumably from an upbringing favoring self-indulgence and low self-discipline.

The $H$ dimension, parmia versus threctia, seems to represent a proneness to situational anxiety and the strength of threat at the same time, a role also represented by the guilt-depression factor, $O$. At the threctic pole, $H(-)$, a ready autonomic responsiveness to threat is found which has a clear association with anxiety ($r$ of 0.33), indicating a predisposition of timidity (for $H$ has a high constitutional determination, Cattell, Blewett, & Beloff, 1955). High ergic tension (the $Q_4$ component), another cornerstone among the six primaries supporting the general anxiety factor prominent in neuroticism, is best interpreted as undischarged instinctual energy. Ergic tension has consistently been found substantially correlated with the sex drive (Cattell, 1957a; Cattell & Scheier, 1961; Rosenthal, I., 1955), agreeing with Freud's theory that sex is prominent among the undischarged drives (Delhees, 1975b).

The last of our neuroticism contributory factors is $M$, or autia, high subjectivity and disregard for reality. It is, however, not the withdrawing autism of some schizophrenic expressions. The autious person lacks practical concern, disregards security and social necessities, and is absorbed in his own thoughts. $M$ is most central among the primaries in the second-order introversion factor.

This pattern of neuroticism is distinct from that found for psychotics, except for the "central pathological pattern" of ego-weakness, $C-$ (along with $E-$ and $F-$). This pattern has been convincingly verified in the studies of Gleser and Gottschalk (1967), Cattell, Tatro, and Komlos (1968). As for

---

[1] This term is essentially equivalent to neurosis but emphasizes that neurotic deviation is factorially complex and varies continuously in amount throughout the population.

neuroticism, we may summarize that (a) neuroticism is a quite complex functional breakdown, in terms of personality processes common to all people and (b) anxiety, though highly characteristic of neurotic behavior, accounts only for part of the deviant variance.

## 3 PERSONALITY STRUCTURES IN THE VARIETIES OF NEUROTICS AND DELINQUENTS

Although neuroticism is relatively sharply visible, it does, of course, show gradations. For practical clinical purposes, the profile of gross neurotic-normal differences based only on general neurotic factor deviations (in a sample that mixes neurotic syndrome groups) the yield of a total level of severity of neuroticism may suffice. This is essentially the type of definition of neuroticism found in the unifactor theory of H. J. Eysenck (1953c) and certain other clinical theorists. However, the importance of profile differences specifying modes of indi-vidual neurotic expression, notably in the anxiety reaction or "anxiety hysteria," depressive reaction, conversion reaction, obsessive compulsive reaction, and psycho-somatic complaints becomes apparent when we wish to refer to real differences in etiology, expression, and course of neurosis. In other words, we need to compare the factor profiles for groups of patients which have been clinically placed in these different neurotic syndrome groups. Figure 2 gives a graphic visual summary of these deviations on the primaries. For comparison, the delin-quent profile has been included.

Each horizontal vector in Fig. 2 can be read as a statement of a particular neurotic expression in questionnaire factors, and each syndrome group is significantly different from the others on a number of distinct personality dimensions. For example, a neu-rotic with high Factor $M$ is predisposed to depressive manifestations of neurosis, while a neurotic with a low score on $M$ shows a leaning toward conversion reactions or psychosomatic disorder, where complaints

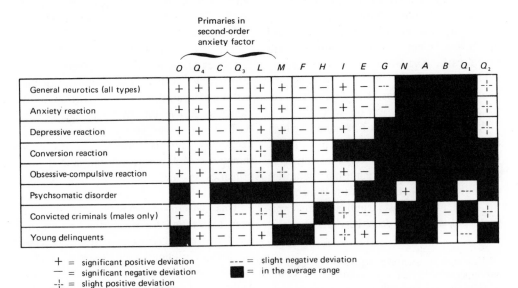

+ = significant positive deviation
− = significant negative deviation
-¦- = slight positive deviation
--- = slight negative deviation
■ = in the average range

**FIGURE 2** Deviations on 16 Personality Factor primaries in various neurotic and delinquent group types.

16 Personality factor primary source traits

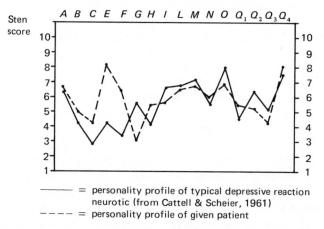

——— = personality profile of typical depressive reaction
        neurotic (from Cattell & Scheier, 1961)
- - - - = personality profile of given patient

**FIGURE 3**  Computational example of the profile similarity coefficient $r_p$ for comparison of two given profiles.

$d$ = difference in Sten scores on each factor of patient from diagnostic profile.

$d$ =  −.3   −.7   −1.5   −4.00  −3.0   +2.5   −1.3   +.9   +.3   +.4   −.4   +1.0   −1.0   −.9   +1.2   +.8   −.6.

$d^2$ =   .09    .49   2.25   16.00   9.00   6.25   1.69   .81   .09   .16   .16   1.00   1.00   .81   1.44   .64   .36.

$\Sigma d^2$ = 41.24.

$$r_p = \frac{122.72 - d^2}{122.72 + d^2} = \frac{122.72 - 41.24}{122.72 + 41.24} = .49.$$ Significant for 16 elements. $r_p$ at p = .01 is .45.

Conclusion: Patient shows significant affiliation to the depression-reaction type.

are mainly of physical symptoms. Similarly, in the person with high ergic frustration, as shown by a high $Q_4$ score, and associated with a strong guilt reaction, expressed by a high $O$ score, the neurotic tendencies are more likely to express themselves as conversion reactions, whereas a person with less tension and feelings of guilt is more prone to psychosomatic manifestations. (Beyond these and other examples, it remains to be noted that neurotic syndrome groups can be located also in terms of second-order factors derivable from the 16 primary factors. The interested reader is referred to Cattell & Scheier, 1961).

One may well ask, "How does a given individual resemble these neurotic syndrome groups?" The clinician can find a precise

answer to this question by using the $r_p$ pattern similarity coefficient (Cattell, 1949) or similar devices to compare the patient's profile with the standard syndrome-norm profiles. Figure 3 provides this comparison between a hypothetical clinical case and a special syndrome group with the neurotic category. The resemblance to the depressive reaction type is significant at the $p < .01$ level by J. L. Horn's (1961b) significance tables. It should be noted that we are examining here the deviation on functionally distinct factor dimensions in terms of total patterns rather than differences of means.

From the profile information in Fig. 2 it will be evident that although important differences between the neurotic and the delinquent personality remain, there exist striking similarities. Indeed, even convicted, hardened criminals have a profile that looks much like the general neurotic profile with less pronounced anxiety and introversion though they still clearly exist ( Knapp, 1963, 1964). In the usual delinquent case there is the problem of high emotionality and uncontrolled impulses and moods (revealed by factor $C-$, ego-weakness) that defeat the criminal's effectiveness in dealing with his life. We may therefore regard the delinquent personality as mostly stemming from failure to acquire normal mechanisms of ego and superego control. As Fig. 2 shows, both are clearly below average in the delinquent, but also somewhat subnormal in the neurotic, supporting Mowrer's position (1966) that neurotics *and* delinquents suffer from superego defect. The delinquent may attempt to solve his problems by resorting to drugs or alcohol or—when frustrated—may impulsively discharge his anger without restraint. Therefore, from the standpoint of practical clinical use of these measurement findings, therapy should aim at building up the superego rather than attempting to reduce anxiety and guilt feelings, as is often the practice in psychoanalytic therapy.

Young delinquents show higher dominance, $E$ factor, and higher surgency, $F$ factor, and no significant deviation from normal on the $O$ factor, guilt-proneness, (Fig. 2). The work of Tyler and Kelly (1963) and Pierson (1964) with the High School Personality Questionnaire (HSPQ, Cattell & Beloff, 1962), dealing with essentially the same primary factors as with adults, brings out the tendency of the young delinquent to be more extraverted. This is independently borne out by a follow-up study by Burt (1948) employing teacher's ratings on— among others—habitual offenders. They were rated "extraverted" in 54% of all cases, and neurotics only in 14%. Further evidence on this comes from the rating and case

history studies on delinquents by Quay (1964a, 1964b), Peterson, Quay, and Cameron (1959), and Peterson, Quay, and Tiffany (1961). Though this may be our first aid in separating delinquents from neurotics and normals, other personality differences exist, notably in a lower self-sentiment ($Q_3$) development and greater individualistic obstructiveness (Factor $J+$) in boys (Karson, 1965). Similar results have been reported for the 16 PF factors on Borstal girls by A. J. W. Taylor (1965) in New Zealand. Aside from these personality differences, there is a 0.3 correlation of intelligence with social status (Cattell, 1966j) and a tendency for less criminal behavior with higher social status, as shown in the studies of Hartshorne, May and Maller (1929). Certainly the impression one gets from consulting room experience in the child guidance clinic and prison wards fits the picture very well as provided by personality factor measurement.

When one weights the scores of young delinquents on the HSPQ according to their significant deviation from the general population on functionally distinct personality factors, one obtains an almost complete separation of the delinquent group from a nondelinquent group. Pierson (1964) has shown that a weighted composite set out in a specification equation (see chapter 1) can be used to predict maximally the liability to delinquency. This work has also resulted in predicting response to treatment, achievement in vocational training, and general achievement in school. It is interesting to see that 42% of the variance of (achievement in) vocational training is due to personality, leaving some doubts about the value of ability and aptitude measures alone as predictors of such achievement. It should not surprise us that, if personality factors contribute so much to the prediction of school achievement, adding measures of motivation and interest strength should predict still more effectively the success of rehabilitating the delinquent. We shall return to the full possibilities of dynamic measurement after an investigatioon of the results from applying objective personality measures to neurosis and delinquency.

## 4 EVIDENCE OF NEUROTICISM AND DELINQUENCY FROM OBJECTIVE-ANALYTIC BATTERIES

Personality factors are in general more easily interpretable in ratings (L data) and questionnaire (Q data) responses than in the T data (objective-analytic) sphere, yet there is empirical evidence for objective-test dimensions that capture aspects of normal personality never before seen in ratings and questionnaires on which clinical psychology has traditionally depended for the diagnosis of neurosis and delinquency (Cattell, 1946, 1957b, 1965c, and chapters 2, 3, and 4).

Granted the reality or existence of these objective-test dimensions, there is still another reason for studying the differences of neurotics, delinquents, and normals by objective test batteries. Unlike question-naires, objective tests tend to measure (in miniature situations) what the patient actually does, rather than what his opinion is about what he does. Furthermore, the risk of faking is considerably reduced here because the person is acting without knowing which aspects of his behavior are in fact being scored. The significance of having such tests is that they can be used as meaningful, standard, objective, and check-able estimates of neuroticism and delinquency and thus define clearly and operationally each of these concepts. In this survey, however, we cannot pursue the technical issues of objective-analytic factors. The interested reader is instead referred to fuller, systematic discussions of their nature and properties elsewhere (Cattell, 1957b; Hundleby, Pawlik, & Cattell, 1965; and chapter 4).

The next question the clinician will naturally want to ask is, What are the dimensions in objective tests on which significant differences exist between neurotics, delinquents, and normals? Table 1 looks at these differences. The personality dimensions on which neurotics differ from normals most con-

**TABLE 1** Comparison of criminals, neurotics, and normals on selected personality factors objectively measured

| Factor index (universal index, U. I) | Source trait | Criminals and normals | | Criminals and neurotics | | Neurotics and normals | |
|---|---|---|---|---|---|---|---|
| | | p value | Higher | p value | Higher | p value | Higher |
| U.I. 16 | Unbound ego | | | .01 | Criminals | .01 | Normals |
| U.I. 22 | Emotional frustration | | | | | .01 | Neurotics |
| U.I. 23 | Mobilization | | | | | .01 | Normals |
| U.I. 24 | Anxiety | .01 | Criminals | | | .01 | Neurotics |
| U.I. 25 | Composed realism | .01 | Normals | .05 | Neurotics | .01 | Normals |
| U.I. 26 | Self-centeredness | .05 | Normals | | | .01 | Normals |
| U.I. 28 | Rigid superego | .01 | Normals | | | .05 | Neurotics |
| U.I. 30 | Independence | .05 | Normals | | | | |
| U.I. 32 | Extraversion | .01 | Normals | | | .01 | Normals |
| U.I. 33 | Dourness | .05 | Normals | | | | |
| U.I. 35 | Disillusionment | .05 | Criminals | | | | |

sistently and at a high level of significance have been called the neurotic process factors (Universal Index, *U.I.*): *U.I.* 22(–), 29(–), 16(–), 23(–), and 24(–). The factors *U.I.* 19(–), 21(–), 32(–), 25(–) and possibly 28 and 34, on which neurotics differ from normals at a lesser but still significant level, have been called the neurotic-contributory factors (Cattell & Scheier, 1961). What stands out on the face of things in Table 1 is that the diagnosis of neuroticism and delinquency can only be understood, as in the previously discussed questionnaire responses, by considering several of these specifically defined and measurable source-trait dimensions. In fact, as Cattell and Scheier (1961) showed, the degree of separation of neurotics from normals by multiple discriminant function weights, applied to the factor scores of 7 or 8 significantly different dimensions, is impressive.

The way in which particular factors in neurosis operate makes good psychological sense. Consider, for example, the regression factor *U.I.* 23. It was discovered independently by Cattell (1933b, 1948a) and H. J. Eysenck (1947). Eysenck called it *the* "neuroticism factor" because it was found to distinguish significantly between neurotics and normals. Cattell suggested the specific interpretation "mobilization-regression" because the central nature of the responses most highly loading in this factor appeared to be an inability of the person to mobilize possessed habits or skills when facing relatively sudden demands for adjustment. The low score of the neurotic on *U.I.* 23 appears to be—in accordance with general clinical observation—the result of chronic fatigue, lowered coordination, and inability to cope with problems. Among those tests showing a high correlation with the *U.I.* 23 factor (at its negative pole) are high sway suggestibility, high motor-perceptual rigidity, low endurance, low effectiveness of

concentration in calculation, poor immediate memory, and poor two-hand coordination.

*U.I.* 23, however, is not the only sign of the neurotic conflict. The *U.I.* 28 or superego source-trait represents particular dynamic conflict adjustments to social demands (of authority and the superego). Like *U.I.* 23, its negative pole suggests ineffective control of resources, but it differs from the regression factor in being more an ineffectiveness in handling events in the environment. As evidence for this, *U.I.* 28(–) tests involve slow mobilization, low basal metabolic rate, and higher criticalness of evaluation. The internal properties of such tests (tests of the O-A battery), may be studied in the larger Objective Test Compendium by Cattell and Warburton (1967).

The theoretical interpretation as to why these and other dimensions (Table 1) are associated with neuroticism has been discussed fully in connection with the genesis of neurosis by Cattell and Scheier (1961) and Eysenck (1957). It is suggested from the evidence on nature-nurture ratios with the Multiple Abstract Variance Analysis (MAVA) design (see Loehlin's chapter 13) by Cattell, Kristy, and Stice (1952) and Eysenck and Prell (1951) with twins, that a certain kind of constitutional, temperamental predisposition has a higher probability of becoming neurotic than others. The evidence is that *U.I.* 32(–), the inviant tendency to avoid people, *U.I.* 17, the tendency to become inhibited by failure, *U.I.* 21(–), the lack of nervous energy, and *U.I.* 23(–), the regression of interest, come close to intelligence in being substantially constitutionally determined; whereas the importance of environment finds its expression mostly in two neurotic-process factors, *U.I.* 16(–) tendency to make little attempt at decisive and aggressive handling of the enviroment, and *U.I.* 22, the cortertia factor or activation level. The correlation of +.59 between U.I. 24 (anxiety) and presence in an institution for children from "broken homes" (found by Hundleby, 1968) is another important piece of evidence for the link between this personality trait and possibly an early disturbed family relationship.

In glancing back at Table 1 and looking at the comparison of criminals with neurotics and criminals with normals it is of interest to note that where these factors concern personality disorganization, they operate in the same direction for criminals and neurotics, as seen in U.I. 24 (anxiety vs. adjustment) and U.I. 25 (realism vs. inflexibility). But where inhibition is concerned, as in U.I. 16, which has been called unbound, assertive ego versus bound, disciplined ego, there is a significant difference in the direction of the criminals' showing subnormal inhibition and the neurotics' showing abnormally high inhibition. As Burt (1948) long ago brought out, and the observations of Hammer (1958) and D. E. Rose (1949) confirm, normals tend to fall between neurotics and delinquents on certain personality factors. The study by Knapp (1965) on enlisted Navy men in the brig strengthens

this conclusion by showing that the brig sample is conspicuously different on U.I. 20, social conformity (tendency to go with the group); U.I. 24, anxiety and maladjustment; U.I. 26, self-centeredness; U.I. 29, overresponsiveness; and U.I. 30, independence (Delhees, 1972).

It may be of interest here to look at the behavioral tests which come together in the important self-centeredness factor, U.I. 26, so central in delinquency (Cattell, 1965c; Knapp, 1965). The individual high on these measures (Table 2) tends to be highly fluent about his own interests. He takes disapproval badly. He shows great persistence in reaching his goals. Finally, he shows determined control of direct behavior and cultured introspection (Cattell, 1965c; Hundleby, Pawlik, & Cattell, 1965). Unfortunately, the etiology of this dimension is largely unknown. However, because it is one of the most important associations with delinquency, it deserves far more extensive experimental study than has yet been given.

Although the other factors separating delinquents are equally interesting, space permits only a concluding note in that if one uses the multiple discriminant function method to produce a weighted score on the

**TABLE 2**  *U.I.* 26. Self-centeredness or narcissistic self versus low self-command

| Master index (MI) number[a] | Significantly correlating objective tests | Average factor loading |
|---|---|---|
| *M.I.* 273 | Higher proportion of fluency on self | +.33 |
| *M.I.* 167a | Better immediate memory for attitudes checked | +.31 |
| *M.I.* 24 a–d | Higher ratio of final to initial performance: C. M. S.[b] | +.41 |
| *M.I.* 105 | Higher proportion of threatening objects seen in unstructured drawings | +.12 |
| *M.I.* 161 a,b | Higher ratio of performance under approval relative to disapproval | +.25 |
| *M.I.* 2 | More preference for form over color in sorting | −.24 |
| | Higher achievement (grade point average) | +.29 |

[a]The master index number is the means of reproducing in research the exact test operations by reference to the Objective Test Compendium of Cattell and Warburton (1967).

[b]Cursive Miniature Situations Test.

O–A personality traits to give maximum separation on these samples of neurotics, criminals, and normals, a tolerably high separation can be obtained.

## 5  THE CONTRIBUTION OF DYNAMIC MEASUREMENT TO NEUROSIS AND DELINQUENCY

The integration of the personality source trait measurement approach to neuroticism and delinquency on one side and the dynamic approach which attributes everything to a complex conflict on the other occupies us in this section. That neurotics differ significantly on a number of general personality factors (Fig. 1 and Table 1) does not negate the possibility (Rickels, Cattell, Aaronson, Gray, Weise, & Yee, 1966; Hunt, Ewing, LaForge, & Gilbert, 1959) that some of these general personality dimensions, e.g., ego-strength or the self-sentiment, can be changed in the normal direction by the therapist's efforts to untangle a conflict. The task is to find quantitatively where drive tension is high, what particular forces are in conflict, how demanding the superego is, the strength of the ego, etc. The conceptual system in which such research has developed, is known as the *dynamic calculus* (Cattell, 1950a, 1957b, 1959). Such concepts describe a series of motivational components (e.g., the id, the ego, the superego, impulsiveness, complexes); a series of drives (redefined as ergs); a series of acquired dynamic structures, such as sentiment to home, to career, to religion; and notions of conflict and integrated and unintegrated attitudes (Delhees, 1975).

When it comes to investigation of the zones of conflict in neurosis and delinquency, one may determine, at a given moment, the strength of undischarged sex need, need for dependence, aggression, etc., the strength of the self-sentiment, the sen-

timents attaching the individual to home, occupation, religion, etc., by the Motivation Analysis Test (Cattell, Horn, Radcliffe, & Sweney, 1964) for adults or by the School Motivation Analysis Test (SMAT, Cattell, Sweney, & Krug, 1968) for children. These tests use the objective devices found valid for attitude-interest measurement (Cattell, 1935, 1950a; Cattell & Baggaley, 1956; Cattell, Radcliffe, & Sweney, 1963; Cattell, Sweney, & Radcliffe, 1960; Delhees, 1973) to measure 10 independent factors—5 ergs (drives) and 5 sentiments. Table 3 summarizes information of particular dynamic factor sources that tend to have most effect on the conflicts inherent in delinquent behavior. The conclusions that may be drawn from this evidence, regarding differences between young delinquents and normals are (a) that they are expressed by dynamic personality factors affecting the readiness to internalize conflict and to handle conflict by repression, and (b) that the conflict in the delinquent is the result of a morbid self-sentiment and superego structure. This is further supported by the research of Pierson, Barton, & Hay (1964) who used the factors of the SMAT as predictors of academic achievement in delinquent boys. Conclusions concerning the older delinquents are not clear at all. Clinical research with these instruments has only just begun.

Although the common dynamic traits represent those structures which the clinician may have looked for in our preceding discussion of general personality dimensions, to delineate individual interest fixations and conflicts requires that we use the factor analytic method called *P* technique for the study of intraindividual, single-person differences (Cattell, 1963, 1966g; Harris, 1963; and chapter 8). For example, Williams (1960), showed that a conflict index proposed by Cattell (1957b), calculating the

**TABLE 3**  Conflict scores (in Stens) of 3 delinquent groups for 3 selected dynamic structure factors on the Motivation Analysis Test

| Group | $N$ | Conflict career | Conflict superego | Conflict self | Total conflict | Repressed fear |
|---|---|---|---|---|---|---|
| Juvenile delinquents (Sweney, 1957) | 126 | 6.0 | 9.0 | 9.0 | 10.0 | 8.0 |
| Criminals, violence (Coffelt, 1964) | 20 | 7.0 | 6.0 | 7.5 | 7.0 | 7.0 |
| Criminals, stealth (Coffelt, 1964) | 20 | 5.5 | 6.0 | 7.5 | 7.5 | 6.5 |

*Note.* The sigma for the general normative American population is 2.0 Stens on all factors, and the mean is 5.5.

level of internal conflict by cancellation of positive and negative loadings of the main drive and sentiment expressions for a given person over a wide array of life interests, is significantly higher in those with high conflict ratings by psychiatrists, with patient or nonpatient status, with independent 16 PF measures of ego-weakness, and with other criteria of conflict. With the availability of high-speed computers this technique may soon become practical for individual analyses of conflicts. (See subsequent discussion for use of $P$ technique in assessing state neuroticism.)

Another important adjunct of the dynamic calculus, particularly when studying integration and adjustment, is the notion of a series of "dynamic crossroads" and "adjustment paths" schematizing the essentials of the clinicians' experience and observations of human conflicts into a quantifiable system called adjustment process analysis, first systematically represented in Cattell and Scheier (1961). This analytic schema recognizes both the innate individual differences and the ways in which differences are acquired, relating them to any conceivable (for instance, therapeutic) learning or conflict situation. It gives the advantage for clinical discussions of, say, neu-

roticism, that any particular individual's adjustment process or conflict situation can be codified. Along with this, the dynamic crossroads analysis brings out hypothetically what is seldom recognized in clinical discussions of neurosis and delinquency, that cognitive and dynamic inabilities to solve life problems (low intelligence and lack of assertiveness) and temperamental tendencies and dispositions to withdraw and to lack resources (resignation, inhibition, low exuberance) are equally associated with the etiology of neurotic and delinquent deviation.

A further differentiation and development of the dynamic calculus model is the notion of the dynamic lattice, which is a map of the way in which interests within individuals subsidiate to basic "instinctive" (ergic) goals through a series of subgoals. It is really this lattice which the clinician tries to understand as he attempts (in the course of the therapeutic treatment) to bring about readjustment in particular areas of drive satisfaction. Success has been limited since the accuracy of the patient's self-report is clouded by his barred insight. If we employ factor analysis as a way of unlocking the connections in the dynamic lattice, we are in fact getting objective evidence for the very roots of the neurotic troubles. These and other possibilities of the dynamic calculus model must be left, however, to auxiliary reading references (Bischof, 1964; Cattell, 1957b; Cattell & Scheier, 1961; Cross, 1951; Lindzey, 1958; Madsen, 1961).

## 6  THE PHASE STATE DIMENSIONS OF NEUROTICISM

Let us now turn to the relation between the expression of permanent (trait) and momentary (state) neuroticism. The experimental strategy with which we are concerned is measuring individuals on variables, characteristic of neurotic behavior, then allowing some time to lapse, measuring them again, and finally correlating the changes found in these variables. This can be done in two ways which have been named, respectively, $P$ technique and differential $R$ technique (Cattell, 1952a, 1957b, 1966g; Harris, 1963b). The outcome of such correlated $P$- and $dR$-technique studies has been to show that neurotic states such as neurotic traits fall into a distinct group of neuroticism-involved factors (Cattell & Scheier, 1961). The theoretical significance and methodological advances of these factors of change are discussed in Nesselroade's chapter 8 and by Cattell (1963, 1966g), Harris (1963b), and others. Here, we are mostly trying to show the experimental evidence for the existence of neurotic state factors, that they require measurement, and that their scores always need to be included in any prediction to complete the picture of neuroticism.

A series of experiments (Cattell, 1957b; Cattell & Scheier, 1961) using both psychological and physiological measures has revealed some nine dimensions of day-to-day variation in psychological states, such as anxiety, elation-depression, effort-stress, and so on. Some of these unmistakably have the

same general character as the corresponding trait dimensions obtained by $R$ technique, but with some interesting modifications from the trait pattern. The neurotic states are a subset within the total dimensions of change, the most clinically pertinent of which have been called neurotic phase factors (Cattell & Scheier, 1961). At least five or six of these factors have no corresponding characterological dimensions; thus, unless trait dimensions also contribute simultaneously to his neurosis, a person whose states are in a neurotic phase may still not be a neurotic as defined by the total neurotic type profile. Thus we may speak of a person low on $P$-technique-derived (or phase) Universal Index $(P.U.I.)$ 2, 8, 9, 11, etc. (the neurotic phase factors which fluctuate under the impact of daily criterion events), but unless he is also chronically low on the source traits $U.I.$ 16, 21, 24, etc., his condition still is not congruent to the clinical definition of neuroticism as a trait. In other words, when only his neurotic phase dimensions are high, a person may only be in a state of temporary neuroticism. How similar this concept is to the psychoanalyst's idea of traumatic neurosis will be appreciated by the clinician.

The important neurotic phase states are anxiety, pathemia, subduedness, regression, torpor, and effort-stress, the first four of which, it will be remembered from our discussion of $T$ data factors of neuroticism, are importantly neurotic-contributory in their temperamental trait forms. Batteries have been constructed for these factors, notably in the Scheier and Cattell Eight Parallel Form Objective Battery for repeated anxiety measures (1961) and the Institute for Personality and Ability Testing (IPAT) Seven Factor State Battery, of which only three important states are shown here in Table 4. Counting all sources of evidence, we can perceive, in a fragmentary way, confir-

**TABLE 4** Loading pattern of 3 important state dimensions

| State title and index number | Variables saliently loading | Loading direction |
| --- | --- | --- |
| Anxiety (P.U.I. 9) | Willingness to admit common failings | Higher |
| | Susceptibility to annoyance | Higher |
| | Confidence in untried performance | Lesser |
| | Systolic pulse pressure | Higher |
| | Electrical skin resistance | Lower |
| | Metabolic rate | Higher |
| Effort-Stress (P.U.I. 4) | Memorizing ease | Better |
| | Number of threatening objects seen in unstructured drawings | Greater |
| | Verbal fluency | Lower |
| | Size of galvanic skin response (GSR) deflections | Smaller |
| | Heart rate | Faster |
| | Smaller size of myokinetic movement | |
| Pathemia (P.U.I. 2) | Reaction time (simple) | Longer |
| | Rate of reversible perspective | Slower |
| | Reduced fluency on self | |
| | Cholinesterase in blood serum | Lower |
| | Small amount of GSR conditioning | |
| | Large body movement tempo | Slower |

mation of these factors in the work of Herrington (1942), Wenger (1948), and others. The pattern of effort-stress (*P.U.I.* 4) is—next to anxiety—one of the most widely and thoroughly investigated state dimensions in the well-known work of Selye (1952, 1953), Hoagland (1944), and others.

One of the most valuable contributions of the *P*-technique experiments has been the differentiation between the stress pattern and the anxiety pattern. The stress response has, as Table 4 shows, much the same ketosteroid, blood pressure, and other responses as anxiety, but it lacks the anxiety content and has only a sense of effort without any emotionality. We can recognize this response as what Hoagland and others found when they were studying the response of airmen to endurance tests of flying, and

that Scheier encountered in a student group as being associated with hard intellectual effort. However, as one investigates the stress response he finds that several of its physiological features have been confused in the literature with effects of anxiety. For example, it has often been suggested that anxiety generates cholesterol and is thus a determiner of heart attacks. Investigations on 100 women by Brandt (cited in Cattell & Scheier, 1961) show zero correlation between blood cholesterol and anxiety. On the other hand the *P*-technique studies show a substantial correlation between stress and cholesterol. This and other physiological associations give the *P.U.I.* 4 effort stress pattern a decided resemblance to the General Adaptation Syndrome as decribed by Selye (1953), but it seems that the Selye pattern is broader, varying somewhat with the nature of the stress (Mefferd, Hale, & Loefer, 1953).

Because of the numerous connections found in neuroses and physiological conditions of psychosomatic appearance, e.g., stomach ulcers, colitis, or hypertension, it is of special interest to look briefly at the relationship between neurosis and psychosomatic symptoms. There is a noticeable difference of personality factor patterns between psychosomatics and the varieties of neurotics. Psychosomatics, relative to neurotics, show higher degrees of control (higher scores on questionnaire factors $C$, $E$, $Q_2$, and $Q_3$) and lower anxiety (Cattell & Scheier, 1961). It is our suggestion that the effort-stress type of response ($P.U.I.$ 4), rather than anxiety, would be their most frequent response. The data on personality profiles (see Figs. 1 and 2) indicates indeed that the neurotic is more inclined to react to challenges with withdrawal (low ego-strength, $C$ −; low will power, $Q_3$ − ; and high anxiety), whereas the psychosomatic meets them with adaptation stress (higher effort-stress, lower anxiety) though it should be remembered that the person with psychosomatic complaints sometimes may be at a high anxiety level for situational reasons. We may conclude (a more extensive discussion is provided in Fahrenberg's chapter 25) from the differences of profile and from the physiological reaction pattern shown by Cattell and Scheier (1961) of the psychosomatic and the neurotic that psychosomatics do not truly belong in the neurotic class.

It will be noted that the number of clinically important dimensions is not quite so large in states as in traits, but it leaves no doubt that there is more than a single neurotic mood. While the variables (in Table 4) defining the state factors are not inclusive, they represent a battery of half a dozen

tests of demonstrated validity. Significant changes of these factor state battery measured by Grinker, Basowitz, Peosky, and Korchin, (1955), Sells, Trites, and Parish (1957), and others are said to occur in response to events in daily life such as examinations, stressful plane flights, and accidents to relatives. Some questionnaire factors (e.g., $C$−, ego-weakness; $O$+, guilt-proneness; $Q_4$, ergic tension) behave as they did in individual temperamental differences. Indeed, it may very well be that in individual-trait-difference work we are picking up neurotic state factors at the same time overlying the trait factors where they exist, because at any given moment we seize everyone at a different level on a state, and unless we measure people repeatedly and average the measures we cannot be sure that we are dealing with only a trait (Cattell & Scheier, 1961). There is some tendency, however, for the neurotic phase dimensions to differ slightly but systematically from their corresponding trait-loading patterns. This difference is shown by anxiety, in which small body build, correlating in the trait pattern, obviously cannot load the state; while respiration rate, which markedly loads the state, loads the trait only slightly. Moreover, neurotic phase dimensions show bigger effects on the physiological variables. For example, electrical skin resistance goes up and down more with excitement as a state. Some of these physiological variables for the different neurotic states have been listed in Table 4, but a more systematic discussion of the meaning of physiological associations with personality differences is given in chapter 25.

What is important in this distinction between trait and state dimensions of neuroticism is, first, that there is a common trait structure which is found from factoring individual scores on one occasion by $R$ technique. Secondly, when one examines difference scores as in *P* technique and differential *R* technique there is on the one hand a trait-change factor and on the other a state factor. The trait-change factor will be recognized by changing continuously in one direction, whereas the state will fluctuate, rising and falling over time (Cattell, 1963, 1966g). Yet there is enough evidence that the state and the trait patterns of neuroticism are two distinct sources of variance, though similar in their effect on certain variables.

## 7  THE DISTINCTION OF NEUROTICISM, ANXIETY, AND DEPRESSION

Whereas some psychologists have confused neuroticism with anxiety, others have allowed its definition to become too broad by including depressive tendencies, stress reactions, fatigue, and similar concepts. It is our task to demonstrate that clinical concepts such as anxiety, depression, and, peripherally, stress, which was discussed in the preceding section, attach each to its own factor; and this factor is not the same as neuroticism.

The typical profile difference for neurotics on the 16 PF is shown in Table 1. There it will be seen that neurotics are higher on the components of the second-order anxiety factor in addition to being lower on dominance (Factor *E*), lower on surgency (Factor *F*), and higher on premsia (Factor *I*). This differentiation of neurotics and normals is supported by the findings of Rickels, Cattell, Weise, Gray, Yee, Mallin, and Aaronson (1966) that when neurotics change under psychotherapy they shift in the normal direction on all these factors. Accordingly, although Freud made anxiety the "central problem of the neuroses," it remains that neurotics differ from normals on much more than anxiety. This is shown even more

clearly in the objective test-factor realm where six source traits distinguish between neurotics and normals at the 1% level of significance, and anxiety, being only one of them, shows less magnitude of difference than the others. The significance of these findings for theories of neuroticism has been discussed by Cattell and Scheier (1961).

Much of the confusion of anxiety with neuroticism has resulted from theories and tests that fail to separate the two concepts. It is true that neurotics are more anxious than normals. Nevertheless, one cannot validate measures of anxiety by demonstrating that neurotics score higher on them. The Taylor Manifest Anxiety Scale (1953), for example, by its derivation from items that distinguish neurotics from normals, mixes various neurotic dimensions into anxiety. The Eysenck Neuroticism Scale (1956), on the other hand, takes too much anxiety into neuroticism and comes close to being an anxiety scale. Recognizing these contradictions inherent in the use of certain definitions and measurements of neuroticism and anxiety, Scheier and Cattell have constructed two distinct scales, the IPAT Neuroticism Scale Questionnaire (NSQ) and the IPAT Anxiety Scale (1959). For these scales it has been shown that the NSQ has a significantly and decidedly lower correlation with the IPAT Anxiety Scale than does the Eysenck Neuroticism Scale (Cattell & Scheier, 1961). The significance of having such tests is that they can be used as meaningful estimates of anxiety and neuroticism, whereas the clinical practitioner may otherwise be measuring anxiety when the scale is labeled "neuroticism" and may be measuring neuroticism when the scale is labeled "anxiety."

The results of multivariate experimental methods have been markedly clear and consistent in regard to neuroticism and anxiety. But they are complex and still partly obscure in relation to depression. When a wide range of normal and pathological depression manifestations—introspective, behavioral, and physiological—was measured in normal subjects and mental hospital subjects and the subsequent multivariate (factor-analytic) and bivariate (dependent-independent) analyses were carried out, they showed no fewer than seven or eight distinct varieties in the questionnaire area of response (Cattell & Bjerstedt, 1967). This finding was confirmed by Cattell's refactoring of behavior ratings on depressives by Kiloh and Garside (1963). Furthermore, in the Cattell-Bjerstedt research the depression factors were shown to occupy "new space" in relation to the previously known questionnaire dimensionality in the 16 PF, except to a certain relation of one of the depression factors with the self-sentiment questionnaire factor, $Q_3$. By their item content, the depression factors have been called exhaustion hypochondria, suicidal disgust, restless, brooding discontent, anxious depression, low-energy depression, guilt and resentment, and bored depression and withdrawal. Even at the second order the structure is not simply that of a single, general depression factor, comparable with the general anxiety factor, $U.I.$ 24, but appears rather to require two and possibly three different sources of variance to account for all manifestations. Broadly, one can see meaning in terms of an anxious depression; a depression associated with exhaustion; and a purely psychogenic, dynamic depression concerned with self-punishment (Delhees & Cattell, 1971a, c). Research on these dimensions is presently being undertaken by the author. Meanwhile, the emerging generalizations are that the understanding of neuroticism requires reference to a fairly complex structure of first and second orders in relation to anxiety and depression.

## 8  THE CONSTRICTIVE AND RECIPROCAL EFFECTS OF AGE, HEREDITY, OCCUPATION, AND THE SOCIOCULTURAL GROUP

Now that the major factor dimensions describing neuroticism have been discussed, we propose to concentrate on the ways in which these response dimensions can be influenced. For when we want to investigate the causes and functions of neuroticism and its response to therapeutic treatment, we need to know whether the pattern is one produced largely by constitutional influences or by environmental attachments. The step of separating those neurotic dimensions that are largely modifiable and those that are mostly constitutional deserves to come first in any economical expenditure of research effort directed toward understanding personality maturation and learning.

The nature-nurture researches with the MAVA method by Cattell and his associates have already given evidence of the nature-nurture ratios for many primary personality factors in $Q$ data (Cattell, Blewett, & Beloff, 1955), and in objective tests (Cattell, Kristy, & Stice, 1951). Allowing for sampling errors when only some 500 cases are taken (which may account for overestimating the environmental contribution—see Loehlin's chapter 13) and for some mislabeling of factors originally found at the child level, the evidence on questionnaire factors that distinguish between neurotics and normals points to a substantial environmental determination of $C$, ego-strength; $F$, surgency; $G$, superego; $O$, guilt-proneness; and $Q_4$, ergic tension level. A fairly marked hereditary determination exists for $D$, excitability (not found in adults); $E$, dominance; and $Q_3$, self-sentiment. The highest hereditary determination, probably 70% to 80% variance, occurs for $B$, intelligence; and $H$, parmia. Anxiety level tends to be more environmentally than hereditarily determined, and somewhat more connected with accidents of individual environment than with differences of environmental atmosphere between families.

Among the neurotic process and neurotic contributory personality factors measured by objective tests (4½ hours of the O–A Battery on 647 boys and girls), the MAVA method showed most environmental determination of ego-strength (U.I. 16), cortertia (U.I. 22), regression (U.I. 23), narcisstic self-concept (U.I. 26), asthenia (U.I. 28). Some predominance of hereditary determination occurred in inhibition (U.I. 17), independence (U.I. 19), and exuberance (U.I. 21). The two source traits with the highest constitutional determination were intelligence (Culture Fair Test, U.I. 1) and comention (U.I. 20), willingness to conform. With these indications of the importance of environment in certain known neuroticism factors, it becomes profitable to investigate the effect of family atmosphere, the individual history within the family, the dynamics of mate selection and compatibility, early child development, etc. For this, the interested reader is referred to Cattell (1957b), Cattell, Blewett, and Beloff (1955), Cattell and Scheier (1961), H. J. Eysenck (1953c), H. J. Eysenck and Prell (1951), and chapter 13.

After nature-nurture ratios, the next important information about neuroticism is the normal distribution of neuroticism and its separate components over age. Fortunately, through the systematic way in which factoring has been carried out with similar variables at different age levels (Cattell & Coan, 1958; Cattell & Gruen, 1954; Cattell & Peterson, 1959; Cattell & Scheier, 1961; Sealy & Cattell, 1966), comparative developmental studies have become possible and evidence on factor trends is clear. From the available data (Cattell & Scheier, 1961),

the normal age-trend curve for neuroticism conveys the general impression that neuroticism stays steady until about age 15 and that it regularly falls off from late adolescence throughout middle age to somewhere around 60 years of age. The results of Byrd (1959) suggest, however, that neuroticism (and anxiety) scores tend to show a steep rising again. Since the extremes of this curve still need strengthening by larger samples, it is too early to say whether this is a situational effect of retirement or some biological causation.

As we come now to examine the findings concerning neuroticism in relation to occupation and culture, it is important to remember that two people may reach the same level of neuroticism but with different contributions from the various components, e.g., one through a deficient ego development, another through higher guilt feelings, and another through greater development of anxiety. In fact, significant negative correlations are found between the criteria of job performance and such measured components in neuroticism as ego-weakness, overprotected, oversensitive, dependent attitudes, and proneness to anxiety. For example, occupations of professional and executive status have shown systematically higher ego-strength (C factor) scores than lower status groups, e.g., janitors (Cattell & Scheier, 1961). It can be said that the neurotic in general performs below the level indicated by his intelligence test and other indications of his ability (Tsushima, 1957). He becomes more maladjusted in human relations and changes his job more frequently (H. J. Eysenck, 1944, 1947).

The mean neuroticism scores on the 16 PF (or the NSQ—derived from it) for various occupations show a large range of differences, as shown in Table 5. The higher-than-average neuroticism score in certain occupations could be due to one of two reasons or

**TABLE 5**  Average tested neuroticism levels in 26 occupational groups[a]

| Neuroticism level | Occupational group |
| --- | --- |
| Relatively higher neuroticism (60th–80th percentile) | Male clerks (bank, insurance); housewives; editorial workers (publishing house office); waitresses; U.S. Navy underwater demolition team; janitors; secretaries; female nurses; cooks (kitchen help, female); hairdressers, barbers (male); psychiatric technicians. |
| Middle ranges of neuroticism (40th–60th percentile) | Executives (business, managerial); elementary school teachers; house painters; clerks (female, filing and typing); policeman; priests. |
| Relatively lower neuroticism (20th–40th percentile) | Electricians; researchers (physics, biology, psychology); mechanics (garage); time-study engineers; aircraft engineering apprentices (no college degree); firemen (city fire engines); U.S.A.F. pilot cadets in training; engineers (mechanical); Olympic athletes; salesman. |

[a]Data from Cattell and Scheier, 1961.

both, either that some occupations tend to attract people who are more neurotic or that they tend to make people more neurotic. One might guess that in some cases both may happen. Some light might be shed on this from the difference between anxiety level and the neurosis level. The latter, as pointed out earlier, is more than anxiety and includes constitutional aspects of personality structure which would be unlikely to be produced by the occupational environment. When this is done (anxiety factor scores for the occupational groups by the IPAT Anxiety Scale are available—Cattell & Scheier, 1961), the rank order of occupations is, in the main, roughly the same for anxiety and neuroticism, but there are a few exceptions. For example, young air pilots in training are well below average in neuroticism but above average on anxiety. Olympic athletes are decidedly nonneurotic, but of average anxiety. Also, a discrepancy of anxiety and neuroticism levels in the

opposite direction is found in some occupations. For example, restaurant cooks and psychiatric technicians are more neurotic than they are anxious. All in all it is not susprising that the neurotic person achieves less, and that, other things being equal, neurotics appear with greater frequency in lower social strata.

One of the most interesting developments in recent years with the advent of objective and conceptually meaningful measurements of anxiety and neuroticism level has been the introduction of cross-cultural comparisons in psychology (see also Izard's chapter 20). Independent factor analyses carried out in the United States, Brazil, Britain, China, Germany, France, Italy, Japan, and India have given evidence of considerable similarity of basic personality dimensions across cultures, though with divergent loading patterns. To illustrate these findings the highest anxiety scores (on the 16 PF) were obtained in Poland and

India, then followed France, Italy and Japan in that order. The two lowest scores, both on anxiety and neuroticism, were made by samples from Britain and the United States, with the United States the lowest (Cattell & Scheier, 1961). Support for these results comes from the work of Morris and Jones (1955). Cattell and Warburton (1961), Rose (1955) as well as others. Obviously, since socioeconomic status is also likely to be important, the next step is to sample people at different levels across countries and compare them on all known personality dimensions.

It is interesting to speculate what these differences mean. Cattell and Scheier (1961) put forward the hypothesis that anxiety and neuroticism are inversely related to economic level and directly related to the number of cultural schisms within the national life. Thus Britain presents a relatively monolithic culture, whereas India has many differences in speech, religion, and caste groups. The possibility has to be considered that part of the frequency of neuroticism in a country could be due to real socioeconomic differences between groups, and vice versa. We may thus reason that neuroticism in nations does as much to pull down the general economic level as poverty contributes to the neuroticism score. From experiments with closely observed performances of small groups in solving their group problems, it is evident that the volume of complaints, the number of noncooperative actions, the number of deadlocks in group action, etc., increase rapidly with the average neuroticism score of the people forming the group (Cattell & Stice, 1960a).

## 9  MEASUREMENT OF THERAPEUTIC CHANGE AND DRUG ACTION

The main evidence of change that a patient experiences under psychotherapy or as the result of drug action resides in the extent to which such restructuring and relearning finally results in significant changes—toward normal—on those components of neuroticism, (e.g., ego-strength and anxiety level), so that we now distinguish the neurotic from the normal person (see Figs. 1 and 2 and Table 2). This postulate of the multidimensionality of therapeutic change departs radically from premetric clinical theory in determining—through measurements of separate personality dimensions—how much of the neuroticism contribution is constitutionally determined, how much is due to early life developments, how much from recent regressions, etc., thus ending up with a definite therapeutic strategy for each case. Since personality factor batteries are now available, it is possible to determine the degree of recovery at any moment in the course of therapy.

Systematic studies (Hunt, Ewing, LaForge, & Gilbert, 1959; Rickels, Cattell, Weise, Gray, Yee, Mallin, & Aaronson, 1966) measuring change on personality factors under therapy have been conducted in different media of observation. For example, Hunt, Ewing LaForge, and Gilbert (1959) investigated the change in students with relatively severe emotional difficulties who were tested on the 16 PF before and after therapy. They found that therapeutic improvement is accompanied by a rising $C$ factor (increased ego-strength), a shift toward surgency (Factor $F$), a shift toward dominance ($E$), a drop on the ergic tension factor ($Q_4$), and an increase in $H$ (moving away from "sizothyme withdrawal"), accompanied by a drop in the anxiety factor and an increase in extraversion. (Cattell (1966d), suggested that dominance and surgency increments could be due to a particular method of therapy. In other words, the changes found in the different personality dimensions will depend on the type of therapy or therapist, the stage of therapy reached, the type of patient, etc. The manipulation of the patient's situation in therapy plays a different role in different therapeutic systems.

As to chemotherapy, information on the combined effect of psychotherapy and chemotherapy on the O–A Battery (Cattell, 1955a) and the IPAT Eight Parallel Form Anxiety Scale (Scheier & Cattell, 1961) for the regression factor *U.I.* 23 and the anxiety factor *U.I.* 24 has come from the research of Rickels, Cattell, Weise, Gray, Yee, Mallin, and Aaronson (1966), shown in Table 6. Here the tests give evidence of a significant two-dimensional change on anxiety and on the regression factor, where presumably some procedures might have reduced anxiety without reducing regression. Rickels, Cattell, Weise, Gray, Yee, Mallin, & Aaronson (1966), who compared two neurotic groups, one on drug and one on placebo, with both groups obtaining therapy and compared them with a group of controls who received neither drugs nor therapy, showed that there is a radical reduction of anxiety by the psychotherapy

with the drug; yet, there is also an almost equally large reduction by psychotherapy without the drug. This would seem to indicate that psychotherapy can produce a decline in anxiety. However, the possibility of some self-healing return to normality for the patients, so ardently proclaimed by H. J. Eysenck (1952a), is not entirely ruled out. (See chapter 25 for further discussion of drug effects.)

As pointed out earlier, we can turn to objective measurement of individual conflicts and individual fixations as a supplement to the general and dynamic common traits by using the *P*-technique method. It also plays an indispensable role as a practical device for measuring therapeutic change and individual conflicts. By measuring an adequate sample of persons on personality factors before and after a set of complex learning experiences (of which therapy is one), one can, without actual manipulative separation of the learning influences, determine the effect of each learning experience on particular personality factors. This constitutes a great challenge for the clinician. However, the chief resulting implications for

**TABLE 6**  Source trait changes on anxiety and regression source traits by therapy

| Measure[a] | Mean pretherapy score | Mean posttherapy score | Mean difference | Significance |
|---|---|---|---|---|
| Anxiety source trait, *U.I.* 24 | | | | |
| By 40-item Verbal Anxiety Scale (IPAT) | 46.09 | 43.02 | −3.07 | $p < .05$ |
| By 8 subtest O–A Personality Battery | .361 | .198 | − .163 | $p < .05$ |
| Regression source trait, *U.I.* 23 | | | | |
| By 4 subtest O–A Personality Battery | .440 | .114 | − .326 | $p < .001$ |

*Note.*  These results are on 46 private patient neurotics. A normal and untherapized group showed no significant change over the same 6-week period. Particulars of groups, measures, therapists, procedures, etc., are given in Rickels, Cattell, Weise, Gray, Yee, Mallin, & Aaronson (1966).

[a]*U.I.* = Universal index; IPAT = Institute for Personality and Ability Testing; O–A = Objective-Analytic.

clinical practice and for therapy are drawn in Cattell (1957b, 1963, 1966d), Cattell and Scheier (1961), and Delhees (1968).

Our major conceptual propositions for measuring therapeutic change concern not only the patient's personality, but also the personality and attitudes of those regularly interacting with him, and the various conflict-provoking emotional situations in his life. Measures on parents, siblings, etc., can be made on the same unitary factors of personality as those of the neurotic patient. Research by Karson (1965) with parents of behavior-problem children shows that these parents have a 16 PF profile which resembles the standard one for clinically diagnosed neurotics (as shown in Fig. 1). They have lower ego-strength $(C-)$, greater autia $(M+)$, and greater ergic tension $(Q_4+)$. The second-order factors reveal that they are both more anxious and more introverted than general adults, but they are at the same time lower on superego strength $(G-)$ and self-sentiment strength $(Q_3-)$. This shows that the maximum utilization of tests in clinical situations calls for measurement of a broad spectrum of personality dimensions in relation to an equally broad spectrum of dimensions and situations of the "inner circle" of the patient's environmental attachments.

## 10 A MULTIFACTOR THEORY OF NEUROSIS AND ITS CLINICAL USEFULNESS

It is our claim that the source-traits, the dynamic ergs, and the dimensions of mood change found by multivariate experimental methods are from the beginning the primary demonstrable entities with which a clinical theory of neurosis should be concerned. By a source-trait, an erg, or a state we mean a replicated maximally simple-structure rotated, oblique factor, which we suppose to be an influence on the measurement vari-

ables. Consequently the aim of any multifactorial theory of neurosis is to arrive at experimental statements of how many and what kind of dimensions account for the observed changes in neurotic deviation. This is not to deny that apart from this, practically every sufferer from a neurosis has certain concurrent troubles that manifest themselves on a physical plane, and for which he may receive ordinary, palliative physical treatment.

Comparison of factor analyses of neurotics and normals shows that although the same source-trait patterns are discoverable (using communalities and simple-structure rotated resolutions) in both, yet they exist at different mean levels in these two groups. The questionnaire general neurosis pattern is clear and consistent. It is characterized by a high anxiety (the second-order pattern of $C$, $O$, $L$, $Q_3$, and $Q_4$); marked introversion (mainly Factors $F$, $H$, and $M$); cultured, overprotected sensitivity $(I+)$; and submissiveness $(E-)$. The neurotic syndrome groups show differences with these factors. For example, obsessive-compulsive and conversion hysteric subgroups seem to differ from the general neurotic profile in lacking detectable differences in $G$, $Q_2$, and $M$.

When these experimental findings are brought into a set of explanatory principles of neurosis formation, we can see that anxiety in the neurotic is the consequence of undischarged drive tension, $Q_4+$; guilt-proneness, $O+$; ego-weakness, $C-$; and poor self-sentiment growth, $Q_3$. One can see that guilt-proneness ($O$ factor) would raise anxiety in the neurotic in that with two equally serious infringements of conscience the person with higher guilt-proneness is largely independent of the extent of development of the $G$ factor (superego), from which we may conclude that Factor $O$ must, like $H$, be regarded as a temperamental "magnifier" of a reaction based on other origins. The role of $Q_4$, ergic tension, interpreted in Cattell and Scheier (1961) as the level of stimulated but unsatisfied drive of any kind, not merely libido, might easily be expected to transform itself into anxiety, as in the transference neuroses. The strength of the measurement of $Q_3$ indicates the degree to which the person has built up a conscious self-concept as a guiding schema in behavior and the extent to which that schema is followed. The amount of anxiety experienced by the individual is likely to be proportional to the weakness of the ego, and we tend to think that ego-weakness is a cause of anxiety and a contributor to neuroticism, insofar as the person with a weak ego is unable to handle his impulses and the stresses between the internal and external environment. Only in the case of the $L$ factor, protension, do we seem to have a relationship where anxiety is the cause of the projected behavior, rather than conversely. When putting primary factors into the causal position we nevertheless recognize that there is, in every case, some circular feedback causal action. For example, a child with a high anxiety level is unable to achieve proper ego growth in stability and security.

Among questionnaire factors, we find the neurotic to be high on Factor $M$ and low on Factors $F$ and $H,$ three of the four main components in the higher-order organization of factors forming the concept of introversion (which is directly scorable from the 16 PF). The inner-directed life and imaginative tension of Factor $M$ seem to place the person in an isolated position, with anxiety arising as a consequence, to be followed by a moving away from the group and the actual dissociative tendency which appear in the content of a neurosis. Indeed, in the case of the $H$ factor one almost has to accept this direction in which those primary factors are contributors to a common pool of anxiety. For the $H$ factor, parmia versus threctia,

shows a high constitutional determination (Cattell, Blewett, & Beloff, 1955). It would seem obvious that a person of a constitutionally more timid disposition would, in general, experience more anxiety than another, less threctic individual from the same amount of conflict or threat.

Proceeding now from introversion to other dimensions of neuroticism, we note that Factor $I$ is at its overprotected, cultured sensitivity pole, which has repeatedly been shown to be strongly associated with proneness to neuroticism. Its generally accepted psychological meaning is derived from an upbringing favoring self-indulgence and low self-discipline and leading to anxious sensitivity and lack of realism. Thus we find in the neurotic a naturally excessive sympathetic responsiveness to threat (threctia, $H-$) raised with effects of an overindulgent and unduly protective environment (Factor $I+$).

A few points in relation to delinquency are worth noting here. Factor $I$ tends to be low in the "tough guys." This tendency is accompanied by low superego strength, Factor $G$, not especially characteristic of neurotics, and is thus considered to be another useful diagnostic indicator of delinquency. Factor $E$ (dominance) also has great use in diagnosis, for it separates the neuroses and general character disorders, where it is definitely $E-$ or low, in contrast to the $E+$ dominance-hostility of the antisocial disorders. The finding of low dominance in neurotics is particularly characteristic of obsessional-compulsives.

By use of objective test batteries, put together from several distinct types of performance subtests selected by their duly calculated factor loadings on these differing personality source-trait factors, it is also possible to aid practical clinical diagnosis of neurosis. According to Eysenck, *U.I.* 23 and *U.I.* 24 are significantly higher in neurotics;

and according to Cattell and Scheier (1961), these and four other factors differ from normals at the $p < .01$ level of significance. Neurotics are, for example, more regressed, more anxious, lower on the cortertia or arousal factor (*U.I.* 22) and the ego factor, *U.I.* 16, which gives support for the Freudian concept of ego-strength and ego-weakness. Anxiety, the *U.I.* 24 factor (which correlates, incidentally, unity with the second-order anxiety factor in the questionnaire realm) in objective laboratory measures, accounts for only part of the variance in the neuroticism pattern in the objective test realm; other personality factors are equally prominent therein, e.g., *U.I.* 16, *U.I.* 23, *U.I.* 30, and others. This again shows how important it is always to study a particular aspect of neurosis in the context of the total dimensionality of known personality source traits.

Our study can now be aided by dynamic measures, derived from developments in the dynamic calculus, such as the Motivation Analysis Test (MAT) measuring through objective tests the strength of interest in a variety of attitudes that are known to be associated with particular drives (e.g., sex, gregariousness, pugnacity) and sentiments (e.g., to the home, to religion, occupation). But more exact experiment in this area is necessary before theorizing can go further. The stage is now set for some important work in the neurosis field in which the types of measurement we have described can be brought into the front line for a direct attack on the problems of etiology, diagnosis, and the treatment of neurosis.

## 11  SUMMARY

1. The first demand in any strategic experimental approach in clinical psychology is for structural research, e.g., to ana-lyze such concepts as ego-strength and guilt-proneness, the trait structure of deviant behavior patterns, and the measurement of states and mood changes in unitary dimensions. It is in this region that the emphasis of the study of neurosis and delinquency in this chapter lies.

2. Neurotics and delinquents differ from normals not in a single factor but in several factors (found by correlational studies of the normal personality). Descriptions of these factor differences can be derived from ratings (*L* data), questionnaire (*Q*), and objective test (*T*) data in the personality and the dynamic measurement realm; and in terms of first-order and higher-order resolutions. Factor-based measurements such as the Sixteen Personality Factor Questionnaire (16 PF), the Guilford-Zimmerman, or the Motivation Analysis Test (MAT), substantially cover the principal personality or motivation dimensions.

3. In terms of the first-order questionnaire components, neuroticism is shown in ego-weakness ($C-$), low dominance ($E-$), low surgency ($F-$), low threctia ($H-$), high premsia ($I+$), high protension ($L+$), high autism ($M+$), high guilt-proneness ($O+$), and high ergic tension ($Q_4+$). Additionally, the neurotic is high on anxiety, which is a product (in terms of a second-order factor) of $C-$, $Q_4+$, $O+$, $Q_3-$, $H-$, and $L+$. The different neurotic syndrome groups are clearly recognizable by different questionnaire factor profiles. The resemblance of a given individual to one or the other syndrome categories can be determined by using the $r_p$ pattern-similarity coefficient.

4. There exist striking similarities between the neurotic and the delinquent personality, though important differences remain. Criminals have a personality profile that looks much like the general neurotic profile, with less pronounced anxiety and introversion. Both show also lower superego

development. However, the young delinquent is notably lower in self-sentiment development ($Q_3$) and greater individualistic obstructiveness (factor $J+$, in boys). He shows higher dominance ($E$ factor) and higher surgency ($F$). Aside from personality differences there is a positive correlation of intelligence with social status and a tendency for less criminal behavior with higher social status.

5. Besides the main questionnaire dimensions, factors in objective tests can be found which differentiate neurotics and delinquents from normals. They have been divided into five first-order neurotic processes (*U.I.* 22, 29, 16, 23, and 24) and four to six neurotic-contribution factors (*U.I.* 19, 21, 32, 25, 28, and 34). Some of these factors (e.g., regression, *U.I.* 23; anxiety, *U.I.* 24) correspond to concepts familiar to the clinician; others (e.g., cortertia, *U.I.* 22; composed realism, *U.I.* 25) do not. Factors that concern personality disorganization (*U.I.* 24 and 25) are seen to operate in the same direction for criminals and neurotics; where inhibition is concerned, as in *U.I.* 16 (unbound, assertive ego), criminals show subnormal and neurotics supernormal inhibition.

6. An additional source of evidence on differences in neurotic, normal and delinquent behavior patterns is that concerned with motivational and dynamic factors. Distinct drive (e.g., sex, pugnacity, gregariousness) and sentiment (e.g., to religion, career, home) factors can be isolated and measured, and a measurement of drive level and of conflict of these drives (e.g., by the Motivation Analysis Test, the MAT) shows marked differences among clinical and other deviation patterns.

7. By multivariate analysis over time (*P* technique), a number of independent neurotic state patterns have emerged, notably anxiety, pathemia, subduedness, regression, torpor, and effort-stress. Some of these are importantly neurotic-contributory also in their temperamental trait forms. Significant physiological connections have been demonstrated for these neurotic mood dimensions, and a clear distinction from other, sometimes confused concepts has been gained. Batteries have been constructed for the state factors, notably in the Eight Parallel Form Objective Battery and the IPAT Seven Factor State Battery.

8. Significant differences in neuroticism levels, measured in terms of source trait factors, exist for various occupations, ages, nations, etc. Some of the neuroticism factors are largely innate (e.g., $H$, parmia; intelligence, $B$; comention, *U.I.* 20); others largely environmentally determined (e.g., $G$, superego; $O$, guilt-proneness; *U.I.* 26, narcissistic self-concept); some are about equal.

9. Neuroticism factors change significantly with experimentally applied conditions, for example, psychotherapy and chemotherapy. Therapeutic improvement is accompanied by changes in personality in the normal direction, such as in the $C$ factor (increased ego-strength), in the $F$ factor (becoming more surgent), a shift toward dominance ($E$), and a drop on the ergic-tension factor ($Q_4$). The multidimensionality of therapeutic change is viewed as a definite advantage over premetric clinical theory.

# 28

## Multivariate Research on the Psychoses

**Lawrence F. Van Egeren**
*Michigan State University, East Lansing*

## 1 INTRODUCTION

The study of psychosis is a hybrid product of three major historical traditions: the clinical, the univariate experimental, and the multivariate experimental. The present chapter surveys research conducted in the third tradition.

Clinical studies led to formulations of the psychoses in terms of such concepts as primary process (unconscious) mentation; primary narcissism (Freud) and autism (Bleuler); unconscious complexes and introversion-extraversion orientations of mental life (Jung); ego boundaries (Federn) and distributions of energy in mental life (Janet); dissociation, overinclusion, and other pathologies of thinking (Bleuler, Cameron); cyclothymic-schizothymic personality development (Kretschmer); distorted interpretations of interpersonal relations and social withdrawal (Sullivan); and concrete orientations of mental life and accompanying catastrophic reactions to stress (Goldstein). This tradition led to important theoretical formulations of psychosis but neglected reliable classification and measurement of clinical phenomena. The univariate experimental tradition introduced careful measurement but did not deal with comprehensive systems of variables. The lack of integrative research plans and models in this tradition has led to a confusing pottage of disconnected findings, as is painfully evident in reviews of research on schizophrenia (Buss, A. H., & Lang, 1965; Lang & Buss, 1965).

Multivariate research differs from univariate research in that it deals with multiple variables related to psychosis simultaneously rather than separately or singly. Comprehensive systems of measures are studied rather than single measures. Since multiple observations reflecting different facets of psychotic functioning are believed to be dependent on one another, they are treated as an integrated system rather than in isolation. Differences between univariate and multivariate research strategies in the study of psychosis can be viewed in the following way. Suppose that we have made $p$ observations on each of $N$ psychotic patients. Quantitative information on the $N$ patients will form a $p \times N$ matrix having $p$ (for the means of the variables) plus $p$ (for variances) plus $p(p - 1)/2$ (for covariances) statistical parameters. The $p(p - 1)/2$ covariances indicate the organizational (integrative) aspects of the empirical system, that is, precisely what makes it a "system." Univariate analyses ignore this information, whereas multivariate analyses deal with it directly. The major question in the latter research tradition is, "What is the organization of the psychotic system, that is, the system of cognitive, affective, and behavioral measures made on psychotic patients?"

Most multivariate research on psychosis has attempted to determine empirically the underlying organization of psychotic symptoms by means of factor analysis. Psychotic patients may differ on $p$ symptoms forming an observational basis for classification (into paranoid schizophrenia, manic-depressive psychosis, etc.). The problem, as formulated by factor analysis, is to find a reduced mathematical basis for classifying patients by resolving $p$ correlated symptoms into $k$ uncorrelated symptom "factors." Each underlying factor (of psychosis) is a linear composite of manifest psychotic symptoms. That is

$$F_m = \sum_{j=1}^{p} a_j z_j \qquad (1)$$

where $F_m(m = 1, 2 \ldots k)$ is a factor of symptoms, $z_j(j = 1, 2 \ldots p)$ a symptom and $a_j$ its linear coefficient. $F_m$ is a (linear) aggregate of symptoms on which patients can be compared. If $k$ (the number of factors) is considerably smaller than $p$ (the number of symptoms), and it usually is, the set of $k$ symptom factors may provide an economical basis for classifying patients.

Manifest psychotic symptoms can be confusing. Determining their factors can introduce simplicity and clarity. The simplest linear model of the symptoms is constructed. Factor analysis can be a useful mathematical device for fitting data (psychotic symptoms) to abstract constructs (factors), thus aiding in theory construction in this area of research. It may do more than that by pointing to ideas concerning the source (origin or etiology) of manifest symptom structures and thus of psychosis itself. Constructs derived by factor analysis may provide the foundation for a mathematical model of psychosis or some restricted aspect of psychosis. A purpose of this chapter is to indicate the extent to which we have reached this objective. Technical aspects of factor analysis are treated in Harman (1976).

## 2 LIFE DATA: THE ORGANIZATION OF PSYCHOTIC SYMPTOMS

The basic data of research on psychosis are obtained from three principal sources, designated elsewhere as $L$ (life record), $Q$ (questionnaire), and $T$ (objective test) (Cattell, 1957a). Selected findings from these sources will be described.

In $L$ data on psychosis, behavior is found rather than controlled. The aim is to follow the patient through his waking day and record his behaviors without controling them. Research of this kind has been based on time samplings of patient behaviors and focused on determining the organization of these behaviors. T. V. Moore (1933) was the first to collect such time samplings (in the form of symptom ratings) and to submit them to a quantitative analysis. He believed that a table of "associations" among psychotic symptoms would reveal the essential syndromes of psychosis and its functional organization. Symptoms functionally interconnected in reality should be highly intercorrelated. Physicians and nurses rated 367 psychotic patients for the presence of 32 psychiatric symptoms. Tetrachoric coefficients were calculated, and the correlation table was submitted to a complex form of cluster analysis. Seven syndrome clusters were found: (a) Catatonic, (b) Deluded and Hallucinated, (c) Paranoid Irritabilities, (d) Manic, (e) Cognitive Defect, (f) Constitutional Hereditary Depression, and (g) Retarded Depression. These seven clusters were intercorrelated to form the Schizophrenic factor, from clusters (a), (b), and (e), and the Circular Insanity factor, from clusters (d), (f), and (g).

Moore's data were reanalyzed with more modern methods by Thurstone (1947) who found five well-defined factors and by Degan (1952). Degan interpreted nine primary factors: *A*, Hallucination-Delusion; *B*, Depression; *C*, Hyperexcitability; *D*, Catatonia; *E*, Schizophrenic Dissociation; *F*, Psychotic Shock; *G*, Hyperirritability; *H*, Deterioration; and *I*, Neurasthenia. The primary factors were correlated and four second-order factors extracted: Factor *W* (loading *G, C, H,* and *I*—), Factor *X* (*E, F, A,* and *H*), Factor *Y* (*I, B, G*—, and *A*—), and Factor *Z* (*D, F, G, H,* and *B*—). Degan interpreted Factor *W* as representing a condition of "mania . . . and sustained hyperexcitability." Factor *X* is aligned with hebephrenic schizophrenia and Factor *Z* with catatonic schizophrenia. Factor *Y* is identified with a paranoid condition with marked depressive features. H. J. Eysenck (1961c) tentatively associated Factor *Y* with the Introversion-Extraversion personality dimension. As is evident from Thurstone's and Degan's analyses of Moore's data, the same correlation matrix can yield different factors and different interpretations of symptom structure (organization), depending on the factor-analysis principles employed. The method affects the message.

Many later studies (Bostian, Smith, Lasky, Hover, & Ging, 1959; A. H. Buss, Fischer, & Simmons, 1962; Dahlstrom, 1949; Guertin, 1952a, 1955, 1961; Guertin & Krugman, 1959; E. Klein & Spohn, 1962; Lorr, 1966; Lorr, Jenkins, & O'Connor, 1955; Lorr & Klett, 1968, 1969 a, b; Lorr, Klett, & Cave, 1967; Lorr, McNair, Klett, & Lasky, 1962; Lorr & O'Connor, 1957, 1962; Lorr, O'Connor, & Stafford, 1957; Mariotto & Paul, 1974; Martorano & Nathan, 1972; Overall, 1962; Overall, Gorham, & Shawver, 1961; Overall, Hollister, & Pichot, 1967; Wittenborn, 1951, 1962; Wittenborn & Holzberg, 1951) also attempted to under-stand the symptom structure of psychotic patients. A number of these studies, and related research, have been reviewed elsewhere (Eysenck, H. J., 1961; Lorr, 1961; Lorr, Klett, & McNair, 1963; Phillips, L., & Draguns, 1971; Zubin, 1967).

The extensive research by Lorr and his associates on psychotic symptoms deserves special attention. Their work was based on symptom ratings by ward aides, nurses, psychologists, and psychiatrists of hundreds of patients observed during interviews and on hospital wards in the United States, Europe, and Japan. A detailed account of this program was published in two monographs (Lorr, 1966; Lorr, Klett, & McNair, 1963). These investigators developed an instrument for rating patients known as the Inpatient Multidimensional Psychiatric Scales (IMPS). Ten primary factors (syndromes) of symptoms measured by these scales found by Lorr and his colleagues appear in Table 1. Correlation analyses indicated that these primary syndromes combined to form three broader (second-order) syndromes, which in turn combined to form a single (third-order) syndrome of schizophrenia. The overall organization of syndromes is shown in Fig. 1. Later analyses (Lorr & Klett, 1968, 1969a) added Obsessional-Phobic, Functional Impairment, and Somatic Complaints symptom clusters to the list of primary syndromes. The 13 primary syndromes are reported (Lorr & Klett, 1968) to be organized into four broader (second-order) symptom clusters, Disorganized Hyperactivity (characterized by excitment and conceptual disorganization), Anxious Depression (anxious depression, depressive mood, and somatic complaints), Schizophrenic Disorganization (psychomotor retardation, disorientation, and motor disturbances) and Paranoid Process (paranoid delusions and hallucinations), which were found in male and female sam-

**TABLE 1**  Primary factors of the Inpatient Multidimensional Psychiatric Scales

| Factor | Loading | Factor | Loading |
|---|---|---|---|
| Excitement | | Motor Disturbance (*continued*) | |
| Hurried speech | .58 | Giggling | .34 |
| Excess of speech | .58 | Overt tension | .32 |
| Dominates interview | .55 | Startled glances | 30 |
| Elevated mood | .50 | Talks to self | .24 |
| Self-dramatization | .50 | Hostile Belligerence | |
| Loud and boisterous | .49 | Verbal hostility | .76 |
| Unrestrained | .40 | Hostile attitude | .74 |
| Overactive | .38 | Bitter and resentful | .70 |
| Attitude of superiority | .34 | Bitter and irritability | .68 |
| | | Complains and gripes | .61 |
| Paranoid Projection | | Suspicious of people | .58 |
| Ideas of conspiracy | .53 | Blames others | .54 |
| People controlling him | .53 | Attitude of contempt | .42 |
| Ideas of reference | .52 | | |
| Delusional beliefs | .44 | Retardation and Apathy | |
| Ideas of persecution | .41 | Slowed speech | .61 |
| Forces controlling him | .38 | Slowed movements | .60 |
| | | Fixed facies | .55 |
| Disorientation | | Whispered speech | .54 |
| As to state | .67 | Failure to answer | .54 |
| As to year | .67 | Apathy | .50 |
| As to age | .67 | Speech blocking | .45 |
| As to hospital | .60 | Lack of goals | .41 |
| As to season | .56 | | |
| Knows no one | .55 | Grandiose Expansiveness | |
| | | Divine mission | .69 |
| Anxious Intropunitiveness | | Great person | .59 |
| Self-depreciating | .80 | Voices praise him | .49 |
| Blames self | .74 | Has unusual powers | .42 |
| Guilt and remorse | .71 | Attitude of superiority | .36 |
| Vaguely apprehensive | .68 | | |
| Depressed in mood | .68 | Perceptual Distortion | |
| Anxiety (specific) | .65 | Accusing voices | .72 |
| Ideas of sinfulness | .62 | Threatening voices | .65 |
| Suicidal thoughts | .61 | Hallucinatory voices | .54 |
| Recurring thoughts | .46 | Voices order him | .52 |
| Shows insight | −.44 | Other hallucinations | .44 |
| Morbid fears | .40 | Visions | .42 |
| | | Conceptual Disorganization | |
| Motor Disturbance | | Incoherent answers | .60 |
| Grimacing | .68 | Irrelevant answers | .54 |
| Repetitive movements | .64 | Neologisms | .42 |
| Rigid posture | .59 | Steroetyped speech | .42 |
| Slovenly appearance | .36 | Rambling answers | .38 |

*Note*. After Cohen, J., 1966.

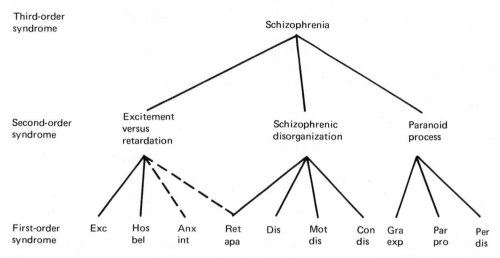

**FIG. 1** Hierarchical model of schizophrenic symptoms. Dotted line indicates negative relationship. From Lorr, Klett, and McNair, 1963.

ples in England, France, Germany, Italy, Sweden, Japan, and the United States.

The linear models of psychotic symptoms developed by Lorr and his colleagues contain either 13 (for 13 "minor" syndromes) or 4 (for 4 "major" syndromes) theoretical constructs (factors). These constructs indicate the distinct ways in which psychotic patients differ maximally. Theories of psychosis, whether genetic, biochemical, or behavioral, should take such symptom organizations into account explicitly. For example, if psychotic patients differ in four relatively independent ways, that is, there are four distinct dimensions characterizing psychotic symptoms, it makes little sense to ask simply, "Is psychosis inherited?" The question should be asked four times, once for each symptom organization.

## 3  LIFE DATA: THE ORGANIZATION OF PSYCHOTIC PATIENTS

The preceding section deals with the linear structure of psychotic symptoms. The present section concerns the distribution of patients on major dimensions of symtomatology. A psychotic symptom space of 13 dimensions can be formed by the minor syndromes (as coordinate axes). A patient's symptom profile will be a unique point in this space. The "organization of psychotic patients" refers to the dispersion of points (patients) in this space. The points may "smear" uniformly throughout the space or form high density swarms. Since far different biological and environmental determinants may operate in different symptom subspaces, finding the boundaries of subspaces and locating patients within them is crucial to the study of psychosis.

Typing of patients involves a number of steps: (a) rating patients on symptom dimensions, (b) forming a matrix having patients as border elements (rather than variables, as in the case of correlation analysis), (c) placing into cells of the matrix quantities which express the (symptom) resemblance of patients denoted by the respective rows and columns, and (d) applying a cluster search method to this resemblance-coefficients matrix. Many methods exist for expressing symptom profile resemblance (distance squared $D^2$; intraclass correlation, Haggard, 1958; Kendall's Tau, Kendall, 1948; profile similarity index $r_p$, Cattell, 1949) and for clustering patients on the basis of symptom resemblance (transpose, Q technique, factor analysis; Latent Structure Analysis, Lazarsfeld, 1950; Linkage Analysis, McQuitty, 1957; Boolean cluster search method of the Taxonome Program, Cattell & Coulter, 1966). Cluster search methodology is reviewed by Cattell, Coulter, and Tsujioka (1966) and by Bolz (1972) and Bolz in this volume (chapter 11). Some substantive results in the area of psychosis have been reviewed by Lorr, Klett, and McNair (1963).

A typical study (Lorr & Klett, 1969b) is examined here to illustrate results. Scores on IMPS factors (Table 1) were obtained for 1,100 psychotic patients from six countries (England, France, Germany, Italy, Sweden, and Japan) between the ages 18 and 55 years who were undrugged or on minimum maintenance dosages. Each patient's symptom (factor) profile was correlated with symptom profiles of all other patients, and the correlations were submitted to a cluster search routine (described in Lorr & Klett, 1969b). Twelve samples, males and females from each of six countries, were analyzed separately. Patients were distributed into five main types, which were equivalent in men and women: Excited (patients with high Excitement and to a lesser extent, Grandiosity, IMPS scores, 15% of men, 14% of women), Anxious-Depressed (high Anxious Intropunitiveness and to a lesser extent, Retardation, IMPS scores, 41% of men, 44% of women), Grandiose Paranoids (high Grandiosity and to a lesser extent, Paranoid Projection and Perceptual Distortion, IMPS scores, 7% of men, 9% of women), Hallucinated Paranoids (high Paranoid Projection and Perceptual Distortion, IMPS scores, 25% of men, 22% of women), and Retarded-

Motor Disturbed (high Retardation and Apathy and Motor Disturbance and to a lesser extent, Disorientation, IMPS scores, 11% of men, 11% of women). These results indicate that most patients are located at the extremes of one of six or seven symptom dimensions.

## 4 QUESTIONNAIRE MEASURES OF PSYCHOSIS

Personality questionnaires have long been a common source of information about psychotic patients because they are easy to administer and score. The patient, in this case, essentially rates himself on selected function dimensions. Use of the questionnaire with the psychotic patient poses special problems in that he may not know himself well and may not respond honestly even if he does. This remains a problem even when responses are treated as behavior rather than self-revelation, insofar as it results in random responding. Susceptibility of questionnaires to distortion has been noted frequently by Edwards (1957) and D. N. Jackson and Messick (1958) and treated in a novel way by Cattell and Digman (1964).

The Minnesota Multiphasic Personality Inventory (MMPI) is the most frequently used questionnaire for psychotic patients. There have been many studies of the linear structure of MMPI items to better understand the organization of the phenomena of psychosis and the nature of the instrument itself. Factor analyses of the MMPI have been reviewed elsewhere (Dahlstrom, Walsh, & Dahlstrom, 1975). The best linear model of MMPI-expressed psychotic phenomena is still far from settled. Major issues remain concerning the number of factors and their meaning.

Many studies have determined two main sources of MMPI scale variance, which Welsh (1956) labeled Factors $A$ and $R$. The $A$

factor, to which *Pt* and *Sc* contributed positively and *K* negatively, was believed to represent primarily subjective anxiety, discomfort, and distress. The *R* factor, to which *Hs, D* and *Hy* contributed positively and *Ma* negatively, was identified with poor self-insight and the use of denial and repression as defense mechanisms. Kassebaum, Couch, and Slater (1959) reinterpreted *R* as Introversion rather than Repression. If this interpretation is acceptable, the two main sources of MMPI scale variance would be the same as the major sources of variance found frequently in personality questionnaires used with normals, namely, Anxiety and Introversion (Cattell, 1957a). However, the meaning of Factors *A* and *R* is still disputable. Factor *A* was interpreted as Anxiety (Welsh, 1956), Psychoticism (Cattell, 1957a), Acquiescence (Jackson, D. N., & Messick, 1961), and Social Desirability (Edwards, A. L., & Diers, 1962).

There have been attempts to relate psychosis to personality processes discovered in normal subjects, to determine the psychotic's tolerance for frustration and his capacity to manage anxiety, dependency, dominance, ego-strength, sources of motivation, and conflict, etc. Cattell and Scheier (1961) published Sixteen Personality Factor (16 PF) Questionnaire results on 480 psychotics, 201 neurotics, and a sample of normal adults. The psychotic patients were males and females, acutely disturbed, and medicated. Compared with normal adults the psychotics had less Intelligence (Factor *B*) and Ego-strength (Factor *C*) and greater Trust (Factor *L*). The psychotics were closer to the average normal profile than were the neurotics, suggesting initially that neurosis was more woven into the fabric of personality than was psychosis or, more likely, that the psychotics had responded more randomly, attenuating their profiles toward the means of the factor scales. Whereas psy-chotics and neurotics differed from normals in the same direction on some personality traits (particularly Ego-strength), they differed from them in a different direction on Trust (Factor *L*). Low Ego-strength (Factor *C*) is found empirically in many forms of psychopathology (neurosis, psychosis, alcoholism, drug addiction, and sexual deviations, Cattell, 1965c) and has been explored clinically as the central quantitative variable in psychosis by Bellak (1958). It is difficult to interpret the findings on Trust (Factor *L*) in psychotic patients, unless it reflects their faith in, and dependence on, the mental hospital as a protective institution.

An experiment by Cattell, Tatro, and Komlos (1964) casts some light on the unexpected "normality" of the psychotics' personality profiles. They contrasted 16 PF scores of 22 paranoid schizophrenics, 41 nonparanoid schizophrenics, and 96 adult controls matched for age, sex, social class, education, and geographical residence. When tests were given to groups of patients on the ward, their scores were within normal limits; when given individually on admission, differences from normal profiles were significant. The authors speculated that the personality factors were sensitive to different stages of schizophrenia and therefore tested newly admitted undrugged patients. The results appear in Fig. 2.

In comparison with normal controls, the nonparanoid patients were introverted (Factor *A*), less intelligent (Factor *B*), and less controlled emotionally (Factor *C*), more submissive (Factor *E*), and more concerned with self-control and social reputation (Factor $Q_3$). In comparison with nonparanoid patients the paranoid patients were more intelligent (Factor *B*) and less tense (Factor $Q_4$). Factor $Q_3$ was interpreted as the capacity to "bind" anxiety, leading to the interesting hypothesis that one of the schizophrenic's major personality problems

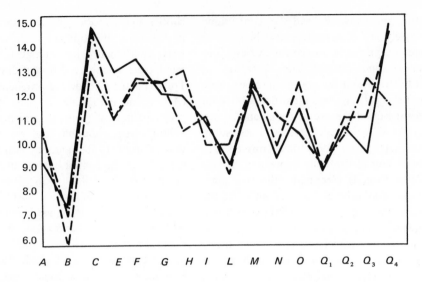

Factor scores:

| | A | B | C | E | F | G | H | I | L | M | N | O | $Q_1$ | $Q_2$ | $Q_3$ | $Q_4$ | |
|---|---|---|---|---|---|---|---|---|---|---|---|---|---|---|---|---|---|
| Paranoid | 10.1 | | 14.6 | | 12.7 | | 12.9 | | 9.9 | | 11.1 | | 9.2 | | 12.7 | | —·—·— |
| schizophrenics | | 7.0 | | 11.0 | | 12.4 | | 9.9 | | 12.4 | | 10.5 | | 10.6 | | 11.5 | |
| Nonparanoid | 10.6 | | 12.9 | | 12.6 | | 10.6 | | 8.7 | | 10.0 | | 9.0 | | 11.2 | | — — — |
| schizophrenics | | 5.6 | | 10.9 | | 12.4 | | 11.1 | | 12.6 | | 12.5 | | 11.2 | | 14.5 | |
| Normal | 9.1 | | 14.7 | | 13.4 | | 11.9 | | 9.1 | | 9.4 | | 9.0 | | 9.6 | | ———— |
| controls | | 7.2 | | 12.8 | | 12.0 | | 10.8 | | 12.2 | | 11.4 | | 10.7 | | 14.8 | |

**FIG. 2** 16 Personality Factor profiles of paranoid schizophrenics, nonparanoid schizophrenics, and normal controls. *A, B, C,* etc. are Cattell's personality factors. From Cattell, Tatro, and Komlos (1964).

is his excessive use of this capacity to bind anxiety rather than to tolerate it and examine its sources adaptively (Cattell, Tatro, & Komlos, 1964).

Questionnaire results on psychotic patients indicate that there are at least two major ways in which psychotic patients differ from one another in symptomatology and some four or five ways in which psychotic patients differ from normal adults. The latter give some indication of the personality processes on which psychotic symptoms appear most frequently to settle, namely, intelligence, emotional control, and social withdrawal.

## 5 OBJECTIVE TEST MEASURES OF PSYCHOSIS

Objective tests (e.g., reaction time, verbal fluency, finger tapping, and body tempo) offer a radically different approach to the study of psychosis, compared with questionnaires and observer ratings. Studies of the relations of these tests to personality have a relatively long history (Downey, 1923; Flugel, 1929; Goldberg, L. R., 1974). Their relationship to psychosis has been studied in the multivariate tradition by Cattell (1957a) and H. J. Eysenck (1961) and their colleagues. Psychomotor aspects of psychosis were studied in univariate experiments (Hunt, J. McV., 1944); but, as noted earlier, these results lacked integration and led to considerable confusion.

Research by Eysenck and his colleagues is reviewed elsewhere (Eysenck, H. J., 1961) and is not examined here. Cattell and Tatro (1966) reported a major study of psychomotor functions in psychotic patients. Fifty-two objective tests believed to measure 18 personality constructs in normal people (Hundleby, Pawlik, and Cattell, 1965) were administered to 138 psychotic patients (24 paranoid schizophrenics, 57 nonparanoid schizophrenics, and 57 affective disorders) and 96 normal adults, who were matched with the patients for age, sex, social status, and education. The patients were recently admitted, undrugged males and females between the age 18 and 55 years, who had clear staff diagnoses.

They were tested in groups of four to six patients on four consecutive days in testing sessions lasting 2 hours each. In comparison with the normal adults the patients had less Ego-strength (Universal Index Factor *U.I.* 16), Independence (*U.I.* 19), Exuberance (*U.I.* 21) and Realism (*U.I.* 25), and more Inhibition (*U.I.* 17), Regression (*U.I.* 23), Pessimism (*U.I.* 33) and Dissofrustance (*U.I.* 30). These factors are described verbally in Table 2. No psychomotor factor differences between paranoid and nonparanoid patients were significant statistically. The authors concluded,

Our general theoretical position is supported in that psychotics (a) like neurotics differ from normals not on one dimension but on a whole pattern of dimensions; (b) share some dimensions of significant deviation in the *same* direction as neurotics; but (c) manifest

**TABLE 2** Principal objective personality factors distinguishing psychotics from normals

| Factor | Title | Psychological description of positive pole |
|--------|-------|--------------------------------------------|
| *U.I.* 16 | Developed ego versus Unassertiveness | Fast speed and action tempo; self-assertive in competitive situations; strong body physique. |
| *U.I.* 17 | Timid distrust versus Trust | High caution and timidity; tendency toward inhibiting overt action; unalert. |
| *U.I.* 19 | Independence versus Subduedness | Accurate, competent performance; critical of others; low social suggestibility. |
| *U.I.* 21 | Exuberance versus Restraint | Fast speed of social and perceptual judgement; high verbal fluency; sensitive to threat and emotional stimulation; high physiological activity. |
| *U.I.* 23 | Mobilization versus Regression | Low rigidity; less dependence on environment; less extremity of viewpoint; able to endure stress. |
| *U.I.* 25 | Realism versus Tensinflexia | Less imaginative cognition; high accuracy and speed in well-structured tasks; reality-directed attitudes; reduced emotional tensions. |
| *U.I.* 30 | Mature Stolidness versus Dissofrustance | Slow psychomotor speed and tempo; careless; independent attitude; restricted emotionality. |
| *U.I.* 33 | Pessimism versus Optimism | Slow in warming to new tasks; inhibited; compulsive; advanced in intelligence. |

significant deviations quite peculiar to themselves (Cattell & Tatro, 1966, p. 50).

In contrast to views of the London group (Eysenck, H. J., 1960b; Eysenck, H. J., 1961c; Eysenck, S. B. G., 1956) Cattell and Tatro viewed neurosis and psychosis as each involving multidimensional, rather than unidimensional, deviations from normality which overlap with respect to some personality factors but are unique with respect to others. The findings by Cattell and Tatro were in general agreement with the results of a similar study by Killian (1965).

Understanding psychotic disorders from a factor-analytic standpoint ultimately translates into a problem of factor interpretation. The latter is an arduous, painstaking process (Burt, 1939; Cattell, 1962a) that involves studying variables that load the factor highly as well as those appearing in its hyperplane, matching factor patterns, examining age trends and nature-nurture ratios of factors, and examining the forms of a factor in different cultures and the effects on it of experimental and clinical treatments. According to these standards the factors appearing in Table 2 are incompletely understood. There are some interesting leads. Cattell, Stice, and Kristy (1957) found a substantial genetic component for two factors (*U.I.* 19 and *U.I.* 21) separating psychotics from normals, using the quantitative genetic methodology known as Multiple Abstract Variance Analysis (MAVA). Evidence for interpretations given other objective test factors (Hundleby, Pawlik, & Cattell, 1965) suggests that psychotic patients do not differ from normal adults on anxiety (*U.I.* 24) nor on problems associated with social authority and superego control (*U.I.* 22, 28, and 29). They are reported to share with the neurotic difficulties in regulating impulses in line with realistic possibilities for satisfaction in the environment

(Factor *U.I.* 16) and excessive inhibition (*U.I.* 17, 19, and 21). Hundleby, Pawlik, and Cattell (1965) speculated that *Dissofrustance* (*U.I.* 30) represents a tendency to disintegrate under stress or, more specifically, to resolve conflict problems by dissociating the cognitive systems involved. Cattell and Tatro (1966), therefore, concluded,

It may be that we have here an inability to handle conflict by moderate compromise and integrative procedures which could lie at the root of those ultimate dissociations recognized in psychosis (p. 49).

Tatro (1966) examined the factor organization of 100 objective test measures obtained on 85 male and 143 female psychotic patients. It has been established that psychotics and normals differ in factor level (as noted previously); the question now is whether they also differ in factor organization. Are linear structural relations among objective personality tests the same for psychotic patients and normal adults? Will the same factor model adequately describe the two samples of individuals? It is conceivable that the psychotic process involves a significant reorganization of psychomotor functions and that this is important for understanding psychosis psychologically. The 100 test measures were resolved into 21 factors that were similar to factors found in normal adults (Hundleby, Pawlik, & Cattell, 1965). Factor solutions for the two sets of individuals were quite similar, as indicated by Burt's congruency coefficient for factor patterns (Harman, 1967). Cattell, Dubin, and Saunders (1954) arrived at the same conclusion after factoring 100 objective measures obtained on 104 psychotic patients.

Of Tatro's (1966) patients, 130 were studied clinically. The patients' social competence; expression of affect; use of defense mechanisms; developmental maturity; relative strengths of ego, superego, and drive forces; quality of interpersonal relations; and psychiatric status were estimated by rating interview and case history material using 102 clinical scales. These scales were reduced to 71, intercorrelated, and resolved into 15 (principal axis) factors. The first factor extracted is presented in Table 3 for illustrative purposes. This factor is a composite of clinical scales suggesting the presence of inhibited, blocked affect, which is maladaptive in that it arises from excessive superego control but is also adaptive in that it appears to control the expression of extreme psychotic symptoms.

Tatro (1966) also related clinical factors to personality factors by computing multiple correlations. The results indicated that roughly 30%–50% of differences in the patients' clinical condition (factors) could be predicted by differences in personality factors. This finding is similar to what was found for questionnaires (Specht, 1966). A major aim of this chapter is to relate psychotic clinical conditions to personality factors. There is a relationship, but it is incomplete. A complete account of psychotic symptomatology will have to consider more than the patient's personality. Some other important influences are considered in the last section of this chapter.

## 6 INTENSIVE STUDIES OF INDIVIDUAL PATIENTS

Psychotic patients are different from one another. Factor-analytic studies (reviewed earlier) develop linear models for these differences. There is considerable merit to studying intensively the individual patient quantitatively. All so-called "universals" of psychosis can be discovered in a *single* psychotic patient who has been properly classified. In addition, background factors affecting the clinical course of psychotic conditions can be examined in exquisite detail in the individual patient. Findings can be generalized about the patient and all patients like him (Chassan, 1960). Some relationships between symptoms and determinants are impossible to discover in principle using a group design (Chassan, 1960; Mefferd, Moran, & Kimble, 1960). Advances in time-series analysis (Holtzman, 1963; Quenouille, 1957) and associated computer software (Shiskin & Eisenpress, 1957) have

**TABLE 3**  Criterion factor 1: Constrictive self-control versus expansive self-abandon

| Variable | Loading | Variable | Loading |
|---|---|---|---|
| Overemotionality | −.58 | Feeling of persecution | −.35 |
| Psychomotor retardation | .43 | Hallucination | −.35 |
| Excitement | −.43 | Delusion | −.32 |
| Apathy | .43 | Elation | −.32 |
| Superego strength | .42 | Feeling of grandeur | −.31 |
| Isolation of affect | −.42 | Objective, outer-oriented | .29 |
| Blocking | .42 | Fantasy | −.29 |
| Feeling of influence | −.40 | Displacement | −.28 |
| Thought disorganization | −.39 | Acting-out | −.25 |
| Compulsive behavior | .37 | | |

*Note.* From Tatro, 1966.

enabled the study of time-related observations that support statistical inferences. The analysis of multiple time series has been useful for the detailed study of neurotic patients (Cattell & Luborsky, 1950), psychotic patients (Mefferd, Moran, & Kimble, 1960; Williams, J. R., 1959), a mentally defective girl (Shotwell, Hurley, & Cattell, 1961), and the physiological states of normal adults (Cattell & Williams, 1953; Wieland & Mefferd, 1970).

In principle, a pair of variables measured on many occasions on one person may be correlated just as they may be correlated when measured on many people on one occasion. A matrix of such correlations may be transformed (e.g., factor analyzed) just like any other correlation matrix, and inferences may be made with respect to a population of occasions, rather than the more familiar population of subjects. The single case is the universe, and many inferences may be made concerning it (and all cases like it).

Mefferd, Moran, and Kimble (1960) estimated the psychiatric condition, using ratings, a word-association test, and serum copper levels of a chronic schizophrenic patient on each of 246 consecutive days. Serum copper is of special interest clinically because nearly all of it is bound as ceruloplasmin (White, A., Handler, & Smith, 1968), a plasma globulin often elevated during acute schizophrenia (Abood, 1960). On 120 days the patient received 400 mg chlorpromazine. During this period there was a definite inverse relationship ($r = -.72$) between the patient's psychiatric condition and levels of serum copper. A striking finding was that throughout this period of time the patient's serum copper remained within normal limits. Had he been a member of a group of patients like himself and compared with normal controls, the researchers would have concluded (wrongly, in the case of this patient) that there was no relationship between psychiatric condition and serum copper.

In an interesting longitudinal study, J. R. Williams (1959) explored the amount and type of conflict in 6 hospitalized psychiatric patients and 6 controls. He measured 14 attitudes on 40 occasions for the 6 individuals. The attitudes were intercorrelated over the occasions of measurement and 6 centroid factors were extracted and rotated separately for each person. The author reasoned that conflict would be indicated by the appearance of *both* positive and negative (loading) attitudes in the same attitude factor. When such occurred, the individual was able to take action implied by the attitude factor only at the cost of losing emotional satisfactions invested in the negative (loading) attitudes. He would thus be in an approach-avoidance conflict with respect to taking the action. There were 6 areas of possible conflict, represented quantitatively by the 6 attitude organizations (factors). Williams developed a formula to express the total conflict in an individual and related this quantitative index to hospitalization status and the psychiatrists' subjective ratings of conflict in the 12 subjects. The psychiatric patients had significantly more (quantitatively estimated) conflict than the normal controls, ($p < .01$ by a Mann-Whitney $U$ test), and the quantitatively estimated conflict was positively related to the psychiatrists' ratings of conflict. This method is a promising technique for the quantitative study of conflict in individual patients.

Despite its obvious importance, little is known about the process of change in psychotic patients. Psychosis is a multidimensional clinical condition. The dimensions of psychosis, as revealed by factor analysis of the behavior of psychotic patients, have been reviewed. Change in psychosis can conveniently be referred to as a movement along these behavior dimensions. Specifying a definite *state* of psychosis would mean locating the patient on all major behavior dimensions at some point of time, and *change* would refer to the propagation of states of psychosis through time. Currently, little is known about the states of psychosis, about what in the environment or the body triggers these states, and about diurnal variations of states and their natural clinical course over longer periods of time.

The author has completed intensive longitudinal studies of four chronic schizophrenic patients. Two younger patients (age 35 and 36 years) were hospitalized almost continuously for 8 and 14 years, respectively, with diagnoses of acute undifferentiated schizophrenia and simple schizophrenia. Two older patients (age 46 and 52 years) had been hospitalized for 30 years with diagnoses of catatonic schizophrenia and paranoid schizophrenia. Three patients received antipsychotic tranquilizers (Mellaril) during the course of the study, while the fourth patient was unmedicated; all four patients were paid for participating in the study. Three patients were seen on 95 occasions and the fourth on 78 occasions covering a 3-month period. On each occasion the patient was administered a battery of tests sampling affective, cognitive, psychomotor, and physiological aspects of functioning; and each was interviewed. His behavior on the ward was rated daily, using standard scales. All unusual incidences on the ward and extrahospital contacts were noted and recorded. A total of 102 observations (44 objective test and 58 clinical) were collected on each patient on each occasion. These multiple time series are typical of what may be expected from the intensive quantitative study of the individual patient. There are a number of statistical models for studying such time series (Holtzman, 1963).

One approach is to partition the total change in behavior into its distinct orthogonal components by means of factor analysis (*P*-technique factor analysis). A linear composite

$$F_m = \sum_{j=1}^{p} a_j z_j, \qquad (2)$$

where $F_m (m = 1, 2 \ldots k)$ is a factor of change, $z_j(j = 1, 2 \ldots p)$ is a test measure (or clinical rating), and $a_j$ its linear coefficient, is found such that the variance of $F_m$ over time is maximized. There may be $k$ dimensions of maximum change, each constituting a distinct form of patient states. Two such linear composites (states) are shown in Table 4 and 5. The linear coefficients (factor loadings) for each patient constitute a column of the tables. Only the largest loading variables are presented.

Factor I (Table 4) is a composite of test measures having a strong linear change across the duration of the study in all four patients. The major elements of the state (variables having large loadings) vary from patient to patient, but nearly all are test measures affected by learning and practice. The word-association test loadings, and clinical ratings which were analyzed separately and are not shown, suggest that Factor I reflects a linear improvement in clinical condition during the study as well as improvement in test performance due to practice.

Factor II (Table 5) is a composite of measures related to motivation (narcissism and fear). Narcissism and fear measures (a preference test, Cattell, 1957a) tended to be inversely related in all patients. On the occasions when fear was high, narcissism was low, and vice versa. The remaining composition of the state varies considerably from patient to patient. Patient 1 had more

**TABLE 4** Dimensions of change in chronic schizophrenia: Factor I

| Variable | Loading | | | |
| | P(1) | P(2) | P(3) | P(4) |
| --- | --- | --- | --- | --- |
| Occasion number | .90 | .90 | .80 | .71 |
| Speed of closure (RPM) | .83 | .32 | .69 | .72 |
| Serial subtraction | .77 | .77 | .04 | .22 |
| Breath-holding time | −.77 | −.03 | .59 | .10 |
| Rapid cancellation | .76 | .44 | .66 | .78 |
| Number facility (RPM) | .66 | .29 | .48 | .50 |
| Alternating perspective | −.58 | .84 | −.46 | −.25 |
| Remote word associations | −.39 | −.62 | −.10 | −.18 |
| Delayed recall | −.04 | .56 | .15 | .31 |
| Word-association latency | −.06 | −.24 | −.88 | −.51 |
| Word-association refusals | −.06 | −.03 | −.71 | −.18 |
| Performance estimate | .30 | −.42 | −.45 | .82 |
| Unwarned reaction time | .15 | −.13 | −.12 | −.81 |
| Negative afterimage duration | −.15 | −.26 | −.13 | −.77 |

remote word associations on occasions when he reported being afraid and less interested in sensual pleasure (narcissism). Patient 2 reported being afraid when sexual interest was strong and he wished to be with others (gregariousness), and he was unconcerned about social reputation (self-sentiment motivation) and less interested in nonsexual pleasure (narcissism). Patient 3 reported little interest in narcissistic pleasure late in the week (weekends). In Patient 4 fear was associated with his need for social contact with others (gregariousness); less interest in narcissistic pleasure; and deterioration of performance on two measures requiring careful concentration, serial subtraction, and speed of (perceptual) closure. These results indicate interesting differences in motivation states among the four patients. These differ-

ences could not be explored in detail in group studies.

It is interesting to note the broad similarities of the preceding analysis of behavior and psychoanalysis. In factor analysis, individual behaviors are analyzed into elemental parts shared by different people (common factors), plus a part unique to the person plus an unanalyzable part (error) lying outside the factor model. One attempts to peek behind manifest behavior to understand underlying behavior constructs (factors), using the classic simplicity and power of mathematics. In psychoanalysis, individual behaviors (symptoms, parapraxes) are analyzed into elemental personality forces (id, ego, superego) that have common forms, forms unique to the individual, and forms that are unanalyzable in the individual case.

The resolution of symptoms into factors has a number of important implications. One

**TABLE 5** Dimensions of change in chronic schizophrenia: Factor II

| Variable | Loading | | | |
| | P(1) | P(2) | P(3) | P(4) |
| --- | --- | --- | --- | --- |
| Narcissistic motivation | −.85 | −.95 | −.40 | −.49 |
| Fear motivation | .75 | .95 | .19 | .49 |
| Remote word associations | .35 | −.10 | −.05 | −.06 |
| Elated mood | −.35 | .07 | −.02 | .12 |
| Sexual motivation | .02 | .98 | .05 | −.20 |
| Self-sentiment motivation | −.06 | −.81 | −.11 | −.03 |
| Gregariousness motivation | .08 | .58 | .19 | .73 |
| Day of week | .10 | .12 | .83 | −.02 |
| Number facility (RPM) | .12 | −.04 | .34 | −.05 |
| Speed of closure (RPM) | .04 | .12 | −.29 | −.25 |
| Serial subtraction, errors | .02 | −.03 | −.01 | .73 |
| Speed of closure (RPM), errors | .22 | .15 | .06 | .56 |

is that a symptom expression at any point in time can originate in multiple ways by means of difference combinations of factors. Symptoms may be changing from occasion to occasion because underlying factors are changing on those occasions, and the latter changes will be reflected in changing factor scores. These changes (in factor scores) for two patients and two factors are shown in Fig. 3. There were large day-to-day fluctuations in psychomotor performances (Factor I) and a general linear trend indicating improvement during the study. Patient 2 dropped in motivation (Factor II) on occasion 2 and changed very little thereafter. Patient 1 dropped in motivation on Occa-

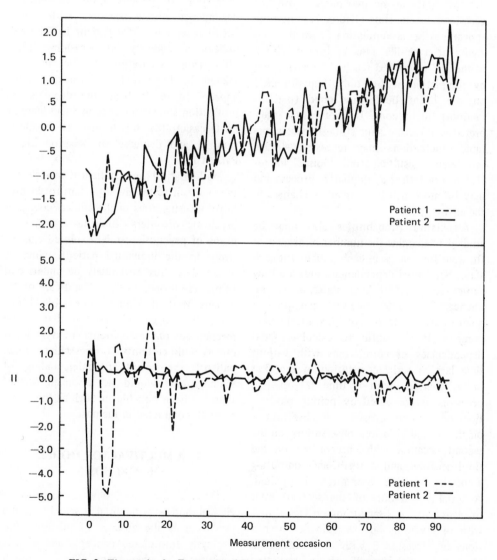

**FIG. 3** Time series for Factors I and II of two chronic schizophrenic patients.

sions 6, 7, and 8 and showed occasional large changes thereafter. The propagation of these two multiform patient states indicates that different aspects of functioning in the same patient can change quite differently over time and that different patients can change differently over time.

Figure 3 also describes the sequences of the two states in the two patients over 95 occasions. In one state (Factor I) something appears to be accumulating in small increments at a similar rate in both patients, neither of which has reached an asymptote by completion of the study. Superimposed on the linear trends are rapid (perhaps random) fluctuations. If Factor I is interpreted as involving some storage process, the rapid fluctuations may represent storage interference resulting from "noise." Factor II does not reflect a cumulative process and may be more tightly coupled to changes in the environment.

Associative probabilities also may be studied to examine the number of degrees of freedom for change in each patient for each state. Sequential dependencies indicate how earlier states affect later states in the sequence. Time-series analysis can provide quantitative indexes of historical phenomena. It is helpful to calculate serial dependencies or correlations with various time lags. A serial correlation of the first order, that is, with a time lag of one occasion, is computed by pairing observations on the first occasion with observations on the second occasion, observations on the second occasion with observations on the third occasion, and so forth, and computing a correlation across observations thus paired. A serial correlation of the second order involves pairing observations on Occasion 1 with observations on Occasion 3, observations on Occasion 2 with observations on Occasion 4, and so forth. These correlation coefficients indicate how phenomena with

various time separations are connected and how the presence of rhythms can be detected.

Serial correlations can be plotted as a function of time lag, forming a "correlogram" as shown in Fig. 4 for Factor II and Patients 1 and 2. The results indicate little occasion-to-occasion dependence in motivation state for patient 2 but considerable dependence among occasions with a one-occasion separation for Patient 1. They also indicate a tendency for occasions with 10-occasion separation to be inversely related in Patient 1. The latter finding appears to result from the decrease (in motivation state) on Occasion 8 and increase on Occasion 18, and the increase on Occasion 11 and decrease on Occasion 21, in Patient 1.

Mathematical and statistical models for the study of states are important for quantitative investigations of the clinical course of psychotic disorders. Biobehavioral mechanisms of psychosis can be explored exhaustively in the individual patient, which is where they must ultimately be understood to provide proper treatment and care of the patient. Mefferd, Moran, and Kimble (1960) made the cogent observation that if the mechanisms of schizophrenia could be determined with certainty in *one* schizophrenic patient, the scientific understanding of schizophrenia would be advanced further than has been possible through all the group research conducted in the past.

## 7  A MULTIFACTOR MODEL OF PSYCHOSIS

One of the most obvious features of clinical and experimental research on the psychoses is the absence of precisely and explicitly formulated concepts and models for psychotic phenomena. There is much discussion of schizophrenic types, depressive

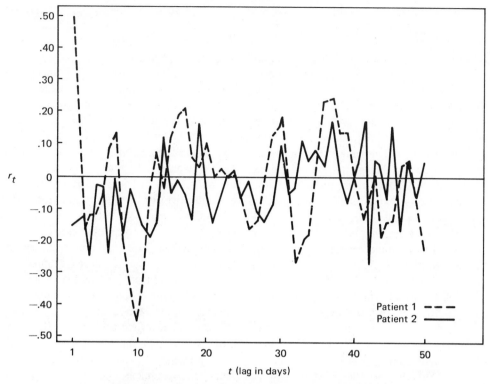

**FIG. 4**  Correlograms for Factor II of two chronic schizophrenic patients.

or catatonic states, the psychotic process, psychodynamic mechanisms, and patient roles without a clear conceptualization of the formal mathematico-statistical, logical, and operational properties of types, states, processes, mechanisms, and roles. Models for these concepts are discussed elsewhere in this book, as well as in Cattell (1966e).

In principle, it is possible to resolve a symptom of a psychotic patient completely into its determinants; in practice, it is painfully obvious that this currently cannot be done. A multifactor model of psychosis may be helpful, however, in indicating how far multivariate research on psychosis has advanced and whether there are glaring lacunae in our understanding. Symptoms may be translated into factors according to the specification equation

$$
\begin{aligned}
a_{ji} = {}& b_{jA_1}A_{1i} + \cdots + b_{jA_x}A_{xi} \\
& + b_{jT_1}T_{1i} + \cdots + b_{jT_y}T_{yi} \\
& + b_{jD_1}D_{1i} + \cdots + b_{jD_z}D_{zi} \\
& + b_{jS_1}S_{1i} + \cdots + b_{jS_k}S_{ki} \\
& + b_{jR_1}R_{1i} + \cdots + b_{jR_m}R_{mi} \\
& + b_{jP_1}P_{1i} + \cdots + b_{jP_n}P_{ni} \\
& + e_{ji}, \hspace{3.5cm} (3)
\end{aligned}
$$

where $a_{ji}$ is a symptomatic behavior of Patient 1 in situation $j$; $A$ is a set of terms for the patient's ability factors; $T$, terms for temperament (or characterological) factors; $D$, terms for drives or motivation; $S$, terms for momentary states; $R$, terms for social roles; $P$, terms for mental and perceptual sets; and $e_{ji}$, is a term for error or changes in the symptom in the situation that are not accounted for by the model. There is no specific term for genetic factors, since it is assumed that all factors in Equation (3) are to some extent heritable. The $b$ coefficients represent the relations between the symptom and the factors.

Equation 3 assumes that the behavioral expression of a symptom is a function of the patient's abilities, temperament, motivation, physiological and behavioral states (diurnal rhythms, etc.), social roles, and mental and perceptual sets that interact with the particular situation (as indicated by $b$ coefficients) in a manner that is linear and additive and involves multiple causation. It may be argued without difficulty that terms for important unknowns affecting the expression of psychotic symptoms are missing in the model and that a linear function is inadequate for expressing the complexity of the relations between symptoms and their determinants. The model may be incomplete, in which case the error $e_{ji}$ will be large. However, some evidence (Tatro, 1966) suggests that nearly 50% of psychotic symptom variations can be predicted by temperament $(T)$ factors alone. There may be special roles (e.g., the "patient" role), states, and motivation conditions which are peculiar to psychotic patients or to certain forms of psychosis; special terms may be needed for these factors. Where this possibility has been tested, namely, for personality traits (Cattell, Dubin, & Saunders, 1954; Tatro, 1966), the results suggested that new terms were not needed for personality factor organizations peculiar to psychotic patients. They may be needed for other classes of factor variables, however, particularly for roles and states.

An additive model for psychotic symptoms may be unsatisfactory. Let us suppose that the symptom is the expression of delusions of grandeur in a specific setting.

The expression of the symptom may be more probable in patients who are Cyclothymic $(T_1)$, Dominant $(T_2)$, and Self-assertive $(D_1)$ in an additive fashion. However, the probability of expressing the symptom may increase greatly whenever the patient perceives that he has just suffered insults to his sense of self-esteem $(P_1)$, is feeling anxious $(S_1)$ and assumes a patient role $(R_1)$. The relations among $P_1$, $S_1$ and $R_1$, with respect to their combined effects on expression of the symptom, may be multiplicative or a power function. The relationship may be "permissive," in the sense that one response may not be conditionally related to expression of the symptom until some other response (say, anxiety) reaches a certain critical value. Conjunctive models (Coombs & Kao, 1955) or permissive models (Cattell, 1957a) may be more suitable than a linear (additive) model. However, until it is shown that some more complicated polynomial is necessary, it is useful to accept a simple linear model.

Equation 3 may offer a framework for examining where multivariate research on psychosis has been primarily directed and how far this research has advanced toward understanding the symptomatic behavior of psychotic patients. This understanding might involve the following: (a) discovering the structure (organization) of psychotic symptoms, (b) discovering estimatable determinants of psychotic symptoms, (c) developing efficient instruments for measuring factors relevant to psychosis, (d) examining the environment with respect to its capacity to elicit psychotic symptoms, and (e) exploring different polynomials for relating symptoms to determinants. Multivariate research on psychosis has been restricted almost exclusively to step (a), that is, studying the organization of behavior on the left-hand side of Equation 3. There has been some research at steps (b) and (c) and virtually no research at steps (d) and (e). There has been virtually no multivariate research on what multidimensional stimuli lead to those multidimensional responses, which we call "psychotic behavior," and very little research on relating symptom factors to nonsymptom factors. The multivariate organization of psychotic symptoms and the organization of psychotic patients in psychiatric symptom space have been given considerable attention, perhaps too much attention in relation to other areas of psychosis that need research. Taxonomy, the topic which stimulated T. V. Moore's (1933) pioneering work, is still the major interest of most multivariate researchers. Perhaps, after decades of research on the problems of classification, the field can now move on to the other problems that are pressing for solutions.

## 8  SUMMARY

1. Research on the psychoses has evolved through three main investigative traditions: the clinical, the univariate experimental, and the multivariate experimental. This chapter presented substantive findings, methods, and models associated with the multivariate research tradition. The aim of this research is not only improved classification of patients but the development of multivariate models for some aspects of psychosis stated in precise, mathematical terms.

2. Multivariate research on psychosis started with exploration of the organization of psychotic symptoms and the organization of psychotic patients in psychiatric symptom space, using factor analysis and multivariate cluster search methods. The former method resolves manifest symptoms into idealized symptoms (symptom factors), and the latter method resolves individual patients into idealized patients (patient categories). This research has been obstructed by the wide diversity of methods and lists of symptoms used.

3. The study of psychosis through the use of questionnaires has been restricted primarily to the MMPI. Research on questionnaires developed for use with normal adults suggests that in comparison with normal adults, nonparanoid schizophrenic patients are more introverted, less intelligent, less controlled emotionally, more concerned with self-control, more submissive and more concerned with social reputation.

4. Studies using objective tests indicated that in comparison with normal adults, psychotic patients had less ego-strength, independence, exuberance, and realism, and more inhibition, regression, pessimism, and dissofrustance. Psychosis appears to be a multidimensional, rather than a unidimensional, deviation from normality. It has been estimated that roughly 30%–50% of the variance in the clinical condition of psychotic patients can be accounted for on the basis of differences in objectively measured personality factors.

5. There are certain unique advantages to studying intensively the individual psychotic patient quantitatively. Recent advances in mathematical and statistical models for time-series observations enable the researcher to discover relationships that were impossible to discover in the past and are impossible in principle to discover by means of research on groups of patients. Three illustrative experiments on individual patients were described.

6. Research on psychosis has been generally lacking in precisely formulated concepts and models. Application of a linear model for psychotic symptoms suggested that multivariate research on psychosis has been rather narrowly confined to the problem of classifying patients. This field of research requires a fuller application of multivariate methodology for a more complete understanding of the psychotic patient.

# Section 7

## Integrations of Personality Concepts

# 29

## Personality and Socio-Ethical Values: The Structure of Self and Superego

**Richard L. Gorsuch**
*University of Texas at Arlington*

**Raymond B. Cattell**
*University of Hawaii, Honolulu*

## 1 OPERATIONAL CONCEPTS OF THE SELF

The great bulk—and it is a very great bulk—of psychological writing on the self has been until recently nonquantitative. Despite the obvious importance of understanding the final integration of the response behavior that psychology studies, experimentalists have avoided it—frightened off by the futility of attacking by pedestrian bivariate classical experimental methods something that obviously demanded imaginative, new multivariate methods. Those methods must combine broad perspectives with hard-headed precision of concepts and methods.[1]

The present chapter combines two topics that at first may not seem organically united: the structure of the self and the psychology of values. Actually, we plan to show that ethical values, the relation of

personality to society, and the development of the self-structure are best studied together. When W. James (1892) and McDougall (1923) spoke of material, social, and spiritual selves and the role of self-esteem (McDougall's "self assertive propensity") in relation to all of them, they also were recognizing this *plexus* of self, society, and values. As Wylie (1960) showed, most discussions have woven a path in and out of these areas.

A definition of the self must emerge as we proceed, but a preliminary definition of *values* is necessary (even though we elaborate more in section 6 of this chapter) to avoid a common misunderstanding at the outset. In dictionary English, a *value* is "that which is worthwhile, important, or esteemed" and as such it could be the goal of any drive or interest whatsoever. The sooner we put aside this wide meaning—synonymous with already available terms such as *incentive, valence,* or *interest*—the better. (Unfortunately, this meaning continues in such tests as the *Allport-Vernon Study of Values,* 1951.) A more restricted, useful, and centrally intended meaning of

---

[1] A second reason, perhaps, why objective methods, bivariate *or* multivariate, have avoided this field, is that it is a raucous marketplace for all manner of loose clinical, philosophical, and humanist dogma, in which working with quiet precision is ignored.

values is a set of moral or artistic standards or beliefs, that is, attitudes and interests in one particular area.

Like values, the self is also a culturally confused concept or, at the least, one on which there is much semantic disagreement; but in this case our approach to a definition is that of a naturalist or an explorer. We are going to ask what structures exist in the general area semantically indicated and then converge on descriptive definitions for each entity found. This descriptive separation of what is often popularly covered by the same word must begin with the more obvious semantic separation of a trinity of meanings: (a) the *experienced or felt self,* which every man knows by immediate introspection; (b) the purely *cognitive self-concept*—an idea such as the individual entertains about any object but now develops about himself; and (c) the *structural, acting self* inferred by an observer from patterns of behavior.

Before behavioristic standards prevailed, psychologists at the beginning of this century, such as Titchener, Stout, Ward, Buhler, Ach, Michotte, Kulpe, James, Aveling, and others, threw what light they could on the first of these phenomena by introspective methods. For example, Aveling (see Cattell, 1930) showed that subjective awareness of the acting self waxed intense in decisions and acts of will. He and Cattell (1930) also showed that in the temporal course of an act of perception, as Plato had surmised, an undifferentiated *pathemic* experience splits in a fraction of a second into awareness of self and object, the self-object separation being greater when stronger dynamic response is involved, as shown by magnitude of the galvanic skin reflex. There are numerous introspective protocols handed down from the structuralism period in which "I see a blue book" is stated to consist of a field of consciousness in which the sensation of blue, in certain relations, coexists with

kinesthetic sensations, in the chest which constitute the felt "I."

Although the present chapter is concerned beyond this point with the felt self ("somewhere back of the eyes and in the chest"), the fact cannot be overlooked, at a common-sense level, that the mystery of consciousness at its most acute expressions is peculiarly linked with adaptive behavior by the self. Furthermore, useful hunches about the behavioral structural self (i.e., as inferred from behavior patterns) might be gained (with the advantages of a foot placed on independent ground, ulterior to behavior) from the extensive past work on the introspected self, including the more recent work of C. R. Rogers and Dymond (1954).

Even when this felt, subjective self has been firmly set aside from any strict behavioral science study of the self, a major current confusion persists regarding one of the two remaining concepts—the *self-concept plexus* and the *structural dynamic, coordinating self*. The phrase "self-concept plexus" will be used or implied here when dealing with behavior associated with the self-concept because we must accept the fact, evident from the beginning, that this is more than a purely cognitive entity—a concept. It is immediately the focus of such powerful attitudes that, unlike most perceived concepts, it locates also a major dynamic *sentiment*. It is this plexus of cognitive and dynamic response potentials that we must pursue to further definition by experimental approaches.

On looking a little more closely at this self-concept, one immediately encounters the absurd situation that what one set of psychologists is defining as "the self-perceived self" another group is pursuing as "the total personality." The second and the third conceptions are, without evidence, run together. For example, questionnaires are made up in studies allegedly of the self-concept which differ in no discernible way from ordinary personality questionnaires. They ask such questions as "Are you shy?" "Do you like to play football?" and "Do you consider yourself a sensitive person?" Should not a line be drawn, one asks, between these total general descriptions of the individual's behavior as the person sees himself and a more restricted entity called the self-concept? For if we do not, then both in regard to a person's concept of himself, and the experimenting observer's conceptual inference about[2] the individual's structural self, there is no distinction between *self* and the total personality.

Despite this embarrassment, psychologists, like the man in the street, have remained obstinately addicted to talking of the self as something different from the total personality. Yet it is still possible that we may have to apply Occam's razor to a superfluous term. As pointed out later, some psychologists, for example, G. A. Kelly (1955), have tried to make a distinction on grounds of content, in terms of more central and more peripheral aspects of personality, as William James once did. Unless this can be backed by operational separation, it is arbitrary and must be rejected. Fortunately, in sections 2 and 3 in this chapter, means for operational separation, mostly not concerned with content, but rather with the manner of the subject's perception of and reaction to the

content are brought forward. By contrast with this self, the mere self-description (with certain corrections, as discussed in trait-view theory) is essentially the total personality. That is to say, it is a panorama of a score or more of largely independent source-trait structures defining the personality, just as height, weight, and so forth, define a box. One of the main expressions of the self arises in the manner of the individual's perception of his personality, and this exerts a pattern of effects on his behavior that can be recognized as a behavioral structure and one different from those due to his general temperament traits or dynamic dispositional traits. We return later to the notion that the self-concept is not merely of cognitive importance but becomes important as the focus and origin of a whole dynamic trait structure.

Later we ask the question of whether this definition is the same as the third meaning of self mentioned earlier. In this purely behavioristic approach we ask if there is something the external observer believes he can infer from behavior as a separate self-system, or subset of phenomena within the total personality behavior. Our first natural inquiry is whether it would be expected to appear, for example, by factor analysis or other evidence of unitariness, say, as one more trait structure. There seems some reluctance, especially among philosophical psychologists, to accept this hypothesis of the self as one more structure among other peer source traits. They want the self to be something more than an addition to a trait series, or just a special dimension of personality. They prefer some notion of a superordinate concept—perhaps some effect of *total constellation* of all the trait parts. If the philosopher means what he says— literally a constellation or pattern of relations among the other traits—it is actually no different from what the structural psychol-

[2] It is not proposed *at this point* to make any distinction (as can ultimately be made) between the actual structural self of the subject and the abstraction that the observer succeeds in making of the subject's self from his total behavior. This would be like drawing a distinction between the structure of the atom and the present world physicist's conception thereof—which is a matter of degree of scientific error. On the other hand the person's *own* concept of his self, as something distinct from what emerges in his total behavior, needs no special technique or justification for its separation.

ogist means by the total integrated personality, when he writes down a profile or places a unique personality as a unique point in multidimensional space. Admittedly, in any system, the relations are different from the fundaments, but there is no real point in calling the relations of traits the *self*.

Nevertheless, the vague philosophical aspirations for a concept of the self—as something different from the obvious totality of dimensional measures we can properly call the personality—can surely better be met in this behavioral field (i.e., additionally to the self-perception world already discussed) by the search for a dimension of behavior that proves peculiarly associated with control and coordination (e.g., the psychoanalytic ego structure). Alternatively, we might study process (Cattell, 1966e; Tucker, 1966) patterns instead of individual difference patterns, for example, by *P* technique, and locate some pattern or style in the dynamic flow of management of the personality resources (resident in other traits) that could properly be called the *active self*. Conceivably we might have the scientific good fortune to unearth the unusually simple solution that the *R*-technique structural control factor, the *P*-technique *process* factor, and the source trait of the *self-concept plexus* are all aspects of the same thing. However, before examining further, let us summarize the chief semantic concepts that have long been in the field.

There are four common semantic usages of *the self* that are related to definitions from observables. They are the following:

1. *Felt-introspected self*. The acting self as introspected at the moment (Ach, Michotte, Kulpe).

2. *Cognized self-concept*. The set of ideas about the self, in all its expression, possessions, and comparisons with others (James, McDougall, Rogers).

3. *Structural self-sentiment*. A unitary factor structure ($Q_3$ in the *L*- and *Q*-data series) found in objective measures of attitudes about the self (see item 2). Item 3 can be considered as the dynamic development about the cognitive, item 2.

4. *Ego structure*. A unitary factor structure (*C* in the *L*- and *Q*-data series) appearing in control and expressions of needs, discussed at a clinical level of Freud's "ego" and at a psychometric level as the *C* factor of Cattell, Eber, and Tatsuoka (1970).

## 2 METHODOLOGY

Having set aside the *felt* introspected self, and indicated two meanings for intensive investigation—the self-concept plexus and the behaviorally observed regulating self—let us discuss the type of observation and the forms of analysis that can effectively be used.

Although our methodological aims require that we achieve a behaviorist concept of the self, the introspective approach can be used as a means of reconnoitering. Here we may explore the meaning of dividing (e.g., James, W., 1892; Kelly, G. A., 1955; McDougall, 1932) the total self-concept into peripheral and core concepts. Intuitively one feels that a person's view of his religious attitudes is more centrally connected with his *self* than are his feelings about the pruning of bushes on his front lawn. If this means something, however, we should be able to demonstrate it along some revelatory continuum of actual measurement. Certainly one thing to guard against in current research fashions is the notion that the self-concept consists purely of social content. Not only are the physical self and the behavioral self equally involved, but also the dealings between a person and nature (which may include his God) and a person and his social world are not fundamentally different.

Equally serious consequences can follow, for example, from lack of attention to and misconceptions about "How wide a brook can I jump?" "Is my constitution immune to bronchitis in London or Los Angeles smog?" and "How heavy a surf can I master when swimming?" as from "Am I too shy to be a good chairman?" or "Do people consider me a fair-minded person?" Concern with all of these fields has importance for well-integrated behavior, as discerning psychologists from James and McDougall to Fitts (1965b) have recognized.

Granted that the factorial dimensions of the introspectively viewed *self-concept* extend across relations to physical and social worlds, we are bound to recognize that they will provide essentially the same dimensions as in any personality assessment. They will yield in the *A, B, C, D,* and so forth, general personality dimensions of the 16 Personality Factor Questionnaire (16 PF) and the Clinical Analysis Questionnaire (CAQ), and in dynamics, the interest dimensions of the Strong Interest Blank, the Guilford analysis (1959), or the Motivational Analysis Test (MAT; Cattell, Horn, and Sweney, 1964). When then do we look for dimensions particularly indicative of the self as here circumscribed?

A priori one may consider the following possible attributes of this more central self-concept on which people might differ as through some unitary structure:

1. With the same content and emphasis (rank order of importance to the self) they might differ in the *strength of their concern* about it. That is, one person might be far more interested in this self-concept than another. (Breadth and intensity of interests we may consider, for the moment, probably substantially correlated.)

2. There could be differences in the *accuracy* (realism, precision) of this self-concept, as examined by agreement with ratings or by an index derived from trait-view theory.

3. There could be differences in the individual's *satisfaction* with his self-concept, primarily as indicated by the perceived gap between actual and ideal self and actual and perceived socially desired pattern, but also by dynamic indexes of satisfaction.

4. There could be differences in *the frequency and force with which the person invokes this self-concept* in bringing his daily behavior into consistency.

5. The stability or instability in the face of mood or drug or other changes of the self and its attitudes and values.

Others may be thought of. Much research, notably by Rogers and his students and by Edwards in regard to *social desirability*, has operated among these concepts in the last 30 years. But such basic questions as how general these behaviors are across content, and what their structural relations are, have not always been asked. Our hypothesis would be, for example, that strength of interest and accuracy of conception would be positively related, and that a low social desirability relative to an ideal self would be not so much a cause as a perceptual consequence of high anxiety and other, (e.g., guilt prone) personality traits. (This was recently confirmed.) The methodology in regard to the self-concept plexus therefore calls for (a) clear hypotheses; (b) priority to careful multivariate checks on structural hypotheses; and (c) relation of self-concept data to a broad array of existing well-checked personality dimensions, that is, to the known general personality and motivation factors, rather than endless comparisons of ideal, true, and social lists of purely cognitive self-concepts. Although evidence to be shown later favors the view that a distinct self-concept structure can be factor analytically found in this "introspective" questionnaire field, let us defer it until we have covered the self as a behaviorally observable, correlationally analyzable, coordinating and controlling source trait. Here the best evidence is obtained by operating in miniature situation objective tests, in objective motivation measures, and in life observations. In all of these the choice of variables must be dynamic (which means behavior directed to control of emotional impulse; to restraint aimed at such possible coordination of goal behaviors as might otherwise mutually interfere; and, in general, to "future directed organization favoring survival").

In the light of much clinical and general evidence, one would not, at this stage, restrict our search to ethically directed behavior, because *self* and *superego* have clinically, pragmatically proved separable. Well-integrated selves have, indeed, existed with criminally deficient superegos, and one does not have to be a cynic to recognize that some proportion of socially desirable and approved behavior could derive from motivations purely directed to self-survival. Indeed, the evidence *does* split interests in social approval into those from the self, and those from the organization of conscience; initially, therefore, we are safer starting with both.

Granted that the area of content for searching for a self-structure is as indicated— controlling, integrating, value stabilizing—the requirements in method are, again, the strategic requirement of first clarifying structure by multivariate experiment before proceeding to bivariate manipulative methods or studies of development. Our first question then, is, What is the evidence for any kind of unitary controlling influence (or distinct unitary influen*ces*) when individual differences are correlated over a wide spectrum of behavior? In section 4 of this chapter, the

evidence is in fact rich and yields well-replicated patterns.

The third methodological approach noted previously—that of the extraction of a self-structure from a sophisticated analysis of *processes*—is ideally required, too, but is no easy path. At least, few follow it. By multivariate patterns, there is Cross's (Cattell & Cross, 1952) 40-day, 80-occasion study showing a set of attitudes about the self changing consistently together. There is J. R. William's study (1959) on psychotics and normals showing that poor integration over time distinguishes the psychotics. Other studies (see Cattell, 1957a, p. 617), show the factors we identify as the Self (*U.I.* 16) and Superego (*U.I.* 29) to exhibit a unitary process of development, rising steadily to adolescence. But in terms of demonstrating over minutes a process of dynamic controls of impulse, defining some characteristic pattern of action of an organized ego, nothing is yet available.

## 3  REPLICATED FINDINGS ON THE SELF–SENTIMENT STRUCTURE

At this point we turn from general questions of history of ideas, and growth of methods, to the positive, replicated findings that lead to a certain amount of integration of the field. We begin with the evidence, on the one hand residing in "introspective, self-concept" views in questionnaires and, on the other, in objective motivational measures of dynamic structures, for the existence of what is commonly named the *self-sentiment structure*.

That the individual forms an idea of himself, just as he does about any environmental object, has been a common theme of discussion among psychologists at least since the time of James and McDougall. Because a self-concept lends itself easily to brief experiments, an enormous output of not too systematic research has appeared in the last 30 years. Studies have covered (see especially Rogers, C. R., 1942, and his students) agreements and disagreements of the numerous varieties of self-concept that one can differentiate. For example, the person's idea of his actual self, society's idea of him, his idea of society's idea of him, his ideal self, his idea of society's conception of the ideal self, and so on. A good notation for formulation and calculation in this realm is needed and might be begun in terms of $TS$ (for True Self, as an abstraction from objective tests), $SPS$ (for Self-perceived Self), $OPS$ (for Other-perceived Self), $SIS$ (for Self-recorded Ideal Self) and $ACIS$ (for Actual Community Ideal Self) and $PCIS$ (for the given individual's Perception of Society's Ideal Self Concepts).

Part of the lack of prior regard for structure and sampling of behavior has shown itself in a neglect of the individual's interactions with the physical world and its demanding standards. The disparities of self and ideal self, which in $Q$-sort and other experiments were "accurately" measured in so much work in the 1950s, were almost meaningless, being as much a function of the sample of variables as of the given individual. And when all is said, probably most of the concepts that contributed to psychologists' analyses at that period were contained in the poet's version:

There were three men went down the road
  As down the road went he
The man he was; the man they saw;
  And the man he wished to be.

However, it was demonstrated at least that this $SPS$ (Self-perceived Self) tends to bear a resemblance to the $TS$ (True Self) or $OPS$ (Other-perceived Self) far beyond

chance. Furthermore, an expression of one kind of maladjustment—that reaching its apogee in the psychotic—can be seen to be closely related to the discrepancy of the self-perceived and the true self.

The most systematic model for studying these differences has so far been that in trait-view theory. Therein the discrepancies of self-concept and real self (obtained from factoring behavior) have proved expressible as a function of the individual's real self source trait profile and the situation in which self-appraisal occurs. However, this is not concerned with the extent of gross, unpredictable error as such. If we measure such *random error* then, along with other maladjustment variables, it would be expected in a factor analysis to yield a general psychoticism factor, such as is known to exist from other data (Eysenck, H. J., 1965; Cattell, 1973a).

The programmatic studies of various manifestations of concern with the self-image that tried first to lay a foundation of known structure (before contrasting structures) led to the discovery of two major replicable patterns, one in objective motivation strength measures (which for various reasons has been indexed as $SS$, for Self-sentiment), and one in the questionnaire domain (which for other reasons became indexed as $Q_3$, e.g., in the 16 PF, the HSPQ, the Child Personality Questionnaire [CPQ], and other questionnaires).

The pattern we designate $SS$ was found using *objective* (nonquestionnaire) measures of motivation strength, for example, galvanic skin response (GSR), reaction time, memory, and word fluency, validated as described in Dielman and Krug's chapter 5 of this book and by the work of Baggaley, Cattell, Horn, Radcliffe, Sweney, and others. These workers (Cattell & Baggaley, 1958; Cattell & Miller, 1952; Cattell, Sweney, &

Radcliffe, 1960; Sweney & Cattell, 1961) covering a sufficient array of attitudes and interests in a wide sampling of the *dynamic sphere* of investments, demonstrated, among a dozen or more dynamic factors, the existence of a particular structure which from content they named the *self-sentiment*. In other words, in terms of individual differences, there appears a real functional unity demonstrable across strength of interest in attitudes concerning the social and physical preservation of the self, and the maintenance of effective control and functioning in regard to the total personality. The attitudes involved in what has since been set out (as the *SS*, Self-sentiment, pattern) in a widely used motivation test, the MAT, are shown in Table 1. A careful study of what is brought together by the

correlations in this table, compared with the patterns of other dynamic structures reported here (notably in Dielman and Krug's chapter 5 on dynamic structures generally or set up in the MAT and the School Motivational Analysis Test [SMAT]) show that it is an entirely distinctive response pattern.

For fuller demonstration of the functional unity of this actual reaction pattern with the cognitive self-concept, different research approaches are needed to cover a number of fronts. First, the dynamic unity itself logically must be checked in other settings and at other ages. As to one other important setting, namely, the *P*-technique and *dR*-technique examination of persisting functional unity over development and daily change with internal condition, definite supporting experimental results already exist

**TABLE 1** The structure of the Self-sentiment: The attitude loading pattern underlying measurement of *SS* development by the Motivation Analysis Test (MAT)

| Item | Loading |
|------|---------|
| 1. I like to have good control over all my mental processes—my memory, impulses, and general behavior. | .4 |
| 2. I want never to do anything that would damage my sense of self-respect. | .4–.9 |
| 3. I want to understand myself better. | .4 |
| 4. I want to be first-rate in my job. | .3–.5 |
| 5. I want to maintain a reputation for honesty and high principles among my fellows. | .3–.6 |
| 6. I want to achieve a full normal sex relationship to a loved person. | .3–.5 |
| 7. I want to take part in citizenship activities in the community in which I live. | .3 |
| 8. I like commanding men and taking the responsibilities of a leader.[a] | .3 |
| 9. I want never to be an insane patient in a mental hospital. | .3–.8 |
| 10. I want to satisfy my sense of duty to my country. | .3 |
| 11. I do *not* want to spend more time in sleep (i.e., to be lazy). | .3 |
| 12. I want to give my wife the good things she should have. | .3–.4 |
| 13. I want to spend more time in reading. | .3 |
| 14. I want to do a good job of looking after my family. | .2–.4 |
| 15. I want to know more about science, art, and literature. | .2–.4 |
| 16. I want to grow up normally. | .2–.4 |
| 17. I want my parents to be proud of me. | .2–.4 |

*Note.* The loadings are rounded to 1 decimal place from the mean value for several researches. It should be kept in mind that these results are not from verbal statement checklists, but from objective measures of attitude strength. Psychologically, the reinforcement of the Self-sentiment structure is here demonstrated to arise from satisfaction of needs to preserve the physical, social, economic, and controlling self as a precondition for all general ergic satisfactions.

[a]This particular attitude is from a study of officers in training.

**TABLE 2** The Self-sentiment as Factor $Q_3$ in the questionnaire medium: Some consistently well-loaded items

| Item | Loading |
|---|---|
| 1. The effort taken in planning ahead: | |
|    (a) is not worth it | |
|    (b) *is never wasted.* | .5 |
| 2. However difficult and unpleasant the obstacles, I always persevere and stick to my original intentions. *Yes* | .5 |
| 3. Many people believe my views on politics and society to be: | |
|    (a) *very sound* | |
|    (b) a little odd or unusual | .5 |
| 4. I am careful and practical about things, so that I have fewer accidents than most people. *Yes* | .4 |

*Note.* The loading refers to the italicized part of the item. Tables 2, 3, and 4 are derived, by kind permission of Institute for Personality and Ability Testing (IPAT), from earlier indexed researches. They are now part of the copyrighted 16 Personality Factor Questionnaire and High School Personality Questionnaire scales.

(Cattell, 1957a; Cattell & Cross, 1952). Additionally, however, this dynamic Self-sentiment strength pattern needs to be related to (a) any possibly similar pattern emerging in *questionnaire* measures of the self-concept; (b) the measures in areas (1), (2), (4) and (5) in Table 1 (strength, correctness, frequency, and stability, p. 679) of self-reference, and (c) such self-manifestations as the clinician or applied psychologist studies, as well as to the various difference scores of self and ideal self, and so forth.

In the first area–Q data–investigation quickly struck oil with the discovery of the pattern located as $Q_3$. This, from its content, has every claim to be called the Self-sentiment. The only rival for such identification (though it is not serious) is the C factor, which is easily recognizable from clinical evidence, as Ego-strength. Ego-strength is considered separately in the next section, on the structural self. Although the items in the $Q_3$ pattern, as shown in Table 2, clearly deal with concerns about the self similar to those picked out in objective motivation tests by the SS factor, we must not, on content alone (especially because of the difference in instrument), assume that

they are the same thing. It could be, for example, that because the SS measures deal with the *strength* of concern, and the $Q_3$ with what conscious standards and behaviors the person has adopted, they are actually uncorrelated. In $Q_3$ (Table 2), the empirical observations (items) can be considered mainly to operate in area (4) in section 2, that is, frequency and strength of self-standard reference. The items that are significantly loaded are those showing a response on the part of the individual as he attempts to make his behavior conform with that held up as desirable (especially morally) *by society*, as illustrated in items from $Q_3$ in the 16 PF and the HSPQ.

Further research on $Q_3$ is necessary to explore how far its content may be equated with *total* interest in the self (the SS correlations of $Q_3$ support this, anyway), and also with elements of the socially ideal self, and so on. Also, why is $Q_3$ so consistently negative in correlations with Anxiety? Its other criterion correlations (high in Achievement, low in Neurosis, low in Delinquency), are thoroughly in accord with the general meaning of the self-sentiment and one could argue that the same is true of the Anxiety correlation. More evidence is needed on its relation to behavior in areas (1) and (2), that is, strength and accuracy of self-reference—and to impulse control experimentally measured. In any case, Self-sentiment applies to both $Q_3$ and the attitude factor, $SS$, for they correlate significantly and substantially (.3–.6). (See the evidence on the objective motivation test Self-sentiment factor, $SS$, in the MAT; Cattell, Horn, & Sweney, 1964.)

Although this is encouraging evidence that we are on the right track, that is, that the cognitive self-concept is the center of some sort of functionally unitary dynamic reaction structures, the present level of validity of the two factor batteries (and the uncertainty on size of instrument factors) is such that we must ask (a) if $Q_3$ and $SS$ (in MAT) are *partially* the same, and (b) if they are an *identical* personality structure expressed in two different media. Theoretically, one might expect the former, because the degree to which one is concerned about self-standards (as shown by $Q$ data) and about making one's self-sentiment image reach the socially desired pattern ($Q_3$) would depend partly on the strength of motivation with the self as a whole ($SS$ in the MAT), but partly also on certain limiting capacities to foresee and restrain one's own actions (possibly in $Q_3$, but not in $SS$). Indeed, there is already evidence (Cattell, Blewett, & Beloff, 1955) of a constitutional component in $Q_3$, concerned with some quality of distractibility ($Q_3$ –) versus capacity to assimilate restraints, and this genetic component finally attained $Q_3$ level. A similar genetic component is hypothesized (but unexamined) also in $SS$. Higher order factoring, as discussed later, also supports the view that $SS$ and $Q_3$ are only different aspects of the same structure (in the individual-difference domain) appearing with two different instrument expressions.

Parenthetically, if the theory is correct (see Becker, 1960; Cattell, 1957a; Cattell & Digman, 1964; Schaie, 1963) that $L$- and $Q$-medium factors are identical when instrument factors are set aside, an equivalent to $Q_3$ should exist in rating studies. By content, this might be the factor indexed as $K$ (Cattell, 1957a). However, it has now been demonstrated that $Q_3$ does come out in ratings ($L$-data) and questionnaires ($Q$-data) properly aligned in the study of Cattell, Pierson, Brim and Finkbeiner (1976). Apart from this, no other known personality factor or factors from a careful study of the 30 or more replicated and indexed (Cattell, 1973a; Hundleby, Pawlik, & Cattell, 1965) have any serious claim to theoretical consideration as the self-pattern. However, $C$, Ego-strength, and $G$, Superego strength, in the $Q$ data series (16 PF, HSPQ, etc.) have significant and special relations to $Q_3$, which are studied in section 4, this chapter.

## 4 EMPIRICAL EVIDENCE FOR THE CONTROLLING EGO STRUCTURE

Our purpose now is to turn to the third of the semantic meanings of the self as listed in section 1 of this chapter, namely, that of an impulse-coordinating entity inferred from behavior. Structural research by actual behavior correlation may or may not show this to be related to the self-concept plexus, identified in $Q_3$ and $SS$, as just recognized. The concept of some unitary functioning structure that is mainly concerned with impulse control, and good coordination of subgoals under conditions of conflict, stress, or frustration, engaged in referring behavior to future consequences, is widespread in individual difference *and* process studies. This concept appears in clinical theory, in brain damage research, in comparisons of animal learning at diverse phylogenetic levels, and various other areas. Its most discussed form is the Freudian ego concept. These do not suppose any deliberate conscious conceptualization of the self, as in the *self-sentiment*. Integration observed in animal behavior (inhibition in the interests of maximum future satisfaction) almost certainly does not require it. Perhaps, the Freudian ego concept, as used by most clinicians, would not totally exclude conscious self-reference from ego action, but it is not central.

In any of these fields of observation of control, inhibition, and future reference (orientation) of immediate behavior, it would generally be agreed by clinicians and experimentalists that ego strength is largely acquired by trial and error, noninsightful behavior, in which the individual learns that certain controls, suppressions, and confluence learnings are ultimately more rewarding than immediate or different responses (meaning, thereby (Cattell, 1950c), compromising in a path of behavior that gives some satisfaction to each of several conflicting needs). Consequently, by ordinary learning laws, one would expect that there would gradually develop new, learned dynamic systems to effect such control. One notes in passing that the self-concept-developed Self-sentiment, $Q_3$ above, and the Ego-strength integration as now being studied (though assumed to be different) are anything but *incompatible* in their action. However, even initially, one suspects that $Q_3$ is more involved with what is good for the social reputation and is more self-conscious, whereas the acting ego is more concerned with maximizing long circuited total individual reward and the maintenance of control, through any means whatever. It just happens that long-circuited behavior also tends to be socially accepted behavior. Thus, at any rate, these concepts are best pursued initially to higher clarity,

each in its own framework of theory and experimental findings.

Now behavior of a kind that has to do with control and coordination has actually been studied intensively for the past 30 years both in ratings and in the 400 or so objective miniature situational tests described by Cattell and Warburton (1967). Hundleby, Pawlik, and Cattell (1965) summarized the evidence for the emergence of various dimensions of *self* action arising out of the thorough, imaginative, and experimentally resourceful work of many psychologists (Bolz & Cattell, 1976; Cattell & Baggaley, 1958; Cattell, Dubin, & Saunders, 1954; Cattell & Gruen, 1955; Cattell & Howarth, 1964; Coan & Cattell, 1958; Delhees, 1968; Digman, 1963a; Eysenck, H. J., 1960b; Gorsuch, 1965; Horn, J. L., 1961a; Hundleby, Pawlik, & Cattell, 1965; Luborsky & Cattell, 1947; Pawlik, 1968; Peterson, 1960; Rickels & Cattell, 1965; Scheier, 1958; Sweney, 1961a; Tsujioka & Cattell, 1965a,b; Warburton & Cattell, 1961; to name the more prominent). The patterns in $Q$ and $L$ data have been summarized by Cattell (1973a). There is, in fact, every evidence that a *functioning self* pattern has already been available for our consideration in one of the earliest factors from the broad (personality sphere) net of programmatic behavioral analyses. In fact, the proof of the theory was there before the theorist asked his question.[3]

---

[3] Indeed, it has happened again and again in the history of personality research that some concept conceived at some late period in an armchair has been shown to be already present and closely discussed in the indexed surveys of personality-sphere factorings (Cattell, 1946, 1957a, 1977; Hundleby, Pawlik, & Cattell, 1965) presenting replicated factor patterns. The same has happened in other sciences, as when chemists found that supposed blanks in the periodic table were really filled by elements overlooked in reported experiments.

Because empirical results have shown that Q- and L-data factors, on the one hand, and objective test (T data) source traits on the other do not have a simple alignment (the latter usually being second order to the former), let us first study the Q- and L-data patterns, which match mutually in an intelligible fashion. In seeking a behavioral self or ego-strength pattern, we would look over the available empirical factors for something matching (in the low pole) the clinical concept of low ego strength, or the kind of behavior seen with injury to the frontal lobe association areas. This pattern should include instinctual impulsiveness, higher general emotionality, evasiveness and immaturity, much use of neurotic defense mechanisms, instability, behavioral undependability, anxiety, and so forth. When one looks for such a pattern in factored L and Q data, the search is quickly rewarded. A factor pattern excellently confirming the psychoanalytic picture has long been in the published data (Cattell, 1946) and has now been repeatedly replicated, in what has been indexed in L- and Q-data source trait lists as Factor C. Factor C is discussed in both L and Q data (see chapters 2 and 3 of this book).

Furthermore, through the use of the 16 PF, HSPQ, CPQ, and other tests in clinical work (all of which include a C measure), it has been shown that this C factor crystallizes out at all ages and that its score has precisely the relationship to life criteria that one would expect of ego-strength and weakness. Thus it shows an almost universal low mean value in all psychopathological syndrome groups, and a specific negative relation to anxiety level. It should be said at once, however, that these criterion relations differ sharply in meaning from those of $Q_3$, discussed previously as the Self-sentiment, for it has negligible reference to social standards of behavior. In ratings, one finds (at the positive pole of C) lack of emotional upset, steady control, frustration tolerance, and evidence of accumulated facility in simply handling impulse and stressful situations under any conditions, as shown by the loadings in Table 3; it is essentially a confident *ability to cope* as contrasted to a generalized emotional dissatisfaction, fear of one's own impulses, and (perhaps secondarily) a general neurotic fatigue. This factor, C, is shown by countless studies in which both have appeared to be distinct from factor $Q_3$. For example, C is not low in several shrewd antisocial types.

The search for a controlling ego-structure pattern is thus successful in Q and L data, but the multivariate experimental approach in the objective test domain (T data) presents us with some difficulties. One must remember that the process of defining a personality factor pattern is iterative: The

TABLE 3   The nature of the Ego-strength source trait as shown by loadings in the Q medium

| Item | Loading |
|------|---------|
| 1. I get impatient and begin to fume and fret when people delay me unnecessarily. (b) *No* | .4 |
| 2. I always have a lot of energy at times when I need it. (a) *Yes* | .7 |
| 3. I feel that my emotions are: | |
|   (a) *well satisfied* | |
|   (b) very little satisfied | .5 |
| 4. I have vivid dreams, disturbing my sleep. *No* | .5 |
| 5. When I get up in the morning I feel I can hardly face the day. *No* | .5 |

*Note.*   The loading refers to the italicized part of the item.

experimenter begins with a tentative definition of his concept at a relatively descriptive
level, demarcating some main properties; and
with his luck finds some pattern of covariation in data that, more than any other, give
some hope of support and the beginning of
reality for his concept.[4] He then reforms his
subjective concept in the light of the evidence, reenters experiment for another
check-up, and so converges finally (in what
Cattell [1966e] called the inductive-
hypothetico-deductive spiral [IHS] to the
most viable concept. This methodology is
classically illustrated in individual-difference
research by Thurstone's (1944) approach to
primary ability concepts or Scheier's (Cattell
& Scheier, 1961) convergence on uniquely
definable concepts and measurements for
anxiety and stress (beginning with popular
and psychiatric indications of the domain
represented by 800 alleged relevant variables).

The problem of locating a pattern—
especially one corresponding to so complex
a concept as the ego—becomes an unusually
subtle one in the realm of objective tests,
where relating of specific laboratory performances to those traits we commonly
recognize and perceive easily in the wide
everyday and clinical $L$ and $Q$ data seems to
require unusual powers. In the name of
caution, therefore, we should give a trial of
identity to a fair number of discovered
$T$-data factors, including some that have
only slender claims.

The need for this strategy has greatly

increased the required breadth and the labor
of such researches as those of J. L. Horn
(1961a) and Gorsuch (1965) seeking the
ego-strength pattern of expression. The
breadth of the search has been further
increased in $T$ data by the hypotheses of
some investigators (Pawlik, 1968; Scheier,
1958) that *ego strength* is a pattern appearing only at the *second or third order* in $T$
data factors. Such a solution is somewhat
unlikely because there has been much evidence to suggest that the first stratum in $T$
data corresponds to the second stratum in $L$
and $Q$ data, as just indicated.[5] On this basis,
the $C$ (Ego-strength) factor should lie even
*below* the first (primary factor) level in $T$
data. Spurred by this paradox, one may
begin to doubt that the ego structure lies at
higher strata in $T$ data and return to re-
examine the known roster of first-order
$T$-data factors. Here one must examine
broadmindedly the claims of *U.I.* 16, Assertiveness; *U.I.* 17, General Inhibition; *U.I.* 19,
Independence; *U.I.* 22, Cortertia; *U.I.* 23,
Mobilization; *U.I.* 25, Reality Contact; *U.I.*
33(−) and *U.I.* 36, Self-sentiment Activity.
On general grounds of present interpretations, not one of them, unless it is *U.I.* 16,
satisfies the condition of being a really good
match or a decidedly better match than the
others.

As far as replication of patterns at the
second stratum is concerned, good congruences have been accumulated among

---

[4] This is a principle of methodology and theory
construction, perhaps still insufficiently appreciated among students of personality, namely, that a
psychologist commonly cannot simply define his
concept in all its polished elaborations from an
armchair, and then expect to find precisely that in
experiment. Except for quite exceptional instances, a continuing intelligent adjustment of
initial hypotheses or concept to the verdict of data
produces a rapid evolution in the early stages.

[5] In psychological research, one must constantly
guard against the notion, begotten of some
statistical or Pythagorean mysticism, that the
higher order factor (a) stands at the head of a
hierarchy, and (b) is *more important* than lower
order factors. In general, the factoring of primaries
as such (a) does not lead to a true pyramid (Cattell,
1971), but to a network, and (b) is just as likely to
move back, in the causal chain, right *outside*
psychology, to turn up broad physiological and
sociological influences having comparatively slight
influence on the primaries.

three independent researches in *T*-data personality factors (Cattell & Scheier, 1961; Knapp, 1961b; Pawlik & Cattell, 1964) yielding seven second-stratum patterns. One of these, *U.I.*(*T*)II, which is marked by positive loadings on *U.I.* 16, Assertivenesss; *U.I.* 1, Intelligence; *U.I.* 19, Independence; *U.I.* 23, Mobilization; and *U.I.* 36, Self-sentiment, deserves serious consideration as an ego-strength pattern, equivalent to *C* in the *Q*- and *L*-data realm, despite being at the wrong stratum.

Some investigators have even been tempted to go to the third stratum, to the Factor $\gamma$ which loads the *U.I.*(*T*)II most saliently (Pawlik & Cattell, 1964) in search of the final ego pattern of control. If we examine the *T* data factors at any level on the basis of (a) some consistent correlations with the *C* factor in the 16 PF and (b) significant differences between normals, on the one hand, and neurotics and psychotics, on the other (Cattell & Schmid, 1972), the objective primaries with remaining claims to show an ego-strength, impulse-control character are only seven, namely, *U.I.* 16(+), 19(+), 22(+), 24(−), 25(+), 33(−), and, perhaps, *U.I.* 21 and *U.I.* 36. A core of these occurs in second-order objective test factors II and VII; both of these are, again, loaded on third-order $\gamma$. All this work urgently calls for replication on new samples and with the improved test batteries now available.

The problem that has to be resolved by this theory is the higher than expected order of $\gamma$ in the *Q* and *L* media. However, it has been noted that (a) $\gamma$ affects more variables, that is, has a lower hyperplane count, than one would expect of a first-order factor and (b) that some higher order *Q*-data studies have shown $\gamma$ and $Q_3$ together in a higher order factor (and it is noteworthy that the *U.I.*s that correlate with $\gamma$ also correlate with $Q_3$).

Every indication remains that the *C* factor in ratings and the 16 PF is the ego. What the ego is in the objective test domain—*U.I.* 16, or *U.I.*(*T*)II, or *U.I.*(*T*)$\gamma$—remains for research to clarify. But it is certain that it is something different from (though persistently positively correlated with) the Self-sentiment as marked by the $Q_3$ and *SS*. Furthermore, as seen by its questionnaire, rating, and the tentative objective test associations, it is expressed in stability in the face of stressful or tempting situations that usually provoke emotionality, by competitiveness of an assured kind, by independence of judgment, control of speed, fatigability, perceptual processes, and so forth; by low anxiety; by respect for reality and refusal to substitute imaginative constructions for it; and by good morale (as opposed to pessimism), low rigidity, moderation in judgments, and realistic estimation of time. (In *T* data the latter are taken from the tests loading the primary factors [*U.I.* 16, etc.], but should later be estimated as projections of second-order Factor II [or possibly third order $\gamma$] directly on the tests.)

Interpretively, these behaviors can be considered to represent the acquisition of a good dynamic integration structure, reached in a learning process. However, this capacity to bring about confluence by learning is partly limited by some genetic parameter (since the Multiple Abstract Variance Analysis [MAVA] researches show *C* with a genetic component) having to do with *span*. (This genetic component of control span is seen in grosser form in the interspecies differences in capacity to inhibit response and to respond to delayed rewards.)

The expression *dynamic integration* used here can be given a more precise operational meaning in the light of the dynamic calculus. It is pointed out in the next section of this chapter and elsewhere in this volume that the amount of enduring conflict in some course of action $a_j$ can be represented by the sum of negative, *cancelled* drive—in the dynamic specification equation, as by $(.3 + .4 + .4)$ in the following:

$$a_j = .7E_1 - .3E_2 + .6E_3 - .4E_5 - .4E_6, (1)$$

where the $E$s are the drive levels on ergs.

Now, as Williams (1959) showed, the sum of such negative values across a representative sample of courses of action (attitudes) is significantly greater in mental hospital patients than in normals. If ego strength is success in finding *confluent* modes of action that give the largest total satisfaction to the needs brought into the compromise, then it can be measured by the integration index $I = (1 - C)$ where $C$ is *conflict* as measured previously by the sum of negative loadings. Actually, this sum correlates negatively with the $C$ factor, measured in the 16 PF (Williams, 1959). It would seem, then, that we have a conception and a measurement for ego strength that have unitary factor property and are distinct from the Self-sentiment factor, $Q_3$.

## 5  EVIDENCE FOR THE SUPEREGO STRUCTURE AND ITS RELATION TO CONTROL

Inasmuch as our study of the self is planned to include the development of values that psychologists such as McDougall, James, and Freud have always connected with it, we must attend next to the concept of conscience or superego. These have been most analytically studied by clinicians, but since the clinical view of the superego is familiar let us turn, as with the ego concept, to see what the empirical multivariate experimental evidence for its existence may be. So far our search for a self-structure has turned

up a duality of factors—$C$ and $Q_3$ in questionnaire responses and elsewhere—consequently, one may wonder whether the supposed unitary superego will also prove to be one or several things.

In $Q$ and $L$ data the evidence is clear for a single factor (indexed $G$ in the alphabetic order according to declining variance), the content of which excellently supports the common-sense and psychoanalytic notions of a moral and irrationally imperative source of pressure toward ethical behavior (see Table 4). The obvious claim of the $G$ pattern to be matched with the clinical superego concept meets any rivalry at all only from $Q_3$, the self-sentiment, and $O$, guilt proneness. From the first of these, separation is actually easy, since its social value side concerns social reputation and even manners, rather than morals. Separation of $G$ from $O$, on the other side, is not difficult for anyone familiar with the history of religious and ethical concepts, wherein one detects a stern and even aggressive pattern—as in, say, Savonarola and the Old Testament prophets—looking much like $G$ and a second more elusive pattern. The factor $G$ is the positive action conscience with definite injunctions to good works and to avoidance of wickedness and damnation. It is categorical, whereas $O$ is a softer feeling of unworthiness, weltschmerz, and what William James called the oceanic identification with human suffering and a loving principle in the universe. This is the pattern of *conscience* in Tolstoy, Dostoyevsky, and, of course, many interpreters of Christianity. In the modern era, the writings of Mowrer (1964, 1967) approached this distinction, for Mowrer argued that guilt, which could be identified either with the $O$ factor or the second-order Anxiety factor, is not, as Freud argued, a function of the strong superego per se, but of failure to express it. Mowrer's position is

**TABLE 4**  The nature of Superego Strength as shown in items loading the $Q$ medium Factor $G$

| Item | Loading |
|---|---|
| 1. I always make a point in deciding anything to refer to basic rules of right and wrong. *Yes* | .6 |
| 2. I find it desirable to make plans to avoid waste of time between jobs. *Yes* | |
| 3. I always check very carefully the condition in which borrowed property is returned *to* me or *by* me to others. *Yes* | .7 |
| 4. I think that plenty of freedom is more important than good manners or respect for the law. *Yes* | .7 |
| 5. I am a fairly strict person, insisting on always doing things as correctly as possible. *True* | .4 |

*Note.*  The loading refers to the italicized part of the item.

in agreement with the more complex picture we draw here, at least to the extent that our theory is supported by evidence of a strong and well-expressed $G$ being significantly *negatively* correlated with Anxiety (Cattell & Child, 1975; Gorsuch, 1965; Horn, J. L., 1961a).

We do not yet known enough about the $G$ pattern developmentally to fill out the picture, but one suspects that this pattern we identify here with the clinical and Old Testament superego is associated with patriarchalism, with fear of authority, and introjection of a fiercely punitive set of standards. (There is some evidence from measurement that it falls off in periods of material ease, as in the present epoch, and that it is weaker in upper than lower middle-class people.) Although $O$ has complex associations with expressions of conscience, all the clear evidence in regard to superego-like behavior turns on $G$; it is this we shall consider centrally.

Technically, psychometrically, the only issue likely to require debate in regard to this $G$ structure is a rather academic one—namely, whether $G$ is strictly a first- or a second-order factor. At the second order there is a Factor $QVIII$ (Cattell, 1973a; Cattell & Nichols, 1972a; Delhees, 1968; Gorsuch & Cattell, 1967) that has positive loadings on $C$, $G$ and $Q_3$, but which we shall

interpret here (but see Cattell & Child, 1973) as Good Moral Upbringing, extending beyond the begetting of the Superego, $G$.

Turning from the $Q$ and $L$ media to that of objective tests, we encounter, as with the ego structure, a less easily resolvable picture in terms of recognizing the pattern from immediate behavior content (see $U.I.$ (T) source traits in chapter 4). Actually, an enormous amount of research on the structure of values that was intended to be *objective* and might be expected to help here has to be set aside because it is built on the morass which is called *opinionnaire* checking. In an area—morality—where verbal behavior is notoriously hypocritical, asking a person the exact extent to which he considers various behaviors to be moral or ethical (e.g., Bryan, L. L., 1956; Crissman, 1942; Grunes, 1956; Rettig & Pasamanick, 1959), is research that can be justified in its own right only as the investigation of verbal response. But it cannot be presumed a priori that it is an adequate approach to the essential structure of behavior. Such verbal statements are all too likely to represent only verbal learning that has occurred in a social setting regarding this particular area of behavior, and it is likely to bear little relationship to overt behavior. Research on delinquents, for example, has found little difference between them and nondelinquents regarding moral-knowledge-evaluating tests of this kind (Gorsuch, 1965). Superego structure must rest on something more than verbal checklists of values.

Although we are dealing in $G$ with something that does not directly reflect the person's adult concern with adjustment to purely social demands, as does the Self-sentiment factor ($Q_3$), yet in infancy this deeper pattern has arisen from the socio-religious culture, and is therefore not morality in the abstract, but still an image of a particular culture. A factor pattern, for example, might be expected, as to its content of injunctions, to vary with cultures and class subcultures frustrating to factor matching. Nevertheless, even though there are obvious cross-cultural differences, often stressed for student interest by cultural anthropologists, more seasoned observers recognize a massive functional similarity of ethics and morality across different backgrounds, as noted by Linton (1956) and other sociologists.

Among psychologists, Cattell and Gorsuch (1965) presented empirical data on the moral structure in societies themselves showing that a general morality factor *does* exist extending across behavior in some 52 countries of quite varied cultures. Although it varies in some social content, and the Biblical 10 commandments are certainly not the explicit core in all the earth's religious traditions, yet the necessary moral conditions for societies to cohere and live generate a sufficiently basic similarity of prohibitions. At any rate, as these investigators show, there is a single factor across these countries loading high (negatively) on syphilis death rate, illegitimate births, death rate from alcholism, and various basic crime incidence rates. Though cultural anthropologists naturally insist on the varieties they have found, there is concrete evidence of some important common, transcendent values.

However, the factoring of $G$ items in the 16 PF for (a) a group of 600 older adults (Cattell, 1974) and (b) a group of undergraduate students (Vaughan, G. M., & Burdsall, in preparation, b), shows a fairly strong difference of emphasis, with a congruence of only about .2.

Nevertheless, it is clear that the $G$ pattern appearing in the medium of $Q$- and $L$-data observations of personality reflects learning of some stable and central values in our culture. As Table 4 shows, it brings together such characteristics as perseverance, determination, responsibility, conscientiousness, emotionality control, and attentiveness to the needs of others (Cattell, 1957a, p. 22). It should also be noted that a similar behavior rating factor reflecting moral character is supported by data in the work of Peck and co-workers (Peck, Havighurst, Cooper, Ruch, Lilienthal, & More, 1960). Various patterns resembling this were also seen in the various questionnaire researches summarized elsewhere (Cattell, 1946) from which the 16 PF was developed, as well as in more recent factor analyses of rating (Norman, 1963a) and questionnaire (Sells, Demaree, & Will, 1970) data. The items from this factor presented in Table 4 are in part from the $G$ factor at lower age levels (High School and Child Personality Questionnaires).

Now when one turns from the questionnaire self-evaluation and more cognitively oriented (morality-aware) responses, as seen in $Q$ data, to the functional behavior responses of the superego, as seen in $T$ data, the identification, as usual with objective tests, is not too easy. We are now looking for evidence of transcendent values being in operation within a person whether or not he can directly verbalize them. It is not perhaps overemphatic to bring out here the crucial point that one only knows an important value is truly adopted if the person is almost willing to give his life for it. To provide such behavioral evidence is a long way from the questionnaire method (and some way from the possible miniature situations of objective tests), though, conceivably, such a value system can show itself distantly in behavior in the miniature situations. For example, self-transcendent values might be expected to show in action where there is no foreseeable short- or long-range personal benefit from some difficult course of action. In a sense, then, one can only be sure that the person has ethical values when these values cause him some personal loss or discomfort in the ordinary sense, even though they must obviously be in some way psychologically rewarding; that is, they must follow a dynamic principle and subsidiate to the superego.

As personality experimenters are aware, the history of search in $T$ data for the superego, that is, honest, self-sacrificing, and morally determined reactions, begins with the classical research of Hartshorne and May (Hartshorne, May, et al., 1928, 1929, 1930). In their test of cheating, for example, there was no way for the child to know that noncheating behavior would benefit him in any way. As students of psychology are told, Hartshorne and May's low intercorrelations forced them to conclude that ethical behavior is not at all general but is highly situational and specific. However, those correlations were examined by relatively primitive methods, before multivariate experimental techniques had developed. When some of their data was later reanalyzed (Maller, 1934; Burton, A., 1965) it was found that a general factor did indeed extend across their various tests. Although the factors did not account for all the variance (a discrepancy expected by any factor analyst who realizes the magnitude of influences from unreliability of the measurements and of the situational aspects upon all behavior), it was found that common vari-

ance was sufficiently large to suggest the existence of a definite superego structure at the functional level.

In view of the obvious influence of a superego structure in everyday life behavior, the early result of the Hartshorne and May research was surprising. Fortunately, the wide net of diverse variables in the objective tests in the Cattell, Hundleby, Pawlik, Eysenck, Bolz, and Schuerger researches cited earlier, and summarized by Ishikawa (chapter 4) presents us instead, as in the case of the ego here, by an *embarras de richesse* of candidates. These we will consider after first looking at the comparatively easily identified factor in the domain of dynamic attitude variables (by objective motivation tests).

The reader should perhaps be reminded that the search for patterns in the dynamic structure area begins with objective (see chapter 4) measurement devices validated both conceptually (*construct validity*) and concretely (*real-life criteria*). By these means a wide variety of single attitude-interests (strength of interests in various courses of action) are measured and factored, yielding eight or nine basic drives (ergs) and several sentiments. Among the latter is one we have already recognized (Table 2) as the Self-sentiment factor (*SS*). Inspection of the remainder at once yields a pattern, shown in Table 5, that seems fully to express the superego concept.

In Table 5 we see some of the attitudes most strongly loaded both in the *SE* factor for adults (and now placed in the MAT test), and for schoolchildren (as entered now in the SMAT, using six objective devices). Their similarity warrants a hypothesis that they are both measuring aspects of the superego structure, although in attitudes appropriately changing with age. If now we have evidence of a superego-like factor in $Q$ data, namely, $G$, and another in objective dynamic

**TABLE 5** The structure of the Superego Sentiment as shown by loadings on objectively measured attitude motivation strengths (from the basis of the Motivation Analysis Test)

| Item | Loading |
| --- | --- |
| I want to avoid impropriety and vice. | .8 |
| I want to satisfy my sense of duty to my parents and my country. | .6 |
| I want never to be selfish in my acts. | .7 |
| I do *not* want to spend more on luxuries, drinking and smoking. | .4 |
| I wish to avoid what are essentially immoral expressions of sex needs. | .3 |
| I want to maintain good self-control. | .3 |
| I want to stick with my job despite any difficulties. | .3 |
| I admire and respect my parents. | .2 |
| I wish to be in touch with God or some principle that gives me moral help. | .2 |

attitudes, namely, *SE*, it is natural to ask here, as we did regarding a similar pair in the Self-sentiment factor, if these may be the same structure in two dresses (instruments). The answer was soon given, by experiment, that *SE* scores correlate positively and significantly with *G*, as measured in the questionnaire. However, the correlation appears not to be as good as that between *SS* and $Q_3$, and we must discuss further evidence as to whether the identity is good enough when one allows for two different instrument-factor intrusions.

Meanwhile, in the domain of objective test factors, it must be recognized that perhaps not enough behavioral measures of honesty versus dishonesty and other central behaviors in the superego have yet been devised (despite a reasonable extensive incursion into the area of *intellectual honesty* [Cattell & Warburton, 1967]). Nevertheless, an array of persistence and cooperation measures surely has been tried enough by now to encompass this factor. On the basis of content, and some degree of correlation with the questionnaire *G* factor, the objective test *U.I.* patterns that a liberal initial search for *G* matches should cover are *U.I.* 17, as Inhibition; *U.I.* 19(−), as Subduedness and foregoing of personal ambition; *U.I.* 20(−) as Integrity; *U.I.* 28(−) Self-assuredness; *U.I.* 29, as Persistence and Cooperative-

ness versus Complacency; and *U.I.* 30(−) as Dissofrustance.

From these we might eliminate *U.I.* 19, 20, 29, and 30—at least as really promising first-order matches. *U.I.* 17 also at first looks doubtful because it is a *general* inhibition or responsiveness to threat of any kind, not obviously a moral restraint. However, despite *U.I.* 17's lacking the positive aspects of superego behavior, recent evidence (Cattell & Schuerger, 1976), matching *T* and *Q* data suggests *U.I.* 17 could be a candidate. *U.I.* 19 (like *U.I.* 16) has some criterion claim in that it correlates with school achievement and other superego behaviors involving performances *positively*, but otherwise we reject it. Although *U.I.* 30(−) loads faster tempo, less suggestibility, faster task completion, more critical evaluation, greater endurance in a task, and more people liked (all consistent with superego), it also loads greater emotionality of comment, greater fluctuation of attitudes, less excess of aspiration over performance, and fewer highbrow tastes. This ambiguity and the fact that, as Dissofrustance, it has highly significant associations with pathology (notably simple schizophrenia [Cattell, Komlos, & Tatro, 1968]), seem to justify doubt that it is a superego expression, though experiments should certainly give it another try.

If space permitted, the history of *U.I.* 20

and *U.I.* 28 as possible superego concepts would deserve a chapter illustrating the erratic course of personality psychologists' research hunches. *U.I.* 20 was first called Sociable, Emotional Evasiveness, purely descriptive, on content. Then, as increasing evidence of social conformity, response to punishment, suggestibility to authority, and so forth accumulated, it was called Comentive Superego, the emphasis on *comentive* or "thinking and acting with the group" implying an immature form of the superego (at least a Riesmanian "other directed" conscience). However, it was soon found that cheating tests correlated *positively* with *U.I.* 20, fitting better the hypocritical "evasiveness" perceived in the first groping interpretation. *U.I.* 20 does not distinguish clinical groups. And then Knapp's (1965) and other delinquency studies showed significantly higher *U.I.* 20 scores in delinquents, notably in group delinquency. Consequently, *U.I.* 20 was given simply the label Comention, designating "mentally going with the group" and, one might add, with emphasis on lack of any real individual conscience.

A similar peculiar ambiguity besets *U.I.* 28, called descriptively Asthenia versus Self-assuredness and interpreted as a massive defense against an attempt by parents to apply rigid superego standards too early. This theory is fully set out elsewhere (Cattell, 1964); but in sheer present content (tendency to agree, higher severity of judgment, more extremity of viewpoint, more shift to attitudes of people called successful), *U.I.* 28 seems at best an immature, insincere, social conformity and does not relate to the life criterion performances (on existing evidence at least) considered affected by the superego. Incidentally, *U.I.* 20 and *U.I.* 28 are factors most frequently mistaken in psychiatric interview for Anxiety (Cattell & Scheier, 1961) and have sometimes been called Bound Anxiety, a

concept with relations to the Superego. Certainly, in some studies high *U.I.* 28 has been found related (Cattell & Schmid, 1972) to Neuroticism. Unfortunately (Gorsuch, 1965; Horn, J. L., 1961a), *U.I.* 20 and 28 (which are mutually positively correlated) have shown a joint negative relation to superego criterion behavior in life.

This leaves only *U.I.* 17 and 29, unless one goes beyond primaries and seeks for some superego pattern at the second order in the *T*-data domain. There he will find rather unimpressive patterns in second-stratum factors I and IV, which involve mild superego-like behavior. However, they are understood better as the *tied socialization* and *inhibition* influences assigned at present (Cattell & Scheier, 1961) as the best interpretations (similarly for $\beta$ at the third stratum).

On the bases so far discussed, many will be prepared to hypothesize factor *U.I.* 29 (as shown in Table 6) as the superego factor. Its match could be with the straight *G* primary or with the second-order *Q*VIII Good Upbringing source trait (*G*, with slight $Q_3$ loadings), which fits the usual rule of second-order *Q* data's being a first-order *T*-data match. Decision awaits extension of variables in *U.I.* 17. Meanwhile, further research should also study *U.I.* 30(−), and perhaps factorings of new variables designed explicitly for superego.

## 6  THEORETICAL EXPECTATIONS

We shall pursue further the empirical research evidence after some clarification here of explicit theoretical expectations. Empirically, we have definite evidence that three structures—an operating ego, a self-sentiment and a superego—can now be recognized, some at the primary, one possibly at the secondary level. At the theoretical level, a number of nonquantitative writers on dynamics, notably Allport, Freud, and

**TABLE 6** Hypothesized ($G$ and $SE$ correlated) factor expressing Superego in objective tests—$U.I.$ 29

| Item | Loading |
|------|---------|
| Less oscillation in steady task | .3 |
| Larger upward drift of skin resistance when told to relax from task | .3 |
| Less impairment of performance by discomfort and threat | .3 |
| Lower motor rigidity, i.e., better self-control | .3 |
| Larger percentage of correct decisions on the Cursive Miniature Situation Test | .3 |
| Less slowing of reaction time by complex instructions | .3 |
| Less extremity of viewpoint (attitudes) | .2 |
| Faster speed in letter comparison task | .2 |
| Higher aspiration for improvement (coding) | .2 |
| Greater preference for tidiness in drawings | .2 |
| Higher ratio of accuracy to speed | .2 |

*Note.* The loadings, averaged over 10 published and some unpublished studies, are intended only as approximations. They need correction for attenuation for brevity of experimental forms of tests used. Collectively (as now published in the O-A Battery; Cattell & Schuerger, 1976), they offer about a .8 multiple $R$ for estimation of the factor.

McDougall, asked what the ultimate relation of the ego to the superego (or to the ideal self or the self-sentiment) would be. They developed the esthetically attractive notion, for which Cattell (1950c) also suggested a model that the ultimate integration of the harmonious personality (which Allport saw in great religious leaders and in some social reformers such as Tolstoy) is one where ego and superego become one. Freud seems to dissent from this, leaving the two structures always separated.

On the independent basis of factor-analytic concepts, the notion of the dynamic lattice, and the tri-vector learning theory (chapter 7), Cattell (1957a) presented, at the 15th International Congress of Psychology, a conception of ultimate integration different from these and involving some rather complex dynamics, developed in this chapter. This conception differs from that of Allport and McDougall in supposing that self-sentiment and superego remain apart, and from the Freudian view in recognizing the self-sentiment as an extra structure beyond the ego.

The construction of a relatively *tight*

theory is hindered at this stage because research on the ego structure has given ambiguous results, as we found in the case of the Self-sentiment and Superego structures. Our evidence so far is that Ego-strength—as identified by the $C$ factor in the 16PF, HSPQ, and perhaps the Objective Analytic (O-A) Batteries (Schuerger, Hundleby)—seems to be the capacity to maximize ergic satisfactions by being able flexibly to work out and firmly to maintain compromise activities. To reach what are in the end maximally ergically satisfying *confluences* of what were formerly more fragmented behaviors, the individual must have the capacity to tolerate deferment of satisfactions, to control emotional impulses, and to dissolve irrational rigidities.

The structural question that arises is whether the rewards of obtaining any one such improved solution—through compromise and control—merely strengthen the habit system in question or contribute also to some generalized capacity to control. That there exists such a generalized capacity to control and defer immediate impulse satisfaction for greater ultimate gains is evidenced by the $C$ factor, perhaps by the pattern discussed tentatively in the objective behavioral batteries, by the evidence of generalized attitude consistency and generalized attitude stability factors, and by William's study showing that the ergic integration index (obverse of the conflict score $\Sigma \bar{b}^2$) is well correlated with $C$. Its nature is, of course, more readily seen by the average reader through the direct questionnaire item than through the inferences from behavior; and there we see a freedom from emotionality (especially of the dissatisfied, frustrated kind), a feeling of capacity to cope, a freedom from neurotic symptoms, a higher energy level, and so forth.

In asking how this structure arises and functions, we should realistically begin (as usual) by asking if there is a genetic foundation. The answer is clearly (Cattell, Blewett, & Beloff, 1955) that a quite appreciable hereditary component exists in the $C$ factor, and since intelligence may also be involved in finding these good behavioral compromises, one expects some contribution also from the heredity in intelligence. On the environmental side, we can see from the work of Burt (1925) that inconsistent discipline, lack of parental guidance and models, and cultural rifts could hinder ego growth, while the Freudian and clinical evidence points out that early trauma, excessive superego demand, and the locking up of energy in early fixations must also have the same role. These connections are documented by the substantial loading, about .6, of low score on $C$ in the second-order Anxiety factor. In the general operation of such influences, one can see a positive feedback effect. "Nothing succeeds like success" where ego strength is concerned. For each successful dynamic compromise, expression brings more resources into the ego structure and aids success in further control. Each setback is likely to produce

more *locked* energy, as measured by the conflict index $\Sigma \bar{b}^2$, inimical to solving the next problem.

Now the main theoretical question about these three structures ($C, G,$ and $Q_3$ in the personality source-trait domain) concerns what their roots are in the dynamic lattice—and, therefore, mutually. It is generally agreed clinically that the superego is an engram that is more like a complex than a sentiment, in that its roots are deep in early life and largely unconscious and unalterable thereafter.

For the biologist there remains the formidable problem of accounting for a satisfaction so powerful that it overrules all ergic (or *other* ergic) gratifications and thus can militate against the survival of the organism. This can perhaps be explained by evolutionary geneticists. Presumably the gains in group survival in group competition succeed in making self-sacrifice pay off biologically for the taxons producing self-sacrificing types (Cattell, 1954).

Granted sufficient genetic endowment for superego formation—which places the superego in the same general category as ergs, though an erg of a special kind—some appropriate educational influence in the early years, perhaps involving the oedipal mechanisms described by psychoanalysis, leaves the 5-year-old child typically with a superego function largely unconscious in its roots. Probably some further altruistic orientation is given to it in adolescence. The developmental aspect cannot be our subject of study here, and we sketch it only to describe the position we finally accept: The typical adult possesses a superego structure that has the continuous demanding quality of an erg (see Dielman and Krug, chapter 5), and invested in objects that, learned as goals by early imprinting, are virtually immune to later conscious relearning. The Superego must therefore be placed proximally, close

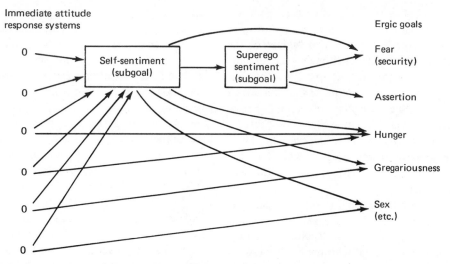

**FIG. 1** Statement of hypothesis of self-sentiment, superego, and ergic goal structure relations in the dynamic lattice.

to the ergic goals, in the dynamic lattice, as in Fig. 1; furthermore, since Self-sentiment has been placed, as in our earlier discussion, decidedly to the distal end, the general dynamics is clear as regards these two. The Self-sentiment must be what it is by virtue of its being a structure set up for the satisfaction both of Ergic and Superego goals; and since most of the subsidiation to the Superego must come from the Self-sentiment, we should expect substantial correlation between them.

Precisely the kind of correlation we should expect, with largest loading on G, Superego, is evidenced in the repeatedly replicated second-order factor shown in Table 7. What remains unclear is the subsidiation of the third member of the trio, Ego. As Table 7 shows, Ego has a comparatively slight positive loading here, suggesting that only part of its variance is contributed to by the individual's having a strong self-sentiment and superego, which one must suppose (except for Freudian trauma in the case of the latter) normally provide orderly situations favorable to the growth of ego

strength. In this connection one expects that the self-sentiment will frequently be brought to the assistance of the ego, in that the conscious integration and value systems in the former should often tip the scales in a

**TABLE 7** The second-order Control or Good Upbringing factor equatable to superego

| Factor | Loading |
| --- | --- |
| Affectia, $A$ | 00 |
| Intelligence, $B$ | 04 |
| Ego-strength, $C$ | **15** |
| Excitability, $D$ | 01 |
| Dominance, $E$ | −02 |
| Surgency, $F$ | **−51** |
| Superego, $G$ | **64** |
| Parmia, $H$ | 00 |
| Premsia, $I$ | 08 |
| Asthenia, $J$ | 09 |
| Guilt Proneness, $O$ | −07 |
| Self-sufficiency, $Q_2$ | 01 |
| Self-sentiment, $Q_3$ | **60** |
| Ergic Tension, $Q_4$ | −03 |

*Note.* This is at the 12–18-year level on the High School Personality Questionnaire and is the mean of 7 samples (see Cattell, *Personality and Mood Structure by Questionnaire*, 1973a).

conflict of ego and erg. However, the learning reinforcement of successful control, as such, is surely the principal builder of the ego as such. And although this learning occurs—at least after the first 2 or 3 years—with conscious perception of the alternatives and of "the discipline of natural consequences" that will ensue, *it need not involve explicit reference to the self-concept.* Thus, the growth of the ego, at least initially, would be independent of that of the self-sentiment.

At this point one recognizes that the structure of the Ego is a subtle thing, not simply parallel to the typical sentiment structure of the Self-sentiment or the (partly *complex*) nature of the superego. One would not expect in the attitude domain to pick it up as a factor among attitudes, for it has no concrete attitude object, but only the general and quite abstract goal of controlling in the best interests of total satisfaction. It is not surprising that with variables used so, it has not been picked up along with Self-sentiment and Superego in, say, the MAT set of attitudes. But one would expect it, as a general *style* of behavior, to be picked up in the objective personality source trait domain.

Certainly we must expect the Ego to appear as a very broad factor indeed (and this checks with the relatively meager hyperplane found for the $C$ factor, and certain difficulties in rotating it from $O$ and $Q_4$). Since the ideal of control becomes incorporated in the Self-sentiment, the Ego is going to *use* the Self-sentiment as something capable of assisting in this larger control. Indeed, as infancy passes we should expect more Ego growth in those in whom there is more Self-sentiment development. Two-way causality must be recognized here; for constant experience of failure to maintain control must prevent the formation, so long as reality contact is maintained, of a self-

respecting Self-sentiment.[6] However, although this hypothesis requires, again, some positive correlation to be found between the $SS$ and the Ego measures, in later childhood, the relation is more complex than for Ego and Superego and one could encounter situations where $SS$ and Ego developments are actually negatively related, because they are complementary. An intriguing instance is the finding in some schizophrenic groups (Cattell, Komlos, & Tatro, 1968) of high $Q_3$ (Self-sentiment) along with the low $C$ (Ego-strength) characteristic of all pathologies. The hypothesis that seems best to meet these observations is that when $C$ deteriorates (possibly, by some theories of schizophrenia, largely through biochemical failure), the patient's experience of his own increasingly wayward and uncontrolled behavior causes him to turn more and more to conscious consideration of his own self-concept for guidance. This would lead to increasing investment in the Self-sentiment (visible in $Q_3$ scores, but even more, one would hypothesize, in $SS$ scores) in an attempt to regain control by what is normally only a secondary and complementary mechanism.

To recapitulate on the learning growth of the Self-sentiment itself, the point is that we have to account for the latter's rise and maintenance by some ergic reward arising therefrom. That is to say, the attitudes in the $SS$ must subsidiate to sentiments and

---

[6] Clearly, a person with a good endowment in Ego-strength can build up a different set of expectations in the Self-concept ($SS$) from one who has not. He can also aim at higher degrees of integration of the Self-sentiment, confident that his neurological-cum-learning acquired apparatus will support that behavior. However, insofar as the Ego structure is capable of being raised to a higher level of integration by learning, there will be a feedback effect in that the expectations in the Self-sentiment will reward the more successfully integrated kinds of Ego action.

ergs by some necessary means-end relation. (Many, many discussions of the self have made no attempt whatever to justify it as a reward-bringing device, such as it must undoubtedly be if it is to be learned.) The theory here is that the individual perceives that the maintenance of the intact self—physically, psychologically, and in social standing—is a necessary prerequisite for all other satisfactions, that is, for all sentiments and ergs. The nature of the attitudes loaded on the Self-sentiment in Table 1 is clearly of this kind, for they are concerned about equally with the person's being alive and well tomorrow, with his sanity, and with his social standing. These are the prerequisites to the other satisfactions he has more unconsciously come to enjoy.

This hypothesis of dynamics needs to be considered in relation to the supposed parameters of the Self-sentiment set out previously. Will greater ultimate satisfaction for the organism be aided by the strength of total investment in the $SS$, by the accuracy of the self-concept, by the frequency of referral of proposed behavior to it, and so on? The answer would seem to be that by acting as a clearinghouse for proposed behaviors (suggested by impulse and passing stimuli), examining their ultimate satisfaction value; by maintaining an accurate, realistic concept of the self; and by referral, the $SS$ maximizes long-term satisfaction.

On this basis we should expect measures of these different aspects of the $SS$ functions to correlate as a single factor, since it grows as a single entity. We might also expect, as with the Ego, that its development would be somewhat positively correlated with intelligence (as seems verified, at a low positive correlation level). For in many everyday matters, no matter how restrained and foresighted about his affairs the individual may wish to be, intelligence is required to perceive the relationships. Attempts at foresight

that are merely punishing because of lack of intelligent perception of connections are not likely to reinforce attitudes of foresight.

It would also follow—if the $SS$ is to be really effective in ordinary ergic impulse conflict—that the magnitude of the $SS$ as a factor, that is, its variance contribution to a representative range of behaviors, should be greater than those of most other dynamic structures. For example, in the behavioral equation for most acts,

$$a_{ij} = b_{je1}E_{1i} + \ldots + b_{jep}E_{pi}$$
$$+ b_{jm1}M_{1i} + \ldots + b_{jm1}M_{1i}$$
$$+ b_{jm_{SS}}M_{SSi}, \qquad (2)$$

we should expect $b_{jm_{SS}}$ to be sufficient to outweigh an average accumulation of ergic ($E$) and other sentiment ($M$) demands. This role of $SS$ as moderately effective control, even in the absence of the Ego-structure action is a matter for empirical investigation.

## 7  TESTS BY MULTIVARIATE, MULTIMEDIA EXPERIMENTS

The theoretical model just presented leads to an appreciable number of inferences that can be put forthwith to the test of experiment. We shall follow up here two or three such experiments already completed. However, psychologists not actually immersed in this area of research may justifiably feel that they want first to check the foundation, namely, that three main structures—$C$, $G$ ($SE$), and $Q_3$ ($SS$)—are central in the area of behavior control and value orientation, and that they correlate positively in the manner stated.

Two major researches (Gorsuch, 1965; Horn, J. L., 1961a) were planned and executed to throw light on the general viability of the theory of structure just mentioned. They were designed at the same time for comprehensive reconnoitering of some alternative possibilities that need to be positively set aside as blind alleys if they are in fact misleading. Hopefully, their completion has established the general nature of the main patterns, and rules out alternatives sufficiently to make possible now more exact experiments capable of penetrating more deeply into the heart of the problem.

The experiments in question and certain related studies cover three samples of adults (more than 400 cases) and two samples of high school children (more than 300 cases), with two independent factor analyses. A careful strategic overlap of variables between experiments has made desirable cross checks possible between these two independent experiments, as well as comparisons of age effect and so forth. The fact that they concurred in outcome on the broader features of structure gives a firm platform for certain conclusions and for the design of the more exactly oriented researches that are now possible.

The plan in both of these researches was the following:

1. To check the reality of the Self and Superego structures as found in the different media (section 5 of this chapter). That is to say, they aimed to check the essential identity across media of (a) the $Q_3$ found in $Q$ data, and the $SS$ of $T$ data, in the case of the Self-sentiment; (b) of the $G$ of $Q$ data and the $SE$ of $T$ data in the case of the Superego; and (c) of the $C$ and $TII$ measures of Ego-strength.

2. To examine the possible claims as further representatives of Self and Superego structures, of claimants among personality factors found in the *objective* test series— *U.I.* 16, 19, 20, 23, 29, and so forth.

3. To introduce several new concepts and associated measures of socially conforming and Superego value behavior,

couched in $Q$ data for exploratory purposes, so as to test certain hypotheses about the distribution of values between the Self-sentiment and Superego structures ($Q_3$, $SS$, $G$, and $SE$).

4. To find how all these primary and suspected primary factors would interrelate at higher factor order levels, especially in terms of ultimate relations of Self and Superego.

The last question concerning the higher order structure embedded in the relations, of course is, Do the Self and Superego structures remain ultimately independent, as theory would require, though with some positive correlation (through the Superego's being one of the main dynamic investors in the Self) or do they come together in a higher order factor that would lend support to the "fully integrated personality" of Allport, McDougall and others? Insofar as it is possible briefly to summarize so vast an amount of measurement (about 6 hours for each subject), the following conclusions can be drawn (see Gorsuch, 1965; Horn, J. L., 1961a).

1. The main previously known questionnaire primary factors ($G$ and $Q_3$), dynamic-structure-in-objective-motivation factors ($SE$ and $SS$), and $T$ data factors ($U.I.$ 16, 17, 20, 24, 26, 27, 28, 30, 32, 34, 35, and 36)— including such abilities as Intelligence, Fluency, and Memory—are verified once more as independent entities at the primary factor level (thus indicating that we are in the required standard empirical "universe of discourse").

2. Some of the new value concepts expressed by Horn, Gorsuch, and others as questionnaire scales in the Self and Superego region—reality acceptance (Gorsuch), perfectionism (Gorsuch), religious interest (Gorsuch), hypocrisy and Machiavellianism

(Horn and Gorsuch), devotion to what is right (Horn), social conformity (Horn), and so forth, also formed distinct but narrow factors of value judgment at the primary level. However, they had substantial correlations with Superego and Self-sentiment factors. The best interpretation at present, however, is that they are not distinct personality factors but only expressions of the presently known Self-sentiment and Superego factors through special instrument factors (refraction factors in the sense of chapter 2).

3. A majority of the $T$-data (O-A Battery) personality factors, which had been included as having even the slightest claim to being expressions of Self or Superego, proved *not* to relate with any significant indications to the general behavior covered in Self-sentiment or Superego.

The central connections in the $T$ data positively and consistently found by both investigators were as follows:

1. The exception to this majority is $U.I.$ 17. The factor $G$ (Superego in $Q$ data) and $U.I.$ 17 (Lack of Inhibition) formed (with slight $Q_3$ and $C$ loadings) a structure that could definitely be called a *transmedium superego primary*. New loadings here include "correcting wrongs," "doing one's best," and "scorning cheating."

2. That Superego, $SE$, in the objective *dynamic* tests (in the MAT, for example), tends to *correlate* positively with ($U.I.$ $29 + G$) in item 1, but nevertheless to segregate therefrom as a distinct primary in the Horn experiment. Horn also found social conformity and low Machiavellianism values to correlate, yet to be distinct. Gorsuch found in $SE$ also "fluency on ethical questions," low rating of popular "everyday" goals, and a peer rating as "independent."

3. The Self-sentiment, $SS$, settles more

clearly into a unitary pattern. A single factor exists binding $SS$ in the dynamic structure factors, to $Q_3$ in the $Q$ data, and to $U.I.$ 36 in the O-A (actually, $U.I.$ 36 is largely marked by $SS$ types of tests). This also has (Gorsuch) some "perfectionism" scale loading and (Horn) some "reward for parents" and "respect and admiration for others." It may be noted that here, as in other work, a "low self-concept" (actually low self-approval and high social undesirability) as well as low score relative to the self ideal, belong on the Anxiety factor, not the Self-sentiment factor.

4. When the previous primaries are taken to the second order, the main findings in relation to our present interest are the following. (a) A "second-order" Superego factor which brings the central superego manifestation together on the positive side and Anxiety ($U.I.$ 24) on the negative side. Although other researches (see Cattell, Eber, & Tsujioka, 1970, p. 122) consistently give a negative correlation of Anxiety with both $G$ and the second-order $G + Q_3 + C$ Upbringing factor, the correlations are sometimes small. Gorsuch, however, found the ($U.I.$ 17, 29, and $G$) Superego and the dynamic $SE$ (MAT) Superego still not merged at the second order, though correlating positively. (b) The Self-sentiment remains distinct from Superego. $SS$ unites $U.I.$ 36, some MAT $SS$, $Q_3$, and also about half the items in the "conforming superego" (also some Introversion and $U.I.$ 16 [negative], i.e., conforming restraint). Conformity per se belongs to $Q_3$ rather than to $G$. (c) As to the Ego, while $C$ preserves its character and the second-order objective test factor, $TII$ (which has been tentatively hypothesized as Ego-strength in the objective medium), is verified as a unity, the *connection* of these two is not established. As to $TII$ itself, both researches yielded a second order $T$ data Ego factor with the general

nature originally found by Cattell and Scheier (1961), that is, *U.I.* 16(+), *U.I.* 1(+), *U.I.* 19(+), *U.I.* 26(+) and *U.I.* 36(+). Additionally, from the new and extensive data on social status variables introduced by Gorsuch, it became evident that this Ego-strength pattern has strong social status and educational level associations. (d) Some of the fringe candidates for Superego like *U.I.* 20 and 28 come together in some kind of "character weakness" pattern. These *evasiveness* and *pseudoconforming* patterns are now shown to have association with cheating tests and delinquency, but they do not seem closely connected with Self and Superego as defined by all other variables. This is a new development in the behavior control and values field that needs to be followed up.

5. By the time the third order is reached in these pioneer researches, the structure is too loosely determined to permit positive conclusions about new structures. However, there is no suggestion, even at the third order, that the Self-sentiment and Superego factors come together in a single broad "integrating" factor, as several psychologists have hypothesized. There is, nevertheless, an indication of a significant tendency to moderate positive correlation of Self-sentiment with Ego and Superego. In any case, it seems that at present the third-order factors are better interpreted as sociological or physiological background influences producing some moderate correlations among the first- and second-stratum-level factors, which are true personal structures.

The main conceptual conclusions at this stage of research may be summarized in Table 8.

Hopefully, with this stripping down to significant possibilities, and the throwing overboard of much junk (that an open mind hitherto required us to carry), research can now enter on the measurements of essential factors necessary to make the higher order structures precise.

## 8 FUNCTIONING OF VALUES IN THE EGO–SUPEREGO–SELF-SENTIMENT STRUCTURES

It remains to relate the domain of values to these structures. The typical form of a

TABLE 8  Ego, Self-sentiment, and Superego structures appearing at first- and second-order in Cross-media factoring

| Primaries verified in separate media and correlated enough for possible identity | Check on identity in terms of inclusive second-order factors across media | | |
|---|---|---|---|
| | Ego structure[a] | Self-sentiment structure[b] | Superego structure |
| *L* data (ratings) | *C* | *K* or $Q_3$ | *G* |
| *Q* data (questionnaires) | *C* | $Q_3$ | *G* |
| *T* data (objective tests): | | | |
| (a) General | Possibly *U.I.* 16 | *U.I.* 36 | *U.I.* 17 |
| (b) Motivational | None | *SS* | *SE* |

*Note.* The measures gathered in the second-order columns might, with some supplementation from Horn (1965b) and Gorsuch (1965), be taken as main entries in a design for experimental check on the hypotheses.

[a]If better matched to a second-order factor, it would be Factor *T*II comprising, in loading order: *U.I.* 16, 1, 18(−), 19, 23, 36. Also social status measure.

[b]If better matched to a second order, it would be $Q_3$, *U.I.* 36, and *SS*–all strong–plus *U.I.* 26(−), 20(−), and 28(−) weak.

value statement, verbally, is "I believe in"— referring to such things as honesty, tidiness, abstractness in art, modernity in music, or whatever. Obviously, we are caught here in a manner of speech, which does not follow through in many languages, for the person does not mean by this the same as he means by "I believe in a round earth" or "I believe two and two make four."

What he means is that honesty seems to him a good thing, of which he would like to see more, and, if he is more truthful than tactful, he would probably add "This means more from you as well as more from me." If he worships absolutely the value of tolerance he *may* restrict himself to the belief that only *he* should show more, but the common meaning of a value is that the person believes it should be increased wherever it exists. In fact, the first important thing to recognize about a value is that it is not a cognitive[7] "belief in the existence of" and the second is that its more important part is not cognitive at all but dynamic. The verbal value statement, in fact, connotes an attitude that can be defined in paradigm of the dynamic calculus (chapter 5) as "I want so much that this value be made more prevalent."

Let us assume that the mere verbal statement of the value attitude has been confirmed by objective motivation measures so that the typical attitude structure can be properly inferred. The problem now becomes that of finding motivational roots for the attitude, in ergs and sentiments, as one does for any attitude. A value attitude is obviously remote from any simple ergic satisfaction; the special problem, in view of its abstractness, is to subsidiate it to any

personal psychological gain or reward.

If the psychologist examines the desire "that this abstract quality shall increase" he will find, of course, that it is less abstract, more personal, and hedged with local situationed conditions than he at first supposed. Esthetically, for example, he may state the value that he likes wind on the heath, but it turns out he does not want a hurricane. Or he admires and desires tactical skill in his fellow soldiers, but does not desire it in the enemy's soldiers. Or he considers sexual allure desirable in his wife but questionable in his daughter. In short, the abstract statement is rarely the pure abstraction it appears to be as a verbal statement.

The word *value* can, of course, be legitimately used in a far wider sense than here, to mean *valence* or the emotional meaning of any object. That, in its precise form, is what in chapter 18 is called the *ergic investment* in an object, calculable exactly as a vector. In this sense the value of a beef steak is its capacity to satisfy hunger and the valence of a thunderstorm is that it is terrifying. But here, by literary convention, the term *value* is restricted to more abstract ethical, sociological, philosophical, religious, and artistic things. We must in fact suppose that when a man says he places courage or perhaps the classical quality in music high in his value system, he is implicitly referring to a score we could get—an *ergic investment* score—if we summed the ergic vectors of his attitudes (averaging of the dynamic rewards) across the many different situations in which people's behavior could show that quality.

The riddle of the motivational roots of values therefore solves itself along these lines—that for many of the individual's needs a certain ethical or artistic behavior in other people or himself contributes to his satisfactions in so many situations and sentiments that he, by an act of abstraction, perceives its general, average usefulness. Thus, with

[7] The validity shown for autism (believing what fits one's wishes) among objective motivation measurement devices may be the clue to the habit of calling values *beliefs*. In this tenuous realm, *belief* is the surest way of expressing a conviction of desirability.

time and enough lost toys, even children will achieve a positive attitude toward the value of *tidiness*. The cognitive abstraction itself is culturally assisted by semantics; and though the less intelligent are less likely to make new perceptions of useful abstract ideal values, they acquire by absorption suitable dynamic emotional investments in common values. No research exists to show whether lower intelligence occasions less total ergic investment in abstract values, but it is likely.

The problem that remains is why these investments in abstractions are as dynamically powerful in social and individual behavior as they sometimes become. Before approaching this, it is desirable to broaden the discussion from the particular realm of socio-ethical-artistic values to which we have otherwise agreed to confine ourselves, so that we may take a glance at the wider field of what better may be called positive and negative valences. The important empirical fact in this area is that many years of rather simple research sum up to the conclusion that it is possible to construct measures for the principal dynamic and general dimensions of personality by testing largely in this area of valences—that is, among items showing what the person "likes" and "does not like." It is a commonplace idea that most of personality can show itself in this way, and literary men use such behavior to sketch in character. The number of dimensions found from factoring *like* and *dislike* items approaches that from more sophisticated measurement, for example, objective miniature situation tests (*T* data). Many of these dimensions can be recognized as those found in general personality research, for example, factoring the Strong Interest Blank likes and dislikes yields a large Affectothymesizothyme, *A*, factor, among other known personality factors; this is true of temperament as well as

merely dynamic, interest factors where it would be expected.

As Cattell has discussed more fully elsewhere, this phenomenon can be explained best by the principle of *personality as a hidden premise*. Ask two people whether their likes are for having the office window open or shut and the implicit syllogism in the mind of one might run as follows: "If rooms are cold I cannot work in them. If the window is opened this room will be cold. Therefore opening the window will upset my work." The reasoning is likely to be found equally in both, but because one has a subthyroid temperament condition he accepts and proceeds on the second premise, whereas the other, more temperamentally robust, does reject it. Experimentally, one could now generate a whole series of items that in one way or another would hinge on the acceptance of this second premise, and one would then expect by factor analysis to obtain a factor running across them corresponding to this temperamental premise. That is to say, one should obtain from these various value judgments a factor that is essentially a hyperthyroid temperament factor.

There is perhaps no need to labor the point, with additional illustrations, that if people possess a similar logic—the purely causal logic of real-world connections that most people must more or less accept—the main differences in desired actions and liked objects among people will ultimately be traceable to differences in temperament (as William James pointed out). The behavior should be factor-analytically traceable to such deeply underlying personal premises given by the temperamental condition and dynamic needs of the person. Indeed, using this approach through syllogisms, it should be readily possible to set up, by hypothesis, what these differing underlying premises might be and to work out logically the resultant groups of valences in everyday-life items that would follow. Such hypotheses would be susceptible to checks by factor analysis, since any such single assumption (on which people had sufficient variance) should show up as a single factor. The ergic source traits found by attitude factoring, in fact, can be considered essentially as factors of this kind: "I feel hungry" is a premise with a wide array of consequences when attached to various second premises, and most of these consequent reactions could be measured as valences, that is, values in the coarser sense.

If this *hidden premise* principle is the correct theoretical approach to values, then we should expect that moral values, like valencies in general but less pervasively, would tend to factor down to a moderate variety of dimensions that would be of a *personality* nature. For a value like "I believe in courage" is surely rooted partly in temperamental capacities and dispositions (perhaps low Timidity) which make it more practical for the person to adopt this value, as well as in his reasonings about the importance of courage for the well-being of society. However, so long as we keep to socio-ethical-artistic values in the sense defined as most important here, it is surely most likely that most of their variance will be accounted for by the two main factors that have already shown substantial loadings on such attitudes, namely, the Self-sentiment and the Superego. It is these that are most concerned with social and ethical behavior (though not with artistic values).

It is, in experimental fact, these two factors, plus certain specific sentiment factors, such as those to religion and career, which seem to account for most of the variance in such value attitudes as "wishing to see moral values maintained," "avoiding damage to one's self-respect," "retaining a reputation for honesty and dependability,"

"maintaining the values of patriotism and duty to one's country," "keeping in touch with God or some principle of moral guidance," "becoming first rate at one's job versus puttering about," and "being unselfish in behavior to others."

On closer scrutiny, one is able to see some sorting out of these by the source-trait analysis which, in fact, we have already begun to notice, namely, (a) comparatively high segregation into the Superego factor of such attitudes as unselfishness, avoiding sin, requiring higher moral values in society, communion with God, duty to country, and reputation and self-respect; (b) comparatively larger emphasis in the Self-sentiment on reputation and self-respect, care for one's family, social position, self-control, knowing oneself better, joining citizenship activities, showing good manners; (c) an equal sharing of some values, such as interest in God and desire for good reputation, between Superego and religious sentiments, of self-respect by Self-sentiment and Superego, of being esteemed for a good job by Self-sentiment and by career sentiment.

That moral values, over and above manners and maintaining social reputation, actually get into the *SS* as well as the *SE* could be explained partly by the subsidiation of the former to the latter (along with other purely ergic goals as already discussed). It could also be partly due to the fact that in most societies, having moral values is also a condition of approval by society; that is, it is a necessary aspect of the Self-sentiment. (Some comparisons of totalitarian countries and those with distinct government-ethical and ethical-religious systems would be revealing here.)

If, scanning the whole psychological field, one were asked what most distinguishes man from animals, and the research on man from research on animals, he would probably go beyond such things as differences in intelligence and problem-solving behavior to the difference in the investments found in values such as are defined here. These abstract value systems in the *SS* and *SE* acquired sentiment structures are so remote from powerful, biological ergic goals, and yet so powerful in determining behavior with life or death consequences, that one becomes aware almost of a difference of quality or total growth *phase* rather than of quantitative parameters alone, between human and animal behavior. This difference can nevertheless be understood only if we recognize (a) the unmistakable common human animal bondage to ultimate subsidiation (of the *SS* in humans) to the whole gamut[8] of ergic satisfaction, and (b) that the *SE* is comparatively immune to conscious manipulation after early childhood and therefore not practically *rational*. Many values, from those of liberty, which sent John Brown's body to molder in the grave, to those of patriotism, which sustained the Japanese kamikaze pilots, receive motivation endowments from both *SS* and *SE* sources. Accordingly, it is not surprising as Equation (2) suggests, that adherence to these values is able to control—in some highly developed persons—the sum of immediate ergic demands for contrary *purely instinctual* action.

## 9  SUMMARY

1. Semantically, three main uses of *the self* can be recognized in psychology, which cover (a) the felt, experienced, introspected immediately acting self; (b) the cognitive

concept that a person has of himself, and which proves to be associated with a plexus of dynamic attitudes; and (c) the self as a controlling coordinated structure inferred from observed behavior, where it is understood as that which accounts for integration of behavior. Our concern here is with the last two.

2. Methodologically, the vitally required strategy is first to determine the number and nature of the structures in a domain, by multivariate, representative, experimental designs. This makes possible the ensuing application of manipulative designs or analyses of development over time. Such a strategy is particularly indicated in so complex a structural problem as that of the self, and it is in this phase of research that substantial progress can be reported.

3. Factor analyses are being pursued both cross sectionally, to reveal the self as a structure, and longitudinally, to recognize coordination as a process, though the latter has received less attention. In regard to the self-concept plexus—which is best called the Self-sentiment, *SS*, because it concerns a factor of acquired attitudes around the cognitive concept as a focus—a pattern has been found in *L* and *Q* data, labeled $Q_3$, and another in objective motivation measures (actually labeled *SS*) with fairly sound evidence of being expressions of the same factor in different media.

4. A second structure, which has all the qualities assigned to the psychoanalytic Ego is found in rating (*L* data) and questionnaire (*Q* data) and labeled *C*. In objective tests (*T* data) there is still doubt, however, as to which pattern expresses *C*; thus, a second-order factor, *T*II, is tentatively indicated.

5. A third structure in this general domain, having the essential nature of the psychoanalytic Superego, has been factor-analytically isolated in four domains—as *G* in *L* and *Q* data; as *U.I.* 17 or 29 in *T*-data; and

---

[8] It is noteworthy that when the ergic content of such sentiments is evaluated (see chapter 5), a major role has to be recognized for such ergs as self-assertion, gregariousness, and exploration that are not always listed among animal biological drives and apparently have evolved to altogether higher levels of motivational strength and predominance in man.

as *SE*, a pattern of attitude loadings in objective motivation measures. The first three correlate mutually consistently with this identification as a single primary; but the third, though positively related, is apparently still contaminated with some extraneous *instrument* variance.

6. The theory proposed to explain the rise of these three structures, their dynamics, and their further observed empirical relations to other variables is rooted in the model of the dynamic lattice and the dynamic calculus, as follows.

The Self-sentiment is a typical sentiment in being a means to ergic goals, but is unique in its breadth, since the maintenance of the physically and socially intact self is a prerequisite to most satisfactions. The factor is produced by covariances due to individual differences in the strength (and in some analysis, the accuracy) of the attitudes in this sentiment.

The Superego we tentatively suppose to originate, as psychoanalysis indicates, from early introjection of the beloved parent, becoming unconscious in its roots. The *SE* is thus more toward the proximal (ergic) end of the dynamic lattice as the *SS* is at the distal end. The subsidiation of the *SS*, in part, to the needs of the *SE* accounts for their observed correlation.

The controlling Ego, *C* factor, begins as a process of arranging such inhibition, deferment, and compromise of impulses in confluent courses of action as will maximize the long-term ergic satisfaction. It has a genetic component of capacity to integrate and to tolerate deflection strain, but grows by learning which, in some way not yet fully worked out, permits reward to reinforce *generalized* control behavior. A second-order factor is found (Upbringing, $T$VIII) which loads in descending order $G$, $Q_3$, and $C$. It suggests that the growth of Ego-strength is aided by influences which strengthen the

Self-sentiment and the Superego. The clinical finding of some negative correlation of Superego and $C$ must be peculiar to pathology, for here both $G$ and $C$ are substantially negatively correlated with Anxiety.

7. Comprehensive investigations simultaneously measuring all the primary factors that have any claim to Self or Superego identity now exist on sufficient samples for initial conclusions about the higher order structures in this domain—though more refined and definitive studies are still needed. They show that the three structures here discussed remain independent even at higher orders and do not collapse as Allport's and McDougall's a priori theories required. Consistent with the theory in item 6, however, there does appear a moderate positive correlation of the coordinating Self, Self-sentiment, and the Superego. However, particularly in the case of the Superego, structural and development separation continues. A theory of complementary action of the controlling Ego (*C*, $T$II) and the Self-sentiment ($Q_3$, *SS*) is discussed. The substantial negative correlation found to exist between Anxiety and Superego development, is explained in terms of integrating action of the latter on Ego and Self-sentiment formation. A substantial positive correlation exists between Ego-strength and social status, intelligence, and educational influences. A number of partly independent *value system* substructures, related to different cultural influences, are to be seen within the Superego structure.

8. If values are defined more restrictively than valences, namely, to mean concern *only* with moral, artistic, and similar cultural values, then it appears that they exist as attitudes (rather than beliefs) with a course of action favoring "the increase of such styles of behavior by everyone." They draw their dynamic support from the subsidiation

that the intelligent person can see to ergic satisfaction generally but especially to the needs of the Self-sentiment and the Superego. Introducing the principle that "the personality is a hidden premise" in reasoning to actual valences (likes and dislikes) we can see why it is that most personality dimensions can be located and studied through factoring valences. Variance on most attitudes dealing with values in the higher sense is split mainly between *SS* and *SE* sources, but also involves such sentiments as career and religion. The splitting shows moral, altruistic, and self-abnegating values more largely supported by the Superego, and social respectability, self-control, manners, prudence, repute, and status associated values loaded more on the Self-sentiment.

# 30

## The Effective Utilization of Personality Constructs in Applied Situations

**David C. Thompson**
*Consulting Psychologist, Philadelphia, Pennsylvania*

### 1  FACTOR ANALYSIS AND THE APPLICATION

Historically, many problems in utilization of personality data in applied situations have derived from measurement problems. Recent developments in the factor analytic approach to personality measurement, for all practical purposes, have solved a key problem in personality measurement—the problem of measuring independent facets of personality with nonoverlapping, "pure" measures (Cattell & Eber, 1957; Guilford, J. P., & Zimmerman, 1956)—creating new possibilities for application and utilization. Before we can fully appreciate these new application possibilities and their attendant potential pitfalls, we must first see clearly that measurement and application are, respectively, the inductive and deductive, or perhaps the analytic and synthetic aspects, of one general data cycle.

### 2  THE DATA CYCLE—ASSUMPTIONS

The data cycle goes something like this. We elect a domain of interest—let us agree on personality. We decide on a set of measures that we expect will tell us what we want to know about the domain in question. We are aware, as we select our set of measures, that our selection is totally arbi-trary and that, in the true Kantian sense, we are imposing categories of understanding on our domain. We agree to standardize, exter-nalize, and perhaps even automate our mea-sures to be "objective" about what we record. Sometimes we are seduced by our objectivity into the belief that it allows us to see what really is. In our rational moments, we realize that while our objectivity will not guarantee that we will see what really is, at least it will improve the probability that we will see things as others see them. The attain-ment of such common vision is important, since it allows us to move our attention from the level of basic data to a higher level of generalization. We should recognize that we accomplish this movement by reducing inter-personal dispute and conflict rather than by coming closer to reality as such.

Almost never do we pursue the possibility that reality is created by our imposition of categories. We settle for the naive assump-tions of the empiricist philosophers that imply a single reality "out there", i.e., a reality someplace independent of the per-ceiver and largely unresponsive to his at-tempts to perceive it. Notions of the separateness of subject and object—notions that appear to pervade our language, lead us in this way to a metaphysical and an epistemological theory.

We feel fairly comfortable with these theories as philosophical underpinnings, and holding the banners of operationalism high, we go on about our psychological business. But to some small extent, we feel that we may have somehow violated reality with our attempts to perceive it. After all, isn't that what Heisenberg pointed out? We settle for our categorizations because we are practical men, and because we implicitly believe that although our measures will never be truly isomorphic to the "old devil" external reality, neither will they be totally unresponsive to his arcane ways. In place of isomorphism between measure and reality, we assume some degree of correlation. It is at this point that our ultimate reliance on assumptions and faith becomes clear. But we do not falter. Rather, we draw ourselves up to our full scientific height, and move out of philosophy into religion in the name of psychology.

The religion of which I speak is the ceremonial collection of data in accordance with commandments of population specifications, sampling, operationalization of concepts, describing distributions, comparing distributions, and generalizing on sets of observed comparisons between distributions. These commandments have been carefully developed over psychological generations, and are passed down as a set of inductive dogmas—or, as a set of psychological genes.

The least that can be said about this collection of dogma is that it is impressive; so impressive, in fact, that we are prone to forget Hume's warnings about empirical proof. By *inductive* I mean what Popper (1961) meant when he said, "It is usual to call an inference inductive if it passes from singular statements, such as accounts of the result of observations or experiments, to universal statements, such as hypotheses or theories."

Gathering and factoring personality data is certainly an inductive process. The intermediate inferences are mathematical rather than verbal, but the end result is the same, since we arrive at universals (factors). And so it is—we can reduce and simplify our perceptions and measurements of human phenomena. But to what end? Some of us value only this inductive process—as some religious persons favor abstract theology with its attendant simplification of life. Others, granting the beauties of induction, want to move from generalities through a process of implications of a deductive nature back to applications at the level of observables.

## 3   THE DATA CYCLE—SOME PARTICULARS AND PROBLEMS

What goes up should come down. Induction is not an end in itself. We also need to work back deductively from our scientific generalizations. But rules and canons of a deductive sort are much fewer in number and harder to find. This scarcity is unfortunate. All the value of our newer, more powerful measures can be quickly lost in careless application. The absence of canons of application leaves considerable room for subjectivity and guesswork in the application process.

Psychologists are often accused of building sand castles and other assorted irrelevant structures. Some argue that the major part of what psychologists do is irrelevant. And anyone who has lived where large numbers of tests are administered and stored may secretly share this haunting suspicion. We have perfected a series of beautiful and fairly straightforward methods for working inductively with our data—for going from observations to multiple observations to distributions to correlations and/or factors, etc. We do this with creditable accuracy, and thanks to the advent of electronic data-processing devices, with great speed. We are masters at gathering, relating, and generalizing our data. We are less skilled, however, at moving down the data cycle.

All theoretical disciplines have a "data cycle" with some kind of content and some type of implication system. Most disciplines, like medicine and law, for example, have some trouble coming down the deductive side of this cycle. Psychology, with its statistical complexity, has considerable difficulty at this point in its data cycle. Being able to complete the data cycle and make "scientific" individual predictions is obviously desirable. Such ability is to the psychologist what the profit and loss sheet is to the business man or the batting average to the baseball player.

Perhaps some diagrams will clarify what my sentences can only approximate. Figure 1 shows the data-cycle concept in specific dress; i.e., that of the factor theorist in the area of personality. A few comments about this figure are in order.

First, the main benefit in using tests, as represented by the lines at 7 o'clock, is that

they lend standardization; repeatability; and thereby, something close to indisputability—something usually called objectivity—to our observations of individuals. Tests also provide a convenient means of changing facts to figures according to definite principles. The score matrix at 8 o'clock in the cycle diagram is a $t$ by $i$ matrix of tests $t$ and individuals $i$. This is a two-dimensional score matrix with which we attempt—no matter how imperfectly—to summarize happenings in our dimensional domain $x$. At best, this score matrix is a distorted representation of the domain.

There are a variety of ways for further summarizing and reducing this score matrix. The $t$ by $t$ correlation matrix shown would first be computed in an $R$ type factor analysis where each test is correlated with every other test, producing a matrix of correlations between tests which, in turn, is factored. Again, this would be a two-dimensional matrix. Half of this correlation matrix is shown in dotted lines, since the matrix is symmetrical around its diagonal axis.

Factor analysis of a matrix of correlations between tests produces "test factors," represented in the data cycle by the multi-dimensional, many-branched figure at 10 o'clock. It is important to notice that at this stage we are once again in more than two dimensions. Factor analysis takes the two-dimensional correlation matrix and isolates the $f$ sources of "true variance" in that matrix. The logic of factor analysis argues that these are the real dimensions in the underlying domain—those that our earlier conceptualizations and categorizations may have violated. This logic is of great importance; since, in essence, it means that our epistemology is a matter of convenience, and that no matter how we violate reality in our cognitive dealings with it, we can rest at ease because the powerful

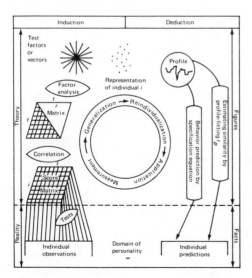

**FIG. 1**  Factor theorist's personality data cycle.

logic of factor analysis promises to restore to reality its rightful dimensionality and structure. Such a promise seems suspect if not downright misleading, but this is subject to empirical proof, at least in synthetic domains where we know the actual dimensions such as in Thurstone's (1947) famous "box problem."

Another question at this level has to do with the appropriate number of tests to represent our domain. While there are rules of thumb that relate the number of factors to the size of the correlation matrix, there are no well-known rules for determining the size of the test battery. No one seriously contends to know the number of basic tests needed to appropriately reflect that underlying variance in any domain. Nevertheless, we deal with this problem, again with a certain degree of arbitrariness. However, having been rescued by factor analysis from our anxiety about arbitrariness in conceptualization and categorization, we are somehow able to tolerate arbitrariness, at least for the time being, with respect to number of tests. The general rule applied to this situation is to use many tests and many observations.

At 12 o'clock on our data-cycle model we see a set of dots representing the placement of persons on the $f$-test factors. At this point, the factor theorist has reduced the persons in question to an irrelevant set of unrelated atomistic points in hyperspace. We are not quite sure at this point whether we want to factor people or to people factors. We are sure, however, that this collection of points, while interesting, is neither an end in itself nor an aesthetically satisfactory way to represent persons. We want to say something about them in the real world—in the world where each functions as an organized totality. The problem now is to put our person back together again in such a way that we can predict something about him that we did not know before. Making these

predictions is what the application half of the data cycle is all about.

This abbreviated review of the factor analyst's creed—the essential features, fundamental assumptions, arbitrary decisions, and various rules and canons that comprise his philosophy of science—is news to no one. It is presented here with tongue somewhat in cheek, but also with a great deal of respect. The techniques and logic that make up the inductive portion of the data cycle are, in and of themselves, things of beauty. They also depend, however, on assumptions that should be clearly stated. Similar arbitrary decisions and questionable assumptions characterize the deductive (application) portion of the data cycle as well.

## 4  BASIC PSYCHOMETRIC DATA MODEL

Another feature that characterizes both portions of the data cycle is a general data model. Personality concepts are applied to two basic problems: prediction and classification. Both problems require separate application techniques; these techniques in turn depend on one psychometric data model. This data model has two important characteristics: relativity and relevance.

Psychological measures basically are simple. They are not absolute measures. A psychological test is a device that compares an individual with a population on some trait or ability. Interpretation of a test score inevitably requires reference to the population used as a baseline—its appropriateness, size, and makeup. Psychological tests, then, are ultimately relative measures. A test score conveys information about an individual's standing relative to a group on some test dimension.

Test dimensions themselves have varying degrees of relationship to other variables. An important aspect of test development is the demonstration of a "respectable" level of correlation between test dimensions and external criteria of some type. This relationship is usually referred to as the validity of the test. Validity, however, is a word that has taken on overtones over the years. Tests are seen as valid or not valid. Validity tends to be seen as an all-or-nothing quality of a test. As the word is usually used, it implies a discrete dichotomy rather than a continuum. Tests tend to be evaluated and assigned status in the test-oriented community only in terms of their validity coefficients. Whereas this means of evaluating a test is not totally unreasonable, the fact that a "respectable" level of validity had not been found for that test does not mean that that particular test is useless. Taking liberty with an old positivist maxim, we might say, "If a measure exists, it can be thinged." A test that does not predict one criterion may still predict another.

In this discussion, the degree of relationship between test scores and some specific set of observables will be referred to as the relevance of the test. The tradition of respecting only tests with high relevance derives from the days when psychologists attempted to predict specific behaviors using tests that overlapped and measured a good deal of common criterion variance. Only tests with rather substantial validities measured enough unique criterion variance to survive partial and multiple correlation analyses. So a high degree of validity becomes a *sine qua non* in the psychometric world.

It is important to recognize that in applying factored measures, even those with low relevance are useful precisely because of their ability to predict an independent slice of criterion variance. Accounting for even a small bite of the independent slice is a step in the right direction.

The relativity of test scores and the relevance of test dimensions are important considerations whether one is moving up or down the data cycle. These notions are offered in spite of their obviousness, because they should help to show the essential similarity between two techniques of "reindividualization" of data.

## 5 REINDIVIDUALIZATION: TWO TYPES

We will refer to the act of applying abstract laws, rules, and findings to separate persons in applied situations as reindividualization. Since it depends on relevance and relativity, we might call reindividualization the "third R of applied psychology."

In the law, the reindividualization process goes on in the courts. The techniques are interpretation, precedent, and persuasion. In psychology, reindividualization is required in any applied situation. Regrettably, the techniques often boil down to "clinical feel," or some kind of "subjective regression equation." One of the reasons for this is that the data we would apply is all too often overlapping and redundant. Combining such data to predict a specific criterion is a complicated process. Multiple correlation is the method of choice, but few applied decision makers have the time or the facilities to make these computations in a systematic fashion. So vague configural and/or impressionistic methods have evolved to fill this gap. Such reindividualization methods are not notably precise or accurate. Although a trained psychologist can do a relatively good job in going from test data to predictions, there still remains a definite need for improvement.

Applied psychologists are asked to do many things with their data. They may be asked to predict delinquency or diagnose pathology, to predict speed of acquisition of some new skill, or to provide vocational counsel. If we take the totality of such questions that might be asked of an applied psychologist in any of the situations in which he might be found, we can imperfectly but approximately sort these questions into problems of specific behavior prediction (*BP*) on the one hand, and estimation of class similarity (*ES*) on the other. For example, in a clinic we might be interested in prediction of response to psychotherapy (*BP*), or in making a differential diagnosis (*ES*); in industry we might wish to predict sales "efficiency" (*BP* on an efficiency criterion) or sales "adjustment" (*ES* in terms of personality similarity to a class of known to be successful, durable, and "happy" salesmen); in a school setting we might want to know a student's ability to learn mathematics (*BP* on a learning criterion) or his best vocational choice (*ES* in terms of relative personality or interest similarity to various vocational groupings). *BP* and *ES* problems ask related but different kinds of questions and require different methods of applying the concepts of relativity and relevance.

## 6  BEHAVIOR PREDICTION: THE SPECIFICATION EQUATION

By behavior prediction we mean the prediction of the placement of a particular individual, relative to others, on a specific, concrete, measurable criterion-dimension. Such predictions constitute the real firing-line problems in psychology.

Any psychologist who has ever worked in a situation where a number of items of test data are regularly gathered on people will be familiar with the problem of applying such data, particularly in combination, to the prediction of the behavior of an individual. Suppose, for example, that a youngster is brought into a psychological clinic because of a school phobia. As part of the general intake process, he is given an intelligence test, a personality questionnaire, and a Thematic Apperception Test. This would not be uncommon. When the child is being staffed, someone asks the psychologist how the child will respond to psychotherapy. This is clearly a *BP*-type question. Our psychologist now has two choices. He can guess, or he can look to his test data for guidance. In the typical case, he will make an educated and sometimes fairly good guess. But it is somehow ironic that after going to the ends of the earth to develop our tests on appropriate groups, using special statistical checks and balances, and developing reliable scoring methods and powerful analytic techniques, we regularly destroy much of the value gained through application of these refinements by using our test results intuitively—by applying them by "rule of thumb." In most testing situations, data are gathered with rigid perfectionism and applied with casual indifference. "Having a clinical feel for the individual" or "taking his situation into consideration" constitute poor methods for bringing data to bear on applied predictions. Predictions made in this fashion are notoriously unreliable and inaccurate. Meehl (1954) demonstrated quite conclusively some years ago that the trained clinician's predictions made from test data by "clinical hunch" were far less accurate than the predictions generated by the actuarial combination of the same data in accordance with fundamental statistical rules. While it is regrettably true that the typical psychologist in the average applied situation has neither the time nor the facilities necessary for making even simple statistical combinations of data between the time of their collection and application, it is equally true that "subjective beta weights" are poor substitutes for computed measures of relationship.

Factor analysis has made great strides in providing workable solutions to this problem. It is interesting to note, however, that along with the advent of factor-analytic methods and the tests derived from them, has come an increased sense of frustration on the part of many practitioners who seem to feel farther away than ever from their test data. This sense of distance and lack of understanding obtains despite the fact that the formidable mathematical operations in factor analysis that isolate and partition variance in computing factor loadings actually make it much simpler to go from factored test data to applied predictions than it was before the development of these techniques. In the modern measurement world, test dimensions derived by factor analysis measure unique, nonoverlapping variance. Consequently, the complex partial correlation techniques are not required to arrive at the predictive implications of factor score patterns. There is now available a much simpler model that can be used in this situation—the specification equation.

The specification equation derives both in form and name from factor analysis. The general argument presented below comes from Harman (1967) and gives an insight into factor analysis that should help to clarify the derivation and meaning of the specification equation. Suppose that we have a variable $(x_j)$ that is to be analyzed in an $R$-type factor analysis of $n$ variables and $N$ individuals. For any individual $i$ we can find an observed value on $x_j$ that we shall designate $x_{ji}$. This observed value can be changed into a standardized value $(z_{ji})$ by the formula $z_{ji} = x_{ji}/\sigma_j$, where $\sigma_j$ is the standard deviation of variable $j$.

Now the set of all standardized observed values $Z_{ji}$ is called a statistical variable $Z_j$ in standard form. Such a variable has a variance of unity. If we now employ the notation $F_1$, $F_2, \ldots, F_m$ for $m$ common factors and $U_1$, $U_2, \ldots, U_n$ for $n$ unique factors, the complete linear expression for any standardized variable $Z_j$ may be written as

$$Z_j = a_{j1}F_1$$
$$+ a_{j2}F_2 + \ldots + a_{jm}F_m + d_jU_j$$

This expression is a model of the original variable $x_j$ in which the totality of variance in $x_j$ can be associated with a number of common and one unique factors. The mathematics looks complex, but the logic is clear. This equation simply states that the variances in $x_j$, when expressed in standard form $Z_j$, can be separated into discrete portions. The coefficients $(a_1, \ldots, a_m)$ of the common factors have two subscripts, the first indicating the variable involved and the second indicating the particular common factor to which the coefficient is attached. The coefficient of the unique factor requires only one subscript, which designates the variable number and the unique factor corresponding to that variable. The coefficients of the factors are usually called "loadings." They are the correlations of the observed variable with the hypothetically derived factors.

Obviously, this equation can be written for individual $i$ as

$$Z_{ji} = a_{j1}F_{1i}$$
$$+ a_{j2}F_{2i} + \ldots + a_{jm}F_{mi} + d_jU_{ji}$$

This equation implies that an individual's standard score on the criterion variable $(Z_{ji})$ can be derived if the loadings or relevance coefficients $(a_{ji}, \ldots, a_{jm})$ and the person's standard factor scores $(F_{1i}, \ldots, F_{mi})$, or relative position on the test factors, are known. Note that this model is an additive one, that it is linear (first degree), and that it contains one unique factor, $U_{ji}$, which describes a unique interaction between the person $i$ and the variable (observed behavior) $j$. This equation is the prototype of the specification equation.

In practice, modern personality measures provide us with individual factor scores in standard units $(F_{1i}, \ldots, F_{mi})$. Our aim is to predict individual criterion performance $(Z_{ji})$. To do so, we need the set of loadings, or relevance correlations $(a_{j1}, \ldots, a_{jm})$, that describe the relationships between the criterion variable $(j)$ except for the unique term $d_j U_{ji}$ which is the residual error term in factor analysis. In practice, this term is dropped from the specification equation. Since it is unique, it cannot be measured by psychometric methods. Its variance is retained as error of prediction. These errors function to reduce the predictive efficiency of the specification equation. They represent presently unmeasurable individual and/or situational factors. Awareness of this inevitability of error in prediction by specification equations is appropriate. Specification equations provide criterion estimates, which should be treated as estimates.

A further source of inexactness in specification equations derives from the fact that while factors are never "pure," i.e., they are to some extent intercorrelated, the specification equation combines an individual's situation weighted factor scores as if they were uncorrelated. Although more complex models could be developed to adjust for factor intercorrelations, good predictions can be achieved with the simpler model.

The specification equation (Cattell, 1957a) is designed to reflect the influence both of the specific situation and of the idiosyncracies of the individual. The influence of the situation is expressed by the relevance correlations, which indicate the importance of any particular personality trait in a specific situation. Put another way, these correlations represent the requirements that a particular situation puts on the individuals in it. The person's relative scores on the various factors are measures of specific individual differences. In this sense, the specification can be seen as an extension of the $R = f(O, S)$ model of the S–R theorist

where $O$ is replaced by a set of $f$s representing a set of individual characteristics and $S$ is replaced by a set of $a$s representing dimensions of stimulus control in the criterion situation. Other improvements over the simple S–R model (see also chapter 1) are implied by this formulation. For example, although the S–R model suggests a dynamic environment acting on a passive "conditioned" organism, the specification equation formulation clearly suggests the contribution of the unique characteristics of the organism both to response probability and to response strength. This model spotlights the multiple determination of responses of which S–R theorists usually fail to speak. And finally, it points to the fact that if one wishes to change behavior, he must consider not only multiple dimensions of the situation, but also multiple dimensions of the individual. The improvement of the specification equation methodology over other more simplistic formulations is demonstrated by the fact that by combining both the situational requirements and the specific individual differences in this manner, the specification equation generates highly efficient predictions.

Constructing a specification equation is straightforward. The first step is to determine the correlation between each of the individual factors and the response dimension in question. This might be done by actual computation or by searching the literature for related studies. Once these correlations are known, a person's relative scores on each separate factor are weighted by the appropriate relevance correlation. The resulting weighted scores are summed over all factors. The result represents the individual's position, again relative to others, on the response dimension in question. It can be seen that this formulation deals with the relative aspect of data, in that it works from a person's position on the individual factors relative to the population. The relevance aspect of this formulation is expressed in the correlations computed between factors and the response dimension. Each factor is relevant to predicting that dimension to the degree that it is correlated with that dimension.

The principle and the equations can be extended indefinitely. As long as we know the correlation between each independent factor that we have measured and some criterion dimension, we can predict any individual's placement on the criterion with a good degree of accuracy from his factor scores alone. There is some question as to the appropriateness of simple addition as a means of combining factor scores. It is quite possible that some factors combine multiplicatively and that others work together in more complex ways. But the research that has been done on this problem suggests that additive methods are an adequate combinational device.

It should be clear to the perceptive reader that a variety of personality types can receive identical criterion placement when specification equations are applied. For example, suppose we know the specification equation for criterion $K$ to be $K = .7A + .4B - .2C + .3D$. Individual $x$ may have scores of 4, 5, 7, and 3 on factors $A$ through $D$ respectively. Thus, his score on $K$ would be $K = .7 \times 4 + .4 \times 5 - .2 \times 7 + .3 \times 3 = 4.3$. Individual $y$ could have very different scores on personality factors $A$ through $D$. He might be a very different type of person. Nevertheless, the specification would indicate a placement on $K$ for $y$ identical to that predicted for $x$ if $y$'s scores on the same four factors were 6, 2, 5, and 1 since $K = .7 \times 6 + .4 \times 2 - .2 \times 5 + .3 \times 1 = 4.3$. (Some lay writers fear that psychologists are bent on selecting persons who have the same "conformist" personality for jobs in industry. These fears should be quieted

by this feature of specification equation methodology.)

It should also be clear that a specification equation will predict only one criterion situation. Personality factors have different degrees of relevance in different settings. There is a unique set of relevance correlations or loadings for each different criterion and therefore, a different specification equation.

A final point must be made. Although we can quite effectively predict a person's criterion placement relative to others in a variety of performance situations using simple-minded specification equations, we cannot, using these techniques, say anything about his overall adjustment in that performance situation. For example, we might want to predict "selling effectiveness" of salesmen candidates. The sales records of current salesmen could be used as the criterion. Personality data on those salesmen could be correlated with sales records to provide loadings. These loadings, in turn, would provide the necessary means of predicting candidates' sales effectiveness from their personality data. However, although a specification equation constructed in this manner would tell us a good deal about the probable selling efficiency or effectiveness of a candidate, it would tell us little, if anything, about how well the candidate in question would fit in or adjust as a salesman. The question of fitting in is a separate issue, which we will now consider under the topic of estimation of similarity.

## 7 ESTIMATION OF SIMILARITY

Operationally, similarity estimates are made by profile matching—a process that proceeds from the assumption "that the mean profile of people who have long stayed in an occupation and are presumably stably adjusted to it, is an ideal pattern in selecting new followers to that occupation" (Cattell &

Eber, 1957, p. 20). On a more general level, the assumption is that the mean profile of a group, whether it be a normal or an abnormal group, is a suitable baseline against which to define an individual's membership in that group. If we know the mean profile of psychopaths, we should be able, through profile matching, to determine whether any particular person should be classified as a psychopath.

The rationale of reindividualization by profile fitting can be seen to relate to the general data model concepts of relevance and relativity in the sense that the mean profile represents the relevant standard for the specified population relative to which an individual is measured. Although the specification equation proceeds to an individually predicted standard score on some performance criterion, profile matching provides a numerical estimate of the degree of congruence between an individual personality profile and a representative profile. As with other diagnostic techniques, it is important to clearly distinguish between naming and explaining. Establishing that the degree of agreement between an individual's profile and that of some representative group is sufficiently high to qualify the person for group membership is in no way explaining why the individual is the way he is. Unlike specification equation techniques, profile-fitting procedures do not illuminate the dynamic or process aspects of personality functioning. Estimations of similarity are non-explanatory.

The utility of such techniques, particularly for psychological diagnosis and vocational counseling, is obvious. One should keep in mind, however, that when class membership is established on a "fit" or "assumed adjustment" basis, the current or modal group, taken with all of its idiosyncracies, inadequacies, and shortcomings, serves as the criterion. This is not a particularly

worrisome problem as far as diagnosis is concerned, but it raises the concern that in vocational counseling applications, profile fitting may result in selecting for mere endurance rather than for performance.

Numerous methods of determining profile similarity have been proposed (Burt, 1937; Zubin, 1936). Careful reviews of profile comparison methods together with empirical studies of their comparative utilities are to be found in the literature (Helmstadter, 1957; Mosel & Roberts, 1954; Muldoon & Kay, 1958). These methods differ in the aspect of profile similarity they emphasize—size, shape, slope, etc. Pure correlation of profiles is a poor comparison method, since profiles of similar shape will correlate highly regardless of differences in profile height or size. An index of "absolute" agreement called $r_p$ was developed some years ago by Cattell (1949). That is, $r_p$ reflects both size and shape elements of similarity. Computation is straightforward. So that all profile scales weigh equally in $r_p$, standard scores are utilized. Deviations from the representative profile on each scale are squared and these squares summed. With the "sum of deviations squared" figure in hand, one refers to a nomograph (see Fig. 2), which translates a $\Sigma d^2$ figure into an $r_p$ figure. Note that it is possible to make such translations where different numbers of elements or dimensions have been compared in computing the $\Sigma d^2$.

Interpretation of $r_p$ is quite similar to interpretation of a correlation coefficient. It ranges from $+1$ (maximum similarity) to $-1$ (maximum dissimilarity), and in essence quantifies the overall degree of similarity between two profiles.

## 8  APPLICATION PROSPECTS

Possibilities for application of these two techniques are limited only by the creativity of the user. The specification equation and the $r_p$ technique are not the only reindividualization methods in use. Their virtues are mainly that both utilize not only group norms and averages but also individual deviations from those averages. Resulting judgments, then, consider not only what is typical, but also what is unique about a particular person. In the usual applied situation, these reindividualization techniques offer almost limitless application possibilities, particularly in the era of electronic data processing equipment. As various types of research are completed, libraries of relevance correlations and representative profiles will be collected. Work in this direction is well on its way (Cattell, Eber, & Tatsuoka, 1970) and the possibilities are indeed exciting.

Applied psychologists should recognize opportunities to collect such data for later predictive application. It would be entirely possible, for example, for an industrial psychologist to collect relevance correlations for response to management training, effectiveness as a supervisor, persuasiveness,

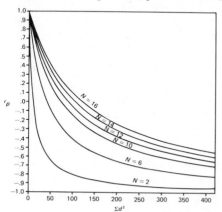

**FIG. 2** Nomograph for rapid calculation of $r_p$. From *The Sixteen Personality Factor Questionnaire* (3rd ed.), by R. B. Cattell and H. W. Eber, Champaign, Ill., Institute for Personality and Ability Testing, 1957. Copyright 1957 by Institute for Personality and Ability Testing. Reprinted by permission.

leader emergence in unstructured situations, and so on. Career counseling might be refined by comparing the specification-equation predictions for different career (marketing vs. public relations; line vs. staff; individual vs. group effort) channels. In addition to straight criterion prediction, it no doubt would be possible to establish the desirable range of $r_p$ for workable superior-subordinate relationships or for ideal work group composition. In the school setting, the questions are somewhat different. Ideally, schools should have access to large data banks, which would allow comparisons to be made between the personality data on any school child and any career group. School class composition based on tracking, not by intellectual ability but by personality type, would present interesting research possibilities. School classes based on one specific typology might prove to be unworkable, and a certain sprinkling of various types might make for more fruitful composition. A simple piece of research would answer this question. A school vocational counselor might want to differentially predict effectiveness in auto mechanics, dentistry, and forest management. At any rate, the application possibilities here are as numerous as the research opportunities are interesting.

Various clinical applications are also possible. Comparing the therapy progress of client/therapist pairs with varying $r_p$ ratios would have considerable theoretical interest. On a more pragmatic level, a clinical researcher might want to know how to predict interpersonal perceptiveness, ability to be assertive, or probability of suicide. He might also want to measure changes in specification equation predictions of these dimensions as a function of treatment. And finally, the possibility of using an increase of $r_p$ against a normal profile to evaluate overall therapeutic effectiveness and progress would be a fascinating application.

The basic requirements are the same in all applied settings. Representative profiles and established relevance correlations are needed. Once these are available, progress is unavoidable. Although the mathematics involved in these procedures is elementary, the power of the procedures in application is great.

The two methods of reindividualization reviewed here are, in a sense, the other side of our well-known methods of getting factor scores and deriving group profiles. These methods allow us to utilize our knowledge of group trends and processes and also to bring to bear what is most unique about the person in arriving at a predictive or descriptive statement. With these new tools, personality data for an individual can be used in exciting and effective new ways. Applied psychologists in all settings will find that they can save time while doing a more accurate and scientific job if these methods are systematically utilized.

## 9  SUMMARY

1. Today's powerful statistical techniques for generalizing and summarizing data require the development of specific application techniques.

2. The observations used to describe a domain are arbitrary. The important thing is that everyone can make the same observations and arrive at the same findings. To insure this kind of objectivity and/or agreement among observers, the ways and means of data collection have been fully formulated. The resulting formulations constitute a set of very tight procedural rules of observation in social science.

3. The rules guiding the application of findings are not well formulated. We need such rules and procedures to complete the data cycle and to apply the findings to individuals. As with the development of rules of data collection, the development of rules of application requires that we make certain arbitrary decisions as to procedure.

4. All psychological measures are relative, either to some population or to other measures made on the same person. Such measures differ in relevance, that is, the degree of correspondence between test dimensions and some independent criteria.

5. The questions asked about individuals in applied situations fall into two classes: specific behavior prediction ($BP$) and class membership ($ES$). Each requires separate reindividualization techniques.

6. Behavior prediction ($BP$) from factored personality measures is best achieved with specification equations. These equations are simple yet powerful. They complete the data cycle with respect to criterion prediction.

7. Estimating similarity ($ES$) to determine class membership is accomplished by profile fitting. Profile fitting is a technique for comparing a person's set of scores on several factor dimensions to the set of scores known to characterize a particular reference group. This comparison yields a "degree of agreement score," which can be used to approximate the degree of personality similarity among individuals, or between an individual and a group norm.

8. There are many application possibilities for specification equation and profile-fitting techniques. The basic requirements, regardless of the particular situation, involve the collection of criterion data for the development of relevance correlations and the collection of normative data for the development of representative profiles.

# 31

# The Formal Properties
# of Cattellian Personality Theory
# and Its Relationship to
# Other Personality Theories

**K. B. Madsen**
*Royal Danish School of Educational Studies, Copenhagen*

## 1  INTRODUCTION

### 1.1  The Task of This Chapter

As stated in the opening chapter and reiterated in the title, this chapter was intended to be a taxonomy of all theories presented in this *Handbook*. After accepting this task and making a closer study of the theoretical chapters in this book, this author, for several reasons, believed it necessary to change the nature of the contribution. First, since most of the workers who contributed to this volume have been associated in some way with Raymond B. Cattell, most, if not all, of the substantive aspects of their work may be conceived of as theoretical differentiations or empirical applications of one theory that may be designated *Cattellian personality theory*. This is not to say that other theories are not represented or that the various authors follow Cattell's model slavishly. (It should be evident, even to the casual reader, that many theoretical positions find representation in this book; and, as for any sycophantic following of Cattell, it will be obvious that the authors definitely have minds and positions of their own.) Nevertheless, the unitary character of the basic position, stemming from a requirement for being asked to participate in the volume, namely, that authors meet the

standard of treating psychology as "a quantitative, rational science" (to borrow Thurstone's expression, which now graces the dedication page of *Psychometrika*), emerges as one reads the chapters of this book.

A second reason for confining the following discussion to Cattellian theory and its comparison with other theories is that though there exists that unity of basic position just mentioned, there are so many other theories alluded to that it would be a hopeless task to encompass in just one chapter all the theories. For an extensive treatment of many theories, from the standpoint of this chapter, the reader should consult this author's text on modern theories of motivation (Madsen, 1974).

Therefore, it seems appropriate to concentrate on the core of the developments in personality theory as a whole in the writings of Cattell and his co-workers and compare it with other theories. Although the writer recognizes the special theoretical differentiations and local, substantive applications in every chapter, he believes that it is best referred to as *Cattellian theory*.

In several places Cattell has stressed the importance and potential utility of a taxonomy of theories. The importance of the task is partly illustrated by the opinion expressed by the senior editor—with which the present writer agrees—"Science is

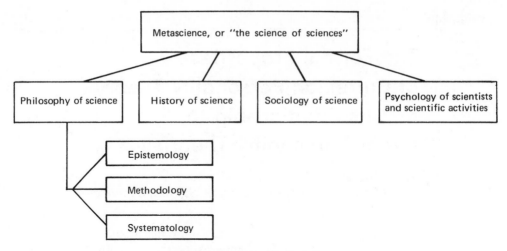

**FIG. 1** Metascientific disciplines.

theory." Furthermore, the importance of the task is influenced by the fact that in all fields of psychology, competing theories are presented that possess some similarities and some differences, both real and apparent. Consequently, the student and the research worker in psychology have to choose from among several theories to find one or, perhaps, must integrate several theories. It may be of some help to be able to refer to a taxonomy of theories, so that this selection among theories may be made on a rational basis. This taxonomy should not be the only basis for selection. It should be an instrument for the first survey and rough selection of those theories that then may be tested in various ways. And, in some cases, the result of the taxonomy may be that the psychologist selects certain aspects of all the theories and integrates them in a new theory.

If the reader is not convinced of the utility of a taxonomy of theories, perhaps this special application of a taxonomy is inadequate, or the author's taxonomy is too narrow for this special task.[1] It is also

possible that another taxonomy of theories might be useful.

## 1.2  Some Definitions

Before we present the results of our study of Cattell's theory, it is necessary to define some fundamental terms. What Cattell has called a *taxonomy of theories* is really the descriptive frame of reference for a special discipline within the larger field of *metascience*. This discipline is a part of the *philosophy of science*, which sometimes has been called *metatheory*, or, more unfortunately, *methodology*, a term that should be confined to a study of the empirical methods of science. The present author (Madsen, 1968a) suggested *systematology* as a more convenient term. This term designates the comparative study of scientific systems (theories, models, etc.). The relationship of this discipline to other meta-

---

[1] This taxonomy has evolved from an original comparative study of 20 theories of motivation, learning and personality (Madsen, 1959, 1968).

Among these theories was Cattell's early version (Cattell, 1950c). The comparative study continued with 22 new theories (among which is the later version of Cattell's theory). The results are presented in *Modern Theories of Motivation* (Madsen, 1974).

scientific disciplines is shown in Fig. 1. The relationships among the metascientific disciplines are shown in Figs. 2 and 3.

One of the tasks of systematology is to create a taxonomy of theories that can be applied in comparative studies of theories, and be improved as a result of such studies. We present some elements of such a taxonomy in this chapter. First, we need to agree about a definition of the term *theory*. This term has been used in many ways, but the writer is inclined to accept Cattell's definition given in chapter 1, which we repeat here for convenience:

A theory may be defined as an integrated set of explicit definitions and explanations. It satisfies the conditions of (a) maintaining internal, syntactical, and logical consistency; (b) bringing about external consistency, in that it bridges more than one set of data, introducing a single coherent explanatory framework; and (c) permitting deduction

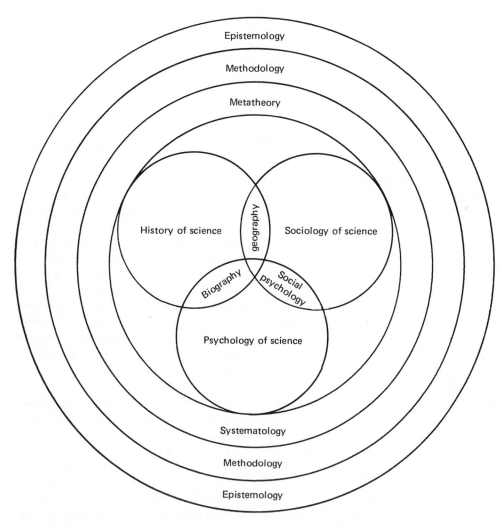

FIG. 2  The systematic organization of the different disciplines constituting the metascience.

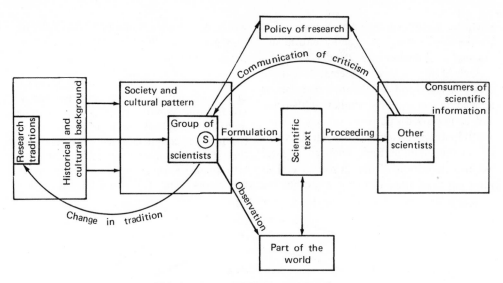

**FIG. 3**  The world of science—metascience.

and extrapolation to several new testable hypotheses, applicable to as yet uninvestigated phenomena.

Cattell regarded this definition as a representative conceptualization of a modern philosophy of science. But even this broad definition excludes some products of scientists, otherwise called *theories*. Therefore, we need a broader defintion; and I suggest the term *scientific discourse* or *text*, including all texts that may be defined as scientific if they satisfy the following criteria:

A scientific text consists of descriptive and explanatory propositions and perhaps some metapropositions about philosophy-of-science problems. Further, it must be noted that this definition of a scientific text is the basis for a stratification of a scientific discourse, or text, into three strata, or levels of abstraction, as presented in Fig. 4. [This conception of a scientific discourse as consisting of strata is borrowed from the Swedish philosopher of science. Hakon Törnebohm, and his collaborator, the Swedish psychologist, Carl Lesche, who applied Törnebohm's *discourse-analytical* philoso-

phy of science to psychology. A detailed, systematic and thought-provoking application of this approach to metascience was presented by Radnitzky (1968).]

After surveying this figure and making a comparison with Cattell's definition of a theory, the reader may notice that they are in agreement—except on two points: (a) Cattell's definition of theory stresses the importance of the *hypothetical* or *explanatory stratum* as the main part of a theory (which agrees with common usage). (b) His definition of theory requires some formal criteria for a text to be counted a theory. Cattell also requires formal development for using the term *model*, but we return to these problems of theory classification in "Dimensions of a Taxonomy," section 2.1 of this chapter, in which we study the formal properties or structure of the theory as a whole.

Before going to that part, it should be pointed out that a systematological study is not only confined to the structure of the theories, but also may deal with the components or elements of a theory. In other words, it is the *content* of explanatory

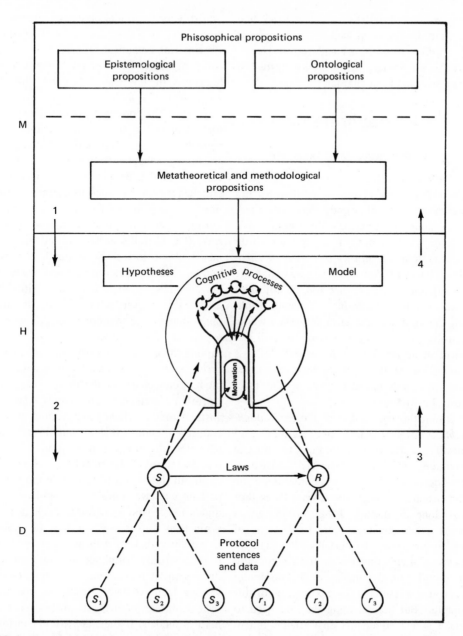

**FIG. 4** The hierarchical structure of a theory: the three strata of a scientific text. M = M level or metastratum; H = H level or hypothetical stratum; D = D level or descriptive stratum. The four arrows (1, 2, 3, 4) indicate that the top level influences the formation of the next level, which in turn influences the bottom level. But there is also a feedback of influence from the D level to the H level and the M level (otherwise it would *not* be a *scientific* theory). From *Modern Theories of Motivation* by K. B. Madsen, Copenhagen and New York, Munksgaard and Wiley, 1974. Copyright 1974 by Wiley. Reprinted by permission.

propositions (hypotheses and laws) and their explanatory terms, as well as the more basic *descriptive* propositions and terms. We return to the content of the theory in the last main section of our chapter.

## 2  STRUCTURE OF THE THEORY

### 2.1  Dimensions for a Taxonomy

Cattell (in chapter 1) used the term *dimensions* for a taxonomy of theories and presented and discussed some of these dimensions. The phrase, dimensions for a taxonomy of theories, is a good substitute for the term *classification system of theories.* The word *dimension* suggests that the classifications usually are not dichotomies with only two classes in each classification. On the contrary, the term suggests a whole continuum of categories with only differences in degree. The terms used to define a dimension are, therefore, thought of as *polar concepts,* defining the ends of the categorical continuum.

From this conception of the term *dimension* follows the task of describing and classifying theories according to such a taxonomy of theories. The task consists of making rank order of the theories along the dimensions. (At least, this is what the author has done in Madsen, 1968b, 1974, where some other dimensions are used, some of which are similar to Cattell's.) We shall try to use Cattell's dimensions for a taxonomy of theories on the theory in this book and present the results in the next section of this chapter. But before doing that, we need to make a few comments on Cattell's dimensions and supplement them with a new dimension.

The first dimension, *Precise model versus purely verbal formulation*, introduces the distinction between a model and a theory, where a theory is the purely verbal formula-

tion to which a model may be connected. A model may vary from abstract mathematical systems (mathematical models) to concrete two- or three-dimensional constructions (diagrams or physical structures). But the verbal formulations of the theory may also vary from the loosely formulated explanatory sketches to the formal *deductive systems*, which may be verbal formulations, but are often connected to a mathematical or a concrete model. Perhaps vague explanatory sketches are not included in Cattell's definition of theory, but we have included them in our more general term *scientific discourse* or *text*. (Cf. Cattell's definition and his comments about logical or syntactical consistencies, which "must be assumed always to be adequate.") In accordance with this usage, we suggest reformulating the first dimension of the taxonomy to a *dimension of formal development of scientific texts,* varying from *explanatory sketches* over *verbal, deductive systems* (with or without a model connected), to the most precise and consistent mathematical models. To the abstract mathematical models must also be connected some verbal formulations, which have the function of presenting semantic interpretations of the model.

In our dimension of formal development, perhaps we have combined two independent dimensions: One dimension of logical or syntactical *consistency* that may be applied to purely verbal, as well as other symbolic (mathematical) formulations, and another dimension of *preciseness of representation*, varying from verbally formulated *analogies* over *concrete models* to abstract mathematical models. If there are two dimensions, then they often covary, so that we sometimes regard them as only one dimension.

The second dimension for a taxonomy of theories is called *Local construct properties versus imported metaphorical properties*, which Cattell explicitly relates to the distinction between *intervening variables* and *hypothetical constructs*. In this way he stressed that this dimension is a continuum, with degrees of differences rather than kinds of differences. In this conception of the continuum of differences between I.V. and H.C., Cattell is in accordance with Tolman, who in his last major paper (in Koch, S., 1959) also took this position. The present author suggested (Madsen, 1959) combining the two variables by using the term *hypothetical variable.*

If we extend the dimension to include at one end the purely descriptive S-R theories, and at the other end the theories with a heavy load of hypothetical constructs (H.C.), we are still in agreement with Cattell. Between them we find theories that employ intervening variables (I.V.), which are completely defined operationally and without any *surplus meaning*. Thus we have the following diagram of the second dimension:

S-R theories | I.V. theories | H.C. theories

Dimension of Abstractness

This dimension may be developed further by dividing the category of H.C. theories into three subcategories according to the kind of imported metaphorical properties or surplus meaning involved:

1. S-O-R theories: These are theories containing explanatory terms that have surplus meaning borrowed or imported from neurophysiology (*O* standing for *organism*). These theories were previously called *reductive theories*, but it seems better to substitute the term *physiological, explanatory theories* or *physiological models* to show that they make use of hypothetical constructs. These constructs may be influenced by neurophysiological research, but the S-O-R theories are not deduced from a phy-

siological theory, which was a presupposition in the original conception of reduction.

2. S-M-R theories: These are theories containing explanatory terms that have surplus meaning borrowed from phenomenological or introspective observation of experiences, consciousness, or mental phenomena (*M* standing for *mind* or *mental*).

3. S-H-R theories: These are theories containing explanatory terms that have surplus meaning imported from such fields as cybernetics and information theory. These theories normally presuppose a neutral conception of, or attitude toward, the old mind-body or psychosomatic problem. In opposition, the other two theories frequently presuppose either a materialistic or a dualistic conception of the psychosomatic problem; in other words, they include as a presupposition a specific, philosophical conception of ultimate reality, while the neutral conception is a genuine hypothetical theory (therefore, the *H* stands for *hypothetical*).

The dimension of abstractness is thus developed into a classification of types of theories. This classification is illustrated by Figs. 5 and 6. The reader will find all the categories of theories mentioned, except for the I.V. theories (which are included in the S-H-R theories, as there is only a difference of degree between I.V. and H.C. with a *neutral* surplus meaning). In addition, in the upper left of Fig. 5 is an illustration of a complete (nonexisting) reductive theory, as well as an illustration of a pure *Geisteswissenschaftliches Verstehen-psychologie* in the lower right of Fig. 5.

The third Cattellian dimension, *Few areas connected versus many areas connected*, may be called the *dimension of applicability*, which, of course, is an important dimension, but no further comments are necessary.

The fourth dimension, *Low complexity versus high intricacy of formulation*, may be

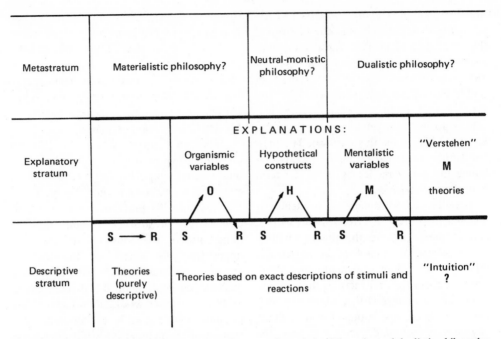

**FIG. 5**  Types of theories: Materialistic philosophy, neutral-monistic philosophy and dualistic philosophy.

equal to the often-discussed dichotomy, *Mechanistic theories contra dynamic theories* (or field theories). This dimension is related to the complexity of the hypotheses: from the simple (including only two variables: cause and effect) to the complex (including several variables, which are interrelated as causes in determining an effect).

The fifth dimension, *Mathematical starkness versus physical enrichment of model*, requires no further comment.

The sixth dimension, *Few deductions possible versus many deductions possible*, is related to the explanatory power of the theory. This is an important dimension for a taxonomy of theories; perhaps it is the most important for selecting one from among many, because this dimension is related to the old and widely accepted epistemological principle of parsimony (or *Occam's Razor*). The present author (Madsen, 1959) invented a formula that makes it possible to calculate the explanatory power or, in other words, to

estimate the number of explanatory propositions in proportion to the number of descriptive propositions. This formula is called the *t/e ratio* or the *Hypotheses Quotient* (HQ):

$$HQ = \frac{(H\text{-}H)}{(S\text{-}H) + (H\text{-}R)} .$$

Using this formula, the author calculated the HQ for 24 theories by dividing the number of purely theoretical hypotheses (H-H) by the sum of the partly empirical hypotheses (S-H and H-R). This procedure presupposes that theories are formulated so explicitly and precisely that it is possible to count the number of hypotheses. Otherwise, it is necessary to reconstruct the theories before calculating the HQ. That introduces a source of error due to the systematologist's lack of skill and objectivity when performing this task. A graduate student, Svend Jorgen-

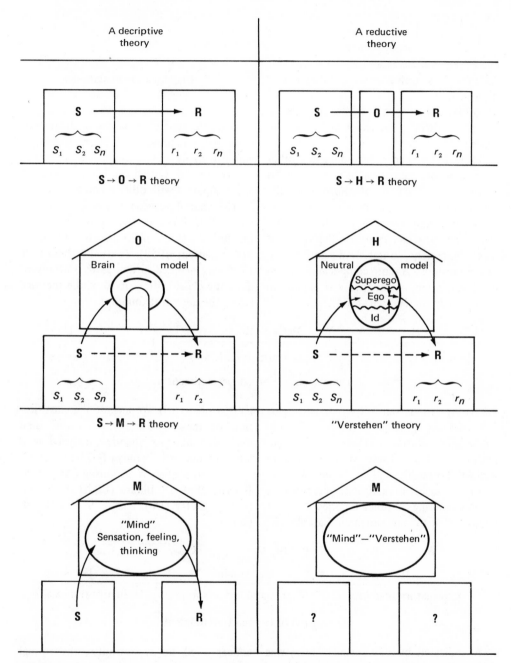

**FIG. 6** Types of theories: A descriptive theory and a reductive theory. S = stimuli; R = reactions; O = organismic variables; H = hypothetical constructs; M = mentalistic variables.

sen, applying Hull's theory, developed (Madsen, 1974) a computer program that measures the content of purely hypothetical, explanatory terms, as well as the content of empirical, descriptive terms, and then makes the calculation. Such a program makes this important task of estimating the explanatory power of theories an exact and objective procedure.

There is no need to introduce any other dimension for a taxonomy of theories in this chapter. In *Theories of Motivation* the author worked with two additional dimensions: *molecular versus molar* theories and *statistical versus deterministic* theories. But these dimensions do not seem significant in this connection. A more complicated system of classification of theories was applied in the later edition (Madsen, 1974).

We are ready to apply our taxonomy of theories.

## 2.2 Classification of Cattellian and Other Theories

After the general discussion of the dimensions for a taxonomy of theories, we are going to apply this taxonomy to a specific theory, that of Cattell and his co-workers,[2] and compare it with other theories.

The first dimension is *Formal development*. This dimension was also included in the author's study of 20 theories of motivation (Madsen, 1959). (Cattell's theory of 1950 was included in that study.) We reproduce the classification of 10 of the theories (using the present taxonomy):

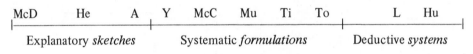

Dimension of Formal Development

The abbreviations stand, from left to right, for: McDougall, Hebb, Allport, Young, McClelland, Murray, Tinbergen, Tolman, Lewin, and Hull. These 10 theories were studied thoroughly and a chapter was devoted to each. In addition, there was a chapter covering 10 other theories. The best known of these are probably Cattell's (C)

and Skinner's (S). We include the classification of these two theories on the same dimension and six theories analyzed in a later comparative study (Madsen, 1973, 1974): those of J. W. Atkinson (At), D. E. Berlyne (Be), D. Bindra (Bi), J. S. Brown (Br), E. Duffy (Du), and R. S. Woodworth (W).

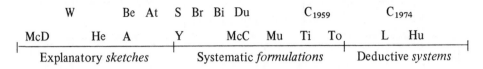

Dimension of Formal Development

As indicated, in 1959 Cattell's theory was classified according to formal development in the rank order between Tinbergen and Tolman. But since Cattell's *comprehensive learning theory*, as presented in this book, is

concentrated in 22 formulas, the formal development has been brought up to the

---

[2] From here on we will refer to this as Cattell's theory.

same level as Lewin's and Hull's theories. We indicated this change by using the years 1959 and 1974 as indexes for our older and newer classifications.

If we look at *preciseness of representation* (in accordance with Fig. 5) instead of syntactical consistency, the picture looks like this:

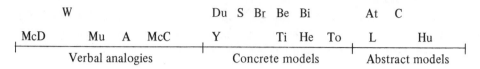

Dimension of Preciseness of Representation

As can be seen, Cattell's theory is among those with abstract models. Others have also changed places.

We now turn to the second, that is, the *dimension of Abstractness,* which Cattell calls *Local "construct" properties versus imported metaphorical properties.* To this dimension we added the purely descriptive theories at the left end of the dimension. At the right end we made a further differentiation of theories with imported metaphorical properties into three subgroups. Thus, we concluded with classifying them into types of theories. In the following list the 18 representative theories are placed according to type of theory.[3]

1. S–R theories: Skinner.

2. S–O–R theories: Berylne, Bindra, Duffy, Hebb, Tinbergen, Young.

3. S–H–R theories: Atkinson, Brown, Cattell, Hull, Lewin, McClelland, Murray, Tolman, Woodworth.

4. S–M–R theories: Allport, McDougall.

The third dimension introduced by Cattell (*Few areas connected versus many areas connected*) was renamed the *dimension of Applicability.* This is a new dimension and was not used in the present author's previous comparative studies.[4] Consequently, we only tentatively indicate the possible classification of some of the typical theories:

Dimension of Applicability

Tinbergen and McClelland are placed at the left, because their *Miniature systems* only set out to cover a small area (consistent with the authors' programs). On the other hand, Lewin, Cattell, and Murray cover the whole personality. Lewin and, to some extent, Cattell also try to cover social psychology.

The fourth dimension is the *dimension of*

*Complexity,* which has already been described as being more or less equal to the old dichotomy of mechanistic versus dynamic theories. But Cattell's definition of this dimension makes it more precise and useful, because with this definition it is possible to

[3] This classification is a combination of two classifications in Madsen (1959); therefore, the original classifications are not reproduced here.

[4] Perhaps there is some relationship—if not identity—between the *dimension of applicability* and the classification into *molecular* and *molar* theories introduced by Tolman and used by the present author (Madsen, 1959).

conceive of it as a continuous dimension. Thus, it is an improvement over the present author's classification of 10 theories, which we reproduce here:

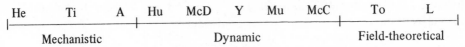

| He | Ti | A | Hu | McD | Y | Mu | McC | To | L |
|----|----|---|----|-----|---|----|-----|----|----|
| Mechanistic | | | | Dynamic | | | | Field-theoretical | |

In the following dimension we see the position of Cattell's and Skinner's theories in the old classification; and, in addition, we indicate the classification of the six new theories according to the renamed dimension of complexity:

|  | S | Be | Bi | Du | $C_{1959}$ | Br | W |  | At | $C_{1974}$ |  |
|---|---|----|----|----|------|----|---|--|----|------|--|
| He | Ti |  | A | Hu |  | McD | Y | Mu | McC | To | L |
| Low | | | | Medium | | | | | High | | |

Dimension of Complexity

Cattell's position has changed the classification from 1959 to 1974, because recent versions of Cattell's theory now belong to the most complex theories in psychology.

We now turn to the fifth classification, *Mathematical starkness versus physical enrichment of model.* This is the only one of the classifications that does not represent a continuous dimension. Rather, it is a real dichotomy, perhaps representing two independent dimensions, as demonstrated by the fact that some theories can be both high in mathematical starkness and physical enrichment. Thus, Lewin's theory may be placed in both categories, as his topological representations may be conceived of as containing both a mathematical and physical model. Nevertheless, we have tentatively tried to indicate the position of some typical theories:

| Hu | C | L | At |  | He | Ti | L | To |
|----|---|---|----|--|----|----|---|----|
| High | | | | Low | Low | | | High |

Mathematical Starkness versus Physical Enrichment of Model

The sixth and last dimension is that of *Few versus many deductions*, or as we have renamed it, the *dimension of Explanatory Power*. This is the only dimension in which it is not necessary to base our classification on more or less subjective, or at least qualitative, judgments, but have the possibility of making quantitative estimations by calculating the t/e ratio or HQ for each theory. We have made such estimations for 24 theories, which we have treated as main motivational theories (Madsen, 1959, 1974). This classification is reproduced in the following label from Madsen (1974):

| Modern theories | HQ | Modern theories | HQ |
|-----------------|------|-----------------|------|
| Cattell | 0.09 | Berlyne | 0.38 |
| Maslow | 0.13? | Brown | 0.38 |
| Duffy | 0.14 | Konorski | 0.54 |
| Miller (I) | 0.20 | Woodworth | 0.57 |
| Pribram | 0.29 | Miller (II) | 0.60 |
| Bindra | 0.30 | Festinger | 0.84 |
| Aktinson and Birch | 0.33 | Atkinson | 0.86 |

| Earlier theories | HQ | Earlier theories | HQ |
|---|---|---|---|
| Tinbergen | 0.11 | Lewin | 0.50 |
| Hebb | 0.13 | Murray | 0.71 |
| McClelland | 0.14 | Young | 0.82 |
| Hull | 0.36 | Allport | 1.00 |
| McDougall | 0.43 | Tolman | 1.43 |

Inspection of this label shows that Cattell's theory has the lowest HQ (which means the highest explanatory power).

The reader may have noticed that there are some relationships among the different dimensions. Thus, Cattell's theory is among the most advanced in formal development, preciseness, applicability, complexity, mathematical starkness, and explanatory power (with a low HQ). But not all theories fit together in this way at all points (especially in the comparison of Cattell's theory with those of Hull, Tolman, and Lewin). Therefore, this author postulates that these dimensions are really independent systematological dimensions. And despite the present subjective qualitative rank-order procedures, we hope that these systematological methods may be developed in the direction of more objective and quantitative procedures, with the help of computer-assisted text analysis, as presented in Stone, P. J., Dunphy, Smith, and Ogilvie (1966), *The General Inquirer*, which inspired our own computer program.

## 3  CONTENT OF THE THEORY

### 3.1  Classification of Terms

In the preceding section, we analyzed and compared the structure of the Cattellian personality theory, as a whole, with that of others. In this section we analyze the content of the theory, especially its terms. We first introduce some classifications of terms and later apply these classifications to the terms in this *Handbook*.

Theories of scientific texts contain explanatory propositions (hypotheses), as well as descriptive propositions, but these propositions are composed of terms, which are the most basic elements contained in scientific texts. Therefore, we shall concentrate on these elements here. Furthermore, some of the important aspects of propositions, especially hypotheses, have been a foundation for some of the dimensions for a taxonomy of theories that were applied in the previous section (especially Dimensions 4 and 6). For clarity, we make an effort to use the often-interchangeable words *term, concept,* and *variable* in this way: *Term* stands for the words in the scientific text; *concept* represents the corresponding structure in the head of the writer (and reader) of the text; and *variable* represents the processes, states, and structures in the organism to which the text refers.

### 3.1.1  The Stratification of Terms

The most important classification of terms (and propositions) is the division of the scientific text into the metastratum, the hypothetical or explanatory stratum, and the descriptive stratum. From this classification we obtain three categories of terms (and propositions):

1. The *metaterms* (and propositions) that deal with epistemologic, systematologic, and methodologic problems.[5]

[5] The metastratum of the theory is not analyzed here, although it is an important part of every theory—what shapes the theory. But limits of time and space have forced the author to concentrate on the other parts. Furthermore, the metapropositions are precisely formulated by Cattell in chapter 1. See also an analysis of Cattell's theory in Madsen (1974).

2. The *hypothetical or explanatory terms* (and propositions) that are used in explanations and predictions, or, more precisely: These terms and propositions are the logical basis for the deductions of the descriptive propositions. These explanatory terms may be classified in several ways and are illustrated later. However, the only classification mentioned here is the distinction between hypothetical constructs and intervening variables, which may be thought of as a classification according to levels of abstraction.

3. The *descriptive terms* (and propositions), which are the only part of the text representing, symbolizing, or referring directly to the described (and observed) events and objects. But although all descriptive terms and propositions refer directly to the observed world, some are concrete and others are abstract. To the concrete terms belong such expressions as *turning right* (in a maze), and to the abstract terms belong such expressions as *goal-directed behavior*. Thus, it may be possible to divide the descriptive terms and propositions into two or three levels of abstraction, or rather a continuum of abstraction.

Another important classification of descriptive terms is the classification into *dependent variables* and *independent variables*. The dependent variables in most modern psychological texts are actually categories or aspects of behavior. The independent variables encompass all the descriptive terms representing the observable variables that are causal or in other ways functionally related to behavior. These independent variables include, besides the actual *stimuli*, the antecedent *conditions*; possibly, some observable processes in the *organism* are also included in these independent variables.

The concept that a scientific text contains not one but several levels of abstraction may be illustrated by examples from factor-

analytical psychology: In the lowest, concrete stratum of the text we find the descriptions of test performances. Somewhat higher, in the continuum of abstraction, but still in the descriptive stratum, we have correlations between test scores. In the explanatory stratum we find those personality factors that may be inferred from the correlations. Still higher in the explanatory stratum we find the higher order factors.

This classification into a stratification of terms is a formal, systematological classification, like the classification of hypothetical constructs according to their surplus meaning, which we have already discussed.

### 3.1.2  Dispositions and Functions

This is an important psychological classification of variables according to the *duration of their existence*. Cattell mentions this classification in his introductory chapter when discussing the terms *personality and process concepts*. What Cattell calls personality concepts can be equated with what others call structure and what the present author prefers to call disposition variables. This is a common term for both inherited dispositions and later acquired (learned) dispositions. The dispositions evolve into enduring structures that influence the processes of functions that are going on in the structures. Thus, the *function* variables are of shorter duration, varying from seconds to hours. There are some longer enduring states or modes (fatigue, intoxication, and so forth) that may last several days and, therefore, influence many on-going processes and functions. Despite these in-between cases (the enduring states) it is easy to distinguish between dispositions and functions. Nevertheless, many psychologists do not distinguish between these categories of variables, and they use the same term for both the disposition and the function, which may be confusing. For example, the term *need* has often been used to designate both enduring dispositions and shorter functions (processes or states). More confusion is created by the lack of a clear distinction between this classification and the next one.

### 3.1.3 Dynamic and Directive Variables

This is a classification of variables according to their effect on behavior. Some variables (dispositions, as well as functions) have a regulative, organizing, or directive effect on behavior, while other variables (both dispositions and functions) have an energy-mobilizing, activating, or dynamic effect on behavior. Furthermore, there are variables that have a combination of both dynamic and directive effects. These variables may be designated *vectorial variables* (or vectors). (Unclear terms that do not clearly differentiate between these two effects may also be counted as *vectorial variables*.)

An illustration is Hull's definition of the term $_sE_r$ (*reaction potential*), which he defines as a function of the dynamic variable *drive D* and the directive variable *habit* $_sH_r$, in this way (for simplicity, all other variables in Hull's formula are omitted):

$$_sE_r = f(D \times {_sH_r}).$$

Unfortunately, Hull's formula also demonstrates the confusion between the two classifications, as his $_sH_r$ is a disposition variable (the acquired habit structure), that is activated by the dynamic function, drive. But there is no term to designate the function corresponding to the disposition ($_sH_r$), nor is there any term to designate the disposition corresponding to the function, drive. Of course, it is possible to interpret Hull's formula this way: The directive disposition $_sH_r$ is activated by the dynamic disposition $D$, and the result is the vectorial function $_sE_r$. But this is a simple theory, and other theories contain the differentiated terminology corresponding to the classifications proposed here.

### 3.1.4 Combined Classifications

On several occasions we have indicated the possibility of combining these two psychological classifications into one. Thus, we have an integrated classification scheme, as shown in Fig. 7. We have filled out the scheme with terms from several modern theories (none from this book).

It is possible to combine these two psychological classifications with the systematological classification into *strata of terms*. We then get a more complicated classification scheme, as illustrated in Fig. 8,

| Effect \ Existence | Directive variables | Dynamic variables | Vectorial variable |
|---|---|---|---|
| Dispositions | Freud's *ego* and *superego* Hull's $_sH_r$ | Atkinson's *motive* | Freud's *id* Murray's *need* (=personality factor) |
| Functions | Atkinson's *expectation* Young's *set* | Atkinson's *value* Freud's *energy* Lewin's *tension* Hull's *drive* | Atkinson's *tendency* Freud's *drive* Lewin's *force* Hull's $_sE_r$ Murray's *need* (=drive) |

**FIG. 7** Classification of hypothetical variables: A combined classification.

Classification of psychological variables. Columns represent Hypothetical variables (Neutral-formal, Neurophysiological, Phenomenological), bounded on the left by Empirical variables (independent, antecedent variables) and on the right by Behavior variables (dependent, consequent variables). Rows represent Disposition variables (Vector, Directive, Dynamogenic) and Function variables (Vector, Directive, Dynamogenic).

| | Empirical variables (independent, antecedent variables) | Neutral-formal | Neurophysiological | Phenomenological | Behavior variables (dependent, consequent variables) |
|---|---|---|---|---|---|
| **Disposition variables — Vector** | | 4 variables (e.g., Murray's *need*) | | | |
| **Disposition variables — Directive** | | 3 variables (e.g., Young's *attitude*) | Tinbergen's *instinct* | | |
| **Disposition variables — Dynamogenic** | | 4 variables (e.g., McDougall's *propensity* Cattell's *erg*) | | | |
| **Function variables — Vector** | 2 variables (e.g., Masserman's *need*) | 7 variables (e.g., Murray's *need* Tolman's *drive* (1932)) | 3 variables (e.g., Stagner's *drive*) | Young's *desire* | |
| **Function variables — Directive** | 2 variables (e.g., Hull's *drive stimulus*) | 5 variables (e.g., Young's *set*) | 2 variables (e.g., Freeman's *set*) | | |
| **Function variables — Dynamogenic** | 11 variables (e.g., Tolman's *drive* (1951) Young's *need* Hull's *need* (CD)) | 8 variables (e.g., Hull's *drive* Tolman's *need* (1951) Lewin's *tension*) | 3 variables (e.g., Young's *drive*) | 2 variables (e.g., Moore's *impulse*) | |

**FIG. 8** Classification of psychological variables.

which is used in the author's comparative study of 20 theories of motivation.

## 3.2 Terms in Cattell's Theory

### 3.2.1 Historical Evaluation

We are going to apply the classifications of terms previously introduced to Cattell's theory. Therefore, it may be convenient to make a survey of the principal terms (variables or concepts) in Cattell's theory (based on Cattell, 1950, 1957, 1959, 1965, and chapter 18 in this book). There are three main components of personality: (a) *cognitive* or ability traits; (b) stylistic or *temperamental* traits; and (c) *dynamic* traits, which include attitudes, sentiments, and ergs. The last category, ergs, is the basic dynamic

component of personality and is made up of several subcomponents according to the following formula:

$$E = (S + k) [C + H + (P - aG) - bG].$$

In this formula, the symbols designate the following: $E$ = the ergic tension, $S + k$ = the stimulus situation, $C$ = the constitutional component in need strength, $H$ = the (personal) historical component in need strength ($C + H$ constitutes the need strength), $P$ = the physiological condition component ($C + H + P$ = drive strength), $G$ = gratification level ($-G$ = absence of gratification), and $k$, $a$, and $b$ = personal constants.

We can summarize the main variables in Cattell's theory by the following hierarchical scheme:

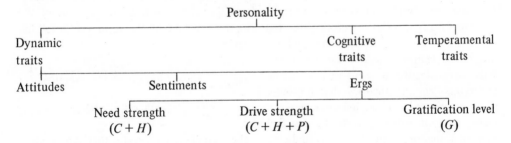

At this point, let us add those terms included in the *comprehensive learning theory*, presented in chapter 18 of this handbook. Through this expanded theory, Cattell makes it possible to integrate personality and motivation theory with learning theory. As far as the present author knows, this is a unique event in the history of psychology. One of the most comprehensive theories—Freud's—lacks hypotheses about learning, as stressed by Rapaport (1960), among others. And K. Lewin's theory is also weak regarding its hypotheses about learning (reflected by the fact that Hilgard omitted Lewin in the third edition of his standard work; see Hilgard, E. R., & Bower, 1966). There has

been integration starting at the bottom. Psychologists have tried to explain personality development on the basis of experimental learning theory. But even the classical contributions from those attempting this integration—for example, Dollard and Miller in *Personality and Psychotherapy* (1950)—have not satisfied personality theorists (see, e.g., Rapaport, 1960). Cattell's comprehensive learning theory should have a good chance of becoming widely accepted, because like Freud's, it starts with the most complex: *personality*. However, unlike Freud, Cattell treats it in an exacting and systematic manner. From this beginning the theory has been developed to integrate motivation and learning in mathematical form, which is clearly in agreement with modern learning theory since Hull.

### 3.2.2  Systematologic Analysis

After this historical evaluation of Cattell's comprehensive learning theory, we turn to a systematologic analysis. For the convenience of the reader, we start with a concentrated summary:

Learning is one of three possible kinds of change $C$:

$C_l$ = learning or modification by experience,

$C_c$ = capacity changes by direct physiological modification, and

$C_e$ = endogenous change or genetical maturation

*Learning,* in turn, comprises three main categories: (a) classical conditioning, (b) instrumental (means-end) learning, and (c) integration learning (or goal modification). This last category is compared with the traditional learning theories that normally allow no change in motivation or personality factors (except, perhaps, for K. Lewin's and Tolman's theories, but they only indicate the possibilities and do not elaborate them into a precise and systematic theory). The revolutionary aspect of Cattell's theory is that it deals with learning as a multidimensional change in a multidimensional situation.

Thus, learning, according to the comprehensive theory, is a function of the following factors at the beginning of the learning sequence:

$E$ = ergic tension level, subdivided into the constant, $E_T$, and a variable, $E_S$ or *ergic sensitivity index,*

$M$ = engram action level (including sentiments and complexes), subdivided into

the constant $M_T$ and the variable $M_S$, or *sentiment sensitivity index,* and

$S$ = state level (arousal, anxiety, etc.).

In addition to these factors, learning is influenced by the following factors at the *end* of a learning sequence:

$E_d$ = drop in ergic level, which is a function of:

$G$ = consummatory gratification or reward magnitude,

$r_{ht}$ = reverbatory level of the cognitive process from situation $h$ at time $t$,

$d_r$ = decline rate of the cognitive reverbatory process, and

$f$ = frequency of repetition after the first sequence.

All these factors, or variables, are functionally related as indicated by one of the most important of the formulas Cattell has devised:

$$a_{hj(tft_1)} = \mathrm{Log}\, f\,[r_{hxt_1} - d_r(t_1 - t_2)]$$
$$\cdot\, [E_{Si}(S_{h_x}es - S_g)]\,.$$

The formula demonstrates that this comprehensive learning theory is also an integrative theory or a synthesis of hypotheses from contemporary learning theories integrated into Cattell's personality (and motivation) theory. Cattell states: "Thus frequency, reward, and 'goal distance' consolidation are brought into a single theory."

### 3.2.3  Systematologic Classification

We are now ready to consider the systematologic classifications of the terms in Cattell's theory. (A comparison between Cattell's and Hull's theories is presented in an appendix in this chapter.) The first classification introduced was the *stratification of terms,* which is roughly equal to the usual division into independent (or $S$) variables, intervening (or $H$) variables, and dependent (or $R$) variables. If we apply this classification to Cattell's variables, we obtain the following results:

1. $S$ variables: stimulus situation $S$, the physiological condition $P$, and the gratification level $G$. (It is with some doubt that $G$ is placed among the $S$ variables, and not the $H$ variables, but $-G$ is conceived of as equal to *deprivation*, which is an experientially controlled variable, just as is $P$.)

2. $H$ variables: abilities, temperament, and *dynamic* traits, including sentiments, attitudes and ergs, which contain $C + H$ (the constitutional and the historical components of need strength), as well as two $S$ variables ($P$ and $G$). From Cattell's comprehensive learning theory we should add the following: learning change $C_l$; state level $S$; the ergic tension variables $E_T$, $E_S$, and $E_d$; the engram variables $M_T$ and $M_S$; and the reverbatory process variables $r_{ht}$ and $d_r$.

3. $R$ variables: The measurable aspects of behavior, which operationally define *ergic tension level* (or other $H$ variables).

The second classification introduced was the division into *dispositions* (structures, factors, or traits) and *functions* (states and processes). Although the author was satisfied with this dichotomal classification in his earlier comparative studies of theories, he thinks it must be changed here for these reasons: First, this book, especially chapters 1, 2, and 8, contains such a precise and operational definition of the term *state S* that it must be constituted as a special category of terms separate from *processes*. Second, the comprehensive learning theory contains precisely defined terms for *change*. There are terms for the general categories of change: $C_l$, $C_c$, and $C_e$, as well as for the special categories: $E_d$ and $d_r$.

Consequently, the author suggests a new and more differentiated classification of terms according to the *duration of the existence* of their corresponding variables, or according to a *time dimension*. We suggest that the dimension be divided into four steps according to increase in time duration, each succeeding step incorporating the one preceding:

$$\underset{o}{\vdash} \quad \overset{p}{\vert} \quad \overset{s}{\vert} \quad \overset{c}{\vert} \quad \overset{d}{\vert} \longrightarrow$$

Dimension of Time for
Duration of Variables

Roughly, $o$ = origin, $p$ = processes, $s$ = states, $c$ = changes, and $d$ = dispositions.

If we apply this new classification to Cattell's theory, we obtain these results:

1. Process variables: Variables with a short duration of existence (from seconds to hours), for example, momentary stimuli, the physiological condition component of ergs, the reverbatory level of the cognitive process, a behavior sequence or action.

2. State variables: Variables with somewhat longer duration (from hours to days), for example, state levels, such as arousal, anxiety, depression, and fatigue; the gratification level; and, perhaps, the physiological condition of ergs and, in addition, the new sensitivity indexes: $E_S$, $M_S$, and perhaps $E_d$.

3. Change variables: Variables that change over varying periods, from seconds to years, for example, learning, capacity change, endogenous change, and decline rate of the reverbatory process.

4. Disposition variables: Variables with the longest duration of existence (from years to a lifetime). Here the term *variables* should, perhaps, be substituted by *factors* or *structures*, for example, ability traits, temperamental traits, and dynamic traits, the latter including $E_T$ and $M_T$, and the special

| Effect / Duration | Dynamic variables | Vectorial variables | Directive variables |
|---|---|---|---|
| Processes | Physiological conditions? | | Reverbatory processes $(r_{ht})$ |
| States | Physiological conditions? arousal anxiety depression gratification level $E_S$ and $E_d$ | | $M_S$ (sentiment sensitivity index) |
| Changes | | $C_l$, learning $C_c$, capacity change $C_e$, endogenous change | Declinerate of reverbatory processes $(d_r)$ |
| Dispositions | Dynamic Traits: $E_T$, $C$, $H$ | Temperamental traits Attitudes | Ability traits $M_T$ (sentiment engram) |

FIG. 9  Combined classification of variables. A short inspection of this classification scheme shows that Cattell's theory has very few process terms. But it can be explained by the fact that it was originally a personality theory that has been expanded to include motivation and learning.

components of ergs: $C$ and $H$, as well as the personal constants $k$, $a$, and $b$ in the defining formula for an erg.

We shall now turn to the third classification of terms, a classification according to the *effect on behavior* of the corresponding variables. This is the classification into dynamic, directive and vectorial variables. When this classification is applied to Cattell's theory, the following results are seen:

1. Dynamic variables: It should be easy to put all the so-called *dynamic traits* in this category, but the present author thinks that only the ergs and their different components ($E_T$, $E_S$, $C$, $H$, $P$, etc.) deserve this designation. The sentiments, which were originally classified as dynamic traits, possess more cognitive and directive functions, a fact stated by Cattell in chapter 18. The new variables, *State levels*, may also be included in this category.

2. Directive variables: To this category belong the engram variables $M_T$ and $M_S$, as well as all ability or cognitive traits. In addition, we find the new variable— reverbatory level of the cognitive consolidation processes—as well as the decline rate of the reverbatory process.

3. Vectorial variables: This category includes those variables which are clearly defined as possessing a combined dynamic-directive effect, as well as those variables with an unclear, or vague, definition. Therefore, from Cattell's theory we include the following variables: *temperamental traits, sentiments* (conceived of as organizations of engrams $M$ and ergs $E$), and the change-variable, *learning*, which may also be included here, as it influences changes in both dynamic and cognitive traits.

To give the reader an overview, we present the results of the last two classifications in a combined classification scheme in Fig. 9.

### 3.2.4  Classification of Motivational Theories

We conclude this analysis of the contents of Cattell's theory by characterizing its basic motivational hypothesis. The author has made a classification of motivational theories according to the *basic* motivational hypotheses (Madsen, 1973) into:

1. Homeostatic theories, that is, theories containing an hypothesis about homeostasis (biological equilibrium, etc.) as the main basis of motivation.

2. Incentive theories, that is, theories containing an hypothesis about (unlearned or learned) incentives (valences, rewards, reinforcements, etc.) as the main basis of motivation.

3. Cognitive theories, that is, theories containing an hypothesis about cognitive processes as a main basis of motivation (or at least as intrinsically motivating the cognitive processes).

4. Humanistic theories, that is, theories containing an hypothesis about a special humanistic (nonbiological, nonnaturalistic) basis for motivation, as well as other psychological variables.

| Types of theories / Basic hypotheses | S–R theories | S–O–R theories | S–H–R theories | | S–M–R theories |
|---|---|---|---|---|---|
| Homeostatic hypotheses | | Pavlov? Duffy Freeman | Freud Hull Murray (1938) | | |
| Incentive hypotheses | Skinner Bolles | Young Tinbergen Hebb Berlyne Bindra | Murray (1959) Lewin McClelland Atkinson | Cattell Miller Spence Brown | |
| Cognitive hypotheses | | | Tolman Woodworth McV. Hunt Koch Festinger | | |
| Humanistic hypotheses | | | | | Allport Maslow |

FIG. 10  Combined classification of theories of motivation. S = stimulus; R = reactions; O = organismic variables; H = hypothetical constructs; M = mentalistic variables. From "Theories of Motivation" by K. B. Madsen, in *Handbook of General Psychology*, edited by B. Wolman, Englewood Cliffs, N.J., Prentice-Hall, 1973. Copyright 1973 by Prentice-Hall. Reprinted by permission.

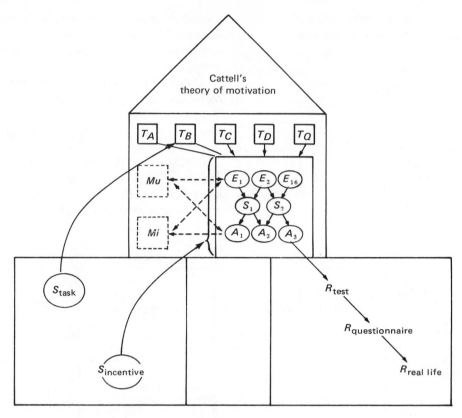

**FIG. 11** The main hypotheses in Cattell's theory of motivation. $T_A$ to $T_Q$ are the *temperamental* traits. One trait, $T_B$, is a cognitive trait, or *ability*, which is influenced by the complexity of the task situation. *Mu* and *Mi* are the Motivational Component factors, which perhaps have another metascientific status (indicated by broken lines symbolizing that these factors are not causal-determining factors similar to all the factors or hypothetical variables in Cattell's theory). The box containing $E_1$ to $E_{16}$ and $S_1$ to $S_2$ and $A_1$ to $A_3$ is the *dynamic lattice*, which is influenced by the incentives in the situation. $E_1$, $E_{16}$ are ergs, $S_1$ and $S_2$ are *sentiments*, $A_1$ to $A_3$ are *attitudes*, which are possibly on the border line between the H level and the D level. From *Modern Theories of Motivation* by K. B. Madsen, Copenhagen and New York, Munksgaard and Wiley, 1974. Copyright 1974 by Wiley. Reprinted by persmission.

This classification of motivational theories is combined with the classification according to types of theories, which has already been discussed. This new combined classification results in the scheme shown in Fig. 10.

From this classification, it is obvious that Cattell's theory is placed in the frame with many other important modern psychological theories and, moreover, that outside its original field (personality), Cattell's theory is

up to date. This chapter is concluded with a graphic model of the variables represented in Cattell's theory (Fig. 11).

## APPENDIX A COMPARISON BETWEEN THE THEORIES OF CATTELL AND HULL

Systematological classifications make possible a general comparison between theories. In addition to what has been presented in this chapter, it seems suitable to compare Cattell's *comprehensive learning theory* with Hull's theory, which is one of the most comprehensive and precise theories among the classic learning theories. For this comparison, we represent the essentials of Hull's theory by his *Postulate VIII, the Constitution of Reaction Potential* ($_sE_r$), which is summarized in this formula (Hull, 1952, p. 7):

$$_sE_r = D \times V \times K \times {_sH_r}.$$

When we compare Hull's formula with Cattell's theory, we find that some terms are systematologically equivalent; that is, they have analogous functions in the two theories without being identical in every aspect. A lesser degree of correspondence is indicated by the term *parallel*. Direct comparisons are made on the following points:

1. $_sE_r$ = reaction evocation potential, which is equivalent to Cattell's $a_{hij}$.

2. $D$ = drive, which parallels, but is not equivalent to Cattell's erg, the latter being more differentiated (among other things, including both a personality factor $E_T$ and a motivational factor $E_S$). In addition, $E$ is made up of many components: constitutional $C$, historical $H$, physiological $P$, as well as a special term for gratification level $G$.

3. $V$ = stimulus intensity dynamism, which is parallel to the many $S_s$ in Cattell's formulas.

4. $K$ = incentive motivation, which is not equivalent or parallel to any term in Cattell's theory. But the *gratification level G* and perhaps the *ergic sensitivity index $E_S$* have analogous functions in Cattell's theory.

5. $_sH_r$ = habit strength. This term is parallel to Cattell's *engram action level M*, which is broader, as it includes not only instrumental skills or habits (like $_sH_r$) but also more cognitive or conceptual variables. It also includes the personality organizing variables, *sentiments* and *complexes*. Perhaps it is a lack of differentiation in Cattell's terminology that there are no special terms for all these subcategories.

6. In addition to the variables quoted in Hull's formula, there is one more important variable, *inhibition*, which is subdivided into *reactive inhibition $I_R$* and *conditioned inhibition $_sI_r$*. But these are thought to be unnecessary in the comprehensive learning theory, according to Cattell (cf. chapter 18).

We may conclude this comparison by stating that there are *some systematological equivalencies and parallels between Cattell's and Hull's theories*. But Hull has one main term (*inhibition*) that Cattell thinks is unnecessary, and Cattell has several terms (especially for personality and motivation variables) that have no equivalent or parallel in Hull's theory. *Cattell's theory may therefore be described as a more comprehensive and differentiated theory than Hull's*, to which it is equal in formal development.

# Bibliography

Abelson, R. P. *Mathematical models of the distribution of attitudes during controversy.* Paper presented at the Educational Testing Service Conference on Contributions to Mathematical Psychology, Princeton, N.J., April 1962.

Abood, I. G. A chemical approach to the problem of mental disease. In D. Jackson (Ed.) *The etiology of schizophrenia.* New York: Basic Books, 1960.

Ach, N. *Uber den Willensakt und das Temperament.* Leipzig: Quellegmeyer, 1910.

Ackerman, S. H., & Sachar, E. J. The lactate theory of anxiety: A review and reevaluation. *Psychosomatic Medicine,* 1974, *36,* 69–80.

Adams, C. R. A new measure of personality. *Journal of Applied Psychology,* 1941, *25,* 141–151.

Adler, A. *The education of children.* London: Allen & Unwin, 1935.

Adorno, T. W., Frenkel-Brunswick, E., Levinson, D. J., & Sanford, R. M. *The authoritarian personality.* New York: Harper & Row, 1950.

Ahmavaara, V. The mathematical theory of factorial invariance under selection. *Psychology,* 1954, *19,* 27–38.

Ainsworth, M. D., & Bell, S. M. Attachment, exploration, and separation: Illustrated by the behavior of one-year-olds in a strange situation. *Child Development,* 1970, *41,* 49–67.

Alexander, F., Flagg, G. W., Foster, S., Clemens, T., & Blahd, W. Experimental studies of emotional stress: I. Hyperthyroidism. *Psychosomatic Medicine,* 1961, *23,* 104–114.

Alker, H. A. Is personality situationally specific or intrapsychically consistent? *Journal of Personality,* 1972, *40,* 1–16.

Allen, K. E., Hart, B., Buell, J. S., Harris, F. R., & Wolf, M. M. Effects of social reinforcement on isolate behavior of a nursery school child. *Child Development,* 1964, *35,* 511–518.

Allen, R. M. *Personality assessment procedures: Psychometric, projective and other approaches.* New York: Harper & Row, 1958.

Allport, G. W. A test for ascendance-submission. *Journal of Abnormal and Social Psychology,* 1928, *23,* 118–136.

Allport, G. W. *Personality: A psychological interpretation.* New York: Holt, 1937.

Allport, G. W. The historical background of modern social psychology. In G. Lindzey (Ed.), *Handbook of social psychology* (Vol. 1). London: Addison-Wesley, 1954.

Allport, G. W., & Allport, F. H. *A-S reaction study.* Boston: Houghton, 1928.

Allport, G. W., & Odbert, H. S. Trait names: A psycholexical study. *Psychological Monographs.* 1936, *47* (Whole No. 211), 1–171.

Allport, G. W., Vernon, P. E., & Lindzey, G. *The Allport-Vernon-Lindzey Study of Values.* Boston: Houghton Mifflin, 1951.

Altman, I., & McGinnies, E. Interpersonal perception and communication in discussion groups of varied attitudinal composition. *Journal of Abnormal and Social Psychology,* 1960, *60,* 390–395.

Amsel, A. Frustrative nonreward in partial reinforcement and discrimination learning: Some recent history and theoretical extension. *Psychological Review,* 1962, *69,* 306–328.

Anastasi, A. *Psychological testing* (1st ed.). New York: Macmillan, 1954.

Anastasi, A. *Differential psychology* (3rd ed.). New York: Macmillan, 1958.

Anastasi, A. *Differential psychology* New York: Macmillan, 1961.

Anastasi, A. *Psychological testing* (3rd & 4th eds.). New York: Macmillan, 1968, 1976.

Anastasi, A., & Foley, J. P. A proposed reorientation in the heredity-environment controversy. *Phychological Review,* 1948, *55,* 239–249.

Anastasi, A. A., Fuller, J. L. Scott, J. P., & Schmitt, J. R. A factor analysis of the performance of dogs on certain learning tests. *Zoologica,* 1955, *40,* 33–46.

Anderson, D. *Application of a behavior modification technique to the control of a hyperactive child.* Unpublished Master's thesis, University of Oregon, 1964.

Anderson, H. H., & Anderson, G. I. *Projective techniques.* New York: Prentice-Hall, 1950.

Anderson, J. E. The prediction of adjustment over time. In I. Iscoe & H. W. Stevenson (Eds.), *Personality development in children.* Austin, Tex.: University of Texas Press, 1960.

Anderson, N. H. Integration theory and attitude change. *Psychological Review,* 1971, *78,* 171–206.

Anderson, T. W. *The use of factor analysis in the statistical analysis of multiple time series* [Tech. Rep. 12, Contract AF 41 (657)–214]. School of Aviation Medicine, Brooks Air Force Base, 1961.

Anderson, V. E., & Siegal, F. Studies of behavior in genetically defined syndromes in man. In S. G. Vandenberg (Ed.), *Progress in human behavior genetics.* Baltimore: Johns Hopkins University Press, 1968.

Angyal, A. *Foundations for a science of personality.* New York: Commonwealth Fund, 1941.

Ansbacher, H. L., & Ansbacher, R. R. (Eds.). *The individual psychology of Alfred Adler: A systematic presentation in selections from his writings.* New York: Basic Books, 1956.

Anthony, W. S. The development of extraversion, of ability, and the relation between the two. *British Journal of Educational Psychology,* 1973, *43,* 223–227.

Appleton, T., Clifton, R., & Goldberg, S. The development of behavioral competence in infancy. In F. D. Horowitz, E. M. Hetherington, S. Scarr-Salapatek, & G. M. Siegel (Eds.), *Review of child development research* (Vol. 4). Chicago: University of Chicago Press, 1974.

Arasteh, J. D. Creativity and related processes in the young child: A review of the literature. *Journal of Genetic Psychology,* 1968, *112,* 77–108.

Arbib, M. P. Memory limitations of stimulus-response models. *Psychological Review,* 1969, *76,* 507–511.

Archer, J. Sex differences in emotional behaviour: A reply to Gray and Buffery. *Acta Psychologica,* 1971, *35,* 415–429.

Argyle, M., & Little, B. R. Do personality traits apply to social behavior? *Journal for the Theory of Social Behavior,* 1972, *2,* 1–35.

Armilla, J. Anxiety in taking the role of the leader. *Journal of Abnormal and Social Psychology,* 1964, *68,* 550–552.

Arnold, A. *Pictures and stories from forgotten children's books.* New York: Dover, 1969.

Aronfreed, J. *Conduct and conscience: The socialization of internalized control over behavior.* New York: Academic Press, 1968.

Aronson, E., & Worchel, P. Similarity versus liking as determinants of interpersonal attractiveness. *Psychonomic Science,* 1966, *5,* 157–158.

Asch, S. E. Forming impressions of personality. *Journal of Abnormal and Social Psychology,* 1946, *41,* 258–290.

Ash, P. The reliability of psychiatric diagnosis. *Journal of Abnormal and Social Psychology,* 1949, *44,* 272–277.

Ashem, B. A., & Poser, E. G. (Eds.). *Adaptive learning: Behavior modification with children.* London: Pergamon Press, 1973.

Montagu, M. F. *Prenatal influences.* Springfield, Ill.: Charles C Thomas, 1962.

Aspy, D. N. *A study of three facilitative conditions and their relationship to the achievement of third grade students.* Unpublished doctoral dissertation, University of Kentucky, 1965.

Aspy, D. N., & Hadlock, W. *The effect of empathy, warmth and genuineness on elementary students' reading achievement.* Unpublished master's thesis, University of Florida, 1966.

Atkinson, J. A. *Nonavailability of mother-attention as an antecedent event for coercive mands in the preschool child.* Unpublished master's thesis, University of Oregon, 1971.

Atkinson, J. W. *An introduction to motivation.* Princeton, N.J.: Van Nostrand, 1964.

Attardi, B., & Ohno, S. Cytosol androgen receptor from kidney of normal and testicular feminized (*Tfm*) mice. *Cell,* 1974, *2,* 205–212.

Atthowe, J. M., Jr., & Krasner, L. A preliminary report on the application of contingent reinforcement procedures (token economy) on a "chronic" psychiatric ward. *Journal of Abnormal Psychology*, 1968, *73*, 37–43.

Attneave, F. Perception and related areas. In S. Koch (Ed.), *Psychology: A study of a science* (Vol. 5). New York: McGraw-Hill, 1962.

Auerbach, S. M. *An investigation of the effects of surgery-induced stress on state and trait anxiety.* Unpublished doctoral dissertation, Florida State University, 1971.

Ausubel, D. P. Relationships between shame and guilt in the socializing process. *Psychological Review*, 1955, *62*, 378–385.

Ausubel, D. P. *Theory and problems of child development.* New York: Grune & Stratton, 1957.

Aveling, F. The psychology of conation and volition. *British Journal of Psychology*, 1926, *16*, 339–353.

Ax, A. F. Goals and methods of psychophysiology. *Psychophysiology*, 1964, *1*, 8–25.

Ayllon, T. Intensive treatment of psychotic behaviour by stimulus sensation and food reinforcement. *Behaviour Research and Therapy*, 1963, *1*, 53–61.

Ayllon, T., & Azrin, N. H. The measurement and reinforcement of behavior of psychotics. *Journal of the Experimental Analysis of Behavior*, 1965, *8*, 356–383.

Ayllon, T., & Azrin, N. H. *The token economy: A motivational system for therapy and rehabilitation.* New York: Appleton-Century-Crofts, 1968.

Ayllon, T., & Michael, J. L. The psychiatric nurse as a behavioral engineer. *Journal of the Experimental Analysis of Behavior*, 1959, *2*, 323–334.

Azrin, N. H., & Lindsley, O. R. The reinforcement of cooperation between children. *Journal of Abnormal and Social Psychology*, 1956, *52*, 100–102.

Back, K. W., & Davis, K. E. Some personal and situational factors relevant to consistency and prediction of conforming behavior. *Sociometry*, 1965, *28*, 227–240.

Bajusz, E. (Ed.). *An introduction to clinical neuroendocrinology.* Basel, N.Y.: Karger, 1967.

Baldwin, A. L. The appraisal of parent behavior. *American Psychologist*, 1946, *41*, 129–135. (a)

Baldwin, A. L. Differences in parent behavior toward three and nine year old children. *Journal of Personality Research*, 1946, *15*, 143–165.

Baldwin, A. L., Kalhorn, J., & Breese, F. H. Patterns of parent behavior. *Psychological Monographs*, 1945, *58*,(3).

Baldwin, J. D. The ontogeny of social behaviour of squirrel monkeys (*Saimiri sciureus*) in a seminatural environment. *Folia Primatologica*, 1969, *11*, 35–79.

Balinsky, B. An analysis of the mental factors of various age groups from nine to sixty. *Genetic Psychology Monographs*, 1941, *23*, 191–234.

Balshan, I. D. Muscle tension and personality in women: A factorial study. *Archives of General Psychiatry*, 1962, *7*, 436–448.

Baltes, P. B. Longitudinal and cross sectional sequences in the study of age and generation effects. *Human Development*, 1968, *11*, 145–171.

Baltes, P. B., & Nesselroade, J. R. Multivariate longitudinal and cross-sectional sequences for analyzing ontogenetic and generational change: A methodological note. *Developmental Psychology*, 1970, *2*, 163–168.

Baltes, P. B., & Nesselroade, J. R. The developmental analysis of individual differences on multiple measures. In J. R. Nesselroade & H. W. Reese (Eds.), *Life-span developmental psychology: Methodological issues.* New York: Academic Press, 1973.

Baltes, P. B., Nesselroade, J. R., & Cornelius, S. Multivariate structural change in developmental and environmental influence patterns. Unpublished manuscript, Division of Individual and Family Studies, Pennsylvania State University, 1976.

Baltes, P. B., Nesselroade, J. R., Schaie, K. W., & LaBouvie, E. W. On the dilemma of regression effects in examining ability-level-related differentials in ontogenetic patterns of intelligence. *Developmental Psychology*, 1972, *6*, 78–84.

Balzas, R. Biochemical effects of thyroid hormones in the developing brain. In D. C. Pease (Ed.), *Cellular aspects of neural growth and differentiation* (UCLA Forum in Medical Sciences No. 14). Los Angeles: University of California Press, 1971.

Bandura, A. Psychotherapist's anxiety level, self insight, and psychotherapeutic competence. *Journal of Abnormal and Social Psychology*, 1956, *52*, 333–337.

Bandura, A. Psychotherapy as a learning process. *Psychological Bulletin*, 1961, *58*, 143–159.

Bandura, A. Social learning through imitation. In M. R. Jones (Ed.), *Nebraska Symposium on Motivation.* Lincoln: University of Nebraska Press, 1962.

Bandura, A. Behavioral modification through modelling procedures. In L. Krasner & L. P. Ullmann (eds.), *Research in behavior modification.* New York: Holt, Rinehart, & Winston, 1965 (a)

Bandura, A. Influences of model's reinforcement contingencies on the acquisition of imitative responses. *Journal of Personality and Social Psychology*, 1965, *1*, 589–595. (b)

Bandura, A. *Psychotherapy conceptualized as a social learning process.* Paper presented at the Centennial Psychotherapy Symposium and Workshop, University of Kentucky, April 1965. (c)

Bandura, A. *Principles of behavior modification.* New York: Holt, Rinehart, & Winston, 1969.

Bandura, A. *Aggression: A social learning analysis.* Englewood Cliffs, N.J.: Prentice-Hall, 1973.

Bandura, A., & Huston, A. C. Identification as a process of incidental learning. *Journal of Abnormal and Social Psychology*, 1961, *63*, 311–318.

Bandura, A., & Kupers, J. Transmission of patterns of self-reinforcement through modeling. *Journal of Abnormal and Social Psychology*, 1964, *69*, 1–9.

Bandura, A., & McDonald, F. J. The influence of social reinforcement and the behavioral models in shaping children's moral judgments. *Journal of Abnormal and Social Psychology*, 1963, *67*, 274–281.

Bandura, A., & Perloff, B. Relative efficacy of self-monitored and externally-imposed reinforcement systems. *Journal of Personality and Social Psychology*, 1967, *7*, 111–116.

Bandura, A., Ross, D., & Ross, S. A. Transmission of aggression through imitation of aggressive models. *Journal of Abnormal and Social Psychology*, 1961, *63*, 575–582.

Bandura, A., Ross, D., & Ross, S. A. *An experimental test of the status envy, social power and the secondary reinforcement theories of identificatory learning.* Unpublished manuscript, Stanford University, 1962.

Bandura, A., Ross, D., & Ross, S. A. Imitation of film-mediated aggressive models. *Journal of Abnormal and Social Psychology*, 1963, *66*, 3–11.

Bandura, A., & Walters, R. H. *Social learning and personality development.* New York: Holt, Rinehart, & Winston, 1963.

Banerjee, U. Influence of pseudopregnancy and sex hormones on conditioned behaviour in rats. *Neuroendocrinology*, 1971, *7*, 278–290.

Banks, C., & Broadhurst, P. L. (Eds.). *Stephanos: Studies in psychology in honour of Sir Cyril Burt.* London: University of London Press, 1965.

Bannister, D., Salmon, P., & Leiberman, D. M. Diagnosis-treatment relationships in psychiatry: A statistical analysis. *British Journal of Psychiatry*, 1964, *110*, 726–732.

Barber, T. X., & Silver, M. J. Fact, fiction, and the experimenter bias effect. *Psychological Bulletin Monograph*, 1968, *70*(6, Pt. 2), 1–29. (a)

Barber, T. X., & Silver, M. J. Pitfalls in data analysis and interpretation: A reply to Rosenthal. *Psychological Bulletin Monograph*, 1968, *70*(6, Pt. 2), 48–62. (b)

Barendregt, J. T. *Research in psychodiagnostics.* The Hague: Mouton, 1961.

Bargmann, R. The statistical significance of simple structure in factor analysis. *Mit. f. Mathematical Stat. Sauderdruck*, Wurzburg: Physica Verlag, 1954.

Barker, R. G. On the nature of the environment. *Journal of Social Issues*, 1963, *19*, 17–38. (a)

Barker, R. G. *The stream of behavior.* New York: Appleton-Century-Crofts, 1963. (b)

Barker, R. G. *Ecological psychology: Concepts and methods for studying the environment of human behavior.* Stanford, Calif.: Stanford University Press, 1968.

Barker, R. G., Kounin, J. S., & Wright, H. F. *Child behavior and development.* New York: McGraw-Hill, 1943.

Barker, R. G., & Wright, H. *Midwest and its children.* New York: Row & Peterson, 1955.

Barnes, B. W. Maternal control of heterosis for yield in drosophila melanogaster. *Heredity*, 1968, *23*, 563–572.

Barnes, E. H. The relationship of biased test responses to psychopathology. *Journal of Abnormal and Social Psychology*, 1955, *51*, 285–290.

Barnes, E. H. Response bias and the MMPI. *Journal of Consulting Psychology*, 1956, *20*, 371–374.

Barnett, P. E., & Benedetti, D. T. *A study in "vicarious conditioning."* Paper presented at the meeting of the Rocky Mountain Psychological Association, Glenwood Springs, Col., May 1960.

Barnette, S. A. *The rat: A study in behavior.* Chicago: Aldine, 1963.

Barraclough, C. A. Modifications in reproductive function after exposure to hormones during the prenatal and early postnatal period. In L. Martini & W. P. Ganong (Eds.), *Neuroendocrin-*

ology (Vol. 2). New York and London: Academic Press, 1967.

Barrett, J. E., & DiMascio, A. Comparative effects on anxiety of the "minor tranquilizers" in "high" and "low" anxious student volunteers. *Diseases of the Nervous System,* 1966, *27,* 483–486.

Barron, F. Some personality correlates of independence of judgment. *Journal of Personality,* 1952, *21,* 287–297.

Barron, F. *Creativity and personal freedom.* Princeton, N.J.: Van Nostrand, 1968.

Bartlett, C. J. Factors affecting forced-choice response. *Personnel Psychology,* 1960, *13,* 399–405.

Barton, K. *The Core Trait and State Battery Handbook.* Champaign, Ill.: Institute for Personality and Ability Testing, 1976.

Barton, K., Bartsch, T., & Cattell, R. B. Longitudinal study of achievement related to anxiety and extroversion. *Psychological Reports,* 1974, *35,* 551–556.

Barton, K., & Cattell, R. B. Personality factor changes related to job promotion and turnover. *Journal of Counseling Psychology,* 1972, *19,* 430–435.

Barton, K., & Cattell, R. B. *The Core Trait and State (CTS) Battery.* Champaign, Ill.: Institute for Personality and Ability Testing, 1976.

Barton, K., Cattell, R. B., & Curran, J. Psychological states: Their definition through *P*-technique and differential *R (dR)* technique factor analysis. *Journal of Behavioral Science,* 1973, *1,* 273–277.

Barton, K., Cattell, R. B., & Vaughan, G. M. Changes in personality as a function of college attendance or work experience. *Journal of Counseling Psychology,* 1973, *20,* 162–165.

Bartsch, T. W. *The influence of instructional material on the temporal stability and structural invariance of certain measures of trait and state anxiety.* Unpublished doctoral dissertation, West Virginia University, 1972.

Bartsch, T. W., A manipulative study of the effect of instructional set on the convergent and discriminant validity of questionnaire measures of trait and state anxiety: A comparative factor analytic approach. *Educational and Psychological Measurement,* 1976, in press.

Bartsch, T. W., & Nesselroade, J. R. Test of the trait state distinction using a manipulative factor analytic design. *Journal of Personality and Social Psychology,* 1973, *27,* 58–64.

Basowitz, H., Persky, H., Korchin, S. J., & Grinker, R. R. *Anxiety and stress.* New York: McGraw-Hill, 1955.

Bass, A. R. Learning transfer and change in ability factors. *Psychological Bulletin,* 1973, *80,* 106–112.

Bass, B. M. Development of a structured disguised personality test. *Journal of Applied Psychology,* 1956, *40,* 393–397.

Bass, B. M. Validity studies of a proverbs personality test. *Journal of Applied Psychology,* 1957, *41,* 158–160.

Bass, B. M. Social behavior and the orientation inventory: A review. *Psychological Bulletin,* 1967, *68,* 260–292.

Bass, B. M., & Dunteman, G. Behavior in groups as a function of self-, interaction-, and task-orientation. *Journal of Abnormal and Social Psychology,* 1963, *66,* 419–428.

Bass, B. M., McGehee, C. R., Hawkins, W. C., Young, P. C., & Gebel, A. S. Personality variables related to leaderless group discussion behavior. *Journal of Abnormal and Social Psychology,* 1953, *48,* 120–128.

Bateson, G., Jackson, D. H., Jr., & Weakland, J. H. Toward a theory of schizophrenia. *Behavioral Science,* 1956, *1,* 251–264.

Bath, K. E., Daley, D. L., & Nesselroade, J. R. Replicability of factors derived from individual *P*-technique analysis. Unpublished manuscript, Division of Individual and Family Studies, Pennsylvania State University, 1976.

Baumgarten, P. Proverb test for attitude measurement. *Personnel Psychology,* 1952, *5,* 249–261.

Baxter, J. D., Becker, J., & Hooks, W. Defensive style in the families of schizophrenics and controls. *Journal of Abnormal and Social Psychology,* 1963, *66,* 512–518.

Bayley, N. Data on the growth of intelligence between 16 and 21 years as measured by the Wechsler-Bellevue scale. *Journal of Genetic Psychology,* 1957, *90,* 3–15.

Beach, F. A. *Hormones and behavior.* New York: Hoeber, 1948.

Beach, F. A. The snark was a boojum. In T. E. McGill (Ed.), *Readings in animal behavior.* New York: Holt, Rinehart, & Winston, 1966.

Beach, F. A. Retrospect and prospect. In F. A. Beach (Ed.), *Sex and behavior.* New York: Wiley, 1968.

Beach, F. A. Hormonal factors controlling the differentiation, development and display of copulatory behavior in the ramstergig and related species. In E. Tobach, L. R. Aronson, & E. Shaw (Eds.), *The biopsychology of development.* New York: Academic Press, 1971.

Beach, F. A., & Holz, M. A. Mating behavior in male rats castrated at various ages and injected with androgen. *Journal of Experimental Zoology,* 1946, *101,* 91–142.

Beach, F. A., & Jaynes, J. Effects of early experience upon the behavior of animals. *Psychological Bulletin,* 1954, *51,* 239–263.

Beatty, W. W., & Beatty, P. A. Hormonal determinants of sex differences in avoidance behavior and reactivity to electric shock in the rat. *Journal of Comparative and Physiological Psychology,* 1970, *73,* 446–455.

Bechtel, G. G. A dual scaling analysis for paired comparisons. *Psychometrika,* 1971, *36,* 135–154.

Becker, W. C. The matching of behavior ratings and questionnaire personality factors. *Psychological Bulletin,* 1960, *57,* 201–211.

Becker, W. C. A comparison of the factor structure and other properties of the 16 PF and the Guilford-Martin personality inventories. *Educational and Psychological Measurement,* 1961, *21,* 393–404.

Becker, W. C. Consequences of different kinds of parental discipline. In M. L. Hoffman & L. W. Hoffman (Eds.), *Review of child development research* (Vol. 1). New York: Russell Sage Foundation, 1964.

Becker, W. C., & Krug, R. S. A circumplex model for social behavior in children. *Child Development,* 1964, *35,* 371–396.

Becker-Carus, C. Zusammenhaenge zwischen EEG, Persoen-lichkeitsvariablen und Vigilanzleistungen. *EEG Clinical Neurophysiology,* 1971, *30,* 519–526.

Behnke, A. R. Quantitative assessment of body build. *American Journal of Physiology,* 1961, *201,* 960–968.

Bell, H. M. *The theory and practice of personal counseling.* Stanford: Stanford University Press, 1939.

Bell, R. Q. Relations between behavior manifestations in the human neonate. *Child Development,* 1960, *31,* 463–477.

Bell, R. Q. A reinterpretation of the direction of effects in studies of socialization. *Psychological Review,* 1968, *75,* 81–95.

Bell, R.Q. Stimulus control of parent or caretaker behavior by offspring. *Developmental Psychology,* 1971, *4,* 63–72.

Bell, R. Q., Weller, G. M., & Waldrop, M. F. Newborn and preschooler: Organization of behavior and relations between periods. *Monographs of the Society for Research in Child Development,* 1971, *36*(1–2), 145 pp.

Bellak, L. *Schizophrenia: A review of the syndrome.* New York: Logos Press, 1958.

Bellows, R. Toward a taxonomy of social situations. In S. B. Sells (Ed.), *Stimulus determinants of behavior.* New York: Ronald Press, 1962.

Belmont, L., & Marolla, F. A. Birth order, family size, and intelligence. *Science,* 1973, *182,* 1096–1101.

Bem, D. J. Constructing cross-situational consistencies in behavior: Some thoughts on Alker's critique of Mischel. *Journal of Personality,* 1972, *40,* 17–26.

Bendig, A. W. Factor analyses of anxiety and neuroticism inventories. *Journal of Consulting Psychology,* 1960, *24,* 161–169.

Benedict, R. *Patterns of culture.* Boston: Houghton Mifflin, 1934.

Benedict, R. *The chrysanthemum and the sword.* Boston: Houghton Mifflin, 1945.

Benedict, R. Continuities and discontinuities in cultural conditioning. In P. Mullahy (Ed.), *A study in interpersonal relations.* New York: Hermitage, 1949.

Bentler, P. Assessment of developmental factor change at the individual and group level. In J. R. Nesselroade & H. W. Reese (Eds.), *Life-span developmental psychology: Methodological issues.* New York: Academic Press, 1972.

Benton, A. I., & Stone, I. R. Consistency of responses to personality inventory items as a function of length of interval between test and retest. *Journal of Social Psychology,* 1937, *8,* 143–153.

Bereiter, C. Some persisting dilemmas in the measurement of change. In C. W. Harris (Ed.), *Problems in measuring change.* Madison: University of Wisconsin Press, 1963.

Bereiter, C. Multivariate analysis of the behavior and structure of groups and organizations. In R. B. Cattell (Ed.), *Handbook of multivariate experimental psychology.* Chicago: Rand McNally, 1966.

Berenson, B. G., & Mitchell, K. M. Therapeutic conditions after therapist-initiated confrontation. *Journal of Clinical Psychology,* 1968, *24,* 363–364.

Berg, I. A. The unimportance of test item content. In B. M. Bass & I. A. Berg *Objective approaches to personality assessment.* Princeton: Van Nostrand, 1959.

Berg, I. A., & Collier, T. S. Personality and group differences in extreme response sets. *Educational and Psychological Measurement,* 1953, *13,* 164–169.

Berger, S. M. Conditioning through vicarious investigation. *Psychological Review,* 1962, *69,* 450–466.

Berkowitz, L. Group standards, cohesiveness and productivity. *Human Relations,* 1954, *7,* 509–519.

Berkowitz, L. Aggression cues in aggressive behavior and hostility catharsis. *Psychological Review,* 1964, *71,* 104–122.

Berkowitz, L. Words and symbols as stimuli to aggressive responses. In J. Knutson (Ed.), *The control of aggression: Implications from basic research.* Chicago, Aldine Press, 1973.

Berkowitz, L., & Knurek, D. A. Label-mediated hostility generalization. *Journal of Personality and Social Psychology,* 1969, *13,* 200–206.

Berlyne, D. E. The arousal and satiation of perceptual curiosity in the rat. *Journal of Comparative and Physiological Psychology,* 1955, *48,* 238–246.

Berlyne, D. E. *Conflict, arousal and curiosity.* New York: McGraw-Hill, 1960.

Berlyne, D. E. Motivational problems raised by exploratory and epistemic behavior. In S. Koch (Ed.), *Psychology: A study of a science* (Vol. 5). New York: McGraw-Hill, 1963.

Berlyne, D. E. *Structure and direction in thinking.* New York: Wiley, 1965.

Berlyne, D. E. Mediating responses: A note on Fodor's criticisms. *Journal of Verbal Learning and Verbal Behavior,* 1966, *5,* 408–411. (a)

Berlyne, D. E. Curiosity and exploration. *Science,* 1966, *153,* 25–33. (b)

Bermann, E., & Miller, D. R. The matching of mates. In R. Jessor & S. Feshback (Eds.), *Cognition, personality, and clinical psychology.* San Francisco: Jossey-Bass, 1967.

Berne, E. *Transactional analysis in psychotherapy.* London: Evergreen Books, 1961.

Bernreuter, R. G. The theory and construction of the personality inventory. *Journal of Social Psychology,* 1933, *4,* 387–405. (a)

Bernreuter, R. G. The validity of the personality inventory. *Personnel Journal,* 1933, *11,* 383–386. (b)

Bernstein, E. Quickness and intelligence. *British Journal of Psychology, Monograph Supplement,* 1924, *3*(Whole No. 7).

Berrien, F. K. *Values of Japanese and American students* (Office of Naval Reaserch Tech. Rep. 14). New Brunswick, N.J.: Rutgers University, 1964.

Betz, B. J. Bases of therapeutic leadership in psychotherapy with the schizophrenic patient. *American Journal of Psychotherapy,* 1963, *17,* 196–212. (a)

Betz, B. J. Differential success rates of psychotherapists with "process" and "non-process" schizophrenic patients. *American Journal of Psychiatry,* 1963, *11,* 1090–1091. (b)

Beumont, P. J. V., Bancroft, J. H. J., Beardwood, C. J., & Russell, G. F. M. Behavioural

changes after treatment with testosterone: Case report. *Psychological Medicine,* 1972, *2,* 70–72.

Bexton, W. H., Heron, W., & Scott, T. H. Effects of decreased variation in the sensory environment. *Canadian Journal of Psychology,* 1954, *8,* 70–76.

Biaggio, A. M. Relationships among behavioral, cognitive, and affective aspects of children's conscience. *Dissertation Abstracts,* 1968, *28*(11-B), 4742.

Bignami, G. Selection for high rates and low rates of conditioning in the rat. *Animal Behavior,* 1965, *13,* 221–227.

Bijou, S. W. A systematic approach to an experimental analysis of young children. *Child Development,* 1955, *26,* 161–168.

Bijou, S. W., & Baer, D. M. *Child development: Readings in experimental analysis.* New York: Appleton-Century-Crofts, 1967.

Bijou, S. W., Birnbrauer, J. S., Kidder, J. D., & Tague, C. Programmed instruction as an approach to teaching of reading, writing, and arithmetic to retarded children. In S. W. Bijou & D. M. Baer (Eds.), *Child development: Readings in experimental analysis.* New York: Appleton-Century-Crofts, 1967.

Bindra, D. *Motivation, a systematic reinterpretation.* New York: Ronald Press, 1959.

Birch, H. G. The relation of previous experience to insightful problem-solving. *Journal of Comparative and Physiological Psychology,* 1954, *38,* 367–383.

Birch, H. G., Thomas, A., Chess, S., & Hertzig, M. E. Individuality in the development of children. *Developmental Medicine and Child Neurology,* 1962, *4,* 370–379.

Birkhill, W. R., & Schaie, K. W. The effect of differential reinforcement of cautiousness in intellectual performance among the elderly. *Journal of Gerontology,* 1975, *30,* 578–583.

Birren, J. E. A factor analysis of the Wechsler-Bellevue given to an elderly population. *Journal of Consulting Psychology,* 1952, *16,* 399–405.

Bischof, L. J. *Interpreting personality theories.* New York: Harper & Row, 1964.

Bishop, B. M. Mother-child interaction and the social behavior of children. *Psychological Monographs,* 1951, (Whole No. 328).

Bitterman, M. E. Learning in animals. In H. Helson & W. Bevan (Eds.), *Contemporary approaches to psychology.* Princeton, N.J.: Van Nostrand, 1967.

Black, M. S. The development of personality factors in children and adolescents. *Dissertation Abstracts,* 1965, *25*(11), 6754.

Black, R. On the combination of drive and incentive motivation. *Psychological Review,* 1965, *72,* 310–317.

Bleda, P. R., Bell, P. A., & Byrne, D. Prior induced affect and sex differences in attraction. *Memory and Cognition,* 1973, *1,* 435–438.

Bleuler, M. Endokrinilogische Psychiatrie. In H. W. Gruhle et al. (Eds.), *Psychiatrie der gegenwart* (Vol. 1). Berlin: Springer, 1964.

Blewett, O. B. An experimental study of the inheritance of intelligence. *Journal of Mental Science,* 1954, *100,* 922–933.

Blizard, D., & Denef, C. Neonatal androgen effects on open-field activity and sexual behavior

in the female rat: The modifying influence of ovarian secretions during development. *Physiology and Behavior,* 1973, *11,* 65–69.

Bloch, A. M. A. Remembrance of feelings past: A study of phenomenological genetics. *Journal of Abnormal Psychology,* 1969, *74,* 340–347.

Bloch, G. J., & Davidson, J. M. Effects of adrenalectomy and experience on postcastration sex behavior in the male rat. *Physiology and Behavior,* 1968, *3,* 461–465.

Block, J. Studies in the phenomenology of emotions. *Journal of Abnormal and Social Psychology,* 1957, *54,* 358–363.

Blodgett, H. C. The effect of the introduction of reward upon the maze performance of rats. *University of California Publications in Psychology,* 1929, *4,* 113–134.

Bloom, B. S. *Research problems of education and culture deprivation.* Paper presented at the Research Conference on Education and Culture Deprivation, 1965.

Bloomfield, L. *Language.* New York: Holt, Rinehart, & Winston, 1933.

Blurton Jones, N. G. An ethological study of some aspects of social behaviour of children in nursery school. In D. Morris (Ed.), *Primate ethology.* London: Weidenfeld & Nicolson, 1967.

Bock, R. D. A family study of spatial visualizing ability. *Proceedings of the 75th Annual Convention of the American Psychological Association,* 2, Washington, D.C., 1967.

Bock, R. D., & Kolakowski, D. Further evidence of sex-linked major-gene influence on human spatial visualizing ability. *American Journal of Human Genetics,* 1973, *25,* 1–14.

Bock, R. D., & Vandenberg, S. G. Components of heritable variation in mental test scores. In S. G. Vandenberg (Ed.), *Progress in human behavior genetics.* Baltimore: Johns Hopkins University Press, 1968.

Bolz, C. R. *The development of cluster analytic theory: An experimental comparison of two models.* Unpublished doctoral dissertation, University of Illinois, 1972. (a)

Bolz, C. R. Personality types. In R. M. Dreger (Ed.), *Multivariate personality research: Contributions to the understanding of personality in honor of Raymond B. Cattell.* Baton Rouge, La.: Claitor, 1972. (b)

Bolz, C. R., & Cattell, R. B. Personality source traits in objective tests, in childrenl Unpublished manuscript, Department of Educational Psychology, University of Texas, 1976.

Borg, W. R., & Tupes, E. C. Personality characteristics related to leadership behavior in two types of small group situational problems. *Journal of Applied Psychology,* 1958, *42,* 252–256.

Borgatta, E. F. Mood, personality, and interaction. *Journal of General Psychology,* 1961, *64,* 105–137. (a)

Borgatta, E. F. Toward a methodological codification: The shotgun and the saltshaker. *Sociometry,* 1961, *24,* 432–435. (b)

Borgatta, E. F., Couch, A. S., & Bales, R. F. Some findings relevant to the great man theory of leadership. *American Sociological Review,* 1954, *19,* 755–759.

Bossard, J. H. S., & Sanger, W. P. The large family system: A research report. *American Sociological Review,* 1952, *17,* 3–9.

Bostian, D. U., Smith, P. A., Lasky, J., Hover, R., & Ging, R. Empirical observation on mental status examination. *Archives of General Psychiatry,* 1959, *1,* 253–262.

Botzum, W. A. A factorial study of reasoning and closure factors. *Psychometrika,* 1951, *16,* 361–386.

Bowers, K. *Situationism in psychology: On making reality disappear* (Research Reports in Psychology, No. 137). Waterloo, Ontario: University of Waterloo, 1972.

Bowers, K. S. Situationalism in psychology: An analysis and a critique. *Psychological Review,* 1973, *80,* 307–336.

Bowlby, J. *Attachment and loss* (Vol. 1). *Attachment.* New York: Basic Books, 1969.

Bowlby, J. *Attachment and loss* (Vol. 2). *Separation: Anxiety and anger.* New York: Basic Books, 1973.

Bradley, R. W. Birth order and school-related behavior: A heuristic review. *Psychological Bulletin,* 1968, *70,* 45–51.

Brady, J. P., & Lind, D. L. Experimental analysis of hysterical blindness. *Archives of General Psychiatry,* 1961, *4,* 331–339.

Brady, J. V. Toward a behavioral biology of emotion. In L. Levi (Ed.), *Emotions: Their parameters and measurement.* New York: Raven Press, 1975.

Bray, C. W. *Psychology and military efficiency.* Princeton: Princeton University Press, 1948.

Breland, H. M. Birth order effects: A reply to Schooler. *Psychological Bulletin,* 1973, *80,* 210–212.

Breland, H. M. Birth order, family size, and intelligence. *Science,* 1974, *184,* 114.

Bridges, K. M. B. A genetic theory of the emotions. *Journal of Genetic Psychology,* 1930, *37,* 514–526.

Bridges, K. M. B. Emotional development in early infancy. *Child Development,* 1932, *3,* 324–341.

Bridges, P. K., & Jones, M. T. Personality, physique and the adrenocortical response to a psychological stress. *British Journal of Psychiatry,* 1967, *113,* 601–605.

Briggs, P. F., Taylor, M., & Tellegren, A. *A study of the Marks and Seeman MMPI profile types as applied to a sample of 2,875 psychiatric patients* (Research Laboratories Rep. PR-66-5). Minneapolis: University of Minnesota, 1966.

Brim, O. G., Jr. Personality development as role-learning. In I. Iscoe & H. W. Stevenson (Eds.), *Personality development in children.* Austin: University of Texas Press, 1960.

Brim, O. G., Jr., & Hoff, D. B. Individual and situational differences in desire for certainty. *Journal of Abnormal and Social Psychology,* 1957, *54,* 225–229.

Broadhurst, P. L. Application of biometrical genetics to behavior in rats. *Nature,* 1959, *184,* 1517–1518.

Broadhurst, P. L. Experiments in psychogenetics: Applications of biometrical genetics to the inheritance of behavior. In H. J. Eysenck (Ed.), *Experiments in personality* (Vol. 1). *Psychogenetics and psychopharmacology.* London: Routledge & Kegan Paul, 1960.

Broadhurst, P. L. The choice of animals for

behaviour studies. *Laboratory Animals Centre Collected Papers,* 1963, *12,* 65–80.

Broadhurst, P. L. Experimental approaches to the evolution of behavior. In J. M. Thoday & A. S. Parkes (Eds.), *Genetic and environmental influences on behaviour.* Edinburgh: Oliver & Boyd, 1968.

Broadhurst, P. L. Psychogenetics of emotionality in the rat. *Annals of the New York Academy of Sciences,* 1969, *159,* 806–824.

Broadhurst, P. L. The Maudsley reactive and nonreactive strains of rats: A survey. *Behavior Genetics,* 1975, *5,* 299–319.

Broadhurst, P. L., Fulker, D. W., & Wilcock, J. Behavioral genetics. *Annual Review of Psychology,* 1974, *25,* 389–415.

Broadhurst, P. L., & Jinks, J. L. Biometrical genetics and behavior: Reanalysis of published data. *Psychological Bulletin,* 1961, *58,* 337–362.

Broadhurst, P. L., & Jinks, J. L. Stability and change in the inheritance of behaviour: A further analysis of statistics from a diallel cross. *Proceedings of the Royal Society, B,* 1966, *165,* 450–472.

Broadhurst, P. L., & Jinks, J. L. Psychogenetics of the dog. (Review of J. P. Scott & J. L. Fuller, *Genetics and social behavior of the dog.*) *Heredity,* 1967, *22,* 153–155.

Broadhurst, P. L., & Jinks, J. L. What genetical architecture can tell us about the natural selection of behavioural traits. In J. H. F. van Abeelen (Ed.), *The genetics of behaviour.* Amsterdam: North Holland Publishing Co., 1974.

Broen, W. E. Ambiguity and discriminating power in personality inventories. *Journal of Consulting Psychology,* 1960, *24,* 174–179.

Brogden, W. J. Sensory pre-conditioning. *Journal of Experimental Psychology,* 1939, *25,* 323–332.

Bronfenbrenner, U. Socialization and social class through time and space. In E. E. Maccoby, T. M. Newcomb, & E. L. Hartley (Eds.), *Readings in social psychology.* New York: Holt, Rinehart, & Winston, 1958.

Bronfenbrenner, U. The changing American child: A speculative analysis. *Journal of Social Issues,* 1961, *17,* 6–18.

Bronson, W. C. Central orientations: A study of behavior organization from childhood to adolescence. *Child Development,* 1966, *37,* 125–155.

Bronson, W. C. Adult derivatives of emotional expressiveness and reactivity-control: Developmental continuities from childhood to adulthood. *Child Development,* 1967, *38,* 801–817.

Bronson, W. C. Stable patterns of behavior: The significance of enduring orientations for personality development. In J. P. Hill (Ed.), *Minnesota symposia on child psychology* (Vol. 2). Minneapolis: University of Minnesota Press, 1969.

Bronson, W. C., Kalten, E. S., & Livson, N. Patterns of authority and affection in two generations. *Journal of Abnormal and Social Psychology,* 1959, *58,* 143–152.

Broverman, D. M., Klaiber, E. L., Kobayashi, Y., & Vogel, W. Roles of activation and inhibition in sex differences in cognitive abilities. *Psychological Review,* 1968, *75,* 23–50.

Brown, A. M., Stafford, R. E., & Vandenberg, S. G. Twins: Behavioral differences. *Child Development,* 1967, *38,* 1055–1064.

Brown, C. C. (Ed.). *Methods in psychophysiology.* Baltimore: Williams & Wilkins, 1966.

Brown, J. L. The effect of drive on learning with secondary reinforcement. *Journal of Comparative and Physiological Psychology,* 1956, *49,* 254–260.

Brown, J. S. The generalization of approach responses as a function of stimulus intensity and strength of motivation. *Journal of Comparative Psychology,* 1942, *33,* 209–226.

Brown, R. *Social psychology.* New York: Free Press, 1965.

Brozek, J. *Human body composition: Approaches and applications.* Oxford: Pergamon, 1965.

Bruell, J. H. Inheritance of behavioral and physiological characters of mice and the problem of heterosis. *American Zoology,* 1964, *4,* 125–138.

Bruell, J. H. Genetics and adaptive significance of emotional defecation in mice. In E. Tobach (Ed.), *Experimental approaches to the study of emotional behavior. Annals of the New York Academy of Sciences,* 1969, *159*(3), 825–830.

Bruner, J. S. Personality dynamics and the process of perceiving. In R. R. Blake & G. V. Ramsey (Eds.), *Perception: An approach to personality.* New York: Ronald Press, 1951.

Bruner, J. S., & Tagiuri, R. The perception of people. In G. Lindzey (Ed.), *Handbook of social psychology* (Vol. 2). Reading, Mass.: Addison-Wesley, 1954.

Brunswik, E. Representative design and probabilistic theory. *Psychological Review,* 1955, *62,* 236–242.

Brunswik, E. *Perception and representative design of psychological experiments.* Berkeley: University of California Press, 1956.

Brunswik, E. Scope and aspects of the cognitive problem. In H. Gruber, R. Jessor, & V. Hammond (Eds.), *Cognition: The Colorado symposium.* Cambridge: Harvard University Press, 1957.

Bryan, J. H. Model affect and children's imitative altruism. *Child Development,* 1971, *42,* 2061–2065.

Bryan, L. L. *A comparative study of moral discrimination in adult male mental patients and adult male Federal prisoners.* Unpublished doctoral dissertation, Indiana University, 1956.

Buchsbaum, M. S. Average evoked response and stimulus intensity in identical and fraternal twins. *Physiological Psychology,* 1974, *2,* 365–370.

Bucio Alanis, L. Environmental and genotype-environmental components of variability: I. Inbred lines. *Heredity,* 1966, *21,* 387–397.

Bucio Alanis, L., & Hill, J. Environmental and genotype-environmental components of variability: II. Heterozygotes. *Heredity,* 1966, *21,* 399–405.

Bucio Alanis, L., Perkins, J. M., & Jinks, J. L. Environmental and genotype-environmental components of variability: V. Segregating generations. *Heredity,* 1969, *24,* 115–127.

Buck, R., Miller, R. E., & Caul, W. F. Sex, personality, and physiological variables in the communication of affect via facial expression. *Journal of Personality and Social Psychology,* 1974, *30*(4), 587–596.

Buck, R., Savin, V. J., Miller, R. E., & Caul, W. F. Nonverbal communication of affect in humans. *Proceedings of the 77th Annual Convention of the*

*American Psychological Association,* 1969, *4,* 367–368.

Buffrey, A. W. H., & Gray, J. A. Sex differences in emotional and cognitive behavior in mammals including man. *Acta Psychologica,* 1971, *35,* 89–111.

Buffrey, A. W. H., & Gray, J. A. Sex differences in the development of spatial and linguistic skills. In F. Ounsted & D. C. Taylor (Eds.), *Gender differences: Their ontogeny and significance.* London: Churchill, 1972.

Burgess, E. W., & Wallin, P. *Engagement and marriage.* New York: Lippincott, 1953.

Burke, W. W. Leadership behavior as a function of the leader, the follower, and the situation. *Journal of Personality,* 1965, *33,* 60–81.

Buros, O. K. *The sixth mental measurements yearbook.* Highland Park, N.J.: Gryphon Press, 1965.

Buros, O. K. *Personality tests and reviews.* Highland Park, N.J.: Gryphon Press, 1970.

Buros, O. K. (Ed.). *The seventh mental measurements yearbook.* Highland Park, N.J.: Gryphon Press, 1972.

Burt, C. L. Experimental tests of general intelligence. *British Journal of Psychology,* 1909, *3,* 94–177.

Burt, C. L. *Distribution and relations of educational abilities.* London: P. S. King, 1917.

Burt, C. L. *The young delinquent.* London: University of London Press, 1925.

Burt, C. L. Correlations between persons. *British Journal of Psychology,* 1937, *28,* 59–96.

Burt, C. L. The factorial analysis of emotional traits. *Character and Personality,* 1939, *9,* 238–254.

Burt, C. L. *The factors of the mind.* London: University of London Press, 1940.

Burt, C. L. *The factors of the mind: An introduction to factor analysis in psychology.* New York: Macmillan, 1941.

Burt, C. L. The factorial study of temperament traits. *British Journal of Psychology, Statistical Section,* 1948, *1,* 178–203. (a)

Burt, C. L. *The young delinquent.* London: University of London Press, 1948. (b)

Burt, C. L. Subdivided factors. *British Journal of Statistical Psychology,* 1949, *2,* 41–63.

Burt, C. L. The differentiation of intellectual abilities. *British Journal of Educational Psychology,* 1954, *24,* 76–90.

Burt, C. L. The inheritance of mental ability. *American Psychologist,* 1958, *13,* 1–15.

Burt, C. L. The factor analysis of the Wechsler scale: II. *British Journal of Statistical Psychology,* 1960, *13,* 82–87.

Burt, C. L. The appropriate use of factor analysis and analysis of variance. In R. B. Cattell (Ed.), *Handbook of multivariate experimental psychology.* Chicago: Rand McNally, 1966. (a)

Burt, C. L. The genetic determination of differences in intelligence: A study of monozygotic twins reared together and apart. *British Journal of Psychology,* 1966, *57,* 137–153. (b)

Burt, C. L. Inheritance of general intelligence. *American Psychologist,* 1972, *27,* 175–190.

Burton, A. *Modern psychotherapeutic practice: Innovations in technique.* Palo Alto, Calif.: Science and Behavior Books, 1965.

Burton, R. V. Validity of retrospective reports assessed by the multitrait-multimethod analysis. *Developmental Psychology Monograph,* 1970, *3*(3), Part 2.

Bush, R. R., & Mosteller, T. A mathematical model for simple learning. *Psychological Review,* 1951, *58,* 313–323.

Bush, R. R., & Mosteller, T. *Stochastic models for learning.* New York: Wiley, 1955.

Bushell, D., Wrobel, P. A., & Michaelis, M. L. Applying "group" contingencies to the classroom study behavior of preschool children. *Journal of Applied Behavior Analysis,* 1968, *1,* 55–61.

Buss, A. H., Fischer, H., & Simmons, A. Aggression and hostility in psychiatric patients. *Journal of Consulting Psychology,* 1962, *26,* 84–89.

Buss, A. H., & Lang, P. J. Psychological deficity in schizophrenia: I. Affect, reinforcement, and concept attainment. *Journal of Abnormal Psychology,* 1965, *70,* 2–24.

Buss, A. R. Multivariate model of quantitative, structural, and quantistructural ontogenetic change. *Developmental Psychology,* 1974, *10,* 190–203.

Buss, A. R. An inferential strategy for determining factor invariance across different individuals and different variables. *Multivariate Behavioral Research,* 1975, *10,* 365–372.

Busse, T. V. Child-rearing antecedents of flexible thinking. *Developmental Psychology,* 1969, *1,* 585–591.

Butcher, H. J. *Human intelligence: Its nature and assessment.* London: Methuen, 1968.

Butcher, H. J. Creativity. In R. M. Dreger (Ed.), *Multivariate personality research: Contributions to the understanding of personality in honor of Raymond B. Cattell.* Baton Rouge, La.: Claitor, 1972.

Butcher, H. J., & Lomax, D. E. (Eds.). *Readings in human intelligence.* London: Methuen, 1972.

Butler, J. M., & Rice, L. N. Adience, self-actualization and drive theory. In J. M. Wepman & R. W. Heine (Eds.), *Concepts of personality.* Chicago: Aldine, 1963.

Butler, R. A. Incentive conditions which influence visual exploration. *Journal of Experimental Psychology,* 1954, *48,* 19–23.

Butt, D. S., & Fiske, D. W. A comparison of strategies in developing scales for dominance. *Psychological Bulletin,* 1968, *70,* 505–519.

Buzby, D. E. The interpretation of facial expression. *American Journal of Psychology,* 1924, *35,* 602–604.

Bykov, K. M., & Kurzin, I. T. [*Kortikoviszerale Pathologie*] (German translation from the Russian). Berlin: Volk & Gesundheit, 1966.

Byrd, E. Measured anxiety in old age. *Psychological Reports,* 1959, *5,* 439–440.

Byrne, D. Interpersonal attraction and attitude similarity. *Journal of Abnormal and Social Psychology,* 1961, *62,* 713–715. (a)

Byrne, D. The repression-sensitization scales: Rationale, reliability, and validity. *Journal of Personality,* 1961, *29,* 334–349. (b)

Byrne, D. Attitudes and attraction. In L. Berkowitz (Ed.), *Advances in experimental social psychology* (Vol. 4). New York: Academic Press, 1969.

Byrne, D. *The attraction paradigm.* New York: Academic Press, 1971.

Byrne, D., Cherry, F., Lamberth, J., & Mitchell, H. E. Husband-wife similarity in response to erotic stimuli. *Journal of Personality,* 1973, *41,* 385–394.

Byrne, D., & Clore, G. L. Predicting interpersonal attraction toward strangers presented in three different stimulus modes. *Psychonomic Science,* 1966, *4,* 239–240.

Byrne, D., & Clore, G. L. Effectance arousal and attraction. *Journal of Personality and Social Psychology Monograph,* 1967, *6*(4, Whole No. 638).

Byrne, D., & Clore, G. L. A reinforcement model of evaluative responses. *Personality: An International Journal,* 1970, *1,* 103–128.

Byrne, D., Clore, G. L., & Worchel, P. The effect of economic similarity-dissimilarity on interpersonal attraction. *Journal of Personality and Social Psychology,* 1966, *4,* 220–224.

Byrne, D., & Erwin, C. R. Attraction toward a Negro stranger as a function of prejudice, attitude similarity, and the stranger's evaluation of the subject. *Human Relations,* 1969, *22,* 397–404.

Byrne, D., & Griffitt, W. Similarity versus liking: A clarification. *Psychonomic Science,* 1966, *6,* 295–296.

Byrne, D., & Griffitt, W. Similarity and awareness of similarity of personality characteristics as determinants of attraction. *Journal of Experimental Research in Personality,* 1969, *3,* 179–186.

Byrne, D., Griffitt, W., & Stefaniak, D. Attraction and similarity of personality characteristics. *Journal of Personality and Social Psychology,* 1967, *5,* 82–90.

Byrne, D., Krivonos, P. D., & Friedrich, G. W. *The effect of interpersonal attraction on task performance.* Paper presented at the meeting of the American Psychological Association, Chicago, August 1975.

Byrne, D., London, O., & Reeves, D. The effects of physical attractiveness, sex, and attitude similarity on interpersonal attraction. *Journal of Personality,* 1968, *36,* 259–271.

Byrne, D., & Nelson, D. Attraction as a linear function of proportion of positive reinforcements. *Journal of Personality and Social Psychology,* 1965, *1,* 659–663.

Byrne, D., & Rhamey, R. Magnitude of positive and negative reinforcements as a determinant of attraction. *Journal of Personality and Social Psychology,* 1965, *2,* 884–889.

Byrne, D., & Wong, T. J. Racial prejudice, interpersonal attraction, and assumed dissimilarity of attitude. *Journal of Abnormal and Social Psychology,* 1962, *65,* 246–253.

Cable, D. *Separation of state and trait anxiety in the context of short term change.* Unpublished doctoral dissertation, West Virginia University, 1972.

Cady, V. The estimation of juvenile incorrigibility. *Journal of Delinquency Monographs,* 1923, No. 2.

Caldwell, B. M. The effects of infant care. In M. L. Hoffman & L. W. Hoffman (Eds.), *Review of child development research* (Vol. 1). New York: Russell Sage Foundation, 1964.

Caldwell, B. M. A new "approach" to

behavioral ecology. In J. P. Hill (Ed.), *Minnesota symposia on child psychology* (Vol. 2). Minneapolis: University of Minnesota Press, 1969.

Calhoun, J. B. A "behavioral skin." In E. Bliss (Ed.), *Roots of behavior.* New York: Harper, 1962.

Callaway, W. R., Jr. Modes of biological adaptation and their role in intellectual development. *Perceptual-Cognitive Development Monographs.* Los Angeles: The Galton Institute, 1970, *1*(1).

Calliotee, J. A. *The effects of a basic encounter group on student teachers' personality traits and subsequent teaching behaviors.* Unpublished doctoral dissertation, St. Louis University, 1970.

Camilleri, S. T. Theory, probability and induction in social research. *American Sociological Review,* 1962, *27,* 170-178.

Campbell, D. T. An error in some demonstrations of the superior social perceptiveness of leaders. *Journal of Abnormal and Social Psychology,* 1955, *51,* 694-695.

Campbell, D. T. Social attitudes and other acquired behavioral dispositions. In S. Koch (Ed.), *Psychology: A study of a science* (Vol. 6). New York: McGraw-Hill, 1963.

Campbell, D. T., & Fiske, D. W. Convergent and discriminant validation by the multitrait-multimethod matrix. *Psychological Bulletin,* 1959, *56,* 81-105.

Cancro, R. *Intelligence: Genetic and environmental influences.* New York: Grune & Stratton, 1971.

Canning, R. R., & Baker, J. M. Effect of the group on authoritarian and non-authoritarian persons. *American Journal of Sociology,* 1959, *64,* 579-581.

Cannon, W. B. *Body changes in pain, hunger, fear and rage.* New York: Appleton-Century-Crofts, 1929.

Canter, S. Personality traits in twins. In G. Claridge, S. Canter, & W. I. Hume. *Personality differences and biological variations: A study of twins.* Oxford: Pergamon, 1973.

Cantor, J. N., & Cantor, G. N. Observing behavior in children as a function of stimulus novelty. *Child Development,* 1964, *35,* 119-128.

Carlsmith, J. M., & Aronson, E. Some hedonic consequences of the confirmation and disconfirmation of expectancies. *Journal of Abnormal and Social Psychology,* 1963, *66,* 151-156.

Carlson, L. A., Levi, L., & Oroe, L. Stressor-induced changes in plasma lipids and urinary excretion of catecholamines, and their modification by nicotinic acid. In L. Levi (Ed.), *Stress and distress in response to psychosocial stimuli.* Oxford: Pergamon, 1972.

Carl-Zeep, A., & Carl, W. Reproduzier barkeit und Faktorenstruktuneiniger klinischer Tests zur vegetativen Diagnostik. *Journal of Neuro-Visceral Relations,* 1969, *31,* 161-170.

Carment, D. W., Miles, C. G., & Cerbin, V. B. Persuasiveness and persuasibility as related to intelligence and extraversion. *British Journal of Social and Clinical Psychology,* 1965, *4,* 1-7.

Carment, D. W., Schwartz, F. S., & Miles, C. G. Persuasiveness and persuasibility as related to intelligence and emotional responsiveness. *Psychological Reports,* 1963, *12,* 767-772.

Carp, A. L., & Shavzin, A. R. The susceptibility to falsification of the Rorschach psychodiagnostic technique. *Journal of Consulting Psychology,* 1950, *14,* 230-233.

Carroll, J. B. Stalking the wayward factors. *Contemporary Psychology,* 1972, *17,* 321-324.

Carter, H. D. Twin-similarities in emotional traits. *Character and Personality,* 1935, *4,* 61-78.

Cartwright, D. S., & Cartwright, C. F. *Psychological adjustment, ego and id.* Chicago: Rand McNally, 1971.

Casler, L. Maternal deprivation: A critical review of the literature. *Monographs of the Society for Research in Child Development,* 1961, *26*(2).

Cass, L. K. Parent-child relationships and delinquency. *Journal of Abnormal and Social Psychology,* 1952, *47,* 101-104.

Cattanach, B. M., Pollard, C. E., & Hawkes, S. G. Sex-reversed mice: XX and XO males. *Cytogenetics,* 1971, *10,* 318-337.

Cattell, R. B. *The subjective character of cognition (British Journal of Psychology Series).* Cambridge: Cambridge University Press, 1930.

Cattell, R. B. The assessment of teaching ability: A survey of professional opinion on the qualities of a good teacher. *British Journal of Educational Psychology,* 1931, *1,* 48-72.

Cattell, R. B. Temperament tests: I. Temperament. *British Journal of Psychology,* 1933, *23,* 308-329. (a)

Cattell, R. B. Temperament tests: II. Tests. *British Journal of Psychology,* 1933, *24,* 20-49. (b)

Cattell, R. B. The measurement of interest. *Character and Personality,* 1935, *4,* 147-169.

Cattell, R. B. Intelligence and fertility. *Eugenics Revue,* 1944, *30,* 126-127.

Cattell, R. B. The principal trait clusters for describing personality. *Psychological Bulletin,* 1945, *42,* 129-161. (a)

Cattell, R. B. Personality traits associated with abilities. *Journal of Educational Psychology,* 1945, *102,* 475-486. (b)

Cattell, R. B. The cultural functions of social stratification. II. Regarding individual and group dynamics. *Journal of Social Psychology,* 1945, *21,* 25-55. (c)

Cattell, R. B. *The description and measurement of personality.* New York: Harcourt Brace Jovanovich; London: Harrap, 1946.

Cattell, R. B. Confirmation and clarification of primary personality factors. *Psychometrika,* 1947, *12,* 197-220. (a)

Cattell, R. B. The ergic theory of attitude and sentiment measurement. *Educational Psychological Measurement,* 1947, *7,* 221-246. (b)

Cattell, R. B. Primary personality factors in the realm of objective tests. *Journal of Personality,* 1948, *16,* 459-487. (a)

Cattell, R. B. Concepts and methods in the measurement of group syntality. *Psychological Review,* 1948, *55,* 48-63. (b)

Cattell, R. B. $r_p$ and other coefficients of pattern similarity. *Psychometrika,* 1949, *14,* 279-298.

Cattell, R. B. The discovery of ergic structure in man in terms of common attitudes. *Journal of Abnormal and Social Psychology,* 1950, *45,* 598-618. (a)

Cattell, R. B. *An introduction to personality study.* London: Hutchinson, 1950. (b)

Cattell, R. B. *Personality: A systematic theoretical and factual study.* New York: McGraw-Hill, 1950. (c)

Cattell, R. B. The principal culture patterns discoverable in the syntal dimensions of modern nations. *Journal of Social Psychology,* 1950, *32,* 215-253. (d)

Cattell, R. B. *Factor analysis: An introduction and manual for the psychologist and social scientist.* New York: Harper, 1952. (a)

Cattell, R. B. The three basic factor analytic research designs—their interrelations and derivatives. *Psychological Bulletin,* 1952, *49,* 499-520. (b)

Cattell, R. B. On the theory of group learning. *Journal of Social Psychology,* 1953, *37,* 27-52. (a)

Cattell, R. B. Research designs in psychological genetics with special reference to the multiple variance method. *American Journal of Human Genetics,* 1953, *5,* 76-93. (b)

Cattell, R. B. Growing points in factor analysis. *Australian Journal of Psychology,* 1954, *6,* 105-140.

Cattell, R. B. *The objective-analytic (O-A) personality factor battery.* Champaign, Ill.: Institute for Personality and Ability Testing, 1955. (a)

Cattell, R. B. *Psychiatric screening of flying personnel: Personality structure in objective tests. A study of 1000 Air Force students in basic pilot training* (Project 21-0202-007, Rep. 9). Randolph Field, Tex.: Air University School of Aviation Medicine, 1955. (b)

Cattell, R. B. Personality and motivation theory based on structural measurement. In J. L. McCary (Ed.), *Psychology of personality.* New York: Logos, 1956. (a)

Cattell, R. B. New developments of personality theory from quantitative factor analytic research. *Revue Internationale de Philosophie,* 1956, *35,* 1-35. (b)

Cattell, R. B. *Personality and motivation structure and measurement.* New York: Harcourt Brace Jovanovich, 1957. (a)

Cattell, R. B. A universal index for psychological factors. *Psychologia,* 1957, *1,* 74-85. (b)

Cattell, R. B. The dynamic calculus: A system of concepts derived from objective motivation measurement. In G. Lindzey (Ed.), *The assessment of human motives.* New York: Holt, Rinehart, & Winston, 1958.

Cattell, R. B. The dynamic calculus: Concepts and crucial experiments. In M. R. Jones (Ed.), *Nebraska symposium on motivation.* Lincoln: University of Nebraska Press, 1959.

Cattell, R. B. The Multiple Abstract Variance Analysis equations and solutions. *Psychological Review,* 1960, *67,* 353-372.

Cattell, R. B. Theory of situational, instrument, second order and refraction factors in personality structure research. *Psychological Bulletin,* 1961, *58,* 160-174.

Cattell, R. B. The basis of recognition and interpretation of factors. *Educational and Psychological Measurement,* 1962, *22,* 667-697. (a)

Cattell, R. B. Personality assessments, based upon functionality unitary personality traits, factor analytically demonstrated. In S. Coopersmith (Ed.), *Personality research.* Copenhagen: Munksgaard, 1962. (b)

Cattell, R. B. Group theory, personality and role: A model for experimental researches. In F. A.

Geldard (Ed.), *Defence psychology*. Oxford and New York: Pergamon, 1962. (c)

Cattell, R. B. Formulating the environmental situation and its perception, in behavior theory. In S. B. Sells (Ed.), *Stimulus determinants of behavior*. New York: Ronald Press, 1963. (a)

Cattell, R. B. The interaction of hereditary and environmental influences. *British Journal of Statistical Psychology*, 1963, *16*, 191–210. (b)

Cattell, R. B. Personality, role, mood, and situation-perception: A unifying theory of modulators. *Psychological Review*, 1963, *70*, 1–18. (c)

Cattell, R. B. The structuring of change by P-technique and incremental R-technique. In C. W. Harris (Ed.), *Problems in measuring change*. Madison: University of Wisconsin Press, 1963. (d)

Cattell, R. B. Teachers' personality description of six-year-olds: A check on structure. *British Journal of Educational Psychology*, 1963, *33*, 219–235. (e)

Cattell, R. B. Theory of fluid and crystallized intelligence: A critical experiment. *Journal of Educational Psychology*, 1963, *54*, 1–22. (f)

Cattell, R. B. Beyond validity and reliability: Some further concepts and coefficients for evaluating tests. *Journal of Experimental Education*, 1964, *33*, 133–143. (a)

Cattell, R. B. Objective personality tests: A reply to Dr. Eysenck. *Occupational Psychology*, 1964, *38*, 69–86. (b)

Cattell, R. B. The parental early repressiveness hypothesis for the authoritarian personality factor, U.I. 28. *Journal of Genetic Psychology*, 1964, *106*, 333–349. (c)

Cattell, R. B. The configurative method for surer identification of personality dimensions, notably in child study. *Psychological Reports*, 1965, *65*, 205–219. (a)

Cattell, R. B. Higher order factor structures and reticular-vs-hierarchical formulae for their interpretation. In C. Banks & P. L. Broadhurst (Eds.), *Studies in psychology in honour of Sir Cyril Burt*. London: University of London Press, 1965. (b)

Cattell, R. B. *The scientific analysis of personality*. Chicago: Aldine; Baltimore, Md., and Harmondsworth, England: Penguin, 1965. (c)

Cattell, R. B. Anxiety and motivation: Theory and crucial experiment. In C. D. Spielberger (Ed.), *Anxiety and behavior*. New York: Academic Press, 1966. (a)

Cattell, R. B. A brief survey of present knowledge and hypotheses on psychophysiological state dimensions. In R. B. Cattell (Ed.), *Handbook of multivariate experimental psychology*. Chicago: Rand McNally, 1966. (b)

Cattell, R. B. The data box: Its ordering of total resources in many possible relational systems. In R. B. Cattell (Ed.), *Handbook of multivariate experimental psychology*. Chicago: Rand McNally, 1966. (c)

Cattell, R. B. Evaluating therapy as total personality change: Theory and available instruments. *American Journal of Psychotherapy*, 1966, *20*, 69–88. (d)

Cattell, R. B. (Ed.). *Handbook of multivariate experimental psychology*. Chicago: Rand McNally, 1966. (e)

Cattell, R. B. The meaning and strategic use of factor analysis. In R. B. Cattell (Ed.), *Handbook of multivariate experimental psychology*. Chicago: Rand McNally, 1966. (f)

Cattell, R. B. Patterns of change: Measurement in relation to state-dimension, trait change, lability, and process concepts. In R. B. Cattell (Ed.), *Handbook of multivariate experimental psychology*. Chicago: Rand McNally, 1966. (g)

Cattell, R. B. The Scree test for the numbers of factors. *Multivariate Behavioral Research*, 1966, *1*, 140–161. (h)

Cattell, R. B. *The trait view theory of perturbations in ratings and self-ratings (L- and Q-data): Its applications to obtaining pure trait scores in questionnaires* (Advance Publication No. 2). Urbana, Ill.: Laboratory of Personality and Group Analysis, 1966. (i)

Cattell, R. B. *The value of measurement approaches to psychiatric and behavior problems in children of lower classes*. In *Mental health and the lower social classes* (Study No. 49). Tallahassee: Florida State University, 1966. (j)

Cattell, R. B. *The theoretically expected role of factors in clinical psychology*. Paper presented at the meeting of the Midwestern Psychological Association, May 1967. (a)

Cattell, R. B. The theory of fluid and crystallized intelligence checked at the 5–6 year-old level. *British Journal of Educational Psychology*, 1967, *37*, 209–224. (b)

Cattell, R. B. Taxonomic principles for locating and using types (and the derived Taxonome computer program). In B. Klieninmuntz (Ed.), *Formal representation of human judgement*. New York: Wiley, 1968. (a)

Cattell, R. B. Trait view theory of perturbations in ratings and self-ratings (*L* (*BR*)- and *Q*-data): Its application to obtaining pure trait score estimates in questionnaires. *Psychological Review*, 1968, *75*, 96–113. (b)

Cattell, R. B. Comparing factor trait and state scores across ages and cultures. *Journal of Gerontology*, 1969, *24*, 348–360.

Cattell, R. B. The isopodic and equipotent principles for comparing scores across different populations. *British Journal of Mathematical and Statistical Psychology*, 1970, *23*, 23–30. (a)

Cattell, R. B. Separating endogenous, exogenous, ecogenic, and epogenic component curves in developmental data. *Developmental Psychology*, 1970, *3*, 151–162. (b)

Cattell, R. B. A factor analytic system for clinicians. In B. R. Maher (Ed.), *New approaches to personality classification*. New York: Columbia University Press, 1970. (c)

Cattell, R. B. *Abilities: Their structure, growth, and action*. Boston: Houghton Mifflin, 1971. (a)

Cattell, R. B. Estimating modulator indices and state liabilities. *Multivariate Behavioral Research*, 1971, *6*, 7–33. (b)

Cattell, R. B. The nature and genesis of mood states: A theoretical model with experimental measurements, concerning anxiety, depression, arousal, etc. Unpublished manuscript, Department of Psychology, University of Illinois, 1971. (c)

Cattell, R. B. The interpretation of Pavlov's typology, and the arousal concept, in replicated trait and state factors. In V. D. Nebylitsyn & J. A. Gray (Eds.), *Biological bases of individual behavior*. New York: Academic Press, 1972. (a)

Cattell, R. B. Real base, true zero factor analysis. *Multivariate Behavioral Research Monograph*, 1972, No. 72–1. (b)

Cattell, R. B. *Personality and mood by questionnaire*. San Francisco: Jossey-Bass, 1973. (a)

Cattell, R. B. Key issues in motivation theory, with special reference to structured learning. In R. Royce (Ed.), *Multivariate analysis and psychological theory*. New York: Academic Press, 1973. (b)

Cattell, R. B. The 16 P.F. and basic personality structure: A reply to Eysenck. *Journal of Behavioral Science*, 1973, *3*, 1–18. (c)

Cattell, R. B. Unravelling maturational and learning developments by the comparative MAVA and structured learning approaches. In J. R. Nesselroade & J. Reese (Eds.), *Life span developmental psychology*. New York: Academic Press, 1973. (d)

Cattell, R. B. Radial parcel factoring-vs.-item factoring in defining personality structure in questionnaires: Theory and experimental checks. *Australian Journal of Psychology*, 1974, *26*, 103–109.

Cattell, R. B. Development of scale vulnerability theory for correcting questionnaire distortion. *Multivariate Behavioral Research*, 1976, in press. (a)

Cattell, R. B. *Comprehensive personality and learning theory*. New York: Springer, 1976. (b)

Cattell, R. B., & Baggaley, A. R. The objective measurement of motivation: Development and evaluation of principles and devices. *Journal of Personality*, 1956, *24*, 401–423.

Cattell, R. B., & Baggaley, A. R. A confirmation of ergic and engram structures in attitudes objectively measured. *Australian Journal of Psychology*, 1958, *10*, 287–318.

Cattell, R. B., Balcar, K. R., Horn, J. L., & Nesselroade, J. Factor matching procedures: An improvement of the S index; with tables. *Educational and Psychological Measurement*, 1969, *27*, 781–792.

Cattell, R. B., & Beloff, H. *The High School Personality Questionnaire*. Champaign, Ill.: Institute for Personality and Ability Testing, 1962.

Cattell, R. B., & Bjerstedt, A. The structure of depression by factoring *Q*-data in relation to general personality source traits. *Scandinavian Journal of Psychology*, 1967, *8*, 17–24.

Cattell, R. B., Blewett, D. B., & Beloff, J. R. The inheritance of personality: A multiple variance analysis determination of approximate nature-nurture ratios for primary personality factors in Q-data. *American Journal of Human Genetics*, 1955, *7*, 122–146.

Cattell, R. B., Boutourline, H. Y., & Hundleby, J. D. Blood groups and personality traits. *American Journal of Human Genetics*, 1964, *16*, 397–402.

Cattell, R. B., Breul, H., & Hartman, H. P. An attempt at more refined definition of the cultural dimensions of syntality in modern nations. *American Sociological Review*, 1952, *17*, 408–421.

Cattell, R. B., & Butcher, H. J. *The prediction of achievement and creativity*. Indianapolis: Bobbs-Merrill, 1968.

Cattell, R. B., Butcher, H. J., Connor, D., Sweney, A. P., & Tsujioka, B. *Prediction and understanding of the effect of children's interest upon school performance*. Urbana, Ill.: Laboratory of Personality Assessment and Group Behavior, University of Illinois, 1962.

Cattell, R. B., Cattell, A. K. S., & Rhymer, R. M. P-technique demonstrated in determining psycho-physiological source traits in a normal individual. *Psychometrika*, 1947, *12*, 267–288.

Cattell, R. B., & Cattell, A. K. S. Factor rotation for proportional profiles: Analytic solution and an example. *British Journal of Statistical Psychology*, 1955, *8*, 83–92.

Cattell, R. B., & Child, D. *Motivation and dynamic structure*. New York & London: Holt, Rinehart, & Winston, 1975.

Cattell, R. B., Child, D., & Delhees, K. H. A check on adult dynamic structure with a large sample. Unpublished manuscript, Department of Psychology, University of Illinois, 1973.

Cattell, R. B., & Coan, R. W. Child personality structure as revealed by teachers' ratings. *Journal of Clinical Psychology*, 1957, *13*, 315–327. (a)

Cattell, R. B., & Coan, R. W. Personality factors in middle childhood as revealed in parents' ratings. *Child Development*, 1957, *28*, 439–458. (b)

Cattell, R. B., & Coan, R. W. Personality dimensions in the questionnaire responses of six- and seven-year-olds. *British Journal of Educational Psychology*, 1958, *28*, 232–242.

Cattell, R. B., & Coulter, M. A. Principles of behavioral taxonomy and the mathematical basis of the taxonome computer program. *British Journal of Mathematical and Statistical Psychology*, 1966, *19*, 237–269.

Cattell, R. B., Coulter, M. A., & Tsujioka, B. The taxonometric recognition of types and functional emergents. In R. B. Cattell (Ed.), *Handbook of multivariate experimental psychology*. Chicago: Rand McNally, 1966.

Cattell, R. B., & Cross, K. Comparison of the ergic and self-sentiment structures found in dynamic traits by R- and P-techniques. *Journal of Personality*, 1952, *21*, 250–271.

Cattell, R. B., & Delhees, K. H. Seven missing normal personality factors in the questionnaire primaries. *Multivariate Behavioral Research*, 1973, *8*, 173–194.

Cattell, R. B., Delhees, K. H., Tatro, D. F., & Nesselroade, J. R. Personality structure checked in primary objective test factors for a mixed normal and psychotic sample. *Multivariate Behavioral Research*, 1971, *6*, 187–214.

Cattell, R. B., & DeVoogd, T. A test of the vulnerability coefficient model for correcting motivational distortion in Q-data personality measurement. Unpublished manuscript, Department of Psychology, University of Illinois, 1973.

Cattell, R. B., De Young, G. E., & Horn, J. L. Human motives as dynamic states: A dR-analysis of objective motivation measures. *Journal of Multivariate Experimental Personality and Clinical Psychology*, 1974, *1*, 58–78.

Cattell, R. B., & Dickman, K. A dynamic model of physical influences demonstrating the necessity of oblique simple structure. *Psychological Bulletin*, 1962, *59*, 389–400.

Cattell, R. B., & Digman, J. M. A theory of the structure of perturbations in observer ratings and questionnaire data in personality research. *Behavioral Science*, 1964, *9*(4), 341–358.

Cattell, R. B., & Dreger, R. M. Personality structure as revealed in questionnaire responses at the preschool level. *Child Development*, 1974, *45*, 49–54.

Cattell, R. B., & Drevdahl, J. E. A comparison of the personality profiles (16 P.F.) of eminent teachers and administrators and of the general population. *British Journal of Psychology*, 1955, *46*, 248–261.

Cattell, R. B., Dubin, S. S., & Saunders, D. R. Personality structure in psychotics by factorization of objective clinical tests. *Journal of Mental Science*, 1954, *100*, 154–176.

Cattell, R. B., & Eber, H. W. *The Sixteen Personality Factor Questionnaire* (3rd ed.). Champaign, Ill.: Institute for Personality and Ability Testing, 1957.

Cattell, R. B., & Eber, H. W. *Handbook for the Sixteen Personality Factor Questionnaire*. Champaign, Ill.: Institute for Personality and Ability Testing, 1964.

Cattell, R. B., & Eber, H. W. *The Sixteen Personality Factor Questionnaire*. Champaign, Ill.: Institute for Personality and Ability Testing, 1966.

Cattell, R. B., Eber, H. W., & Delhees, K. H. A large sample cross validation of the personality trait structure of the 16 P.F. with some clinical implications. *Multivariate Behavioral Research*, 1968, *3*, 107–132. (Special Issue)

Cattell, R. B., Eber, H. W., & Tatsuoka, M. *Handbook for the Sixteen Personality Factor Questionnaire* (3rd ed.). Champaign, Ill.: Institute for Personality and Ability Testing, 1970.

Cattell, R. B., & Gibbons, B. D. Personality factor structure of the combined Guilford and Cattell personality questionnaires. *Journal of Personality and Social Psychology*, 1968, *9*, 107–120.

Cattell, R. B., & Gorsuch, R. L. The uniqueness and significance of simple structure demonstrated by contrasting organic "natural structure" and "random structure" data. *Psychometrika*, 1963, *28*, 55–67.

Cattell, R. B., & Gorsuch, R. L. The definition and measurement of national morale and morality. *Journal of Social Psychology*, 1965, *67*, 77–96.

Cattell, R. B., & Gruen, W. The personality factor structure of 11-year-old children in terms of behavior rating data. *Journal of Clinical Psychology*, 1953, *9*, 255–266.

Cattell, R. B., & Gruen, W. Primary personality factors in the questionnaire medium for children eleven to fourteen years old. *Educational and Psychological Measurement*, 1954, *14*, 50–76.

Cattell, R. B., & Gruen, W. The primary personality factors in eleven year old children, by objective tests. *Journal of Personality*, 1955, *23*, 460–478.

Cattell, R. B., & Horn, J. L. An integrating study of the factor structure of adult attitudes-interests. *Genetic Psychology Monographs*, 1963, *67*, 89–149.

Cattell, R. B., & Horn, J. L. Age differences in fluid and crystallized intelligence. *Acta Psychologica*, 1967, *26*, 107–129.

Cattell, R. B., Horn, J. L., & Butcher, H. J. The dynamic structure of attitudes in adults: A description of some established factors and of their measurement by the Motivation Analysis Test. *British Journal of Psychology*, 1962, *53*, 57–69.

Cattell, R. B., Horn, J. L., Sweney, A. B., & Radcliffe, J. A. *The Motivation Analysis Test, MAT*. Champaign, Ill.: Institute for Personality and Ability Testing, 1964.

Cattell, R. B., & Howarth, E. Verification of objective personality patterns of middle childhood. *Journal of Genetic Psychology*, 1964, *104*, 331–349.

Cattell, R. B., & Jaspars, J. A. General plasmode (No. 30–10–5–2) for factor analytic exercises and research. *Multivariate Behavioral Monograph* (No. 67–3), 1967.

Cattell, R. B., & Killian, L. R. The pattern of objective test personality factor differences in schizophrenia and the character disorders. *Journal of Clinical Psychology*, 1967, *23*, 343–348.

Cattell, R. B., Knapp, R. B., & Scheier, I. H. Second-order personality facture structure in the objective test realm. *Journal of Consulting Psychology*, 1961, *25*, 345–352.

Cattell, R. B., Komlos, E., & Tatro, D. F. Significant differences of affective, paranoid, and nonparanoid schizophrenic psychotics on primary source traits in the 16 P.F. *Multivariate Behavioral Research*, 1968, 33–54. (Special Issue)

Cattell, R. B., Kristy, N., & Stice, G. F. A first approximation to nature-nurture ratios for eleven primary personality factors in objective tests. *Journal of Abnormal and Social Psychology*, 1952, *54*, 143–159.

Cattell, R. B., & Luborsky, L. B. P-technique demonstrated as a new clinical method for determining personality and symptom structure. *Journal of General Psychology*, 1950, *42*, 3–24.

Cattell, R. B., Maxwell, E. F., Light, B. H., & Unger, M. P. The objective measurement of attitudes. *British Journal of Psychology*, 1949, *40*, 81–90.

Cattell, R. B., & Miller, A. A confirmation of the ergic and self-sentiment patterns among dynamic traits (attitude variables) by R-technique. *British Journal of Psychology*, 1952, *43*, 280–294.

Cattell, R. B., & Nesselroade, J. R. Likeness and completeness theories examined by Sixteen Personality Factor measures on stably and unstably married couples. *Journal of Personality and Social Psychology*, 1967, *7*, 351–361.

Cattell, R. B., & Nesselroade, J. R. Note on analyzing personality relations in married couples. *Psychological Reports*, 1968, *22*, 381–382.

Cattell, R. B., & Nesselroade, J. R. The discovery of the anxiety state pattern in Q-data, and its distinction, in the LM model, from depression, effort, stress, and fatigue. *Multivariate Behavioral Research*, 1976, *11*, 27–46.

Cattell, R. B., & Nichols, K. E. A comparison of several cross-cultural analyses of the 16 P.F. second stratum structure. Unpublished manuscript, Department of Psychology, University of Illinois, 1972. (a)

Cattell, R. B., & Nichols, K. E. An improved definition from ten researches of second order personality factors in Q-data (with cross-cultural checks). *Journal of Social Psychology*, 1972, *86*, 187–203. (b)

Cattell, R. B., & Peterson, D. R. Personality structure in 4–5 year olds, by factoring observed, time-sampled behavior. *Rassigna di Psicologia Generale e Clinica*, 1958, *3*, 3–21.

Cattell, R. B., & Peterson, D. R. Personality structure in four and five year olds in terms of objective tests. *Journal of Clinical Psychology*, 1959, *15*, 355-369.

Cattell, R. B., Pierson, G., Brim, T., & Finkbeiner, C. Alignment of primary personality factors in L- and Q-data demonstrated on a common factorization. *Multivariate Experimental and Clinical Research*, 1976, *2*, 1-20.

Cattell, R. B., Pierson, Y. H., Finkbeiner, C., & Brim, B. J. Proof of alignment of personality source trait factors from questionnaire and observer ratings: The theory of instrumental free patterns. *Multivariate Experimental Clinical Psychology*, 1976, *4*, 1-31.

Cattell, R. B., Radcliffe, J. A. Factors in objective motivation measures with children: A preliminary study. *Australian Journal of Psychology*, 1961, *18*, 65-76.

Cattell, R. B., & Radcliffe, J. A. Reliabilities and validities of simple and extended weighted and buffered unifactor scales. *British Journal of Statistical Psychology*, 1962, *15*, 113-128.

Cattell, R. B., Radcliffe, J. A., & Sweney, A. B. The nature and measurement of components of motivation. *Genetic Psychology Monographs*, 1963, *68*, 49-211.

Cattell, R. B., & Rickels, K. Diagnostic power of IPAT objective anxiety and neuroticism tests. *Archives of General Psychiatry*, 1965, *11*, 459-465.

Cattell, R. B., & Rickels, K. The relationship of clinical symptoms and IPAT-factored tests of anxiety, regression, and asthenia: A factor-analytic study. *Journal of Nervous and Mental Disease*, 1968, *146*, 147-160.

Cattell, R. B., Rickels, K., Weise, C., Gray, B., & Yee, R. The effects of psychotherapy upon measured anxiety and regression. *American Journal of Psychotherapy*, 1966, *20*, 261-269.

Cattell, R. B., Saunders, D. R. Interrelations and matching of personality factors from behavior rating, questionnaire, and objective test data. *Journal of Social Psychology*, 1950, *31*, 243-260.

Cattell, R. B., & Saunders, D. R. Beiträge zur Faktoren-Analyse der Persönlichkeit. *Zeitschrift für experimentelle und angewandte Psychologie*, 1954, *2*, 325-357. (a)

Cattell, R. B., & Saunders, D. R. Musical preferences and personality diagnosis: I. A factorization of one hundred and twenty themes. *Journal of Social Psychology*, 1954, *39*, 3-24. (b)

Cattell, R. B., Saunders, D. R., & Stice, G. F. The dimensions of syntality in small groups: I. The neonate group. *Human Relations*, 1953, *6*, 331-356.

Cattell, R. B., & Scheier, I. H. Extension of meaning of objective test personality factors: Especially into anxiety, neuroticism, questionnaire, and physical factors. *Journal of General Psychology*, 1959, *61*, 287-315. (a)

Cattell, R. B., & Scheier, I. H. *The IPAT Anxiety Scale*. Champaign, Ill.: Institute for Personality and Ability Testing, 1959. (b)

Cattell, R. B., & Scheier, I. H. Stimuli relating to stress, neuroticism, excitation, and anxiety response patterns: Illustrating a new multivariate experimental design. *Journal of Abnormal and Social Psychology*, 1960, *60*, 195-204.

Cattell, R. B., & Scheier, I. H. *The meaning and measurement of neuroticism and anxiety*. New York: Ronald Press, 1961.

Cattell, R. B., & Scheier, I. H. *Handbook for the IPAT anxiety scale* (2nd ed.). Champaign, Ill.: Institute for Personality and Ability Testing, 1963.

Cattell, R. B., & Schmidt, L. R., with the assistance of A. Bjerstedt. Clinical diagnosis by the Objective-Analytic personality batteries. *Journal of Clinical Psychology, Special Monograph Supplement*, 1972, *28*, 239-312.

Cattell, R. B., Schmidt, L. R., & Pawlik, K. Cross cultural comparison (U.S.A., Japan, Austria) of the personality structures of 10 to 14 year olds in objective tests. *Social Behavior and Personality*, 1973, *1*, 182-211.

Cattell, R. B., & Schuerger, J. *The O-A (Objective-Analytic) Personality Battery*. Champaign, Ill.: Institute for Personality and Ability Testing, 1976.

Cattell, R. B., Sealy, A. P., & Sweney, A. B. What can personality and motivation source traits measurements add to the prediction of school achievement. *British Journal of Educational Psychology*, 1966, *36*, 280-295.

Cattell, R. B., & Sells, S. B. *The Clinical Analysis Questionnaire*. Champaign, Ill.: Institute for Personality and Ability Testing, 1972.

Cattell, R. B., & Shotwell, A. M. Personality profiles of more successful and less successful psychiatric technicians. *American Journal of Mental Deficiency*, 1954, *58*, 496-499.

Cattell, R. B., & Stice, G. F. *The behavior of small groups*. Champaign, Ill.: Institute for Personality and Ability Testing, 1960. (a)

Cattell, R. B., & Stice, G. F. *The dimensions of groups and their relations to the behavior of members*. Champaign, Ill.: Institute for Personality and Ability Testing, 1960. (b)

Cattell, R. B., Stice, G. F., & Kristy, N. F. A first approximation to nature-nurture ratios for eleven primary personality factors in objective tests. *Journal of Abnormal and Social Psychology*, 1957, *54*, 143-159.

Cattell, R. B., & Sweney, A. B. Measurable components on the structure of conflict manifestations. *Journal of Abnormal and Social Psychology*, 1964, *68*, 479-490.

Cattell, R. B., Sweney, A. B., & Krug, S. E. *The School Motivation Analysis Test, SMAT*. Champaign, Ill.: Institute for Personality and Ability Testing, 1968.

Cattell, R. B., Sweney, A. B., & Radcliffe, J. A. The objective measurement of motivation structure in children. *Journal of Clinical Psychology*, 1960, *16*, 227-232.

Cattell, R. B., & Tatro, D. F. The personality factors, objectively measured, which distinguish psychotics from normals. *Behaviour Research and Therapy*, 1966, *4*, 39-51.

Cattell, R. B., Tatro, D. F., & Komlos, E. The diagnosis and inferred structure of paranoid and nonparanoid schizophrenia from the 16 P.F. profile. *Indian Psychological Review*, 1964, *1*, 52-61.

Cattell, R. B., & Tsujioka, B. The importance of factor-trueness and validity, versus homogeneity and orthogonality, in test scales. *Educational and Psychological Measurement*, 1964, *24*, 3-30.

Cattell, R. B., & Vogelmann, S. A comprehensive set of traits of the Scree test for determining the number of factors. *Psychological Bulletin*, 1976, in press.

Cattell, R. B., & Warburton, F. W. A cross-cultural comparison of patterns of extraversion and anxiety. *British Journal of Psychology*, 1961, *52*, 3-15.

Cattell, R. B., & Warburton, F. W. *Objective personality and motivation tests: A theoretical introduction and practical compendium*. Urbana, Ill.: University of Illinois Press, 1967.

Cattell, R. B., & Wenig, P. Dynamic and cognitive factors controlling misperception. *Journal of Abnormal and Social Psychology*, 1952, *47*, 797-809.

Cattell, R. B., & Williams, H. U. M. *P*-technique, a new statistical device for analyzing functional unities in the intact organism. *British Journal of Preventive and Social Medicine*, 1953, *7*, 141-153.

Cattell, R. B., & Wispe, L. C. The dimensions of syntality in small groups. *Journal of Social Psychology*, 1948, *28*, 57-78.

Cattell, R. B., Young, H. B., & Hundleby, J. D. Blood groups and personality traits. *American Journal of Human Genetics*, 1964, *16*, 397-402.

Cavalli-Sforza, L. L. An analysis of linkage in quantitative inheritance. In E. C. R. Reeve & C. H. Waddington (Eds.), *Quantitative inheritance*. London: His Majesty's Stationer's Office, 1952.

Cavalli-Sforza, L. L., & Bodmer, W. F. *The genetics of human populations*. San Francisco: Freeman, 1971.

Caveny, E., Wittson, C., Hunt, W., & Herman, R. Psychiatric diagnosis, its nature and function. *Journal of Nervous and Mental Disease*, 1955, *121*, 367-380.

Cervin, V. Experimental investigation of behavior in social situations. I. Behavior under opposition. *Canadian Journal of Psychology*, 1955, *9*, 107-116.

Cervin, V. Relationships of ascendant-submissive behavior in dyadic groups of human subjects to their emotional responsiveness. *Journal of Abnormal and Social Psychology*, 1957, *54*, 241-249.

Charlesworth, W. R. Cognition in infancy: Where do we stand in the mid-sixties? *Merrill-Palmer Quarterly*, 1968, *14*, 25-46.

Chassan, J. B. Statistical inference and the single case in clinical design. *Psychiatry*, 1960, *23*, 173-184.

Cheek, D. B. (Ed.). *Human growth. Body composition, cell growth, energy, and intelligence*. Philadelphia: Lea & Febiger, 1968.

Chein, I. Personality and typology. *Journal of Social Psychology*, 1943, *18*, 89-109.

Chessick, R. D., Bassam, M., & Shattan, S. A comparison of the effect of infused catecholamines and certain affect states. *American Journal of Psychiatry*, 1966, *123*, 156-165.

Childs, R. Sir Archibald Garrod's conception of chemical individuality: A modern appreciation. *New England Journal of Medicine*, 1970, *282*, 71-77.

Chomsky, N. *Syntactic structures*. The Hague, Netherlands: Mouton, 1957.

Chomsky, N. Review of *Verbal Behavior*. *Language*, 1959, *35*, 26-58.

Chomsky, N. *Aspects of the theory of syntax*. Cambridge: Massachusetts Institute of Technology Press, 1965.

Chorost, S. B. Parental child-rearing attitudes

and their correlates in adolescent hostility. *Genetic Psychology Monographs*, 1962, *66*, 49–90.

Chudnovskii, V. E. [Studies of the characteristics of type of nervous system in preschool children.] *Voprosy Psikhologii*, 1963, (3), 5–20. (*Psychological Abstracts*, 1965, *39*, 7967.)

Clapp, W. F. Dependence and competence in children: Parental treatment of four-year-old boys. *Dissertation Abstracts*, 1967, *28*(4–B), 1703.

Claridge, G. S. The excitation-inhibition balance in neurotics. In H. J. Eysenck (Ed.), *Experiments in personality* (Vol. 2). London: Routledge & Kegan Paul, 1960.

Claridge, G. S. *Personality and arousal*. Oxford: Pergamon, 1967.

Claridge, G. S., Canter, S., & Hume, W. I. *Personality differences and biological variations: A study of twins*. Oxford: Pergamon, 1973.

Clausen, J. A. (Ed.). *Socialization and society*. Boston: Little, Brown, 1968.

Clemans, W. V. An analytical and empirical examination of some properties of ipsative scores. *Psychometric Monographs No. 21*. Chicago: University of Chicago Press, 1966.

Cleveland, S. E., & Morton, R. B. Group behavior and body image: A follow-up study. *Human Relations*, 1962, *15*, 77–85.

Cliff, N. *Multidimensional scaling and cognition: III. Threat evaluation and subjective organization of simulated raids* (Tech. Rep. No. 3). Los Angeles: University of Southern California, 1966.

Clore, G. L. *Discrimination learning as a function of awareness and magnitude of attitudinal reinforcement*. Unpublished doctoral dissertation, University of Texas, 1966.

Clore, G. L. *Interpersonal attraction–an overview*. Morristown, N.J.: General Learning Press, 1975.

Clore, G. L., & Baldridge, B. Interpersonal attraction: The role of agreement and topic interest. *Journal of Personality and Social Psychology*, 1968, *9*, 340–346.

Clore, G. L., & Byrne, D. A reinforcement-affect model of attraction. In T. L. Huston (Ed.), *Foundations of interpersonal attraction*. New York: Academic Press, 1974.

Clore, G. L., & Gormly, J. B. Knowing, feeling, and liking: A psychological study of attraction. *Journal of Research in Personality*, 1974, *8*, 218–230.

Clyde, D. J. *Manual for the Clyde Mood Scale*. Coral Gables, Fla: University of Miami Biometric Laboratory, 1963.

Coan, R. W. Child personality and developmental psychology. In R. B. Cattell (Ed.), *Handbook of multivariate experimental psychology*. Chicago: Rand McNally, 1966.

Coan, R. W. The changing personality. In R. M. Dreger (Ed.), *Multivariate personality research*. Baton Rouge, La.: Claitor, 1972.

Coan, R. W., & Cattell, R. B. Reproducible personality factors in middle childhood. *Journal of Clinical Psychology*, 1958, *14*, 339–345.

Cofer, C. N., & Appley, M. H. *Motivation: Theory and research*. New York: Wiley, 1966.

Cofer, C. N., Chance, J., & Hudson, A. J. A study of malingering on the Minnesota Multiphasic Personality Inventory. *Journal of Psychology*, 1949, *27*, 491–499.

Cohen, A., Stotland, E., & Wolfe, D. M. An experimental investigation of need for cognition. *Journal of Abnormal and Social Psychology*, 1955, *51*, 291–297.

Cohen, D. J. Justin and his peers: An experimental analysis of a child's social world. *Child Development*, 1962, *33*, 697–717.

Cohen, J. The factorial structure of the WAIS between early adulthood and old age. *Journal of Consulting Psychology*, 1957, *21*, 283–290.

Cohen, J. The factorial structure of the WISC at ages 7–6, 10–6, and 13–6. *Journal of Consulting Psychology*, 1959, *23*, 285–299.

Cohen, J. The impact of multivariate research in clinical psychology. In R. B. Cattell (Ed.), *Handbook of multivariate experimental psychology*. Chicago: Rand McNally, 1966.

Cohen, M. R., & Nagel, E. *An introduction to logic and scientific method*. New York: Harcourt Brace Jovanovich, 1934.

Colby, K. M. Computer simulation of a neurotic process. In S. S. Tomkins & S. Messick (Eds.), *Computer simulation of personality*. New York: Wiley, 1963.

Coleman, J. C. *Abnormal psychology and modern life* (2nd ed.). New York: Appleton, 1950.

Colquhoun, W. P. (Ed.). *Biological rhythms and human performance*. London: Academic Press, 1971.

Comrey, A. L. A factor analysis of items on the *K* scale of the MMPI. *Educational and Psychological Measurement*, 1958, *18*, 633–639.

Comrey, A. L. *Manual for the Comrey Personality Scales*. San Diego: Educational and Industrial Testing Service, 1970.

Comrey, A. L., & Duffy, D. E. Cattell and Eysenck factor scores related to Comrey personality factors. *Multivariate Behavioral Research*, 1968, *4*, 379–392.

Comstock, R. E., & Robinson, J. F. Estimation of average dominance of genes. In J. W. Gowen (Ed.), *Heterosis*. Ames, Iowa: State College Press, 1952.

Conrad, K. *Der Konstitutionstypus* (2nd ed.). Berlin: Springer, 1963.

Cook, P., & Mather, K. Estimating the components of continuous variation: II. Genetical. *Heredity*, 1962, *17*, 211–236.

Cooper, M., & Aronson, L. The effect of adrenalectomy on the sexual behaviour of castrated male cats. *Anatomical Record*, 1958, *131*, 544.

Cooper, R., Osselton, J. W., & Shaw, J. D. *EEG technology*. London: Butterworth, 1969.

Coombs, C. H., & Kao, R. C. *Nonmetric factor analysis* (Bulletin of the Department of Engineering Research, No. 38). Ann Arbor: University of Michigan, 1955.

Corballis, M. C., & Traub, R. E. Longitudinal factor analysis. *Psychometrika*, 1970, *35*, 79–98.

Cornu, F. Psychopharmakotherapie. In H. W. Gruhle et al. (Eds.), *Psychiatrie der Gegenwart* (Vol. 1, Pt. 2). Berlin: Springer, 1963.

Couch, A., & Keniston, K. Yeasayers and naysayers: Agreeing responses set as a personality variable. *Journal of Abnormal and Social Psychology*, 1960, *60*, 151–174.

Courrier, R. Interactions between estrogens and progesterone. *Vitamins and Hormones*, 1950, *8*, 179–214.

Crandall, V., & Preston, A. Verbally expressed needs and overt maternal behavior. *Child Development*, 1961, *32*, 261–270.

Crissman, P. Temporal change and sexual difference in moral judgments. *Journal of Social Psychology*, 1942, *16*, 29–38.

Crisswell, J. H., Solomon, H., & Suppes, P. (Eds.). *Mathematical methods in small group processes*. Stanford: Stanford University Press, 1962.

Crockett, W. Cognitive complexity and impression formation. In B. Maher (Ed.), *Progress in experimental personality research*. New York: Academic Press, 1965.

Cronbach, L. J. Response sets and test validity. *Educational and Psychological Measurement*, 1946, *6*, 475–494.

Cronbach, L. J. *Essentials of psychological testing*. New York: Harper, 1949. (a)

Cronbach, L. J. Statistical methods applied to Rorschach scores: A review. *Psychological Bulletin*, 1949, *46*, 393–429. (b)

Cronbach, L. J. Further evidence on response sets and test design. *Educational and Psychological Measurement*, 1950, *10*, 3–31.

Cronbach, L. J. Processes affecting a score on "understanding of others" and "assumed similarity." *Psychological Bulletin*, 1955, *52*, 177–193.

Cronbach, L. J. The two disciplines of scientific psychology. *American Psychologist*, 1957, *12*, 671–684.

Cronbach, L. J. Proposals leading to analytic treatment of social perception scores. In R. Tagiuri & L. Petrullo (Eds.), *Person perception and interpersonal behavior*. Stanford: Stanford University Press, 1958.

Cronbach, L. J. *Essentials of psychological testing* (3rd ed.). New York: Harper & Row, 1970.

Cronbach, L. J., & Furby, L. How should we measure "change"–or should we? *Psychological Bulletin*, 1970, *74*, 68–80.

Cronbach, L. J., & Gleser, G. C. Assessing similarity between profiles. *Psychological Bulletin*, 1953, *50*, 456–473.

Cronbach, L. J., & Gleser, G. C. *Psychological tests and personal decisions* (Rev. ed.). Urbana: University of Illinois Press, 1965.

Crook, M. N. Intra-family relationship in personality test performance. *Psychological Record*, 1937, *1*, 479–502.

Cross, K. P. *Determination of ergic structure of common attitudes by P-technique*. Unpublished master's thesis, University of Illinois, 1951.

Crow, J. F., & Felsenstein, J. The effect of assortative mating on the genetic composition of a population. *Eugenics Quarterly*, 1968, *15*, 85–97.

Crown, S. Psychological changes following prefrontal leucotomy: A review. *Journal of Mental Science*, 1951, *97*, 49–83.

Crowne, D. P., Holland, C. H., & Conn, L. K. Personality factors in discrimination learning in children. *Journal of Personality and Social Psychology*, 1968, *10*, 420–430.

Crowne, D. P., & Liverant, S. Conformity under varying conditions of personal commitment. *Journal of Abnormal and Social Psychology*, 1963, *66*, 547–555.

Crowne, D. P., & Marlowe, D. *The approval motive: Studies in evaluative dependence*. New York: Wiley, 1964.

Crutchfield, R. S. Assessment of persons

through a quasi group-interaction technique. *Journal of Abnormal and Social Psychology*, 1951, *46*, 577–588.

Crutchfield, R. S. Conformity and character. *American Psychologist*, 1955, *10*, 191–198.

Curran, J. P. *Dimensions of state change in Q-data and chain-P technique, on 20 women.* Unpublished master's thesis, University of Illinois, 1968.

Curran, J., & Cattell, R. B. *The 8-state Questionnaire.* Champaign, Ill.: Institute for Personality and Ability Testing, 1974.

Dabrowski, K. *Personality-shaping through positive disintegration.* Boston: Little, Brown, 1967.

Dahlstrom, W. G. *An exploration of mental status syndromes by a factor analytic technique.* Unpublished doctoral dissertation, University of Minnesota, 1949.

Dahlstrom, W. G. The roles of social desirability and acquiescence in responses to the MMPI. In S. Messick & J. Ross (Eds.), *Measurement in personality and cognition.* New York: Wiley, 1962.

Dahlstrom, W. G., & Welsh, G. *An MMPI handbook.* Minneapolis: University of Minnesota Press, 1960.

Dahlstrom, W. G., Welsh, G. S., & Dahlstrom, L. E. *An MMPI handbook* (Vol. 1). *Clinical interpretation* (Rev. ed.). Minneapolis: University of Minnesota Press, 1972.

Damarin, F. L., Jr., & Cattell, R. B. Personality factors in early childhood and their relation to intelligence. *Monograph of the Society for Research in Child Development*, 1968, *33*(6), 95 pp.

Danzinger, K. *Socialization.* Harmondsworth, England: Penguin, 1971.

Darley, J. G., Gross, N., & Martin, W. E. Studies of group behavior: Stability, change, and interrelations of psychosomatic and sociometric variables. *Journal of Abnormal and Social Psychology*, 1951, *46*, 565–576.

Darley, J. G., & McNamara, W. J. *Manual of directions: Minnesota Personality Scale.* New York: Psychological Corporation, 1941.

Davidson, P. O., Payne, R. W., & Sloane, B. B. Conditionability in normals and neurotics. *Journal of Experimental Research in Personality*, 1968, *3*, 107–113.

Davies, D. R., & Tune, G. S. *Human vigilance performance.* London: Staples, 1970.

Davis, A., & Havighurst, R. J. Social class and color differences in child rearing. *American Sociological Review*, 1946, *11*, 698–710.

Davis, P. C. A factor analysis of the WB scale. *Educational and Psychological Measurement*, 1956, *16*, 127–146.

Deese, J. Behavior and fact. *American Psychologist*, 1969, *24*, 515–523.

Deese, J., Lazarus, R. S., & Kennan, J. Anxiety, anxiety reduction, and stress in learning. *Journal of Experimental Psychology*, 1953, *46*, 55–60.

Degan, J. W. Dimensions of functional psychosis. *Psychometric Monographs*, No. 6. Chicago: University of Chicago Press, 1952.

Delhees, K. H. Die Logik des Messens und Quantifizierens in der klinischen Psychologie. *Schweizer Zeitschrift für Psychologie und ihre Anwendungen*, 1966, *25*, 97–106. (a)

Delhees, K. H. *Die psychodiagnostische Syn-* dromatik der Homosexualität. Bern: Huber, 1966. (b)

Delhees, K. H. Conflict measurement by the dynamic calculus model, and its applicability in clinical practice. *Multivariate Behavioral Research*, 1968, *3*, 73–96.

Delhees, K. H. Hypotheses of origin and nature for the "Somindence-Dissofrustance" personality factor, U.I. 30. *Journal of Genetic Psychology*, 1972, *120*, 189–201.

Delhees, K. H. The objective measurement of intrafamilial attitudes and sentiments. *Archiv für Psychologie*, 1973, *125*, 134–152.

Delhees, K. H. Das Stadium der Persönlichkeit in der modernen Psychologie. *Schweizer Erziehungs-Rundschau*, 1974, *47*, 75–87.

Delhees, K. H. *Motivation und Verhalten.* München: Kindler, 1975.

Delhees, K. H., & Cattell, R. B. Obtaining 16 PF scores from the MMPI, and MMPI scores from the 16 PF. *Journal of Projective Techniques and Personality Assessment*, 1970, *34*, 251–255.

Delhees, K. H., & Cattell, R. B. *The Clinical Analysis Questionnaire. Experimental Form.* Champaign, Ill.: Institute for Personality and Ability Testing, 1971. (a)

Delhees, K. H., & Cattell, R. B. Differences of personality factors, by the O-A battery, in paranoid and non-paranoid schizophrenics, manic-depressives, psychoneurotics, and the personality disorders. *Archiv für Psychologie*, 1971, *123*, 35–48. (b)

Delhees, K. H., & Cattell, R. B. The dimensions of pathology: Proof of their projections beyond the normal 16 P.F. source traits. *Personality*, 1971, *2*, 149–173. (c)

Delhees, K. H., Cattell, R. B., & Sweney, A. B. The structure of parents' intrafamilial attitudes and sentiments measured by objective tests and a vector model. *Journal of Social Psychology*, 1970, *82*, 231–252.

Delhees, K. H., Cattell, R. B., & Sweney, A. B. Objective measures of children's intra-familial attitudes and sentiments and the investment subsidiation model. *Journal of Genetic Psychology*, 1971, *118*, 87–113.

Delius, L., & Fahrenberg, J. *Psychovegetative syndrome.* Stuttgart: Thieme, 1966.

Delius, L., Kottek, L., & Fahrenberg, J. Eine factorenanlytische Untersuchung psychophysiologischer Korrelate. *Archiv für die gesamte Psychologie*, 1968, *120*, 54–73.

Dell, P. C. Some basic mechanisms of the translation of bodily needs into behavior. In G. W. W. Wolsterholme & C. M. O'Connor (Eds.), *Neurological basis of behavior.* Boston: Ciba Foundation, 1958.

Dember, W. N. Alternation behavior. In D. W. Fiske & S. R. Maddi (Eds.), *Functions of varied experience.* Homewood, Ill.: Dorsey Press, 1961.

Dember, W. N., & Earl, R. W. Analysis of exploratory, manipulatory, and curiosity behaviors. *Psychological Review*, 1957, *64*, 91–96.

Dember, W. N., Earl, R. W., & Paradise, N. Response by rats to differential stimulus complexity. *Journal of Comparative and Physiological Psychology*, 1957, *50*, 514–518.

deMolina, A. F., & Hunsperger, R. W. Organization of the subcortical system governing defence and flight reactions in the cat. *Journal* of Physiology (London), 1962, *160*, 200–213.

Denenberg, V. H., & Whimbey, A. E. Behavior of adult rats is modified by the experience their mothers had as infants. *Science*, 1963, *142*, 1192–1193.

Dennis, W., & Najarian, P. Infant development under environmental handicap. *Psychological Monographs*, 1957, *71*(7, Whole No. 436).

Denny, J. P. Effect of anxiety and intelligence on concept formation. *Journal of Experimental Psychology*, 1966, *72*, 596–602.

Denton, J. C., & Taylor, C. W. A factor analysis of mental abilities and personality traits. *Psychometrika*, 1955, *20*, 75–81.

DeVoge, J. T. *Anxiety and complex learning in the absence of response learning.* Unpublished master's thesis, West Virginia University, 1968.

Dewey, J. The reflex arc concept in psychology. *Psychological Review*, 1896, *3*.

Dewey, J., & Bentley, A. F. *Knowing and the known.* Boston: Beacon Press, 1949.

De Young, G. E. Standards of decision regarding personality factors in questionnaires. *Canadian Journal of Behavioral Science*, 1972, *4*, 253–255.

De Young, G. E., & Cattell, R. B. *The effect of underfactoring upon the proportion of pseudo-second order factors in rotational resolutions.* Unpublished manuscript, obtainable from G. E. De Young, St. Louis University, 1974.

Diamond, M. C., Drech, D., & Rosenzweig, M. R. The effects of an enriched environment on the histology of the rat cerebral cortex. *Journal of Comparative Neurology*, 1964, *123*, 111–119.

Diamond, S. *Personality and temperament.* New York: Harper, 1957.

Dickenson, W. A. *Therapist self-disclosure as a variable in psychotherapeutic process and outcome.* Unpublished doctoral dissertation, University of Kentucky, 1965.

Dielman, T. E., Barton, K., & Cattell, R. B. Relationships among family attitude dimensions and child motivation. *Journal of Genetic Psychology*, 1974, *124*, 295–302.

Dielman, T. E., & Cattell, R. B. The prediction of behavior problems in 6- to 8-year-old children from mothers' reports of child-rearing practices. *Journal of Clinical Psychology*, 1972, *28*, 13–17.

Dielman, T. E., & Digman, J. M. *A test of three-factor model of the second-order organization of personality traits in children as seen in teachers' behavior ratings.* Unpublished manuscript, University of Hawaii, 1968.

Dielman, T. E., Schuerger, J. M., & Cattell, R. B. *Prediction of junior high school achievement from I.Q. and objective-analytic factors U.I. 21, 24, 32.* Unpublished manuscript, Department of Psychology, University of Illinois, 1969.

Diers, C. J. Social desirability and acquiescence in response to personality items. *Journal of Consulting Psychology*, 1964, *28*, 71–77.

Digman, J. M. Principal dimensions of child personality as inferred from teachers' judgments. *Child Development*, 1963, *34*, 43–60. (a)

Digman, J. M. *The evidence for complexity.* Paper presented at the symposium *Factor analytic models of child personality: Simplicity vs. complexity* at the Convention of the Society for Research in Child Development, 1963. (b)

Digman, J. M. Child behavior ratings: Further

evidence for a multiple-factor model of child personality. *Educational and Psychological Measurement*, 1965, *25*, 787–799. (a)

Digman, J. M. *A test of multiple-factor model of child personality.* Unpublished manuscript, University of Hawaii, 1965. (b)

Digman, J. M. The structure of child personality as seen in behavior ratings. In R. M. Dreger (Ed.), *Multivariate personality research.* Baton Rouge, La.: Claitor, 1972.

DiMascio, A., Meyer, R. E., & Stifler, L. Effects of imipramine on individuals varying in level of depression. *American Journal of Psychiatry*, 1968, *124*, 55–58.

Diskin, P. A study of predictive empathy and the ability of student teachers to maintain harmonious interpersonal relations in selected elementary classrooms. *Dissertation Abstracts*, 1956, *16*, 1399.

Divesta, F. J., & Cox, L. Some dispositional correlates of conformity behavior. *Journal of Social Psychology*, 1960, *52*, 259–268.

Dollard, J., & Miller, N. E. *Personality and psychotherapy.* New York: McGraw-Hill, 1950.

Donovan, B. T. The extra-hypothalamic control of gonadotrophin secretion. In D. T. Baird & J. A. Strong (Eds.), *Control of gonadal steroid secretions.* Edinburgh: Edinburgh University Press, 1971.

Doob, L. W. The behavior of attitudes. *Psychological Review*, 1947, *54*, 135–156.

Doppelt, J. E. *The organization of mental abilities in the age range thirteen to seventeen.* Unpublished doctoral dissertation, Columbia University, 1950.

Dörner, G. Zur Frage einer neuroendokrinen Pathogenese, Prophylaxe und Therapie angeborener Sexualdeviationen. *Deutsche Medizinische Wochenschrift*, 1969, *94*, 390.

Dörner, G., Döcke, F., & Moustafa, S. Differential localization of a male and a female mating centre. *Journal of Reproduction and Fertility*, 1968, *17*, 583–586.

Dörner, G., & Hinz, G. Induction and prevention of male homosexuality by androgen. *Journal of Endocrinology*, 1968, *40*, 387–388.

Dougherty, F. E., Bartlett, E. S., & Izard, C. E. A cross-cultural comparison of emotion perception responses of schizophrenics. *Journal of Clinical Psychology*, 1976, in press.

Douvain, E. Social status and success strivings. *Journal of Abnormal and Social Psychology*, 1956, *52*, 219–223.

Downey, J. E. *The will-temperament and its testing.* New York: Harcourt Brace Jovanovich, 1923.

Drake, R. M. Test review. In O. K. Puros (Ed.), *The third mental measurements yearbook.* New Brunswick: Rutgers University Press, 1949.

Dreger, R. M. *Fundamentals of personality: A functional psychology of personality.* Philadelphia: Lippincott, 1962.

Dreger, R. M. Just how far can social change change personality? *Journal of Psychology*, 1966, *64*, 167–191.

Dreger, R. M. The establishment of diagnostic categories for the evaluation of specific therapies for children's emotional disorders. *Alabama Journal of Medical Science*, 1970, *7*, 56–60.

Dreger, R. M. (Ed.). *Multivariate personality research: Contributions to the understanding of personality in honor of Raymond B. Cattell.* Baton Rouge, La.: Claitor, 1972.

Dreger, R. M. Intellectual functioning. In K. S. Miller & R. M. Dreger (Eds.), *Comparative studies of blacks and whites in the United States: Psychological, sociological, and physiological.* New York: Seminar Press, 1973.

Dreger, R. M. *Changes in superego contents across a changing decade: 1964–1974.* Unpublished manuscript, Louisiana State University, 1975.

Dreger, R. M., & Barnert, M. Measurement of the custom and conscience functions of the superego. *Journal of Social Psychology*, 1969, *77*, 269–280.

Dreger, R. M., & Dreger, G. E. *Behavioral classification project. Report No. 1* (Proceedings of the Technical Assistance Project held at Jacksonville University, August 16–17, 1962). Jacksonville, Fla.: Behavioral Classification Project, 1962.

Drischel, H. Die vegetative Regulation als theoretisches Problem einer selbsttätigen Regelung. *Acta Neurovegetativa*, 1953, *6*, 318–346.

Drischel, H. Biokybernetische Grundlagen der vegetativen Regulations-prufungen. *Arztliche Forschung*, 1962, *16*, 474–484.

Dudek, F. J., & Kleemeier, R. W. A factorial investigation of flexibility. *Educational and Psychological Measurement*, 1950, *10*, 107–118.

Duffy, E. *Activation and behavior.* New York: Wiley, 1962.

Duffy. E. Activation. In N. S. Greenfield & R. A. Sternbach (Eds.), *Handbook of psychophysiology.* New York: Holt, Rinehart, & Winston, 1972.

Dulany, D. E. Hypotheses and habits in verbal "operant conditioning." *Journal of Abnormal and Social Psychology*, 1961, *63*, 251–263.

Dulany, D. E. The place of hypotheses and intentions: An analysis of verbal control in verbal conditioning. *Journal of Personality*, 1962, *30*, 102–129. (Supplement)

Dulany, D. E. Awareness, rules and propositional controls: A confrontation with S-P behavior theory. In D. Horton & T. Dixon (Eds.), *Verbal behavior and behavior theory.* New York: Prentice-Hall, 1967.

Duncanson, J. P. *Intelligence and the ability to learn.* Princeton: Educational Testing Service, 1964.

Dunn, J. P. Social class gradient of serum uric levels in males. *Journal of the American Medical Association*, 1963, *185*, 431–436.

Dye, N. W., & Very, P. S. Growth changes in factorial structure by age and sex. *Genetic Psychology Monographs*, 1968, *78*, 55–88.

Early, J. C. Attitude learning in children. *Journal of Educational Psychology*, 1968, *59*, 176–180.

Eason, R. G., & Dudley, L. M. Physiological and behavioral indicants of activation. *Psychophysiology*, 1971, *7*, 223–232.

Eaves, L. J. The structure of genotypic and environmental covariation for personality measurements: An analysis of the PEN. *British Journal of Social and Clinical Psychology*, 1973, *12*, 275–282.

Eaves, L. J., & Eysenck, H. J. The nature of extraversion: A genetical analysis. *Journal of Personality and Social Psychology*, 1975, *32*, 102–112.

Eaves, L. J., & Gale, J. S. A method for analyzing the genetic basis of covariation. *Behavior Genetics*, 1974, *4*, 253–267.

Eber, H. W. Toward oblique simple structure: A new version of Cattell's Maxplane Rotation Program for the 7094. *Multivariate Behavioral Research*, 1966, *1*, 112–125.

Eber, H. W., Cattell, R. B., & Delhees, K. H. Allocation of variance by computer synthesis programs: A strategy for improved use of multifactor scales. *Educational and Psychological Measurement*, 1976, in press.

Ebner, M. *An investigation of the role of the social environment in the generalization and persistence of the effect of a behavior modification program.* Unpublished doctoral dissertation, University of Oregon, 1967.

Eccles, J. (Ed.). *Brain and conscious experience.* Berlin: Springer, 1966.

Eckart, C., & Young, G. The approximation of one matrix by another of lower rank. *Psychometrika*, 1936, *1*, 211–218.

Eckehammer, B. Interactionism in personality from a historical perspective. *Psychological Bulletin*, 1974, *81*, 1026–1048.

Edwards, A. L. The relationship between the judged desirability of a trait and the probability that the trait will be endorsed. *Journal of Applied Psychology*, 1953, *37*, 90–93.

Edwards, A. L. *The social desirability variable in personality assessment and research.* New York: Dryden, 1957.

Edwards, A. L. *Edwards Personal Preference Schedule.* New York: Psychological Corporation, 1959. (a)

Edwards, A. L. Social desirability and personality test construction. In B. M. Bass & I. A. Berg (Eds.), *Objective approaches to personality assessment.* Princeton: Van Nostrand, 1959. (b)

Edwards, A. L. The social desirability hypothesis: Theoretical implications for personality measurement. In S. Messick & J. Ross (Eds.), *Measurement in personality and cognition.* New York: Wiley, 1962.

Edwards, A. L., & Diers, C. J. Social desirability and the factorial interpretation of the MMPI. *Educational and Psychological Measurement*, 1962, *22*, 501–510.

Edwards, A. L., & Diers, C. J. Neutral items as a measure of acquiescence. *Educational and Psychological Measurement*, 1963, *23*, 687–698.

Edwards, K. R., Jr. *Psychological changes associated with pregnancy and obstetric complications.* Unpublished doctoral dissertation, University of Miami (Florida), 1969.

Efron, D. H. (Ed.). *Psychopharmacology. A review of progress 1957–1967.* Washington, D.C.: U.S. Government Printing Office, 1968.

Ehrhardt, A. A., Epstein, R., & Money, J. Fetal androgens and female gender identity in the early-treated adrenogenital syndrome. *Johns Hopkins Medical Journal*, 1968, *122*, 160–167.

Ehrhardt, A. A., & Money, J. Progestin-induced hermaphroditism: IQ and psychosexual identity in a study of 10 girls. *Journal of Sex Research*, 1967, *3*, 83–100.

Ehrhardt, K. J. *Neuropsychologie "motivierten" Verhaltens.* Stuttgart: Enke, 1974.

Ehrman, L., Omenn, G. S., & Caspari, E. (Eds.). *Genetics, environment, and behavior*. New York: Academic Press, 1972.

Eisenberg, L., & Kanner, L. Early infantile autism: 1943–1955. *American Journal of Orthopsychiatry*, 1956, *26*, 556–566.

Eisenman, R., & Cherry, H. D. Creativity, authoritarianism, and birth order. *Journal of Social Psychology*, 1970, *80*, 233–235.

Ekman, P. E. Differential communication of affect by head and body cues. *Journal of Personality and Social Psychology*, 1965, *40*, 726–735.

Ekman, P., Friesen, W. V., & Ellsworth, P. *Emotion in the human face: Guidelines for research and an integration of findings*. New York: Pergamon Press, Inc., 1972.

Ekman, P. E., Sorenson, R., & Friesen, W. V. Pancultural elements in facial displays of emotion. *Science*, 1969, *164*, 86–88.

Ekstrand, B. R. A note on measuring response learning during paired-associate learning. *Journal of Verbal Learning and Verbal Behavior*, 1966, *5*, 344–347.

Elias, G. Self evaluation questionnaires as a projective measure of personality. *Journal of Consulting Psychology*, 1951, *15*, 496–500.

Elkes, J. Behavioral pharmacology in relation to psychiatry. In H. W. Gruhle et al. (Eds.), *Psychiatrie der Gegenwart* (Vol. 1, Pt. 1A). Berlin: Springer, 1967.

Elkind, D., Deblinger, J., & Adler, D. Motivation and creativity: The context effect. *American Educational Research Journal*, 1970, *7*, 351–357.

El-Koussey, A. H. *Trends of research in space abilities*. Paper presented at the International Colloquium on Factor Analysis, Paris, 1955.

Elliot, R. Effects of uncertainty about the nature and advent of a noxious stimulus (shock) upon heart rate. *Journal of Personality and Social Psychology*, 1966, *3*, 353–356.

Ellis, A. The validity of personality questionnaires. *Psychological Bulletin*, 1946, *43*, 385–440.

Ellis, A. A comparison of the use of direct and indirect phrasing in personality questionnaires. *Psychological Monographs*, 1947, *61*(3, Whole No. 284).

Ellis, A., & Conrad, H. S. The validity of personality inventories in military practice. *Psychological Bulletin*, 1948, *45*, 385–426.

Ellson, D. G. A method for identifying pattern clusters in test score profiles. *American Psychologist*, 1947, *2*, 425.

Ellsworth, R., Gilbert, A., Kracker, D., & Childers, B. *The outcome of psychiatric evaluation as perceived by staff and families* (Veterans Administration Research Rep. No. 8200). Roseburg, Ore.: Psychology Department, Veterans Administration Hospital, 1967.

Elston, R. C., & Gottesman, I. I. The analysis of quantitative inheritance simultaneously from twin and family data. *American Journal of Human Genetics*, 1968, *20*, 512–521.

Emmerich, W. Family role concepts of children ages six to ten. *Child Development*, 1961, *32*, 609–624.

Emmerich, W. Continuity and stability in early social development. *Child Development*, 1964, *35*, 311–333.

Emmerich, W. Continuity and stability in early social development: II. Teacher ratings. *Child Development*, 1966, *37*, 16–27.

Emmerich, W. Personality development and concepts of structure. *Child Development*, 1968, *39*, 671–690.

Endler, N. S. The person versus the situation—a pseudo issue? A response to Alker. *Journal of Personality*, 1973, *41*, 287–303.

Endler, N. S. The role of person by situation interactions in personality theory. In I. Uzgiris & F. Weizmann (Eds.), *The structuring of experience*. New York: Plenum Press, 1976.

Endler, N. S., & Hunt, J. McV. Sources of behavioral variance as measured by the S–R Inventory of Anxiousness. *Psychological Bulletin*, 1966, *65*, 336–346.

Endler, N. S., Hunt, J. McV. & Rosenstein, A. J. An S–R inventory of anxiousness. *Psychological Monographs*, 1962, *76* (Whole No. 536).

Engel, B. T., & Moos, R. H. The generality of specificity. *Archives of General Psychiatry*, 1967, *16*, 574–581.

Eppinger, H., & Hess, L. [*Vagotonia*]. New York: Nervous and Mental Disorders Publishing Co., 1915. (Originally published, 1910)

Epting, F. *Cognitive complexity and persuasibility across cognitive domains*. Unpublished doctoral dissertation, Ohio State University, 1967.

Eriksen, C. W. The case for perceptual defense. *Psychological Review*, 1954, *61*, 175–182.

Eriksen, C. W. (Ed.). *Behavior and awareness: A symposium of research and interpretation*. Durham, N.C.: Duke University Press, 1962.

Erikson, E. H. *Childhood and society*. New York: Norton, 1950.

Erikson, E. H. *Childhood and society* (2nd ed.). New York: Norton, 1963.

Eron, L. D. Relationship of TV viewing habits and aggressive behavior in children. *Journal of Abnormal and Social Psychology*, 1963, *67*, 193–196.

Escalona, S. K. Patterns of infantile experience and the developmental process. In *The psychoanalytic study of the child* (Vol. 18). New York: International Universities Press, 1963.

Escalona, S. K. *The roots of individuality*. London: Tavistock, 1969.

Essman, W. B. Psychopharmacology. In H. J. Eysenck (Ed.), *Handbook of abnormal psychology*. San Diego: Knapp, 1973.

Estes, W. K. *Modern learning theory*. New York: Appleton-Century-Crofts, 1954.

Estes, W. K., Burke, C. J., Atkinson, R. C., & Frankmann, J. P. Probabilistic discrimination learning. *Journal of Experimental Psychology*, 1957, *54*, 233–239.

Evans, G. C. Validity of ascendance measurements in group interaction. *Psychological Reports*, 1960, *7*, 114.

Everett, J. W. The mammalian female reproductive cycle and its controlling mechanisms. In W. C. Young (Ed.), *Sex and internal secretions* (Vol. 1). Baltimore: Williams & Wilkins, 1961.

Everitt, B. J., & Herbert, J. The effects of dexamethasone and androgens on sexual receptivity of female rhesus monkeys. *Journal of Endocrinology*, 1971, *51*, 575–588.

Everitt, B. J., Herbert, J., & Hamer, J. D. Sexual receptivity of bilaterally adrenalectomized female rhesus monkeys. *Physiology and Behavior*, 1972, *8*, 409–415.

Ewert, O. Erziehungsstile in ihrer Abhängigkeit von soziokulturellen Normen. In T. Herrmann (Ed.), *Psychologie der Erziehungsstile*. Göttingen: Hogrefe, 1966.

Exline, R. V. Interrelations among two dimensions of sociometric status, group congeniality and accuracy of social perception. *Sociometry*, 1960, *23*, 85–101.

Eyferth, K. Methoden zur Erfassung von Erziehungsstilen. In T. Herrmann (Ed.), *Psychologie der Erziehungsstile*. Göttingen: Hogrefe, 1966.

Eysenck, H. J. Critical notice of "Primary Mental Abilities" by L. L. Thurstone. *British Journal of Educational Psychology*, 1939, *9*, 270–275.

Eysenck, H. J. Types of personality: Factorial study of seven hundred neurotics. *Journal of Mental Science*, 1944, *90*, 851–861.

Eysenck, H. J. *Dimensions of personality*. London: Kegan Paul, 1947.

Eysenck, H. J. Criterion analysis: An application of the hypotheticodeductive method to factor analysis. *Psychological Review*, 1950, *57*, 38–53.

Eysenck, H. J. The effects of psychotherapy—an evaluation. *Journal of Consulting Psychology*, 1952, *16*, 319–324. (a)

Eysenck, H. J. *The scientific study of personality*. London: Methuen, 1952. (b)

Eysenck, H. J. (Ed.). *Experiments with drugs*. Oxford: Pergamon, 1953. (a)

Eysenck, H. J. Fragebogen als messmittel der personlichkeit. *Zeitschrift für Experimentelle und Angewante Psychologie*, 1953, *1*, 291–335. (b)

Eysenck, H. J. *The structure of human personality*. London: Methuen, 1953. (c)

Eysenck, H. J. The inheritance of extraversion-introversion. *Acta Psychologia*, 1956, *12*, 95–110. (a)

Eysenck, H. J. The questionnaire measurement of neuroticism and extraversion. *Rivista di Psicologia*, 1956, *50*, 113–140. (b)

Eysenck, H. J. *The dynamics of anxiety and hysteria*. London: Routledge & Kegan Paul, 1957.

Eysenck, H. J. *Manual of the Maudsley Personality Inventory*. London: University of London Press, 1959.

Eysenck, H. J. *Experiments in personality* (2nd ed.). London: Methuen, 1960. (a)

Eysenck, H. J. *The structure of human personality* (2nd ed.). London: Methuen, 1960. (b)

Eysenck, H. J. Classification and the problem of diagnosis. In H. J. Eysenck (Ed.), *Handbook of abnormal psychology*. New York: Basic Books, 1961. (a)

Eysenck, H. J. Eysenck on Cattell. A review of R. B. Cattell and I. H. Scheier, *The meaning and measurement of neuroticism and anxiety*. *Occupational Psychology*, 1961, *35*, 253–256. (b)

Eysenck, H. J. (Ed.). *Handbook of abnormal psychology*. New York: Basic Books, 1961. (c)

Eysenck, H. J. Conditioning and personality. *British Journal of Psychology*, 1962, *53*, 229–305.

Eysenck, H. J. The biological basis of personality. *Nature*, 1963, *199*, 1031–1034.

Eysenck, H. J. Biological factors in neurosis and crime. *Scientia*, 1964, December, 1–11. (a)

Eysenck, H. J. *Crime and personality.* Boston: Houghton Mifflin, 1964. (b)

Eysenck, H. J. Principles and methods of personality description, classification and diagnosis. *British Journal of Psychology,* 1964, *55,* 284–294. (c)

Eysenck, H. J. *The structure of human personality* (2nd ed.). London: Methuen, 1965.

Eysenck, H. J. *The biological basis of personality.* Springfield, Ill.: Charles C Thomas, 1967.

Eysenck, H. J. *The structure of human personality* (3rd ed.). London: Methuen, 1970.

Eysenck, H. J. (Ed.). *Readings in extraversion-introversion* (Vol. 3). *Bearings on psychological processes.* London: Staples, 1971.

Eysenck, H. J. Human typology, higher nervous activity, and factor analysis. In V. D. Nebylitsyn & J. A. Gray (Eds.), *Biological bases of individual behavior.* New York: Academic Press, 1972.

Eysenck, H. J. (Ed.). *Handbook of abnormal psychology* (2nd ed.). San Diego: Knapp, 1973.

Eysenck, H. J., & Eysenck, S. B. G. *Manual for the Eysenck Personality Inventory.* San Diego: Educational and Industrial Testing Service, 1963.

Eysenck, H. J., & Eysenck, S. B. G. On the unitary nature of extraversion. *Acta Psychologia,* 1967, *26,* 383–390.

Eysenck, H. J., & Eysenck, S. B. G. *Personality structure and measurement.* San Diego: Knapp; London: Routledge & Kegan Paul, 1969.

Eysenck, H. J., & Prell, D. B. The inheritance of neuroticism: An experimental study. *Journal of Mental Science,* 1951, *97,* 441–465.

Eysenck, H. J., & Rachman, S. *The causes and cures of neuroses.* London: Routledge & Kegan Paul, 1965.

Eysenck, S. B. G. Neurosis and psychosis: An experimental analysis. *Journal of Mental Science,* 1956, *102,* 517–529.

Eysenck, S. B. G. Personality dimensions in children. In H. J. Eysenck & S. B. G. Eysenck, *Personality structure and measurement.* San Diego: Knapp, 1969.

Eysenck, S. B. G., & Eysenck, H. J. The measurement of psychoticism: A study of factor stability and reliability. *British Journal of Social and Clinical Psychology,* 1968, *7,* 286–294.

Eysenck, S. B. G., & Eysenck, H. J. Scores on three personality variables as a function of age, sex, and social class. *British Journal of Social and Clinical Psychology,* 1969, *8,* 69–76.

Eysenck, S. B. G., & Eysenck, H. J. A comparative study of criminals and matched controls on three dimensions of personality. *British Journal of Social and Clinical Psychology,* 1971, *10,* 362–366.

Eysenck, S. B. G., & Eysenck, H. J. The questionnaire measurement of psychoticism. *Psychological Medicine,* 1972, *2,* 50–55.

Fahrenberg, J. *Psychophysiologische Personlichkeitsforschung.* Gottingen: Hogrefe, 1967.

Fahrenberg, J. Körperlich-funktionelle Beschwerden und Personlichkeitsmerkmale. *Nervenarzt,* 1969, *40,* 111–116.

Fahrenberg, J. Die Freiburger Beschwerdeliste FBL. *Zeitschrift für Klinische Psychologie,* 1975, *4,* 79–100.

Fahrenberg, J., Kuhn, M., Kulick, B., & Myrtek. Methodenentwicklung für psychologische Zeitreihenstudien. Unpublished manuscript, Department of Psychology, University of Freiburg, 1976.

Fahrenberg, J., & Myrtek, M. Ein kritischer Beitrag zur psychophysiologischen Persönlichkeitsforschung. *Zeitschrift für angewandte und experimentelle Psychologie,* 1966, *13,* 222–247.

Falconer, D. S. *Introduction to quantitative genetics.* Edinburgh: Oliver & Boyd, 1960.

Fantz, R. L., Ordy, J. M., & Udelf, M. S. Maturation of pattern vision in infants, during the first six months. *Journal of Comparative and Physiological Psychology,* 1962, *55,* 907–917.

Farber, I. E. The things people say to themselves. *American Psychologist,* 1963, *18,* 185–197.

Farber, I. E., & Spence, K. W. Complex learning and conditioning as a function of anxiety. *Journal of Experimental Psychology,* 1953, *45,* 120–125.

Fargo, G. A., Behrns, C., & Nolen, P. *Behavior modification in the classroom.* Belmont, Calif.: Wadsworth, 1970.

Faterson, H. F. Articulateness of experience: An extension of the field-dependence-independence concept. In S. Messick & J. Ross (Eds.), *Measurement in personality and cognition.* New York: Wiley, 1962.

Faterson, H. F., & Witkin, H. A. Longitudinal study of the development of the body concept. *Developmental Psychology,* 1970, *2,* 429–438.

Feigenbaum, K. D. A pilot investigation of the effects of training techniques designed to accelerate children's acquisition of conservation of discontinuous quantity. *Journal of Genetic Psychology,* 1971, *119,* 13–23.

Feigl, H. The "mental" and the "physical." In H. Feigl, M. Scriven, & G. Maxwell (Eds.), *Concepts, theories, and the mind-body problem* (Vol. 2). *Minnesota studies in the philosophy of science.* Minneapolis: University of Minnesota Press, 1958.

Feigl, H., & Brodbeck, M. *Readings in the philosophy of science.* New York: Appleton-Century-Crofts, 1953.

Feigl, H., & Scriven, M. *The foundations of science and the concepts of psychology and psychoanalysis.* Minneapolis: University of Minnesota Press, 1956.

Feld, S. C. Longitudinal study of the origins of achievement striving. *Journal of Personality and Social Psychology,* 1967, *7,* 408–414.

Feldman, S. M., & Underwood, B. J. Stimulus recall following paired-associate learning. *Journal of Experimental Psychology,* 1957, *53,* 11–15.

Feledy, A. M. The expression of the emotions. *Psychological Review,* 1914, *21,* 33–34.

Fenichel, O. *The psychoanalytic theory of neurosis.* New York: Norton, 1945.

Ferguson, G. A. On transfer and the abilities of man. *Canadian Journal of Psychology,* 1956, *10,* 121–131.

Ferster, C. B. Positive reinforcement and behavioral deficits in autistic children. *Child Development,* 1961, *32,* 437–456.

Ferster, C. B. *Classification of behavioral pathology.* Unpublished manuscript, Institute for Behavioral Research, Silver Spring, Md., 1964.

Ferster, C. B., & Perrott, M. C. *Behavior principles.* New York: Appleton-Century-Crofts, 1968.

Festinger, L. Informal social communication. *Psychological Review,* 1950, *57,* 271–282.

Festinger, L. A theory of social comparison processes. *Human Relations,* 1954, *7,* 117–140.

Festinger, L. *A theory of cognitive dissonance.* New York: Row, Peterson, 1957.

Fiedler, F. E., & Meuwise, W. A. T. Leader's contribution to task performance in cohesive and uncohesive groups. *Journal of Abnormal and Social Psychology,* 1963, *67,* 83–87.

Fine, B. J., & Sweeney, D. R. Personality traits, and situational factors, and catecholamine excretion. *Journal of Experimental Research in Personality,* 1968, *3,* 15–27.

Fischer, G. H., & Roppert, J. (Eds.). *Lineare Strukturen in Mathematik und Statistik.* Wuerzburg: Physika, 1965.

Fishbein, M., & Ajzen, I. Attitudes and opinions. *Annual Review of Psychology,* 1972, *23,* 487–544.

Fishbein, M., & Ajzen, I. *Belief, attitude, intention, and behavior: An introduction to theory and research.* Reading, Mass.: Addison-Wesley, 1975.

Fisher, R. A. The correlation between relatives on the supposition of Mendelian inheritance. *Transactions of the Royal Society (Edinburgh),* 1918, *52,* 399–433.

Fiske, D. W. Consistency of factorial structures of personality ratings from different sources. *Journal of Abnormal and Social Psychology,* 1949, *44,* 329–344.

Fiske, D. W. *Measuring the concepts of personality.* Chicago: Aldine, 1971.

Fitts, W. H. *The experience of psychotherapy: What it's like for client and therapist.* Princeton: Van Nostrand, 1965. (a)

Fitts, W. H. *Manual: Tennessee Self-Concept Scale.* Nashville, Tenn.: Counselor Recordings and Tests, 1965. (b)

Fitzgerald, J. M., Nesselroade, J. R., & Baltes, P. B. Emergence of adult intellectual structure: Prior to or during adolescence? *Developmental Psychology,* 1973, *9,* 114–119.

Flanagan, J. C. *Factor analysis in the study of personality.* Stanford: Stanford University Press, 1935.

Flavell, J. H. *The developmental psychology of Jean Piaget.* Princeton, Toronto: Van Nostrand, 1963.

Fleishman, E. A. A comparative study of aptitude patterns in unskilled and skilled motor performance. *Journal of Applied Psychology,* 1957, *41,* 263–272.

Fleishman, E. A. *The structure and measurement of physical fitness.* Englewood Cliffs, N.J.: Prentice-Hall, 1964.

Fleishman, E. A. Human abilities and the acquisition of skill. In E. A. Bilodeau (Ed.), *Acquisition of skill.* New York: Academic Press, 1966.

Fleishman, E. A. Individual differences in motor learning. In R. B. Gagne (Ed.), *Learning and individual differences.* Columbus, Ohio: Merrill, 1967.

Fleishman, E. A., & Hempel, W. E. The relation between abilities and improvement with practice in a visual discrimination reaction task. *Journal of Experimental Psychology,* 1955, *49,* 301–312.

Fleiss, J. G., & Zubin, J. On the methods and

theory of clustering. *Multivariate Behavioral Research*, 1969, *4*, 235–250.

Flugel, J. C. Practice, fatigue and oscillation. *British Journal of Psychology* (Monograph Supplement 4, No. 13), 1929.

Fodor, J. A. Could meaning be an $r_m$? *Journal of Verbal Learning and Verbal Behavior*, 1965, *4*, 73–81.

Fodor, J. A. More about mediators: A reply to Berlyne and Osgood. *Journal of Verbal Learning and Verbal Behavior*, 1966, *5*, 412–415.

Foulds, G. The reliability of psychiatric, and the validity of psychological diagnosis. *Journal of Mental Science*, 1955, *101*, 851–862.

Fowler, H. *Curiosity and exploratory behavior*. New York: Macmillan, 1965.

Fowler, R. D. Purposes and usefulness of the Alabama program. In *Three approaches to the automatic interpretation of the MMPI*. Symposium presented at the meeting of the American Psychological Association, Chicago, September 5, 1965.

Fowler, W. Sequence and styles in cognitive development. In I. Uzgiris & F. Weizmann (Eds.), *The structuring of experience*. New York: Plenum Press, 1976.

Fox, H. M., Gifford, S., Valenstein, A. F., & Murawski, B. J. Psychophysiological correlation of 17-ketosteroids and 17-hydroxycorticosteroids in 21 pairs of monozygotic twins. *Journal of Psychosomatic Research*, 1970, *14*, 71–79.

Fox, S. Self-maintained sensory input and sensory deprivation in monkeys: A behavioral and neuro-pharmacological study. *Journal of Comparative and Psyiological Psychology*, 1962, *55*, 438–444.

Frank, J. D. *The role of hope in psychotherapy*. Paper presented at the Kentucky Centennial Psychotherapy Symposium, University of Kentucky, 1965.

Frankenhaeuser, M. Experimental approaches to the study of catecholamines and emotion. In L. Levi (Ed.), *Emotions: Their parameters and measurement*. New York: Raven, 1975. (a)

Frankenhaeuser, M. Sympathetic-adrenomedullary activity, behaviour and the psychosocial environment. In P. H. Venables & M. J. Christie (Eds.), *Research in psychophysiology*. New York: Wiley, 1975. (b)

Frankenhaeuser, M., Mellis, I., Rissler, A., Björkvall, C., & Pátkai, P. Catecholamine excretion as related to cognitive and emotional reaction patterns. *Psychosomatic Medicine*, 1968, *30*, 109–120.

Franks, C. M. Personality and eyeblink conditioning seven years later. *Acta Psychologica*, 1963, *21*, 295–312.

Franks, C. M. Individual differences in conditioning and associated techniques. In J. Wolpe, A. Slater, & L. J. Reyna (Eds.), *The conditioning therapies*. New York: Holt, Rinehart, & Winston, 1964.

Franks, C. M. (Ed.). *Behavior therapy: Appraisal and status*. New York: McGraw-Hill, 1969.

Franks, C. M., & Franks, V. "Conditionability" as a general factor of man's performance in different conditioning situations. In V. D. Nebylitsyn (Organizer), *Physiological bases of individual psychological differences*. Symposium presented at

the 18th International Congress of Psychology, Moscow, 1966.

Frazee, H. E. Children who later become schizophrenic. *Smith College Studies in Social Work*, 1953, *23*, 125–149.

Frederiksen, N. Toward a taxonomy of situations. *American Psychologist*, 1972, *27*, 114–123.

Frederiksen, N., & Messick, S. Response set as a measure of personality. *Educational and Psychological Measurement*, 1959, *19*, 137–157.

Freedman, D. G., & Keller, B. Inheritance of behavior in infants. *Science*, 1963, *140*, 196–198.

Freeman, F. S. *Theory and practice of psychological testing*. New York: Holt, Rinehart, & Winston, 1955.

Freeman, R. V., & Grayson, H. M. Maternal attitudes in schizophrenia. *Journal of Abnormal and Social Psychology*, 1955, *50*, 45–52.

French, E. G. A note on the Edwards Personal Preference Schedule for use with basic airmen. *Educational and Psychological Measurement*, 1958, *18*, 109–115.

French, J. W. The description of aptitude and achievement tests in terms of rotated factors. *Psychometric Monographs*, No. 5. Chicago: University of Chicago Press, 1951.

French, J. W. *The description of personality measurements in terms of rotated factors*. Princeton, N.J.: Educational Testing Service, 1953.

French, J. W., Ekstrom, R. B., & Price, L. A. *Manual for kit of reference tests for cognitive factors*. Princeton, N.J.: Educational Testing Service, 1963.

Freud, A. The concept of developmental lines. In *The Psychoanalytic Study of the Child* (Vol. 18). New York: International Universities Press, 1963.

Freud, S. The dynamics of transference. In E. Jones (Ed. and trans.), *Collected papers* (Vol. 2). London: Hogarth, 1924.

Freud, S. *A general introduction to psychoanalysis*. New York: Liveright, 1935.

Freud, S. *The problem of anxiety*. New York: Norton, 1936.

Freud, S. *An outline of psychoanalysis* (Translated). New York: Norton, 1949.

Freud, S. *The ego and the id* (J. Riviere, trans.). London: Hogarth, 1957. (Originally published, 1927.)

Friedman, H. S., Rubin, Z., Jacobson, J., & Clore, G. L. *Induced affect and attraction toward dating partners and opposite-sex strangers*. Unpublished manuscript, Harvard University, 1975.

Friedman, N. *The social nature of psychological research*. New York: Basic Books, 1967.

Friedrich, L. K., & Stein, A. H. Aggressive and prosocial television programs and the natural behavior of preschool children. *Monographs of the Society for Research in Child Development*, 1973, *38*(4, Serial No. 151).

Frois-Wittman, J. The judgment of facial expression. *Journal of Experimental Psychology*, 1930, *13*, 113–151.

Fromkin, H. L. Feelings of interpersonal undistinctiveness: An unpleasant affective state. Unpublished manuscript, Purdue University, 1972.

Fromkin, H., Dipbaye, R. L., & Pyle, M. *Reversal of the attitude similarity-dissimilarity*

effect by uniqueness deprivation. Unpublished manuscript, Purdue University, 1971.

Fromm, E. *Escape from freedom*. New York: Farrar & Rinehart, 1941.

Fromm, E. *The sane society*. New York: Holt, Rinehart, & Winston, 1955.

Fry, C. L. Personality and acquisition factors in the development of co-ordination strategy. *Journal of Personality and Social Psychology*, 1965, *2*, 403–407.

Fulker, D. W. Maternal buffering of rodent genotypic responses to stress: A complex genotype-environment interaction. *Behavioral Genetics*, 1970, *1*, 119–124.

Fulker, D. W. Applications of a simplified triple-test cross. *Behavioral Genetics*, 1972, *2*, 185–197.

Fuller, G. B. *Research in alcoholism with the 16 P.F.* (IPAT Information Bulletin No. 12). Champaign, Ill.: Institute for Personality and Ability Testing, 1966.

Fuller, J. L., & Thompson, W. R. *Behavior genetics*. New York: Wiley, 1960.

Furneaux, W., & Gibson, H. B. A children's personality inventory designed to measure neuroticism and extraversion. *British Journal of Educational Psychology*, 1961, *31*, 204–207.

Gagné, R. M. *The conditions of learning*. New York: Holt, Rinehart, & Winston, 1965.

Gagné, R. M. (Ed.). *Learning and individual differences*. Columbus, Ohio: Merrill, 1967.

Gaier, E. L., Lee, M. C., & McQuitty, L. L. Response patterns in a test of logical inference. *Educational and Psychological Measurement*, 1953, *13*, 550–567.

Gale, A. The psychophysiology of individual differences: Studies in extraversion and the EEG. In P. Kline (Ed.), *New approaches to psychological measurement*. London: Wiley, 1973.

Galton, F. *Hereditary genius*. New York: D. Appleton, 1870.

Galton, F. Measurement of character. *Fortnightly Review*, 1884, *42*, 179–185.

Garai, J. E., & Scheinfeld, A. Sex differences in mental and behavioral traits. *Genetic Psychology Monographs*, 1968, *77*, 169–299.

Gardner, R. L., & Lyon, M. F. X chromosome inactivation studied by injection of a single cell into the mouse blastocyst. *Nature*, 1971, *231*, 385–386.

Gardner, R. W., Holzman, P. E., Klein, G. S., Linton, H., & Spence, D. D. Cognitive control: A study of individual consistencies in cognitive behavior. *Psychological Issues*, 1959, *1*, 1–186.

Garrett, H. E. A developmental theory of intelligence. *American Psychologist*, 1946, *1*, 372–378.

Garron, D. C. Sex-linked recessive inheritance of spatial and numerical abilities, and Turner's syndrome. *Psychological Review*, 1970, *77*, 147–152.

Gates, G. S. An experimental study of the growth of social perception. *The Journal of Educational Psychology*, 1923, *14*, 449–461.

Gates, G. S. A test for ability to interpret facial expressions. *Psychological Bulletin*, 1925, *22*, 120.

Gazzaniga, M. S., & Blakemore, C. (Eds.). *Handbook of psychobiology*. New York: Academic Press, 1975.

Gebel, A. S. Self-perception and leaderless

group discussion status. *Journal of Social Psychology*, 1954, *40*, 309–318.

Geddes, L. A. *Electrodes and the measurement of bioelectric events*. New York: Wiley, 1972.

Geer, J. H., & Turteltaub, A. Fear reduction following observation of a model. *Journal of Personality and Social Psychology*, 1967, *6*, 327–331.

Gehring, U., Tomkins, G. M., & Ohno, S. Effect of the androgen-insensitivity mutation on a cytoplasmic receptor for dihydrotestosterone. *Nature, New Biology*, 1971, *232*, 106–107.

Geidt, H. F., & Downing, L. An extraversion scale for the MMPI. *Journal of Clinical Psychology*, 1961, *17*, 156–159.

Gellhorn, E. Motion and emotion: The role of proprioception in the physiology and pathology of the emotions. *Psychological Review*, 1964, *71*(6), 457–472.

Gellhorn, E. *Principles of autonomic-somatic integrations*. Minneapolis: University of Minnesota Press, 1967.

Gellhorn, E. The emotions and the ergotropic and trophotropic systems. *Psychologische Forschung*, 1970, *34*, 48–94.

Gengerelli, J. A., & Butler, B. V. A method for comparing the profiles of several population samples. *Journal of Psychology*, 1955, *40*, 247–268.

Gerall, A. A., Hendricks, S. E., Johnson, L. L., & Brounds, W. T. Effects of early castration in male rats on adult sexual behavior. *Journal of Comparative and Physiological Psychology*, 1967, *64*, 206–212.

Gerard, H. B. Emotional uncertainty and social comparison. *Human Relations*, 1954, *7*, 117–140.

Gerard, H. B., & Miller, N. Group dynamics. *Annual Review of Psychology*, 1967, *18*, 287–332.

Gergen, K. J., & Jones, E. E. Mental illness, predictability, and affective consequences as stimulus factors in person perception. *Journal of Abnormal and Social Psychology*, 1963, *67*, 95–104.

Gershon, S., & Raskin, A. *Genesis and treatment of psychologic disorders in the elderly*. New York: Raven Press, 1975.

Gesell, A., & Amatruda, C. S. *Developmental diagnosis*. New York: Paul B. Hoeber, 1947.

Gesell, A., & Ilg, F. L. *Infant and child in the culture of today*. New York: Harper, 1943.

Gesell, A., Ilg, F., Ames, L. B., & Rodell, J. L. *Infant and child in the culture of today: The guidance of development in home and nursery school* (Rev. ed.). New York: Harper & Row, 1974.

Getzels, J. W., & Jackson, P. W. *Creativity and intelligence: Explorations with gifted students*. London, New York: Wiley, 1962.

Gewirtz, H., & Gewirtz, J. Caretaking settings, background events and behavior differences in four Israeli child-rearing environments: Some preliminary trends. In B. Foss (Ed.), *Determinants of infant behavior* (Vol. 4). London: Methuen, 1967.

Gibb, C. Changes in culture patterns of Australia, 1906–1944, as determined by *P*-technique. *Journal of Social Psychology*, 1956, *43*, 225–238.

Gibbons, B. D. *A study of the relationships between factors found in Cattell's Sixteen Personality Factor Questionnaire and factors found in the Guilford personality inventories*. Unpublished doctoral dissertation, University of Southern California, 1966.

Gibson, D. C. The young child's awareness of affect. *Child Development*, 1969, *40*(2), 629–640.

Gibson, J. J. A critical review of the concept of set in contemporary experimental psychology. *Psychological Bulletin*, 1941, *38*, 781–817.

Gibson, J. J. The concept of the stimulus in psychology. *American Psychologist*, 1960, *15*, 694–703.

Gilberstadt, H. Construction and application of MMPI cookbooks. In J. N. Butcher (Ed.), *MMPI: Research developments and clinical applications*. New York: McGraw-Hill, 1969.

Gilberstadt, H., & Duker, J. *A handbook for clinical and actuarial MMPI interpretation*. Philadelphia: Saunders, 1965.

Ginott, H. G. *Group psychotherapy with children: The theory and practice of play-therapy*. New York: McGraw-Hill, 1961.

Glanzer, M. The role of stimulus satiation in spontaneous alternation. *Journal of Experimental Psychology*, 1953, *45*, 387–393.

Glanzer, M. Individual performance, R–R theory and perception. In R. M. Gagne (Ed.), *Learning and individual differences*. Columbus: Merrill, 1967.

Glass, D. C. (Ed.). *Environmental influences: Proceedings of a conference under the auspices of Russell Sage Foundation, the Social Science Research Council, and the Rockefeller University*. New York: Rockefeller University Press, 1968. (a)

Glass, D. C. (Ed.). *Genetics*. New York: Rockefeller University Press, 1968. (b)

Gleser, G., & Gottschalk, L. A. Personality characteristics of schizophrenics in relationship to sex and current functioning. *Journal of Clinical Psychology*, 1967, *23*, 349–354.

Gloor, P. A., & Feindel, M. Affective behaviour and temporal lobe. In M. Monnier (Ed.), *Physiologie und Pathophysiologie des vegetativen Nervensystems*. Stuttgart: Hippokrates, 1963.

Glueck, B. C. Current personality assessment research. *International Psychiatry Clinics*, 1966, *3*, 205–227.

Glueck, S., & Glueck, E. Working mother and delinquency. *Mental Hygiene*, 1957, *41*, 327–352.

Goldberg, L. R. A model of item ambiguity in personality assessment. *Educational and Psychological Measurement*, 1963, *23*, 467–492.

Goldberg, L. R. Simple models or simple processes? Some research on clinical judgments. *American Psychologist*, 1968, *23*, 483–496.

Goldberg, L. R. Some recent trends in personality assessment. *Journal of Personality Assessment*, 1972, *36*, 547–560.

Goldberg, L. R. Parameters of personality inventory construction and utilization: A comparison of prediction strategies and tactics. *Multivariate Behavioral Research Monographs*, 1972, *7*, No. 2.

Goldberg, L. R. Objective diagnostic tests and measurements. *Annual Review of Psychology*, 1974, *25*, 343–366.

Goldberg, L. R. *Language and personality: Toward a taxonomy of trait descriptive terms*. Paper presented at the annual meeting of the Society for Multivariate Experimental Psychology, Oregon, Nov. 1975.

Goldberg, S. C., Hunt, R. G., Cohen, W., & Meadow, A. Some personality correlates of perceptual distortion in the direction of group conformity. *American Psychologist*, 1954, *9*, 378. (Abstract)

Goldfarb, W. Infant rearing as a factor in foster home placement. *American Journal of Orthopsychiatry*, 1944, *14*, 162–167.

Goldfarb, W. Psychological privation in infancy and subsequent adjustment. *American Journal of Orthopsychiatry*, 1945, *15*, 247–255.

Goldfoot, D. A., Feder, H. H., & Goy, R. W. Development of bisexuality in the male rat treated neonatally with androstenedione. *Journal of Comparative and Physiological Psychology*, 1969, *67*, 41–45.

Goldfried, M. R., & Merbaum, M. (Eds.). *Behavior change through self-control*. New York: Holt, Rinehart, & Winston, 1973.

Goldin, P. C. A review of children's reports of parent behaviors. *Psychological Bulletin*, 1969, *71*, 222–236.

Goldstein, A. P. Interpersonal attraction: Social psychological perspectives on the psychotherapeutic relationship. In M. J. Feldman (Ed.), *Buffalo studies in psychotherapy and behavioral change*. Buffalo, N.Y.: State University of New York at Buffalo Press, 1968.

Golightly, C., & Byrne, D. Attitude statements as positive and negative reinforcements. *Science*, 1964, *146*, 798–799.

Goodenough, F. L. Expression of the emotions in a blind-deaf child. *Journal of Abnormal and Social Psychology*, 1932–33, *27*, 328–333.

Goodfellow, L. D. The human element in probability. *Journal of General Psychology*, 1940, *23*, 201–205.

Goodman, C. H. Factorial analysis of Thurstone's seven primary abilities. *Psychometrika*, 1943, *8*, 121–129.

Goodstein, L. D. Behavior theoretical views of counseling. In B. Steffbel (Ed.), *Theories of counseling*. New York: McGraw-Hill, 1965.

Gordon, L. V. Validities of the forced-choice and questionnaire methods of personality measurement. *Journal of Applied Psychology*, 1951, *35*, 407–412.

Gordon, L. V. Some interrelationships among personality item characteristics. *Educational and Psychological Measurement*, 1953, *13*, 264–272.

Gordon, L. V., & Stapleton, E. S. Fakability of a forced choice personality test under realistic high school employment conditions. *Journal of Applied Psychology*, 1956, *40*, 258–262.

Gorfein, D. Conformity behavior and the "authoritarian personality." *Journal of Social Psychology*, 1961, *53*, 121–125.

Gormly, J. Sociobehavioral and physiological responses to interpersonal disagreements. *Journal of Experimental Research in Personality*, 1971, *5*, 216–222.

Gorsuch, R. L. *The clarification of some superego factors*. Unpublished doctoral dissertation, University of Illinois, 1965.

Gorsuch, R. L. *Factor analysis*. Philadelphia: Saunders, 1974.

Gorsuch, R. L., & Cattell, R. B. *An experimental clarification of the superego structure* (Advance reprint). Champaign, Ill.: Laboratory of Personality and Group Analysis, 1966.

Gorsuch, R. L., & Cattell, R. B. Second-stratum personality factors defined in the questionnaire realm by the 16 P.F. *Multivariate Behavioral Research*, 1967, *2*, 211–224.

Goslin, D. A. (Ed.). *Handbook of socialization theory and research.* Chicago: Rand McNally, 1969.

Goss, A. E. Early behaviorism and verbal mediating responses. *American Psychologist*, 1961, *16*, 285–298.

Gottesman, I. I. Heritability of personality: A demonstration. *Psychological Monographs*, 1963, 77(9, Whole No. 572).

Gottesman, I. I. Personality and natural selection. In S. G. Vandenberg (Ed.), *Methods and goals in human behavior genetics.* New York: Academic Press, 1965.

Gottesman, I. I. Genetic variance in adaptive personality traits. *Journal of Child Psychology and Psychiatry*, 1966, *7*, 199–208.

Gottschalk, L. A. Phasic circulating biochemical reflections of transient mental content. In A. J. Mandell & M. P. Mandell (Eds.), *Psychochemical research in man.* New York: Academic Press, 1969.

Gottschalk, L. A., & Gleser, G. G. *The measurement of psychological states through the content analyses of verbal behavior.* Berkeley: University of California Press, 1969.

Gouaux, C. Induced affective states and interpersonal attraction. *Journal of Personality and Social Psychology*, 1971, *20*, 27–43.

Gough, H. G. An additional study of food aversions. *Journal of Abnormal and Social Psychology*, 1946, *41*, 86–88.

Gough, H. G. *California Psychological Inventory.* Palo Alto: Consulting Psychologists Press, 1956.

Gouldner, A. W. (Ed.). *Studies in leadership.* New York: Harper, 1950.

Goulet, L. R. Anxiety (drive) and verbal learning: Implications for research and some methodological considerations. *Psychological Bulletin*, 1968, *69*, 235–247.

Goulet, L. R., & Mazzei, J. Verbal learning and confidence thresholds as a function of test anxiety, intelligence, and stimulus similarity. *Journal of Experimental Research in Personality*, 1969, *3*, 247–252.

Govallo, V. I. [On the stability of the typological properties of the higher nervous activity in young children.] *Doklady Akademii Nauk SSSR*, 1961, *136*, 737–740. (*Psychological Abstracts*, 1962, *36*, IFD34V.)

Gowan, J. C. Relationship between leadership and personality measures. *Journal of Educational Research*, 1955, *48*, 623–627.

Goy, R. W. Organising effects of androgen on the behaviour of rhesus monkeys. In R. P. Michael (Ed.), *Endocrinology and human behaviour.* London: Oxford University Press, 1968.

Graesser, R. F. Guessing on multiple choice tests. *Educational and Psychological Measurement*, 1958, *18*, 617–620.

Graffam, D. T. Dickinson College personality changes. *The Dickinson Alumnus*, 1967, *44*, 2–7.

Graham, D. T. Psychosomatic medicine. In N. S. Greenfield & R. A. Sternbach (Eds.), *Handbook of psychophysiology.* New York: Holt, Rinehart, & Winston, 1972.

Graham, F. K., & Clifton, R. K. Heart-rate change as a component of the orienting response. *Psychological Bulletin*, 1966, *65*, 305–320.

Graham, W. R. An experimental comparison of methods to control faking of inventories. *Educational and Psychological Measurements*, 1958, *18*, 387–401.

Gray, J. A. *Pavlov's typology.* Oxford: Pergamon; New York: Macmillan, 1964.

Gray, J. A. Strength of the nervous system, introversion-extraversion, conditionability and arousal. *Behaviour Research and Therapy*, 1967, *5*, 151–169.

Gray, J. A. The Lister Lecture, 1967: The physiological basis of personality. *Advancement of Science*, 1968, *24*, 293–305.

Gray, J. A. Sex differences in emotional behaviour in mammals including man: Endocrine bases. *Acta Psychologica*, 1971, *35*, 29–46.

Gray, J. A. The structure of the emotions and the limbic system. In J. Knight (Ed.), *Physiology, emotion, and psychosomatic illness.* Amsterdam: Associated Scientific Publishers, 1972.

Gray, J. A. Causal theories of personality and how to test them. In J. R. Royce (Ed.), *Multivariate analysis and psychological theory.* London: Academic Press, 1973.

Gray, J. A. The behavioural inhibition system: A possible substrate for anxiety. In P. Feldman & A. M. Broadhurst (Eds.), *Theoretical and experimental bases of behaviour modification.* London: Wiley, 1976.

Gray, J. A. Drug effects on fear and frustration: Possible limbic site of action of minor tranquilizers. In L. Iversen, S. Iversen, & S. Snyder (Eds.), *Handbook of psychopharmacology.* New York: Plenum Press, in press.

Gray, J. A., & Ball, G. G. Frequency-specific relation between hippocampal theta rhythm, behavior, and amobarbital action. *Science*, 1970, *168*, 1246–1248.

Gray, J. A., & Buffery, A. W. H. Sex differences in emotional and cognitive behavior in mammals including man: Adaptive and neural bases. *Acta Psychologica*, 1971, *35*, 89–111.

Gray, J. A., Drewett, R. F., & Lalljee, B. Effects of neonatal castration and testosterone injection on adult open-field behaviour in rats with atypical sex differences in defecation. *Animal Behaviour*, 1975, *23*, 733–778.

Gray, J. A., & Lalljee, B. Sex differences in emotional behavior in the rat: Correlation between open-field defecation and active avoidance. *Animal Behaviour*, 1974, *22*, 856–861.

Gray, J. A., Lean, J., & Keynes, A. Infant androgen treatment and adult open-field behaviour: Direct effects and effects of injections to siblings. *Physiology and Behavior*, 1964, *4*, 177–181.

Gray, J. A., Levine, S., & Broadhurst, P. L. Gonadal hormone injections in infancy and adult emotional behaviour. *Animal Behaviour*, 1965, *13*, 33–45.

Gray, J. A., McNaughton, N., James, D. T. D., & Kelly, P. H. Effect of minor tranquillisers on hippocampal theta rhythm mimicked by depletion of forebrain noradrenaline. *Nature*, 1975, *258*, 424–425.

Gray, S. W. Perceived similarity to parents and adjustment. *Child Development*, 1959, *30*, 91–107.

Graziano, A. M. A factor analytic investigation of the concept of personality rigidity. *Dissertation Abstracts*, 1962, *22*(7), 2465.

Green, R. F. Does a selection situation induce testees to bias their answers on interest and temperament tests? *Educational and Psychological Measurement*, 1951, *11*, 503–515.

Green, R. F. *The measurement of mood* (Technical Report, Office of Naval Research). Washington, D.C.: U.S. Government Printing Office, 1964.

Green, R. F., & Nowlis, V. *A factor analytic study of the domain of mood with independent experimental validation of the factors.* Paper presented at the meeting of the American Psychological Association, New York, September, 1957.

Greenberg, D. J., & Weizmann, F. The measurement of visual attention in infants: A comparison of two methodologies. *Journal of Experimental Child Psychology*, 1971, *3*, 235–243.

Greenberg, H., Guerino, R., Lashen, M., Mayer, D., & Piskowski, D. Order of birth as a determinant of personality and attitudinal characteristics. *Journal of Social Psychology*, 1963, *60*, 221–230.

Greenberger, E., O'Connor, J., & Sorenson, A. Personality, cognitive, and academic correlates of problem-solving flexibility. *Developmental Psychology*, 1971, *4*, 416–424.

Greenfield, N. S., & Sternbach, R. A. (Eds.). *Handbook of psychophysiology.* New York: Holt, Rinehart, & Winston, 1972.

Greenspoon, J. *The effect of verbal and nonverbal stimuli on the frequency of members of two verbal response classes.* Unpublished doctoral dissertation, Indiana University, 1950.

Greer, F. L. *Small group effectiveness.* Philadelphia: Institute for Research in Human Relations, 1955.

Greer, F. L., Galanter, E. H., & Nordlie, P. G. Interpersonal knowledge and individual and group effectiveness. *Journal of Abnormal and Social Psychology*, 1954, *49*, 411–414.

Griffitt, W. B. Interpersonal attraction as a function of self-concept and personality similarity-dissimilarity. *Journal of Personality and Social Psychology*, 1966, *4*, 581–584.

Griffitt, W. B. Attraction toward a stranger as a function of direct and associated reinforcement. *Psychonomic Science*, 1968, *11*, 147–148.

Griffitt, W. B., & Guay, P. "Object" evaluation and conditioned affect. *Journal of Experimental Research in Personality*, 1969, *4*, 1–8.

Griffitt, W. B., & Veitch, R. Hot and crowded: Influence of population density and temperature on interpersonal affective behavior. *Journal of Personality and Social Psychology*, 1971, *17*, 92–98.

Grinder, R. E. Relationship between behavioral and cognitive dimensions of conscience in middle childhood. *Child Development*, 1964, *35*, 881–891.

Grinder, R. E., & McMichaels, R. E. Cultural influence on conscience development: Resistance to temptation and guilt among Samoans and American Caucasians. *Journal of Abnormal and Social Psychology*, 1963, *66*, 503–507.

Grinder, R. E., & McMichaels, R. E. Guilt and resistance to temptation in Japanese and white Americans. *Journal of Social Psychology*, 1964, *64*, 217–223.

Grinder, R. E., & McMichaels, R. E. Children's guilt after transgression: Combined effect of exposure to American culture and ethnic background. *Child Development,* 1966, *37*(2), 425–431.

Grinker, R. R., Basowitz, H., Peosky, H. J., & Korchin, S. J. *Anxiety and stress.* New York: McGraw-Hill, 1955.

Grossman, B. D., & Levy, P. S. A factor analytic study of coping behavior in preschool children. *Journal of Genetic Psychology,* 1974, *124,* 287–294.

Grossman, S. P. *A textbook of physiological psychology.* New York: Wiley, 1967.

Grosz, H. J., & Farmer, B. B. Blood lactate in the development of anxiety symptoms. *Archives of General Psychiatry,* 1969, *21,* 611–619.

Groves, P. M., & Thompson, R. F. Habituation: A dual-process theory. *Psychological Review,* 1970, *77,* 419–450.

Grunes, M. Some aspects of conscience and their relationship to intelligence. *Dissertation Abstracts,* 1956, *16,* 1282–1283.

Grunt, J. A., & Young, W. C. Differential reactivity of individuals and the response of the male guinea pig to testosterone propionate. *Endocrinology,* 1952, *51,* 237–248.

Grush, J., Clore, G. L., & Costin, F. Dissimilarity and attraction: When difference makes a difference. *Journal of Personality and Social Psychology,* 1975, *32,* 783–789.

Guertin, W. H. A factor-analytic study of schizophrenic symptoms. *Journal of Consulting Psychology,* 1952, *16,* 308–312. (a)

Guertin, W. H. An inverted factor-analytic study of schizophrenia. *Journal of Consulting Psychology,* 1952, *16,* 371–375. (b)

Guertin, W. H. A factor analysis of schizophrenic ratings on the Hospital Adjustment Scale. *Journal of Clinical Psychology,* 1955, *10,* 70–73.

Guertin, W. H. Schizophrenics as psychiatrists diagnose them. *Psychological Reports,* 1956, *2,* 279–282.

Guertin, W. H. A transposed analysis of paranoid schizophrenics. *Psychological Reports,* 1958, *4,* 591–594.

Guertin, W. H. Empirical syndrome groupings of schizophrenic hospital admissions. *Journal of Clinical Psychology,* 1961, *17,* 268–275. (a)

Guertin, W. H. Medical and statistical psychological models for research in schizophrenia. *Behavioral Science,* 1961, *6,* 200–204. (b)

Guertin, W. H. The search for recurring patterns among individual profiles. *Educational and Psychological Measurement,* 1966, *26,* 151–165.

Guertin, W. H. Typing ships with transposed factor analysis. *Educational and Psychological Measurement,* 1971, *31,* 397–405.

Guertin, W. H., & Bailey, J. P., Jr. *Introduction to modern factor analysis.* Ann Arbor, Mich.: Edwards Brothers, 1970.

Guertin, W. H., & Krugman, A. D. A factor analytically derived scale for rating activities of psychiatric patients. *Journal of Clinical Psychology,* 1959, *15,* 32–35.

Guilford, J. P. Introversion-extroversion. *Psychological Bulletin,* 1934, *31,* 331–354.

Guilford, J. P. *Psychometric Methods* (2nd ed.). New York: McGraw-Hill, 1954.

Guilford, J. P. *Personality.* New York: McGraw-Hill, 1959. (a)

Guilford, J. P. Three faces of intellect. *American Psychologist,* 1959, *14,* 469–479. (b)

Guilford, J. P. *The nature of human intelligence.* New York: McGraw-Hill, 1967.

Guilford, J. P. *Intelligence, creativity, and their educational implications.* San Diego: Robert R. Knapp, 1968.

Guilford, J. P. Factors and factors of personality. *Psychological Bulletin,* 1975, *82,* 802–814.

Guilford, J. P., & Christensen, P. R. *A factor-analytic study of verbal fluency* (Psychological Laboratory Report No. 17). Los Angeles: University of Southern California, 1956.

Guilford, J. P., Christensen, P. R., Frick, J. W., & Merrifield, P. R. *The relations of creative-thinking aptitudes to non-aptitude personality traits* (Psychological Laboratory Report No. 20). Los Angeles: University of Southern California, 1957.

Guilford, J. P., Frick, J. W., Christensen, P. R., & Merrifield, P. R. *A factor-analytic study of flexibility in thinking* (Psychological Laboratory Report No. 18). Los Angeles: University of Southern California, 1957.

Guilford, J. P., & Hoepfner, R. *The analysis of intelligence.* New York: McGraw-Hill, 1971.

Guilford, J. P., & Michael, W. B. Approaches to univocal factor scores. *Psychometrika,* 1948, *13,* 1–22.

Guilford, J. P., & Zimmerman, W. S. *The Guilford-Zimmerman Temperament Survey: Manual.* Beverly Hills, Calif.: Sheridan Supply Co., 1949.

Guilford, J. P., & Zimmerman, W. S. *The Guilford-Zimmerman Aptitude Survey.* Beverly Hills, Calif.: Sheridan Supply Co., 1956.

Guilford, J. S. Maturation of values in young children. *Journal of Genetic Psychology,* 1974, *124,* 241–248.

Gulliksen, H. *Theory of mental tests.* New York: Wiley, 1950.

Guthrie, E. R. *Psychology of human conflict.* New York: Harper, 1938.

Guttman, L. *Communalities that maximize determinancy* (Res. Dept. 16, Control No. AF 41 (657)-76). Berkeley: University of California, 1957.

Guttman, L. What lies ahead for factor analysis? *Educational Psychological Measurement,* 1958, *18,* 497–515.

Guttman, L. A structural theory for intergrouping beliefs and actions. *American Sociological Review,* 1959, *24,* 318–328.

Guttman, L. A faceted definition of intelligence. *Scripta Hierosoymitana,* 1965, *14,* 166–181.

Gynther, M. D. *Different cultures . . . different norms?* Paper presented at the 6th Annual MMPI Symposium, Minneapolis, Minn., April 7–8, 1971.

Haber, R. N. (Ed.). *Current research in motivation.* New York: Holt, Rinehart, & Winston, 1966.

Haggard, E. A. *Intraclass correlation and the analysis of variance.* New York: Dryden, 1958.

Hake, H. W. Form discrimination and the invariance of form. In L. Uhr (Ed.), *Pattern recognition.* New York: Wiley, 1966.

Hakstian, A. R. *Some notes on the factor analytic treatment of measures obtained on two different occasions* (Research and Information Rep. 71-10). Edmonton, Canada: Division of Educational Research, 1971.

Hakstian, A. R., & Cattell, R. B. The checking of primary ability structure on a broader basis of performances. *British Journal of Psychology,* 1974, *44,* 140–154.

Hall, B. *Anxiety, stress, task difficulty and achievement via programmed instruction.* Unpublished doctoral dissertation, Florida State University, 1969.

Hall, C. S. The inheritance of emotionality. *Sigma Chi Quarterly,* 1938, *26,* 17–27, 37. Reprinted in W. F. Martin & C. B. Stendler (Eds.), *Readings in child development.* New York: Harcourt, Brace, 1954.

Hall, C. S. The genetics of behavior. In S. S. Stevens (Ed.), *Handbook of experimental psychology.* New York: Wiley, 1951.

Hall, R. L. *Predicting bomber crew performance from the aircraft commander's role.* San Antonio, Texas: Lackland Air Force Base, 1956.

Hallworth, H. J. The dimensions of personality among children of school age. *British Journal of Mathematical and Statistical Psychology,* 1965, *18,* 45–56.

Hammer, A. G. Contemporary theorizing in abnormal psychology. *Australian Journal of Psychology,* 1958, *10,* 69–84.

Hammond, D. R. Probabilistic functioning and the clinical method. *Psychological Review,* 1955, *62,* 255–262.

Hammond, K. R. Measuring attitude by error choice: An indirect method. *Journal of Abnormal and Social Psychology,* 1948, *43,* 38–48.

Hammond, S. B. *Some invariant factors from rating studies.* Unpublished manuscript, University of Melbourne, 1965.

Hammond, S. B. *Boy and man: Explanations of general intelligence.* Unpublished manuscript, Department of Psychology, Melbourne University, 1975.

Hammond, W. H. The constancy of physical types as determined by factor analysis. *Human Biology,* 1957, *29,* 40–61.

Hand, J., & Reynolds, H. H. Suppressing distortion in temperament inventories. *Journal of Consulting Psychology,* 1961, *25,* 180–181.

Haney, C. A. Status group membership and the perception of deviancy. *Florida State University Studies.* Tallahassee, Florida: Florida State University, 1967.

Hardy, K. R. Determinants of conformity and attitude change. *Journal of Abnormal and Social Psychology,* 1957, *54,* 289–294.

Hare, A. P. *Handbook of small group research.* New York: Glencoe Free Press, 1962.

Harleston, B. W. Task difficulty, anxiety level, and ability level as factors affecting performance in a verbal learning situation. *Journal of Psychology,* 1963, *55,* 165–168.

Harleston, B. W., & Cunningham, S. M. Task difficulty and anxiety level as factors affecting performance in a verbal learning situation. *Journal of Psychology,* 1961, *52,* 77–86.

Harlow, H. F. The formation of learning sets. *Psychological Review,* 1949, *56,* 51–65.

Harlow, H. F. The nature of love. *American Psychologist,* 1958, *13,* 673–685.

Harlow, H. F., & Harlow, M. K. Social deprivation in monkeys. *Scientific American,* 1962, *207,* 136–146.

Harlow, H. F., & Harlow, M. K. The affectional systems. In A. M. Schrier, H. F. Harlow, & F. Stollnitz (Eds.), *Behavior of non-human primates* (Vol. 2). New York and London: Academic Press, 1965.

Harman, H. H. *Modern factor analysis* (2nd ed.). Chicago: University of Chicago Press, 1967.

Harman, H. H. *Modern factor analysis* (3rd ed.). Chicago: University of Chicago Press, 1976.

Harms, J. Y., & Staats, A. W. *Food-deprivation and the reinforcing value of food-words: Interaction of Pavlovian and instrumental conditioning.* Unpublished manuscript, Department of Psychology, University of Hawaii, 1976.

Harper, L. V. The young as a source of stimuli controlling caretaker behavior. *Developmental Psychology,* 1971, *4,* 73–88.

Harris, C. W. Canonical factor models for the description of change. In C. W. Harris (Ed.), *Problems in measuring change.* Madison: University of Wisconsin Press, 1963. (a)

Harris, C. W. *Problems in measuring change.* Madison: University of Wisconsin Press, 1963. (b)

Harris, F. R., Johnston, M. K., Kelley, C. S., & Wolf, M. M. Effects of positive social reinforcement on regressed crawling of a nursery school child. *Journal of Educational Psychology,* 1964, *55,* 35–41.

Harris, G. W., & Campbell, H. J. The regulation of the secretion of luteinizing hormone and ovulation. In G. W. Harris & B. T. Donovan (Eds.), *The pituitary gland* (Vol. 2). London: Butterworth, 1966.

Harris, G. W., & Jacobsohn, D. Functional grafts of the anterior pituitary gland. *Proceedings of the Royal Society, Series B,* 1952, *139,* 263–276.

Harris, I. D. *Normal children and mothers.* Glencoe, Ill.: Free Press, 1959.

Harrison, A. A. Response competition, frequency, exploratory behavior and liking. *Journal of Personality and Social Psychology,* 1968, *9,* 363–368.

Harrower, M. *Diagnostic psychological testing.* Springfield, Ill.: Charles C Thomas, 1950.

Hart, B. L. Manipulation of neonatal androgen: Effects on sexual responses and penile development in male rats. *Physiology and Behavior,* 1972, *8,* 841–845.

Hartmann, H. *Ego psychology and the problem of adaptation.* New York: International Universities Press, 1939.

Hartshorne, H., & May, M. A. *Studies in deceit* (Vol. 1). *Studies in the nature of character by the Character Education Inquiry.* New York: Macmillan, 1928.

Hartshorne, H., May, M. A., & Maller, J. B. *Studies in service and self-control* (Vol. 2). *Studies in the nature of character by the Character Education Inquiry.* New York: Macmillan, 1929.

Hartshorne, H., May, M. A., & Shuttleworth, F. K. *Studies in the organization of character* (Vol. 3). *Studies in the nature of character by the Character Education Inquiry.* New York: Macmillan, 1930.

Hartshorne, H., May, M. A., & Shuttleworth, F. K. *Studies in the nature of character by the*

*Character Education Inquiry* (3 vols.). New York: Macmillan, 1928–30.

Hartup, W. Nurturance and nurturance withdrawal in relation to the dependence behavior of young children. *Child Development,* 1958, *29,* 191–201.

Harvey, O. J., Hunt, D. E., & Schroder, H. M. *Conceptual systems and personality organization.* New York: Wiley, 1961.

Hase, E. D., & Goldberg, L. R. Comparative validity of different strategies of constructing personality inventory scales. *Psychological Bulletin,* 1967, *67,* 231–248.

Hathaway, S. R. Increasing clinical efficiency. In B. M. Bass & I. A. Berg (Eds.), *Objective approaches to personality assessment.* Princeton: Van Nostrand, 1959.

Hawkes, G. R., Burchinal, L. G., & Gardner, B. Pre-adolescents' views of some of their relations with their parents. *Child Development,* 1957, *28,* 393–399.

Hawkes, G. R., & Egbert, R. L. Personal values and the empathic response: Their interrelationships. *Journal of Educational Psychology,* 1954, *45,* 469–476.

Hayes, K. J. Genes, drives and intellect. *Psychological Reports,* 1962, *10,* 299–342.

Hayman, B. I. The analysis of variance of diallel crosses. *Biometrics,* 1954, *10,* 235–244.

Haythorn, W. The influence of individual members on the characteristics of small groups. *Journal of Abnormal and Social Psychology,* 1953, *48,* 276–284.

Haythorn, W., Couch, A., Haefner, D., Langham, P., & Carter, L. F. The behavior of authoritarian and equalitarian personalities in groups. *Human Relations,* 1956, *9,* 51–74. (a)

Haythorn, W., Couch, A., Haefner, D., Langham, P., & Carter, L. F. The effects of varying combinations of authoritarian and equalitarian leaders and followers. *Journal of Abnormal and Social Psychology,* 1956, *53,* 210–219. (b)

Hebb, D. O. The effects of early experience on problem-solving at maturity. *American Psychologist,* 1947, *2,* 306–307.

Hebb, D. O. *The organization of behavior.* New York: Wiley, 1949.

Hebb, D. O. Drives and the C. N. S. (Conceptual nervous system). *Psychological Review,* 1955, *62,* 243–254.

Hebb, D. O. The American Revolution. *American Psychologist,* 1960, *15,* 735–745.

Heider, F. Attitudes and cognitive organization. *Journal of Psychology,* 1946, *21,* 107–112.

Heider, F. *The psychology of interpersonal relations.* New York: Wiley, 1958.

Heilbrun, A. B., & McKinley, R. Perception of maternal child rearing attitudes, personality of the perceiver, and incipient psychopathology. *Child Development,* 1962, *33,* 73–83.

Held, R., & Hein, A. Movement-produced stimulation in the development of visually guided behavior. *Journal of Comparative and Physiological Psychology,* 1963, *56,* 872–875.

Heller, K., & Marlatt, G. A. Verbal conditioning, behavior therapy, and behavior change: Some problems in extrapolation. In C. M. Franks (Ed.), *Behavior therapy: Appraisal and status.* New York: McGraw-Hill, 1969.

Helm, C. E., & Tucker, L. R. Individual

differences in the structure of color perception. *American Journal of Psychology,* 1962, *75,* 437–444.

Helmstadter, G. C. Procedures for obtaining separate set and content components of a test score. *Psychometrika,* 1957, *22,* 381–393.

Helmstadter, G. C. The empirical comparison of methods for estimating profile similarity. *Educational and Psychological Measurement,* 1967, *17,* 71–82.

Helson, H. Adaptation level as the basis for a quantitative theory of frame of reference. *Psychological Review,* 1948, *55,* 297–313.

Helson, H. Adaptation level theory. In S. Koch (Ed.), *Psychology: A study of a science.* New York: McGraw-Hill, 1969.

Helson, H., & Bevan, W. (Eds.). *Contemporary approaches to psychology.* Princeton: Van Nostrand, 1967.

Hendricks, B. C. *The sensitivity of the dynamic calculus to short term change in interest structure.* Unpublished master's thesis, University of Illinois, 1971.

Hendrickson, A. E., & White, P. O. Promax: A quick method for rotation to oblique simple structure. *British Journal of Statistical Psychology,* 1964, *17,* 65–70.

Henry, E. M., & Rotter, J. B. Situational influences on Rorschach responses. *Journal of Consulting Psychology,* 1956, *20,* 547–562.

Henshel, A-M. The relationship between values and behavior. *Child Development,* 1971, *42,* 1997–2007.

Herjanic, B., Herjanic, M., Brown, F., & Wheatt, T. Are children reliable reporters? *Journal of Abnormal Child Psychology,* 1975, *3,* 41–48.

Hernandez-Peon, R., Scherrer, H., & Jouvet, M. Modification of electrical activity in the cochlear nucleus during "attention" in unanesthetized cats. *Science,* 1956, *123,* 331–332.

Heron, A. The effect of real-life modification of questionnaire response. *Journal of Applied Psychology,* 1956, *40,* 65–68. (a)

Heron, A. A two-part personality measure for use as a research criterion. *British Journal of Psychology,* 1956, *47,* 243–251. (b)

Herrington, L. P. The relation of physiological and social indices of activity level. In Q. McNemar & M. A. Merrill (Eds.), *Studies in personality.* New York: McGraw-Hill, 1942.

Herrmann, Th. (Ed.). *Psychologie der Erziehungsstile.* Göttingen: Hogrefe, 1966.

Herrmann, Th. *Lehrbuch der empirischen Persönlichkeitsforschung.* Göttingen: Hogrefe, 1969.

Herrmann, Th., Schwitajewski, E., & Ahrens, H. J. Untersuchungen zum elterlichen Erziehungsstile: Strenge und Unterstützung. *Archiv für die gesamte Psychologie,* 1968, *120,* 74–105.

Herrmann, Th., & Stapf, A. *Elterliche Erziehungsstile: Strenge und Unterstützung.* Unveröff. Bericht für die Deutsche Forschungsgemeinschaft, Marburg, 1971. (a)

Herrmann, Th., & Stapf, K. H. Über theoretische Konstruktionen in der Psychologie. *Psychologische Beiträge,* 1971, *13,* 336–354. (b)

Herrmann, Th., Stapf, A., & Deutsch, W. Datensammeln ohne Ende? Anmerkungen zur Erziehungsstilforschung. *Psychologische Rundschau,* 1975, *26,* 176–182.

Herrmann, Th., Stapf, A., & Krohne, H. W. Die Marburger Skalen zur Erfassung des elterlichen Erziehungsstile. *Diagnostica,* 1971, *17,* 118–131.

Hess, R. D. *Maternal teaching styles and socialization of educability.* Paper presented at the meeting of the American Psychological Association, Los Angeles, September 1964.

Hess, W. R. *Uber die Wechselbeziehungen zwischen und vegetativen Funktionen.* Zurich: O. Füssli, 1925.

Hess, W. R. *Psychologie in biologischer Sicht* (2nd ed.). Stuttgart: Thieme, 1968.

Hetrick, S. H., Lilly, R. S., & Merrifield, P. R. Figural creativity, intelligence, and personality in children. *Multivariate Behavioral Research,* 1968, *3,* 173–187.

Heymans, G., & Wiersma, E. Beiträge zur speziellen Psychologie auf Grund einer Masseununtersuchung. *Zeitschrift für Psychologie,* 1906, *42,* 81–127; 1906, *43,* 321–373; 1907, *45,* 1–42; 1908, *46,* 321–333; 1908, *49,* 414–439; 1909, *51,* 1–72.

Hildebrand, E. P. A factorial study of introversion-extraversion. *British Journal of Psychology,* 1958, *49,* 1–11.

Hildreth, H. M. A battery of feeling and attitude scales for clinical use. *Journal of Clinical Psychology,* 1946, *2,* 214–221.

Hilgard, E. R., & Bower, G. H. *Theories of learning.* New York: Appleton-Century-Crofts, 1966.

Hilgard, J. R. Sibling rivalry and social heredity. *Psychiatry,* 1951, *14,* 375–385.

Hills, Y. The influence of instructions on personality inventory scores. *Journal of Counseling Psychology,* 1961, *8,* 43–48.

Hilton, I. Differences in the behavior of mothers toward first- and later-born children. *Journal of Personality and Social Psychology,* 1967, *7,* 282–290.

Himmelweit, H. T. Socio-economic background and personality. *International Social Science Bulletin,* 1955, *7,* 29–35.

Hinde, R. A. *Animal behavior.* New York: McGraw-Hill, 1966.

Hinde, R. An overview of ethologic approaches. In J. DeWit & W. Hartup (Eds.), *Determinants and origins of aggressive behavior.* The Hague, Netherlands: Mouton Press, 1975.

Hindley, C. B. Stability and change in abilities up to five years: Group trends. *Journal of Child Psychology and Psychiatry,* 1965, *6,* 85–99.

Hinkle, D. M. *The changes of personal constructs from the viewpoint of a theory of implications.* Unpublished doctoral dissertation, Ohio State University, 1965.

Hirsch, J. (Ed.). *Behavior-genetic analysis.* New York: McGraw-Hill, 1967.

Hirsch, J. Genetics and competence: Do heritability indices predict educability? In J. McV. Hunt (Ed.), *Human intelligence.* New Brunswick, N.J.: Transaction Books, 1972.

Hirsch, J., & Erlenmeyer-Kimling, L. Studies in experimental behavior genetics: IV. Chromosome analyses for geotaxis. *Journal of Comparative and Physiological Psychology,* 1962, *55,* 732–739.

Hitt, J. C., Hendricks, S. E., Ginsberg, S. I., & Lewis, J. H. Disruption of male, but not female, sexual behavior in rats by medial forebrain bundle lesions. *Journal of Comparative and Physiological Psychology,* 1970, *73,* 377–384.

Hoagland, H. J. Adventures in biological engineering. *Science,* 1944, *100,* 63–67.

Hoch, P., & Zubin, J. *Current problems in psychiatric diagnosis.* New York: Grune & Stratton, 1953.

Hodges, W. F. *The effects of success, threat of shock, and failure on anxiety.* Unpublished doctoral dissertation, Vanderbilt University, 1967.

Hodges, W. F., & Felling, J. P. Types of stressful situations and their relation to trait anxiety and sex. *Journal of Consulting and Clinical Psychology,* 1970, *34,* 333–337.

Hodges, W. F., & Spielberger, C. D. The effects of threat of shock on heart rate for subjects who differ in manifest anxiety and fear of shock. *Psychophysiology,* 1966, *2,* 287–294.

Hoffeld, D. R., Thompson, R. F., & Brogden, W. J. Effect of stimuli-time relations during pre-conditioning training upon the magnitude of sensory pre-conditioning. *Journal of Experimental Psychology,* 1958, *56,* 437–442.

Hoffman, L. R., & Maier, N. R. F. Quality and acceptance of problem solutions by members of homogeneous and heterogeneous groups. *Journal of Abnormal and Social Psychology,* 1961, *62,* 401–407.

Hoffman, L. W. *Effects of maternal employment on the child.* Paper presented at the meeting of the National Council on Family Relations, Ames, Iowa, 1959.

Hoffman, M. L. Some psychodynamic factors in compulsive conformity. *Journal of Abnormal and Social Psychology,* 1953, *48,* 383–393.

Hoffman, M. L. Child-rearing practices and moral development: Generalizations from empirical research. *Child Development,* 1963, *34,* 295–318.

Hofstaetter, P. R., & O'Connor, G. P. Anderson's overlap hypothesis and the discontinuities of growth. *Journal of Genetic Psychology,* 1956, *88,* 95–106.

Hofstätter, P. R. *Sozialpsychologie.* Berlin: de Gruyter, 1964.

Hogben, L. *Mathematics for the millions.* New York: Norton, 1937.

Holland, J. G., & Skinner, B. F. *The analysis of behavior: A program of self-instruction.* New York: McGraw-Hill, 1961.

Hollander, E. P. Authoritarianism and leadership choice in a military setting. *Journal of Abnormal and Social Psychology,* 1954, *49,* 365–370.

Hollander, E. P. *Principles and methods of social psychology.* New York: Oxford, 1971.

Hollander, E. P., & Willis, R. H. Some current issues in the psychology of conformity and nonconformity. *Psychological Bulletin,* 1967, *68,* 62–76.

Hollingshead, A. B. Cultural factors in the selection of marriage mates. *American Sociological Review,* 1950, *15,* 619–627.

Holloway, F. A., & Parsons, O. A. Habituation of the orienting reflex in brain damaged patients. *Psychophysiology,* 1971, *8,* 623–634.

Holt, B-G. Some family life correlates of social behavior in young children. *Dissertation Abstracts,* 1967, *27*(12-A), 4362–4363.

Holtzman, W. H. Methodological issues in P-technique. *Psychological Bulletin,* 1962, *59,* 248–255.

Holtzman, W. H. Statistical models for the study of change in the single case. In C. W. Harris (Ed.), *Problems in measuring change.* Madison: University of Wisconsin Press, 1963.

Holtzman, W. H. Personality structure. In *Annual Review of Psychology* (Vol. 16). Palto Alto, Calif.: Annual Reviews, 1965.

Holzinger, K. J., & Harman, H. H. Comparison of two factorial analyses. *Psychometrika,* 1938, *3,* 45–60.

Homans, G. C. *The human group.* New York: Harcourt, Brace, 1950.

Homskaya, E. D. The human frontal lobes and their role in the organization of activity. *Acta Neurobiologica Experimentalis,* 1973, *33,* 509–522.

Honkavaara, S. The psychology of expression. *British Journal of Psychology, Monograph Supplement,* No. 33, 1961.

Honzik, M. P. Environmental correlates of mental growth: Prediction from the family setting at 21 months. *Child Development,* 1967, *38,* 337–364.

Hopkins, B. L., Schutte, B. C., & Garton, K. L. The effects of access to a playroom on the rate and quality of printing and writing of first- and second-grade students. *Journal of Applied Behavior Analysis,* 1971,*,4,* 77–87.

Hopkins, K. D., & Bibelheimer, M. Five-year stability of intelligence quotients from language and nonlanguage group tests. *Child Development,* 1971, *42,* 645–649.

Horn, J. L. *Structure in measures of self-sentiment, ego, and super ego concepts.* Unpublished master's thesis, University of Illinois, 1961. (a)

Horn, J. L. Significance tests for use with $r_p$ and related profile statistics. *Educational and Psychological Measurement,* 1961, *21,* 363–370. (b)

Horn, J. L. The discovery of personality traits. *Journal of Educational Research,* 1963, *56,* 460–465.

Horn, J. L. *Fluid and crystallized intelligence: A factor analytic and developmental study of the structure among primary mental abilities.* Unpublished doctoral dissertation, University of Illinois, 1965. (a)

Horn, J. L. Second order factors in questionnaire data. *Educational and Psychological Measurement,* 1965, *23,* 117–134. (b)

Horn, J. L. *Final Report: Short period fluctuations in intelligence.* (NASA NSG-518, Project No. DRI-614). Denver, Col.: University of Denver, 1966. (a)

Horn, J. L. Integration of structural and developmental concepts in the theory of fluid and crystallized intelligence. In R. B. Cattell (Ed.), *Handbook of multivariate experimental psychology.* Chicago: Rand McNally, 1966. (b)

Horn, J. L. Motivation and dynamic calculus concepts from multivariate experiment. In R. B. Cattell (Ed.), *Handbook of multivariate experimental psychology.* Chicago: Rand McNally, 1966. (c)

Horn, J. L. On subjectivity in factor analysis. *Educational Psychological Measurement,* 1967, *27,* 811–820. (a)

Horn, J. L. Intelligence—why it grows, why it declines. *Trans-Action,* 1967, 23–31. (b)

Horn, J. L. Organization of abilities and the development of intelligence. *Psychological Review,* 1968, *79,* 242–259.

Horn, J. L. Organization of data on life-span development of human abilities. In L. R. Goulet & P. B. Baltes (Eds.), *Life-span development psychology.* New York: Academic Press, 1970. (a)

Horn, J. L. Review of Guilford's "The nature of human intelligence." *Psychometrika,* 1970, *35,* 273–277. (b)

Horn, J. L. The structure of intellect: Primary abilities. In R. M. Dreger (Ed.), *Multivariate Personality Research.* Baton Rouge, La.: Claitor, 1972. (a)

Horn, J. L. State, trait and change dimensions of intelligence. *British Journal of Educational Psychology,* 1972, *42,* 159–185. (b)

Horn, J. L. The Porteus Maze Test. In O. K. Buros (Ed.), *Seventh mental measurements yearbook* (Rev. 429, 753–756). Highland Park, N.J.: Gryphon, 1972. (c)

Horn, J. L. Theory of functions represented among auditory and visual test performances. In J. R. Royce (Ed.), *Multivariate analysis and psychological theory.* New York: Academic Press, 1973.

Horn, J. L. Educability and group differences: The prima facie case for the heritability of intelligence and associates. *American Journal of Psychology,* 1974, *87,* 546–551.

Horn, J. L. *Human abilities: A review of research and theory in the early 1970's.* Expanded manuscript from the *Annual Review of Psychology,* University of Denver, 1976.

Horn, J. L., & Bramble, W. J. Second-order ability structure revealed in rights and wrongs scores. *Journal of Educational Psychology,* 1967, *58,* 115–122.

Horn, J. L., & Cattell, R. B. Refinement and test of the theory of fluid and crystallized intelligence. *Journal of Educational Psychology,* 1966, *57,* 253–270. (a)

Horn, J. L., & Cattell, R. B. Age differences in primary mental ability factors. *Journal of Gerontology,* 1966, *21,* 210–220. (b)

Horn, J. L., & Cattell, R. B. Age differences in fluid and crystallized intelligence. *Acta Psychologica,* 1967, *26,* 107–129.

Horn, J. L., & Knapp, J. R. The subjective character of the empirical base of the structure of intellect model. *Psychological Bulletin,* 1973, *80,* 33–43.

Horn, J. L., & Little, K. B. Isolating change and invariance in patterns of behavior. *Multivariate Behavioral Research,* 1966, *2,* 219–228.

Horn, J. L., & Sweney, A. B. The dynamic calculus model for motivation and its use in understanding the individual case. In A. R. Mahrer (Ed.), *New approaches to personality classification.* New York: Columbia University Press, 1970.

Horn, J. M., Plomin, R., & Rosenman, R. Heritability of personality traits in adult male twins. *Behavior Genetics,* 1976, *6,* 17–30.

Horne, G., & Hinde, R. A. (Eds.). *Short-term changes in neural activity and behaviour.* Cambridge: Cambridge University Press, 1970.

Horney, K. *Neurosis and human growth.* New York: Norton, 1950.

Horowitz, L. M. Associative matching and intralist similarities. *Psychological Reports,* 1962, *10,* 751–757.

Horst, P. *Matrix algebra for social scientists.* New York: Holt, Rinehart, & Winston, 1963.

Horst, P. *Factor analysis of data matrices.* New York: Holt, Rinehart, & Winston, 1965.

Horst, P. *Psychological measurement and prediction.* Belmont, Calif.: Wadsworth, 1966.

Hotelling, H. The generalization of student's ratio. *Annals of Mathematical Statistics,* 1931, *2,* 360–378.

House, S. D. A mental hygiene inventory. *Archives of Psychology,* 1926, *14,* 1–112.

Howarth, E. A factor analysis of selected markers for objective personality factors. *Multivariate Behavioral Research,* 1972, *7,* 451–476. (a)

Howarth, E. A source of independent verification: Convergencies and divergencies in the work of Cattell and Eysenck. In R. M. Dreger (Ed.), *Multivariate personality research.* Baton Rouge, La.: Claitor, 1972. (b)

Howarth, E., & Browne, A. An item-factor analysis of the 16 P.F. Personality Questionnaire. *Personality: An International Journal,* 1971, *2,* 117–139.

Hull, C. L. Knowledge and purpose as habit mechanisms. *Psychological Review,* 1930, *37,* 511–525.

Hull, C. L. *Principles of behavior.* New York: Appleton-Century, 1943.

Hull, C. L. The place of innate individual and species differences in a natural science theory of behavior. *Psychological Review,* 1945, *52,* 55–60.

Hull, C. L. *Essentials of behavior.* New Haven: Yale University Press, 1951.

Hull, C. L. *A behavior system.* New Haven: Yale University Press, 1952.

Humm, D. G., & Humm, K. A. The Humm-Wadsworth Temperament Scale. *American Journal of Psychiatry,* 1935, *92,* 163–200.

Humphreys, L. G. Characteristics of type concepts with special reference to Sheldon's typology. *Psychological Bulletin,* 1957, *54,* 218–228.

Humphreys, L. G. Investigations of the simplex. *Psychometrika,* 1960, *25,* 313–323.

Humphreys, L. G. *On derived scores.* Unpublished manuscript, University of Illinois, c. 1961.

Humphreys, L. G. The organization of human abilities. *American Psychologist,* 1962, *17,* 475–483. (a)

Humphreys, L. G. *Hierarchical factors in course grades in an aviation high school* (PRL-TDR-62–23). Lackland Air Force Base, Tex.: 6570th Personnel Research Laboratory, 1962. (b)

Humphreys, L. G. Critique of "Theory of fluid and crystallized intelligence: A critical experiment." *Journal of Educational Psychology,* 1967, *58,* 129–136.

Humphreys, L. G. The fleeting nature of the prediction of college academic success. *Journal of Educational Psychology,* 1968, *59,* 375–380.

Humphreys, L. G., Ilgen, D., McGrath, D., & Montanelli, R. Capitalization on chance in rotation of factors. *Educational and Psychological Measurement,* 1969, *29,* 259–271.

Hundal, P. S. Organization of mental abilities at successive grade levels. *Indian Journal of Psychology,* 1966, *41,* 65–72.

Hundleby, J. D. The trait of anxiety, as defined by objective performance and indices of emotional disturbance in middle childhood. *Multivariate Behavioral Research,* 1968, Special Issue, 7–14.

Hundleby, J. D., & Cattell, R. B. Personality structure in middle childhood and the prediction of school achievement and adjustment. *Monographs of the Society for Research in Child Development,* 1968, *33*(5), 61 pp.

Hundleby, J. D., Pawlik, K., & Cattell, R. B. *Personality factors in objective test devices: A critical integration of a century's research.* San Diego: Knapp, 1965.

Hunt, A. M. A study of the relative value of certain ideals. *Journal of Abnormal Psychology,* 1935, *30,* 222–228.

Hunt, H. F. The effect of deliberate deception on Minnesota Multiphasic Personality Inventory performance. *Journal of Consulting Psychology,* 1948, *12,* 396–402.

Hunt, J. McV. (Ed.). *Personality and the behavior disorders.* New York: Ronald Press, 1944.

Hunt, J. McV. Experience and the development of motivation: Some reinforcement. *Child Development,* 1960, *31,* 489–504.

Hunt, J. McV. *Intelligence and experience.* New York: Ronald Press, 1961.

Hunt, J. McV. Motivation inherent in information processing and action. In O. J. Harvey (Ed.), *Motivation and social interaction.* New York: Ronald Press, 1963.

Hunt, J. McV. Intrinsic motivation and its role in psychological development. In D. Levine (Ed.), *Nebraska Symposium on Motivation, 1965.* Lincoln: University of Nebraska Press, 1965. (a)

Hunt, J. McV. Traditional personality theory in the light of recent evidence. *American Scientist,* 1965, *53,* 80–96. (b)

Hunt, J. McV. Intrinsic motivation: Information and circumstance. In H. M. Schroder & P. Suedfeld (Eds.), *Personality theory and information processing.* New York: Ronald Press, 1971.

Hunt, J. McV. (Ed.). *Human intelligence.* New Brunswick, N.J.: Transaction Books, 1972. (a)

Hunt, J. McV. The role of experience in the development of competence. In J. McV. Hunt (Ed.), *Human intelligence.* New Brunswick, N.J.: Transaction Books, 1972. (b)

Hunt, J. McV., Ewing, T. N., LaForge, R., & Gilbert, W. M. An integrated approach to research on therapeutic counseling with samples of results. *Journal of Counseling Psychology,* 1959, *6,* 46–54.

Hunt, W. H., & Stevenson, I. Psychological testing in military clinical psychology: II. Personality testing. *Psychological Review,* 1946, *53,* 107–115.

Hurley, J. R., & Cattell, R. B. The Procrustes Program: Producing direct rotation to test a hypothesized factor structure. *Behavioral Science,* 1962, *7,* 258–262.

Hursch, C. L., Hammond, D. R., & Hursch, J. L. Some methodological considerations in multiple-cue probability studies. *Psychological Review,* 1964, *71,* 42–60.

Hurst, J. G. A factor analysis of the Merrill-Palmer with reference to theory and test construction. *Educational and Psychological Measurement,* 1960, *20,* 519–532.

Hurst, J. G. Factor analyses of the Merrill-Palmer at two age levels: Structure and comparison. *Journal of Genetic Psychology,* 1963, *102,* 231–244.

Husén, T. *Psychological twin research.* Stockholm: Almqvist & Wiksell, 1959.

Hutchinson, R. R., & Renfrew, J. W. Stalking, attack and eating behaviors elicited from the same sites in the hypothalamus. *Journal of Comparative and Physiological Psychology,* 1966, *61,* 360–367.

Hutt, M. L. The use of projective methods of personality measurement in army medical installations. *Journal of Clinical Psychology,* 1945, *1,* 134–140.

Ingersoll, H. L. A study of the transmission of authority patterns in the family. *Genetic Psychology Monographs,* 1949, *38,* 225–302.

Inhelder, B., & Piaget, J. *The growth of logical thinking from childhood to adolescence* (Anne Parsons & S. Milgram, trans.). New York: Basic Books, 1958.

Ippolitov, F. V. Interanalyzer differences in the sensitivity-strength parameter for vision, hearing and cutaneous modalities. In V. D. Nebylitsyn & J. A. Gray (Eds.), *Biological bases of individual behavior.* New York: Academic Press, 1972.

Isaacs, S. *Intellectual growth in young children.* Routledge & Kegan Paul, 1930.

Isaacson, R. L., McKeachie, W. J., & Milholland, J. E. A correlation of teacher personality variables and student ratings. *Journal of Educational Psychology,* 1963, *54,* 110–117.

Ismail, A. H., Falls, H. B., & MacLeod, D. F. Development of a criterion for physical fitness tests from factor analysis results. *Journal of Applied Physiology,* 1965, *20,* 991–999.

Izard, C. E. Projective responses of paranoid schizophrenic and normal subjects to photographs of human faces. *Journal of Consulting Psychology,* 1959, *23,* 119–124.

Izard, C. E. The effects of role-played emotion on Ss' affective reactions, intellectual functioning, and evaluative ratings of the actress. *Journal of Clinical Psychology,* 1964, *4,* 444–446.

Izard, C. E. *The face of emotion.* New York: Appleton-Century-Crofts, 1971.

Izard, C. E. *Patterns of emotions: A new analysis of anxiety and behavior.* New York: Academic Press, 1972.

Izard, C. E., Cherry, E. S., Arnold, A., & Fox, J. The Picture Description Test: Reliability and validity of a homogeneous scale (Tech. Rep. No. 23, Vanderbilt University, 1965; Contract ONR 2149(03) NR 171–609, Office of Naval Research).

Izard, C. E., Kotsch, W., Kidd, D., & Izard, C. E., Jr. *The facial expression of anger as an activator of the subjective experience of anger.* Unpublished manuscript, Vanderbilt University, 1974.

Izard, C. E., & Nunnally, J. C. Evaluative responses to affectively positive and negative facial photographs: Factor structure and construct validity. *Educational and Psychological Measurement,* 1965, *25,* 1061–1071.

Izard, C. E., & Tomkins, S. S. Affect and behavior: Anxiety as a negative affect. In C. D. Spielberger (Ed.), *Anxiety and behavior.* New York: Academic Press, 1966.

Jackson, D. N. Desirability judgments as a method of personality assessment. *Educational and Psychological Measurement,* 1964, *24,* 223–238.

Jackson, D. N. Comments on evaluation of multi-method factor analysis. *Psychological Bulletin,* 1971, *75,* 421–423.

Jackson, D. N. The High School Personality Questionnaire. In O. K. Buros (Ed.), *Seventh mental measurements yearbook.* Highland Park, N.J.: Gryphon Press, 1972.

Jackson, D. N., & Messick, S. Content and style in personality assessment. *Psychological Bulletin,* 1958, *55,* 243–252.

Jackson, D. N., & Messick, J. Acquiescence and desirability as response determinants on the MMPI. *Educational and Psychological Measurement,* 1961, *21,* 771–790.

Jackson, D. N., and Messick, S. Response styles and the assessment of psychopathology. In S. Messick & J. Ross (Eds.), *Measurement in personality and cognition.* New York: Wiley, 1962.

Jackson, M. A. The factor analysis of the Wechsler scale. I. *British Journal of Statistical Psychology,* 1960, *73,* 79–82.

Jakobovits, L. A. Mediation theory and the "single-stage" S-R model: Different. *Psychological Review,* 1966, *73,* 376–381.

James, G., & Lott, A. J. Reward frequency and the formation of positive attitudes toward group members. *Journal of Social Psychology,* 1964, *62,* 111–115.

James, W. *Principles of psychology.* 2 vols. New York: Holt, 1890.

James, W. *Psychology: Briefer course.* New York: Holt, 1892 (1920).

James, W. *The principles of psychology* (Vol. 1). New York: Dover, 1950.

James, W. H. The distribution of coitus within the human intermenstruum. *Journal of Biosocial Science,* 1971, *3,* 159–171.

Janis, I. L. Personality correlates of susceptibility to persuasion. *Journal of Personality,* 1954, *22,* 504–518.

Janis, I. L., Mahl, G. F., Kagan, J., & Holt, R. R. *Personality: Dynamics, development, and assessment.* New York: Harcourt, Brace, Jovanovitch, 1969.

Jeffrey, W. E. Early stimulation and cognitive development. In J. P. Hill (Ed.), *Minnesota Symposium on child psychology* (Vol. 3). Minneapolis: University of Minnesota Press, 1969.

Jellinek, E. Some principles of psychiatric classification. *Psychiatry,* 1939, *2,* 161–165.

Jellison, J. M., Mills, J. Effect of similarity and fortune of the other on attraction. *Journal of Personality and Social Psychology,* 1967, *5,* 459–463.

Jennings, E. E. *The anatomy of leadership: Princes, heroes, and supermen.* New York: Harper, 1960.

Jensen, A. R. Extraversion, neuroticism and serial learning. *Acta Psychologica,* 1962, *20,* 66–67.

Jensen, A. R. Varieties of individual differences in learning. In R. M. Gagné (Ed.), *Learning and individual differences.* Columbus, Ohio: Merrill, 1967. (a)

Jensen, A. R. Estimation of the limits of heritability of traits by comparison of monozygotic and dizygotic twins. *Proceedings of the National Academy of Sciences,* 1967, *58,* 149–156. (b)

Jensen, A. R. The culturally disadvantaged and the heredity-environment uncertainty. In J. Hellmuth (Ed.), *The culturally disadvantaged child.* Seattle, Wash.: Special Child Publication, 1968.

Jensen, A. R. How much can we boost IQ and scholastic achievement? *Harvard Educational Review,* 1969, *39,* 1–23.

Jensen, A. R. A theory of primary and secondary familial mental retardation. *International Review of Research in Retardation,* 1970, *4,* 33–105.

Jessor, R. Phenomenological personality theory and the data language of psychology. *Psychological Review,* 1956, *63,* 173–200.

Jessor, R., & Feshbach, S. *Cognition, personality and clinical psychology.* San Francisco: Jossey-Bass, 1967.

Jinks, J. L., & Broadhurst, P. L. Diallel analysis of litter size and body weight in rats. *Heredity,* 1963, *18,* 319–336.

Jinks, J. L., & Broadhurst, P. L. The detection and estimation of heritable differences in behaviour among individuals. *Heredity,* 1965, *20,* 97–116.

Jinks, J. L., & Fulker, D. W. Comparison of the biometrical genetical, MAVA and classical approaches to the analysis of human behavior. *Psychological Bulletin,* 1970, *73,* 311–349.

Jinks, J. L., & Jones, R. M. Estimation of the components of heterosis. *Genetics,* 1958, *43,* 223–234.

Jinks, J. L., & Perkins, J. M. A general method for the detection of additive, dominance and epistatic components of variation: III. $F_2$ and backcross populations. *Heredity,* 1970, *25,* 419–429.

Jinks, J. L., Perkins, J. M., & Breese, E. L. A general method of detecting additive, dominance and epistatic variation for metrical traits: II. Application of inbred lines. *Heredity,* 1969, *24,* 45–57.

Joffe, J. M. Genotype and prenatal and premating stress interact to affect adult behavior in rats. *Science,* 1965, *150,* 1844–1845.

Joffe, J. M. *Prenatal determinants of behaviour.* Oxford: Pergamon, 1969.

Johansson, G., Frankenhaeuser, M., & Magnusson, D. Catecholamine output in school children as related to performance and adjustment. *Scandinavian Journal of Psychology,* 1973, *14,* 20–28.

Johnson, D. M. Applications of standard score IQ to social statistics. *Journal of Social Psychology,* 1948, *27,* 217–227.

Johnson, R. C., & Medinnus, G. R. *Child psychology.* New York: Wiley, 1965.

Johnson, R. C., Weiss, R. L., & Zelhart, P. F. Similarities and differences between normal and psychotic subjects in response to verbal stimuli. *Journal of Abnormal and Social Psychology,* 1964, *68,* 221–226.

Johnson, R. M. On a theorem stated by Eckart and Young. *Psychometrika,* 1963, *28,* 259–263.

Johnson, S. C. Hierarchical clustering schemes. *Psychometrika,* 1967, *32*(3), 241–254.

Jonassen, C. T., & Peres, S. H. *Interrelationships of dimensions of community systems.* Columbus: Ohio State University Press, 1960.

Jones, E. E., & Gerard, H. B. *Foundations of social psychology.* New York: Wiley, 1967.

Jones, H. E. The galvanic skin reflex as related to overt emotional expression. *American Journal of Psychology,* 1935, *47,* 241–251.

Jones, H. E. The study of patterns of emotional expression. In L. Reymert (Ed.), *Feelings and emotions.* New York: McGraw-Hill, 1950.

Jones, H. E. Perceived differences among twins. *Eugenics Quarterly*, 1955, *2*, 98–102.

Jones, H. E. Intelligence and problem-solving. In J. E. Birrens (Ed.), *Aging and the individual*. Chicago: University of Chicago Pres, 1959.

Jones, L. V. A factor analysis of the Stanford-Binet at four age levels. *Psychometrika*, 1949, *14*, 299–331.

Jones, M. B., & Fennell, R. S. Runway performance by two strains of rats. *Quarterly Journal of the Florida Academy of Science*, 1965, *28*, 289–296.

Jones, M. C. The elimination of children's fears. *Journal of Experimental Psychology*, 1924, *7*, 380–390.

Jones, R. M. Linkage distributions and epistacy in quantitative inheritance. *Heredity*, 1960, *15*, 153–159.

Jones, R. M., & Mather, K. Interaction of genotype and environment in continuous variation: II. Analysis. *Biometrics*, 1958, *14*, 489–498.

Jones, R. R., Reid, J. B., & Patterson, G. R. Naturalistic observations in clinical assessment. In P. McReynolds (Ed.), *Advances in psychological assessment* (Vol. 3). San Francisco: Jossey-Bass, 1975.

Jones, S. C., & Regan, D. T. Ability evaluation through social comparison. *Journal of Experimental Social Psychology*, 1974, *10*, 133–146.

Jonsson, C. O. *Questionnaire and interviews; experimental studies concerning concurrent validity on well-motivated subjects.* Stockholm: The Swedish Council for Personnel Administration, 1957.

Jordan, T. E. Early developmental adversity and the first two years of life. *Multivariate Behavioral Research Monographs*, 1971, *6*, 1–80.

Jöreskog, K. G., & Sörbom, D. *Statistical models and methods for analysis of longitudinal data* (Research Rep. 75-1). Department of Statistics, University of Uppsala, Sweden, 1975.

Joslyn, W. D. Androgen-induced social dominance in infant female rhesus monkeys. *Journal of Child Psychology and Psychiatry and Allied Disciplines*, 1973, *14*, 137–145.

Jost, A. Problems of fetal endocrinology: The gonadal and hypophyseal hormones. *Recent Progress in Hormone Research*, 1953, *8*, 379–418.

Jost, A. The role of fetal hormones in prenatal development. *The Harvey Lectures*, 1961, *55*, 201–226.

Juel-Nielsen, N. Individual and environment: A psychiatric-psychological investigation of monozygous twins reared apart. *Acta Psychiatrica et Neurologica Scandinavica*, 1965. (Supplement 183)

Jung, C. G. *Two essays on analytical psychology*. New York: Pantheon, 1953.

Jung, C. G. *Psychological types.* New York: Harcourt, Brace, Jovanovitch, 1963.

Jung, J. Two stages of paired-associate learning as a function of intralist response similarity (IRS) and response meaningfulness (M). *Journal of Experimental Psychology*, 1965, *70*, 371–378.

Jung, R. Neurophysiologie und Psychiatrie. In H. W. Gruhle et al. (Eds.), *Psychiatrie der Gegenwart* (Vol. 1, Pt. 1A). Berlin: Springer, 1967.

Kaada, B. R. Stimulation and regional ablation of the amygdaloid complex with reference to functional representations. In B. E. Eleftheriou (Ed.), *The neurobiology of the amygdala*. New York: Plenum Press, 1972.

Kagan, J. American longitudinal research on psychological development. *Child Development*, 1964, *35*, 1–32.

Kagan, J. Reflection-impulsivity and reading ability in primary grade children. *Child Development*, 1965, *36*, 609–628.

Kagan, J. On the need for relativism. *American Psychologist*, 1967, *22*, 131–142.

Kagan, J., & Garn, S. M. A constitutional correlate of early intellective function. *Journal of Genetic Psychology*, 1963, *102*, 83–89.

Kagan, J., Hosken, B., & Watson, S. Child's symbolic conceptualization of parents. *Child Development*, 1961, *32*, 625–636.

Kagan, J., & Kogan, N. Individual variation in cognitive processes. In P. H. Mussen (Ed.), *Carmichael's manual of child psychology* (Vol. 1). New York: Wiley, 1970.

Kagan, J., & Moss, H. A. The stability of passive and dependent behavior from childhood through adulthood. *Child Development*, 1960, *31*, 577–591.

Kagan, J., & Moss, H. A. *Birth to maturity: A study in psychological development.* New York: Wiley, 1962.

Kaiser, H. F. The varimax criterion for analytic rotation in factor analysis. *Psychometrika*, 1958, *23*, 187–200.

Kaiser, H. F. *Relating factors between studies based upon different individuals.* Unpublished manuscript, University of Illinois, 1960.

Kaiser, H. F., & Caffrey, J. Alpha-factor analyses. *Psychometrika*, 1965, *30*, 1–14.

Kaiser, H. F., Hunka, S., & Bianchini, J. Relating factors between studies based upon different individuals. *Multivariate Behavioral Research*, 1971, *6*, 409.

Kalish, H. I., Garmezy, N., Rodnick, E. H., & Blake, R. C. The effects of anxiety and experimentally-induced stress on verbal learning. *Journal of General Psychology*, 1958, *59*, 87–95.

Kanfer, F. H. Verbal conditioning: Reinforcement schedules and experimenter influence. *Psychological Reports*, 1958, *4*, 443–452.

Kanfer, F. H., & Marston, A. R. Conditioning of self-reinforcement responses: An analogue to self-confidence training. *Psychological Reports*, 1963, *13*, 63–70. (a)

Kanfer, F. H., & Marston, A. R. Determinants of self-reinforcement in human learning. *Journal of Experimental Psychology*, 1963, *66*, 245–254. (b)

Kanfer, F. H., & Phillips, J. S. *Learning foundations of behavior therapy.* New York: Wiley, 1970.

Kanfer, F. H., & Saslow, G. Behavioral analysis: An alternative to diagnostic classification. *Archives of General Psychiatry*, 1965, *12*, 529–538.

Kangas, J., & Bradway, K. Intelligence at middle age: A thirty-eight-year follow-up. *Developmental Psychology*, 1971, *5*, 333–337.

Kaplan, A. R. (Ed.). *Human behavior genetics.* Springfield, Ill.: Charles C Thomas, 1975.

Kaplan, B. (Ed.). *Studying personality cross-culturally.* New York: Harper & Row, 1961.

Kardiner, A., Linton, R., DuBois, C., & West, J. *The psychological frontiers of society.* New York: Columbia University Press, 1945.

Kardiner, A., & Preble, E. *They studied man.* New York: New American Library, 1963.

Karli, P., Vergnes, M., & Didiergeorges, F. Rat–mouse interspecific aggressive behaviour and its manipulation by brain ablation and by brain stimulation. In S. Garattini & E. B. Sigg (Eds.), *Aggressive behaviour.* Amsterdam: Excerpta Medica Foundation, 1969.

Karsch, F. J., Dierschke, D. J., & Knobil, E. Sexual differentiation of pituitary function: Apparent difference between primates and rodents. *Science*, 1973, *179*, 484–486.

Karson, S. Primary factor correlates of boys with personality and conduct problems. *Journal of Clinical Psychology*, 1965, *21*, 16–18.

Karson, S., & Pool, K. B. Second-order factors in personality measurement. *Journal of Consulting Psychology*, 1958, *22*, 299–303.

Kassebaum, G. G., Cough, A. S., & Slater, P. E. The factorial dimensions of the MMPI. *Journal of Consulting Psychology*, 1959, *23*, 226–236.

Katahn, M. Effect of anxiety (drive) on the acquisition and avoidance of a dominant intratask response. *Journal of Personality*, 1964, *32*, 542–550.

Katahn, M., & Dean, S. Anxiety and the learning of responses varying in initial rank in the response hierarchy. *Journal of Personality*, 1966, *34*, 287–299.

Katkin, E. S. The relationship between manifest anxiety and two indices of autonomic response to stress. *Journal of Personality and Social Psychology*, 1965, *2*, 324–333.

Katz, D. *Productivity, supervision, and morale in an office situation.* Ann Arbor: Institute for Social Research, University of Michigan, 1950.

Katz, D., Maccoby, N., & Morse, N. C. *Productivity, supervision, and morale in an office situation. Part I.* Ann Arbor: Institute for Social Research, University of Michigan, 1950.

Katz, D., & Stotland, E. A preliminary statement to a theory of attitude structure and change. In S. Koch (Ed.), *Psychology: A study of a science* (Vol. 3). New York: McGraw-Hill, 1959.

Katz, M. M. A phenonenological typology of schizophrenia. In M. M. Katz, J. O. Cole, & W. E. Barton (Eds.), *The role and methodology of classification in psychiatry and psychopathology.* Washington, D.C.: U.S. Government Printing Office, 1968.

Kausler, D. H., Lair, C. V., & Matsumoto, R. Interference transfer paradigms and the performance of schizophrenics and controls. *Journal of Abnormal and Social Psychology*, 1964, *69*, 584–587.

Kawi, A., & Pasamanick, B. Association of factors of pregnancy with disorders in childhood. *Journal of American Medical Association*, 1968, *166*, 1420–1423.

Kay, P. Psychoanalytic theory of development in childhood and preadolescence. In B. B. Wolman (Ed.), *Handbook of child psychoanalysis: Research, theory, and practice.* Princeton, N.J.: Van Nostrand, 1972.

Kearsey, M. J., & Jinks, J. L. A general method of detecting additive, dominance and epistatic variation for metrical traits: I. Theory. *Heredity*, 1968, *23*, 403–409.

Keenan, B. S., Meyer, W. J., III, Hadjian, A. J., Jones, H. W., & Migeon, C. J. Syndrome of an androgen insensitivity in man: Absence of 5-α-dihydrotestosterone binding protein in skin fibroblasts. *Journal of Clinical Endocrinology and Metabolism*, 1974, *38*, 1143–1146.

Keller, F. S. *Learning: Reinforcement theory* (2nd ed.). New York: Random House, 1969.

Keller, F. S., & Schoenfeld, W. N. *Principles of psychology*. New York: Appleton, 1950.

Kelly, E. L. A preliminary report on psychological factors in assortative mating. *Psychological Bulletin*, 1937, *34*, 749.

Kelly, E. L., & Fiske, D. W. *The prediction of performance in clinical psychology*. Ann Arbor: University of Michigan Press, 1951.

Kelly, G. A. *The psychology of personal constructs* (Vol. 1). New York: Norton, 1955.

Kelly, G. A. *A theory of personality*. New York: Norton, 1963.

Kemp, C. G. *Perspectives on the group process*. Boston: Houghton, Mifflin, 1964.

Kempthorne, O., & Osborne, R. H. The interpretation of twin data. *American Journal of Human Genetics*, 1961, *13*, 320–339.

Kendall, M. G. *Rank correlation methods*. London: Griffin, 1948.

Kendler, H. H. Some specific reactions to general S–R theory. In T. R. Dixon & D. L. Horton (Eds.), *Verbal behavior and general behavior theory*. Englewood Cliffs, N.J.: Prentice-Hall, 1968.

Kendler, T. S. Verbalization and optional reversal shifts among kindergarten children. *Journal of Verbal Learning and Verbal Behavior*, 1964, *3*, 428–436.

Kennedy, G. C. Hypothalamic control of the endocrine and behavioural changes associated with oestrus in the rat. *Journal of Physiology*, 1964, *172*, 383–392.

Kent, R., O'Leary, K. D., Diament, C., & Dietz, A. Expectation biases in observational evaluations of therapeutic change. *Journal of Consulting and Clinical Psychology*, 1974, *42*, 774–780.

*Kentucky Symposium on learning theory, personality theory and clinical research*. New York: Wiley, 1954.

Kerr, W. A., & Speroff, B. J. *Manual for the empathy test*. Chicago: Psychometric Affiliates, 1951.

Khatena, J. Teaching disadvantaged preschool children to think creatively with pictures. *Journal of Educational Psychology*, 1971, *62*, 384–386.

Kiessling, R. J., & Kalish, R. A. Correlates of success in leaderless group discussion. *Journal of Social Psychology*, 1961, *54*, 359–366.

Killian, L. Objective personality factor differences between normals and schizophrenics. Unpublished master's thesis, University of Illinois, 1965.

Kiloh, L. G., & Garside, R. F. The independence of neurotic depression and endogenous depression. *British Journal of Psychiatry*, 1963, *109*, 451–463.

Kimber, J. A. M. The insight of college students into the items on a personality test. *Educational and Psychological Measurement*, 1947, *7*, 411–420.

Kimble, D. P. (Ed.). *The organization of recall*. New York: New York Academy of Science, 1967.

Kimble, G. A., Hilgard, E. L., & Marquis, D. G. *Conditioning and learning*. New York: Appleton-Century, 1961.

King, G. Research with neuropsychiatric samples. *Journal of Psychology*, 1954, *38*, 383–387.

Kingsley, R. C., & Hall, V. C. Training conservation through the use of learning sets. *Child Development*, 1967, *38*, 1111–1126.

Kinsey, A. C., Pomeroy, W. B., & Martin, C. E. *Sexual behavior in the human male*. Philadelphia: Saunders, 1948.

Kinsey, A. C., Pomeroy, W. B., Martin, C. E., & Gebhard, P. H. *Sexual behavior in the human female*. Philadelphia: Saunders, 1953.

Kipnis, D., & Wagner, C. Character structure and response to leadership power. *Journal of Experimental Research in Personality*, 1967, *2*, 16–24.

Kirkpatrick, C. Familial development, selective needs, and predictive theory. *Journal of Marriage and the Family*, 1967, *29*, 229–236.

Kistiakovskaia, M. I. Stimulus evoking positive emotions in infants in the first months of life. *Soviet Journal of Psychiatry*, 1965, *3*, 39–48.

Kitana, H. L. H. Adjustment of problem and nonproblem children to specific situations: A study in role theory. *Child Development*, 1962, *33*, 229–233.

Klatskin, E. H., Jackson, E. B., & Wilkin, L. C. The influence of degree of flexibility in maternal child care practices on early child behavior. *American Journal of Orthopsychiatry*, 1956, *26*, 79–93.

Klein, E., & Spohn, H. Behavioral dimensions of chronic schizophrenia. *Psychological Reports*, 1962, *11*, 777–783.

Klein, G. S., Barr, H. L., & Wolitsky, D. L. Personality. *Annual Review of Psychology*, 1967, *18*, 467–560.

Kling, A. Effects of amygdalectomy on social-affective behaviour in non-human primates. In B. E. Eleftheriou (Ed.), *The neurobiology of the amygdala*. New York: Plenum Press, 1972.

Knapen, M. L. Some results of an inquiry into the influence of child-training practices on the development of personality in a Bacongo society (Belgian Congo). *Journal of Social Psychology*, 1958, *47*, 223–229.

Knapp, R. R. *Criterion predictions in the Navy from the O-A personality test battery*. Paper presented at the meeting of the American Psychological Association, New York, September 1961. (a)

Knapp, R. R. Objective personality tests and sociometric correlates of frequency of sick bay visits. *Journal of Applied Psychology*, 1961, *45*, 104–110. (b)

Knapp, R. R. Personality correlates of delinquency rate in a Navy sample. *Journal of Applied Psychology*, 1963, *47*, 68–71.

Knapp, R. R. Value and personality difference between offenders and nonoffenders. *Journal of Applied Psychology*, 1964, *48*, 59–62.

Knapp, R. R. Delinquency and objective personality test factors. *Journal of Applied Psychology*, 1965, *49*, 8–10.

Koch, H. Attitudes of young children toward their peers as related to certain characteristics of their siblings. *Psychological Monographs*, 1956, *70*(19, Whole No. 323).

Koch, H. The relation of certain formal attributes of siblings to attitudes held toward each other and toward their parents. *Monographs of the Society for Research in Child Development*, 1960, *25*(4).

Koch, H. L. *Twins and twin relations*. Chicago: University of Chicago Press, 1966.

Koch, S. Epilogue. In S. Koch (Ed.), *Psychology: A study of a science* (Vol. 3). New York: McGraw-Hill, 1959.

Koch, S. Psychology and emerging conceptions of knowledge as unitary. In T. R. Wann (Ed.), *Behaviorism and phenomenology*. Chicago: University of Chicago Press, 1965.

Kogan, N., & Pankove, E. *Creative ability over a five-year span* (RB-71-57). Princeton, N.J.: Educational Testing Service, 1971.

Kohlberg, L. *The role of early experience in the study of conscience*. Paper presented at the meeting of the Western Psychological Association, San Francisco, April, 1962.

Kohlberg, L. Early education: A cognitive-developmental view. *Child Development*, 1968, *39*, 1014–1062.

Kohlberg, L. Moralization: The cognitive developmental approach. In P. B. Baltes & K. W. Schaie (Eds.), *Life-span developmental psychology: Personality and socialization*. New York: Academic Press, 1973.

Kohn, M. L. Social class and parental values. *American Journal of Sociology*, 1959, *64*, 337–351. (a)

Kohn, M. L. Social class and the exercise of parental authority. *American Sociological Review*, 1959, *24*, 352–366. (b)

Kohn, M. L. Social class and parent-child relationships. *American Journal of Sociology*, 1963, *68*, 471–480.

Kohn, M. L. The child as a determinant of his peers' approach to him. *Journal of Genetic Psychology*, 1966, *109*, 91–100.

Kopel, S., & Arkowitz, H. The role of attribution and self-perception in behavior change: Implications for behavior therapy. *Genetic Psychology Monographs*, 1975, *92*, 175–212.

Kopfstein, D. The effects of accelerating and decelerating consequences on the social behavior of trainable retarded children. *Child Development*, 1972, *43*, 800–809.

Korenchevsky, V. *Physiological and psychological aging*. New York: Hafner, 1962.

Koriat, A., Averill, J. R., & Malmstrom, E. J. Individual differences in habituation: Some methodological and conceptual issues. *Journal of Research in Personality*, 1973, *7*, 88–101.

Krasner, L. Studies of the conditioning of verbal behavior. *Psychological Bulletin*, 1958, *55*, 148–170.

Krasner, L., & Ullmann, L. P. *Research in behavior modification*. New York: Holt, Rinehart, & Winston, 1965.

Krause, M. S. The measurement of transitory anxiety. *Psychological Review*, 1961, *68*, 178–189.

Krause, M. S. Corroborative results and subsequent research commitments. *Journal of General Psychology*, 1971, *84*, 219–227.

Kreitman, N., Sainsbury, P., Morrissey, J., Towers, J., & Scrivener, J. The reliability of psychiatric assessment: An analysis. *Proceedings of the Royal Society of Medicine*, 1960, *53*, 1047–1052.

Kretschmer, E. *Physique and character.* New York: Harcourt, Brace, 1925.

Kretschmer, E. *Koerperbau und Charakter* (25th ed.). Berlin: Springer, 1967.

Kreuz, L. E., & Rose, R. M. Assessment of aggressive behavior and plasma testosterone in a young criminal population. *Psychosomatic Medicine,* 1972, *34,* 321–332.

Krug, S. E. *A test of Cattell's "trait-view" theory of distortion in measurement of personality by questionnaire.* Unpublished master's thesis, University of Illinois, 1968.

Krug, S. E., & Cattell, R. B. A test of the "trait-view" theory of distortion in measurement of personality by questionnaire. *Educational and Psychological Measurement,* 1971, *31,* 721–734.

Krug, S. E., & Cattell, R. B. Persönlichkeit: die Ansicht des Experimentators. In H. Gadamev & P. Voglev. (Eds.), *Neue Anthropologie* (Vol. 5). Stuttgart: Thieme, 1975.

Krumboltz, J. D., & Thoresen, C. E. (Eds.). *Behavioral counseling: Cases and techniques.* New York: Holt, Rinehart, & Winston, 1969.

Kryshova, N. A., Beliaeva, Z. V., Dmitrieva, A. F., Zhilinskaya, M. A., & Pervov, L. G. Investigations of the higher nervous activity and of certain vegetative features in twins. *Soviet Psychology and Psychiatry,* 1963, *1,* 36–41.

Kubany, A. J. A validation study of the error-choice technique using attitudes on national health insurance. *Educational and Psychological Measurement,* 1953, *13,* 157–163.

Kuder, G. F. *The Kuder Preference Record.* Chicago: Science Research Associates, 1953.

Kuder, G. F. *Preference Record: Occupational.* Chicago: Science Research Associates, 1956.

Kuhn, T. S. *The structure of scientific revolutions.* Chicago: University of Chicago Press, 1962.

L'Abate, L. Manifest anxiety and the learning of syllables with different associative values. *American Journal of Psychology,* 1959, *72,* 107–110.

Labouvie, E. W., & Schaie, K. W. Personality structure as a function of behavioral stability in children. *Child Development,* 1974, *45,* 252–255.

Labouvie, G. V., Frohring, W. R., Baltes, P. B., & Goulet, L. R. Changing relationships between recall performance and abilities as a function of stage of learning and timing of recall. *Journal of Educational Psychology,* 1973, *64,* 191–198.

Lacey, J. Somatic response patterning in stress: Some revisions of activation theory. In M. H. Appley & R. Trumbull (Eds.), *Psychological stress: Issues in research.* New York: Appleton-Century-Crofts, 1967.

Lacey, J. I., & Lacey, B. C. Verification and extension of the principle of autonomic response-stereotypy. *American Journal of Psychology,* 1958, *71,* 50–73.

Lachman, R. The model in theory construction. *Psychological Review,* 1960, *67,* 113–129.

Lader, M. H. Palmar skin conductance measure in anxiety and phobic states. *Journal of Psychosomatic Research,* 1967, *11,* 271–281.

Lader, M. H., & Tyrer, D. J. Central and peripheral effects of propranolol and sotalol in normal human subjects. *British Journal of Pharmacology,* 1972, *45,* 557–560.

Lader, M. H., & Wing, L. *Physiological measures, sedative drugs and morbid anxiety.* London: Oxford University Press, 1966.

Laffal, J., Lenkoski, L. D., & Ameen, L. "Opposite speech" in a schizophrenic patient. *Journal of Abnormal and Social Psychology,* 1956, *52,* 409–413.

Lagerspetz, K. M. J., & Lagerspetz, K. Y. H. Changes in the aggressiveness of mice resulting from selective breeding, learning, and social isolation. *Scandinavian Journal of Psychology,* 1971, *12,* 241–248.

Laing, R. D., Phillipson, H., & Lee, A. R. *Interpersonal perception: A theory and method of research.* London: Tavistock Publications, 1966.

Laird, D. A. Detecting abnormal behavior. *Journal of Abnormal and Social Psychology,* 1925, *20,* 128–141.

Laird, J. D. Self attribution of emotion: The effects of expressive behavior on the quality of emotional experience. *Journal of Personality and Social Psychology,* 1974, *29,* 475–486.

Lamb, D. H. *The effects of public speaking on self-report, physiological and behavioral measures of anxiety.* Unpublished doctoral dissertation, Florida State University, 1969.

Landis, C. Studies of emotional reactions. I. A preliminary study of facial expression. *Journal of Experimental Psychology,* 1924, *7,* 325–341.

Landis, C. The interpretation of facial expression in emotion. *Journal of General Psychology,* 1929, *2,* 59–72.

Landis, C. An attempt to measure emotional traits in juvenile delinquency. In K. S. Lashley (Ed.), *Studies in the dynamics of behavior.* Chicago: University of Chicago Press, 1932.

Landis, J. T. The trauma of children when parents divorce. *Marriage and Family Living,* 1960, *22,* 7–13.

Lang, P. J. Psychotherapy, pseudotherapy and behavior therapy. In *The implications of conditioning techniques for interview therapy.* Symposium presented at the meeting of the Midwestern Psychological Association, Chicago, 1965.

Lang, P. J., & Buss, A. H. Psychological deficit in schizophrenia: II. Interference and activation. *Journal of Abnormal and Social Psychology,* 1965, *70,* 77–106.

Lang, P. J., & Lazovik, A. D. Experimental desensitization of a phobia. *Journal of Abnormal and Social Psychology,* 1963, *66,* 519–525.

Lang, P. J., & Luoto, K. Mediation and associative facilitation in neurotic, psychotic and normal subjects. *Journal of Abnormal and Social Psychology,* 1962, *64,* 113–120.

Langfeld, H. S. The judgment of emotion from facial expression. *Journal of Abnormal and Social Psychology,* 1918, *13,* 173–184.

Lanzetta, J. T., & Driscoll, J. M. Preference for information about an uncertain but unavoidable outcome. *Journal of Personality and Social Psychology,* 1966, *3,* 96–102.

Lanzetta, J. T., & Kleck, R. Encoding and decoding of facial affect in humans. *Journal of Personality and Social Psychology,* 1970, *16*(1), 12–19.

Larsson, K. Individual differences in reactivity to androgen in male rats. *Physiology and Behavior,* 1966, *1,* 255–258.

Lasko, J. K. Parent behavior toward first and second children. *Genetic Psychology Monographs,* 1954, *49,* 97–137.

Lassner, J. (Ed.). Hypnosis and psychosomatic medicine. In *Proceedings of the International Congress on Hypnosis and Psychosomatic Medicine,* Paris (France), 1965. Berlin: Springer, 1967.

Laughlin, J. *Prediction of action decisions from the dynamic calculus.* Unpublished master's thesis, University of Illinois, 1972.

Lawlis, F. *The motivational aspects of the chronically unemployed.* Paper presented at the meeting of the Southwestern Psychological Association: Houston, Tex., 1967.

Lazarus, A. A. (Ed.). *Clinical behavior therapy.* New York: Bruner-Mazel, 1972.

Lazarus, A. A., & Abramovitz, A. The use of "emotive imagery" in the treatment of children's phobias. *Journal of Mental Science,* 1962, *108,* 191–195.

Lazarus, R. S., Deese, J., & Hamilton, R. Anxiety and stress in learning: The role of intra-list duplication. *Journal of Experimental Psychology,* 1954, *47,* 111–114.

Lazarsfeld, P. F. The logical and mathematical foundation of latent structure analysis. In S. Stouffer (Ed.), *Measurement and prediction* (Vol. 4), Princeton: Princeton University Press, 1950.

League, B. J., & Jackson, D. N. Conformity, veridicality and self-esteem. *Journal of Abnormal and Social Psychology,* 1964, *68,* 113–115.

Learmonth, G. J., Ackerly, W., & Kaplan, M. Relationships between palmar skin potential during stress and personality variables. *Psychosomatic Medicine,* 1959, *21,* 150–157.

Leary, T., & Coffey, H. Interpersonal diagnosis, some problems of methodology and validation. *Journal of Abnormal and Social Psychology,* 1955, *50,* 110–126.

Lebo, M. A. *Intra-individual mood structure and change: A P-technique analysis of five pregnant women.* Unpublished doctoral dissertation, West Virginia University, 1972.

Leeper, R. W. The role of motivation in learning: A study of the phenomenon of differential motivational control of the utilization of habits. *Journal of Genetic Psychology,* 1935, *46,* 3–40.

Leeper, R. W. Some needed developments in the motivational theory of emotions. In D. Levine (Ed.), *Nebraska Symposium on Motivation (1964).* Lincoln: University of Nebraska Press, 1965.

Leeper, R., & Madison, P. *Toward understanding human personalities.* New York: Appleton-Century-Crofts, 1959.

Legewie, H. *Persoenlichkeitstheorie und Psychopharmaka.* Meisenheim, Glan: Hain, 1968.

Lenneberg, E. H. On explaining language. (The development of language in children can best be understood in the context of developmental biology.) *Science,* 1969, *164,* 635–643.

Lentz, F. T. Acquiescence as a factor in the measurement of personality. *Psychological Bulletin,* 1938, *35,* 659.

Leontieff, B. *The nature of conditioning.* Presidential Address, 21st International Congress of Psychology, Moscow, 1966.

Leontiev, A. N. Ponyatie ostrazheniya; ego znachenie dlya psikhologii. *Voprosy Filosofii,* 1966, *20,* 48–56.

Leslie, G. R. *The family in social context.* New York: Oxford University Press, 1967.

Leton, D. A. A study of the validity of parent attitude measurement. *Child Development,* 1958, *29,* 515–520.

Levene, H. I., Engel, B. T., & Schulkin, F. R. Patterns of autonomic responsivity in identical schizophrenic twins. *Psychophysiology,* 1967, *3,* 363–370.

Levi, L. (Ed.). *Society, stress and disease* (Vol. 1). *The environment and psychosomatic disease.* London: Oxford University Press, 1971.

Levi, L. (Ed.). *Stress and distress in response to psychosocial stimuli.* Oxford: Pergamon, 1972.

Levi, L. (Ed.). *Emotions: Their parameters and measurement.* New York: Raven Press, 1975.

Levine, S. The effects of differential infantile stimulation on emotionality at weaning. *Canadian Journal of Psychology,* 1959, *13,* 243–247.

Levine, S. Sex differences in the brain. *Scientific American,* 1966, *214*(4), 84–90.

Levine, S., & Mullins, R. F. J. Hormonal influences on brain organization in infant rats. *Science,* 1966, *152,* 1585–1592.

Levinger, G., & Breedlove, J. Interpersonal attraction and agreement: A study of marriage partners. *Journal of Personality and Social Psychology,* 1966, *3,* 367–372.

Levinson, E. J. The modification of intelligence by training in verbalization of word definitions and simple concepts. *Child Development.* 1971, *42,* 1361–1380.

Levis, D. J. (Ed.). *Learning approaches to therapeutic behavior change.* Chicago: Aldine Press, 1970.

Levitt, E. E. A brief commentary on the "psychiatric break through" with emphasis on the hematology of anxiety. In C. D. Spielberger (Ed.), *Anxiety: Current trends in theory and research* (Vol. I). New York: Academic Press, 1972.

Levitt, H., & Goss, A. E. Stimulus attributes and drive in paired-associate learning. *Journal of Experimental Psychology,* 1961, *62,* 243–252.

Levy, D. M. *Maternal overprotection.* New York: Columbia University Press, 1943.

Levy, L. H. *Conceptions of personality: Theories and research.* New York: Random House, 1970.

Levy, N., & Schlosberg, H. Woodworth scale values of the Lightfoot pictures of facial expression. *Journal of Experimental Psychology,* 1960, *60,* 121–125.

Lévy-Schoen, A. *L'image d'autrui chez l'enfant.* Paris: Presses Universitaires de France, 1964.

Lewin, K. *A dynamic theory of personality.* New York: McGraw-Hill, 1935.

Lewin, K. *Field theory in social science.* New York: Harper, 1951.

Lewis, M. Infants' responses to facial stimuli during the first year of life. *Developmental Psychology,* 1969, *1,* 75–86.

Lewis, M. State as an infant-environment interaction: An analysis of mother-infant behavior as a function of sex (RB-71-29). Princeton, N.J.: Educational Testing Service, 1971.

Lewis, N. A., & Taylor, J. A. Anxiety and extreme response preferences. *Educational and Psychological Measurement,* 1955, *15,* 111–116.

Lichtenberg, P., & Norton, D. C. *Cognitive and mental development in the first five years of life: A review of recent research* (U.S. Public Health Service Publication No. 2057). Rockville, Md.: National Institute of Mental Health, 1970.

Lichtenwalner, J. S., & Maxwell, J. The relationship of birth order and socioeconomic status to the creativity of preschool children. *Child Development,* 1969, *40,* 1241–1247.

Lidz, R. W., & Lidz, T. The family environment of schizophrenic patients. *Journal of American Psychiatry,* 1949, *106,* 332–345.

Lidz, T., Cornelison, A., Fleck, S., & Terry, D. The intra-familial environment of schizophrenic patients: II. Marital schism and marital skew. *American Journal of Psychiatry,* 1957, *114,* 241–248.

Lienert, G. A. *Belastung und Regression.* Meisenheim, Glan: Hain, 1963.

Likert, R. A technique for the measurement of attitudes. *Archives of Psychology,* 1932, (No. 140), 55.

Lindegard, B., & Nyman, G. E. *Interrelations between psychologic, somatologic and endocrine dimensions.* Lunds Universitets Årsskrift. Lund: Gleerup, 1956.

Lindsley, D. B. Psychophysiology and motivation. In M. R. Jones (Ed.), *Nebraska Symposium on Motivation (1957).* Lincoln: University of Nebraska Press, 1957.

Lindsley, D. B. The role of nonspecific reticulo-thalamo-cortical-systems in emotion. In P. Black (Ed.), *Physiological correlates of emotion.* New York: Academic Press, 1970.

Lindsley, O. R. Operant conditioning methods applied to research in chronic schizophrenia. *Psychiatric Research Reports,* 1956, *5,* 118–153.

Lindsley, O. R. Direct measurement and prosthesis of retarded behavior. *Journal of Education,* 1964, *147,* 62–81.

Lindzey, G. *Assessment of human motives.* New York: Rinehart, 1958.

Lindzey, G., & Byrne, D. Measurement of social choice and interpersonal attractiveness. In G. Lindzey & E. Aronson (Eds.), *Handbook of social psychology* (Vol. II). Reading, Mass.: Addison-Wesley, 1968.

Lindzey, G., Loehlin, J. C., Manosevitz, M., & Thiessen, D. D. Behavioral genetics. *Annual Review of Psychology,* 1971, *22,* 39–94.

Lindzey, G., & Thiessen, D. D. (Eds.). *Contributions to behavior-genetic analysis: The mouse as a prototype.* New York: Appleton-Century-Crofts. 1970.

Lingoes, J. C., & Vandenberg, S. G. A nonmetric analysis of twin data based on a multifaceted design. *Louisville twin study* (Rep. No. 17). Louisville, Ky.: University of Louisville School of Medicine, 1966.

Linton, R. Status and role. In E. Borgatta & H. J. Meyer (Eds.), *Sociological theory.* New York: Knopf, 1956.

Lippitt, R., & Radke, M. New trends in the investigation of prejudice. *Annals of the American Academy of Political and Social Science,* 1946, *244,* 167–176.

Locke, E. A. The relationship of task success to task liking and satisfaction. *Journal of Applied Psychology,* 1965, *49,* 379–385.

Loehlin, J. C. A computer program that simulates personality. In S. Tomkins & S. Messick (Eds.), *Computer simulation of personality.* New York: Wiley, 1963.

Loehlin, J. C. Some methodological problems in Cattell's Multiple Abstract Variance Analysis. *Psychological Review,* 1965, *72,* 156–161. (a)

Loehlin, J. C. A heredity-environment analysis of personality inventory data. In S. G. Vandenberg (Ed.), *Method and goals in human behavior genetics.* New York: Academic Press, 1965. (b)

Loehlin, J. C., Lindzey, G., & Spuhler, J. N. *Race differences in intelligence.* San Francisco: Freeman, 1975.

Loehlin, J. C., & Nichols, R. C. *Heredity, environment, and personality.* Austin: University of Texas Press, 1976.

Loehlin, J. C., & Vandenberg, S. G. Genetic and environmental components in the covariation of cognitive abilities. In S. G. Vandenberg (Ed.), *Progress in human behavior genetics.* Baltimore: Johns Hopkins University Press, 1968.

Logan, F. A., & Wagner, A. R. *Reward and punishment.* Boston: Allyn & Bacon, 1965.

Lombardo, J. P., Weiss, R. F., & Buchanan, W. Reinforcing and attracting functions of yielding. *Journal of Personality and Social Psychology,* 1972, *21,* 359–368.

London, P. *Behavior control.* New York: Harper & Row, 1969.

Longstaff, R. P., & Jurgensen, C. E. Fakability of the Jurgensen Classification Inventory. *Journal of Applied Psychology,* 1953, *37,* 86–89.

Longstreth, L. E., Longstreth, G. V., Ramirez, C., & Fernandez, G. The ubiquity of big brother. *Child Development,* 1975, *46,* 769–772.

Loraine, J. A., Ismail, A. A. A., Adamopoulos, D. A., & Dove, G. A. Endocrine function in male and female homosexuals. *British Medical Journal,* 1970, *4,* 406–408.

Lord, F. M. Elementary models for measuring change. In C. W. Harris (Ed.), *Problems in measuring change.* Madison: University of Wisconsin Press, 1963.

Lorge, I. Gen-like: Halo or reality? *Psychological Bulletin,* 1937, *34,* 545–546.

Lorr, M. Classification of the behavior disorders. *Annual Review of Psychology,* 1961, *2,* 195–216.

Lorr, M. *Explorations in typing psychotics.* London: Pergamon, 1966.

Lorr, M. Dimensions and categories for assessment of psychotics. In P. McReynolds (Ed.), *Advances in psychological assessment* (Vol. 2). Palo Alto, Calif.: Science and Behavior Books, 1971.

Lorr, M., Daston, P., & Smith, I. R. An analysis of mood states. *Educational and Psychological Measurement,* 1967, *27,* 89–96.

Lorr, M., & Jenkins, R. L. Three factors in parent behavior. *Journal of Consulting Psychology,* 1953, *17,* 306–308.

Lorr, M., Jenkins, R. L., & O'Connor, J. P. Factors descriptive of psychopathology and behavior of hospitalized psychotics. *Journal of Abnormal and Social Psychology,* 1955, *50,* 78–86.

Lorr, M., & Klett, C. J. Major psychotic disorders. *Archives of General Psychiatry,* 1968, *19,* 652–658.

Lorr, M., & Klett, C. J. Cross-cultural comparisons of psychotic syndromes. *Journal of Abnormal Psychology,* 1969, *74,* 531–543. (a)

Lorr, M., & Klett, C. J. Psychotic behavioral types. *Archives of General Psychiatry*, 1969, *20*, 592-597. (b)

Lorr, M., Klett, C. J., & Cave, R. Higher level psychotic syndromes. *Journal of Abnormal Psychology*, 1967, *72*, 74-77.

Lorr, M., Klett, C. J., & McNair, D. M. *Syndromes of psychosis*. New York: Macmillan & Pergamon, 1963.

Lorr, M., McNair, D. M., Klett, C. J., & Lasky, J. Evidence of ten psychotic syndromes. *Journal of Consulting Psychology*. 1962, *26*, 185-189.

Lorr, M., & O'Connor, J. P. The relation between neurosis and psychosis: A re-analysis. *Journal of Mental Science*, 1957, *103*, 375-380.

Lorr, M., & O'Connor, J. P. Psychotic symptom patterns in a behavior inventory. *Educational and Psychological Measurement*, 1962, *22*, 139-146.

Lorr, M., O'Connor, J. P., & Stafford, J. W. Confirmation of nine psychotic symptom patterns. *Journal of Clinical Psychology*, 1957, *13*, 252-257.

Lorr, M., O'Connor, J. P., & Stafford, J. W. The psychotic reaction profile. *Journal of Clinical Psychology*, 1960, *16*, 241-245.

Losse, H., Kretschmer, W., Kuban, G., & Böttger, K. Die vegetativ Struktur des Individuums. *Acta Neurovegativativa*, 1956, *13*, 337-339.

Lott, A. J. *Learning and liking.* Paper presented at the meeting of the Southwestern Psychological Association, Arlington, Tex., 1966.

Lott, A. J., Aponte, J. F., McGinley, W. H., & Lott, B. E. The effect of delayed reward on the development of interpersonal attraction. *Journal of Experimental Social Psychology*, 1969, *5*, 101-113.

Lott, A. J., Bright, M. A., Weinstein, P., & Lott, B. E. Liking for persons as a function of incentive and drive during acquisition. *Journal of Personality and Social Psychology*, 1970, *14*, 66-76.

Lott, A. J., & Lott, B. E. Group cohesiveness as interpersonal attraction: A review of relationships with antecedent and consequent variables. *Psychological Bulletin*, 1965, *64*, 259-309.

Lott, A. J., & Lott, B. E. Group cohesiveness and individual learning. *Journal of Educational Psychology*, 1966, *57*, 61-73.

Lott, A. J., & Lott, B. E. A learning theory approach to interpersonal attitudes. In T. C. Brock, A. G. Greenwald, & T. M. Ostrom (Eds.), *Attitude change theory and research*. New York: Academic Press, 1968.

Lott, A. J., Lott, B. E., & Matthews, G. Interpersonal attraction among children as a function of vicarious reward. *Journal of Educational Psychology*, 1969, *60*, 274-283.

Lott, B. E., & Lott, A. J. The formation of positive attitudes toward group members. *Journal of Abnormal and Social Psychology*, 1960, *61*, 297-300.

Lovaas, O. I., Berberich, J. P., Perloff, B. F., & Schaeffer, B. Acquisition of imitative speech by schizophrenic children. *Science*, 1966, *151*, 705-707.

Lovibond, S. H. Intermittent reinforcement in behavior therapy. *Behaviour Research and Therapy*, 1963, *1*, 127-132.

Lovibond, S. H. Personality and conditioning. In B. A. Maher (Ed.), *Progress in experimental personality research*. New York: Academic Press, 1964.

Lovitt, T. C., Guppy, T. E., & Blattner, J. E. The use of a free-time contingency with fourth graders to increase spelling accuracy. *Behaviour Research and Therapy*, 1969, *7*, 151-156.

Luborsky, L. B., & Cattell, R. B. The validation of personality factors in humor. *Journal of Personality*, 1947, *15*, 283-291.

Luborsky, L., & Mintz, J. The contribution of P-technique to personality, psychotherapy, and psychosomatic research. In R. M. Dreger (Ed.), *Multivariate personality research: Contributions to the understanding of personality in honor of Raymond B. Cattell*. Baton Rouge, La.: Claitor, 1972.

Lucas, J. D. The interactive effects of anxiety, failure, and intra-serial duplication. *American Journal of Psychology*, 1952, *65*, 59-66.

Lukesch, H. (Ed.). *Auswirkungen elterlicher Erziehungsstile*. Göttingen: Hogrefe, 1975.

Lund, R. Personality factors and desynchronization of circadian rhythms. *Psychosomatic Medicine*, 1974, *36*, 224-228.

Lundin, R. W. *Personality: An experimental approach*. New York: Macmillan, 1961.

Luria, A. R. *The mind of a mnemonist*. New York: Basic Books, 1968.

Lushene, R. E. *The effects of physical and psychological threat on the autonomic, motoric, and ideational components of state anxiety*. Unpublished doctoral dissertation, Florida State University, 1970.

Luthe, W. (Ed.). *Autogenic therapy* (6 vols.). New York: Grune & Stratton, 1969-1973.

Lykken, D. T. Neuropsychology and psychophysiology in personality research. In E. F. Borgatta & W. W. Lambert (Eds.), *Handbook of personality theory and research*. Chicago: Rand McNally, 1968.

Lykken, D. T., Tellegen, A., & Thorkelson, K. Genetic determination of EEG frequency spectra. *Biological Psychology*, 1974, *1*, 245-259.

Lynn, R. *Attention, arousal and the orientation reaction*. Oxford: Pergamon, 1966.

Lynn, R. *Personality and national character*. Oxford: Pergamon, 1971.

Lyon, M. F. Gene action in the X-chromosome of the mouse (*Mus musculus* L.). *Nature*, 1961, *190*, 372-373.

Lyon, M. F. The activity of the sex chromosomes in mammals. *Science Progress*, 1970, *58*, 117-130.

Lyon, M. F., & Hawkes, S. G. X-linked gene for testicular feminization in the mouse. *Nature*, 1970, *227*, 1217-1219.

Lysk, R. D. Diencephalic placement of estradiol and sexual receptivity in the female rat. *American Journal of Physiology*, 1962, *203*, 493-496.

Lytton, H. Observational studies of parent-child interaction: A methodological review. *Child Development*, 1971, *42*, 651-684.

Maccoby, E. E. The choice of variables in the study of socialization. *Sociometry*, 1961, *24*, 357-371.

Maccoby, E. E. (Ed.). *The development of sex differences*. Stanford: Stanford University Press, 1966.

Maccoby, E. E., Dowley, E. M., Hagen, J. W., & Degerman, R. Activity level and intellectual functioning in normal preschool children. *Child Development*, 1965, *36*, 761-770.

Maccoby, E. E., & Gibbs, P. K. Methods of child-rearing in two social classes. In W. E. Martin & C. B. Stendler (Eds.), *Readings in child development*. New York: Harcourt, Brace, 1954.

Maccoby, E. E., & Jacklin, C. N. *The psychology of sex differences*. London: Oxford University Press, 1975.

MacCorquodale, K., & Meehl, P. E. On a distinction between hypothetical constructs and intervening variables. *Psychological Review*. 1948, *55*, 95-107.

MacDonald, A. P., Jr. Birth order and personality. *Journal of Consulting and Clinical Psychology*, 1971, *36*, 171-176.

MacDonald, D. G., Johnson, L. C., & Hord, D. J. Habituation of the orienting response in alert and drowsy subjects. *Psychophysiology*, 1964, *1*, 163-173.

Macfarlane, J. W., Allen, L., & Honzik, M. P. *A developmental study of the behavioral problems of normal children between 21 months and 14 years*. Berkeley, Calif.: University of California Press, 1962.

Mack, J. C. The attitudes of mothers of male schizophrenics toward child behavior. *Journal of Abnormal and Social Psychology*, 1953, *48*, 485-489.

Mackay, H. A., & Inglis, J. *The reinforcement of simple responses in elderly psychiatric patients with and without memory disorder*. Paper presented at the meeting of the Eastern Psychological Association, Atlantic City, N.J., April, 1965.

Mackintosh, N. J. *The psychology of animal learning*. London: Academic Press, 1974.

Maddi, S. Affective tone during environmental regularity and change. *Journal of Abnormal and Social Psychology*, 1961, *62*, 338-345.

Madsen, K. B. *Theories of motivation*. Copenhagen: Munksgaard, 1959.

Madsen, K. B. *Theories of motivation*. Cleveland: Howard Allen, 1961.

Madsen, K. B. *Theories of motivation*. Cleveland: Howard Allen, 1964.

Madsen, K. B. *Theories of motivation* (4th ed.; Spanish ed.). Buenos Aires: Paidos, 1967.

Madsen, K. B. *Integration through metascience*. Wien: Akten des XIV Internationalen Kongres für Philosophie, 1968. (a)

Madsen, K. B. *Theories of motivation*. (4th ed.) Copenhagen and Kent, Ohio: Munksgaard and Kent State University Press, 1968. (b)

Madsen, K. B. Theories of motivation. In B. Wolman (Ed.), *Handbook of general psychology*. Englewood Cliffs, N.J.: Prentice-Hall, 1973.

Madsen, K. B. *Theories of motivation*. Copenhagen and New York: Munksgaard and Wiley, 1974.

Mahalanobis, P. C. On the generalized distance in statistics. *Proceedings of the India National Institute of Science*, Calcutta, 1936, *2*, 49-55.

Mahler, M. S., Pine, F., & Bergman, A. *The psychological birth of the human infant: Symbiosis and individuation*. New York: Basic Books, 1975.

Malinowski, B. *The father in primitive psychology*. New York: Norton, 1927.

Maller, J. B. General and specific factors in character. *Journal of Social Psychology*, 1934, *5*, 97-102.

Malmo, R. B. Measurement of drive: An unsolved problem in psychology. In M. R. Jones (Ed.), *Nebraska symposium on motivation (1957-1958)*. Lincoln: University of Nebraska Press, 1958.

Malmo, R. B. Activation: A neuropsychological dimension. *Psychological Review*, 1959, *66*, 367-386.

Maltzman, I. Theoretical conceptions of semantic conditioning and generalization. In T. R. Dixon & D. L. Horton (Eds.), *Verbal behavior and general behavior theory*. Englewood Cliffs, N.J.: Prentice-Hall, 1968.

Mandler, G. Emotion. In R. Brown, E. Galanter, E. H. Haas, & G. Mandler (Eds.), *New directions in psychology*. New York: Holt, Rinehart, & Winston, 1962.

Mandler, G. Organization and memory. In K. W. Spence & J. T. Spence (Eds.), *The psychology of learning and motivation: Advances in research and theory*. New York: Academic Press, 1968.

Mandler, G. *Mind and emotion*. New York: Wiley, 1975.

Mandler, G., & Sarason, S. B. A study of anxiety and learning. *Journal of Abnormal and Social Psychology*, 1952, *47*, 166-173.

Mangan, G. L. Studies of the relationships between neo-Pavlovian properties of higher nervous activity and Western personality dimensions: IV. A factor-analytic study of extraversion and flexibility and the sensitivity and mobility of the nervous system. *Journal of Experimental Research in Personality*, 1967, *2*, 124-127.

Mangan, G. L., & O'Gorman, J. G. Initial amplitude and rate of habituation of orienting reaction in relation to extraversion and neuroticism. *Journal of Experimental Research in Personality*, 1969, *3*, 275-282.

Mangan, G. L., Quartermain, D., & Vaughn, G. M. Relationship between Taylor MAS scores and group conformity. *Perceptual and Motor Skills*, 1959, *9*, 207-209.

Mangan, G. L., Quartermain, D., & Vaughn, G. M. Taylor MAS and group conformity pressure. *Journal of Abnormal and Social Psychology*, 1960, *61*, 146-147.

Mann, R. D. A review of the relationships between personality and performance in small groups. *Psychological Bulletin*, 1959, *56*, 241-270.

Manning, A. Selection for mating speed in *Drosophila melanogaster* based on the behaviour of one sex. *Animal Behaviour*, 1963, *11*, 116-120.

Manosevitz, M., Lindzey, G., & Thiessen, D. D. *Behavioral genetics: Method and research*. New York: Appleton-Century-Crofts, 1969.

Mariotto, M. J., & Paul, G. L. A multimethod validation of the Inpatient Multidimensional Psychiatric Scale with chronically institutionalized patients. *Journal of Consulting and Clinical Psychology*, 1974, *42*, 497-508.

Mark, V. H., Ervin, F. R., & Sweet, W. H. Deep temporal lobe stimulation in man. In B. E. Eleftheriou (Ed.), *The neurobiology of the amygdala*. New York: Plenum Press, 1972.

Marke, S., & Nyman, G. E. *Perception of parental identification, parental dominance, and anxiety in young adults*. Lund: CWK Gleerup, 1963.

Marks, P. A., & Seeman, W. *The actuarial description of abnormal personality: An atlas for use with the MMPI*. Baltimore: Williams & Wilkins, 1963.

Marston, A. R. Response strength and self-reinforcement. *Journal of Experimental Psychology*, 1964, *68*, 537-540. (a)

Marston, A. R. Variables affecting incidence of self-reinforcement. *Psychological Reports*, 1964, *14*, 879-884. (b)

Marston, A. R. Imitation, self-reinforcement, and reinforcement of another person. *Journal of Personality and Social Psychology*, 1965, *2*, 255-261. (a)

Marston, A. R. *Self-reinforcement research: Analogue to psychotherapy*. Unpublished manuscript, University of Wisconsin, 1965. (b)

Martin, B. The assessment of anxiety by physiological behavioral measures. *Psychological Bulletin*, 1961, *58*, 234-255.

Martin, I. Somatic reactivity: Methodology. In H. J. Eysenck (Ed.), *Handbook of abnormal psychology* (2nd ed.). San Diego: Knapp, 1973. (a)

Martin, I. Somatic reactivity: Interpretation. In H. J. Eysenck (Ed.), *Handbook of abnormal psychology* (2nd ed.). San Diego: Knapp, 1973. (b)

Martin, I. Psychophysiology and conditioning. In P. H. Venables & M. J. Christie (Eds.), *Research in psychophysiology*. London: Wiley, 1975.

Martin, I., & Levey, A. B. *The genesis of the classical conditioned response*. London: Pergamon, 1969.

Martin, J. C., Carkhuff, R. R., & Berenson, B. G. Process variables in counseling and psychotherapy: A study in counseling and friendship. *Journal of Counseling Psychology*, 1966, *13*, 356-359.

Martin, L., & Adkins, D. C. A second-order analysis of reasoning abilities. *Psychometrika*, 1954, *19*, 71-78.

Martorano, R. D., & Nathan, P. E. Syndromes of psychosis and nonpsychosis: Factor analysis of a systems analysis. *Journal of Abnormal Psychology*, 1972, *80*, 1-10.

Marx, N. H., & Hillix, W. *Systems and theories in psychology*. New York: McGraw-Hill, 1963.

Masica, D. N., Money, J., Ehrhardt, A. A., & Lewis, V. G. I.Q., fetal sex hormones and cognitive patterns: Studies in the testicular feminizing syndrome of androgen insensitivity. *Johns Hopkins Medical Journal*, 1969, *124*, 33-43.

Masling, J. The influence of situational and interpersonal variables in projective testing. *Psychological Bulletin*, 1960, *57*, 65-85.

Maslow, A. H. A dynamic theory of human motivation. *Psychological Review*, 1943, *50*, 370-396.

Maslow, A. H. *Motivation and personality*. New York: Harper & Row, 1954.

Mason, J. W. Organization of psychoendocrine mechanisms: A review and reconsideration of research. In N. S. Greenfield & R. A. Sternbach (Eds.), *Handbook of Psychophysiology*. New York: Holt, Rinehart, & Winston, 1972.

Mason, J. W. Emotion as reflected in patterns of endocrine integration. In L. Levi (Ed.), *Emotions: Their parameters and measurement*. New York: Raven Press, 1975.

Masters, W. H., & Johnson, V. E. *Human sexual response*. London: Churchill, 1967.

Masuda, M. Adaptational individuality. In A. J. Mandell & M. P. Mandell (Eds.), *Psychochemical research in man*. New York: Academic Press, 1969.

Mather, K. *Biometrical genetics: The study of continuous variation*. London: Methuen, 1949.

Mather, K., & Jinks, J. L. Correlations between relatives arising from sex-linked genes. *Nature* (London), 1963, *198*, 314-315.

Mather, K. & Jinks, J. L. *Biometrical genetics: The study of continuous variation* (2nd ed.). London: Chapman & Hall, 1971.

Matthews, C. G., Guertin, W. H., & Reitan, R. M. Wechsler-Bellevue subtest mean rank orders in diverse diagnostic groups. *Psychological Reports*, 1962, *11*, 3-9.

Mattock, J., & Mackinnon, P. C. B. Changes in the amygdala at puberty. *Journal of Anatomy*, 1975, *119*, 414.

Maurer-Groeli, Y. Blutgruppen, Persoenlichkeit und Schulabschluss: Eine Untersuchung mittels FPI. *Schweizerische Zeitschrift für Psychologie*, 1974, *33*, 407-410.

May, J. M., & Sweney, A. B. *Personality and motivational changes observed in the treatment of psychotic patients*. Paper presented at Southwestern Psychological Association meeting, 1965.

May, R. *The meaning of anxiety*. New York: Ronald Press, 1950.

Mazzei, J. *Two stages of paired-associate learning as a function of intralist response similarity, response meaningfulness, and anxiety*. Unpublished master's thesis, West Virginia University, 1969.

McAdoo, W. G. *The effects of success and failure feedback on A-State for subjects who differ in A-Trait*. Unpublished doctoral dissertation, Florida State University, 1969.

McArthur, R. T., & Elley, W. B. The reduction of socioeconomic bias in intelligence testing. *British Journal of Educational Psychology*, 1963, *33*, 107-119.

McCall, R. B., Appelbaum, M. I., & Hogarty, P. S. Developmental changes in mental performance. *Monographs of the Society for Research in Child Development*, 1973, *38*, (3, Serial No. 150).

McCance, R. A., Luff, M. C., & Widdowson, E. E. Physical and emotional periodicity in women. *Journal of Hygiene*, 1937, *37*, 571-611.

McCartin, R. A., & Meyers, C. E. An exploration of six semantic factors at 1st grade. *Multivariate Behavioral Research*, 1966, *1*, 74-94.

McClearn, G. E. Genotype and mouse activity. *Journal of Comparative and Physiological Psychology*, 1961, *54*, 674-676.

McClearn, G. E., & DeFries, J. C. *Introduction to behavioral genetics*. San Francisco: Freeman, 1973.

McClearn, G. E., & Meredith, W. Behavioral genetics. *Annual Review of Psychology*, 1966, *17*, 515-550.

McClelland, D. *The achieving society*. Princeton, N.J.: Van Nostrand, 1961.

McClelland, D. O., Atkinson, J. W., Clark, R. A., & Lowell, E. I. *The achievement motive*. New York: Appleton-Century-Crofts, 1953.

McCrary, J. W., Jr., & Hunter, W. S. Serial position curves in verbal learning. *Science*, 1953, *117*, 131-134.

McCreary, J. B., & Bendig, A. W. Comparison of two forms of the Manifest Anxiety Scale. *Journal of Consulting Psychology*, 1954, *18*, 206.

McDavid, J. W. Personality and situational

determinants of conformity. *Journal of Abnormal and Social Psychology,* 1959, *58,* 241–246.

McDavid, J. W., & Sistrunk, F. Personality correlates of two kinds of conforming behavior. *Journal of Personality,* 1964, *32,* 420–435.

McDonald, D. G., Johnson, L. C., & Hord, D. J. Habituation of the orienting response in alert and drowsy subjects. *Psychophysiology,* 1964, *1,* 163–173.

McDonald, R. D. *The effect of reward-punishment and affiliation need on interpersonal attraction.* Unpublished doctoral dissertation, University of Texas, 1962.

McDougall, W. *Outline of psychology.* London: Methuen, 1923.

McDougall, W. *Energies of men.* London: Methuen, 1932.

McDougall, W. B. *Outline of psychology* (6th ed.). London: Methuen, 1933.

McGrath, J. E., & Altman, I. *Small group research.* New York: Holt, Rinehart, & Winston, 1966.

McGuire, W. J. Attitudes and opinions. *Annual Review of Psychology,* 1966, *17,* 475–514.

McLaughlin, R. J., & Eysenck, H. J. Extraversion, neuroticism, and paired-associates learning, *Journal of Experimental Research in Personality,* 1967, *2,* 128–132.

McMichael, R. E., & Grinder, R. E. Guilt and resistance to temptation in Japanese- and white Americans. *The Journal of Social Psychology,* 1964, *64,* 217–223.

McMichael, R. E., & Grinder, R. E. Children's guilt after transgression: Combined effect of exposure to American culture and ethnic background. *Child Development,* 1966, *37,* 425–431.

McNair, D. M., & Lorr, M. An analysis of mood in neurotics. *Journal of Abnormal and Social Psychology,* 1964, *69,* 620–627.

McNair, D. M., Lorr, M., & Droppleman, L. F. *Test manual for the Profile of Mood States (POMS).* San Diego, Calif.: Educational and Industrial Testing Service, 1971.

McNemar, Q. On growth measurement. *Educational and Psychological Measurement,* 1958, *18,* 47–55.

McQuitty, L. L. Elementary linkage analysis for isolating orthogonal and oblique types and typal relevances. *Educational and Psychological Measurement,* 1957, *17,* 207–229.

McQuitty, L. L. A method for selecting patterns to differentiate categories of people. *Educational and Psychological Measurement,* 1961, *21,* 85–94.

McQuitty, L. L. Multiple hierarchical classification of institutions and persons with reference to union-management relations and psychological well-being. *Educational and Psychological Measurement,* 1962, *22,* 513–531.

McQuitty, L. L. A mutual development of some typological theories and some pattern-analytic methods. *Educational and Psychological Measurement,* 1967, *27,* 21–46.

Mead, M. *Coming of age in Samoa.* New York: Morrow, 1928.

Mead, M. *Growing up in New Guinea.* New York: Morrow, 1930.

Mead, M. *Sex and temperament in three primitive societies.* New York: Morrow, 1935.

Mead, M. *Cooperation and competition among primitive peoples.* New York: McGraw-Hill, 1937.

Mead, M. *Male and female: A study of the sexes in a changing world.* New York: Morrow, 1949.

Mead, M. Social change and cultural surrogates. In C. Kluckhohn & H. A. Murray (Eds.), *Personality in nature, society, and culture* (2nd ed.). New York: Knopf, 1956.

Medinnus, G. R., & Johnson, R. C. *Child and adolescent psychology: Behavior and development.* New York: Wiley, 1969.

Mednick, S. A. A learning theory approach to research in schizophrenia. *Psychological Bulletin,* 1958, *55,* 316–327.

Mednick, S. A. The associative basis of the creative process. *Psychological Review,* 1962, *69,* 220–232.

Mednick, S. A., & DeVito, R. *Associative response competition in verbal learning of acute and chronic schizophrenics.* Paper presented at the meeting of the Eastern Psychological Association, Philadelphia, April 1958.

Meehl, P. E. The dynamics of "structured" personality tests. *Journal of Clinical Psychology,* 1945, *1,* 296–303.

Meehl, P. E. On the circularity of the law of effect. *Psychological Bulletin,* 1950, *47,* 52–75.

Meehl, P. E. *Clinical vs. statistical prediction.* Minneapolis: University of Minnesota Press, 1954.

Meehl, P. E., & Hathaway, S. R. The K-factor as a suppressor variable in the Minnesota Multiphasic Personality Inventory. *Journal of Applied Psychology,* 1946, *30,* 525–564.

Mefford, H. B., Jr., Hale, H. B., & Loefer, J. B. *Individual excretion patterns of rats during chronic exposure to adverse conditions.* Paper presented at the XIXth Congress of International Physiology, Montreal, August–September 1953.

Mefford, R. B. Structuring physiological correlates of mental processes and states: The study of biological correlates of mental processes. In R. B. Cattell (Ed.), *Handbook of multivariate experimental psychology.* Chicago: Rand McNally, 1966.

Mefford, R. B. Some experimental implications of change. In P. H. Venables & M. J. Christie (Eds.), *Research in psychophysiology.* London: Wiley, 1975.

Mefford, R. B., Moran, L. J., & Kimble, J. P. Methodological considerations in the quest for a physical basis of schizophrenia. *Journal of Nervous and Mental Disease,* 1960, *131,* 354–359.

Megargee, E. I. *The California Psychological Inventory Handbook.* San Francisco: Jossey-Bass, 1972.

Mehlman, B. The reliability of psychiatric diagnosis. *Journal of Abnormal and Social Psychology,* 1952, *47,* 577–587.

Meichenbaum, D., & Goodman, J. Reflection-impulsivity and verbal control of motor behavior. *Child Development,* 1969, *40,* 785–797.

Meissner, W. H. Intervening constructs: The problem of functional validity. *Psychological Review,* 1961, *11,* 355–364.

Mellone, M. S. A factorial study of picture tests for young children. *British Journal of Psychology,* 1944, *35,* 9–16.

Meltzoff, J. The effect of mental set and item structure upon response to a projective test. *Journal of Abnormal and Social Psychology,* 1951, *46,* 177–189.

Menninger, K. The practice of psychiatry. *Digest of Neurological Psychiatry,* 1955, *23,* 101.

Meredith, G. M. Observations on the acculturation of Sansei Japanese Americans in Hawaii. *Psychologia,* 1965, *8,* 41–49.

Meredith, G. M. Observations of the origins and current status of the ego assertive personality factor, *U.I.* 16. *Journal of Genetic Psychology,* 1967, *110,* 269–286. (a)

Meredith, G. M. *Effect of instructional conditions on the 16 P.F. questionnaire.* Unpublished manuscript, University of Hawaii, 1967. (b)

Meredith, W. Rotation to achieve factorial invariance. *Psychometrika,* 1964, *29*(2), 187–208.

Meredith, W. A model for analyzing heritability in the presence of correlated genetic and environmental effects. *Behavior Genetics,* 1973, *3,* 271–277.

Merrifield, P. R., Guilford, J. P., & Gershon, A. *The differentiation of divergent-production abilities at the sixth-grade level (Psychological Laboratory Report No. 27).* Los Angeles: University of Southern California, 1963.

Messick, S. J. Dimensions of social desirability. *Journal of Consulting Psychology,* 1960, *24,* 279–287.

Messick, S. J., & Jackson, D. N. Authoritarianism or acquiescence in Bass' data. *Journal of Abnormal and Social Psychology,* 1957, *54,* 424–426.

Messick, S. J., & Jackson, D. N. The measurement of authoritarian attitudes. *Educational and Psychological Measurement,* 1958, *18,* 241–253.

Messick, S. J., & Kogan, N. Personality consistencies in judgment: Dimensions of role constructs. *Multivariate Behavioral Research,* 1966, *1,* 165–175.

Meyer, H. H. Factors related to success in the human relations aspect of work-group leadership. *Psychological Monographs.* 1951, *65,* (3, Whole No. 320).

Michael, R. P. Gonadal hormones and the control of primate behaviour. In R. P. Michael (Ed.), *Endocrinology and human behaviour.* London: Oxford University Press, 1968.

Michael, R. P., & Wilson, M. Effects of castration and hormone replacement in fully adult male rhesus. *Endocrinology,* 1974, *95,* 150–159.

Michael, W. B., Barth, G., & Kaiser, H. F. Dimensions of temperament in three groups of music teachers. *Psychological Reports,* 1961, *9,* 701–704.

Michotte, A. The emotions as functional connections. In M. L. Reymert (Ed.), *Feelings and emotions.* New York: McGraw-Hill, 1950.

Midlarsky, E., & Bryan, J. H. Training charity in children. *Journal of Personality and Social Psychology,* 1967, *5,* 408–415.

Miles, D. M. The efficiency of a high speed screening procedure in detecting the neuropsychiatrically unfit at a U.S. Marine Corps recruit training depot. *Journal of Psychology,* 1946, *21,* 243–268.

Miller, D. R., & Swanson, G. E. *The changing American parent.* New York: Wiley, 1958.

Miller, G. A. The magical number seven, plus or minus two: Some limits on our capacity for processing information. *Psychological Review,* 1956, *63,* 81–97.

Miller, G. A., & Frick, F. C. Statistical

behavioristics and sequences of responses. *Psychological Review*, 1949, *56*, 311–324.

Miller, G. A., Galanter, E., & Pribram, K. H. *Plans and the structure of behavior*. New York: Holt, 1960.

Miller, N. E. Learnable drives and rewards. In S. S. Stevens (Ed.), *Handbook of experimental psychology*. New York: Wiley, 1951.

Miller, N. E. Liberalization of basic S-R concepts: Extensions to conflict behavior, motivation, and social learning. In S. Koch (Ed.), *Psychology: A study of a science* (Vol. 2). New York: McGraw-Hill, 1959.

Miller, N. E., & Dollard, J. *Social learning and imitation*. New Haven: Yale University Press, 1941.

Miller, N. E., & Murray, E. J. Displacement and conflict: Learnable drives as a basis for the steeper gradient of avoidance than of approach. *Journal of Experimental Psychology*, 1952, *43*, 227–231.

Miller, R. E., Murphy, J. V., & Mirsky, I. A. Relevance of facial expression and posture as cues in communication of affect between monkeys. *Archives of Genetic Psychiatry*, 1959, *1*, 480–488.

Milner, E. Effects of sex role and social status on the early adolescent personality. *Genetic Psychology Monographs*, 1949, *40*, 231–325.

Milner, E. A study of the relationship between reading readiness in grade one school children and patterns of parent-child interaction. *Child Development*, 1951, *22*, 95–112.

Milton, G. A. A. A factor analytic study of child-rearing behaviors. *Child Development*, 1958, *29*, 381–392.

Mischel, W. *Personality and assessment*. New York: Wiley, 1968.

Mischel, W. Continuity and change in personality. *American Psychologist*, 1969, *24*, 1012–1018.

Mischel, W. *Introduction to personality*. New York: Holt, Rinehart, & Winston, 1971.

Mischel, W. Direct versus indirect personality assessment: Evidence and implications. *Journal of Consulting Psychology*, 1972, *38*, 319–324.

Mischel, W. Toward a cognitive social learning reconceptualization of personality. *Psychological Review*, 1973, *80*, 252–283.

Mischel, W. *Introduction to personality* (2nd ed.). New York: Holt, Rinehart, & Winston, 1976.

Mittler, P. *The study of twins*. Harmondsworth, England: Penguin Books, 1971.

Mizuno, M., Lobotsky, J., Lloyd, C. W., Kobayashi, T., & Murasawa, Y. Plasma androstenedione and testosterone during pregnancy and in the newborn. *Journal of Clinical Endocrinology and Metabolism*, 1968, *24*, 1133–1142.

Moeller, G., & Applesweig, M. H. A motivational factor in conformity. *Journal of Abnormal and Social Psychology*, 1957, *55*, 114–120.

Moir, D. J. Egocentrism and the emergence of conventional morality in preadolescent girls. *Child Development*, 1974, *45*, 299–304.

Money, J. Components of eroticism in man: The hormones in relation to sexual morphology and sexual desire. *Journal of Nervous and Mental Disease*, 1961, *132*, 239–248.

Money, J. Sexual dimorphism and homosexual gender identity. *Psychological Bulletin*, 1970, *74*, 425–440.

Money, J., & Ehrhardt, A. A. Prenatal hormonal exposure: Possible effects on behavior in man. In R. P. Michael (Ed.), *Endocrinology and human behavior*. London: Oxford University Press, 1968.

Monnier, M. (Ed.). *Physiologie und Pathophysiologie des vegetativen Nervensystems* (2 vols.). Stuttgart: Hippokrates, 1963.

Montague, E. K. The role of anxiety in serial rote learning. *Journal of Experimental Psychology*, 1953, *45*, 91–96.

Moor, L. Niveau intellectuel et polygonosomie: Confrontation du caryotype et du niveau mental de 374 malades dont le caryotype comporte un excess de chromosomes X ou Y. *Revue de Neuropsychiatrie Infantile et d'Hygiene Mentale de l'Enfance*, 1967, *15*, 325–348.

Moore, O. K. *Autotelic responsive environments and exceptional children*. Unpublished manuscript, Rutgers University, 1964.

Moore, T. V. The essential psychoses and their fundamental syndromes. *Studies in Psychology and Psychiatry*, 1933, *3*(1), 1–128.

Moreno, J. L. *The first book on group psychotherapy (3rd ed.)*. New York: Beacon Hill, 1957.

Moriarty, A. E. Coping patterns of preschool children in response to intelligence test demands. *Genetic Psychology Monographs*, 1961, *64*, 3–127.

Morris, C., & Jones, L. V. Value scales and dimensions. *Journal of Abnormal and Social Psychology*, 1955, *51*, 523–535.

Morris, W. W. Rorschach estimates of personality attributes in the Michigan Assessment Project. *Psychological Monographs*, 1952, *66*(6, Whole No. 338).

Mosel, J. N., & Roberts, J. B. The comparability of measures of profile similarity: An empirical study. *Journal of Consulting Psychology*, 1954, *18*, 61–66.

Moss, H. A. Sex, age, and state as determinants of mother-infant interaction. In K. Danzinger (Ed.), *Readings in child socialization*. Oxford: Pergamon, 1970.

Moss, H. A., & Kagan, J. Report on personality, consistency and change from the Fels Longitudinal Study. *Vita Humana*, 1964, *7*, 127–138.

Mowrer, O. H. A stimulus-response analysis of anxiety and its role as a reinforcing agent. *Psychological Review*, 1939, *46*, 553–565.

Mowrer, O. H. *Learning theory and personality dynamics*. New York: Ronald Press, 1950.

Mowrer, O. H. *Learning theory and behavior*. New York: Wiley, 1960. (a)

Mowrer, O. H. *Learning theory and the symbolic processes*. New York: Wiley, 1960. (b)

Mowrer, O. H. *The new group therapy*. Princeton, N.J.: Van Nostrand, 1964.

Mowrer, O. H. Abnormal reactions or actions? An autobiographical answer. In J. Vernon (Ed.), *A general introduction to psychology*. Dubuque, Iowa: Brown, 1966.

Mowrer, O. H. Communication, conscience and the unconscious. *Journal of Communication Disorders*, 1967, *1*, 109–135.

Mowrer, O. H., & Ullman, A. D. Time as a determinant in integrative learning. *Psychological Review*, 1945, *52*, 61–90.

Muchow, H. H. *Jugend und Zeitgeist*. Hamburg: Rowohlt, 1962.

Mudd, S. A. Group sanction severity as a function of degree of behavior deviation and relevance of norm. *Journal of Personality and Social Psychology*, 1968, *8*, 258–260.

Mueller, E. F., & Beimann, M. Die Beziehung der Harnsäure zu Testwerten der nach Heckhausen gemessenen Leistungsmotivation. *Zeitschrift für experimentelle und angewandte Psychologie*, 1969, *16*, 295–306.

Muldoon, J. F., & Ray, O. S. A comparison of pattern similarity as measured by six statistical techniques and eleven clinicians. *Educational and Psychological Measurement*, 1958, *18*, 775–781.

Mullahy, P. *Psychoanalysis and interpersonal psychiatry; The contributions of Harry Stack Sullivan*. New York: Science House, 1970.

Mundy-Castle, A. C. The electroencephalogram and mental activity. *Electroencephalography and Clinical Neurophysiology*, 1957, *9*, 643–655.

Munkelt, P. Persönlichkeitsmerkmale als Bedingungsfaktoren der psychotropen Arzneimittelwirkung. *Psychologische Beiträge*, 1965, *8*, 98–183.

Munn, N. L. The effect of knowledge of the situation upon judgment of emotion from facial expressions. *Journal of Abnormal and Social Psychology*, 1940, *35*, 324–338.

Munroe, R., & Munroe, R. *Cross-cultural human development*. California: Brooks/Cole, 1975.

Munsinger, H., & Kessen, W. Uncertainty, structure, and preference. *Psychological Monographs*, 1964, *78*(9, Whole No. 586).

Murdock, G. P. *Social structure*. New York: Macmillan, 1949.

Murphy, G. *Personality: A biosocial approach to origins and structure*. New York: Harper, 1947.

Murphy, L. B. *The widening world of childhood: Paths toward mastery*. New York: Basic Books, 1962.

Murphy, L. B. Discussion of papers by Brill et al. In M. M. Katz, J. O. Cole, & W. E. Barton (Eds.), *The role and methodology of classification in psychiatry and psychopathology*. Chevy Chase, Md.: U.S. National Institute of Mental Health, 1967.

Murray, E. J., & Berkun, M. M. Displacement as a function of conflict. *Journal of Abnormal and Social Psychology*, 1955, *51*, 47–56.

Murray, H. A. *Explorations in personality*. New York: Oxford University Press, 1938.

Murstein, B. I. The complementary need hypothesis in newlyweds and middle-aged married couples. *Journal of Abnormal and Social Psychology*, 1961, *63*, 194–197.

Mussen, P. H., & Kagan, J. Group conformity and perception of parents. *Child Development*, 1958, *29*, 57–60.

Mussen, P. H., & Porter, L. W. Personal motivations and self-conceptions associated with effectiveness and ineffectiveness in emergent groups. *Journal of Abnormal and Social Psychology*, 1959, *59*, 23–27.

Myers, R. D. (Ed.). *Methods in psychobiology* (2 vols.). London: Academic Press, 1971.

Myrdal, A. *Nation and family*. London: Harper & Row, 1945.

Myrtek, M. Fehlerkoeffizienten bei klinisch-physiologischen und klinisch-chemischen Analysen. *Die Medicinische Welt*, 1975, *26*, 2144–2149. (a)

Myrtek, M. Ergebnisse der psychosomatischen Korrelations-forschung. *Zeitschrift für Klinische*

*Psychologie und Psychotherapie*, 1975, *23*, 316–330. (b)

Myrtek, M., Foerster, F., & Wittmann, W. Das Ausgangswertproblem. Theoretische Ueberlegungen und empirische Untersuchungen. *Zeitschrift für experimentelle und angewandte Psychologie*, 1976, in press.

Nadler, E. B. Yielding, authoritarianism, and authoritarian ideology regarding groups. *Journal of Abnormal and Social Psychology*, 1959, *58*, 408–410.

Nakamura, C. Y. *The relation between conformity and problem-solving* (Contract No. 25125). Stanford: Department of Psychology, Stanford University, 1955.

Nakao, H. [Brain stimulation and learning.] *Abhandlungen aus dem Gebiet der Hirnforschung und Verhaltenphysiologie*, East Germany, 1976, *3*.

Namenek, A. A., & Schuldt, W. J. Differential effects of experimenters' personality and instructional sets on verbal conditioning. *Journal of Counseling Psychology*, 1971, *18*, 170–172.

Nauta, W. J. H. The problem of the frontal lobe: A reinterpretation. *Journal of Psychiatric Research*, 1971, *8*, 167–187.

Nebylitsyn, V. D. [The structure of the fundamental properties of the nervous system.] *Voprosy Psikholojii*, 1963, *4*, 21–34.

Nebylitsyn, V. D. *Fundamental properties of the human nervous system*. New York: Plenum Press, 1972.

Nebylitsyn, V. D., & Gray, J. A. (Eds.). *Biological bases of individual behavior*. New York: Academic Press, 1972.

Neimark, E. D. Longitudinal development of formal operations thought. *Genetic Psychology Monographs*, 1975, *91*, 171–225.

Nelson, D. *The cue-approval hypothesis*. Paper presented at the meeting of the Southwestern Psychological Association, Arlington, Tex., April 1967.

Nelson, P. D. Similarities and differences among leaders and followers. *Journal of Social Psychology*, 1964, *63*, 161–167.

Nesselroade, J. R. *A comparison of cross product and differential-R factoring regarding cross study stability of change patterns*. Unpublished doctoral dissertation, University of Illinois, 1967.

Nesselroade, J. R. Application of multivariate strategies to problems of measuring and structuring long term change. In L. R. Goulet & P. B. Baltes (Eds.), *Life-span developmental psychology: Research and theory*. New York: Academic Press, 1970.

Nesselroade, J. R. Note on "the longitudinal factor analysis model." *Psychometrika*, 1972, *37*, 187–191.

Nesselroade, J. R. Faktorenanalyse von Kreuzprodukten zur Beschreibung von Veränderrungsphänomenen (Change). *Zeitschrift für Experimentelle und Angewandte Psychologie*, 1973, *20*, 92–106.

Nesselroade, J. R. Application of multivariate analysis procedures to the study of aging and behavioral changes. In J. E. Birren & K. W. Schaie (Eds.), *The handbook of the psychology of aging*. New York: Van Nostrand Reinhold, 1976, in press.

Nesselroade, J. R., & Cable, D. G. "Sometimes, it's okay to factor difference scores"—the separation of trait and state anxiety. *Multivariate Behavioral Research*, 1974, *9*, 273–282.

Nesselroade, J. R., & Cattell, R. B. The discovery of the anxiety state pattern in Q-data, and its distinction, in the LM model from depression, effort, stress and fatigue. *Multivariate Behavioral Research*, 1976, *11*, 27–40.

Nesselroade, J. R., & Delhees, K. H. Methods and findings in experimentally based personality theory. In R. B. Cattell (Ed.), *Handbook of multivariate experimental psychology*. Chicago: Rand McNally, 1966.

Nesselroade, J. R., & Reese, J. (Eds.). *Life span developmental psychology*. New York: Academic Press, 1973.

Nesselroade, J. R., Schaie, K. W., & Baltes, P. Ontogenetic and generational components of structural and quantitative change in adult behavior. *Journal of Gerontology*, 1972, *27*, 222–228.

Nesselroade, J. R., Schneewind, K., & Cattell, R. B. *Personality factors in objective tests in childhood years*. Unpublished manuscript, University of Illinois, 1970.

Neumann, F., Steinbeck, H., & Hahn, J. D. Hormones and brain differentiation. In L. Martini, M. Motta, & F. Fraschini (Eds.), *The hypothalamus*. New York: Academic Press, 1970.

Neuringer, C., & Michael, J. L. (Eds.). *Behavior modification in clinical psychology*. New York: Appleton-Century-Crofts, 1970.

Newcomb, T. M. An approach to the study of communicative acts. *Psychological Review*, 1953, *60*, 393–404.

Newcomb, T. M. The prediction of interpersonal attraction. *American Psychologist*, 1956, *11*, 575–586.

Newcomb, T. M. Dyadic balance as a source of clues about interpersonal attraction. In B. I. Murstein (Ed.), *Theories of attraction and love*. New York: Springer, 1971.

Newman, H. H., Freeman, F. N., & Holzinger, K. J. *Twins: A study of heredity and environment*. Chicago: University of Chicago Press, 1937.

Newton, J. R. Judgment and feedback in a quasi-clinical situation. *Journal of Personality and Social Psychology*, 1965, *1*, 336–342.

Nichols, R. C. The National Merit twin study. In S. G. Vandenberg (Ed.), *Methods and goals in human behavior genetics*. New York: Academic Press, 1965.

Nichols, R. C. The resemblance of twins in personality and interests. In M. Manosevitz, G. Lindzey, & D. D. Thiessen (Eds.), *Behavioral genetics: Method and research*. New York: Appleton-Century-Crofts, 1969.

Nicholson, W. M. The influence of anxiety upon learning: Interference of drive increment? *Journal of Personality*, 1958, *26*, 303–319.

Nissen, H. W. A study of exploratory behavior in the white rat by means of the obstruction method. *Journal of Genetic Psychology*, 1930, *37*, 361–376.

Norman, W. T. Toward an adequate taxonomy of personality attributes: Replicated factor structure in peer nomination personality ratings. *Journal of Abnormal and Social Psychology*, 1963, *66*, 574–583. (a)

Norman, W. T. Relative importance of test item content. *Journal of Consulting Psychology*, 1963, *27*, 166–174. (b)

Norman, W. T. *2800 personality trait descriptors* (NIMH Grant Report No. MH07195). Ann Arbor: University of Michigan, no date.

Norman, W. T., & Goldberg, L. Raters, ratees, and randomness in personality structure. *Journal of Personality and Social Psychology*, 1966, *4*, 681–691.

Norman, W. T., & Harshbarger, T. R. Matching components of self-report and peer nomination personality measures. *Psychometrika*, 1965, *30*, 481–490.

Norris, V. *Mental illness in London* (Maudsley Monograph, No. 6). London: Chapman & Hall, 1959.

Notterman, J. M. *Behavior: A systematic approach*. New York: Random House, 1971.

Nowlis, V. Methods for studying mood changes produced by drugs. *Revue de Psychologie Appliquée*, 1961, *11*, 373–386.

Nowlis, V. Research with the Mood Adjective Check List. In S. S. Tomkins & C. E. Izard (Eds.), *Affect, cognition and personality*. New York: Springer, 1965.

Nowlis, V., & Green, R. F. *Factor analytic studies of the Mood Adjective Check List* [Tech. Rep. No. 11, NR 171-342, ONR Contract 68 (12)]. Office of Naval Research, 1965.

Noyes, A. *Modern clinical psychiatry*. Philadelphia: Saunders, 1953.

Nunnally, J. C. *Tests and measurement, assessment and prediction*. New York: McGraw-Hill, 1959.

Nunnally, J. C. The analysis of profile data. *Psychological Bulletin*, 1962, *59*, 311–319.

Nunnally, J. C., & Husek, T. R. The phoney language examination: An approach to the measurement of response bias. *Educational and Psychological Measurement*, 1958, *18*, 275–282.

Nunnally, J. C., Stevens, D. A., & Hall, G. F. Association of neutral objects with rewards: Effect on verbal evaluation and eye movements. *Journal of Experimental Child Psychology*, 1965, *2*, 44–57.

Nuttin, J., & Greenwald, A. G. *Reward and punishment in human learning*. New York: Academic Press, 1968.

Nye, F. J. *Employment status and maternal adjustment to children*. Paper presented at the meeting of the American Sociological Society, Chicago, 1959.

Obrist, P. A., Black, A. H., Brener, J., & Dicara, L. V. (Eds.). *Cardiovascular psychophysiology*. Chicago: Aldine, 1974.

Odom, L., & Lemond, M. Developmental differences in the perception and production of facial expression. *Child Development*. 1972, *43*, 359–369.

Oeser, O. A., & Hammond, S. B. *Social structure and personality in a city*. New York: MacMillan, 1954.

Ogburn, W. F. *Technology and the changing family*. Boston: Houghton Mifflin, 1955.

Ohno, S. Evolution of sex chromosomes in mammals. *Annual Review of Genetics*, 1969, *3*, 495–524.

Ohno, S. Simplicity of mammalian regulatory systems inferred by single gene determination of sex phenotypes. *Nature*, 1971, *234*, 134–137.

Olds, J. Satiation effects in self-stimulus of the

brain. *Journal of Comparative and Physiological Psychology*, 1958, *51*, 675–678.

Olds, J., & Milner, P. M. Positive reinforcement produced by electrical stimulation of septal area and other regions of rat brains. *Journal of Comparative and Physiological Psychology*, 1954, *47*, 419–427.

Olds, J., & Olds, M. E. Drives, rewards, and the brain. In F. Barron (Ed.), *New directions in psychology* (Vol. 2). New York: Holt, Rinehart, & Winston, 1965.

O'Leary, K. D., & O'Leary, S. G. (Eds.). *Classroom management: The successful use of behavior modification*. London: Pergamon, 1972.

Olmsted, D. W., & Monachesi, E. D. *MMPI trends of small group leaders and members*. Minneapolis: University of Minnesota Press, 1955.

O'Neil, H. F., Jr. *Effects of stress on state anxiety and performance in computer-assisted learning*. Unpublished doctoral dissertation, Florida State University, 1969.

O'Neil, H. F., Jr., Spielberger, C. D., & Hansen, D. N. The effects of state-anxiety and task difficulty on computer-assisted learning. *Journal of Educational Psychology*, 1969, *60*, 343–350.

Opler, M. K. Cultural perspectives in research on schizophrenia: A history with examples. *Psychiatric Quarterly*, 1959, *33*, 506–524.

Oppelt, W., & Vossius, G. (Eds.). *Der Mensch als Regler*. Berlin: VEB Verlag Technik, 1970.

Orlando, R., & Bijou, S. W. Single and multiple schedules of reinforcement in developmentally retarded children. *Journal of Experimental Analysis of Behavior*, 1960, *3*, 339–348.

Orne, M. T. On the social psychology of the psychological experiment: With particular reference to demand characteristics and their implications. *American Psychologist*, 1962, *17*, 776–783.

Orne, M. T., & Evans, F. J. Social control in the psychological experiment: Anti-social behavior and hypnosis. *Journal of Personality and Social Psychology*, 1964, *1*, 189–200.

Orne, M. T., & Scheibe, K. E. The contribution of nondeprivation factors in the production of sensory deprivation effects: The psychology of the "panic button." *Journal of Abnormal and Social Psychology*, 1964, *68*, 3–12.

Orpet, R. E., & Meyers, C. E. Six structure-of-intellect hypotheses in six-year-old children. *Journal of Educational Psychology*, 1966, *57*, 341–346.

Orr, W. C., & Stern, J. A. The relationship between stimulus information, reaction time and cortical habituation. *Psychophysiology*, 1971, *7*, 445–484.

Osborne, J. G. Free-time as a reinforcer in the management of classroom behavior. *Journal of Applied Behavior Analysis*, 1969, *2*, 113–118.

Osborne, R. T. Factor structure of the Wechsler Intelligence Scale for Children at pre-school level and after first grade: A longitudinal analysis. *Psychological Reports*, 1965, *16*, 637–644.

Osborne, R. T., Anderson, H. E., Jr., & Bashaw, W. L. The stability of the WISC factor structure at three age levels. *Multivariate Behavioral Research*, 1967, *2*, 443–451.

Osborne, R. T., & Lindsay, J. M. A longitudinal investigation of change in the factorial composition of intelligence with age in young school children. *Journal of Genetic Psychology*, 1967, *110*, 49–58.

Osburn, H. G., Lubin, A., Loeffler, J. C., & Tye, V. M. The relative validity of forced choice and single stimulus self description items. *Educational and Psychological Measurement*, 1954, *14*, 407–417.

Osgood, C. E. *Method and theory in experimental psychology*. New York: Oxford University Press, 1953.

Osgood, C. E. Motivational dynamics of language behavior. In M. R. Jones (Ed.), *Nebraska Symposium on Motivation, 1957*. Lincoln: University of Nebraska Press, 1957.

Osgood, C. E. Studies on the generality of affective meaning systems. *American Psychology*, 1962, *17*, 10–28.

Osgood, C. E. Psycholinguistics. In S. Koch (Ed.), *Psychology: A study of a science* (Vol. 6). New York: McGraw-Hill, 1963.

Osgood, C. E. Meaning cannot be $r_m$? *Journal of Verbal Learning and Verbal Behavior*, 1966, *5*, 402–407.

Osgood, C. E. Towards a wedding of insufficiencies. In T. R. Dixon & D. L. Horton (Eds.), *Verbal behavior and general behavior theory*. Englewood Cliffs, N.J.: Prentice-Hall, 1968.

Osgood, C. E., Suci, G. J., & Tannenbaum, P. H. *The measurement of meaning*. Urbana: University of Illinois press, 1957.

Osgood, C. E., & Tannenbaum, P. The principle of congruity and the prediction of attitude change. *Psychological Review*, 1955, *62*, 42–55.

Osler, W. *A way of life*. New York: Oxford University Press, 1951.

Osofsky, J. D. Children's influences upon parental behavior: An attempt to define the relationship with the use of laboratory tasks. *Genetic Psychology Monographs*, 1971, *83*, 147–169.

Othmer, E., Netter-Munkelt, P. Golle, R., & Meyer, A. E. Autonome Steuerung bei psychischen und vegetativen Extremlagen. *Zeitschrift für experimentelle und angewandt Psychologie*, 1969, *16*, 307–333.

Ounsted, C., & Taylor, D. C. (Eds.). *Gender differences: Their ontogeny and significance*. London: Churchill, 1972. (a)

Ounsted, C., & Taylor, D. C. The Y chromosome message: A point of view. In C. Ounsted & D. C. Taylor (Eds.), *Gender differences: Their ontogeny and significance*. London: Churchill, 1972. (b)

Overall, J. E. Dimensions of manifest depression. *Journal of Psychiatric Research*, 1962, *1*, 239–245.

Overall, J. E., Gorham, D., & Shawver, J. Basic dimensions of change in the symptomatology of chronic schizophrenics. *Journal of Abnormal and Social Psychology*, 1961, *63*, 597–602.

Overall, J. E., Hollister, L. E., Johnson, M., & Pennington, V. Nosology of depression and differential response to drugs. *Journal of the American Medical Association*, 1966, *195*, 946–948.

Overall, J. E., Hollister, L. E., & Pichot, P. Major psychiatric disorders. *Archives of General Psychiatry*, 1967, *16*, 146–151.

Owens, W. A. Age and mental abilities: A longitudinal study. *Genetic Psychology Monographs*, 1953, *48*, 3–54.

Owens, W. A. Age and mental ability: A second adult follow-up. *Journal of Educational Psychology*, 1966, *57*, 311–325.

Pagano, D. F. Effects of test anxiety on acquisition and retention of material resembling the content of college courses. *Journal of Experimental Research in Personality*, 1970, *4*, 213–221.

Pagano, D. F., & Katahn, M. Effects of test anxiety on acquisition and retention of psychological terms and single letter stimulus-response pairs. *Journal of Experimental Research in Personality*, 1967, *2*, 260–267.

Papousek, H. Genetics and child development. In J. N. Spuhler (Ed.), *Genetic diversity and human behavior*. Chicago: Aldine, 1967.

Pare, D. D. *Accurate Empathy Scale: Relative or absolute?* Unpublished doctoral dissertation, University of Florida, 1970.

Parr, A. E. In search of theory. In H. M. Proshansky, W. H. Ittelson, & L. G. Rivlin (Eds.), *Environmental psychology: Man and his physical setting*. New York: Holt, Rinehart, & Winston, 1970.

Parrino, J. J. *The effects of pre-therapy information on learning in psychotherapy*. Unpublished doctoral dissertation, Louisiana State University, 1969.

Parsons, P. A. Behavioural homeostasis in mice. *Genetica*, 1967, *38*, 134–142.

Parsons, T. *The social system*. Glencoe, Ill.: Free Press, 1938.

Parsons, T. Family structure and the socialization of the child. In T. Parsons & R. F. Bales (Eds.), *Family, socialization, and interaction process*. Glencoe, Ill.: Free Press, 1955.

Parsons, T., & Bales, R. F. (Eds.). Family, socialization, and interaction process. Glencoe, Ill.: Free Press, 1955.

Partanen, J., Brunn, K., & Markkanen, T. *Inheritance of drinking behavior*. Helsinki: Finnish Foundation for Alcohol Studies, 1966.

Pasamanick, B., & Knoblock, C. A. Brain and behavior: Session II-2. Brain damage and reproductive casualty. *American Journal of Orthopsychiatry*, 1960, *30*, 298–305.

Passini, F. T., & Norman, W. T. A universal conception of personality structure? *Journal of Personality and Social Psychology*, 1966, *4*, 44–49.

Patterson, G. R. *An application of conditioning techniques to the control of a hyperactive child*. Unpublished manuscript, University of Oregon, 1963.

Patterson, G. R. An empirical approach to the classification of disturbed children. *Journal of Clinical Psychology*, 1964, *20*, 326–327.

Patterson, G. R. Prediction of victimization from an instrumental conditioning procedure. *Journal of Consulting Psychology*, 1967, *31*, 147–152.

Patterson, G. R. Behavioral intervention procedures in the classroom and in the home. In A. E. Bergin & S. Garfield (Eds.), *Handbook of psychotherapy and behavior change: An empirical analysis*. London: Wiley, 1971.

Patterson, G. R. Changes in status of family members as controlling stimuli: A basis for describing treatment process. In L. A. Hamerlynck, L. C. Handy, & E. J. Mash (Eds.), *Behavior change: Methodology, concepts and practice*. Champaign, Ill.: Research Press, 1973.

Patterson, G. R. A basis for identifying stimuli which control behaviors in natural settings. *Child Development,* 1974, *45,* 900–911.

Patterson, G. R. The aggressive child: Victim and architect of a coercive system. In L. A. Hamerlynck, E. J. Mash, & L. C. Handy (Eds.), *Behavior modification and families: I. Theory and research.* New York: Brunner/Mazell, 1975.

Patterson, G. R., & Cobb, J. A. A dyadic analysis of "aggressive" behaviors. In J. P. Hill (Ed.), *Minnesota Symposium on Child Psychology* (Vol. 5). Minneapolis: University of Minnesota Press, 1971.

Patterson, G. R., & Cobb, J. A. Stimulus control for classes of noxious behaviors. In J. F. Knutson (Ed.), *The control of aggression: Implications from basic research.* Chicago: Aldine, 1973.

Patterson, G. R., & Harris, A. *Some methodological considerations for observation procedures.* Paper presented at the annual meeting of the American Psychological Association, San Francisco, 1968.

Patterson, G. R., Jones, R., Whittier, J., & Wright, M. A. A behavior modification technique for the hyperactive child. *Behaviour Research and Therapy,* 1965, *2,* 217–226.

Patterson, G. R., Littman, R., & Bricker, W. Assertive behavior in children: A step toward a theory of aggression. *Monographs of the Society for Research in Child Development,* 1967, *32*(5 & 6), 36 pp.

Patterson, G. R., Maerov, S., Garber, L., Brummett, B., & Reid, J. B. A manual for coding family interactions. *Oregon Research Institute Research Bulletin,* 1976, in press.

Patterson, G. R., Ray, R. S., Shaw, D. A., & Cobb, J. A. *Manual for coding family interactions, 1969 revision* (Document 01234). New York: Microfiche Publications, 1969.

Patterson, G. R., & Reid, J. B. Reciprocity and coercion: Two facets of social systems. In C. Neuringer & J. D. Michael (Eds.), *Behavior modification in clinical psychology.* New York: Appleton-Century-Crofts, 1970.

Patterson, G. R., Reid, J. B., Jones, R. R., & Conger, R. F. *A social learning approach to family intervention* (Vol. 1). *Families with aggressive children.* Eugene, Ore.: Castalia Press, 1975.

Patterson, G. R., Shaw, D. A., & Ebner, M. Teachers, peers, and parents as agents of change in the classroom. In F. A. M. Benson (Ed.), *Modifying deviant social behaviors in various classroom settings.* Eugene, Ore.: University of Oregon Press, 1969.

Pauker, J. D. Identification of MMPI profile types in a female, inpatient, psychiatric setting using the Marks and Seeman rules. *Journal of Consulting Psychology,* 1966, *30,* 90.

Paul, G. L. *Insight vs. densensitization in psychotherapy: An experiment in anxiety reduction.* Stanford, Calif.: Stanford University Press, 1966.

Paul, G. L. Behavior modification research: Design and tactics. In C. M. Franks (Ed.), *Behavior therapy: Appraisal and status.* New York: McGraw-Hill, 1969.

Pavlov, I. P. *Conditioned reflexes: An investigation of the physiological activity of the cerebral cortex* (G. V. Anrep, Ed. and trans.). London: Oxford University Press, 1927.

Pawlik, K. *Educational prediction from objective personality test dimensions.* Paper presented at the annual meeting of the American Psychological Association, New York, September 1961.

Pawlik, K. Concepts and calculations in human cognitive abilities. In R. B. Cattell (Ed.), *Handbook of multivariate experimental psychology.* Chicago: Rand McNally, 1966.

Pawlik, K. *Dimensions des Verhaltens.* Bern: Huber, 1968.

· Pawlik, K., & Cattell, R. B. Third-order factors in objective personality tests. *British Journal of Psychology,* 1964, *55,* 1–18.

Pawlik, K., & Cattell, R. B. The relationship between certain personality factors and measures of cortical arousal. *Neuropsychologia,* 1965, *3,* 129–151.

Payne, A. P., & Swanson, H. H. Agonistic behaviour between pairs of hamsters of the same and opposite sex in a neutral observation area. *Behaviour,* 1970, *36,* 259–269.

Payne, R. W. Cognitive abnormalities. In H. J. Eysenck (Ed.), *Handbook of abnormal psychology.* New York: Basic Books, 1961.

Pearson, K. Assortative mating in man. *Biometrika,* 1903, *2,* 481–498.

Peck, R. F., Havighurst, R. J., Cooper, R., Lilienthal, J., & More, O. *The psychology of character development.* New York: Wiley, 1960.

Pederson, D. M. The measurement of individual differences in perceived personality-trait relationships and their relation to certain determinants. *Journal of Social Psychology,* 1965, *65,* 233–258.

Peeke, H. V. S., & Herz, M. J. *Habituation* (Vol. 1). *Behavioral studies.* New York: Academic Press, 1973.

Peiper, A. *Cerebral function in infancy and childhood.* New York: Consultants Bureau, 1963.

Pemberton, C. The closure factors related to temperament. *Journal of Personality,* 1952, *21,* 159–175.

Penk, W. Developmental patterns in children's inkblot responses. *Developmental Psychology,* 1969, *1,* 55–64.

Penrose, L. S. Some recent trends in human genetics. *Caryologia,* 1954, *6,* 521–530. (Supplement)

Penrose, L. S. Medical significance of fingerprints and related phenomena. *British Medical Journal,* 1968, *2,* 321–325.

Peretz, E., Goy, R. W., Phoenix, C. H., & Resko, J. A. Influence of hormones on the nervous system. *Proceedings of the International Society for Psychoneuroendocrinology* (Brooklyn, 1970). Basel: Karger, 1971.

Perkins, J. M., & Jinks, J. L. Environmental and genotype-environmental components of variability: III. Multiple lines and crosses. *Heredity,* 1968, *23,* 339–356.

Perry, D. K. Forced-choice versus LID response items in vocational interests measurement. *Journal of Applied Psychology,* 1955, *39,* 256–262.

Persky, H., Zuckerman, M., & Curtis, G. C. Endocrine function in emotionally disturbed and normal men. *Journal of Nervous and Mental Disease,* 1968, *146,* 488–497.

Pervin, L. A. The need to predict and control under conditions of threat. *Journal of Personality,* 1963, *31,* 570–587.

Peterson, D. R. The age generality of personality factors derived from ratings. *Educational and Psychological Measurement,* 1960, *20,* 461–474.

Peterson, D. R. The scope and generality of verbally defined personality factors. *Psychological Review,* 1965, *72,* 48–59.

Peterson, D. R. *The clinical study of social behavior.* New York: Appleton-Century-Crofts, 1968.

Peterson, D. R., Becker, W., Shoemaker, D., Luria, Z., & Hellmer, L. Child behavior problems and parental attitudes. *Child Development,* 1961, *32,* 151–162.

Peterson, D. R., & Cattell, R. B. Personality factors in nursery school children as derived from parent ratings. *Journal of Consulting and Clinical Psychology,* 1958, *14,* 346–355.

Peterson, D. R., & Catell, R. B. Personality factors in nursery school children as derived from teachers' ratings. *Journal of Consulting and Clinical Psychology,* 1959, *23,* 562.

Peterson, D. R., Quay, H. C., & Cameron, G. R. Personality and background factors in juvenile delinquency as inferred from questionnaire response. *Journal of Consulting and Clinical Psychology,* 1959, *23,* 395–399.

Peterson, D. R., Quay, H. C., & Tiffany, T. L. Personality factors related to juvenile delinquency. *Child Development,* 1961, *32,* 355–372.

Pfaff, D. W., & Zigmond, R. E. Neonatal androgen effects on sexual and non-sexual behavior of adult rats tested under various hormone regimes. *Neuroendocrinology,* 1971, *7,* 129–145.

Phelps, R. E., & Meyer, M. E. Personality and conformity, and sex differences. *Psychological Reports,* 1966, *18,* 730.

Philipp, R. L., & Wilde, G. J. S. *Stimulation seeking behavior and extraversion.* Paper presented at the Annual Convention of the Canadian Psychological Association, Calgary, Alberta, June 5–7, 1968.

Philipp, R. L., & Wilde, G. J. S. Stimulation seeking behavior and extraversion, *Acta Psychologica,* 1970, *32,* 269–280.

Phillipps, E. L., & Wiener, D. M. *Short-term psychotherapy and structural behavioral change.* New York: McGraw-Hill, 1966.

Phillips, J. D., & Delhees, K. H. *A personality analysis of drug addicts by the 16 P.F. and evaluation of the influence of rehabilitation* (Advanced Publication No. 9). Urbana: The Laboratory of Personality and Group Analysis, University of Illinois, April 1967.

Phillips, L., & Draguns, J. G. Classification of the behavior disorders. *Annual Review of Psychology,* 1971, *22,* 447–482.

Phillips, L., & Rabinovitch, M. Social role and patterns of symtomatic behaviors. *Journal of Abnormal and Social Psychology,* 1958, *57,* 181–186.

Phoenix, C. H., Slob, A. K., & Goy, R. W. Effects of castration and replacement therapy on sexual behavior of adult male rhesuses. *Journal of Comparative and Physiological Psychology,* 1973, *84,* 472–481.

Piaget, J. *The moral judgment of the child.* London: Kegan Paul, 1932.

Piaget, J. *The psychology of intelligence.* London: Routledge & Kegan Paul, 1950.

Piaget, J. *The origins of intelligence in children.*

New York: International Universities Press, 1952.

Piaget, J., & Inhelder, B. *The psychology of the child.* New York: Basic Books, 1969.

Piechowski, M. M. A theoretical and empirical approach to the study of development. *Genetic Psychology Monographs,* 1975, *92,* 231-297.

Piers, G., & Singer, M. *Shame and guilt: A psychoanalytic and a cultural study.* Springfield, Ill.: Charles C Thomas, 1953.

Pierson, G. R. *Current research in juvenile delinquency with IPAT factored instruments* (IPAT Information Bulletin No. 4). Champaign, Ill.: Institute for Personality and Ability Testing, 1964.

Pierson, G. R., Barton, V., & Hey, G. SMAT motivation factors as predictors of academic achievement of delinquent boys. *Journal of Psychology,* 1964, *57,* 243-249.

Piezko, H. J. *Global perceptiveness as a process common to synthetization-repression and the factors of independence, commentive, superego, and asthenia.* Unpublished master's thesis, University of Illinois, 1967.

Pinneau, S. The infant disorders of hospitalism and anaclitic depression. *Psychological Bulletin,* 1955, *52,* 429-452.

Pinzka, O., & Saunders, D. R. Analytic rotation to simple structure II: Extension to an oblique solution (Research Bulletin RB-54-a31). Princeton: Educational Testing Sercvice, 1954.

Pitts, F. N., & McClure, J. N. Lactate metabolism in anxiety neurosis. *New England Journal of Medicine,* 1967, *277,* 1329-1336.

Plomin, R., Willerman, L., & Loehlin, J. C. Resemblance in appearance and the equal environments assumption in twin studies of personality traits. *Behavior Genetics,* 1976, *6,* 43-52.

Ploog, D. Verhaltensforschung und Psychiatrie. In H. W. Cruhle et al. (Eds.), *Psychiatrie der Gegenwart* (Vol. 1, pt. 1B). Berlin: Springer, 1964.

Polani, P. E. Abnormal sex chromsomes and mental disorder. *Nature,* 1969, *223,* 680-686.

Popper, K. R. *The logic of scientific discovery.* New York: Science Editions, 1961.

Porter, R. B., & Cattell, R. B. *Children's Personality Questionnaire.* Champaign, Ill.: Institute for Personality and Ability Testing, 1963.

Postman, L. Transfer of training as a function of experimental paradigm and degree of first-list learning. *Journal of Verbal Learning and Verbal Behavior,* 1962, *1,* 109-118.

Premack, D. Prediction of the comparative reinforcement values of running and drinking. *Science,* 1963, *139,* 1062-1063.

Premack, D. Reinforcement theory. In D. Levine (Ed.), *Nebraska Symposium on Motivation, 1965.* Lincoln: University of Nebraska Press, 1965.

Pribram, K. H. The new neurology and the biology of emotion. *American Psychologist,* 1967, *22,* 830-838.

Pribram, K. H., & Luria, A. R. (Eds.). *Psychophysiology of the frontal lobes.* New York: Academic Press, 1973.

Prideaux, E. Expression of the emotions in cases of mental disorders. *British Journal of Medical Psychology,* 1922, *2,* 45.

Proshansky, H. N., Ittelson, W. H., & Rivlin, L. G. (Eds.). *Environmental psychology: Man and his physical setting.* New York: Holt, Rinehart, & Winston, 1970.

Quay, H. C. Personality dimensions in delinquent males as inferred from the factor analysis of behavior ratings. *Journal of Research in Crime and Delinquency,* 1964, *1,* 33-37. (a)

Quay, H. C. Dimensions of personality in delinquent boys as inferred from the factor analysis of case history data. *Child Development,* 1964, *35,* 479-484. (b)

Quenouille, M. H. *The analyses of multiple time series.* New York: Hafner, 1957.

Qureshi, M. Y. Pattern of intellectual development during childhood and adolescence. *Genetic Psychology Monographs,* 1973, *87,* 313-334.

Rabin, A. J. Some psychosexual differences between kibbutz and non-kibbutz Israeli boys. *Journal of Projective Techniques,* 1958, *22,* 328-332.

Rachman, S. Extraversion and neuroticism in childhood. In H. J. Eysenck & S. B. G. Eysenck, *Personality structure and measurement.* San Diego: Knapp, 1969.

Radnitzky, G. *Contemporary schools of metascience.* Copenhagen: Munksgaard, 1968.

Raisman, G., & Field, P. M. Sexual dimorphism in the neuropil of the preoptic area of the rat and its dependence on neonatal androgen. *Brain Research,* 1973, *54,* 1-29.

Rapaport, D. The structure of psychoanalytic theory. *Psychological Issues,* 1960, *2,* Monograph 6.

Rath, R., & Misra, S. K. Change of attitudes as a function of some personality factors. *Journal of Social Psychology,* 1963, *60,* 311-317.

Raush, H. L. Interaction sequences. *Journal of Personality and Social Pscyhology,* 1965, *2,* 487-499.

Raymond, M. Case of fetishism treated by aversion therapy. *British Medical Journal,* 1956, *2,* 854-57.

Read, H. H. Parents' expressed attitudes and children's behavior. *Journal of Consulting Psychology,* 1945, *9,* 95-100.

Reaser, G. P. (Ed.). *Child health and development: Research progress* (DHEW Publication No. (NIH) 72-39). Washington, D.C.: U.S. Government Printing Office, 1972.

Rees, A. H., & Palmer, F. H. Factors related to change in mental test performance. *Developmental Psychology Monograph,* 1970, *3*(2, Pt. 2).

Rees, L. Constitutional factors and abnormal behavior. In H. J. Eysenck (Ed.), *Handbook of abnormal psychology* (2nd ed.). San Diego: Knapp, 1973.

Reinhart, G. Comparative factor analytic studies of intelligence throughout the human life-span. In L. R. Goulet & P. B. Baltes (Ed.), *Life-span development psychology.* New York: Academic Press, 1970.

Reitman, W. R. *Cognition and thought: An information processing approach.* New York: Wiley, 1965.

Rescorla, R. A., & Solomon, R. L. Two-process learning theory: Relationships between Pavlovian conditioning and instrumental learning, *Psychological Review,* 1967, *74,* 151-182.

Resko, J. A. Androgen secretion by the fetal and neonatal rhesus monkey. *Endocrinology,* 1970, *87,* 680-687.

Restle, F. *Learning: Animal behavior and human cognition.* New York: McGraw-Hill, 1975.

Rettig, S., & Pasamanick, B. Changes in moral values over three decades, 1929-1958. *Social Problems,* 1959, *6,* 320-328.

Reznikoff, M., & Honeyman, M. S. MMPI profiles of monozygotic and dizygotic twin pairs. *Journal of Consulting Psychology,* 1967, *31,* 100.

Rheingold, H. L. The modification of social responsiveness in institutional babies. *Monographs of the Society for Research in Child Development,* 1956, *21*(2, Serial No. 63).

Rheingold, H. L. The measurement of maternal care. *Child Development,* 1960, *31,* 565-575.

Rheingold, H. L. The effect of environmental stimulation upon social and exploratory behavior in the human infant. In B. M. Foss (Ed.), *Determinants of infant behavior.* New York: Wiley, 1961.

Rhine, W. R. Birth order differences in conformity and level of achievement arousal. *Child Development,* 1968, *39,* 987-996.

Ribble, M. A. *The rights of infants.* New York: Columbia University Press, 1943.

Ribble, M. A. Infantile experience in relation to personality development. In J. McV. Hunt (Ed.), *Personality and the behavior disorders* (Vol. 2). New York: Ronald Press, 1944.

Ricciuti, H. N. Social and emotional behavior in infancy: Some developmental issues and problems. *Merrill-Palmer Quarterly,* 1968, *14,* 82-100.

Rickels, K., & Cattell, R. B. The clinical factor validity and trueness of the IPAT verbal and objective batteries for anxiety and regression. *Journal of Clinical Psychology,* 1965, *21,* 257-264.

Rickels, K., Cattell, R. B., Weise, C., Gray, B., Yee, R., Mallin, A., & Aaronson, H. G. Controlled psychopharmacological research in private psychiatric practice. *Psychopharmacologia,* 1966, *9,* 288-306.

Rickles, W. H. Central nervous system substrates of some psychophysiological variables. In N. S. Greenfield & F. A. Sternbach (Eds.), *Handbook of psychophysiology.* New York: Holt, Rinehart, & Winston, 1972.

Riesen, A. H. Plasticity of behavior: Psychological aspects. In H. F. Harlow & C. N. Woolsey (Eds.), *Biological and biochemical bases of behavior.* Madison: University of Wisconsin Press, 1958.

Riesen, A. H. *Critical stimulation and optimum period.* Paper presented at the meeting of the American Psychological Association, New York, 1961.

Riesman, D. *The lonely crowd.* New Haven: Yale University Press, 1950.

Rimoldi, H. J. A. The central intellective factor. *Psychometrika,* 1951, *16,* 75-101.

Rivarola, M. A., Forest, M. G., & Migeon, C. J. Testosterone, androstenedione and dehydroepiandrosterone in plasma during pregnancy and at delivery: Concentration and protein binding. *Journal of Clinical Endocrinology and Metabolism,* 1968, *28,* 34-40.

Rodd, W. G. *A cross-cultural study of Taiwan's schools.* Unpublished doctoral dissertation, Western Reserve University, 1958.

Roe, A. Integration of personality theory and clinical practice. *Journal of Abnormal and Social Psychology,* 1941, *44,* 36-41.

Roesler, F. Die Abhaengigkeit des Elektroenzephalogramms von den Persoenlichkeitsdimensionen E und N sensu Eysenck und unterschiedlich aktivierenden Situationen. *Zeitschrift für experimentelle und angewandte Psychologie, 1975, 22,* 630–667.

Roff, M. A factorial study of the Fels Parent Behavior Scales. *Child Development,* 1949, *20,* 29–45.

Roff, M. Some properties of the communality in multiple factor theory. *Psychometrika,* 1936, *1,* 1–6.

Roff, M. A. A factorial study of tests in the perceptual area. *Psychometric Monographs,* No. 8. Chicago: University of Chicago Press, 1952.

Rogers, C. R. *Counseling and psychotherapy.* Boston: Houghton Mifflin, 1942.

Rogers, C. R. *Client centered therapy: Its current practice, implications and theory.* Boston: Houghton-Mifflin, 1951.

Rogers, C. R., & Dymond, R. T. *Psychotherapy and personality change.* Chicago: University of Chicago Press, 1954.

Rogers, T. B. The process of responding to personality items: Some issues, a theory and some research. *Multivariate Behavioral Research Monographs,* 1971, *6*(2).

Rorer, L. G. The great response-style myth. *Psychological Bulletin,* 1965, *63,* 129–156.

Rose, A. M. The adequacy of woman's expectations for adult roles. *Social Forces,* 1951, *30,* 69–77.

Rose, A. M. *Mental health and mental disorder.* New York: Norton, 1955.

Rose, D. E. Social factors in delinquency. *Australian Journal of Psychology,* 1949, *1,* 1–8.

Rose, R. M., Gordon, T. P., & Bernstein, I. S. Plasma testosterone levels in the male rhesus: Influences of sexual and social stimuli. *Science,* 1972, *178,* 643–645.

Rose, R. M., Holaday, J. W., & Bernstein, I. S. Plasma testosterone, dominance rank and aggressive behaviour in male rhesus monkeys. *Nature,* 1971, *251,* 366–368.

Rosen, B. C. Family structure and achievement motivation. *American Sociological Review,* 1961, *26,* 574–585.

Rosen, B. C., & D'Andrade, R. G. The psychosocial origins of achievement motivation. *Sociometry,* 1959, *22,* 185–218.

Rosen, H., & Rosen, R. A. H. The validity of undecided answers in questionnaire responses. *Journal of Applied Psychology,* 1955, *39,* 178–181.

Rosenblatt, P. C., & Skoogberg, E. L. Birth order in cross-cultural perspective. *Developmental Psychology,* 1974, *10,* 48–54.

Rosenfeld, H. Relationships of ordinal position and affiliation to achievement motives: Direction and generality. *Journal of Personality,* 1966, *34,* 467–479.

Rosenthal, D. *Genetic theory and abnormal behavior.* New York: McGraw-Hill, 1970.

Rosenthal, I. *A factor analysis of anxiety variables.* Unpublished doctoral dissertation, University of Illinois, 1955.

Rosenthal, R. *Experimenter effects in behavioral research.* New York: Appleton-Century-Crofts, 1966.

Rosenthal, R. Experimenter expectancy and the reassuring nature of the null hypothesis procedure. *Psychological Bulletin Monographs,* 1968, *70*(No. 6, Pt. 2), 30–47.

Rossman, B. B., & Horn, J. L. Cognitive, motivational and temperamental indicants of creativity and intelligence. *Journal of Educational Measurement,* 1972, *9,* 265–286.

Rotter, J. B. *Social learning and clinical psychology.* Englewood Cliffs, N.J.: Prentice-Hall, 1954.

Rotter, J. B. The role of the psychological situation in determining the direction of human behavior. In M. R. Jones (Ed.), *The Nebraska Symposium of Motivation, 1955.* Lincoln: University of Nebraska Press, 1955.

Roudabush, G. E. Analyzing dyadic relationships. In S. G. Vandenberg (Ed.), *Progress in human behavior genetics.* Baltimore: Johns Hopkins University Press, 1968.

Routtenberg, A. The two-arousal-hypothesis: Reticular formation and limbic system. *Psychological Review,* 1968, *75,* 51–80.

Royce, J. R. *Multivariate analysis and psychological theory.* New York: Academic Press, 1963.

Royce, J. R. Concepts generated in comparative and physiological observations. In R. B. Cattell (Ed.), *Handbook of multivariate experimental psychology.* Chicago: Rand McNally, 1966.

Royce, J. R. The conceptual framework for a multifactor theory of individuality. In J. R. Royce (Ed.), *Multivariate analysis and psychological theory.* London: Academic Press, 1973.

Royce, J. R. Psychology is multi: Methodological variate, epistemic, theoretic and disciplinary. In W. J. Arnold (Ed.), *Nebraska Symposium on the conceptual foundations of theory and method in psychology.* Lincoln: University of Nebraska Press, 1976.

Rozeboom, W. W. Dynamic analysis of multivariate process data. *Psychometric Monographs,* in press. Chicago: University of Chicago Press, 1976.

Rozhdestvenskaia, V. I., Neblytsin, V. D., Borisova, M. N., & Ermolaeva-Tomina, L. [Comparative study of various indicators of the strength of the nervous system.] Voprosy Psikhologii, 1960, no. 5, 41–56.

Rubin, K. H., & Schneider, F. W. The relationship between moral judgment, egocentrism, and altruistic behavior. *Child Development,* 1973, *44,* 661–665.

Ruch, F. L. A technique for detecting attempts to fake performance on a self-inventory type of personality test. In Q. McNemar & M. A. Merrill (Eds.), *Studies in personality,* New York: McGraw-Hill, 1942.

Ruckmick, C. A. A preliminary study of emotions. *Psychological Monographs,* 1921, *136,* 30–35.

Rummel, R. J. Dimensions of conflict behavior within and between nations. *Yearbook of Society for General Systems Research,* 1963, *8,* 1–50.

Rummel, R. J. *Applied factor analysis.* Evanston: Northwestern University Press, 1970.

Rundquist, E. A. Form of statement in personality adjustment. *Journal of Educational Psychology,* 1940, *31,* 135–147.

Rundquist, E. A., & Sletto, R. F. *Personality in the depression.* Minneapolis: University of Minnesota Press, 1936.

Rusalow, V. M. Absolute sensitivity of the anlyzers and somatotype in man. In V. D.

Nebylitsyn & J. A. Gray (Eds.), *Biological bases of individual behavior.* New York: Academic Press, 1972.

Rushmore, J. T. Fakability of the Gordon Personal Profile. *Journal of Applied Psychology,* 1956, *40,* 175–177.

Russell, E. W. The power of behavior control: A critique of behavior modification methods. *Journal of Clinical Psychology,* 1974, *30,* 111–136. (Special Monograph Supplement)

Russell, W. A. Purpose and the problem of associative selectivity. In C. N. Cofer & B. S. Musgrove (Eds.), *Verbal behavior and learning.* New York: McGraw-Hill, 1963.

Rutter, M. Psychological development—predictions from infancy. *Journal of Child Psychology and Psychiatry,* 1970, *11,* 49–62.

Rychlak, J. F. Personality correlates of leadership among first level managers. *Psychological Reports,* 1963, *12,* 43–52.

Sachs, D. H., & Byrne, D. Differential conditioning of evaluative responses to neutral stimuli through association with attitude statements. *Journal of Experimental Research in Personality,* 1970, *4,* 181–185.

Saltz, E. Manifest anxiety: Have we misread the data? *Psychological Review,* 1970, *77,* 568–573.

Saltz, E., & Hoehn, A. J. A test of the Taylor-Spence theory of anxiety. *Journal of Abnormal and Social Psychology,* 1957, *54,* 114–117.

Salzinger, K., Feldman, R. S., & Portnoy, S. The effects of reinforcement on verbal and non-verbal responses. *Journal of General Psychology,* 1964, *70,* 225–234.

Salzinger, K., Portnoy, S., & Feldman, R. S. Experimental manipulation of continuous speech in schizophrenic patients. *Journal of Abnormal and Social Psychology,* 1964, *68,* 508–516.

Salzinger, S., Salzinger, K., Portnoy, S. Eckman, J., Bacon, P. M., Deutsch, M., & Zubin, J. Operant conditioning of continuous speech in young children. *Child Development,* 1962, *33,* 683–695.

Sampson, E. E. Birth order, need achievement, and conformity. *Journal of Abnormal and Social Psychology,* 1962, *64,* 155–159.

Sander, J., Tausch, R., Bastine, R., & Nagel, K. *Die Äuswirkung experimenteller Änderungen des psychotherapeuten Verhaltens auf Klienten in psychotherapeutischen Gesprächen.* Unpublished manuscript, University of Hamburg, 1968.

Santostefano, S., & Baker, A. H. Research in child psychopathology: The contributions of developmental psychology. In B. B. Wolman (Ed.), *The manual of child psychopathology.* New York: McGraw-Hill, 1970.

Saploskey, A. Effects of interpersonal relationships upon verbal conditioning. *Journal of Abnormal and Social Psychology,* 1960, *60,* 241–246.

Sarason, I. G. Effect of anxiety, motivational instructions, and failure on serial learning. *Journal of Experimental Psychology,* 1956, *51,* 253–260.

Sarason, I. G. Effect of anxiety and two kinds of failure on serial learning. *Journal of Personality,* 1957, *25,* 383–392. (a)

Sarason, I. G. Effect of anxiety and two kinds of motivating instructions on verbal learning. *Journal of Abnormal and Social Psychology,* 1957, *54,* 166–171. (b)

Sarason, I. G. Effects on verbal learning of anxiety, reassurance, and meaningfulness of material. *Journal of Experimental Psychology,* 1958, *56,* 472-477.

Sarason, I. G. Empirical findings and theoretical problems in the use of anxiety scales. *Psychological Bulletin,* 1960, *57,* 403-415.

Sarason, I. G. Experimental approaches to test anxiety: Attention and the uses of information. In C. D. Spielberger (Ed.), *Anxiety: Current trends in theory and research* (Vol. 2). Washington and New York: Academic Press, 1972.

Sarason, I. G. Test anxiety, attention and the general problem of anxiety. In C. D. Spielberger & I. G. Sarason (Eds.), *Stress and anxiety* (Vol. 1). Washington, D.C.: Hemisphere/Wiley, 1975.

Sarason, S. B. The measurement of anxiety in children: Some questions and problems. In C. D. Spielberger (Ed.), *Anxiety and behavior.* New York: Academic Press, 1966.

Sarason, S. B., Davidson, K. S., Lighthall, F. F., Waite, R. R., & Ruebush, B. K. *Anxiety in elementary school children.* New York: Wiley, 1960.

Sargent, F., & Weinman, K. P. Physiological individuality. *Annals of the New York Academy of Science,* 1966, *134,* 696-719.

Saunders, D. R. On the dimensionality of the WAIS battery for two groups of normal males. *Psychological Reports,* 1958, *5,* 529-541.

Saunders, D. R., & Schuman, H. *Syndrome analysis: An efficient procedure for isolating meaningful subgroups in a non-random sample of a population.* Paper presented at the meeting of the Psychonomic Society, St. Louis, 1962.

Savitsky, J. C., & Izard, C. E. Developmental changes in the use of emotion cues in a concept formation task. *Developmental Psychology,* 1970, *3,* 350-357.

Savitsky, J. C., & Sim, M. Trading emotions. Equity theory of rewards and punishment. *Journal of Communication,* 1974, *24,* 140-146.

Sawrey, W. L., Keller, L., & Conger, J. J. An objective method of grouping profiles by distance functions and its relation to factor analysis. *Education and Psychological Measurement,* 1960, *20,* 651-673.

Scarr, S. Genetic factors in activity motivation. *Child Development,* 1966, *37,* 663-673.

Scarr, S. Environmental bias in twin studies. *Eugenics Quarterly,* 1968, *15,* 34-40.

Scarr, S. Social introversion-extraversion as a heritable response. *Child Development,* 1969, *40,* 823-832.

Scarr-Salapatek, S. Genetics and the development of intelligence. In F. D. Horowitz, E. M. Hetherington, S. Scarr-Salapatek, & G. M. Siegel (Eds.), *Review of child development research* (Vol. 4). Chicago: University of Chicago Press, 1975.

Schacter, S. *The psychology of affiliation.* Stanford: Stanford University Press, 1959.

Schachter, S. *Emotion, obesity, and crime.* New York: Academic Press, 1971.

Schachter, S., Ellertson, T., & Gregory, D. An experimental study of cohesiveness and productivity. *Human Relations,* 1951, *4,* 229-238.

Schachter, S., & Latané, B. Crime, cognition, and the autonomic nervous system. In D. Levine (Ed.), *Nebraska symposium on motivation, 1964.* Lincoln: University of Nebraska Press, 1964.

Schaefer, E. S. A circumplex model for maternal behavior. *Journal of Abnormal and Social Psychology,* 1959, *59,* 226-235.

Schaefer, E. S., & Bayley, N. Maternal behavior, child behavior, and their intercorrelations from infancy through adolescence. *Monographs of the Society for Research in Child Development,* 1963, *28,* 127 pp.

Schaeffer, H. H., & Martin, P. L. *Behavioral therapy.* New York: McGraw-Hill, 1969.

Schaffer, H. R. Activity level as a constitutional determinant of infantile deprivation. *Child Development,* 1966, *37,* 595-602.

Schaffer, H. R. *The growth of sociability.* Middlesex: Penguin, 1971.

Schaffer, H. R., & Emerson, P. E. The development of social attachments in infancy. *Monographs of the Society for Research in Child Development,* 1964, *29*(3).

Schaie, K. W. A test of behavioral rigidity. *Journal of Abnormal and Social Psychology,* 1955, *51,* 604-610.

Schaie, K. W. Rigidity-flexibility and intelligence: A cross-sectional study of the adult life-span from 20 to 70 years. *Psychological Monographs,* 1958, *72*(9, Whole No. 462).

Schaie, K. W. On the equivalence of questionnaire and rating data. *Psychological Reports,* 1962, *10,* 521-522.

Schaie, K. W. *Equivalence or chaos: A hypothesis testing factor analysis study of the role of behavior rating, questionnaire and instrument factors in personality structure research.* Paper presented at the meeting of the Society for Multivariate Experimental Psychology, Boulder, Col., 1963.

Schaie, K. W. A general model for the study of developmental problems. *Psychological Bulletin,* 1965, *64,* 92-107.

Schaie, K. W. Year-by-year changes in personality from six to eighteen years. *Multivariate Behavioral Research,* 1966, *1,* 293-305.

Schaie, K. W. Methodological problems in descriptive developmental research on adulthood and aging. In J. R. Nesselroade & H. W. Reese (Eds.), *Life-span developmental psychology: Methodological issues.* New York: Academic Press, 1973.

Schaie, K. W., Anderson, V. E., McClearn, G. E., & Money, J. (Eds.). *Developmental human behavior genetics.* Lexington, Mass.: Heath, 1975.

Schaie, K. W., & Nesselroade, J. R. *Equivalence or chaos revisited: A factor analysis study of the effects of role of behavior rating, questionnaire and instrument factors in personality structure research.* Paper presented at the meeting of the Society of Multivariate Experimental Psychology, Austin, Tex., 1968.

Schaie, K. W., & Parham, I. A. *Manual for the Test of Behavioral Rigidity.* Palo Alto, Calif.: Consulting Psychologists Press, 1975.

Schaie, K. W., & Strother, C. R. The effect of time and cohort differences on the interpretation of age changes in cognitive behavior. *Multivariate Behavioral Research,* 1968, *3,* 259-293.

Schalling, D., Cronholm, B., & Asberg, M. Components of state and trait anxiety as related to personality and arousal. In L. Levi (Ed.), *Emotions: Their parameters and measurement.* New York: Raven, 1975.

Scheibel, M. E., & Scheibel, A. B. Anatomical basis of attention mechanisms in vertebrate brains. In G. Quarton, J. Melnechuk, & F. Schmitt (Eds.), *The neurosciences.* New York: Rockefeller University Press, 1967.

Scheier, I. H. What is an "objective test"? *Psychological Reports,* 1958, *4,* 147-157.

Scheier, I. H., & Cattell, R. B. Confirmation of objective test factors and assessment of their relation to questionnaire factors: A factor analysis of 113 rating, questionnaire and objective test measurements of personality. *Journal of Mental Science,* 1958, *104,* 608-624.

Scheier, I. H., & Cattell, R. B. *Handbook and test kit for the IPAT 8 Parallel Form Anxiety Battery.* Champaign, Ill.: Institute for Personality and Ability Testing, 1960.

Scheier, I. H., & Cattell, R. B. *Handbook for the Neuroticism Scale Questionnaire, "the NSC."* Champaign, Ill.: Institute for Personality and Ability Testing, 1961. (a)

Scheier, I. H. & Cattell, R. B. *The Eight-Parallel Form Anxiety Scale.* Champaign, Ill.: Institute for Personality and Ability Testing, 1961. (b)

Scheier, I. H., Cattell, R. B., & Horn, J. L. Objective test factor U. I. 23: Its measurement and its relation to clinically-judged neuroticism. *Journal of Clinical Psychology,* 1960, *16,* 135-145.

Scheier, I. H., & Ferguson, G. A. Further factorial studies of tests of rigidity. *Canadian Journal of Psychology,* 1952, *6,* 18-30.

Schelsky, J. *Wandlungen des deutschen Familie in der Gegenwart.* Stuttgart: Enke, 1954.

Schick, C. P. Konstitutionelle Diagnostik. In R. Heiss (Ed.), *Psychologische Diagnostik: Handbuch der Psychologie* (Vol. 6). Gottingen: Hogrefe, 1964.

Schlesser, G. E. Improving the validity of personality measurements by use of overrating. *Educational and Psychological Measurement,* 1953, *13,* 77-86.

Schmidt, G. [Personality evaluation of infants and children.] *Archiv für die Gesamte Psychologie,* 1966, *118,* 195-228. (*Psychological Abstracts,* 1967, *41,* 8671.)

Schmidt, H. O. Notes on the Minnesota Multiphasic Personality Inventory: The K-factor. *Journal of Consulting Psychology,* 1948, *12,* 337-342.

Schneewind, K. A., & Cattell, R. B. A contribution to the problem of factor identification: Distribution and confidence intervals of congruence coefficients as far as objective-analytic tests are concerned. *Psychologische Beitrage,* 1970, *12,* 214-226.

Schoenemann, P. H. *A solution of the orthogonal Procrustes problem with applications to orthogonal and oblique rotation.* Unpublished doctoral dissertation, University of Illinois, 1964.

Schoenfeldt, L. F. The hereditary components of the Project TALENT two-day test battery. *Measurement in Evaluation and Guidance,* 1968, *1,* 130-140.

Schonberg, W. B. Modification of attitudes of college students over time: 1923-1970. *Journal of Genetic Psychology,* 1974, *125,* 107-117.

Schonpflug, W. (Ed.). *Methoden der Aktivierungsforschung.* Bern: Huber, 1969.

Schooler, C. Birth order effects: Not here, not now! *Psychological Bulletin,* 1972, *78,* 161-175.

Schooley, M. Personality resemblances of married couples. *Journal of Abnormal and Social Psychology*, 1936, *31*, 340–347.

Schreider, E. Typology and biometrics. *Annals of the New York Academy of Sciences*, 1966, *134*, 789–803.

Schroder, H. M., Driver, M. J., & Streuffert, S. *Human information processing*. New York: Holt, Rinehart, & Winston, 1967.

Schroder, H. M., & Hunt, D. E. Dispositional effects upon conformity at different levels of discrepancy. *Journal of Personality*, 1958, *26*, 243–258.

Schroder, H. M., & Suedfeld, P. (Eds.). *Personality theory and information processing*. New York: Ronald Press, 1971.

Schuerger, J. M., & Cattell, R. B. A check on the structure of fourteen personality factors in objective tests, in children, at the 14–16-year level. In preparation.

Schuerger, J. M., Dielman, T. E., & Cattell, R. B. Objective analytic personality factors (U.I. 16, 17, 19, and 20) as correlates of school achievement. *Personality*, 1970, *1*, 95–101.

Schulman, R. E., Shoemaker, D. J., & Moelis, I. Laboratory measurement of parental behavior. *Journal of Consulting Psychology*, 1962, *26*, 109–114.

Schumacher, G., & Cattell, R. B. Faktorenanalyse des Deutschen HSPQ. *Zeitschrift für Experimentelle und Angewandte Psychologie*, 1974, *21*, 621–636.

Schutz, W. C. *FIRO: A three-dimensional theory of interpersonal behavior*. New York: Holt, 1958.

Schwartz, G. E., Fair, P. L., Greenberg, P. S., Friedman, M. J., & Klerman, G. L. Facial electomyography in the assessment of emotion. Paper presented at the meeting of the Society for Psychophysiological Research, Galveston, Tex., October 1973.

Schwartz, M., & Beach, F. A. Effects of adrenalectomy upon mating behavior in castrated male dogs. *American Psychologist*, 1954, *9*, 467.

Schwebel, A. I. Effects of impulsivity on performance of verbal tasks in middle- and lower-class children. *American Journal of Orthopsychiatry*, 1966, *36*, 13–21.

Scodel, A., & Mussen, P. H. Social perceptions of authoritarians and non-authoritarians. *Journal of Abnormal and Social Psychology*, 1953, *48*, 181–184.

Scott, J. P., & Fuller, J. L. *Genetics and social behavior of the dog*. Chicago: University of Chicago Press, 1965.

Scott, W. Research definitions of mental health and mental illness. *Psychological Bulletin*, 1958, *55*, 1–45.

Sealy, A. P. The influence of children's personality and interests on school performance. *American Psychologist*, 1963. *1*, 377.

Sealy, A. P., & Cattell, R. B. Adolescent personality trends in primary factors measured on the 16 P. F. and the HSPQ questionnaire through ages 11 to 23. *British Journal of Social and Clinical Psychology*, 1966, *5*, 172–184.

Sears, P. S. Child-rearing factors related to playing of sex-typed roles. *American Psychologist*, 1953, *8*, 431.

Sears, R. R. Ordinal position in the family as a psychological variable. *American Sociological Review*, 1950, *15*, 397–401.

Sears, R. R. A theoretical framework for personality and social behavior. *American Psychologist*, 1951, *6*, 476–483.

Sears, R. R. Comparison of interviews with questionnaires for measuring mother's attitudes toward sex and aggression. *Journal of Personality and Social Psychology*, 1965, *2*, 37–44.

Sears, R. R., Maccoby, E. E., & Levin, H. *Patterns of child rearing*. Evanston, Ill.: Row, Peterson, 1957.

Sears, R. R., Rau, L., & Alpert, R. *Identification and child rearing*. Stanford: Stanford University Press, 1965.

Sechrest, L., & Jackson, D. N. The generality of deviant response tendencies. *Journal of Consulting Psychology*, 1962, *26*, 395–401.

Secord, P. F., & Backman, C. W. *Social psychology*, New York: McGraw-Hill, 1964.

Secord, P. F., & Backman, C. W. An interpersonal approach to personality. In B. A. Maher (Ed.), *Progress in experimental personality research* (Vol. 2). New York: Academic Press, 1965.

Seeman, W. The concept of "subtlety" in structured psychiatric and personality tests: An experimental approach. *Journal of Abnormal and Social Psychology*, 1953, *48*, 239–247.

Sells, S. B. *A research program on the psychiatric selection of flying personnel. I. Methodological introduction and experimental design*. Randolph Field, Tex.: Air University School of Aviation Medicine, 1952.

Sells, S. B. (Ed.). *Stimulus determinants of behavior*. New York: Ronald Press, 1963.

Sells, S. B., Demaree, R. B., & Will, D. P. *A taxonomic investigation of personality conjoint factor structure of Guilford and Cattell trait markers*. Fort Worth: Institute of Behavioral Research, Texas Christian University, August 1968.

Sells, S. B., Demaree, R. G., & Will, D. P. Dimensions of personality: I. Conjoint factor structure of Cattell and Guilford trait markers. *Multivariate Behavioral Research*, 1970, *5*, 391–422.

Sells, S. B., Demaree, R. G., & Will, D. P. Dimensions of personality: II. Separate factor structures in Guilford and Cattell trait markers. *Multivariate Behavioral Research*, 1971, *6*, 135–185.

Sells, S. B., & Roff, M. *Peer acceptance-rejection and personality development* (Final Report, Project OE 5-0417). Washington, D.C.: Office of Education, U.S. Department of Health, Education, and Welfare, 1967.

Sells, S. B., Trites, D. K., & Parish, H. S. Correlates of manifest anxiety in beginning pilot trainees. *Journal of Aviation Medicine*, 1957, *28*, 583–588.

Selye, H. *The physiology and pathology of exposure to stress*. Montreal: Acta, 1950.

Selye, H. *The story of the adaptation syndrome*. Montreal: Acta, 1952.

Selye, H. The general adaptation syndrome in its relationship to neurology, psychology, and psychopathology. In A. Weider (Ed.), *Contributions toward medical psychology*. New York: Ronald Press, 1953.

Sewell, W. H., & Mussen, P. H. The effect of feeding, weaning, and scheduling procedures on childhood adjustment and the function of oral symptoms. *Child Development*, 1952, *23*, 185–191.

Sewell, W. H., Mussen, P. H., & Harris, C. W. Relationships among child training practices. *American Sociological Review*, 1955, *20*, 137–148.

Shagass, C. Electrical activity of the brain. In N. S. Greenfield & R. A. Sternbach (Eds.), *Handbook of psychophysiology*. New York: Holt, Rinehart, & Winston, 1972.

Shagass, C. *Eelctrophysiological parameters and methods*. New York: Raven Press, 1975.

Shapiro, A. P., Nicotero, J., Sapira, J., & Scheib, E. Analysis of the variability of blood pressure, pulse rate, and catecholamine responsivity in identical and fraternal twins. *Psychosomatic Medicine*, 1968, *30*, 506–520.

Shapiro, J. G. Relationships between expert and neophyte ratings of therapeutic conditions. *Journal of Consulting Psychology*, 1968, *32*, 87–89. (a)

Shapiro, J. G. Perception of therapeutic conditions from different vantage points. *Journal of Consulting Psychology*, 1968, *15*, 346–350. (b)

Shapiro, J. G., Foster, C. P., & Powell, K. Facial and bodily cues of genuineness, empathy, and warmth. *Journal of Clinical Psychology*, 1968, *24*, 233–236.

Shapiro, J. G., Krauss, H. H., & Truax, C. B. Therapeutic conditions and disclosure beyond the therapeutic encounter. *Journal of Counseling Psychology*, 1969, *16*, 290–294.

Shapiro, S., & Stine, J. The figure drawings of three-year-old children: A contribution to the early development of body image. In *The Psychoanalytic study of the child* (Vol. 20). New York: International Universities Press, 1965.

Shaw, M. E. A note concerning homogeneity of membership and group problem solving. *Journal of Abnormal and Social Psychology*, 1960, *60*, 448–450.

Sheldon, M. S. Conditions affecting the fakability of teacher-selection inventories. *Educational and Psychological Measurement*, 1959, *19*, 207–219.

Sheldon, W. H. *The varieties of temperament: A psychology of constitutional differences*. New York: Harper, 1942.

Sherif, C. W., & Sherif, M. (Eds.). *Attitude, ego involvement and change*. New York: Wiley, 1967.

Sherif, M. *Social interaction, process and products*. Chicago: Aldine, 1967.

Sherif, M., & Sherif, C. W. *An outline of social psychology*. New York: Harper & Row, 1956.

Sherman, J. A., & Baer, D. M. Appraisal of operant therapy techniques with children and adults. In C. M. Franks (Ed.), *Behavior therapy: Appraisal and status*. New York: McGraw-Hill, 1969.

Shields, J. *Monozygotic twins*. Oxford: Oxford University Press, 1962.

Shields, J. Heredity and psychological abnormality. In H. J. Eysenck (Ed.), *Handbook of abnormal psychology* (2nd ed.). San Diego: Knapp, 1973.

Shipley, W. C., Gray, F. S., & Newbert, N. The Personal Inventory—its derivation and validation. *Journal of Clinical Psychology*, 1946, *2*, 318–322.

Shiskin, J., & Eisenpress, H. Seasonal adjustments by electronic computer methods. *Journal of* the American Statistical Association, 1957, 52, 415–449.

Shoben, E. J. A learning theory interpretation of psychotherapy. Harvard Educational Review, 1948, 18, 129–145.

Shoben, E. J. Psychotherapy as a problem in learning theory. Psychological Bulletin, 1949, 46, 366–392.

Shotwell, A. M., Hurley, J. B., & Cattell, R. B. Motivational structure of a hospitalized mental defective. Journal of Abnormal and Social Psychology, 1961, 62, 422–426.

Shucard, D. W., & Horn, J. L. Cortical evoked potentials and measurement of human abilities. Journal of Comparative and Physiological Psychology, 1972, 78, 59–68.

Shuey, A. M. Improvement in scores on the American Council Psychological Examination from freshman to senior year. Journal of Educational Psychology, 1948, 38, 417–426.

Shuter, R. The psychology of music ability. London: Methuen, 1968.

Siddle, D. A. T., Morrish, R. B., White, K. D., & Mangan, G. L. Relation of visual sensitivity to extraversion. Journal of Experimental Research in Personality, 1969, 3, 264–267.

Siegel, B. J. High anxiety levels and cultural integration: Notes on a psycho-cultural hypothesis. Social Forces, 1955, 39, 42–48.

Siegelman, M. Evaluation of Bronfenbrenner's questionnaire for children concerning parental behavior. Child Development, 1965, 36, 163–174.

Siegelman, M. Loving and punishing parental behaviors and introversion tendencies in sons. Child Development, 1966, 37, 985–992.

Sigall, H., & Landy, D. Radiating beauty: Effects of having a physically attractive partner on person perception. Journal of Personality and Social Psychology, 1973, 28, 218–224.

Sigel, I. E., Roeper, A., & Hooper, T. H. A training procedure for acquisition of quantity: A pilot study and its replication. British Journal of Educational Psychology, 1966, 36, 301–311.

Sigg, E. B. The organization and functions of the central sympathetic nervous system. In L. Levi (Ed.), Emotions: Their parameters and measurement. New York: Raven Press, 1975.

Silverstein, A. B. Faking on the Rosenzweig Picture Frustration study. Journal of Applied Psychology, 1957, 41, 191–194.

Simon, H. A. Motivational and emotional controls of cognition. Psychological Review, 1967, 74, 29–39.

Simpson, G. G. The crisis in biology. American Scholar, 1967, 36, 363–377.

Simsarian, F. P. Case histories of five thumb-sucking children breast fed on unscheduled regimes, without limitations of nursing time. Child Development, 1947, 18, 180–184.

Sines, J. O. Behavior correlates of genetically enhanced susceptibility to stomach lesion development. Journal of Psychosomatic Research, 1961, 5, 120–126.

Sines, J. O. Actuarial methods in personality assessment. In B. R. Maher (Ed.), Progress in experimental personality research. New York: Academic Press, 1966.

Singer, J. D. Human behavior and international politics. Chicago: Rand McNally, 1965.

Singer, J. L., & Singer, D. G. Personality. In

P. E. Mussen & M. R. Rosenzweig (Eds.), Annual review of psychology. Palo Alto, Calif.: Annual Reviews, Inc., 1972.

Singer, J. J. Hypothalamic control of male and female sexual behavior in female rats. Journal of Comparative and Physiological Psychology, 1968, 66, 738–742.

Sinha, D. Position effect in the readministration of an anxiety scale. Journal of General Psychology, 1964, 70, 305–309.

Sitkei, E. G., & Meyers, C. Comparative structure of intellect in middle and lower-class 4-year-olds of two ethnic groups. Developmental Psychology, 1969, 1, 592–604.

Sixtl, F. Messmethoden der Psychologie. Weinheim: Beltz, 1967.

Sixtl, R. Ein verfahren zuz Rotation von Faktorenladung nach einem vorgegebenen Kriterium. Archiv für die Gesamte Psychologie, 1964, 116, 92–97.

Skager, R. W., Schultz, C. B., & Klein, S. P. The multidimensional scaling of a set of artistic drawings: Perceived structure and scale correlates. Multivariate Behavioral Research, 1966, 1, 425–436.

Skard, A. G., Inhelder, B., Noelting, G., Murphy, L. B., & Thomas, H. Longitudinal research in personality development. In H. P. David & J. C. Brengelmann (Eds.), Perspectives in personaltiy research. New York: Springer, 1960.

Skeels, H. M., & Dye, H. B. A study in the effects of differential stimulation on mentally retarded children. Proceedings of the American Association of Mental Deficiency, 1939, 44, 114–136.

Skinner, B. F. The behavior of organisms: An experimental analysis. New York: Appleton, 1938.

Skinner, B. F. Are theories of learning necessary? Psychological Review, 1950, 57, 193–216.

Skinner, B. F. Science and human behavior. New York: Macmillan, 1953.

Skinner, B. F. Verbal behavior. New York: Appleton-Century-Crofts, 1957.

Skinner, B. F. Behaviorism at fifty. In T. W. Wann (Ed.), Behaviorism and phenomenology. Chicago: University of Chicago Press, 1964.

Skinner, B. F. Contingencies of reinforcement. New York: Appleton-Century-Crofts, 1969.

Skinner, B. F. The steep and thorny way to a science of behavior. American Psychologist, 1975, 30, 42–49.

Skinner, J. E., & Lindsley, D. B. The non-specific mediothalamic-frontocortical system: Its influence on electrocortical activity and behavior. In K. H. Pribram & A. R. Luria (Eds.), Psychophysiology of the frontal lobes. New York: Academic Press, 1973.

Skinner, N. S. J. F., & Howarth, E. Cross-media independence of questionnaire and objective-test personality factors. Multivariate Behavioral Research, 1973, 8, 23–40.

Slovic, P. The consistency and cue utilization in judgment. American Journal of Psychology, 1966, 79, 427–434.

Small, D. O., & Campbell, D. T. The effect of acquiescence response set upon the relationship of the F-scale and conformity. Sociometry, 1960, 23, 69–71.

Smelser, W. T. Dominance as a factor in achievement and perception in cooperative prob-

lem solving interaction. Journal of Abnormal and Social Psychology, 1961, 62, 535–542.

Smith, H. T. A comparison of interview and observation measures of mother behavior. Journal of Abnormal and Social Psychology, 1958, 57, 278–282.

Smith, K. H. Ego strength and perceived competence as conformity variables. Journal of Abnormal and Social Psychology, 1961, 62, 169–171.

Smith, R. T. A comparison of socioenvironmental factors in monozygotic and dizygotic twins, testing an assumption. In S. G. Vandenberg (Ed.), Methods and goals in human behavior genetics. New York: Academic Press, 1965.

Smith, S. T. Extraversion and sensory threshold. Psycholophysiology, 1968, 5, 293–299.

Smith, W. G. A model for psychiatric diagnosis. Archives of General Psychiatry, 1966, 14, 521–529.

Sokolov, E. N. Neuronal models and the orienting reflex. In M. A. B. Brazier (Ed.), The central nervous system and behavior. New York: Josiah Macey Foundation, 1960.

Sokolov, E. N. Perception and the conditioned reflex (S. W. Waydenfeld, trans.). New York: Macmillan, 1963. (a)

Sokolov, E. N. Higher nervous functions: The orienting reflex. Annual Review of Physiology, 1963, 25, 545–580. (b)

Sollberger, A. Biological rhythm research. Amsterdam: Elsevier, 1965.

Solomon, A. Authoritarian attitude changes and group homogeneity. Journal of Social Psychology, 1963, 59, 129–135.

Sommer, R., Dewar, R., & Osmond, H. Is there a schizophrenic language? Archives of General Psychiatry, 1960, 3, 665–673.

Sontag, L. W. The history of longitudinal research: Implications for the future. Child Development, 1971, 42, 987–1002.

Sontag, L. W., & Wallace, R. F. The effect of cigarette smoking during pregnancy on fetal heart rate. American Journal of Obstetrics and Gynecology, 1935, 29, 77–82. (a)

Sontag, L. W., & Wallace, R. F. The movement response of the human fetus to sound stimuli. Child Development, 1935, 6, 253–258. (b)

Sontag, L. W., & Wallace, R. F. Changes in the rate of human fetal heart in response to vibratory stimuli. American Journal of Disturbed Children, 1936, 56, 583–589.

Sopolsky, A. Effect of interpersonal relationship upon verbal conditioning. Journal of Abnormal and Social Psychology, 1960, 60, 241–246.

Soueif, M. I. Extreme response sets as a measure of intolerance of ambiguity. British Journal of Psychology, 1958, 49, 329–334.

Soueif, M. I., Eysenck, H. J., & White, P. O. A joint factorial study of the Guilford, Cattell and Eysenck scales. In H. J. Eysenck & S. B. G. Eysenck, Personality structure and measurement. London: Routledge & Kegan Paul, 1969.

Southwick, C. H. The population dynamics of confined house mice supplied with unlimited food. Ecology, 1955, 36, 212–225.

Spearman, C. E. General intelligence objectively measured and determined. American Journal of Psychology, 1904, 15, 201.

Spearman, C. E. *The abilities of man.* London: Macmillan, 1927.

Spearman, C. E. Thurstone's work reworked. *Journal of Educational Psychology,* 1939, *30,* 1–16.

Specht, L. L. *A comparison of the domains of the 16 P.F. items and items in the MMPI.* Unpublished manuscript, University of Illinois, 1966.

Spence, J. T. Learning theory and personality. In J. Wepman & R. W. Heine (Eds.), *Concepts of personality.* Chicago: Aldine, 1963.

Spence, J. T., & Lair, C. V. Associative interference in the verbal learning performance of schizophrenics and normals. *Journal of Abnormal and Social Psychology,* 1964, *68,* 204–209.

Spence, J. T., & Spence, K. W. The motivational components of manifest anxiety: Drive and drive stimuli. In C. D. Spielberger (Ed.), *Anxiety and behavior.* New York: Academic Press, 1966.

Spence, K. W. The nature of theory construction in contemporary psychology. *Psychological Review,* 1944, *51,* 47–68.

Spence, K. W. *Behavior theory and conditioning.* New Haven: Yale University Press, 1956.

Spence, K. W. A theory of emotionally based drive (D) and its relation to performance in simple learning situations. *American Psychologist,* 1958, *13,* 131–141.

Spence, K. W. Anxiety (drive) level and performance in eyelid conditioning. *Psychological Bulletin,* 1964, *61,* 129–141.

Spence, K. W., & Spence, J. T. *The psychology of learning and motivation.* New York: Academic Press, 1967–1968.

Spielberger, C. D. The effects of manifest anxiety on the academic achievement of college students. *Mental Hygiene,* 1962, *46,* 420–426.

Spielberger, C. D. Theoretical and epistemological issues in verbal conditioning. In S. Rosenberg (Ed.), *Directions in psycholinguistics.* New York: Macmillan, 1965.

Spielberger, C. D. Theory and research on anxiety. In C. D. Spielberger (Ed.), *Anxiety and behavior.* New York: Academic Press, 1966. (a)

Spielberger, C. D. The effects of anxiety on complex learning and academic achievement. In C. D. Spielberger (Ed.), *Anxiety and behavior.* New York: Academic Press, 1966. (b)

Spielberger, C. D. (Ed.). *Anxiety and behavior.* New York: Academic Press, 1966. (c)

Spielberger, C. D. Anxiety as an emotional state. In C. D. Spielberger (Ed.), *Anxiety: Current trends in theory and research.* New York: Academic Press, 1971. (a)

Spielberger, C. D. Trait-state anxiety: and motor behavior. *Journal of Motor Behavior,* 1971, *3,* 265–279. (b)

Spielberger, C. D. Anxiety as an emotional state. In C. D. Spielberger (Ed.), *Anxiety: Current trends in theory and research* (Vol. 1). New York: Academic Press, 1972. (a)

Spielberger, C. D. Conceptual and methodological issues in research on anxiety. In C. D. Spielberger (Ed.), *Anxiety: Current trends in theory and research* (Vol. 1). New York: Academic Press, 1972. (b)

Spielberger, C. D. *Anxiety: Current trends in theory and research* (Vol. 1). New York: Academic Press, 1972. (c)

Spielberger, C. D. Anxiety: State-trait-process. In C. D. Spielberger & I. G. Sarason (Eds.), *Stress and anxiety* (Vol. 1). Washington, D.C.: Hemisphere/Wiley, 1975.

Spielberger, C. D. State-trait anxiety and interactional psychology. In D. Magnusson & N. S. Endler (Eds.), *Interactional psychology: Current issues and future prospects.* New York: LEA/Wiley, 1976.

Spielberger, C. D., Anton, W., & Bedell, J. The nature and treatment of test anxiety. In M. Zuckerman & C. D. Spielberger (Eds.), *Emotions and anxiety: New concepts in methods and applications.* New York: LEA/Wiley, 1976.

Spielberger, C. D., Auerbach, S. M., Wadsworth, A. P., Dunn, T. M., & Taulbee, E. S. Emotional reactions to surgery. *Journal of Consulting and Clinical Psychology,* 1973, *40,* 33–38.

Spielberger, C. D., & Gorsuch, R. L. *Mediating processes in verbal conditioning.* Report to the National Institute of Mental Health, 1966.

Spielberger, C. D., Gorsuch, R., & Lushene, R. *The State-trait Anxiety Inventory (STAI) test manual, form X.* Palo Alto, Calif.: Consulting Psychologists Press, 1969.

Spielberger C. D., Gorsuch, R. L., & Lushene, R. E. *Manual for the State-trait Anxiety Inventory.* Palo Alto, Calif.: Consulting Psychologists Press, 1970.

Spielberger, C. D., O'Neil, H. F., & Hansen, D. N. Anxiety, drive theory, and computer-assisted learning. In B. A. Maher (Ed.), *Progress in experimental personality research* (Vol. 6). New York: Academic Press, 1972.

Spielberger, C. D., & Smith, L. H. Anxiety (drive), stress, and serial-position effect in serial-verbal learning. *Journal of Experimental Psychology,* 1966, *72,* 589–595.

Spiro, M. Social systems, personality, and functional analysis. In B. Kaplan (Ed.), *Studying personality cross-culturally.* New York: Harper & Row, 1961.

Spitz, R. A. Hospitalism: An inquiry into the genesis of psychiatric conditions in early childhood. In *The psychoanalytic study of the child* (Vols. 1 & 2). New York: International Universities Press, 1945, 1946.

Spuhler, J. N. (Ed.). *Genetic diversity and human behavior.* Chicago: Aldine, 1967.

Staats, A. W. Learning theory and "opposite speech." *Journal of Abnormal and Social Psychology,* 1957, *55,* 268–269.

Staats, A. W. Comments on Professor Russell's paper. In C. N. Cofer & B. S. Musgrave (Eds.), *Verbal behavior and learning.* New York: McGraw-Hill, 1963.

Staats, A. W. (Ed.). *Human learning.* New York: Holt, Rinehart, & Winston, 1964.

Staats, A. W. *Learning, language, and cognition.* New York: Holt, Rinehart, & Winston, 1968. (a)

Staats, A. W. Social behaviorism and human motivation: Principles of the attitude-reinforcer-discriminative system. In A. G. Greenwald, T. C. Brock, & T. M. Ostrom (Eds.), *Psychological foundations of attitudes.* New York: Academic Press, 1968. (b)

Staats, A. W. *Child learning, intelligence, and personality.* New York: Harper & Row, 1971.

Staats, A. W. *Social behaviorism.* Homewood, Ill.: Dorsey Press, 1975.

Staats, A. W., Finley, J. R., Minke, K. A., & Wolf, M. M. Reinforcement variables in the control of unit reading responses. *Journal of the Experimental Analysis of Behavior,* 1964, *7,* 139–149.

Staats, A. W., Gross, M. C., Guay, P. F., & Carlson, C. C. Personality and social systems and attitude-reinforcer-discriminative theory: Interest (attitude) formation, function, and measurement. *Journal of Personality and Social Psychology,* 1973, *26,* 251–261.

Staats, A. W., & Hammond, O. W. Natural words as physiological conditioned stimuli: Food-word-elicited salivation and deprivation effects. *Journal of Experimental Psychology,* 1972, *96,* 206–208.

Staats, A. W., & Staats, C. K. Effect of number of trials on the language conditioning of meaning. *Journal of General Psychology,* 1959, *61,* 211–223.

Staats, A. W., & Staats, C. K. *Complex human behavior: A systematic extension of learning principles.* New York: Holt, Rinehart, & Winston, 1963.

Staats, A. W., Staats, C. K., Heard, W. G., & Finley, J. R. Operant conditioning of factor analytic personality traits. *Journal of General Psychology,* 1962, *66,* 101–114.

Staats, A. W., Staats, C. K., Schutz, R. E., & Wolf, M. M. The conditioning of reading responses using "extrinsic" reinforcers. *Journal of the Experimental Analysis of Behavior,* 1962, *5,* 33–40.

Staats, A. W., & Warren, D. R. Motivation and three-function learning: Deprivation-satiation and approach-avoidance to food words. *Journal of Experimental Psychology,* 1974, *103,* 1191–1199.

Stafford, R. E. Sex differences in spatial visualization as evidence of sex-linked inheritance. *Perceptual and Motor Skills,* 1961, *13,* 428.

Stager, P. Conceptual level as a composition variable in small-group decision making. *Journal of Personality and Social Psychology,* 1967, *5,* 152–161.

Standish, R. R., & Champion, R. A. Task difficulty and drive in verbal learning. *Journal of Experimental Psychology,* 1960, *59,* 361–365.

Stankov, L., & Horn, J. L. *Ability structure in auditory performances.* Unpublished manuscript, University of Denver, 1973.

Stapert, J., & Clore, G. L. Attraction and disagreement-produced arousal. *Journal of Personality and Social Psychology,* 1969, *13,* 64–69.

Stapf, A. *Elterliche Erziehung in Befragung und Experiment. Überprüfung eines zweidimensionalen Konzepts der elterlichen Bekräftigung.* Unpublished doctoral dissertation, Unversity of Marburg, 1973.

Stapf, A. Neuere Untersuchungen zur elterlichen Strenge un Ünerstützung. In H. Lukesch (Ed.), *Auswirkungen elterlicher Erziehungsstile.* Göttingen: Hogrefe, 1975.

Stapf, K. H., Herrmann, T., Stapf, A., & Stäcker, K. H. *Psychologie des elterlichen Erziehungsstils.* Stuttgart: Huber, 1972.

Starkweather, E. K., & Cowling, F. G. The measurement of conforming and nonconforming behavior in preschool children. *Proceedings of the Oklahoma Academy of Sciences,* 1964, *44,* 168–180. (*Psychological Abstracts,* 1965, *39,* 9803.)

Stein, M. I. Explorations in typology. In R. W. White (Ed.), *The study of lives: Essays on personality in honor of Henry A. Murray.* New York: Atherton, 1963.

Stein, M. I. *Volunteers for peace.* New York: Wiley, 1966.

Steiner, I. D. Group dynamics. *Annual Review of Psychology,* 1964, *15,* 421–446.

Steiner, I. D., & Johnson, H. H. Authoritarianism and conformity. *Sociometry,* 1963, *26,* 21–34.

Steiner, I. D., & Rogers, E. D. Alternative response to dissonance. *Journal of Abnormal and Social Psychology,* 1963, *66,* 128–136.

Stellar, E., & Sprague, J. M. *Progress in physiological psychology* (Vol. 1). New York: Academic Press, 1966.

Stephenson, W. The inverted factor technique. *British Journal of Psychology.* 1936, *26,* 344–361.

Stephenson, W. *The study of behavior.* Chicago: University of Chicago Press, 1953.

Stern, C. S., Caldwell, B. M., Hersher, L., Lipton, E. L., & Richmond, J. B. A factor analytic study of the mother-infant dyad. *Child Development,* 1969, *40,* 163–181.

Stern, W. *Die differentielle Psychologie in ihren methodischen Grundlagen.* Leipzig: Barth, 1921.

Sternbach, R. A. *Principles of psychophysiology.* New York: Academic Press, 1966.

Stevenson, I. Is the human personality more plastic in infancy and childhood? *American Journal of Psychiatry,* 1957, *114,* 152–161.

Stewart, J., Skvarenina, A., & Pottier, J. Effects of neonatal androgens on open-field behavior and maze learning in the prepubescent and adult rat. *Physiology and Behavior,* 1975, *14,* 291–295.

Stimpson, D., & Bass, B. M. Dyadic behavior of self-interaction-, and task-oriented subjects in a test situation. *Journal of Abnormal and Social Psychology,* 1964, *68,* 558–562.

Stogdill, R. M. Personal factors associated with leadership: A survey of the literature. *Journal of Psychology,* 1948, *25,* 35–71.

Stogdill, R. M. Leadership, emembership, and orgaanization. *Psychological Bulletin,* 1950, *47,* 1014.

Stolurow, L. M. Social impact of programmed instruction: Aptitudes and abilities revisited. In J. P. DeCeddo (Ed.), *Educational technology.* New York: Holt, Rinehart, & Winston, 1964.

Stolz, L. M. Effects of maternal employment on children. *Child Development,* 1960, *31,* 749–782.

Stone, J. L., Murphy, L. B., & Smith, H. T. (Eds.). *The competent infant.* New York: Basic Books, 1973.

Stone, P. J., Dunphy, O. C., Smith, M. S., & Ogilivie, D. M. *The General Inquirer–a computer approach to content analysis.* Cambridge: Massachusetts Institute of Technology Press, 1966.

Stotland, E., & Dunn, R. E. Identification, "oppositeness," authoritarianism, self-esteem, and birth order. *Psychological Monographs,* 1962, *76*(9, Whole No. 528).

Stotland, E., Thorley, S., Thomas, E., Cohen, A. R., & Zander, A. The effects of group expectations and self-esteem upon self-evaluation. *Journal of Abnormal and Social Psychology,* 1957, *54,* 55–63.

Stott, L. H. Personality at age four. *Child Development,* 1962, *33,* 287–311.

Stott, L. H. & Ball, R. S. Infant and preschool mental tests: Review and evaluation. *Monographs*

*of the Society for Research in Child Development,* 1965, *30*(Serial No. 101).

Stouffer, S. A., Guttman, L., Suchman, F. A., Lazarsfeld, P. F., Star, S. A., & Clausen, J. A. *Measurement and prediction.* Princeton, N.J.: Princeton University Press, 1950.

Strauss, A. A. *George Herbert Mead on social psychology.* Chicago: University of Chicago Press, Phoenix Books, 1964.

Strickland, B. R., & Crowne, D. P. Conformity under conditions of simulated group pressure as a function of the need for social approval. *Journal of Social Psychology,* 1962, *58,* 171–181.

Strodtbeck, F. L. *Family interaction and the transmission of achievement related attitudes.* Unpublished manuscript, University of Chicago, 1954.

Strodtbeck, F. L. Family interaction, values, and achievement. In D. C. McClelland, A. L. Baldwin, U. Bronfenbrenner, & F. L. Strodtbeck (Eds.), *Talent and society.* Princeton, N.J.: Van Nostrand, 1958.

Stroebel, C. F. Psychophysiological pharmacology. In N. S. Greenfield & R. A. Sternbach (Eds.), *Handbook of psychophysiology.* New York: Holt, Rinehart, & Winston, 1972.

Strong, E. K. *Vocational interests of men and women.* Palo Alto, Calif.: Stanford University Press, 1943.

Strong, P. *Biophysical measurements.* Beaverton, Ore.: Tektronix, 1970.

Stroup, A. L. Marital adjustment of the mother and the personality of the child. *Marriage and Family Living,* 1956, *18,* 109–113.

Studer, R. G. The dynamics of behavior-contingent physical systems. In H. M. Proshansky, W. H. Ittelson, and L. G. Rivlin (Eds.), *Environmental psychology: Man and his physical setting.* New York: Holt, Rinehart, & Winston, 1970.

Stumpf, C. Drug action on the electrical activity of the hippocampus. *International Review of Neurobiology,* 1965, *8,* 77–138.

Sturm, A., & Birkmayer, W. (Eds.). *Klinische Pathologie des vegetativen Nervensystems.* Stuttgart: G. Fischer, 1976.

Sudak, H. S., & Maas, J. W. Behavioral-neurochemical correlation in reactive and nonreactive strains of rats. *Science,* 1964, *146,* 418–420.

Suedfeld, P. Sensory deprivation stress: Birth order and instructional set as interacting variables. *Journal of Personality and Social Psychology,* 1969, *11,* 70–74.

Sullivan, E. V., McCullough, G., & Stagner, M. A developmental study of the relationship between conceptual, ego, and moral development. *Child Development,* 1970, *41,* 399–411.

Sullivan, H. S. *The interpersonal theory of psychiatry.* New York: Norton, 1953.

Sulman, F. G. Einfuss der Hormone auf Persönlichkeit und Verhalten. In H. Meng (Ed.), *Psyche und Hormon.* Bern: Huber, 1960.

Summers, S. A. The learning of responses to multiple weighted cues. *Journal of Experimental Psychology,* 1962, *64,* 29–34.

Suomi, S. J., Collins, M. L., & Harlow, H. F. Effects of permanent separation from mother on infant monkeys. *Developmental Psychology,* 1973, *9,* 376–384.

Suppes, P. Stimulus-response theory of auto-

mata in TOTE hierarchies: A reply to Arbib. *Psychological Review,* 1969, *76,* 511–515.

Sutherland, E. H., & Cressey, D. R. *Principles of criminology* (5th ed.). Chicago: Lippincott, 1955.

Sutton-Smith, B., Rosenberg, B. G., & Morgan, E. F., Jr. Historical changes in the freedom with which children express themselves on personality inventories. *Journal of Genetic Psychology,* 1961, *99,* 309–315.

Swanson, H. H. Alteration of sex-typical behaviour of hamsters in open-field and emergence tests by neo-natal administration of androgen or oestrogen. *Animal Behaviour,* 1967, *15,* 209–216.

Sweney, A. B. Faktorenanalytische methoden in der motivations-forschung Cattells. *Archiv gesamte Psychologie,* 1961, *8,* 136–147. (a)

Sweney, A. B. *Repression or denial mechanisms operationally defined through factor analytic techniques.* Paper presented at the meeting of the Society for Multivariate Experimental Psychology, Fort Worth, Tex., 1961. (b)

Sweney, A. B. Objective measurement of strength of dynamic structure factors. In R. B. Cattell & F. W. Warburton (Eds.), *Objective personality and motivation tests.* Urbana, Ill.: University of Illinois Press, 1967.

Sweney, A. B. *Individual assessment with the MAT.* Champaign, Ill.: Institute for Personality and Ability Testing, 1968.

Sweney, A. B. *A preliminary descriptive manual for individual assessment of the Motivation Analysis Test.* Champaign, Ill.: Institute for Personality and Ability Testing, 1969.

Sweney, A. B., & Cartwright, D. S. Relations between conscious and unconscious manifestations of motivation in children. *Multivariate Behavioral Research,* 1966, *1,* 447–459.

Sweney, A. B., & Cattell, R. B. Dynamic factors in twelve-year-old children as revealed in measures of integrated motivation. *Journal of Clinical Psychology,* 1961, *17,* 360–369.

Sweney, A. B., & Cattell, R. B. Relationships between integrated and unintegrated motivation structure examined by objective tests. *Journal of Social Psychology,* 1962, *57,* 217–226.

Sewney, A. B., Cattell, R. B., & Krug, S. E. *The School Motivation Analysis Test.* Champaign, Ill.: Institute for Personality and Ability Testing, 1970.

Symonds, P. M. *Diagnosing personality and conduct.* New York: Century Croft, 1931.

Symonds, P. M. *The dynamics of parent-child relationships* (2nd ed.). New York: Appleton-Century-Crofts, 1949.

Talbot, E. *The effect of note taking upon verbal responses and its implications for the interview.* Unpublished doctoral dissertation, University of California, Los Angeles, 1954.

Tallman, J. Adaptability: A problem solving approach to assessing child-rearing practices. *Child Development,* 1961, *32,* 651–661.

Tanner, J. M. Inheritance of morphological and physiological traits. In A. Sorsby (Ed.), *Clinical genetics.* London: Butterworth, 1953.

Tapp, J. *An examination of hypotheses concerning the motivational components of attitude strength.* Unpublished master's thesis, University of Illinois, 1958.

Tatro, D. F. *The interpretation of objectively measured personality factors in terms of clinical data and concepts.* Unpublished doctoral dissertation, University of Illinois, 1966.

Tateishi, K. [Behavior of washing baits in Formosan monkeys (*Macaca cyclopis*).] (In Japanese.) *Annual of Animal Psychology,* 1958, *8,* 89–94.

Tatsuoka, M. M. *Multivariate analysis: Techniques for educational and psychological research.* New York: Wiley, 1971.

Taylor, A. J. W. The significance of "darls" or "special relationships" for Borstal girls. *British Journal of Criminology,* 1965, *15,* 406–418.

Taylor, D. A., Wheeler, L., & Altman, I. Stress reactions in socially isolated groups. *Journal of Personality and Social Psychology,* 1968, *9,* 369–376.

Taylor, F. K. The three-dimensional basis of emotional interactions in small groups. I. *Human Relations,* 1954, *7,* 441–471.

Taylor, F. K. The three-dimensional basis of emotional interactions in small groups. II. *Human Relations,* 1955, *8,* 3–28.

Taylor, J. A. The relationship of anxiety to the conditioned eyelid response. *Journal of Experimental Psychology,* 1951, 41, 81–92.

Taylor, J. A. A personality scale of manifest anxiety. *Journal of Abnormal and Social Psychology,* 1953, *48,* 285–290.

Taylor, J. A. Drive theory and manifest anxiety. *Psychological Bulletin,* 1956, *53,* 303–320.

Taylor, J. A. The effects of anxiety level and psychological stress on verbal learning. *Journal of Abnormal and Social Psychology,* 1958, *57,* 55–60.

Teitelbaum, H. A. *Psychosomatic neurology.* New York: Grune & Stratton, 1964.

Terman, L. M., & Miles, C. C. *Sex and personality: Studies in masculinity and femininity.* New York & London: McGraw-Hill, 1936.

Tharp, R. G. Psychological patterning in marriage. *Psychological Bulletin,* 1963, *60,* 97–117.

Thayer, S., & Schiff, W. *Stimulus factors in observer judgment of social interaction. I. Facial expression and motion pattern.* Unpublished manuscript, The City College of the City University of New York, 1967.

Thoday, J. M. New insights into continuous variation. *Proceeding of the 3rd International Congress of Human Genetics,* 1966, 339–350.

Thomas, A., Birch, H. G., Chess, S., & Robbins, L. C. Individuality in responses of children to similar environmental situations. *American Journal of Psychiatry,* 1961, *117,* 798–803.

Thomas, A., Chess, S., Birch, H. G., & Hertig, M. A longitudinal study of primary reaction patterns in children. *Comprehensive Psychiatry,* 1960, *1,* 103–112.

Thompson, J. Development of facial expression of emotion in blind and seeing children. *Archives of Psychology,* 1941, No. 264.

Thompson, R. F. *Foundations of physiological psychology.* New York: Harper, 1967.

Thompson, R. F., & Patterson, M. M. (Eds.). *Bioelectric recording techniques.* Part B. *Electroencephalography and human brain potentials.* New York: Academic Press, 1974.

Thompson, W. R. Multivariate experiment in behavior genetics. In R. B. Cattell (Ed.), *Handbook of multivariate experimental psychology.* Chicago: Rand McNally, 1966.

Thompson, W. R. Genetics and social behavior. In D. C. Glass (Ed.), *Genetics: Proceedings of a Conference under the Auspices of Russell Sage Foundation, the Social Science Research Council, and the Rockefeller University.* New York: Rockefeller University Press, 1968. (a)

Thompson, W. R. Development and the biophysical bases of personality. In E. F. Borgatta & W. W. Lambert (Eds.), *Handbook of personality theory and research.* Chicago: Rand McNally, 1968. (b)

Thompson, W. R., & Heron, W. The effects of restricting early experiences on the problem-solving capacity of dogs. *Canadian Journal of Psychology,* 1954, *8,* 17–31.

Thompson, W. R., & Wilde, G. J. S. Behavior genetics. In B. B. Wolman (Ed.), *Handbook of general psychology.* Englewood Cliffs, N.J.: Prentice-Hall, 1973.

Thorndike, R. L. Critical note on the Pressey Interest Attitudes Test. *Journal of Applied Psychology,* 1938, *22,* 657–658.

Thorne, F. Back to fundamentals. *Journal of Clinical Psychology,* 1953, *9,* 89–91.

Thorne, F. C. Theory of the psychological state. *Journal of Clinical Psychology,* 1966, *22,* 127–235.

Thurstone, L. L. Multiple factor analysis. *Psychological Review,* 1931, *38,* 406–427.

Thurstone, L. L. *The vectors of the mind.* Chicago: University of Chicago Press, 1935.

Thurstone, L. L. A new rotational method in factor analysis. *Psychometrika,* 1938, *3,* 199–218. (a)

Thurstone, L. L. Primary mental abilities. *Psychometric Monographs,* No. 1. Chicago: University of Chicago Press, 1938. (b)

Thurstone, L. L. An experimental study of simple structure. *Psychometrika,* 1940, *5,* 153–168.

Thurstone, L. L. A factorial study of perception. *Psychometric Monograph, No. 4.* Chicago University of Chicago Press, 1944.

Thurston, L. L. *Multiple factor analysis.* Chicago: University of Chicago Press, 1947.

Thurstone, L. L. *Thurstone Temperament Schedule.* Chicago: Science Research Associates, 1950.

Thurstone, L. L. The dimensions of temperament. *Psychometrika,* 1951, *16,* 11–20.

Thurstone, L. L., & Jenkins, R. L. Birth order and intelligence. *Journal of Educational Psychology,* 1929, *20,* 641–651.

Thurstone, L. L., & Thurstone, T. G. A neurotic inventory. *Journal of Social Psychology,* 1930, *1,* 3–30.

Thurstone, L. L., & Thurstone, T. G. Factorial studies of intelligence. *Psychometric Monographs,* No. 2. Chicago: University of Chicago Press, 1941.

Timmons, E. O., & Noblin, C. D. The differential performance of orals and anals in a verbal conditioning paradigm. *Journal of Consulting Psychology,* 1963, *27,* 383–386.

Tobias, M., & Michael, W. B. Dimensions of biological and psychological functions in two samples of children in the third grade. *Psychological Reports,* 1963, *12,* 759–762.

Todd, F. *A methodological analysis of clinical judgment.* Unpublished doctoral dissertation, University of Colorado, 1954.

Tollefson, D. *Response to humor in relation to other measures of personality.* Unpublished doctoral dissertation, University of Illinois, 1961.

Tolman, C. W., & Bainsley, R. H. Effects of verbal reinforcement on conformity and deviant behavior: Replication report. *Psychological Reports,* 1966, *19,* 910.

Tolman, E. C. *Purposive behavior in animals and men.* New York: Appleton-Century-Crofts, 1932.

Tolman, E. C. The determiners of behavior at a choice point. *Psychological Review,* 1938, *45,* 1–41.

Tolman, E. C. Principles of purposive behavior. In S. Koch (Ed.), *Psychology: A study of a science.* New York: McGraw-Hill, 1959.

Toman, W. *An introduction to the psychoanalytic theory of motivation.* New York: Pergamon Press, 1960.

Tolman, W. Über Familienkonstellationen. *Psychological Research,* 1961, *12,* 237–250.

Tomkins, S. S. *Affect, imagery, consciousness* (Vol. 1). *The positive affects.* New York: Springer, 1962.

Tomkins, S. S. *Affect, imagery, consciousness* (Vol. 2). *The negative affects.* New York: Springer, 1963.

Tomkins, S. S., & McCarter, R. What and where are the primary affects? Some evidence for a theory. *Perceptual and Motor Skills,* 1964, *18,* 119–158.

Tomkins, S. S., & Messick, S. *Computer simulation of personality.* New York: Wiley, 1963.

Torgerson, W. S. *Theory and methods of scaling.* New York: Wiley, 1958.

Torrance, E. P. *Guiding creative talent.* Englewood Cliffs, N.J.: Prentice-Hall, 1962.

Torres, A. A. Sensitization and association in alpha blocking "conditioning." *EEG Clinical Neurophysiology,* 1968, *24,* 297–306.

Traisman, A. S., & Traisman, H. S. Thumb- and finger-sucking: A study of 2650 infants and children. *Journal of Pediatrics,* 1958, *53,* 566–572.

Trapold, M. A., & Winokur, S. W. Transfer from classical conditioning and extinction to acquisition, extinction, and stimulus generalization of a positively reinforced instrumental response. *Journal of Experimental Psychology,* 1967, *63,* 7–11.

Traver, R. M. W. Rational hypotheses in the construction of tests. *Educational and Psychological Measurement,* 1951, *11,* 128–137.

Triandis, H. C., Malpass, R. S., & Davidson, A. R. Psychology and culture. *Annual Review of Psychology,* 1973, *24,* 355–378.

Trouton, D., & Eysenck, H. J. The effects of drugs on behaviour. In H. J. Eysenck (Ed.), *Handbook of abnormal psychology.* London: Pitman, 1960.

Truax, C. B. Reinforcement and nonverbal reinforcement in Rogerian psychotherapy. *Journal of Abnormal and Social Psychology,* 1966, *71,* 1–9.

Truax, C. B. Therapist interpersonal reinforcement of client self-exploration and therapeutic outcome in group psychotherapy. *Journal of Counseling Psychology,* 1968, *15,* 225–231.

Truax, C. B., & Carkhuff, R. R. Concreteness: A neglected variable in the psychotherapeutic process. *Journal of Clinical Psychology,* 1964, *20,* 264–267. (a)

Truax, C. B., & Carkhuff, R. R. The old and the new: Theory and research in counseling and psychotherapy. *Personnel and Guidance Journal*, 1964, *42*, 860–866. (b)

Truax, C. B., & Carkhuff, R. R. Personality change in hospitalized mental patients during group psychotherapy as a function of alternate sessions and vicarious therapy pre-training. *Journal of Clinical Psychology*, 1965, *21*, 225–228.

Truax, C. B., & Carkhuff, R. R. *Toward effective counseling and psychotherapy: Training and practice.* Chicago: Aldine, 1967.

Truax, C. B., & Mitchell, K. M. Research on certain therapist intervention skills in relation to process outcome. In A. E. Bergin & S. L. Garfield (Eds.), *Handbook of psychotherapy and behavior change: An empirical analysis.* New York: Wiley, 1971.

Truax, C. B., Mitchell, K. M., Bozarth, J. Wargo, D. G., & Krauft, C. The effect of therapeutic conditions on patient outcome in public and private practice. *University of Arkansas Discussion Papers*, May 1971.

Truax, C. B., & Shapiro, J. C. *Personality disturbance and the perception of empathy, warmth, and genuineness.* Unpublished manuscript, Arkansas Rehabilitation Research and Training Center, University of Arkansas, 1969.

Truax, C. B., & Tatum, C. R. An extension from the effective psychotherapeutic model to constructive personality change in preschool children. *Childhood Education*, 1966, *42*, 456–462.

Truax, C. B., Tunnell, B. T., Jr., & Glenn, A. W. *Accurate empathy, nonpossessive warmth, genuineness and patient outcome in silent and verbal patients.* Unpublished manuscript, Arkansas Rehabilitation Research and Training Center, University of Arkansas, 1966.

Truax, C. B., & Wargo, D. G. Antecedents to outcome in group psychotherapy with juvenile delinquents: Effects of therapeutic conditions, alternate sessions, vicarious pre-training and patient self-exploration. *Discussion papers* (Vol. 1, No. 14). Arkansas Rehabilitation Research and Training Center, University of Arkansas, 1968. (a)

Truax, C. B., & Wargo, D. G. Effects of therapeutic conditions, alternate sessions, vicarious therapy pre-training, and patient self-exploration on hospitalized mental patients during group therapy. *Discussion papers* (Vol. 1, No. 15). Arkansas Rehabilitation Research and Training Center, University of Arkansas, 1968. (b)

Truax, C. B., Wargo, D. G., Frank, J. D., Imber, S. D., Battle, C., Hoehn-Saric, R., Nash, E. H., & Stone, A. R. Therapist empathy, genuineness, and warmth and patient therapeutic outcome. *Journal of Consulting Psychology*, 1966, *30*, 395–401.

Truax, C. B., Wargo, V., & Volksdorf, N. Antecedents to outcome and group counseling with institutionalized juvenile delinquents: Effects of therapeutic conditions, patient's self-exploration, alternate sessions and vicarious therapy pretraining. *Journal of Abnormal Psychology*, 1970, *76*, 235–242.

Truax, C. B., & Wittmer, J. The effects of therapist focus on patient anxiety source and the interaction with therapist level of accurate empathy. *Journal of Clinical Psychology*, 1971, *27*, 297–299.

Tryon, R. C. *Cluster analysis: Correlation profile and orthometric (factor) analysis for the isolation of unities in mind and personality.* Ann Arbor: Edwards Brothers, 1938.

Tryon, R. C. Genetic differences in maze-learning ability in rats. *Yearbook of the National Society for the Study of Education*, 1940, *39*, 111–119.

Tryon, R. C. Cumulative communality cluster analysis. *Educational and Psychological Measurement*, 1958, *18*, 3–35.

Tsujioka, B. *Illustration of a state model, dynamic and general.* Paper presented at the 19th International Congress of Psychology, London, 1970.

Tsujioka, B., & Cattell, R. B. Constancy and difference in personality structure and mean profile, in the questionnaire medium, from applying the 16 P.F. test in America and Japan. *British Journal of Social and Clinical Psychology*, 1965, *4*, 287–297. (a)

Tsujioka, B., & Cattell, R. B. A cross-cultural comparison of second-stratum questionnaire personality factor structures—anxiety and extraversion—in America and Japan. *Journal of Social Psychology*, 1965, *65*, 205–219. (b)

Tsushima, Y. *Failure stress in examinations related to anxiety inventory scores.* Unpublished master's thesis, University of Illinois, 1957.

Tucker, L. R. The role of correlated factors in factor analysis. *Psychology*, 1940, *5*, 141, 152.

Tucker, L. R. *A method for synthesis of factor analysis studies.* (Personnel Research Section Rep. No. 984). Washington, D.C.: Department of the Army, 1951.

Tucker, L. R. An inter-battery method of factor analysis. *Psychometrika*, 1958, *23*, 111–137.

Tucker, L. R. Implications of factor analysis of three-way matrices for measurement of change. In C. W. Harris (Ed.), *Problems in measuring change.* Madison: University of Wisconsin Press, 1963.

Tucker, L. R. The extension of factor analysis to three-dimensional matrices. In N. Fredriksen & H. Gulliksen (Eds.), *Contributions to mathematical psychology.* New York: Holt, Rinehart, & Winston, 1964. (a)

Tucker, L. R. Systematic differences between individuals in perceptual judgments. In M. Shelly & G. Bryan (Eds.), *Human judgments and optimality.* New York: Wiley, 1964. (b)

Tucker, L. R. Learning theory and multivariate experiment: Illustration by determination of generalized learning curves. In R. B. Cattell (Ed.), *Handbook of multivariate experimental psychology.* Chicago: Rand McNally, 1966.

Tucker, L. R., Damarin, F., & Messick, S. A base-free measure of change. *Psychometrika*, 1966, *31*, 457–473.

Tucker, L. R., & Messick, S. An individual differences model for multidimensional scaling. *Psychometrika*, 1963, *28*, 333–367.

Tuckman, B. W. Personality structure, group composition, and group functioning. *Sociometry*, 1964, *27*, 469–487.

Tuckman, B. W. Group composition and group performance of structured and unstructured tasks. *Journal of Experimental Social Psychology*, 1967, *3*, 25–40.

Tuddenham, R. D. Correlates of yielding to a distorted norm. *Journal of Personality*, 1959, *27*, 272–284.

Tulving, E., & Donaldson, W. *Organization of memory.* New York: Academic Press, 1972.

Tupes, E. C. Relationships between behavior trait ratings by peers and later officer performance of USAF officer candidate school graduates (Rep. No. AFPTRC-TN-57-125). Lackland Air Force Base, Tex.: USAF Personnel and Training Research Center, 1957. (ASTIA Doc. No. 134257).

Tupes, E. C., & Christal, R. C. *Stability of personality trait rating factors obtained under diverse conditions* (USAF WADC Tech. Note No. 58-61). Wright-Patterson Air Force Base, Ohio, 1958.

Tupes, E. C., & Christal, R. C. *Recurrent personality factors based on trait ratings* (Rep. No. ASD-TR-61-97). Lackland Air Force Base, Tex.: Aeronautical Systems Development Personnel Laboratory, 1961.

Tupes, E. C., & Kaplan, M. N. *Similarity of factors underlying peer ratings of socially acceptable, socially unacceptable, and bipolar personality traits* (Rep. No. ASD-TN-61-48). Lackland Air Force Base, Tex.: Aeronautical Systems Development Personnel Laboratory, 1961.

Turiel, E. An experimental test of the sequentiality of developmental stages in the child's moral judgments. *Journal of Personality and Social Psychology*, 1966, *3*, 611–618.

Turner, F. J. *The frontier in American history.* New York: Henry Holt, 1921.

Tyler, F., T., & Dimichaelis, J. U. K scores applied to the MMPI scales for college women. *Educational and Psychological Measurement*, 1953, *13*, 459–466.

Tyler, L. E. *The psychology of human differences.* London: Methuen, 1950, 1960.

Tyler, V., & Kelly, R. *Cattell's HSPQ as a predictor of the behavior of institutionalized delinquents* (Psychology Research Rep. No. 2). Port Townsend, Wash.: Fort Worden School, 1963.

Udry, J. R., & Morris, N. M. Distribution of coitus in the menstrual cycle. *Nature, 1968, 220,* 593–596.

Uhr, L., & Miller, J. G. (Eds.). *Drugs and behavior.* New York: Wiley, 1960.

Ullmann, L. P., & Krasner, L. (Eds.). *Case studies in behavior modification.* New York: Holt, Rinehart, & Winston, 1965.

Ullmann, L. P., & Krasner, L. *A psychological approach to abnormal behavior.* Englewood Cliffs, N.J.: Prentice-Hall, 1969.

Underwood, B. J. Stimulus selection in verbal learning. In C. Cofer & B. Musgrave (Eds.), *Verbal behavior and learning.* New York: McGraw-Hill, 1963.

Underwood, B. J., Runquist, W. N., & Schulz, R. W. Response learning in paired-associate lists as a function of intralist similarity. *Journal of Experimental Psychology*, 1959, *58*, 70–78.

Underwood, B. J., & Schulz, R. W. *Meaningfulness and verbal learning.* Philadelphia: Lippincott, 1960.

Uno, T., & Grings, W. W. Autonomic components of orienting behavior. *Psychophysiology*, 1965, *1*, 311–321.

Valenstein, E. S. Steroid hormones and the neuropsychology of development. In R. L.

Isaacson (Ed.), *The neuropsychology of development.* New York: Wiley, 1968.

Valenstein, E. S., Cox, V. C., & Kakolewski, J. W. Sex differences in hyperphagia and body weight following hypothalamic damage. *Annals of the New York Academy of Sciences,* 1970, *157,* 1030–1046.

Vandenberg, S. G. The primary mental abilities of Chinese students: A comparative study of stability of a factor structure. *Annals of the New York Academy of Science,* 1959, *79,* 257–304.

Vandenberg, S. G. The hereditary abilities study. *American Journal of Human Genetics,* 1962, *14,* 220–237.

Vandenberg, S. G. Innate abilities: One or many? *Acta Geneticae Medicae et Gemellologiae,* 1965, *14,* 41–47. (a)

Vandenberg, S. G. (Ed.). *Methods and goals in human behavior genetics.* New York: Academic Press, 1965. (b)

Vandenberg, S. G. Contributions of twin research to psychology. *Psychological Bulletin,* 1966, *66,* 327–352.

Vandenberg, S. G. Hereditary factors in normal personality traits (as measured by inventories). In J. Wortis (Ed.), *Recent advances in biological psychiatry* (Vol. 9). New York: Plenum Press, 1967. (a)

Vandenberg, S. G. Hereditary factors in psychological variables in man, with a special emphasis on cognition. In J. H. Spuhler (Ed.), *Genetic diversity and human behavior.* Chicago: Aldine, 1967 (b)

Vandenberg, S. G. The nature and nurture of intelligence. In D. C. Glass (Ed.), *Genetics: Proceedings of a conference under the auspices of Russell Sage Foundation, the Social Science Research Council, and the Rockefeller University.* New York: Rockefeller University Press, 1968. (a)

Vandenberg, S. G. (Ed.). *Progress in human behavior genetics.* Baltimore: Johns Hopkins University Press, 1968. (b)

Vandenberg, S. G., Clark, P. J., & Samuels, I. Psychological reactions of twins: Hereditary factors in galvanic skin resistance, heartbeat, and breathing rates. *Eugenics Quarterly,* 1965, *12,* 7–10.

Vandenberg, S. G., Comrey, A. L., & Stafford, R. E. *Hereditary factors in personality and attitude scales: A twin study* (Res. Rep. No. 16, Louisville Twin Study). Louisville, Ky.: University of Louisville School of Medicine, 1967.

Vandenbergh, J. G. The effects of gonadal hormones on the aggressive behavior of adult golden hamsters (Mesocricetus auratus). *Animal Behaviour,* 1971, *19,* 589–594.

Vanden Bos, G. R. *Therapist conditions in psychoanalytic psychotherapy.* Michigan State Psychotherapy Research Project Bulletin, June 1970, (11), 1–17.

Van Den Daele, L. A developmental study of the ego-ideal. *Genetic Psychology Monographs,* 1968, *78,* 191–256.

Van der Veen, J. M. The 2 × 2 genotype-environmental table. *Heredity,* 1959, *13,* 123–126.

Van Egeren, L. F. *Experimental determination by P-technique of functional unities of depression and other psychological states.* Unpublished manuscript, University of Illinois, 1963.

Van Egeren, L. F. Multivariate statistical analysis. *Psychophysiology,* 1973, *10,* 517–532.

Vannoy, J. S. Generality of cognitive complexity-simplicity as a personality construct. *Journal of Personality and Social Psychology,* 1965, *2,* 385–396.

Van Olst, E. H. *The orienting reflex.* The Hague: Mouton, 1971.

Van Zelst, R. H. Worker pupularity and job satisfaction. *Personnel Psychology,* 1951, *4,* 405–412.

Van Zelst, R. H. Validation evidence of the empathy test. *Educational and Psychological Measurement,* 1953, *13,* 474–477.

Vasilev, M. F. [Correlations between type of nervous system and vascular reflexes in 2–3 year old children.] *Doklady Akademii Nauk SSSR,* 1961, *136,* 734–736. (*Psychological Abstracts,* 1962, *36,* IFD34V.)

Vaughan, D. S. The relative methodological soundness of several major personality factor analyses. *Journal of Behavioral Science,* 1973, *1,* 305–313.

Vaughan, G. M. The trans-situational aspect of conforming behavior. *Journal in Personality,* 1964, *32,* 335–354.

Vaughan, G. M., & Burdsall, C. A check on the factor structure of the 16 P. F. by factoring 184 items. In preparation. (a)

Vaughan, G. M., & Burdsall, C. A comparison of the super ego factor pattern across a generation. In preparation. (b)

Vaughan, G. M., & Taylor, A. J. W. Clinical anxiety and conformity. *Perceptual and Motor Skills,* 1966, *22,* 719–722.

Vaughan, G. M., & White, K. D. Conformity and authoritarianism re-examined. *Journal of Personality and Social Psychology,* 1966, *3,* 363–366.

Veitch, R., & Griffitt, W. B. *Good news—bad news: Affective and interpersonal effects.* Unpublished manuscripts, Bowling Green State University, 1975.

Venables, P. H., & Christie, M. J. (Eds.). *Research in psychophysiology.* London: Wiley, 1975.

Venables, P. H., & Martin, I. (Eds.). *Manual of psychophysiological methods.* Amsterdam: North-Holland, 1967.

Vernon, P. E. *The structure of human abilities.* London: Methuen, 1950.

Vernon, P. E. *Intelligence and attainment tests.* London: University of London Press, 1960.

Vernon, P. E. *The structure of human abilities* (2nd ed.). London: Methuen, 1961.

Vernon, P. E. *Personality assessment: A critical survey.* London: Methuen, 1964.

Vernon, P. E. *Intelligence and cultural environment.* London: Methuen, 1972.

Vernon, P. E. Intelligence. In W. B. Dockrell (Ed.), *On intelligence.* London: Methuen, 1970.

Verplanck, W. S. The control of the content of conversation: Reinforcement of statements of opinion. *Journal of abnormal and Social Psychology,* 1955, *51,* 668–676.

Very, P. S. Differential factor structure in mathematical ability. *Genetic Psychology Monographs,* 1967, *75,* 169–207.

Very, P. S., & Iacono, C. H. Differential factor structure of seventh grade students. *Journal of Genetic Psychology,* 1970, *117,* 239–251.

Voas, R. B. A procedure for reducing the effects of slanting questionnaire responses toward social acceptability. *Educational and Psychological Measurement.* 1958, *18,* 337–345.

Vogel, F. Genetische Aspekte des Elektroenzephalogramms. *Deutsche Medizinische Wochenschrift,* 1963, *88,* 1748–1759.

Vogel, W., Broverman, D. M., & Klaiber, E. L. EEG and mental abilities. *Electroencephalography and Clinical Neurophysiology,* 1968, *24,* 166–175.

von Bertalanffy, L. *General system theory: Foundations, development, applications.* New York: George Braziller, 1968.

Von Neumann, J., & Morgenstern, O. *Theory of games and economic behavior.* Princeton: Princeton University Press, 1944.

Vuyk, R. *Das Kind in der Zweikinderfamilie.* Bern and Stuttgart: Huber, 1959.

Vygotsky, L. S. *Thought and language.* (E. Hanfmann & G. Vakar, Eds. and trans.). Cambridge: Massachusetts Institute of Technology Press, 1962.

Wachtel, P. C. Conceptions of broad and narrow attention. *Psychological Bulletin,* 1967, *68,* 417–429.

Wachtel, P. C. Psychodynamics, behavior therapy, and the implicable experimenter: An inquiry into the consistency of personality. *Journal of Abnormal Psychology,* 1973, *82,* 324–344.

Waldrop, M. F., & Bell, R. Q. Relation of preschool dependency behavior and family size and density. *Child Development,* 1964, *35,* 1187–1195.

Waldrop, M. F., & Bell, R. Q. Effects of family size and density on newborn characteristics. *American Journal of Orthopsychiatry,* 1966, *36,* 544–550.

Waldrop, M. F., & Halverson, C. F., Jr. Intensive and extensive peer behavior. *Child Development,* 1975, *46,* 19–26.

Wallach, M. A. Commentary: Active-analytical vs. passive-global cognitive functioning. In S. Messick and J. Ross (Eds.), *Measurement in personality and cognition.* New York: Wiley, 1962.

Wallach, M. A., Green, L. R., Lippsitt, P. D., & Winehart, J. B. Contradiction between overt and projective personality indicators as a function of defensiveness. *Psychological Monographs,* 1962, *76,*(Whole No. 520), 23–120.

Wallach, M. A., & Kogan, N. *Modes of thinking in young children: A study of the creativity-intelligence distinction.* New York: Holt, Rinehart, & Winston, 1965.

Wallbrown, F. H., Blake, J., & Wherry, R. J. The hierarchical factor structure of the Wechsler Preschool and Primary Scale of Intelligence. *Journal of Consulting and Clinical Psychology,* 1973, *41,* 356–362.

Wallen, R. W. Food aversion and behavior disorders. *Journal of Consulting Psychology.* 1948, *12,* 310–312.

Walker, E. L. Psychological complexity as a basis for a theory of motivation and choice. In D. Levine (Ed.), *Nebraska Symposium on Motivation,* 1964. Lincoln: University of Nebraska Press, 1964.

Walker, R. N. Body build and behavior in young children: II. Body build and parents' ratings. *Child Development,* 1963, *34,* 1–23.

Walters, C. E. Prediction of postnatal development from fetal activity. *Child Development,* 1965, *36,* 801–808.

Walters, H. A., & Jackson, D. N. Group and

individual regularities in trait inference: A multidimensional scaling analysis. *Multivariate Behavioral Research,* 1966, *1,* 145–163.

Walters, J., & Stinnett, N. Parent-child relationships: A decade of research. *Journal of Marriage and the Family,* 1971, *33,* 70–111.

Walters, R. H., & Parke, R. D. The role of the distance receptors in the development of social responsiveness. In L. P. Lipsitt & C. C. Spiker (Eds.), *Advances in child development and behavior (Vol. 2).* New York: Academic Press, 1965.

Warburton, F. W. The relationship between personality factors and scholastic attainment. In R. M. Dreger (Ed.), *Multivariate personality research: Contributions to the understanding of personality in honor of Raymond B. Cattell.* Baton Rouge, La.: Claitor, 1972.

Warburton, F. W., & Cattell, R. B. A cross cultural comparison of patterns of extraversion and anxiety. *British Journal of Psychology,* 1961, *52,* 3–16.

Ward, C. H., Beck A. T., Mendelson, M., Mock, J. E., & Erbaugh, J. K. The psychiatric nomenclature: Reasons for diagnostic disagreement. *Archives of General Psychiatry,* 1962, *7,* 198–205.

Ward, W. C. Creativity in young children. *Child Development,* 1968, *39,* 737–754. (a)

Ward, W. C. Reflection-impulsivity in kindergarten children. *Child Development,* 1968, *39,* 867–874. (b)

Ward, W. C. Rate and uniqueness in children's creative responding. *Child Development,* 1969, *40,* 869–878.

Ward, W. C. *Convergent and divergent measurement of creativity in children* (RB-71-40). Princeton, N.J.: Educational Testing Service, 1971.

Warden, C. J., Jenkins, T. N., & Warner, L. H. *Comparative psychology.* New York: Ronald Press, 1940.

Warren, J. B. Birth order and social behavior. *Psychological Bulletin,* 1966, *65,* 38–49.

Warren, R. P., & Aronson, L. R. Sexual behavior in castrated-adrenalectomized hamsters maintained on DCA. *Endocrinology,* 1956, *58,* 293–304.

Wassenaar, C. M. C. *Labiliteit as temperamentsfaktor.* Unpublished doctoral dissertation, University of Stellenbosch, South Africa, 1956.

Waters, E., & Crandall, V. J. Social class and observed maternal behavior from 1940 to 1960. *Child Development,* 1964, *35,* 1021–1032.

Watson, J. B. *Behavior.* New York: Holt, 1914.

Watson, J. B., & Raynor, R. Conditioned emotional reactions. *Journal of Experimental Psychology,* 1920, *3,* 1–14.

Watson, R. I. Historical review of objective personality testing: The search for objectivity. In B. M. Bass & I. A. Berg (Eds.), *Objective approaches to personality assessment.* Princeton: Van Nostrand, 1959.

Waxenberg, S. E., Drellic, M. G., & Sutherland, A. M. The role of hormones in human behavior. 1. Changes in female sexuality after adrenalectomy. *Journal of Clinical Endocrinology and Metabolism,* 1959, *19,* 193–202.

Weber, M. *The Protestant ethic and the spirit of capitalism.* New York: Scribner, 1930.

Weiner, B. Effects of motivation on the availability and retrieval of memory traces. *Psychological Bulletin,* 1966, *65,* 24–37.

Weiner, H., & McGinnies, E. Authoritarianism, conformity, and confidence in a perceptual judgment situation. *Journal of Social Psychology,* 1961, *55,* 77–84.

Weinert, F. Erziehungsstile in ihrer Abhängigkeit von der individuellen Eigenart des Erziehers. In Th. Herrmann (Ed.), *Psychologie der Erziehungsstile.* Göttingen: Hogrefe, 1966.

Weir, M. W. Developmental changes in problemsolving strategies. *Psychological Review,* 1964, *71,* 473–490.

Weisgerber, C. A. Accuracy in judging emotional expressions as related to understanding of literature. *Journal of Social Psychology,* 1957, *46,* 253–258.

Weiss, R. F. Operant conditioning techniques in psychological assessment. In P. McReynolds (Ed.), *Advances in psychological assessment.* Palo Alto, Calif.: Science & Behavior Books, 1968.

Weiss, R. L. Krasner, L., & Ullman, L. P. Responsivity to verbal conditioning as a function of emotional atmosphere and patterning of reinforcement. *Psychological Reports,* 1960, *5,* 415–426.

Weisskopf, E. A., & Dieppa, J. J. Experimentally induced faking of TAT responses. *Journal of Consulting Psychology,* 1951, *15,* 469–474.

Weizmann, F. *A developmental study of preference for novelty.* Unpublished doctoral dissertation, Ohio State University, 1966.

Weizmann, F., & Protter, B. S. The generality of locus of control: A Rep-Grid investigation of personality consistency. *Journal of Clinical and Consulting Psychology,* 1976, *44,* 863.

Welker, W. L. Some determinants of play and exploration in chimpanzees. *Journal of Comparative and Physiological Psychology,* 1956, *49,* 84–89.

Wells, F. L. The systematic observation of the personality in its relation to the hygiene of the mind. *Psychological Review,* 1915, *21,* 295–333.

Welsh, G. S. Factor dimensions *A* and *R.* In G. S. Welsh & W. G. Dahlstrom (Eds.), *Basic readings on the MMPI in psychology and medicine.* Minneapolis: University of Minnesota Press, 1956.

Welsh, G. S., & Dalhstrom, W. G. *Basic readings on the MMPI in psychology and medicine.* Minneapolis: University of Minnesota Press, 1956.

Wenger, M. A. Studies of autonomic balance in Army-Air Forces personnel. *Comparative Psychology Monographs,* 1948, *19,* (4, Whole No. 101).

Wenger, M. A. Studies in autonomic balance: A summary. *Psychophysiology,* 1966, *2,* 173–186.

Wenger, M. A., Clemens, T. L., Darsie, M. L., Engel, B. T., Estess, F. M., & Sonnenschein, R. R. Autonomic response patterns during intravenous infusion of ephinephrine and nor-ephinephrine. *Psychosomatic Medicine,* 1960, *22,* 294–307.

Wenger, M. A., & Cullen, T. D. Studies in autonomic balance in children and adults. In N. S. Greenfield & R. A. Sternbach (Eds.), *Handbook of psychophysiology.* New York: Holt, Rinehart, & Winston, 1972.

Wenger, M. A., Engel, B. T., & Clemens, T. L. Studies in autonomic response patterns: Rationale and methods. *Behavioral Science,* 1957, *2,* 216–221.

Wenig, P. *The relative roles of naive, artistic, cognitive and press compatibility misperception and ego defense operations in tests of misperception.* Unpublished master's thesis, University of Illinois, 1952.

Wepman, J. M., & Heine, R. W. *Concepts of personality.* Chicago: Aldine, 1963.

Werner, E. C., Honzik, M. P., & Smith, R. S. Prediction of intelligence and achievement at ten years from twenty month pediatric and psychologic examinations. *Child Development,* 1968, *39,* 1063–1075.

Werner, E. E. From birth to latency: Behavioral differences in a multiracial group of twins. *Child Development,* 1973, *44,* 438–444.

Werner, H. *Comparative psychology of mental development* (Rev. ed.). New York: International Universities Press, 1948.

Weschler, I. R. A follow-up study of the measurement of attitudes toward labor and management by means of the error-choice method. *Journal of Social Psychology,* 1950, *32,* 63–69. (a)

Weschler, I. R. An investigation of attitudes toward labor and management by means of the error-choice method. *Journal of Social Psychology,* 1950, *32,* 51–62. (b)

Wessman, A. E., & Ricks, D. F. *Mood and personality.* New York: Holt, 1966.

Wessman, A. E., Ricks, D. F., & Tyl, M. Characteristics and concomitants of mood fluctuation in college women. *Journal of Abnormal and Social Psychology,* 1960, *60,* 117–126.

West, S. Sibling configurations of scientists. *American Journal of Sociology,* 1960, *66,* 268–274.

Wezler, K., Thauer, R., & Greven, K. Die vegetative Struktur des Individuums, genessen am Kreislauf und Gasstoffwechsel in Ruhe. *Zeitschrift für experimentelle Medizin,* 1940, *107,* 673–708, 751–784.

Whisler, L. R. "Reliability" of scores on attitude scales as related to scoring method. *Studies in higher education.* West Lafayette, Ind.: Purdue University, 1938.

White, A., Handler, P., & Smith, E. *Principles of biochemistry.* New York: McGraw-Hill, 1968.

White, B. L. An experimental approach to the effects of experience on early human behavior. In J. P. Hill (Ed.), *Minnesota symposium on child psychology* (Vol. 1). Minneapolis: University of Minnesota Press, 1967.

White, K. D., & Vaughan, G. M. Some sex differences in relating trans-situational conformity to personality. *Perceptual and Motor Skills,* 1967, *24,* 190.

White, R. W. Motivation reconsidered: The concept of competence. *Psychological Review,* 1959, *66,* 297–333.

Whitehorn, J. C. Human factor in psychiatry. *Bulletin of the New York Academy of Medicine,* 1964, *40,* 451–466.

Whiting, J. W. M., & Child, I. L. *Child training and personality: A cross-cultural study.* New Haven: Yale University Press, 1953.

Whybrow, P. C., Prange, A. J., & Treadway, C. R. Mental changes accompanying thyroid gland dysfunction. *Archives of General Psychiatry,* 1969, *20,* 48– 63.

Wieland, B. A., & Mefferd, R. B. Systematic changes in levels of physiological activity during a four-month period. *Psychophysiology*, 1970, *6*, 669–689.

Wiener, D. N. Subtle and obvious keys for the MMPI. In G. S. Welsh & W. G. Dahlstrom (Eds.), *Basic readings on the MMPI in psychology and medicine*. Minneapolis: University of Minnesota Press, 1956.

Wiggins, J. S. Interrelationships among MMPI measures of dissimulation under standard and social desirability instructions. *Journal of Consulting Psychology*, 1959, *23*, 419–427.

Wiggins, J. S. Definitions of social desirability and acquiescence in personality inventories. In S. Messick & J. Ross (Eds.), *Measurement in personality and cognition*. New York: Wiley, 1962. (a)

Wiggins, J. S. Strategic, method and stylistic variance in the MMPI. *Psychological Bulletin*, 1962, *59*, 224–242. (b)

Wiggins, J. S. *Personality and prediction: Principles of personality assessment*. London: Addison-Wesley, 1973.

Wiggins, N., & Fishbein, M. Dimensions of semantic space: A problem of individual differences. In J. R. Snider & C. E. Osgood (Eds.), *The semantic differential technique*. Chicago: Aldine, 1969.

Wiggins, N., & Hoffman, P. J. Three models of clinical judgment. *Journal of Abnormal Psychology*, 1968, *73*, 70–77.

Wiggins, N., Hoffman, P. J., & Taber, T. Types of judges and cue utilization in judgments of intelligence. *Journal of Personality and Social Psychology*, 1969, *12*, 52–59.

Wilde, G. J. S. *Neurotische Labiliteit gemeten volgens do vragenlijstmethode*. [The questionnaire measurement of neuroticism.] (With extensive summary in English.) Amsterdam: Van Rossen, 1963.

Wilde, G. J. S. Inheritance of personality traits. *Acta Psychologica*, 1964, *22*, 37–51. (a)

Wilde, G. J. S. Social desirability set, interpersonal differences in item desirability and validity of neuroticism questionnaires. *Acta Psychologica*, 1964, *22*, 145–154. (b)

Wilde, G. J. S. *Self-report and error-choice*. Paper presented at the 29th annual meeting of the Canadian Psychological Association, Montreal, June 1966. (a)

Wilde, G. J. S. The significance of decided and query answers to lie-items in a personality questionnaire. *British Journal of Social and Clinical Psychology*, 1966, *5*, 37–41. (b)

Wilde, G. J. S., & DeWit, O. Self-report and error-choice; Part B: Individual differences in the operations of the error-choice principle and their validity in personality questionnaire items. *British Journal of Psychology*, 1970, *61*, 219–228.

Wilde, G. J. S., & Fortuin, S. Self-report and error-choice; Part A: An application of the error choice principle to the construction of personality test items. *British Journal of Psychology*, 1969, *60*, 101–108.

Wilde, G. J. S., & Tellegen, B. *The dimensional structure of psychiatric diagnoses: A canonical variate analysis of questionnaire measures obtained from psychotics, neurotics and normal controls*. Unpublished manuscript, Queen's University, 1965.

Wilkin, H. A., Dyk, R. B., Faterson, H. F.,

Goodenough, D. R., & Karp, S. A. *Psychological differentiation*. New York: Wiley, 1962.

Wilks, S. S. Certain generalizations in the analysis of variance. *Biometrika*, 1932, *24*, 471–474.

Willerman, L., & Plomin, R. Activity level in children and their parents. *Child Development*, 1973, *44*, 854–858.

Willett, R. A. The effects of psychosurgical procedures on behavior. In H. J. Eysenck (Ed.), *Handbook of abnormal behavior*. New York: Basic Books, 1961.

Williams, J. R. *The definition and measurement of conflict in terms of P-technique: A test of validity*. Unpublished doctoral dissertation, University of Illinois, 1958.

Williams, J. R. A test of the validity of P-technique in the measurement of internal conflict. *Journal of Personality*, 1959, *27*, 418–457.

Williams, S. B. Resistance to extinction as a function of the number of reinforcements. *Journal of Experimental Psychology*, 1938, *23*, 506–522.

Williams, R. J. *Biochemical individuality, the basis for the genetotrophic concept*. New York: Wiley, 1956.

Williams, W. S. A semantic differential study of the meaning of personality test items to children from different socioeconomic groups. *Journal of Psychology*, 1971, *79*, 179–188.

Williamson, E. G., & Hoyt, D. Measured personality characteristics of student leaders. *Educational and Psychological Measurement*, 1952, *12*, 65–78.

Willis, C. B. The effect of primogeniture on intellectual capacity. *Journal of Abnormal and Social Psychology*, 1924, *18*, 375–377.

Willis, M. *The guinea pigs after 20 years*. Columbus, Ohio: Ohio State University press, 1961.

Wilson, R. C., Beem, H. P., & Comrey, A. L. Factors influencing organizational effectiveness: A survey of skilled tradesmen. *Personnel Psychology*, 1953, *6*, 313–325.

Wilson, R. S. Analysis of autonomic reaction patterns. *Psychophysiology*, 1967, *4*, 125–142.

Wilson, R. S. Twins: Patterns of cognitive development as measured on the Wechsler Preschool and Primary Scale of Intelligence. *Developmental Psychology*, 1975, *11*, 126–134.

Wilson, W. P. *Applications of electrencephalography in psychiatry*. Durham, N.C.: Duke University Press, 1965.

Winch, R. F. Theoretische Ansätze in der Untersuchung der Familie. In R. König (Hrsg.), *Soziologie der Familie, Kolner Zeitschrift für Soziologie und Sozialpsychologie*. Sonderheft 14, Opladen: Westdeutscher Verlag, 1970.

Winch, R. F., Ktsanes, T., & Ktsanes, V. The theory of complementary needs in mate-selection: An analytic and descriptive study. *American Sociological Review*, 1954, *19*, 241–249.

Windle, G. Test-retest effects on personality questionnaires. *Educational and Psychological Measurement*, 1954, *14*, 617–633.

Winterbottom, M. R. The relation of need for achievement to learning experiences in independence and mastery. In J. W. Atkinson (Ed.), *Motives and fantasy, action and society*. Princeton, N.J.: Van Nostrand, 1958.

Winthrop, H. Relations between appeal value and highbrow status on some radio and television programs. *Psychological Reports*, 1958, *4*, 53–54.

Wiseman, S. *Intelligence and ability: Selected readings*. Baltimore: Penguin, 1967.

Witkin, H. A. The preception of the upright. In D. N. Jackson & S. Messick (Eds.), *Problems of human assessment*. New York: McGraw-Hill, 1967.

Witkin, H. A., Dyk, R. B., Faterson, H. F., Goodenough, D. R., & Karp, S. A. *Psychological differentiation*. New York: Wiley, 1962.

Wittenborn, J. R. A new procedure for evaluating mental hospital patients. *Journal of Consulting Psychology*, 1950, *14*, 500–501.

Wittenborn, J. R. Symptom patterns in a group of mental hospital patients. *Journal of Consulting Psychology*, 1951, *15*, 290–302.

Wittenborn, J. R. The behavioral symptoms for certain organic psychoses. *Journal of Consulting Psychology*, 1952, *16*, 104–106.

Wittenborn, J. R. The dimensions of psychosis. *Journal of Nervous and Mental Disease*, 1962, *134*, 117–128.

Wittenborn, J. R., & Bailey, C. The symptoms of involutional psychosis. *Journal of Consulting Psychology*, 1952, *16*, 13–17.

Wittenborn, J. R., & Holzberg, J. D. The generality of psychiatric syndromes. *Journal of Consulting Psychology*, 1951, *15*, 372–380.

Wittenborn, J. R., & Weiss, W. Patients diagnosed manic psychosis, manic state. *Journal of Consulting Psychology*, 1952, *16*, 193–198.

Wittman, P., & Sheldon, W. A proposed classification of psychotic behavior reactions. *American Journal of Psychiatry*, 1948, *105*, 124–128.

Witty, P. (Ed.). *The gifted child*. Boston: Heath, 1951.

Wolf, M. M., Giles, D. K., & Hall, V. R. Experiments with token reinforcement in a remedial classroom. *Behaviour Research and Therapy*, 1968, *6*, 51–64.

Wolk, M. M., Risley, T., & Mees, H. Application of operant conditioning procedures to the behaviour problems of an autistic child. *Behaviour Research and Therapy*, 1964, *1*, 305–312.

Wolman, B. B. (Ed.). *Handbook of child psychoanalysis: Research, theory, and practice*. New York: Van Nostrand, 1972. (a)

Wolman, B. B. Psychoanalytic theory of infantile development. In B. B. Wolman (Ed.), *Handbook of child psychoanalysis: Research, theory, and practice*. New York: Van Nostrand, 1972. (b)

Wolpe, J. *Psychotherapy by reciprocal inhibition*. Stanford: Stanford University Press, 1958.

Wolpe, J. *The practice of behavior therapy*. New York: Pergamon, 1969.

Wolpe, J., & Lazarus, A. A. *Behavior therapy techniques: A guide to the treatment of neuroses*. Oxford: Pergamon Press, 1966.

Woodger, J. H. *The technique of theory construction*. Chicago: University of Chicago Press, 1939.

Woodrow, H. Factors in improvement with practice. *Journal of Psychology*, 1939, *7*, 55–70.

Woodworth, R. S. *Dynamics of behavior*. New York: Holt, Rinehart, & Winston, 1958.

Woodworth, R. S., & Schlosberg, H. S.

*Experimental psychology*. New York: Henry Holt, 1956.

Woody, R. H. *Behavioral problem children in the schools: Recognition, diagnosis, and behavioral modification*. New York: Appleton-Century-Crofts, 1969.

Worchel, W., & Byrne, D. (Eds.). *Personality change*. New York: Wiley, 1964.

Wright, H. Observational child study. In P. Mussen (Ed.), *Handbook of research methods in child development*. New York: Wiley, 1960.

Wright, S. Systems of mating: II. The effects of inbreeding on the genetic composition of a population. *Genetics*, 1921, *6*, 124–143.

Wrigley, C. Theory construction or fact finding in a computer age? *Behavioral Science*, 1960, *5*, 183–186.

Wurzbacher, G. *Leitbilder gegenwärtigen deutschen Familienlebens*. Stuttgart: Enke, 1954.

Wyckoff, L. B., Jr. The role of observing responses in discrimination learning, Part I. *Psychological Review*, 1952, *59*, 431–442.

Wyer, R. S., Jr. *Cognitive organization and change: An information processing approach*. Potomac, Md.: Erlbaum, 1974.

Wylie, R. C. *The self concept: Critical survey of pertinent literature*. Lincoln: University of Nebraska Press, 1960.

Wynne, J. D., & Brogden, W. J. Effect upon sensory pre-conditioning of backward, forward and track pre-conditioning training. *Journal of Experimental Psychology*, 1962, *64*, 422–423.

Wynne, L. C., Ryckoff, J. M., Day, J., & Hirsch, S. J. Pseudomutuality in the family relations of schizophrenics. *Psychiatry*, 1958, *21*, 205–220.

Wynne, R. D. *Can schizophrenics give the associations that "most people" do?* Paper presented at the meeting of the Eastern Psychological Association, New York, April 1963.

Wyss, D. *Die tiefenpsychologischen Schulen von den Anfängenbis zur Gegenwart*. Göttingen: Vandenhoeck & Ruprecht, 1961.

Yarrow, L. J. Maternal deprivation: Toward an empirical and conceptual re-evaluation. *Psychological Bulletin*, 1961, *58*, 459–490.

Yarrow, L. J. Separation from parents during early childhood. In M. L. Hoffman & L. W. Hoffman (Eds.), *Child development research* (Vol. 1). New York: Russell Sage Foundation, 1964.

Yarrow, L. J., & Yarrow, M. Y. Personality continuity and change in the family context. In P. Worchel & D. Byrne (Eds.), *Personality change*. New York: Wiley, 1964.

Yarrow, M. R., Campbell, J. D., & Burton, R. V. *Child rearing: An inquiry into research and methods*. San Francisco: Jossey-Bass, 1968.

Yarrow, M. R., Campbell, J. D., & Burton, R. V. Reliability of maternal retrospection: A preliminary report. In K. Danzinger (Ed.), *Readings in child socialization*. Oxford: Pergamon, 1970.

Yarrow, M. R., Waxler, C. A., & Scott, P. M. Child effects on adult behavior. *Developmental Psychology*, 1971, *5*, 300–311.

Young, P. T., & Shuford, E. H., Jr. Quantitative control motivation through sucrose solution of different concentration. *Journal of Comparative and Physiological Psychology*, 1955, *48*, 114–118.

Young, R. D. Developmental psychopharmacology: A beginning. *Psychological Bulletin*, 1967, *67*, 73–86.

Young, R. K. Tests of three hypotheses about the stimulus in serial learning. *Journal of Experimental Psychology*, 1962, *63*, 307–313.

Young, W. C. Hormones and mating behavior. In W. C. Young (Ed.). *Sex and internal secretions* (Vol. 2). Baltimore: Williams & Wilkins, 1961.

Young, W. C. Goy, R. W., & Phoenix, C. H. Hormones and sexual behavior. *Science*, 1964, *143*, 212–218.

Zajonc, R. B. *Social psychology: An experimental approach*. Belmont, Calif.: Wadsworth, 1966.

Zajonc, R. B. Attitudinal effects of mere exposure. *Journal of Personality and Social Psychology, Monograph Supplement*, 1968, *9*(No. 2, Pt. 2).

Zajonc, R. B., & Markus, G. B. Birth order and intellectual development. *Psychological Bulletin*, 1975, *82*, 74–88.

Zener, K. The significance of behavior accompanying conditioned salivary secretion for theories of the conditioned response. *American Journal of Psychology*, 1937, *50*, 384–403.

Zern, D. Competence reconsidered: The concept of secondary process development as an explanation of "competence" phenomena. *Journal of Genetic Psychology*, 1973, *122*, 135–162.

Zerssen, D. von. Physique and personality. In A. R. Kaplan (Ed.), *Human behavior genetics*. Springfield, Ill.: Charles C Thomas, 1976 (in press).

Zigler, E., & Phillips, L. Psychiatric diagnosis: A critique. *Journal of Abnormal and Social Psychology*, 1961, *63*, 607–618.

Zimbardo, P. G. Involvement and communication discrepancy as determined by opinion conformity. *Journal of Abnormal and Social Psychology*, 1960, *60*, 86–94.

Zimmerman, C. C. *The family of tomorrow: The cultural crisis and the way out*. New York: Harper, 1949.

Zimmerman, D. W. Durable secondary reinforcement: Method and theory. *Psychological Review*, 1957, *64*, 373–383.

Zubin, J. A technique for pattern analysis. *Psychological Bulletin*, 1936, *33*, 733.

Zubin, J. Classification of the behavior disorders. *Annual Review of Psychology*, 1967, *18*, 373–406.

Zubin, J., Sutton, S., Salzinger, K., Salzinger, S., Durdock, E. I., & Peretz, D. A biometric approach to prognosis in schizophrenia. In P. H. Hock & J. Zubin (Eds.), *Comparative epidemiology in the mental disorders*. New York: Grüne & Stratton, 1961.

Zuckerman, J. V. Interest item response arrangement as it affects discrimination between professional groups. *Journal of Applied Psychology*, 1952, *36*, 79–85.

Zuckerman, M. The development of an Affect Adjective Check List for the measurement of anxiety. *Journal of Consulting Psychology*, 1960, *24*, 457–462.

Zuckerman, M., & Biase, D. B. Replication and further data on the Affect Adjective Check List measure of anxiety. *Journal of Consulting Psychology*, 1962, *26*, 291.

Zuckerman, M., & Lubin, B. *Manual for the Multiple Affect Adjective Check List*. San Diego, Calif.: Educational and Industrial Testing Service, 1965.

Zuckerman, M., & Lubin, B. *Bibliography for the Multiple Affect Adjective Check List*. San Diego, Calif.: Educational and Industrial Testing Service, 1968.

Zuckerman, M., Lubin, B., Vogel, L., & Valerius, E. Measurement of experimentally induced affects. *Journal of Consulting Psychology*, 1964, *28*, 418–425.

# Index